BATMAN

KNIGHTFALL

volume one

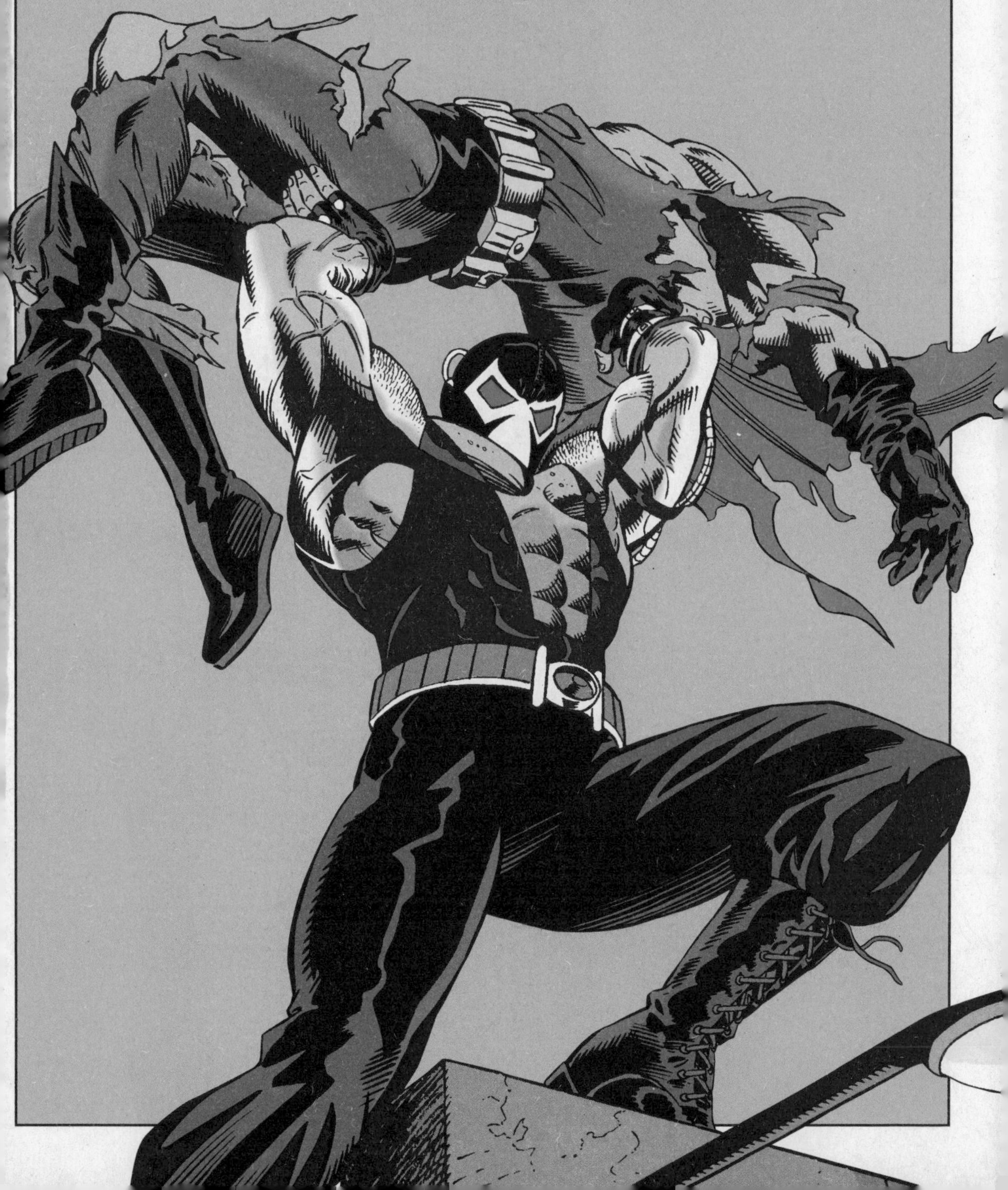

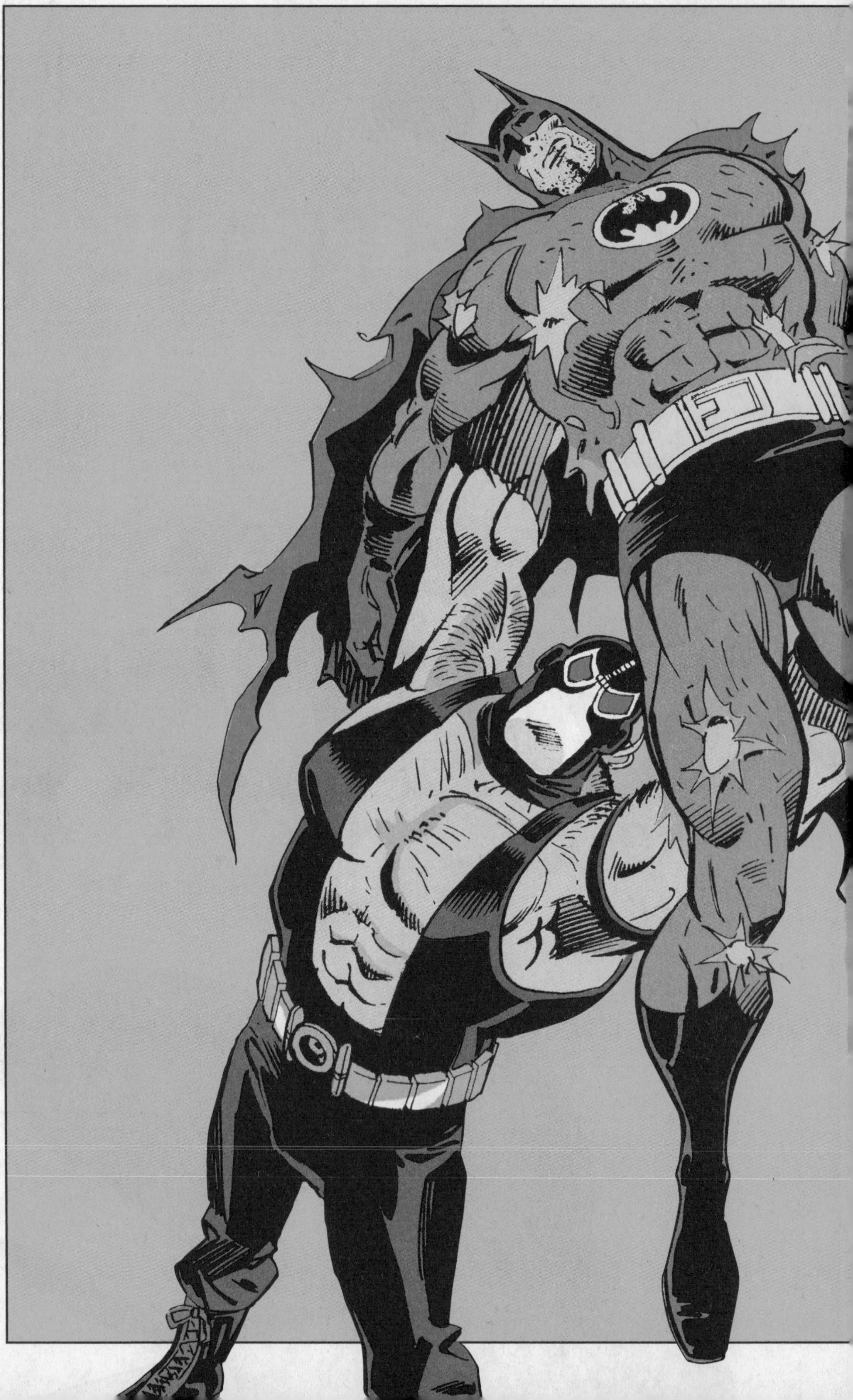

BATMAN

volume one

DOUG **MOENCH** CHUCK **DIXON**
ALAN **GRANT**

writers

JIM **APARO** NORM **BREYFOGLE**
GRAHAM **NOLAN** JIM **BALENT**
BRET **BLEVINS** KLAUS **JANSON**
MIKE **MANLEY**

pencillers

SCOTT **HANNA** NORM **BREYFOGLE**
JIM **APARO** TOM **MANDRAKE**
BOB **WIACEK** JOSEF **RUBINSTEIN**
DICK **GIORDANO** MIKE **MANLEY**
BRET **BLEVINS** STEVE **GEORGE**
TERRY **AUSTIN** RICK **BURCHETT**

inkers

ADRIENNE **ROY**
KLAUS **JANSON**

colorists

RICHARD **STARKINGS** JOHN **COSTANZA**
TIM **HARKINS** KEN **BRUZENAK**
TODD **KLEIN** BOB **PINAHA**

letterers

KELLEY **JONES**

cover artist

Batman created by BOB **KANE**

with BILL **FINGER**

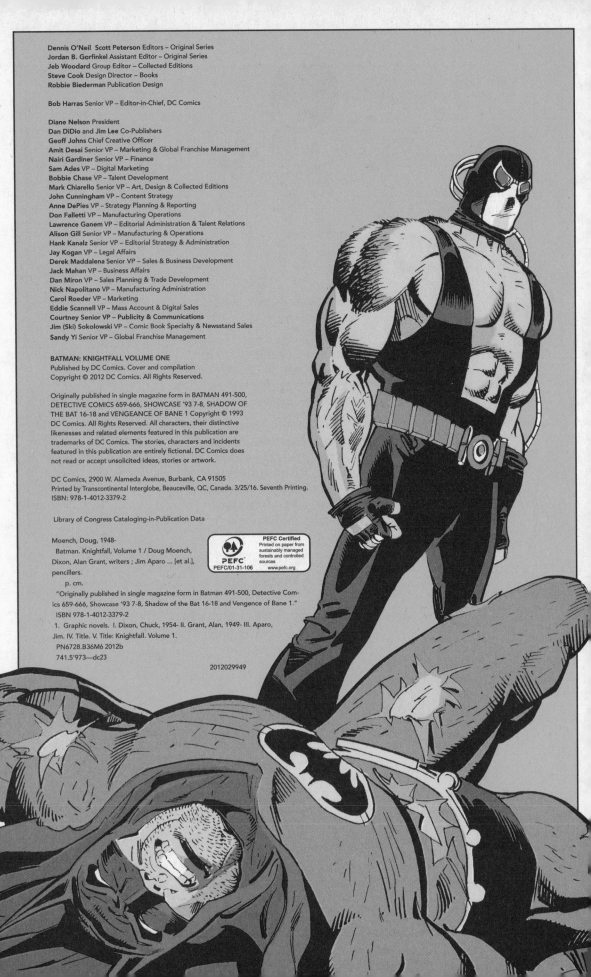

Dennis O'Neil Scott Peterson Editors – Original Series
Jordan B. Gorfinkel Assistant Editor – Original Series
Jeb Woodard Group Editor – Collected Editions
Steve Cook Design Director – Books
Robbie Biederman Publication Design

Bob Harras Senior VP – Editor-in-Chief, DC Comics

Diane Nelson President
Dan DiDio and Jim Lee Co-Publishers
Geoff Johns Chief Creative Officer
Amit Desai Senior VP – Marketing & Global Franchise Management
Nairi Gardiner Senior VP – Finance
Sam Ades VP – Digital Marketing
Bobbie Chase VP – Talent Development
Mark Chiarello Senior VP – Art, Design & Collected Editions
John Cunningham VP – Content Strategy
Anne DePies VP – Strategy Planning & Reporting
Don Falletti VP – Manufacturing Operations
Lawrence Ganem VP – Editorial Administration & Talent Relations
Alison Gill Senior VP – Manufacturing & Operations
Hank Kanalz Senior VP – Editorial Strategy & Administration
Jay Kogan VP – Legal Affairs
Derek Maddalena Senior VP – Sales & Business Development
Jack Mahan VP – Business Affairs
Dan Miron VP – Sales Planning & Trade Development
Nick Napolitano VP – Manufacturing Administration
Carol Roeder VP – Marketing
Eddie Scannell VP – Mass Account & Digital Sales
Courtney Senior VP – Publicity & Communications
Jim (Ski) Sokolowski VP – Comic Book Specialty & Newsstand Sales
Sandy Yi Senior VP – Global Franchise Management

DC Comics, 2900 W. Alameda Avenue, Burbank, CA 91505
Printed by Transcontinental Interglobe, Beauceville, QC, Canada. 3/25/16. Seventh Printing.
ISBN: 978-1-4012-3379-2

Library of Congress Cataloging-in-Publication Data

Moench, Doug, 1948-
   Batman. Knightfall, Volume 1 / Doug Moench,
Dixon, Alan Grant, writers ; Jim Aparo ... [et al.],
pencillers.
   p. cm.
   "Originally published in single magazine form in Batman 491-500, Detective Com-
ics 659-666, Showcase '93 7-8, Shadow of the Bat 16-18 and Vengence of Bane 1."
   ISBN 978-1-4012-3379-2
   1. Graphic novels. I. Dixon, Chuck, 1954- II. Grant, Alan, 1949- III. Aparo,
Jim. IV. Title. V. Title: Knightfall. Volume 1.
   PN6728.B36M6 2012b
   741.5'973—dc23
                                           2012029949

PEFC Certified
Printed on paper from
sustainably managed
forests and controlled
sources
PEFC/01-31-106   www.pefc.org

Cover art by **GLENN FABRY**

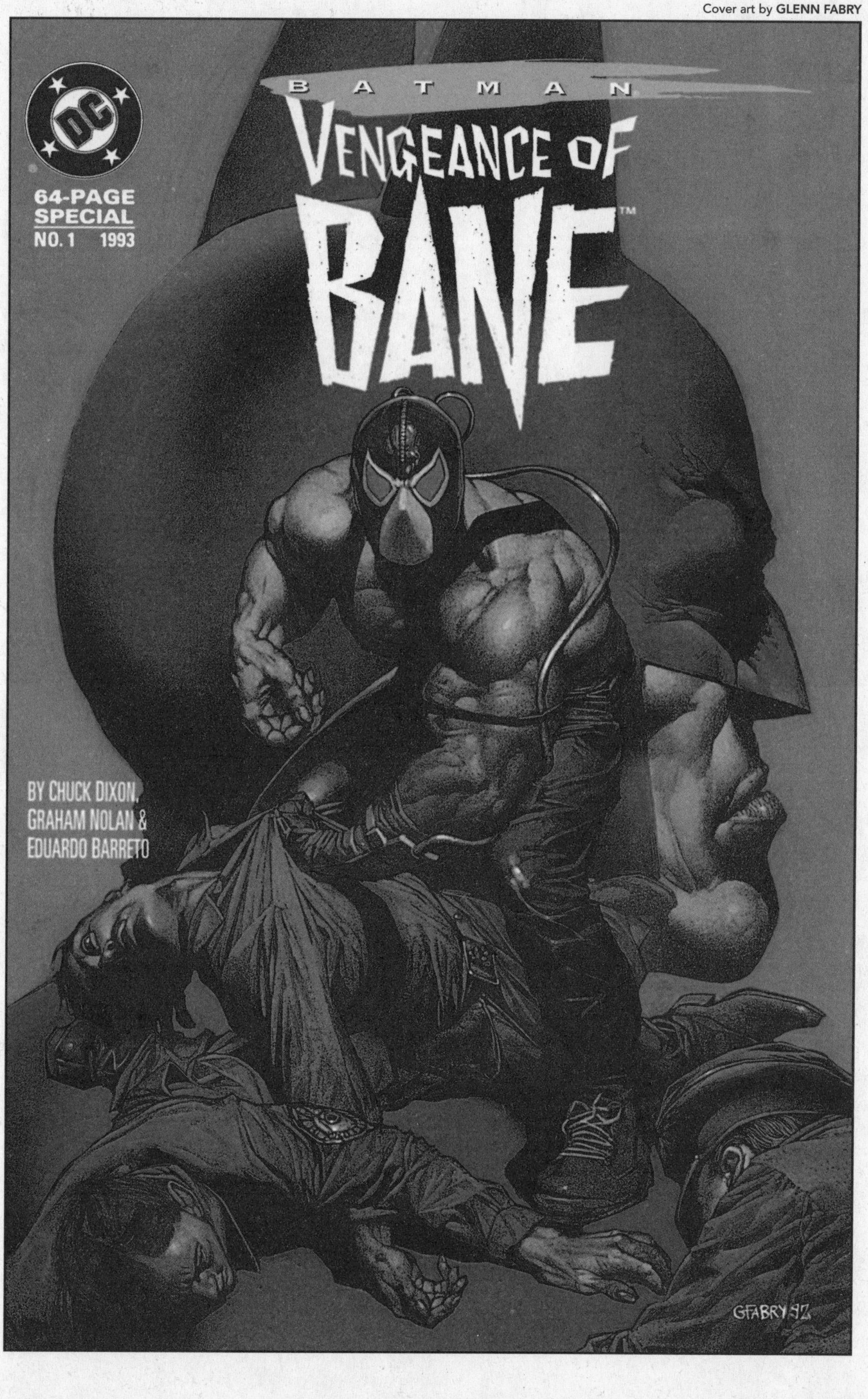

DC
64-PAGE SPECIAL
NO. 1 1993
BATMAN
VENGEANCE OF
BANE™
BY CHUCK DIXON, GRAHAM NOLAN & EDUARDO BARRETO
GFABRY 92

VENGEANCE OF BANE

CHUCK DIXON · GRAHAM NOLAN · EDUARDO BARRETO · ADRIENNE ROY · BILL OAKLEY · SCOTT PETERSON · DENNIS O'NEIL

WRITER · PENCILLER · INKER · COLORIST · LETTERER · ASSISTANT EDITOR · EDITOR

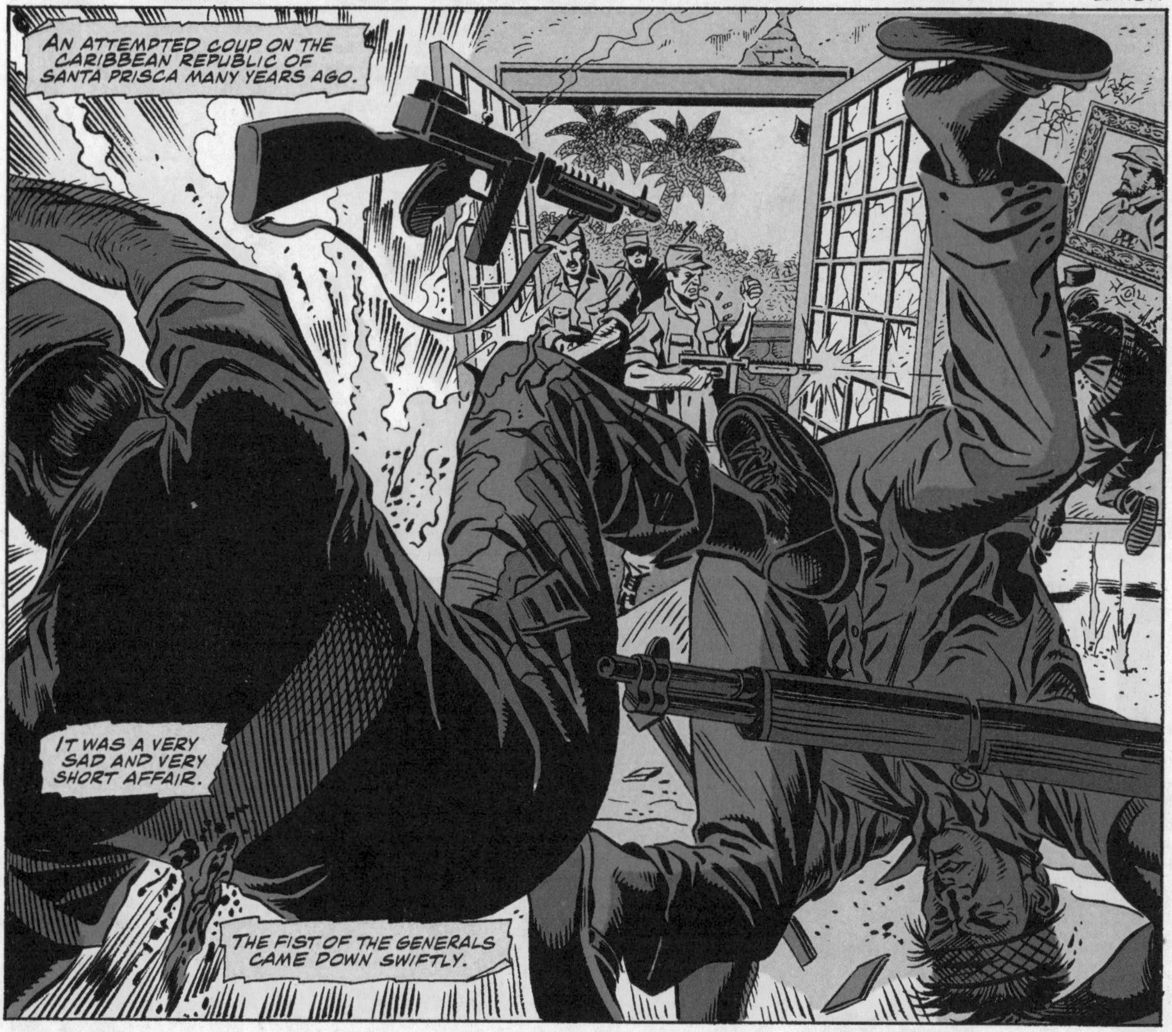
AN ATTEMPTED COUP ON THE CARIBBEAN REPUBLIC OF SANTA PRISCA MANY YEARS AGO.
IT WAS A VERY SAD AND VERY SHORT AFFAIR.
THE FIST OF THE GENERALS CAME DOWN SWIFTLY.

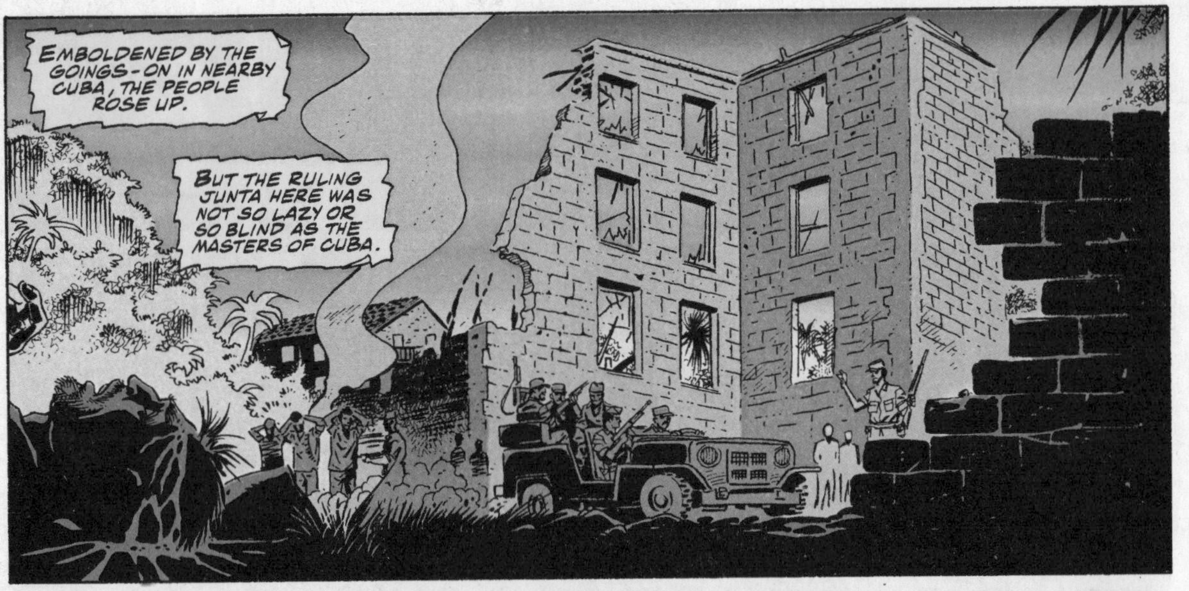
EMBOLDENED BY THE GOINGS-ON IN NEARBY CUBA, THE PEOPLE ROSE UP.
BUT THE RULING JUNTA HERE WAS NOT SO LAZY OR SO BLIND AS THE MASTERS OF CUBA.

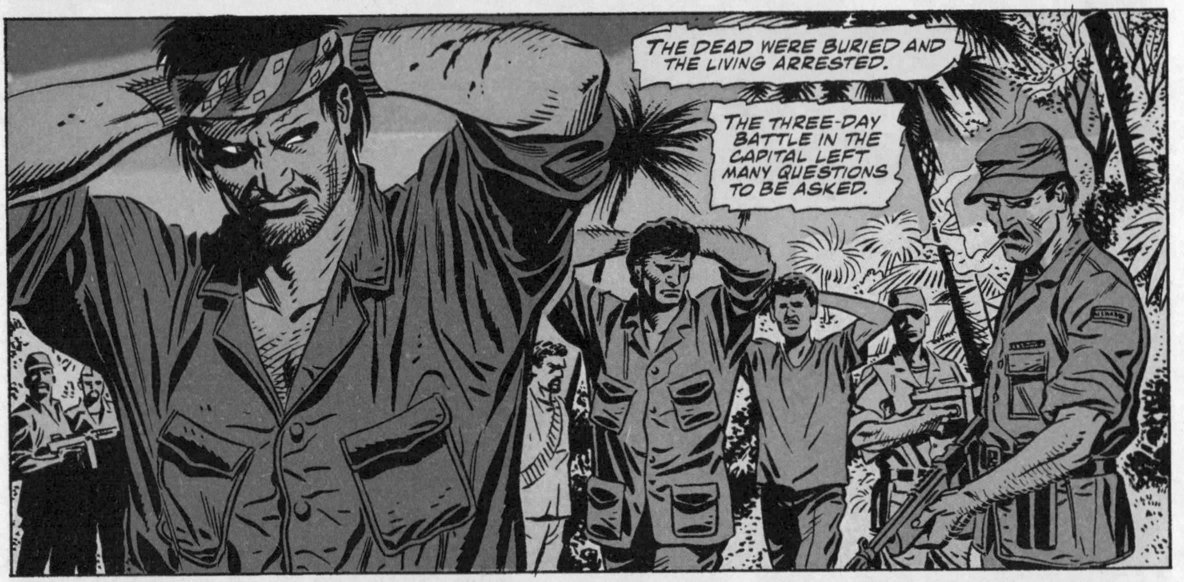
THE DEAD WERE BURIED AND THE LIVING ARRESTED.
THE THREE-DAY BATTLE IN THE CAPITAL LEFT MANY QUESTIONS TO BE ASKED.

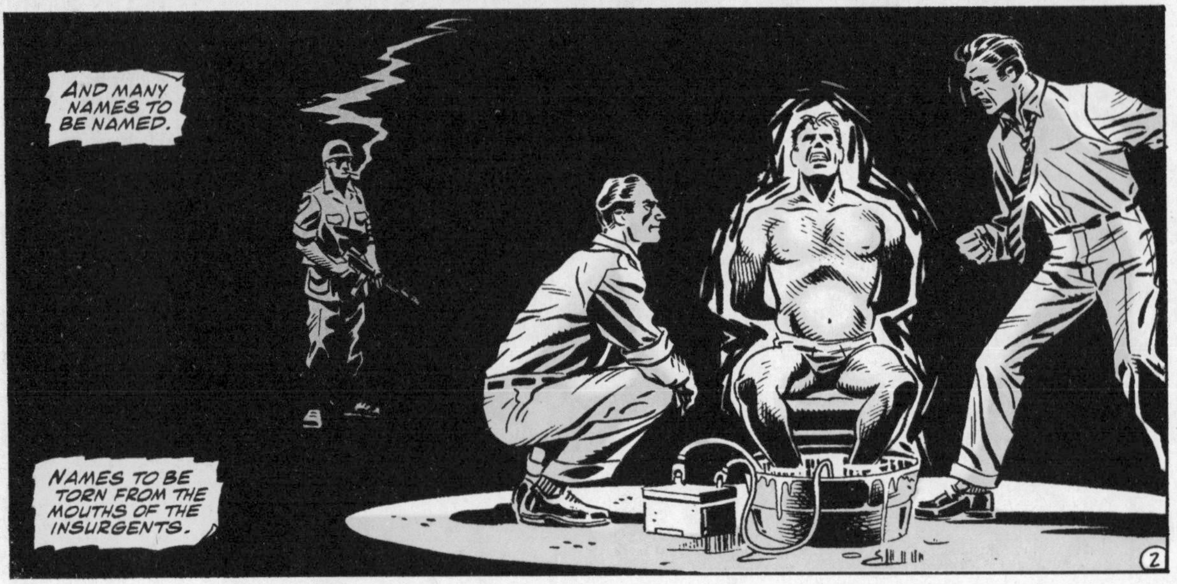
AND MANY NAMES TO BE NAMED.
NAMES TO BE TORN FROM THE MOUTHS OF THE INSURGENTS.
2

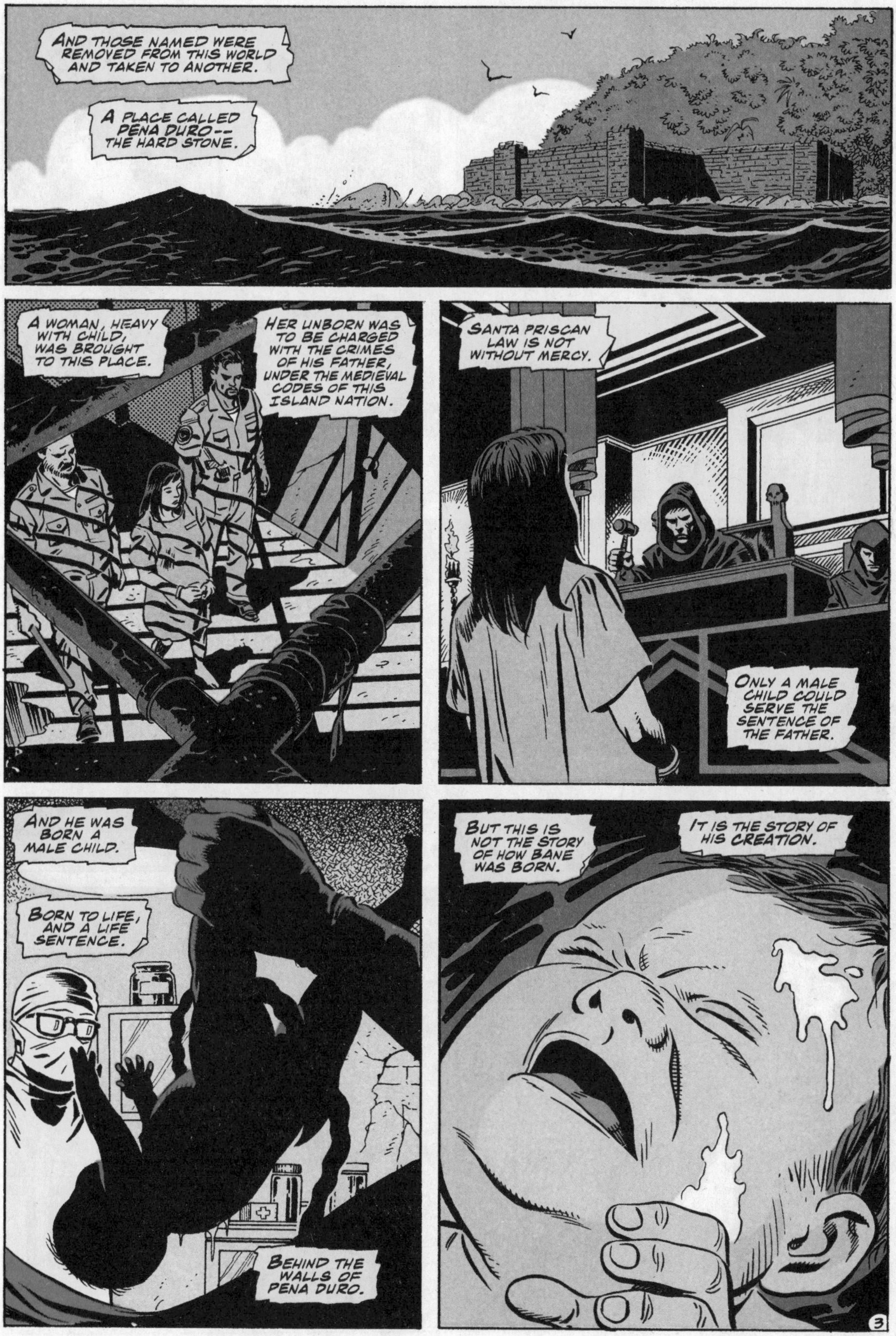

AND THOSE NAMED WERE REMOVED FROM THIS WORLD AND TAKEN TO ANOTHER.
A PLACE CALLED PENA DURO-- THE HARD STONE.
A WOMAN, HEAVY WITH CHILD, WAS BROUGHT TO THIS PLACE.
HER UNBORN WAS TO BE CHARGED WITH THE CRIMES OF HIS FATHER, UNDER THE MEDIEVAL CODES OF THIS ISLAND NATION.
SANTA PRISCAN LAW IS NOT WITHOUT MERCY.
ONLY A MALE CHILD COULD SERVE THE SENTENCE OF THE FATHER.
AND HE WAS BORN A MALE CHILD.
BORN TO LIFE, AND A LIFE SENTENCE.
BEHIND THE WALLS OF PENA DURO.
BUT THIS IS NOT THE STORY OF HOW BANE WAS BORN.
IT IS THE STORY OF HIS CREATION.
3

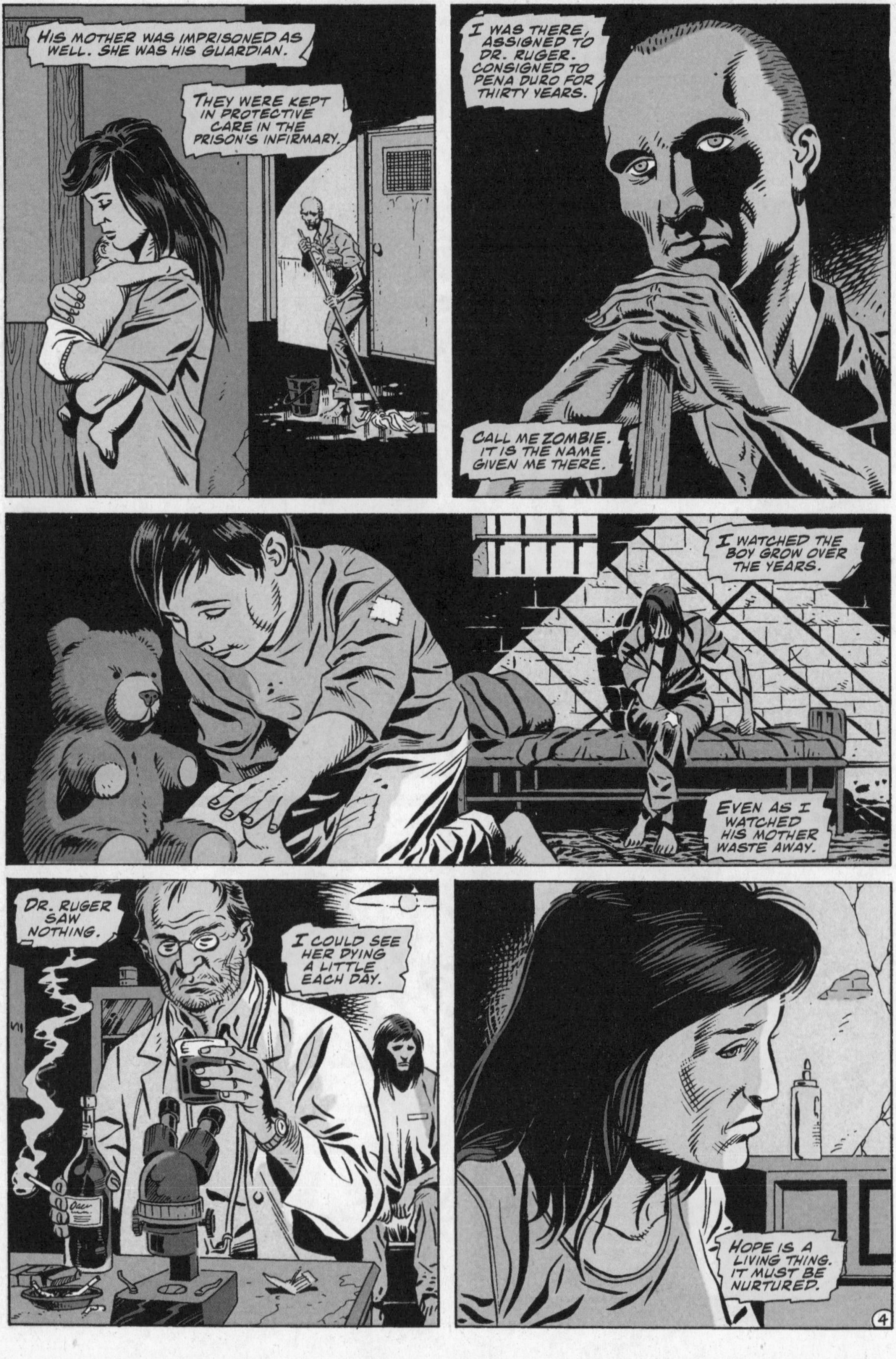

HIS MOTHER WAS IMPRISONED AS WELL. SHE WAS HIS GUARDIAN.
THEY WERE KEPT IN PROTECTIVE CARE IN THE PRISON'S INFIRMARY.
I WAS THERE, ASSIGNED TO DR. RUGER. CONSIGNED TO PENA DURO FOR THIRTY YEARS.
CALL ME ZOMBIE. IT IS THE NAME GIVEN ME THERE.
I WATCHED THE BOY GROW OVER THE YEARS.
EVEN AS I WATCHED HIS MOTHER WASTE AWAY.
DR. RUGER SAW NOTHING.
I COULD SEE HER DYING A LITTLE EACH DAY.
HOPE IS A LIVING THING. IT MUST BE NURTURED.
4

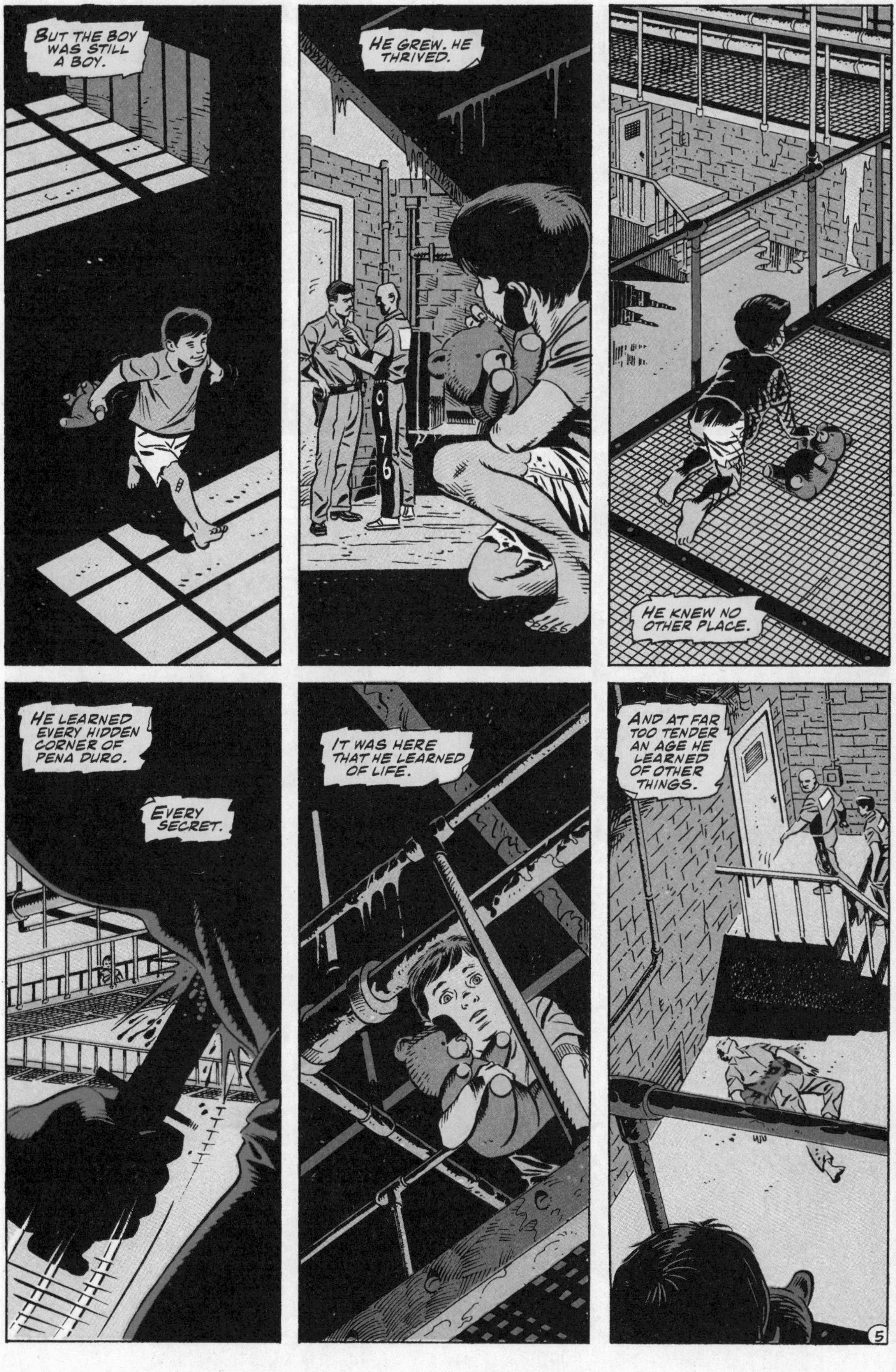
BUT THE BOY WAS STILL A BOY.
HE GREW. HE THRIVED.
0176
HE KNEW NO OTHER PLACE.
HE LEARNED EVERY HIDDEN CORNER OF PENA DURO.
EVERY SECRET.
IT WAS HERE THAT HE LEARNED OF LIFE.
AND AT FAR TOO TENDER AN AGE HE LEARNED OF OTHER THINGS.
5

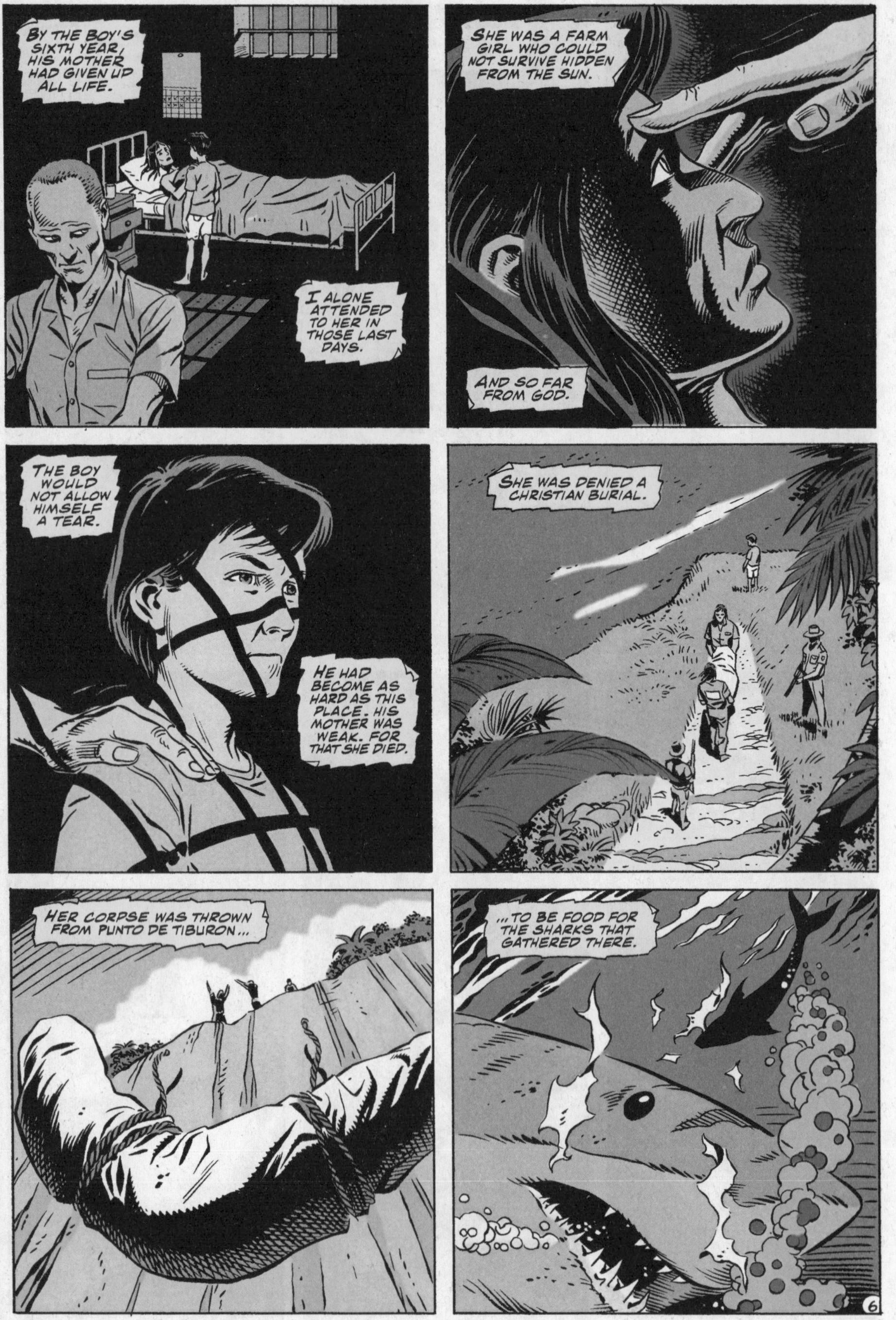
BY THE BOY'S SIXTH YEAR, HIS MOTHER HAD GIVEN UP ALL LIFE.
I ALONE ATTENDED TO HER IN THOSE LAST DAYS.
SHE WAS A FARM GIRL WHO COULD NOT SURVIVE HIDDEN FROM THE SUN.
AND SO FAR FROM GOD.
THE BOY WOULD NOT ALLOW HIMSELF A TEAR.
HE HAD BECOME AS HARD AS THIS PLACE. HIS MOTHER WAS WEAK. FOR THAT SHE DIED.
SHE WAS DENIED A CHRISTIAN BURIAL.
HER CORPSE WAS THROWN FROM PUNTO DE TIBURON...
...TO BE FOOD FOR THE SHARKS THAT GATHERED THERE.
6

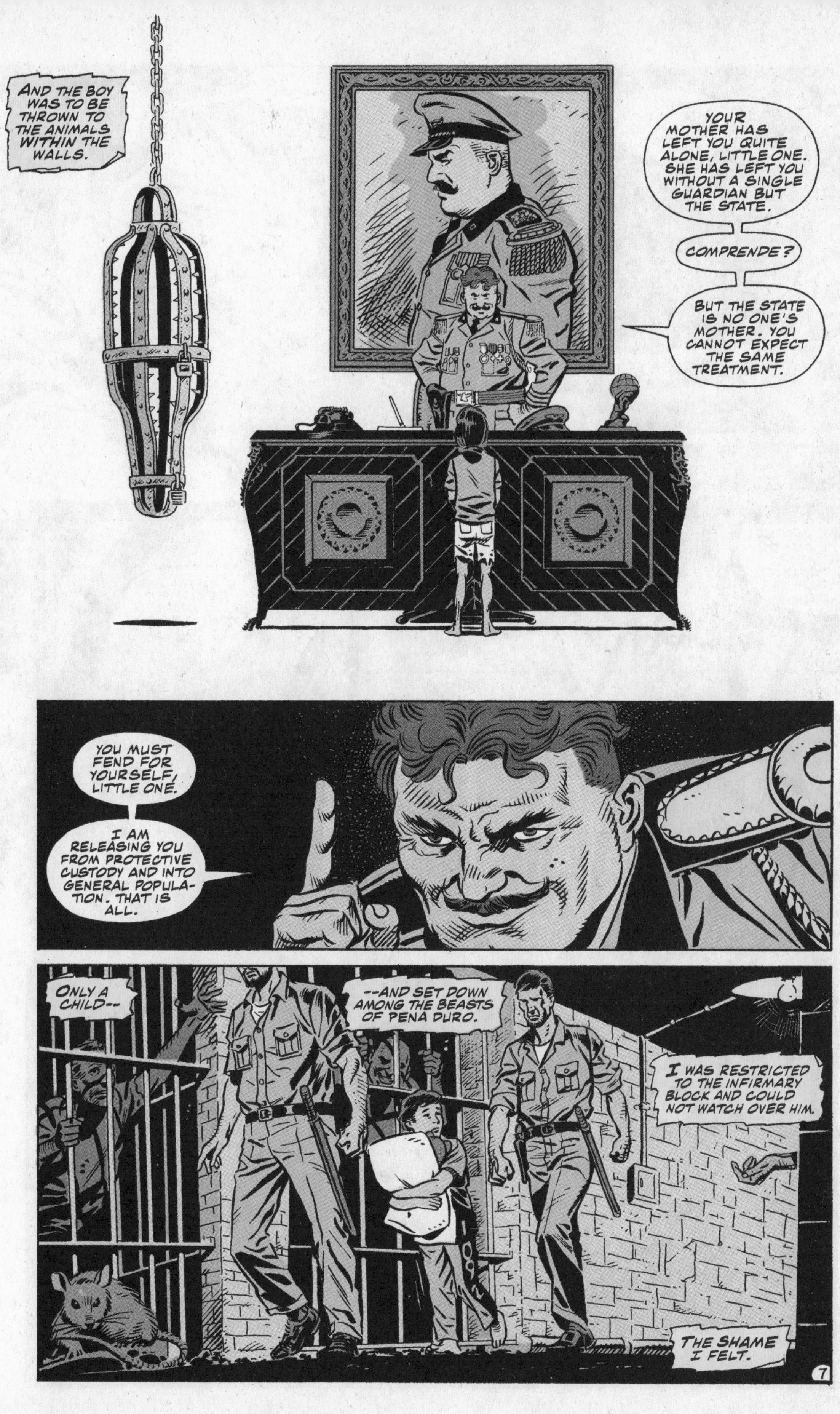

AND THE BOY WAS TO BE THROWN TO THE ANIMALS WITHIN THE WALLS.
YOUR MOTHER HAS LEFT YOU QUITE ALONE, LITTLE ONE. SHE HAS LEFT YOU WITHOUT A SINGLE GUARDIAN BUT THE STATE.
COMPRENDE?
BUT THE STATE IS NO ONE'S MOTHER. YOU CANNOT EXPECT THE SAME TREATMENT.
YOU MUST FEND FOR YOURSELF, LITTLE ONE.
I AM RELEASING YOU FROM PROTECTIVE CUSTODY AND INTO GENERAL POPULATION. THAT IS ALL.
ONLY A CHILD--
--AND SET DOWN AMONG THE BEASTS OF PENA DURO.
I WAS RESTRICTED TO THE INFIRMARY BLOCK AND COULD NOT WATCH OVER HIM.
THE SHAME I FELT.
7

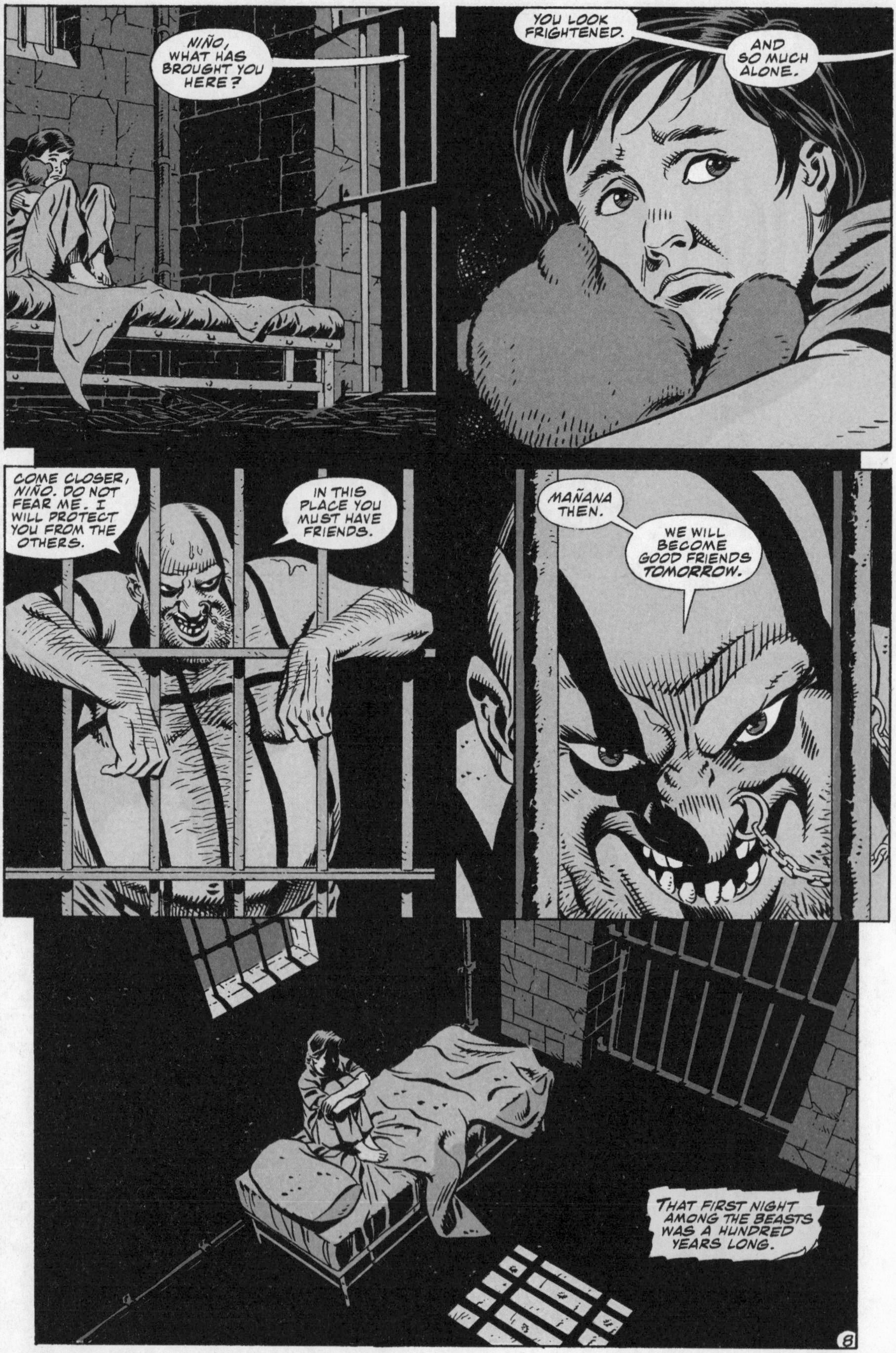
NIÑO, WHAT HAS BROUGHT YOU HERE?
YOU LOOK FRIGHTENED.
AND SO MUCH ALONE.
COME CLOSER, NIÑO. DO NOT FEAR ME. I WILL PROTECT YOU FROM THE OTHERS.
IN THIS PLACE YOU MUST HAVE FRIENDS.
MAÑANA THEN.
WE WILL BECOME GOOD FRIENDS TOMORROW.
THAT FIRST NIGHT AMONG THE BEASTS WAS A HUNDRED YEARS LONG.
8

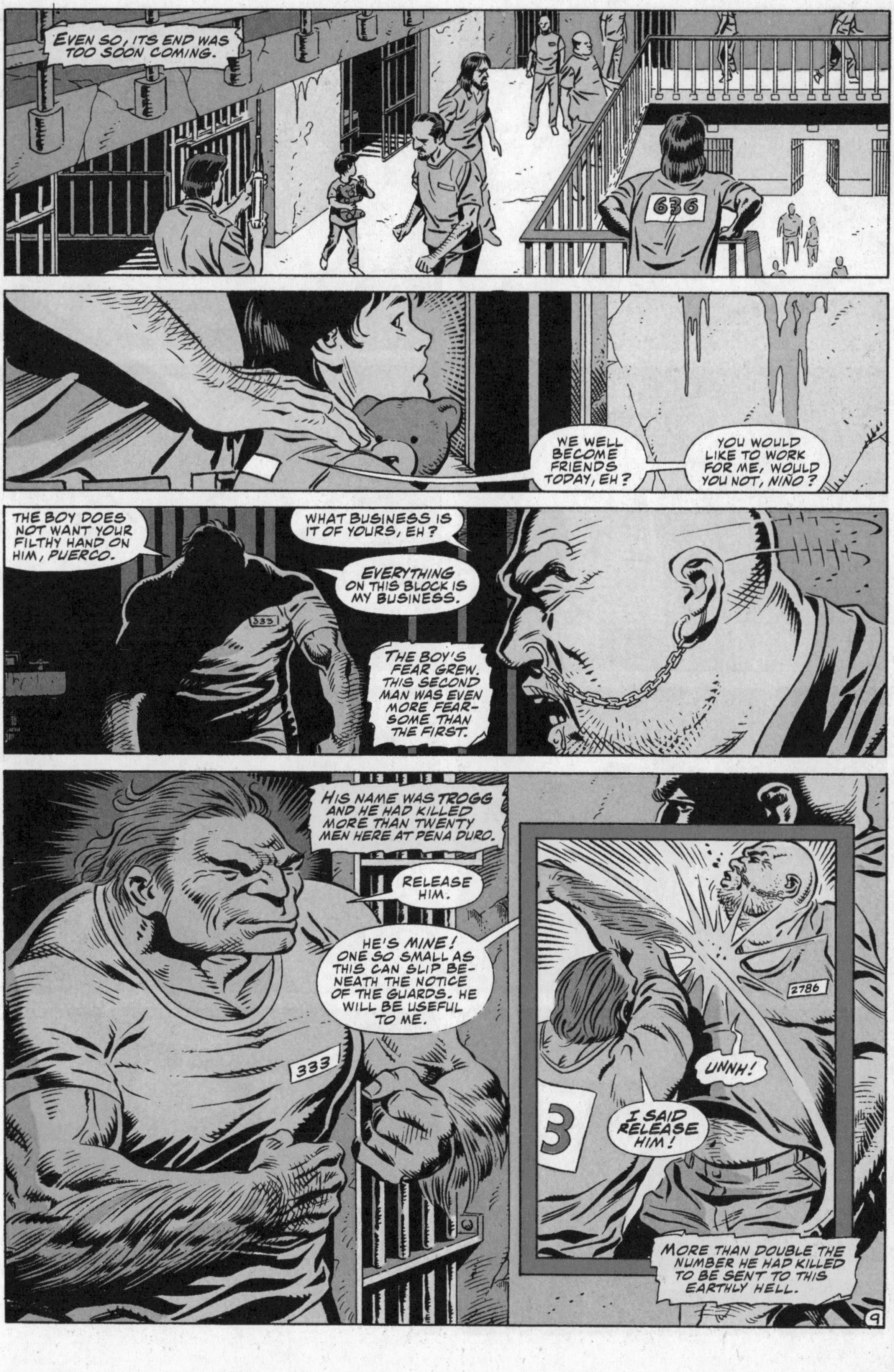

EVEN SO, ITS END WAS TOO SOON COMING.
636
WE WELL BECOME FRIENDS TODAY, EH?
YOU WOULD LIKE TO WORK FOR ME, WOULD YOU NOT, NIÑO?
THE BOY DOES NOT WANT YOUR FILTHY HAND ON HIM, PUERCO.
WHAT BUSINESS IS IT OF YOURS, EH?
EVERYTHING ON THIS BLOCK IS MY BUSINESS.
333
THE BOY'S FEAR GREW. THIS SECOND MAN WAS EVEN MORE FEARSOME THAN THE FIRST.
HIS NAME WAS TROGG AND HE HAD KILLED MORE THAN TWENTY MEN HERE AT PENA DURO.
RELEASE HIM.
HE'S MINE! ONE SO SMALL AS THIS CAN SLIP BENEATH THE NOTICE OF THE GUARDS. HE WILL BE USEFUL TO ME.
333
2786
UNNH!
I SAID RELEASE HIM!
3
MORE THAN DOUBLE THE NUMBER HE HAD KILLED TO BE SENT TO THIS EARTHLY HELL.
9

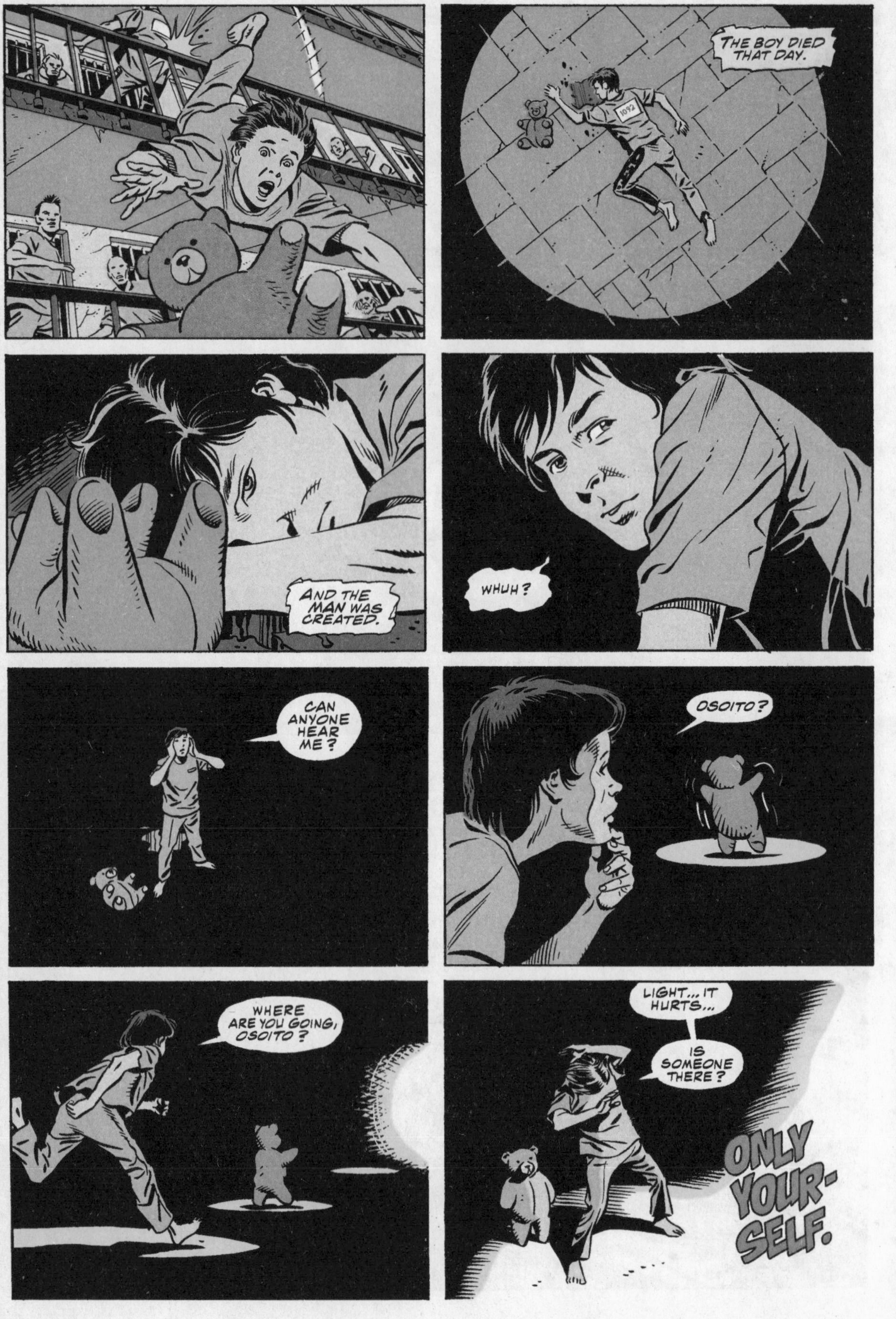
THE BOY DIED THAT DAY.
AND THE MAN WAS CREATED.
WHUH?
CAN ANYONE HEAR ME?
OSOITO?
WHERE ARE YOU GOING, OSOITO?
LIGHT... IT HURTS...
IS SOMEONE THERE?
ONLY YOUR-SELF.

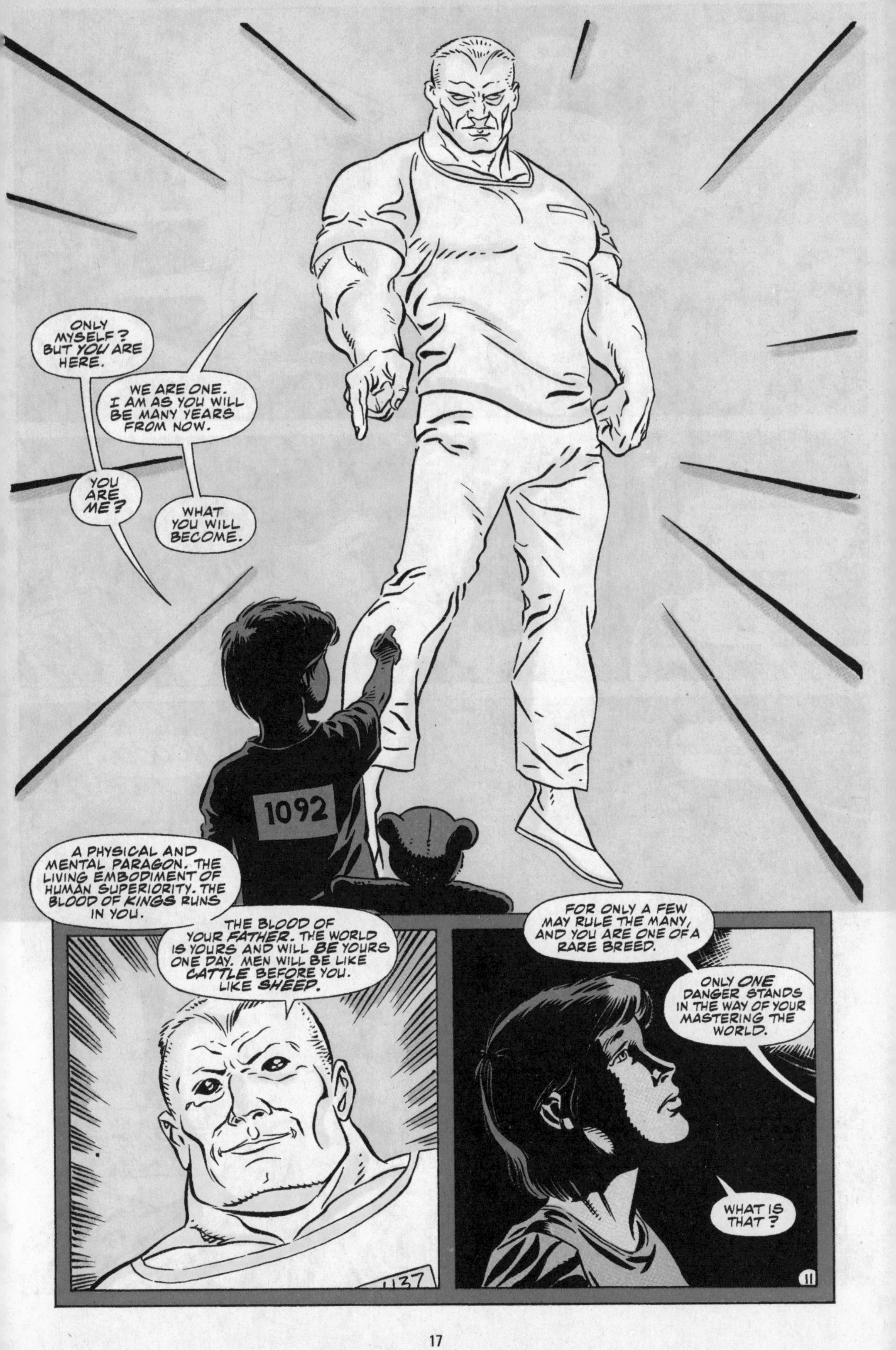
ONLY MYSELF? BUT YOU ARE HERE.
WE ARE ONE. I AM AS YOU WILL BE MANY YEARS FROM NOW.
YOU ARE ME?
WHAT YOU WILL BECOME.
1092
A PHYSICAL AND MENTAL PARAGON. THE LIVING EMBODIMENT OF HUMAN SUPERIORITY. THE BLOOD OF KINGS RUNS IN YOU.
THE BLOOD OF YOUR FATHER. THE WORLD IS YOURS AND WILL BE YOURS ONE DAY. MEN WILL BE LIKE CATTLE BEFORE YOU. LIKE SHEEP.
1137
FOR ONLY A FEW MAY RULE THE MANY, AND YOU ARE ONE OF A RARE BREED.
ONLY ONE DANGER STANDS IN THE WAY OF YOUR MASTERING THE WORLD.
WHAT IS THAT?
11

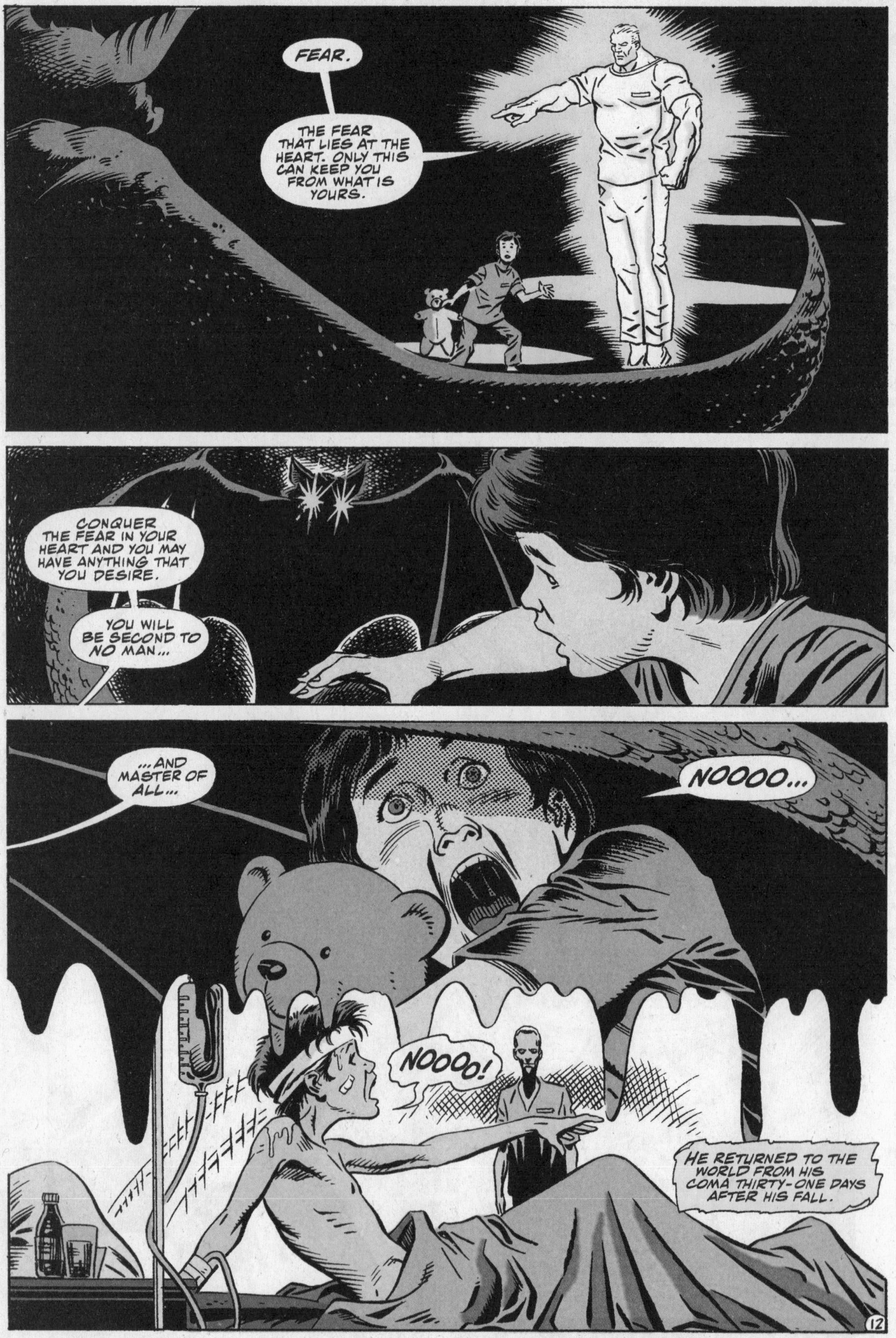
FEAR.
THE FEAR THAT LIES AT THE HEART. ONLY THIS CAN KEEP YOU FROM WHAT IS YOURS.
CONQUER THE FEAR IN YOUR HEART AND YOU MAY HAVE ANYTHING THAT YOU DESIRE.
YOU WILL BE SECOND TO NO MAN...
...AND MASTER OF ALL...
NOOOO...
NOOOO!
HE RETURNED TO THE WORLD FROM HIS COMA THIRTY-ONE DAYS AFTER HIS FALL.
12

HE RETURNED NO LONGER A CHILD.

ARE YOU SLEEPING?

QUE...?

NIÑO? I THOUGHT YOU HAD DIED...

1092

THE NIÑO IS DEAD, PUERCO.

BUT I AM HERE.

DO YOU STILL WANT ME TO WORK FOR YOU?

NO....

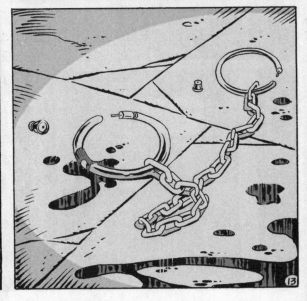

13

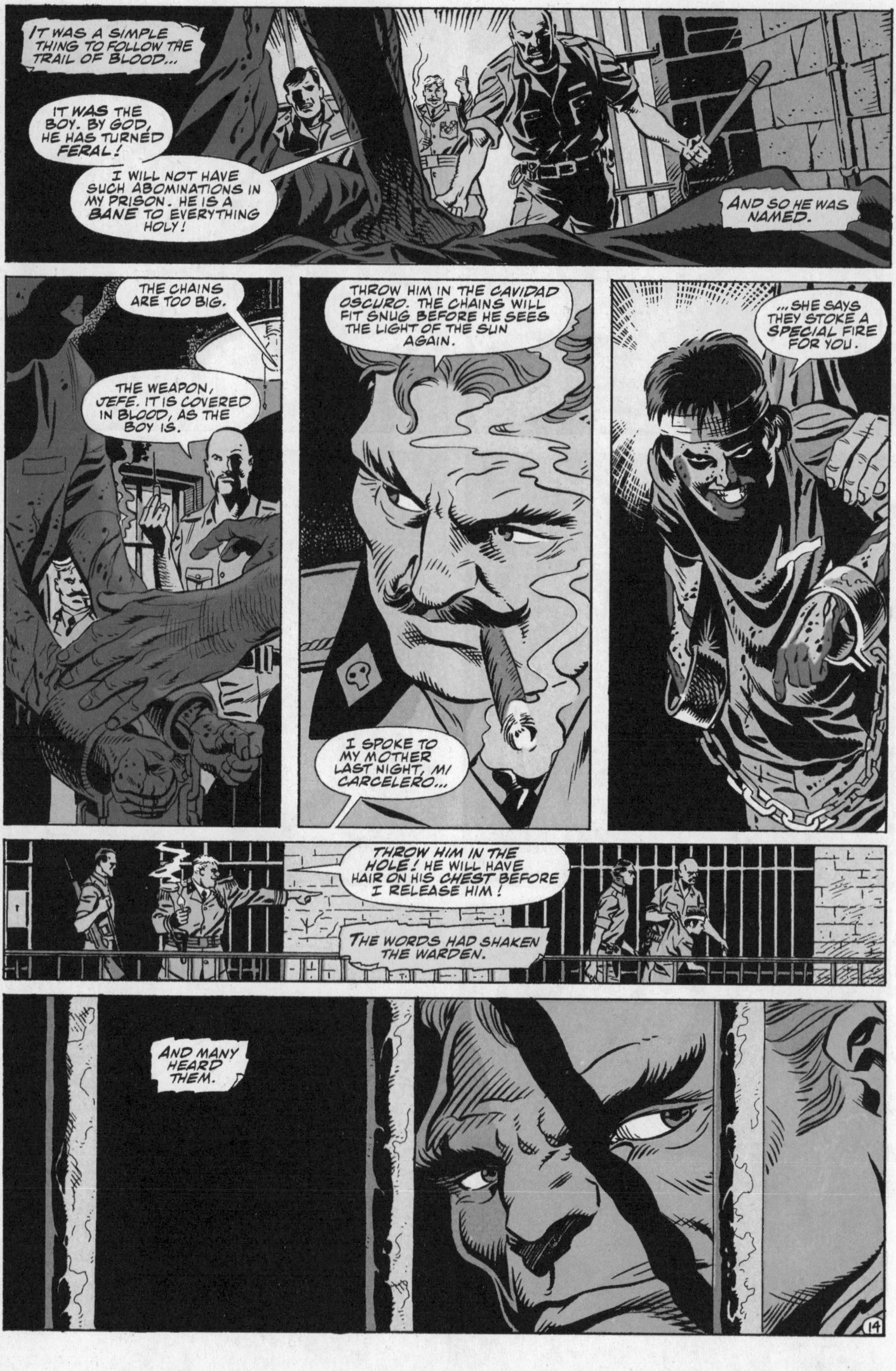
IT WAS A SIMPLE THING TO FOLLOW THE TRAIL OF BLOOD...
IT WAS THE BOY. BY GOD, HE HAS TURNED FERAL!
I WILL NOT HAVE SUCH ABOMINATIONS IN MY PRISON. HE IS A BANE TO EVERYTHING HOLY!
AND SO HE WAS NAMED.
THE CHAINS ARE TOO BIG.
THE WEAPON, JEFE. IT IS COVERED IN BLOOD, AS THE BOY IS.
THROW HIM IN THE CAVIDAD OSCURO. THE CHAINS WILL FIT SNUG BEFORE HE SEES THE LIGHT OF THE SUN AGAIN.
I SPOKE TO MY MOTHER LAST NIGHT, MI CARCELERO...
...SHE SAYS THEY STOKE A SPECIAL FIRE FOR YOU.
THROW HIM IN THE HOLE! HE WILL HAVE HAIR ON HIS CHEST BEFORE I RELEASE HIM!
THE WORDS HAD SHAKEN THE WARDEN.
AND MANY HEARD THEM.
14

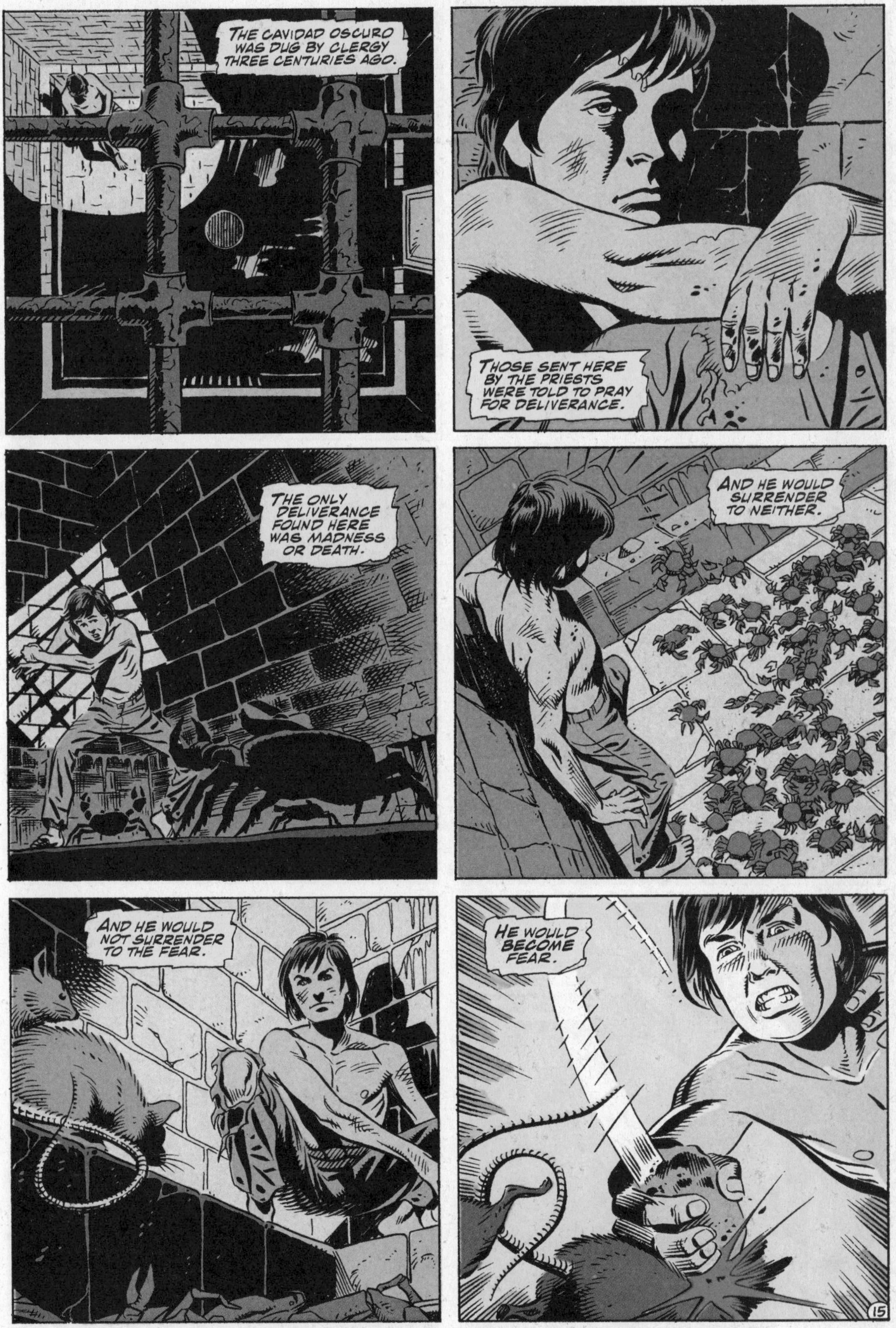
THE CAVIDAD OSCURO WAS DUG BY CLERGY THREE CENTURIES AGO.
THOSE SENT HERE BY THE PRIESTS WERE TOLD TO PRAY FOR DELIVERANCE.
THE ONLY DELIVERANCE FOUND HERE WAS MADNESS OR DEATH.
AND HE WOULD SURRENDER TO NEITHER.
AND HE WOULD NOT SURRENDER TO THE FEAR.
HE WOULD BECOME FEAR.
15

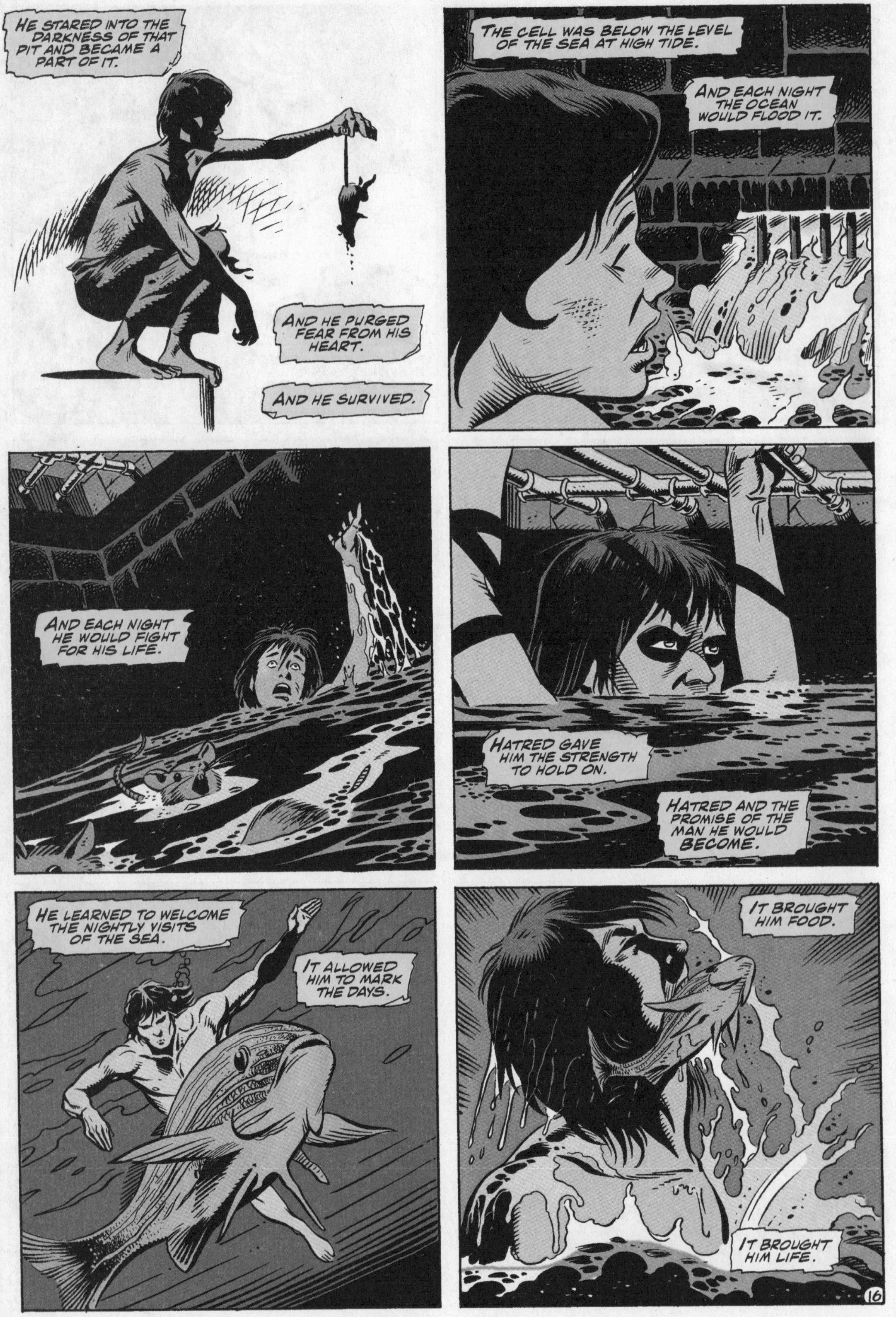
HE STARED INTO THE DARKNESS OF THAT PIT AND BECAME A PART OF IT.
AND HE PURGED FEAR FROM HIS HEART.
AND HE SURVIVED.
THE CELL WAS BELOW THE LEVEL OF THE SEA AT HIGH TIDE.
AND EACH NIGHT THE OCEAN WOULD FLOOD IT.
AND EACH NIGHT HE WOULD FIGHT FOR HIS LIFE.
HATRED GAVE HIM THE STRENGTH TO HOLD ON.
HATRED AND THE PROMISE OF THE MAN HE WOULD BECOME.
HE LEARNED TO WELCOME THE NIGHTLY VISITS OF THE SEA.
IT ALLOWED HIM TO MARK THE DAYS.
IT BROUGHT HIM FOOD.
IT BROUGHT HIM LIFE.
16

AND IN ALL THOSE DAYS HE HEARD NO VOICE BUT HIS OWN.

ANIMALE

WELDED INTO A FIVE-BY-TEN-FOOT CELL.

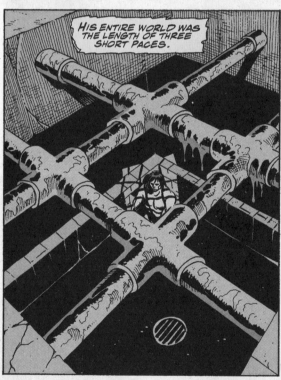

HIS ENTIRE WORLD WAS THE LENGTH OF THREE SHORT PACES.

THEY COULD NOT CONFINE HIS MIND.

IN HIS MIND HE TRAVELLED BEYOND HIS TOMB.

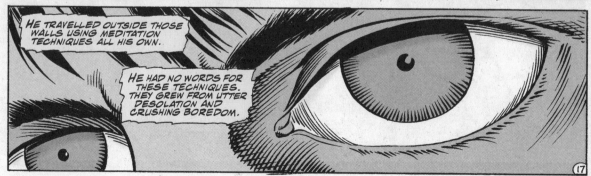

HE TRAVELLED OUTSIDE THOSE WALLS USING MEDITATION TECHNIQUES ALL HIS OWN.

HE HAD NO WORDS FOR THESE TECHNIQUES. THEY GREW FROM UTTER DESOLATION AND CRUSHING BOREDOM.

17

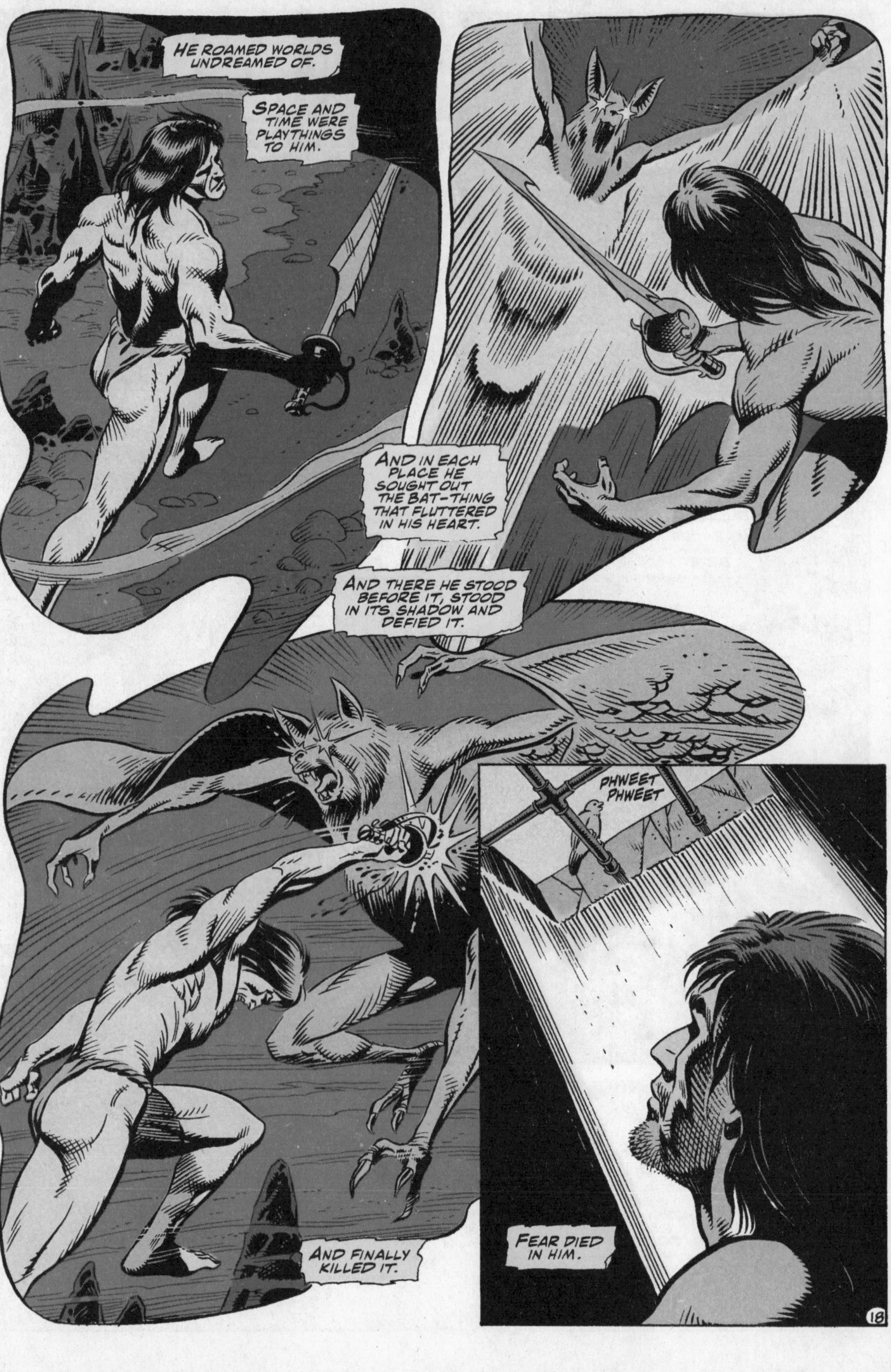
HE ROAMED WORLDS UNDREAMED OF.
SPACE AND TIME WERE PLAYTHINGS TO HIM.
AND IN EACH PLACE HE SOUGHT OUT THE BAT-THING THAT FLUTTERED IN HIS HEART.
AND THERE HE STOOD BEFORE IT, STOOD IN ITS SHADOW AND DEFIED IT.
AND FINALLY KILLED IT.
PHWEET PHWEET
FEAR DIED IN HIM.
18

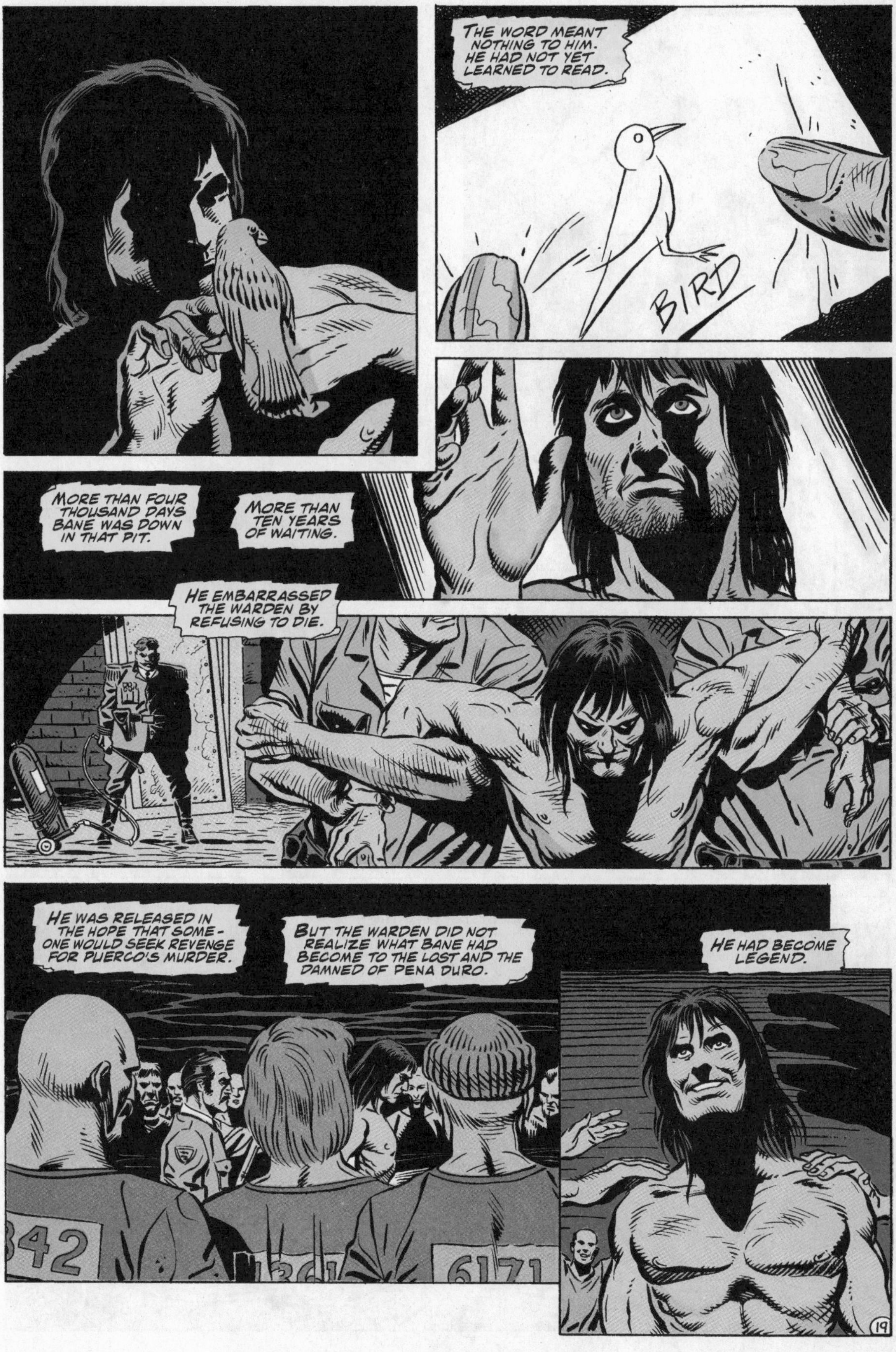
THE WORD MEANT NOTHING TO HIM. HE HAD NOT YET LEARNED TO READ.
BIRD
MORE THAN FOUR THOUSAND DAYS BANE WAS DOWN IN THAT PIT.
MORE THAN TEN YEARS OF WAITING.
HE EMBARRASSED THE WARDEN BY REFUSING TO DIE.
HE WAS RELEASED IN THE HOPE THAT SOME-ONE WOULD SEEK REVENGE FOR PUERCO'S MURDER.
BUT THE WARDEN DID NOT REALIZE WHAT BANE HAD BECOME TO THE LOST AND THE DAMNED OF PENA DURO.
HE HAD BECOME LEGEND.
19

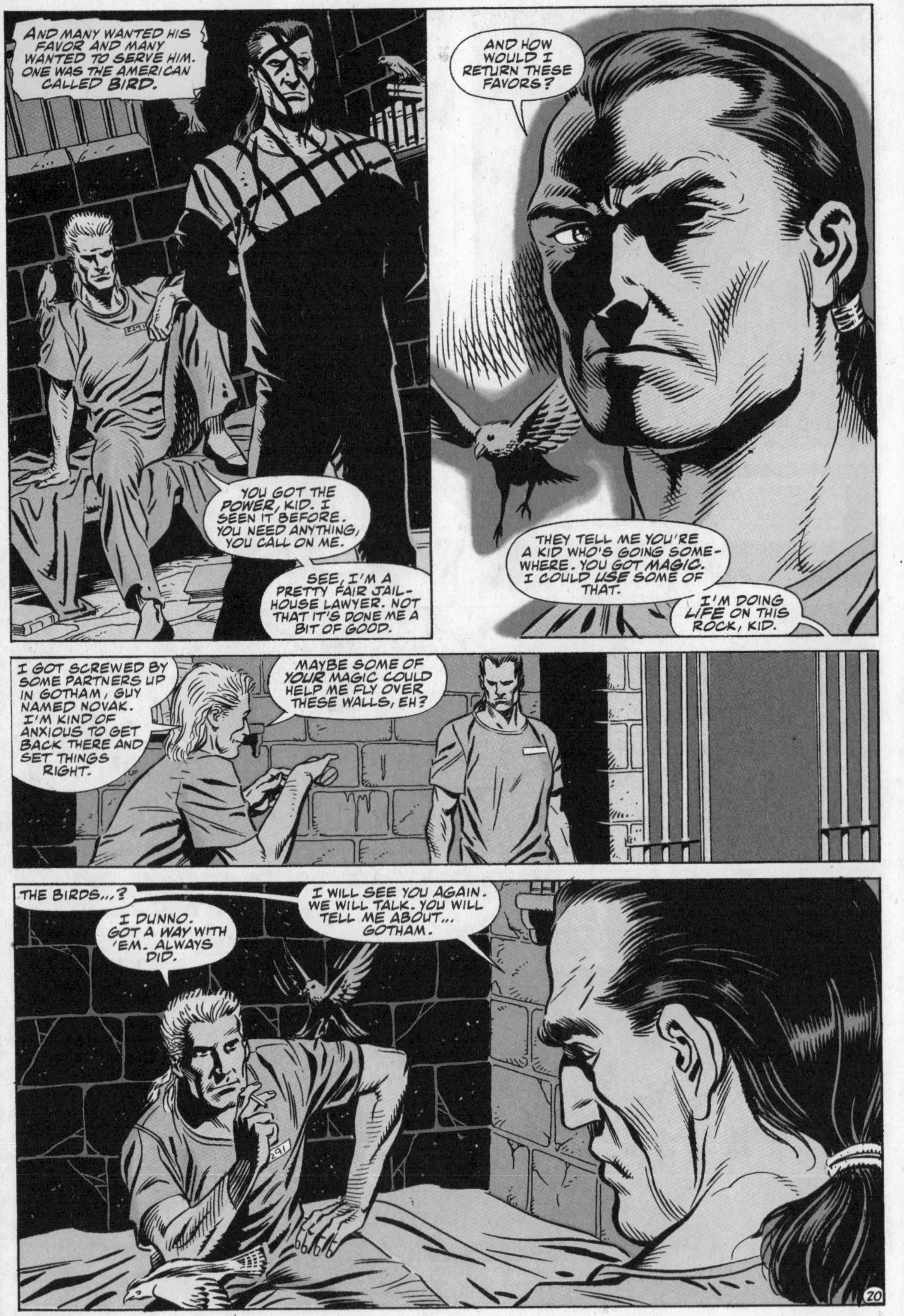
AND MANY WANTED HIS FAVOR AND MANY WANTED TO SERVE HIM. ONE WAS THE AMERICAN CALLED BIRD.
YOU GOT THE POWER, KID. I SEEN IT BEFORE. YOU NEED ANYTHING, YOU CALL ON ME.
SEE, I'M A PRETTY FAIR JAIL-HOUSE LAWYER. NOT THAT IT'S DONE ME A BIT OF GOOD.
AND HOW WOULD I RETURN THESE FAVORS?
THEY TELL ME YOU'RE A KID WHO'S GOING SOME-WHERE. YOU GOT MAGIC. I COULD USE SOME OF THAT.
I'M DOING LIFE ON THIS ROCK, KID.
I GOT SCREWED BY SOME PARTNERS UP IN GOTHAM, GUY NAMED NOVAK. I'M KIND OF ANXIOUS TO GET BACK THERE AND SET THINGS RIGHT.
MAYBE SOME OF YOUR MAGIC COULD HELP ME FLY OVER THESE WALLS, EH?
THE BIRDS...?
I DUNNO. GOT A WAY WITH 'EM. ALWAYS DID.
I WILL SEE YOU AGAIN. WE WILL TALK. YOU WILL TELL ME ABOUT... GOTHAM.
20

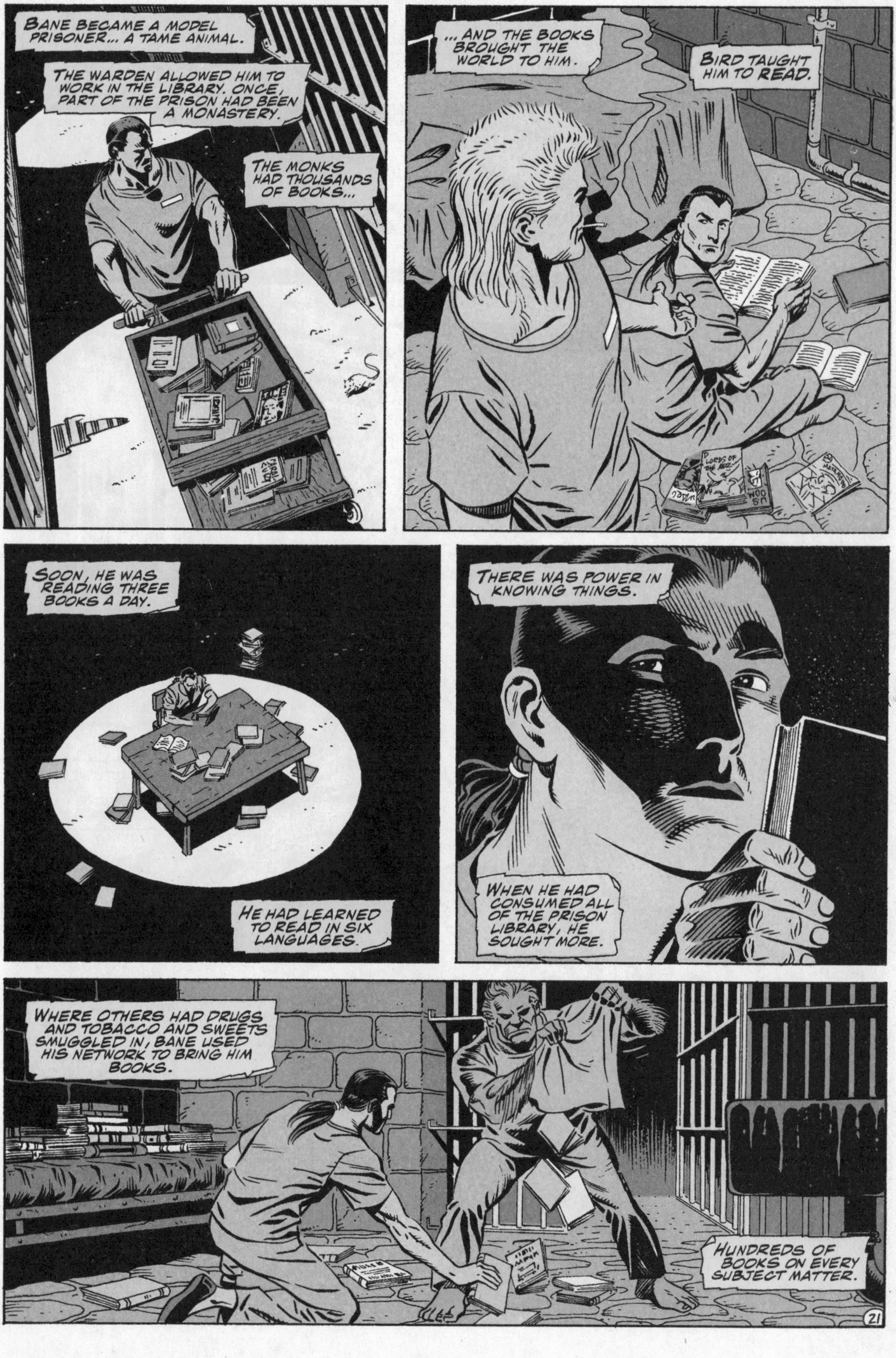
BANE BECAME A MODEL PRISONER... A TAME ANIMAL.
THE WARDEN ALLOWED HIM TO WORK IN THE LIBRARY. ONCE, PART OF THE PRISON HAD BEEN A MONASTERY.
THE MONKS HAD THOUSANDS OF BOOKS...
...AND THE BOOKS BROUGHT THE WORLD TO HIM.
BIRD TAUGHT HIM TO READ.
SOON, HE WAS READING THREE BOOKS A DAY.
HE HAD LEARNED TO READ IN SIX LANGUAGES.
THERE WAS POWER IN KNOWING THINGS.
WHEN HE HAD CONSUMED ALL OF THE PRISON LIBRARY, HE SOUGHT MORE.
WHERE OTHERS HAD DRUGS AND TOBACCO AND SWEETS SMUGGLED IN, BANE USED HIS NETWORK TO BRING HIM BOOKS.
HUNDREDS OF BOOKS ON EVERY SUBJECT MATTER.
21

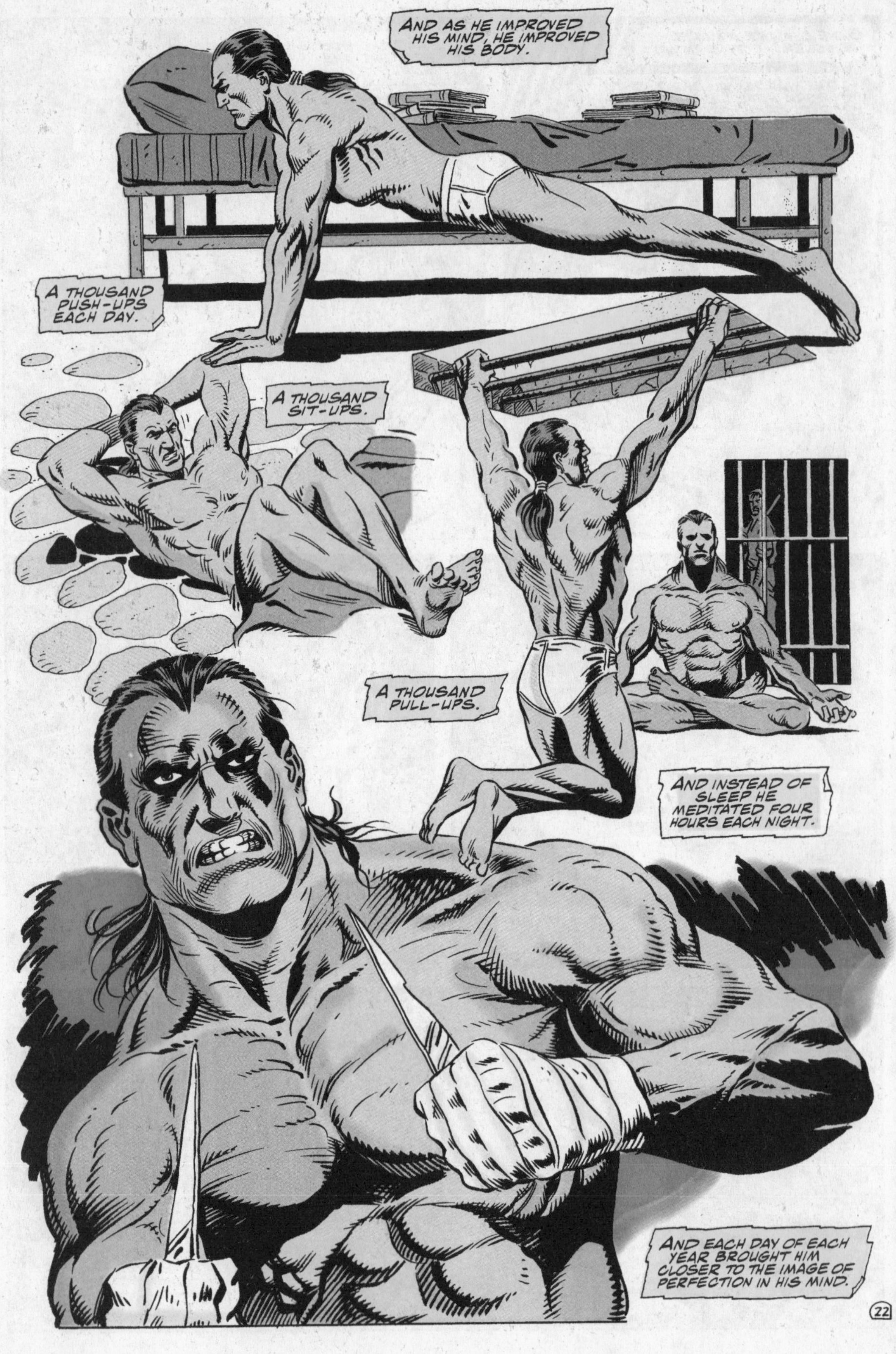
AND AS HE IMPROVED HIS MIND, HE IMPROVED HIS BODY.
A THOUSAND PUSH-UPS EACH DAY.
A THOUSAND SIT-UPS.
A THOUSAND PULL-UPS.
AND INSTEAD OF SLEEP HE MEDITATED FOUR HOURS EACH NIGHT.
AND EACH DAY OF EACH YEAR BROUGHT HIM CLOSER TO THE IMAGE OF PERFECTION IN HIS MIND.
22

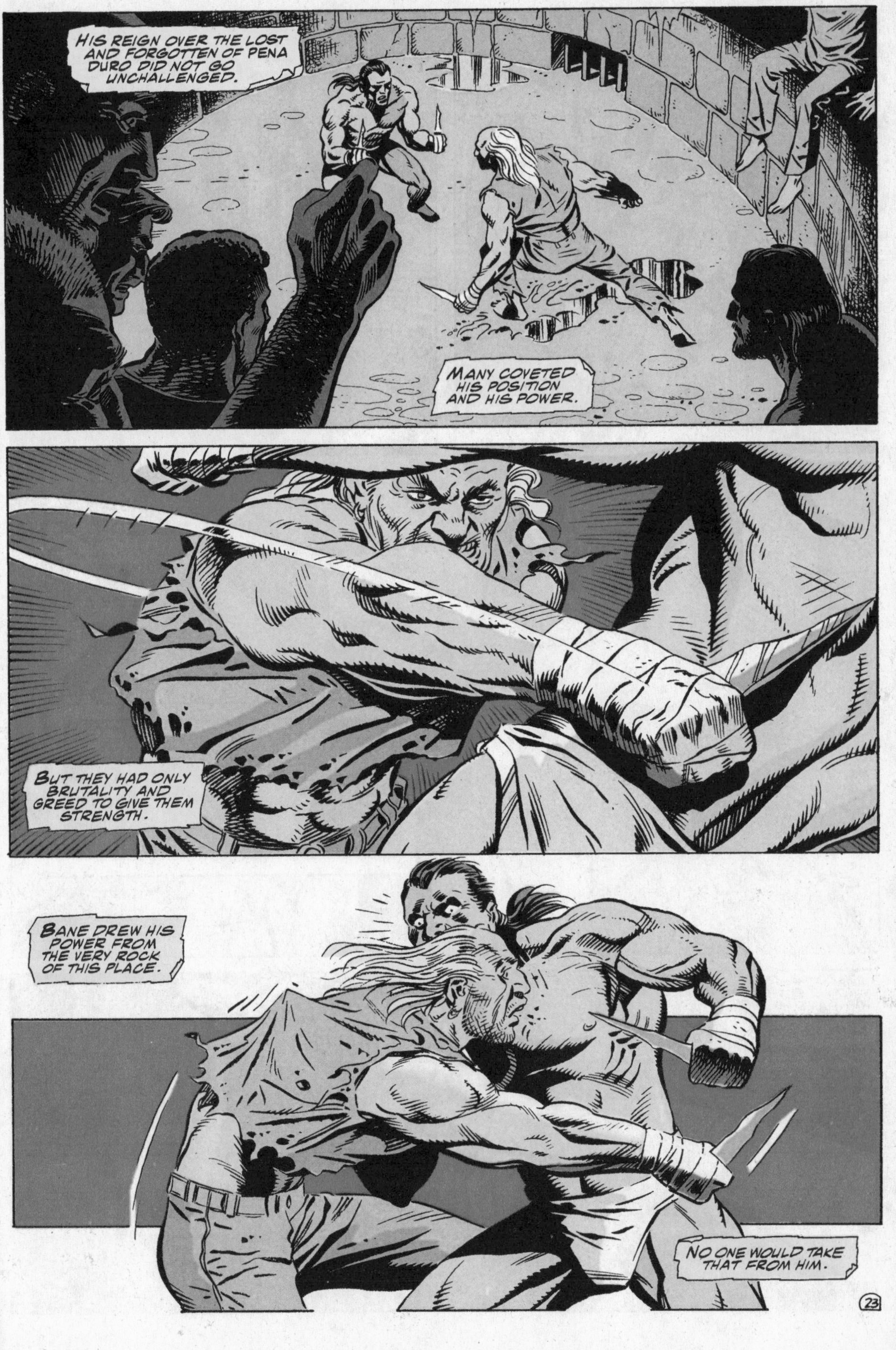
HIS REIGN OVER THE LOST AND FORGOTTEN OF PENA DURO DID NOT GO UNCHALLENGED.
MANY COVETED HIS POSITION AND HIS POWER.
BUT THEY HAD ONLY BRUTALITY AND GREED TO GIVE THEM STRENGTH.
BANE DREW HIS POWER FROM THE VERY ROCK OF THIS PLACE.
NO ONE WOULD TAKE THAT FROM HIM.
23

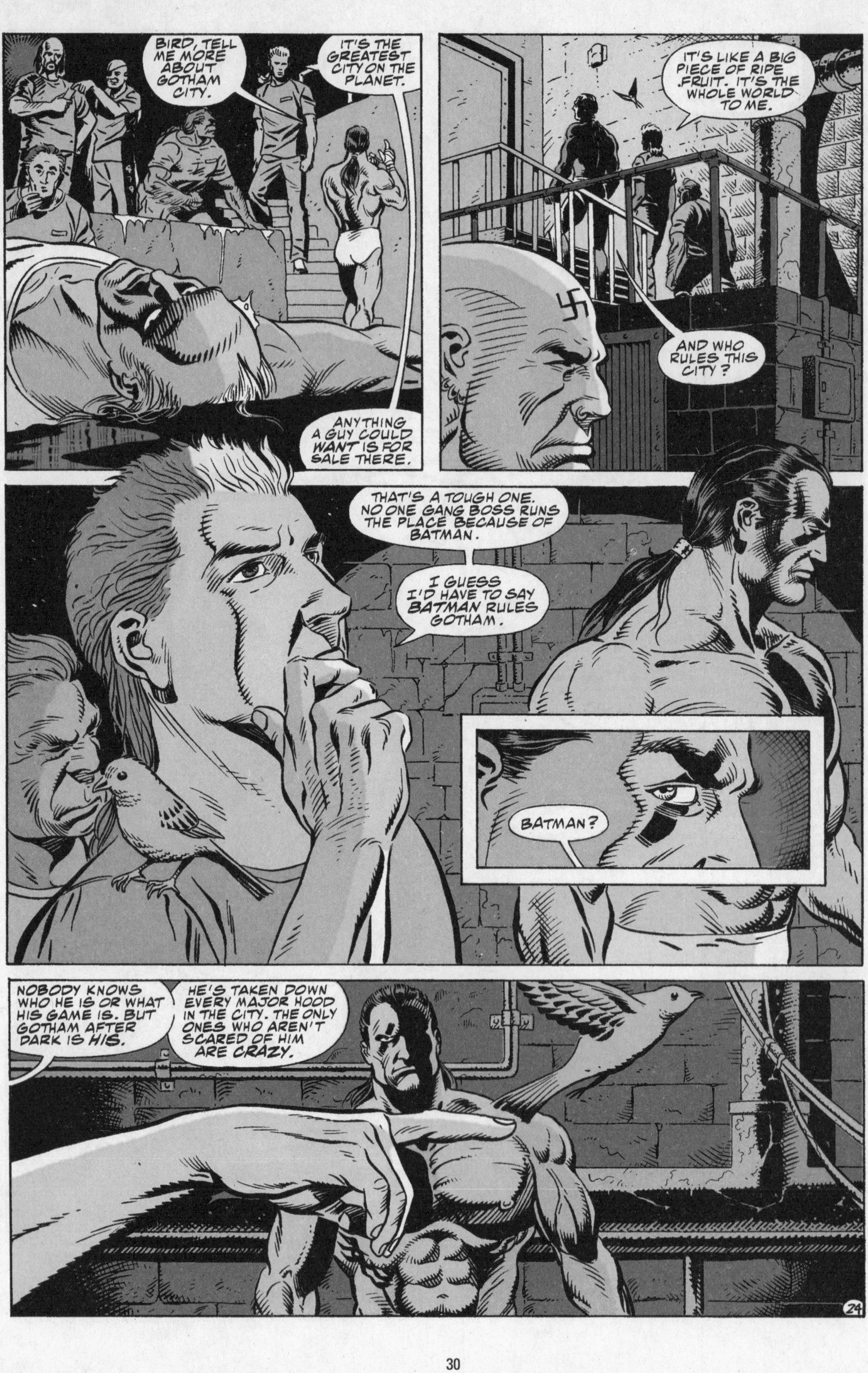
BIRD, TELL ME MORE ABOUT GOTHAM CITY.
IT'S THE GREATEST CITY ON THE PLANET.
ANYTHING A GUY COULD WANT IS FOR SALE THERE.
IT'S LIKE A BIG PIECE OF RIPE FRUIT. IT'S THE WHOLE WORLD TO ME.
AND WHO RULES THIS CITY?
THAT'S A TOUGH ONE. NO ONE GANG BOSS RUNS THE PLACE BECAUSE OF BATMAN.
I GUESS I'D HAVE TO SAY BATMAN RULES GOTHAM.
BATMAN?
NOBODY KNOWS WHO HE IS OR WHAT HIS GAME IS. BUT GOTHAM AFTER DARK IS HIS.
HE'S TAKEN DOWN EVERY MAJOR HOOD IN THE CITY. THE ONLY ONES WHO AREN'T SCARED OF HIM ARE CRAZY.
24

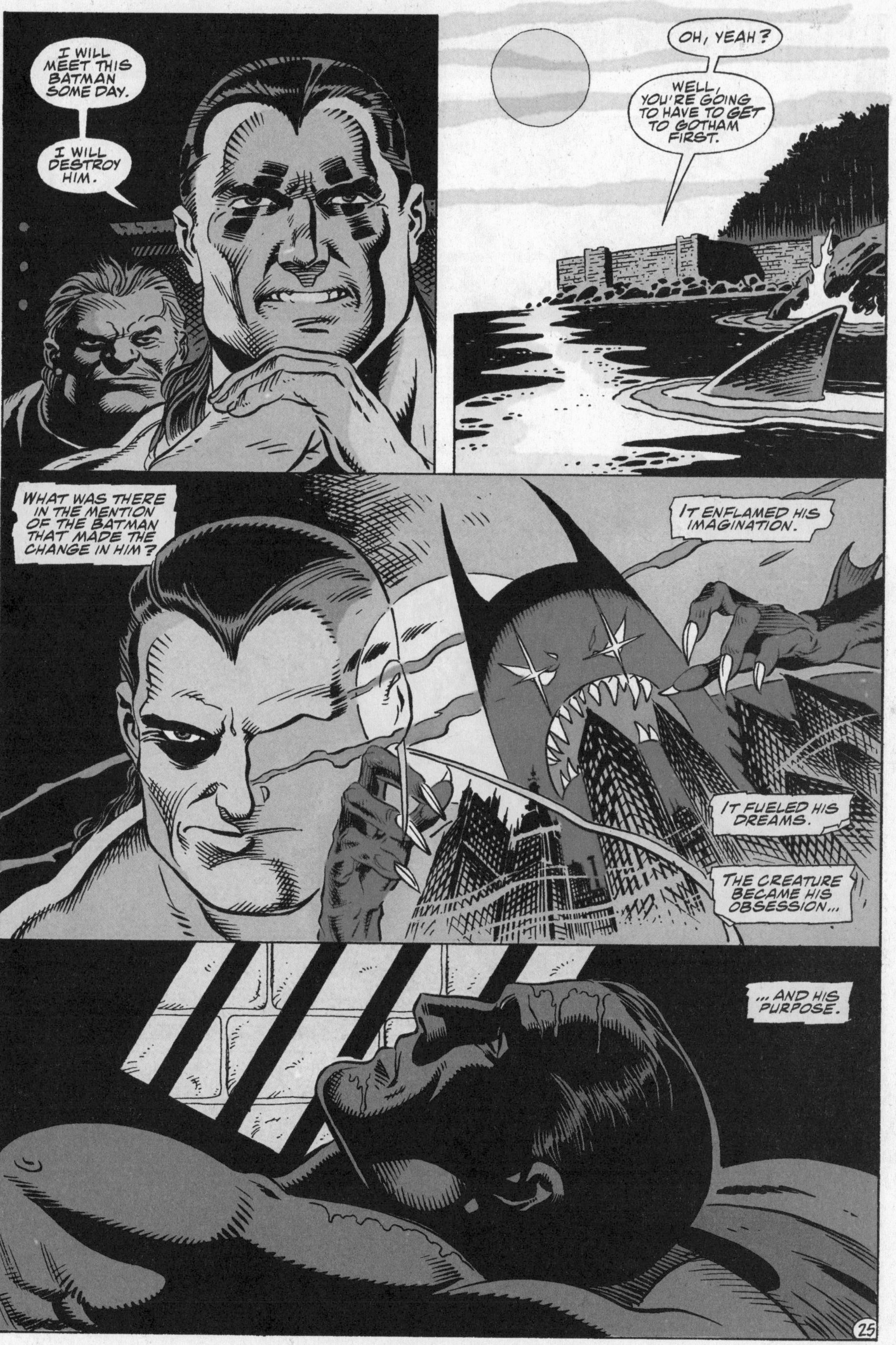
I WILL MEET THIS BATMAN SOME DAY.
I WILL DESTROY HIM.
OH, YEAH?
WELL, YOU'RE GOING TO HAVE TO GET TO GOTHAM FIRST.
WHAT WAS THERE IN THE MENTION OF THE BATMAN THAT MADE THE CHANGE IN HIM?
IT ENFLAMED HIS IMAGINATION.
IT FUELED HIS DREAMS.
THE CREATURE BECAME HIS OBSESSION...
...AND HIS PURPOSE.
25

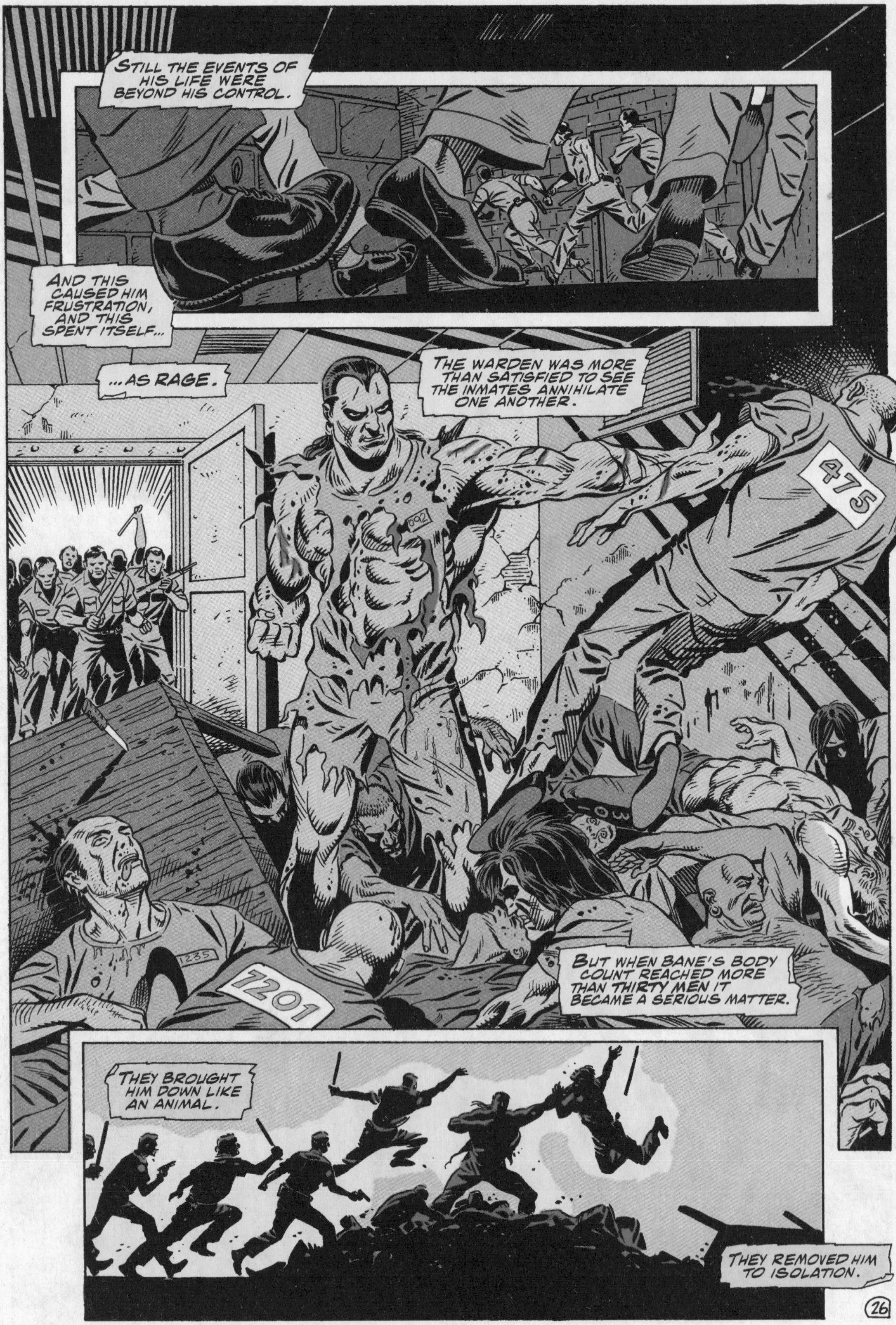

STILL THE EVENTS OF HIS LIFE WERE BEYOND HIS CONTROL.
AND THIS CAUSED HIM FRUSTRATION, AND THIS SPENT ITSELF...
...AS RAGE.
THE WARDEN WAS MORE THAN SATISFIED TO SEE THE INMATES ANNIHILATE ONE ANOTHER.
0092
475
1235
7201
BUT WHEN BANE'S BODY COUNT REACHED MORE THAN THIRTY MEN IT BECAME A SERIOUS MATTER.
THEY BROUGHT HIM DOWN LIKE AN ANIMAL.
THEY REMOVED HIM TO ISOLATION.
26

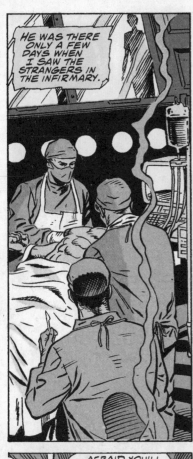

HE WAS THERE ONLY A FEW DAYS WHEN I SAW THE STRANGERS IN THE INFIRMARY.

THIS IS THE FIFTH INMATE WHO HAS DIED FROM THESE INJECTIONS.

WHAT IS THE *OBJECT* OF THESE EXPERIMENTS?

A NEW NERVE TOXIN? THE FORMULA FOR A *SUPER SOLDIER?* SOME MILITARY APPLICATION, I'M CERTAIN.

WHAT IS *YOUR* CONCERN...

...AFRAID YOU'LL RUN OUT OF PRISONERS?

DEAD. THE CRETIN'S HEART EXPLODED.

I'LL NEED ANOTHER SUBJECT IMMEDIATELY. CAN YOU GET ME A *STRONG* ONE THIS TIME, WARDEN? ONE THAT WILL LAST *MORE* THAN THREE DAYS?

I HAVE JUST SUCH A MAN IN ISOLATION AT THE MOMENT.

27

I COULD NOT GET TO BANE TO WARN HIM.

WHAT COULD HE HAVE DONE IN ANY CASE?

THE LAB BUILDING WAS NEW, BUILT BY THE ARMY TO HOUSE THIS EXPERIMENT.

THEY HAD ALREADY KILLED FIVE MEN WITH THEIR DRUGS.

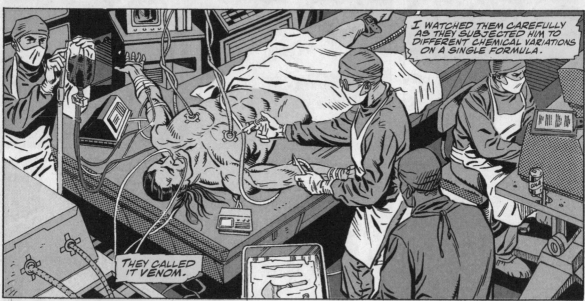

I WATCHED THEM CAREFULLY AS THEY SUBJECTED HIM TO DIFFERENT CHEMICAL VARIATIONS ON A SINGLE FORMULA.

THEY CALLED IT VENOM.

HIS BODY REBELLED AGAINST THE SERIES OF INJECTIONS-- REBELLED AND TRIUMPHED.

SO EASY TO OBTAIN A SAMPLE OF THE DRUG WHILE BANE PROVIDED A DISTRACTION.

28

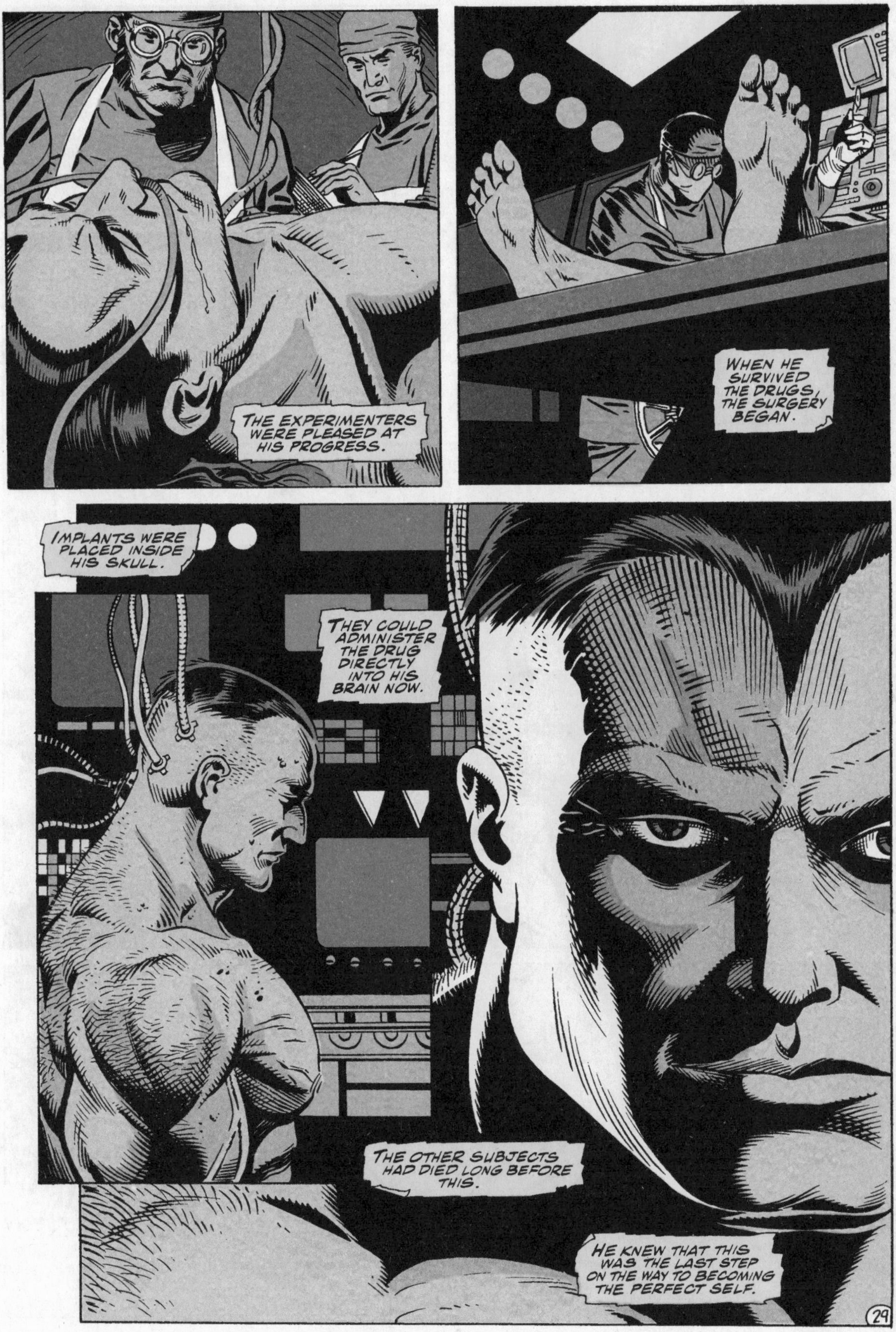
THE EXPERIMENTERS WERE PLEASED AT HIS PROGRESS.
WHEN HE SURVIVED THE DRUGS, THE SURGERY BEGAN.
IMPLANTS WERE PLACED INSIDE HIS SKULL.
THEY COULD ADMINISTER THE DRUG DIRECTLY INTO HIS BRAIN NOW.
THE OTHER SUBJECTS HAD DIED LONG BEFORE THIS.
HE KNEW THAT THIS WAS THE LAST STEP ON THE WAY TO BECOMING THE PERFECT SELF.
29

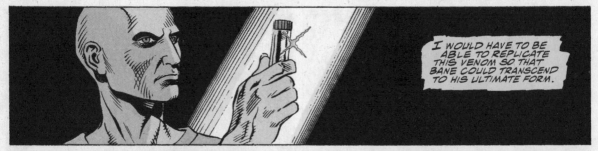

I WOULD HAVE TO BE ABLE TO REPLICATE THIS VENOM SO THAT BANE COULD TRANSCEND TO HIS ULTIMATE FORM.

I HAD DONE THIS MANY TIMES IN DESIGNING NARCOTICS FOR MY FORMER EMPLOYERS.

BUT NEVER HAD I SEEN ANY COMBINATION SO COMPLEX. COMPLEX, BUT EASILY COPIED.

A SUPER STEROID DERIVED FROM A DRUG CODE-NAMED VENOM.

IT ALSO CONTAINED ELEMENTS THAT WOULD STIMULATE THE ADRENAL GLANDS.

ANOTHER INGREDIENT TARGETED THE CORPUS CALLOSUM SEGMENT OF THE BRAIN.

THIS DRUG WOULD ULTIMATELY FUSE THE RIGHT AND LEFT HEMISPHERES OF THE BRAIN.

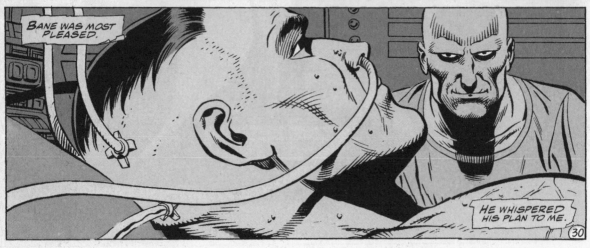

BANE WAS MOST PLEASED.

HE WHISPERED HIS PLAN TO ME.

30

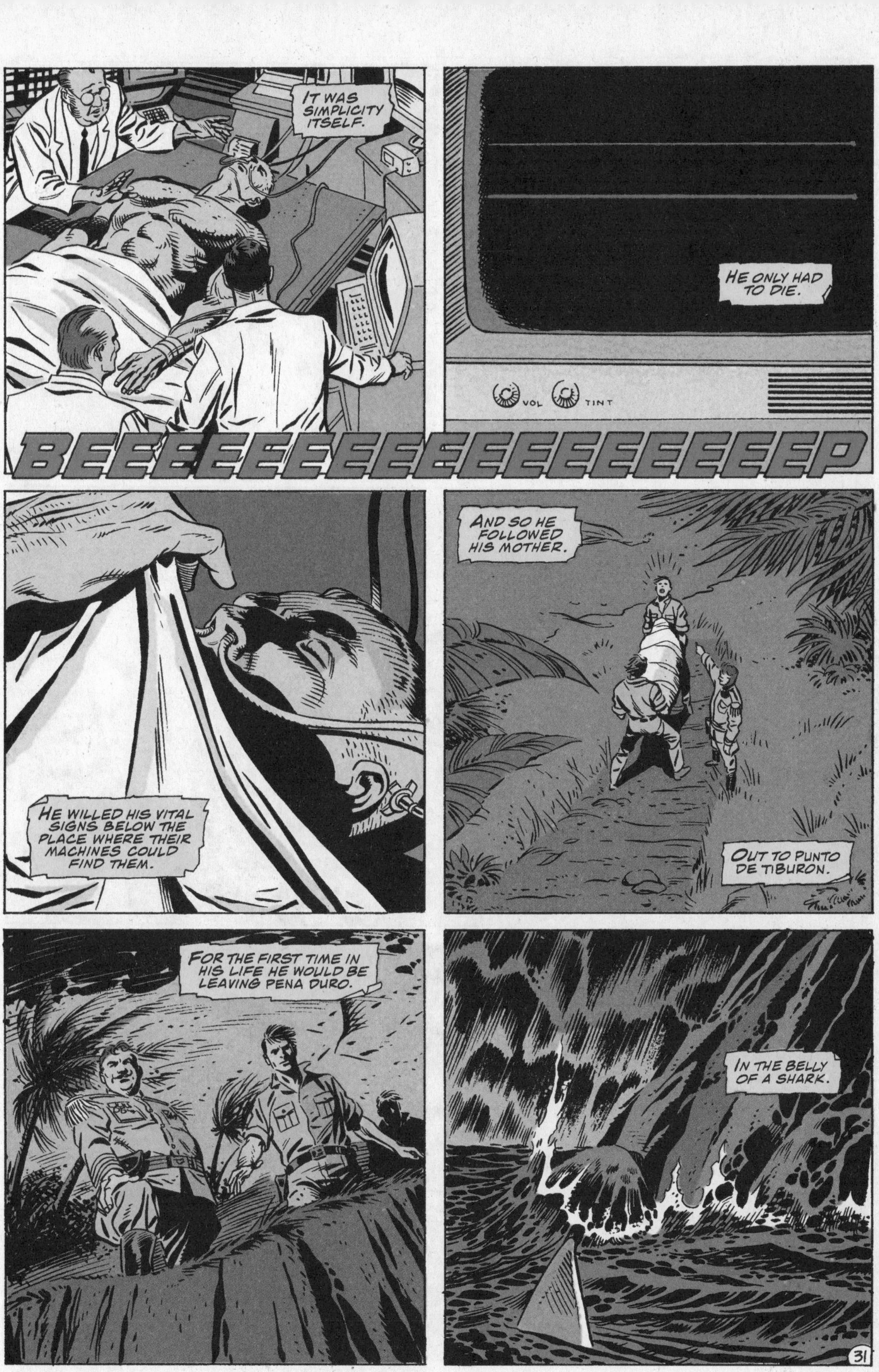
IT WAS SIMPLICITY ITSELF.
HE ONLY HAD TO DIE.
VOL
TINT
BEEEEEEEEEEEEEEEEEP
HE WILLED HIS VITAL SIGNS BELOW THE PLACE WHERE THEIR MACHINES COULD FIND THEM.
AND SO HE FOLLOWED HIS MOTHER.
OUT TO PUNTO DE TIBURON.
FOR THE FIRST TIME IN HIS LIFE HE WOULD BE LEAVING PENA DURO.
IN THE BELLY OF A SHARK.
31

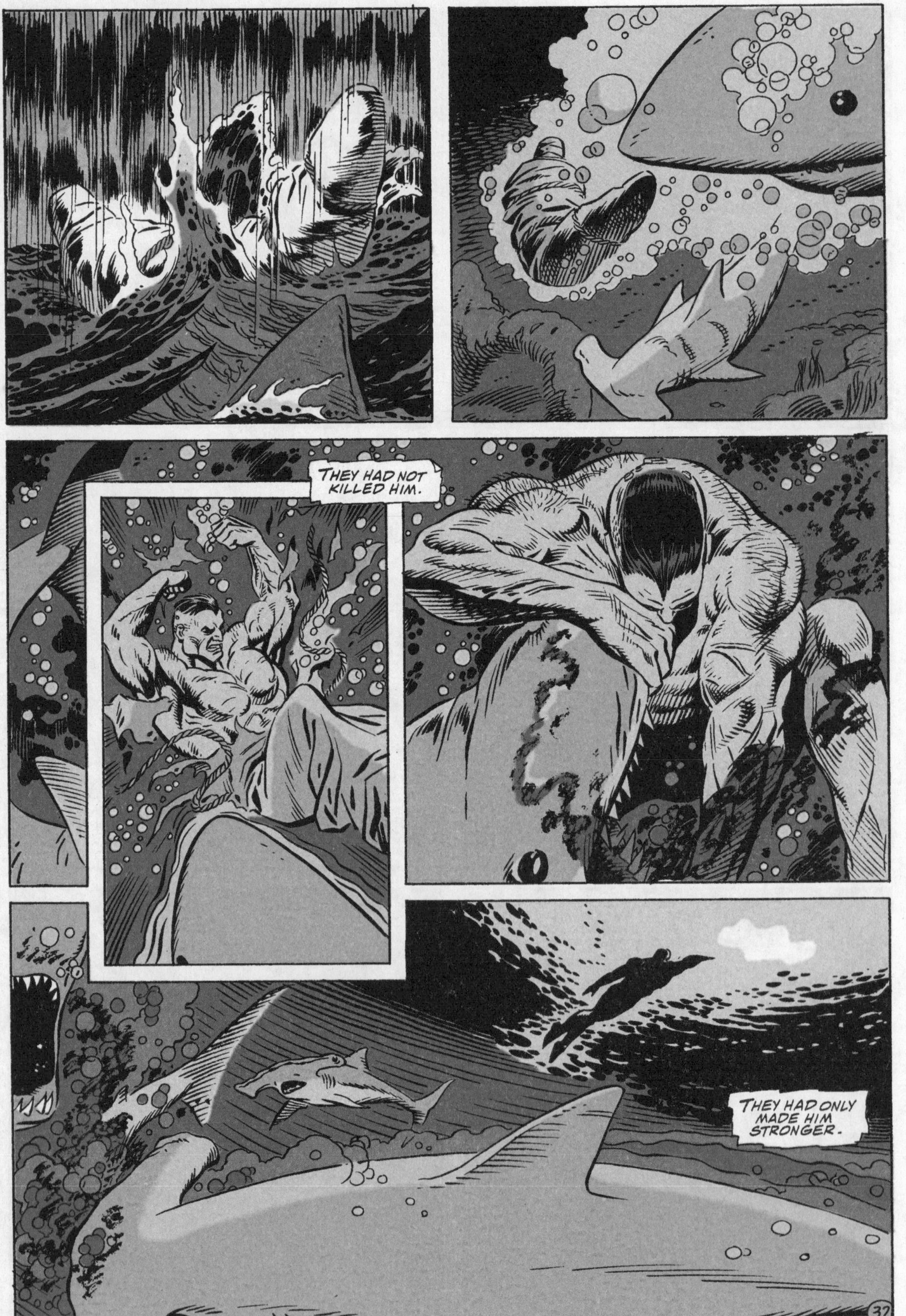
THEY HAD NOT KILLED HIM.
THEY HAD ONLY MADE HIM STRONGER.
32

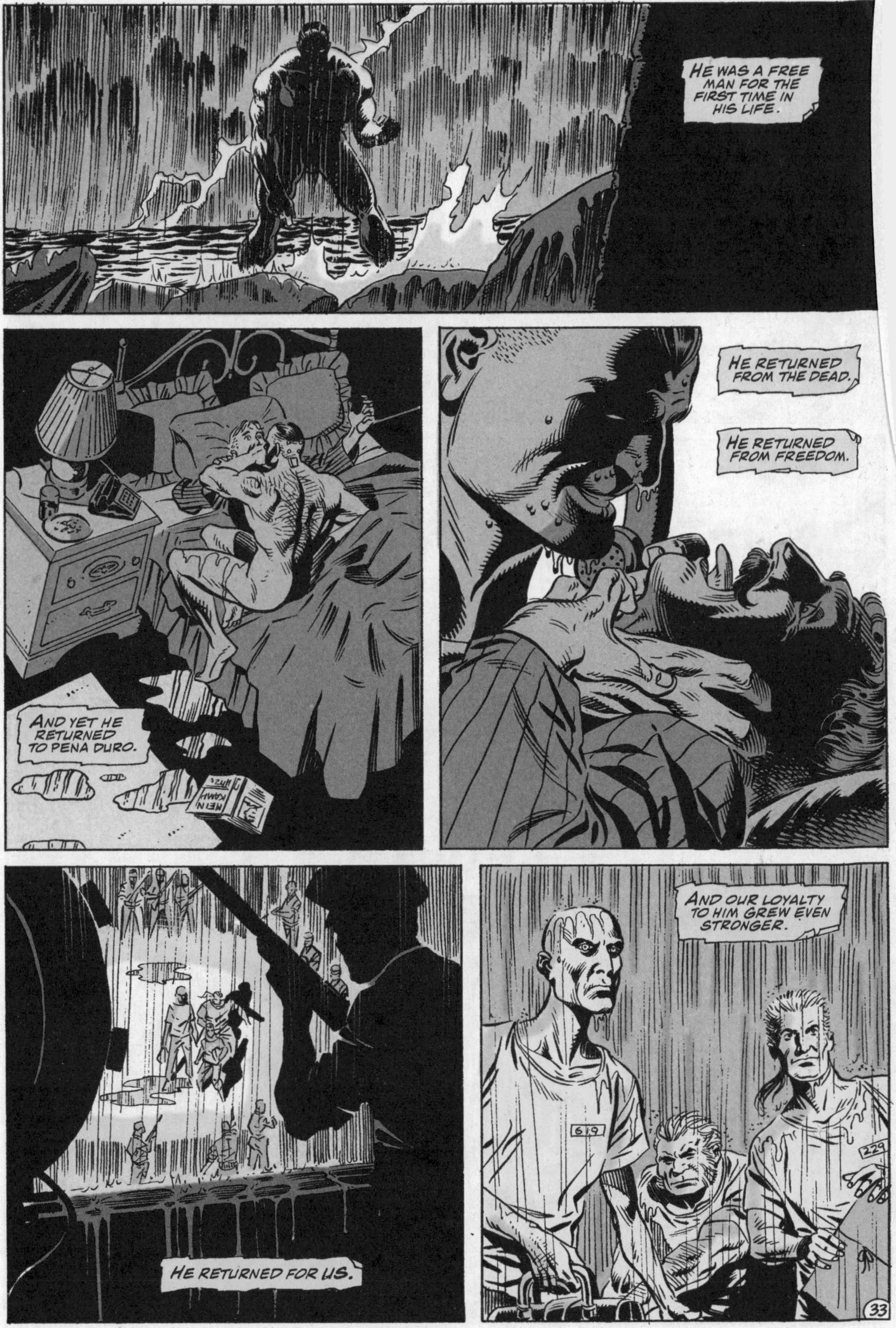
HE WAS A FREE MAN FOR THE FIRST TIME IN HIS LIFE.
AND YET HE RETURNED TO PENA DURO.
HE RETURNED FROM THE DEAD.
HE RETURNED FROM FREEDOM.
HE RETURNED FOR US.
AND OUR LOYALTY TO HIM GREW EVEN STRONGER.
619
229
33

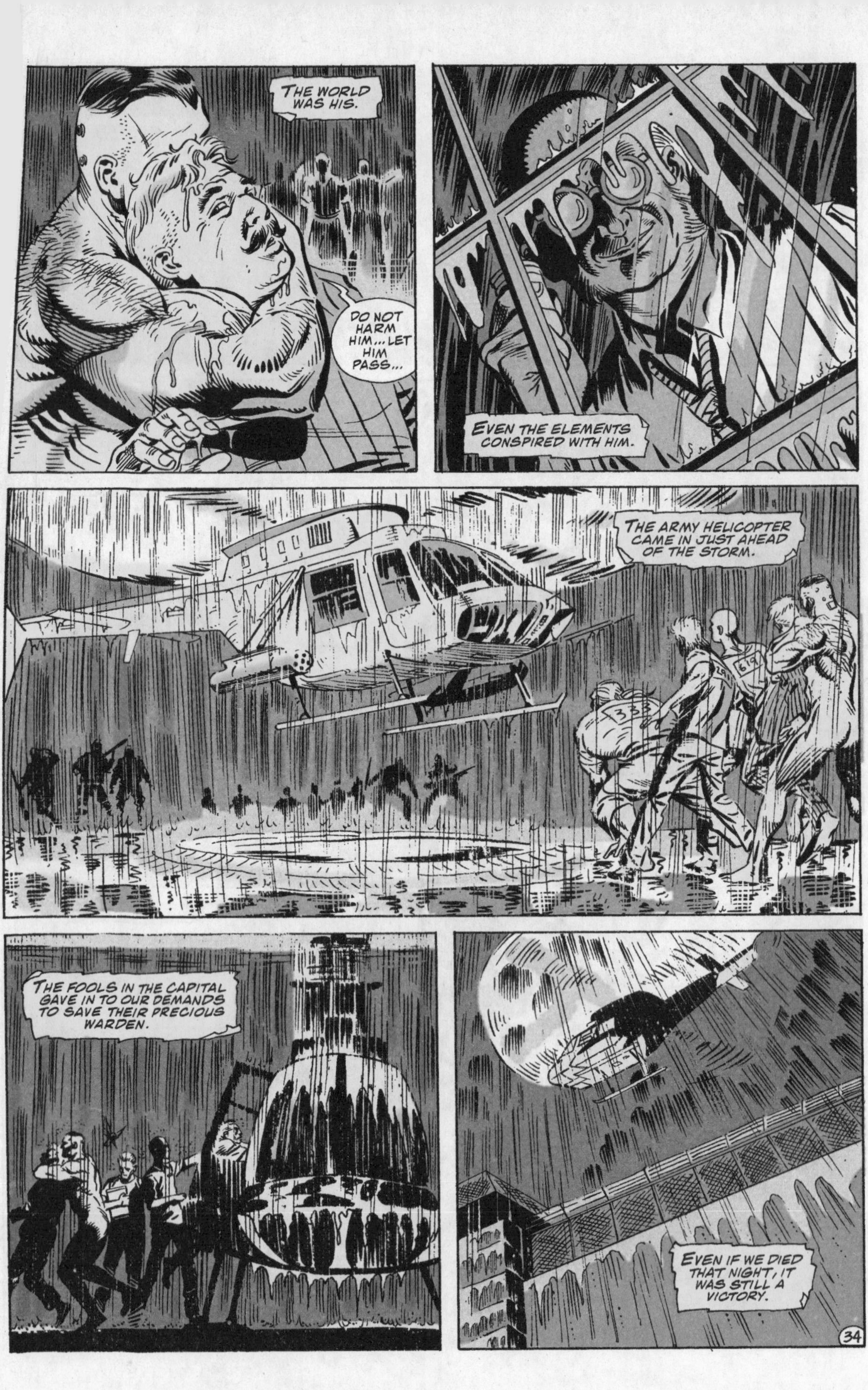
THE WORLD WAS HIS.
DO NOT HARM HIM... LET HIM PASS...
EVEN THE ELEMENTS CONSPIRED WITH HIM.
THE ARMY HELICOPTER CAME IN JUST AHEAD OF THE STORM.
THE FOOLS IN THE CAPITAL GAVE IN TO OUR DEMANDS TO SAVE THEIR PRECIOUS WARDEN.
EVEN IF WE DIED THAT NIGHT, IT WAS STILL A VICTORY.
34

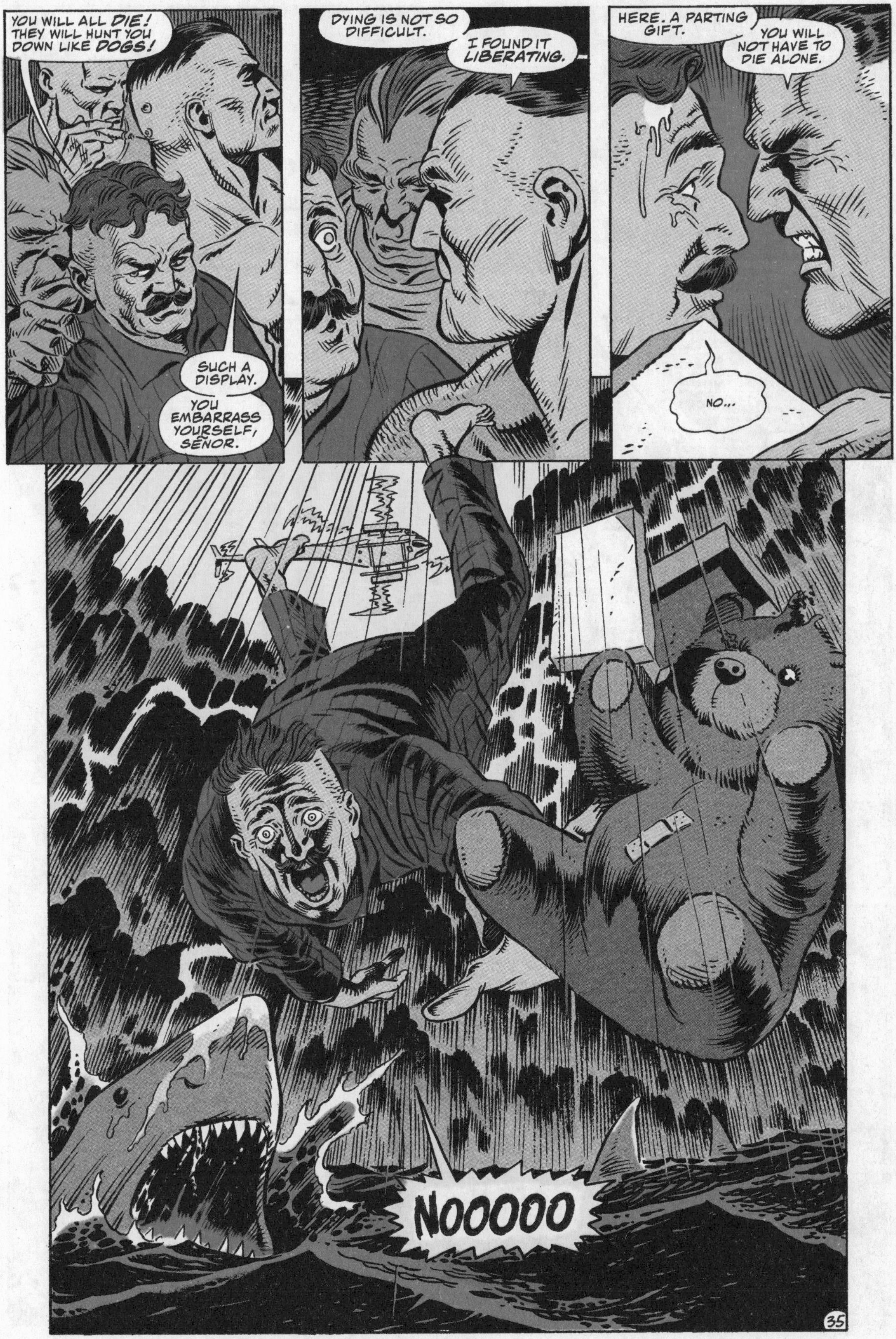
YOU WILL ALL DIE! THEY WILL HUNT YOU DOWN LIKE DOGS!
SUCH A DISPLAY.
YOU EMBARRASS YOURSELF, SEÑOR.
DYING IS NOT SO DIFFICULT.
I FOUND IT LIBERATING.
HERE. A PARTING GIFT.
YOU WILL NOT HAVE TO DIE ALONE.
NO...
NOOOOO
35

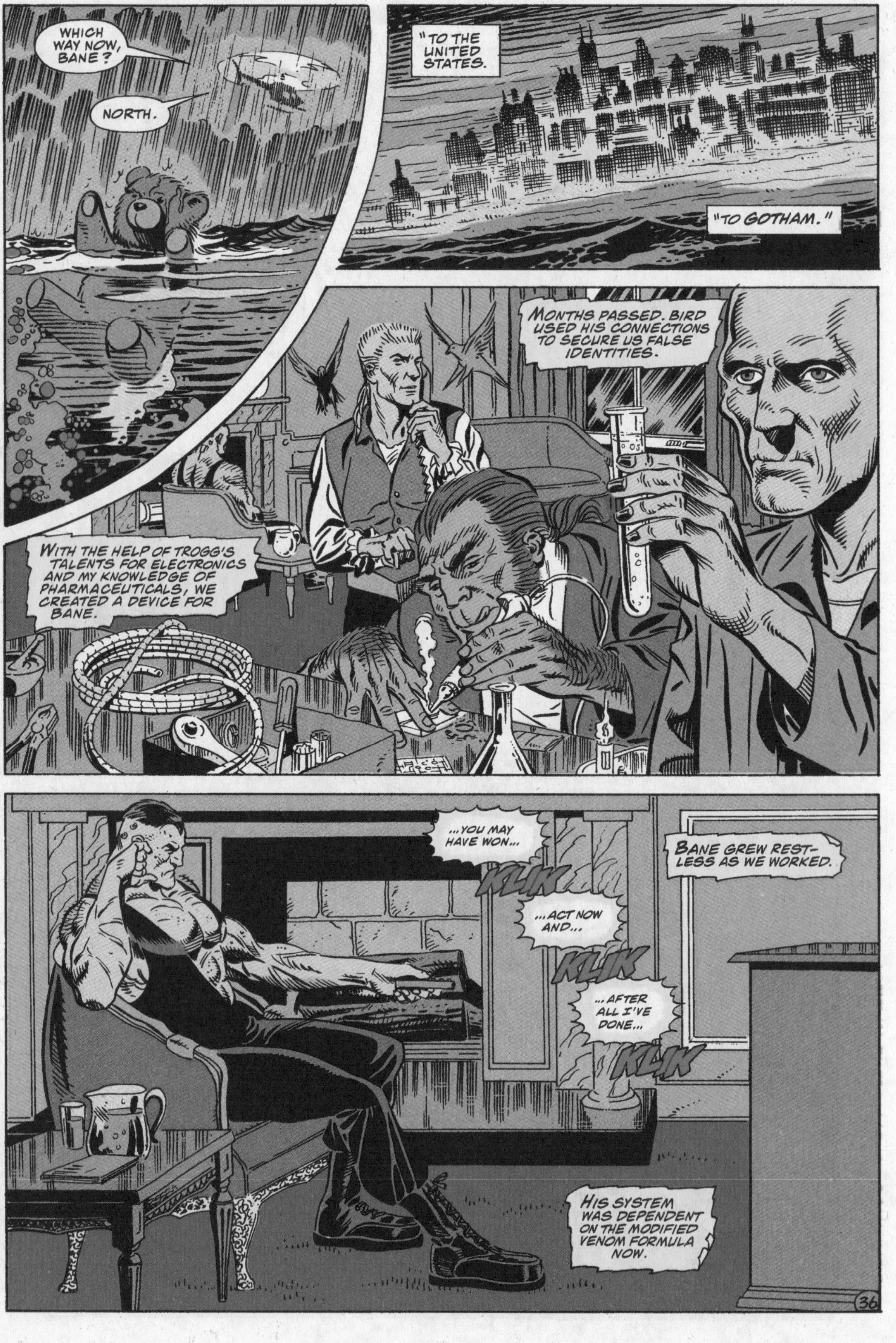
WHICH WAY NOW, BANE?
NORTH.
"TO THE UNITED STATES.
"TO GOTHAM."
MONTHS PASSED. BIRD USED HIS CONNECTIONS TO SECURE US FALSE IDENTITIES.
WITH THE HELP OF TROGG'S TALENTS FOR ELECTRONICS AND MY KNOWLEDGE OF PHARMACEUTICALS, WE CREATED A DEVICE FOR BANE.
BANE GREW RESTLESS AS WE WORKED.
...YOU MAY HAVE WON...
KLIK
...ACT NOW AND...
KLIK
...AFTER ALL I'VE DONE...
KLIK
HIS SYSTEM WAS DEPENDENT ON THE MODIFIED VENOM FORMULA NOW.
36

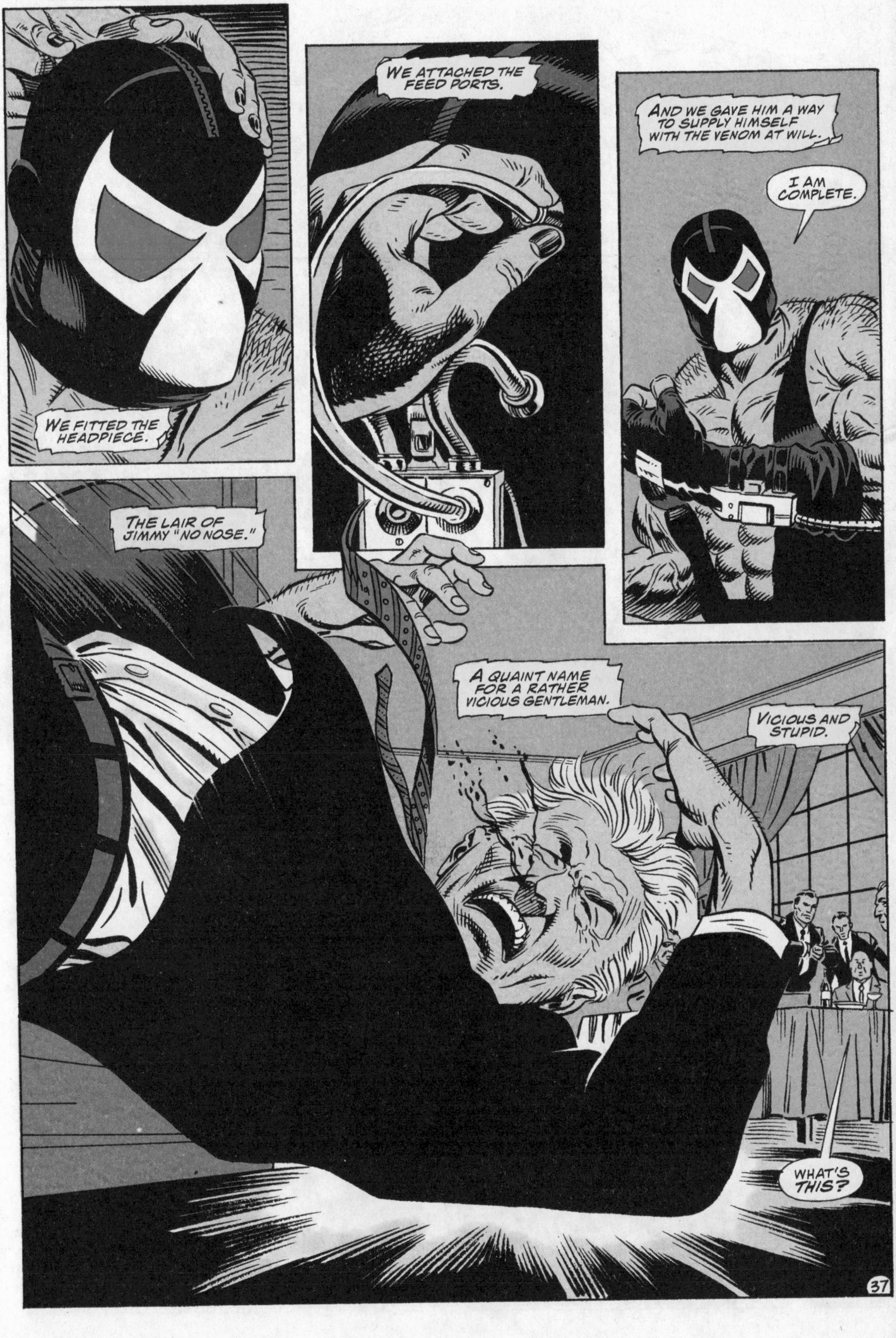
WE FITTED THE HEADPIECE.
WE ATTACHED THE FEED PORTS.
AND WE GAVE HIM A WAY TO SUPPLY HIMSELF WITH THE VENOM AT WILL.
I AM COMPLETE.
THE LAIR OF JIMMY "NO NOSE."
A QUAINT NAME FOR A RATHER VICIOUS GENTLEMAN.
VICIOUS AND STUPID.
WHAT'S THIS?
37

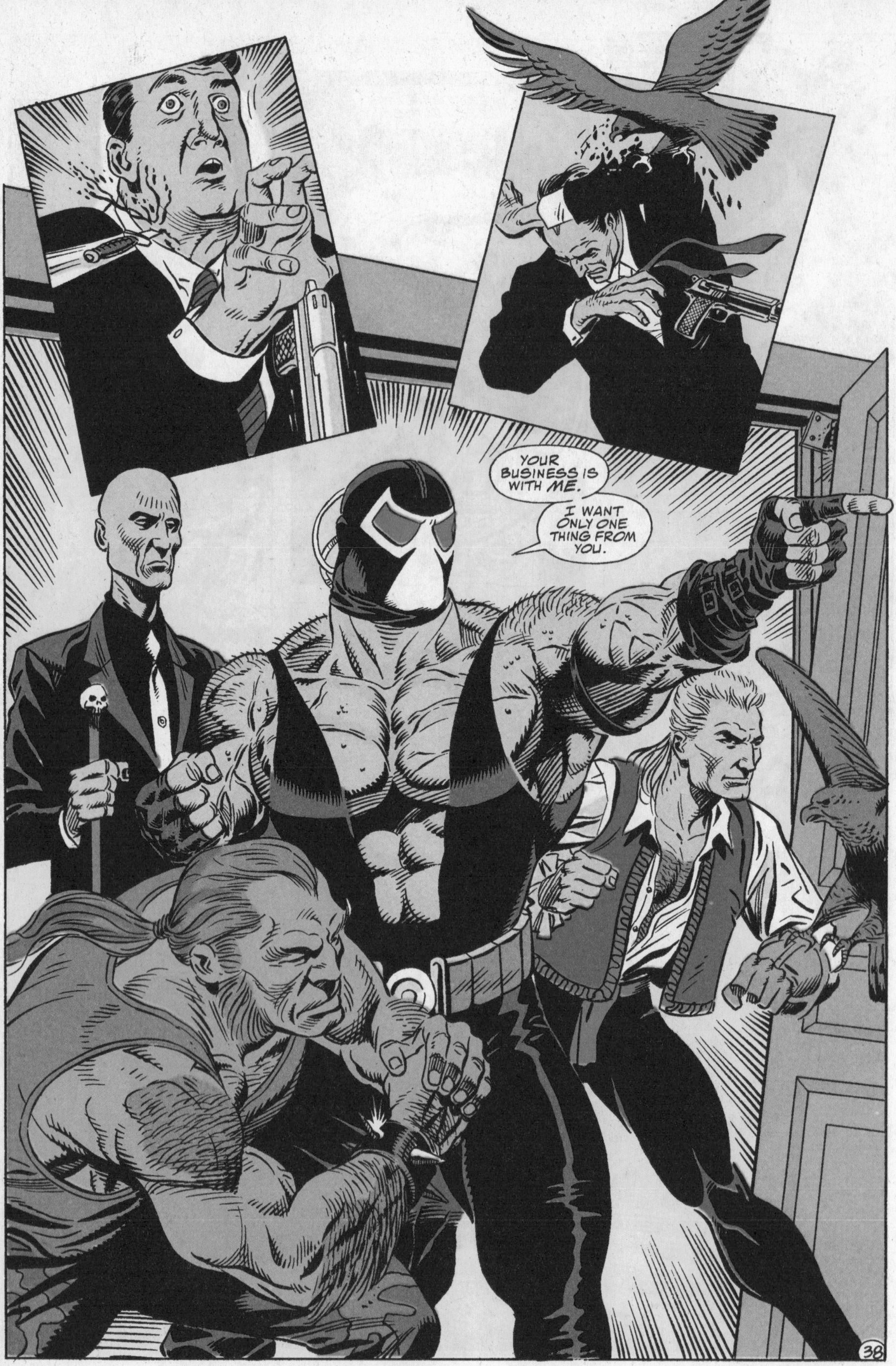
YOUR BUSINESS IS WITH ME.
I WANT ONLY ONE THING FROM YOU.
38

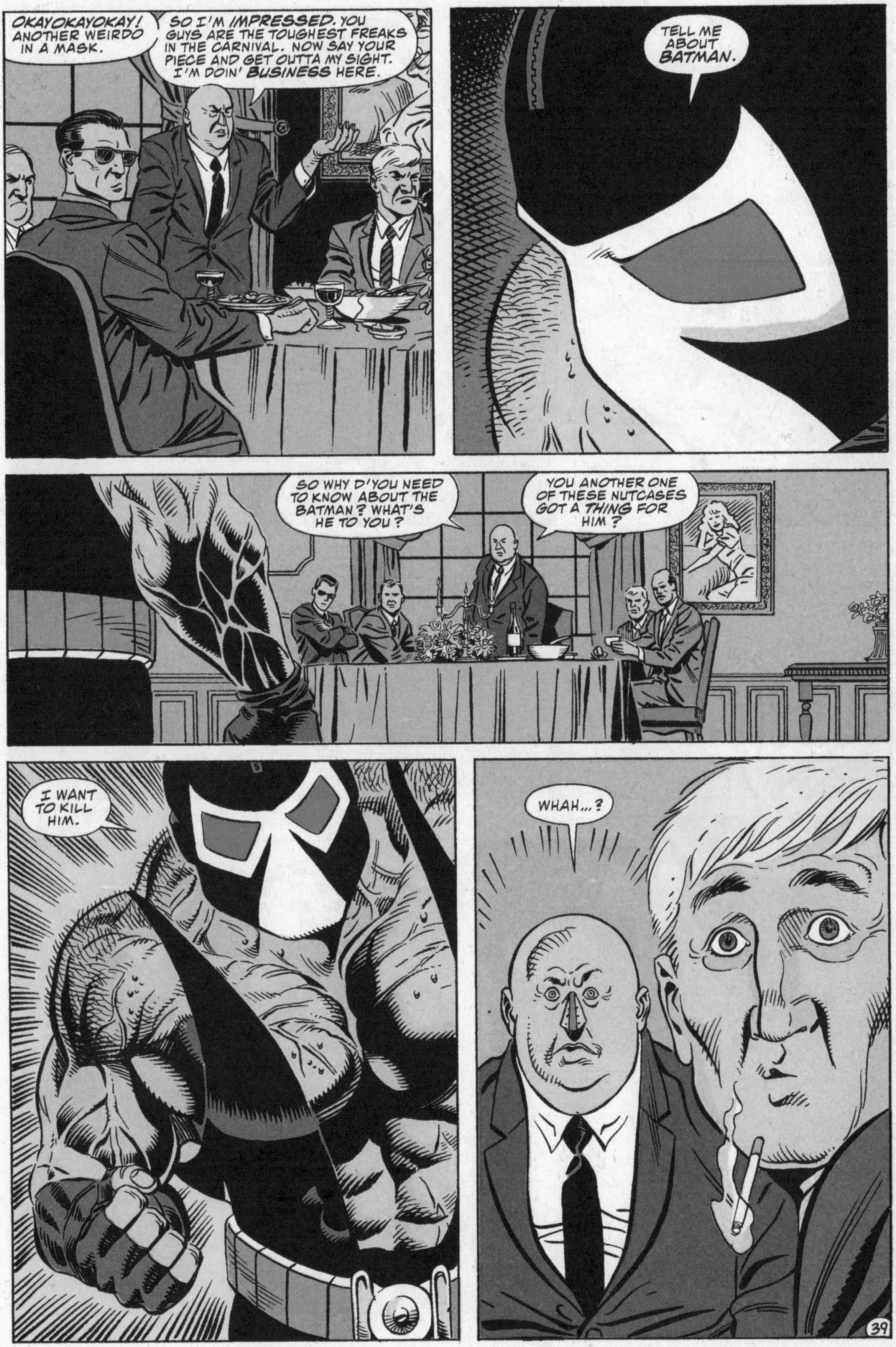
OKAYOKAYOKAY! ANOTHER WEIRDO IN A MASK.
SO I'M IMPRESSED. YOU GUYS ARE THE TOUGHEST FREAKS IN THE CARNIVAL. NOW SAY YOUR PIECE AND GET OUTTA MY SIGHT. I'M DOIN' BUSINESS HERE.
TELL ME ABOUT BATMAN.
SO WHY D'YOU NEED TO KNOW ABOUT THE BATMAN? WHAT'S HE TO YOU?
YOU ANOTHER ONE OF THESE NUTCASES GOT A THING FOR HIM?
I WANT TO KILL HIM.
WHAH...?
39

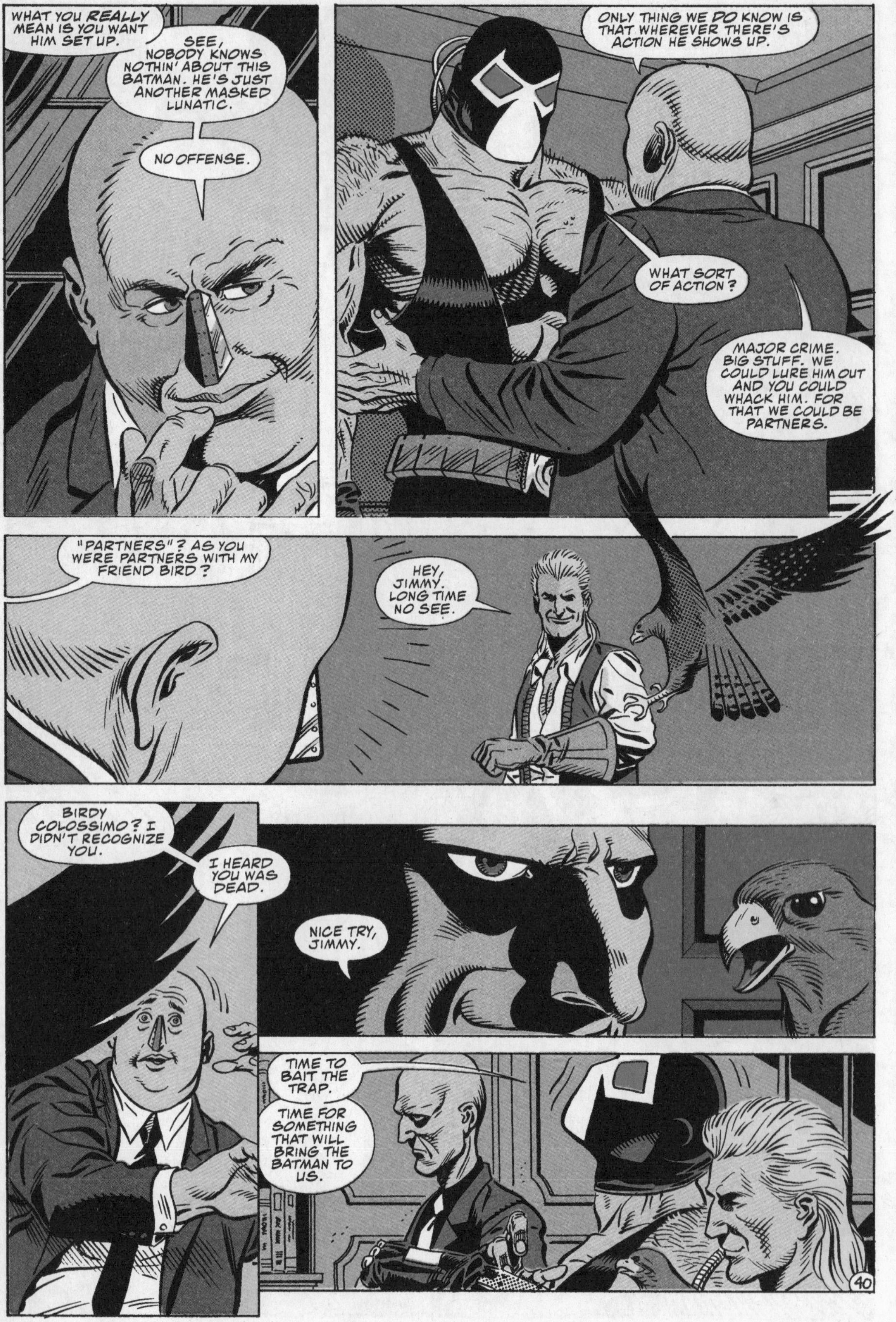
WHAT YOU REALLY MEAN IS YOU WANT HIM SET UP.
SEE, NOBODY KNOWS NOTHIN' ABOUT THIS BATMAN. HE'S JUST ANOTHER MASKED LUNATIC.
NO OFFENSE.
ONLY THING WE DO KNOW IS THAT WHEREVER THERE'S ACTION HE SHOWS UP.
WHAT SORT OF ACTION?
MAJOR CRIME. BIG STUFF. WE COULD LURE HIM OUT AND YOU COULD WHACK HIM. FOR THAT WE COULD BE PARTNERS.
"PARTNERS"? AS YOU WERE PARTNERS WITH MY FRIEND BIRD?
HEY, JIMMY. LONG TIME NO SEE.
BIRDY COLOSSIMO? I DIDN'T RECOGNIZE YOU.
I HEARD YOU WAS DEAD.
NICE TRY, JIMMY.
TIME TO BAIT THE TRAP.
TIME FOR SOMETHING THAT WILL BRING THE BATMAN TO US.
40

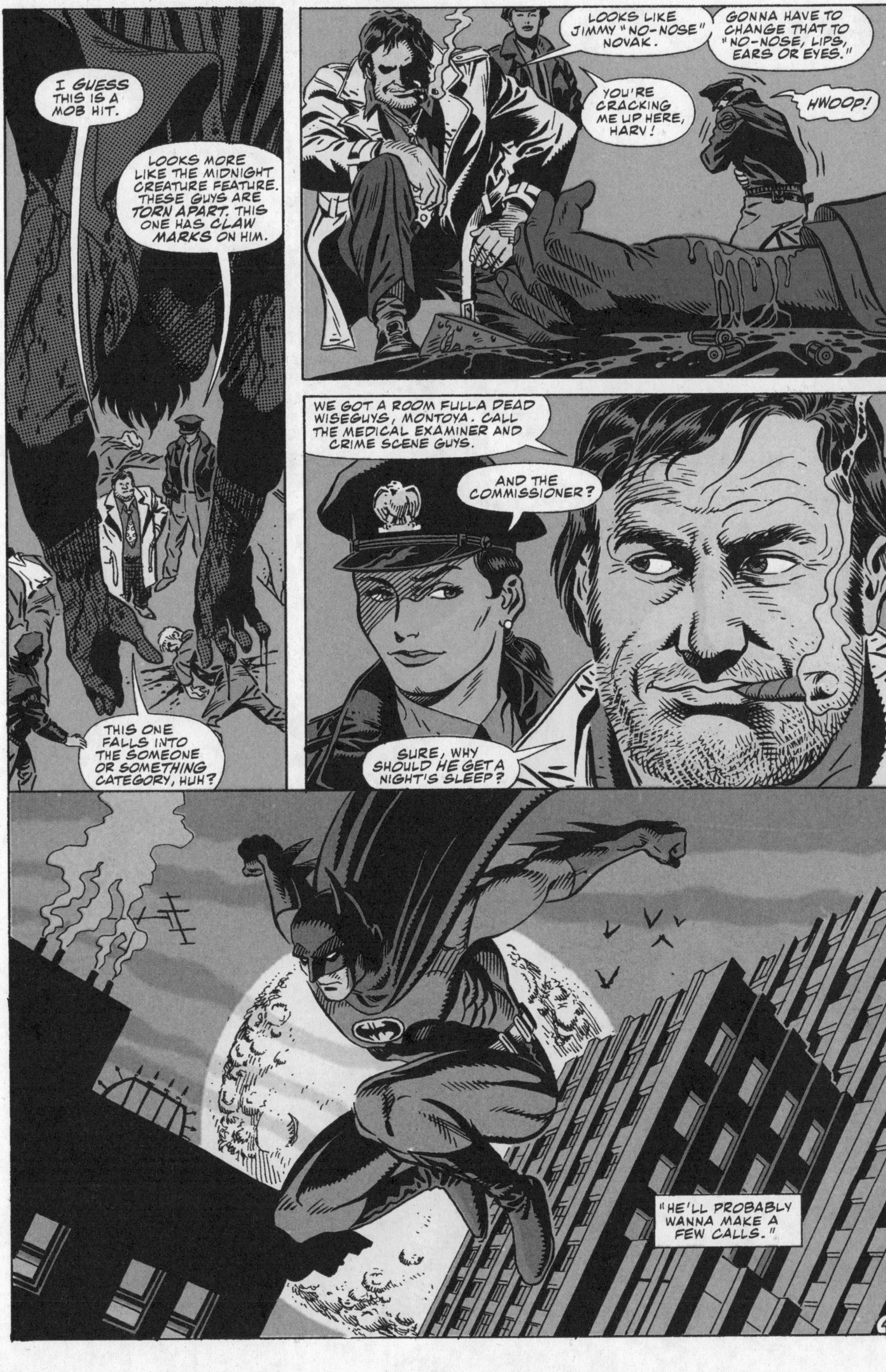
I GUESS THIS IS A MOB HIT.
LOOKS MORE LIKE THE MIDNIGHT CREATURE FEATURE. THESE GUYS ARE TORN APART. THIS ONE HAS CLAW MARKS ON HIM.
THIS ONE FALLS INTO THE SOMEONE OR SOMETHING CATEGORY, HUH?
LOOKS LIKE JIMMY "NO-NOSE" NOVAK.
GONNA HAVE TO CHANGE THAT TO "NO-NOSE, LIPS, EARS OR EYES."
YOU'RE CRACKING ME UP HERE, HARV!
HWOOP!
WE GOT A ROOM FULLA DEAD WISEGUYS, MONTOYA. CALL THE MEDICAL EXAMINER AND CRIME SCENE GUYS.
AND THE COMMISSIONER?
SURE, WHY SHOULD HE GET A NIGHT'S SLEEP?
"HE'LL PROBABLY WANNA MAKE A FEW CALLS."
41

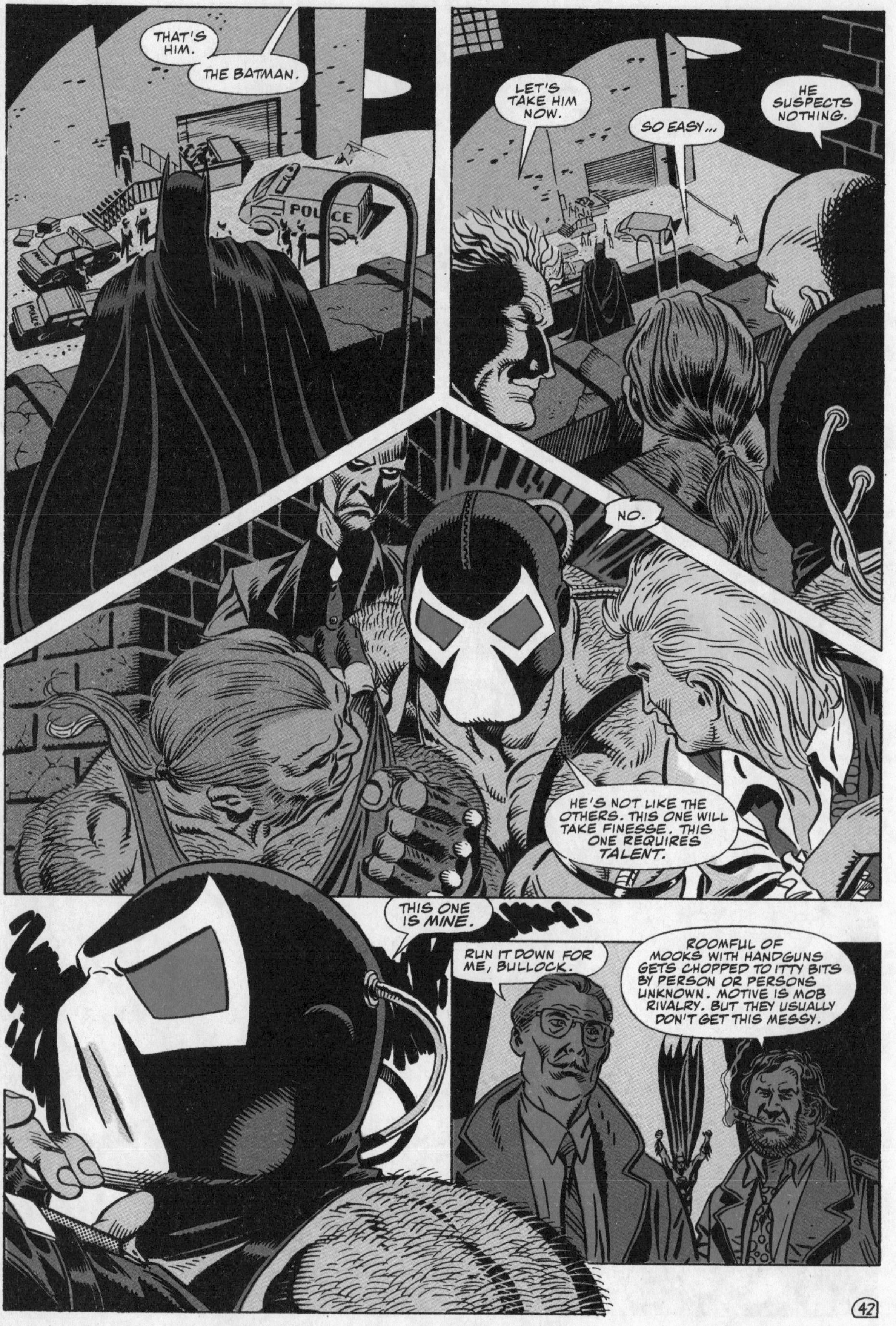
THAT'S HIM.
THE BATMAN.
LET'S TAKE HIM NOW.
SO EASY...
HE SUSPECTS NOTHING.
NO.
HE'S NOT LIKE THE OTHERS. THIS ONE WILL TAKE FINESSE. THIS ONE REQUIRES TALENT.
THIS ONE IS MINE.
RUN IT DOWN FOR ME, BULLOCK.
ROOMFUL OF MOOKS WITH HANDGUNS GETS CHOPPED TO ITTY BITS BY PERSON OR PERSONS UNKNOWN. MOTIVE IS MOB RIVALRY. BUT THEY USUALLY DON'T GET THIS MESSY.
42

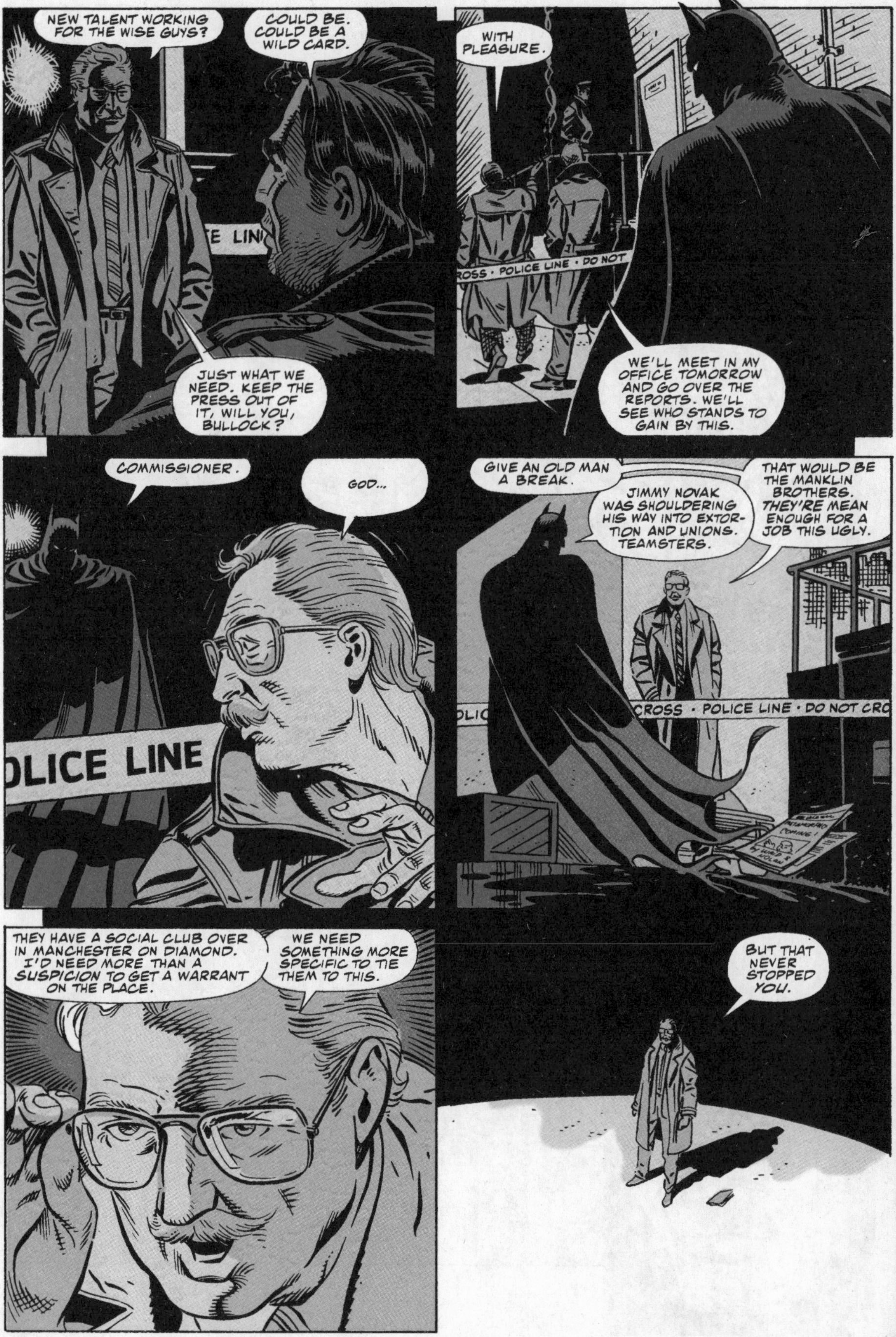
NEW TALENT WORKING FOR THE WISE GUYS?
COULD BE. COULD BE A WILD CARD.
JUST WHAT WE NEED. KEEP THE PRESS OUT OF IT, WILL YOU, BULLOCK?
WITH PLEASURE.
CROSS · POLICE LINE · DO NOT
WE'LL MEET IN MY OFFICE TOMORROW AND GO OVER THE REPORTS. WE'LL SEE WHO STANDS TO GAIN BY THIS.
COMMISSIONER.
GOD...
POLICE LINE
GIVE AN OLD MAN A BREAK.
JIMMY NOVAK WAS SHOULDERING HIS WAY INTO EXTORTION AND UNIONS. TEAMSTERS.
THAT WOULD BE THE MANKLIN BROTHERS. THEY'RE MEAN ENOUGH FOR A JOB THIS UGLY.
CROSS · POLICE LINE · DO NOT CRO
THEY HAVE A SOCIAL CLUB OVER IN MANCHESTER ON DIAMOND. I'D NEED MORE THAN A SUSPICION TO GET A WARRANT ON THE PLACE.
WE NEED SOMETHING MORE SPECIFIC TO TIE THEM TO THIS.
BUT THAT NEVER STOPPED YOU.

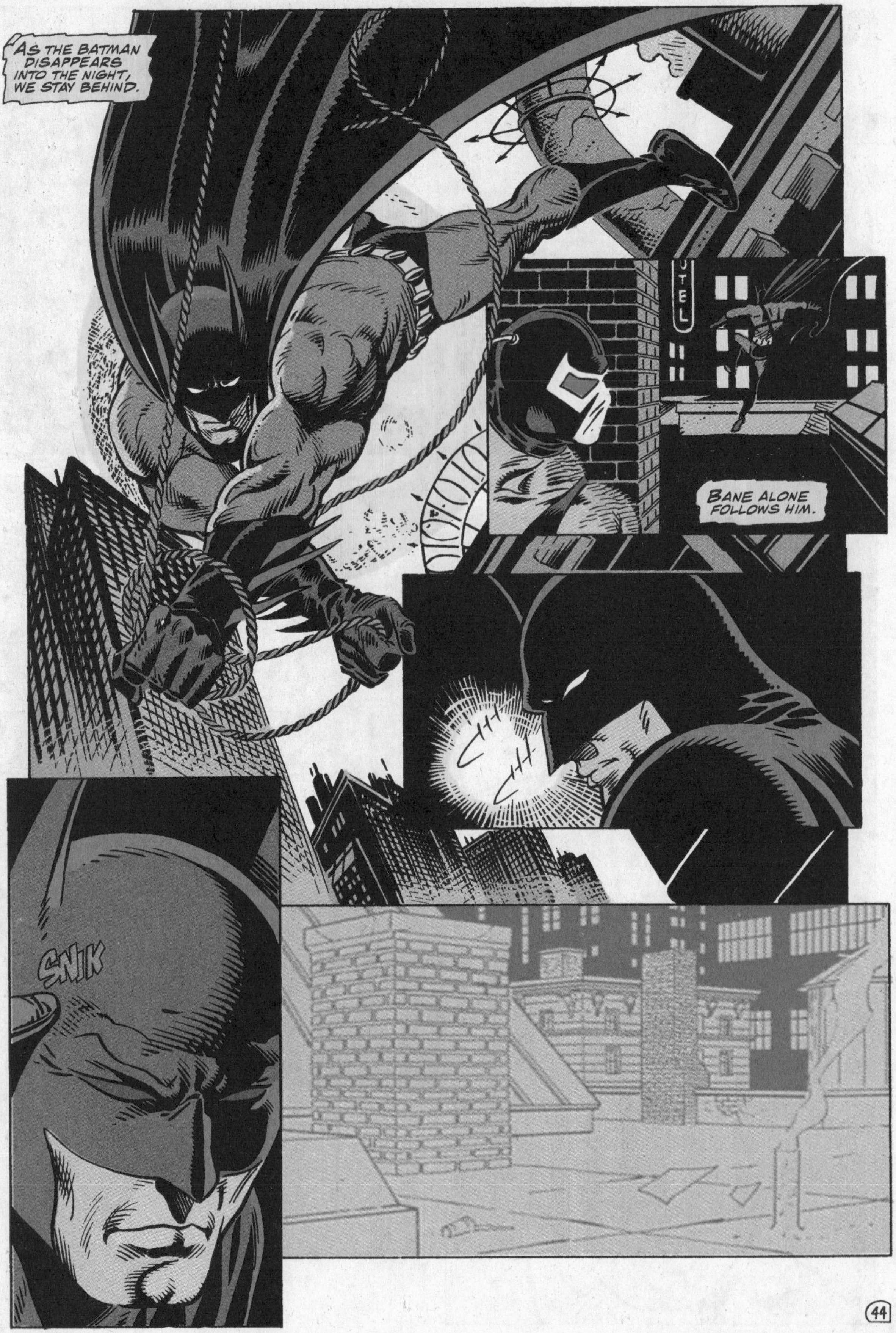
AS THE BATMAN DISAPPEARS INTO THE NIGHT, WE STAY BEHIND.
BANE ALONE FOLLOWS HIM.
SNIK
44

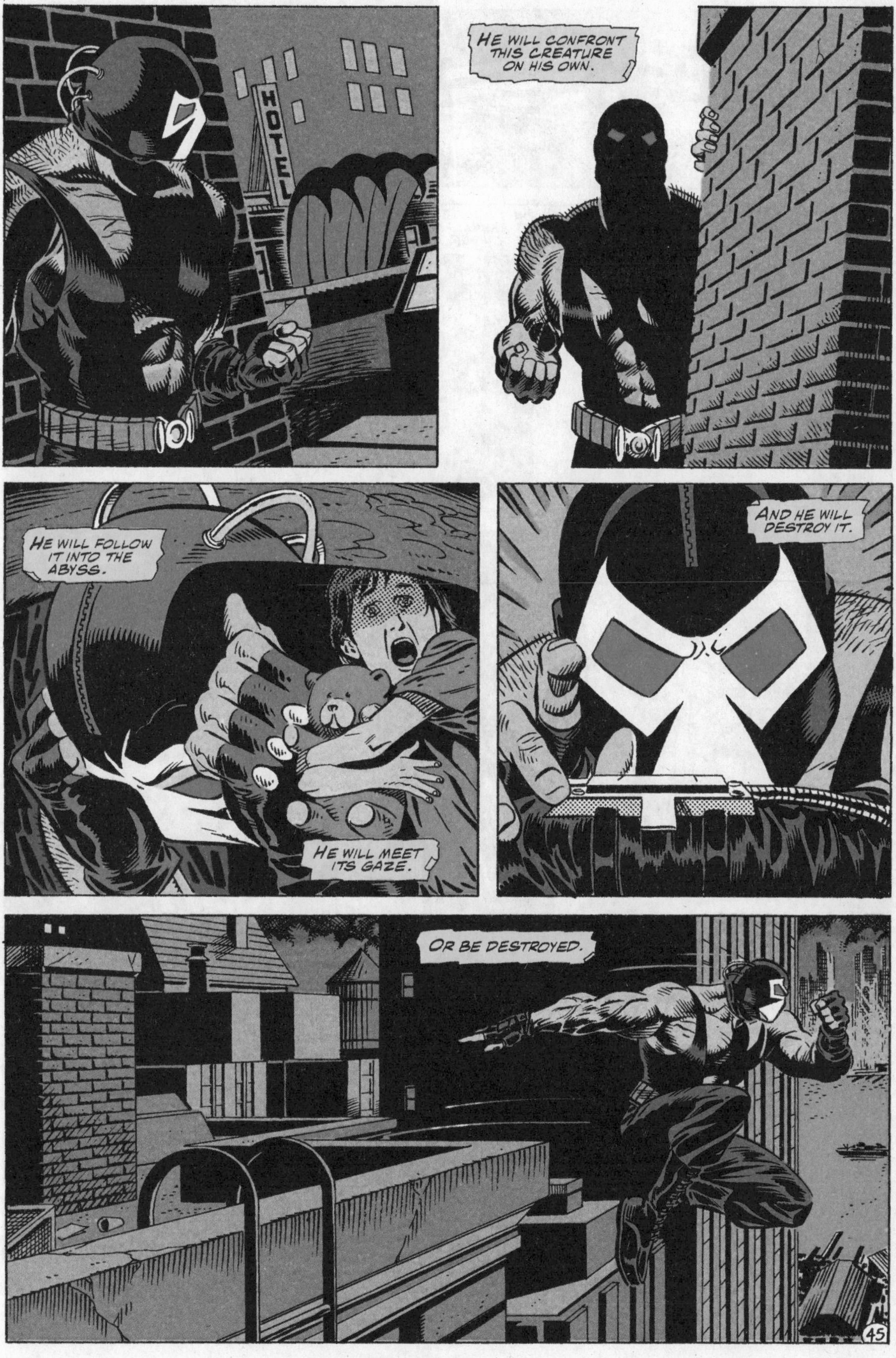
HOTEL
HE WILL CONFRONT THIS CREATURE ON HIS OWN.
HE WILL FOLLOW IT INTO THE ABYSS.
HE WILL MEET ITS GAZE.
AND HE WILL DESTROY IT.
OR BE DESTROYED.
45

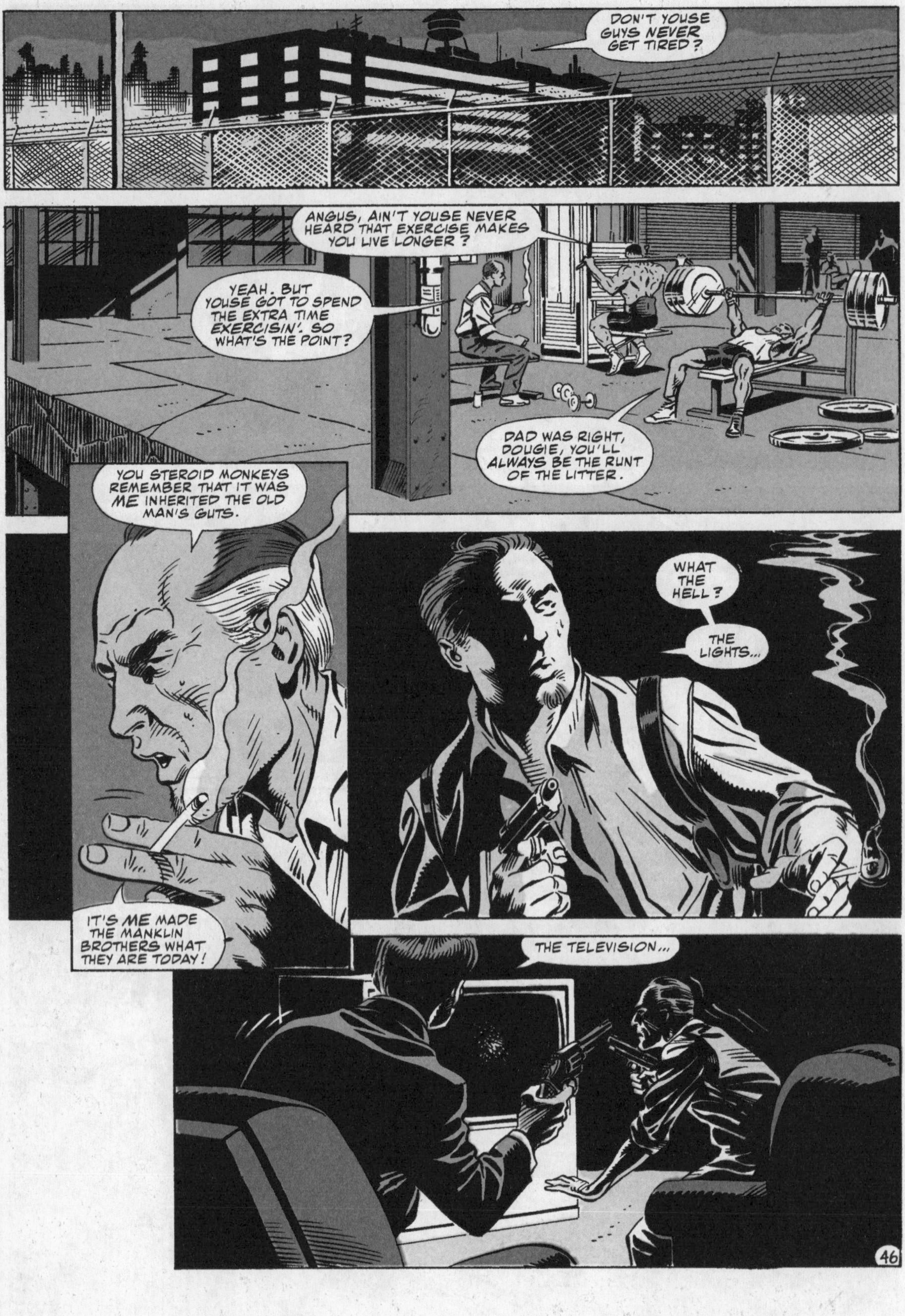
DON'T YOUSE GUYS NEVER GET TIRED?
ANGUS, AIN'T YOUSE NEVER HEARD THAT EXERCISE MAKES YOU LIVE LONGER?
YEAH. BUT YOUSE GOT TO SPEND THE EXTRA TIME EXERCISIN'. SO WHAT'S THE POINT?
DAD WAS RIGHT, DOUGIE, YOU'LL ALWAYS BE THE RUNT OF THE LITTER.
YOU STEROID MONKEYS REMEMBER THAT IT WAS ME INHERITED THE OLD MAN'S GUTS.
IT'S ME MADE THE MANKLIN BROTHERS WHAT THEY ARE TODAY!
WHAT THE HELL?
THE LIGHTS...
THE TELEVISION...
46

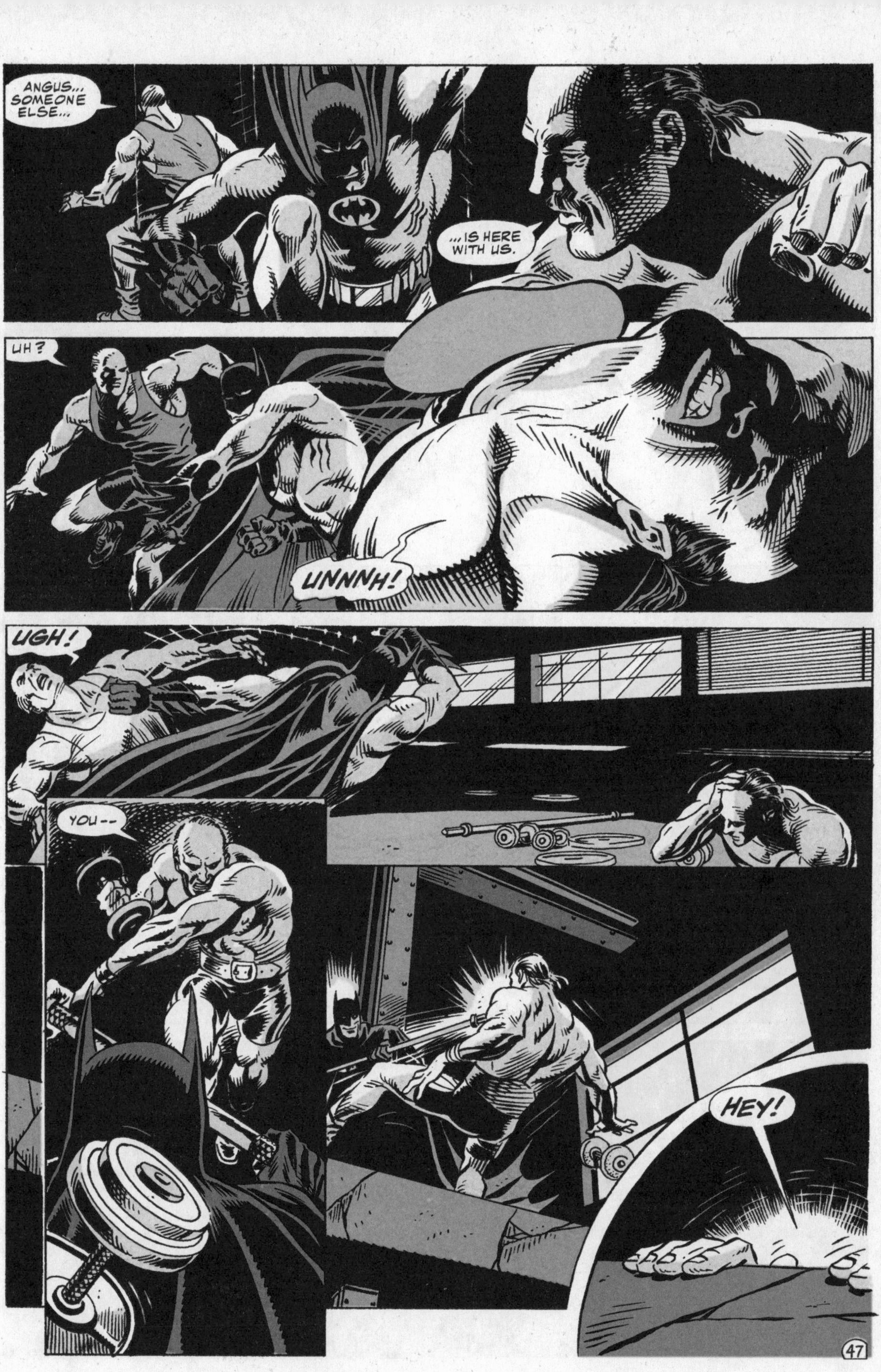
ANGUS... SOMEONE ELSE...
...IS HERE WITH US.
UH?
UNNNH!
UGH!
YOU--
HEY!
47

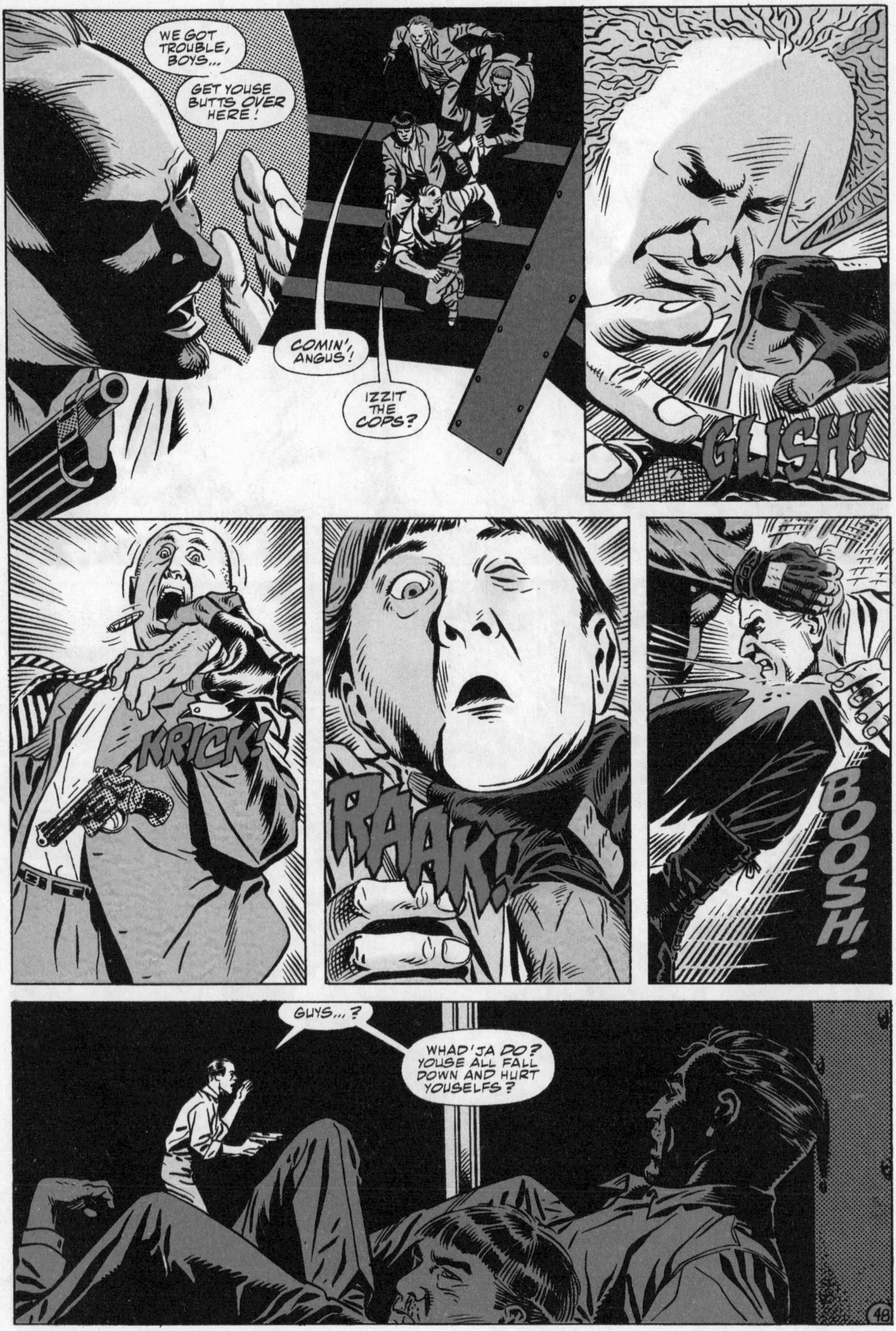
WE GOT TROUBLE, BOYS...
GET YOUSE BUTTS OVER HERE!
COMIN', ANGUS!
IZZIT THE COPS?
GLISH!
KRICK!
RAAK!
BOOSH!
GUYS...?
WHAD'JA DO? YOUSE ALL FALL DOWN AND HURT YOUSELFS?
48

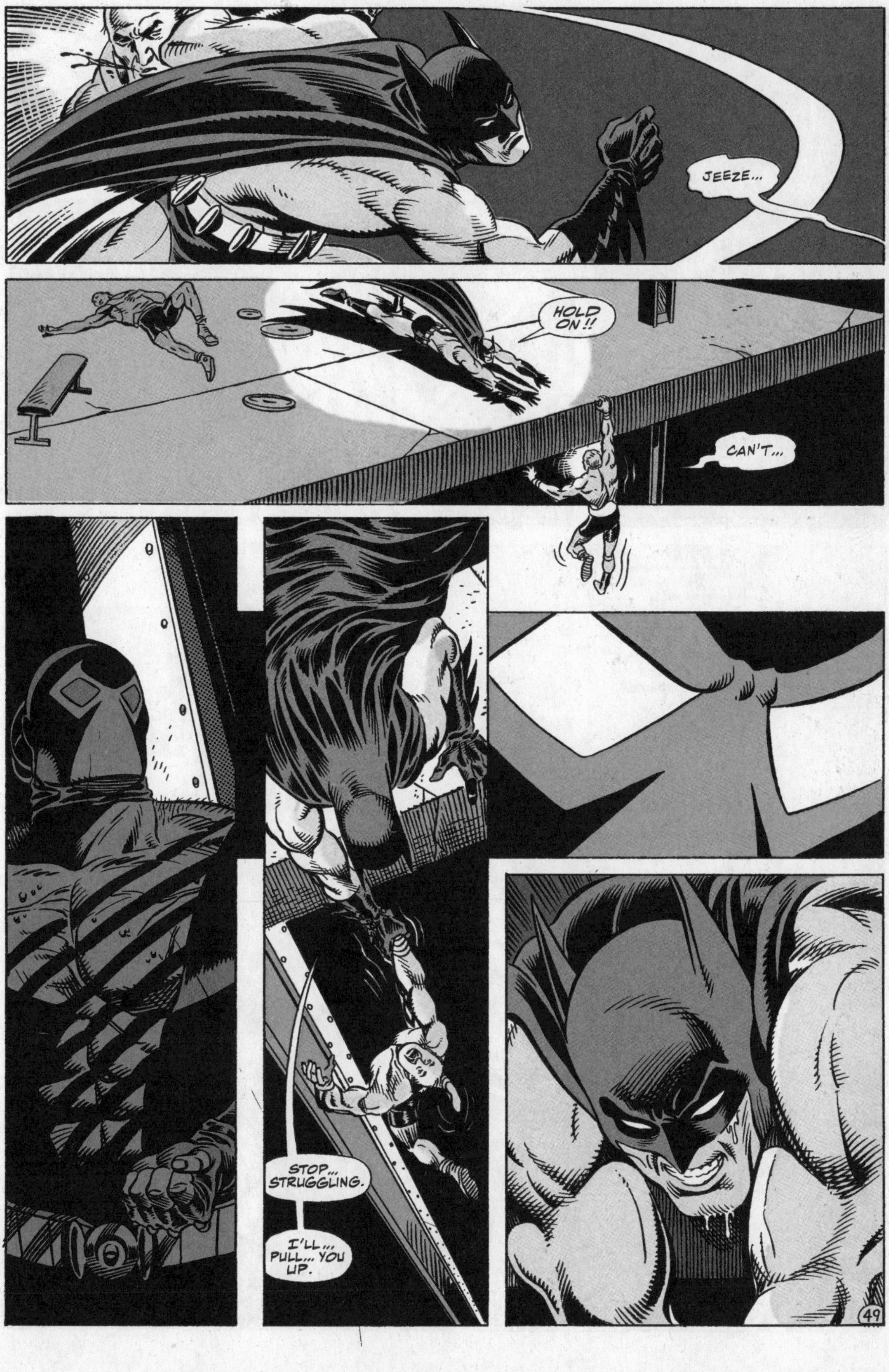
JEEZE...
HOLD ON!!
CAN'T...
STOP... STRUGGLING.
I'LL... PULL... YOU UP.
49

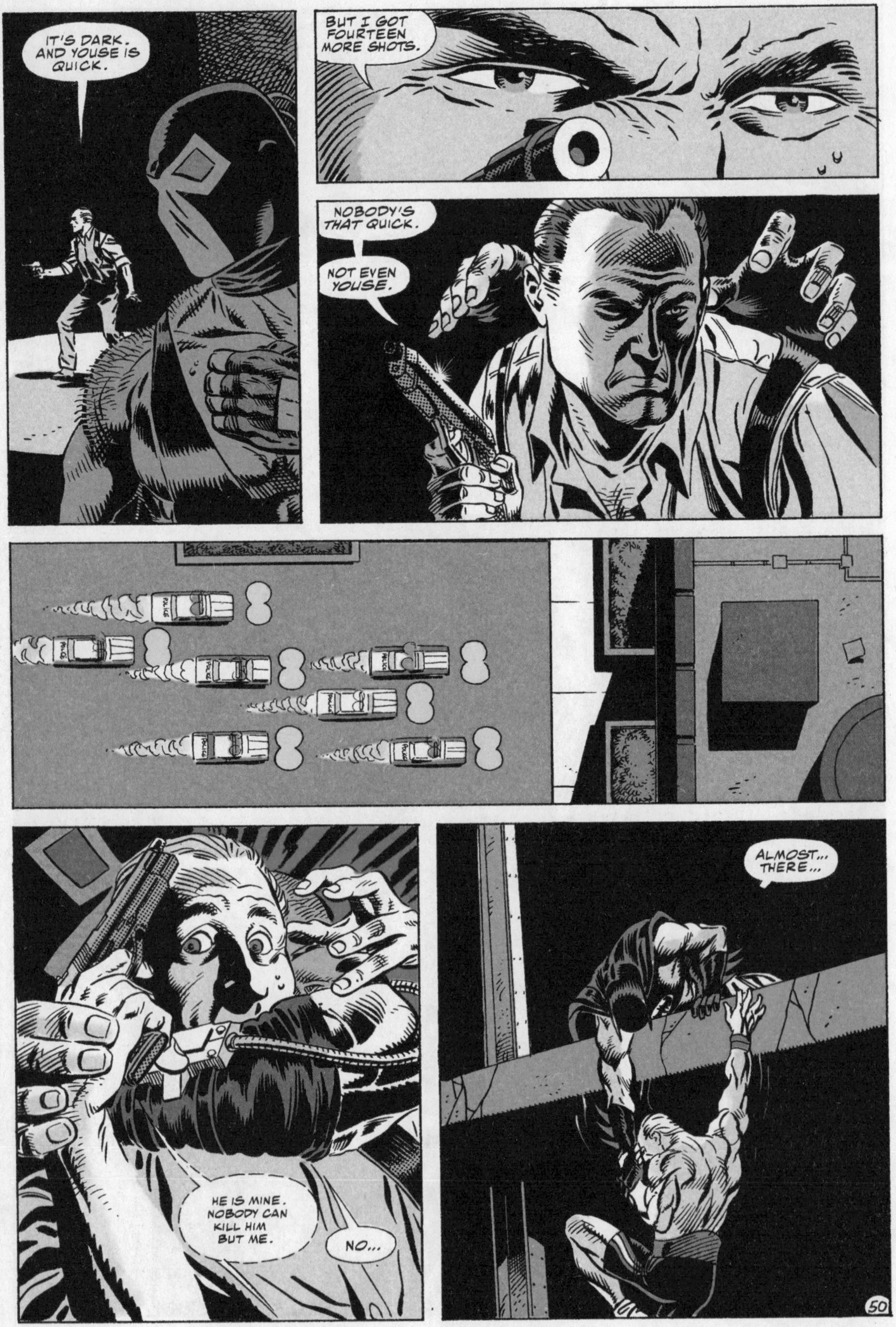
IT'S DARK. AND YOUSE IS QUICK.
BUT I GOT FOURTEEN MORE SHOTS.
NOBODY'S THAT QUICK.
NOT EVEN YOUSE.
HE IS MINE. NOBODY CAN KILL HIM BUT ME.
NO...
ALMOST... THERE...
50

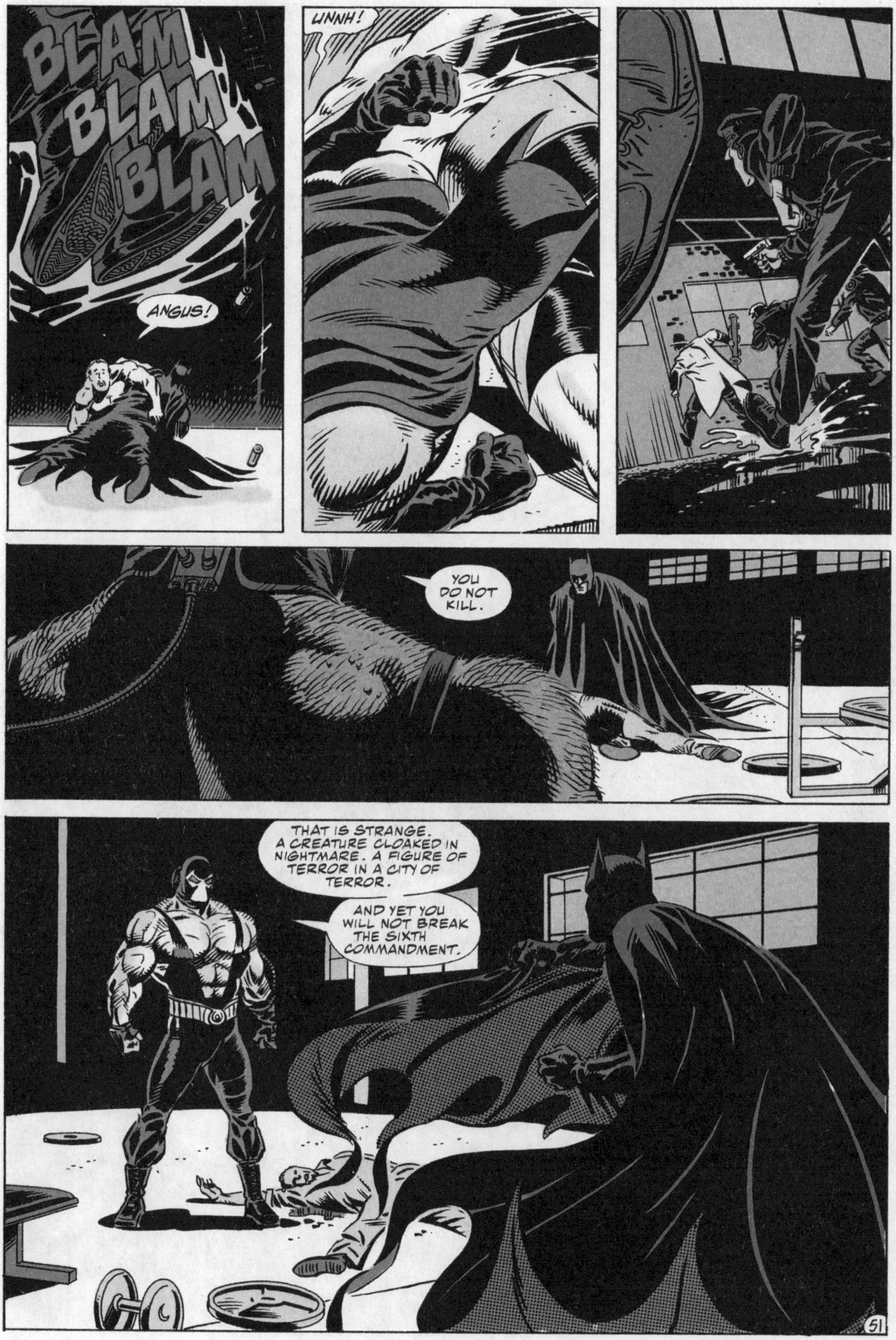
BLAM
BLAM
BLAM
ANGUS!
UNNH!
YOU DO NOT KILL.
THAT IS STRANGE. A CREATURE CLOAKED IN NIGHTMARE. A FIGURE OF TERROR IN A CITY OF TERROR.
AND YET YOU WILL NOT BREAK THE SIXTH COMMANDMENT.
51

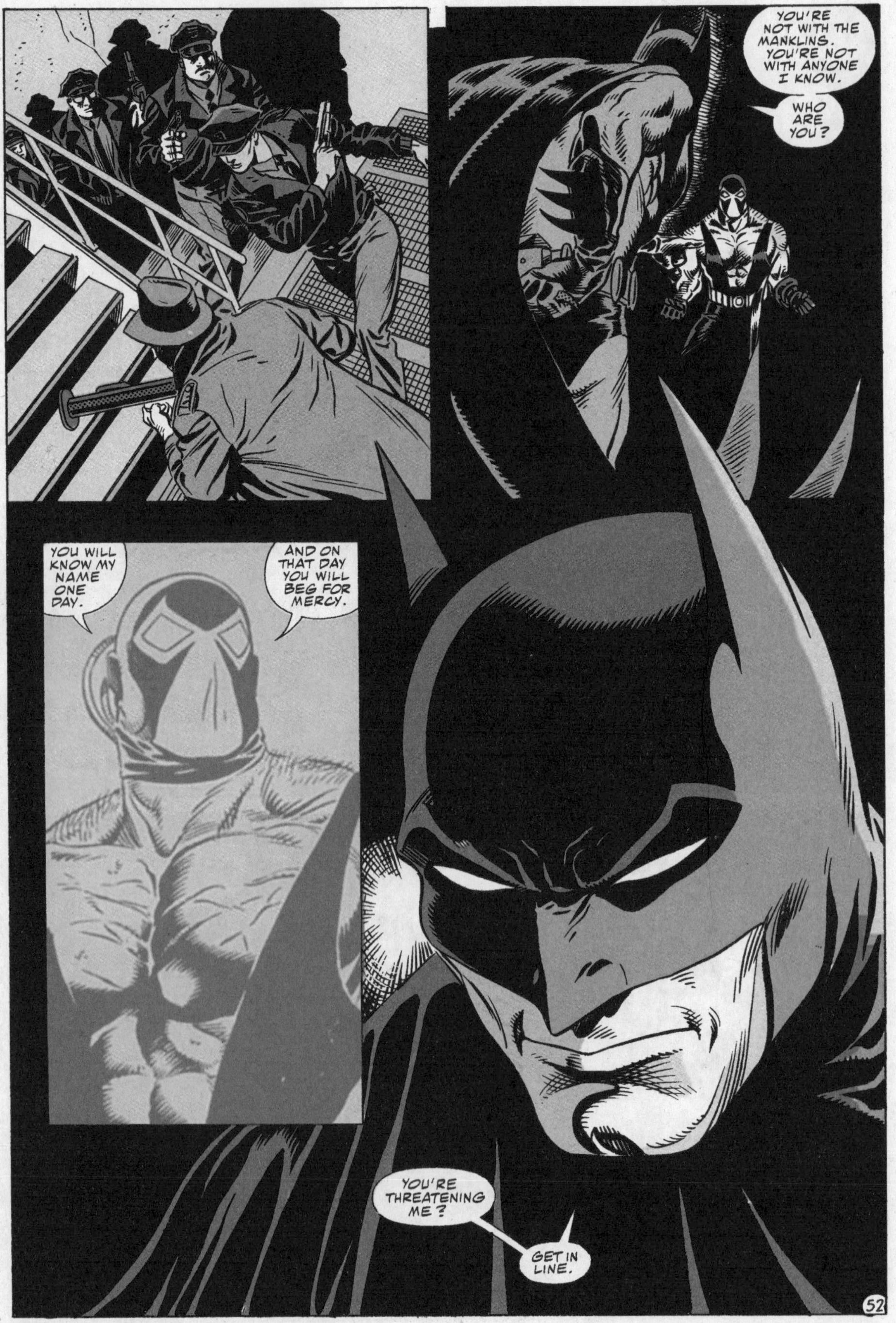
YOU'RE NOT WITH THE MANKLINS. YOU'RE NOT WITH ANYONE I KNOW.
WHO ARE YOU?
YOU WILL KNOW MY NAME ONE DAY.
AND ON THAT DAY YOU WILL BEG FOR MERCY.
YOU'RE THREATENING ME?
GET IN LINE.
52

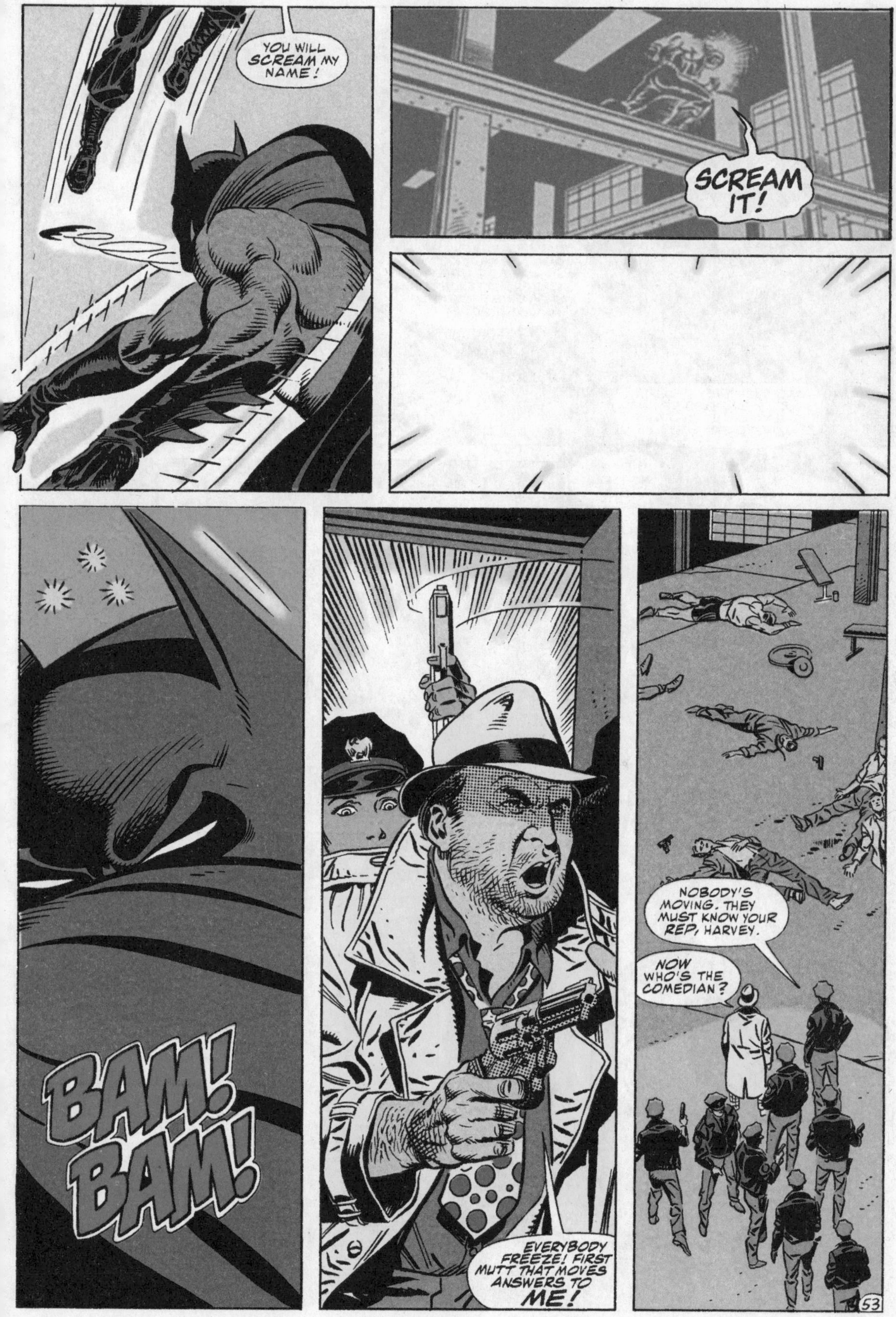
YOU WILL SCREAM MY NAME!
SCREAM IT!
BAM! BAM!
EVERYBODY FREEZE! FIRST MUTT THAT MOVES ANSWERS TO ME!
NOBODY'S MOVING. THEY MUST KNOW YOUR REP, HARVEY.
NOW WHO'S THE COMEDIAN?
53

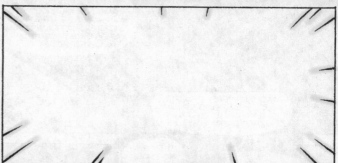

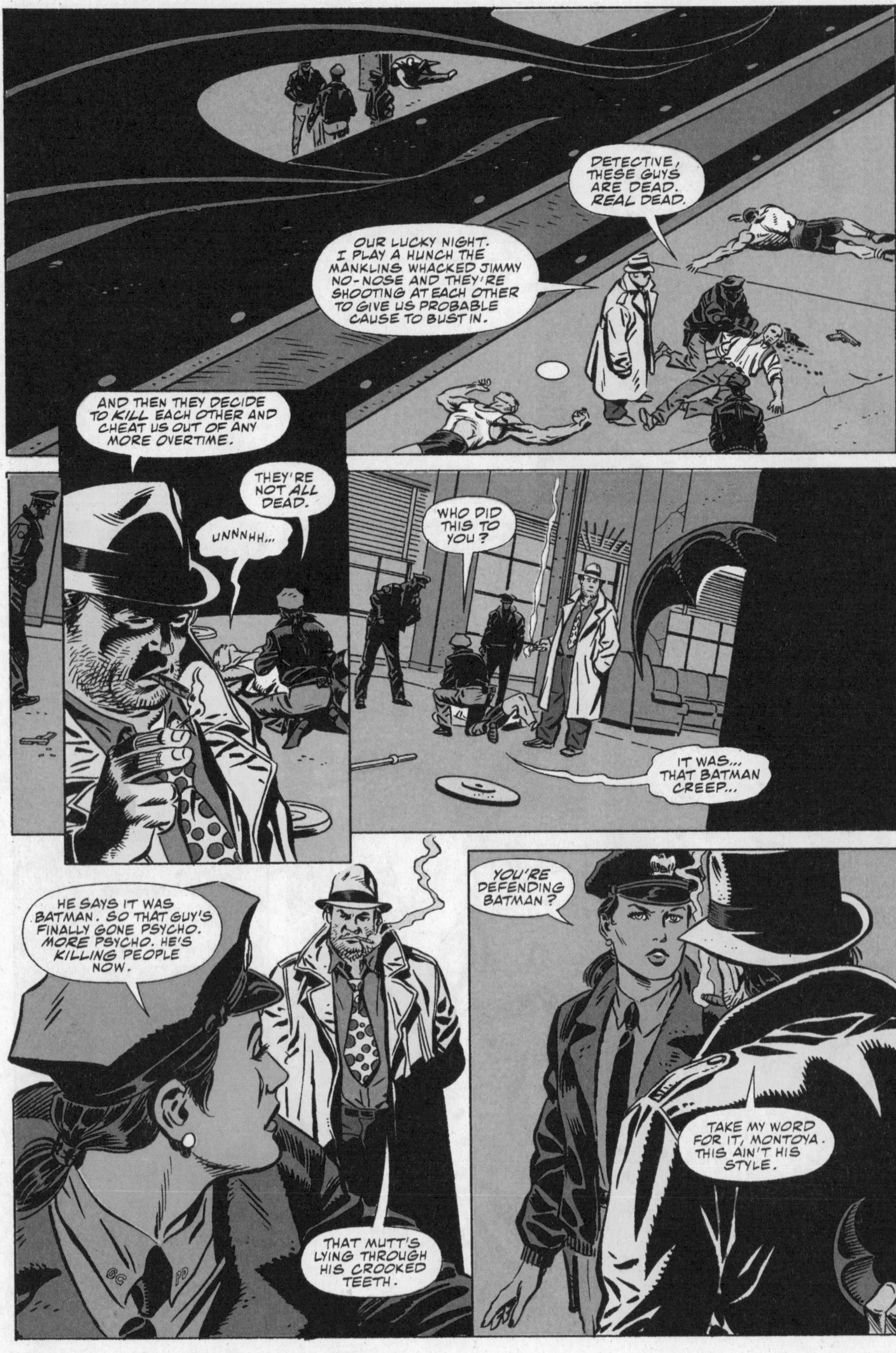
DETECTIVE, THESE GUYS ARE DEAD. REAL DEAD.
OUR LUCKY NIGHT. I PLAY A HUNCH THE MANKLINS WHACKED JIMMY NO-NOSE AND THEY'RE SHOOTING AT EACH OTHER TO GIVE US PROBABLE CAUSE TO BUST IN.
AND THEN THEY DECIDE TO KILL EACH OTHER AND CHEAT US OUT OF ANY MORE OVERTIME.
THEY'RE NOT ALL DEAD.
UNNNHH...
WHO DID THIS TO YOU?
IT WAS... THAT BATMAN CREEP...
HE SAYS IT WAS BATMAN. SO THAT GUY'S FINALLY GONE PSYCHO. MORE PSYCHO. HE'S KILLING PEOPLE NOW.
THAT MUTT'S LYING THROUGH HIS CROOKED TEETH.
YOU'RE DEFENDING BATMAN?
TAKE MY WORD FOR IT, MONTOYA. THIS AIN'T HIS STYLE.

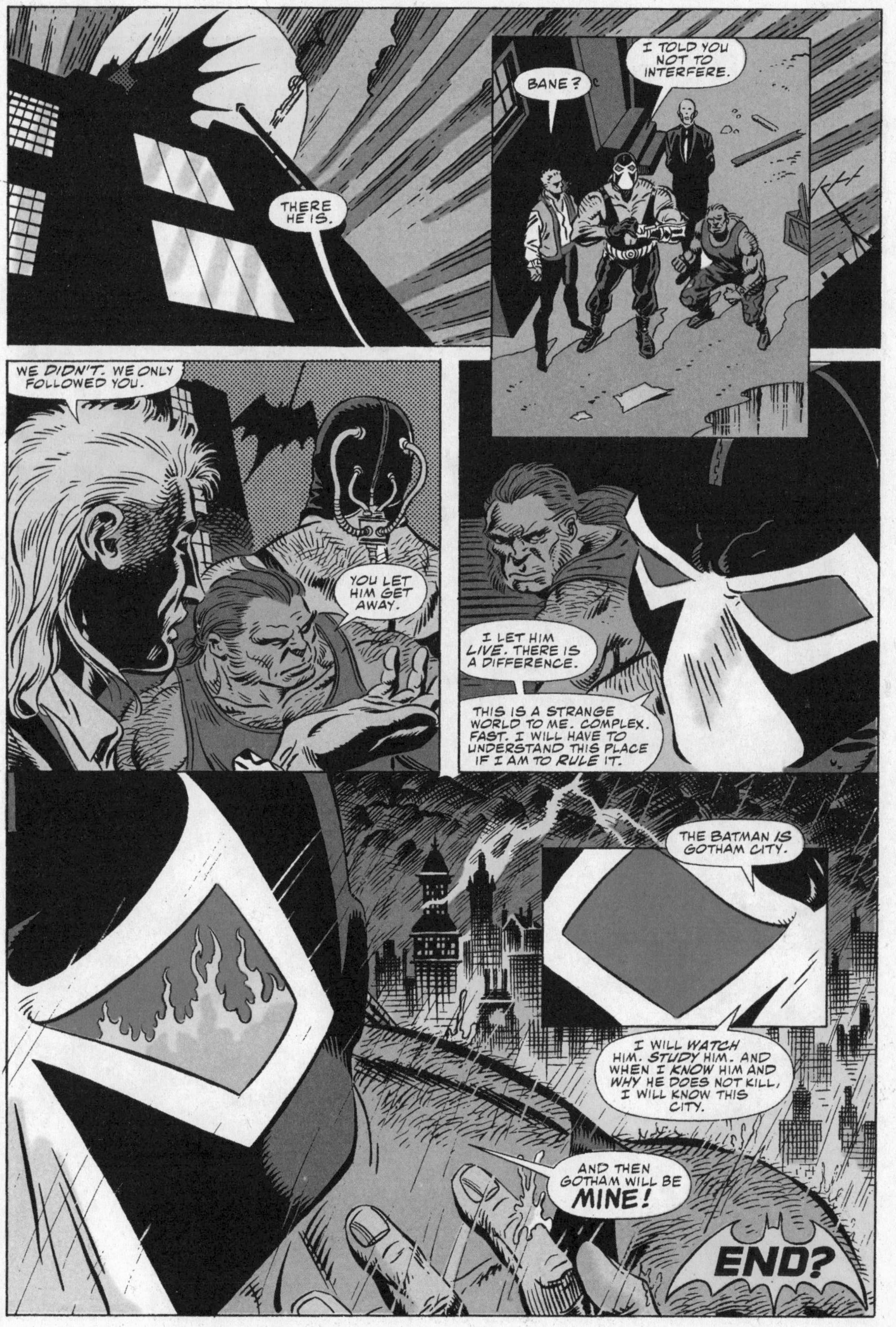
THERE HE IS.
BANE?
I TOLD YOU NOT TO INTERFERE.
WE DIDN'T. WE ONLY FOLLOWED YOU.
YOU LET HIM GET AWAY.
I LET HIM LIVE. THERE IS A DIFFERENCE.
THIS IS A STRANGE WORLD TO ME. COMPLEX. FAST. I WILL HAVE TO UNDERSTAND THIS PLACE IF I AM TO RULE IT.
THE BATMAN IS GOTHAM CITY.
I WILL WATCH HIM. STUDY HIM. AND WHEN I KNOW HIM AND WHY HE DOES NOT KILL, I WILL KNOW THIS CITY.
AND THEN GOTHAM WILL BE MINE!
END?

Cover art by KELLEY JONES

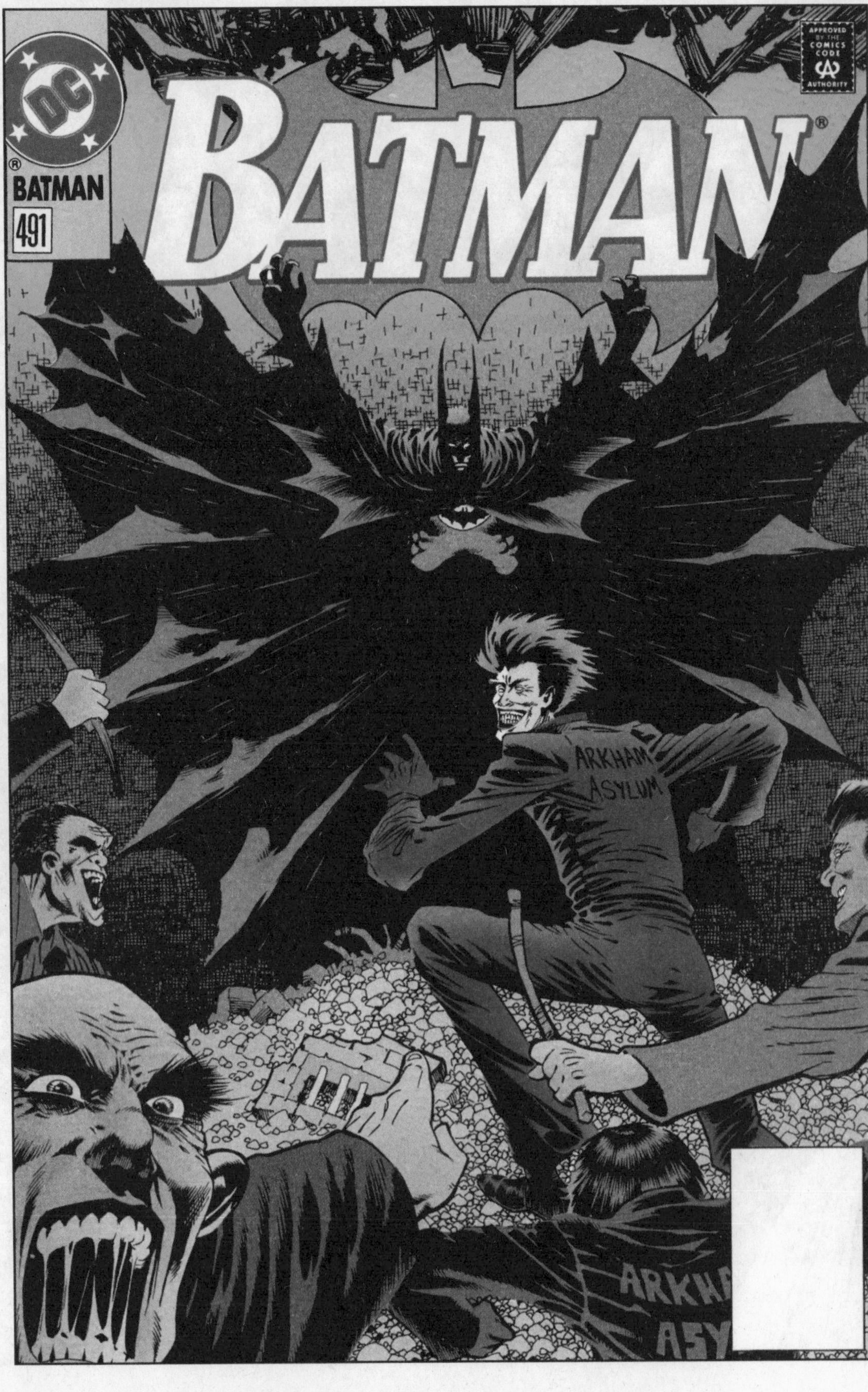
APPROVED BY THE COMICS CODE AUTHORITY
DC
BATMAN
BATMAN
491
ARKHAM ASYLUM
ARKHA
ASY

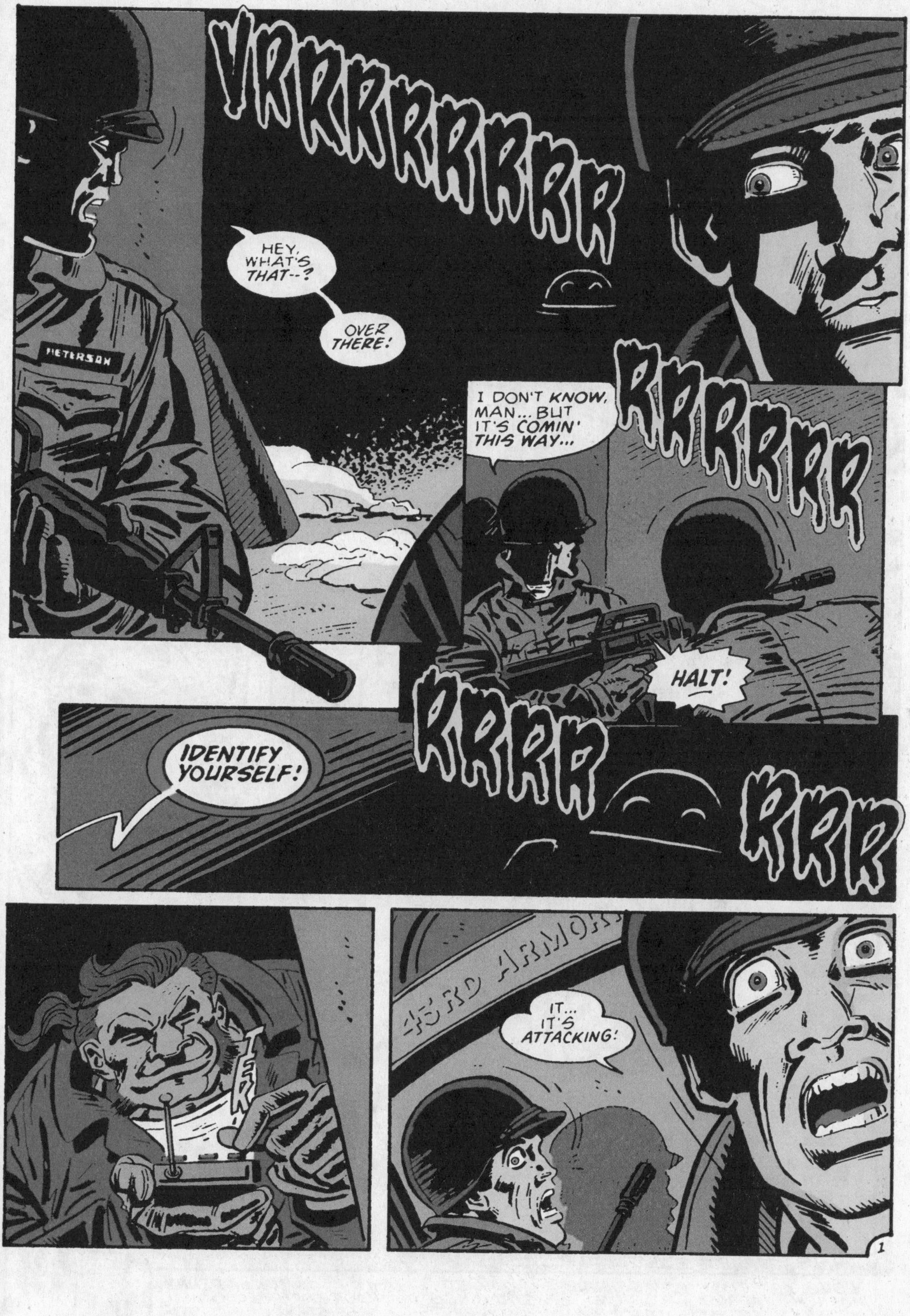
VRRRRRRRRR
HEY, WHAT'S THAT--?
OVER THERE!
PETERSON
RRRRRRR
I DON'T KNOW, MAN... BUT IT'S COMIN' THIS WAY...
HALT!
RRRR
IDENTIFY YOURSELF!
RRR
43RD ARMOR
IT... IT'S ATTACKING!
1

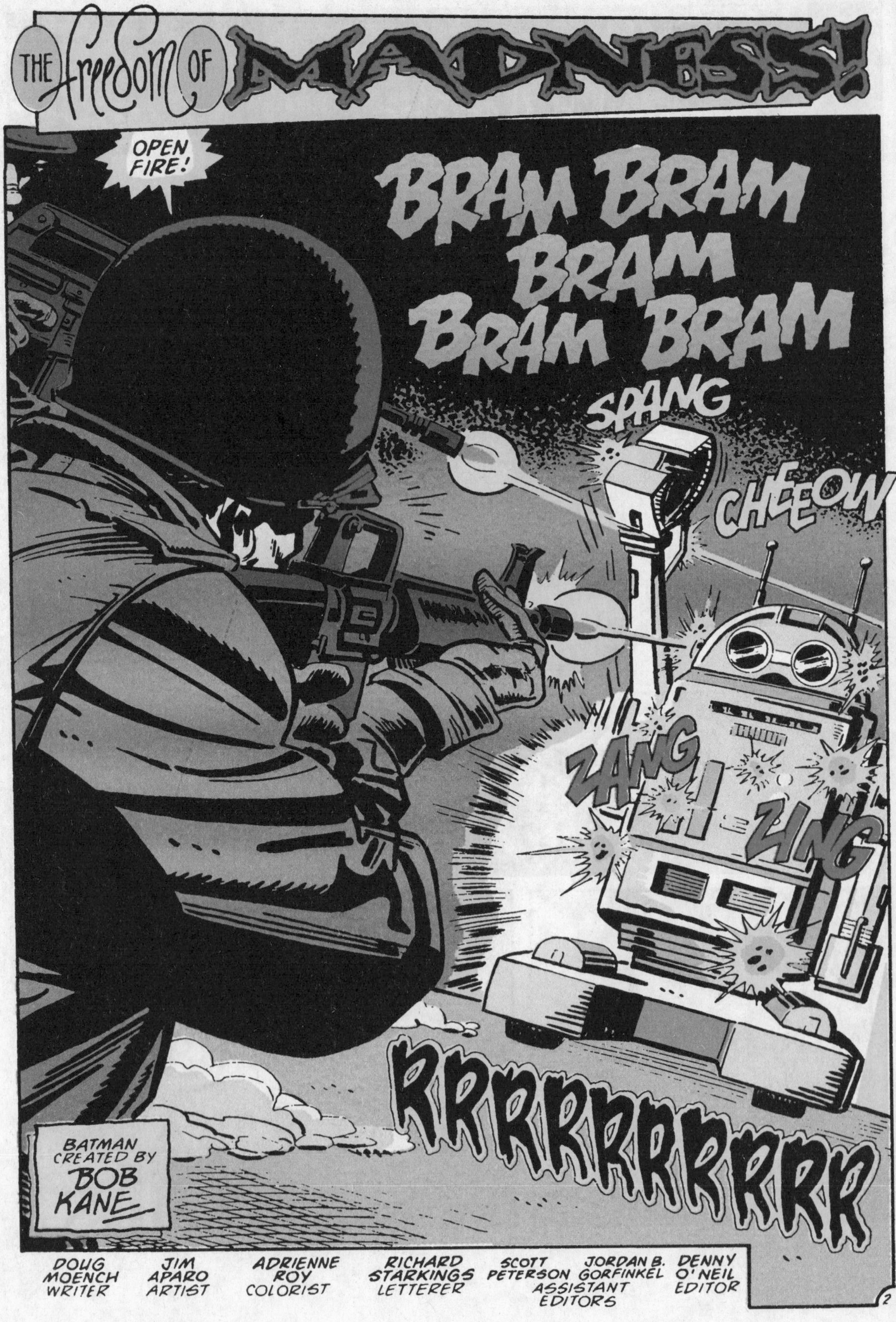
THE Freedom OF MADNESS!
OPEN FIRE!
BRAM BRAM BRAM BRAM BRAM
SPANG
CHEEOW
ZANG
ZING
RRRRRRRRRRRK
BATMAN CREATED BY BOB KANE
DOUG MOENCH WRITER
JIM APARO ARTIST
ADRIENNE ROY COLORIST
RICHARD STARKINGS LETTERER
SCOTT PETERSON JORDAN B. GORFINKEL ASSISTANT EDITORS
DENNY O'NEIL EDITOR
2

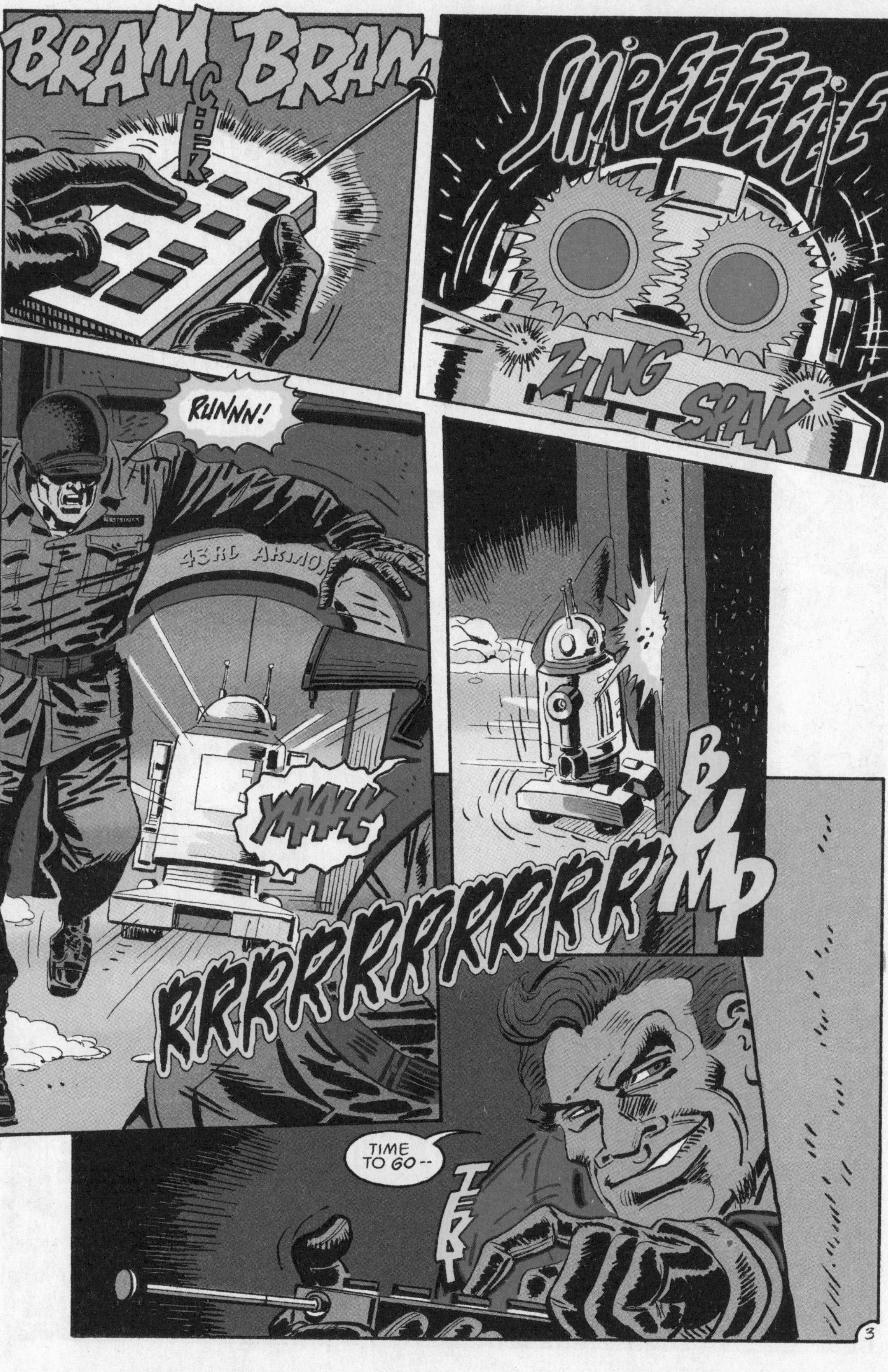

BRAM BRAM
CHEK
SHREEEEEEIE
ZING
SPAK
RUNNN!
YAAAH
BUMP
RRRRRRRRRRRRRRRRR
TIME TO GO --
TEK
3

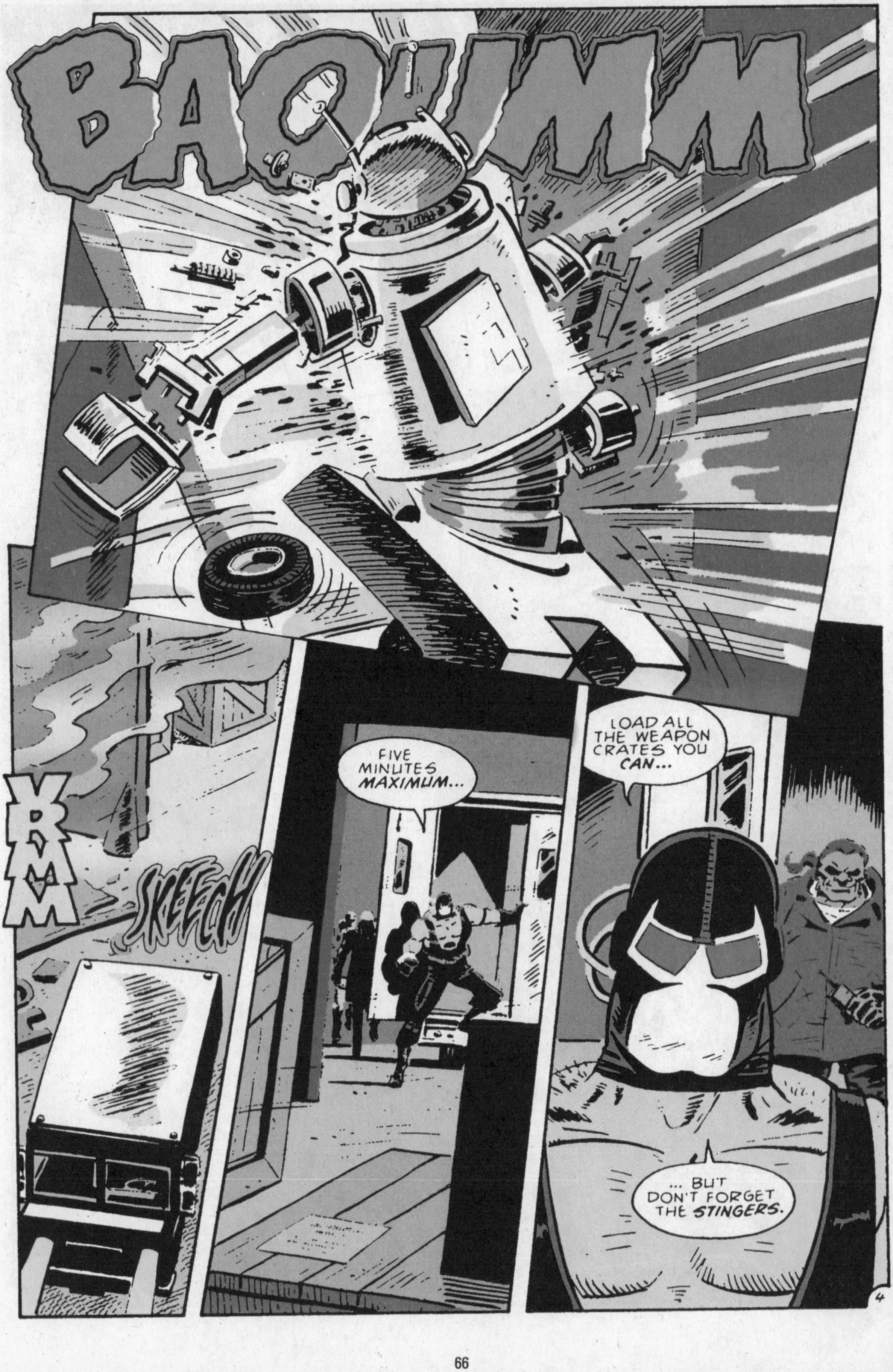
BA-OUMM
VRMM
SKEECH
FIVE MINUTES MAXIMUM...
LOAD ALL THE WEAPON CRATES YOU CAN...
... BUT DON'T FORGET THE STINGERS.
4

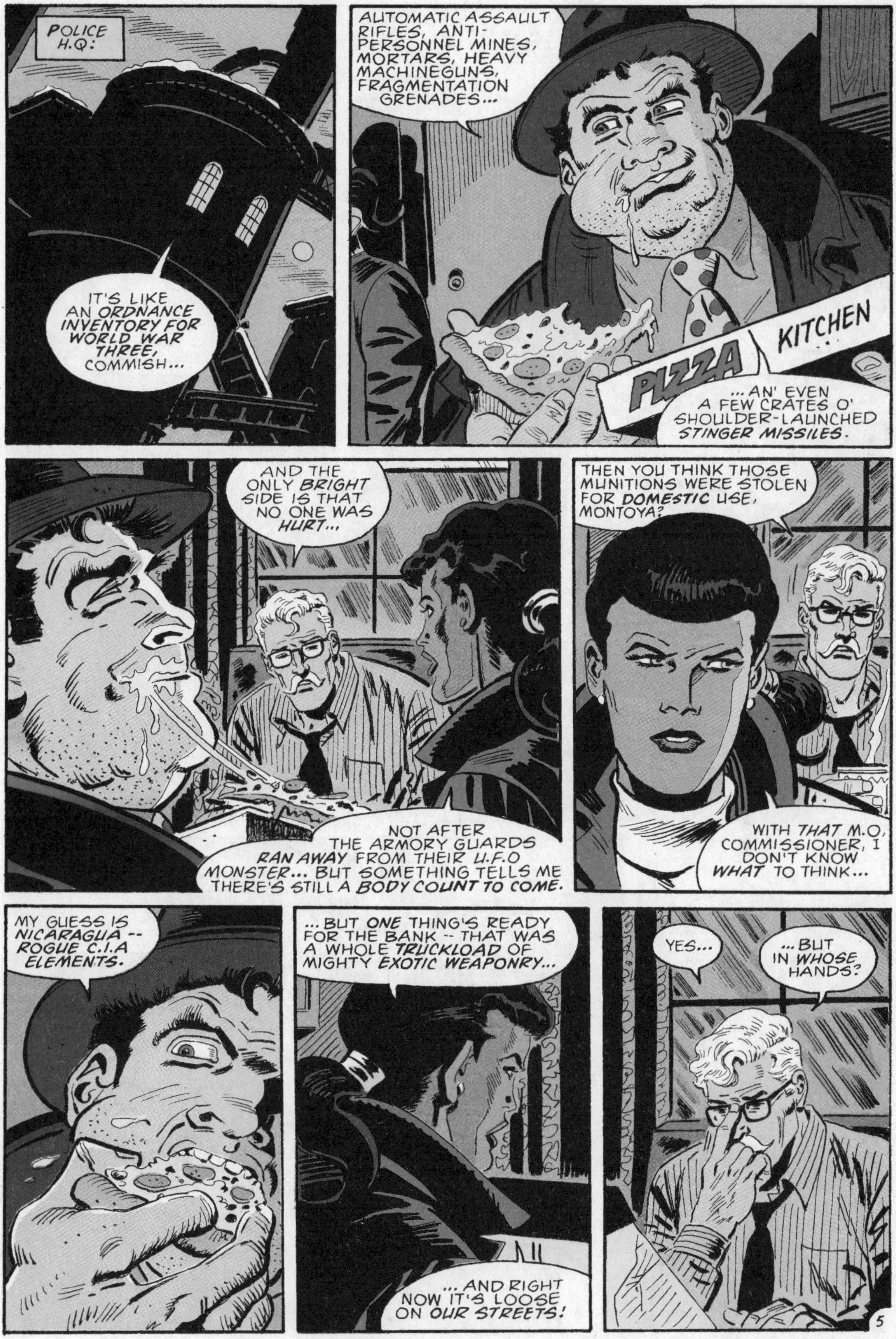

POLICE H.Q:
IT'S LIKE AN ORDNANCE INVENTORY FOR WORLD WAR THREE, COMMISH...
AUTOMATIC ASSAULT RIFLES, ANTI-PERSONNEL MINES, MORTARS, HEAVY MACHINEGUNS, FRAGMENTATION GRENADES...
PIZZA KITCHEN
...AN' EVEN A FEW CRATES O' SHOULDER-LAUNCHED STINGER MISSILES.
AND THE ONLY BRIGHT SIDE IS THAT NO ONE WAS HURT...
NOT AFTER THE ARMORY GUARDS RAN AWAY FROM THEIR U.F.O MONSTER... BUT SOMETHING TELLS ME THERE'S STILL A BODY COUNT TO COME.
THEN YOU THINK THOSE MUNITIONS WERE STOLEN FOR DOMESTIC USE, MONTOYA?
WITH THAT M.O, COMMISSIONER, I DON'T KNOW WHAT TO THINK...
MY GUESS IS NICARAGUA -- ROGUE C.I.A ELEMENTS.
...BUT ONE THING'S READY FOR THE BANK -- THAT WAS A WHOLE TRUCKLOAD OF MIGHTY EXOTIC WEAPONRY...
...AND RIGHT NOW IT'S LOOSE ON OUR STREETS!
YES...
...BUT IN WHOSE HANDS?
5

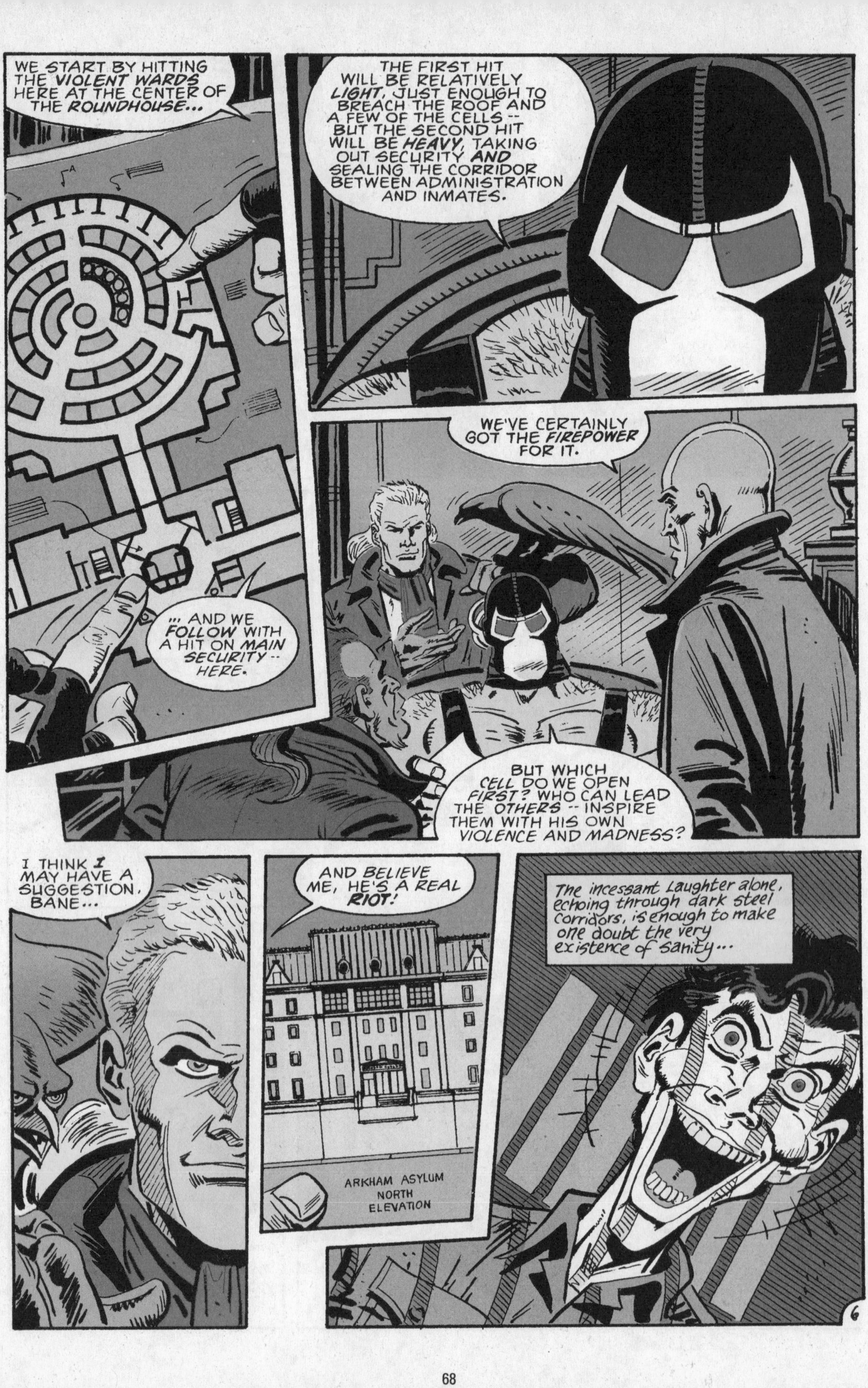
WE START BY HITTING THE VIOLENT WARDS HERE AT THE CENTER OF THE ROUNDHOUSE...
THE FIRST HIT WILL BE RELATIVELY LIGHT, JUST ENOUGH TO BREACH THE ROOF AND A FEW OF THE CELLS -- BUT THE SECOND HIT WILL BE HEAVY, TAKING OUT SECURITY AND SEALING THE CORRIDOR BETWEEN ADMINISTRATION AND INMATES.
... AND WE FOLLOW WITH A HIT ON MAIN SECURITY -- HERE.
WE'VE CERTAINLY GOT THE FIREPOWER FOR IT.
BUT WHICH CELL DO WE OPEN FIRST? WHO CAN LEAD THE OTHERS -- INSPIRE THEM WITH HIS OWN VIOLENCE AND MADNESS?
I THINK I MAY HAVE A SUGGESTION, BANE...
AND BELIEVE ME, HE'S A REAL RIOT!
ARKHAM ASYLUM NORTH ELEVATION
The incessant laughter alone, echoing through dark steel corridors, is enough to make one doubt the very existence of sanity...
6

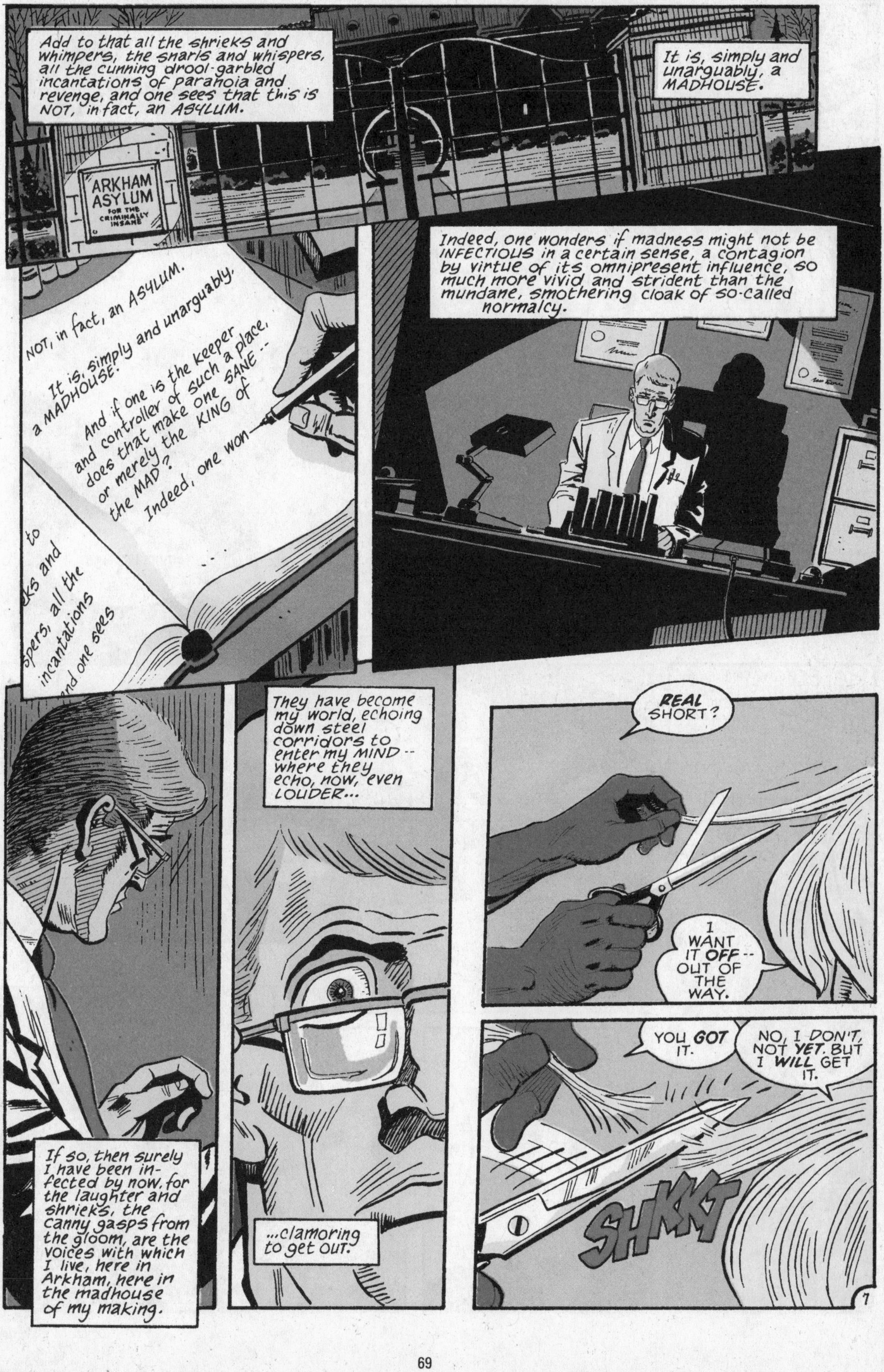
Add to that all the shrieks and whimpers, the snarls and whispers, all the cunning drool-garbled incantations of paranoia and revenge, and one sees that this is NOT, in fact, an ASYLUM.
It is, simply and unarguably, a MADHOUSE.
ARKHAM ASYLUM FOR THE CRIMINALLY INSANE
NOT, in fact, an ASYLUM.
It is, simply and unarguably, a MADHOUSE.
And if one is the keeper and controller of such a place, does that make one SANE -- or merely the KING of the MAD?
Indeed, one won
Indeed, one wonders if madness might not be INFECTIOUS in a certain sense, a contagion by virtue of its omnipresent influence, so much more vivid and strident than the mundane, smothering cloak of so-called normalcy.
If so, then surely I have been infected by now, for the laughter and shrieks, the canny gasps from the gloom, are the voices with which I live, here in Arkham, here in the madhouse of my making.
They have become my world, echoing down steel corridors to enter my MIND -- where they echo, now, even LOUDER...
...clamoring to get out.
REAL SHORT?
I WANT IT OFF -- OUT OF THE WAY.
YOU GOT IT.
NO, I DON'T, NOT YET. BUT I WILL GET IT.
SHKKT
7

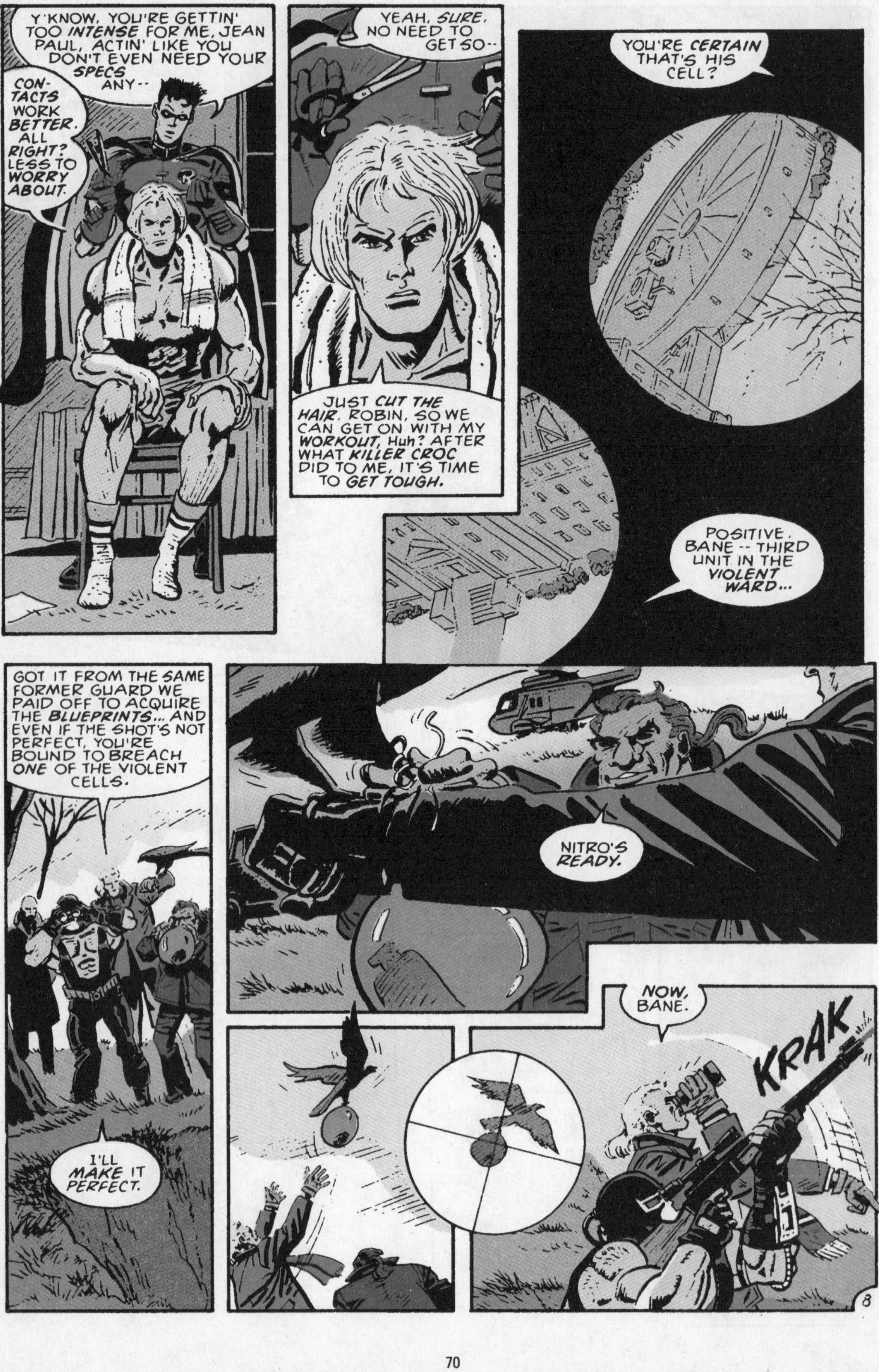
Y'KNOW, YOU'RE GETTIN' TOO INTENSE FOR ME, JEAN PAUL, ACTIN' LIKE YOU DON'T EVEN NEED YOUR SPECS ANY--
CONTACTS WORK BETTER. ALL RIGHT? LESS TO WORRY ABOUT.
YEAH, SURE, NO NEED TO GET SO--
JUST CUT THE HAIR, ROBIN, SO WE CAN GET ON WITH MY WORKOUT, Huh? AFTER WHAT KILLER CROC DID TO ME, IT'S TIME TO GET TOUGH.
YOU'RE CERTAIN THAT'S HIS CELL?
POSITIVE. BANE -- THIRD UNIT IN THE VIOLENT WARD...
GOT IT FROM THE SAME FORMER GUARD WE PAID OFF TO ACQUIRE THE BLUEPRINTS... AND EVEN IF THE SHOT'S NOT PERFECT, YOU'RE BOUND TO BREACH ONE OF THE VIOLENT CELLS.
I'LL MAKE IT PERFECT.
NITRO'S READY.
NOW, BANE.
KRAK
8

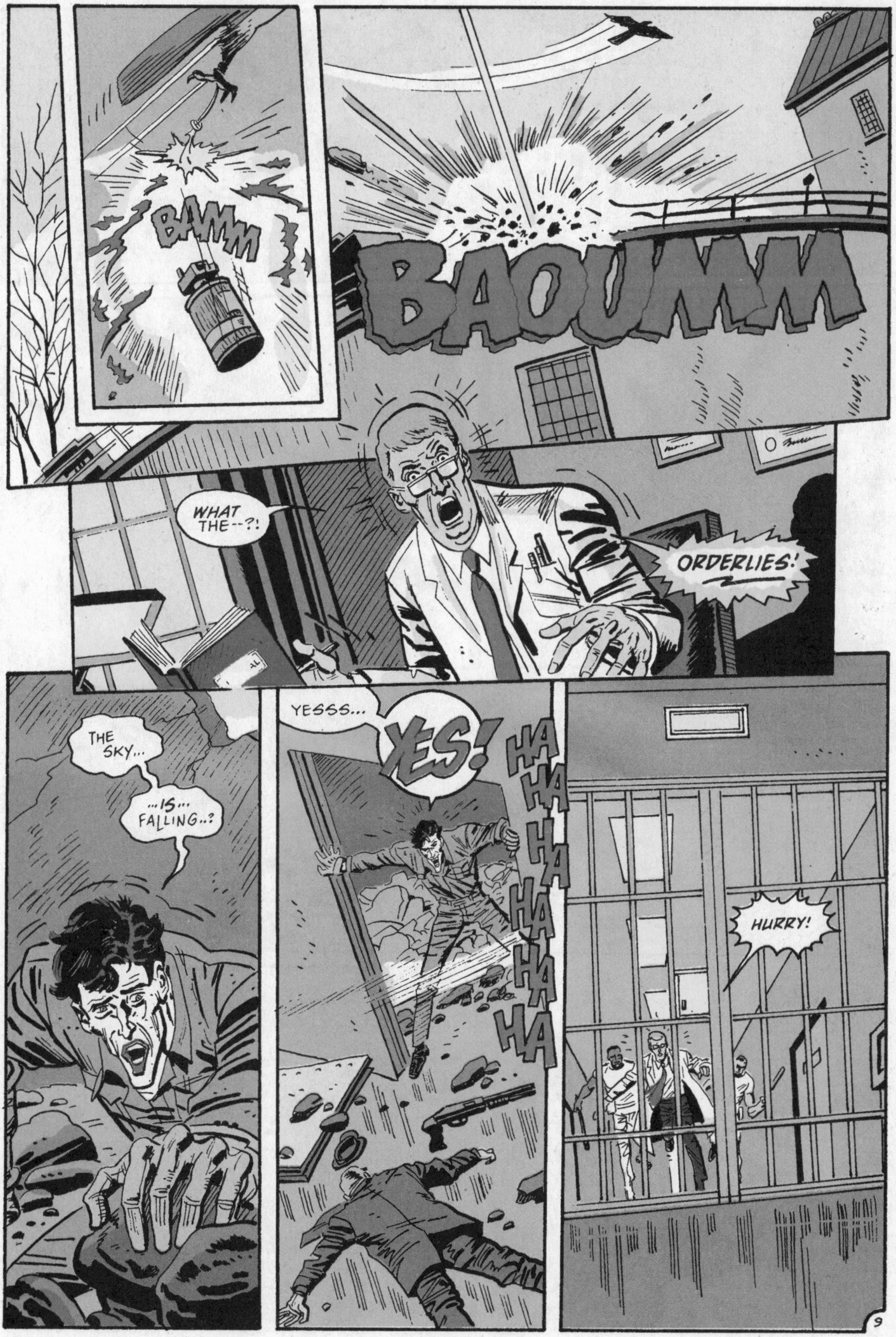
BAMM
BAOUMM
WHAT THE--?!
ORDERLIES!
THE SKY...
...IS... FALLING..?
YESSS...
YES!
HA HA HA HA HA HA HA HA
HURRY!
9

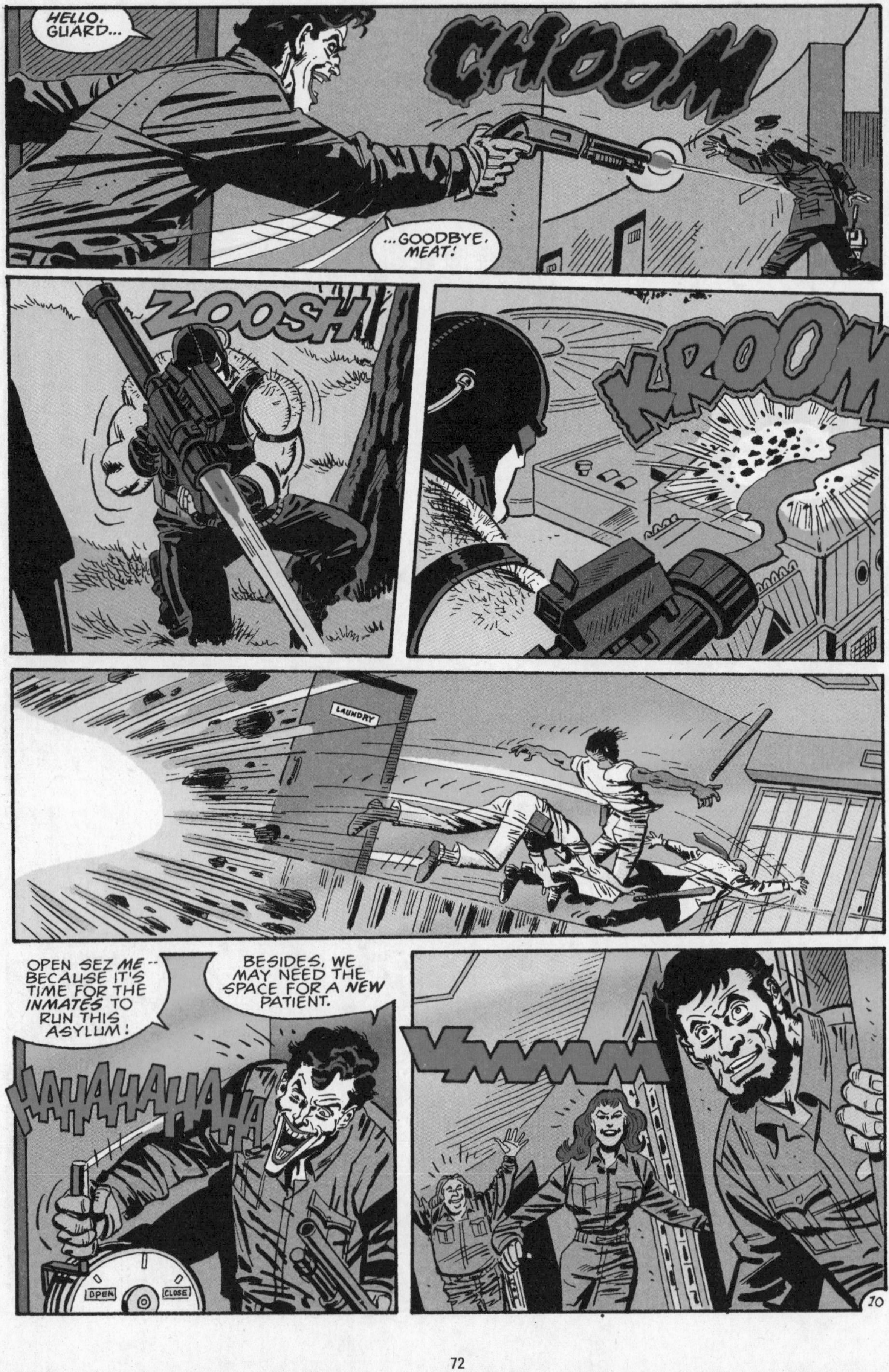
HELLO, GUARD...
CHOOM
...GOODBYE, MEAT!
ZOOSH
KROOM
LAUNDRY
OPEN SEZ ME -- BECAUSE IT'S TIME FOR THE INMATES TO RUN THIS ASYLUM!
BESIDES, WE MAY NEED THE SPACE FOR A NEW PATIENT.
HAHAHAHAHAHA
OPEN
CLOSE
VMMMMM
10

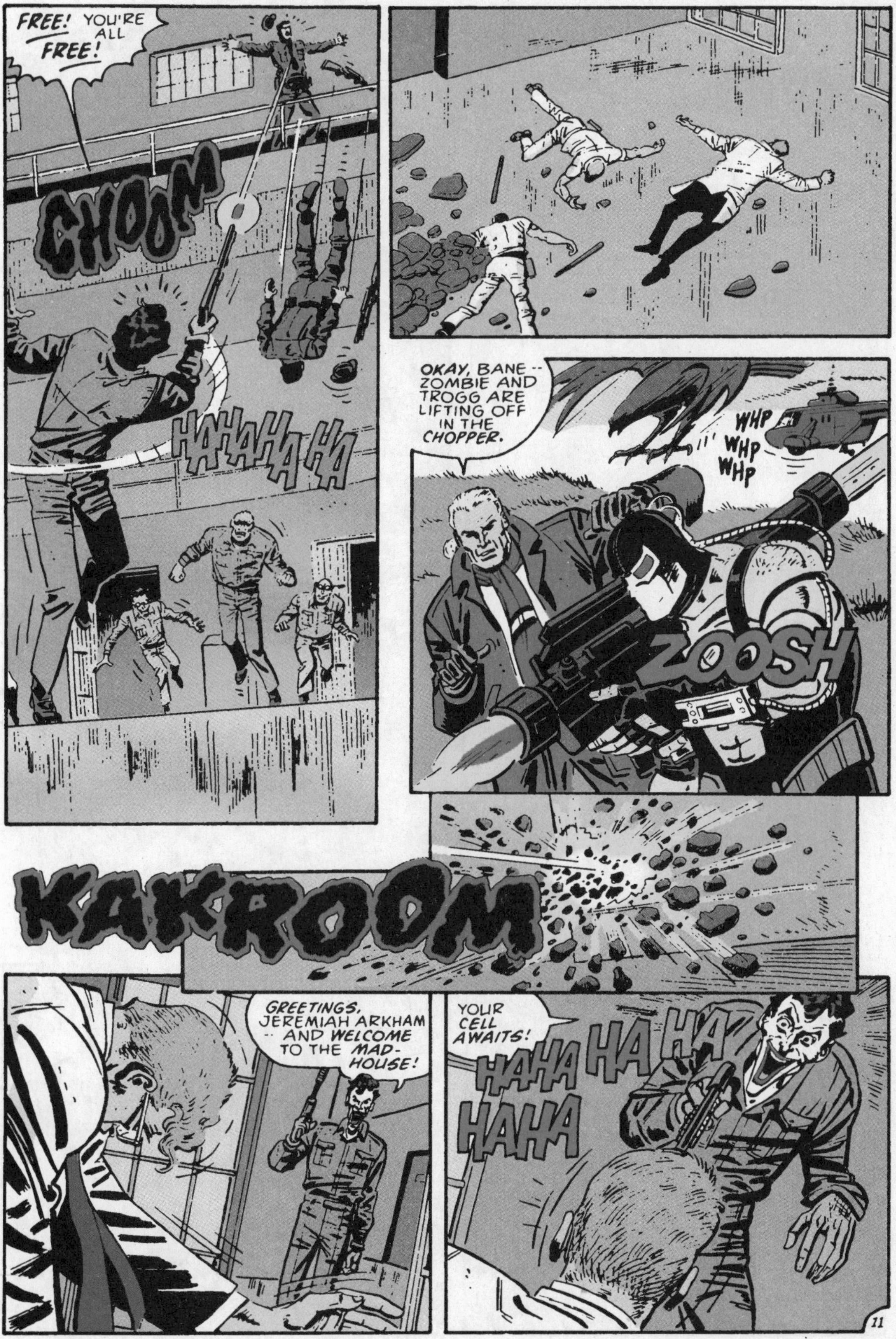

FREE! YOU'RE ALL FREE!
CHOOM
HAHAHAHA
OKAY, BANE -- ZOMBIE AND TROGG ARE LIFTING OFF IN THE CHOPPER.
WHP WHP WHP
ZOOSH
KAKROOM
GREETINGS, JEREMIAH ARKHAM -- AND WELCOME TO THE MAD-HOUSE!
YOUR CELL AWAITS!
HAHA HA HA HAHA
11

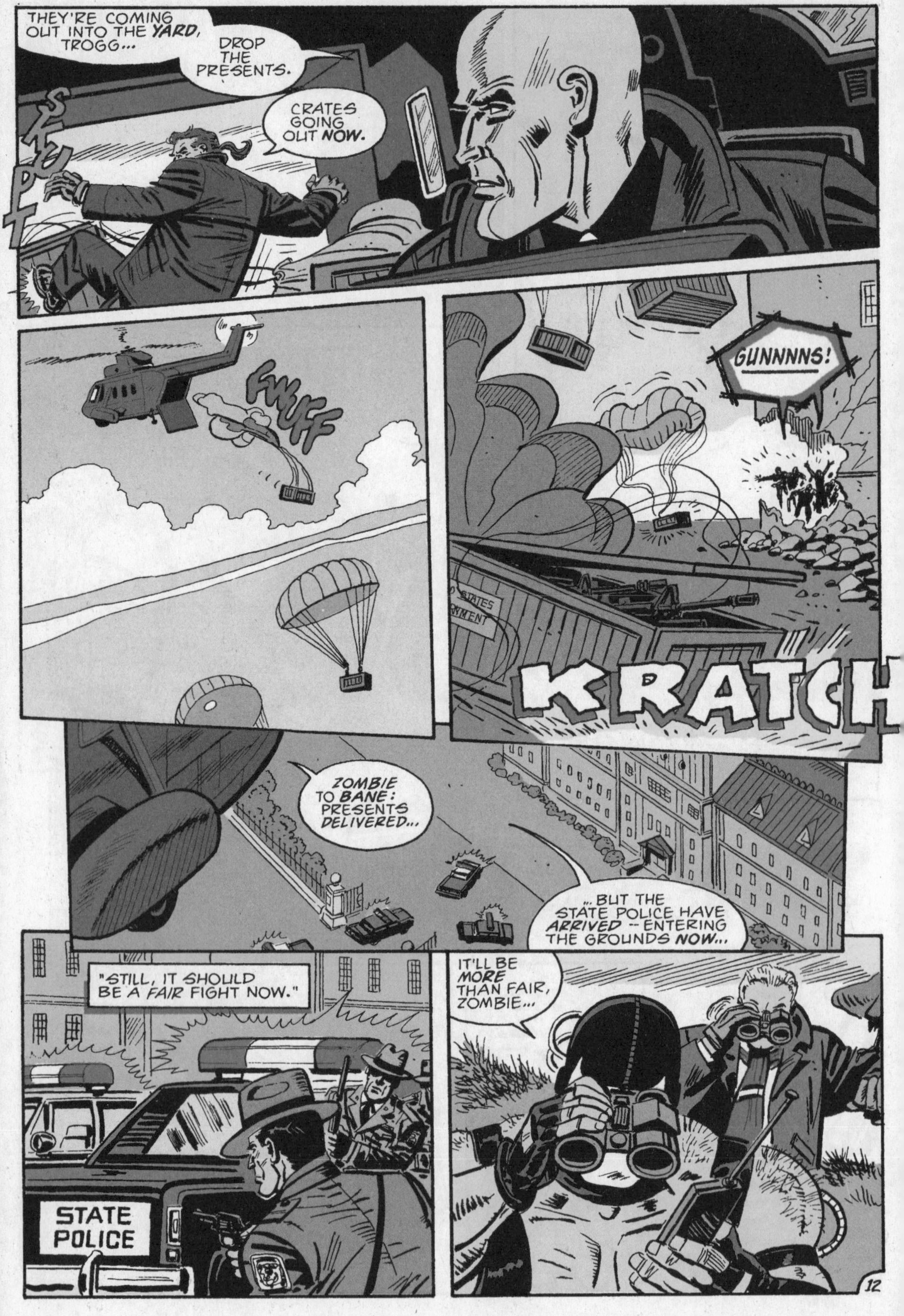
THEY'RE COMING OUT INTO THE YARD, TROGG...
DROP THE PRESENTS.
SKRUPT
CRATES GOING OUT NOW.
FWUFF
GUNNNNS!
KRATCH
ZOMBIE TO BANE: PRESENTS DELIVERED...
...BUT THE STATE POLICE HAVE ARRIVED -- ENTERING THE GROUNDS NOW...
"STILL, IT SHOULD BE A FAIR FIGHT NOW."
IT'LL BE MORE THAN FAIR, ZOMBIE...
STATE POLICE
12

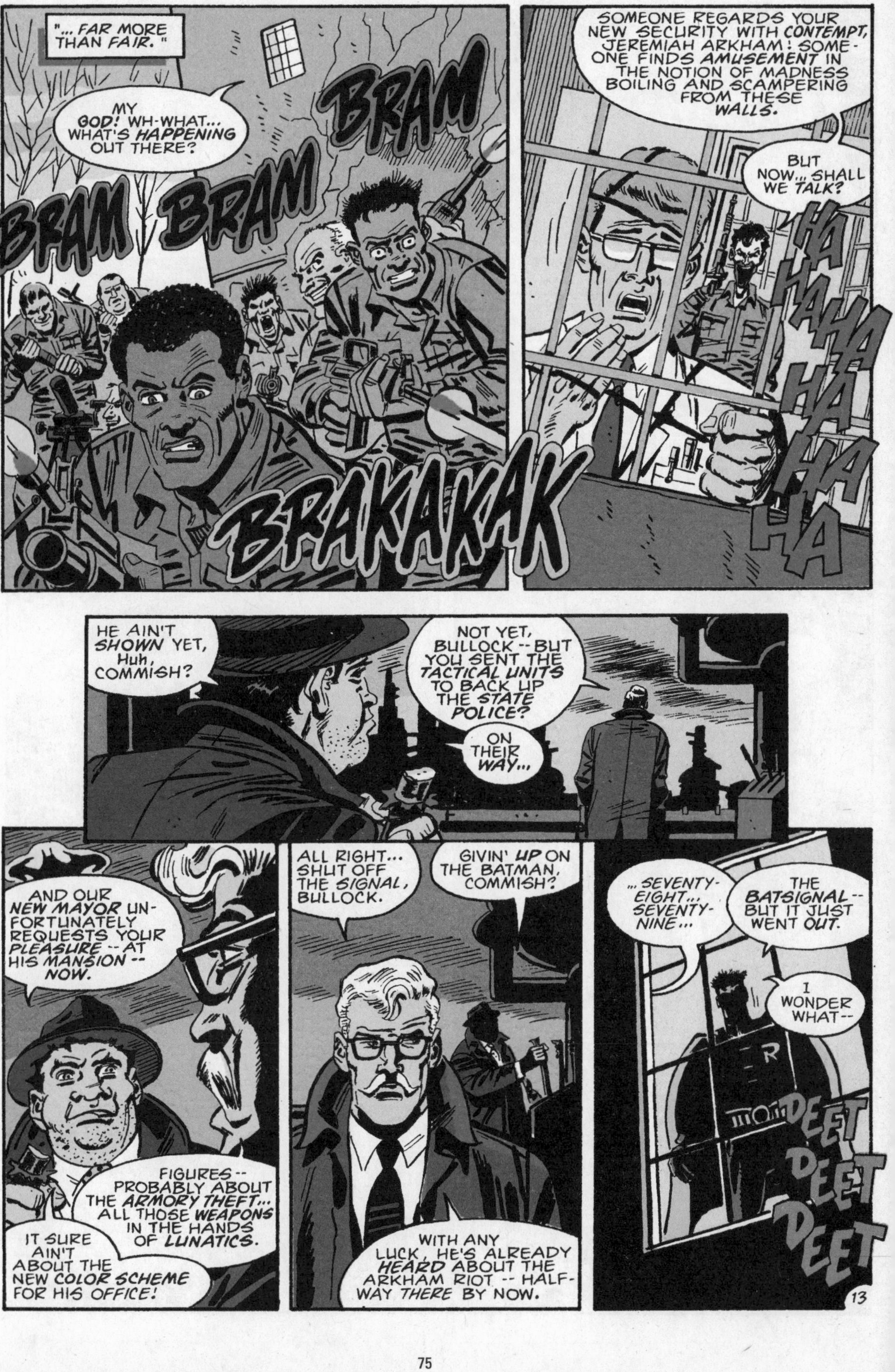
"...FAR MORE THAN FAIR."
MY GOD! WH-WHAT... WHAT'S HAPPENING OUT THERE?
BRAM BRAM BRAM BRAM
BRAKAKAK
SOMEONE REGARDS YOUR NEW SECURITY WITH CONTEMPT, JEREMIAH ARKHAM: SOMEONE FINDS AMUSEMENT IN THE NOTION OF MADNESS BOILING AND SCAMPERING FROM THESE WALLS.
BUT NOW... SHALL WE TALK?
HA HA HA HA HA HA HA
HE AIN'T SHOWN YET, Huh, COMMISH?
NOT YET, BULLOCK -- BUT YOU SENT THE TACTICAL UNITS TO BACK UP THE STATE POLICE?
ON THEIR WAY...
AND OUR NEW MAYOR UNFORTUNATELY REQUESTS YOUR PLEASURE -- AT HIS MANSION -- NOW.
FIGURES -- PROBABLY ABOUT THE ARMORY THEFT... ALL THOSE WEAPONS IN THE HANDS OF LUNATICS.
IT SURE AIN'T ABOUT THE NEW COLOR SCHEME FOR HIS OFFICE!
ALL RIGHT... SHUT OFF THE SIGNAL, BULLOCK.
GIVIN' UP ON THE BATMAN, COMMISH?
WITH ANY LUCK, HE'S ALREADY HEARD ABOUT THE ARKHAM RIOT -- HALFWAY THERE BY NOW.
...SEVENTY-EIGHT... SEVENTY-NINE...
THE BATSIGNAL -- BUT IT JUST WENT OUT.
I WONDER WHAT--
DEET DEET DEET
13

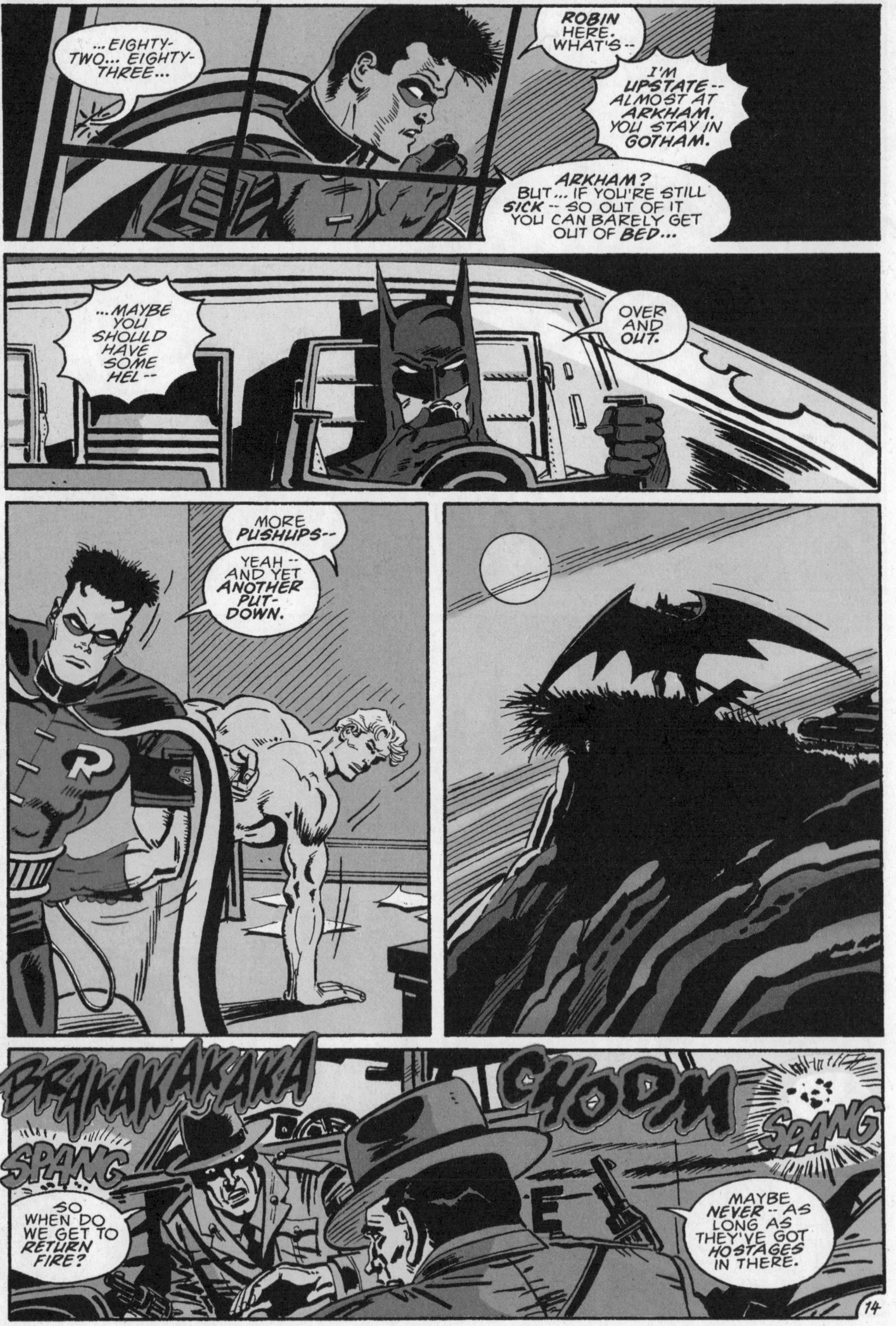
...EIGHTY-TWO... EIGHTY-THREE...
ROBIN HERE. WHAT'S --
I'M UPSTATE -- ALMOST AT ARKHAM. YOU STAY IN GOTHAM.
ARKHAM? BUT... IF YOU'RE STILL SICK -- SO OUT OF IT YOU CAN BARELY GET OUT OF BED...
...MAYBE YOU SHOULD HAVE SOME HEL --
OVER AND OUT.
MORE PUSHUPS--
YEAH -- AND YET ANOTHER PUT-DOWN.
BRAKAKAKAKA
CHOOM
SPANG
SPANG
SO WHEN DO WE GET TO RETURN FIRE?
MAYBE NEVER -- AS LONG AS THEY'VE GOT HOSTAGES IN THERE.
14

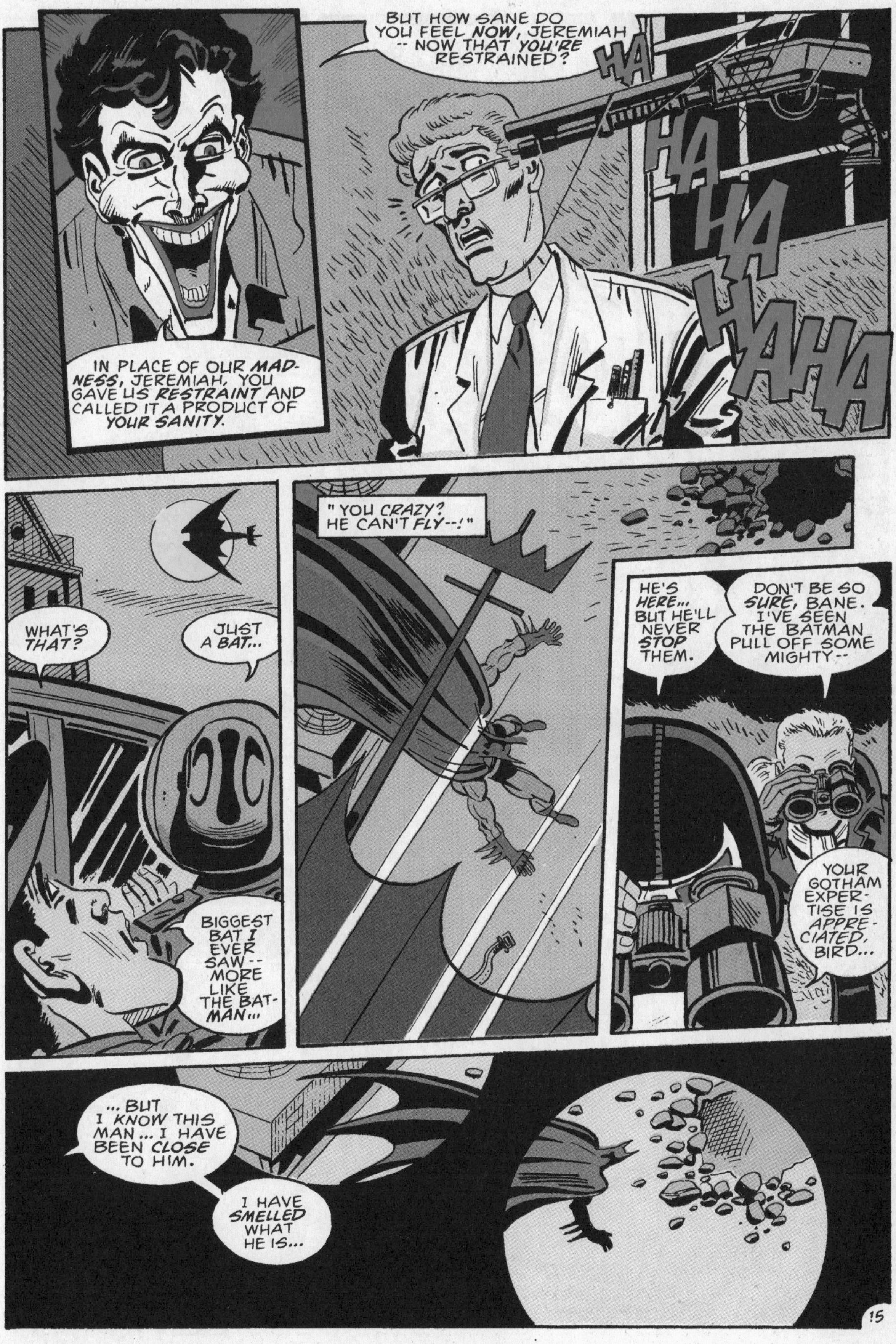
BUT HOW SANE DO YOU FEEL NOW, JEREMIAH -- NOW THAT YOU'RE RESTRAINED?
HA HA HA HA HAHA
IN PLACE OF OUR MADNESS, JEREMIAH, YOU GAVE US RESTRAINT AND CALLED IT A PRODUCT OF YOUR SANITY.
WHAT'S THAT?
JUST A BAT...
BIGGEST BAT I EVER SAW-- MORE LIKE THE BATMAN...
"YOU CRAZY? HE CAN'T FLY--!"
HE'S HERE... BUT HE'LL NEVER STOP THEM.
DON'T BE SO SURE, BANE. I'VE SEEN THE BATMAN PULL OFF SOME MIGHTY--
YOUR GOTHAM EXPERTISE IS APPRECIATED, BIRD...
...BUT I KNOW THIS MAN... I HAVE BEEN CLOSE TO HIM.
I HAVE SMELLED WHAT HE IS...
15

"EVEN IF HE *COULD* STOP THEM, HE *WON'T.*"

"HE WILL CHOOSE THE *SAVING OF LIVES* OVER THE *APPREHENSION* OF *KILLERS...*"

DEAD.

"HE *ALWAYS* DOES."

"AND AS FOR THE *POLICE...* THEY *NEVER* HAD A *CHANCE.*"

HEY-- IT'S THE *CAVALRY!*

STATE POLICE

STATE POLICE

ABOUT *TIME!*

WHAT'S THE *CURRENT* HOSTAGE SITUATION?

MOST OF THE ORDER-LIES HAVE MANAGED TO HOLE UP IN THE *ROUNDHOUSE GARRISON* -- BUT, BE-FORE THE 'PHONE LINES WERE CUT, THEY REPORTED A NUM-BER OF *GUARDS* DOWN...

...AND *JEREMIAH ARKHAM* TAKEN BY THE *JOKER.*

THE JOKER--?

"-- THEN GOD *HELP HIM.*"

ALL YOUR *NEW SECURITY,* JEREMIAH, BREACHED LIKE A *WET PAPER BAG* ... ALL YOUR *HARD WORK,* UN-DONE IN A *TWINKLING* OF *FRENZY.*

I *LIKE* THE WORD *"TWINKLING,"* DON'T *YOU?* WERE YOU *HARD* TO *POTTY TRAIN,* JEREMIAH?

DOESN'T *MATTER* -- BECAUSE *EVERY-THING* YOU'VE *TRAINED* FOR, EVERYTHING YOU'VE *ACCOMPLISHED,* IS *SHATTERED...*

...JUST LIKE YOUR *MIND* RIGHT NOW, JERE-MIAH -- *SHATTERED.*

HAHAHAHA

16

78

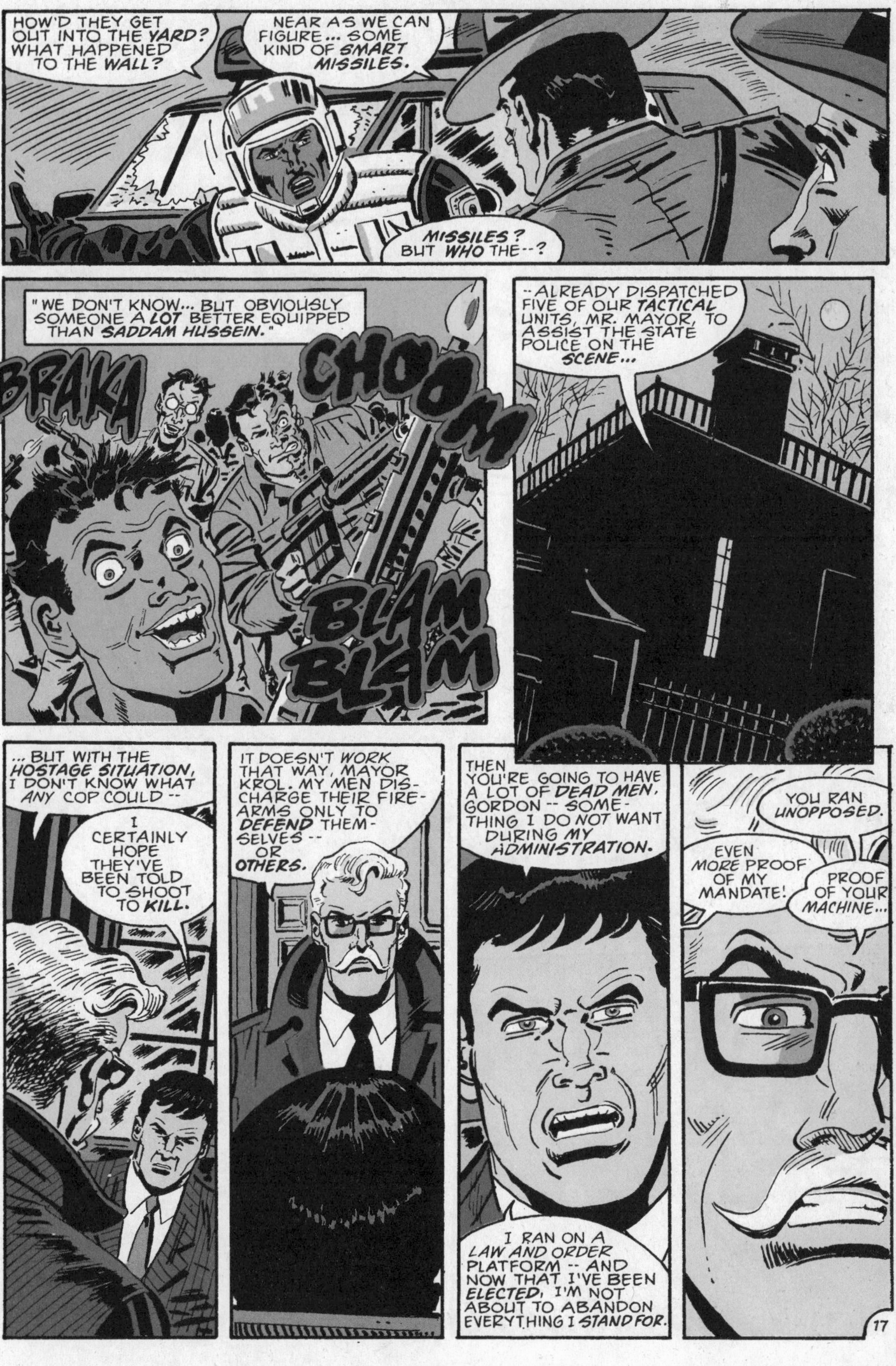
HOW'D THEY GET OUT INTO THE YARD? WHAT HAPPENED TO THE WALL?
NEAR AS WE CAN FIGURE... SOME KIND OF SMART MISSILES.
MISSILES? BUT WHO THE--?
"WE DON'T KNOW... BUT OBVIOUSLY SOMEONE A LOT BETTER EQUIPPED THAN SADDAM HUSSEIN."
BRAKA
CHOOM
BLAM BLAM
--ALREADY DISPATCHED FIVE OF OUR TACTICAL UNITS, MR. MAYOR, TO ASSIST THE STATE POLICE ON THE SCENE...
...BUT WITH THE HOSTAGE SITUATION, I DON'T KNOW WHAT ANY COP COULD --
I CERTAINLY HOPE THEY'VE BEEN TOLD TO SHOOT TO KILL.
IT DOESN'T WORK THAT WAY, MAYOR KROL. MY MEN DISCHARGE THEIR FIREARMS ONLY TO DEFEND THEMSELVES -- OR OTHERS.
THEN YOU'RE GOING TO HAVE A LOT OF DEAD MEN, GORDON -- SOMETHING I DO NOT WANT DURING MY ADMINISTRATION.
I RAN ON A LAW AND ORDER PLATFORM -- AND NOW THAT I'VE BEEN ELECTED, I'M NOT ABOUT TO ABANDON EVERYTHING I STAND FOR.
YOU RAN UNOPPOSED.
EVEN MORE PROOF OF MY MANDATE!
PROOF OF YOUR MACHINE...
17

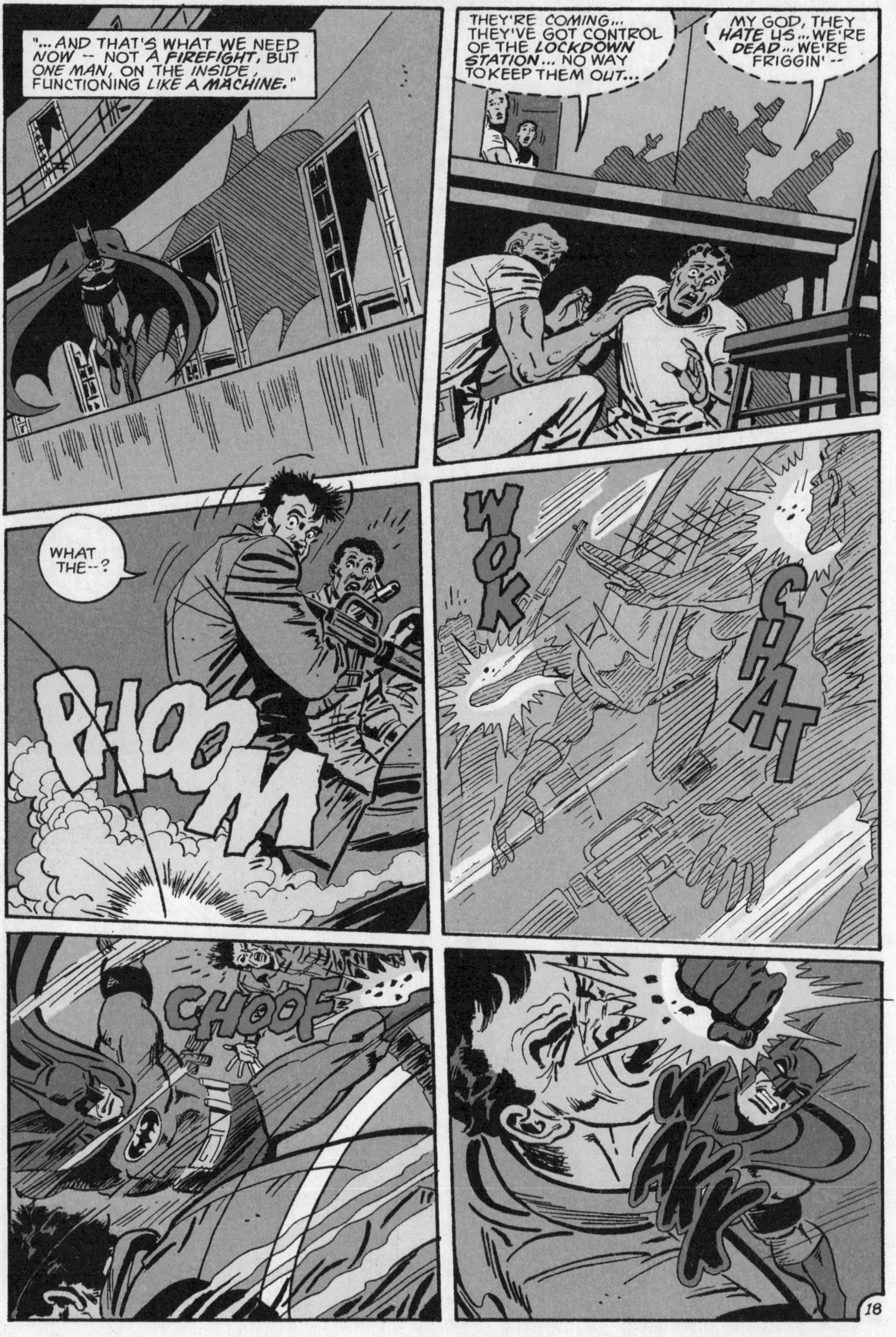
"...AND THAT'S WHAT WE NEED NOW -- NOT A FIREFIGHT, BUT ONE MAN, ON THE INSIDE, FUNCTIONING LIKE A MACHINE."
THEY'RE COMING... THEY'VE GOT CONTROL OF THE LOCKDOWN STATION... NO WAY TO KEEP THEM OUT...
MY GOD, THEY HATE US... WE'RE DEAD... WE'RE FRIGGIN' --
WHAT THE--?
PHOOM
WOK
CHAT
CHOOF
WAKK
18

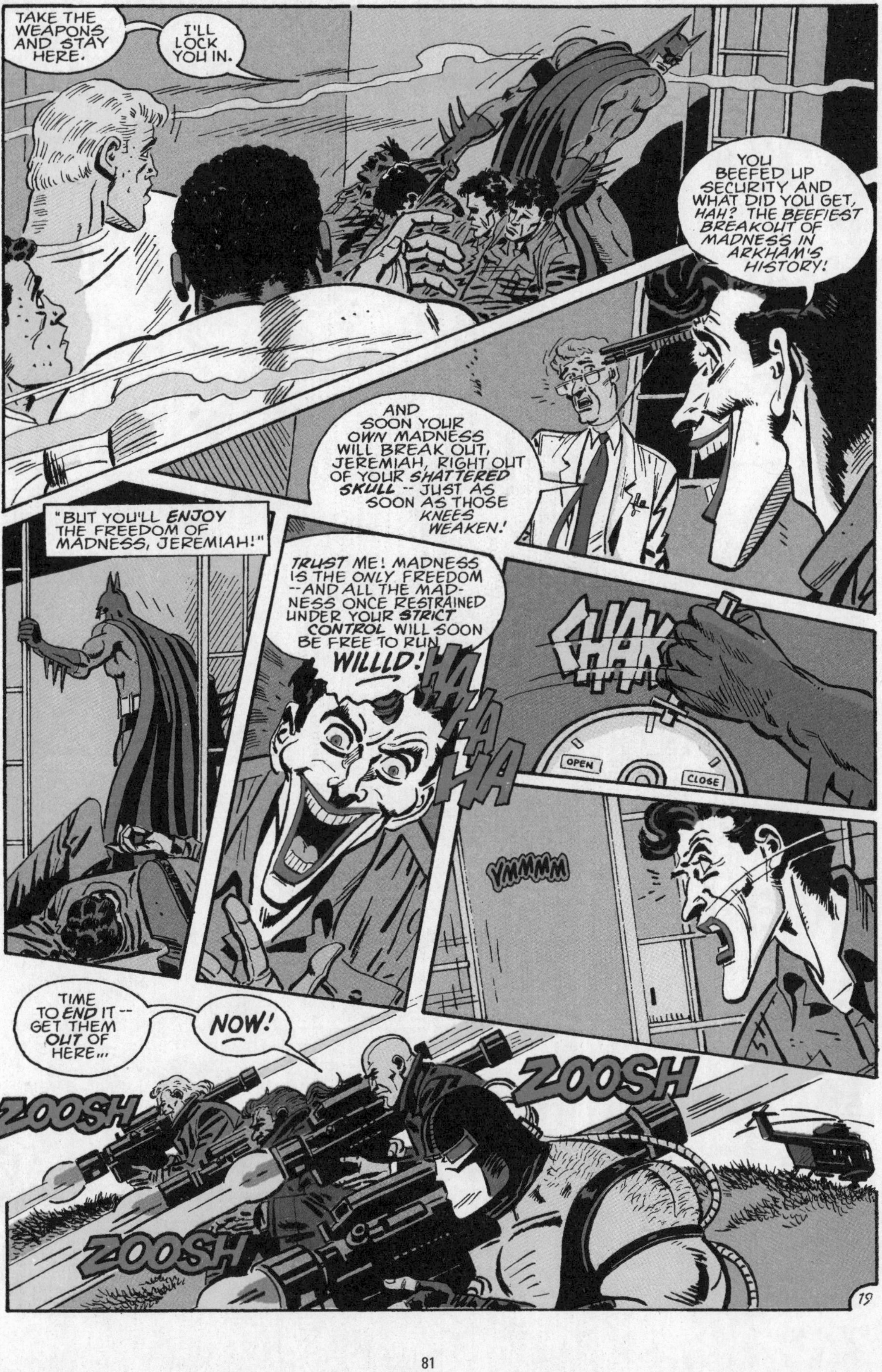
TAKE THE WEAPONS AND STAY HERE.
I'LL LOCK YOU IN.
YOU BEEFED UP SECURITY AND WHAT DID YOU GET, HAH? THE BEEFIEST BREAKOUT OF MADNESS IN ARKHAM'S HISTORY!
AND SOON YOUR OWN MADNESS WILL BREAK OUT, JEREMIAH, RIGHT OUT OF YOUR SHATTERED SKULL -- JUST AS SOON AS THOSE KNEES WEAKEN!
"BUT YOU'LL ENJOY THE FREEDOM OF MADNESS, JEREMIAH!"
TRUST ME! MADNESS IS THE ONLY FREEDOM --AND ALL THE MADNESS ONCE RESTRAINED UNDER YOUR STRICT CONTROL WILL SOON BE FREE TO RUN WILLLD!
HAHAHA
CHAK
OPEN
CLOSE
YMMMM
TIME TO END IT -- GET THEM OUT OF HERE...
NOW!
ZOOSH
ZOOSH
ZOOSH
19

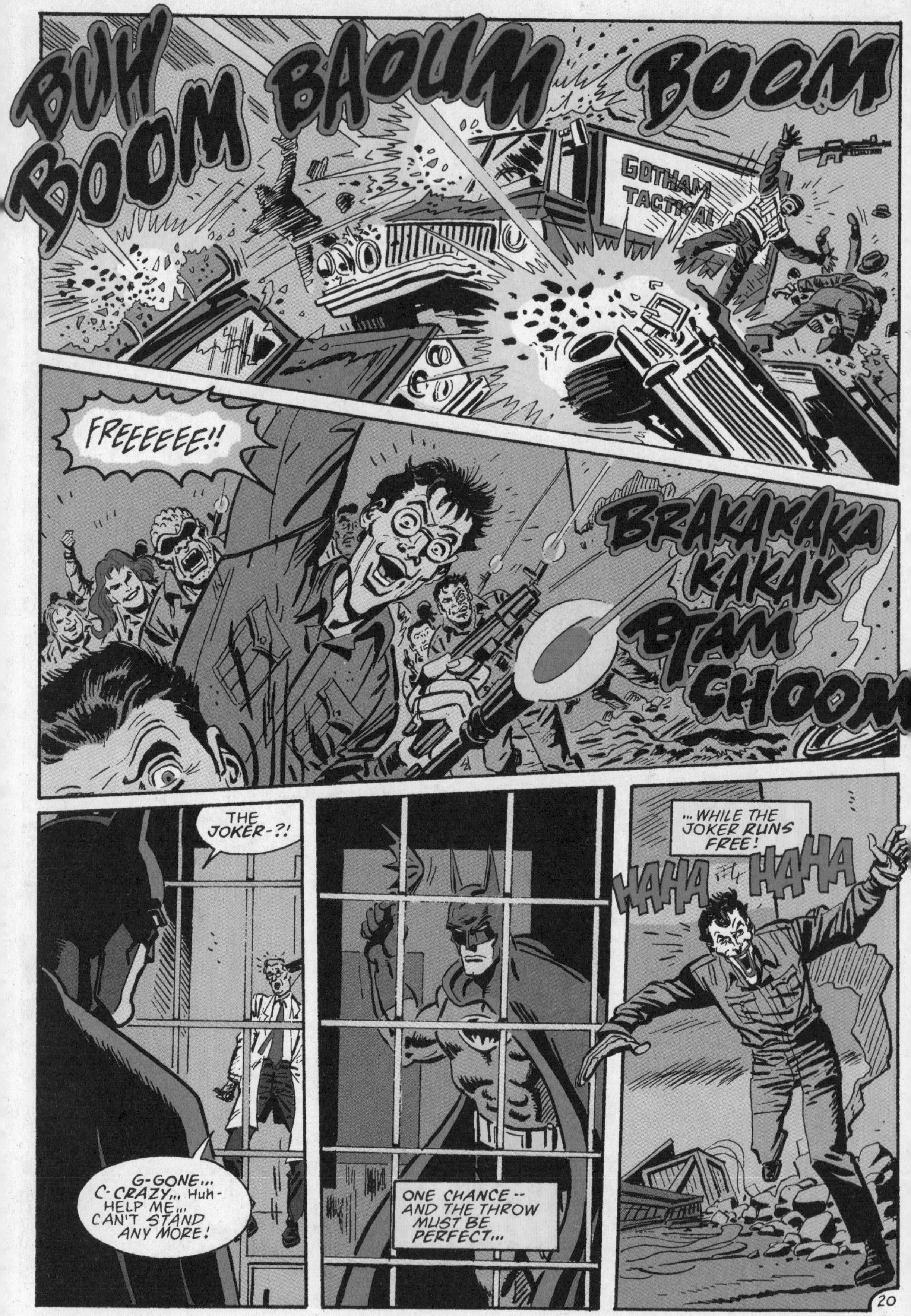
BUH BOOM BAOUM BOOM
GOTHAM TACTICAL
FREEEEEE!!
BRAKAKAKA KAKAK BLAM CHOOM
THE JOKER-?!
G-GONE... C-CRAZY... Huh-HELP ME... CAN'T STAND ANY MORE!
ONE CHANCE -- AND THE THROW MUST BE PERFECT...
...WHILE THE JOKER RUNS FREE!
HAHA HAHA
20

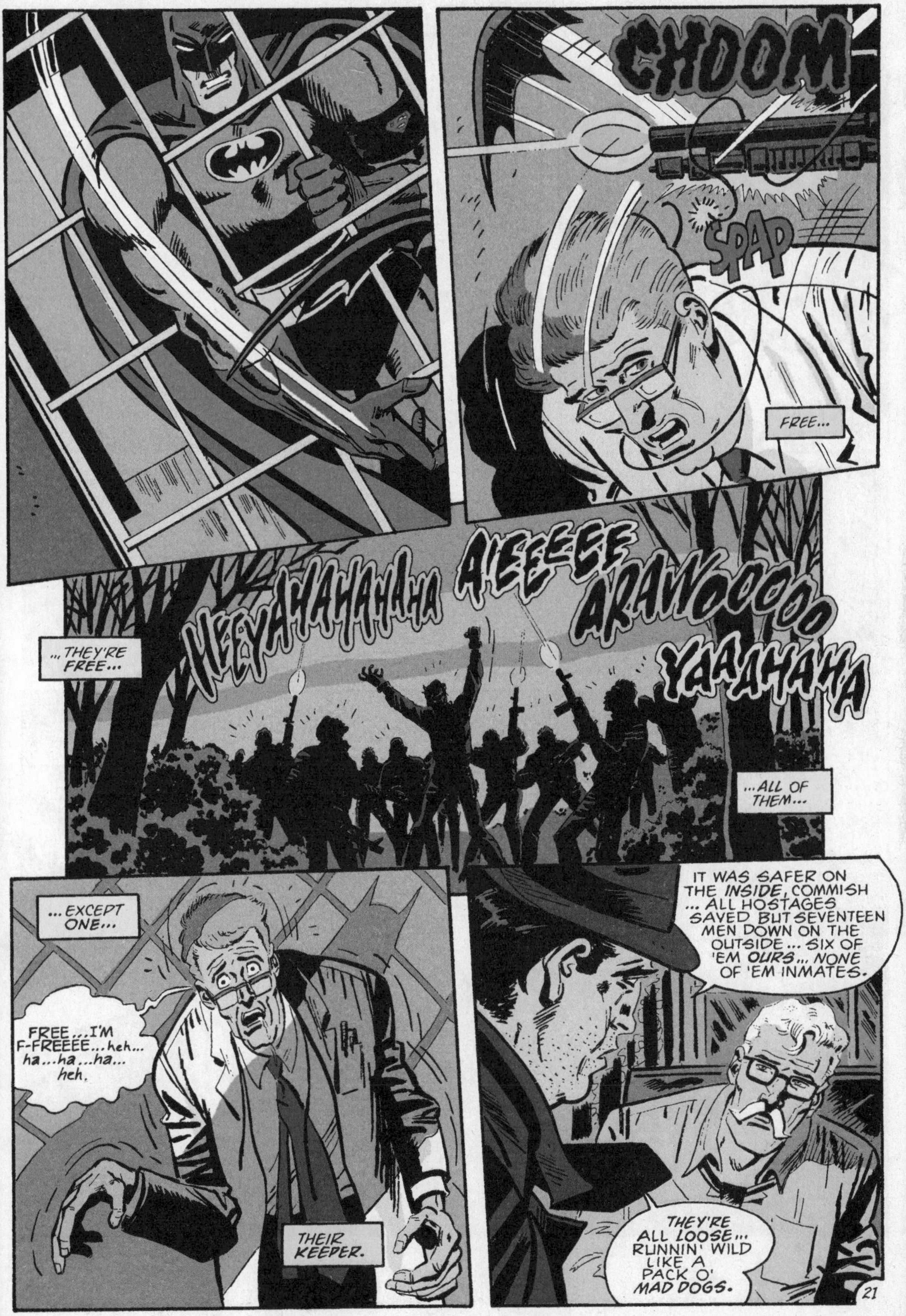
CHOOM
SPAP
FREE...
HEEYAHAHAHAHAHA AIEEEEE ARAWOOOOOO YAAAHAHA
...THEY'RE FREE...
...ALL OF THEM...
...EXCEPT ONE...
FREE...I'M F-FREEEE...heh... ha...ha...ha... heh.
THEIR KEEPER.
IT WAS SAFER ON THE INSIDE, COMMISH ...ALL HOSTAGES SAVED BUT SEVENTEEN MEN DOWN ON THE OUTSIDE...SIX OF 'EM OURS...NONE OF 'EM INMATES.
THEY'RE ALL LOOSE... RUNNIN' WILD LIKE A PACK O' MAD DOGS.
21

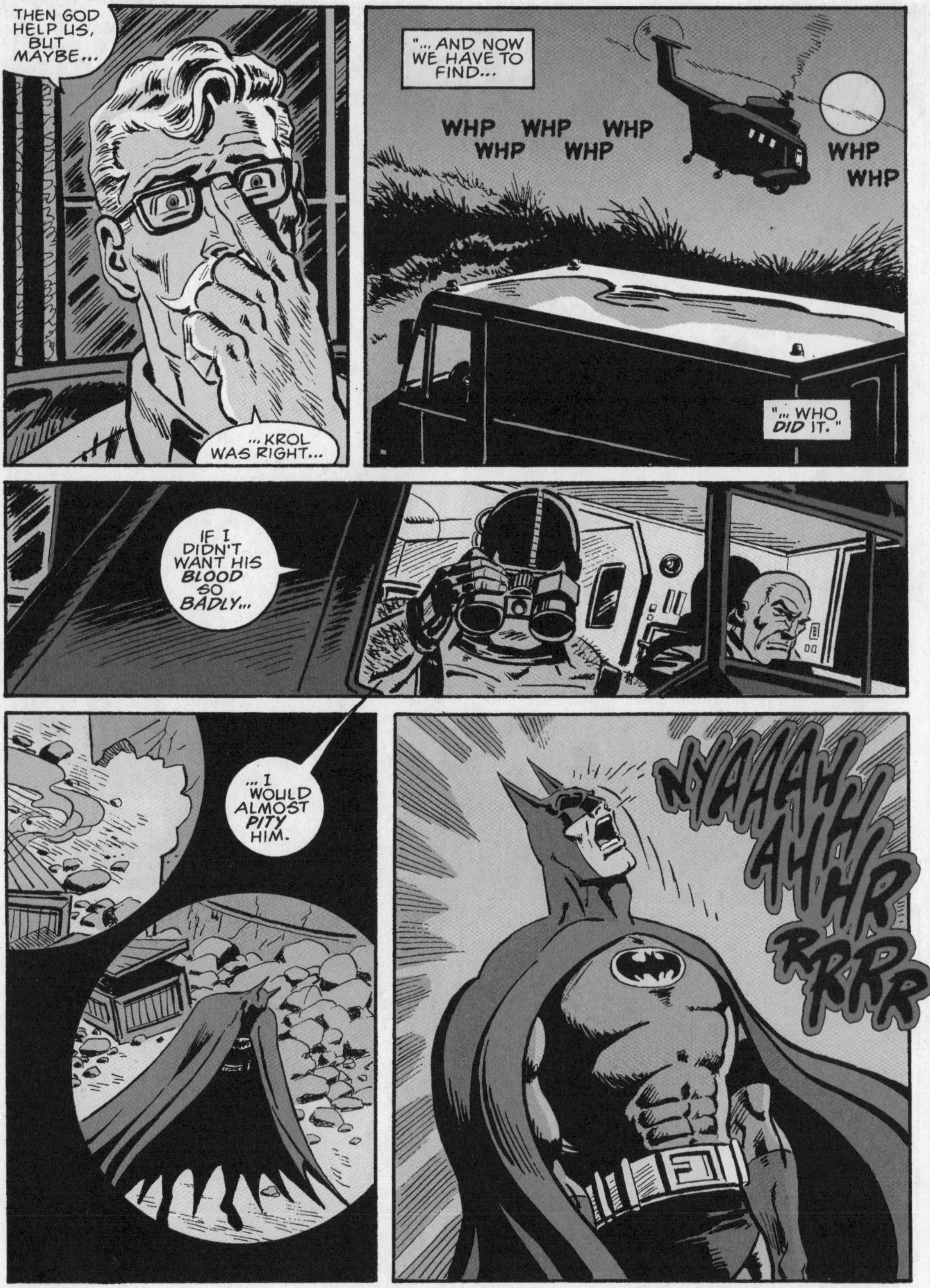
THEN GOD HELP US, BUT MAYBE...
...KROL WAS RIGHT...
"...AND NOW WE HAVE TO FIND...
WHP WHP WHP WHP WHP
WHP WHP
"...WHO *DID* IT."
IF I DIDN'T WANT HIS *BLOOD* SO *BADLY*...
...I WOULD ALMOST *PITY* HIM.
NYAAAAH AHHR RRRR

Cover art by KELLEY JONES

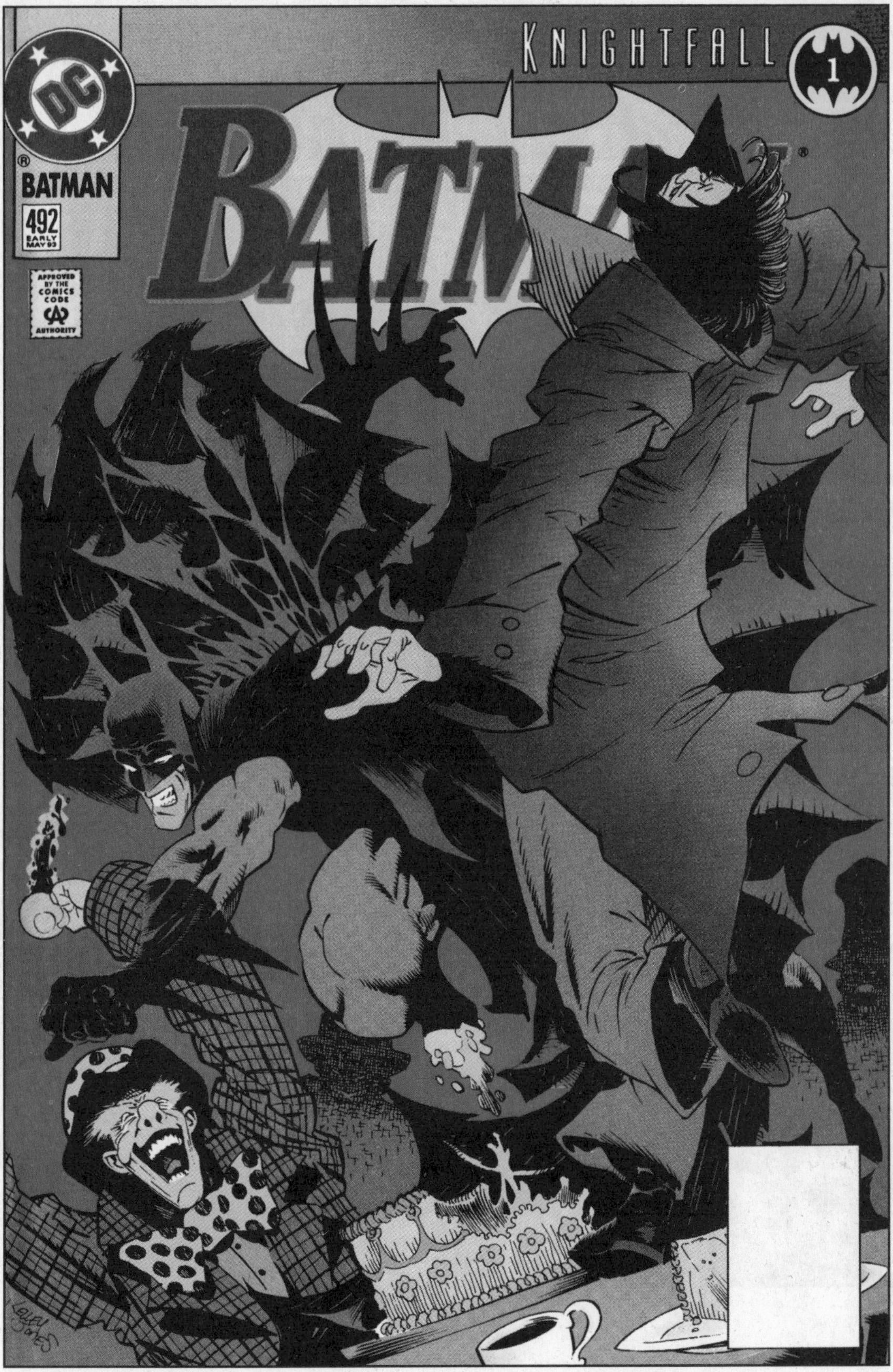

KNIGHTFALL
1
BATMAN
BATMAN
492
EARLY MAY 93
APPROVED BY THE COMICS CODE AUTHORITY

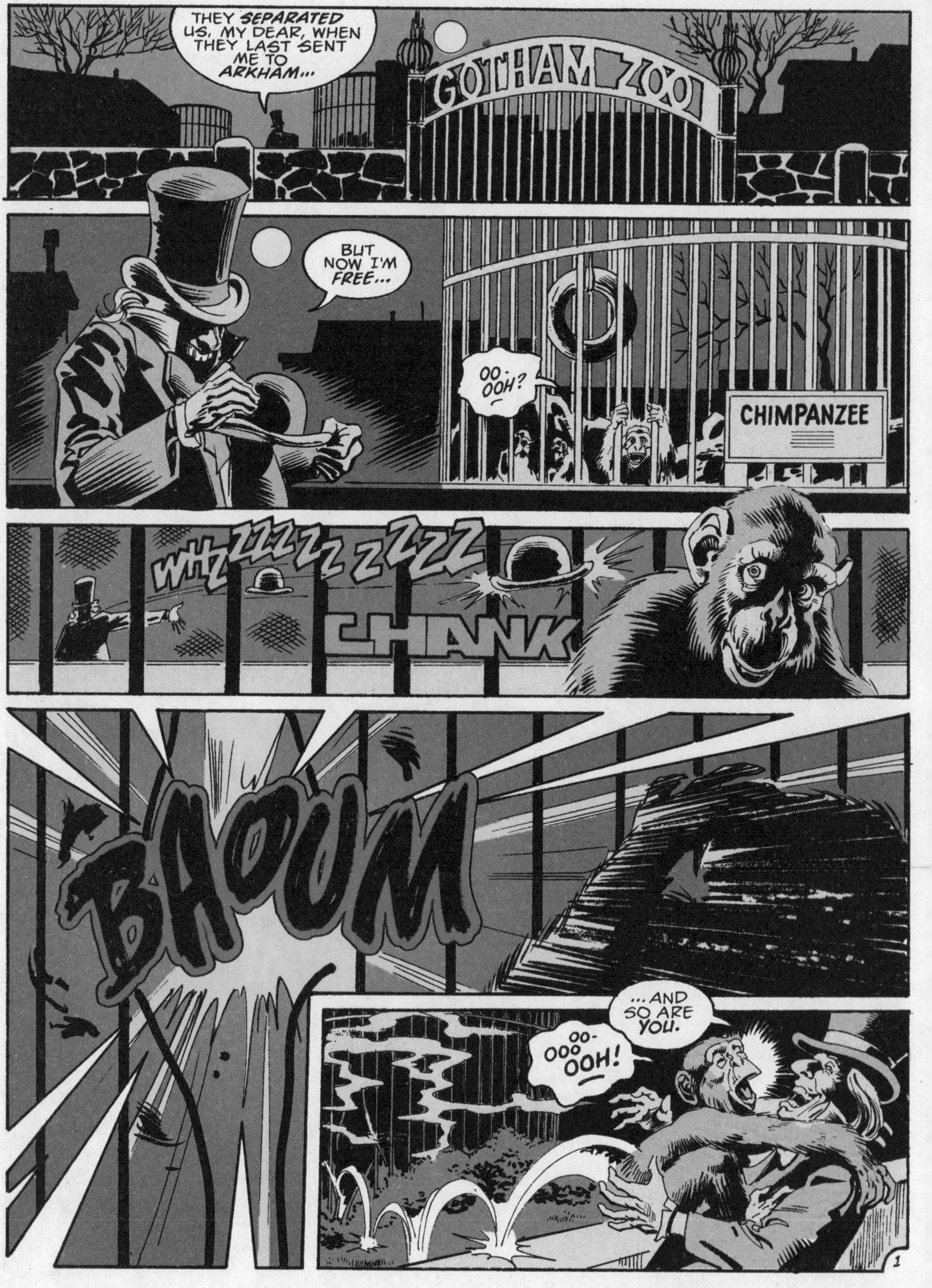
THEY SEPARATED US, MY DEAR, WHEN THEY LAST SENT ME TO ARKHAM...
GOTHAM ZOO
BUT NOW I'M FREE...
OO-OOH?
CHIMPANZEE
WHZZZZZZZZZ
CHANK
BAOUM
...AND SO ARE YOU.
OO-OOO OOH!
1

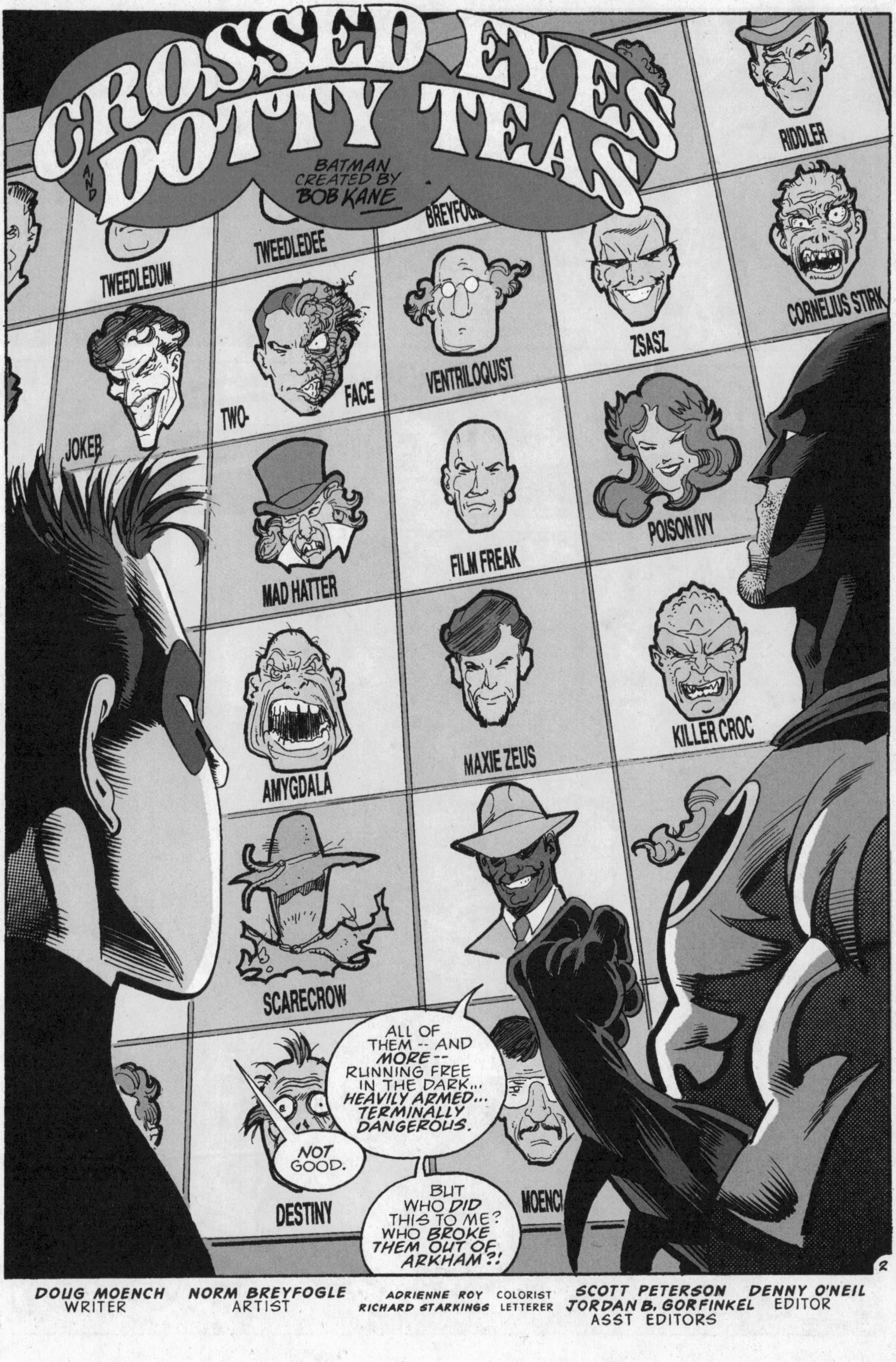
CROSSED EYES AND DOTTY TEAS
BATMAN CREATED BY BOB KANE
RIDDLER
TWEEDLEDUM
TWEEDLEDEE
BREYFOG
CORNELIUS STIRK
ZSASZ
VENTRILOQUIST
TWO-FACE
JOKER
POISON IVY
FILM FREAK
MAD HATTER
KILLER CROC
MAXIE ZEUS
AMYGDALA
SCARECROW
DESTINY
MOENC
ALL OF THEM -- AND MORE -- RUNNING FREE IN THE DARK... HEAVILY ARMED... TERMINALLY DANGEROUS.
NOT GOOD.
BUT WHO DID THIS TO ME? WHO BROKE THEM OUT OF ARKHAM?!
2

DOUG MOENCH WRITER · NORM BREYFOGLE ARTIST · ADRIENNE ROY COLORIST · RICHARD STARKINGS LETTERER · SCOTT PETERSON, JORDAN B. GORFINKEL ASST EDITORS · DENNY O'NEIL EDITOR

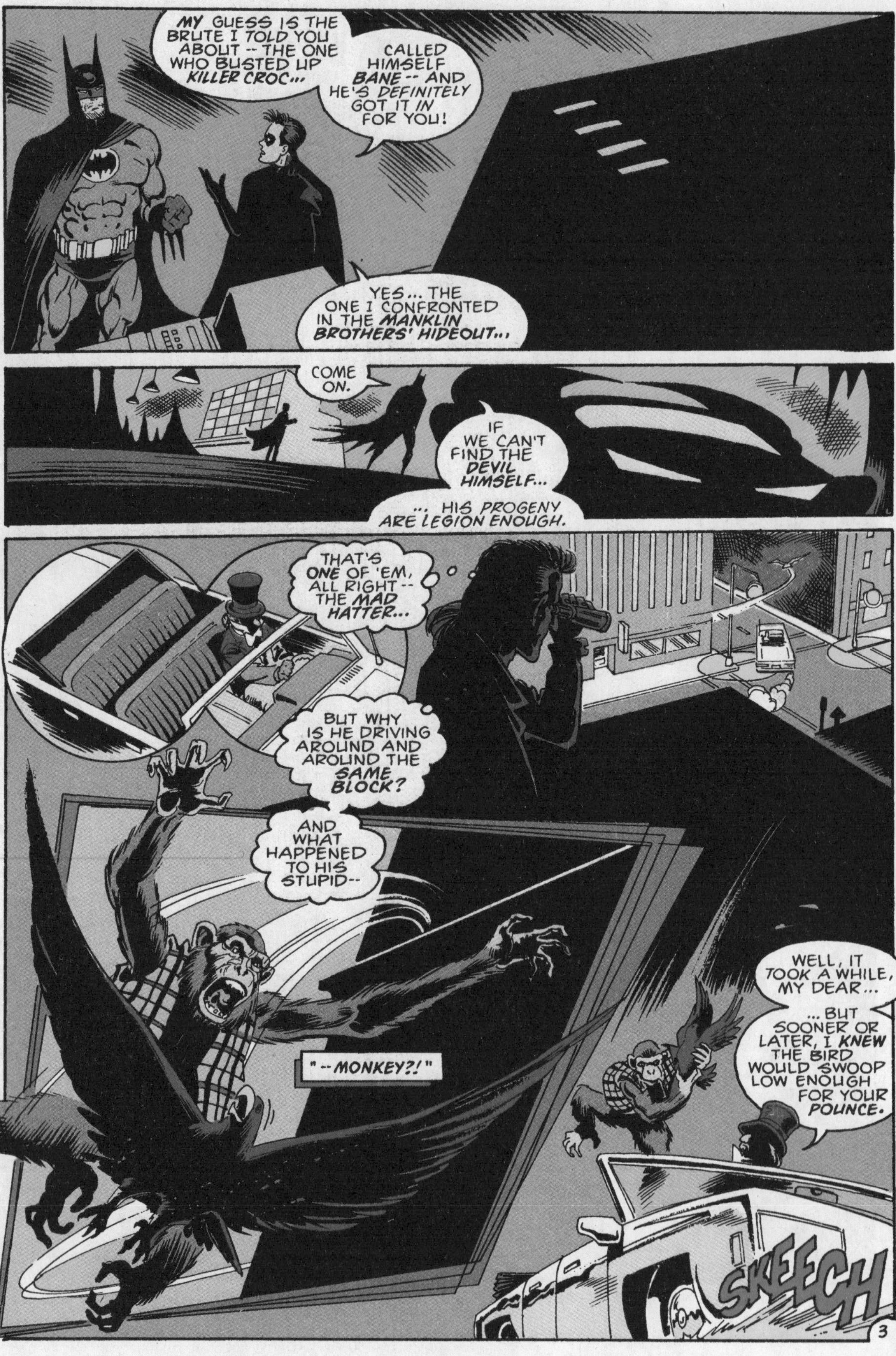
MY GUESS IS THE BRUTE I TOLD YOU ABOUT -- THE ONE WHO BUSTED UP KILLER CROC...
CALLED HIMSELF BANE -- AND HE'S DEFINITELY GOT IT IN FOR YOU!
YES... THE ONE I CONFRONTED IN THE MANKLIN BROTHERS' HIDEOUT...
COME ON.
IF WE CAN'T FIND THE DEVIL HIMSELF...
... HIS PROGENY ARE LEGION ENOUGH.
THAT'S ONE OF 'EM, ALL RIGHT -- THE MAD HATTER...
BUT WHY IS HE DRIVING AROUND AND AROUND THE SAME BLOCK?
AND WHAT HAPPENED TO HIS STUPID--
"--MONKEY?!"
WELL, IT TOOK A WHILE, MY DEAR...
... BUT SOONER OR LATER, I KNEW THE BIRD WOULD SWOOP LOW ENOUGH FOR YOUR POUNCE.
SKEECH
3

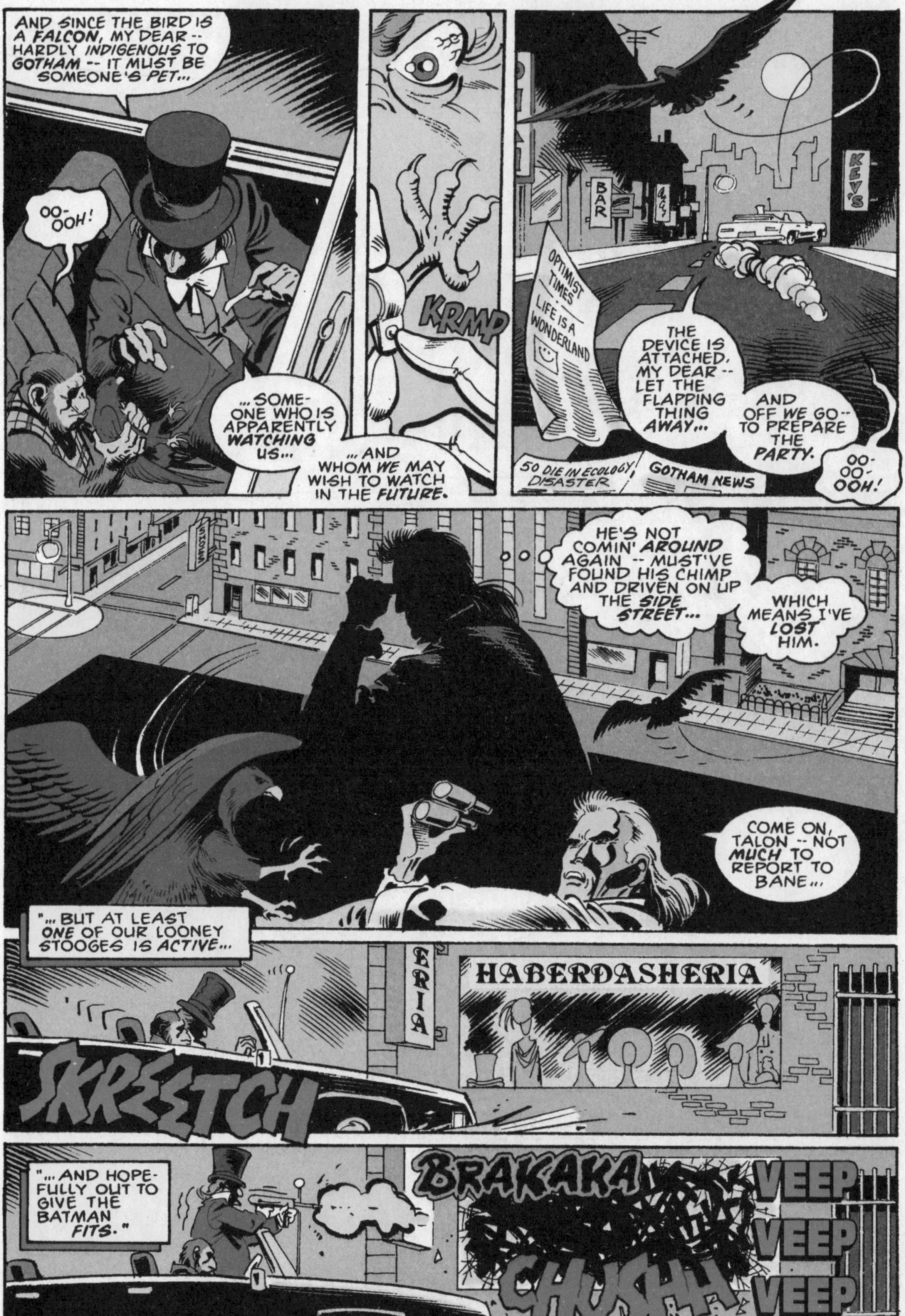
AND SINCE THE BIRD IS A FALCON, MY DEAR -- HARDLY INDIGENOUS TO GOTHAM -- IT MUST BE SOMEONE'S PET...
OO-OOH!
...SOME-ONE WHO IS APPARENTLY WATCHING US...
KRMP
...AND WHOM WE MAY WISH TO WATCH IN THE FUTURE.
BAR
KEV'S
OPTIMIST TIMES
LIFE IS A WONDERLAND
50 DIE IN ECOLOGY DISASTER
GOTHAM NEWS
THE DEVICE IS ATTACHED, MY DEAR -- LET THE FLAPPING THING AWAY...
AND OFF WE GO -- TO PREPARE THE PARTY.
OO-OO-OOH!
HE'S NOT COMIN' AROUND AGAIN -- MUST'VE FOUND HIS CHIMP AND DRIVEN ON UP THE SIDE STREET...
WHICH MEANS I'VE LOST HIM.
COME ON, TALON -- NOT MUCH TO REPORT TO BANE...
"...BUT AT LEAST ONE OF OUR LOONEY STOOGES IS ACTIVE...
HABERDASHERIA
ERIA
SKREETCH
"...AND HOPE-FULLY OUT TO GIVE THE BATMAN FITS."
BRAKAKA
VEEP
VEEP
VEEP
CHUSHH
4

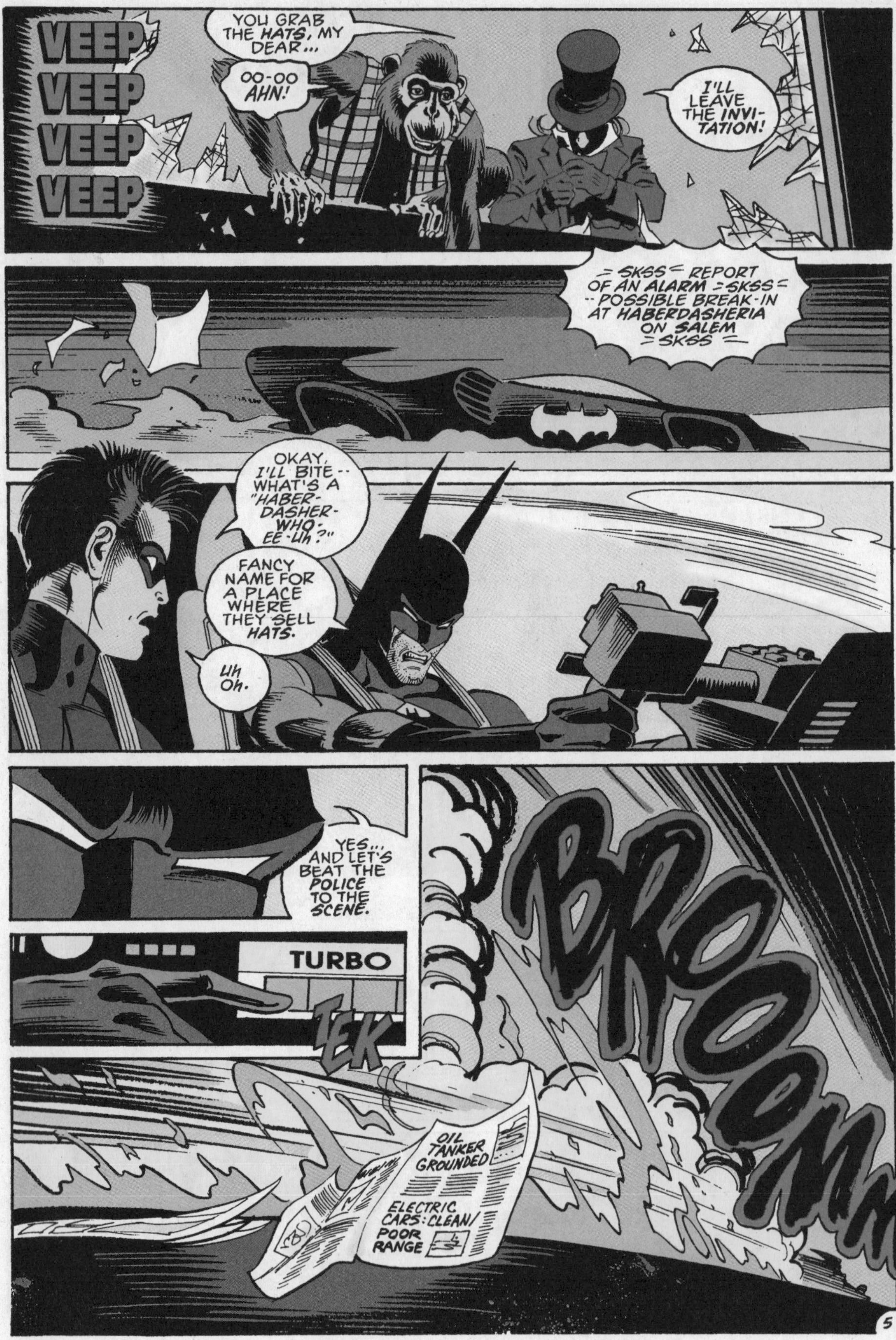
VEEP
VEEP
VEEP
VEEP
YOU GRAB THE HATS, MY DEAR...
OO-OO AHN!
I'LL LEAVE THE INVITATION!
=SKSS= REPORT OF AN ALARM =SKSS= --POSSIBLE BREAK-IN AT HABERDASHERIA ON SALEM =SKSS
OKAY, I'LL BITE-- WHAT'S A "HABER-DASHER-WHO-EE-UH?"
FANCY NAME FOR A PLACE WHERE THEY SELL HATS.
Uh Oh.
YES... AND LET'S BEAT THE POLICE TO THE SCENE.
TURBO
TEK
BROOOMM
OIL TANKER GROUNDED
ELECTRIC CARS: CLEAN/ POOR RANGE
5

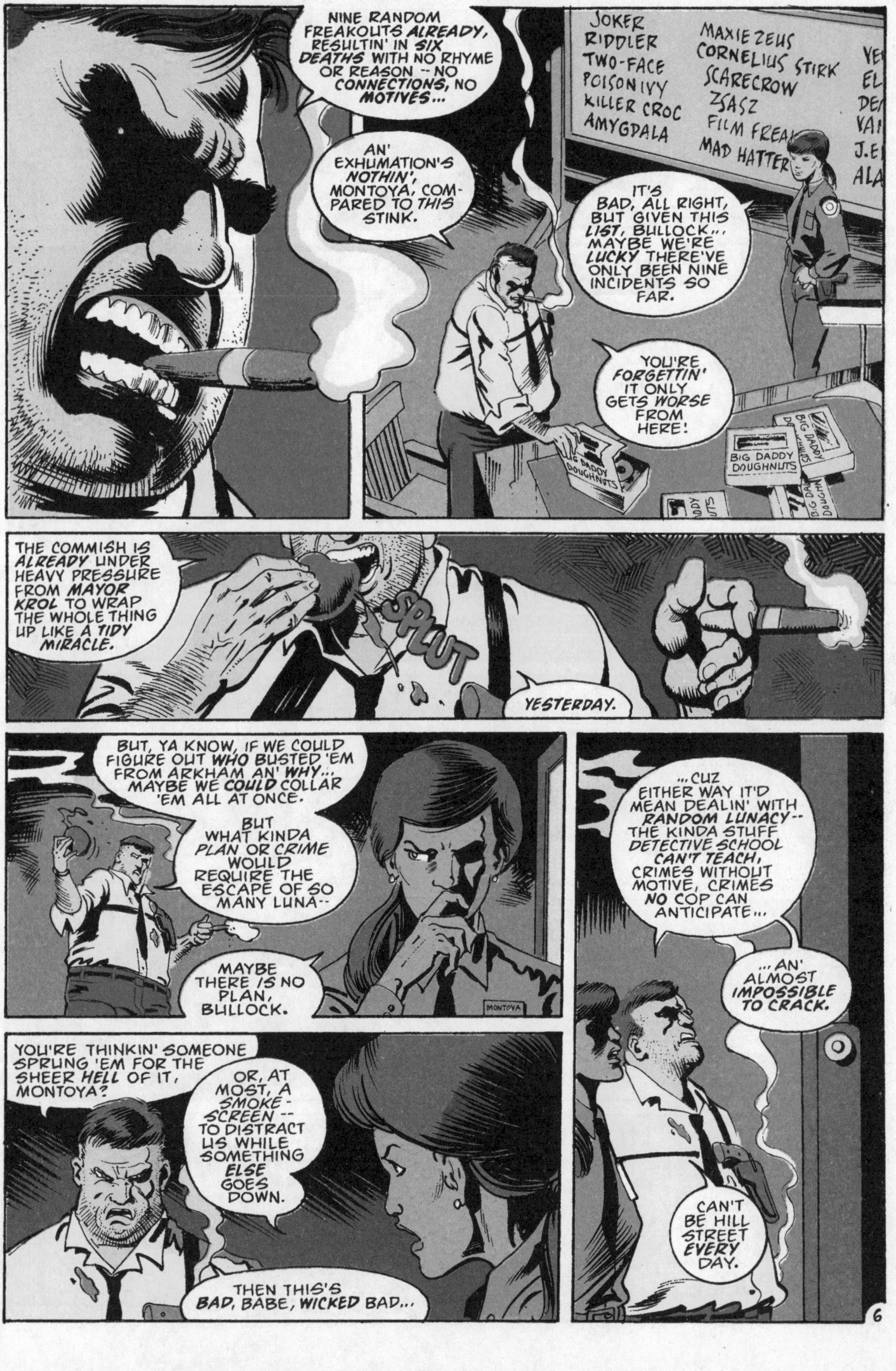
NINE RANDOM FREAKOUTS ALREADY, RESULTIN' IN SIX DEATHS WITH NO RHYME OR REASON -- NO CONNECTIONS, NO MOTIVES...
AN' EXHUMATION'S NOTHIN', MONTOYA, COMPARED TO THIS STINK.
JOKER
RIDDLER
TWO-FACE
POISON IVY
KILLER CROC
AMYGDALA
MAXIE ZEUS
CORNELIUS STIRK
SCARECROW
ZSASZ
FILM FREA
MAD HATTER
IT'S BAD, ALL RIGHT, BUT GIVEN THIS LIST, BULLOCK... MAYBE WE'RE LUCKY THERE'VE ONLY BEEN NINE INCIDENTS SO FAR.
YOU'RE FORGETTIN' IT ONLY GETS WORSE FROM HERE!
BIG DADDY DOUGHNUTS
BIG DADDY DOUGHNUTS
THE COMMISH IS ALREADY UNDER HEAVY PRESSURE FROM MAYOR KROL TO WRAP THE WHOLE THING UP LIKE A TIDY MIRACLE.
SPLUT
YESTERDAY.
BUT, YA KNOW, IF WE COULD FIGURE OUT WHO BUSTED 'EM FROM ARKHAM AN' WHY... MAYBE WE COULD COLLAR 'EM ALL AT ONCE.
BUT WHAT KINDA PLAN OR CRIME WOULD REQUIRE THE ESCAPE OF SO MANY LUNA--
MAYBE THERE IS NO PLAN, BULLOCK.
MONTOYA
YOU'RE THINKIN' SOMEONE SPRUNG 'EM FOR THE SHEER HELL OF IT, MONTOYA?
OR, AT MOST, A SMOKE-SCREEN -- TO DISTRACT US WHILE SOMETHING ELSE GOES DOWN.
THEN THIS'S BAD, BABE, WICKED BAD...
...CUZ EITHER WAY IT'D MEAN DEALIN' WITH RANDOM LUNACY -- THE KINDA STUFF DETECTIVE SCHOOL CAN'T TEACH, CRIMES WITHOUT MOTIVE, CRIMES NO COP CAN ANTICIPATE...
...AN' ALMOST IMPOSSIBLE TO CRACK.
CAN'T BE HILL STREET EVERY DAY.
6

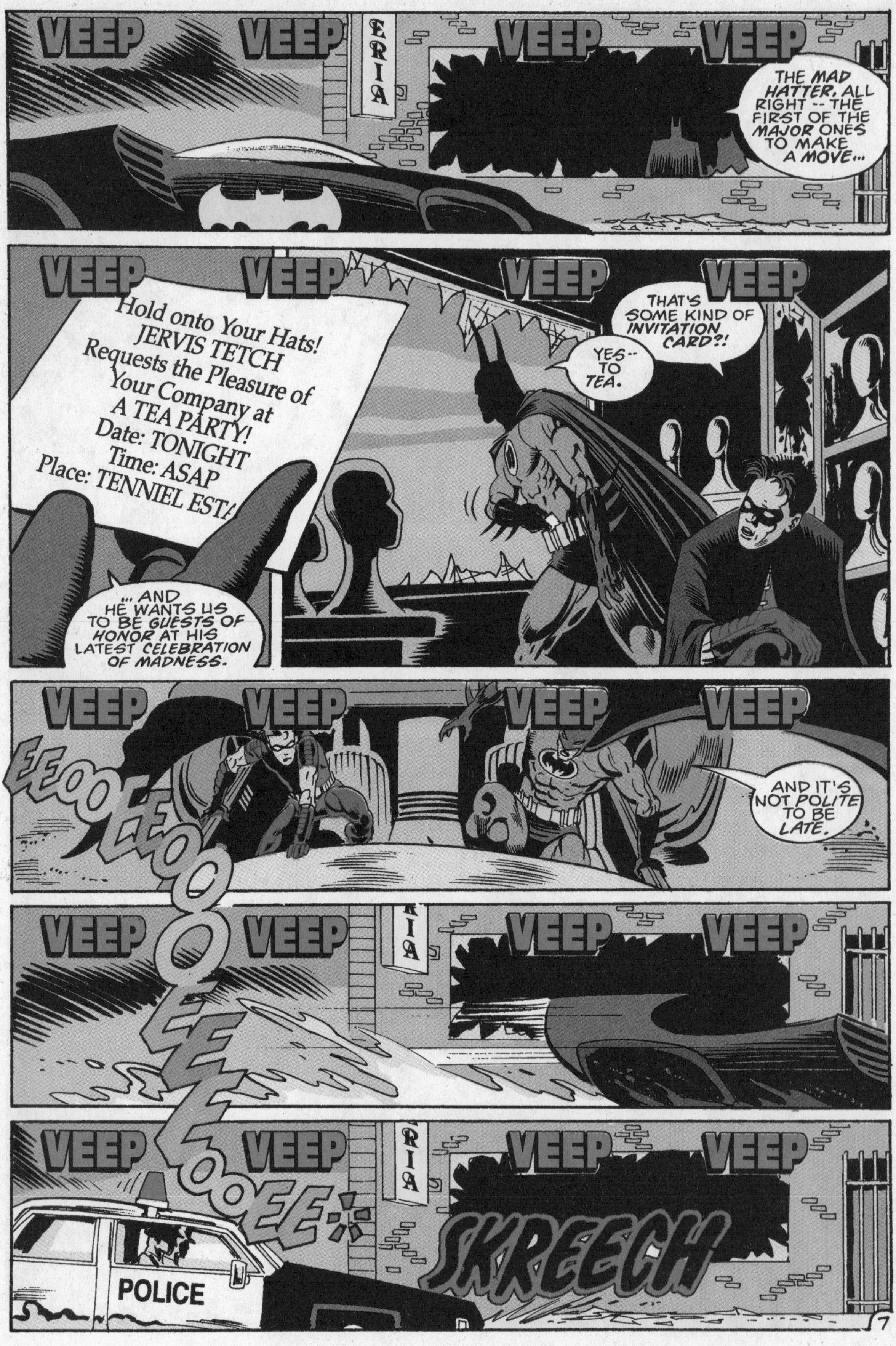
VEEP VEEP VEEP VEEP
ERIA
THE MAD HATTER, ALL RIGHT -- THE FIRST OF THE MAJOR ONES TO MAKE A MOVE...
VEEP VEEP VEEP VEEP
Hold onto Your Hats! JERVIS TETCH Requests the Pleasure of Your Company at A TEA PARTY! Date: TONIGHT Time: ASAP Place: TENNIEL ESTA
THAT'S SOME KIND OF INVITATION CARD?!
YES-- TO TEA.
... AND HE WANTS US TO BE GUESTS OF HONOR AT HIS LATEST CELEBRATION OF MADNESS.
VEEP VEEP VEEP VEEP
EEOOEEOO
AND IT'S NOT POLITE TO BE LATE.
VEEP VEEP VEEP VEEP
RIA
VEEP VEEP VEEP VEEP
RIA
POLICE
EEEOOEE
SKREECH
7

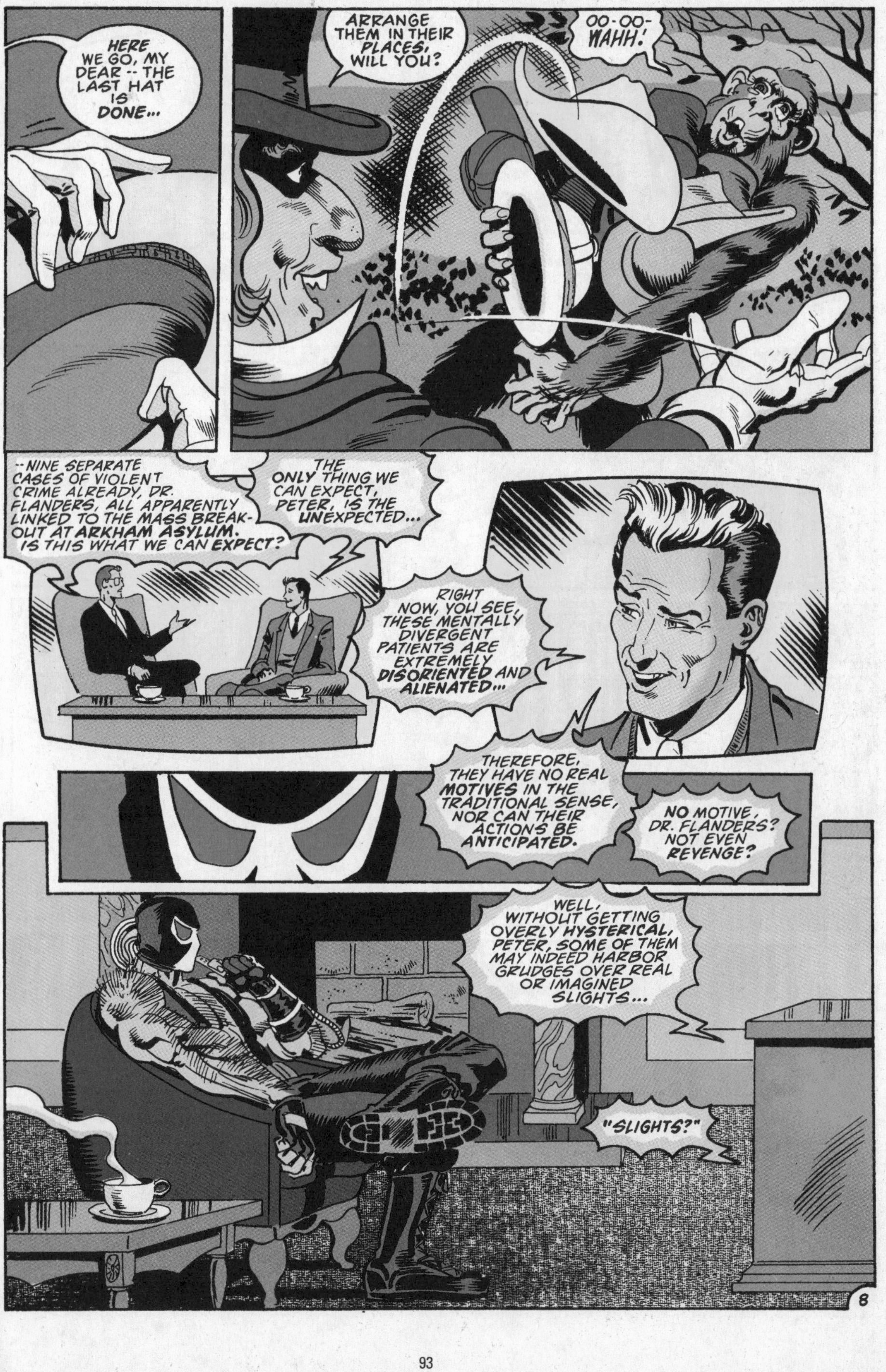
HERE WE GO, MY DEAR -- THE LAST HAT IS DONE...
ARRANGE THEM IN THEIR PLACES, WILL YOU?
OO-OO-WAHH!
--NINE SEPARATE CASES OF VIOLENT CRIME ALREADY, DR. FLANDERS, ALL APPARENTLY LINKED TO THE MASS BREAK-OUT AT ARKHAM ASYLUM. IS THIS WHAT WE CAN EXPECT?
THE ONLY THING WE CAN EXPECT, PETER, IS THE UNEXPECTED...
RIGHT NOW, YOU SEE, THESE MENTALLY DIVERGENT PATIENTS ARE EXTREMELY DISORIENTED AND ALIENATED...
THEREFORE, THEY HAVE NO REAL MOTIVES IN THE TRADITIONAL SENSE, NOR CAN THEIR ACTIONS BE ANTICIPATED.
NO MOTIVE, DR. FLANDERS? NOT EVEN REVENGE?
WELL, WITHOUT GETTING OVERLY HYSTERICAL, PETER, SOME OF THEM MAY INDEED HARBOR GRUDGES OVER REAL OR IMAGINED SLIGHTS...
"SLIGHTS?"
8

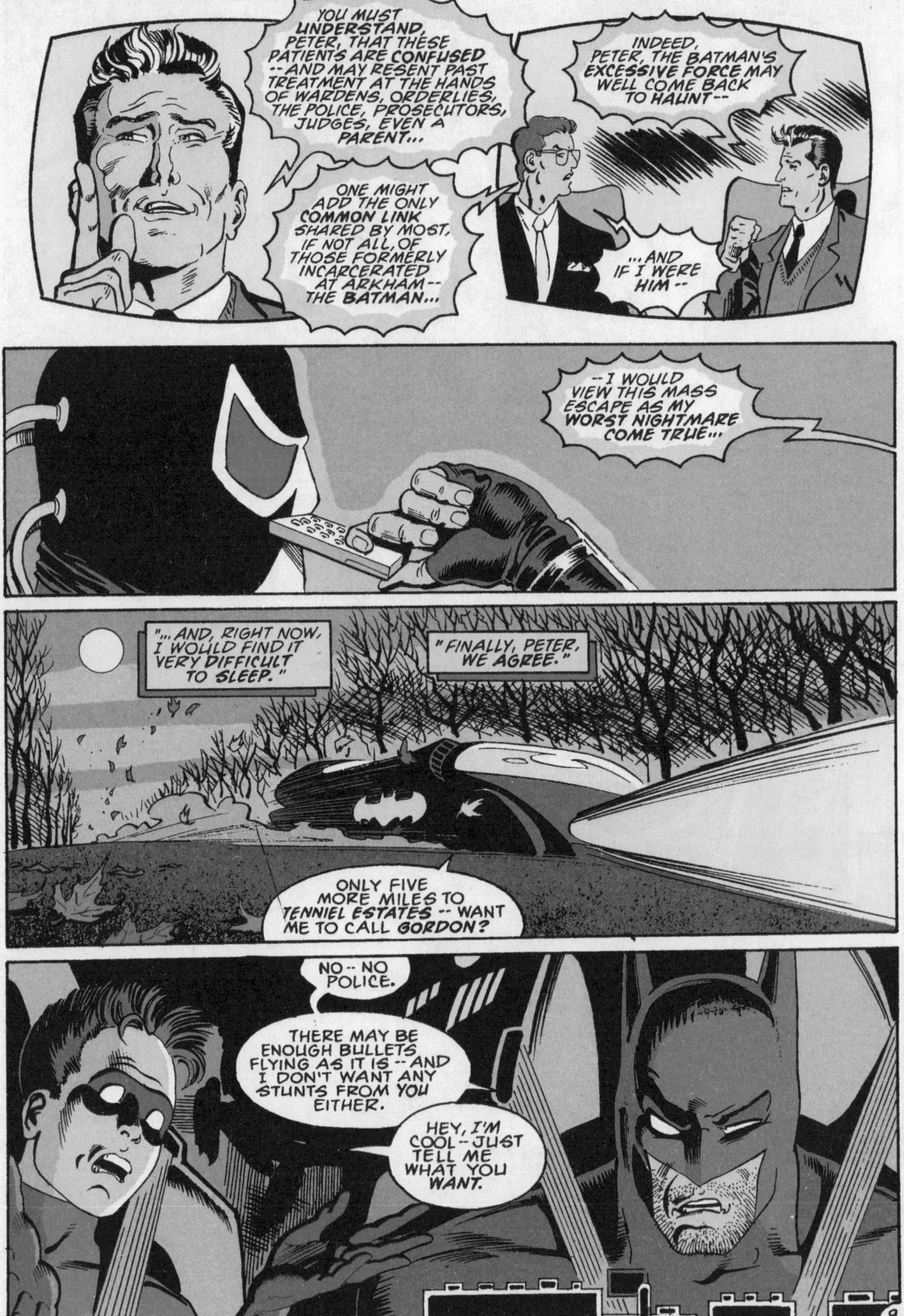
YOU MUST UNDERSTAND, PETER, THAT THESE PATIENTS ARE CONFUSED -- AND MAY RESENT PAST TREATMENT AT THE HANDS OF WARDENS, ORDERLIES, THE POLICE, PROSECUTORS, JUDGES, EVEN A PARENT...
ONE MIGHT ADD THE ONLY COMMON LINK SHARED BY MOST, IF NOT ALL, OF THOSE FORMERLY INCARCERATED AT ARKHAM -- THE BATMAN...
INDEED, PETER, THE BATMAN'S EXCESSIVE FORCE MAY WELL COME BACK TO HAUNT--
...AND IF I WERE HIM --
-- I WOULD VIEW THIS MASS ESCAPE AS MY WORST NIGHTMARE COME TRUE...
"... AND, RIGHT NOW, I WOULD FIND IT VERY DIFFICULT TO SLEEP."
"FINALLY, PETER, WE AGREE."
ONLY FIVE MORE MILES TO TENNIEL ESTATES -- WANT ME TO CALL GORDON?
NO -- NO POLICE.
THERE MAY BE ENOUGH BULLETS FLYING AS IT IS -- AND I DON'T WANT ANY STUNTS FROM YOU EITHER.
HEY, I'M COOL -- JUST TELL ME WHAT YOU WANT.
9

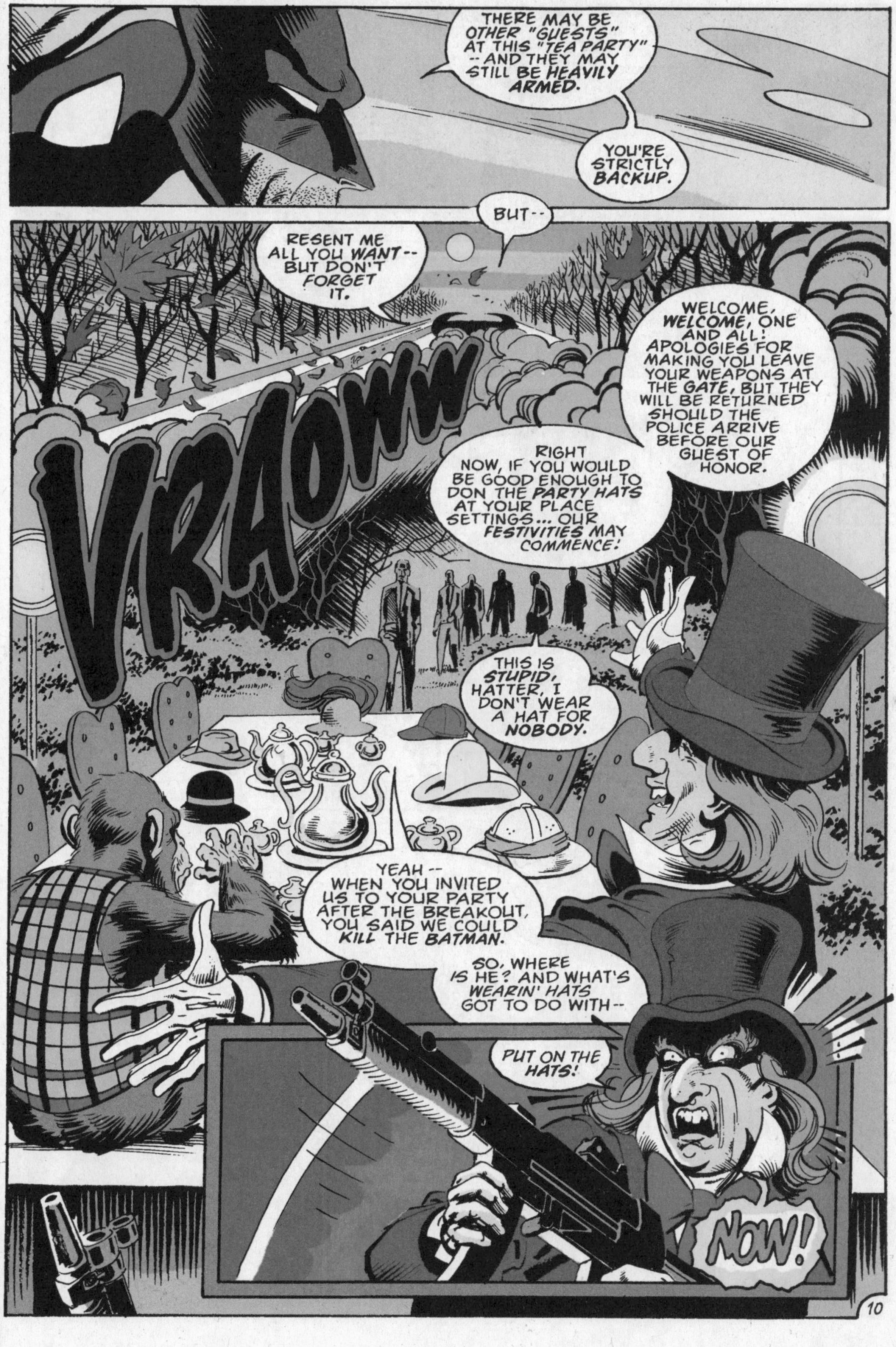
THERE MAY BE OTHER "GUESTS" AT THIS "TEA PARTY" -- AND THEY MAY STILL BE HEAVILY ARMED.
YOU'RE STRICTLY BACKUP.
BUT--
RESENT ME ALL YOU WANT-- BUT DON'T FORGET IT.
VRAOWW
WELCOME, WELCOME, ONE AND ALL! APOLOGIES FOR MAKING YOU LEAVE YOUR WEAPONS AT THE GATE, BUT THEY WILL BE RETURNED SHOULD THE POLICE ARRIVE BEFORE OUR GUEST OF HONOR.
RIGHT NOW, IF YOU WOULD BE GOOD ENOUGH TO DON THE PARTY HATS AT YOUR PLACE SETTINGS... OUR FESTIVITIES MAY COMMENCE!
THIS IS STUPID, HATTER, I DON'T WEAR A HAT FOR NOBODY.
YEAH -- WHEN YOU INVITED US TO YOUR PARTY AFTER THE BREAKOUT, YOU SAID WE COULD KILL THE BATMAN.
SO, WHERE IS HE? AND WHAT'S WEARIN' HATS GOT TO DO WITH--
PUT ON THE HATS!
NOW!
10

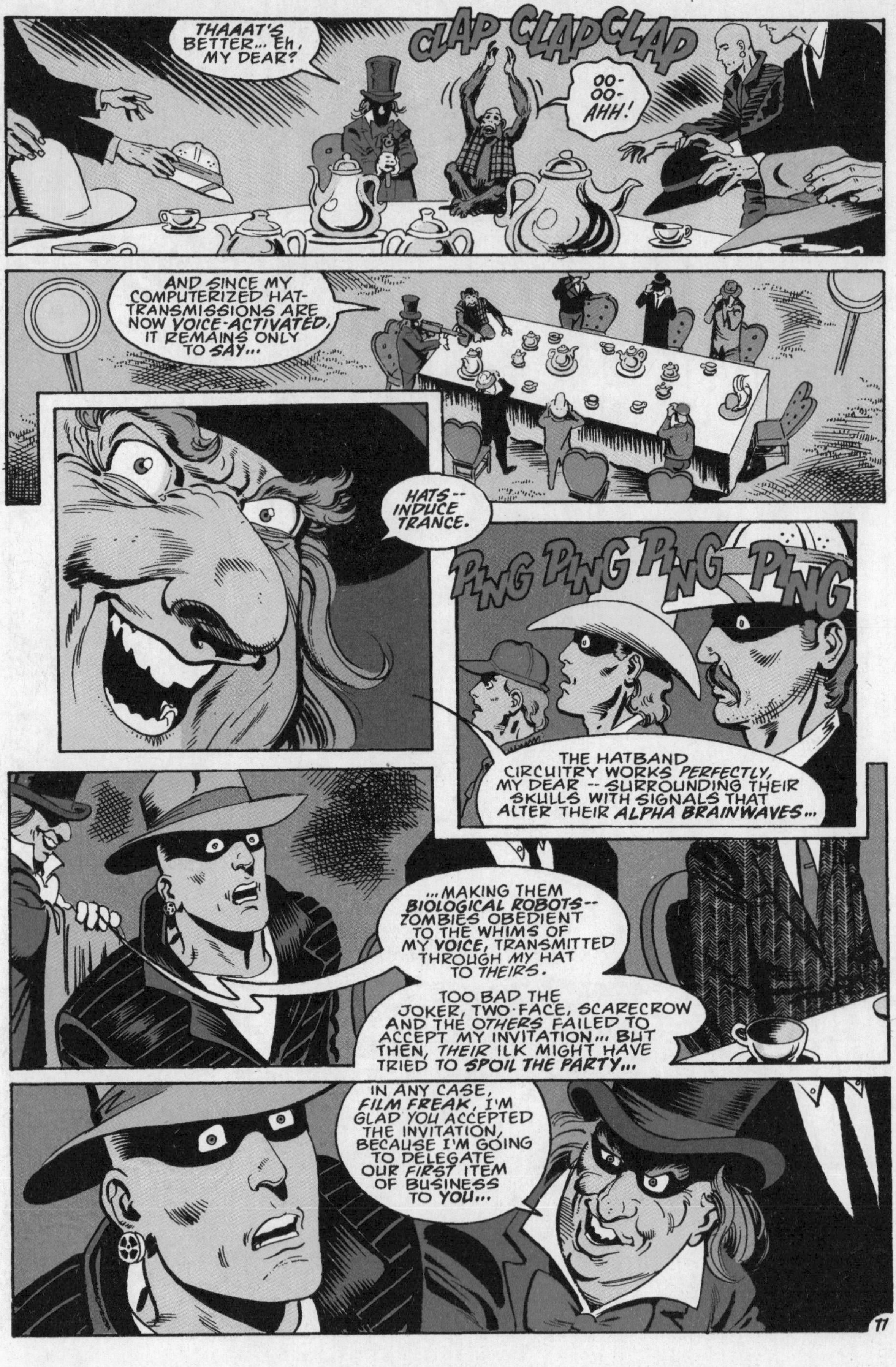
THAAAT'S BETTER... EH, MY DEAR?
CLAP CLAP CLAP CLAP
OO-OO-AHH!
AND SINCE MY COMPUTERIZED HAT-TRANSMISSIONS ARE NOW VOICE-ACTIVATED, IT REMAINS ONLY TO SAY...
HATS -- INDUCE TRANCE.
PING PING PING PING
THE HATBAND CIRCUITRY WORKS PERFECTLY, MY DEAR -- SURROUNDING THEIR SKULLS WITH SIGNALS THAT ALTER THEIR ALPHA BRAINWAVES...
...MAKING THEM BIOLOGICAL ROBOTS -- ZOMBIES OBEDIENT TO THE WHIMS OF MY VOICE, TRANSMITTED THROUGH MY HAT TO THEIRS.
TOO BAD THE JOKER, TWO-FACE, SCARECROW AND THE OTHERS FAILED TO ACCEPT MY INVITATION... BUT THEN, THEIR ILK MIGHT HAVE TRIED TO SPOIL THE PARTY...
IN ANY CASE, FILM FREAK, I'M GLAD YOU ACCEPTED THE INVITATION, BECAUSE I'M GOING TO DELEGATE OUR FIRST ITEM OF BUSINESS TO YOU...
11

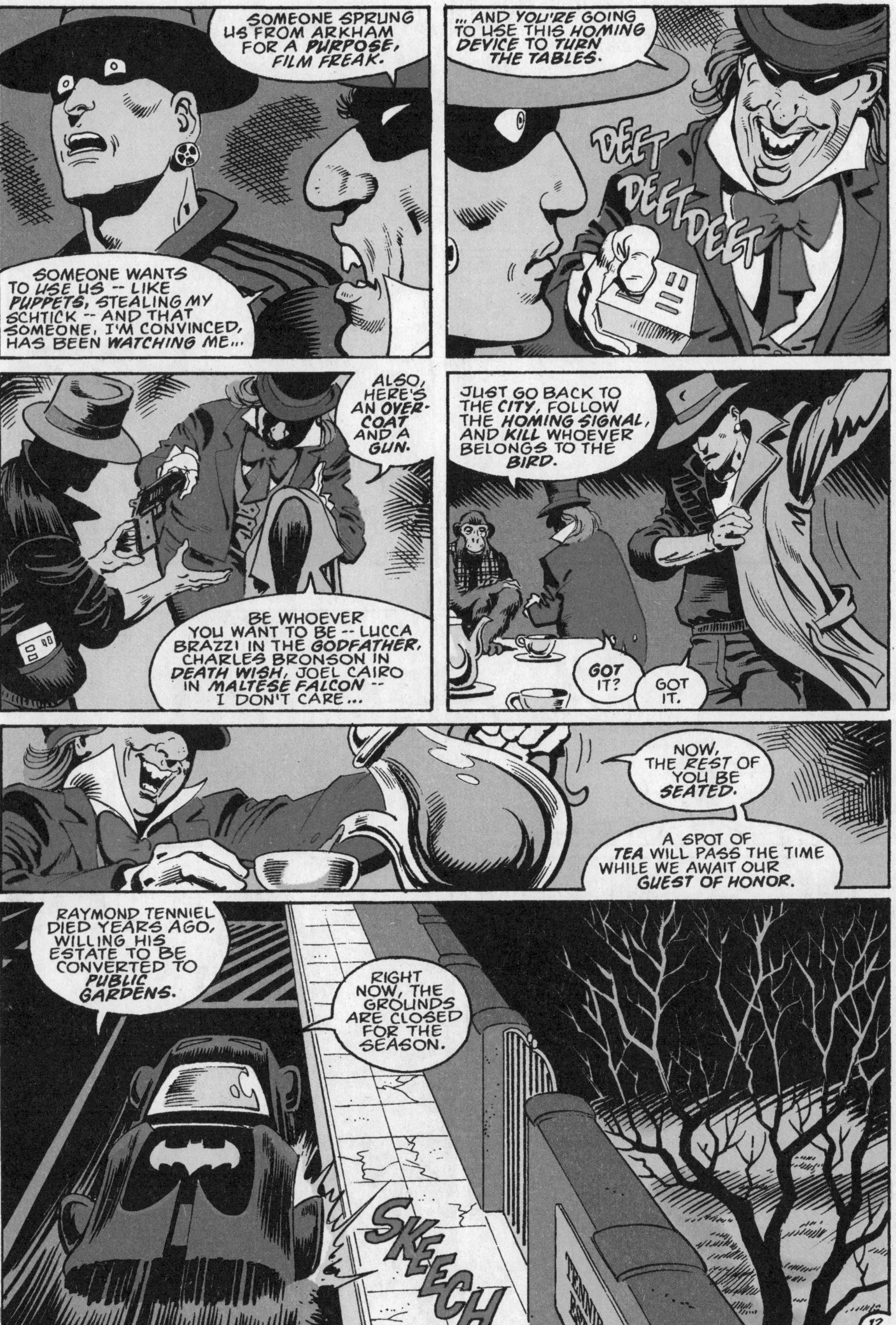
SOMEONE SPRUNG US FROM ARKHAM FOR A PURPOSE, FILM FREAK.
SOMEONE WANTS TO USE US -- LIKE PUPPETS, STEALING MY SCHTICK -- AND THAT SOMEONE, I'M CONVINCED, HAS BEEN WATCHING ME...
...AND YOU'RE GOING TO USE THIS HOMING DEVICE TO TURN THE TABLES.
DEET DEET DEET DEET
ALSO, HERE'S AN OVER-COAT AND A GUN.
BE WHOEVER YOU WANT TO BE -- LUCCA BRAZZI IN THE GODFATHER, CHARLES BRONSON IN DEATH WISH, JOEL CAIRO IN MALTESE FALCON -- I DON'T CARE...
JUST GO BACK TO THE CITY, FOLLOW THE HOMING SIGNAL, AND KILL WHOEVER BELONGS TO THE BIRD.
GOT IT?
GOT IT.
NOW, THE REST OF YOU BE SEATED.
A SPOT OF TEA WILL PASS THE TIME WHILE WE AWAIT OUR GUEST OF HONOR.
RAYMOND TENNIEL DIED YEARS AGO, WILLING HIS ESTATE TO BE CONVERTED TO PUBLIC GARDENS.
RIGHT NOW, THE GROUNDS ARE CLOSED FOR THE SEASON.
SKEECH
12

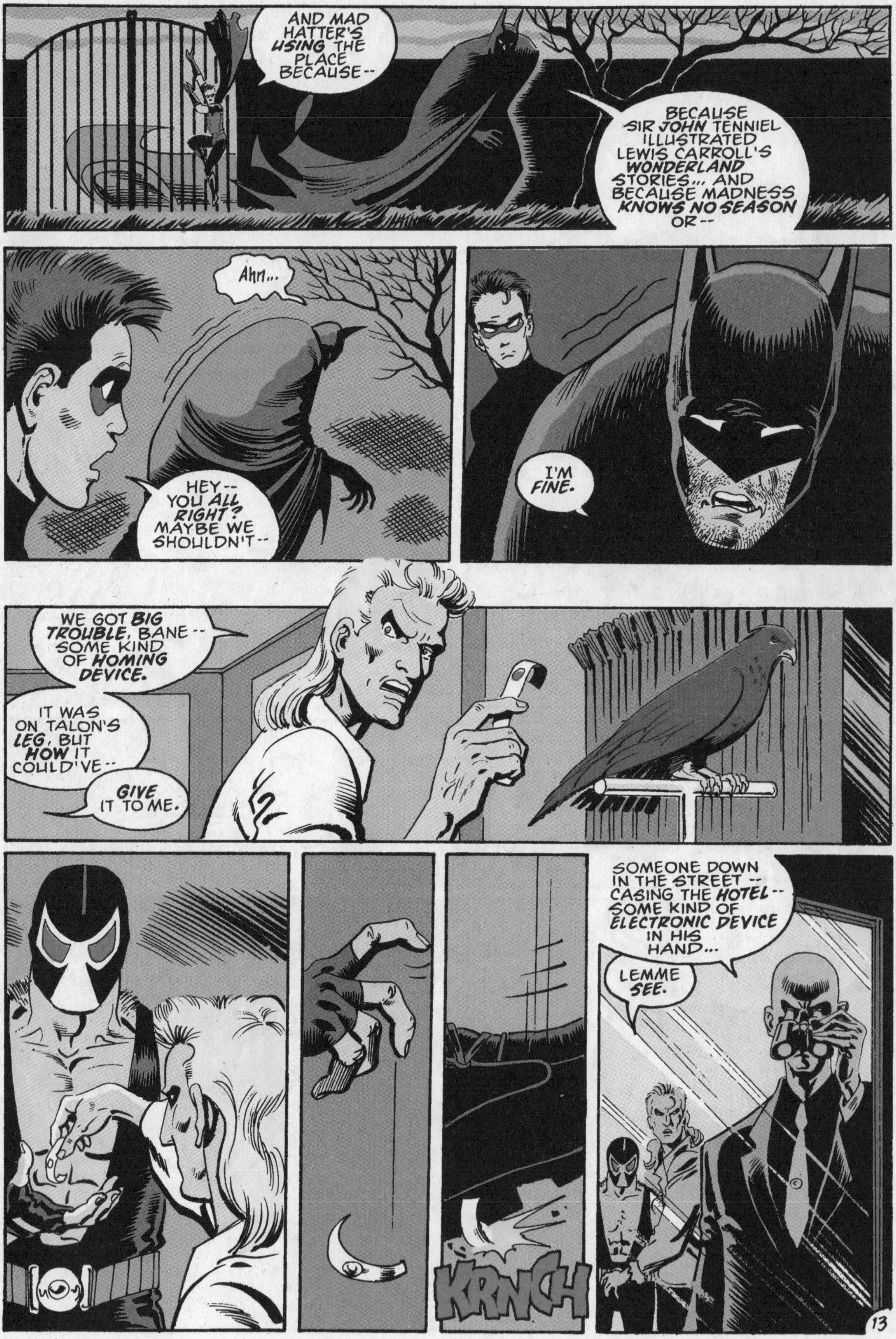
AND MAD HATTER'S USING THE PLACE BECAUSE--
BECAUSE SIR JOHN TENNIEL ILLUSTRATED LEWIS CARROLL'S WONDERLAND STORIES... AND BECAUSE MADNESS KNOWS NO SEASON OR--
Ahh...
HEY-- YOU ALL RIGHT? MAYBE WE SHOULDN'T--
I'M FINE.
WE GOT BIG TROUBLE, BANE-- SOME KIND OF HOMING DEVICE.
IT WAS ON TALON'S LEG, BUT HOW IT COULD'VE--
GIVE IT TO ME.
KRNCH
SOMEONE DOWN IN THE STREET-- CASING THE HOTEL-- SOME KIND OF ELECTRONIC DEVICE IN HIS HAND...
LEMME SEE.
13

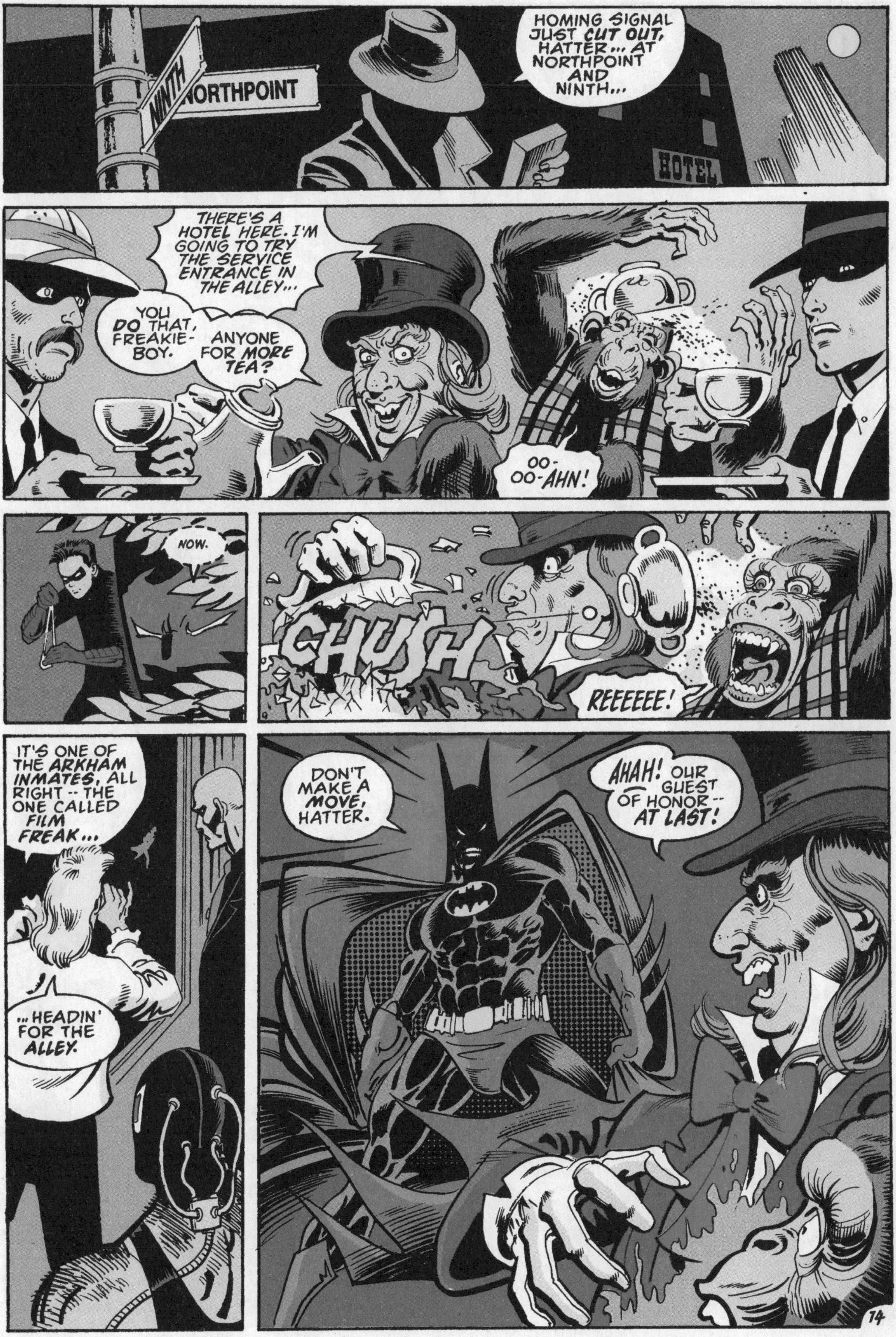
NINTH
NORTHPOINT
HOMING SIGNAL JUST CUT OUT, HATTER... AT NORTHPOINT AND NINTH...
HOTEL
THERE'S A HOTEL HERE. I'M GOING TO TRY THE SERVICE ENTRANCE IN THE ALLEY...
YOU DO THAT, FREAKIE-BOY.
ANYONE FOR MORE TEA?
OO-OO-AHN!
NOW.
CHUSH
REEEEEE!
IT'S ONE OF THE ARKHAM INMATES, ALL RIGHT -- THE ONE CALLED FILM FREAK...
...HEADIN' FOR THE ALLEY.
DON'T MAKE A MOVE, HATTER.
AHAH! OUR GUEST OF HONOR -- AT LAST!
14

YOU STAY **HERE**...

TEK

FWTH *FWTH*

...WHILE I **KILL** HIM.

SIT **DOWN**, BATMAN! HAVE A CUP OF **TEA**...

WHAT'S YOUR GAME **THIS** TIME, HATTER? WHO IS THIS **BANE**?

WHAT'S HE **AFTER** -- AND WHY ARE YOU **HELPING** HIM?

IT'S **LOCKED**, HATTER...

SERVICE ENTRA[NCE]

I MAY **HAVE** TO JUST WATCH THE **FRONT** ENTRANCE.

TRANS-MITTER AND RECEIVER IN YOUR **HAT** -- BUT WHO'S **USING** IT?

OH, JUST **FILM FREAK** -- REPORTING ON GOTHAM'S **NIGHT** LIFE.

ALSO PART OF BANE'S PLAN?

THAT'S THE **SECOND** TIME YOU'VE MENTIONED THAT **NAME**... BUT, IN REPLY, I CAN ONLY SAY...

15

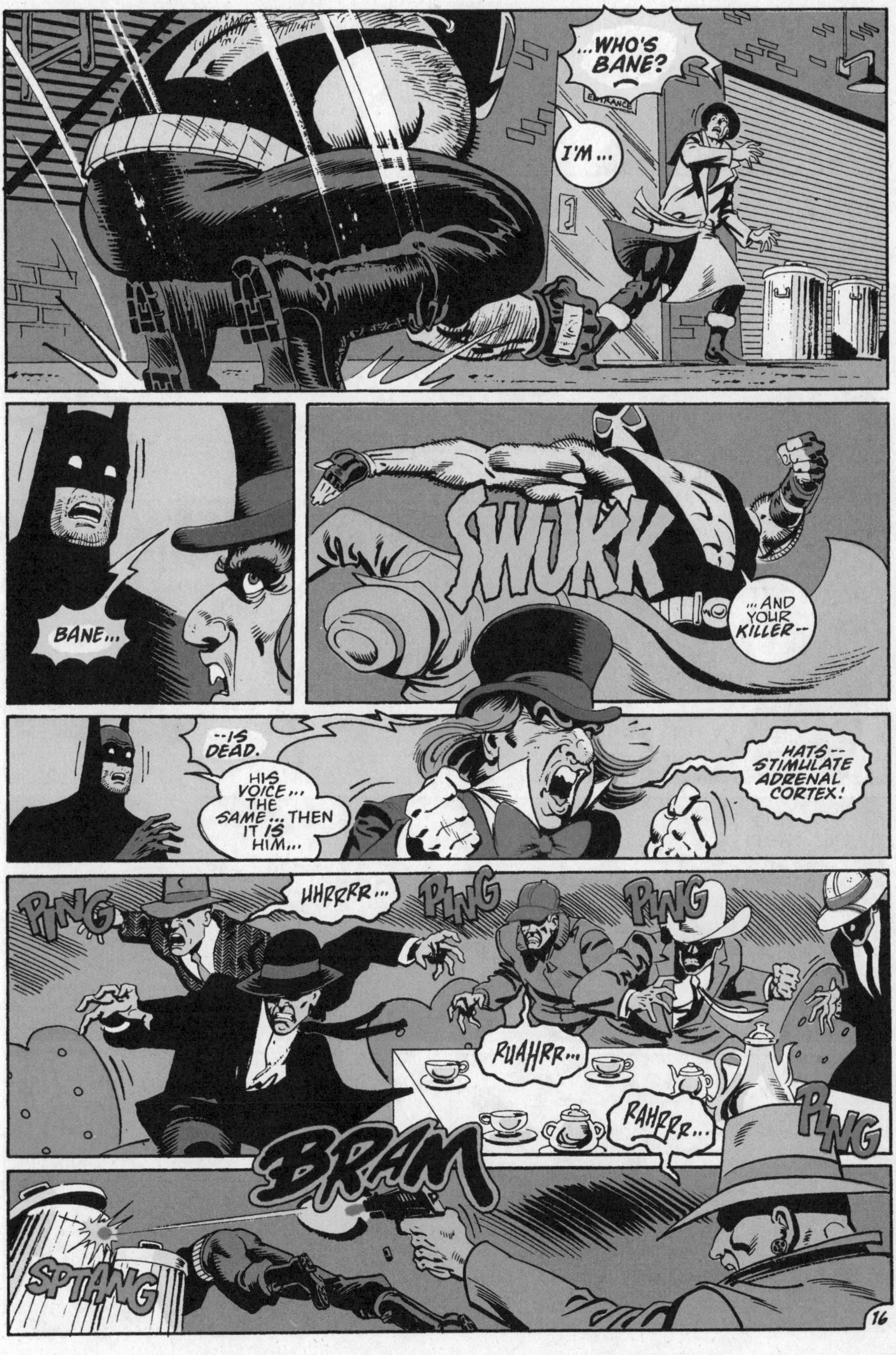
...WHO'S BANE?
ENTRANCE
I'M ...
BANE...
SWUKK
...AND YOUR KILLER--
--IS DEAD.
HIS VOICE... THE SAME... THEN IT IS HIM...
HATS-- STIMULATE ADRENAL CORTEX!
PING
UHRRRR...
PING
PING
RUAHRR...
RAHRRR...
PING
BRAM
SPTANG
16

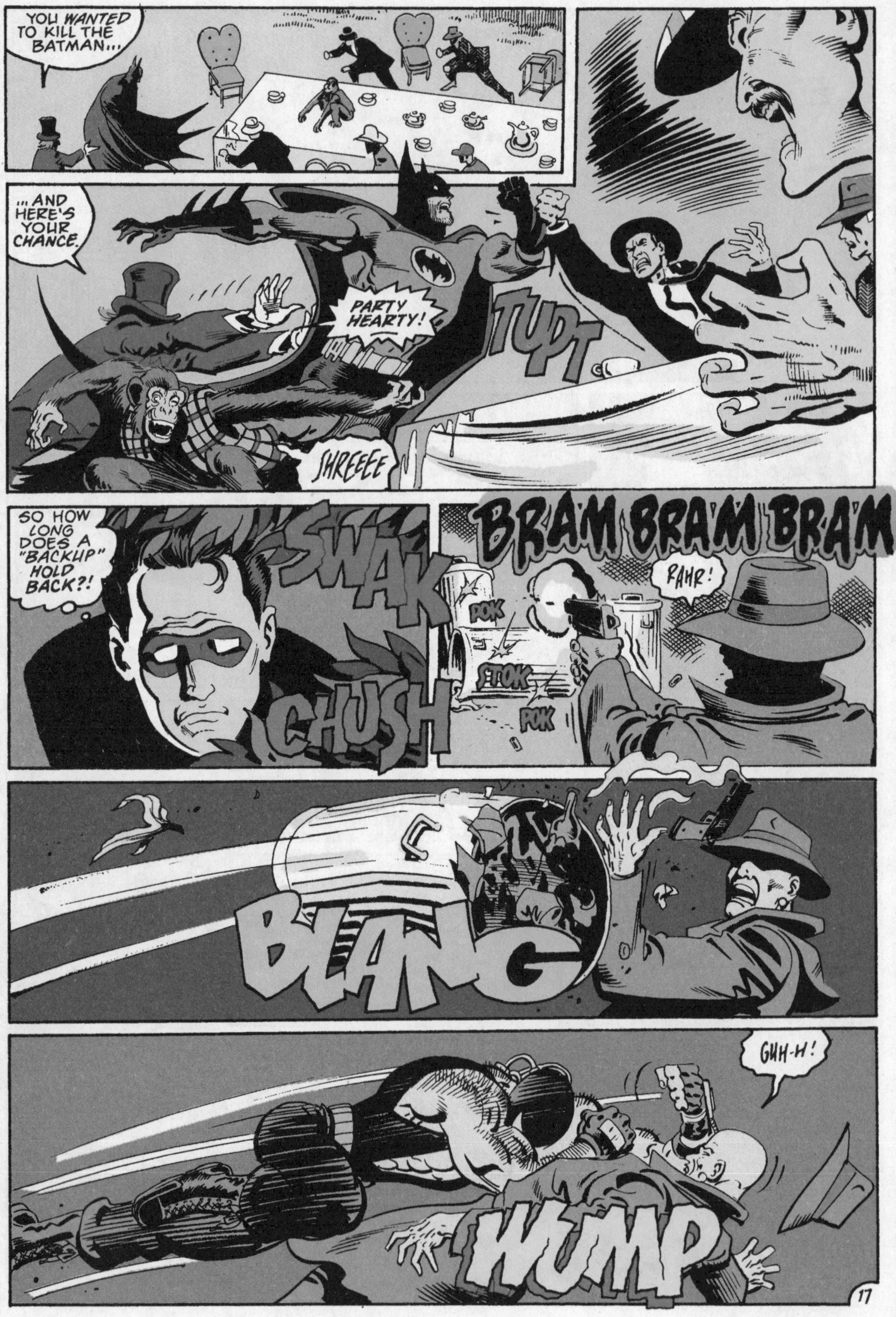
YOU WANTED TO KILL THE BATMAN...
...AND HERE'S YOUR CHANCE.
PARTY HEARTY!
TUPT
SHREEEE
SO HOW LONG DOES A "BACKUP" HOLD BACK?!
SWAK
CHUSH
BRAM BRAM BRAM
RAHR!
POK
STOK
POK
BLANG
GUH-H!
WUMP
17

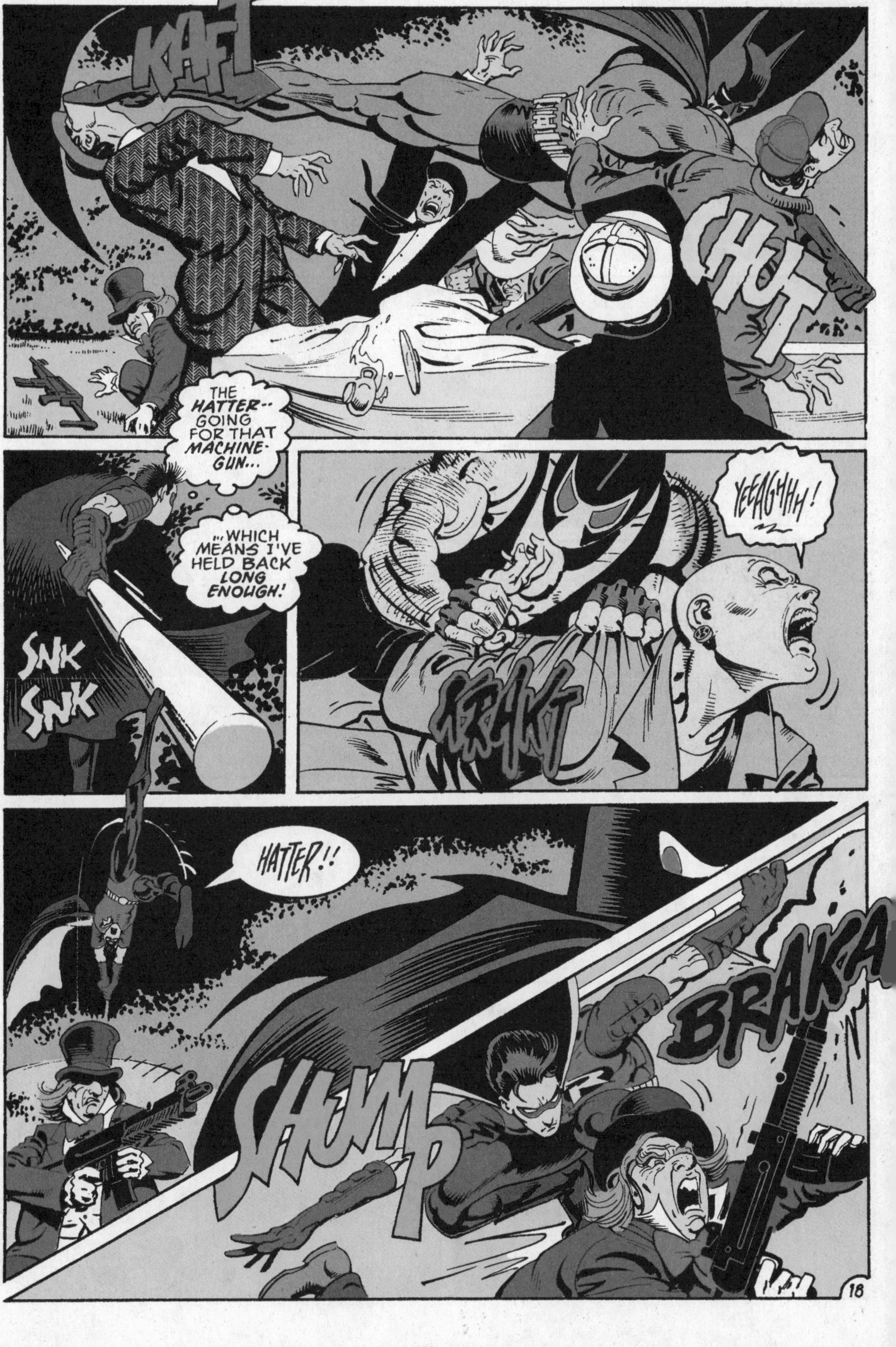
KAFT
CHUT
THE HATTER--GOING FOR THAT MACHINE-GUN...
...WHICH MEANS I'VE HELD BACK LONG ENOUGH!
SNK SNK
YEEAGHHH!
HATTER!!
BRAKA
SHUMP
18

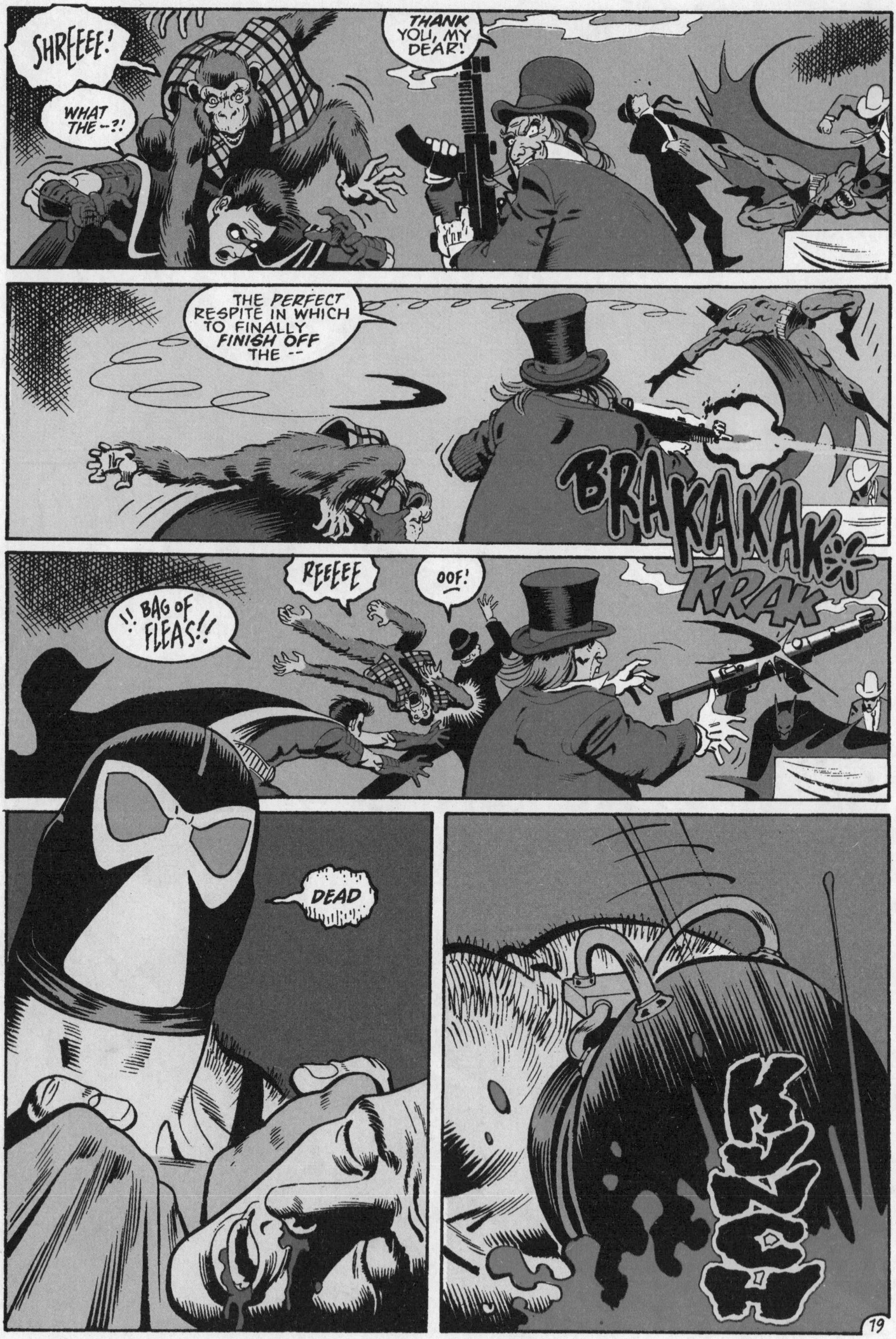
SHREEEE!
WHAT THE--?!
THANK YOU, MY DEAR!
THE PERFECT RESPITE IN WHICH TO FINALLY FINISH OFF THE --
BRAKAKAK
KRAK
!! BAG OF FLEAS!!
REEEEE
OOF!
DEAD
19

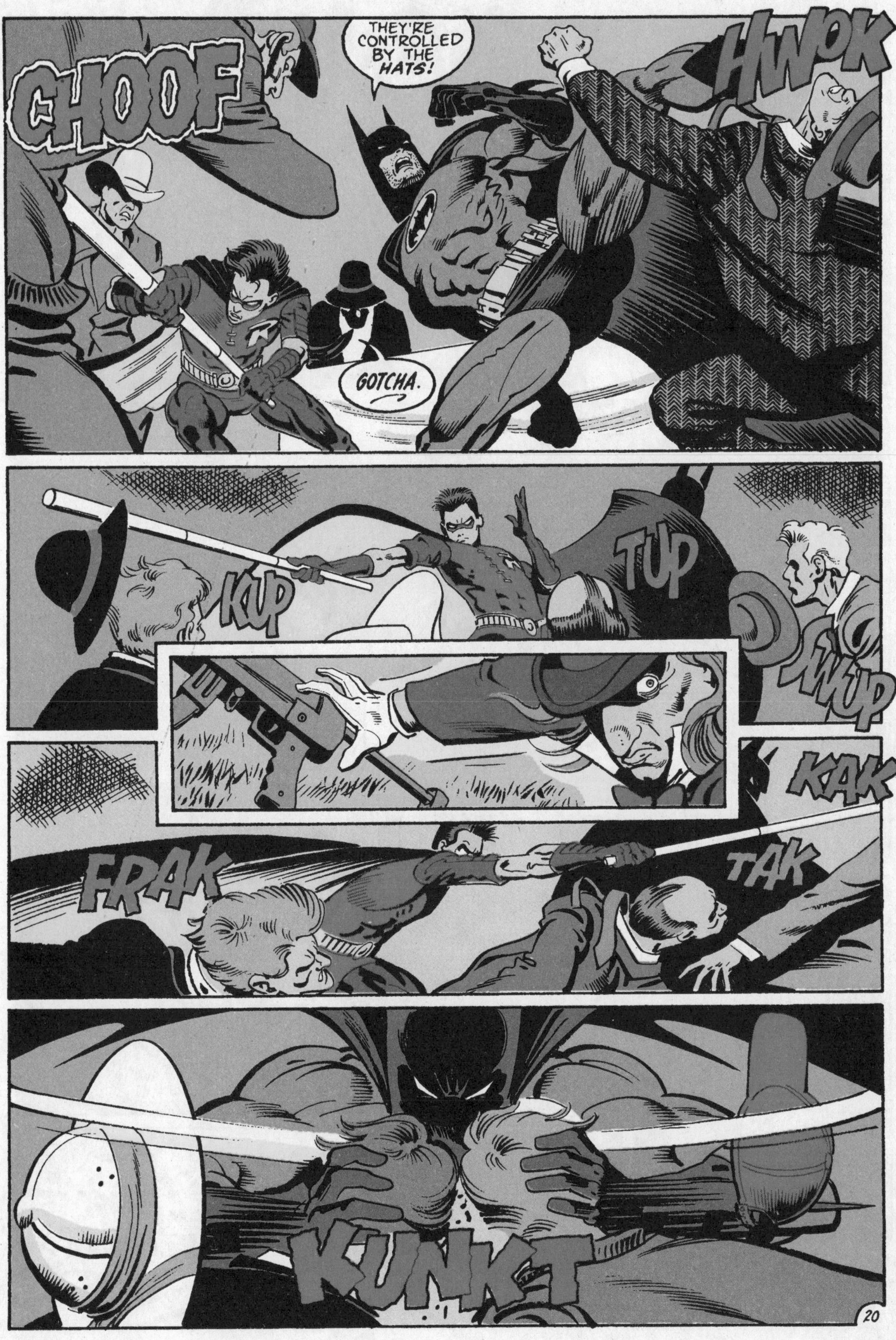

CHOOF
THEY'RE CONTROLLED BY THE HATS!
HWOK
GOTCHA.
KUP
TUP
SWUP
KAK
FRAK
TAK
KUNKT
20

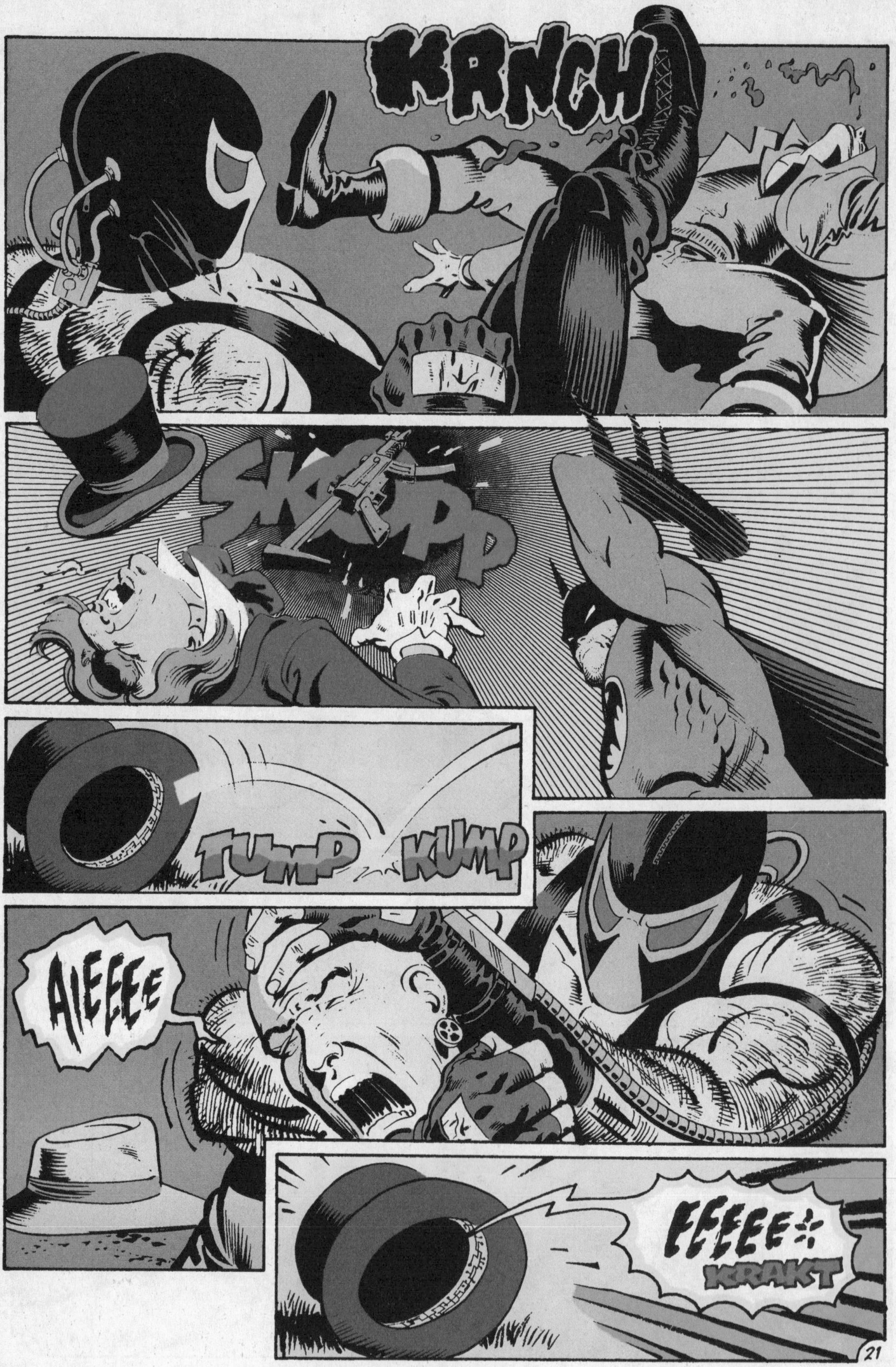
KRNCH
SKLUMP
TUMP
KUMP
AIEEEe
EEEEE
KRAKT
21

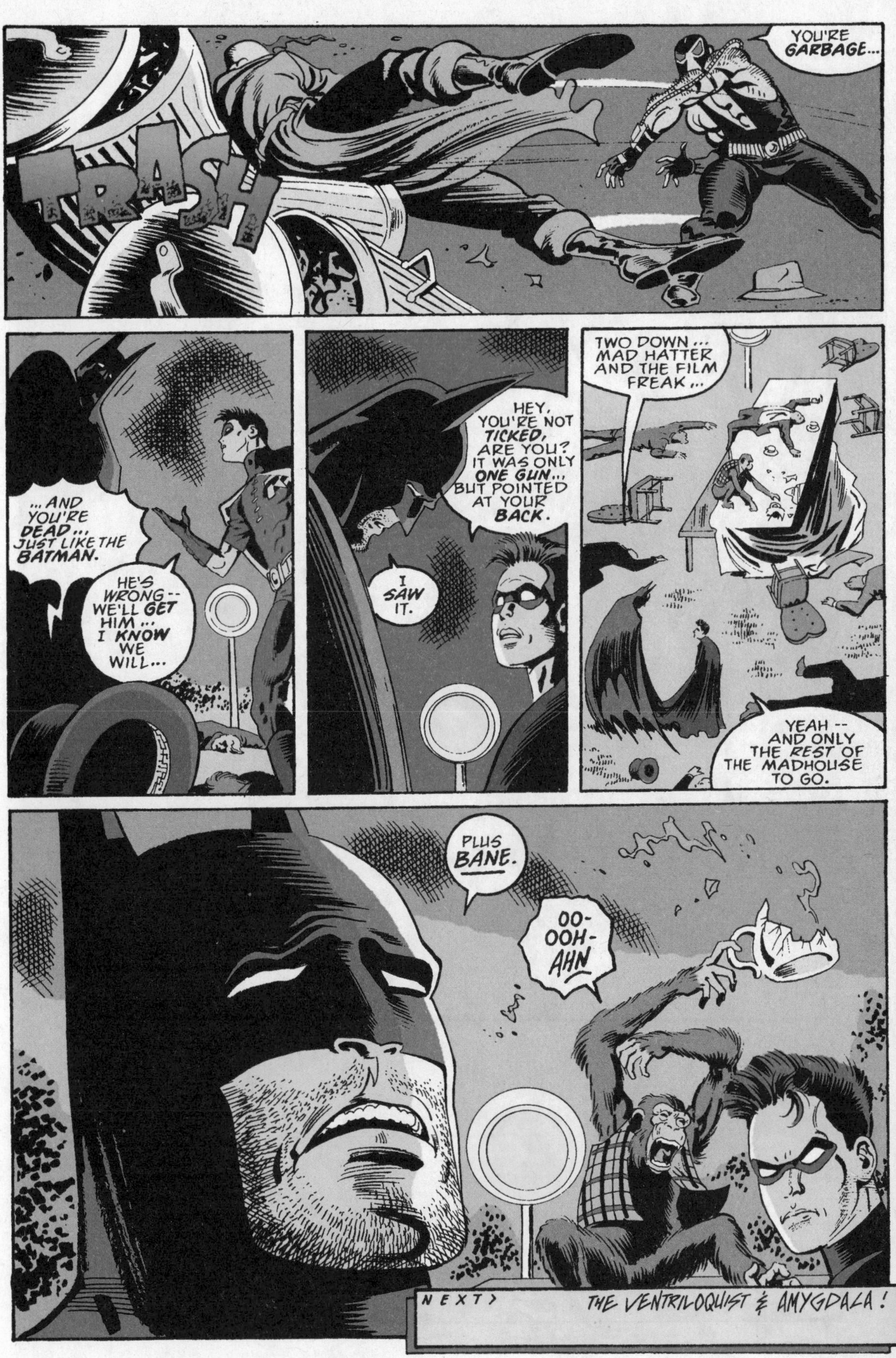
YOU'RE GARBAGE...
TRASH
...AND YOU'RE DEAD... JUST LIKE THE BATMAN.
HE'S WRONG -- WE'LL GET HIM... I KNOW WE WILL...
HEY, YOU'RE NOT TICKED, ARE YOU? IT WAS ONLY ONE GUN... BUT POINTED AT YOUR BACK.
I SAW IT.
TWO DOWN... MAD HATTER AND THE FILM FREAK...
YEAH -- AND ONLY THE REST OF THE MADHOUSE TO GO.
PLUS BANE.
OO-OOH-AHN
NEXT> THE VENTRILOQUIST & AMYGDALA!

Cover art by KELLEY JONES

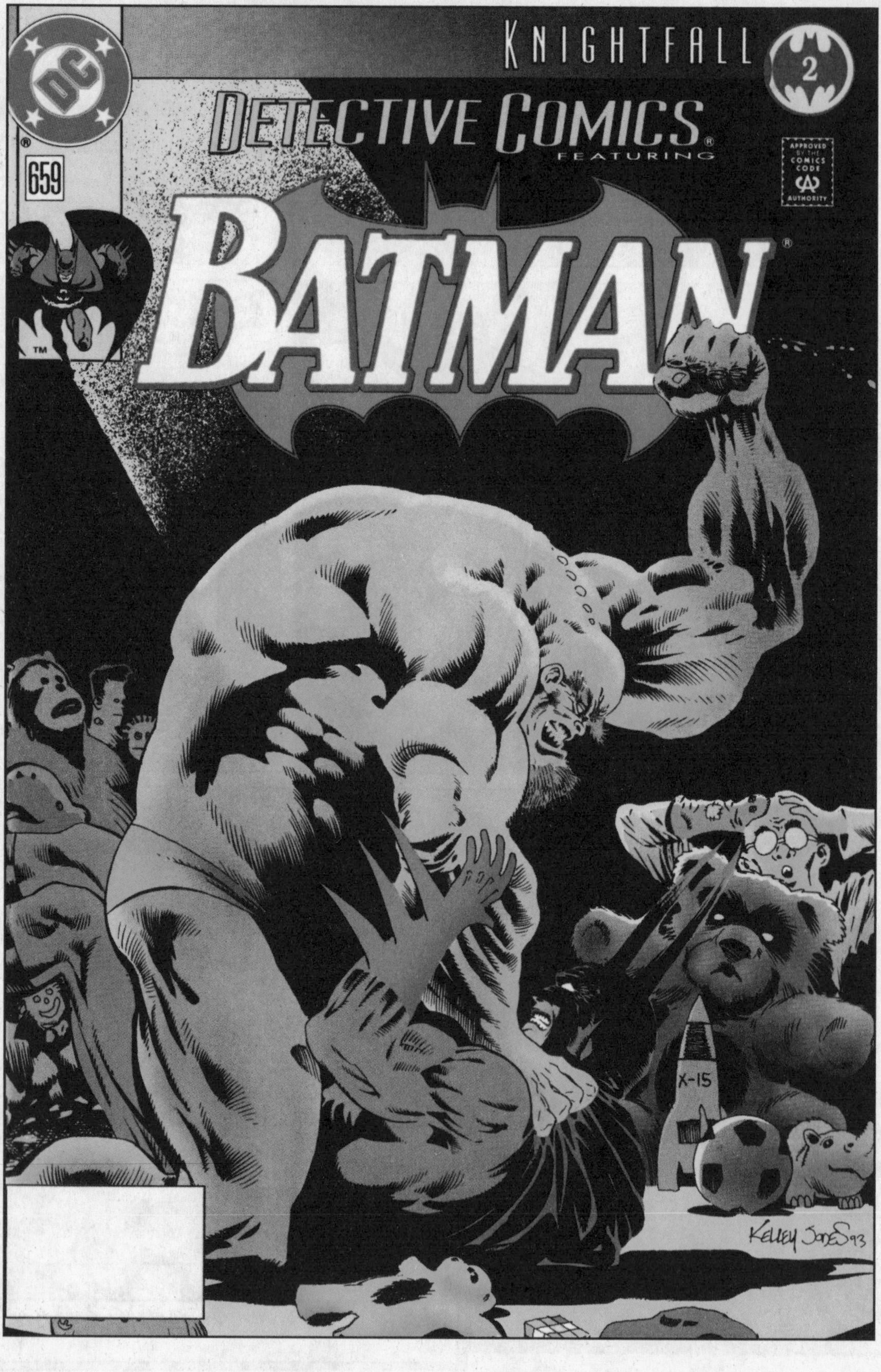

DC
659
KNIGHTFALL
2
DETECTIVE COMICS
FEATURING
BATMAN
APPROVED BY THE COMICS CODE AUTHORITY
X-15
KELLEY JONES 93

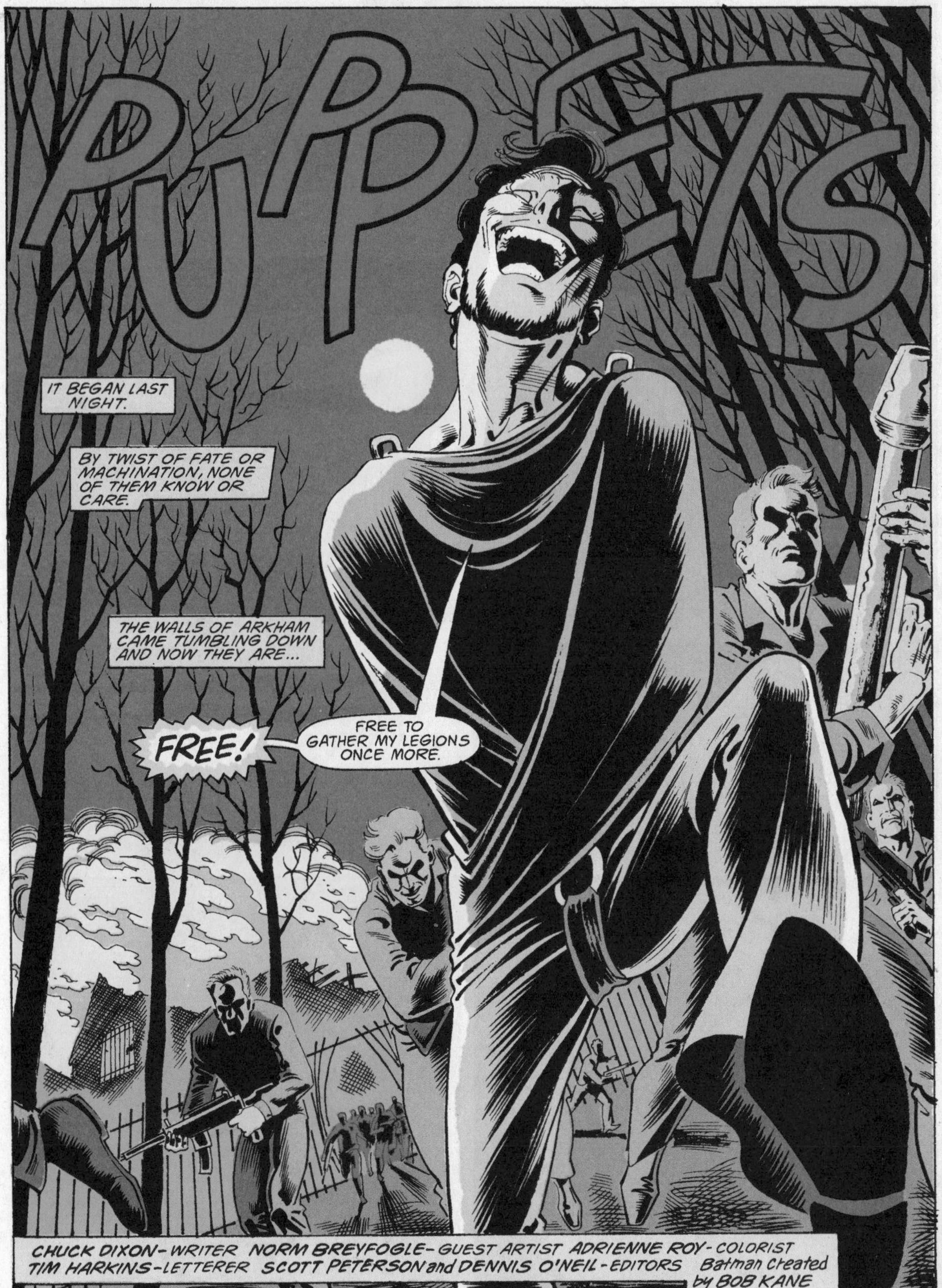
PUPPETS
IT BEGAN LAST NIGHT.
BY TWIST OF FATE OR MACHINATION, NONE OF THEM KNOW OR CARE.
THE WALLS OF ARKHAM CAME TUMBLING DOWN AND NOW THEY ARE...
FREE!
FREE TO GATHER MY LEGIONS ONCE MORE.
CHUCK DIXON-WRITER NORM BREYFOGLE-GUEST ARTIST ADRIENNE ROY-COLORIST
TIM HARKINS-LETTERER SCOTT PETERSON and DENNIS O'NEIL-EDITORS Batman created by BOB KANE

THEY THOUGHT TO *IMPRISON* A *GOD?* TO *CONTAIN* MAXIE ZEUS?

HA! I HAD ONLY TO CALL DOWN *THUNDERBOLTS* TO WREST ME FROM THEIR FEEBLE *GRASP!* FOR AM I *NOT--*

WHUD!

unhhhh...

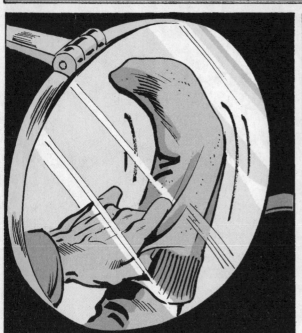

NOOOO, MR. VENTRILOQUIST...

I *HAVEN'T* SEEN YOUR FRIEND MR. SCARFACE...

2

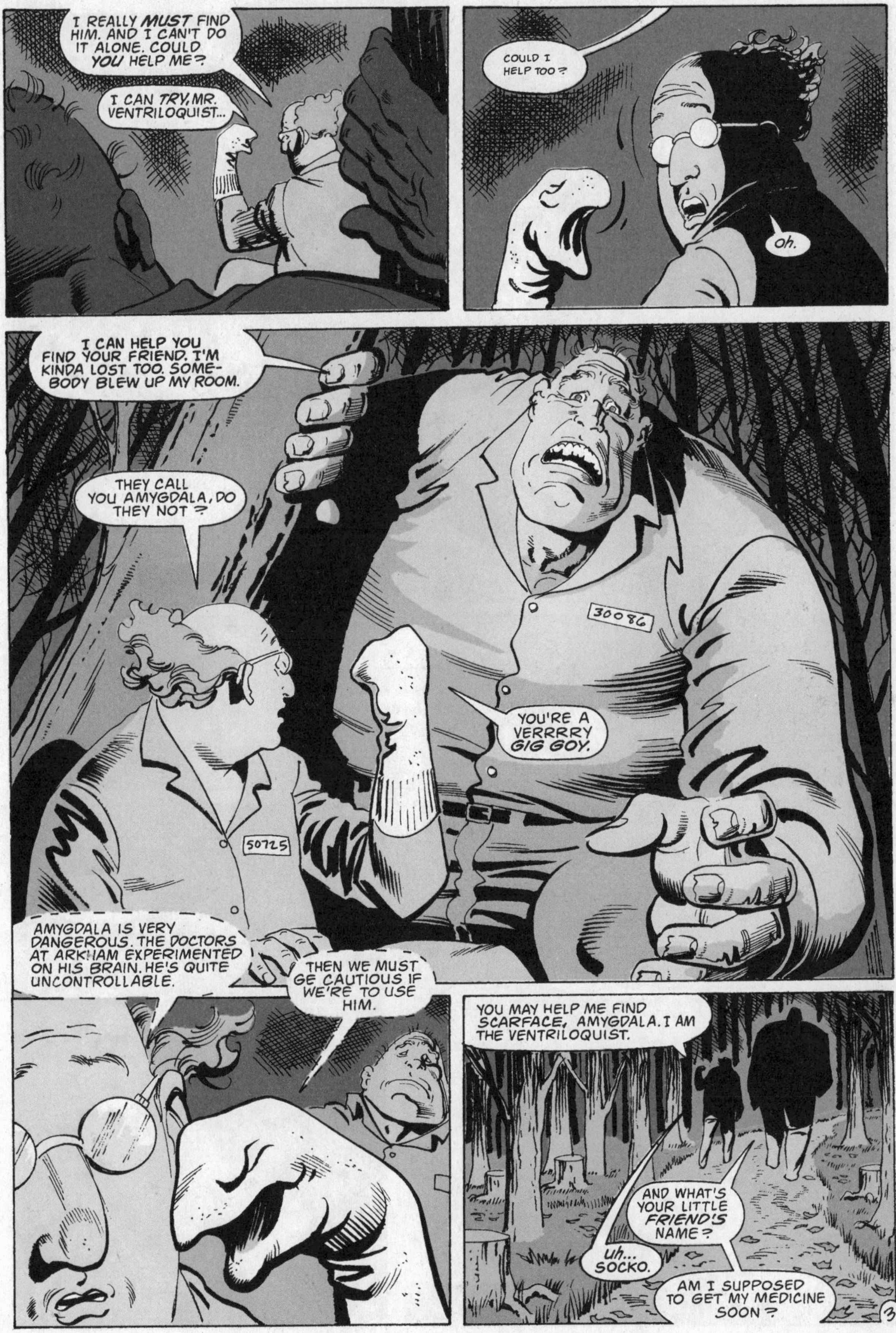
I REALLY MUST FIND HIM. AND I CAN'T DO IT ALONE. COULD YOU HELP ME?
I CAN TRY, MR. VENTRILOQUIST...
COULD I HELP TOO?
Oh.
I CAN HELP YOU FIND YOUR FRIEND. I'M KINDA LOST TOO. SOMEBODY BLEW UP MY ROOM.
THEY CALL YOU AMYGDALA, DO THEY NOT?
30086
YOU'RE A VERRRRY GIG GOY.
50725
AMYGDALA IS VERY DANGEROUS. THE DOCTORS AT ARKHAM EXPERIMENTED ON HIS BRAIN. HE'S QUITE UNCONTROLLABLE.
THEN WE MUST GE CAUTIOUS IF WE'RE TO USE HIM.
YOU MAY HELP ME FIND SCARFACE, AMYGDALA. I AM THE VENTRILOQUIST.
AND WHAT'S YOUR LITTLE FRIEND'S NAME?
uh... SOCKO.
AM I SUPPOSED TO GET MY MEDICINE SOON?
3

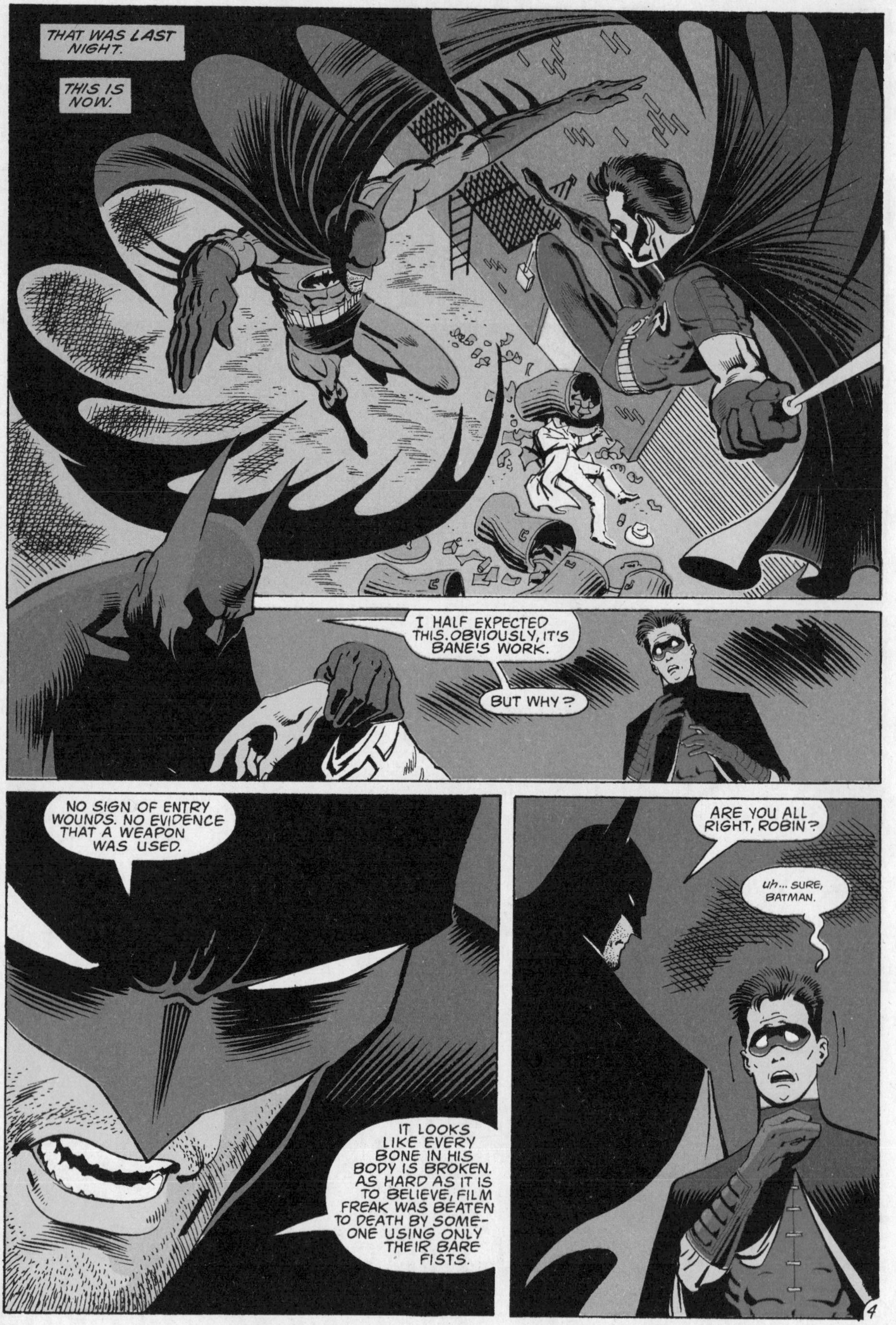
THAT WAS LAST NIGHT.
THIS IS NOW.
I HALF EXPECTED THIS. OBVIOUSLY, IT'S BANE'S WORK.
BUT WHY?
NO SIGN OF ENTRY WOUNDS. NO EVIDENCE THAT A WEAPON WAS USED.
IT LOOKS LIKE EVERY BONE IN HIS BODY IS BROKEN. AS HARD AS IT IS TO BELIEVE, FILM FREAK WAS BEATEN TO DEATH BY SOME-ONE USING ONLY THEIR BARE FISTS.
ARE YOU ALL RIGHT, ROBIN?
uh... SURE, BATMAN.
4

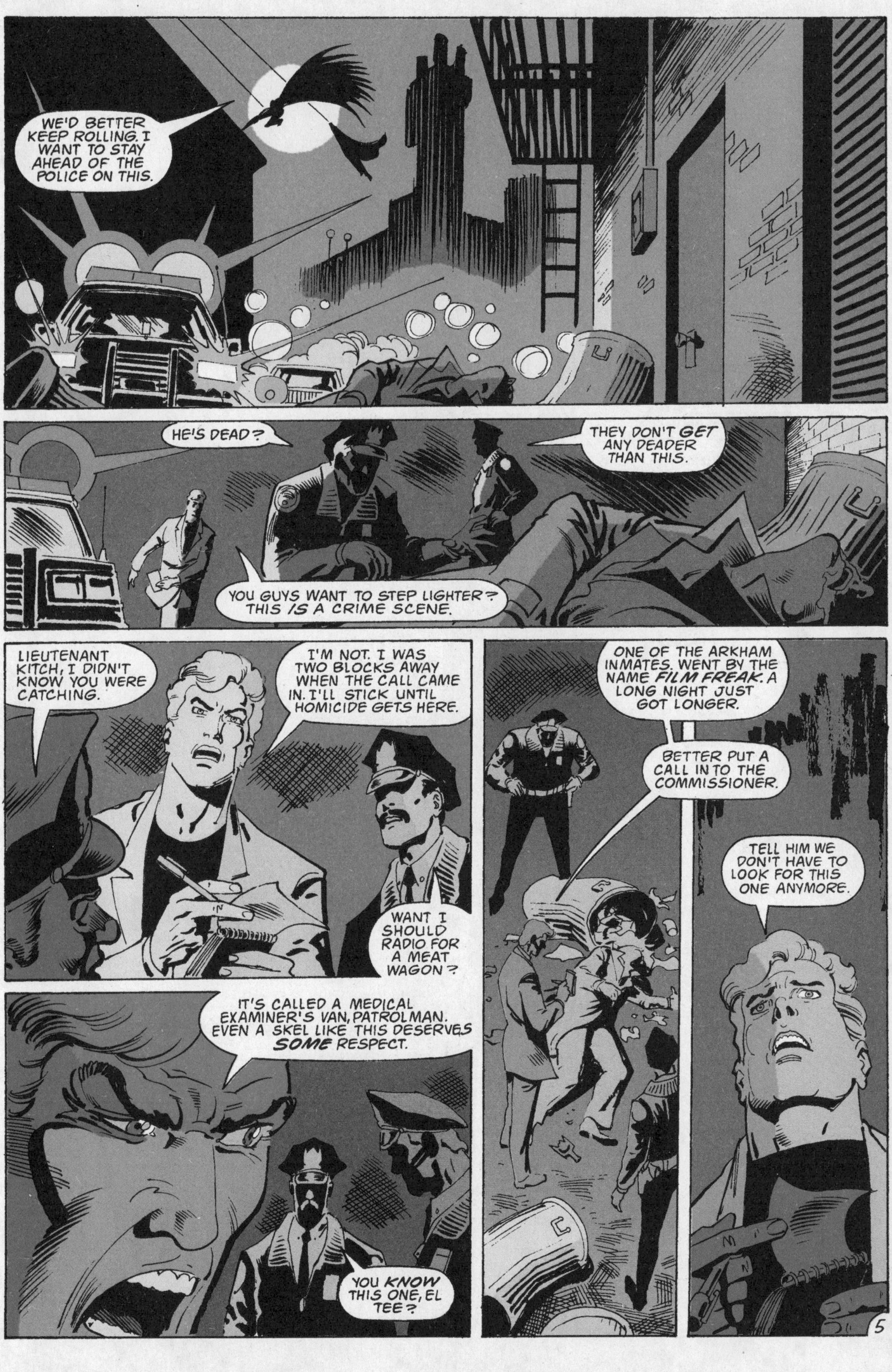
WE'D BETTER KEEP ROLLING. I WANT TO STAY AHEAD OF THE POLICE ON THIS.
HE'S DEAD?
THEY DON'T GET ANY DEADER THAN THIS.
YOU GUYS WANT TO STEP LIGHTER? THIS IS A CRIME SCENE.
LIEUTENANT KITCH, I DIDN'T KNOW YOU WERE CATCHING.
I'M NOT. I WAS TWO BLOCKS AWAY WHEN THE CALL CAME IN. I'LL STICK UNTIL HOMICIDE GETS HERE.
WANT I SHOULD RADIO FOR A MEAT WAGON?
IT'S CALLED A MEDICAL EXAMINER'S VAN, PATROLMAN. EVEN A SKEL LIKE THIS DESERVES SOME RESPECT.
YOU KNOW THIS ONE, EL TEE?
ONE OF THE ARKHAM INMATES. WENT BY THE NAME FILM FREAK. A LONG NIGHT JUST GOT LONGER.
BETTER PUT A CALL IN TO THE COMMISSIONER.
TELL HIM WE DON'T HAVE TO LOOK FOR THIS ONE ANYMORE.
5

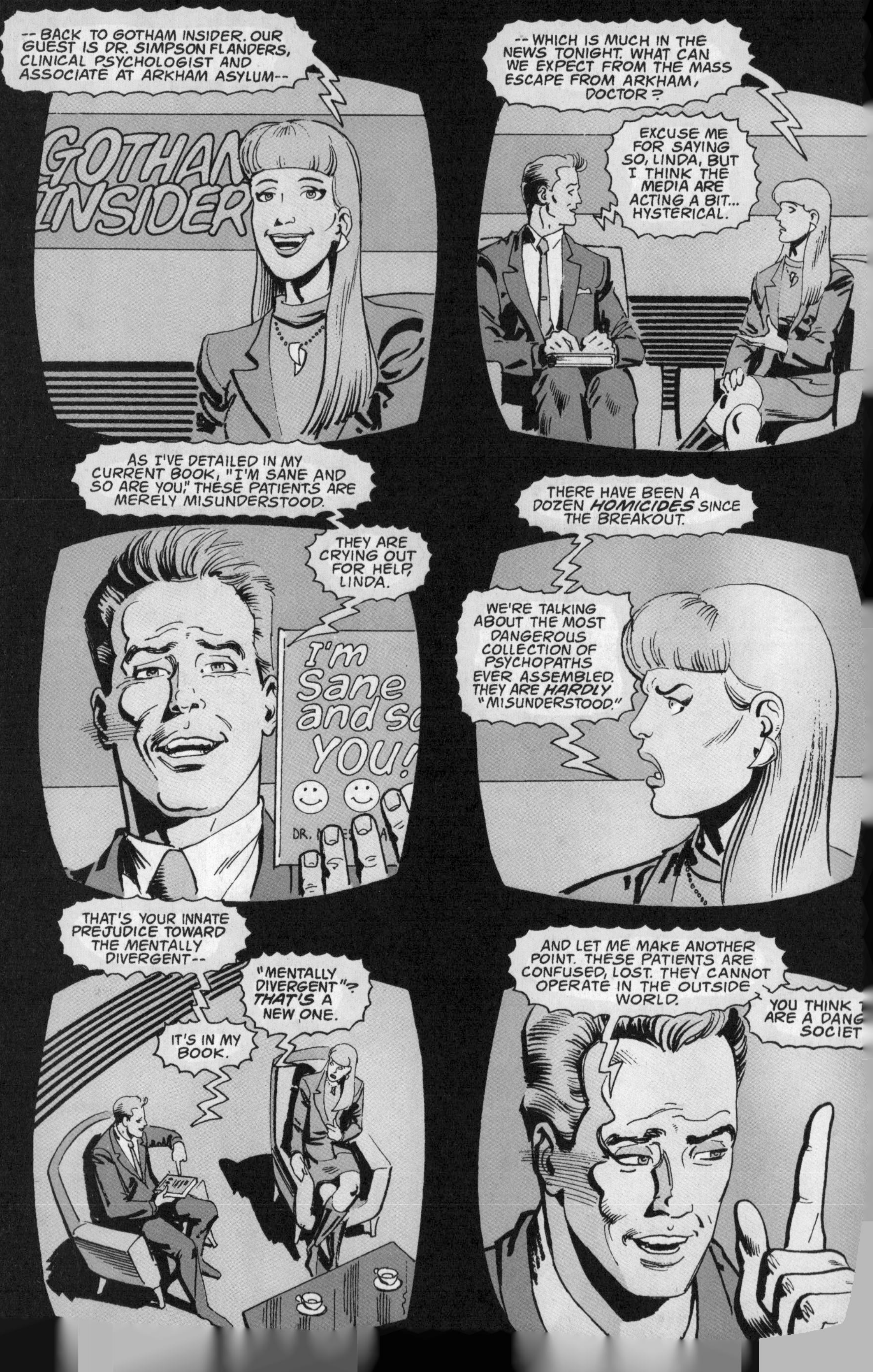
-- BACK TO GOTHAM INSIDER. OUR GUEST IS DR. SIMPSON FLANDERS, CLINICAL PSYCHOLOGIST AND ASSOCIATE AT ARKHAM ASYLUM--
GOTHAM INSIDER
-- WHICH IS MUCH IN THE NEWS TONIGHT. WHAT CAN WE EXPECT FROM THE MASS ESCAPE FROM ARKHAM, DOCTOR?
EXCUSE ME FOR SAYING SO, LINDA, BUT I THINK THE MEDIA ARE ACTING A BIT... HYSTERICAL.
AS I'VE DETAILED IN MY CURRENT BOOK, "I'M SANE AND SO ARE YOU," THESE PATIENTS ARE MERELY MISUNDERSTOOD.
THEY ARE CRYING OUT FOR HELP, LINDA.
I'm Sane
THERE HAVE BEEN A DOZEN *HOMICIDES* SINCE THE BREAKOUT.
WE'RE TALKING ABOUT THE MOST DANGEROUS COLLECTION OF PSYCHOPATHS EVER ASSEMBLED. THEY ARE *HARDLY* "MISUNDERSTOOD."
THAT'S YOUR INNATE PREJUDICE TOWARD THE MENTALLY DIVERGENT--
"MENTALLY DIVERGENT"? *THAT'S* A NEW ONE.
IT'S IN MY BOOK.
AND LET ME MAKE ANOTHER POINT. THESE PATIENTS ARE CONFUSED, LOST. THEY CANNOT OPERATE IN THE OUTSIDE WORLD.
YOU THINK T ARE A DANG SOCIET

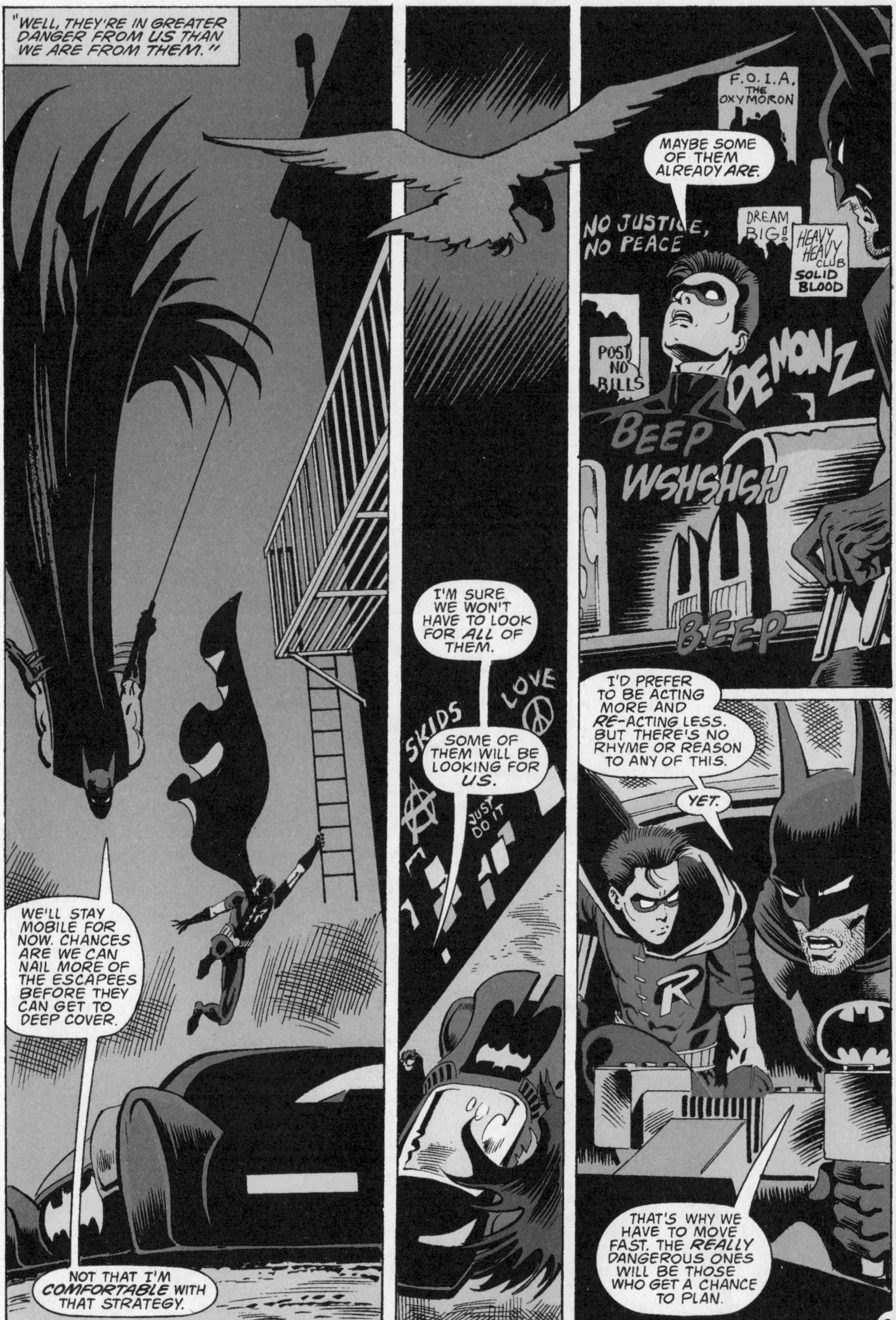

"WELL, THEY'RE IN GREATER DANGER FROM US THAN WE ARE FROM THEM."
WE'LL STAY MOBILE FOR NOW. CHANCES ARE WE CAN NAIL MORE OF THE ESCAPEES BEFORE THEY CAN GET TO DEEP COVER.
NOT THAT I'M COMFORTABLE WITH THAT STRATEGY.
I'M SURE WE WON'T HAVE TO LOOK FOR ALL OF THEM.
SKIDS
LOVE
SOME OF THEM WILL BE LOOKING FOR US.
JUST DO IT
F.O.I.A. THE OXYMORON
MAYBE SOME OF THEM ALREADY ARE.
NO JUSTICE, NO PEACE
DREAM BIG!
HEAVY HEAVY CLUB
SOLID BLOOD
POST NO BILLS
DEMONZ
BEEP
WSHSHSH
BEEP
I'D PREFER TO BE ACTING MORE AND RE-ACTING LESS. BUT THERE'S NO RHYME OR REASON TO ANY OF THIS.
YET.
THAT'S WHY WE HAVE TO MOVE FAST. THE REALLY DANGEROUS ONES WILL BE THOSE WHO GET A CHANCE TO PLAN.
7

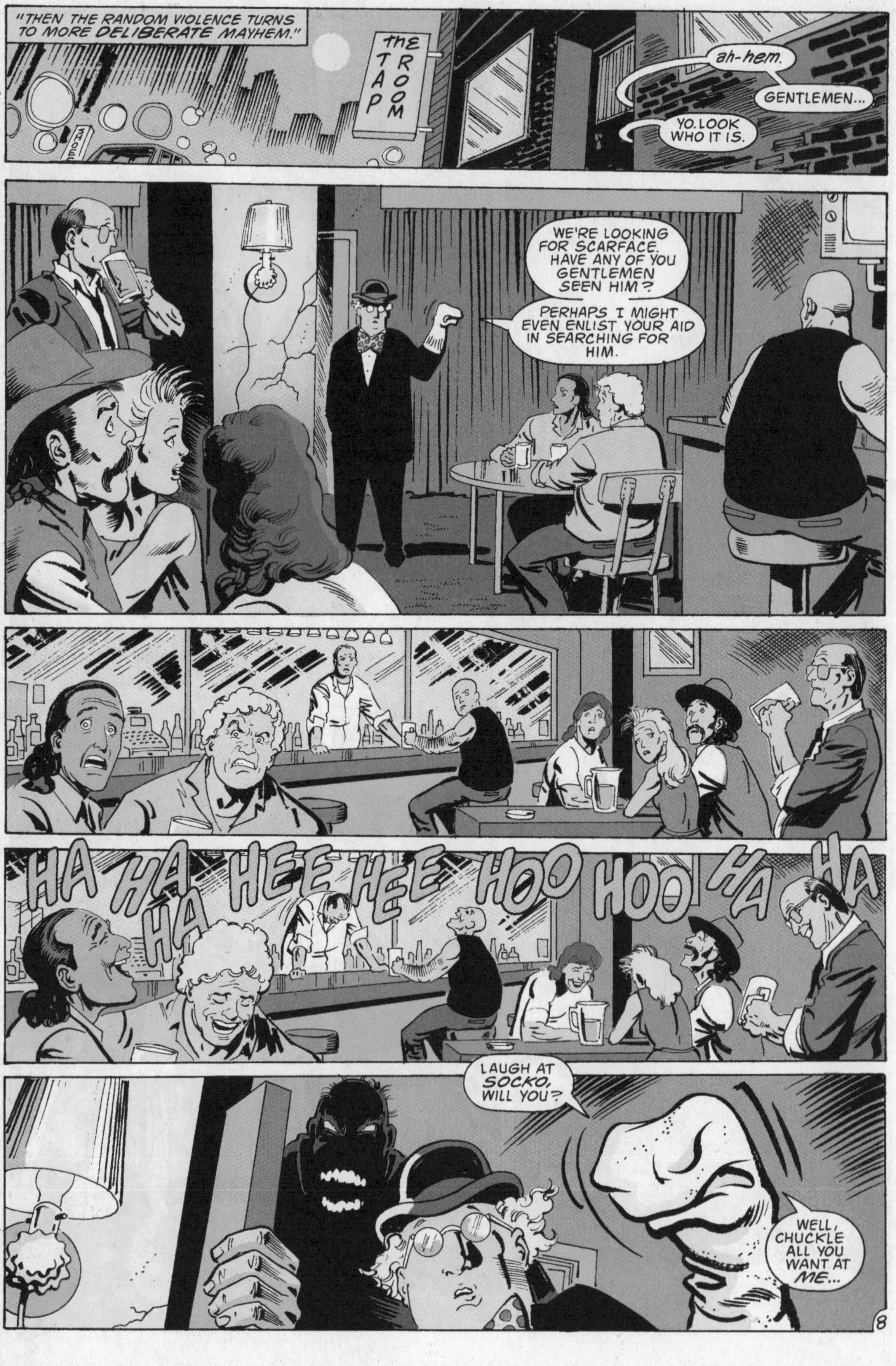
"THEN THE RANDOM VIOLENCE TURNS TO MORE DELIBERATE MAYHEM."
THE TAP ROOM
ah-hem.
GENTLEMEN...
YO. LOOK WHO IT IS.
WE'RE LOOKING FOR SCARFACE. HAVE ANY OF YOU GENTLEMEN SEEN HIM?
PERHAPS I MIGHT EVEN ENLIST YOUR AID IN SEARCHING FOR HIM.
HA HA HA HEE HEE HOO HOO HA HA
LAUGH AT SOCKO, WILL YOU?
WELL, CHUCKLE ALL YOU WANT AT ME...
8

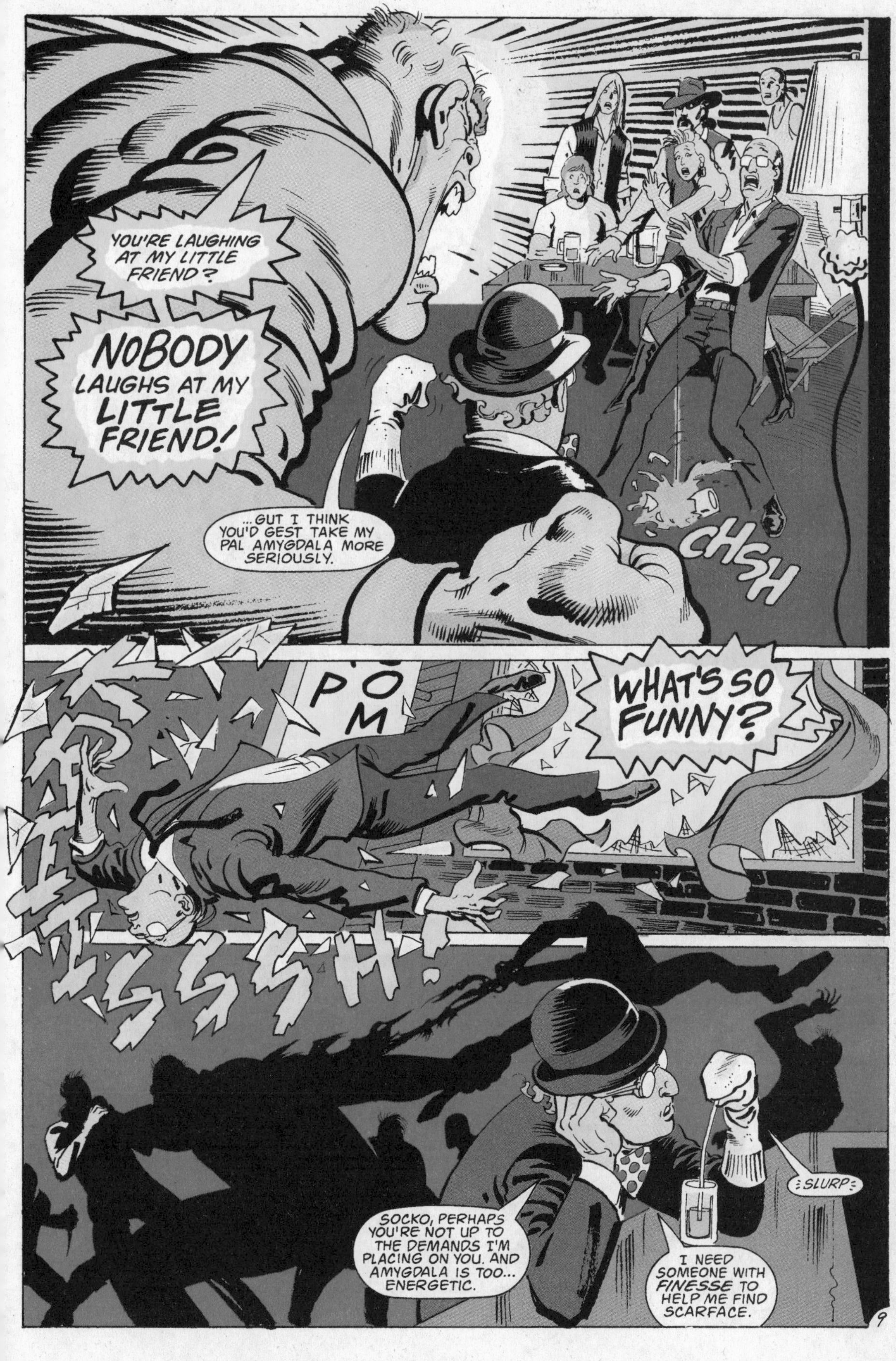
YOU'RE LAUGHING AT MY LITTLE FRIEND?
NOBODY LAUGHS AT MY LITTLE FRIEND!
...GUT I THINK YOU'D GEST TAKE MY PAL AMYGDALA MORE SERIOUSLY.
CHSH
POM
WHAT'S SO FUNNY?
KSSSH!
SLURP
SOCKO, PERHAPS YOU'RE NOT UP TO THE DEMANDS I'M PLACING ON YOU. AND AMYGDALA IS TOO... ENERGETIC.
I NEED SOMEONE WITH FINESSE TO HELP ME FIND SCARFACE.
9

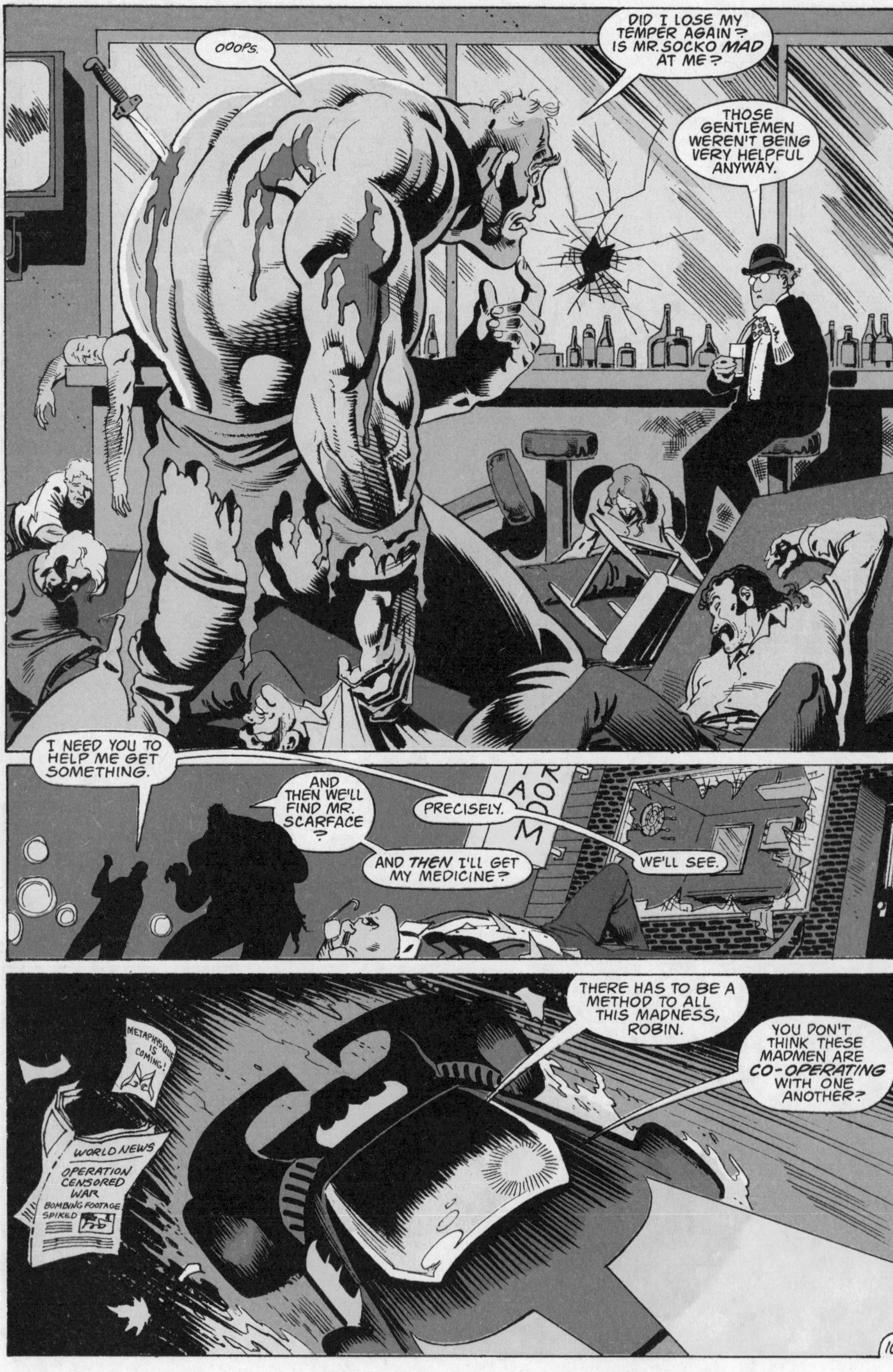
OOOPS.
DID I LOSE MY TEMPER AGAIN? IS MR. SOCKO MAD AT ME?
THOSE GENTLEMEN WEREN'T BEING VERY HELPFUL ANYWAY.
I NEED YOU TO HELP ME GET SOMETHING.
AND THEN WE'LL FIND MR. SCARFACE?
PRECISELY.
AND THEN I'LL GET MY MEDICINE?
WE'LL SEE.
ROOM
METAPHYSIQUE IS COMING!
WORLD NEWS
OPERATION CENSORED WAR
BOMBING FOOTAGE SPIKED
THERE HAS TO BE A METHOD TO ALL THIS MADNESS, ROBIN.
YOU DON'T THINK THESE MADMEN ARE CO-OPERATING WITH ONE ANOTHER?
10

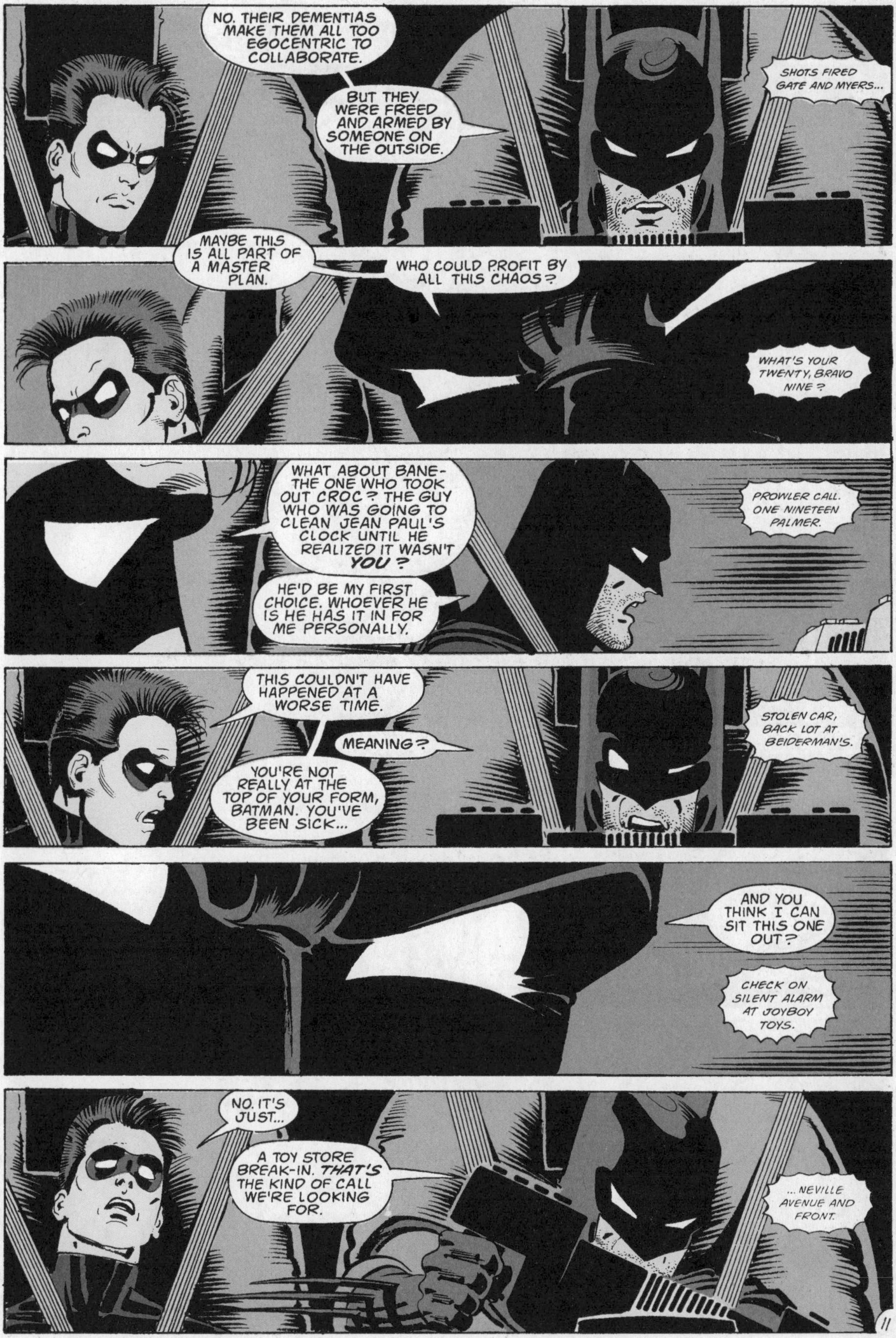
NO. THEIR DEMENTIAS MAKE THEM ALL TOO EGOCENTRIC TO COLLABORATE.
BUT THEY WERE FREED AND ARMED BY SOMEONE ON THE OUTSIDE.
SHOTS FIRED GATE AND MYERS...
MAYBE THIS IS ALL PART OF A MASTER PLAN.
WHO COULD PROFIT BY ALL THIS CHAOS?
WHAT'S YOUR TWENTY, BRAVO NINE?
WHAT ABOUT BANE-THE ONE WHO TOOK OUT CROC? THE GUY WHO WAS GOING TO CLEAN JEAN PAUL'S CLOCK UNTIL HE REALIZED IT WASN'T YOU?
HE'D BE MY FIRST CHOICE. WHOEVER HE IS HE HAS IT IN FOR ME PERSONALLY.
PROWLER CALL. ONE NINETEEN PALMER.
THIS COULDN'T HAVE HAPPENED AT A WORSE TIME.
MEANING?
YOU'RE NOT REALLY AT THE TOP OF YOUR FORM, BATMAN. YOU'VE BEEN SICK...
STOLEN CAR, BACK LOT AT BEIDERMAN'S.
AND YOU THINK I CAN SIT THIS ONE OUT?
CHECK ON SILENT ALARM AT JOYBOY TOYS.
NO. IT'S JUST...
A TOY STORE BREAK-IN. THAT'S THE KIND OF CALL WE'RE LOOKING FOR.
...NEVILLE AVENUE AND FRONT.
11

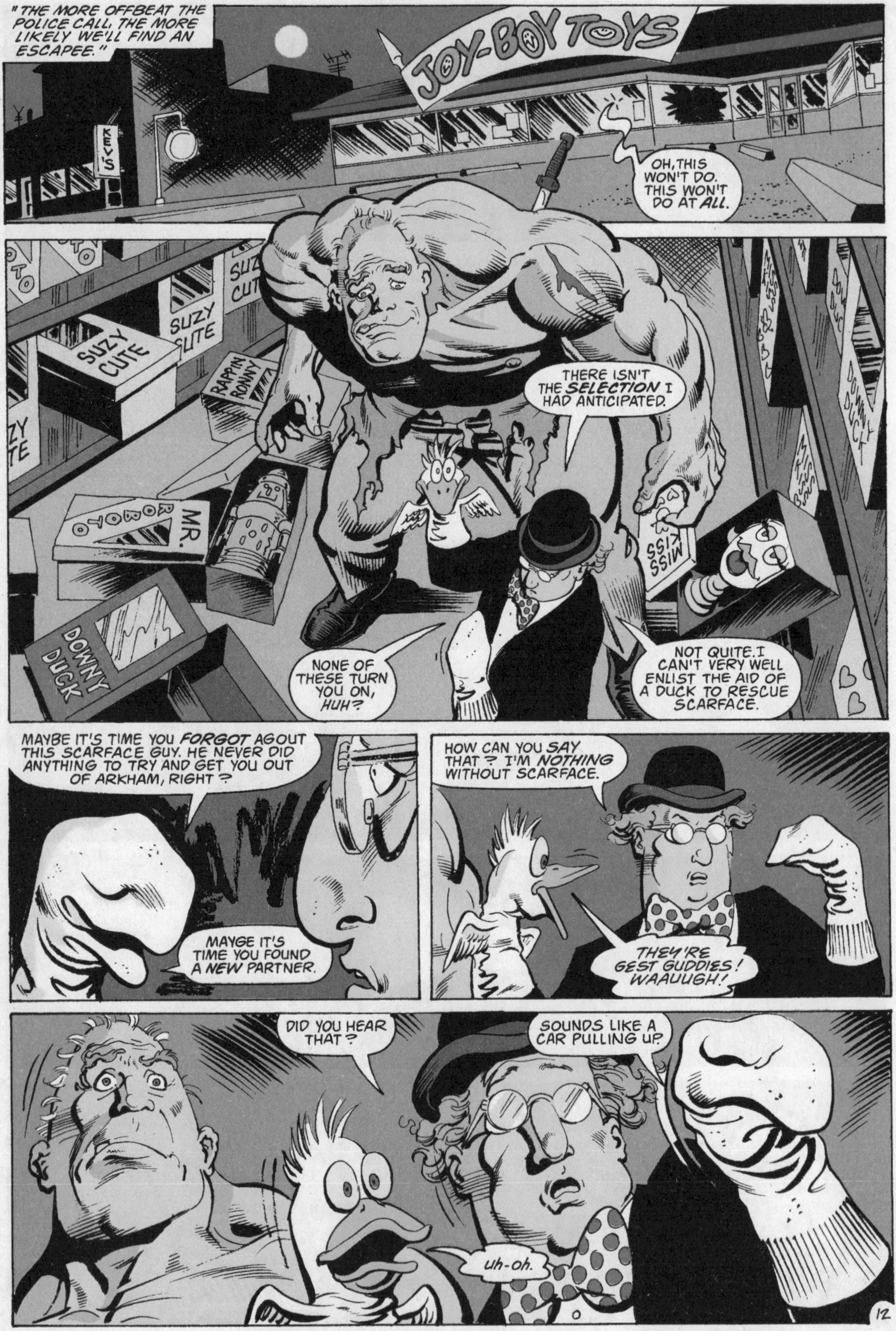
"THE MORE OFFBEAT THE POLICE CALL, THE MORE LIKELY WE'LL FIND AN ESCAPEE."
JOY-BOY TOYS
KEV'S
OH, THIS WON'T DO. THIS WON'T DO AT ALL.
SUZY CUTE
RAPPIN RONNY
MR. ROBOTO
DOWNY DUCK
MISS KISS
THERE ISN'T THE SELECTION I HAD ANTICIPATED.
NONE OF THESE TURN YOU ON, HUH?
NOT QUITE. I CAN'T VERY WELL ENLIST THE AID OF A DUCK TO RESCUE SCARFACE.
MAYBE IT'S TIME YOU FORGOT AGOUT THIS SCARFACE GUY. HE NEVER DID ANYTHING TO TRY AND GET YOU OUT OF ARKHAM, RIGHT?
MAYGE IT'S TIME YOU FOUND A NEW PARTNER.
HOW CAN YOU SAY THAT? I'M NOTHING WITHOUT SCARFACE.
THEY'RE GEST GUDDIES! WAAUUGH!
DID YOU HEAR THAT?
SOUNDS LIKE A CAR PULLING UP.
uh-oh.
12

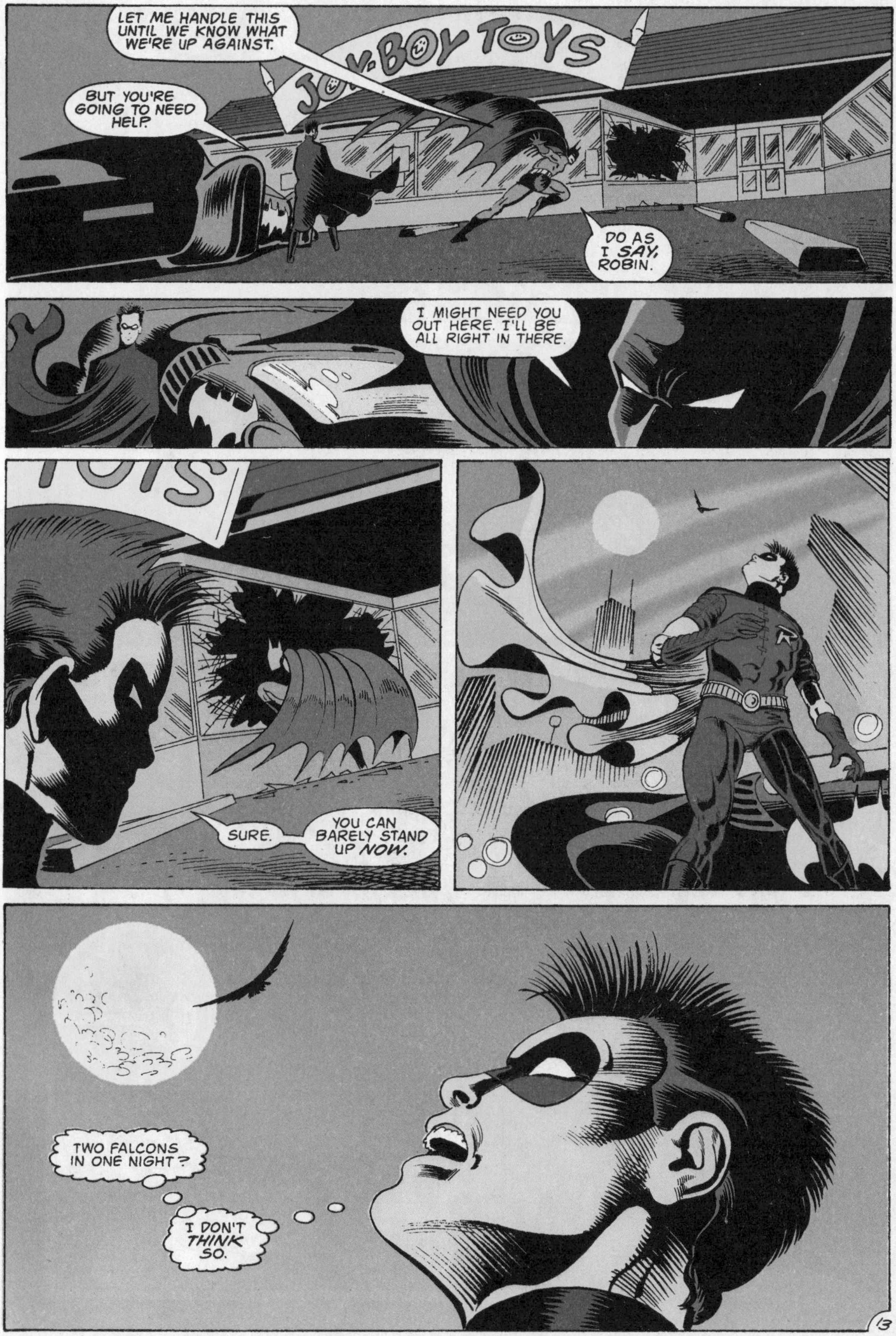
LET ME HANDLE THIS UNTIL WE KNOW WHAT WE'RE UP AGAINST.
JOY-BOY TOYS
BUT YOU'RE GOING TO NEED HELP.
DO AS I SAY, ROBIN.
I MIGHT NEED YOU OUT HERE. I'LL BE ALL RIGHT IN THERE.
SURE.
YOU CAN BARELY STAND UP NOW.
TWO FALCONS IN ONE NIGHT?
I DON'T THINK SO.
13

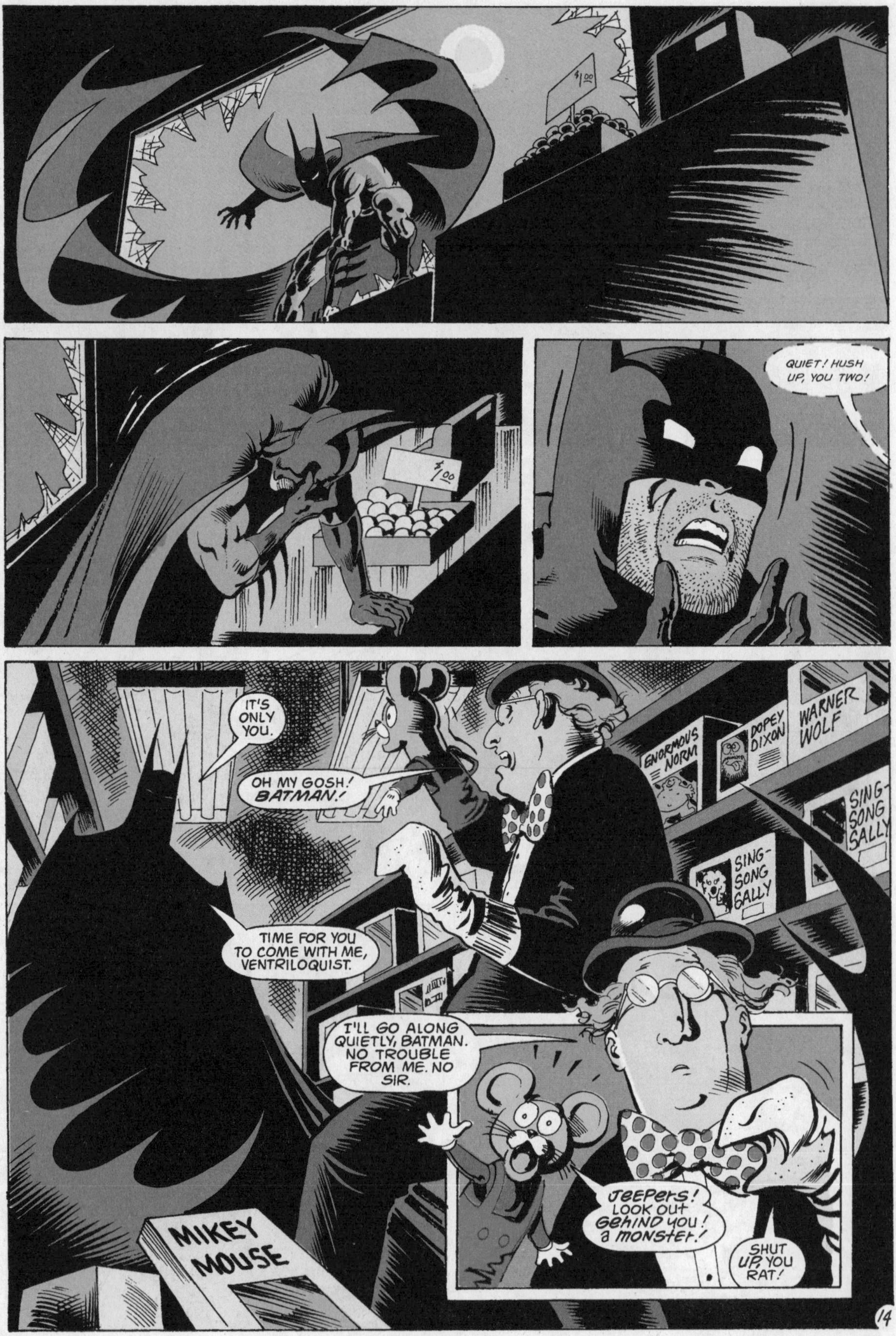

$1.00
$1.00
QUIET! HUSH UP, YOU TWO!
IT'S ONLY YOU.
OH MY GOSH! BATMAN!
ENORMOUS NORM
DOPEY DIXON
WARNER WOLF
SING-SONG SALLY
SING-SONG SALLY
TIME FOR YOU TO COME WITH ME, VENTRILOQUIST.
I'LL GO ALONG QUIETLY, BATMAN. NO TROUBLE FROM ME. NO SIR.
JEEPERS! LOOK OUT BEHIND YOU! A MONSTER!
SHUT UP, YOU RAT!
MIKEY MOUSE
14

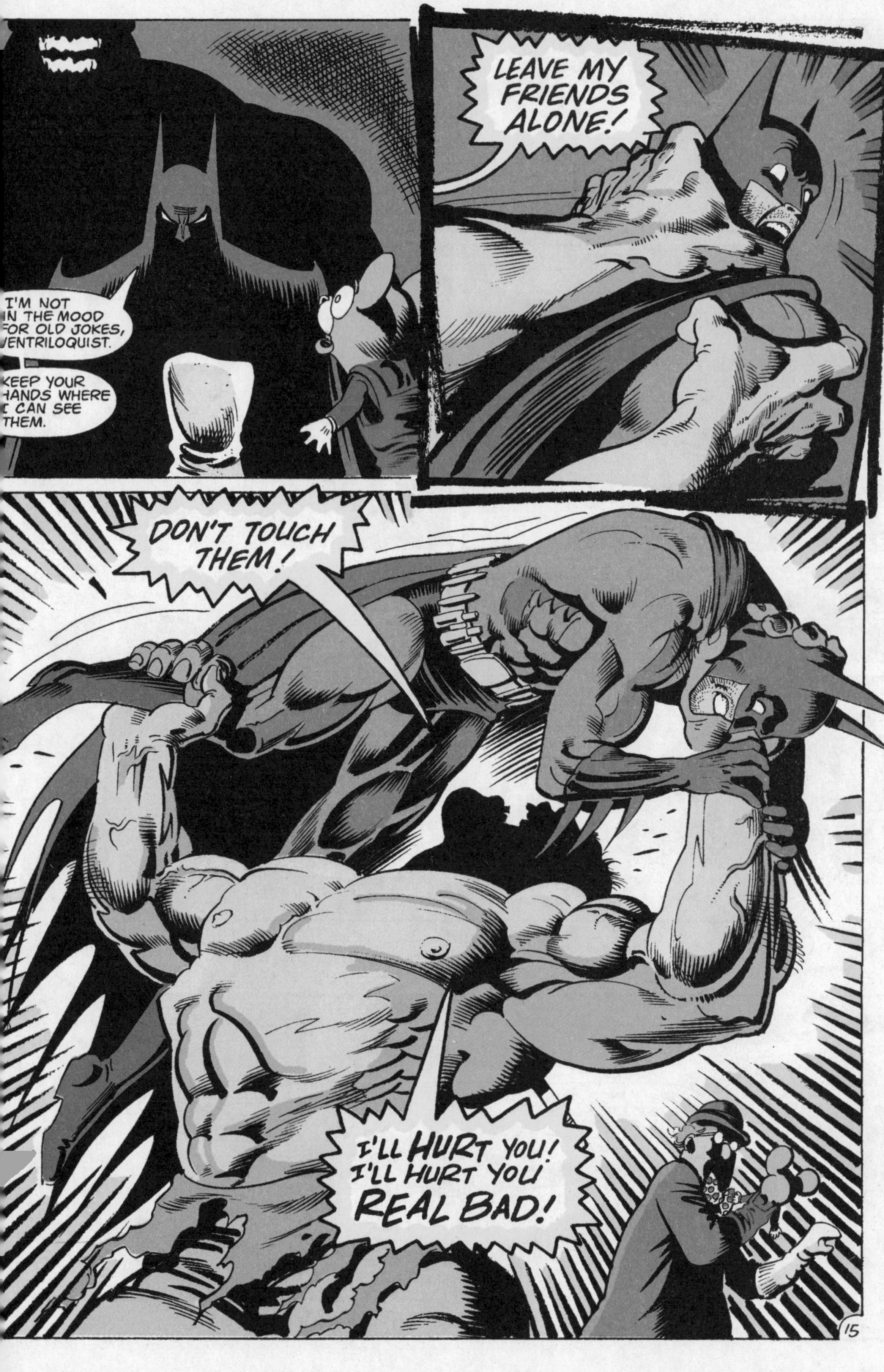
I'M NOT IN THE MOOD FOR OLD JOKES, VENTRILOQUIST.
KEEP YOUR HANDS WHERE I CAN SEE THEM.
LEAVE MY FRIENDS ALONE!
DON'T TOUCH THEM!
I'LL HURT YOU! I'LL HURT YOU REAL BAD!
15

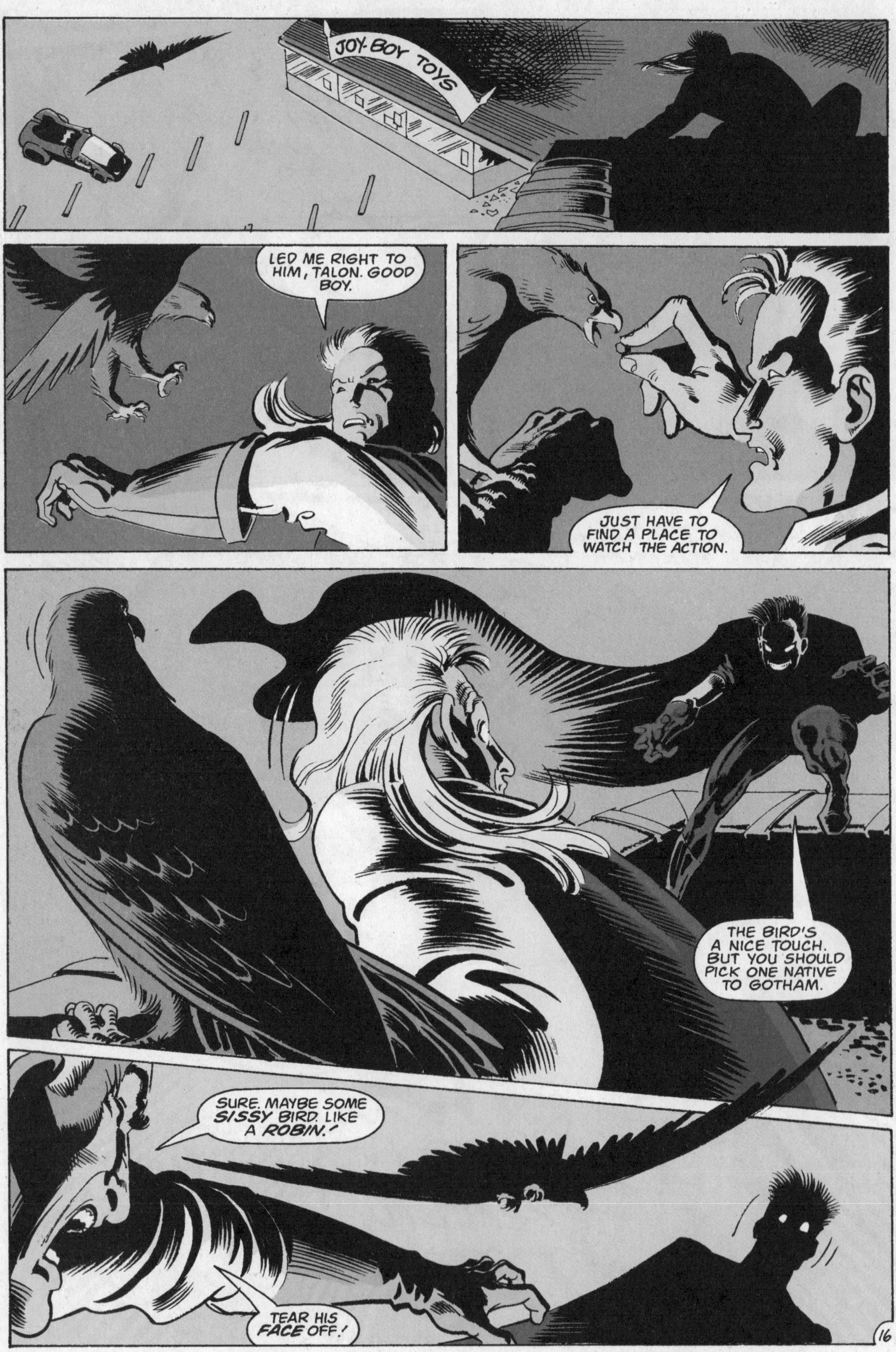
JOY-BOY TOYS
LED ME RIGHT TO HIM, TALON. GOOD BOY.
JUST HAVE TO FIND A PLACE TO WATCH THE ACTION.
THE BIRD'S A NICE TOUCH. BUT YOU SHOULD PICK ONE NATIVE TO GOTHAM.
SURE. MAYBE SOME SISSY BIRD. LIKE A ROBIN.'
TEAR HIS FACE OFF.'
16

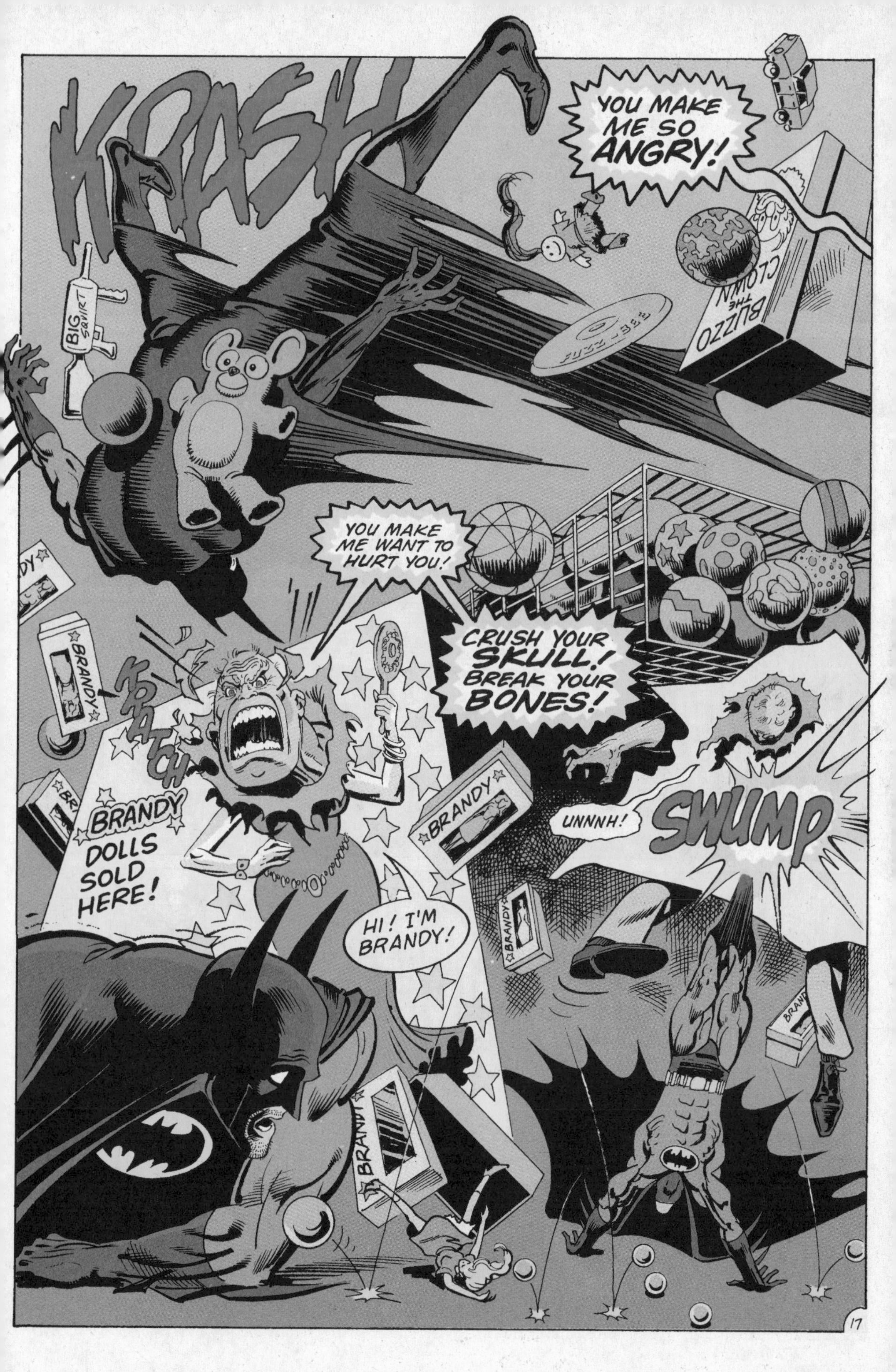
KRASH
YOU MAKE ME SO ANGRY!
BIG SQUIRT
BUZZO THE CLOWN
YOU MAKE ME WANT TO HURT YOU!
CRUSH YOUR SKULL! BREAK YOUR BONES!
KRATCH
BRANDY
BRANDY DOLLS SOLD HERE!
UNNNH!
SWUMP
HI! I'M BRANDY!
17

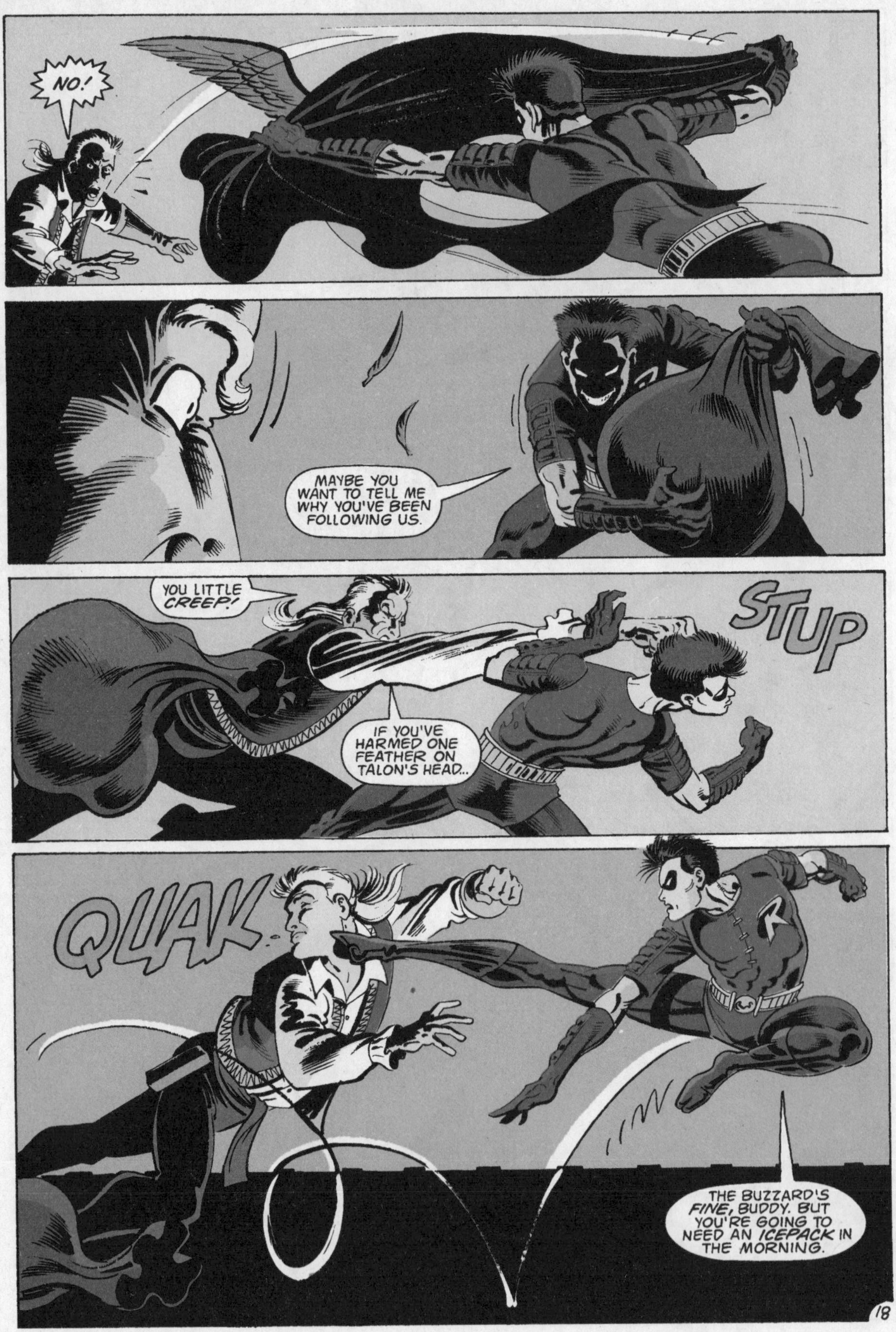
NO!
MAYBE YOU WANT TO TELL ME WHY YOU'VE BEEN FOLLOWING US.
YOU LITTLE CREEP!
IF YOU'VE HARMED ONE FEATHER ON TALON'S HEAD...
STUP
QUAK
THE BUZZARD'S FINE, BUDDY. BUT YOU'RE GOING TO NEED AN ICEPACK IN THE MORNING.
18

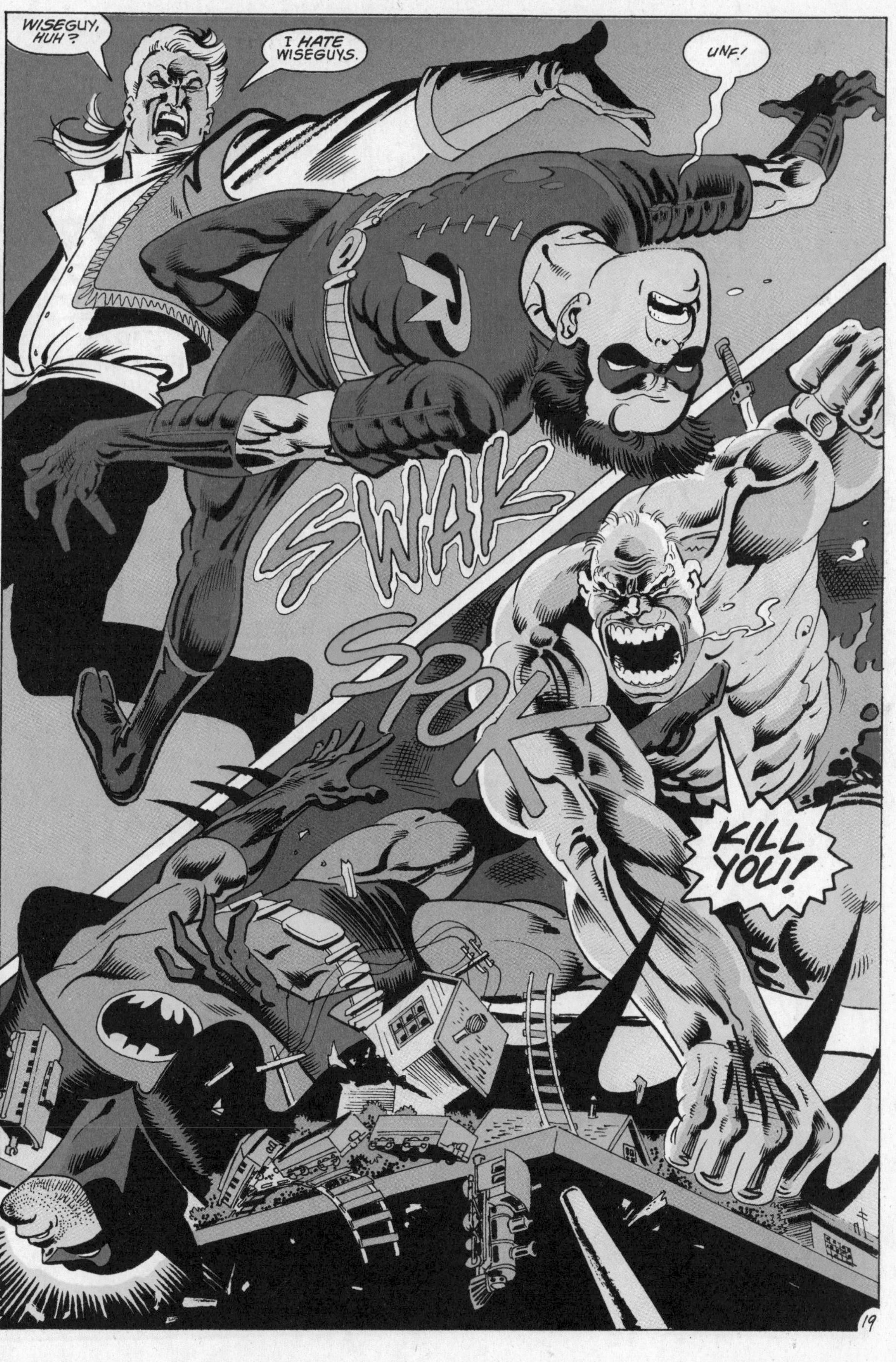
WISEGUY, HUH?
I HATE WISEGUYS.
UNF!
SWAK
SPOK
KILL YOU!
19

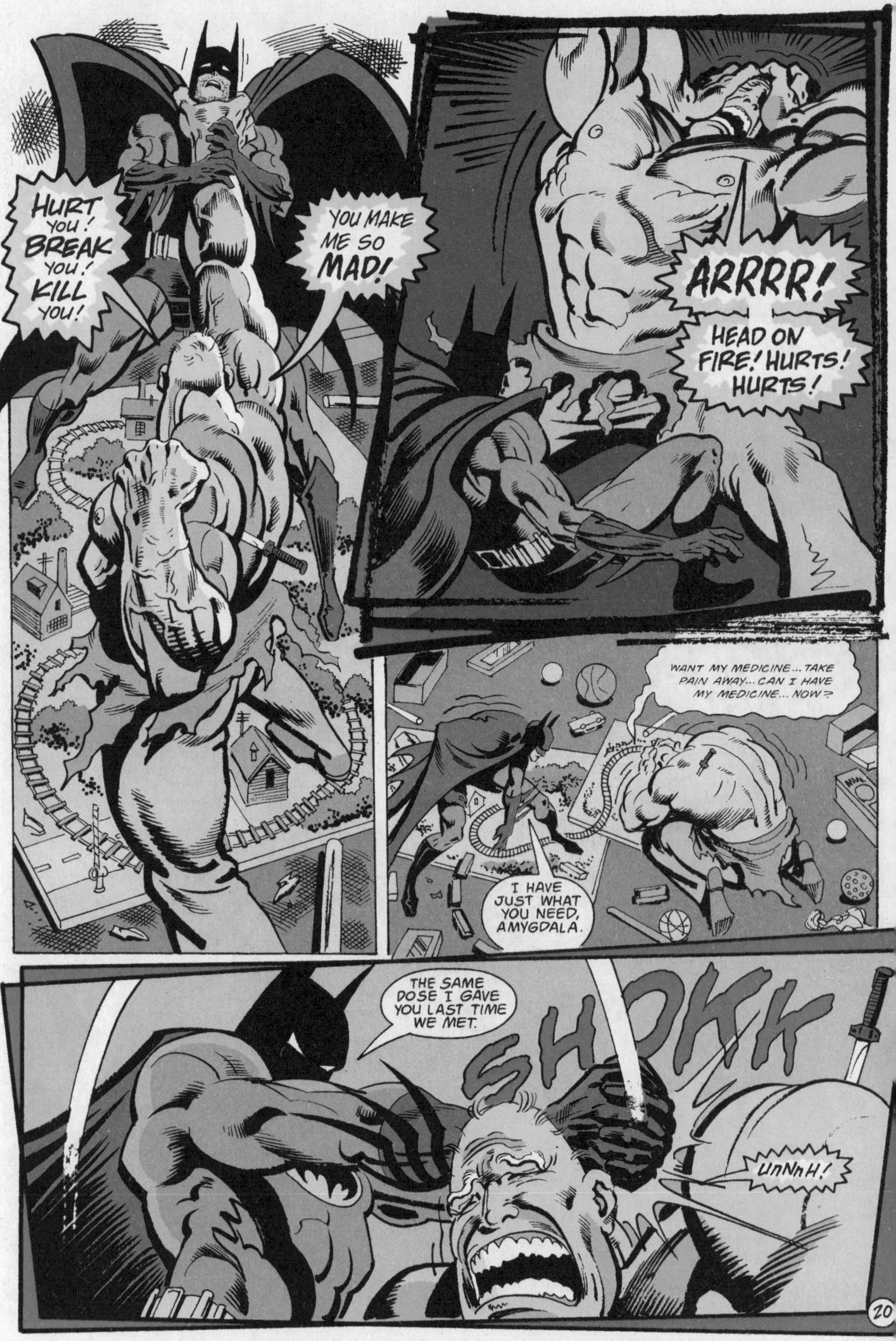

HURT YOU! BREAK YOU! KILL YOU!
YOU MAKE ME SO MAD!
ARRRR!
HEAD ON FIRE! HURTS! HURTS!
WANT MY MEDICINE... TAKE PAIN AWAY... CAN I HAVE MY MEDICINE... NOW?
I HAVE JUST WHAT YOU NEED, AMYGDALA.
THE SAME DOSE I GAVE YOU LAST TIME WE MET.
SHOKK
UnNnH!
20

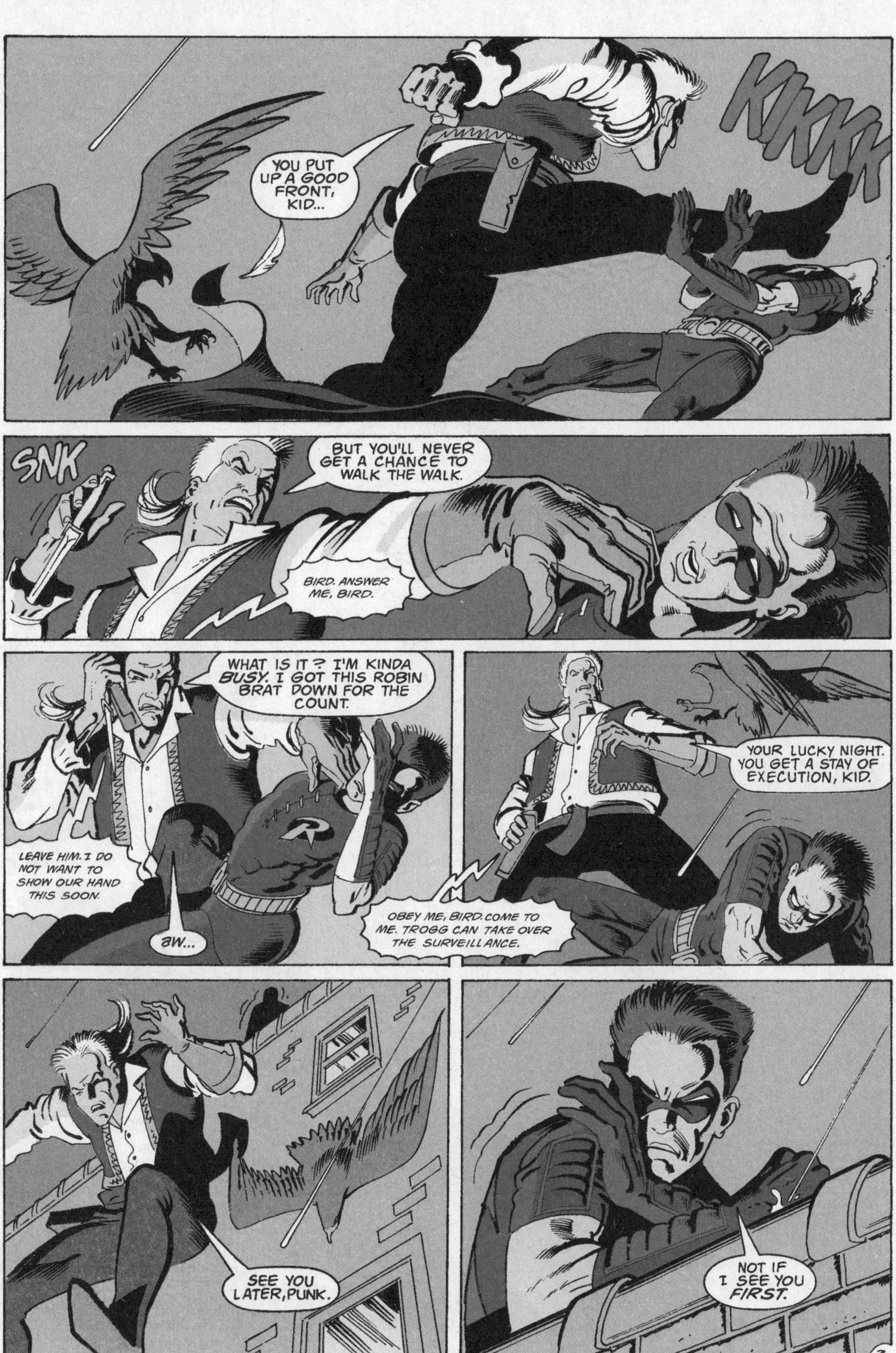

KIKKK
YOU PUT UP A GOOD FRONT, KID...
SNK
BUT YOU'LL NEVER GET A CHANCE TO WALK THE WALK.
BIRD. ANSWER ME, BIRD.
WHAT IS IT? I'M KINDA BUSY. I GOT THIS ROBIN BRAT DOWN FOR THE COUNT.
LEAVE HIM. I DO NOT WANT TO SHOW OUR HAND THIS SOON.
AW...
OBEY ME, BIRD. COME TO ME. TROGG CAN TAKE OVER THE SURVEILLANCE.
YOUR LUCKY NIGHT. YOU GET A STAY OF EXECUTION, KID.
SEE YOU LATER, PUNK.
NOT IF I SEE YOU FIRST.
21

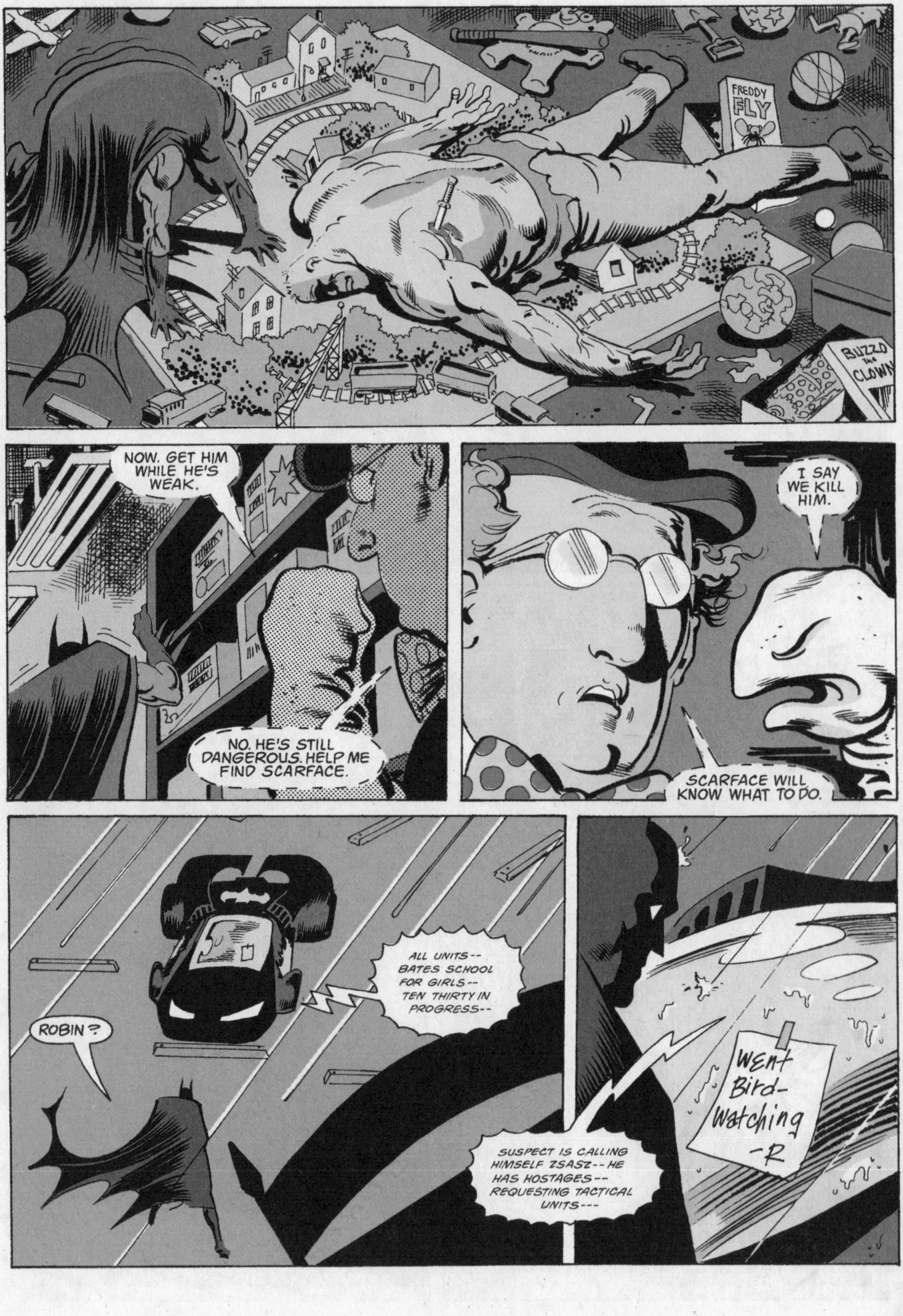
FREDDY FLY
BUZZO the CLOWN
NOW. GET HIM WHILE HE'S WEAK.
NO. HE'S STILL DANGEROUS. HELP ME FIND SCARFACE.
I SAY WE KILL HIM.
SCARFACE WILL KNOW WHAT TO DO.
ALL UNITS-- BATES SCHOOL FOR GIRLS-- TEN THIRTY IN PROGRESS--
ROBIN?
SUSPECT IS CALLING HIMSELF ZSASZ-- HE HAS HOSTAGES-- REQUESTING TACTICAL UNITS---
WENt Bird-Watching -R

Cover art by KELLEY JONES

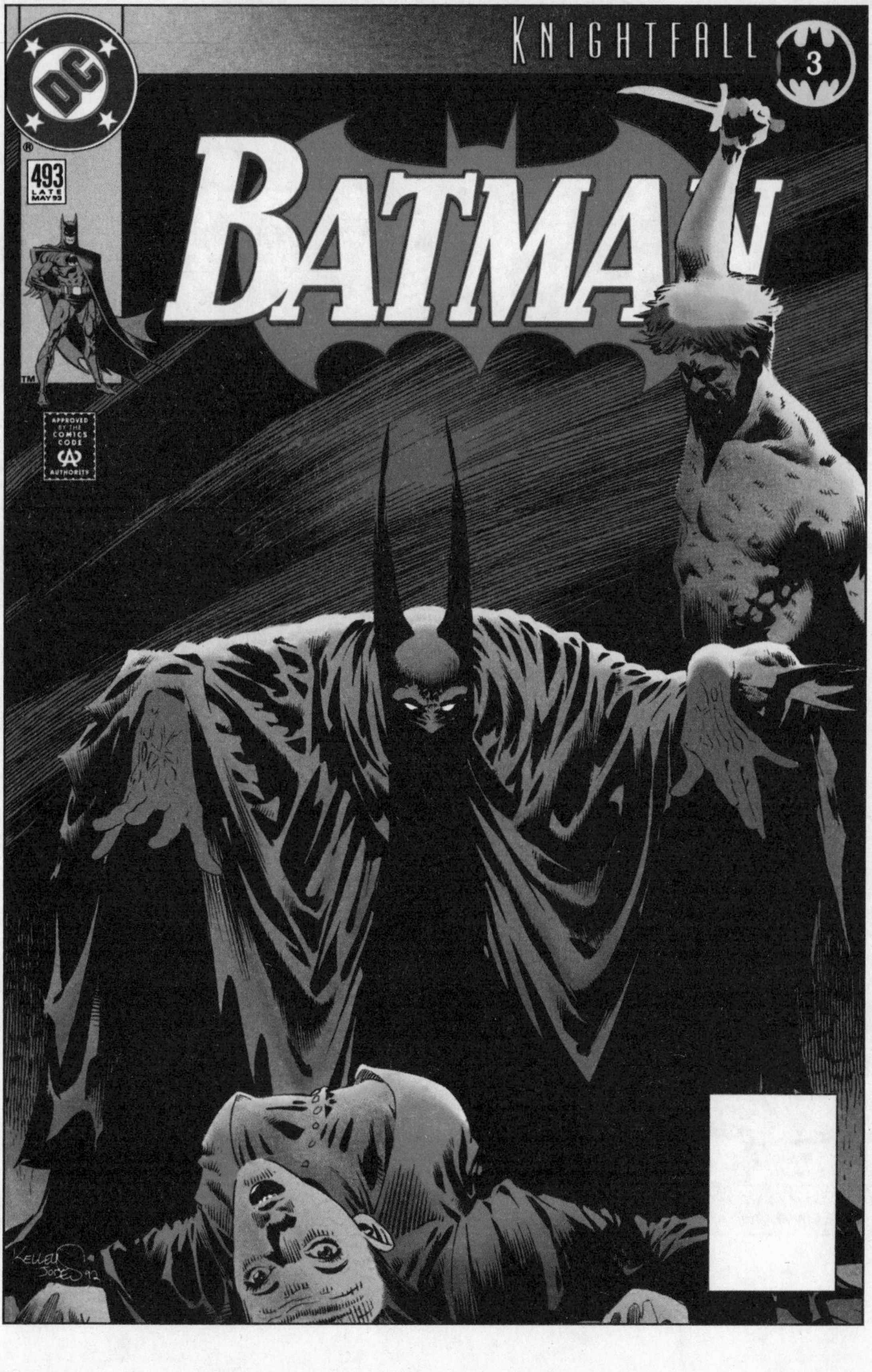

KNIGHTFALL
3
BATMAN
493
LATE MAY 93
APPROVED BY THE COMICS CODE AUTHORITY

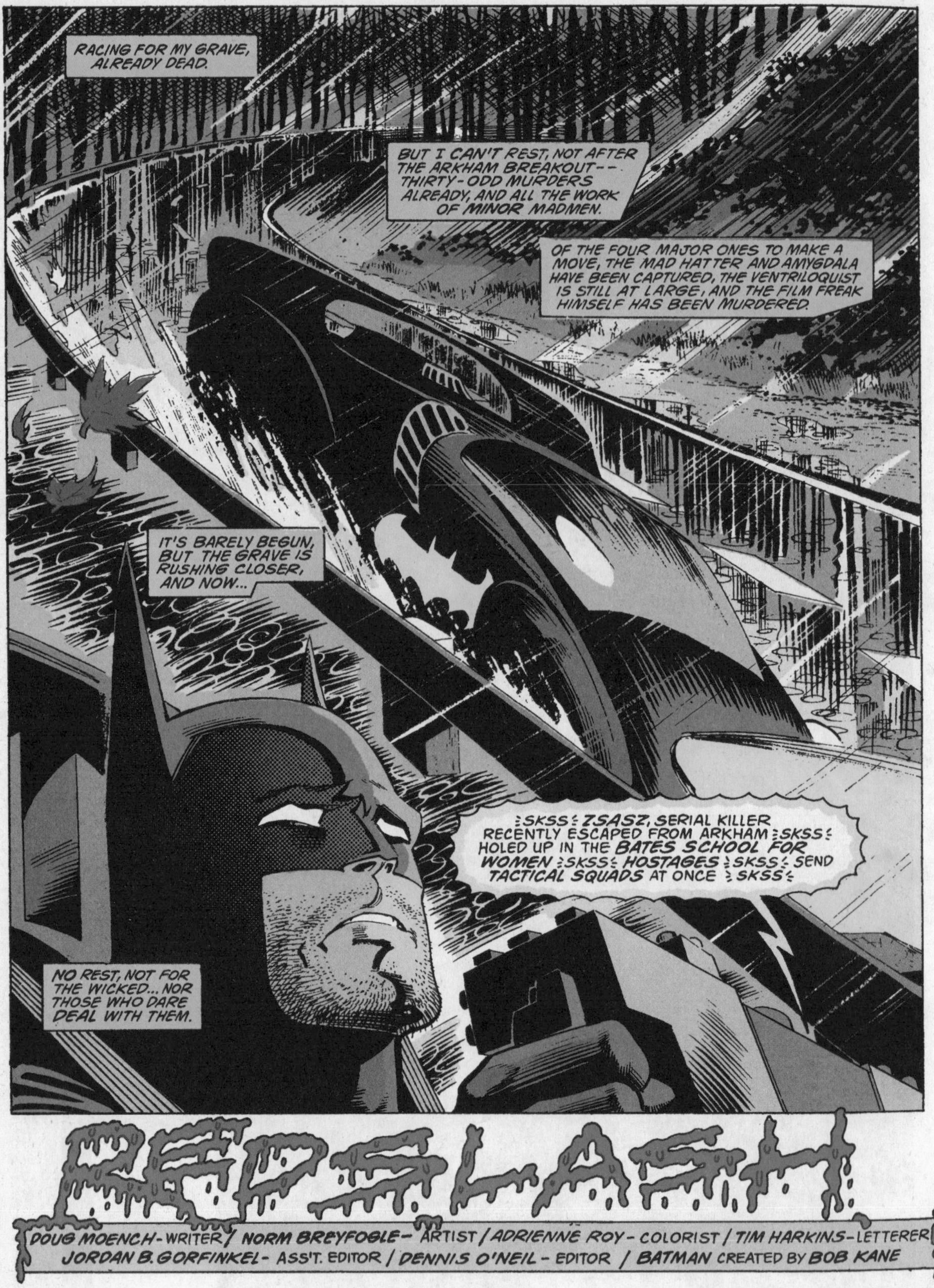
RACING FOR MY GRAVE, ALREADY DEAD.
BUT I CAN'T REST, NOT AFTER THE ARKHAM BREAKOUT-- THIRTY-ODD MURDERS ALREADY, AND ALL THE WORK OF MINOR MADMEN.
OF THE FOUR MAJOR ONES TO MAKE A MOVE, THE MAD HATTER AND AMYGDALA HAVE BEEN CAPTURED, THE VENTRILOQUIST IS STILL AT LARGE, AND THE FILM FREAK HIMSELF HAS BEEN MURDERED.
IT'S BARELY BEGUN, BUT THE GRAVE IS RUSHING CLOSER, AND NOW...
SKSS ZSASZ, SERIAL KILLER RECENTLY ESCAPED FROM ARKHAM SKSS HOLED UP IN THE BATES SCHOOL FOR WOMEN SKSS HOSTAGES SKSS SEND TACTICAL SQUADS AT ONCE SKSS
NO REST, NOT FOR THE WICKED... NOR THOSE WHO DARE DEAL WITH THEM.

RED SLASH

DOUG MOENCH-WRITER / NORM BREYFOGLE-ARTIST / ADRIENNE ROY-COLORIST / TIM HARKINS-LETTERER
JORDAN B. GORFINKEL-ASS'T. EDITOR / DENNIS O'NEIL-EDITOR / BATMAN CREATED BY BOB KANE

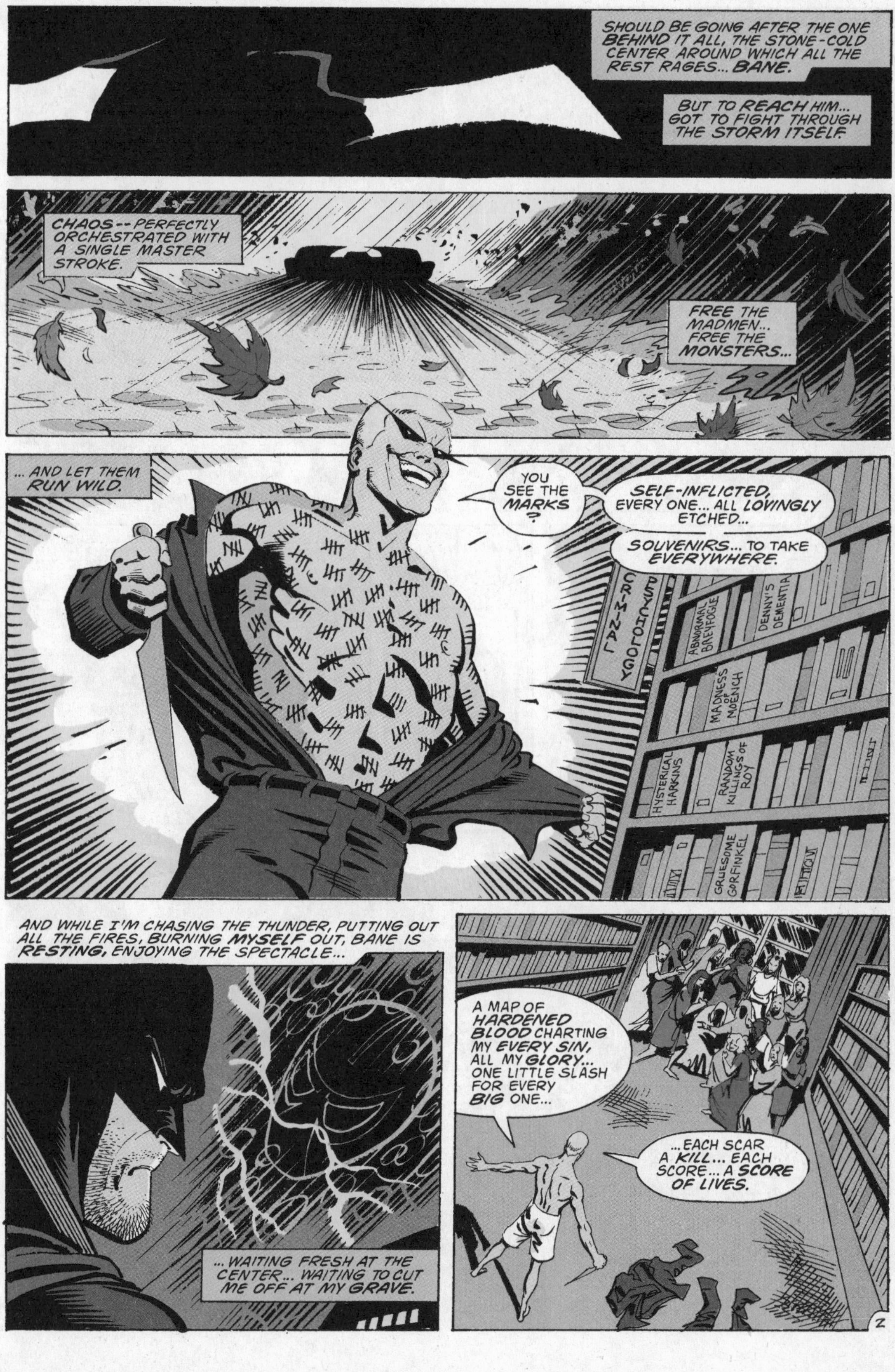
SHOULD BE GOING AFTER THE ONE BEHIND IT ALL, THE STONE-COLD CENTER AROUND WHICH ALL THE REST RAGES... BANE.
BUT TO REACH HIM... GOT TO FIGHT THROUGH THE STORM ITSELF.
CHAOS--PERFECTLY ORCHESTRATED WITH A SINGLE MASTER STROKE.
FREE THE MADMEN... FREE THE MONSTERS...
...AND LET THEM RUN WILD.
YOU SEE THE MARKS?
SELF-INFLICTED, EVERY ONE... ALL LOVINGLY ETCHED...
SOUVENIRS... TO TAKE EVERYWHERE.
CRIMINAL PSYCHOLOGY
ABNORMAL BREYFOGLE
DENNY'S DEMENTIA
MADNESS OF MOENCH
HYSTERICAL HARKINS
RANDOM KILLINGS OF ROY
GRUESOME GORFINKEL
AND WHILE I'M CHASING THE THUNDER, PUTTING OUT ALL THE FIRES, BURNING MYSELF OUT, BANE IS RESTING, ENJOYING THE SPECTACLE...
...WAITING FRESH AT THE CENTER... WAITING TO CUT ME OFF AT MY GRAVE.
A MAP OF HARDENED BLOOD CHARTING MY EVERY SIN, ALL MY GLORY... ONE LITTLE SLASH FOR EVERY BIG ONE...
...EACH SCAR A KILL... EACH SCORE... A SCORE OF LIVES.
2

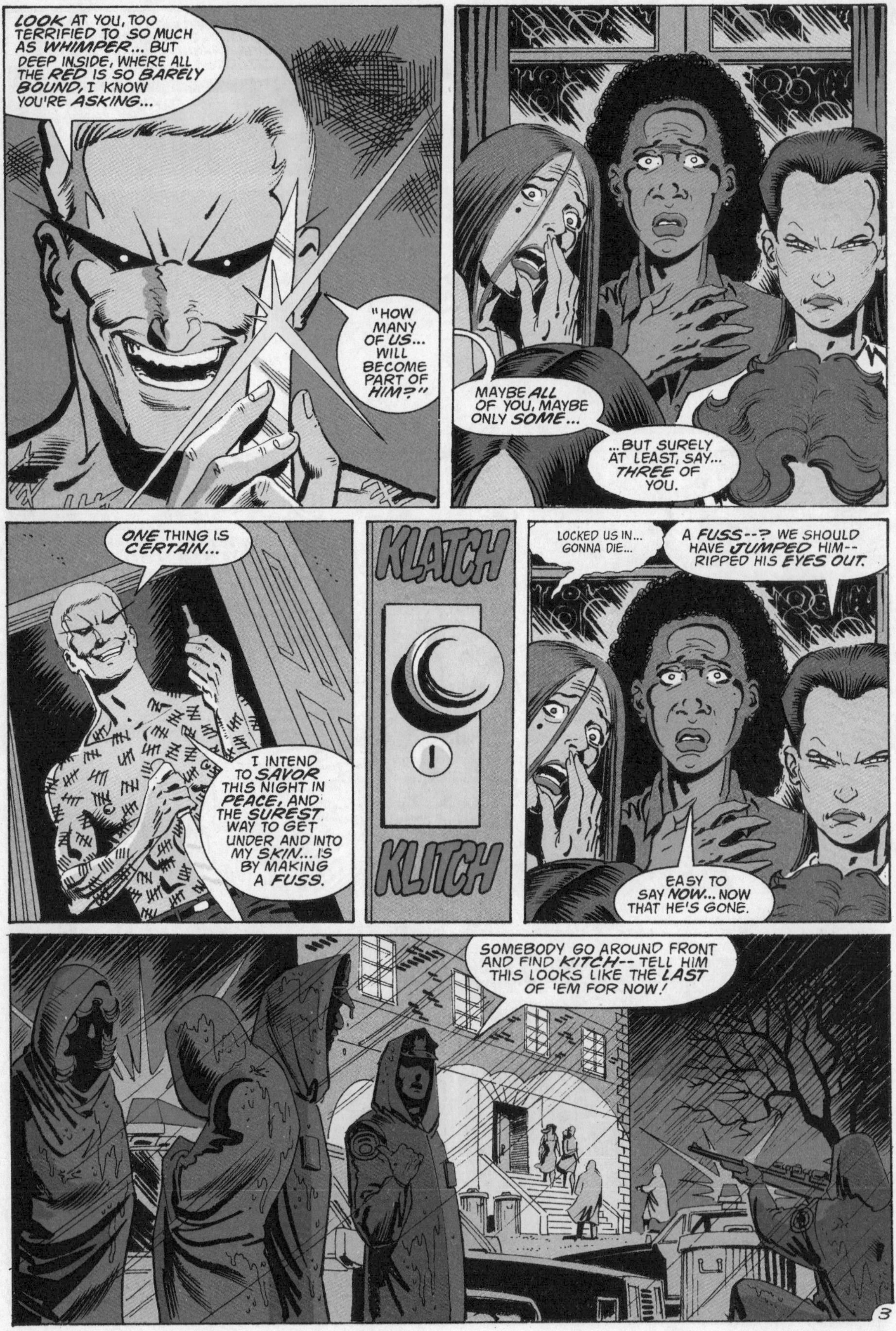
LOOK AT YOU, TOO TERRIFIED TO SO MUCH AS WHIMPER... BUT DEEP INSIDE, WHERE ALL THE RED IS SO BARELY BOUND, I KNOW YOU'RE ASKING...
"HOW MANY OF US... WILL BECOME PART OF HIM?"
MAYBE ALL OF YOU, MAYBE ONLY SOME...
...BUT SURELY AT LEAST, SAY... THREE OF YOU.
ONE THING IS CERTAIN...
I INTEND TO SAVOR THIS NIGHT IN PEACE, AND THE SUREST WAY TO GET UNDER AND INTO MY SKIN... IS BY MAKING A FUSS.
KLATCH
KLITCH
LOCKED US IN... GONNA DIE...
A FUSS--? WE SHOULD HAVE JUMPED HIM-- RIPPED HIS EYES OUT.
EASY TO SAY NOW... NOW THAT HE'S GONE.
SOMEBODY GO AROUND FRONT AND FIND KITCH-- TELL HIM THIS LOOKS LIKE THE LAST OF 'EM FOR NOW!
3

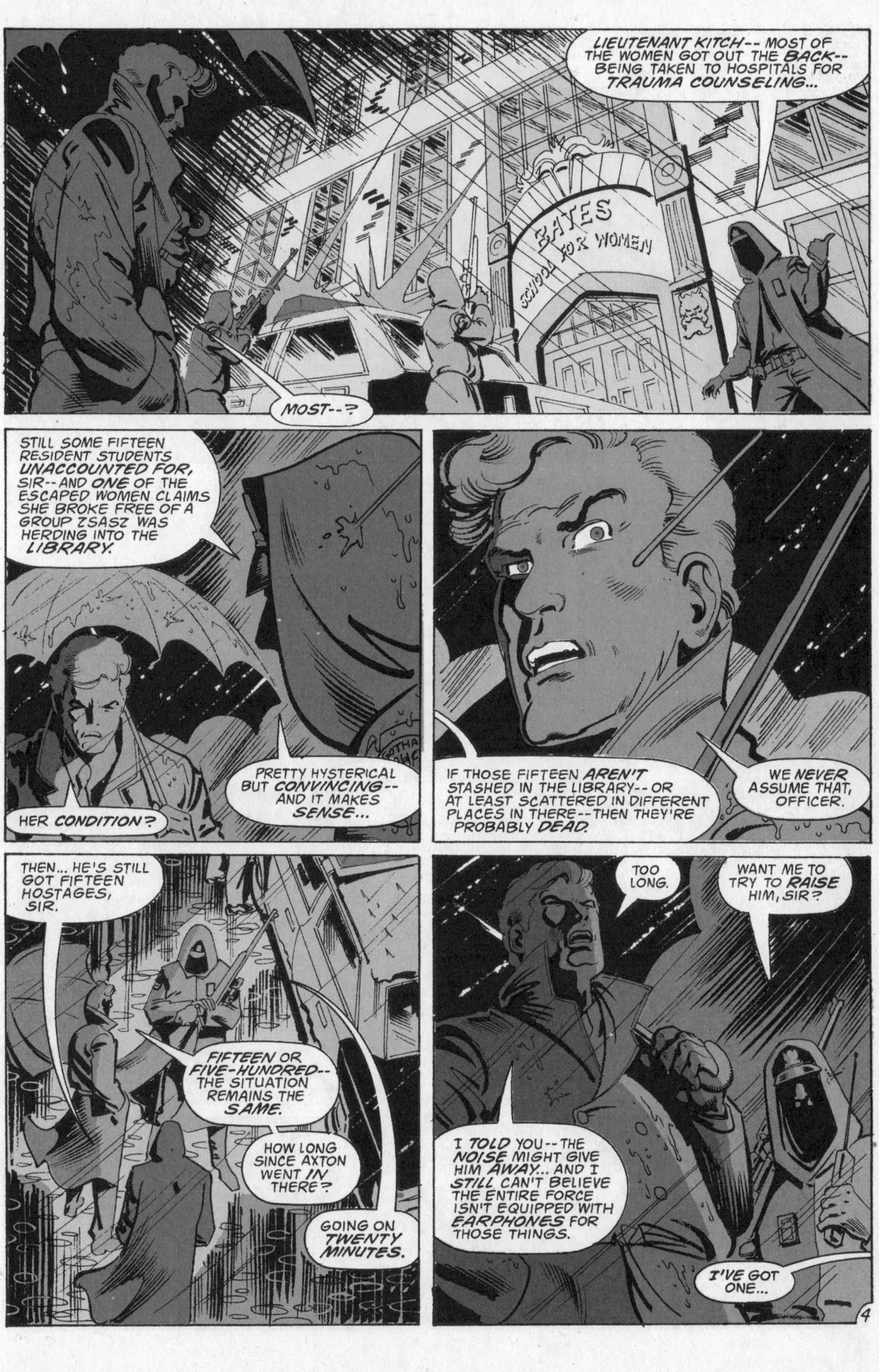
LIEUTENANT KITCH-- MOST OF THE WOMEN GOT OUT THE BACK-- BEING TAKEN TO HOSPITALS FOR TRAUMA COUNSELING...
BATES SCHOOL FOR WOMEN
MOST--?
STILL SOME FIFTEEN RESIDENT STUDENTS UNACCOUNTED FOR, SIR--AND ONE OF THE ESCAPED WOMEN CLAIMS SHE BROKE FREE OF A GROUP ZSASZ WAS HERDING INTO THE LIBRARY.
HER CONDITION?
PRETTY HYSTERICAL BUT CONVINCING--AND IT MAKES SENSE...
IF THOSE FIFTEEN AREN'T STASHED IN THE LIBRARY-- OR AT LEAST SCATTERED IN DIFFERENT PLACES IN THERE--THEN THEY'RE PROBABLY DEAD.
WE NEVER ASSUME THAT, OFFICER.
THEN... HE'S STILL GOT FIFTEEN HOSTAGES, SIR.
FIFTEEN OR FIVE-HUNDRED-- THE SITUATION REMAINS THE SAME.
HOW LONG SINCE AXTON WENT IN THERE?
GOING ON TWENTY MINUTES.
TOO LONG.
WANT ME TO TRY TO RAISE HIM, SIR?
I TOLD YOU--THE NOISE MIGHT GIVE HIM AWAY... AND I STILL CAN'T BELIEVE THE ENTIRE FORCE ISN'T EQUIPPED WITH EARPHONES FOR THOSE THINGS.
I'VE GOT ONE...
4

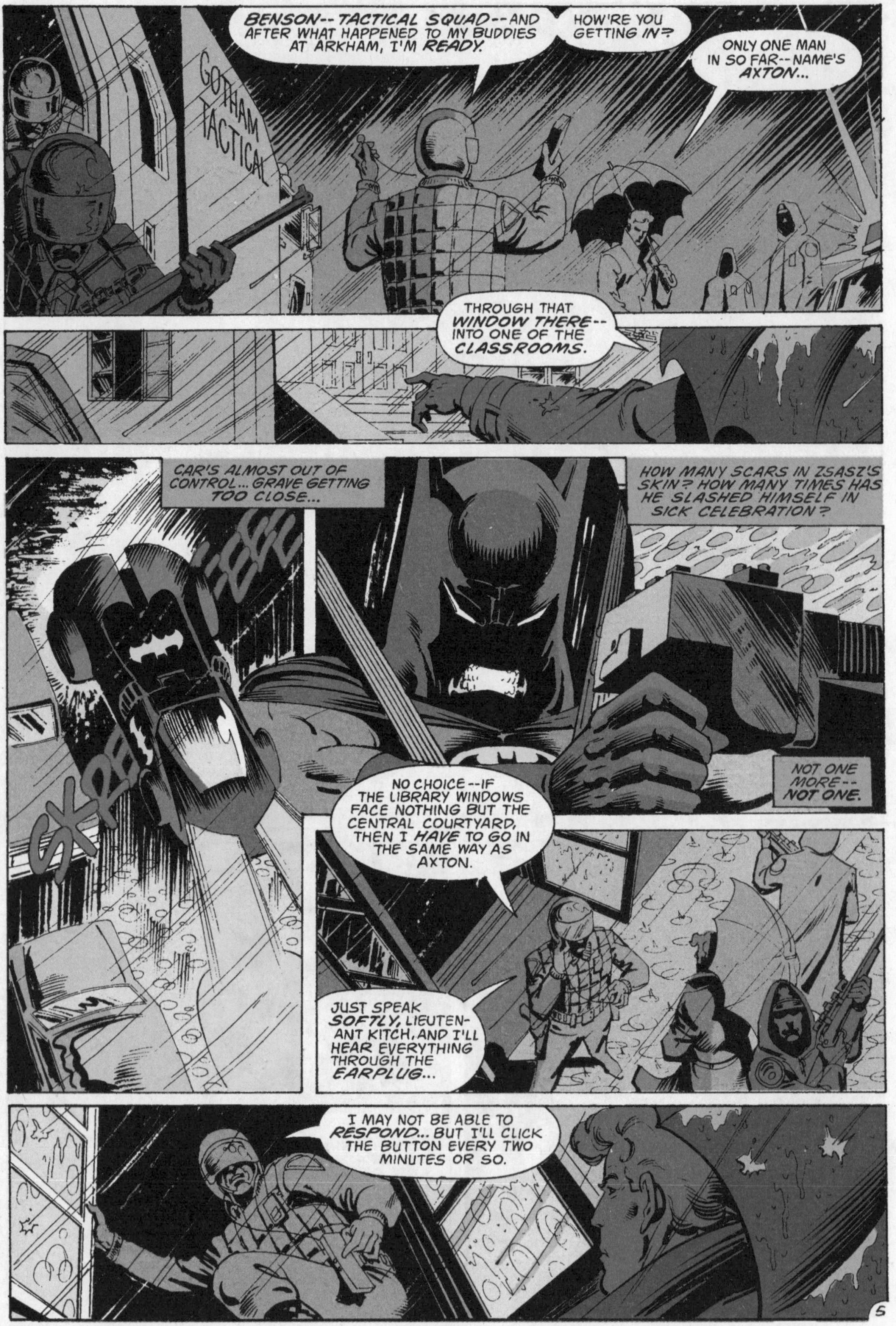
BENSON--TACTICAL SQUAD--AND AFTER WHAT HAPPENED TO MY BUDDIES AT ARKHAM, I'M READY.
HOW'RE YOU GETTING IN?
ONLY ONE MAN IN SO FAR--NAME'S AXTON...
GOTHAM TACTICAL
THROUGH THAT WINDOW THERE--INTO ONE OF THE CLASSROOMS.
CAR'S ALMOST OUT OF CONTROL... GRAVE GETTING TOO CLOSE...
HOW MANY SCARS IN ZSASZ'S SKIN? HOW MANY TIMES HAS HE SLASHED HIMSELF IN SICK CELEBRATION?
NOT ONE MORE--NOT ONE.
NO CHOICE--IF THE LIBRARY WINDOWS FACE NOTHING BUT THE CENTRAL COURTYARD, THEN I HAVE TO GO IN THE SAME WAY AS AXTON.
JUST SPEAK SOFTLY, LIEUTENANT KITCH, AND I'LL HEAR EVERYTHING THROUGH THE EARPLUG...
I MAY NOT BE ABLE TO RESPOND... BUT I'LL CLICK THE BUTTON EVERY TWO MINUTES OR SO.
5

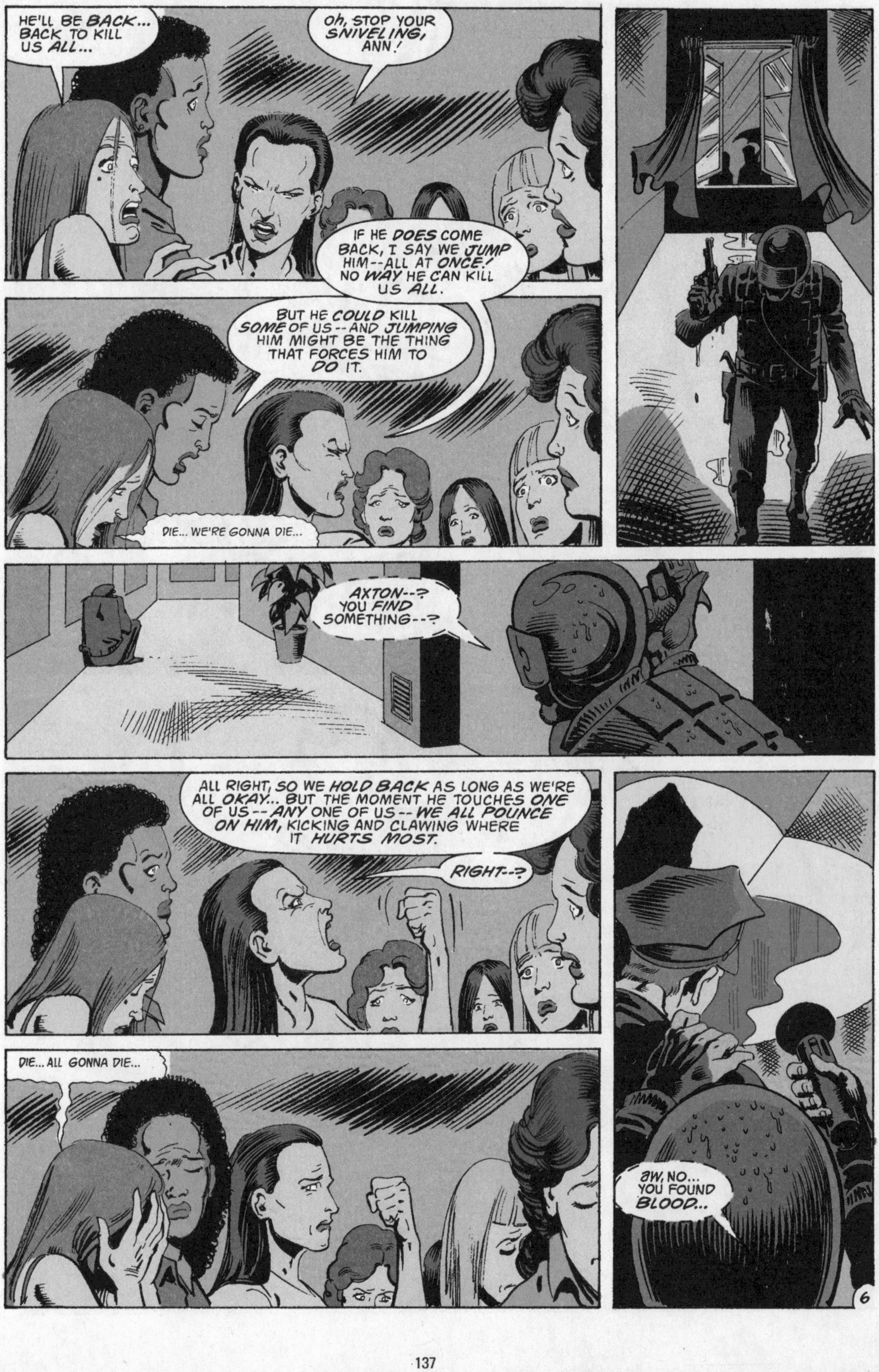
HE'LL BE BACK... BACK TO KILL US ALL...
Oh, STOP YOUR SNIVELING, ANN!
IF HE DOES COME BACK, I SAY WE JUMP HIM--ALL AT ONCE! NO WAY HE CAN KILL US ALL.
BUT HE COULD KILL SOME OF US--AND JUMPING HIM MIGHT BE THE THING THAT FORCES HIM TO DO IT.
DIE... WE'RE GONNA DIE...
AXTON--? YOU FIND SOMETHING--?
ALL RIGHT, SO WE HOLD BACK AS LONG AS WE'RE ALL OKAY... BUT THE MOMENT HE TOUCHES ONE OF US--ANY ONE OF US--WE ALL POUNCE ON HIM, KICKING AND CLAWING WHERE IT HURTS MOST.
RIGHT--?
DIE... ALL GONNA DIE...
aW, NO... YOU FOUND BLOOD...
6

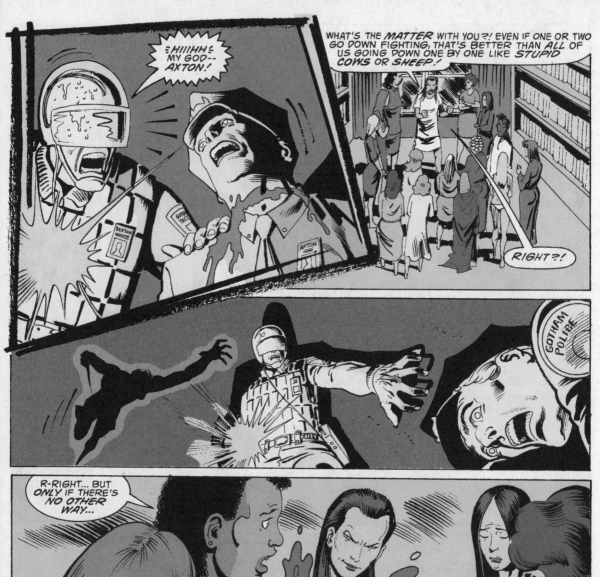

EHIIIHHE MY GOD-- AXTON!

WHAT'S THE *MATTER* WITH YOU?! EVEN IF ONE OR TWO GO DOWN FIGHTING, THAT'S BETTER THAN *ALL* OF US GOING DOWN ONE BY ONE LIKE *STUPID COWS* OR *SHEEP!*

RIGHT?!

R-RIGHT... BUT *ONLY* IF THERE'S *NO OTHER WAY...*

SHREKKK

"...ONLY IF HE'S REALLY *ABOUT* TO USE *THAT KNIFE.*"

YESSS.

7

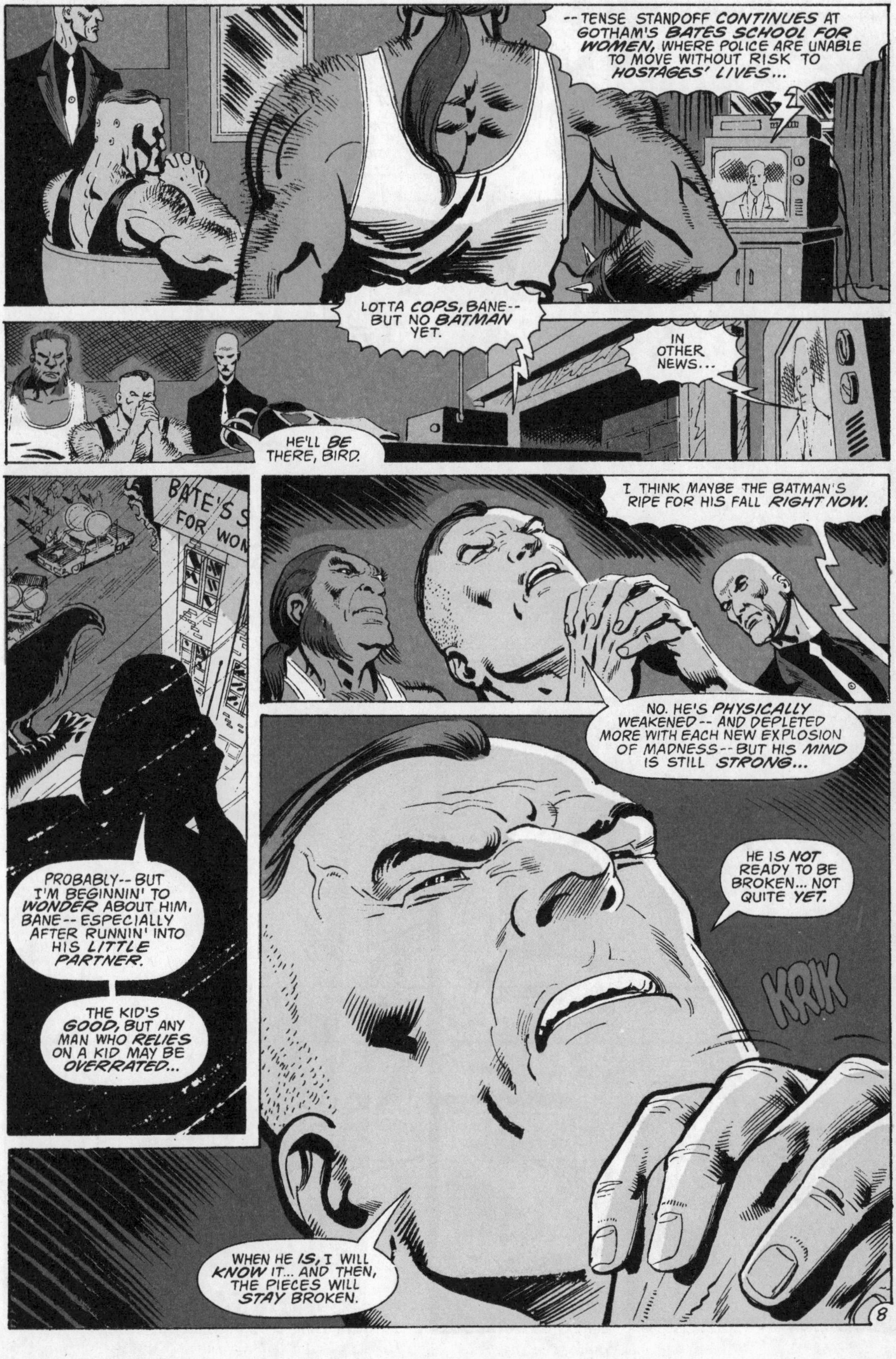
--TENSE STANDOFF CONTINUES AT GOTHAM'S BATES SCHOOL FOR WOMEN, WHERE POLICE ARE UNABLE TO MOVE WITHOUT RISK TO HOSTAGES' LIVES...
LOTTA COPS, BANE-- BUT NO BATMAN YET.
IN OTHER NEWS...
HE'LL BE THERE, BIRD.
BATE'S S
FOR WOM
I THINK MAYBE THE BATMAN'S RIPE FOR HIS FALL RIGHT NOW.
PROBABLY-- BUT I'M BEGINNIN' TO WONDER ABOUT HIM, BANE-- ESPECIALLY AFTER RUNNIN' INTO HIS LITTLE PARTNER.
THE KID'S GOOD, BUT ANY MAN WHO RELIES ON A KID MAY BE OVERRATED...
NO. HE'S PHYSICALLY WEAKENED-- AND DEPLETED MORE WITH EACH NEW EXPLOSION OF MADNESS-- BUT HIS MIND IS STILL STRONG...
HE IS NOT READY TO BE BROKEN... NOT QUITE YET.
KRIK
WHEN HE IS, I WILL KNOW IT... AND THEN, THE PIECES WILL STAY BROKEN.
8

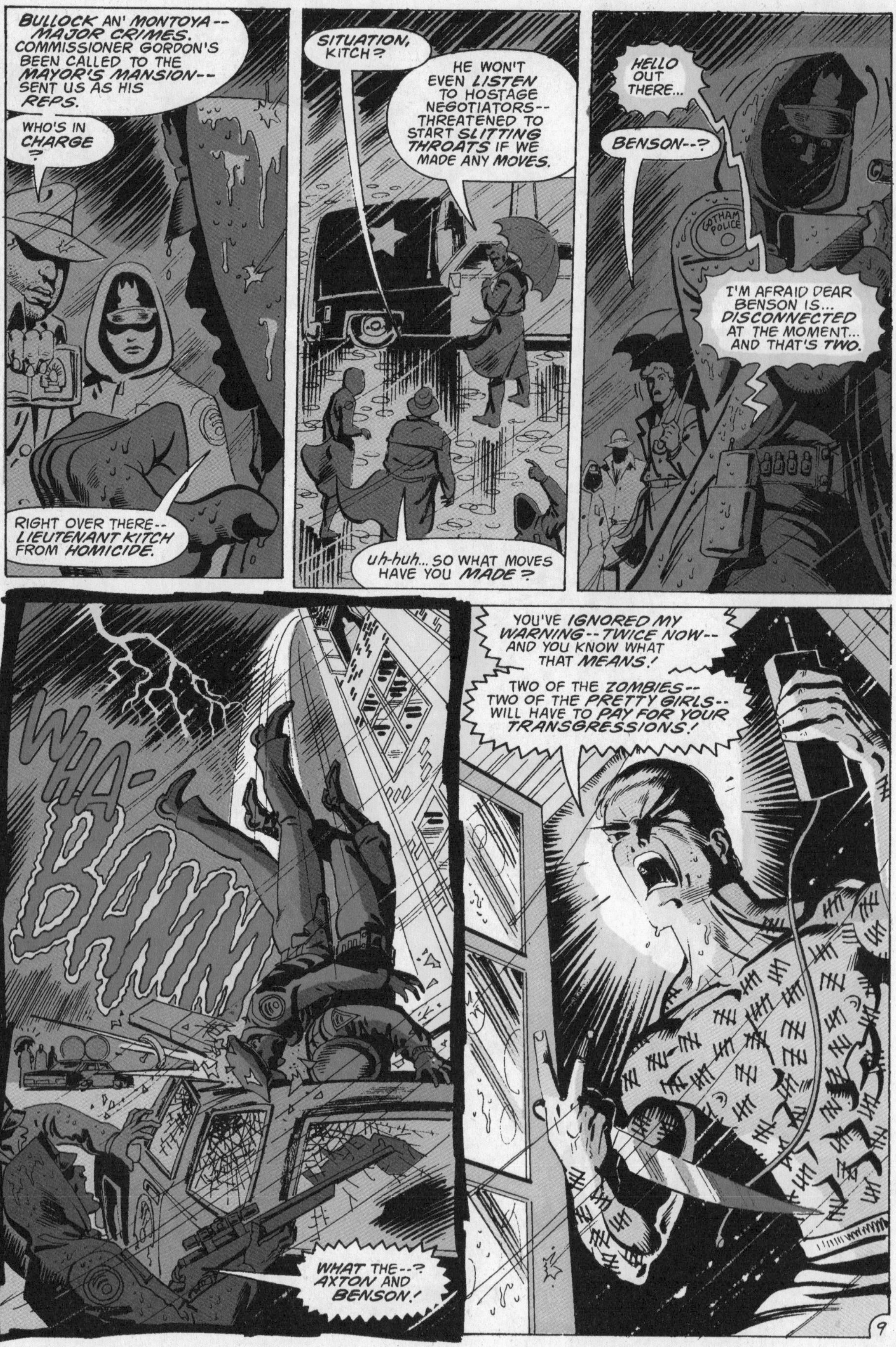
BULLOCK AN' MONTOYA-- MAJOR CRIMES. COMMISSIONER GORDON'S BEEN CALLED TO THE MAYOR'S MANSION-- SENT US AS HIS REPS.
WHO'S IN CHARGE?
RIGHT OVER THERE-- LIEUTENANT KITCH FROM HOMICIDE.
SITUATION, KITCH?
HE WON'T EVEN LISTEN TO HOSTAGE NEGOTIATORS-- THREATENED TO START SLITTING THROATS IF WE MADE ANY MOVES.
uh-huh... SO WHAT MOVES HAVE YOU MADE?
HELLO OUT THERE...
BENSON--?
GOTHAM POLICE
I'M AFRAID DEAR BENSON IS... DISCONNECTED AT THE MOMENT... AND THAT'S TWO.
WHA-BAMM
WHAT THE--? AXTON AND BENSON!
YOU'VE IGNORED MY WARNING--TWICE NOW-- AND YOU KNOW WHAT THAT MEANS!
TWO OF THE ZOMBIES-- TWO OF THE PRETTY GIRLS-- WILL HAVE TO PAY FOR YOUR TRANSGRESSIONS!
9

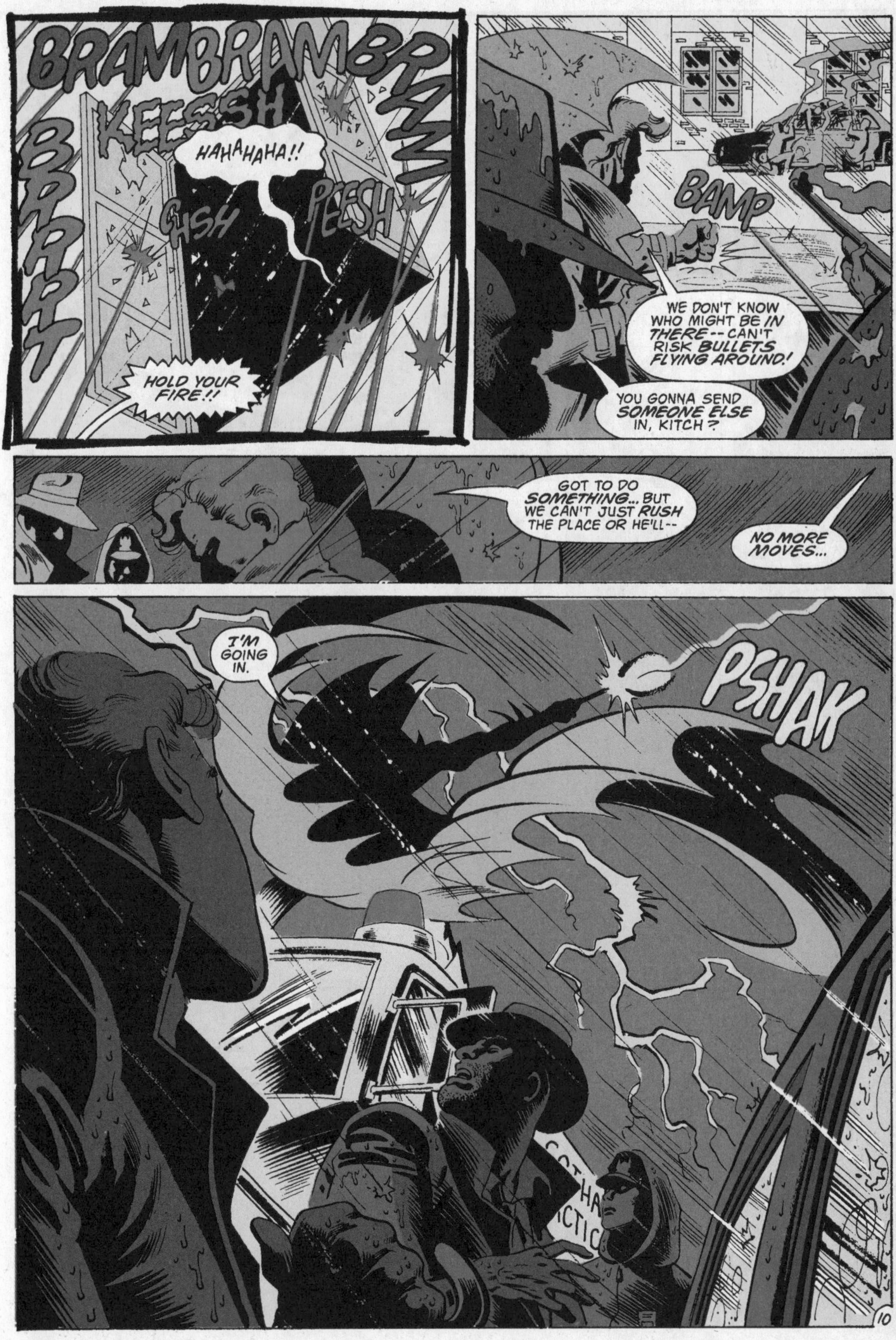
BRAMBRAMBRAMBRAM
BBRRRRT
KEESSH
HAHAHAHA!!
CHSH
PEESH
HOLD YOUR FIRE!!
BAMP
WE DON'T KNOW WHO MIGHT BE IN THERE -- CAN'T RISK BULLETS FLYING AROUND!
YOU GONNA SEND SOMEONE ELSE IN, KITCH?
GOT TO DO SOMETHING... BUT WE CAN'T JUST RUSH THE PLACE OR HE'LL--
NO MORE MOVES...
I'M GOING IN.
PSHAK
10

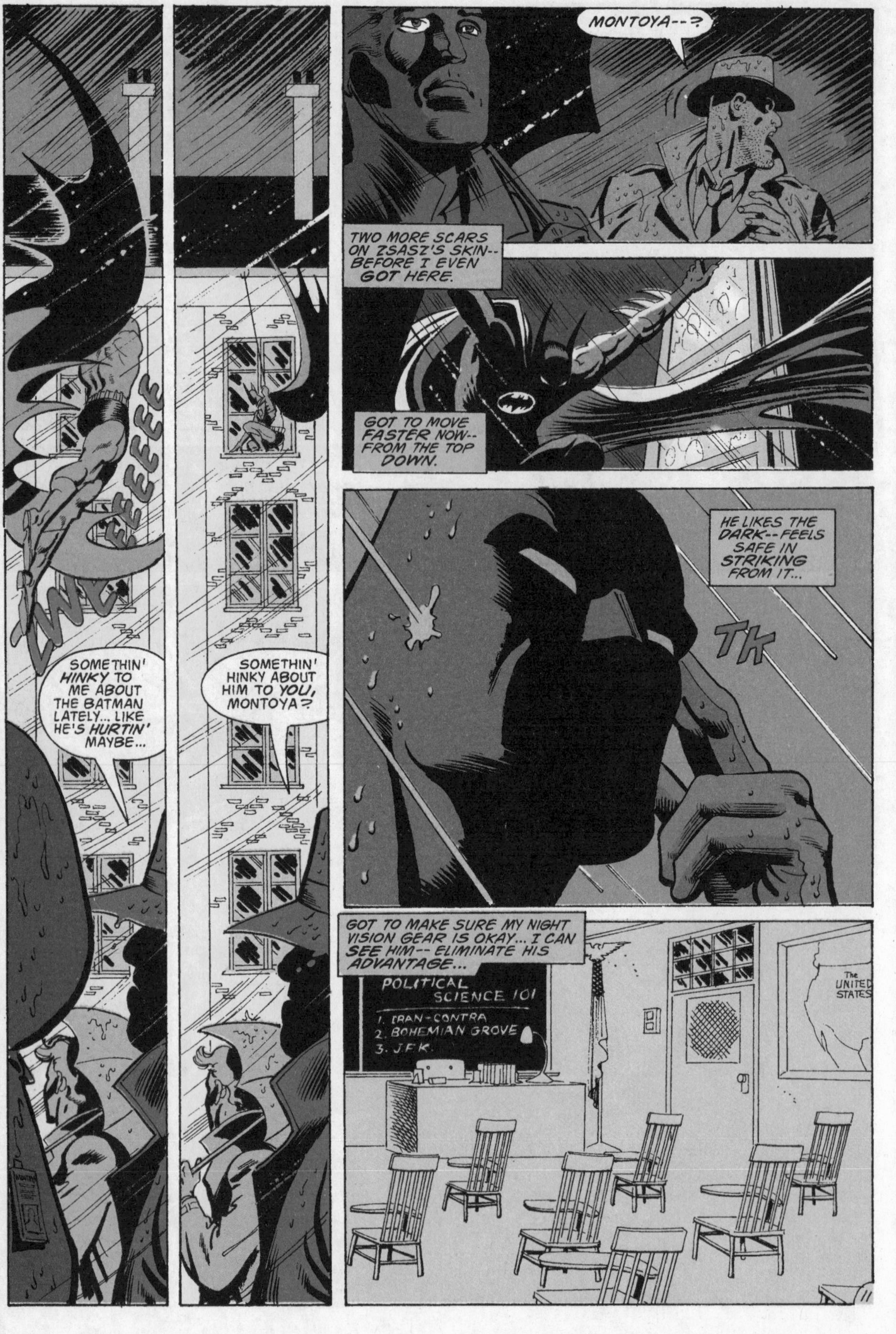
SOMETHIN' HINKY TO ME ABOUT THE BATMAN LATELY... LIKE HE'S HURTIN' MAYBE...
SOMETHIN' HINKY ABOUT HIM TO YOU, MONTOYA?
MONTOYA--?
TWO MORE SCARS ON ZSASZ'S SKIN-- BEFORE I EVEN GOT HERE.
GOT TO MOVE FASTER NOW-- FROM THE TOP DOWN.
HE LIKES THE DARK--FEELS SAFE IN STRIKING FROM IT...
TK
GOT TO MAKE SURE MY NIGHT VISION GEAR IS OKAY... I CAN SEE HIM-- ELIMINATE HIS ADVANTAGE...
POLITICAL SCIENCE 101
1. IRAN-CONTRA
2. BOHEMIAN GROVE
3. J.F.K.
The UNITED STATES
11

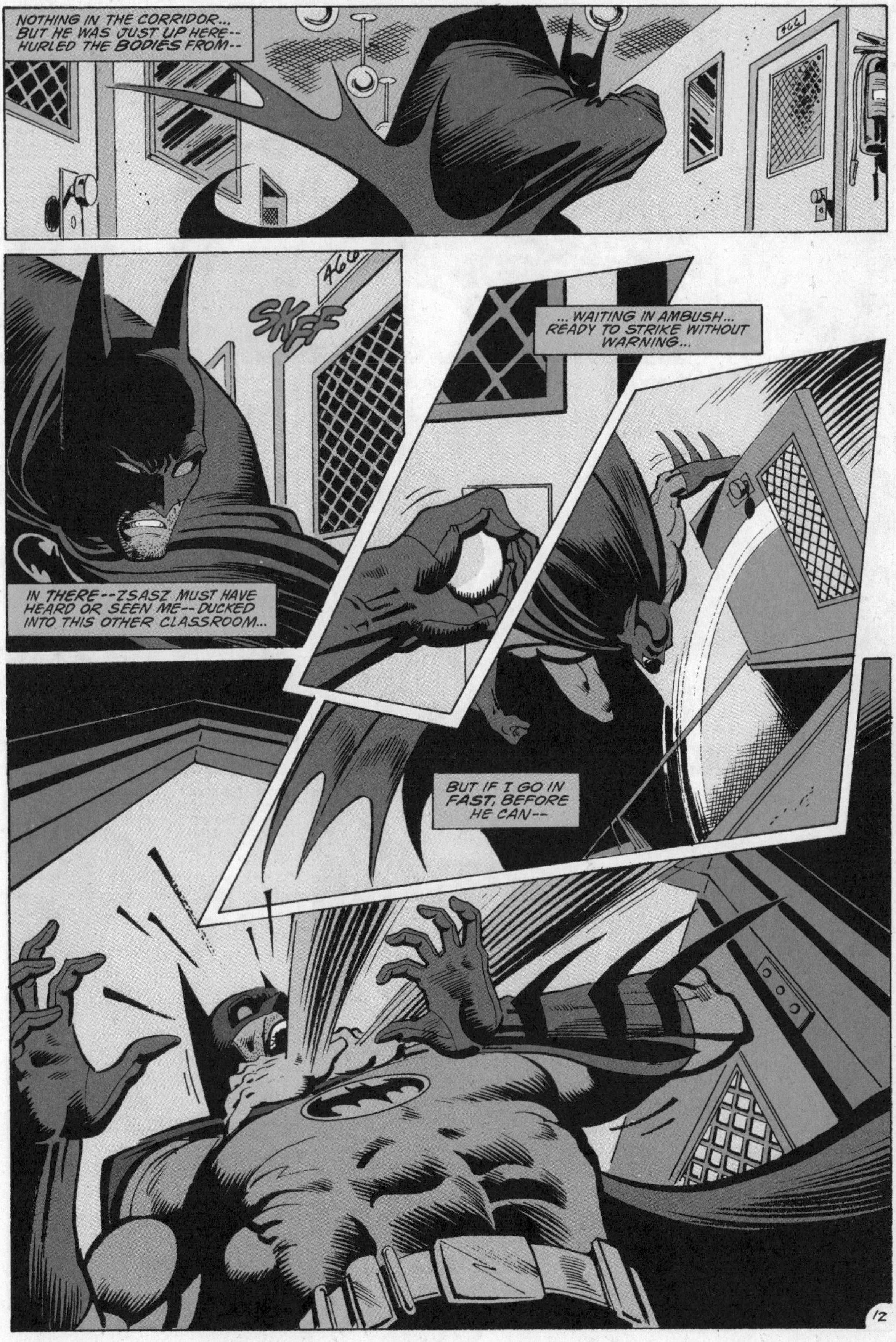
NOTHING IN THE CORRIDOR... BUT HE WAS JUST UP HERE-- HURLED THE BODIES FROM--
SKFF
IN THERE--ZSASZ MUST HAVE HEARD OR SEEN ME--DUCKED INTO THIS OTHER CLASSROOM...
...WAITING IN AMBUSH... READY TO STRIKE WITHOUT WARNING...
BUT IF I GO IN FAST, BEFORE HE CAN--
12

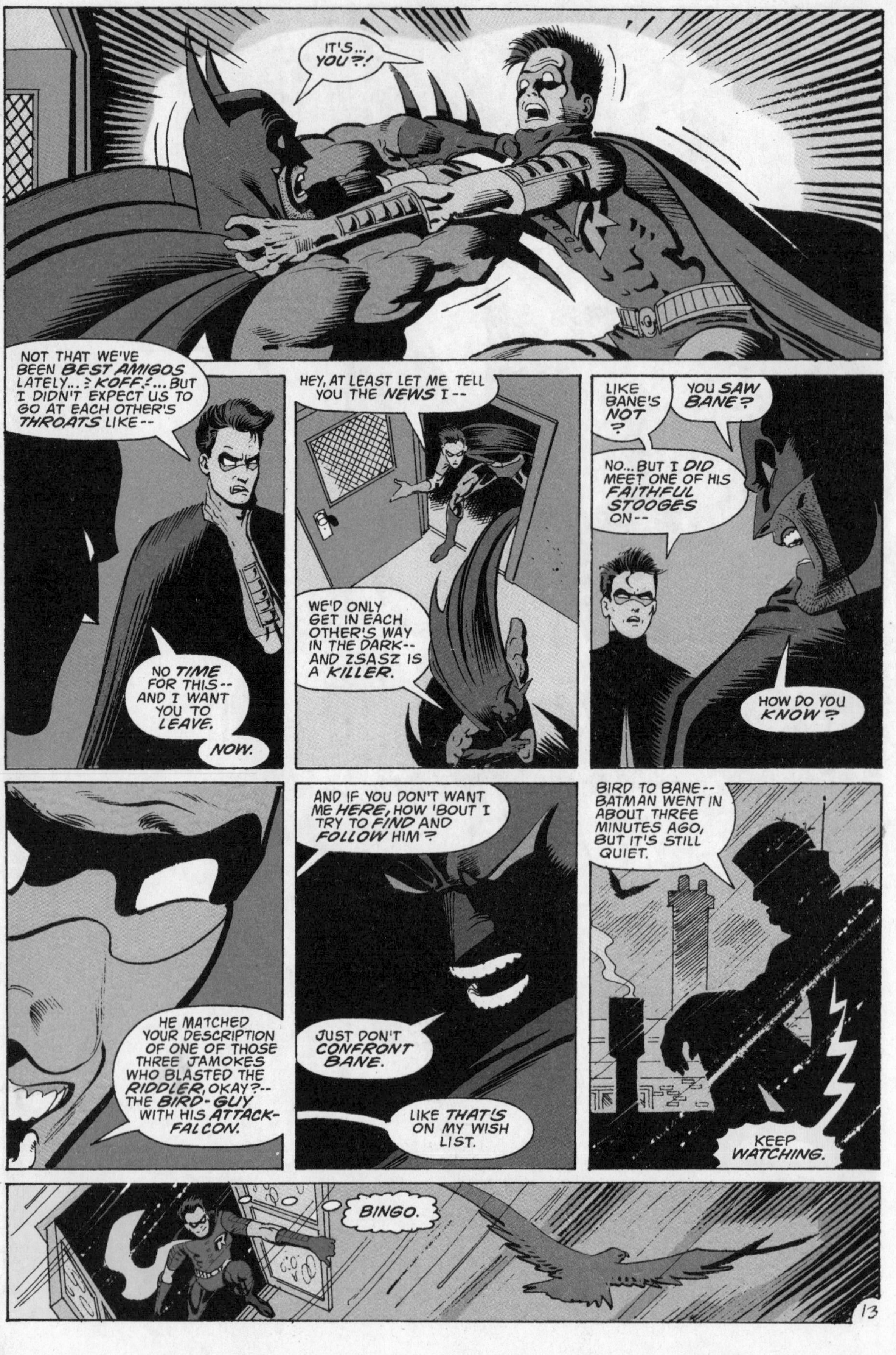

IT'S... YOU?!
NOT THAT WE'VE BEEN BEST AMIGOS LATELY... KOFF ... BUT I DIDN'T EXPECT US TO GO AT EACH OTHER'S THROATS LIKE--
NO TIME FOR THIS-- AND I WANT YOU TO LEAVE.
NOW.
HEY, AT LEAST LET ME TELL YOU THE NEWS I--
WE'D ONLY GET IN EACH OTHER'S WAY IN THE DARK-- AND ZSASZ IS A KILLER.
LIKE BANE'S NOT?
YOU SAW BANE?
NO... BUT I DID MEET ONE OF HIS FAITHFUL STOOGES ON--
HOW DO YOU KNOW?
HE MATCHED YOUR DESCRIPTION OF ONE OF THOSE THREE JAMOKES WHO BLASTED THE RIDDLER, OKAY?-- THE BIRD-GUY WITH HIS ATTACK-FALCON.
AND IF YOU DON'T WANT ME HERE, HOW 'BOUT I TRY TO FIND AND FOLLOW HIM?
JUST DON'T CONFRONT BANE.
LIKE THAT'S ON MY WISH LIST.
BIRD TO BANE-- BATMAN WENT IN ABOUT THREE MINUTES AGO, BUT IT'S STILL QUIET.
KEEP WATCHING.
BINGO.
13

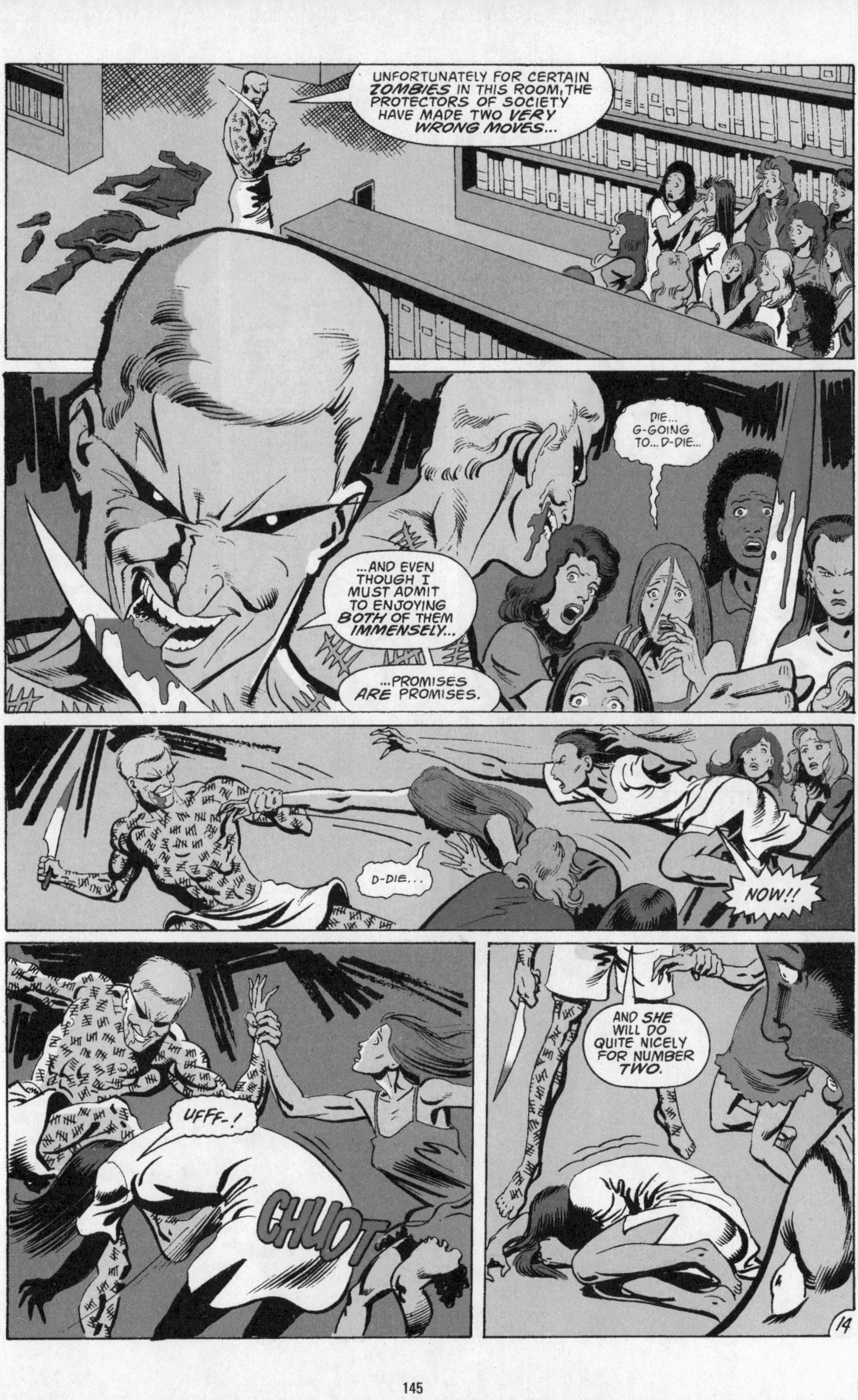
UNFORTUNATELY FOR CERTAIN ZOMBIES IN THIS ROOM, THE PROTECTORS OF SOCIETY HAVE MADE TWO VERY WRONG MOVES...
DIE... G-GOING TO... D-DIE...
...AND EVEN THOUGH I MUST ADMIT TO ENJOYING BOTH OF THEM IMMENSELY...
...PROMISES ARE PROMISES.
D-DIE...
NOW!!
UFFF-!
CHUDT
AND SHE WILL DO QUITE NICELY FOR NUMBER TWO.
14

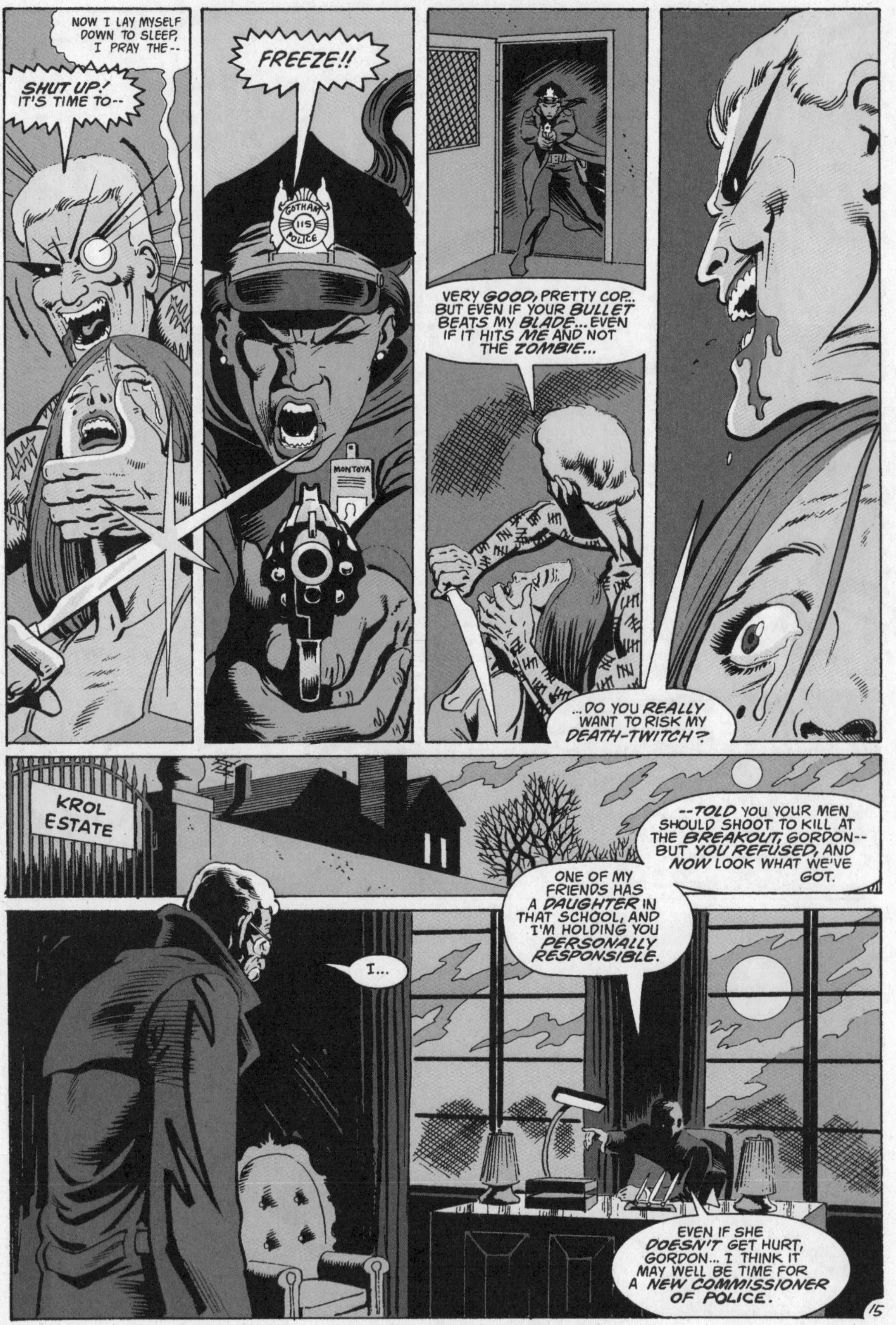
NOW I LAY MYSELF DOWN TO SLEEP, I PRAY THE--
SHUT UP! IT'S TIME TO--
FREEZE!!
GOTHAM 115 POLICE
MONTOYA
VERY GOOD, PRETTY COP... BUT EVEN IF YOUR BULLET BEATS MY BLADE... EVEN IF IT HITS ME AND NOT THE ZOMBIE...
...DO YOU REALLY WANT TO RISK MY DEATH-TWITCH?
KROL ESTATE
--TOLD YOU YOUR MEN SHOULD SHOOT TO KILL AT THE BREAKOUT, GORDON-- BUT YOU REFUSED, AND NOW LOOK WHAT WE'VE GOT.
ONE OF MY FRIENDS HAS A DAUGHTER IN THAT SCHOOL, AND I'M HOLDING YOU PERSONALLY RESPONSIBLE.
I...
EVEN IF SHE DOESN'T GET HURT, GORDON... I THINK IT MAY WELL BE TIME FOR A NEW COMMISSIONER OF POLICE.
15

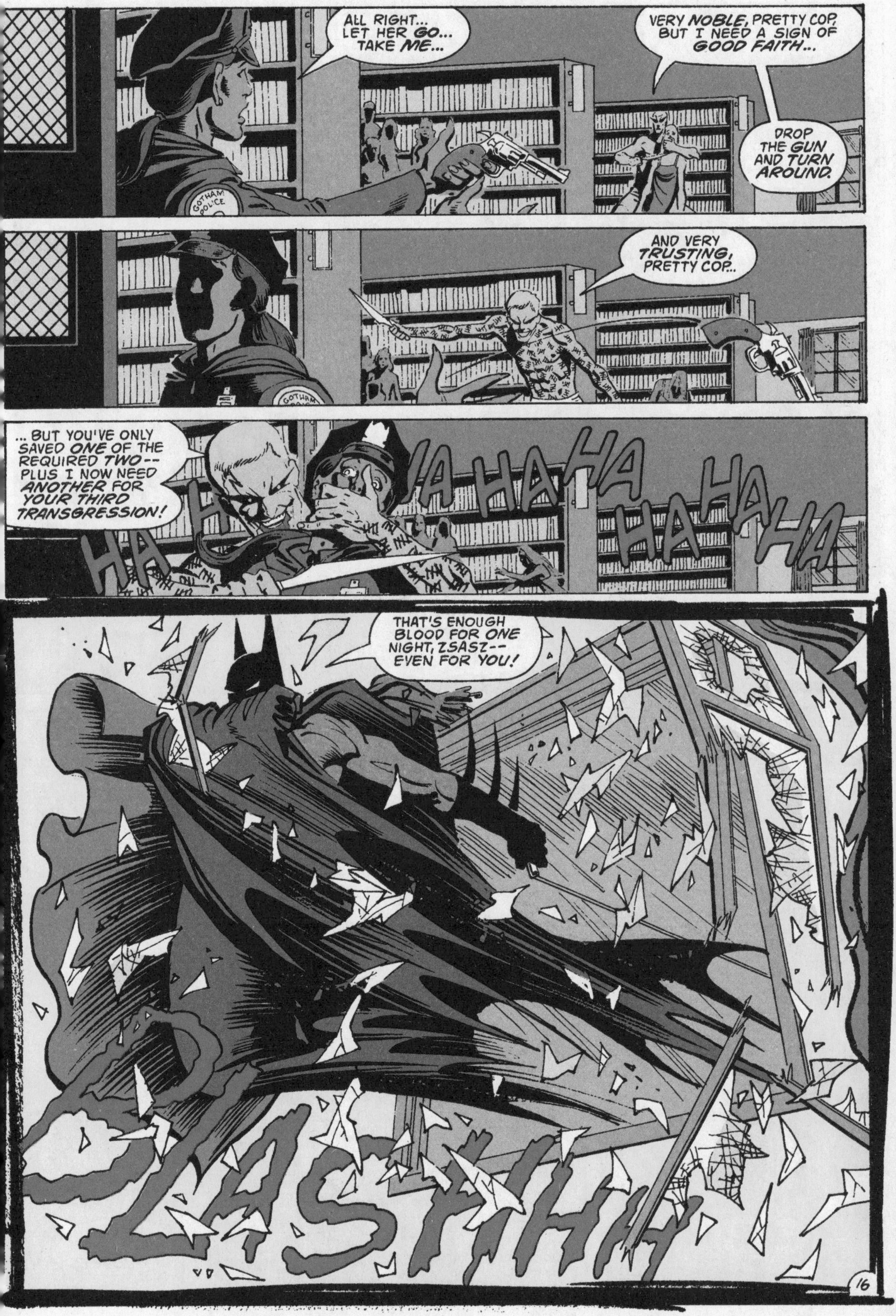

ALL RIGHT... LET HER GO... TAKE ME...
VERY NOBLE, PRETTY COP. BUT I NEED A SIGN OF GOOD FAITH...
DROP THE GUN AND TURN AROUND.
AND VERY TRUSTING, PRETTY COP...
... BUT YOU'VE ONLY SAVED ONE OF THE REQUIRED TWO-- PLUS I NOW NEED ANOTHER FOR YOUR THIRD TRANSGRESSION!
HA HA HA HA HA HA HA HA HA HA HA
THAT'S ENOUGH BLOOD FOR ONE NIGHT, ZSASZ-- EVEN FOR YOU!
SMASHHH
16

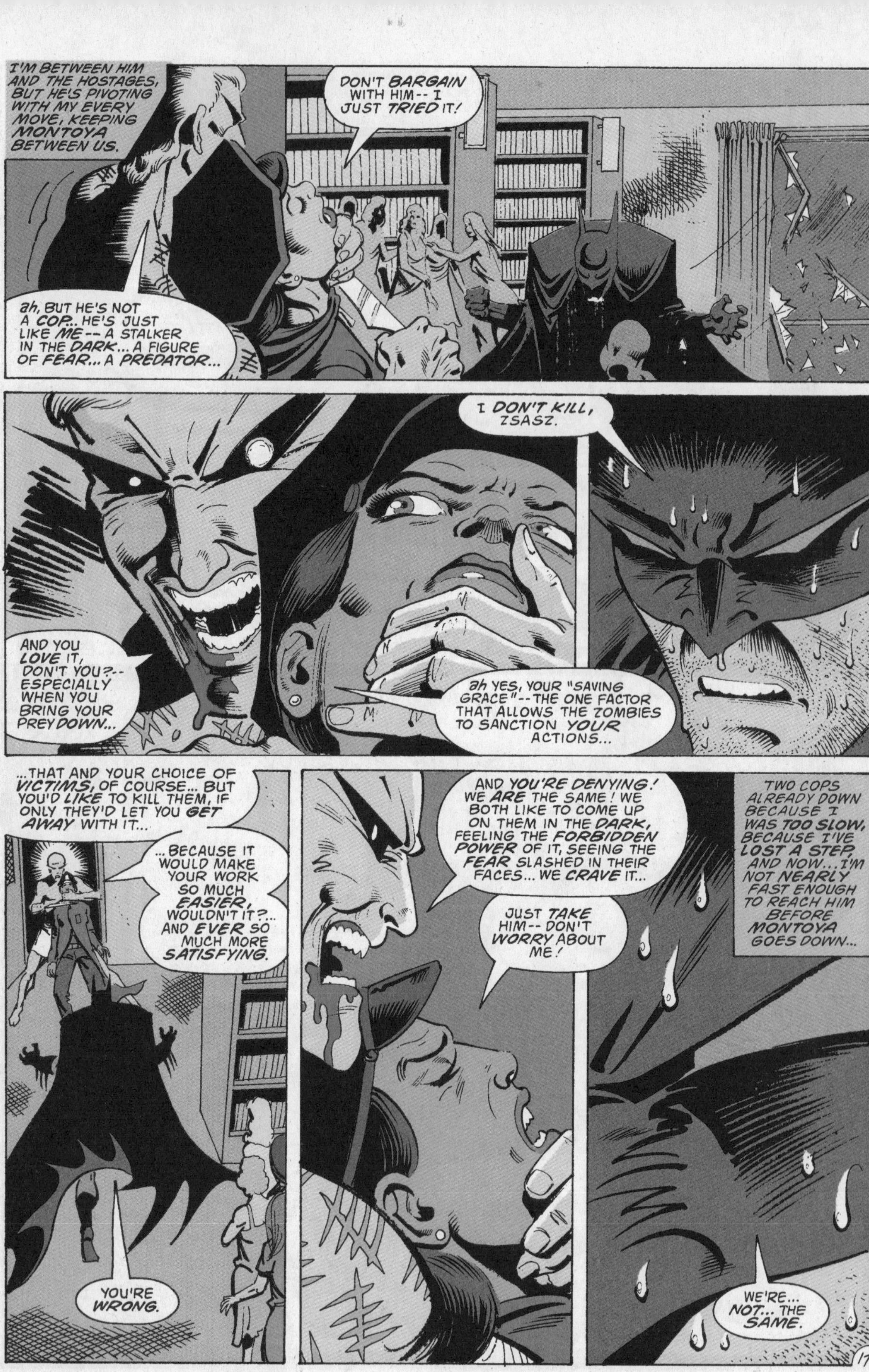
I'M BETWEEN HIM AND THE HOSTAGES, BUT HE'S PIVOTING WITH MY EVERY MOVE, KEEPING MONTOYA BETWEEN US.
DON'T BARGAIN WITH HIM-- I JUST TRIED IT!
ah, BUT HE'S NOT A COP.. HE'S JUST LIKE ME-- A STALKER IN THE DARK... A FIGURE OF FEAR... A PREDATOR...
I DON'T KILL, ZSASZ.
AND YOU LOVE IT, DON'T YOU?-- ESPECIALLY WHEN YOU BRING YOUR PREY DOWN...
ah YES, YOUR "SAVING GRACE"--THE ONE FACTOR THAT ALLOWS THE ZOMBIES TO SANCTION YOUR ACTIONS...
...THAT AND YOUR CHOICE OF VICTIMS, OF COURSE... BUT YOU'D LIKE TO KILL THEM, IF ONLY THEY'D LET YOU GET AWAY WITH IT...
...BECAUSE IT WOULD MAKE YOUR WORK SO MUCH EASIER, WOULDN'T IT?... AND EVER SO MUCH MORE SATISFYING.
YOU'RE WRONG.
AND YOU'RE DENYING! WE ARE THE SAME! WE BOTH LIKE TO COME UP ON THEM IN THE DARK, FEELING THE FORBIDDEN POWER OF IT, SEEING THE FEAR SLASHED IN THEIR FACES... WE CRAVE IT...
JUST TAKE HIM-- DON'T WORRY ABOUT ME!
TWO COPS ALREADY DOWN BECAUSE I WAS TOO SLOW, BECAUSE I'VE LOST A STEP, AND NOW... I'M NOT NEARLY FAST ENOUGH TO REACH HIM BEFORE MONTOYA GOES DOWN...
WE'RE... NOT... THE SAME.
17

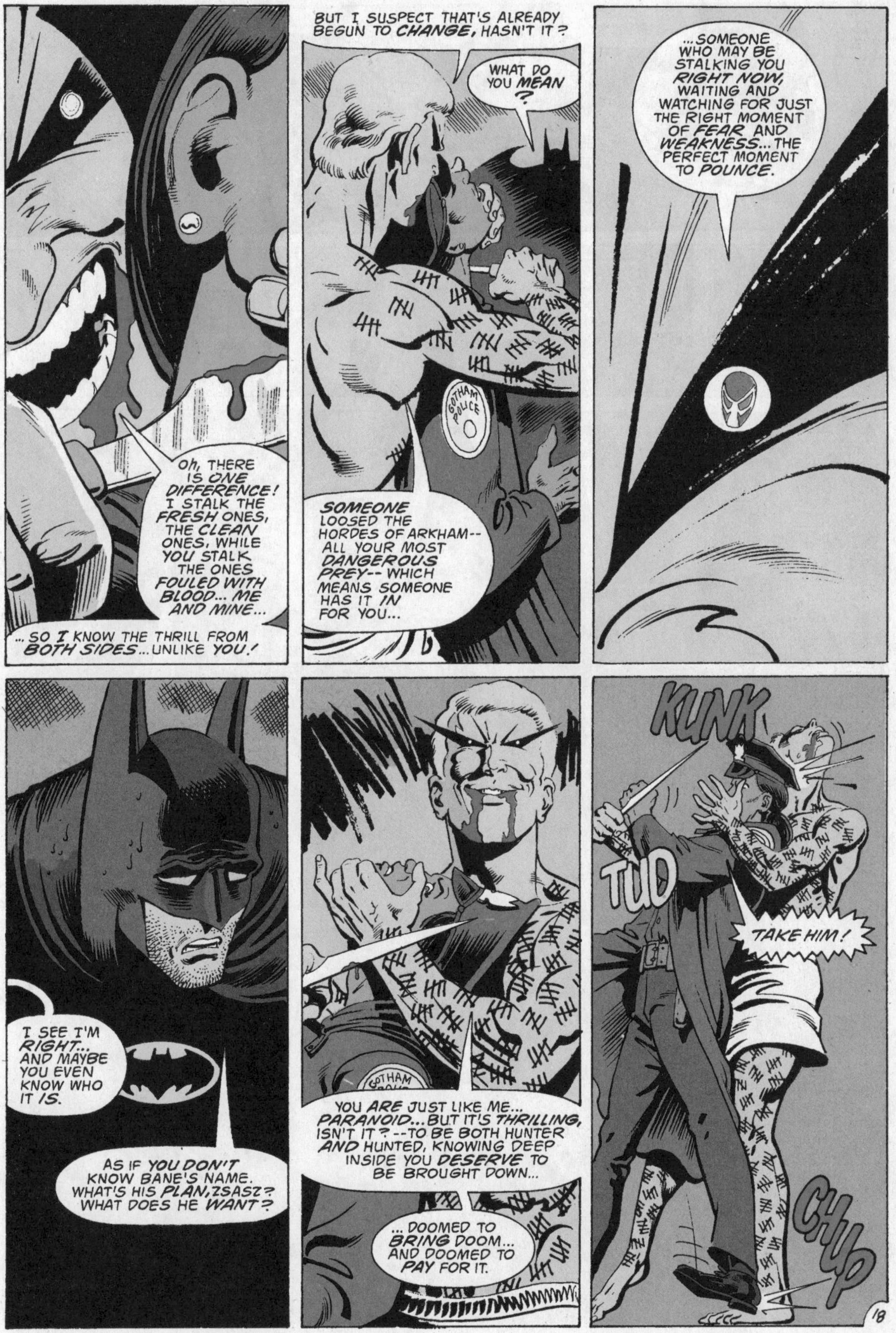
Oh, THERE IS ONE DIFFERENCE! I STALK THE FRESH ONES, THE CLEAN ONES, WHILE YOU STALK THE ONES FOULED WITH BLOOD... ME AND MINE...
... SO I KNOW THE THRILL FROM BOTH SIDES... UNLIKE YOU!
BUT I SUSPECT THAT'S ALREADY BEGUN TO CHANGE, HASN'T IT?
WHAT DO YOU MEAN?
SOMEONE LOOSED THE HORDES OF ARKHAM-- ALL YOUR MOST DANGEROUS PREY-- WHICH MEANS SOMEONE HAS IT IN FOR YOU...
GOTHAM POLICE
...SOMEONE WHO MAY BE STALKING YOU RIGHT NOW, WAITING AND WATCHING FOR JUST THE RIGHT MOMENT OF FEAR AND WEAKNESS... THE PERFECT MOMENT TO POUNCE.
I SEE I'M RIGHT... AND MAYBE YOU EVEN KNOW WHO IT IS.
AS IF YOU DON'T KNOW BANE'S NAME. WHAT'S HIS PLAN, ZSASZ? WHAT DOES HE WANT?
YOU ARE JUST LIKE ME... PARANOID... BUT IT'S THRILLING, ISN'T IT? --TO BE BOTH HUNTER AND HUNTED, KNOWING DEEP INSIDE YOU DESERVE TO BE BROUGHT DOWN...
... DOOMED TO BRING DOOM... AND DOOMED TO PAY FOR IT.
KUNK
TUD
TAKE HIM!
CHUP
18

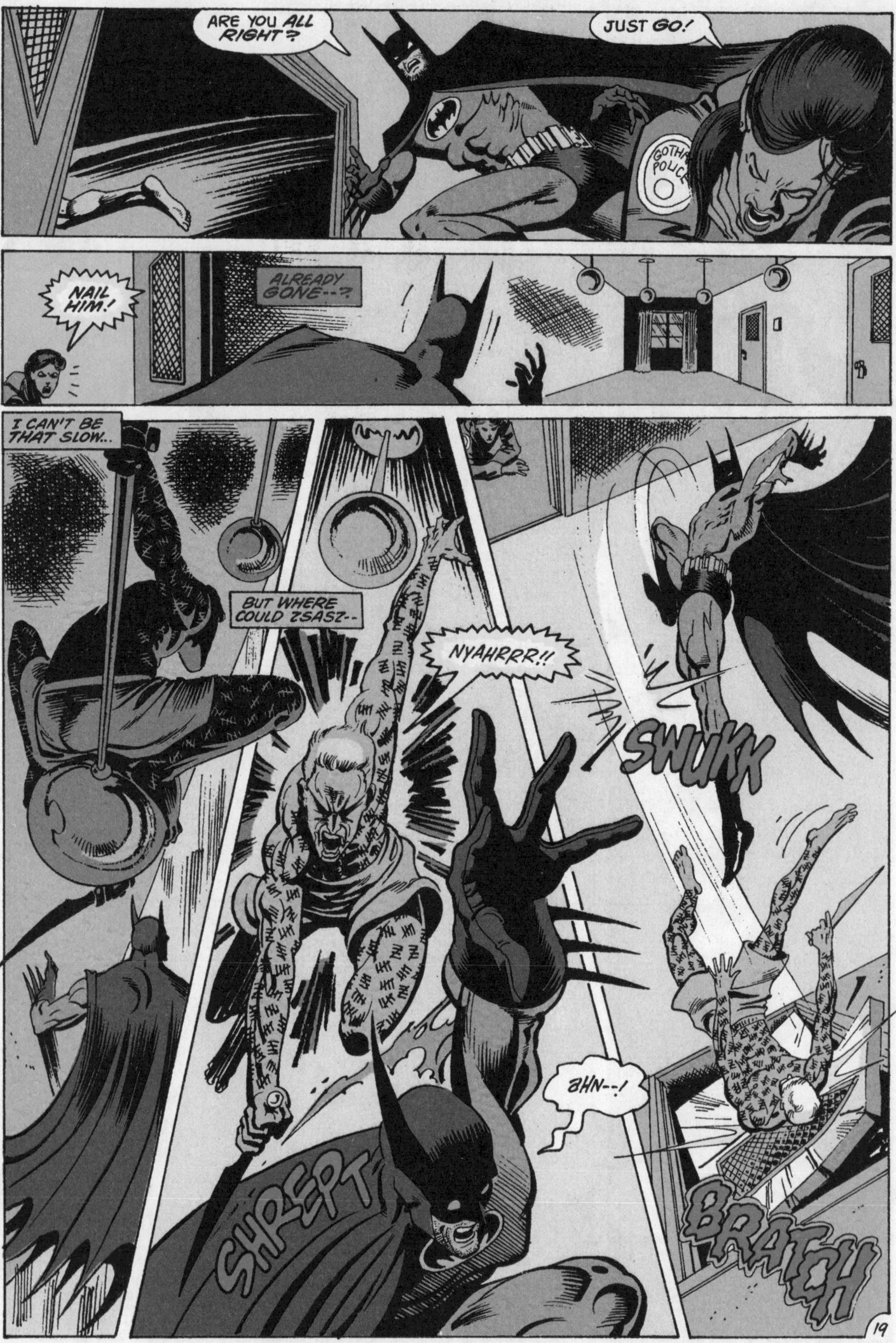
ARE YOU ALL RIGHT?
JUST GO!
NAIL HIM!
ALREADY GONE--?
I CAN'T BE THAT SLOW...
BUT WHERE COULD ZSASZ--
NYAHRRR!!
SWUKK
SHREPT
AHN--!
BRATCH
19

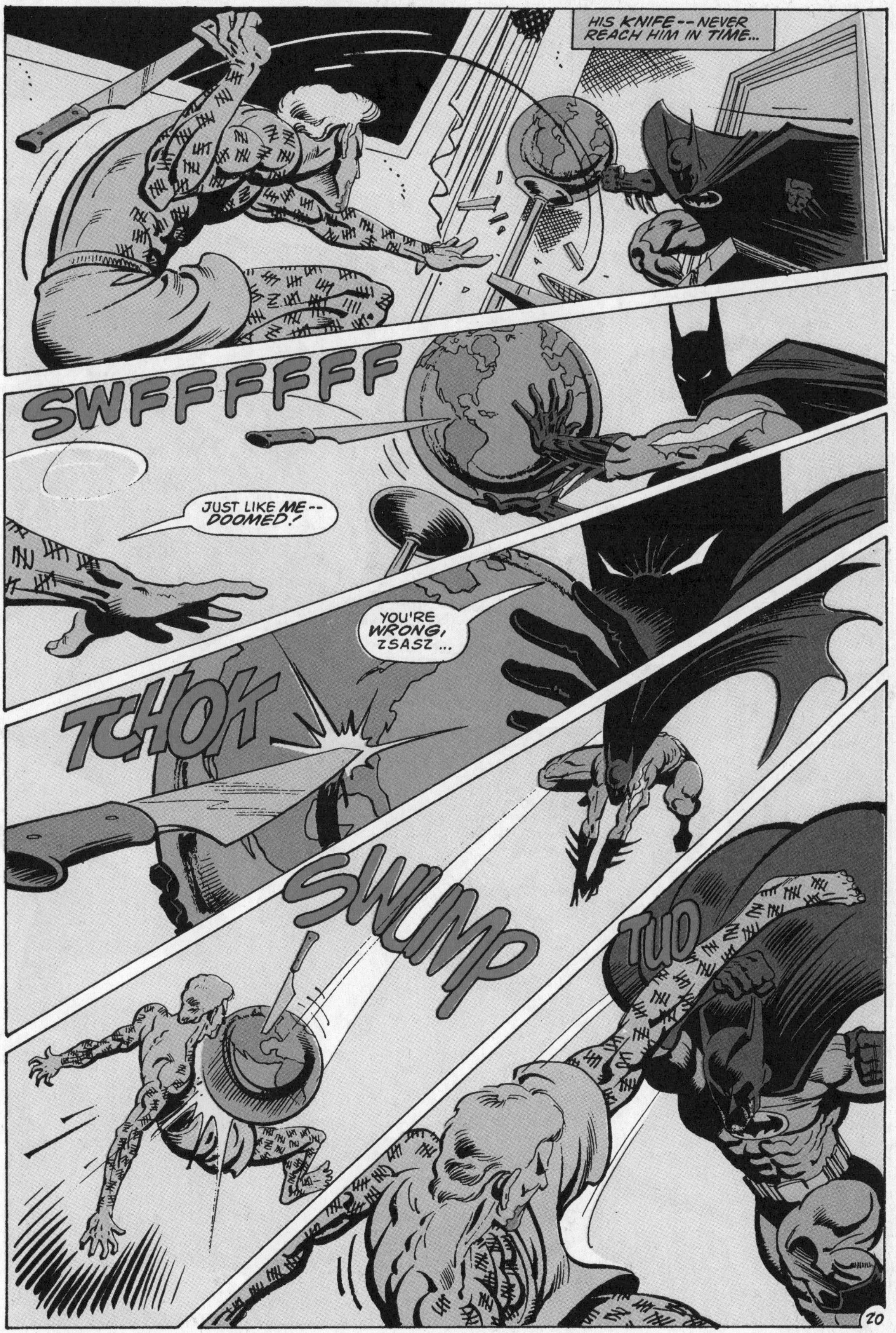
HIS KNIFE--NEVER REACH HIM IN TIME...
SWFFFFFF
JUST LIKE ME--DOOMED!
YOU'RE WRONG, ZSASZ...
TCHOK
SWUMP
TUD
20

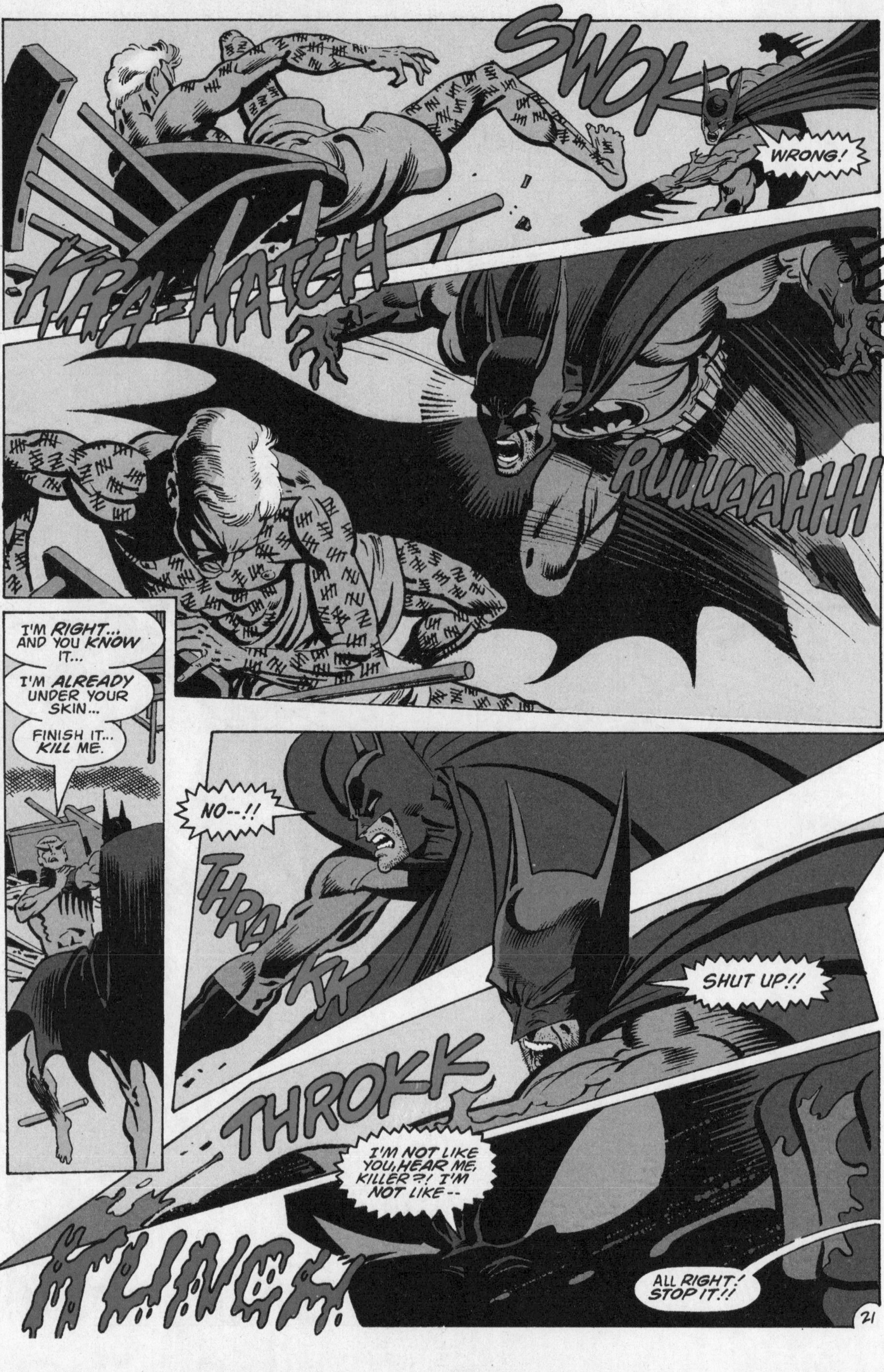
SWOK
WRONG!
KRA-KATCH
RUUUAAHHH
I'M RIGHT... AND YOU KNOW IT...
I'M ALREADY UNDER YOUR SKIN...
FINISH IT... KILL ME.
NO--!!
THRAKK
SHUT UP!!
THROKK
I'M NOT LIKE YOU, HEAR ME, KILLER?! I'M NOT LIKE --
THUNCH
ALL RIGHT! STOP IT!!
21

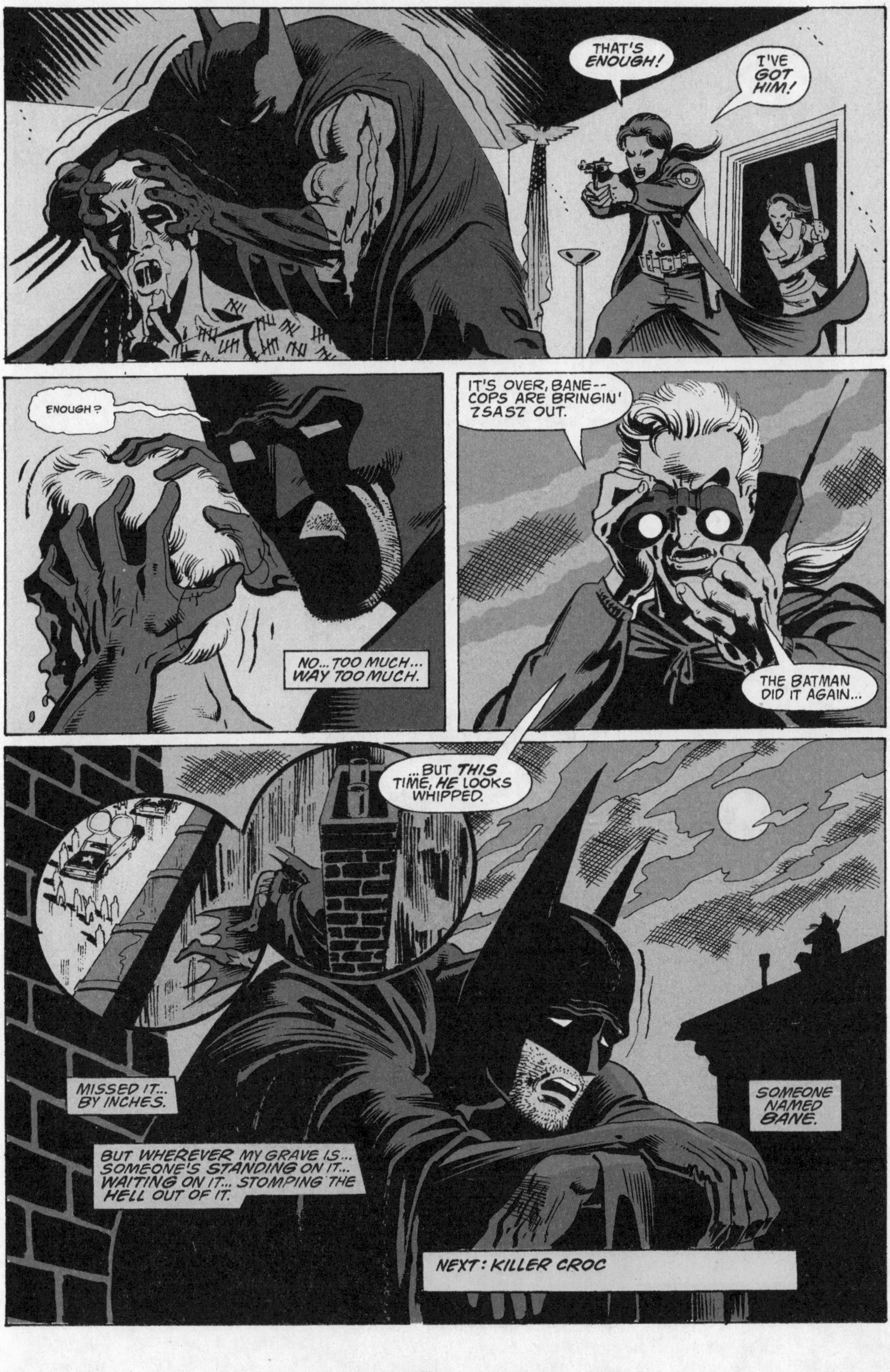
THAT'S ENOUGH!
I'VE GOT HIM!
ENOUGH?
NO... TOO MUCH... WAY TOO MUCH.
IT'S OVER, BANE-- COPS ARE BRINGIN' ZSASZ OUT.
THE BATMAN DID IT AGAIN...
...BUT THIS TIME, HE LOOKS WHIPPED.
MISSED IT... BY INCHES.
BUT WHEREVER MY GRAVE IS... SOMEONE'S STANDING ON IT... WAITING ON IT... STOMPING THE HELL OUT OF IT.
SOMEONE NAMED BANE.
NEXT: KILLER CROC

Cover art by SAM KIETH

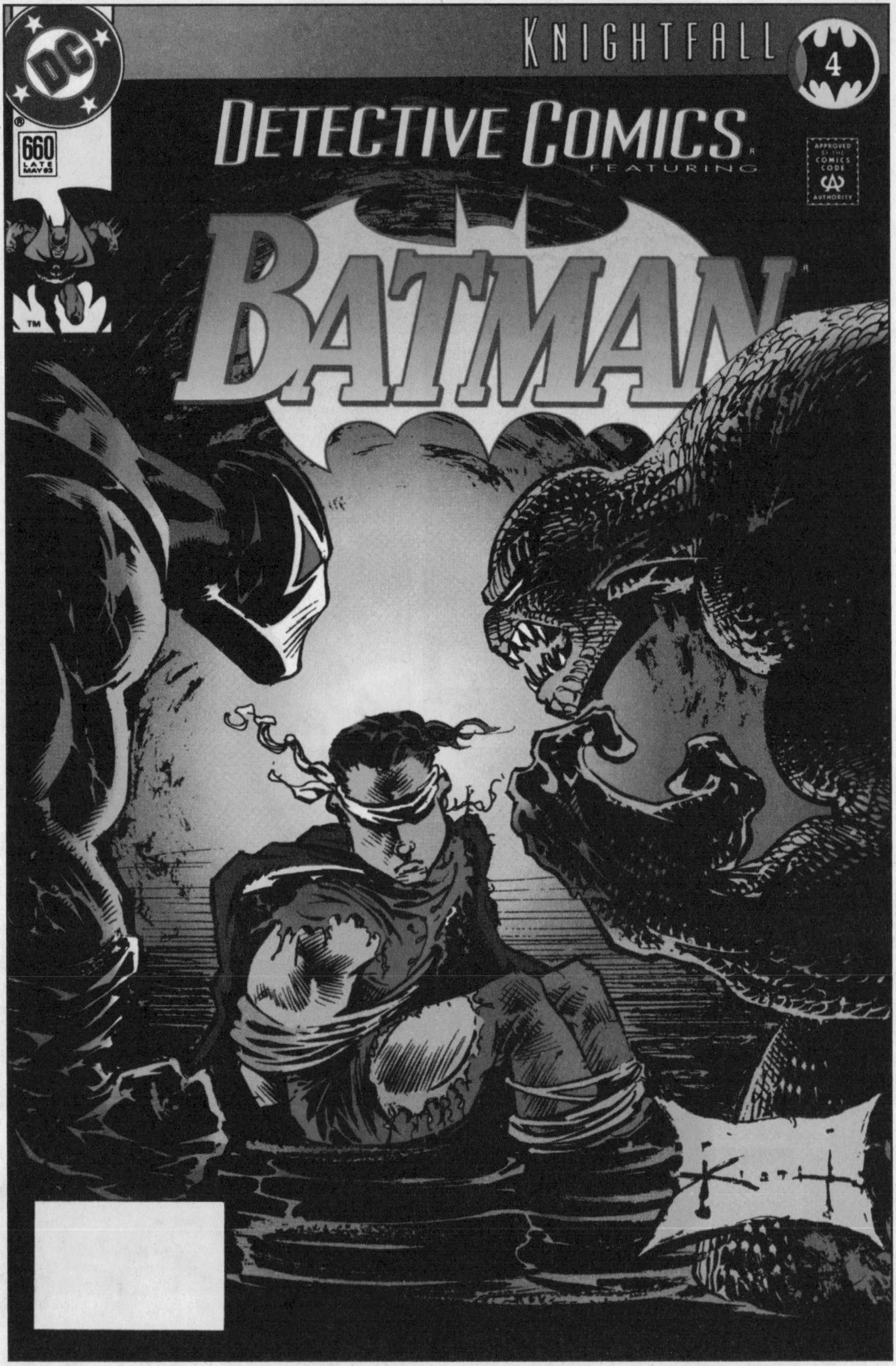
KNIGHTFALL
4
DETECTIVE COMICS
FEATURING
BATMAN
660
LATE MAY 93
APPROVED BY THE COMICS CODE AUTHORITY
Kieth

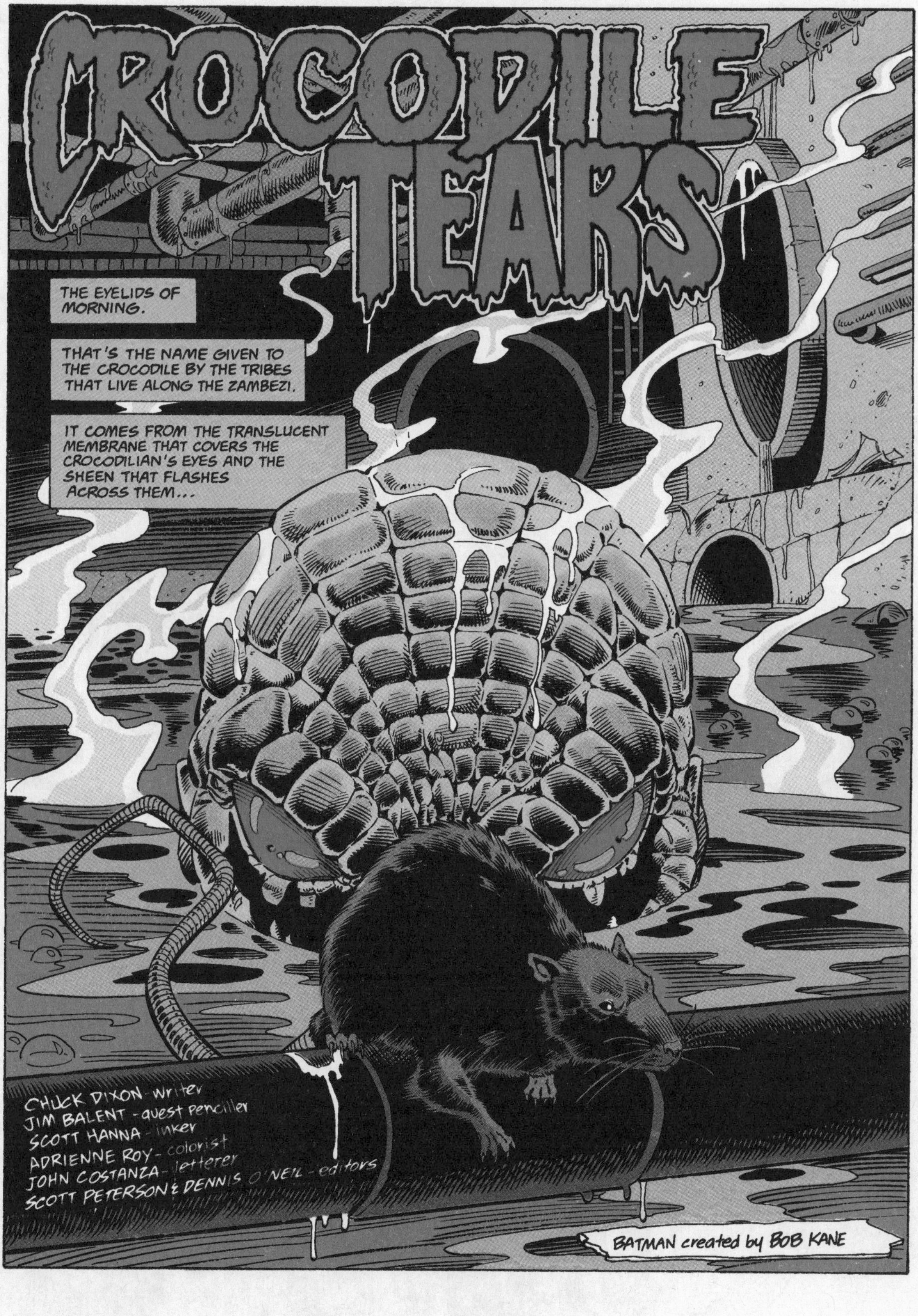
CROCODILE TEARS
THE EYELIDS OF MORNING.
THAT'S THE NAME GIVEN TO THE CROCODILE BY THE TRIBES THAT LIVE ALONG THE ZAMBEZI.
IT COMES FROM THE TRANSLUCENT MEMBRANE THAT COVERS THE CROCODILIAN'S EYES AND THE SHEEN THAT FLASHES ACROSS THEM...
CHUCK DIXON - writer
JIM BALENT - guest penciller
SCOTT HANNA - inker
ADRIENNE ROY - colorist
JOHN COSTANZA - letterer
SCOTT PETERSON & DENNIS O'NEIL - editors
BATMAN created by BOB KANE

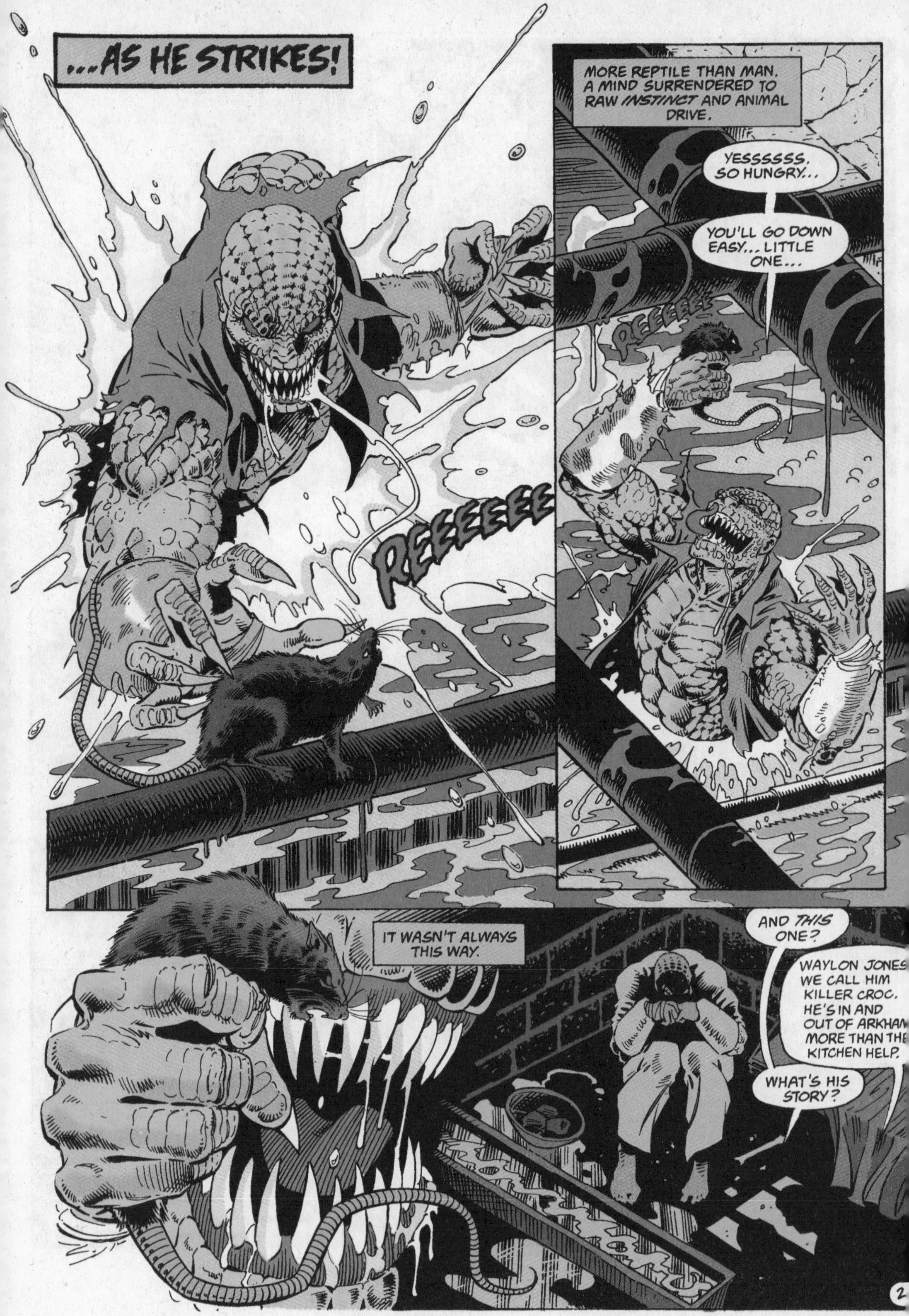
...AS HE STRIKES!
REEEEEE
MORE REPTILE THAN MAN. A MIND SURRENDERED TO RAW INSTINCT AND ANIMAL DRIVE.
YESSSSSS. SO HUNGRY...
YOU'LL GO DOWN EASY... LITTLE ONE...
REEEEEE
IT WASN'T ALWAYS THIS WAY.
AND THIS ONE?
WAYLON JONES WE CALL HIM KILLER CROC. HE'S IN AND OUT OF ARKHAM MORE THAN THE KITCHEN HELP.
WHAT'S HIS STORY?
2

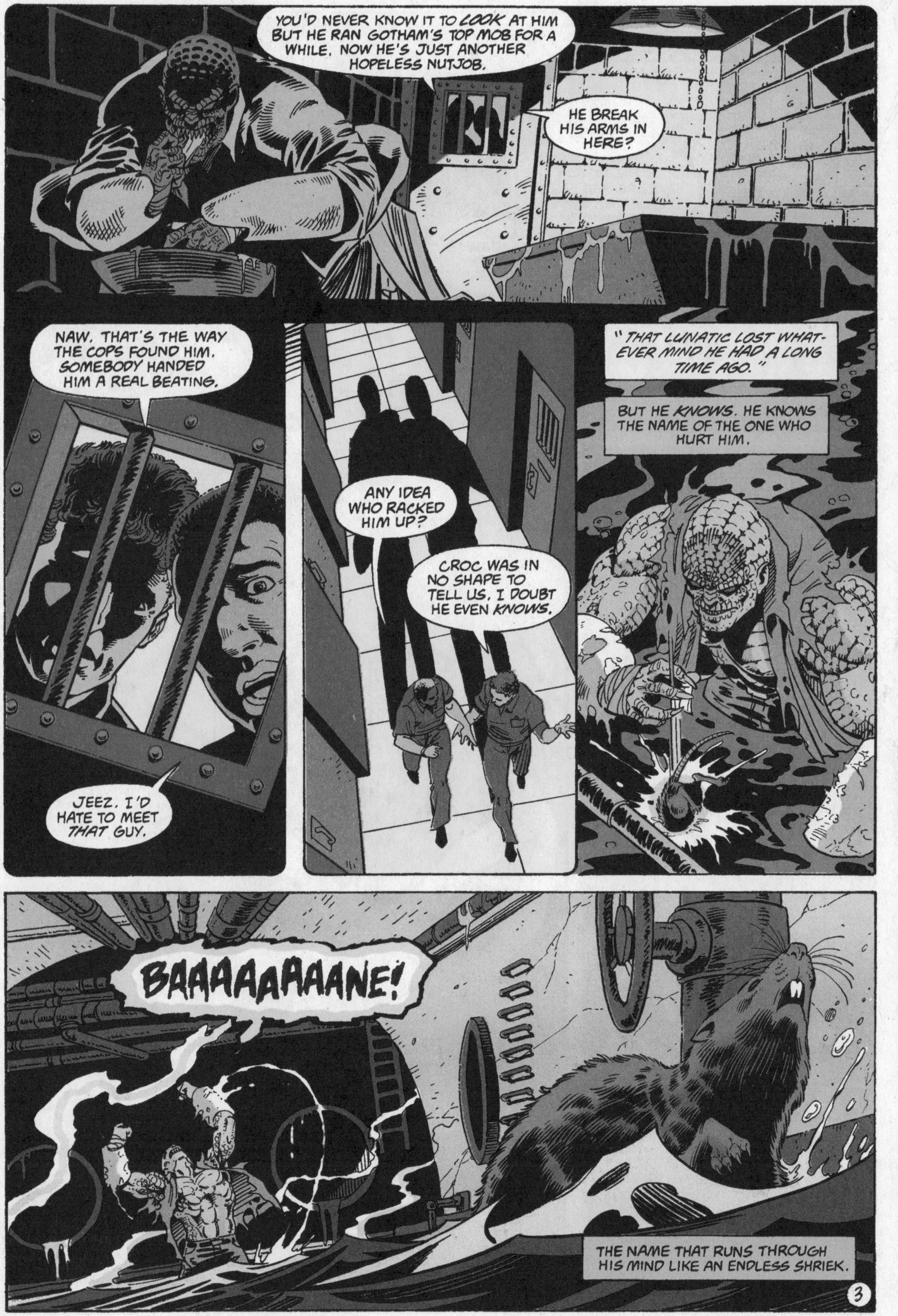
YOU'D NEVER KNOW IT TO LOOK AT HIM BUT HE RAN GOTHAM'S TOP MOB FOR A WHILE. NOW HE'S JUST ANOTHER HOPELESS NUTJOB.
HE BREAK HIS ARMS IN HERE?
NAW. THAT'S THE WAY THE COPS FOUND HIM. SOMEBODY HANDED HIM A REAL BEATING.
JEEZ. I'D HATE TO MEET THAT GUY.
ANY IDEA WHO RACKED HIM UP?
CROC WAS IN NO SHAPE TO TELL US. I DOUBT HE EVEN KNOWS.
"THAT LUNATIC LOST WHAT-EVER MIND HE HAD A LONG TIME AGO."
BUT HE KNOWS. HE KNOWS THE NAME OF THE ONE WHO HURT HIM.
BAAAAAAAANE!
THE NAME THAT RUNS THROUGH HIS MIND LIKE AN ENDLESS SHRIEK.
3

IS IT WISE TO BE THIS *PUBLIC*, BANE?

AND WHAT PURPOSE DOES THE TERROR I HAVE CREATED SERVE IF I CANNOT *SAVOR* IT, ZOMBIE?

LOOK AT THE STREETS. EMPTY. LIFELESS. .

A COMMUNITY COWERS BEHIND LOCKED DOORS. I HAVE CREATED A DARKNESS THAT CHILLS THEIR VERY SOULS.

I HAVE MADE A CITY INURED TO ITS OWN HORRORS KNOW FEAR.

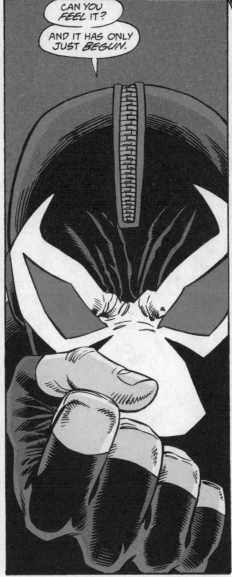

CAN YOU *FEEL* IT?

AND IT HAS ONLY JUST *BEGUN*.

AH, BIRD HAS RETURNED.

4

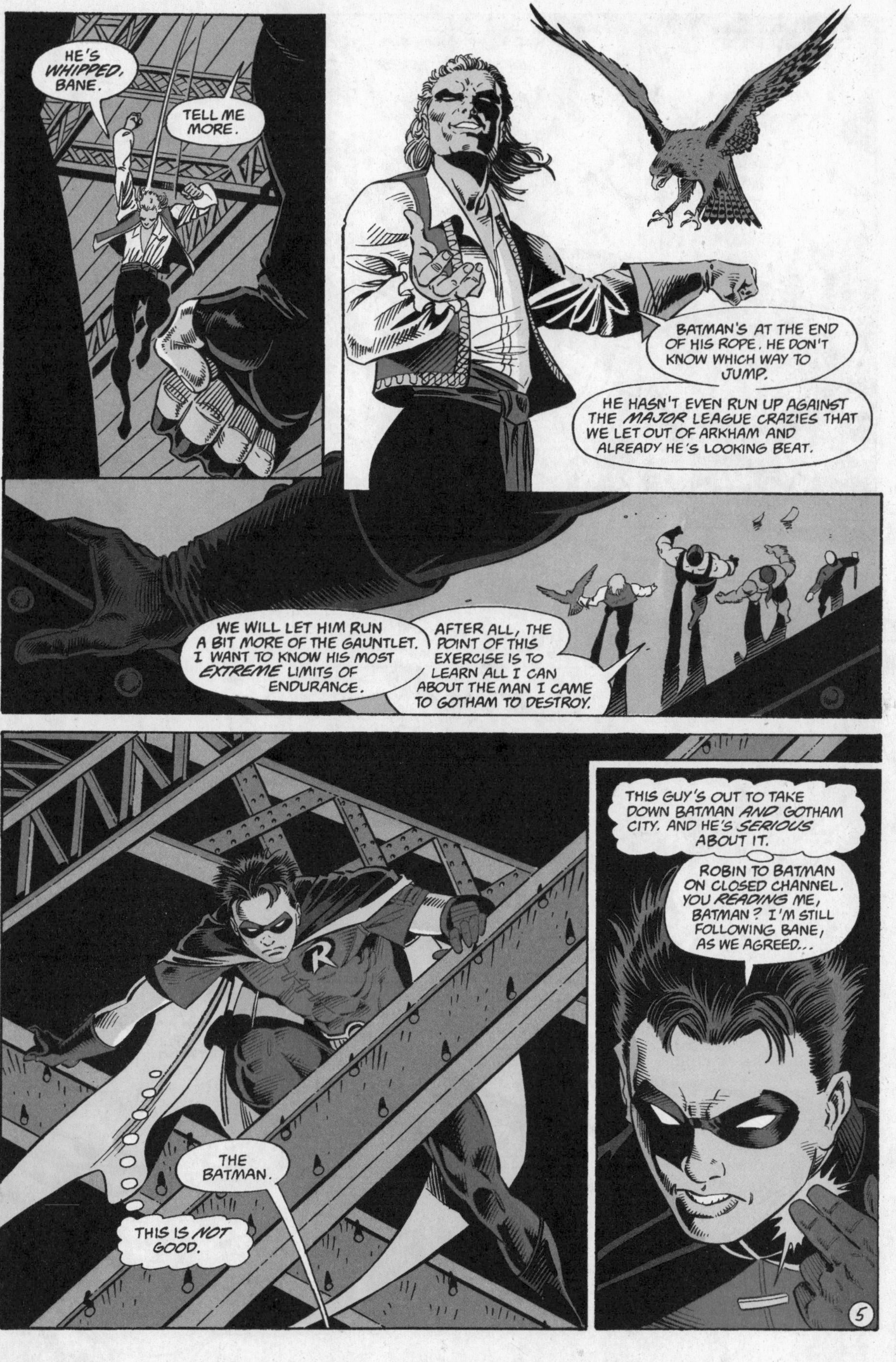
HE'S WHIPPED, BANE.
TELL ME MORE.
BATMAN'S AT THE END OF HIS ROPE. HE DON'T KNOW WHICH WAY TO JUMP.
HE HASN'T EVEN RUN UP AGAINST THE MAJOR LEAGUE CRAZIES THAT WE LET OUT OF ARKHAM AND ALREADY HE'S LOOKING BEAT.
WE WILL LET HIM RUN A BIT MORE OF THE GAUNTLET. I WANT TO KNOW HIS MOST EXTREME LIMITS OF ENDURANCE.
AFTER ALL, THE POINT OF THIS EXERCISE IS TO LEARN ALL I CAN ABOUT THE MAN I CAME TO GOTHAM TO DESTROY.
THE BATMAN.
THIS IS NOT GOOD.
THIS GUY'S OUT TO TAKE DOWN BATMAN AND GOTHAM CITY. AND HE'S SERIOUS ABOUT IT.
ROBIN TO BATMAN ON CLOSED CHANNEL. YOU READING ME, BATMAN? I'M STILL FOLLOWING BANE, AS WE AGREED...
5

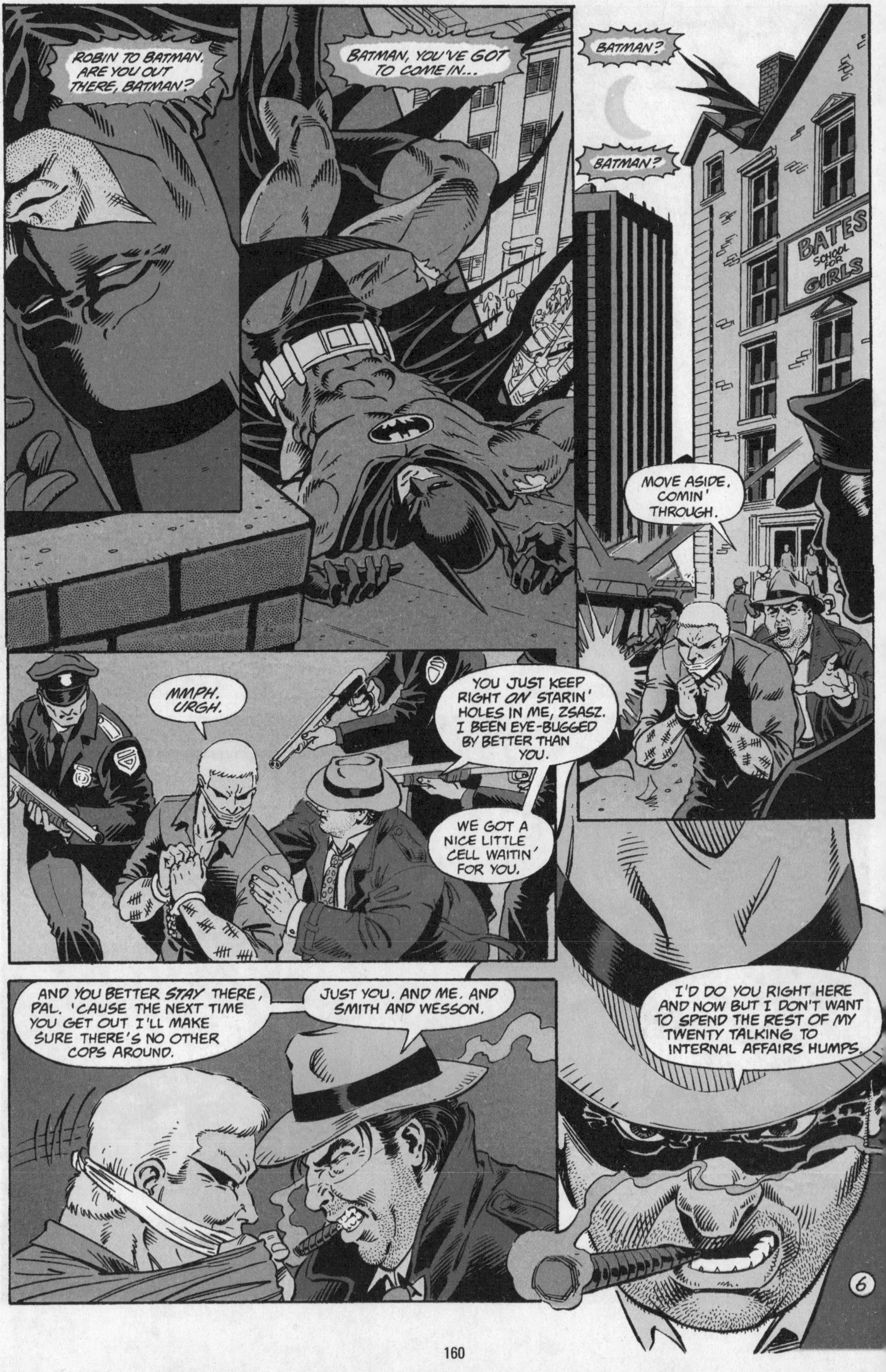
ROBIN TO BATMAN. ARE YOU OUT THERE, BATMAN?
BATMAN, YOU'VE GOT TO COME IN...
BATMAN?
BATMAN?
BATES SCHOOL FOR GIRLS
MOVE ASIDE. COMIN' THROUGH.
MMPH. URGH.
YOU JUST KEEP RIGHT ON STARIN' HOLES IN ME, ZSASZ. I BEEN EYE-BUGGED BY BETTER THAN YOU.
WE GOT A NICE LITTLE CELL WAITIN' FOR YOU.
AND YOU BETTER STAY THERE, PAL. 'CAUSE THE NEXT TIME YOU GET OUT I'LL MAKE SURE THERE'S NO OTHER COPS AROUND.
JUST YOU. AND ME. AND SMITH AND WESSON.
I'D DO YOU RIGHT HERE AND NOW BUT I DON'T WANT TO SPEND THE REST OF MY TWENTY TALKING TO INTERNAL AFFAIRS HUMPS.
6

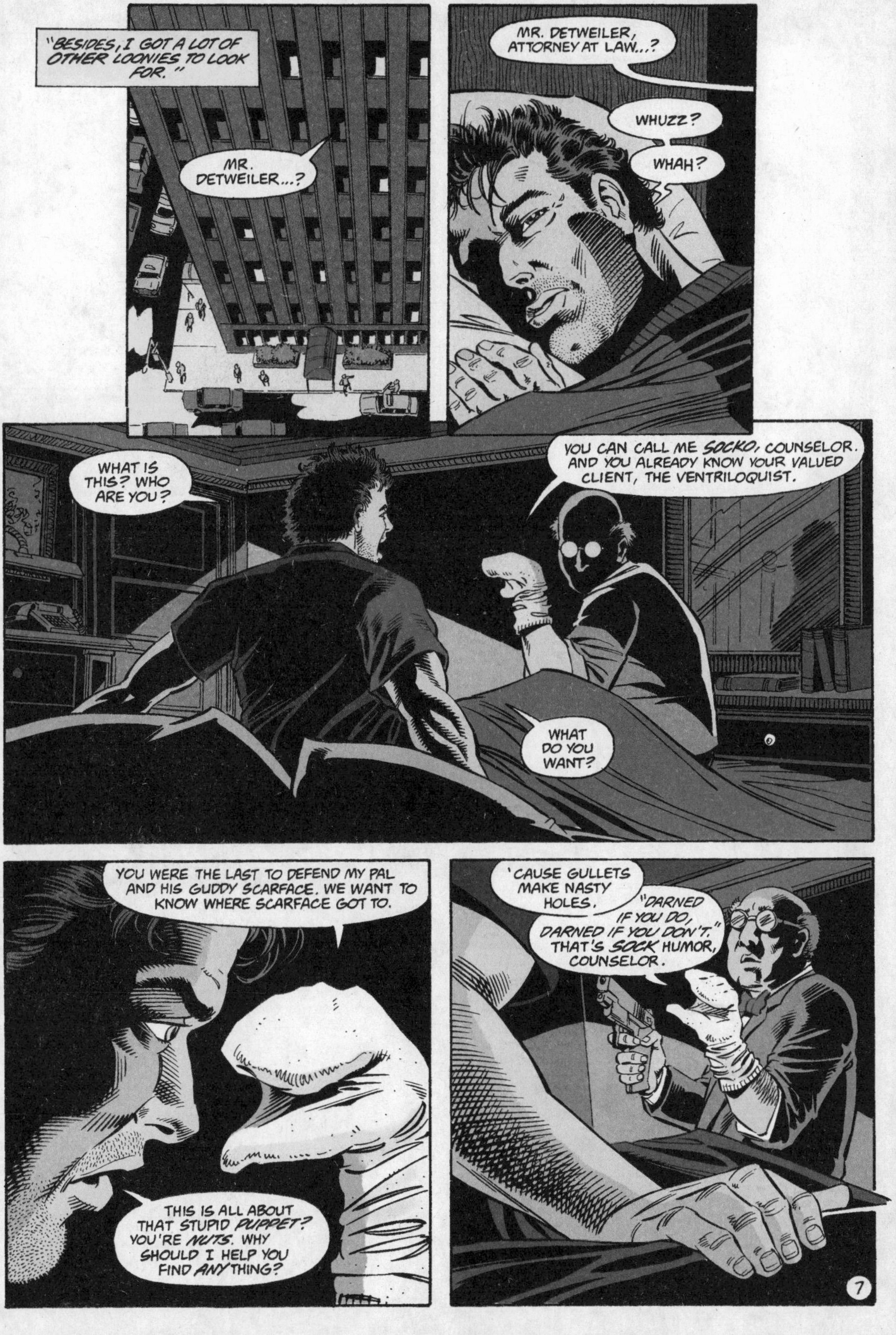
"BESIDES, I GOT A LOT OF OTHER LOONIES TO LOOK FOR."
MR. DETWEILER...?
MR. DETWEILER, ATTORNEY AT LAW...?
WHUZZ?
WHAH?
WHAT IS THIS? WHO ARE YOU?
YOU CAN CALL ME *SOCKO*, COUNSELOR. AND YOU ALREADY KNOW YOUR VALUED CLIENT, THE VENTRILOQUIST.
WHAT DO YOU WANT?
YOU WERE THE LAST TO DEFEND MY PAL AND HIS GUDDY SCARFACE. WE WANT TO KNOW WHERE SCARFACE GOT TO.
THIS IS ALL ABOUT THAT STUPID *PUPPET*? YOU'RE *NUTS*. WHY SHOULD I HELP YOU FIND *ANY*THING?
'CAUSE GULLETS MAKE NASTY HOLES.
"DARNED IF YOU DO, DARNED IF YOU DON'T." THAT'S *SOCK* HUMOR, COUNSELOR.
7

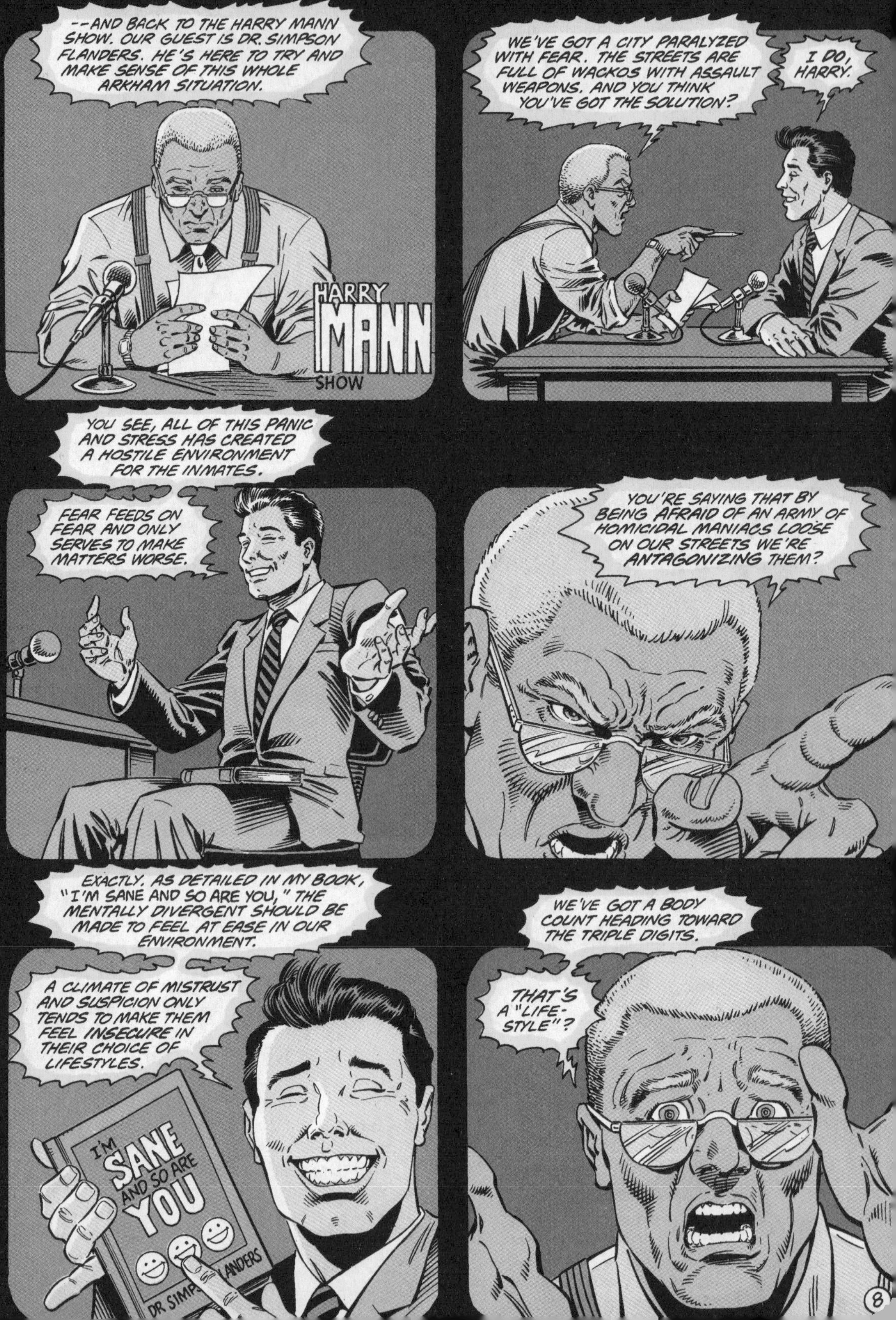
--AND BACK TO THE HARRY MANN SHOW. OUR GUEST IS DR. SIMPSON FLANDERS. HE'S HERE TO TRY AND MAKE SENSE OF THIS WHOLE ARKHAM SITUATION.
HARRY MANN SHOW
WE'VE GOT A CITY PARALYZED WITH FEAR. THE STREETS ARE FULL OF WACKOS WITH ASSAULT WEAPONS. AND YOU THINK YOU'VE GOT THE SOLUTION?
I DO, HARRY.
YOU SEE, ALL OF THIS PANIC AND STRESS HAS CREATED A HOSTILE ENVIRONMENT FOR THE INMATES.
FEAR FEEDS ON FEAR AND ONLY SERVES TO MAKE MATTERS WORSE.
YOU'RE SAYING THAT BY BEING AFRAID OF AN ARMY OF HOMICIDAL MANIACS LOOSE ON OUR STREETS WE'RE ANTAGONIZING THEM?
EXACTLY. AS DETAILED IN MY BOOK, "I'M SANE AND SO ARE YOU," THE MENTALLY DIVERGENT SHOULD BE MADE TO FEEL AT EASE IN OUR ENVIRONMENT.
A CLIMATE OF MISTRUST AND SUSPICION ONLY TENDS TO MAKE THEM FEEL INSECURE IN THEIR CHOICE OF LIFESTYLES.
I'M SANE AND SO ARE YOU
WE'VE GOT A BODY COUNT HEADING TOWARD THE TRIPLE DIGITS.
THAT'S A "LIFE-STYLE"?
8

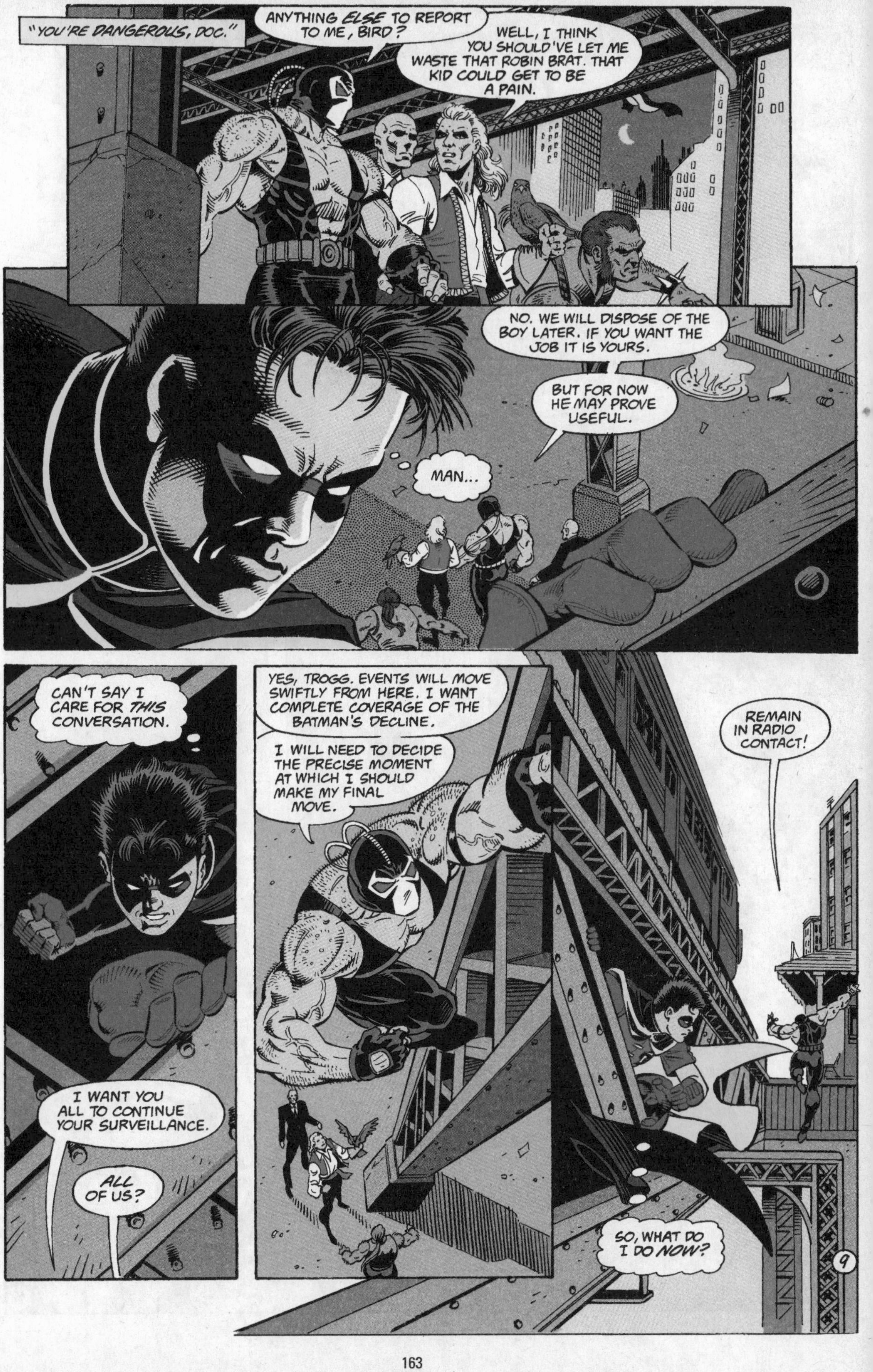

"YOU'RE DANGEROUS, DOC."
ANYTHING ELSE TO REPORT TO ME, BIRD?
WELL, I THINK YOU SHOULD'VE LET ME WASTE THAT ROBIN BRAT. THAT KID COULD GET TO BE A PAIN.
NO. WE WILL DISPOSE OF THE BOY LATER. IF YOU WANT THE JOB IT IS YOURS.
BUT FOR NOW HE MAY PROVE USEFUL.
MAN...
CAN'T SAY I CARE FOR THIS CONVERSATION.
I WANT YOU ALL TO CONTINUE YOUR SURVEILLANCE.
ALL OF US?
YES, TROGG. EVENTS WILL MOVE SWIFTLY FROM HERE. I WANT COMPLETE COVERAGE OF THE BATMAN'S DECLINE.
I WILL NEED TO DECIDE THE PRECISE MOMENT AT WHICH I SHOULD MAKE MY FINAL MOVE.
REMAIN IN RADIO CONTACT!
SO, WHAT DO I DO NOW?
9

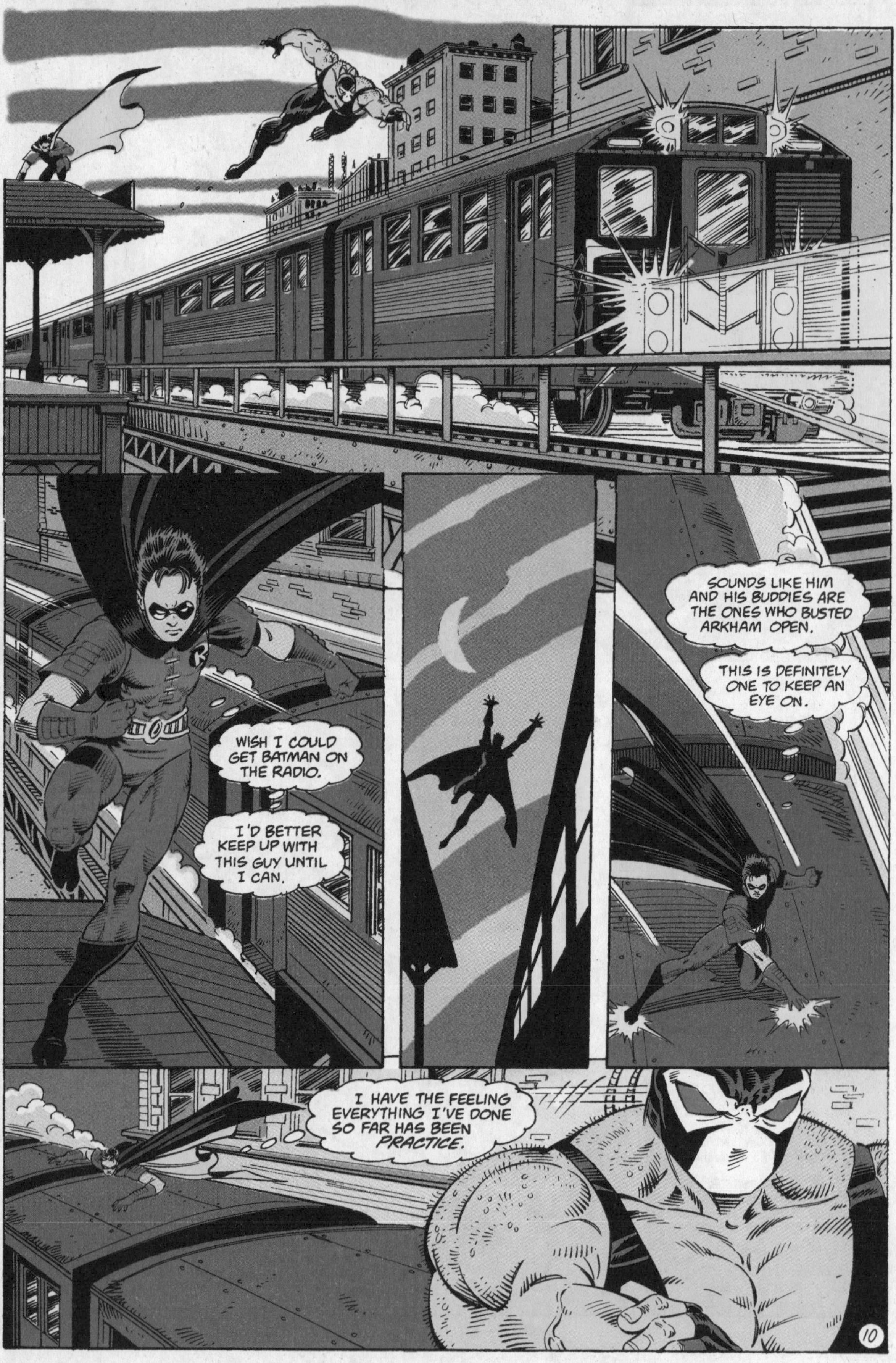
WISH I COULD GET BATMAN ON THE RADIO.
I'D BETTER KEEP UP WITH THIS GUY UNTIL I CAN.
SOUNDS LIKE HIM AND HIS BUDDIES ARE THE ONES WHO BUSTED ARKHAM OPEN.
THIS IS DEFINITELY ONE TO KEEP AN EYE ON.
I HAVE THE FEELING EVERYTHING I'VE DONE SO FAR HAS BEEN PRACTICE.
10

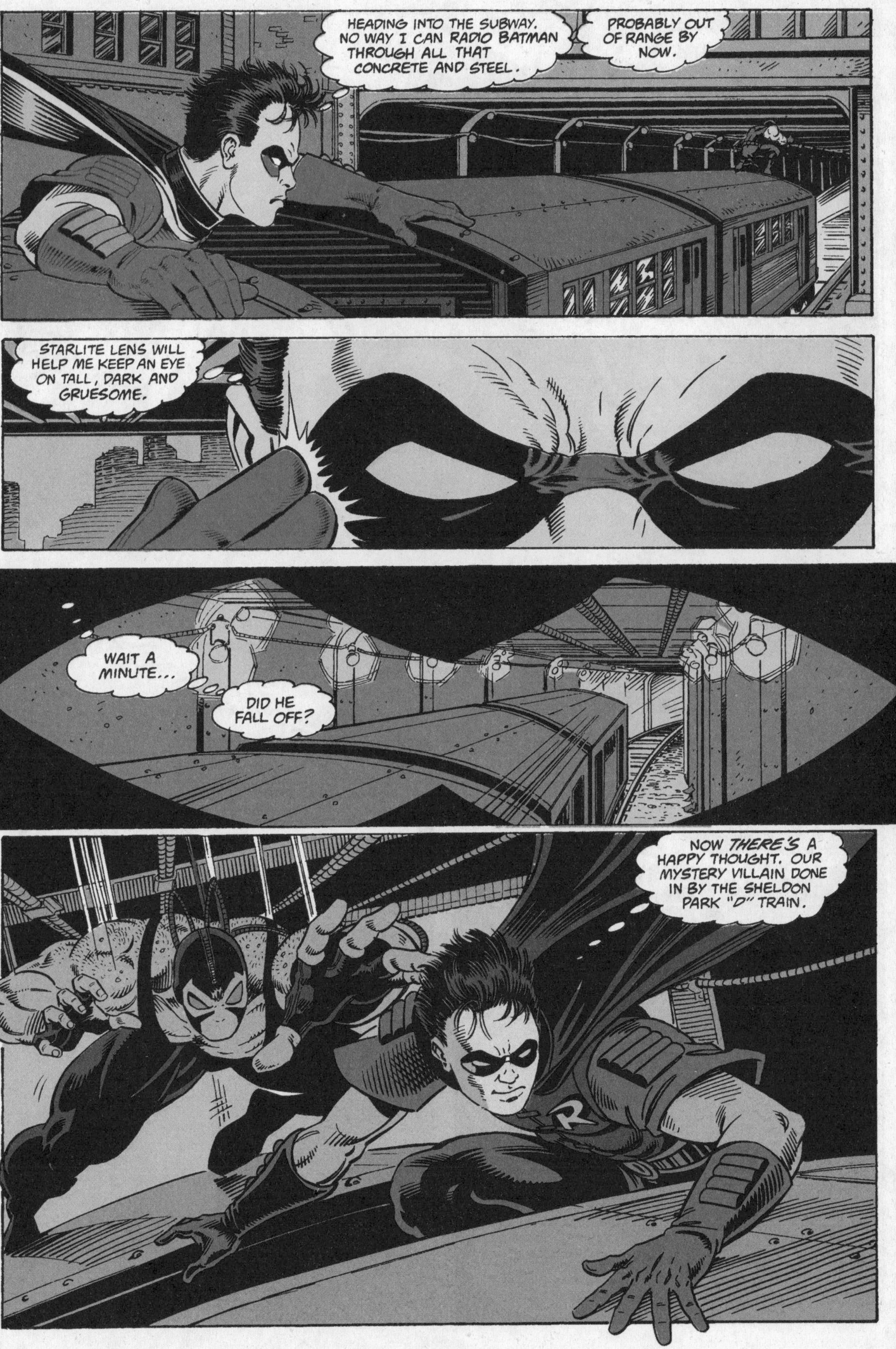
HEADING INTO THE SUBWAY. NO WAY I CAN RADIO BATMAN THROUGH ALL THAT CONCRETE AND STEEL.
PROBABLY OUT OF RANGE BY NOW.
STARLITE LENS WILL HELP ME KEEP AN EYE ON TALL, DARK AND GRUESOME.
WAIT A MINUTE...
DID HE FALL OFF?
NOW *THERE'S* A HAPPY THOUGHT. OUR MYSTERY VILLAIN DONE IN BY THE SHELDON PARK "D" TRAIN.

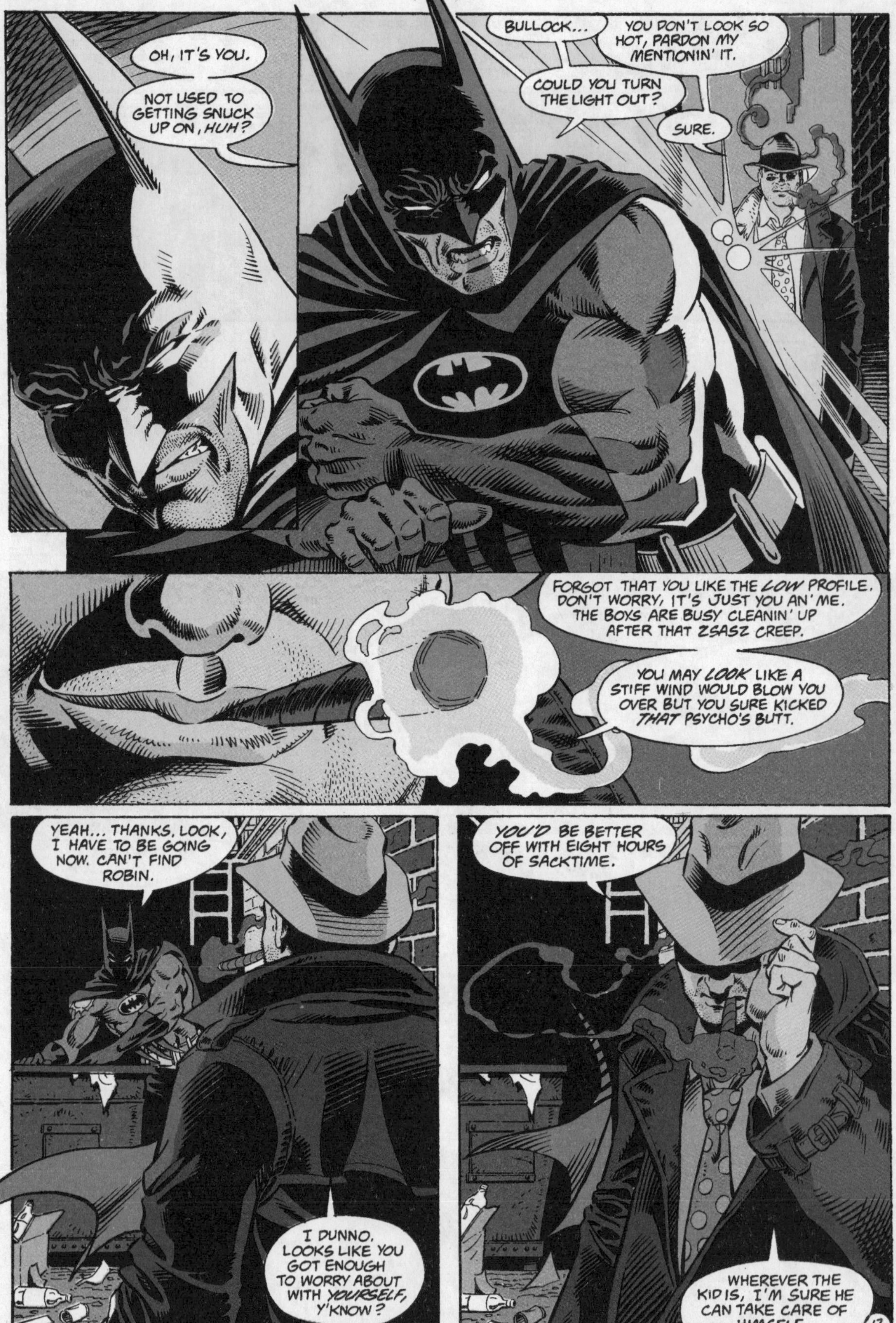
OH, IT'S YOU.
NOT USED TO GETTING SNUCK UP ON, HUH?
BULLOCK...
YOU DON'T LOOK SO HOT, PARDON MY MENTIONIN' IT.
COULD YOU TURN THE LIGHT OUT?
SURE.
FORGOT THAT YOU LIKE THE LOW PROFILE. DON'T WORRY, IT'S JUST YOU AN' ME. THE BOYS ARE BUSY CLEANIN' UP AFTER THAT ZSASZ CREEP.
YOU MAY LOOK LIKE A STIFF WIND WOULD BLOW YOU OVER BUT YOU SURE KICKED THAT PSYCHO'S BUTT.
YEAH... THANKS. LOOK, I HAVE TO BE GOING NOW. CAN'T FIND ROBIN.
I DUNNO. LOOKS LIKE YOU GOT ENOUGH TO WORRY ABOUT WITH YOURSELF, Y'KNOW?
YOU'D BE BETTER OFF WITH EIGHT HOURS OF SACKTIME.
WHEREVER THE KID IS, I'M SURE HE CAN TAKE CARE OF HIMSELF.
12

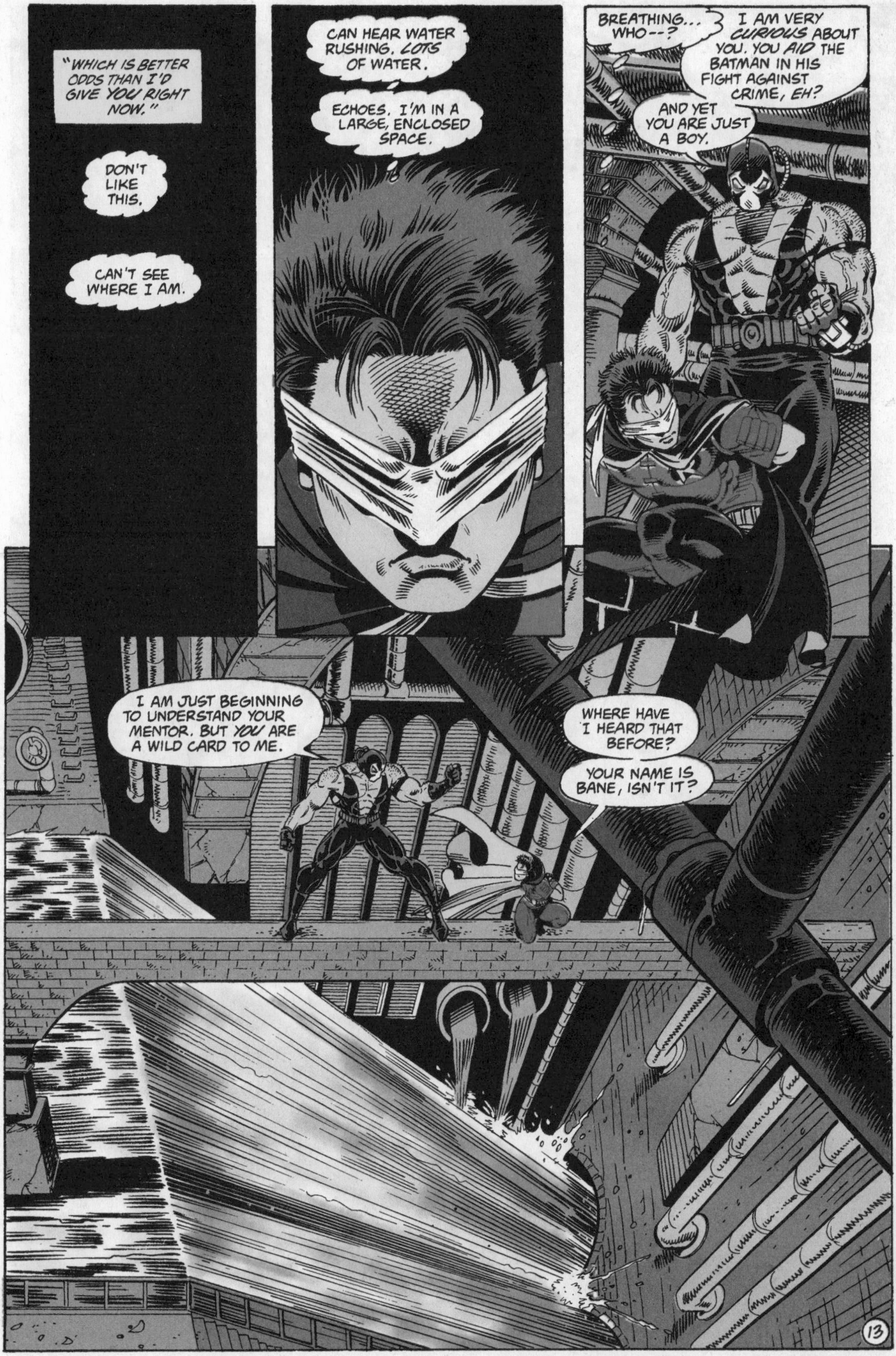
"WHICH IS BETTER ODDS THAN I'D GIVE YOU RIGHT NOW."
DON'T LIKE THIS.
CAN'T SEE WHERE I AM.
CAN HEAR WATER RUSHING. LOTS OF WATER.
ECHOES. I'M IN A LARGE, ENCLOSED SPACE.
BREATHING... WHO--?
I AM VERY CURIOUS ABOUT YOU. YOU AID THE BATMAN IN HIS FIGHT AGAINST CRIME, EH?
AND YET YOU ARE JUST A BOY.
I AM JUST BEGINNING TO UNDERSTAND YOUR MENTOR. BUT YOU ARE A WILD CARD TO ME.
WHERE HAVE I HEARD THAT BEFORE?
YOUR NAME IS BANE, ISN'T IT?
13

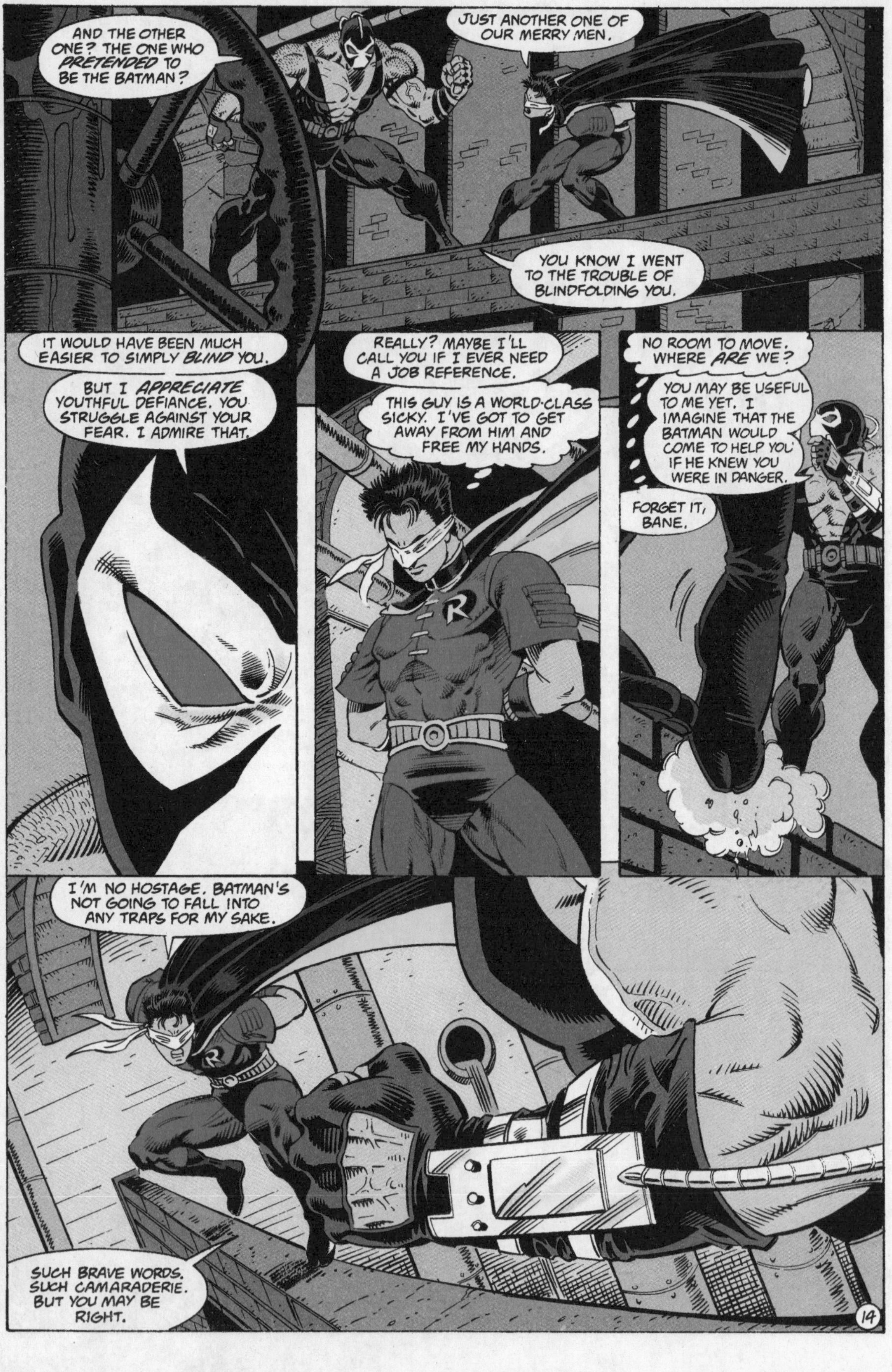
AND THE OTHER ONE? THE ONE WHO PRETENDED TO BE THE BATMAN?
JUST ANOTHER ONE OF OUR MERRY MEN.
YOU KNOW I WENT TO THE TROUBLE OF BLINDFOLDING YOU.
IT WOULD HAVE BEEN MUCH EASIER TO SIMPLY BLIND YOU.
BUT I APPRECIATE YOUTHFUL DEFIANCE. YOU STRUGGLE AGAINST YOUR FEAR. I ADMIRE THAT.
REALLY? MAYBE I'LL CALL YOU IF I EVER NEED A JOB REFERENCE.
THIS GUY IS A WORLD-CLASS SICKY. I'VE GOT TO GET AWAY FROM HIM AND FREE MY HANDS.
NO ROOM TO MOVE. WHERE ARE WE?
YOU MAY BE USEFUL TO ME YET. I IMAGINE THAT THE BATMAN WOULD COME TO HELP YOU IF HE KNEW YOU WERE IN DANGER.
FORGET IT, BANE.
I'M NO HOSTAGE. BATMAN'S NOT GOING TO FALL INTO ANY TRAPS FOR MY SAKE.
SUCH BRAVE WORDS. SUCH CAMARADERIE. BUT YOU MAY BE RIGHT.
14

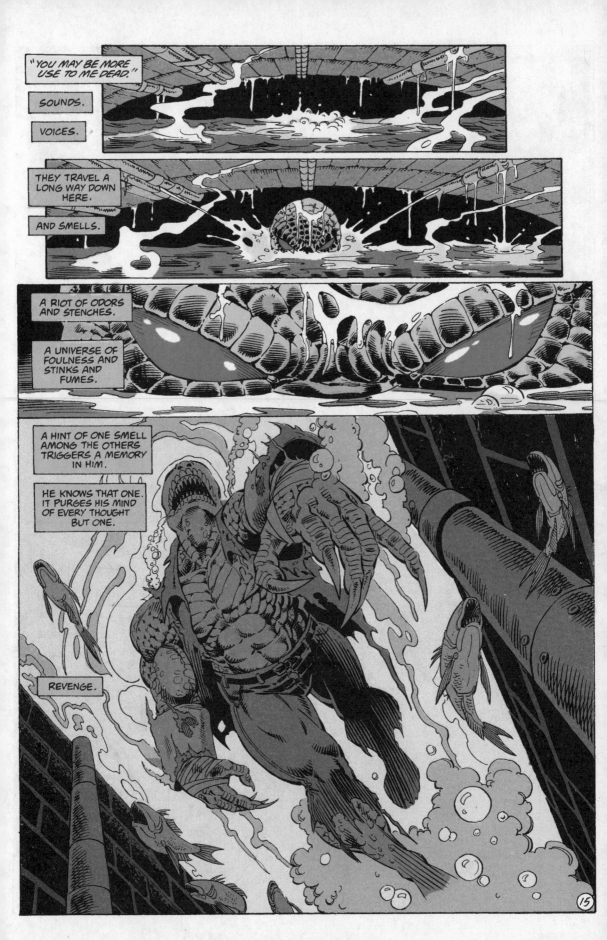

"YOU MAY BE MORE USE TO ME DEAD."

SOUNDS.

VOICES.

THEY TRAVEL A LONG WAY DOWN HERE.

AND SMELLS.

A RIOT OF ODORS AND STENCHES.

A UNIVERSE OF FOULNESS AND STINKS AND FUMES.

A HINT OF ONE SMELL AMONG THE OTHERS TRIGGERS A MEMORY IN HIM.

HE KNOWS THAT ONE. IT PURGES HIS MIND OF EVERY THOUGHT BUT ONE.

REVENGE.

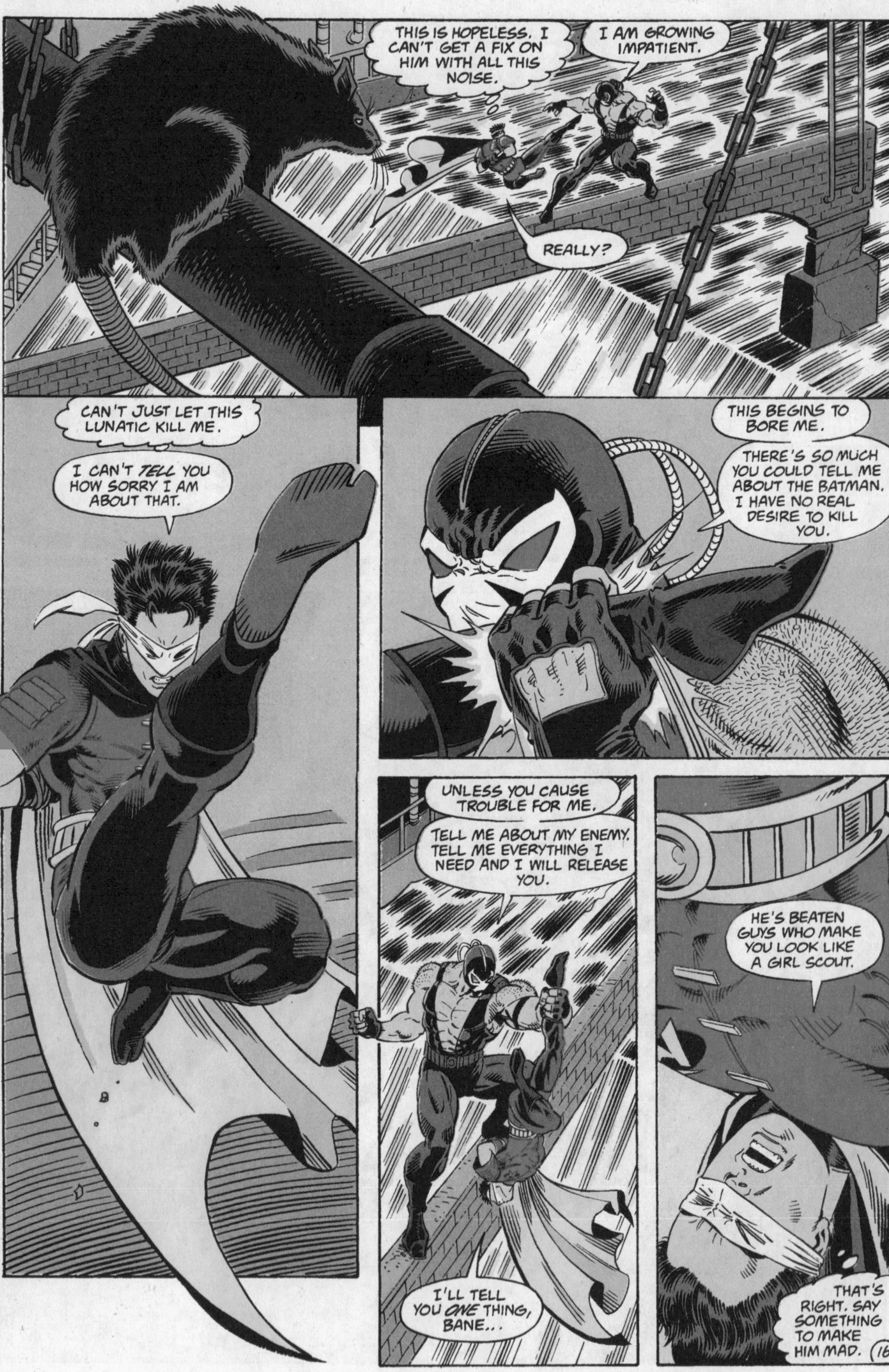
THIS IS HOPELESS. I CAN'T GET A FIX ON HIM WITH ALL THIS NOISE.
I AM GROWING IMPATIENT.
REALLY?
CAN'T JUST LET THIS LUNATIC KILL ME.
I CAN'T TELL YOU HOW SORRY I AM ABOUT THAT.
THIS BEGINS TO BORE ME.
THERE'S SO MUCH YOU COULD TELL ME ABOUT THE BATMAN. I HAVE NO REAL DESIRE TO KILL YOU.
UNLESS YOU CAUSE TROUBLE FOR ME.
TELL ME ABOUT MY ENEMY. TELL ME EVERYTHING I NEED AND I WILL RELEASE YOU.
I'LL TELL YOU ONE THING, BANE...
HE'S BEATEN GUYS WHO MAKE YOU LOOK LIKE A GIRL SCOUT.
THAT'S RIGHT. SAY SOMETHING TO MAKE HIM MAD.
16

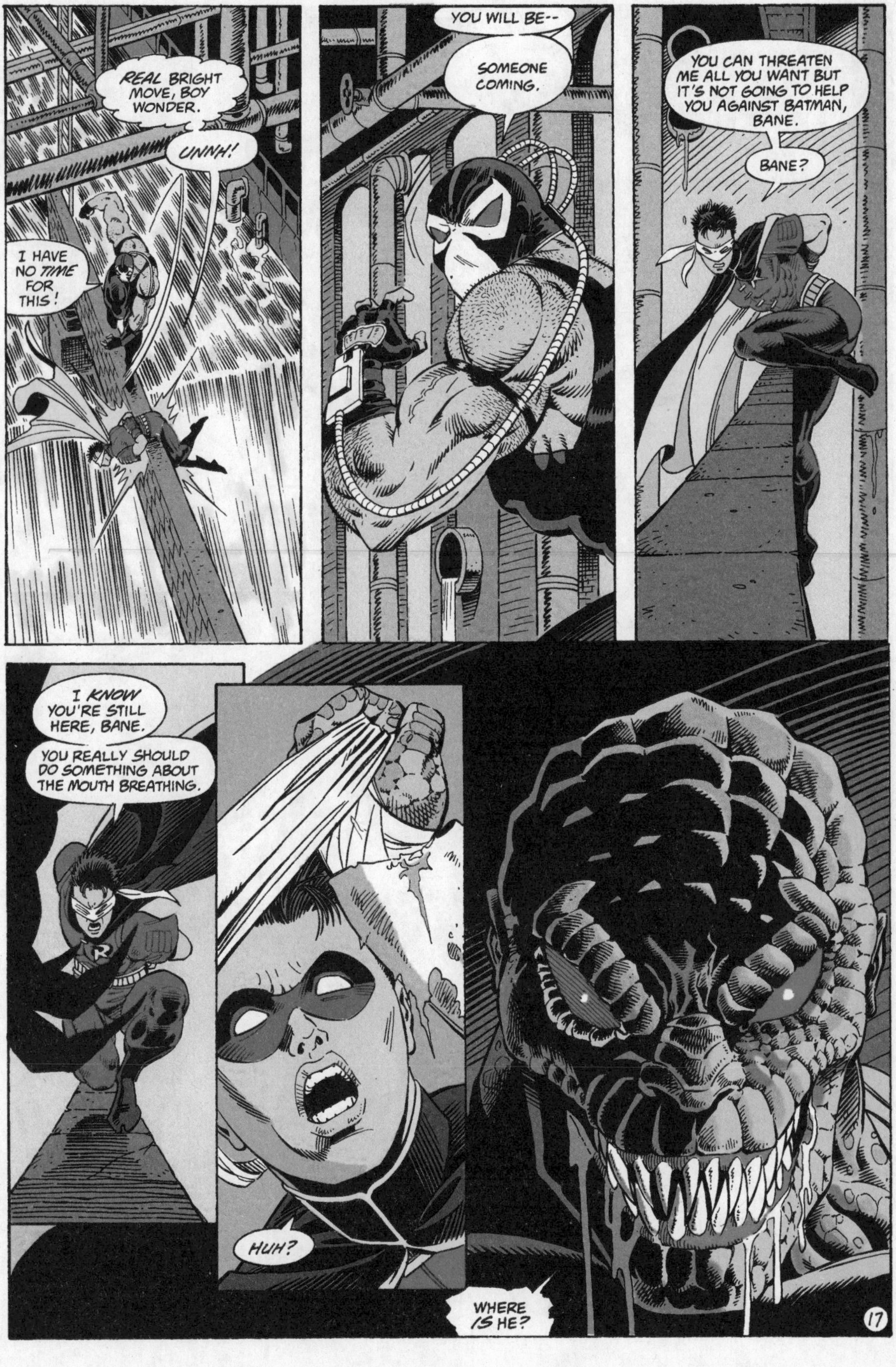
REAL BRIGHT MOVE, BOY WONDER.
UNNH!
I HAVE NO TIME FOR THIS!
YOU WILL BE--
SOMEONE COMING.
YOU CAN THREATEN ME ALL YOU WANT BUT IT'S NOT GOING TO HELP YOU AGAINST BATMAN, BANE.
BANE?
I KNOW YOU'RE STILL HERE, BANE.
YOU REALLY SHOULD DO SOMETHING ABOUT THE MOUTH BREATHING.
HUH?
WHERE IS HE?
17

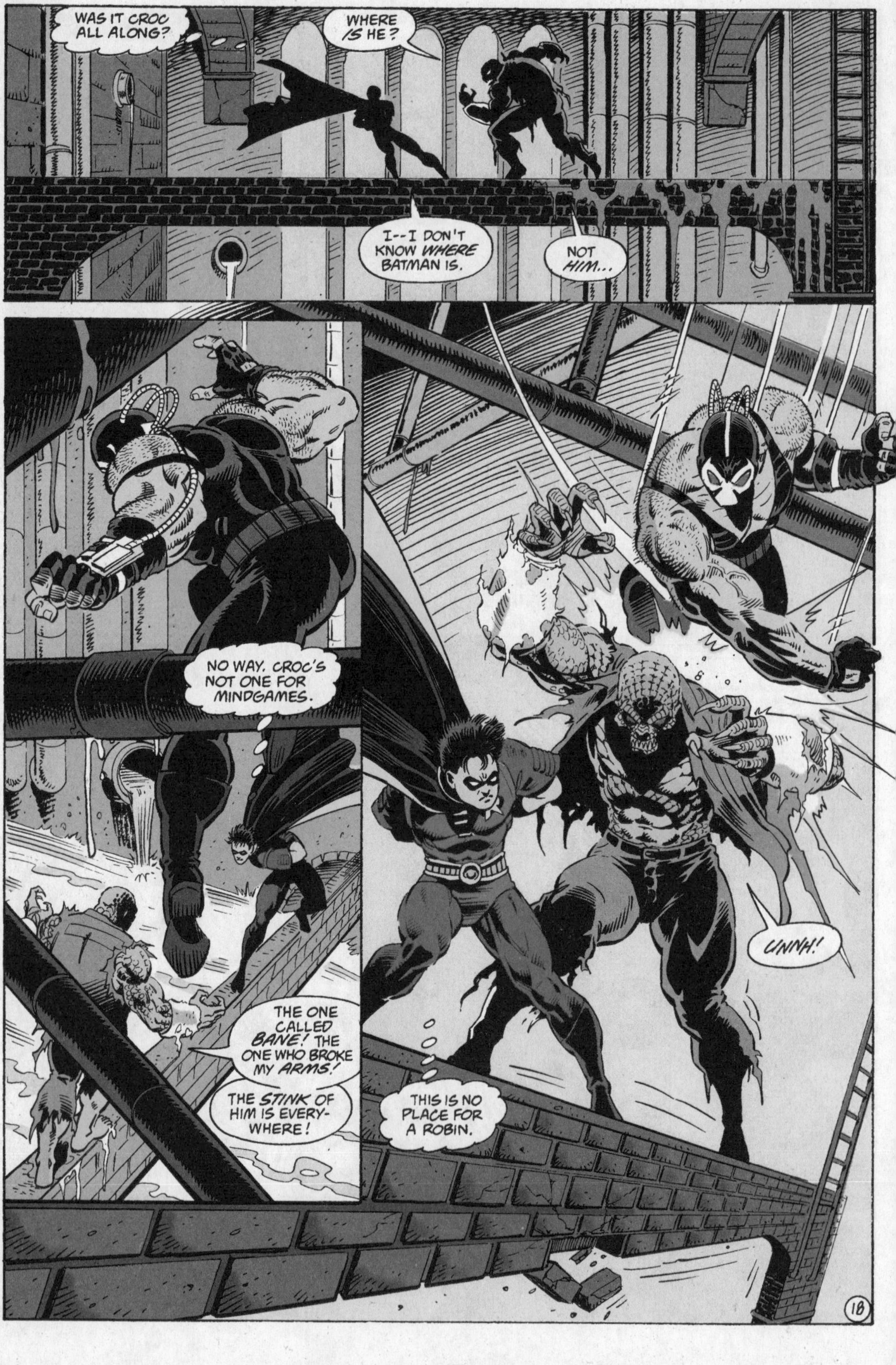

WAS IT CROC ALL ALONG?
WHERE IS HE?
I--I DON'T KNOW WHERE BATMAN IS.
NOT HIM...
NO WAY. CROC'S NOT ONE FOR MINDGAMES.
THE ONE CALLED BANE! THE ONE WHO BROKE MY ARMS!
THE STINK OF HIM IS EVERY-WHERE!
THIS IS NO PLACE FOR A ROBIN.
UNNH!
18

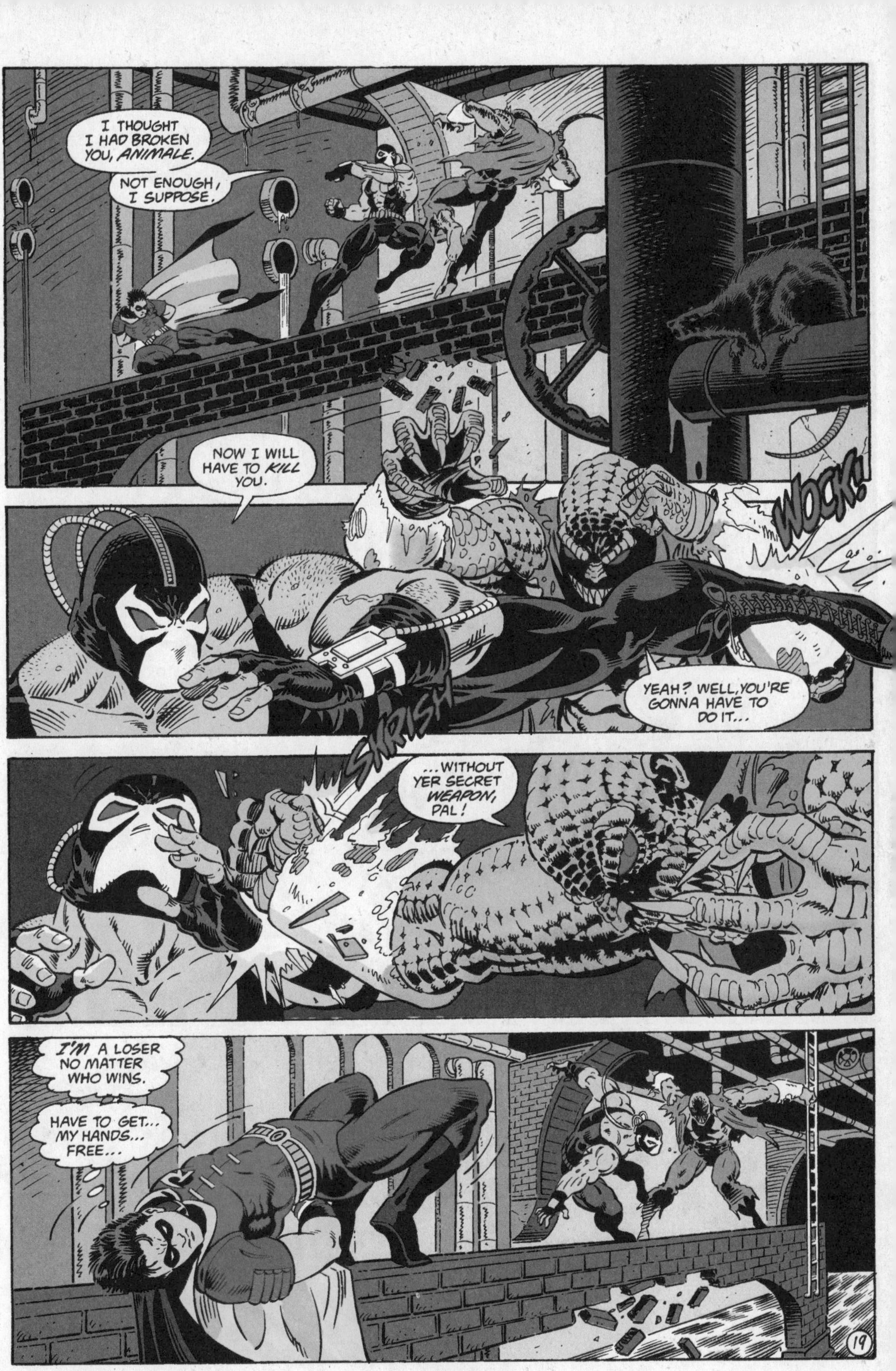
I THOUGHT I HAD BROKEN YOU, ANIMALE.
NOT ENOUGH, I SUPPOSE.
NOW I WILL HAVE TO KILL YOU.
WOCK!
YEAH? WELL, YOU'RE GONNA HAVE TO DO IT...
SKRISH
...WITHOUT YER SECRET WEAPON, PAL!
I'M A LOSER NO MATTER WHO WINS.
HAVE TO GET... MY HANDS... FREE...
19

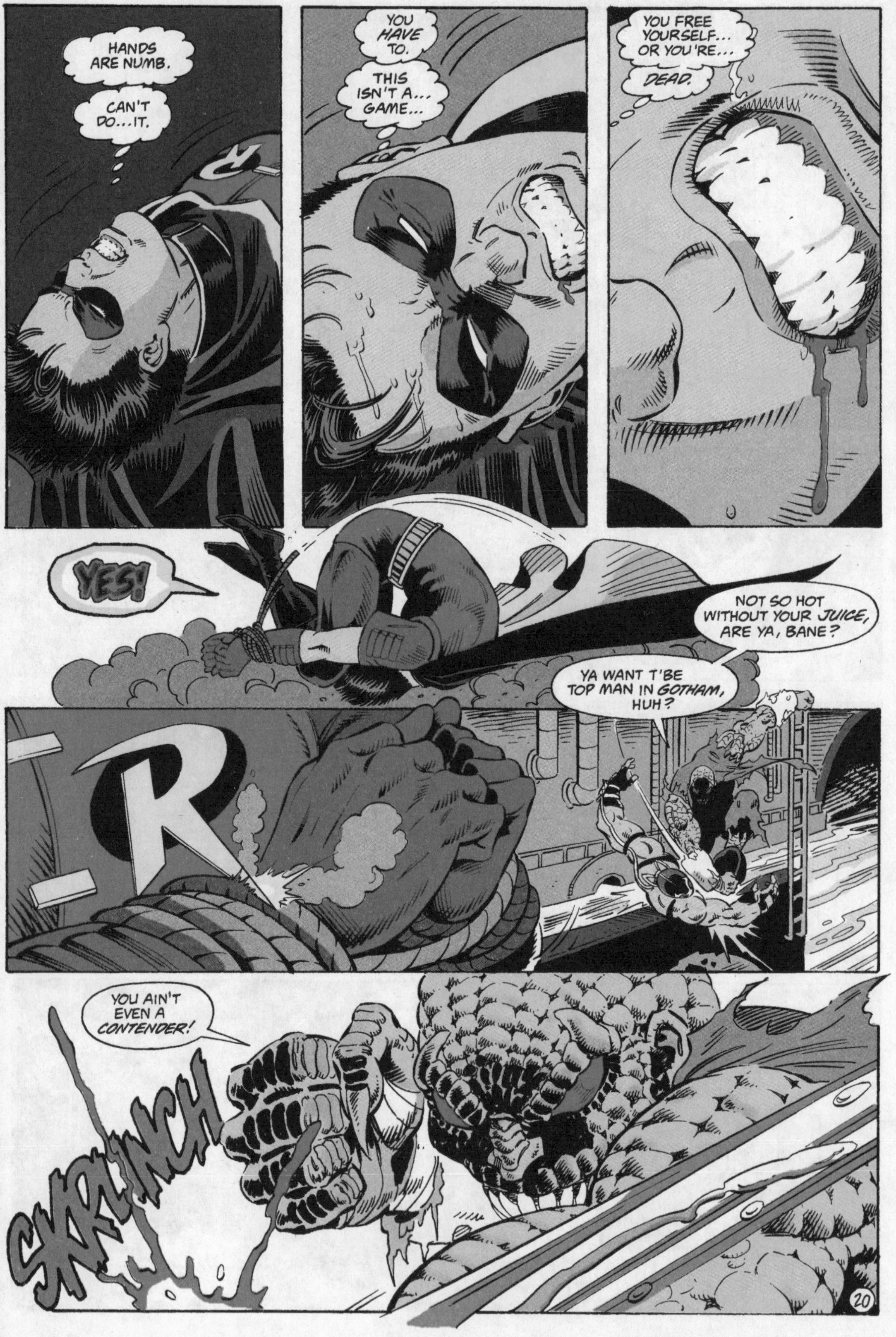
HANDS ARE NUMB.
CAN'T DO... IT.
YOU HAVE TO.
THIS ISN'T A... GAME...
YOU FREE YOURSELF... OR YOU'RE...
DEAD.
YES!
NOT SO HOT WITHOUT YOUR JUICE, ARE YA, BANE?
YA WANT T'BE TOP MAN IN GOTHAM, HUH?
YOU AIN'T EVEN A CONTENDER!
SKRUNCH
20

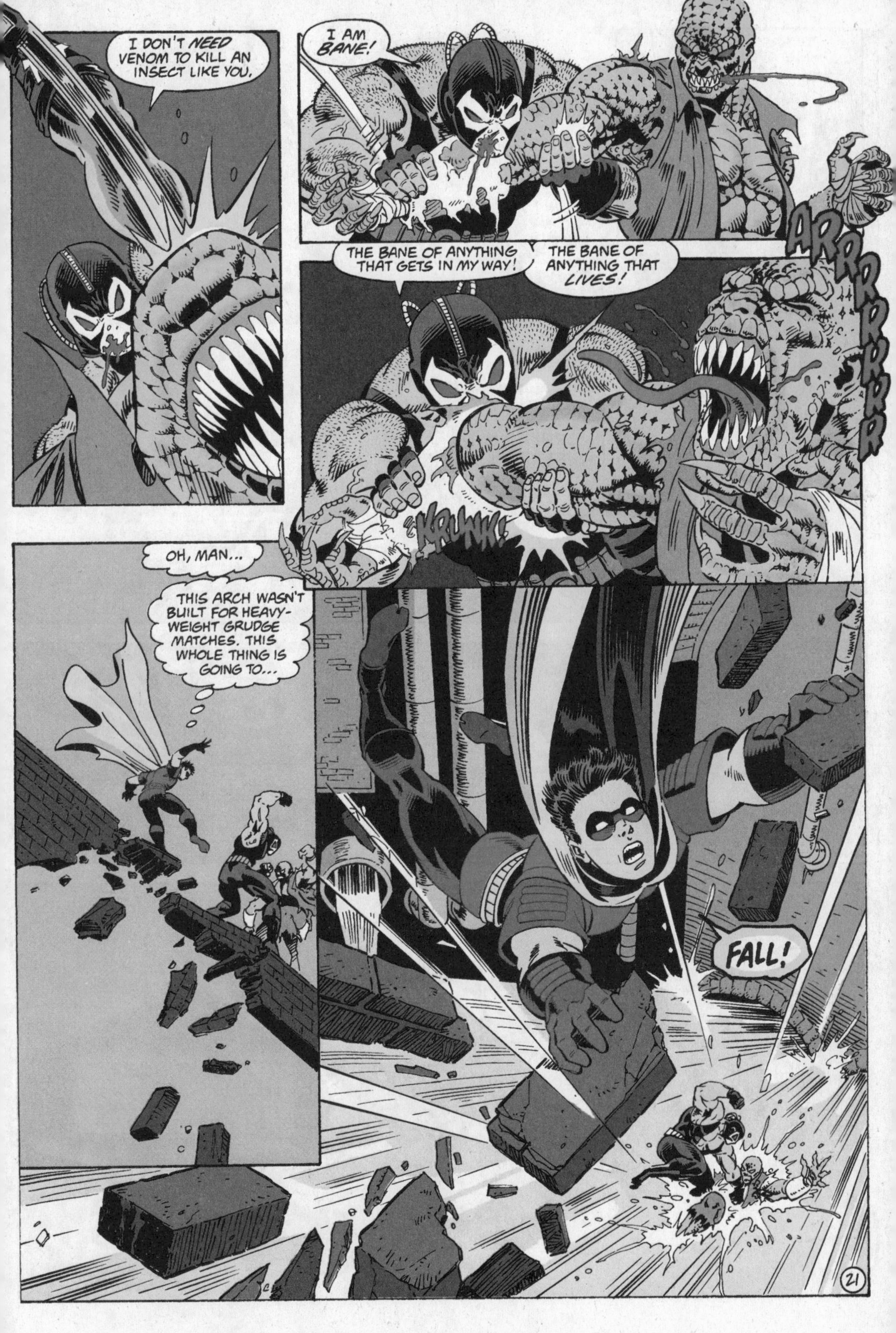
I DON'T NEED VENOM TO KILL AN INSECT LIKE YOU.
I AM BANE!
ARRRRRRRRR
THE BANE OF ANYTHING THAT GETS IN MY WAY!
THE BANE OF ANYTHING THAT LIVES!
KRUNK!
OH, MAN...
THIS ARCH WASN'T BUILT FOR HEAVY-WEIGHT GRUDGE MATCHES. THIS WHOLE THING IS GOING TO...
FALL!
21

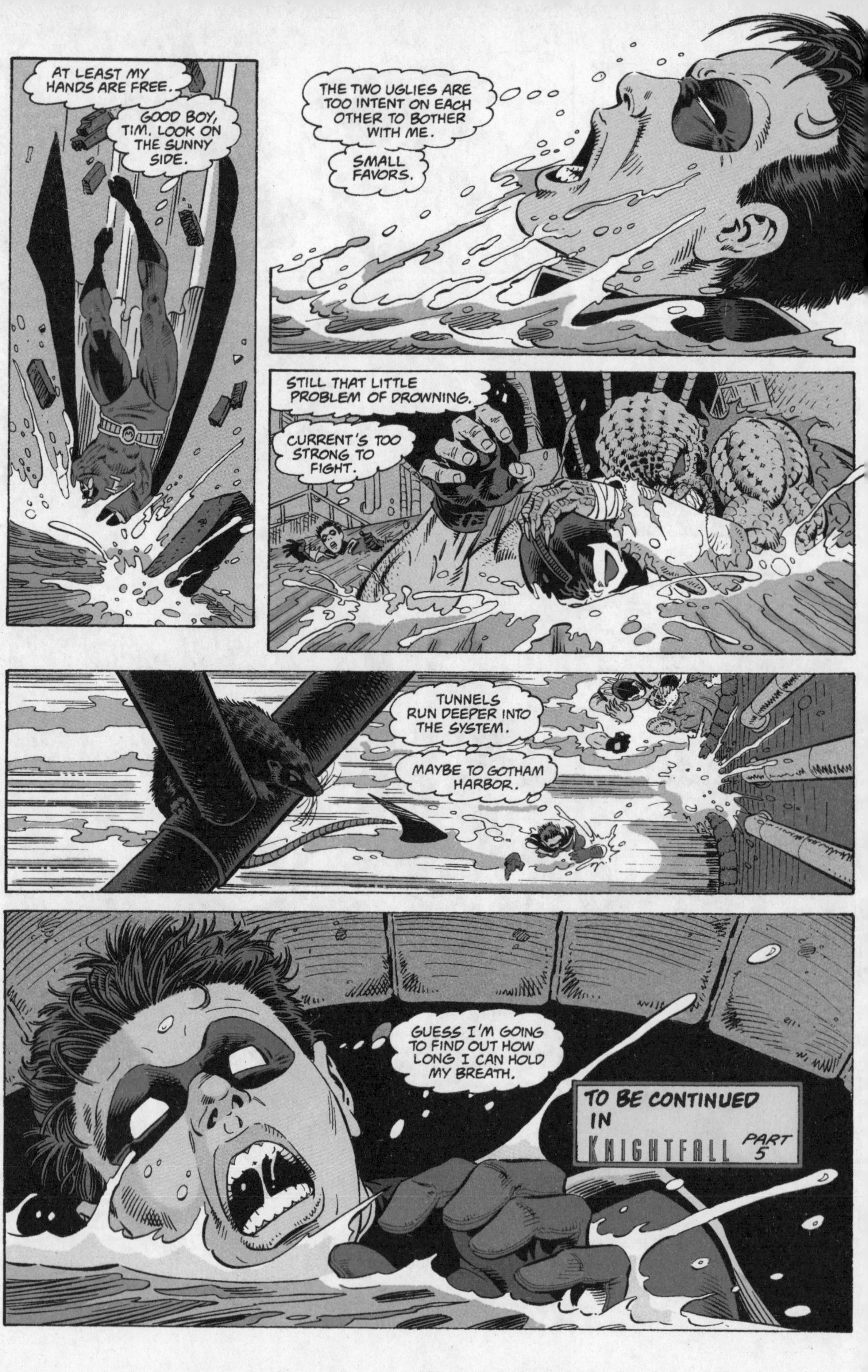
AT LEAST MY HANDS ARE FREE.
GOOD BOY, TIM. LOOK ON THE SUNNY SIDE.
THE TWO UGLIES ARE TOO INTENT ON EACH OTHER TO BOTHER WITH ME.
SMALL FAVORS.
STILL THAT LITTLE PROBLEM OF DROWNING.
CURRENT'S TOO STRONG TO FIGHT.
TUNNELS RUN DEEPER INTO THE SYSTEM.
MAYBE TO GOTHAM HARBOR.
GUESS I'M GOING TO FIND OUT HOW LONG I CAN HOLD MY BREATH.
TO BE CONTINUED IN KNIGHTFALL PART 5

Cover art by KELLEY JONES

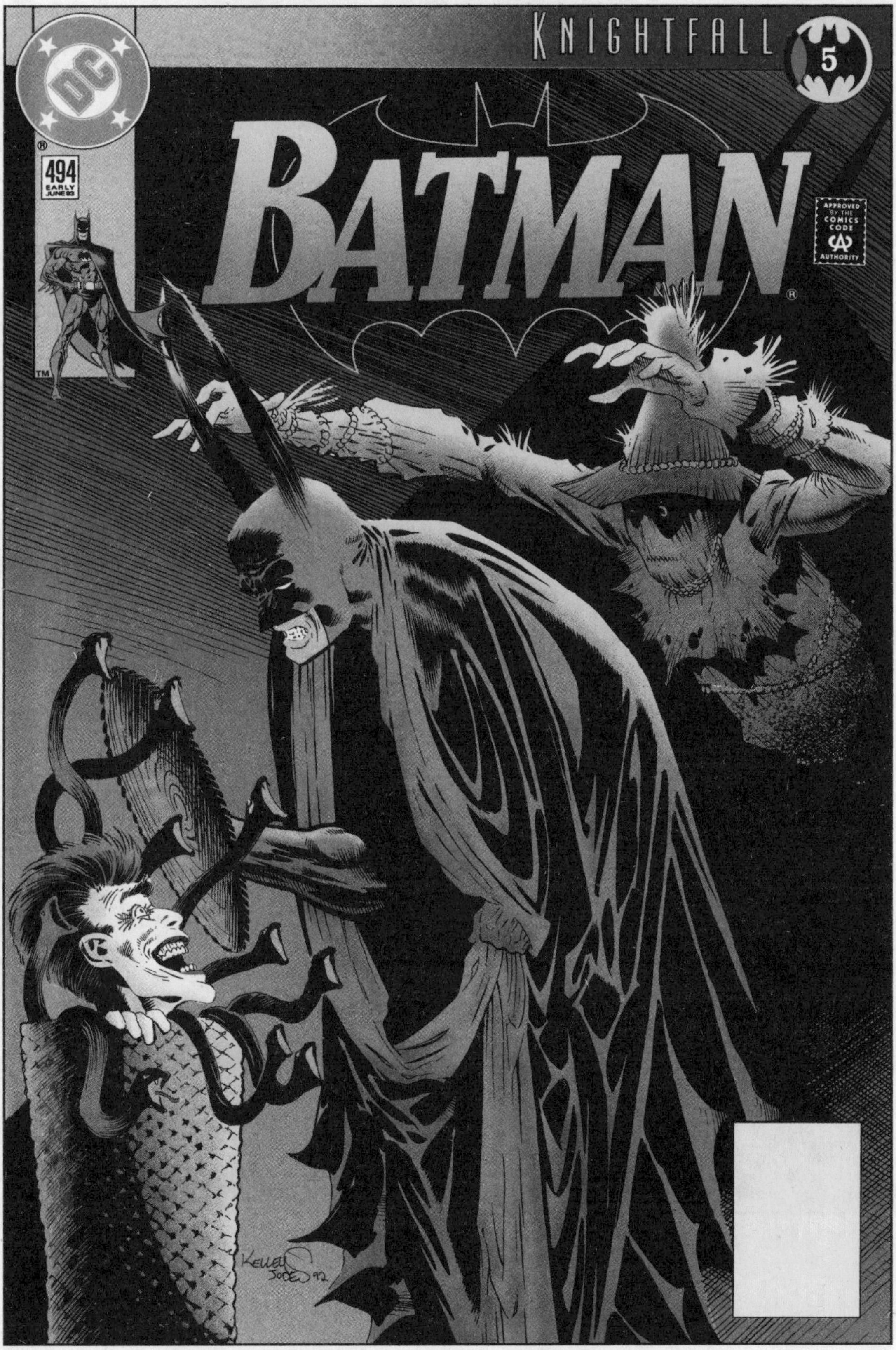

KNIGHTFALL
5
DC
494
EARLY JUNE 93
BATMAN
APPROVED BY THE COMICS CODE AUTHORITY

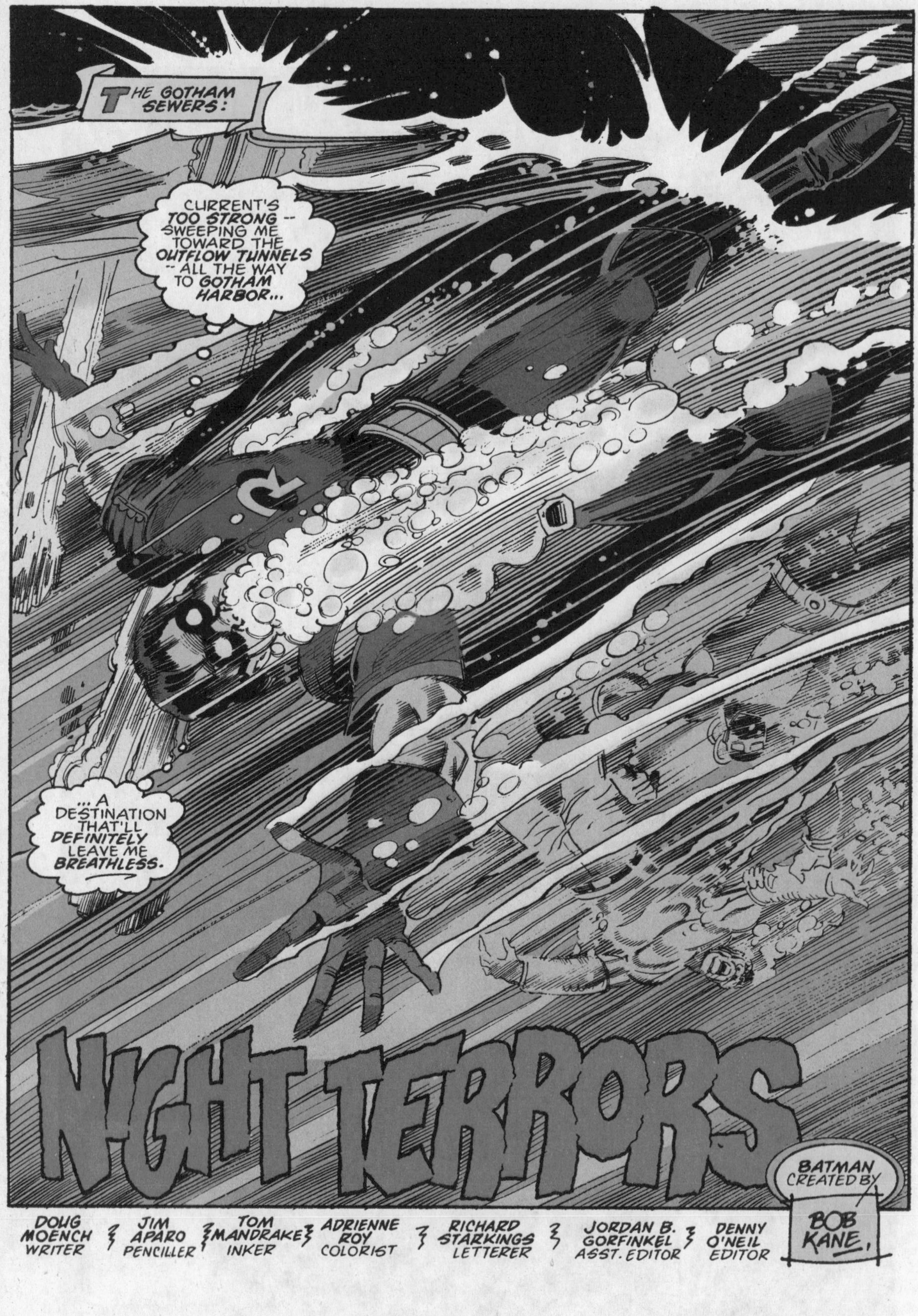
THE GOTHAM SEWERS:
CURRENT'S TOO STRONG -- SWEEPING ME TOWARD THE OUTFLOW TUNNELS -- ALL THE WAY TO GOTHAM HARBOR...
...A DESTINATION THAT'LL DEFINITELY LEAVE ME BREATHLESS.
NIGHT TERRORS
BATMAN CREATED BY BOB KANE
DOUG MOENCH WRITER
JIM APARO PENCILLER
TOM MANDRAKE INKER
ADRIENNE ROY COLORIST
RICHARD STARKINGS LETTERER
JORDAN B. GORFINKEL ASST. EDITOR
DENNY O'NEIL EDITOR

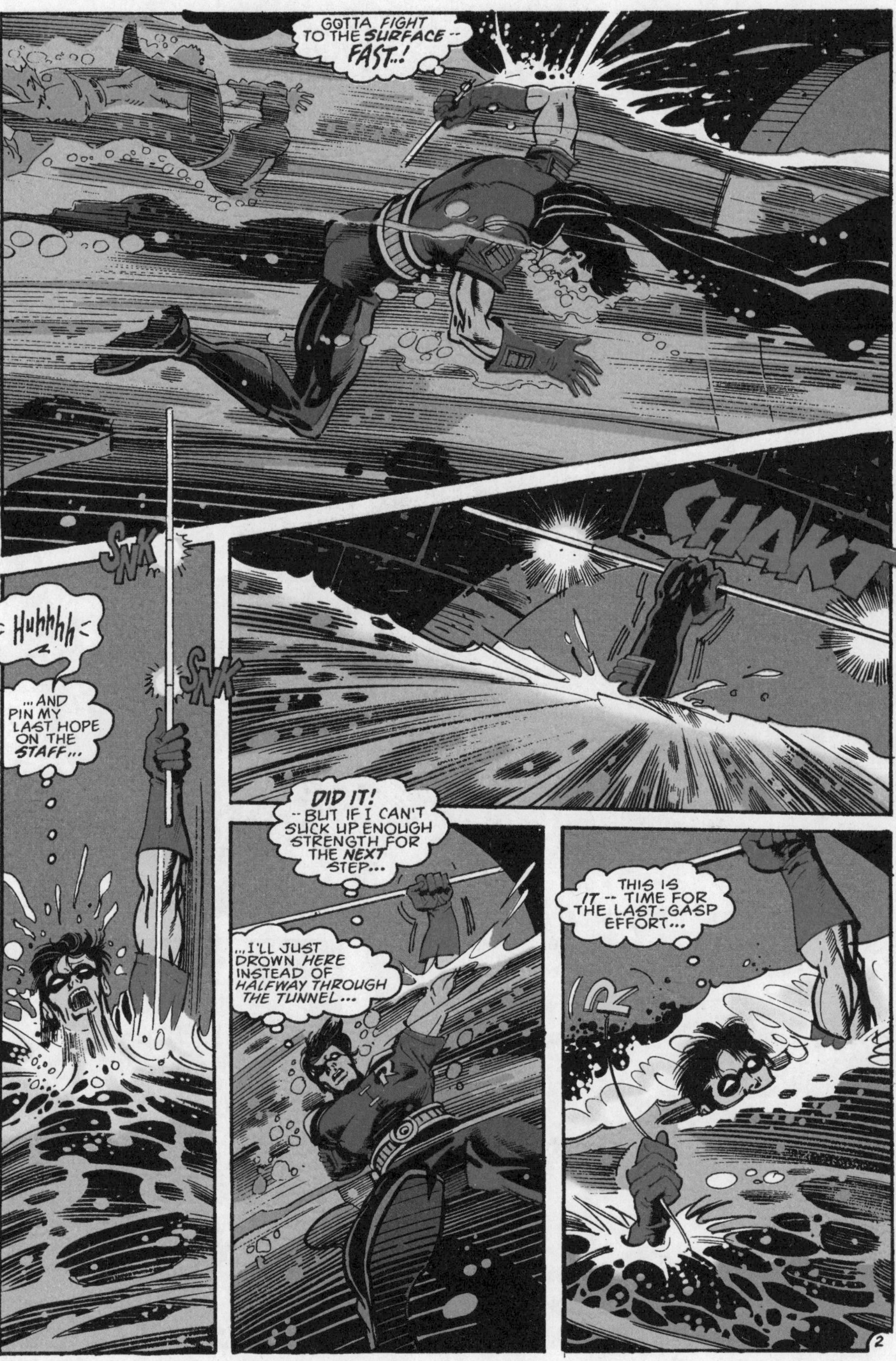
GOTTA FIGHT TO THE SURFACE -- FAST..!
SNK
Huhhhh
...AND PIN MY LAST HOPE ON THE STAFF...
SNK
CHAKT
DID IT! -- BUT IF I CAN'T SUCK UP ENOUGH STRENGTH FOR THE NEXT STEP...
...I'LL JUST DROWN HERE INSTEAD OF HALFWAY THROUGH THE TUNNEL...
THIS IS IT -- TIME FOR THE LAST-GASP EFFORT...
2

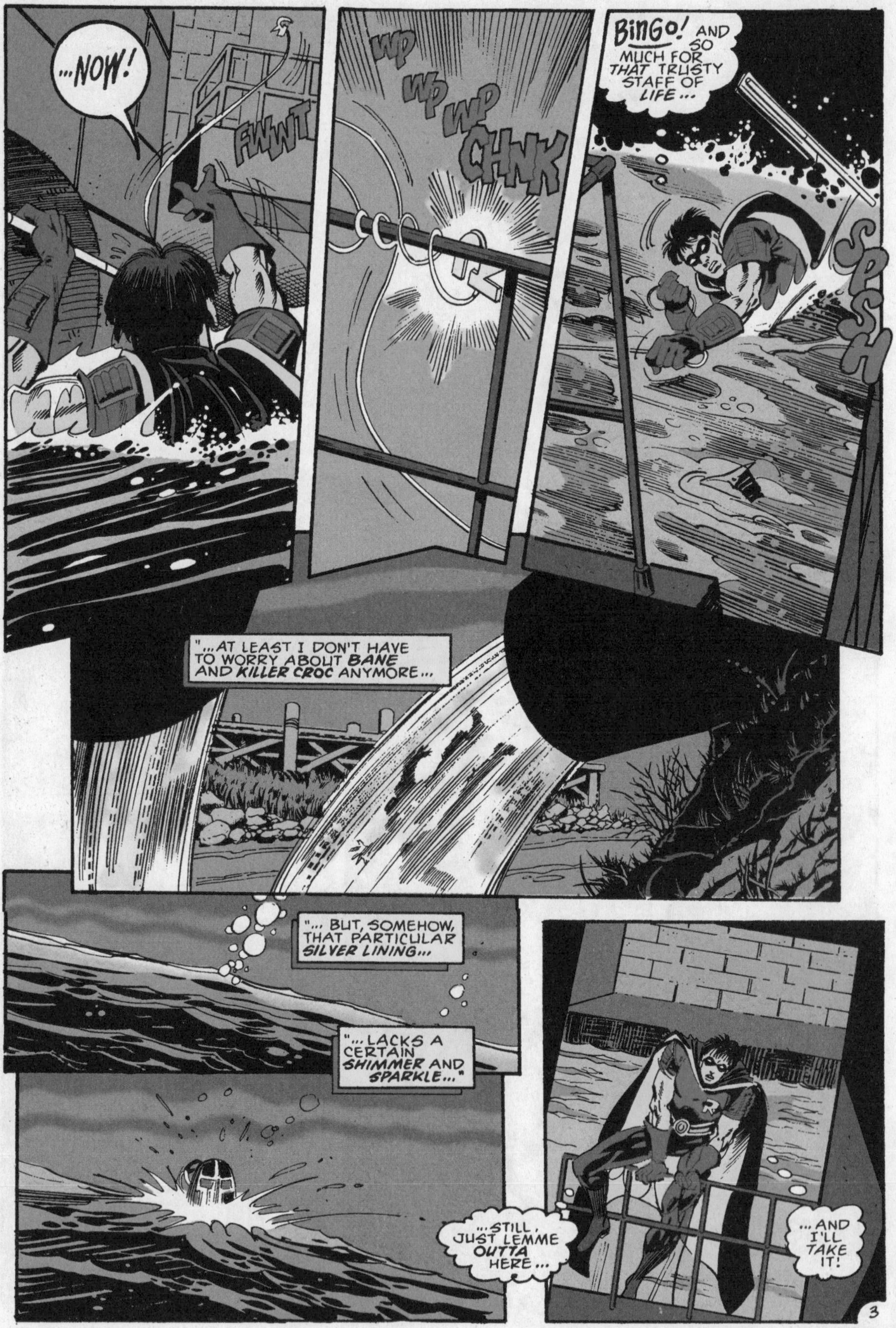
...NOW!
FWWT
WP
WP
WP
WP
CHNK
BINGO! AND SO MUCH FOR THAT TRUSTY STAFF OF LIFE...
SPSH
"...AT LEAST I DON'T HAVE TO WORRY ABOUT BANE AND KILLER CROC ANYMORE...
"... BUT, SOMEHOW, THAT PARTICULAR SILVER LINING...
"...LACKS A CERTAIN SHIMMER AND SPARKLE..."
...STILL, JUST LEMME OUTTA HERE...
...AND I'LL TAKE IT!
3

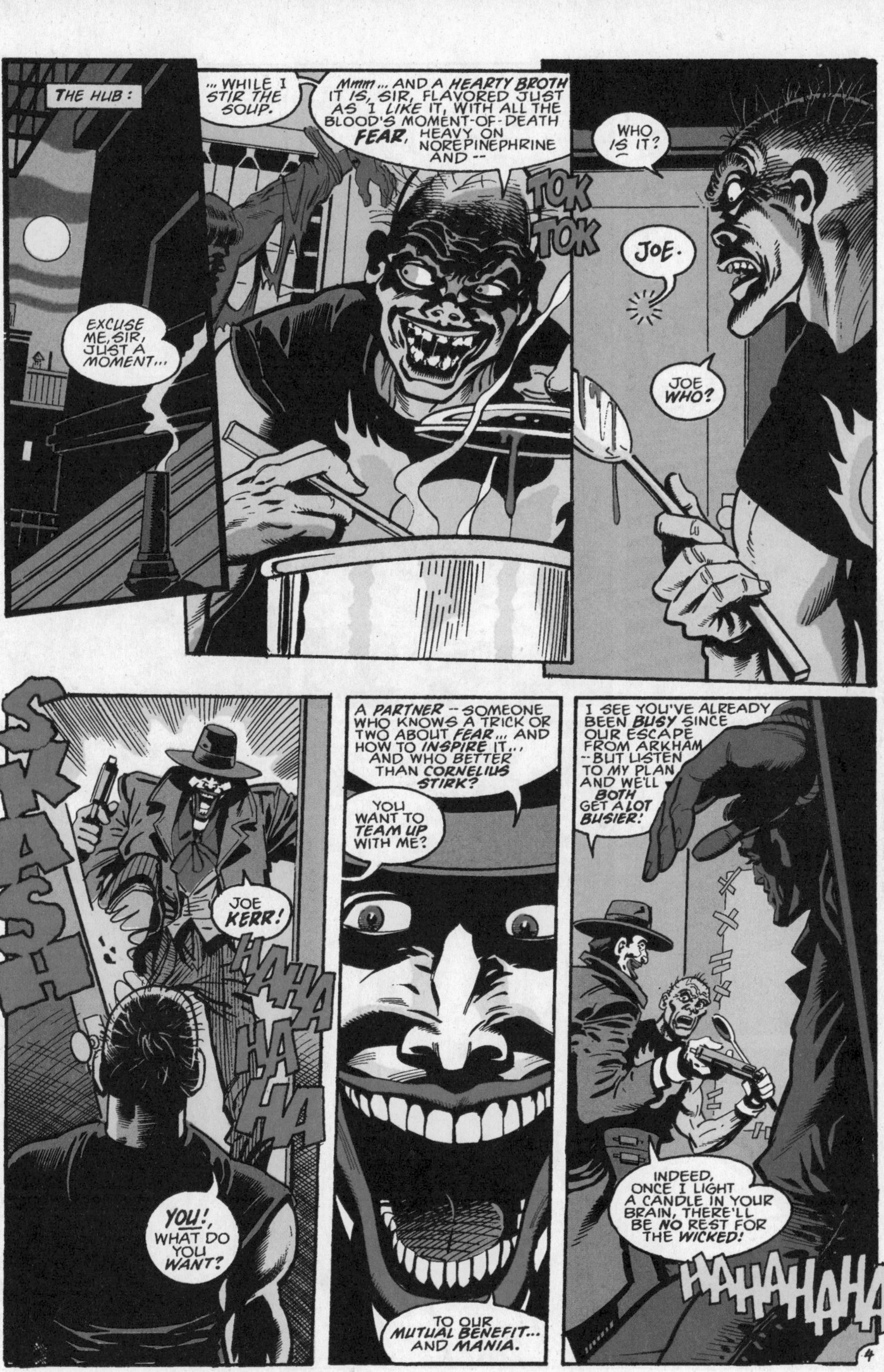
THE HUB:
EXCUSE ME, SIR, JUST A MOMENT...
...WHILE I STIR THE SOUP.
Mmm... AND A HEARTY BROTH IT IS, SIR, FLAVORED JUST AS I LIKE IT, WITH ALL THE BLOOD'S MOMENT-OF-DEATH FEAR, HEAVY ON NOREPINEPHRINE AND --
TOK TOK
WHO IS IT?
JOE.
JOE WHO?
SKASH
JOE KERR!
HAHA HA HA HA
YOU!, WHAT DO YOU WANT?
A PARTNER -- SOMEONE WHO KNOWS A TRICK OR TWO ABOUT FEAR... AND HOW TO INSPIRE IT... AND WHO BETTER THAN CORNELIUS STIRK?
YOU WANT TO TEAM UP WITH ME?
TO OUR MUTUAL BENEFIT... AND MANIA.
I SEE YOU'VE ALREADY BEEN BUSY SINCE OUR ESCAPE FROM ARKHAM -- BUT LISTEN TO MY PLAN AND WE'LL BOTH GET A LOT BUSIER!
INDEED, ONCE I LIGHT A CANDLE IN YOUR BRAIN, THERE'LL BE NO REST FOR THE WICKED!
HAHAHAHA
4

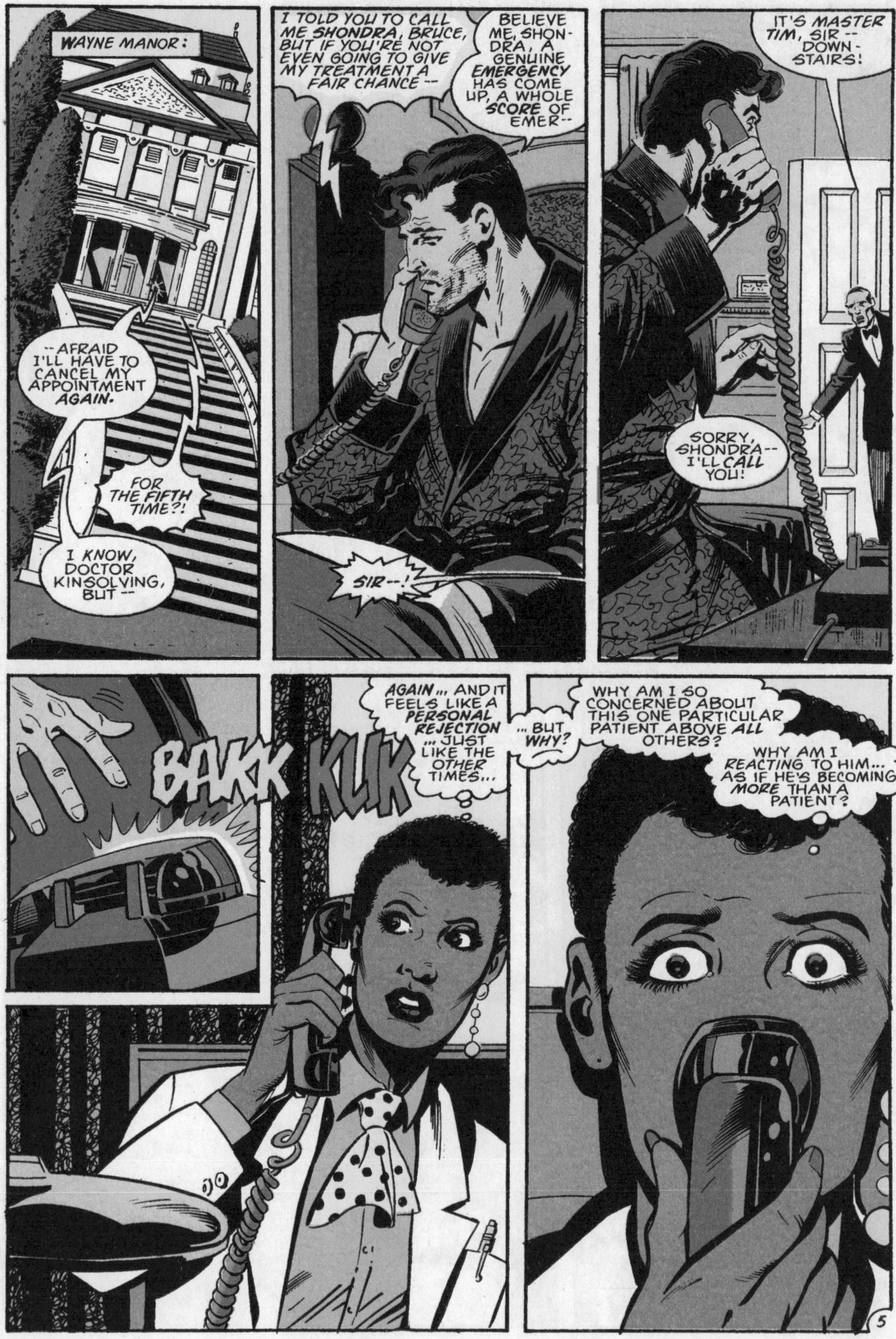
WAYNE MANOR:
--AFRAID I'LL HAVE TO CANCEL MY APPOINTMENT AGAIN.
FOR THE FIFTH TIME?!
I KNOW, DOCTOR KINSOLVING, BUT --
I TOLD YOU TO CALL ME SHONDRA, BRUCE, BUT IF YOU'RE NOT EVEN GOING TO GIVE MY TREATMENT A FAIR CHANCE --
BELIEVE ME, SHONDRA, A GENUINE EMERGENCY HAS COME UP, A WHOLE SCORE OF EMER--
SIR--!
IT'S MASTER TIM, SIR -- DOWNSTAIRS!
SORRY, SHONDRA-- I'LL CALL YOU!
BAKK KLIK
AGAIN... AND IT FEELS LIKE A PERSONAL REJECTION ... JUST LIKE THE OTHER TIMES...
...BUT WHY?
WHY AM I SO CONCERNED ABOUT THIS ONE PARTICULAR PATIENT ABOVE ALL OTHERS?
WHY AM I REACTING TO HIM... AS IF HE'S BECOMING MORE THAN A PATIENT?
5

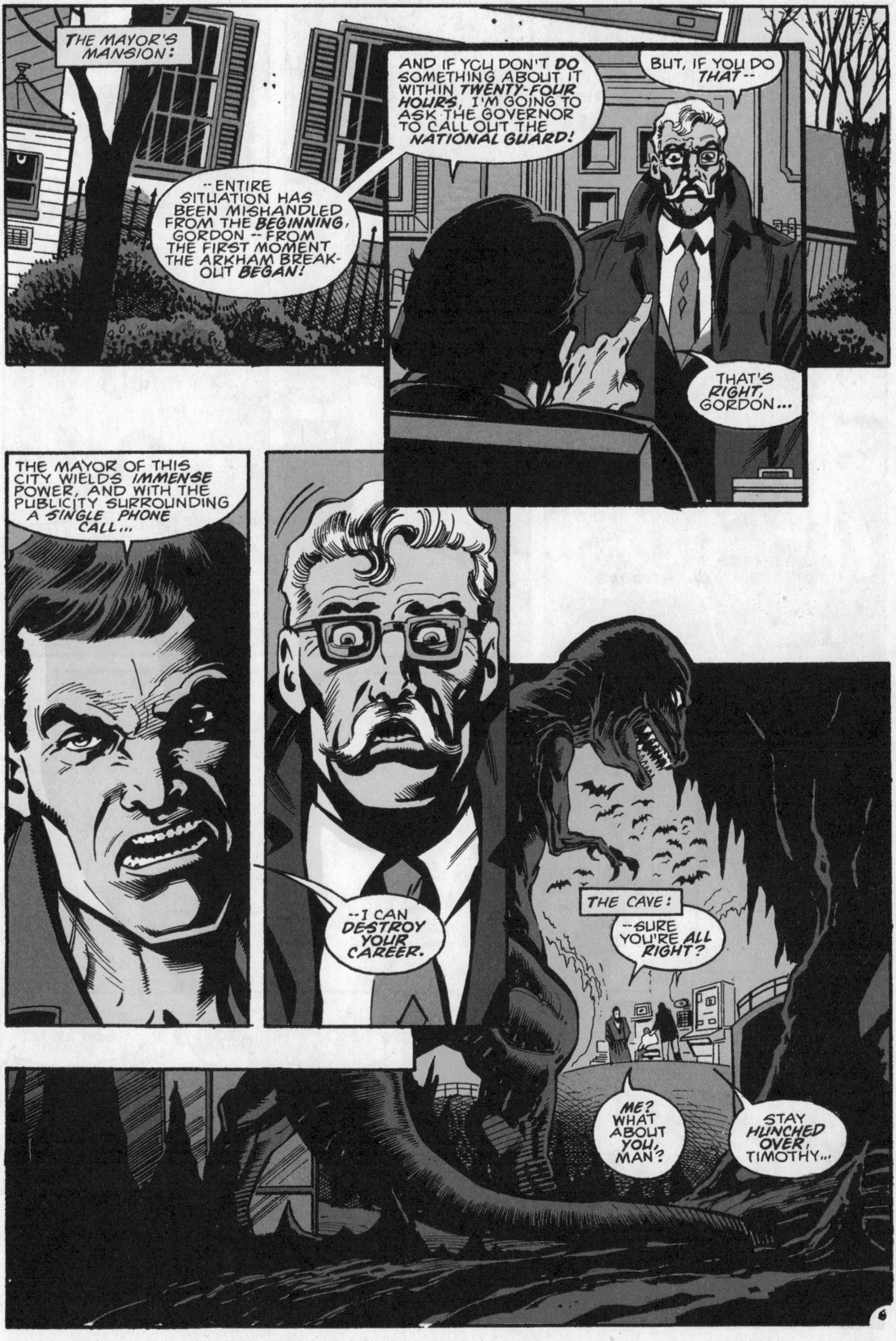
THE MAYOR'S MANSION:
--ENTIRE SITUATION HAS BEEN MISHANDLED FROM THE BEGINNING, GORDON -- FROM THE FIRST MOMENT THE ARKHAM BREAKOUT BEGAN!
AND IF YOU DON'T DO SOMETHING ABOUT IT WITHIN TWENTY-FOUR HOURS, I'M GOING TO ASK THE GOVERNOR TO CALL OUT THE NATIONAL GUARD!
BUT, IF YOU DO THAT --
THAT'S RIGHT, GORDON...
THE MAYOR OF THIS CITY WIELDS IMMENSE POWER, AND WITH THE PUBLICITY SURROUNDING A SINGLE PHONE CALL...
--I CAN DESTROY YOUR CAREER.
THE CAVE:
--SURE YOU'RE ALL RIGHT?
ME? WHAT ABOUT YOU, MAN?
STAY HUNCHED OVER, TIMOTHY...
6

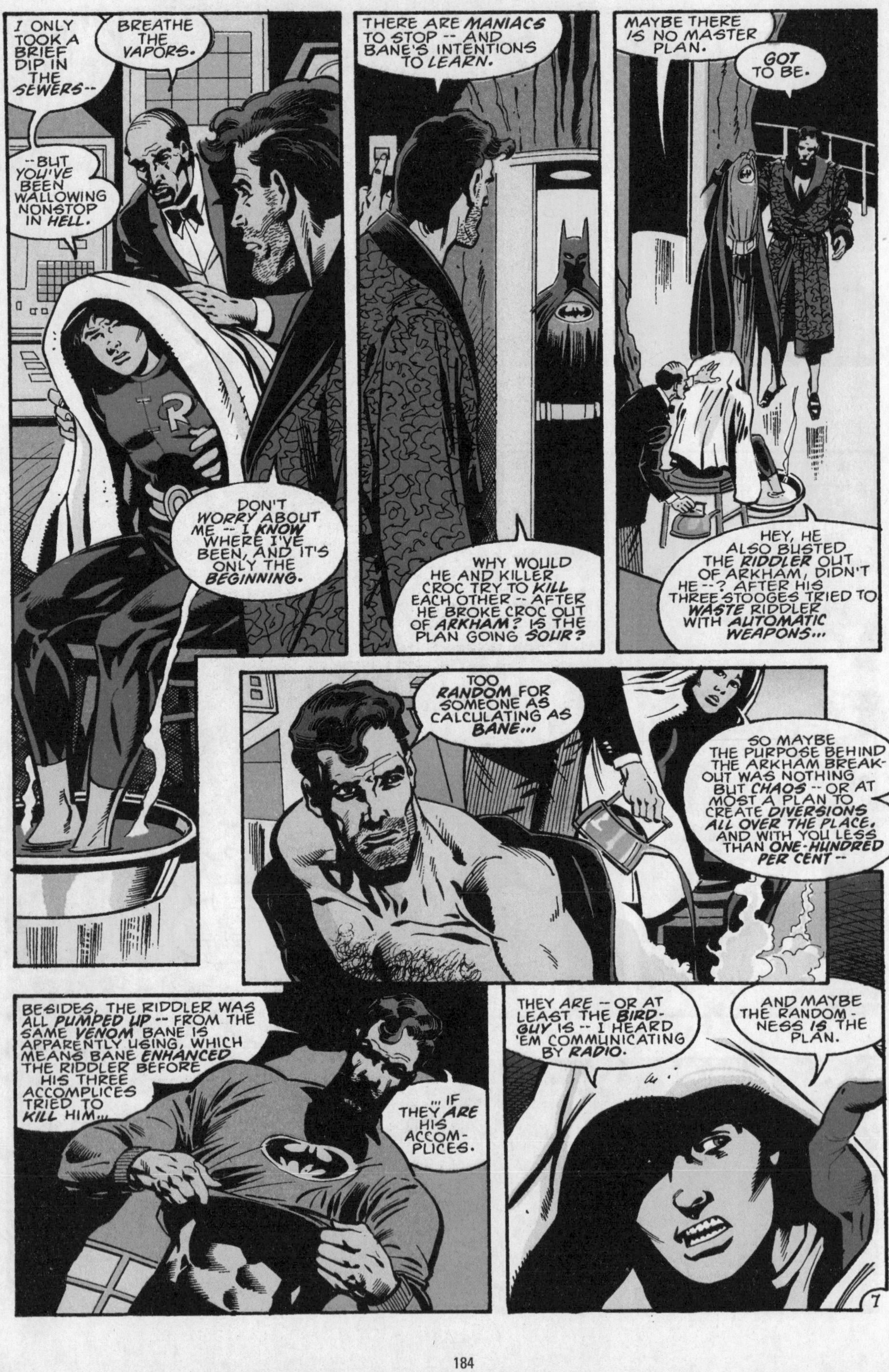
I ONLY TOOK A BRIEF DIP IN THE SEWERS--
BREATHE THE VAPORS.
--BUT YOU'VE BEEN WALLOWING NONSTOP IN HELL.
DON'T WORRY ABOUT ME -- I KNOW WHERE I'VE BEEN, AND IT'S ONLY THE BEGINNING.
THERE ARE MANIACS TO STOP -- AND BANE'S INTENTIONS TO LEARN.
WHY WOULD HE AND KILLER CROC TRY TO KILL EACH OTHER -- AFTER HE BROKE CROC OUT OF ARKHAM? IS THE PLAN GOING SOUR?
MAYBE THERE IS NO MASTER PLAN.
GOT TO BE.
HEY, HE ALSO BUSTED THE RIDDLER OUT OF ARKHAM, DIDN'T HE --? AFTER HIS THREE STOOGES TRIED TO WASTE RIDDLER WITH AUTOMATIC WEAPONS...
TOO RANDOM FOR SOMEONE AS CALCULATING AS BANE...
SO MAYBE THE PURPOSE BEHIND THE ARKHAM BREAK-OUT WAS NOTHING BUT CHAOS -- OR AT MOST A PLAN TO CREATE DIVERSIONS ALL OVER THE PLACE, AND WITH YOU LESS THAN ONE-HUNDRED PER CENT --
BESIDES, THE RIDDLER WAS ALL PUMPED UP -- FROM THE SAME VENOM BANE IS APPARENTLY USING, WHICH MEANS BANE ENHANCED THE RIDDLER BEFORE HIS THREE ACCOMPLICES TRIED TO KILL HIM...
...IF THEY ARE HIS ACCOMPLICES.
THEY ARE -- OR AT LEAST THE BIRD-GUY IS -- I HEARD 'EM COMMUNICATING BY RADIO.
AND MAYBE THE RANDOMNESS IS THE PLAN.
7

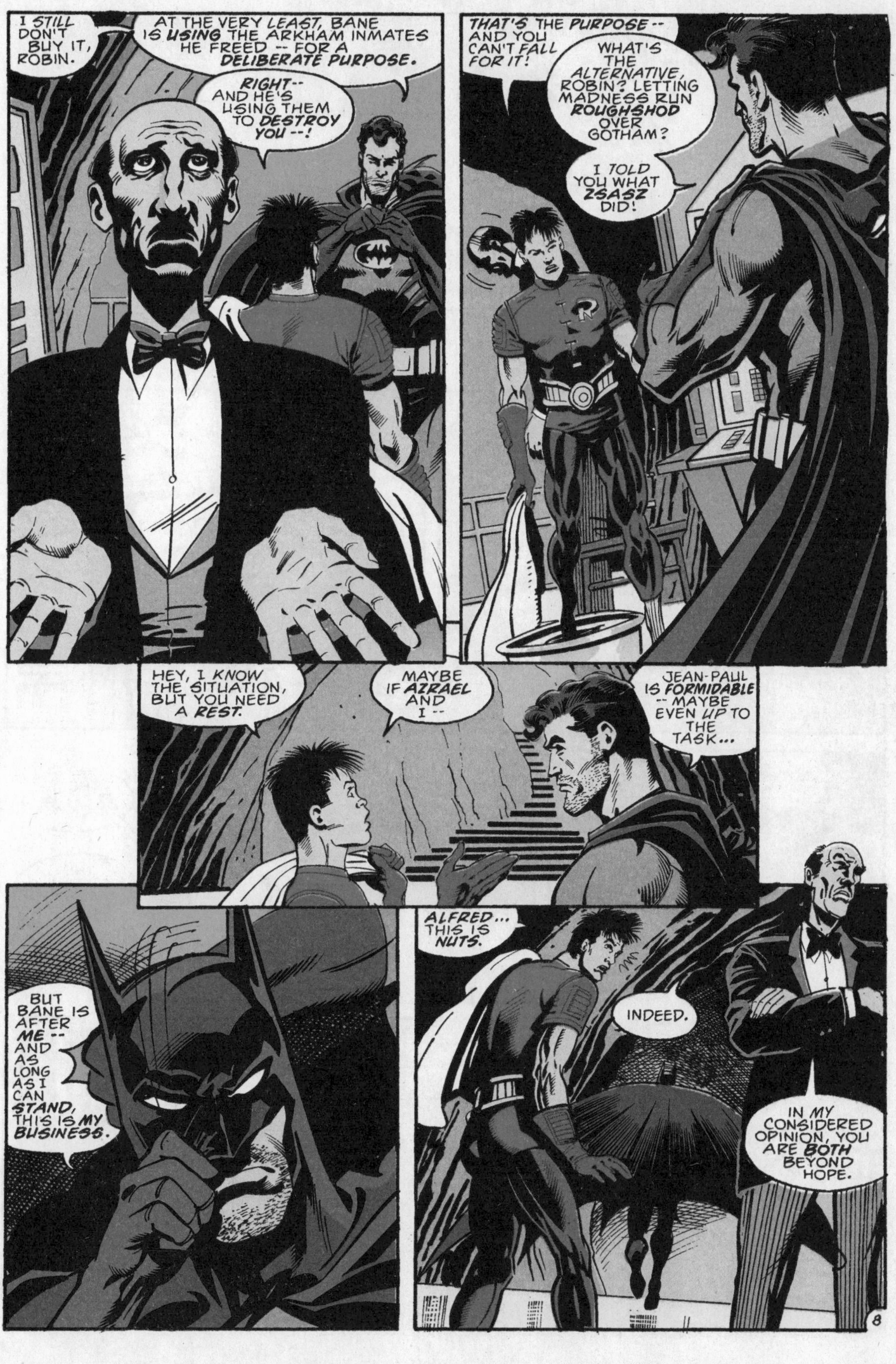
I STILL DON'T BUY IT, ROBIN.
AT THE VERY LEAST, BANE IS USING THE ARKHAM INMATES HE FREED -- FOR A DELIBERATE PURPOSE.
RIGHT-- AND HE'S USING THEM TO DESTROY YOU --!
THAT'S THE PURPOSE -- AND YOU CAN'T FALL FOR IT!
WHAT'S THE ALTERNATIVE, ROBIN? LETTING MADNESS RUN ROUGHSHOD OVER GOTHAM?
I TOLD YOU WHAT ZSASZ DID!
HEY, I KNOW THE SITUATION, BUT YOU NEED A REST.
MAYBE IF AZRAEL AND I --
JEAN-PAUL IS FORMIDABLE -- MAYBE EVEN UP TO THE TASK...
BUT BANE IS AFTER ME -- AND AS LONG AS I CAN STAND, THIS IS MY BUSINESS.
ALFRED... THIS IS NUTS.
INDEED.
IN MY CONSIDERED OPINION, YOU ARE BOTH BEYOND HOPE.
8

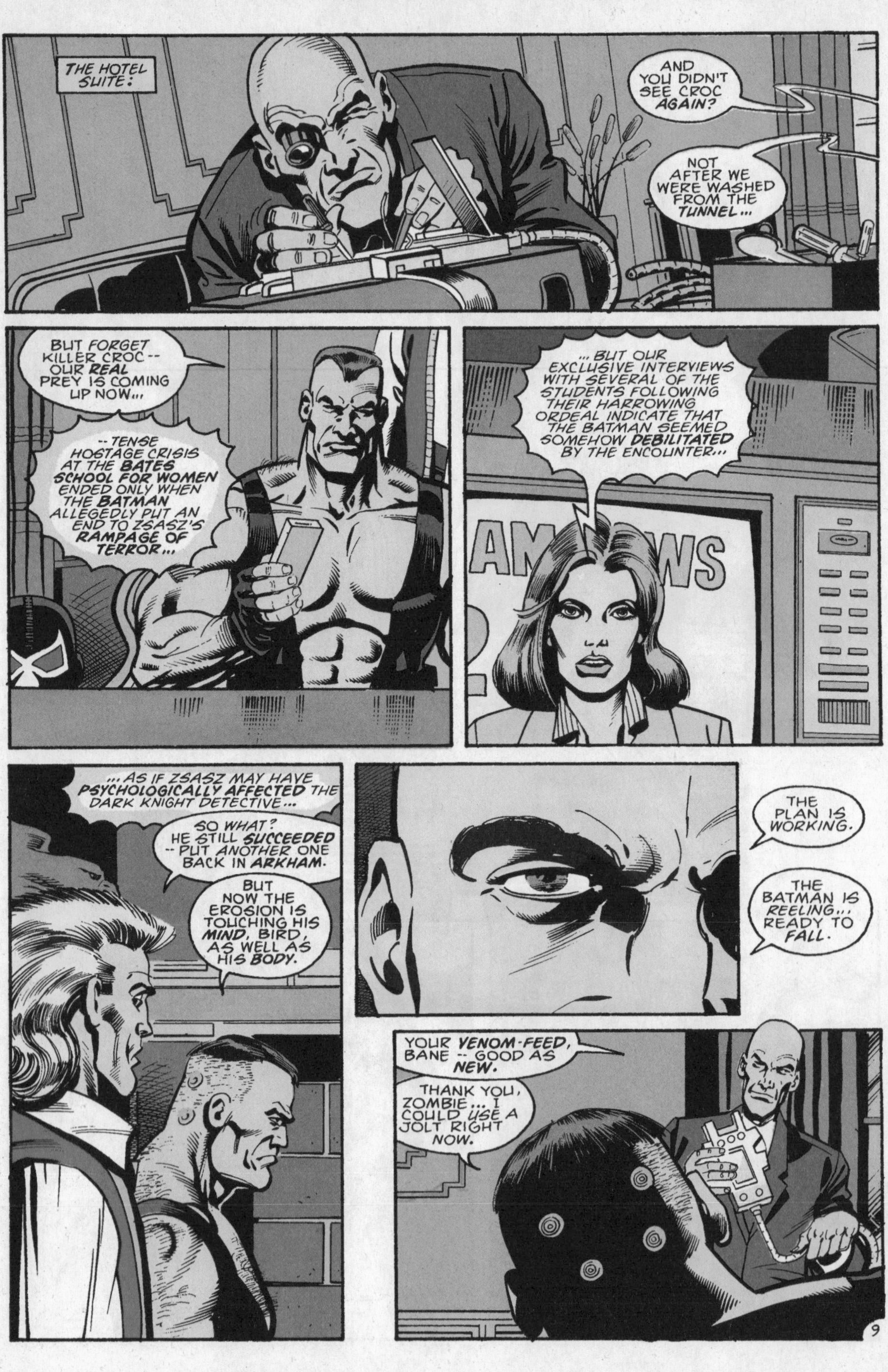

THE HOTEL SUITE:
AND YOU DIDN'T SEE CROC AGAIN?
NOT AFTER WE WERE WASHED FROM THE TUNNEL...
BUT FORGET KILLER CROC -- OUR REAL PREY IS COMING UP NOW...
-- TENSE HOSTAGE CRISIS AT THE BATES SCHOOL FOR WOMEN ENDED ONLY WHEN THE BATMAN ALLEGEDLY PUT AN END TO ZSASZ'S RAMPAGE OF TERROR...
... BUT OUR EXCLUSIVE INTERVIEWS WITH SEVERAL OF THE STUDENTS FOLLOWING THEIR HARROWING ORDEAL INDICATE THAT THE BATMAN SEEMED SOMEHOW DEBILITATED BY THE ENCOUNTER...
... AS IF ZSASZ MAY HAVE PSYCHOLOGICALLY AFFECTED THE DARK KNIGHT DETECTIVE...
SO WHAT? HE STILL SUCCEEDED -- PUT ANOTHER ONE BACK IN ARKHAM.
BUT NOW THE EROSION IS TOUCHING HIS MIND, BIRD, AS WELL AS HIS BODY.
THE PLAN IS WORKING.
THE BATMAN IS REELING... READY TO FALL.
YOUR VENOM-FEED, BANE -- GOOD AS NEW.
THANK YOU, ZOMBIE... I COULD USE A JOLT RIGHT NOW.
9

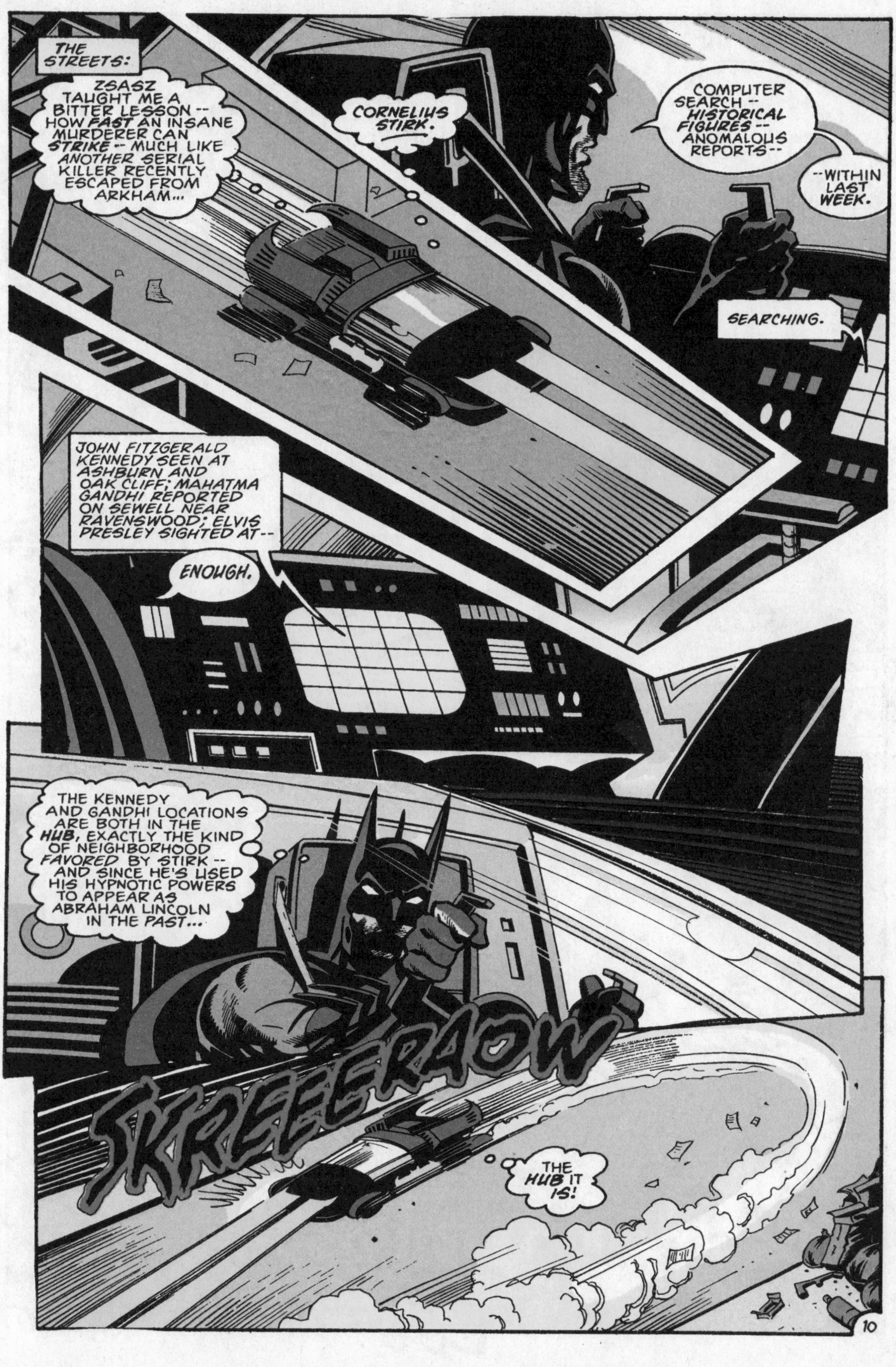
THE STREETS:
ZSASZ TAUGHT ME A BITTER LESSON -- HOW FAST AN INSANE MURDERER CAN STRIKE -- MUCH LIKE ANOTHER SERIAL KILLER RECENTLY ESCAPED FROM ARKHAM...
CORNELIUS STIRK.
COMPUTER SEARCH -- HISTORICAL FIGURES -- ANOMALOUS REPORTS --
--WITHIN LAST WEEK.
SEARCHING.
JOHN FITZGERALD KENNEDY SEEN AT ASHBURN AND OAK CLIFF; MAHATMA GANDHI REPORTED ON SEWELL NEAR RAVENSWOOD; ELVIS PRESLEY SIGHTED AT--
ENOUGH.
THE KENNEDY AND GANDHI LOCATIONS ARE BOTH IN THE HUB, EXACTLY THE KIND OF NEIGHBORHOOD FAVORED BY STIRK -- AND SINCE HE'S USED HIS HYPNOTIC POWERS TO APPEAR AS ABRAHAM LINCOLN IN THE PAST...
SKREEERAOW
THE HUB IT IS!
10

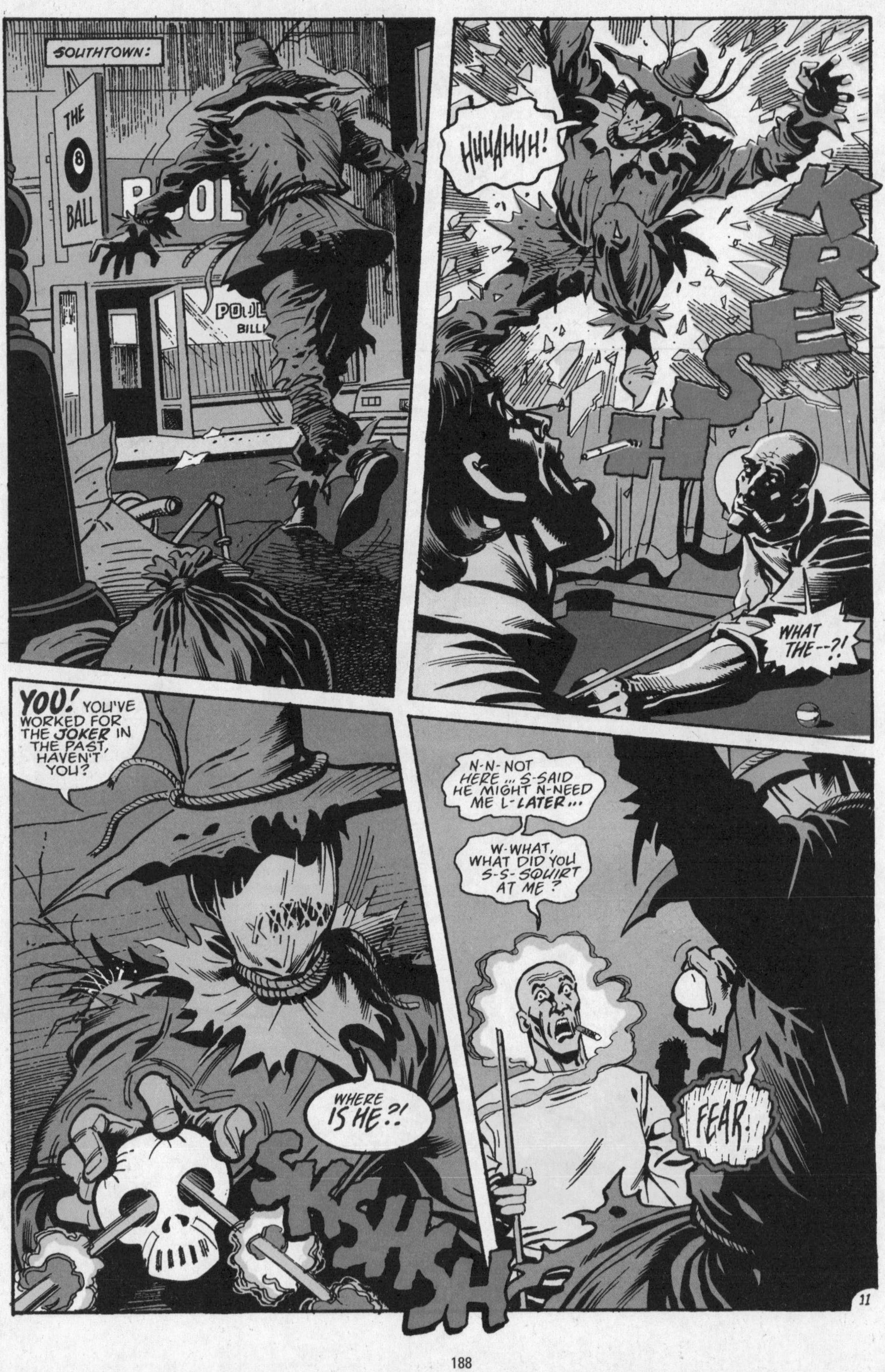

SOUTHTOWN:
THE 8 BALL
POOL
HUUAHHH!
KRESSH
WHAT THE--?!
YOU! YOU'VE WORKED FOR THE JOKER IN THE PAST, HAVEN'T YOU?
WHERE IS HE?!
SSSHHH
N-N-NOT HERE... S-SAID HE MIGHT N-NEED ME L-LATER...
W-WHAT, WHAT DID YOU S-S-SQUIRT AT ME?
FEAR!
11

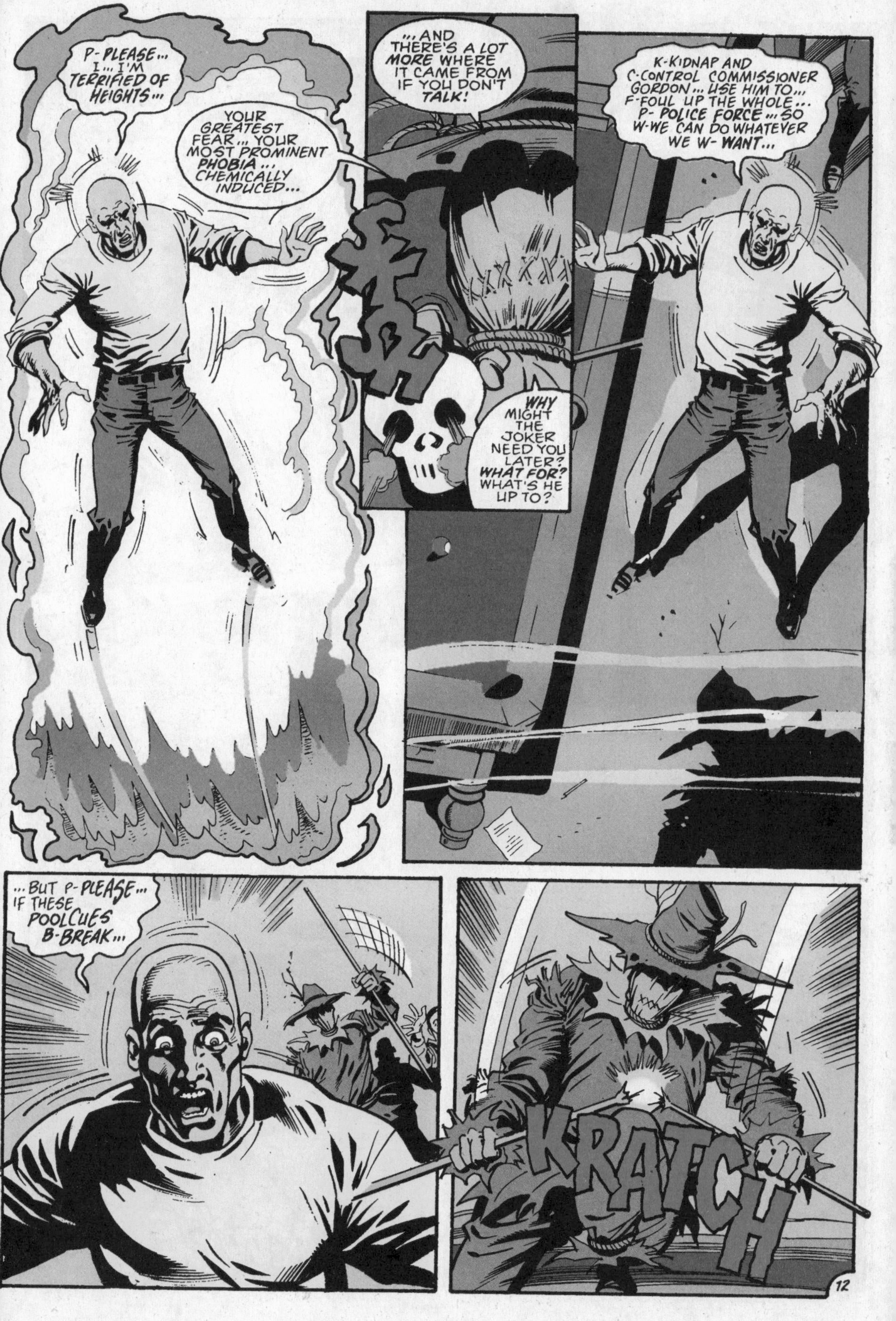
P-PLEASE... I... I'M TERRIFIED OF HEIGHTS...
YOUR GREATEST FEAR... YOUR MOST PROMINENT PHOBIA... CHEMICALLY INDUCED...
..., AND THERE'S A LOT MORE WHERE IT CAME FROM IF YOU DON'T TALK!
WHY MIGHT THE JOKER NEED YOU LATER? WHAT FOR? WHAT'S HE UP TO?
K-KIDNAP AND C-CONTROL COMMISSIONER GORDON... USE HIM TO... F-FOUL UP THE WHOLE... P-POLICE FORCE... SO W-WE CAN DO WHATEVER WE W-WANT...
... BUT P-PLEASE... IF THESE POOLCUES B-BREAK...
KRATCH
12

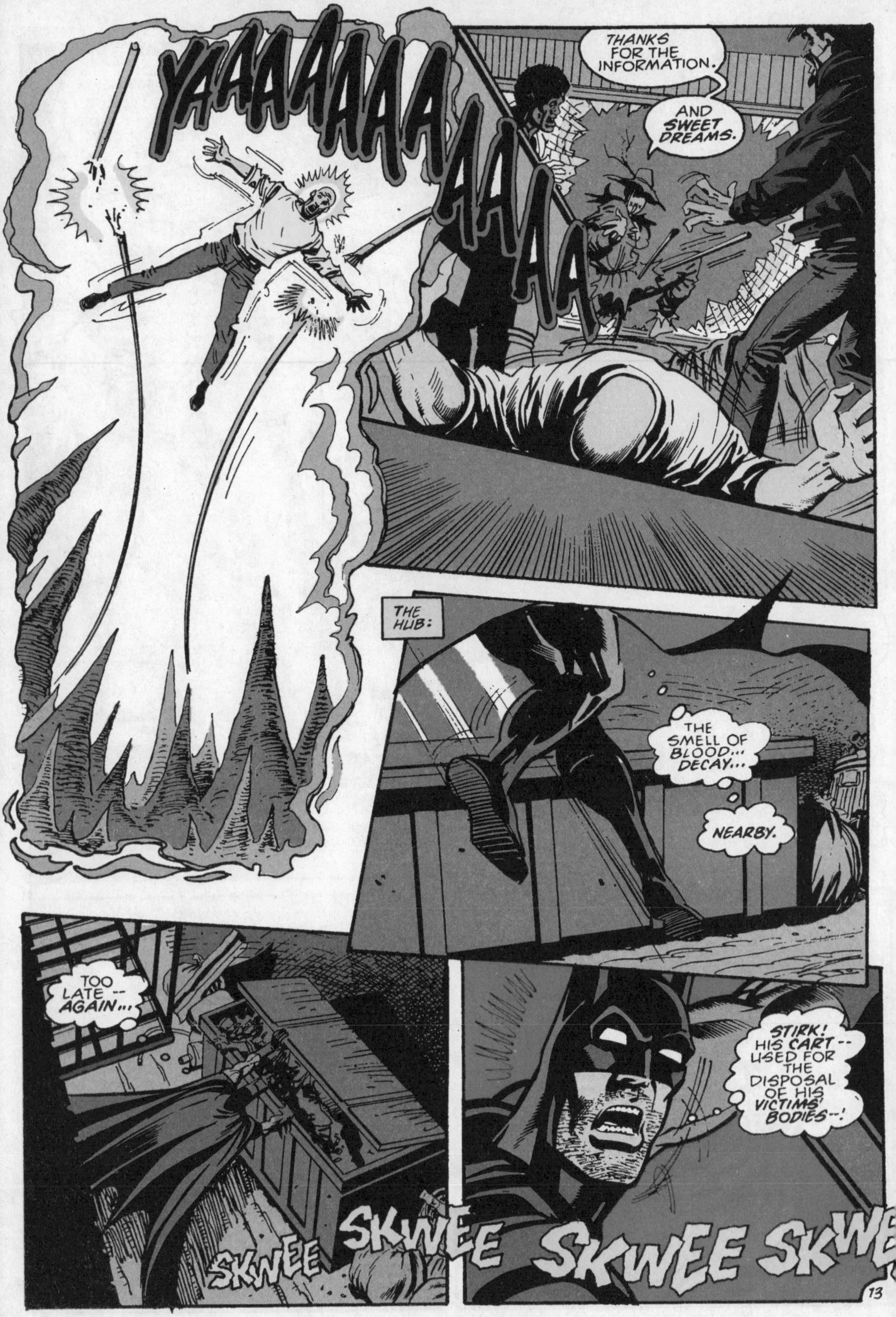
YAAAAAAAAAAAAA
THANKS FOR THE INFORMATION.
AND SWEET DREAMS.
THE HUB:
THE SMELL OF BLOOD... DECAY...
NEARBY.
TOO LATE -- AGAIN...
STIRK! HIS CART -- USED FOR THE DISPOSAL OF HIS VICTIMS' BODIES--!
SKWEE SKWEE
SKWEE SKWE
13

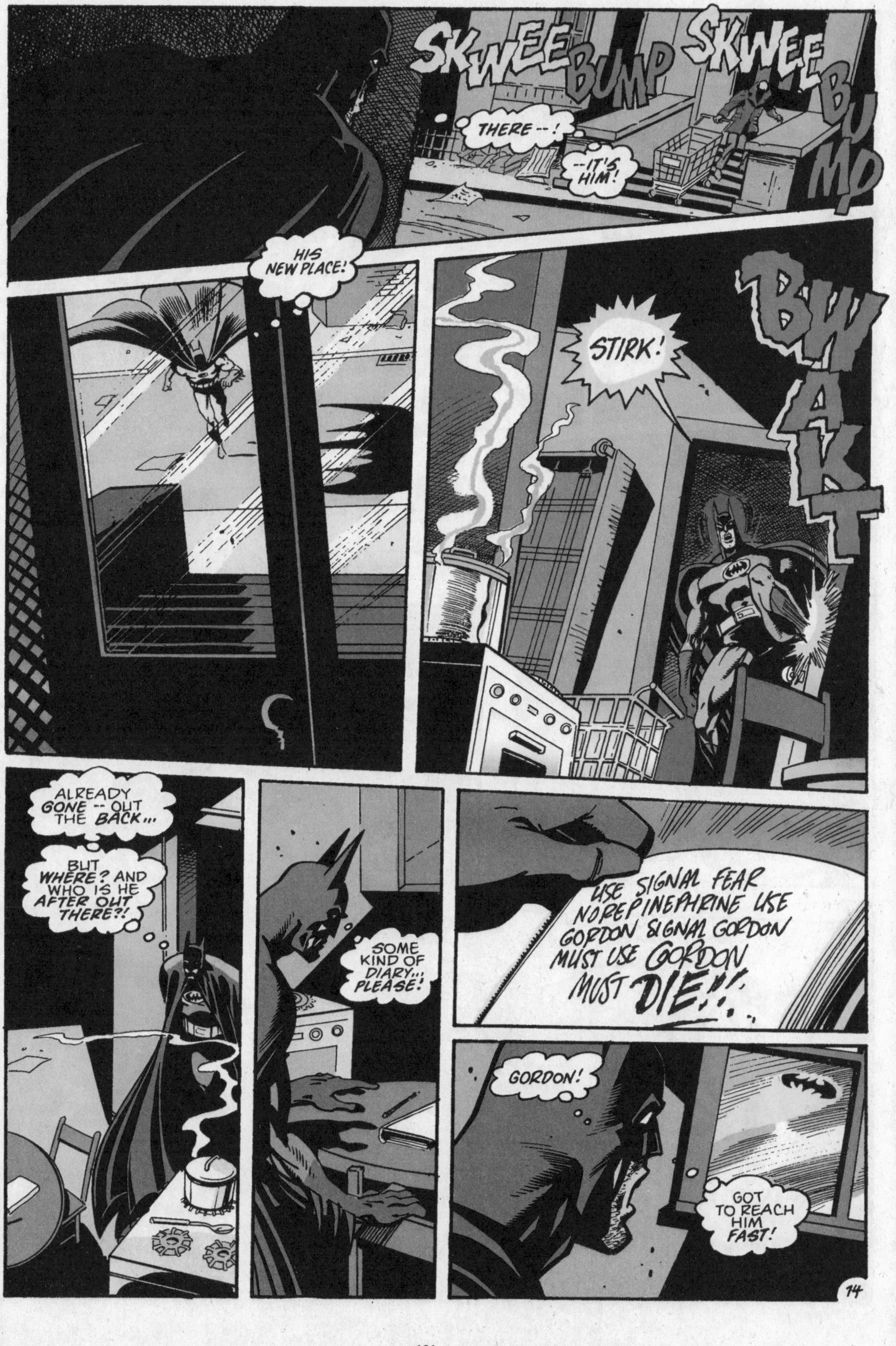
SKWEE BUMP SKWEE BUMP
THERE--!
--IT'S HIM!
HIS NEW PLACE!
BWAKT
STIRK!
ALREADY GONE -- OUT THE BACK...
BUT WHERE? AND WHO IS HE AFTER OUT THERE?!
SOME KIND OF DIARY... PLEASE!
USE SIGNAL FEAR NOREPINEPHRINE USE GORDON SIGNAL GORDON MUST USE GORDON MUST DIE!!!
GORDON!
GOT TO REACH HIM FAST!
14

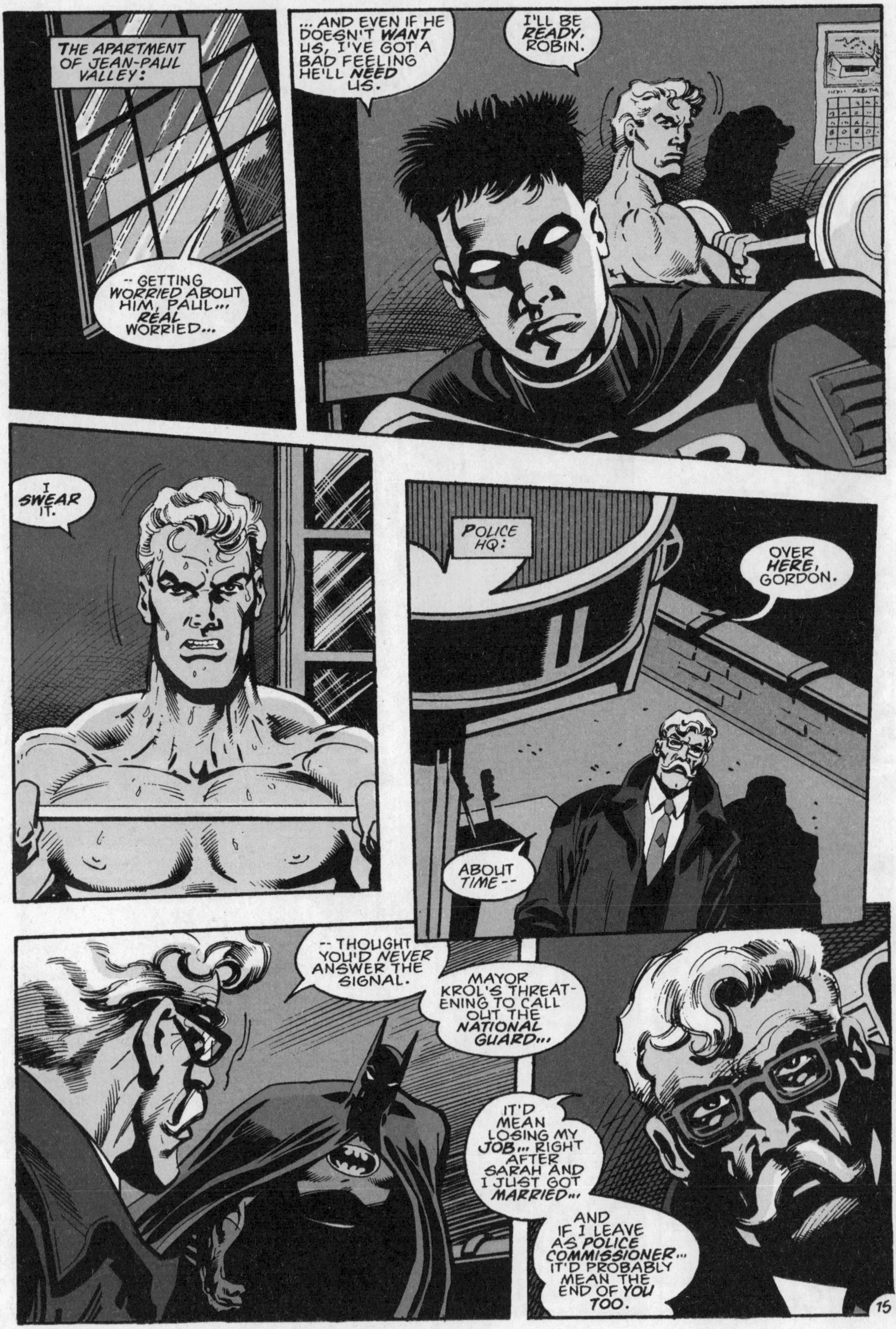
THE APARTMENT OF JEAN-PAUL VALLEY:
-- GETTING WORRIED ABOUT HIM, PAUL... REAL WORRIED...
... AND EVEN IF HE DOESN'T WANT US, I'VE GOT A BAD FEELING HE'LL NEED US.
I'LL BE READY, ROBIN.
I SWEAR IT.
POLICE HQ:
OVER HERE, GORDON.
ABOUT TIME --
-- THOUGHT YOU'D NEVER ANSWER THE SIGNAL.
MAYOR KROL'S THREATENING TO CALL OUT THE NATIONAL GUARD...
IT'D MEAN LOSING MY JOB... RIGHT AFTER SARAH AND I JUST GOT MARRIED...
AND IF I LEAVE AS POLICE COMMISSIONER... IT'D PROBABLY MEAN THE END OF YOU TOO.
15

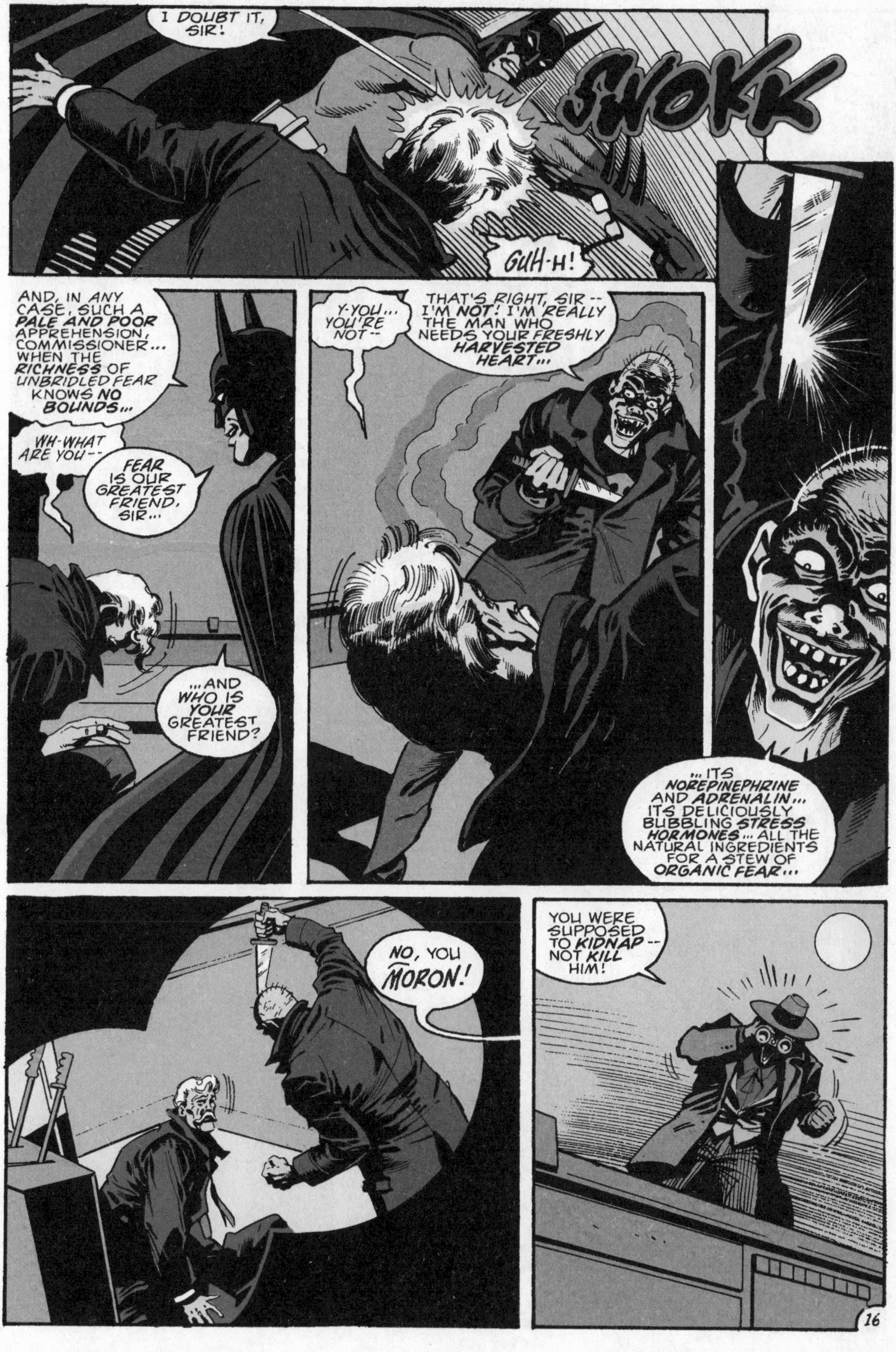
I DOUBT IT, SIR!
SWOKK
GUH-H!
AND, IN ANY CASE, SUCH A PALE AND POOR APPREHENSION, COMMISSIONER... WHEN THE RICHNESS OF UNBRIDLED FEAR KNOWS NO BOUNDS...
WH-WHAT ARE YOU--
FEAR IS OUR GREATEST FRIEND, SIR...
...AND WHO IS YOUR GREATEST FRIEND?
Y-YOU... YOU'RE NOT--
THAT'S RIGHT, SIR -- I'M NOT! I'M REALLY THE MAN WHO NEEDS YOUR FRESHLY HARVESTED HEART...
...ITS NOREPINEPHRINE AND ADRENALIN... ITS DELICIOUSLY BUBBLING STRESS HORMONES... ALL THE NATURAL INGREDIENTS FOR A STEW OF ORGANIC FEAR...
NO, YOU MORON!
YOU WERE SUPPOSED TO KIDNAP -- NOT KILL HIM!
16

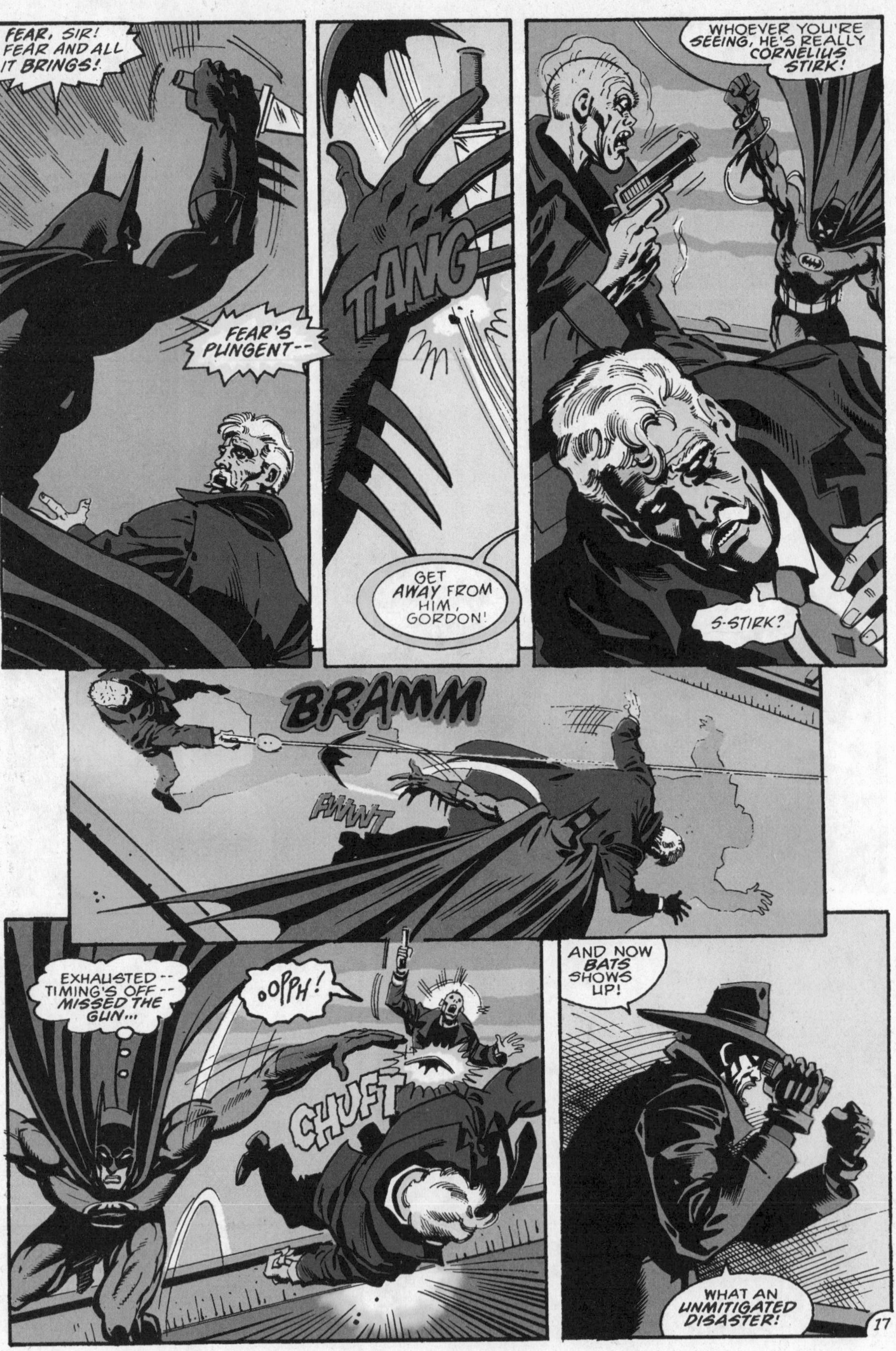
FEAR, SIR! FEAR AND ALL IT BRINGS!
FEAR'S PUNGENT--
TANG
GET AWAY FROM HIM, GORDON!
WHOEVER YOU'RE SEEING, HE'S REALLY CORNELIUS STIRK!
S-STIRK?
BRAMM
FWWNT
EXHAUSTED-- TIMING'S OFF-- MISSED THE GUN...
OOPPH!
CHUFT
AND NOW BATS SHOWS UP!
WHAT AN UNMITIGATED DISASTER!
17

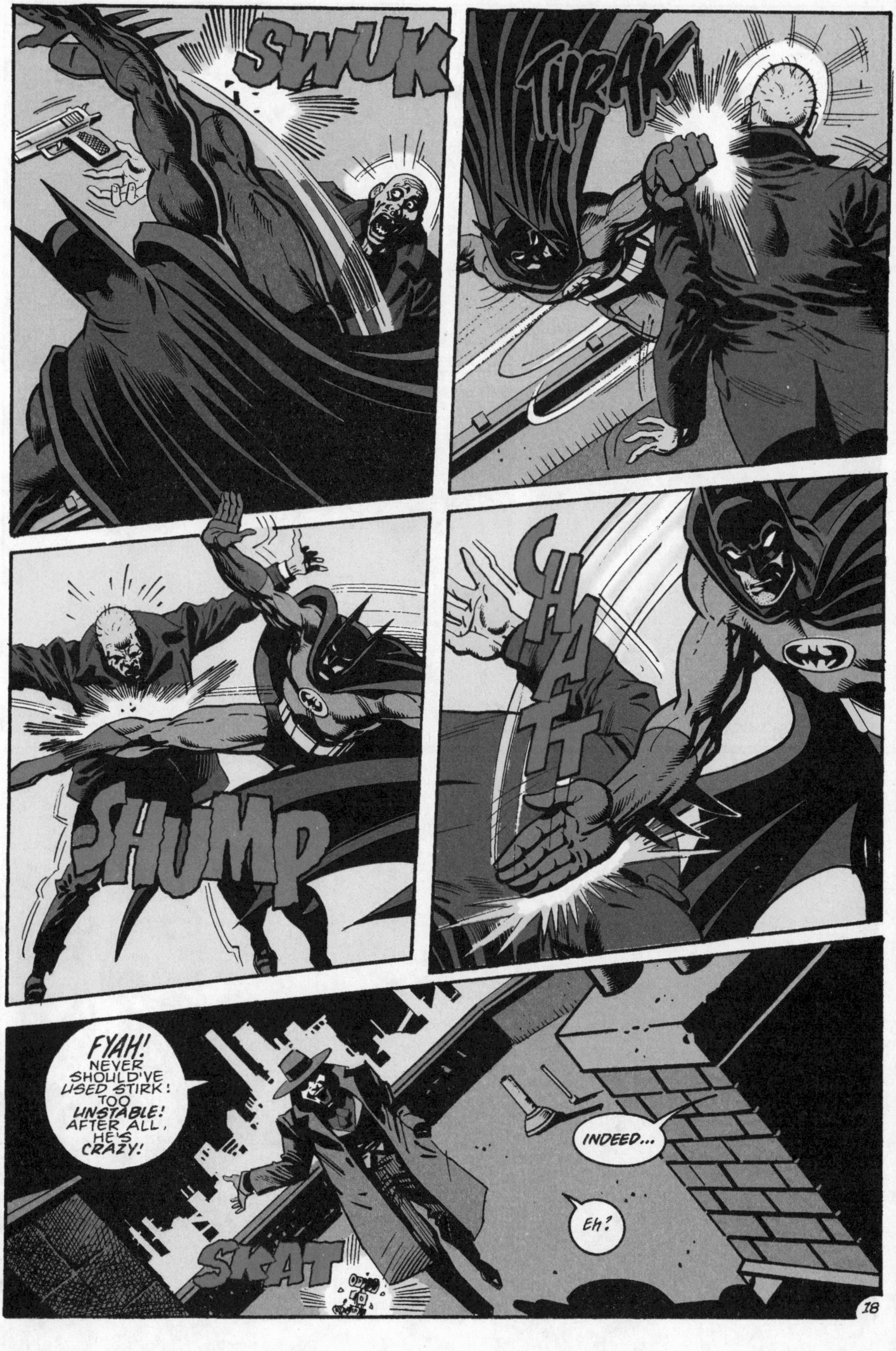

SWUK
THRAK
SHUMP
CHATT
FYAH! NEVER SHOULD'VE USED STIRK! TOO UNSTABLE! AFTER ALL, HE'S CRAZY!
INDEED...
Eh?
SKAT
18

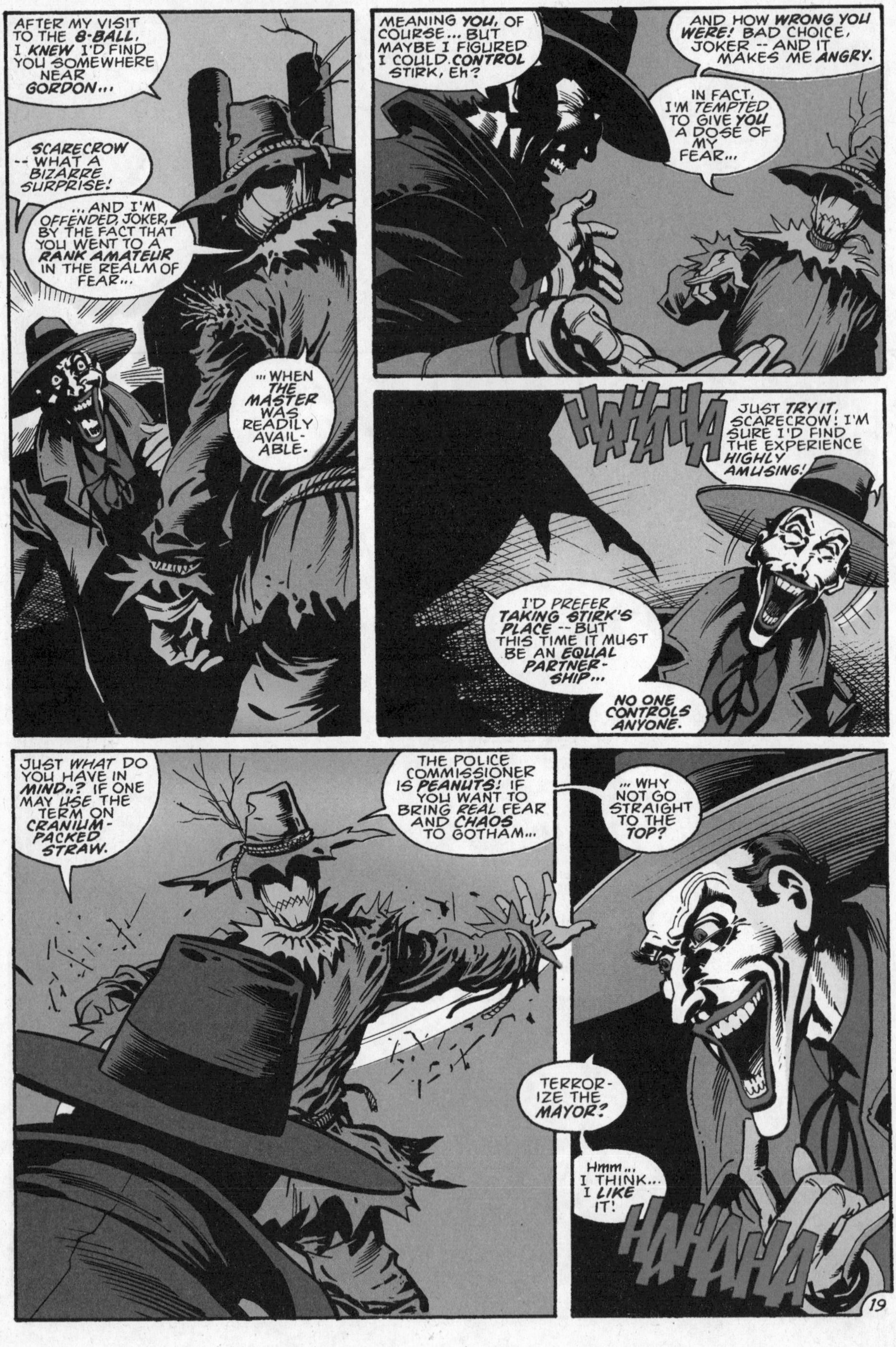

AFTER MY VISIT TO THE 8-BALL, I KNEW I'D FIND YOU SOMEWHERE NEAR GORDON...
SCARECROW -- WHAT A BIZARRE SURPRISE!
...AND I'M OFFENDED, JOKER, BY THE FACT THAT YOU WENT TO A RANK AMATEUR IN THE REALM OF FEAR...
...WHEN THE MASTER WAS READILY AVAIL-ABLE.
MEANING YOU, OF COURSE... BUT MAYBE I FIGURED I COULD CONTROL STIRK, Eh?
AND HOW WRONG YOU WERE! BAD CHOICE, JOKER -- AND IT MAKES ME ANGRY.
IN FACT, I'M TEMPTED TO GIVE YOU A DOSE OF MY FEAR...
HAHAHA
JUST TRY IT, SCARECROW! I'M SURE I'D FIND THE EXPERIENCE HIGHLY AMUSING!
I'D PREFER TAKING STIRK'S PLACE -- BUT THIS TIME IT MUST BE AN EQUAL PARTNER-SHIP...
NO ONE CONTROLS ANYONE.
JUST WHAT DO YOU HAVE IN MIND..? IF ONE MAY USE THE TERM ON CRANIUM-PACKED STRAW.
THE POLICE COMMISSIONER IS PEANUTS! IF YOU WANT TO BRING REAL FEAR AND CHAOS TO GOTHAM...
...WHY NOT GO STRAIGHT TO THE TOP?
TERROR-IZE THE MAYOR?
Hmm... I THINK... I LIKE IT!
HAHAHAHA
19

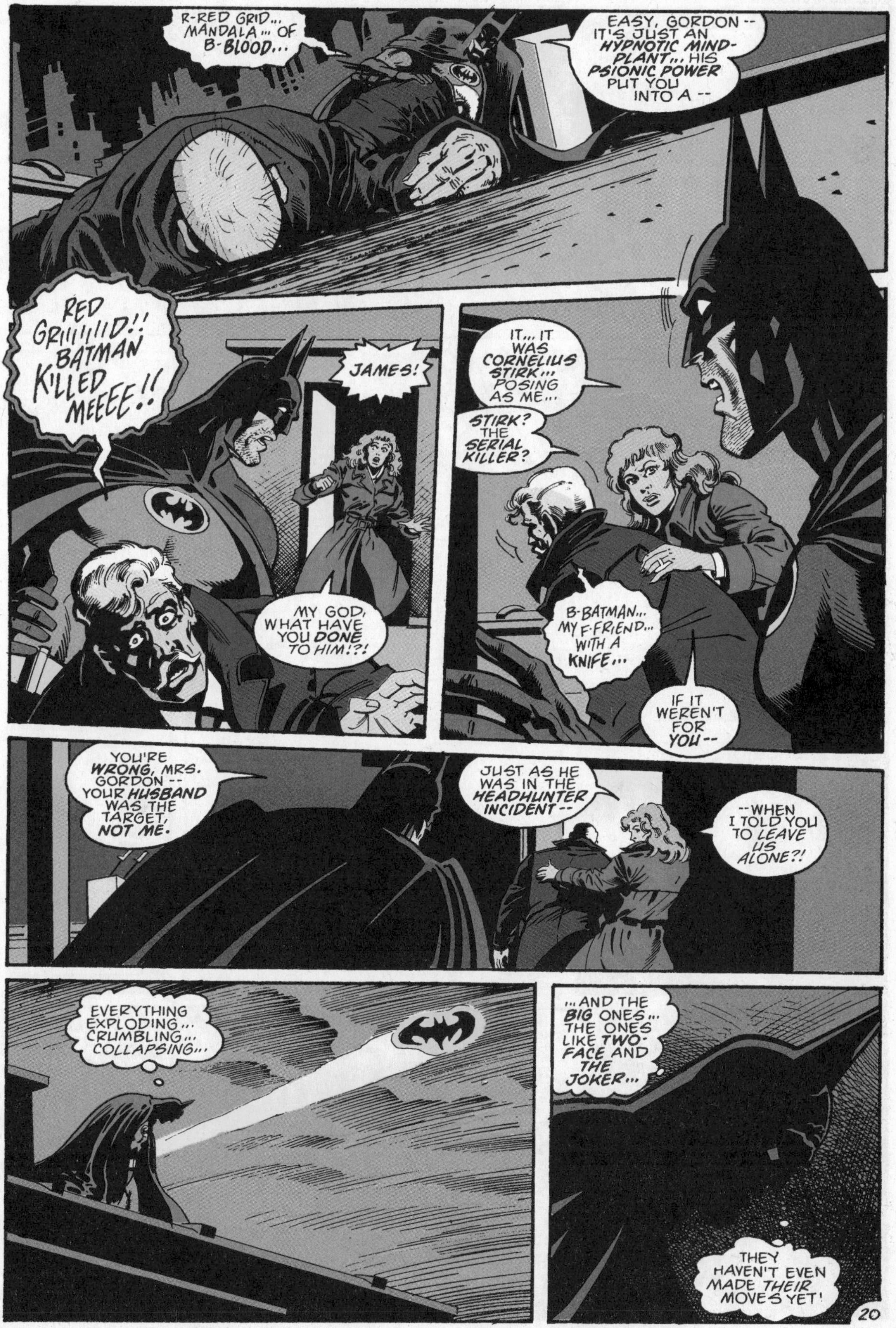
R-RED GRID... MANDALA... OF B-BLOOD...
EASY, GORDON -- IT'S JUST AN HYPNOTIC MIND-PLANT... HIS PSIONIC POWER PUT YOU INTO A --
RED GRIIIIIID!! BATMAN KILLED MEEEE!!
JAMES!
MY GOD, WHAT HAVE YOU DONE TO HIM!?!
IT... IT WAS CORNELIUS STIRK... POSING AS ME...
STIRK? THE SERIAL KILLER?
B-BATMAN... MY F-FRIEND... WITH A KNIFE...
IF IT WEREN'T FOR YOU --
YOU'RE WRONG, MRS. GORDON -- YOUR HUSBAND WAS THE TARGET, NOT ME.
JUST AS HE WAS IN THE HEADHUNTER INCIDENT --
-- WHEN I TOLD YOU TO LEAVE US ALONE?!
EVERYTHING EXPLODING... CRUMBLING... COLLAPSING...
...AND THE BIG ONES... THE ONES LIKE TWO-FACE AND THE JOKER...
THEY HAVEN'T EVEN MADE THEIR MOVES YET!
20

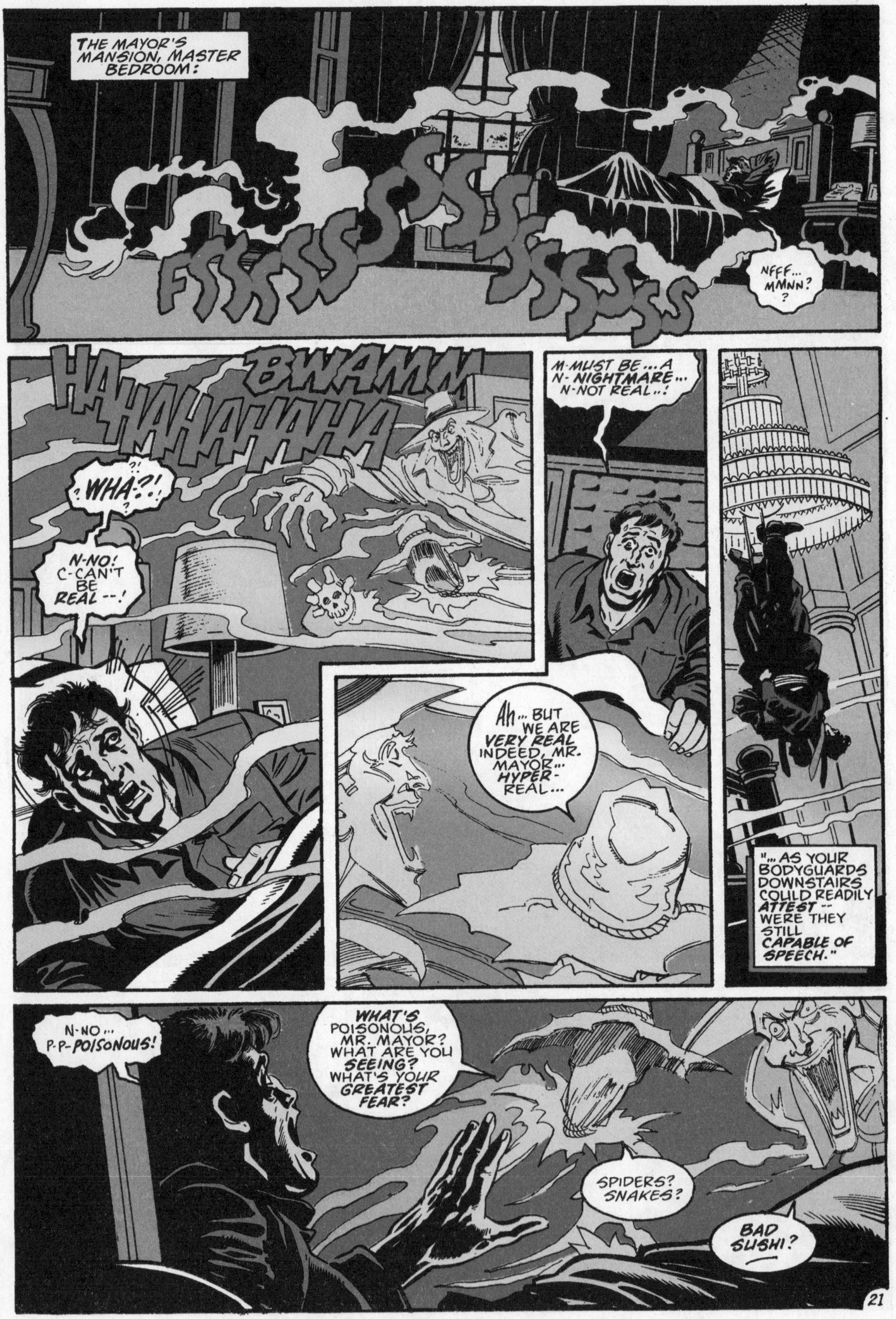
THE MAYOR'S MANSION, MASTER BEDROOM:
FSSSSSSSSSSSSSSSSS
NFFF... MMNN? ?
HAHAHAHAHAHA
BWAMM
WHA?!
N-NO! C-CAN'T BE REAL--!
M-MUST BE... A N-NIGHTMARE... N-NOT REAL..!
Ah... BUT WE ARE VERY REAL INDEED, MR. MAYOR... HYPER-REAL...
"...AS YOUR BODYGUARDS DOWNSTAIRS COULD READILY ATTEST-- WERE THEY STILL CAPABLE OF SPEECH."
N-NO... P-P-POISONOUS!
WHAT'S POISONOUS, MR. MAYOR? WHAT ARE YOU SEEING? WHAT'S YOUR GREATEST FEAR?
SPIDERS? SNAKES?
BAD SUSHI?
21

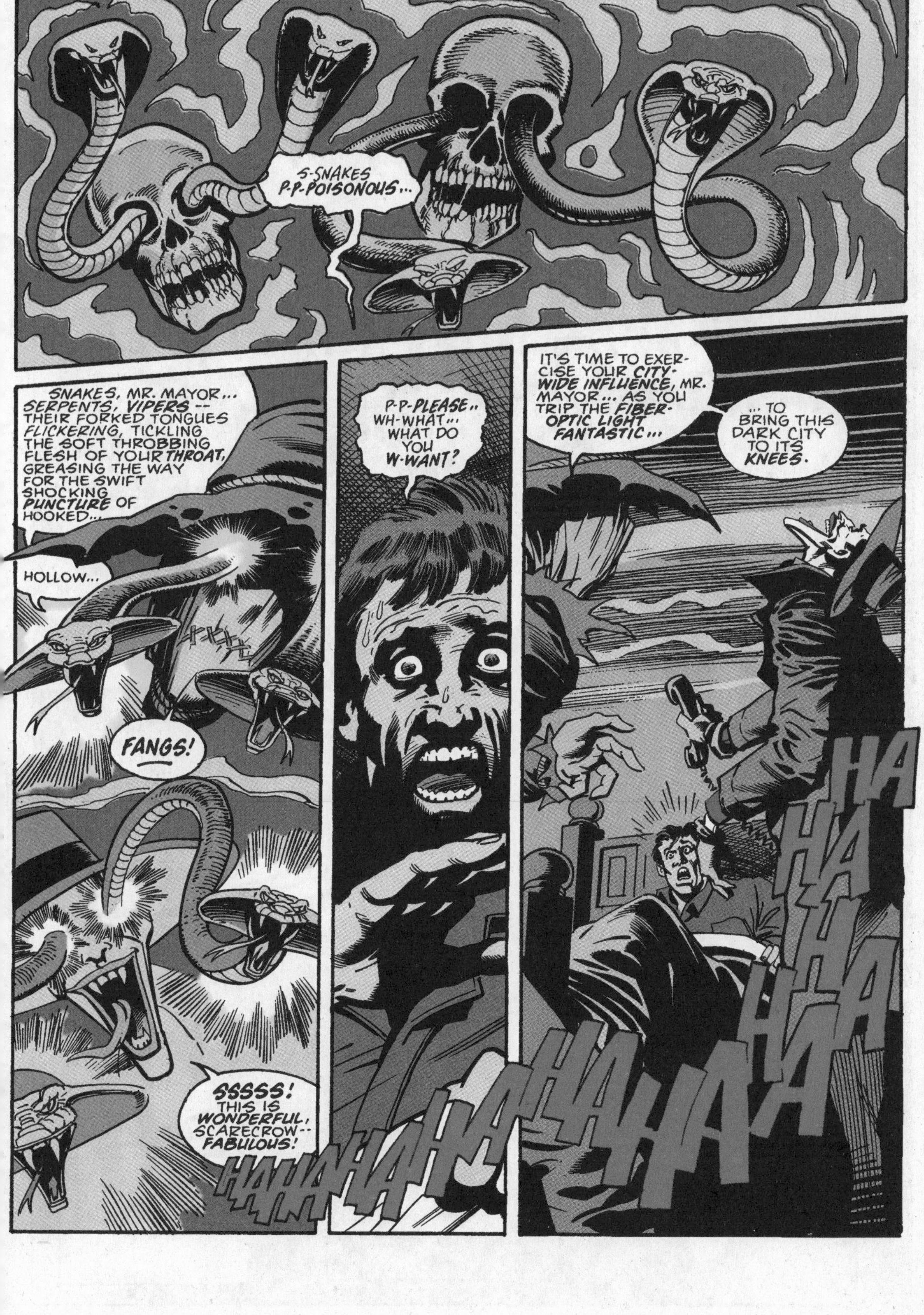
S-SNAKES P-P-POISONOUS...
SNAKES, MR. MAYOR... SERPENTS, VIPERS -- THEIR FORKED TONGUES FLICKERING, TICKLING THE SOFT THROBBING FLESH OF YOUR THROAT, GREASING THE WAY FOR THE SWIFT SHOCKING PUNCTURE OF HOOKED...
HOLLOW...
FANGS!
SSSSS! THIS IS WONDERFUL, SCARECROW-- FABULOUS!
P-P-PLEASE.. WH-WHAT... WHAT DO YOU W-WANT?
IT'S TIME TO EXERCISE YOUR CITY-WIDE INFLUENCE, MR. MAYOR... AS YOU TRIP THE FIBER-OPTIC LIGHT FANTASTIC...
...TO BRING THIS DARK CITY TO ITS KNEES.
HAHAHAHAHAHAHAHAHAHAHAHA
HA HA HA HA HA HA HA

Cover art by KELLEY JONES

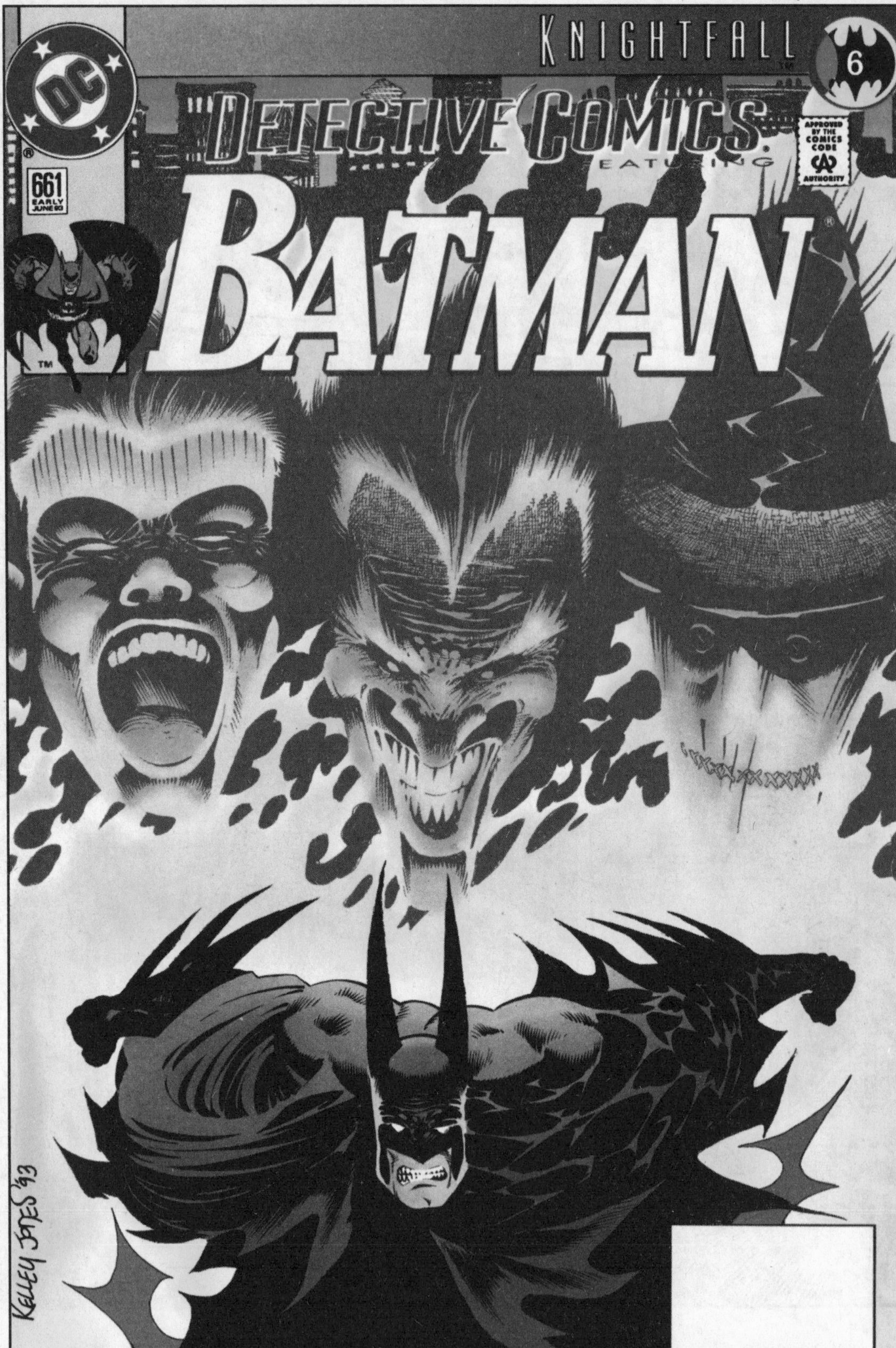
KNIGHTFALL
6
DC
661
EARLY JUNE 93
DETECTIVE COMICS
FEATURING
BATMAN
APPROVED BY THE COMICS CODE AUTHORITY
KELLEY JONES '93

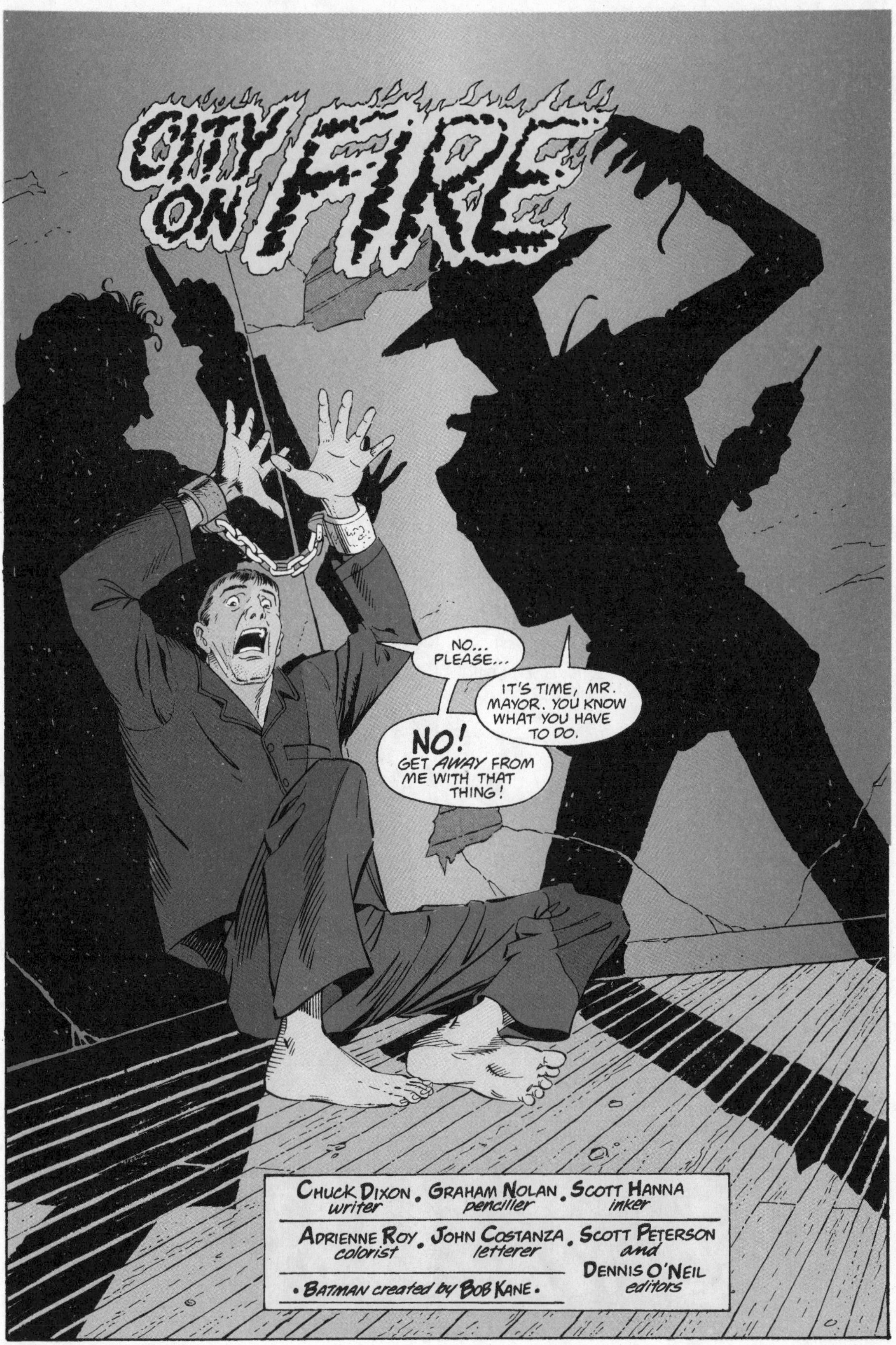
CITY ON FIRE
NO... PLEASE...
IT'S TIME, MR. MAYOR. YOU KNOW WHAT YOU HAVE TO DO.
NO! GET AWAY FROM ME WITH THAT THING!
CHUCK DIXON writer • GRAHAM NOLAN penciller • SCOTT HANNA inker
ADRIENNE ROY colorist • JOHN COSTANZA letterer • SCOTT PETERSON and DENNIS O'NEIL editors
• BATMAN created by BOB KANE •

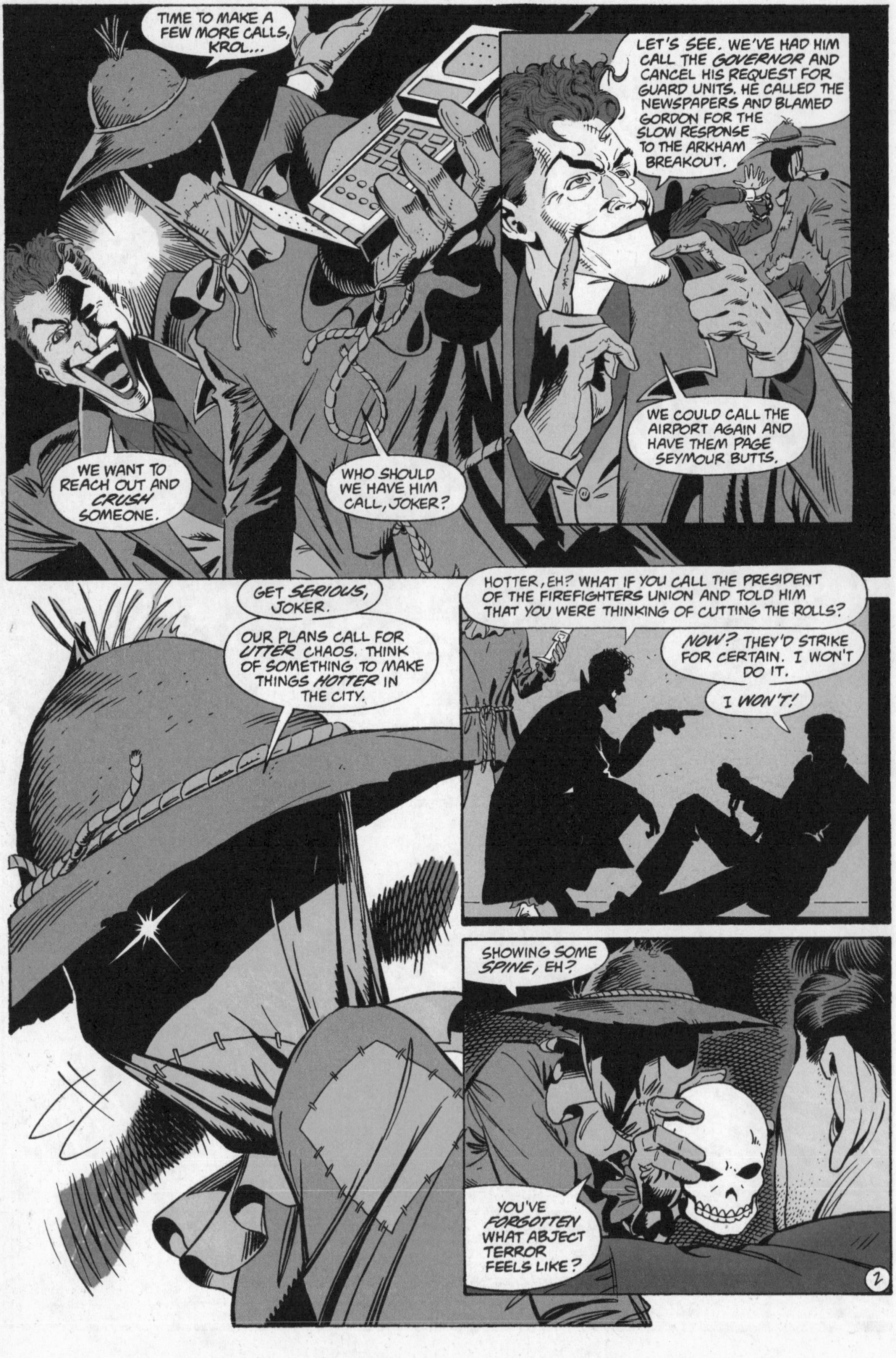
TIME TO MAKE A FEW MORE CALLS, KROL...
WE WANT TO REACH OUT AND CRUSH SOMEONE.
WHO SHOULD WE HAVE HIM CALL, JOKER?
LET'S SEE. WE'VE HAD HIM CALL THE GOVERNOR AND CANCEL HIS REQUEST FOR GUARD UNITS. HE CALLED THE NEWSPAPERS AND BLAMED GORDON FOR THE SLOW RESPONSE TO THE ARKHAM BREAKOUT.
WE COULD CALL THE AIRPORT AGAIN AND HAVE THEM PAGE SEYMOUR BUTTS.
GET SERIOUS, JOKER.
OUR PLANS CALL FOR UTTER CHAOS. THINK OF SOMETHING TO MAKE THINGS HOTTER IN THE CITY.
HOTTER, EH? WHAT IF YOU CALL THE PRESIDENT OF THE FIREFIGHTERS UNION AND TOLD HIM THAT YOU WERE THINKING OF CUTTING THE ROLLS?
NOW? THEY'D STRIKE FOR CERTAIN. I WON'T DO IT.
I WON'T!
SHOWING SOME SPINE, EH?
YOU'VE FORGOTTEN WHAT ABJECT TERROR FEELS LIKE?
2

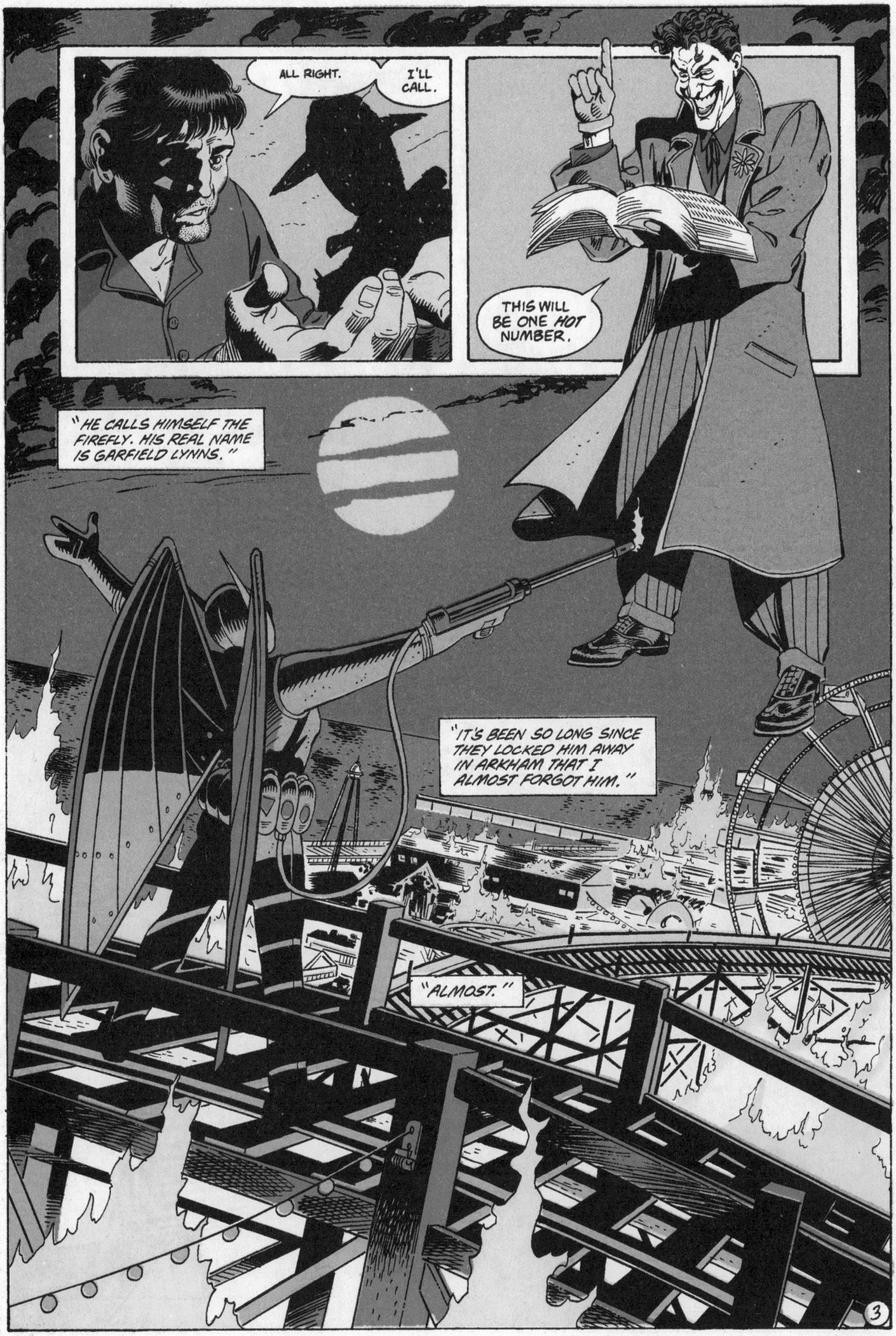
ALL RIGHT.
I'LL CALL.
THIS WILL BE ONE *HOT* NUMBER.
"HE CALLS HIMSELF THE FIREFLY. HIS REAL NAME IS GARFIELD LYNNS."
"IT'S BEEN SO LONG SINCE THEY LOCKED HIM AWAY IN ARKHAM THAT I ALMOST FORGOT HIM."
"ALMOST."
3

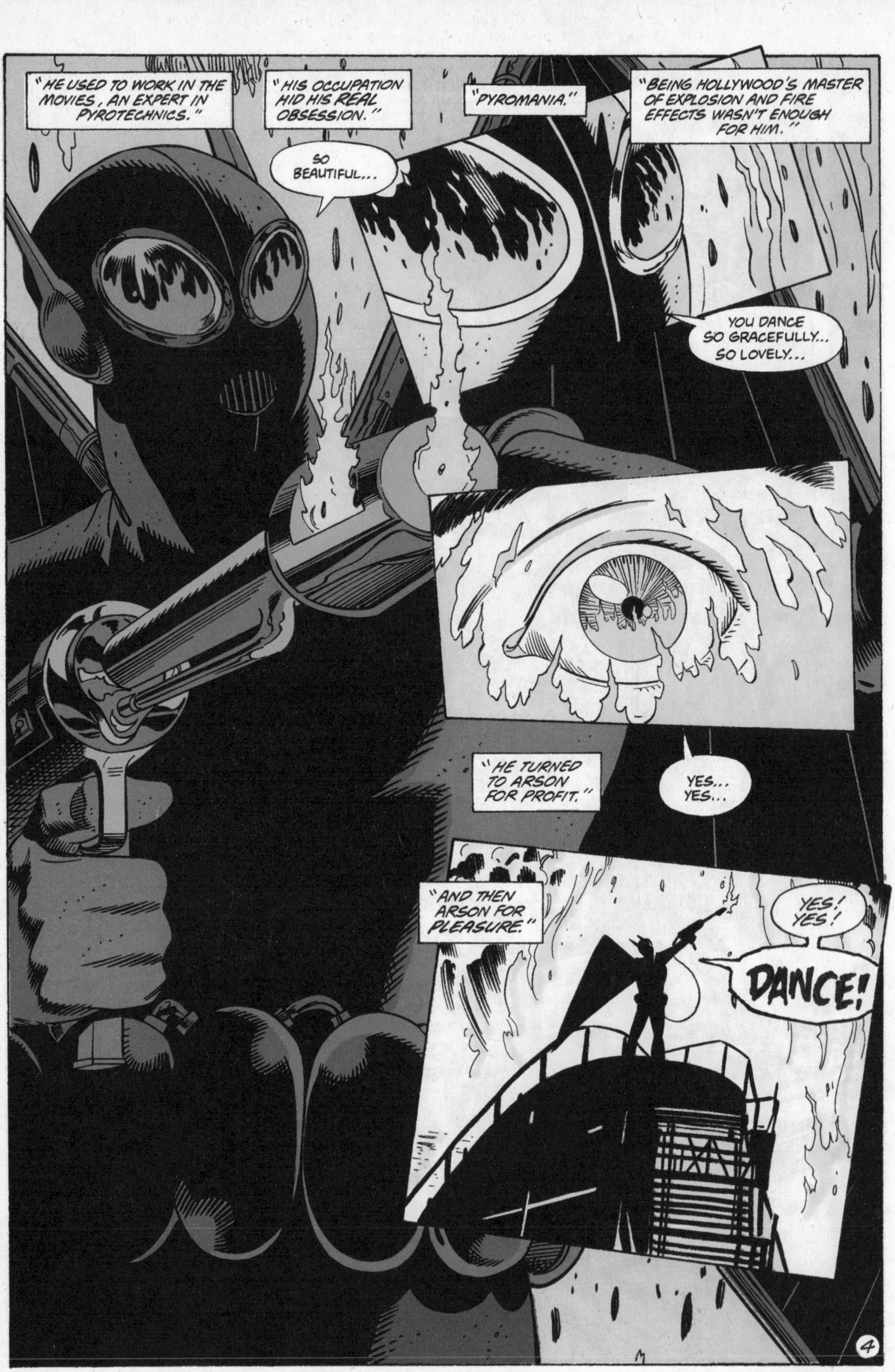
"HE USED TO WORK IN THE MOVIES, AN EXPERT IN PYROTECHNICS."
"HIS OCCUPATION HID HIS REAL OBSESSION."
"PYROMANIA."
"BEING HOLLYWOOD'S MASTER OF EXPLOSION AND FIRE EFFECTS WASN'T ENOUGH FOR HIM."
SO BEAUTIFUL...
YOU DANCE SO GRACEFULLY... SO LOVELY...
"HE TURNED TO ARSON FOR PROFIT."
YES... YES...
"AND THEN ARSON FOR PLEASURE."
YES! YES!
DANCE!
4

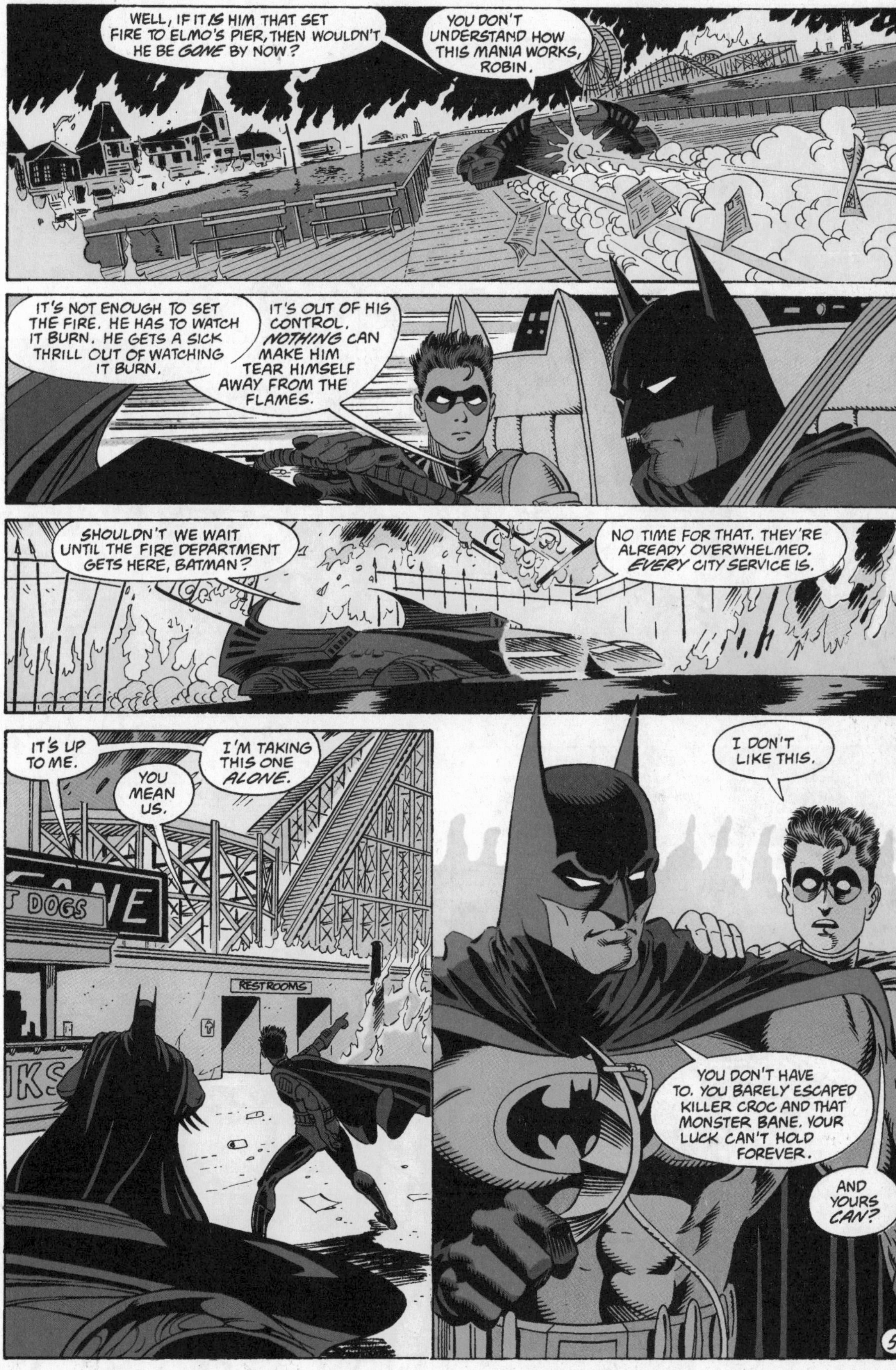
WELL, IF IT IS HIM THAT SET FIRE TO ELMO'S PIER, THEN WOULDN'T HE BE GONE BY NOW?
YOU DON'T UNDERSTAND HOW THIS MANIA WORKS, ROBIN.
IT'S NOT ENOUGH TO SET THE FIRE. HE HAS TO WATCH IT BURN. HE GETS A SICK THRILL OUT OF WATCHING IT BURN.
IT'S OUT OF HIS CONTROL. NOTHING CAN MAKE HIM TEAR HIMSELF AWAY FROM THE FLAMES.
SHOULDN'T WE WAIT UNTIL THE FIRE DEPARTMENT GETS HERE, BATMAN?
NO TIME FOR THAT. THEY'RE ALREADY OVERWHELMED. EVERY CITY SERVICE IS.
IT'S UP TO ME.
YOU MEAN US.
I'M TAKING THIS ONE ALONE.
DOGS
RESTROOMS
I DON'T LIKE THIS.
YOU DON'T HAVE TO. YOU BARELY ESCAPED KILLER CROC AND THAT MONSTER BANE. YOUR LUCK CAN'T HOLD FOREVER.
AND YOURS CAN?
5

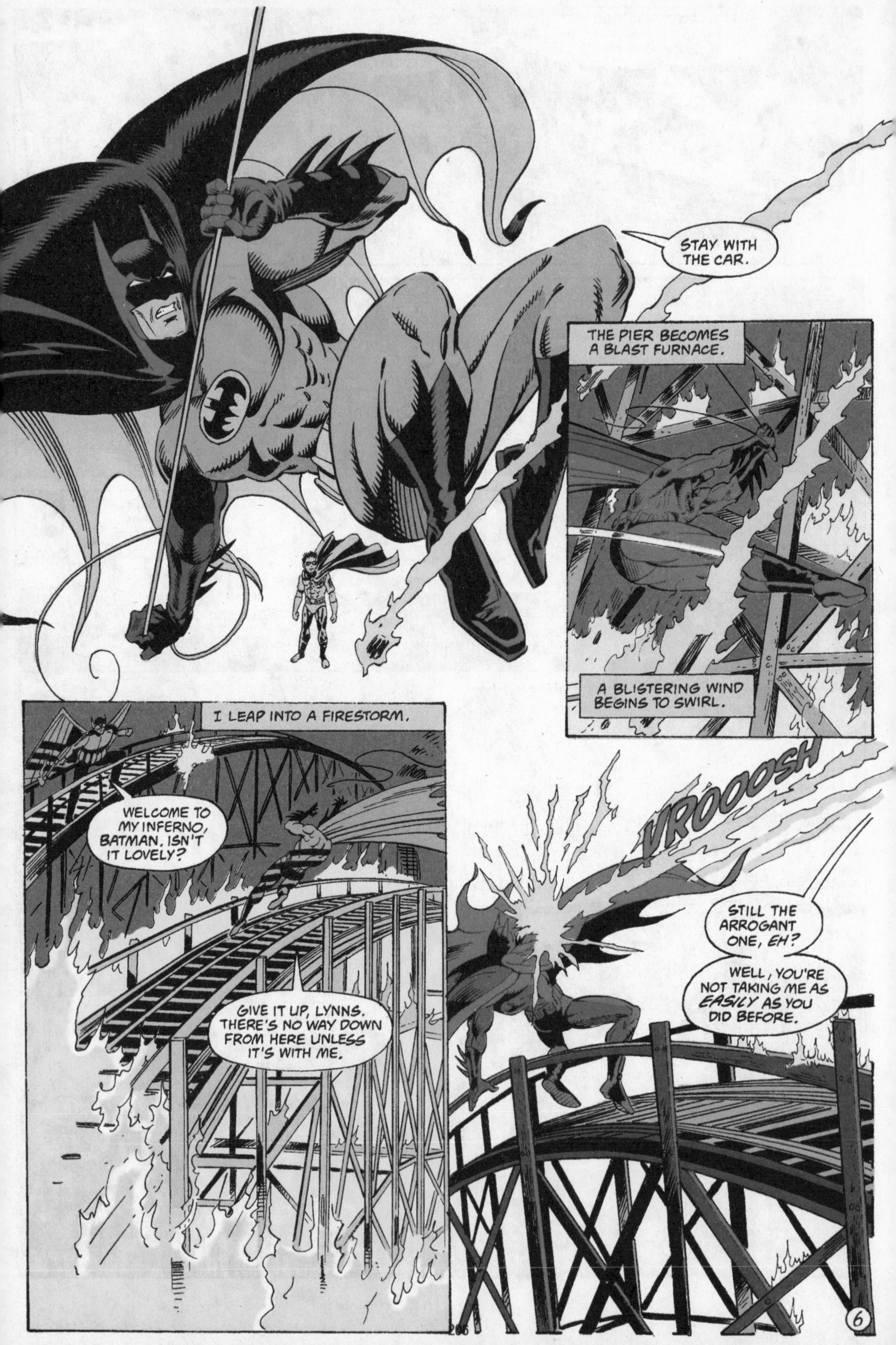
STAY WITH THE CAR.
THE PIER BECOMES A BLAST FURNACE.
A BLISTERING WIND BEGINS TO SWIRL.
I LEAP INTO A FIRESTORM.
WELCOME TO MY INFERNO, BATMAN. ISN'T IT LOVELY?
GIVE IT UP, LYNNS. THERE'S NO WAY DOWN FROM HERE UNLESS IT'S WITH ME.
VROOOOSH
STILL THE ARROGANT ONE, EH?
WELL, YOU'RE NOT TAKING ME AS EASILY AS YOU DID BEFORE.
6

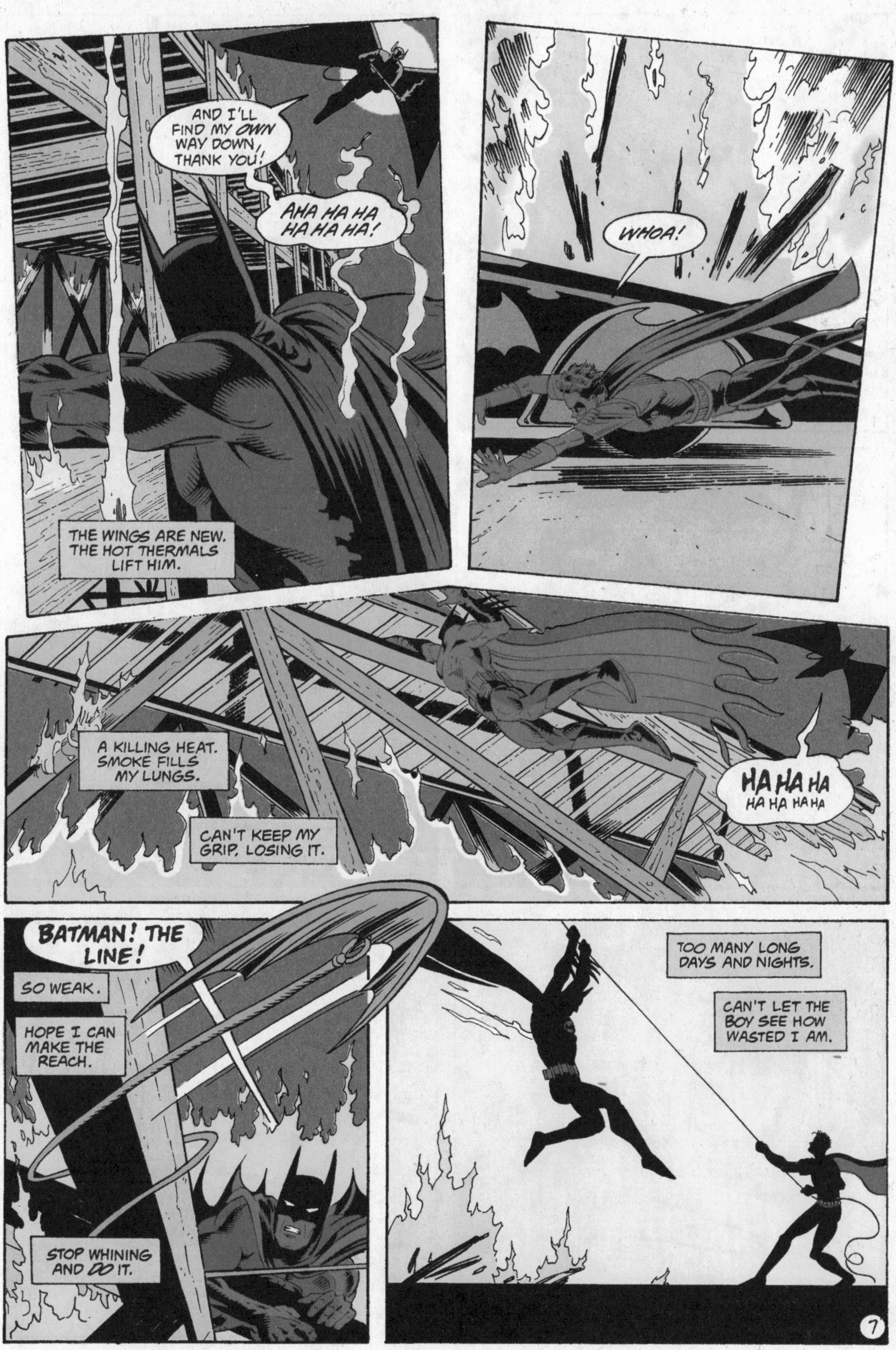
AND I'LL FIND MY OWN WAY DOWN, THANK YOU!
AHA HA HA HA HA HA!
THE WINGS ARE NEW. THE HOT THERMALS LIFT HIM.
WHOA!
A KILLING HEAT. SMOKE FILLS MY LUNGS.
CAN'T KEEP MY GRIP, LOSING IT.
HA HA HA HA HA HA HA
BATMAN! THE LINE!
SO WEAK.
HOPE I CAN MAKE THE REACH.
STOP WHINING AND DO IT.
TOO MANY LONG DAYS AND NIGHTS.
CAN'T LET THE BOY SEE HOW WASTED I AM.
7

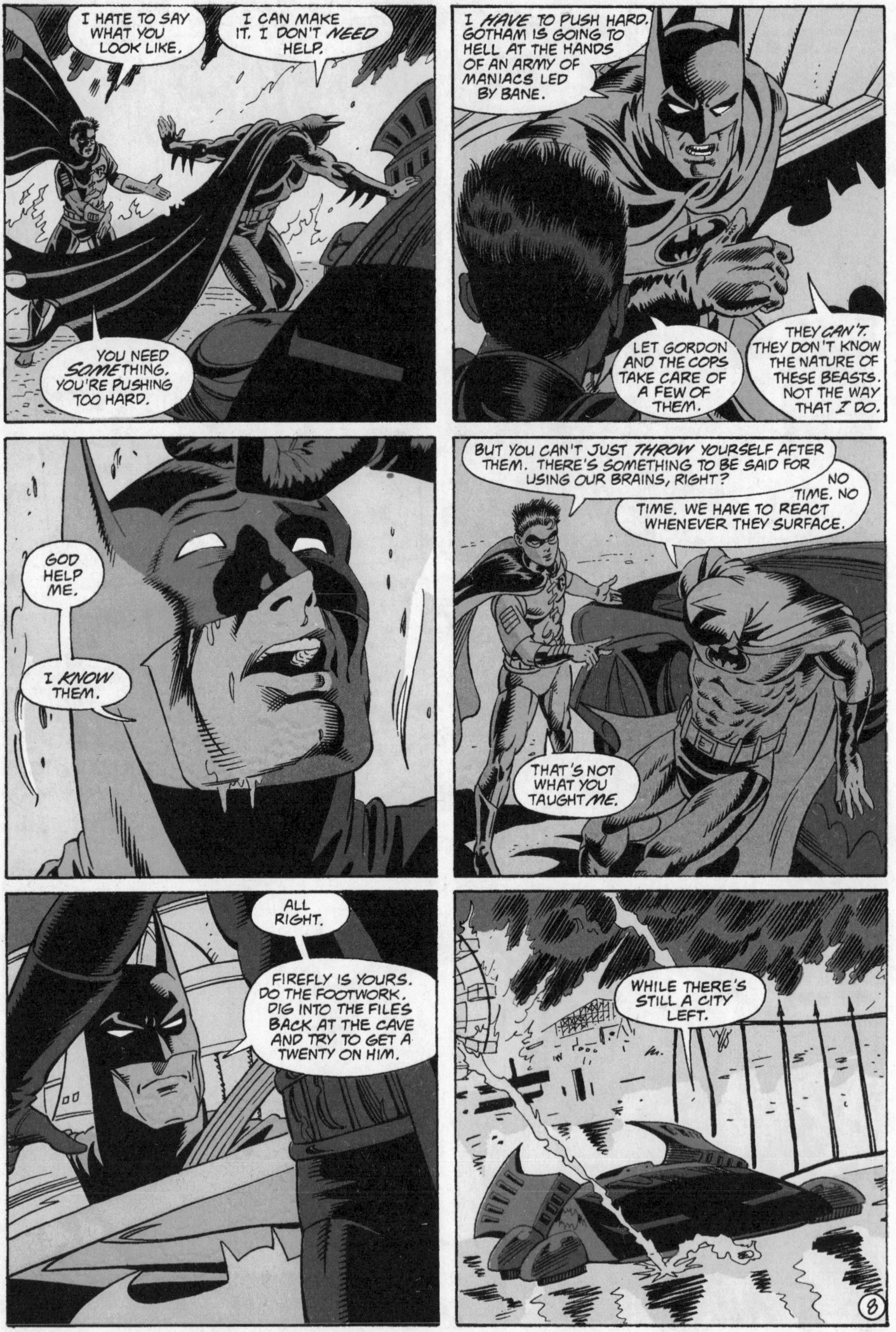

I HATE TO SAY WHAT YOU LOOK LIKE.
I CAN MAKE IT. I DON'T NEED HELP.
YOU NEED SOMETHING. YOU'RE PUSHING TOO HARD.
I HAVE TO PUSH HARD. GOTHAM IS GOING TO HELL AT THE HANDS OF AN ARMY OF MANIACS LED BY BANE.
LET GORDON AND THE COPS TAKE CARE OF A FEW OF THEM.
THEY CAN'T. THEY DON'T KNOW THE NATURE OF THESE BEASTS. NOT THE WAY THAT I DO.
GOD HELP ME.
I KNOW THEM.
BUT YOU CAN'T JUST THROW YOURSELF AFTER THEM. THERE'S SOMETHING TO BE SAID FOR USING OUR BRAINS, RIGHT?
NO TIME. NO TIME. WE HAVE TO REACT WHENEVER THEY SURFACE.
THAT'S NOT WHAT YOU TAUGHT ME.
ALL RIGHT.
FIREFLY IS YOURS. DO THE FOOTWORK. DIG INTO THE FILES BACK AT THE CAVE AND TRY TO GET A TWENTY ON HIM.
WHILE THERE'S STILL A CITY LEFT.
8

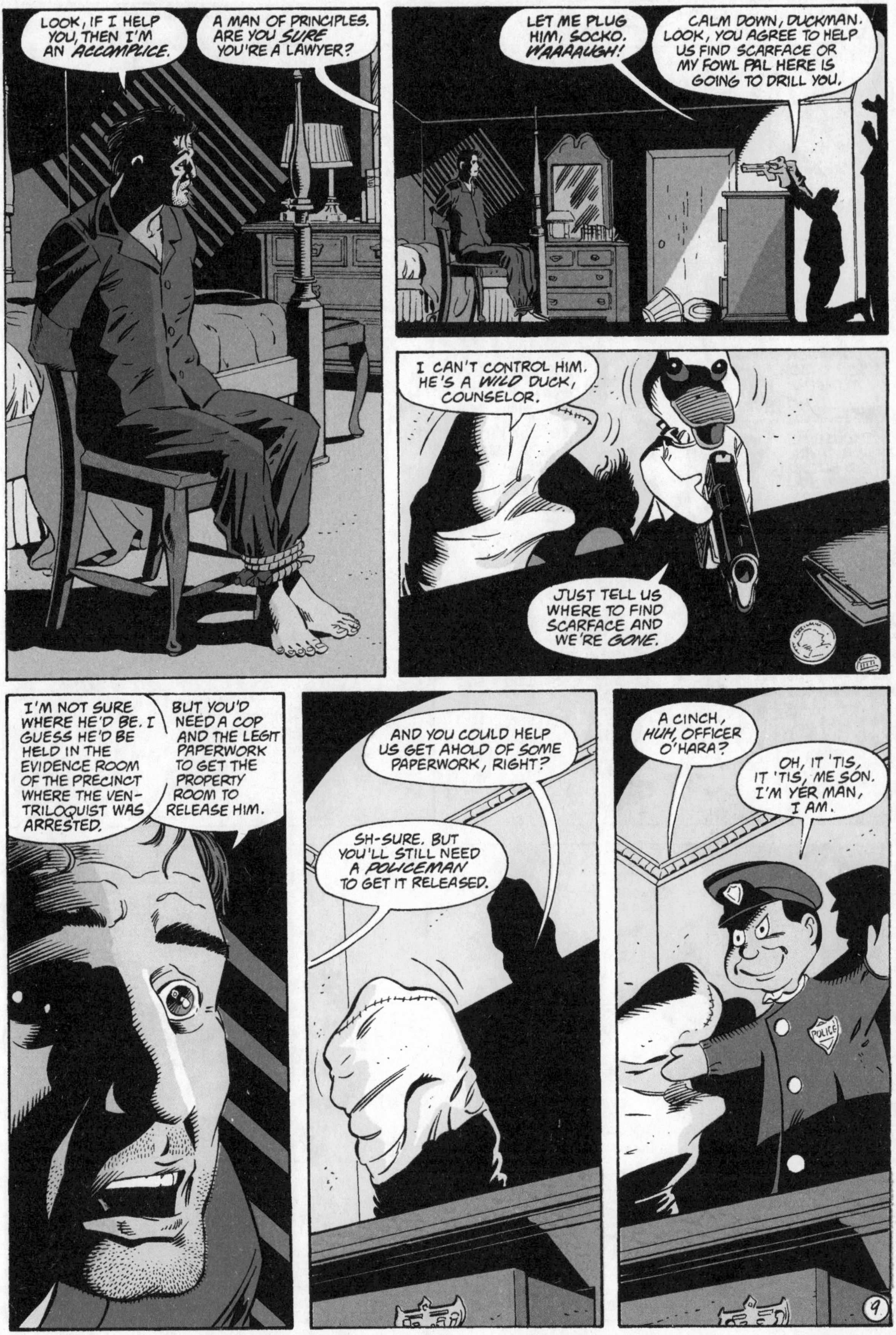
LOOK, IF I HELP YOU, THEN I'M AN ACCOMPLICE.
A MAN OF PRINCIPLES. ARE YOU SURE YOU'RE A LAWYER?
LET ME PLUG HIM, SOCKO. WAAAAUGH!
CALM DOWN, DUCKMAN. LOOK, YOU AGREE TO HELP US FIND SCARFACE OR MY FOWL PAL HERE IS GOING TO DRILL YOU.
I CAN'T CONTROL HIM. HE'S A WILD DUCK, COUNSELOR.
JUST TELL US WHERE TO FIND SCARFACE AND WE'RE GONE.
I'M NOT SURE WHERE HE'D BE. I GUESS HE'D BE HELD IN THE EVIDENCE ROOM OF THE PRECINCT WHERE THE VENTRILOQUIST WAS ARRESTED.
BUT YOU'D NEED A COP AND THE LEGIT PAPERWORK TO GET THE PROPERTY ROOM TO RELEASE HIM.
AND YOU COULD HELP US GET AHOLD OF SOME PAPERWORK, RIGHT?
SH-SURE. BUT YOU'LL STILL NEED A POLICEMAN TO GET IT RELEASED.
A CINCH, HUH, OFFICER O'HARA?
OH, IT 'TIS, IT 'TIS, ME SON. I'M YER MAN, I AM.
POLICE
9

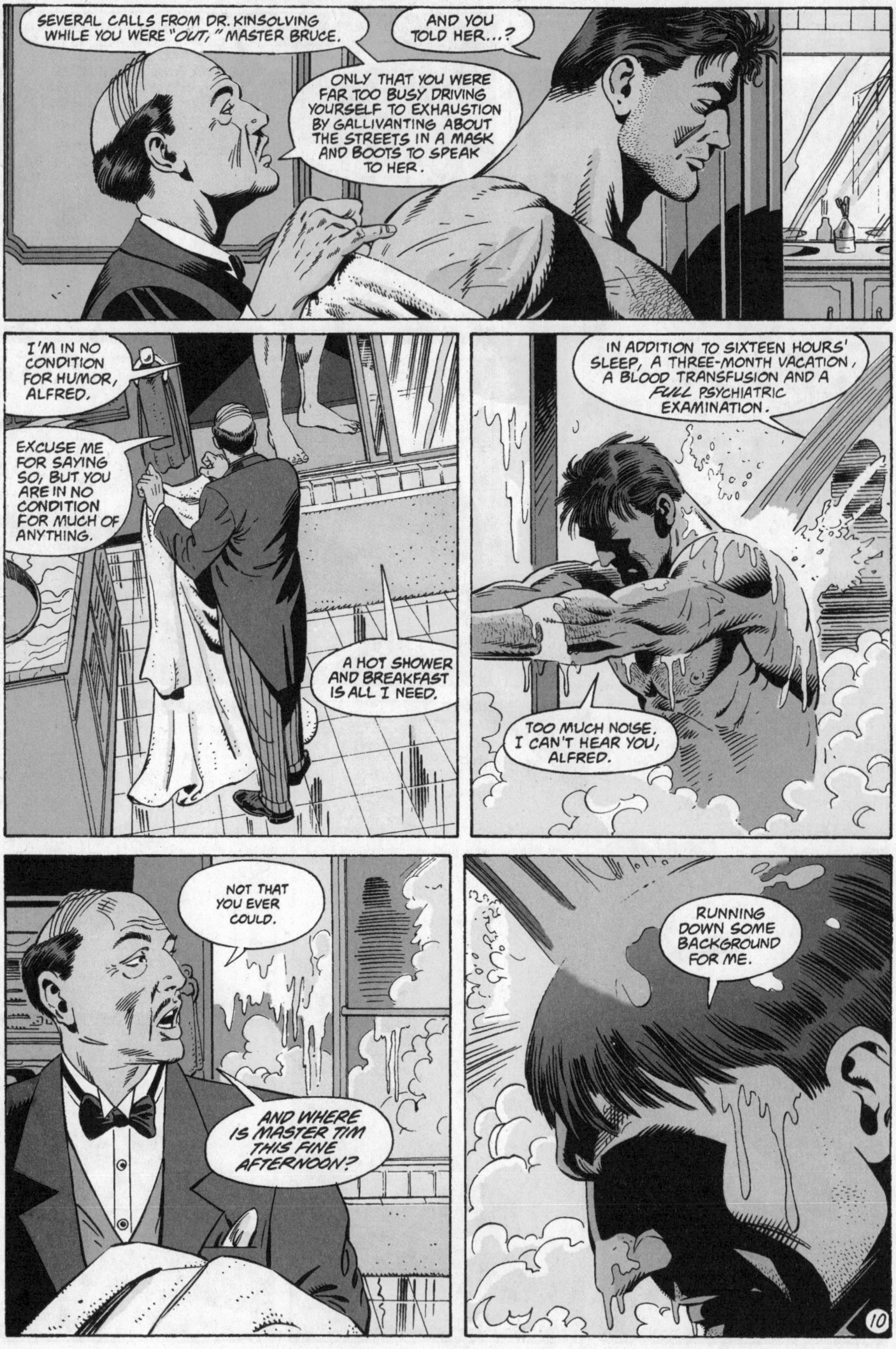

SEVERAL CALLS FROM DR. KINSOLVING WHILE YOU WERE "OUT," MASTER BRUCE.
AND YOU TOLD HER...?
ONLY THAT YOU WERE FAR TOO BUSY DRIVING YOURSELF TO EXHAUSTION BY GALLIVANTING ABOUT THE STREETS IN A MASK AND BOOTS TO SPEAK TO HER.
I'M IN NO CONDITION FOR HUMOR, ALFRED.
EXCUSE ME FOR SAYING SO, BUT YOU ARE IN NO CONDITION FOR MUCH OF ANYTHING.
A HOT SHOWER AND BREAKFAST IS ALL I NEED.
IN ADDITION TO SIXTEEN HOURS' SLEEP, A THREE-MONTH VACATION, A BLOOD TRANSFUSION AND A FULL PSYCHIATRIC EXAMINATION.
TOO MUCH NOISE. I CAN'T HEAR YOU, ALFRED.
NOT THAT YOU EVER COULD.
AND WHERE IS MASTER TIM THIS FINE AFTERNOON?
RUNNING DOWN SOME BACKGROUND FOR ME.
10

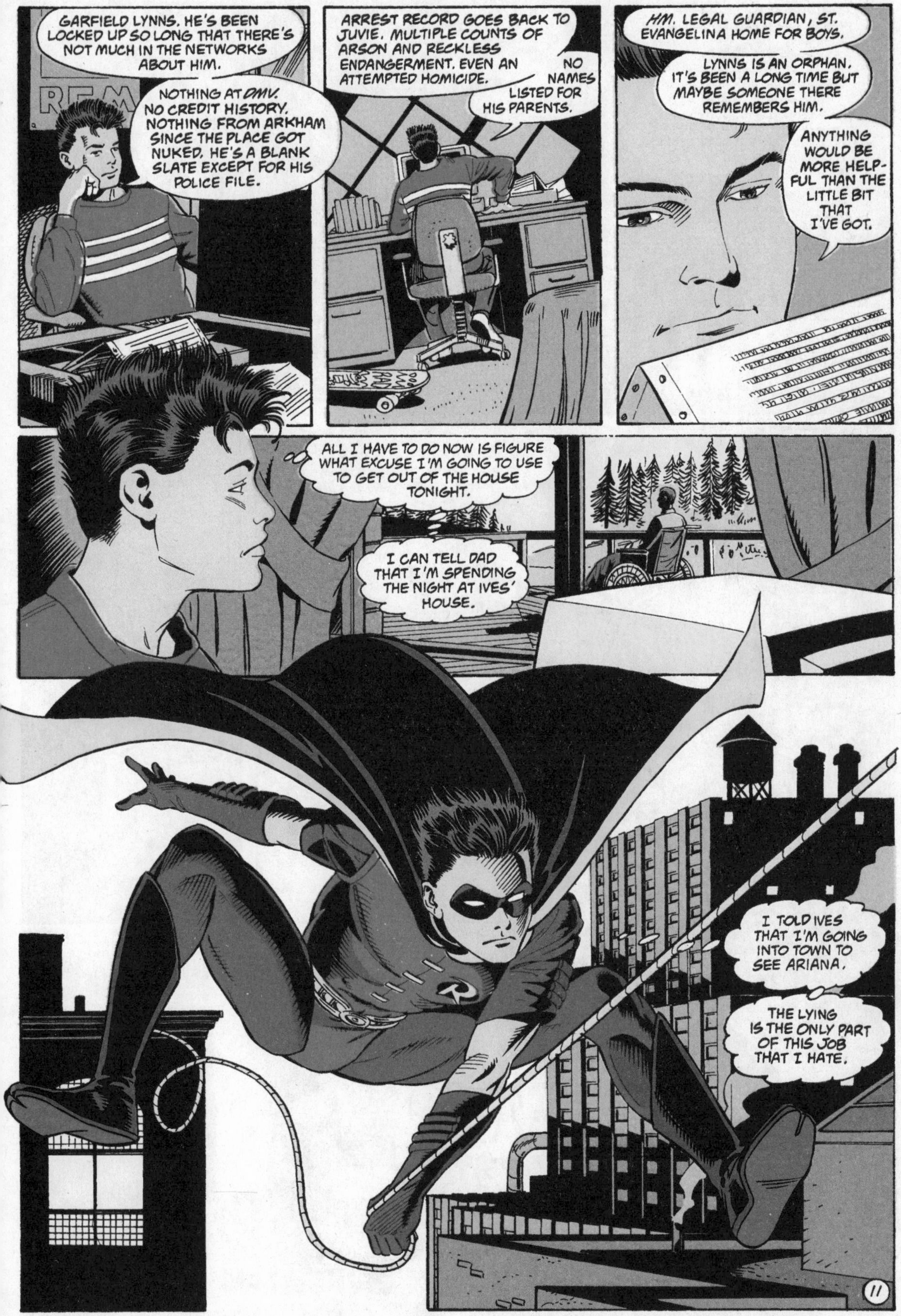
GARFIELD LYNNS. HE'S BEEN LOCKED UP SO LONG THAT THERE'S NOT MUCH IN THE NETWORKS ABOUT HIM.
NOTHING AT DMV. NO CREDIT HISTORY. NOTHING FROM ARKHAM SINCE THE PLACE GOT NUKED. HE'S A BLANK SLATE EXCEPT FOR HIS POLICE FILE.
ARREST RECORD GOES BACK TO JUVIE. MULTIPLE COUNTS OF ARSON AND RECKLESS ENDANGERMENT. EVEN AN ATTEMPTED HOMICIDE.
NO NAMES LISTED FOR HIS PARENTS.
HM. LEGAL GUARDIAN, ST. EVANGELINA HOME FOR BOYS.
LYNNS IS AN ORPHAN. IT'S BEEN A LONG TIME BUT MAYBE SOMEONE THERE REMEMBERS HIM.
ANYTHING WOULD BE MORE HELPFUL THAN THE LITTLE BIT THAT I'VE GOT.
ALL I HAVE TO DO NOW IS FIGURE WHAT EXCUSE I'M GOING TO USE TO GET OUT OF THE HOUSE TONIGHT.
I CAN TELL DAD THAT I'M SPENDING THE NIGHT AT IVES' HOUSE.
I TOLD IVES THAT I'M GOING INTO TOWN TO SEE ARIANA.
THE LYING IS THE ONLY PART OF THIS JOB THAT I HATE.
11

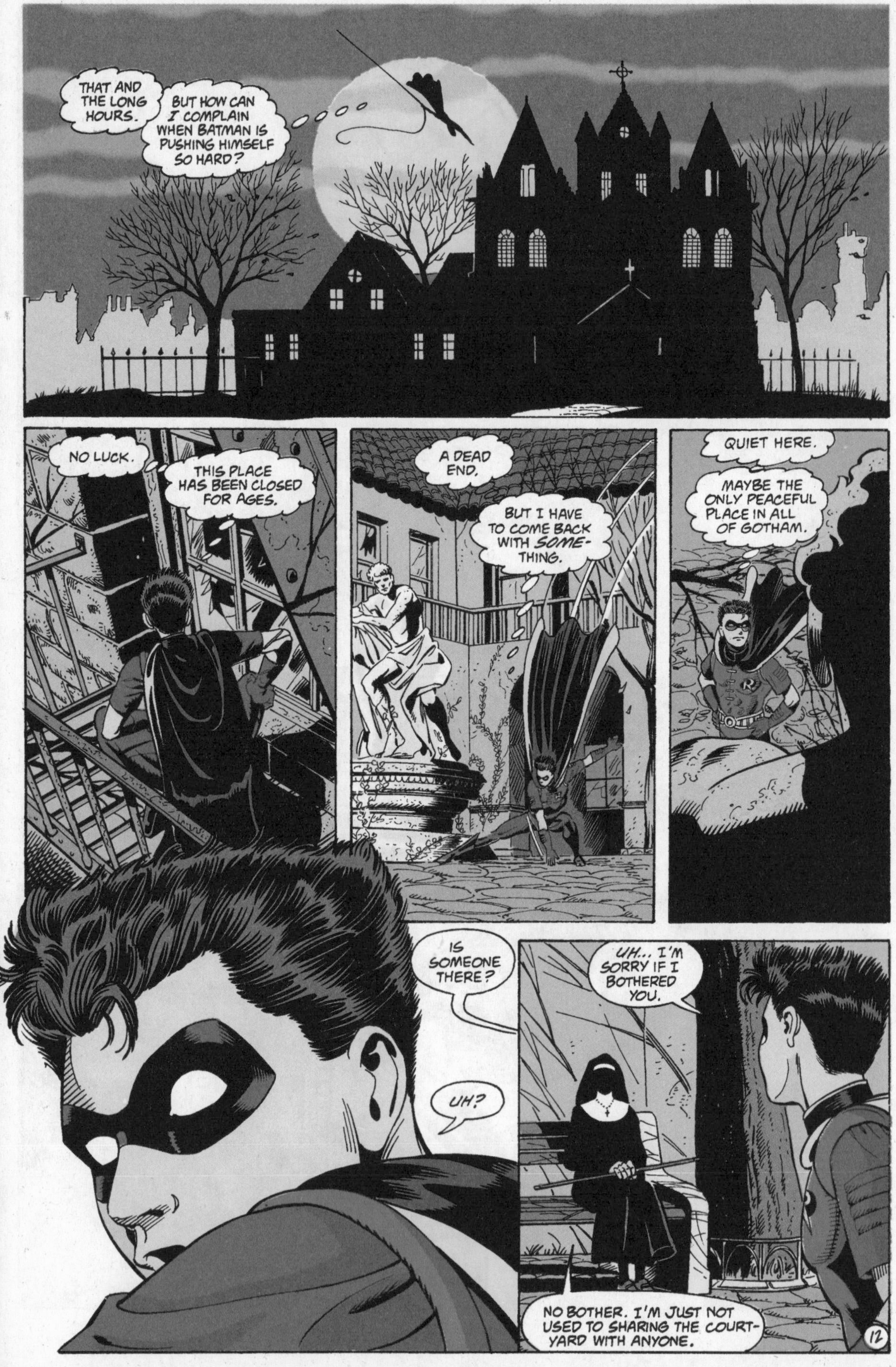
THAT AND THE LONG HOURS.
BUT HOW CAN I COMPLAIN WHEN BATMAN IS PUSHING HIMSELF SO HARD?
NO LUCK.
THIS PLACE HAS BEEN CLOSED FOR AGES.
A DEAD END.
BUT I HAVE TO COME BACK WITH SOME-THING.
QUIET HERE.
MAYBE THE ONLY PEACEFUL PLACE IN ALL OF GOTHAM.
IS SOMEONE THERE?
UH?
UH... I'M SORRY IF I BOTHERED YOU.
NO BOTHER. I'M JUST NOT USED TO SHARING THE COURT-YARD WITH ANYONE.
12

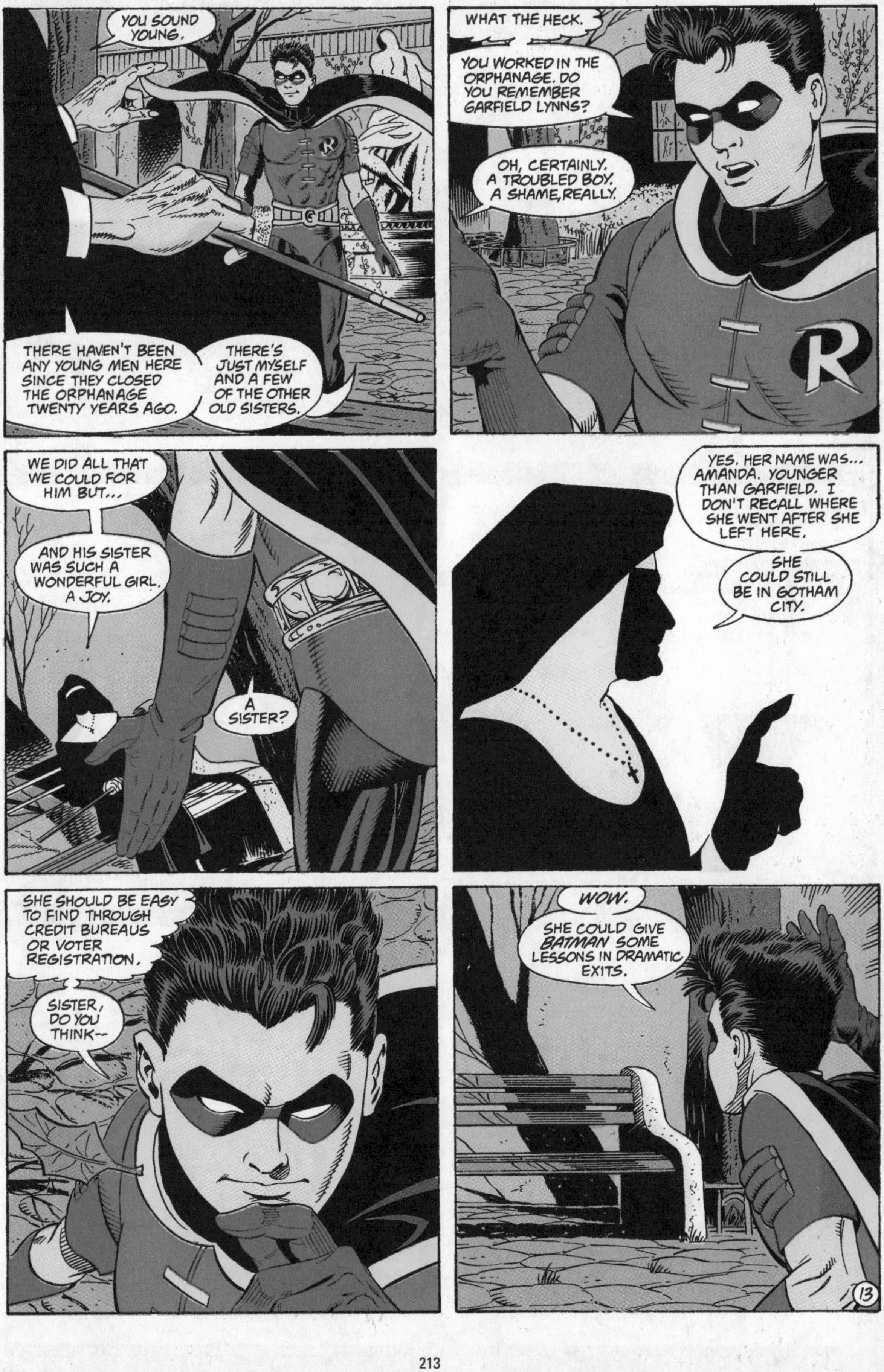
YOU SOUND YOUNG.
THERE HAVEN'T BEEN ANY YOUNG MEN HERE SINCE THEY CLOSED THE ORPHANAGE TWENTY YEARS AGO.
THERE'S JUST MYSELF AND A FEW OF THE OTHER OLD SISTERS.
WHAT THE HECK.
YOU WORKED IN THE ORPHANAGE. DO YOU REMEMBER GARFIELD LYNNS?
OH, CERTAINLY. A TROUBLED BOY. A SHAME, REALLY.
WE DID ALL THAT WE COULD FOR HIM BUT...
AND HIS SISTER WAS SUCH A WONDERFUL GIRL. A JOY.
A SISTER?
YES. HER NAME WAS... AMANDA. YOUNGER THAN GARFIELD. I DON'T RECALL WHERE SHE WENT AFTER SHE LEFT HERE.
SHE COULD STILL BE IN GOTHAM CITY.
SHE SHOULD BE EASY TO FIND THROUGH CREDIT BUREAUS OR VOTER REGISTRATION.
SISTER, DO YOU THINK--
WOW.
SHE COULD GIVE BATMAN SOME LESSONS IN DRAMATIC EXITS.
13

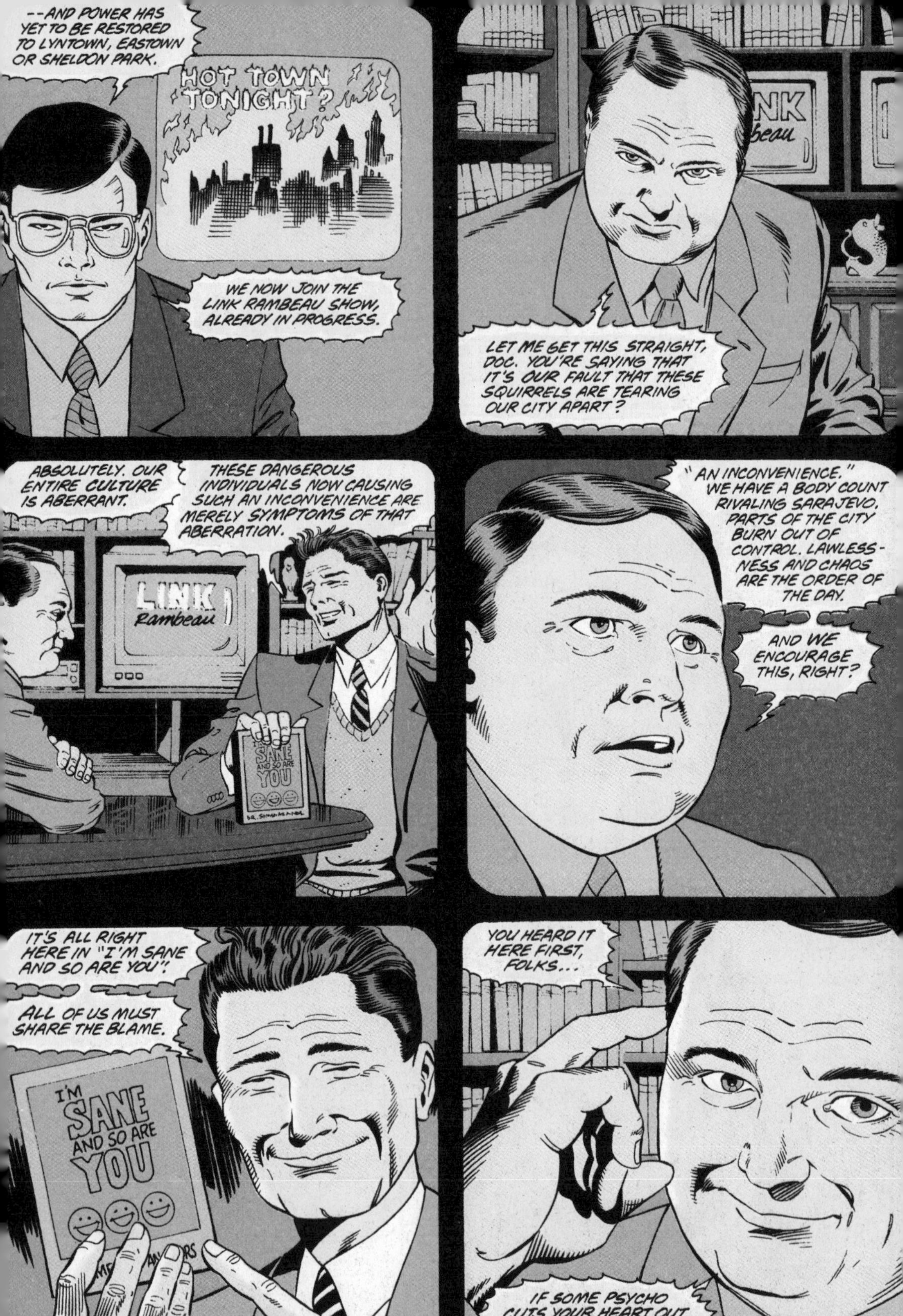
--AND POWER HAS YET TO BE RESTORED TO LYNTOWN, EASTOWN OR SHELDON PARK.
HOT TOWN TONIGHT?
WE NOW JOIN THE LINK RAMBEAU SHOW, ALREADY IN PROGRESS.
LINK Rambeau
LET ME GET THIS STRAIGHT, DOC. YOU'RE SAYING THAT IT'S OUR FAULT THAT THESE SQUIRRELS ARE TEARING OUR CITY APART?
ABSOLUTELY. OUR ENTIRE CULTURE IS ABERRANT.
THESE DANGEROUS INDIVIDUALS NOW CAUSING SUCH AN INCONVENIENCE ARE MERELY SYMPTOMS OF THAT ABERRATION.
LINK Rambeau
"AN INCONVENIENCE." WE HAVE A BODY COUNT RIVALING SARAJEVO. PARTS OF THE CITY BURN OUT OF CONTROL. LAWLESSNESS AND CHAOS ARE THE ORDER OF THE DAY.
AND WE ENCOURAGE THIS, RIGHT?
IT'S ALL RIGHT HERE IN "I'M SANE AND SO ARE YOU".
ALL OF US MUST SHARE THE BLAME.
I'M SANE AND SO ARE YOU
YOU HEARD IT HERE FIRST, FOLKS...
IF SOME PSYCHO CUTS YOUR HEART OUT BECAUSE HIS SALISBURY STEAK TOLD HIM TO...
14

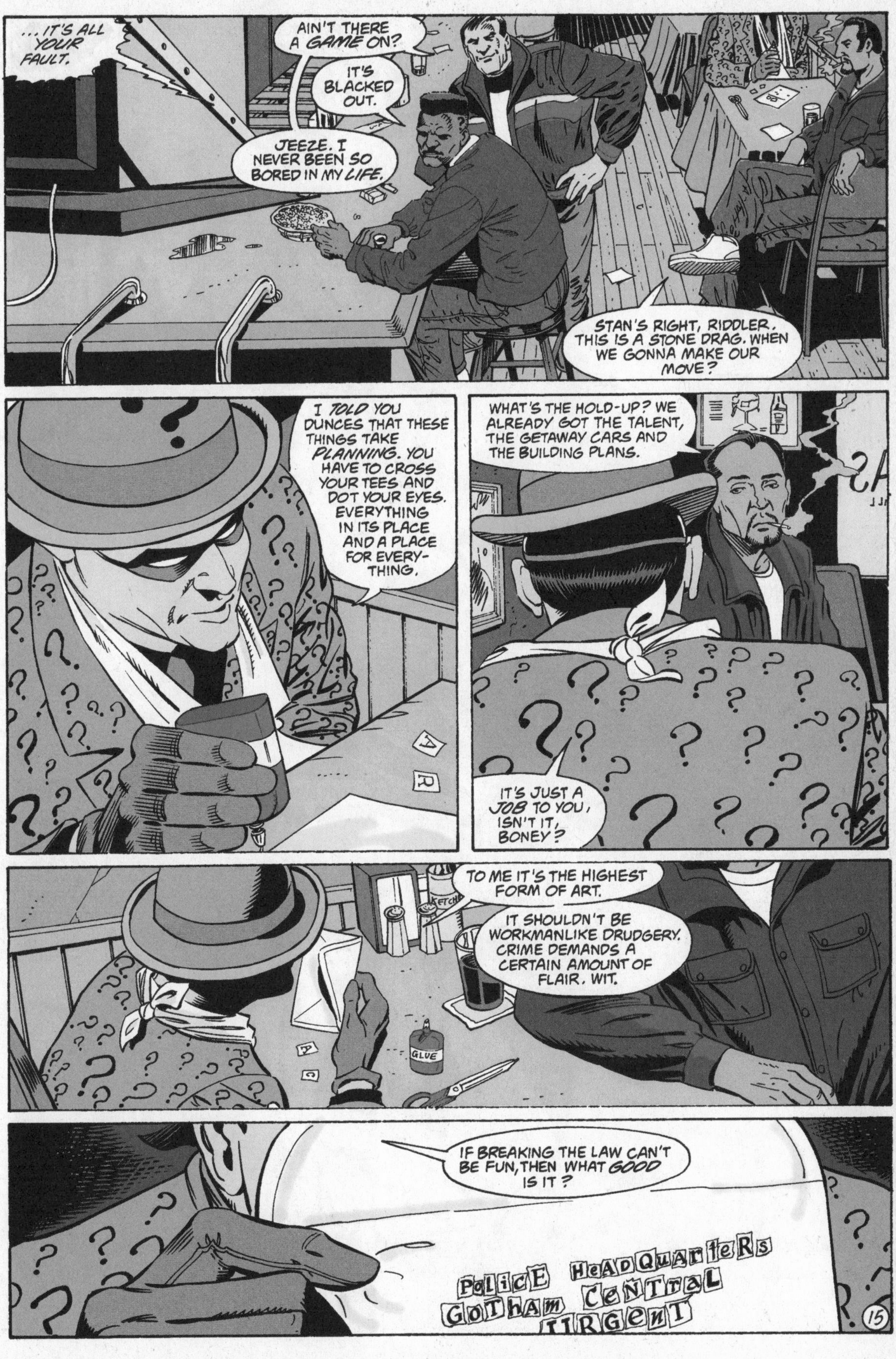
...IT'S ALL YOUR FAULT.
AIN'T THERE A GAME ON?
IT'S BLACKED OUT.
JEEZE. I NEVER BEEN SO BORED IN MY LIFE.
STAN'S RIGHT, RIDDLER. THIS IS A STONE DRAG. WHEN WE GONNA MAKE OUR MOVE?
I TOLD YOU DUNCES THAT THESE THINGS TAKE PLANNING. YOU HAVE TO CROSS YOUR TEES AND DOT YOUR EYES. EVERYTHING IN ITS PLACE AND A PLACE FOR EVERYTHING.
WHAT'S THE HOLD-UP? WE ALREADY GOT THE TALENT, THE GETAWAY CARS AND THE BUILDING PLANS.
IT'S JUST A JOB TO YOU, ISN'T IT, BONEY?
TO ME IT'S THE HIGHEST FORM OF ART.
IT SHOULDN'T BE WORKMANLIKE DRUDGERY. CRIME DEMANDS A CERTAIN AMOUNT OF FLAIR. WIT.
GLUE
IF BREAKING THE LAW CAN'T BE FUN, THEN WHAT GOOD IS IT?
POLICE HEADQUARTERS
GOTHAM CENTRAL
URGENT
15

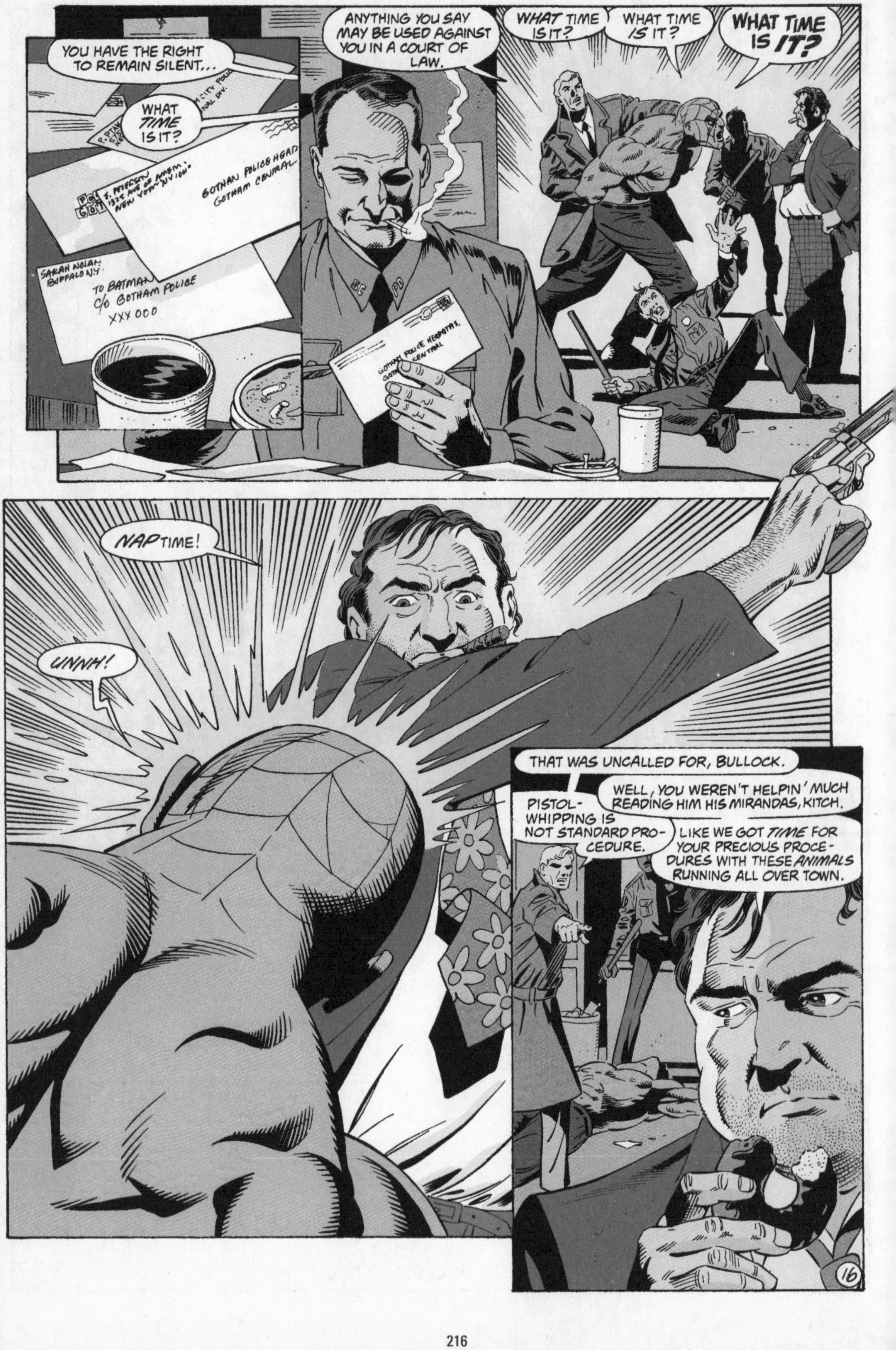
YOU HAVE THE RIGHT TO REMAIN SILENT...
WHAT TIME IS IT?
ANYTHING YOU SAY MAY BE USED AGAINST YOU IN A COURT OF LAW.
WHAT TIME IS IT?
WHAT TIME IS IT?
WHAT TIME IS IT?
NAP TIME!
UNNH!
THAT WAS UNCALLED FOR, BULLOCK.
WELL, YOU WEREN'T HELPIN' MUCH READING HIM HIS MIRANDAS, KITCH.
PISTOL-WHIPPING IS NOT STANDARD PRO-CEDURE.
LIKE WE GOT TIME FOR YOUR PRECIOUS PROCE-DURES WITH THESE ANIMALS RUNNING ALL OVER TOWN.
16

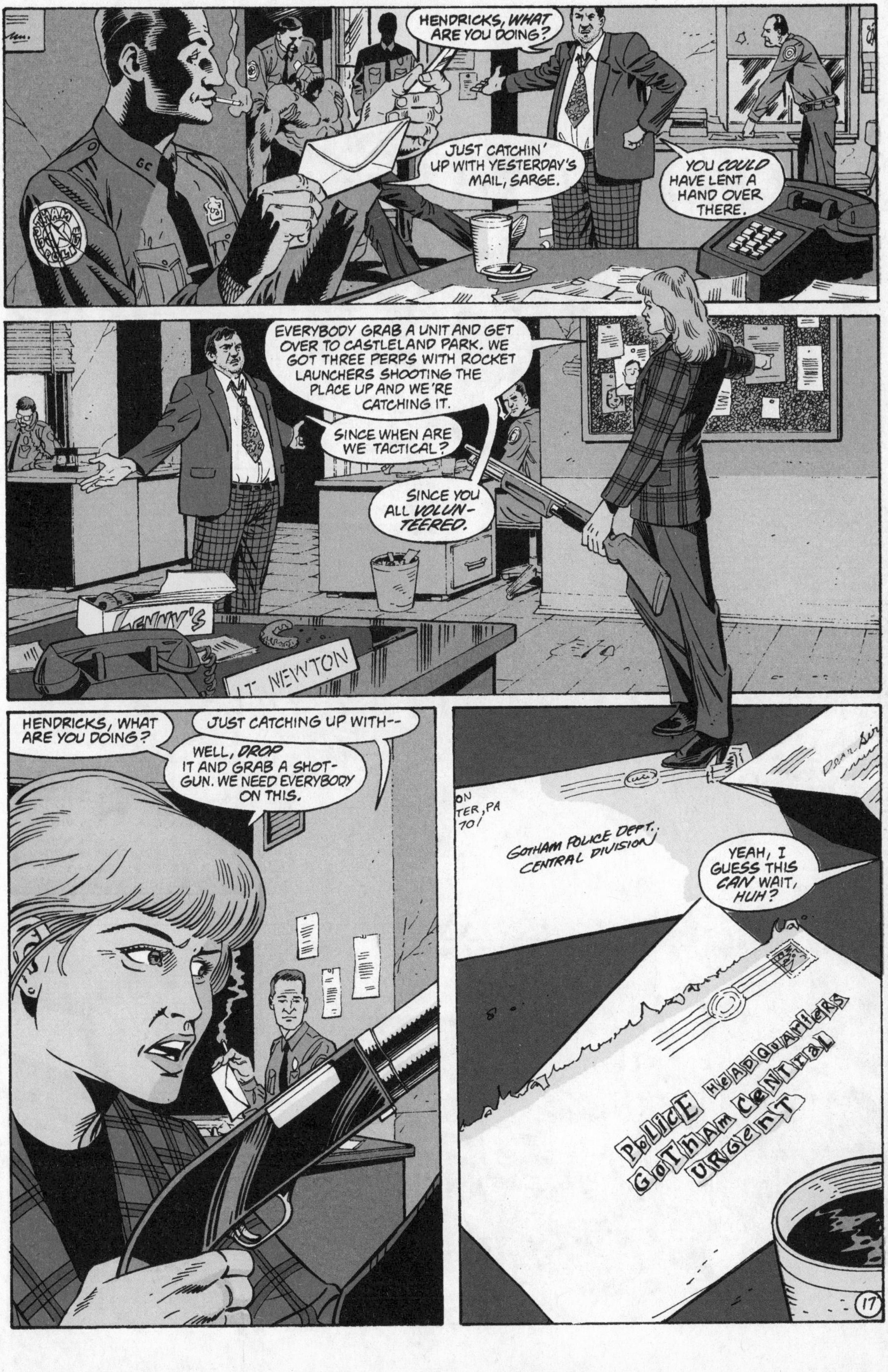
HENDRICKS, *WHAT* ARE YOU DOING?
JUST CATCHIN' UP WITH YESTERDAY'S MAIL, SARGE.
YOU *COULD* HAVE LENT A HAND OVER THERE.
EVERYBODY GRAB A UNIT AND GET OVER TO CASTLELAND PARK. WE GOT THREE PERPS WITH ROCKET LAUNCHERS SHOOTING THE PLACE UP AND WE'RE CATCHING IT.
SINCE WHEN ARE WE TACTICAL?
SINCE YOU ALL *VOLUNTEERED.*
LT. NEWTON
HENDRICKS, WHAT ARE YOU DOING?
JUST CATCHING UP WITH--
WELL, *DROP* IT AND GRAB A SHOTGUN. WE NEED EVERYBODY ON THIS.
GOTHAM POLICE DEPT. CENTRAL DIVISION
YEAH, I GUESS THIS *CAN* WAIT, HUH?
POLICE HEADQUARTERS
GOTHAM CENTRAL
URGENT
17

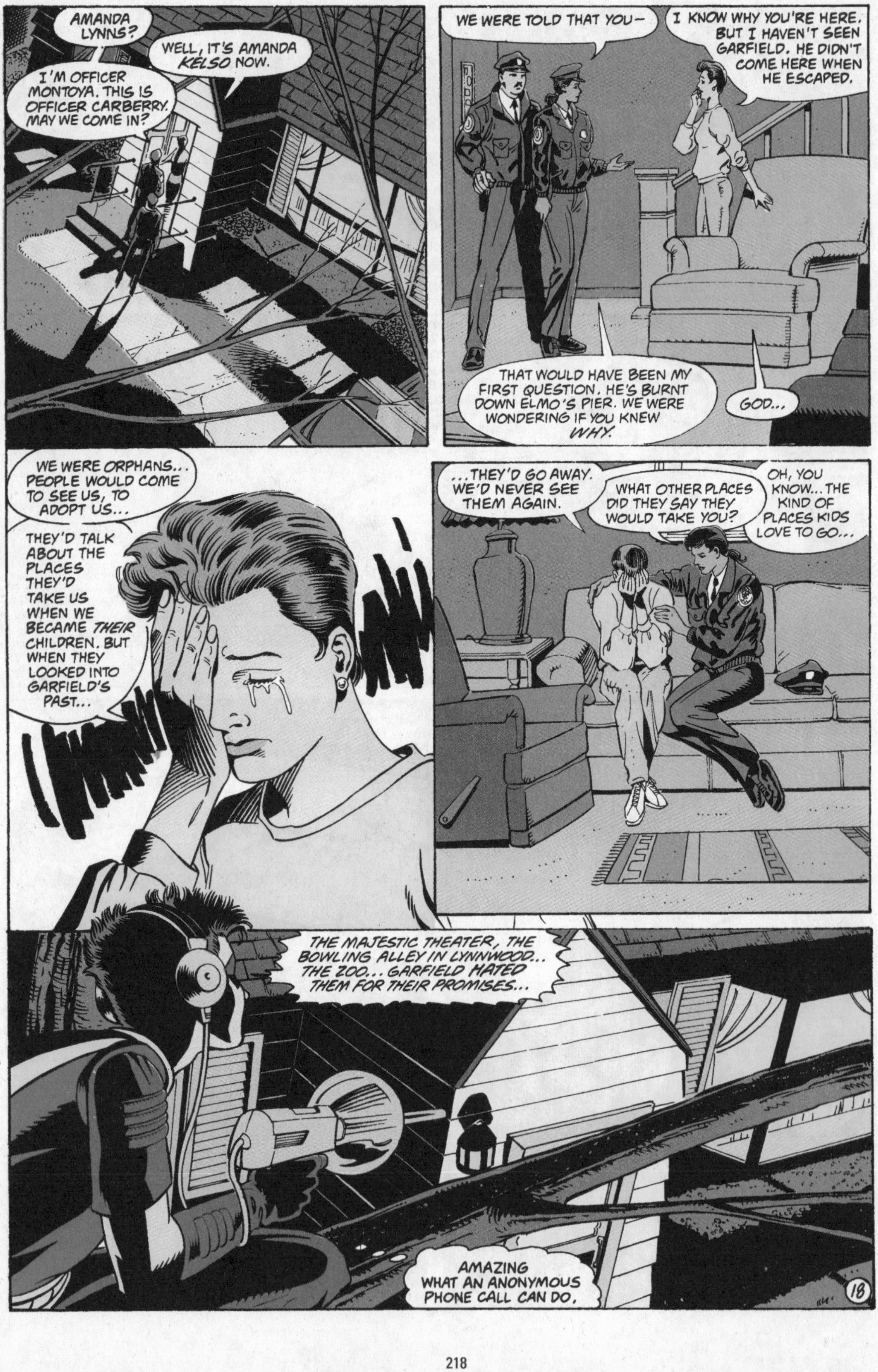
AMANDA LYNNS?
WELL, IT'S AMANDA *KELSO* NOW.
I'M OFFICER MONTOYA. THIS IS OFFICER CARBERRY. MAY WE COME IN?
WE WERE TOLD THAT YOU—
I KNOW WHY YOU'RE HERE. BUT I HAVEN'T SEEN GARFIELD. HE DIDN'T COME HERE WHEN HE ESCAPED.
THAT WOULD HAVE BEEN MY FIRST QUESTION. HE'S BURNT DOWN ELMO'S PIER. WE WERE WONDERING IF YOU KNEW *WHY*.
GOD...
WE WERE ORPHANS... PEOPLE WOULD COME TO SEE US, TO ADOPT US...
THEY'D TALK ABOUT THE PLACES THEY'D TAKE US WHEN WE BECAME *THEIR* CHILDREN. BUT WHEN THEY LOOKED INTO GARFIELD'S PAST...
...THEY'D GO AWAY. WE'D NEVER SEE THEM AGAIN.
WHAT OTHER PLACES DID THEY SAY THEY WOULD TAKE YOU?
OH, YOU KNOW... THE KIND OF PLACES KIDS LOVE TO GO...
THE MAJESTIC THEATER, THE BOWLING ALLEY IN LYNNWOOD... THE ZOO... GARFIELD HATED THEM FOR THEIR PROMISES...
AMAZING WHAT AN ANONYMOUS PHONE CALL CAN DO.
18

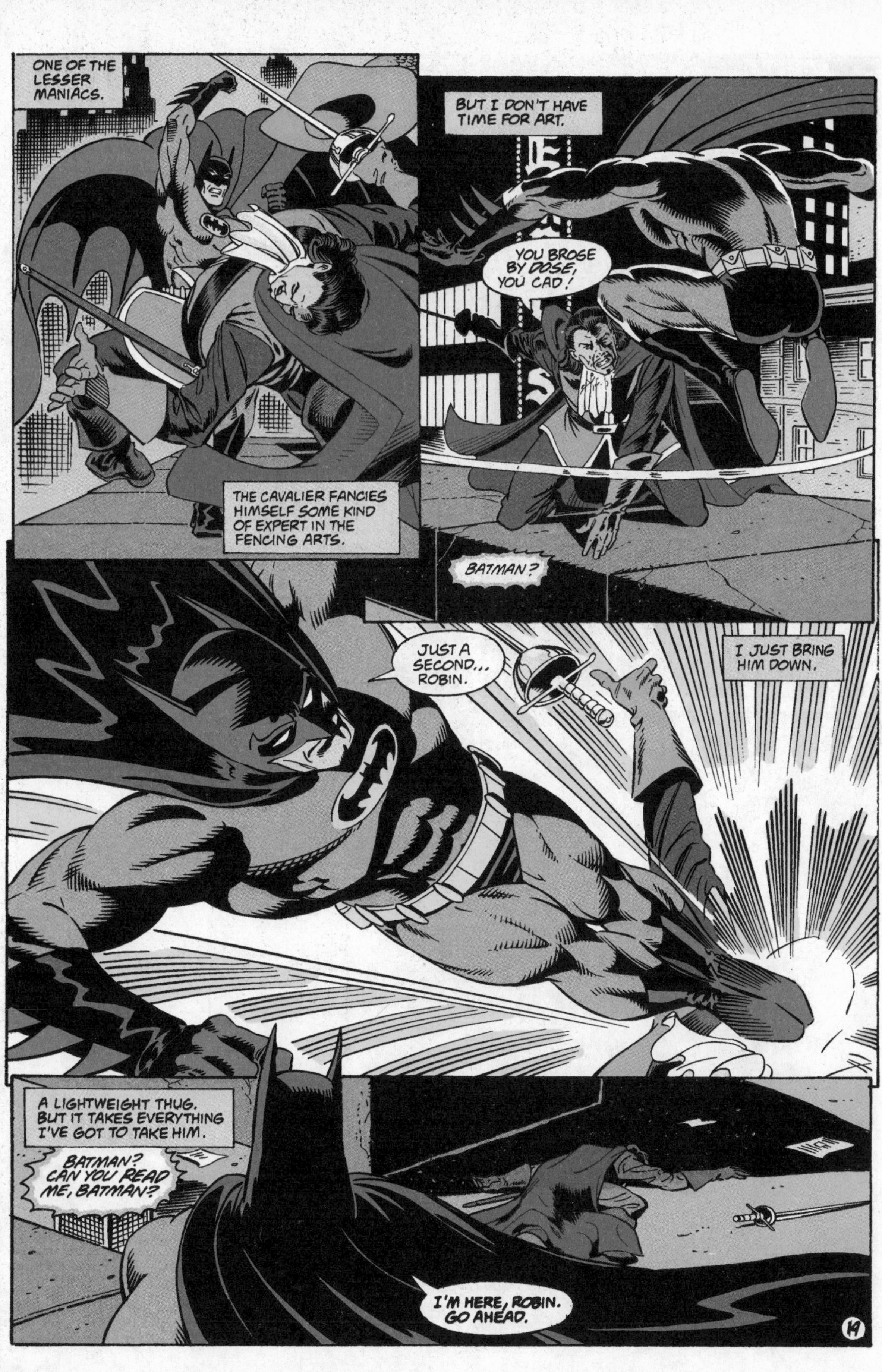

ONE OF THE LESSER MANIACS.
THE CAVALIER FANCIES HIMSELF SOME KIND OF EXPERT IN THE FENCING ARTS.
BUT I DON'T HAVE TIME FOR ART.
YOU BROSE BY DOSE, YOU CAD!
BATMAN?
JUST A SECOND... ROBIN.
I JUST BRING HIM DOWN.
A LIGHTWEIGHT THUG. BUT IT TAKES EVERYTHING I'VE GOT TO TAKE HIM.
BATMAN? CAN YOU READ ME, BATMAN?
I'M HERE, ROBIN. GO AHEAD.
19

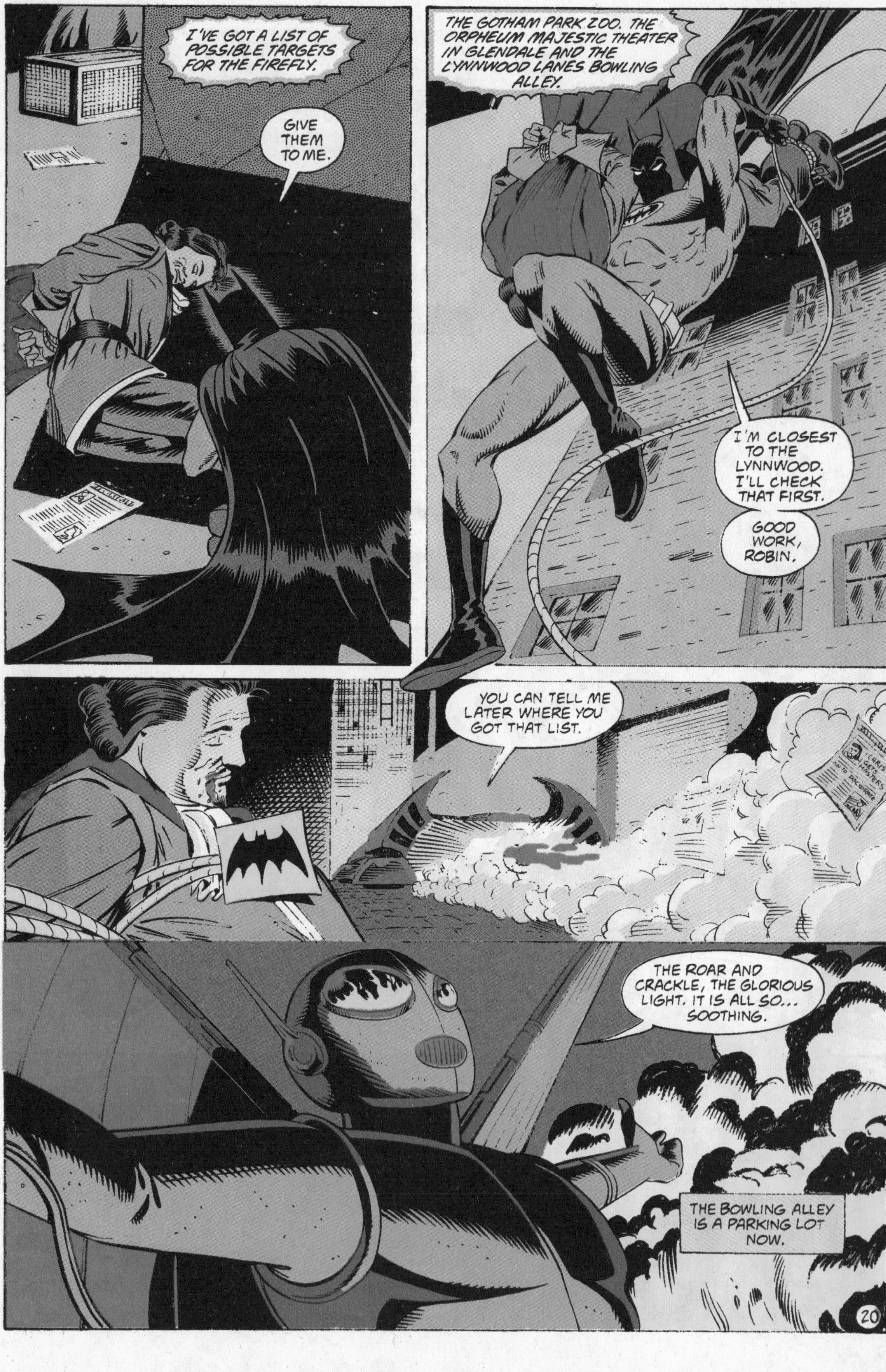
I'VE GOT A LIST OF POSSIBLE TARGETS FOR THE FIREFLY.
GIVE THEM TO ME.
THE GOTHAM PARK ZOO. THE ORPHEUM MAJESTIC THEATER IN GLENDALE AND THE LYNNWOOD LANES BOWLING ALLEY.
I'M CLOSEST TO THE LYNNWOOD. I'LL CHECK THAT FIRST.
GOOD WORK, ROBIN.
YOU CAN TELL ME LATER WHERE YOU GOT THAT LIST.
THE ROAR AND CRACKLE, THE GLORIOUS LIGHT. IT IS ALL SO... SOOTHING.
THE BOWLING ALLEY IS A PARKING LOT NOW.
20

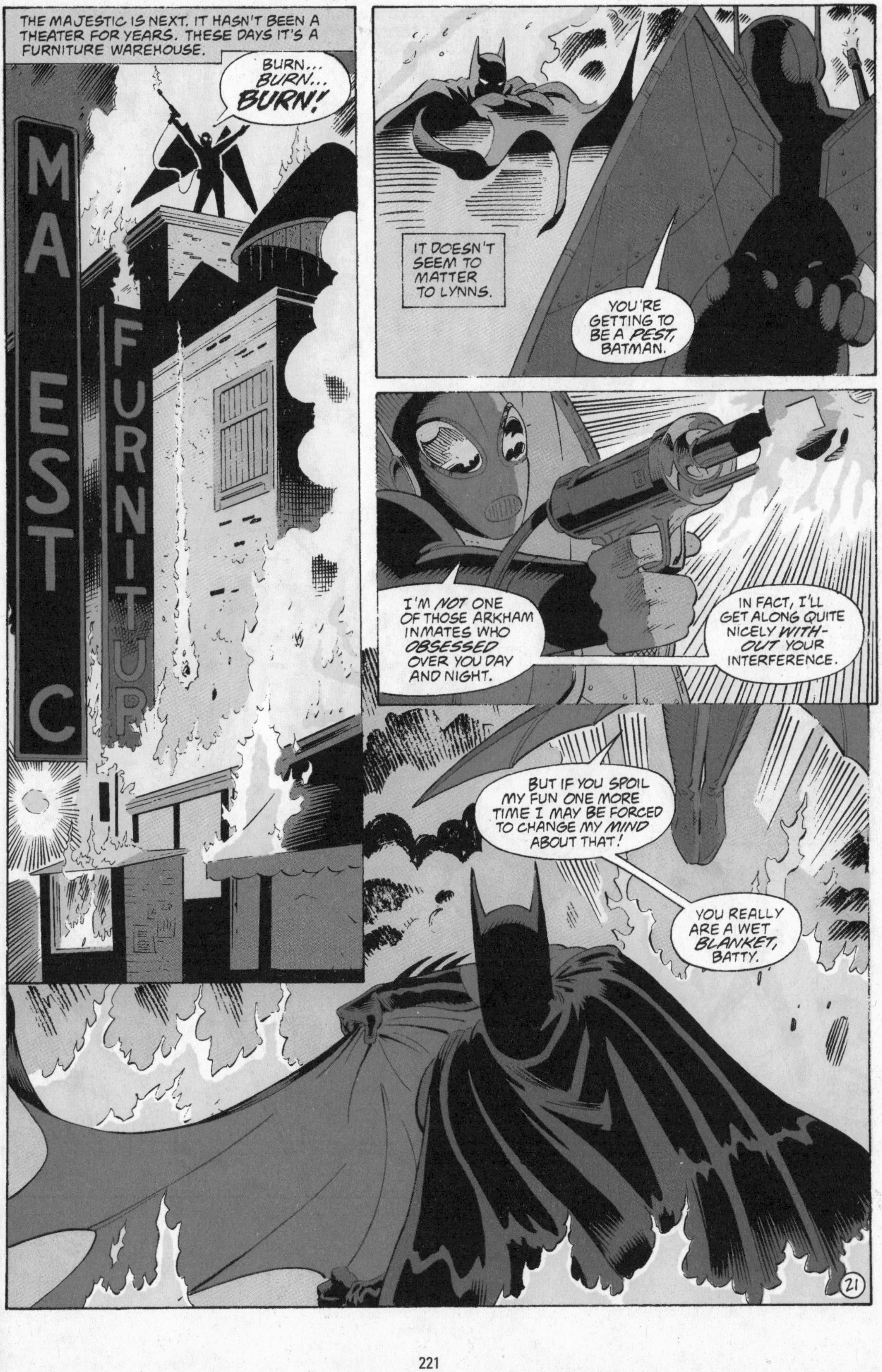
THE MAJESTIC IS NEXT. IT HASN'T BEEN A THEATER FOR YEARS. THESE DAYS IT'S A FURNITURE WAREHOUSE.
BURN... BURN... BURN!
MAJESTIC
FURNITUR
IT DOESN'T SEEM TO MATTER TO LYNNS.
YOU'RE GETTING TO BE A PEST, BATMAN.
I'M NOT ONE OF THOSE ARKHAM INMATES WHO OBSESSED OVER YOU DAY AND NIGHT.
IN FACT, I'LL GET ALONG QUITE NICELY WITHOUT YOUR INTERFERENCE.
BUT IF YOU SPOIL MY FUN ONE MORE TIME I MAY BE FORCED TO CHANGE MY MIND ABOUT THAT!
YOU REALLY ARE A WET BLANKET, BATTY.
21

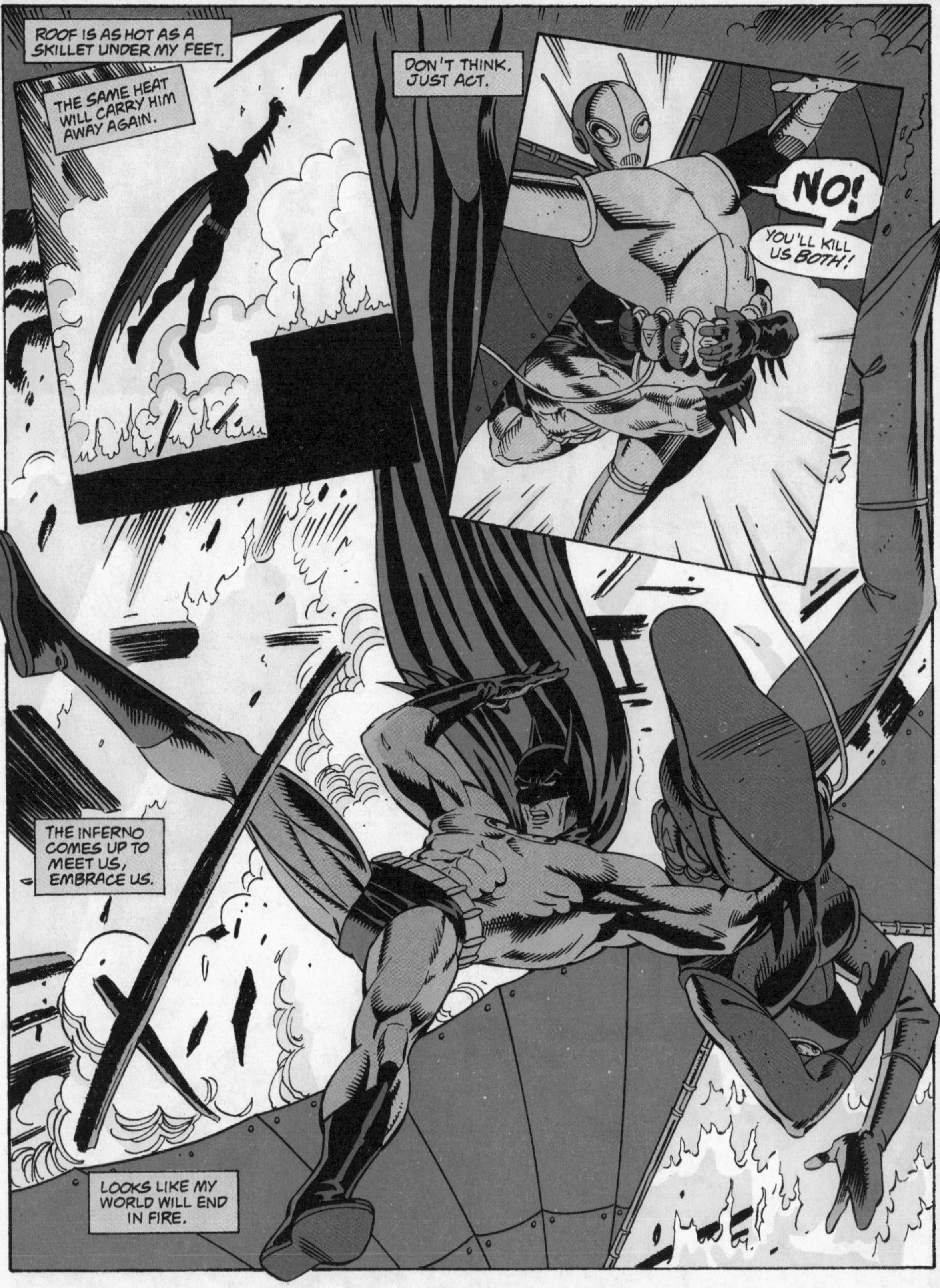

ROOF IS AS HOT AS A SKILLET UNDER MY FEET.
THE SAME HEAT WILL CARRY HIM AWAY AGAIN.
DON'T THINK. JUST ACT.
NO!
YOU'LL KILL US BOTH!
THE INFERNO COMES UP TO MEET US, EMBRACE US.
LOOKS LIKE MY WORLD WILL END IN FIRE.

Cover art by KELLEY JONES

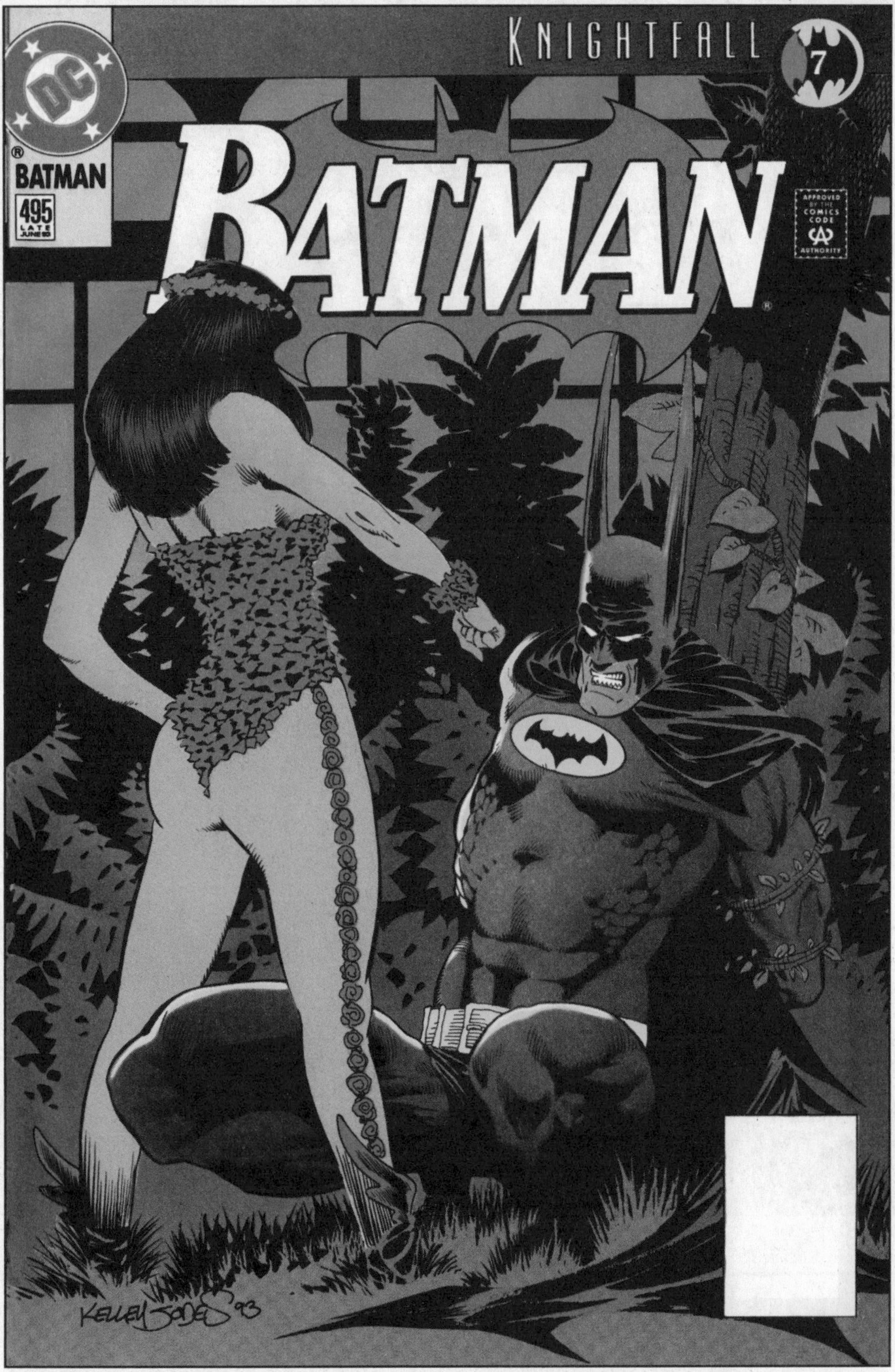
KNIGHTFALL
7
DC
BATMAN
495
LATE JUNE 93
BATMAN
APPROVED BY THE COMICS CODE AUTHORITY
KELLEY JONES '93

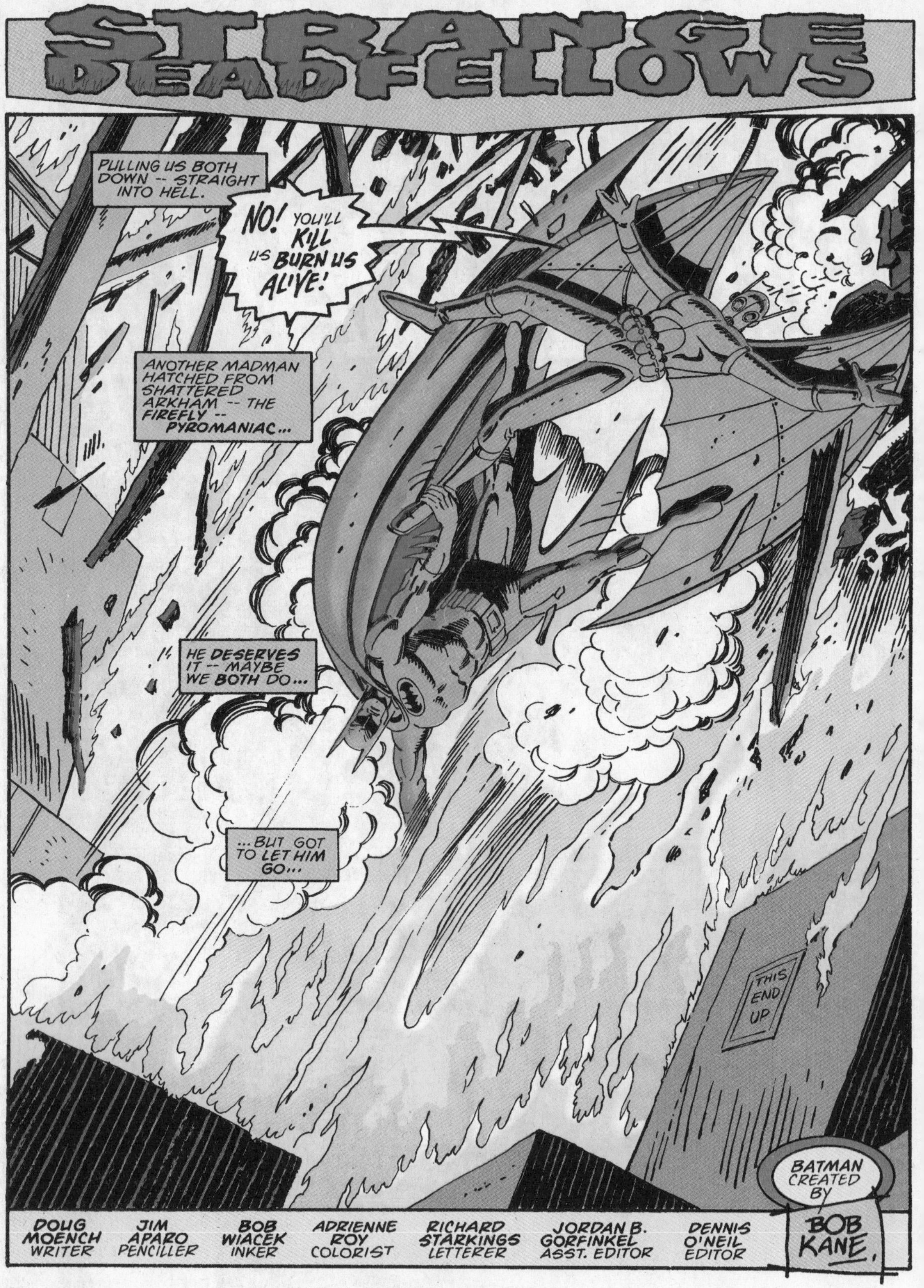
STRANGE DEADFELLOWS
PULLING US BOTH DOWN -- STRAIGHT INTO HELL.
NO! YOU'LL KILL US BURN US ALIVE!
ANOTHER MADMAN HATCHED FROM SHATTERED ARKHAM -- THE FIREFLY -- PYROMANIAC...
HE DESERVES IT -- MAYBE WE BOTH DO...
...BUT GOT TO LET HIM GO...
THIS END UP
BATMAN CREATED BY BOB KANE
DOUG MOENCH WRITER
JIM APARO PENCILLER
BOB WIACEK INKER
ADRIENNE ROY COLORIST
RICHARD STARKINGS LETTERER
JORDAN B. GORFINKEL ASST. EDITOR
DENNIS O'NEIL EDITOR

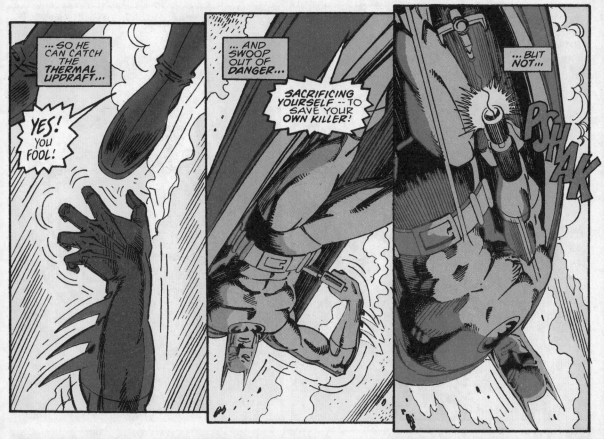

...SO HE CAN CATCH THE THERMAL UPDRAFT...

YES! YOU FOOL!

...AND SWOOP OUT OF DANGER...

SACRIFICING YOURSELF -- TO SAVE YOUR OWN KILLER!

...BUT NOT...

P-SHAK

...OUT OF REACH.

WHAT THE--?!

S-TAK-T

GOT TO HOLD ON -- TOUGH OUT THE IMPACT...

...LET MY CAPE PROTECT ME...

SKRASSH

2

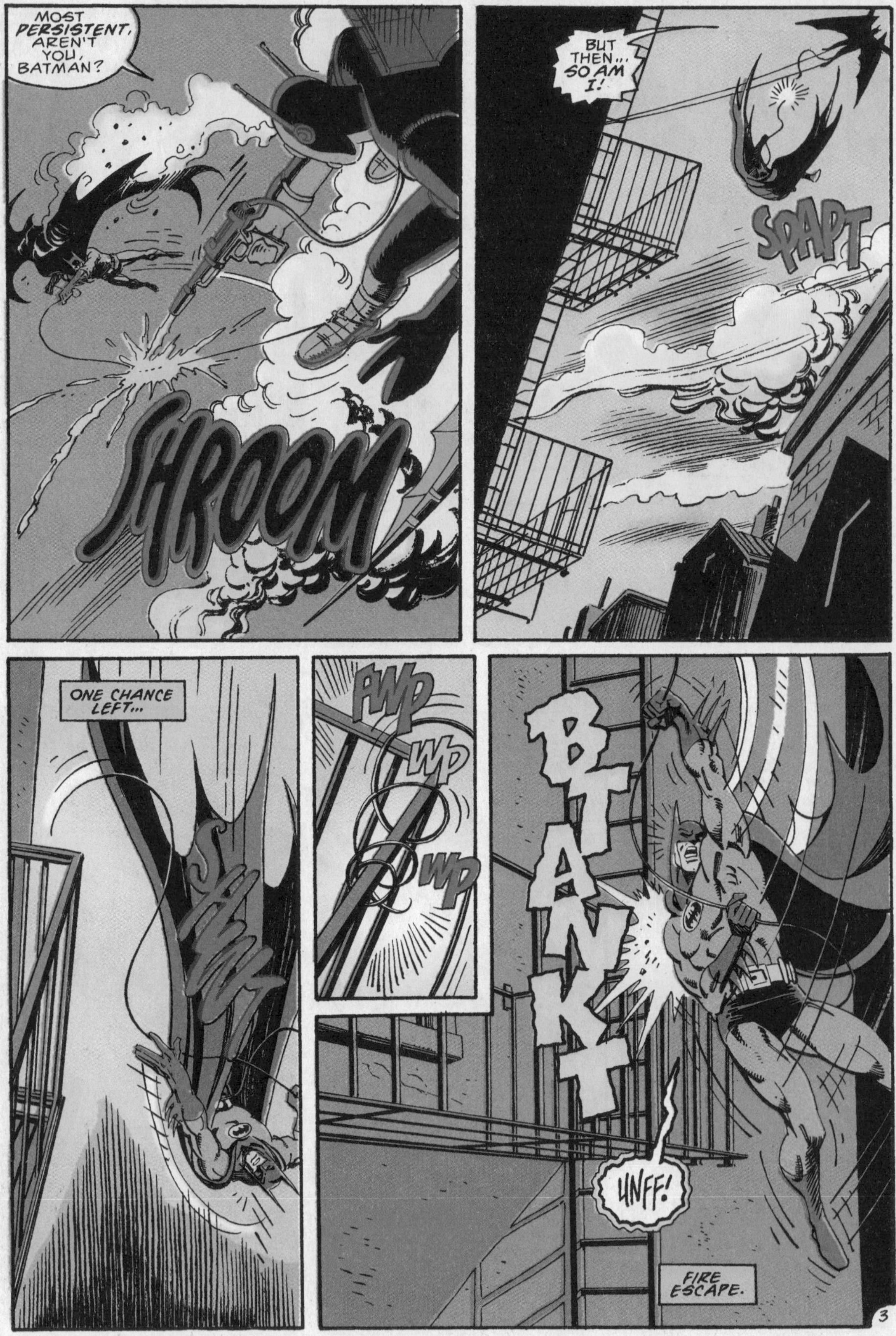
MOST PERSISTENT, AREN'T YOU, BATMAN?
SHROOM
BUT THEN... SO AM I!
SPAPT
ONE CHANCE LEFT...
SHWW
FWP
WP
WP
BTANK
UNFF!
FIRE ESCAPE.
3

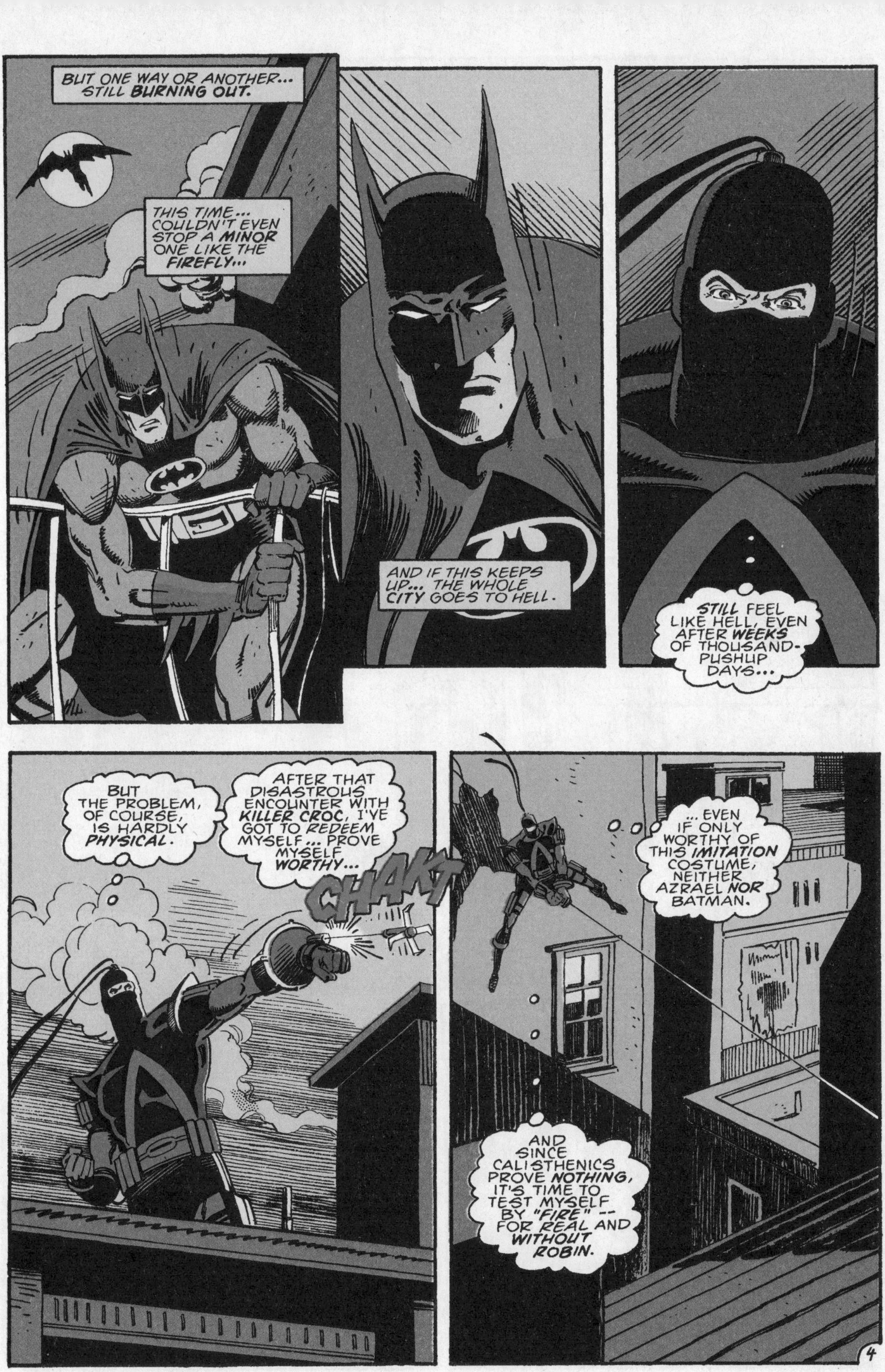
BUT ONE WAY OR ANOTHER... STILL BURNING OUT.
THIS TIME... COULDN'T EVEN STOP A MINOR ONE LIKE THE FIREFLY...
AND IF THIS KEEPS UP... THE WHOLE CITY GOES TO HELL.
STILL FEEL LIKE HELL, EVEN AFTER WEEKS OF THOUSAND-PUSHUP DAYS...
BUT THE PROBLEM, OF COURSE, IS HARDLY PHYSICAL.
AFTER THAT DISASTROUS ENCOUNTER WITH KILLER CROC, I'VE GOT TO REDEEM MYSELF... PROVE MYSELF WORTHY...
CHAKT
... EVEN IF ONLY WORTHY OF THIS IMITATION COSTUME, NEITHER AZRAEL NOR BATMAN.
AND SINCE CALISTHENICS PROVE NOTHING, IT'S TIME TO TEST MYSELF BY "FIRE" -- FOR REAL AND WITHOUT ROBIN.
4

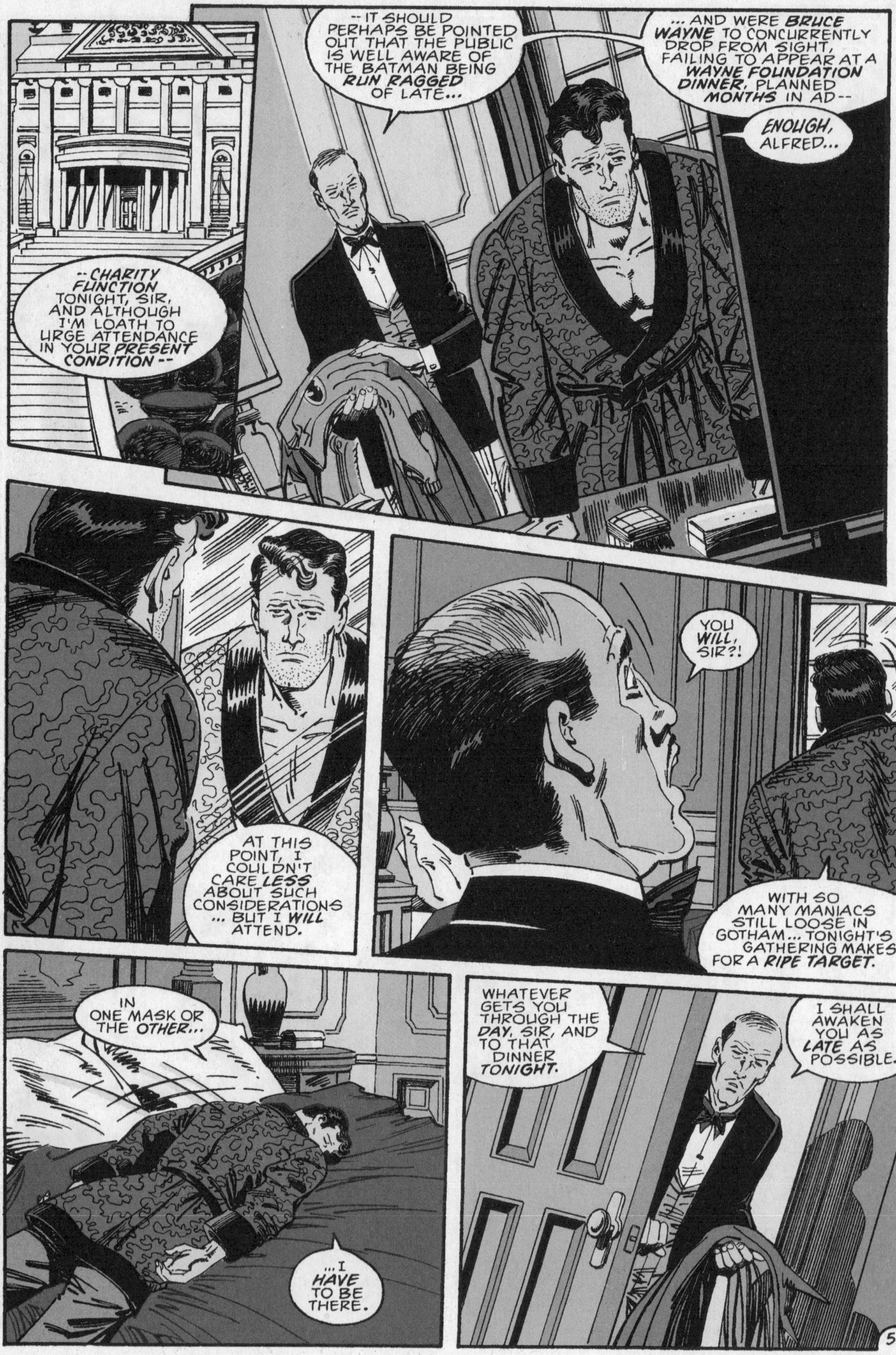
--CHARITY FUNCTION TONIGHT, SIR, AND ALTHOUGH I'M LOATH TO URGE ATTENDANCE IN YOUR PRESENT CONDITION--
--IT SHOULD PERHAPS BE POINTED OUT THAT THE PUBLIC IS WELL AWARE OF THE BATMAN BEING RUN RAGGED OF LATE...
...AND WERE BRUCE WAYNE TO CONCURRENTLY DROP FROM SIGHT, FAILING TO APPEAR AT A WAYNE FOUNDATION DINNER, PLANNED MONTHS IN AD--
ENOUGH, ALFRED...
AT THIS POINT, I COULDN'T CARE LESS ABOUT SUCH CONSIDERATIONS ... BUT I WILL ATTEND.
YOU WILL, SIR?!
WITH SO MANY MANIACS STILL LOOSE IN GOTHAM... TONIGHT'S GATHERING MAKES FOR A RIPE TARGET.
IN ONE MASK OR THE OTHER...
...I HAVE TO BE THERE.
WHATEVER GETS YOU THROUGH THE DAY, SIR, AND TO THAT DINNER TONIGHT.
I SHALL AWAKEN YOU AS LATE AS POSSIBLE.
5

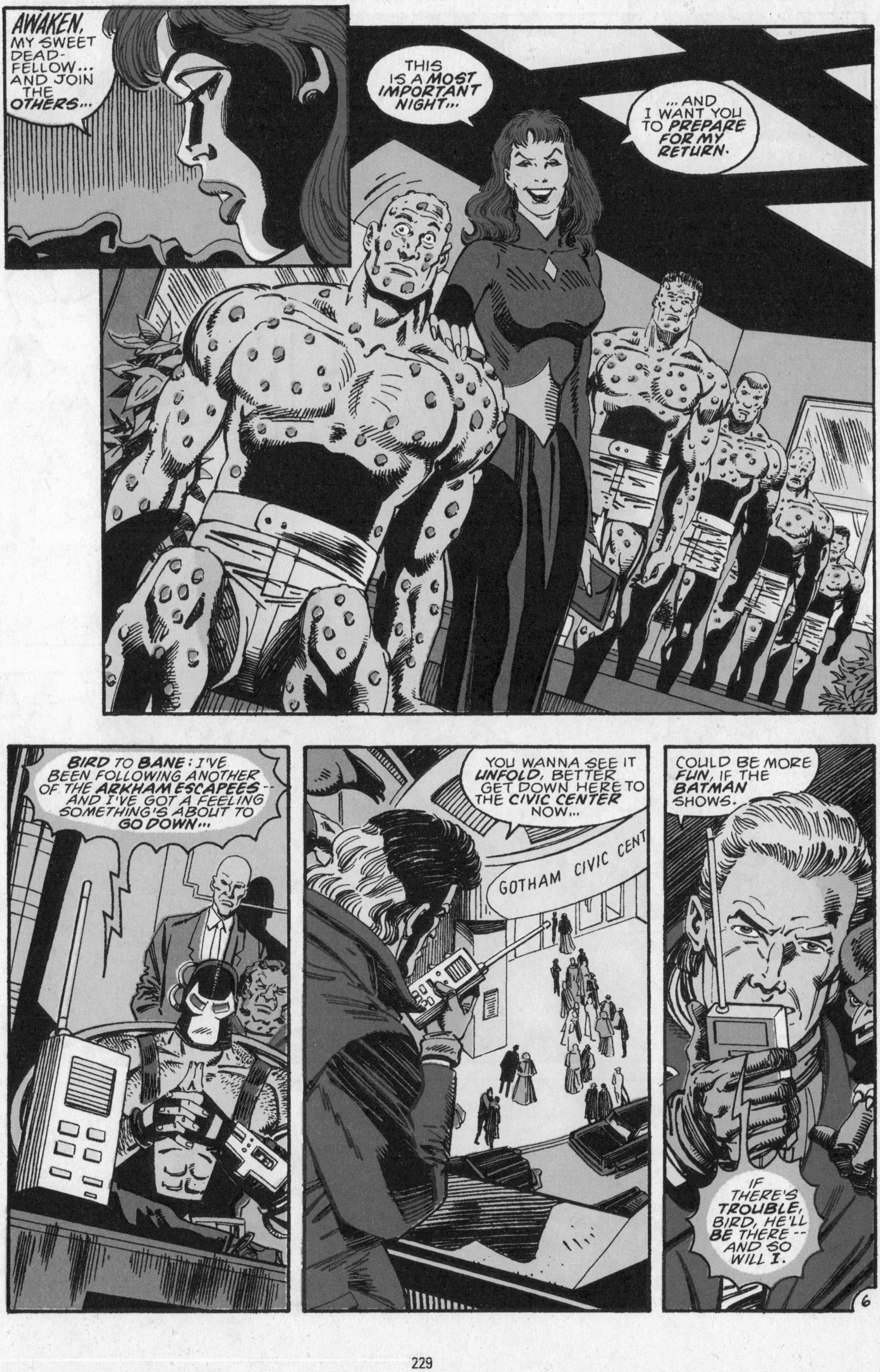
AWAKEN, MY SWEET DEAD-FELLOW... AND JOIN THE OTHERS...
THIS IS A MOST IMPORTANT NIGHT...
...AND I WANT YOU TO PREPARE FOR MY RETURN.
BIRD TO BANE: I'VE BEEN FOLLOWING ANOTHER OF THE ARKHAM ESCAPEES -- AND I'VE GOT A FEELING SOMETHING'S ABOUT TO GO DOWN...
YOU WANNA SEE IT UNFOLD, BETTER GET DOWN HERE TO THE CIVIC CENTER NOW...
GOTHAM CIVIC CENT
COULD BE MORE FUN, IF THE BATMAN SHOWS.
IF THERE'S TROUBLE, BIRD, HE'LL BE THERE -- AND SO WILL I.
6

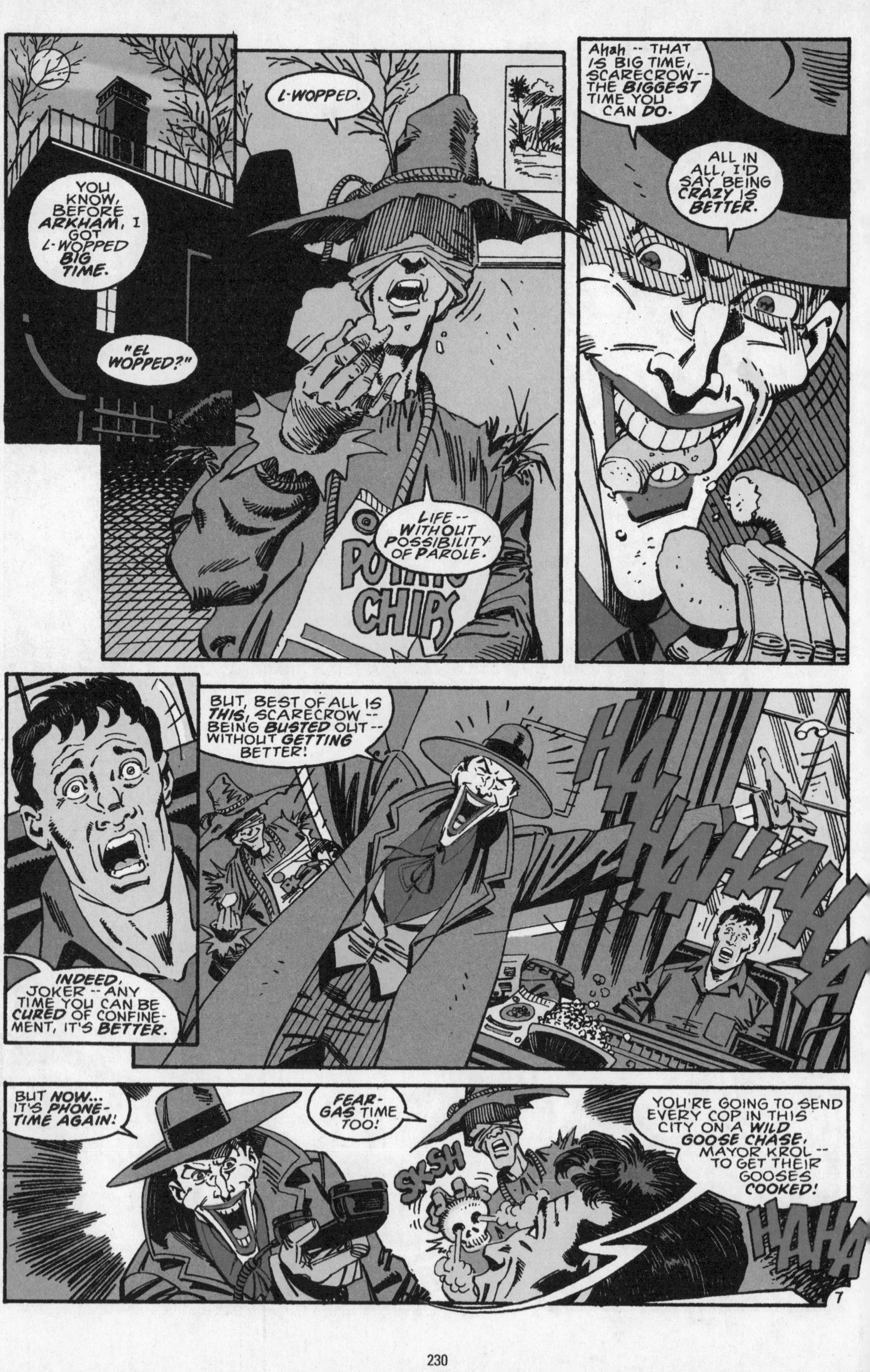
YOU KNOW, BEFORE ARKHAM, I GOT L-WOPPED BIG TIME.
"EL WOPPED?"
L-WOPPED.
LIFE -- WITHOUT POSSIBILITY OF PAROLE.
POTATO CHIPS
Ahah -- THAT IS BIG TIME, SCARECROW -- THE BIGGEST TIME YOU CAN DO.
ALL IN ALL, I'D SAY BEING CRAZY IS BETTER.
BUT, BEST OF ALL IS THIS, SCARECROW -- BEING BUSTED OUT -- WITHOUT GETTING BETTER!
INDEED, JOKER -- ANY TIME YOU CAN BE CURED OF CONFINE-MENT, IT'S BETTER.
HA HAHAHAHA
BUT NOW... IT'S PHONE-TIME AGAIN!
FEAR-GAS TIME TOO!
SKSH
YOU'RE GOING TO SEND EVERY COP IN THIS CITY ON A WILD GOOSE CHASE, MAYOR KROL -- TO GET THEIR GOOSES COOKED!
HAHA
7

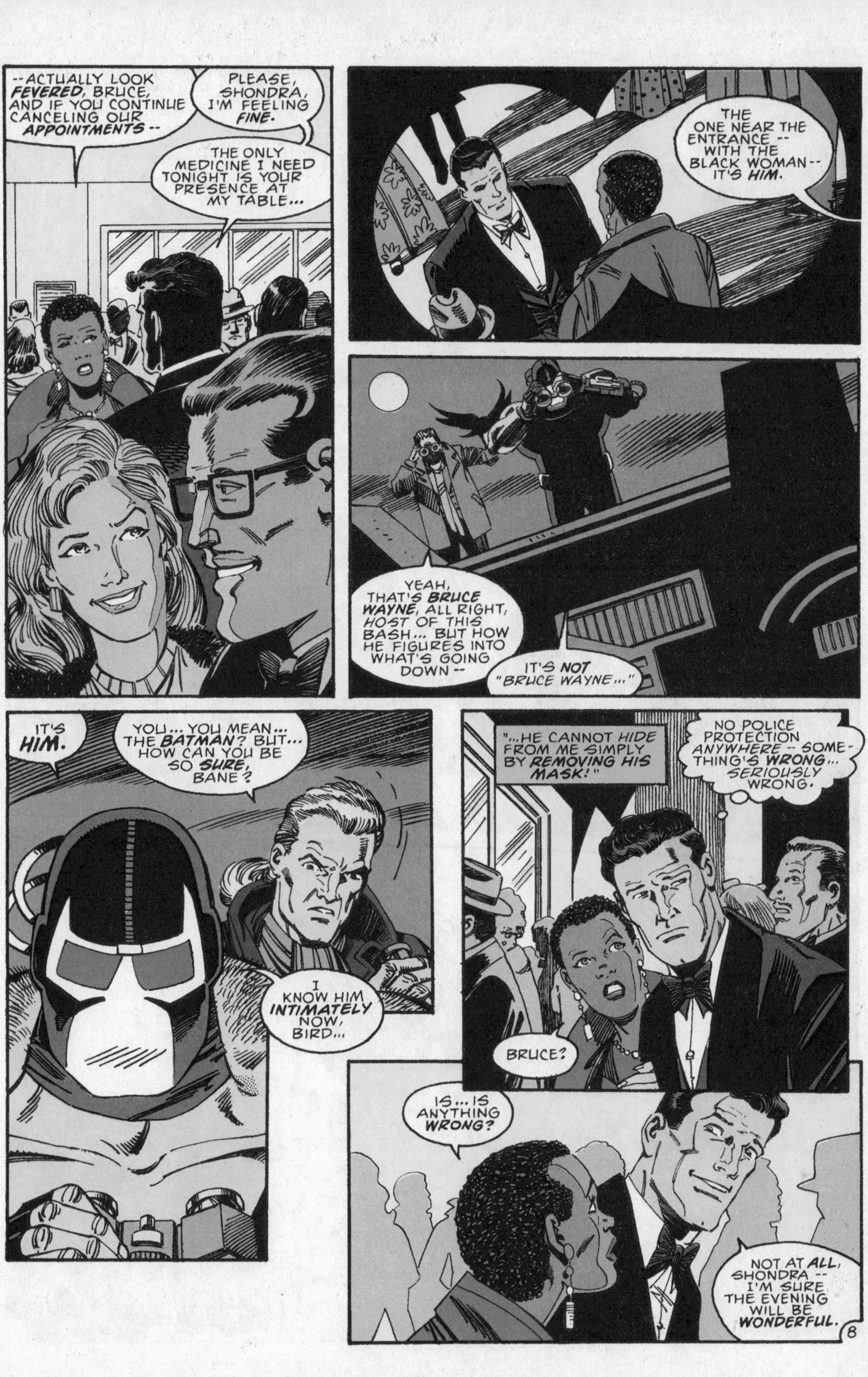
--ACTUALLY LOOK FEVERED, BRUCE, AND IF YOU CONTINUE CANCELING OUR APPOINTMENTS--
PLEASE, SHONDRA, I'M FEELING FINE.
THE ONLY MEDICINE I NEED TONIGHT IS YOUR PRESENCE AT MY TABLE...
THE ONE NEAR THE ENTRANCE -- WITH THE BLACK WOMAN-- IT'S HIM.
YEAH, THAT'S BRUCE WAYNE, ALL RIGHT, HOST OF THIS BASH... BUT HOW HE FIGURES INTO WHAT'S GOING DOWN --
IT'S NOT "BRUCE WAYNE..."
IT'S HIM.
YOU... YOU MEAN... THE BATMAN? BUT... HOW CAN YOU BE SO SURE, BANE?
I KNOW HIM INTIMATELY NOW, BIRD...
"...HE CANNOT HIDE FROM ME SIMPLY BY REMOVING HIS MASK!"
NO POLICE PROTECTION ANYWHERE -- SOMETHING'S WRONG... SERIOUSLY WRONG.
BRUCE?
IS... IS ANYTHING WRONG?
NOT AT ALL, SHONDRA -- I'M SURE THE EVENING WILL BE WONDERFUL.
8

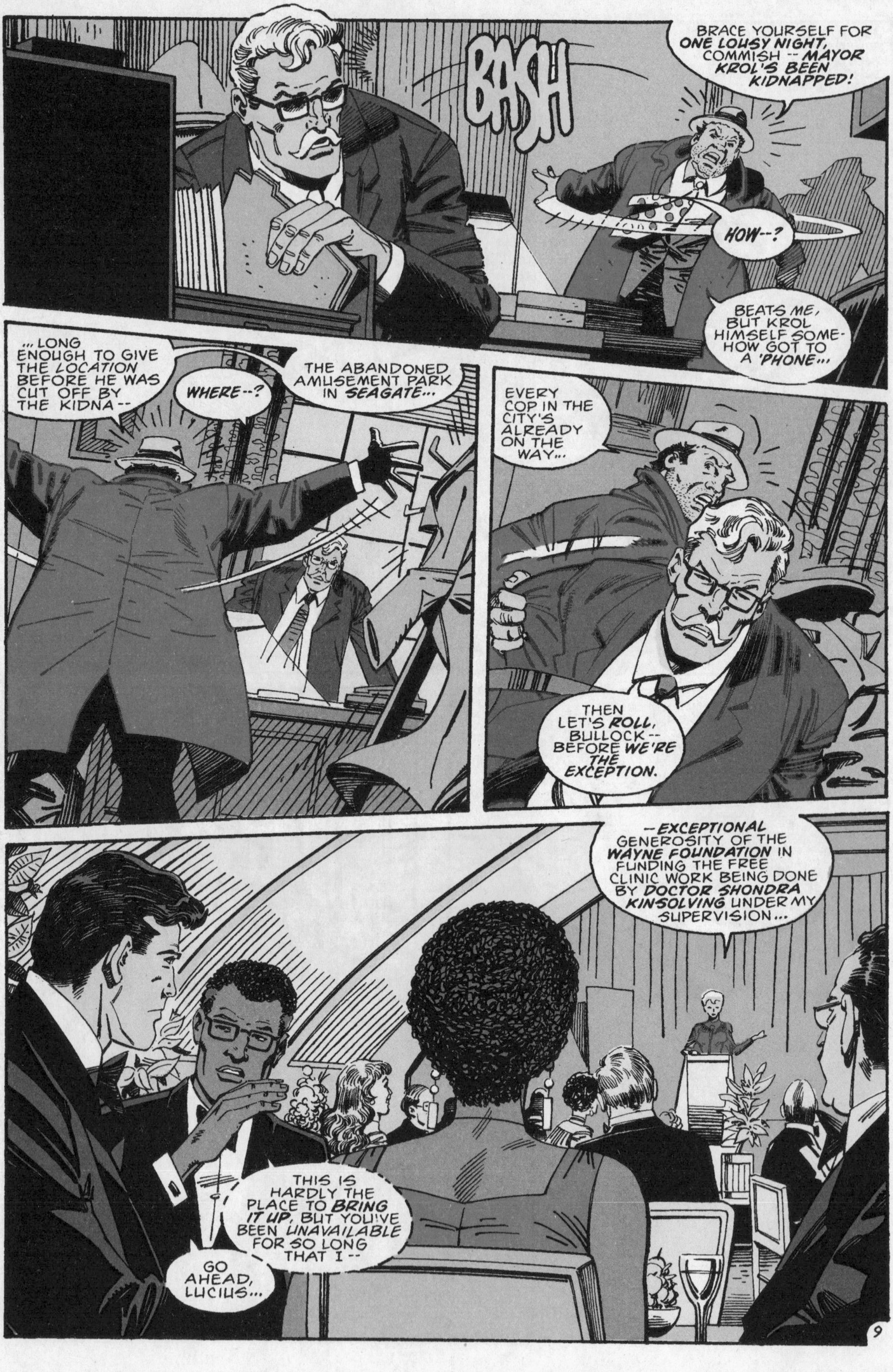
BASH
BRACE YOURSELF FOR ONE LOUSY NIGHT, COMMISH -- MAYOR KROL'S BEEN KIDNAPPED!
HOW--?
BEATS ME, BUT KROL HIMSELF SOMEHOW GOT TO A 'PHONE'...
...LONG ENOUGH TO GIVE THE LOCATION BEFORE HE WAS CUT OFF BY THE KIDNA--
WHERE--?
THE ABANDONED AMUSEMENT PARK IN SEAGATE...
EVERY COP IN THE CITY'S ALREADY ON THE WAY...
THEN LET'S ROLL, BULLOCK -- BEFORE WE'RE THE EXCEPTION.
--EXCEPTIONAL GENEROSITY OF THE WAYNE FOUNDATION IN FUNDING THE FREE CLINIC WORK BEING DONE BY DOCTOR SHONDRA KINSOLVING UNDER MY SUPERVISION...
THIS IS HARDLY THE PLACE TO BRING IT UP, BUT YOU'VE BEEN UNAVAILABLE FOR SO LONG THAT I --
GO AHEAD, LUCIUS...
9

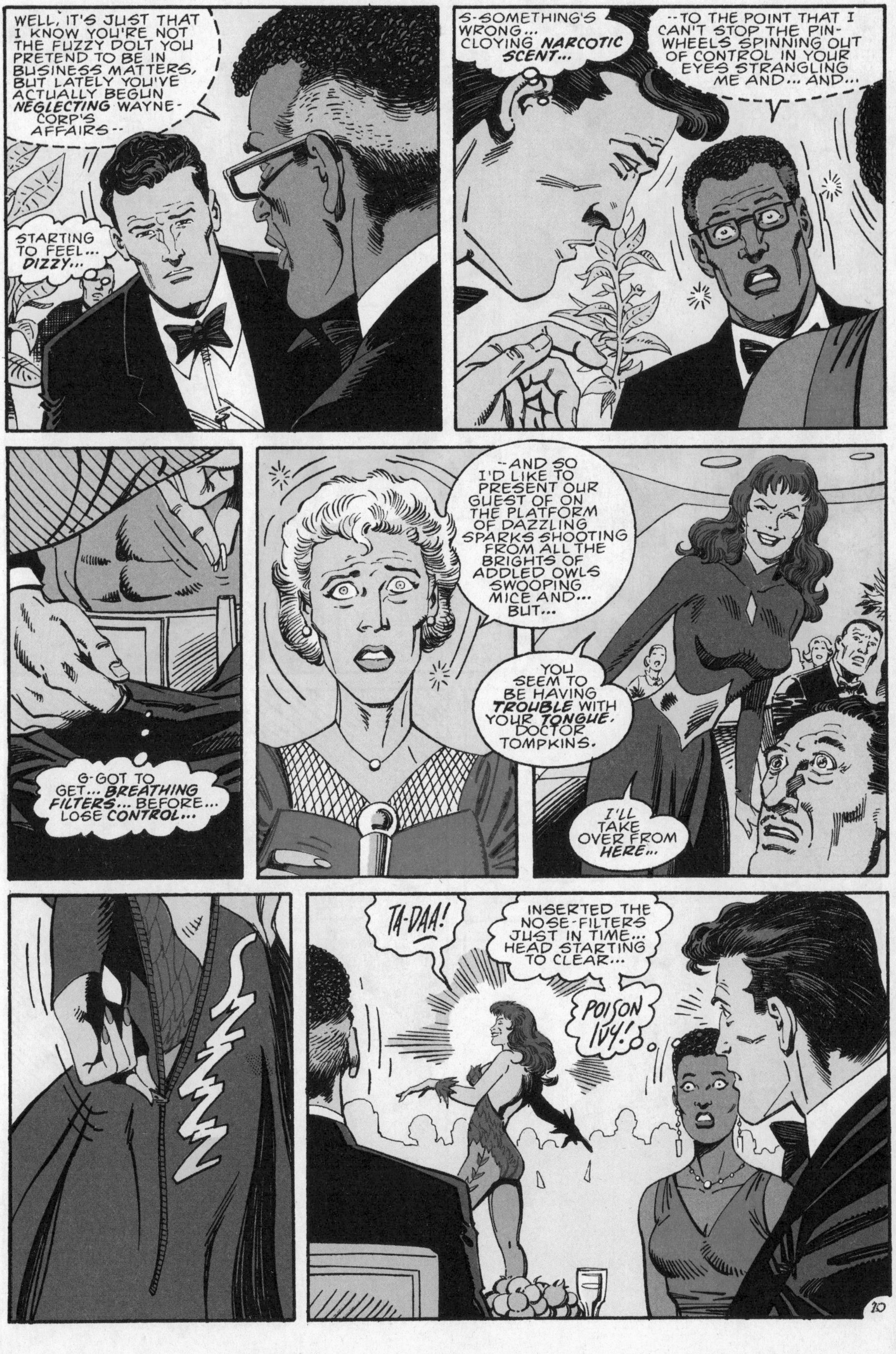
WELL, IT'S JUST THAT I KNOW YOU'RE NOT THE FUZZY DOLT YOU PRETEND TO BE IN BUSINESS MATTERS, BUT LATELY YOU'VE ACTUALLY BEGUN NEGLECTING WAYNE-CORP'S AFFAIRS--
STARTING TO FEEL... DIZZY...
S-SOMETHING'S WRONG... CLOYING NARCOTIC SCENT...
--TO THE POINT THAT I CAN'T STOP THE PIN-WHEELS SPINNING OUT OF CONTROL IN YOUR EYES STRANGLING ME AND... AND...
G-GOT TO GET... BREATHING FILTERS... BEFORE... LOSE CONTROL...
--AND SO I'D LIKE TO PRESENT OUR GUEST OF ON THE PLATFORM OF DAZZLING SPARKS SHOOTING FROM ALL THE BRIGHTS OF ADDLED OWLS SWOOPING MICE AND... BUT...
YOU SEEM TO BE HAVING TROUBLE WITH YOUR TONGUE, DOCTOR TOMPKINS.
I'LL TAKE OVER FROM HERE...
TA-DAA!
INSERTED THE NOSE-FILTERS JUST IN TIME... HEAD STARTING TO CLEAR...
POISON IVY!
10

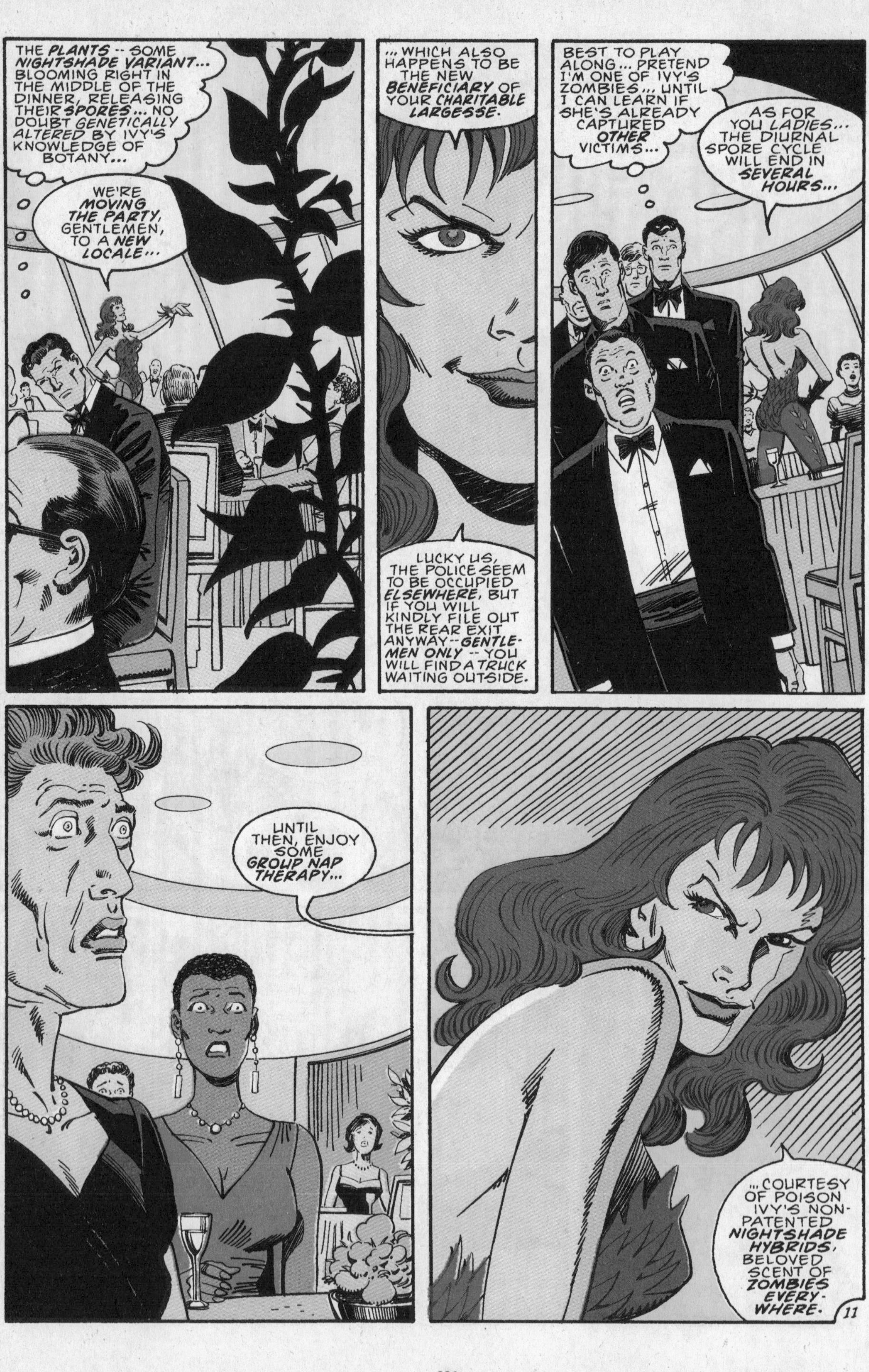
THE PLANTS -- SOME NIGHTSHADE VARIANT... BLOOMING RIGHT IN THE MIDDLE OF THE DINNER, RELEASING THEIR SPORES... NO DOUBT GENETICALLY ALTERED BY IVY'S KNOWLEDGE OF BOTANY...
WE'RE MOVING THE PARTY, GENTLEMEN, TO A NEW LOCALE...
...WHICH ALSO HAPPENS TO BE THE NEW BENEFICIARY OF YOUR CHARITABLE LARGESSE.
LUCKY US, THE POLICE SEEM TO BE OCCUPIED ELSEWHERE, BUT IF YOU WILL KINDLY FILE OUT THE REAR EXIT ANYWAY--GENTLEMEN ONLY -- YOU WILL FIND A TRUCK WAITING OUTSIDE.
BEST TO PLAY ALONG... PRETEND I'M ONE OF IVY'S ZOMBIES... UNTIL I CAN LEARN IF SHE'S ALREADY CAPTURED OTHER VICTIMS...
AS FOR YOU LADIES... THE DIURNAL SPORE CYCLE WILL END IN SEVERAL HOURS...
UNTIL THEN, ENJOY SOME GROUP NAP THERAPY...
...COURTESY OF POISON IVY'S NON-PATENTED NIGHTSHADE HYBRIDS, BELOVED SCENT OF ZOMBIES EVERYWHERE.
11

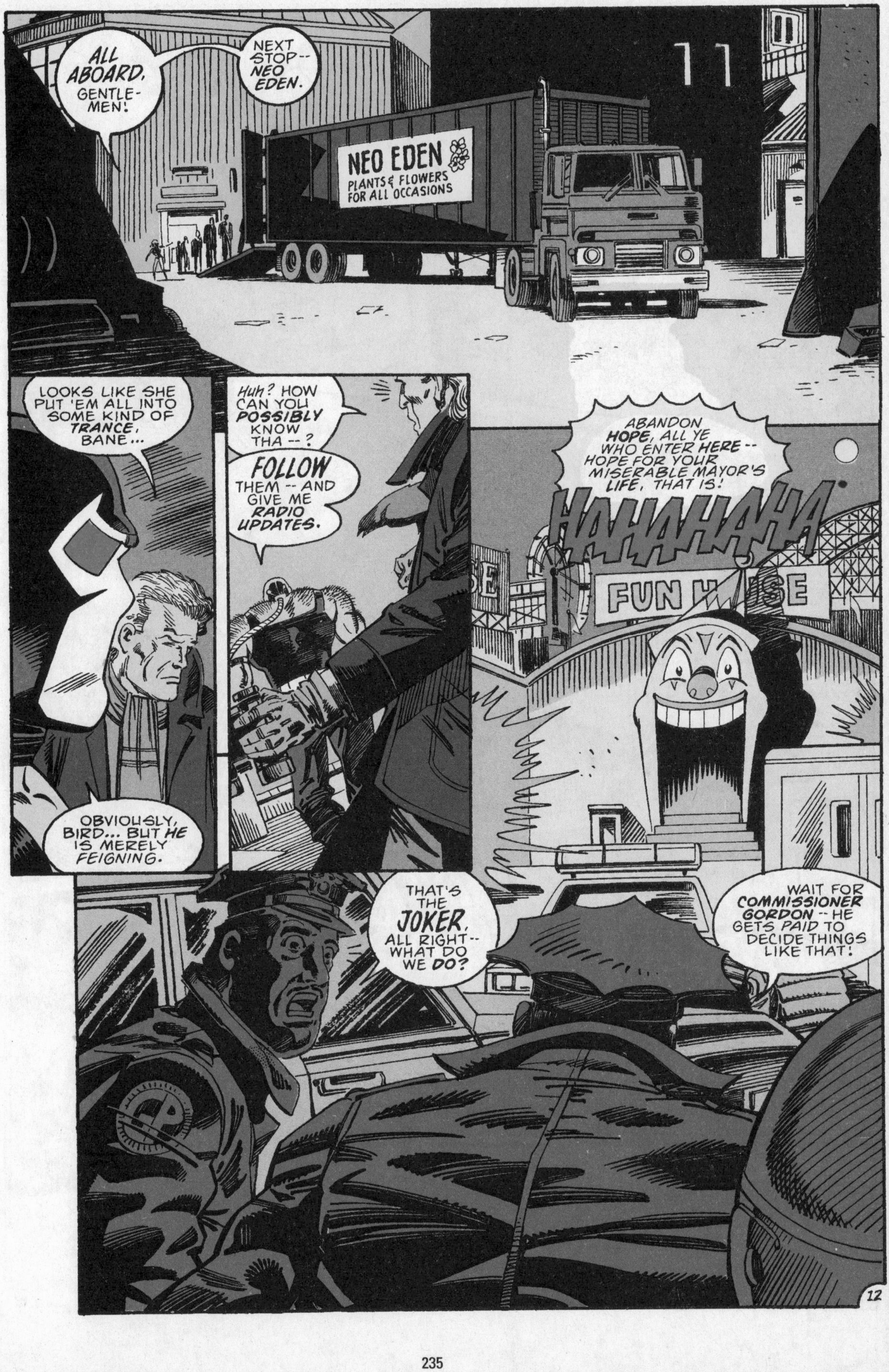
ALL ABOARD, GENTLEMEN!
NEXT STOP-- NEO EDEN.
NEO EDEN PLANTS & FLOWERS FOR ALL OCCASIONS
LOOKS LIKE SHE PUT 'EM ALL INTO SOME KIND OF TRANCE, BANE...
OBVIOUSLY, BIRD... BUT HE IS MERELY FEIGNING.
Huh? HOW CAN YOU POSSIBLY KNOW THA--?
FOLLOW THEM--AND GIVE ME RADIO UPDATES.
ABANDON HOPE, ALL YE WHO ENTER HERE-- HOPE FOR YOUR MISERABLE MAYOR'S LIFE, THAT IS!
HAHAHAHA
FUN H USE
THAT'S THE JOKER, ALL RIGHT-- WHAT DO WE DO?
WAIT FOR COMMISSIONER GORDON-- HE GETS PAID TO DECIDE THINGS LIKE THAT!
12

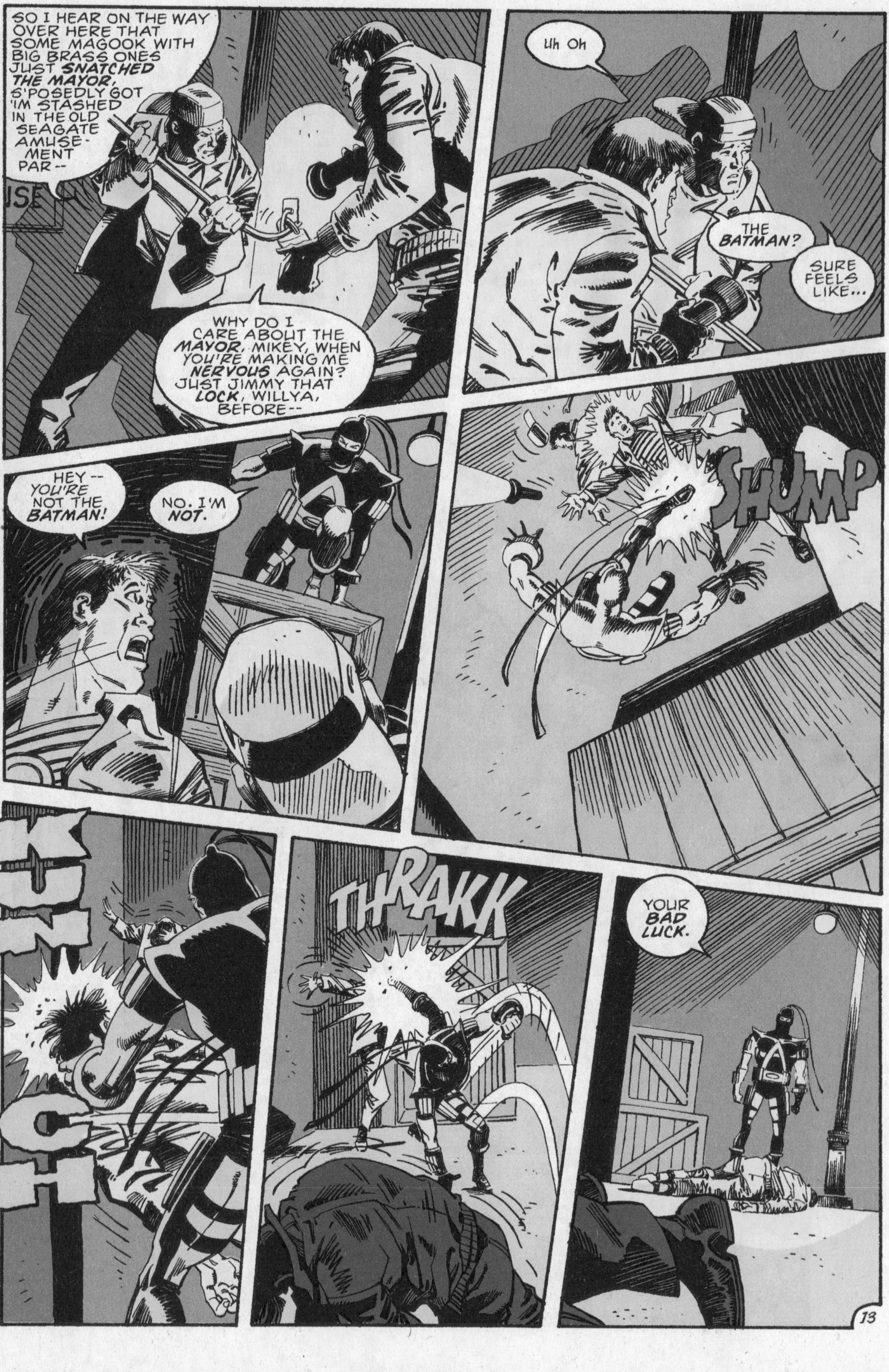
SO I HEAR ON THE WAY OVER HERE THAT SOME MAGOOK WITH BIG BRASS ONES JUST SNATCHED THE MAYOR. S'POSEDLY GOT 'IM STASHED IN THE OLD SEAGATE AMUSEMENT PAR--
WHY DO I CARE ABOUT THE MAYOR, MIKEY, WHEN YOU'RE MAKING ME NERVOUS AGAIN? JUST JIMMY THAT LOCK, WILLYA, BEFORE--
Uh Oh
THE BATMAN?
SURE FEELS LIKE...
HEY -- YOU'RE NOT THE BATMAN!
NO. I'M NOT.
SHUMP
KUNCH
THRAKK
YOUR BAD LUCK.
13

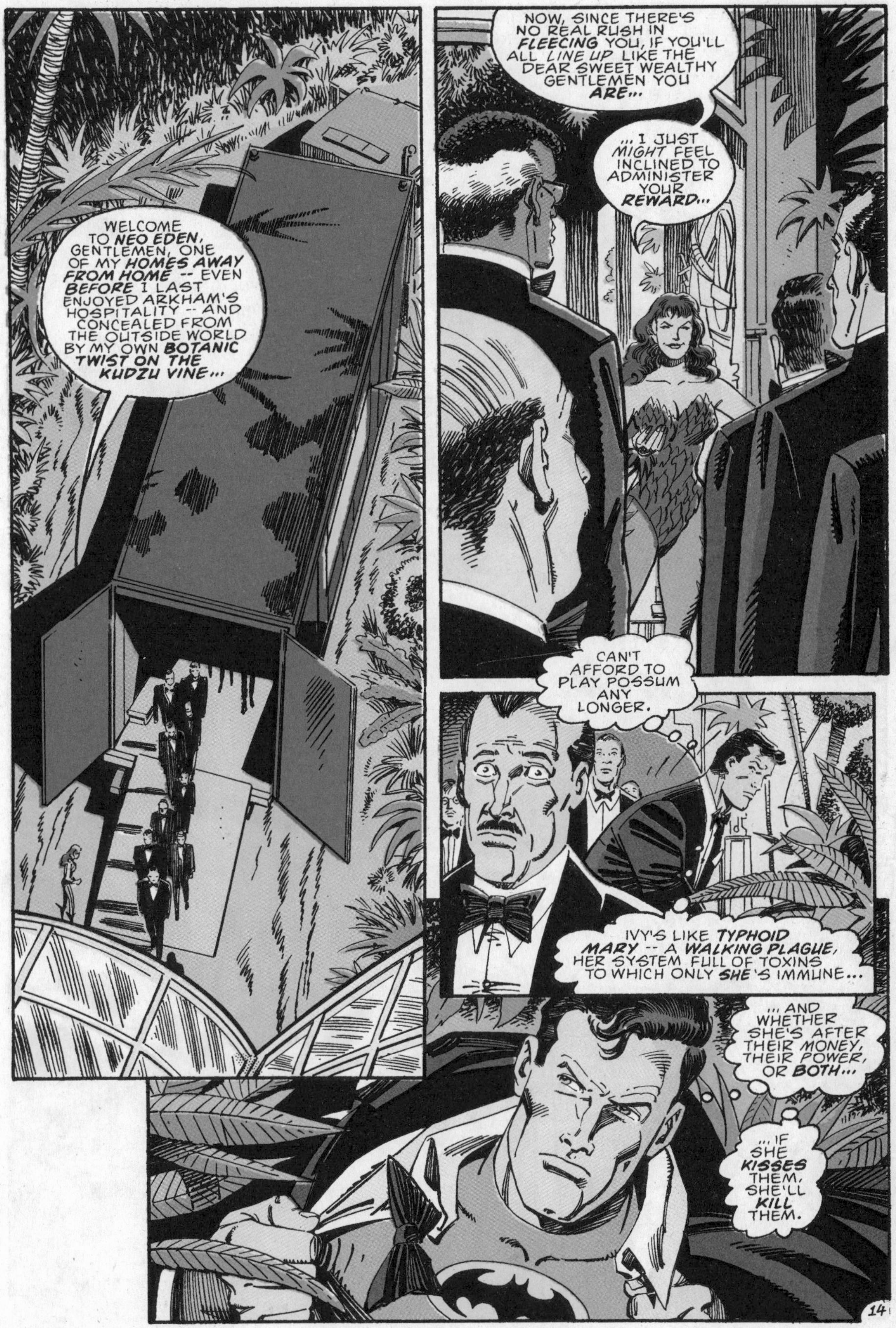
WELCOME TO NEO EDEN, GENTLEMEN, ONE OF MY HOMES AWAY FROM HOME -- EVEN BEFORE I LAST ENJOYED ARKHAM'S HOSPITALITY -- AND CONCEALED FROM THE OUTSIDE WORLD BY MY OWN BOTANIC TWIST ON THE KUDZU VINE...
NOW, SINCE THERE'S NO REAL RUSH IN FLEECING YOU, IF YOU'LL ALL LINE UP LIKE THE DEAR SWEET WEALTHY GENTLEMEN YOU ARE...
...I JUST MIGHT FEEL INCLINED TO ADMINISTER YOUR REWARD...
CAN'T AFFORD TO PLAY POSSUM ANY LONGER.
IVY'S LIKE TYPHOID MARY -- A WALKING PLAGUE, HER SYSTEM FULL OF TOXINS TO WHICH ONLY SHE'S IMMUNE...
...AND WHETHER SHE'S AFTER THEIR MONEY, THEIR POWER, OR BOTH...
...IF SHE KISSES THEM, SHE'LL KILL THEM.
14

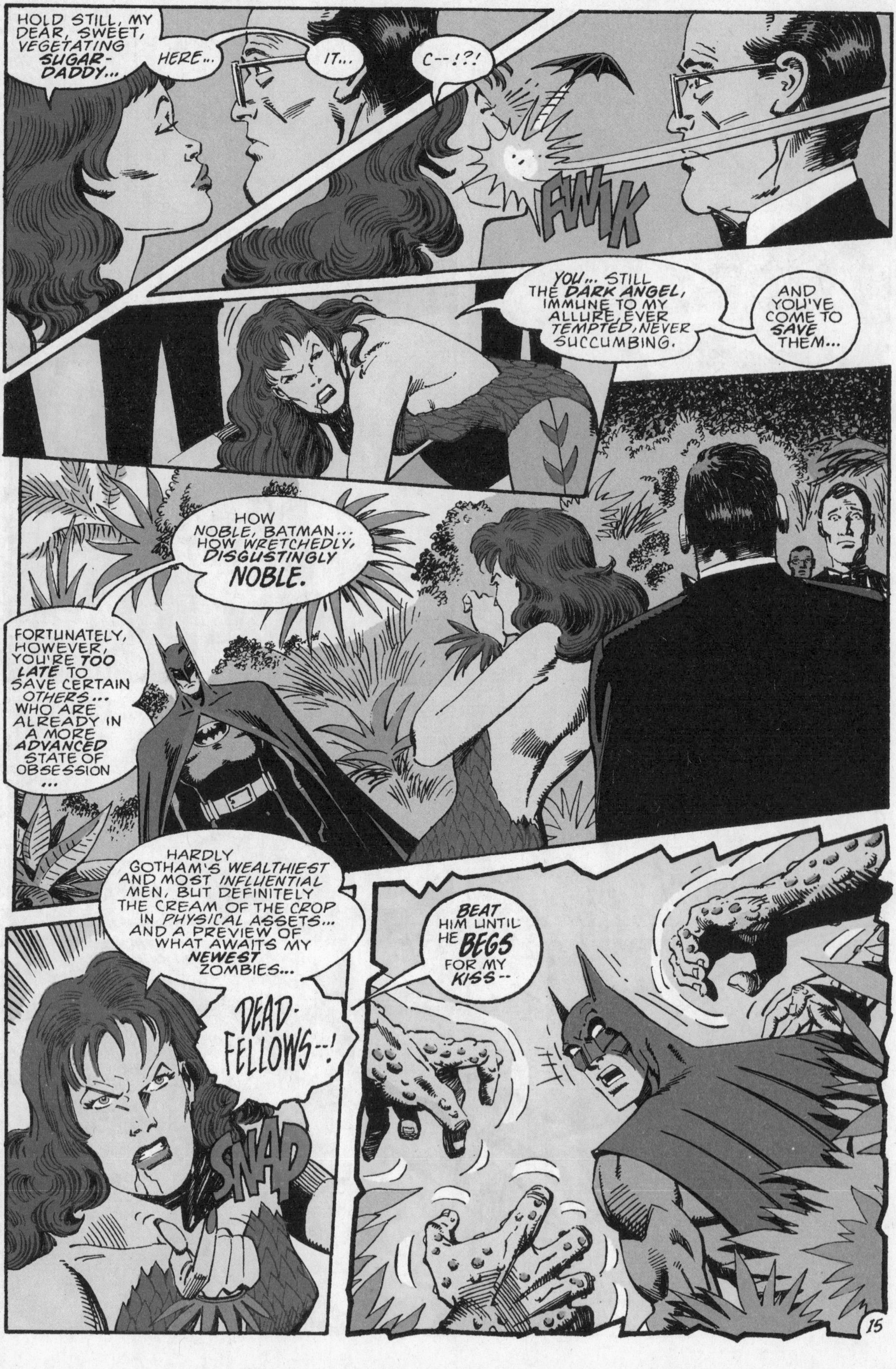
HOLD STILL, MY DEAR, SWEET, VEGETATING SUGAR-DADDY...
HERE...
IT...
C--!?!
FWAK
YOU... STILL THE DARK ANGEL, IMMUNE TO MY ALLURE, EVER TEMPTED, NEVER SUCCUMBING.
AND YOU'VE COME TO SAVE THEM...
HOW NOBLE, BATMAN... HOW WRETCHEDLY, DISGUSTINGLY NOBLE.
FORTUNATELY, HOWEVER, YOU'RE TOO LATE TO SAVE CERTAIN OTHERS... WHO ARE ALREADY IN A MORE ADVANCED STATE OF OBSESSION ...
HARDLY GOTHAM'S WEALTHIEST AND MOST INFLUENTIAL MEN, BUT DEFINITELY THE CREAM OF THE CROP IN PHYSICAL ASSETS... AND A PREVIEW OF WHAT AWAITS MY NEWEST ZOMBIES...
DEAD-FELLOWS--!
SNAP
BEAT HIM UNTIL HE BEGS FOR MY KISS--
15

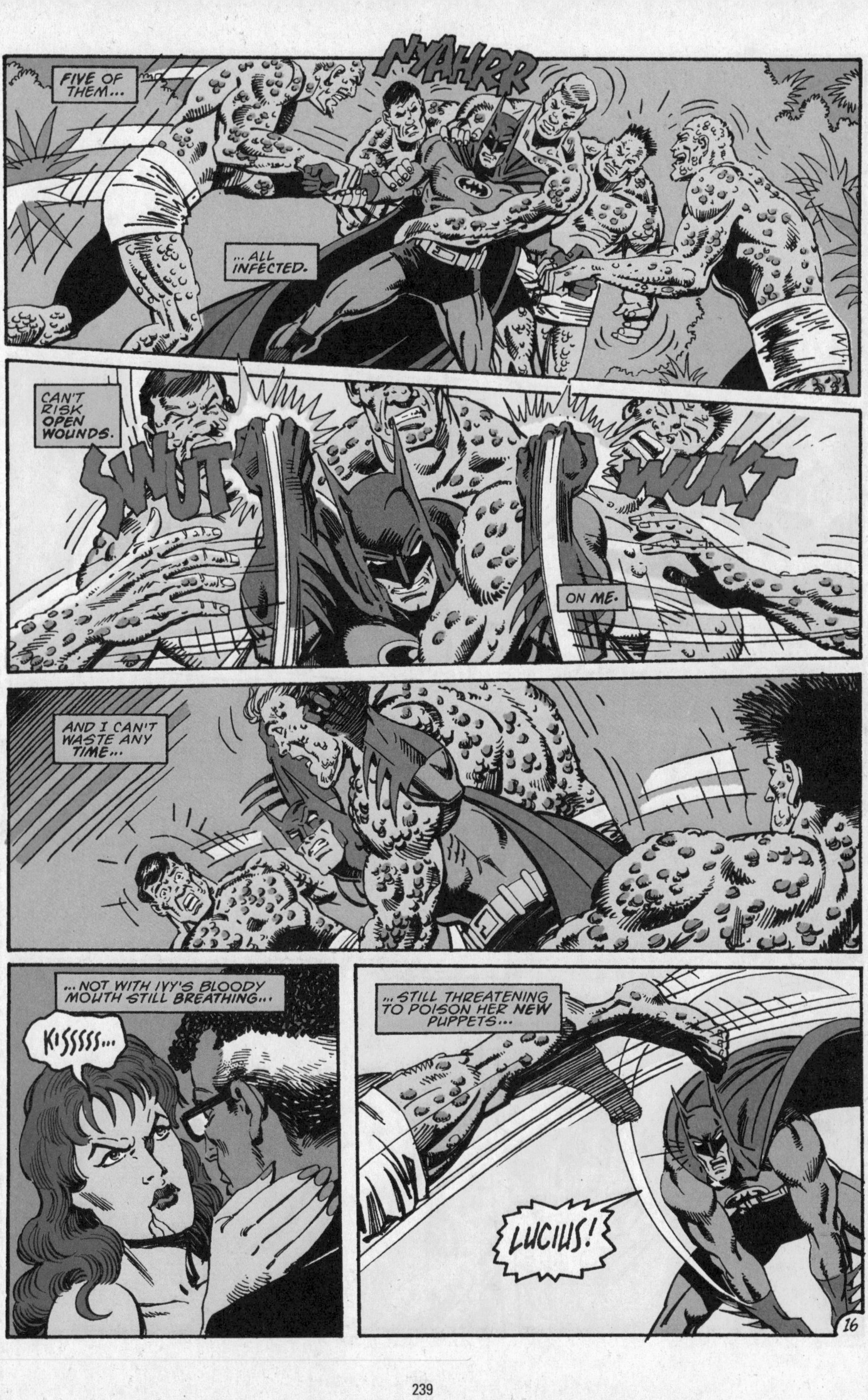
NYAHRR
FIVE OF THEM...
...ALL INFECTED.
CAN'T RISK OPEN WOUNDS.
SWUT
WUKT
ON ME.
AND I CAN'T WASTE ANY TIME...
...NOT WITH IVY'S BLOODY MOUTH STILL BREATHING...
KISSSSS...
...STILL THREATENING TO POISON HER NEW PUPPETS...
LUCIUS!
16

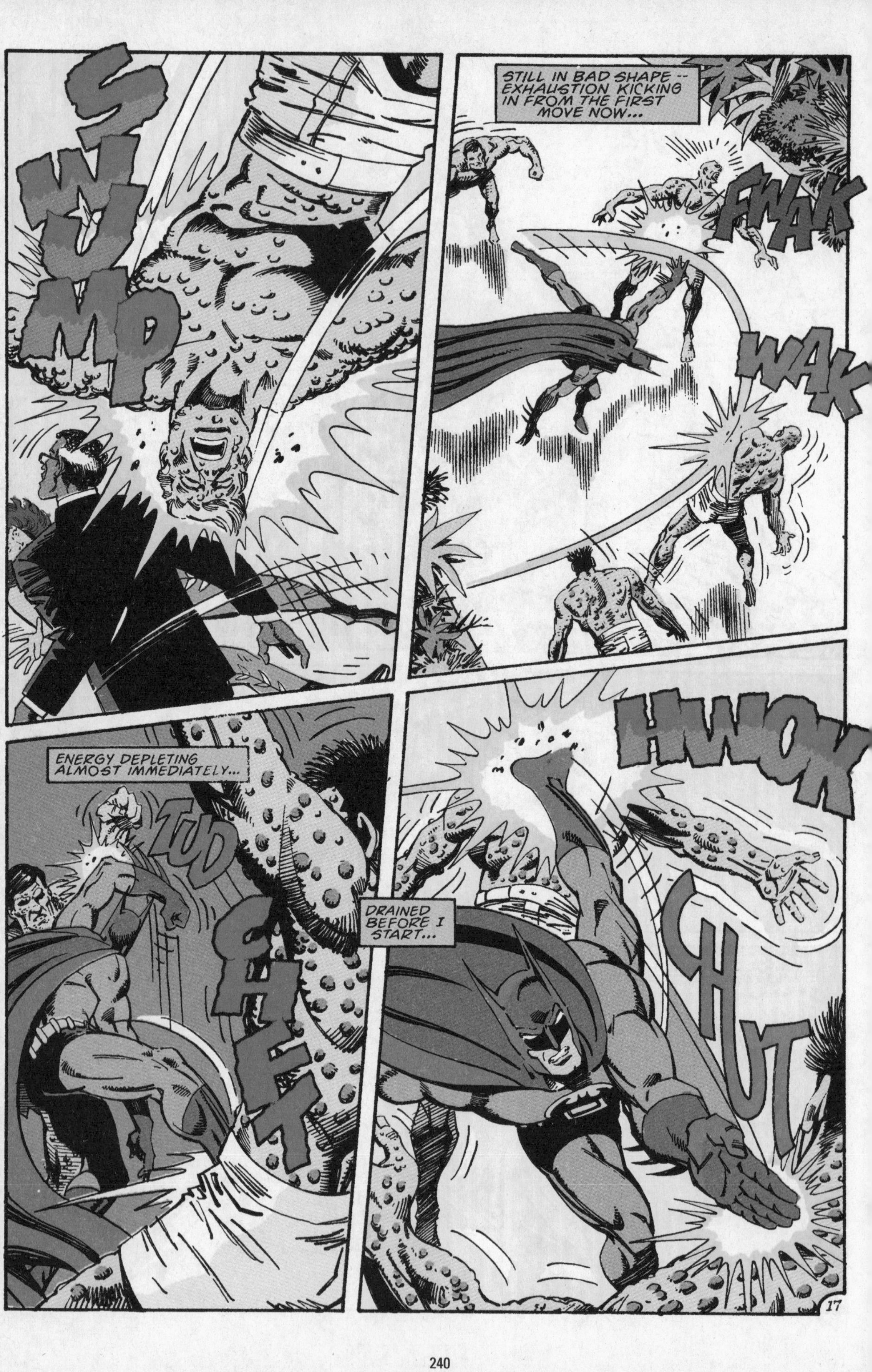
SWUMP
STILL IN BAD SHAPE -- EXHAUSTION KICKING IN FROM THE FIRST MOVE NOW...
FWAK
WAK
ENERGY DEPLETING ALMOST IMMEDIATELY...
TUD
CHEK
DRAINED BEFORE I START...
HWOK
CHUT
17

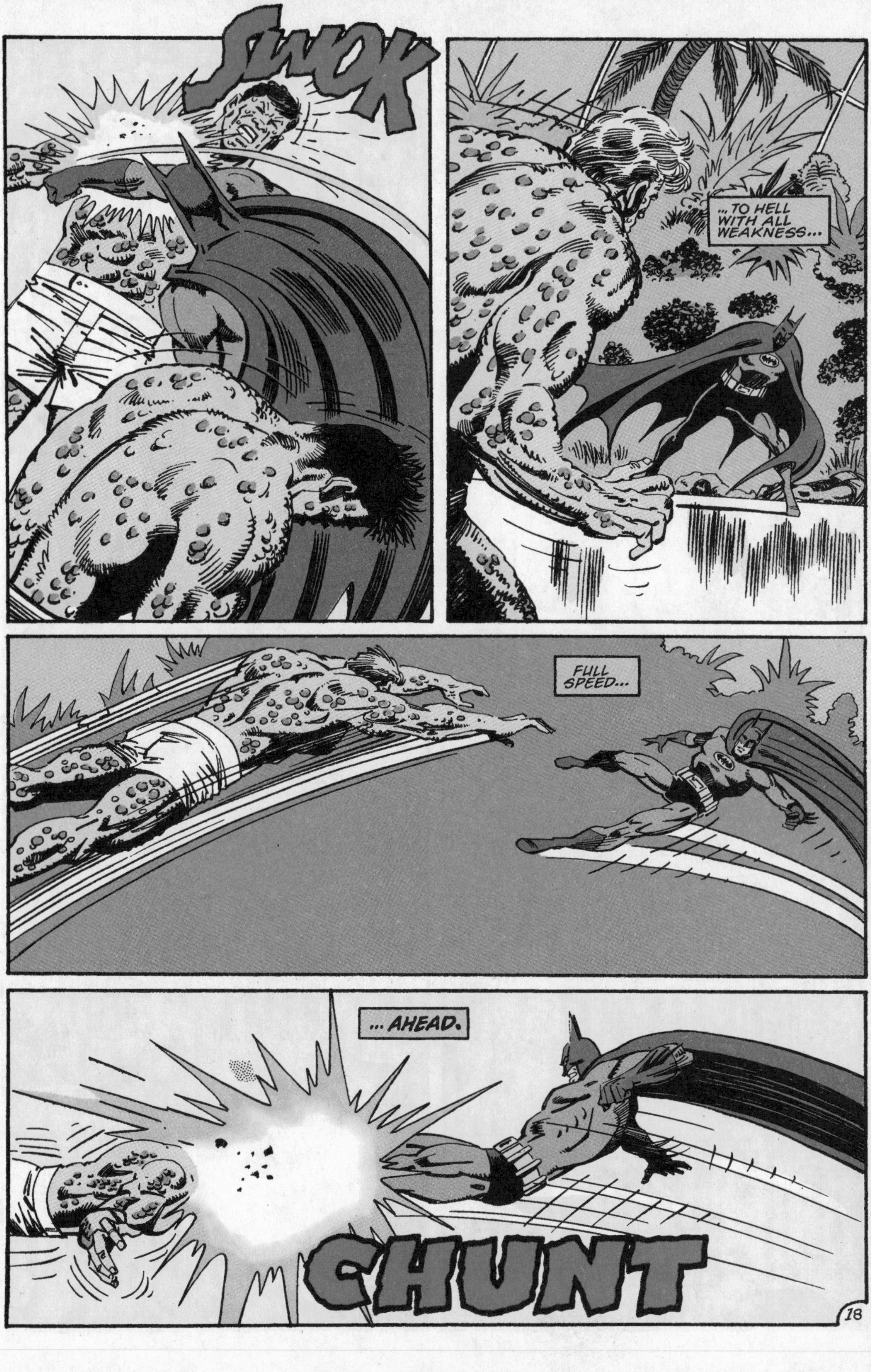
SWOK
...TO HELL WITH ALL WEAKNESS...
FULL SPEED...
...AHEAD.
CHUNT
18

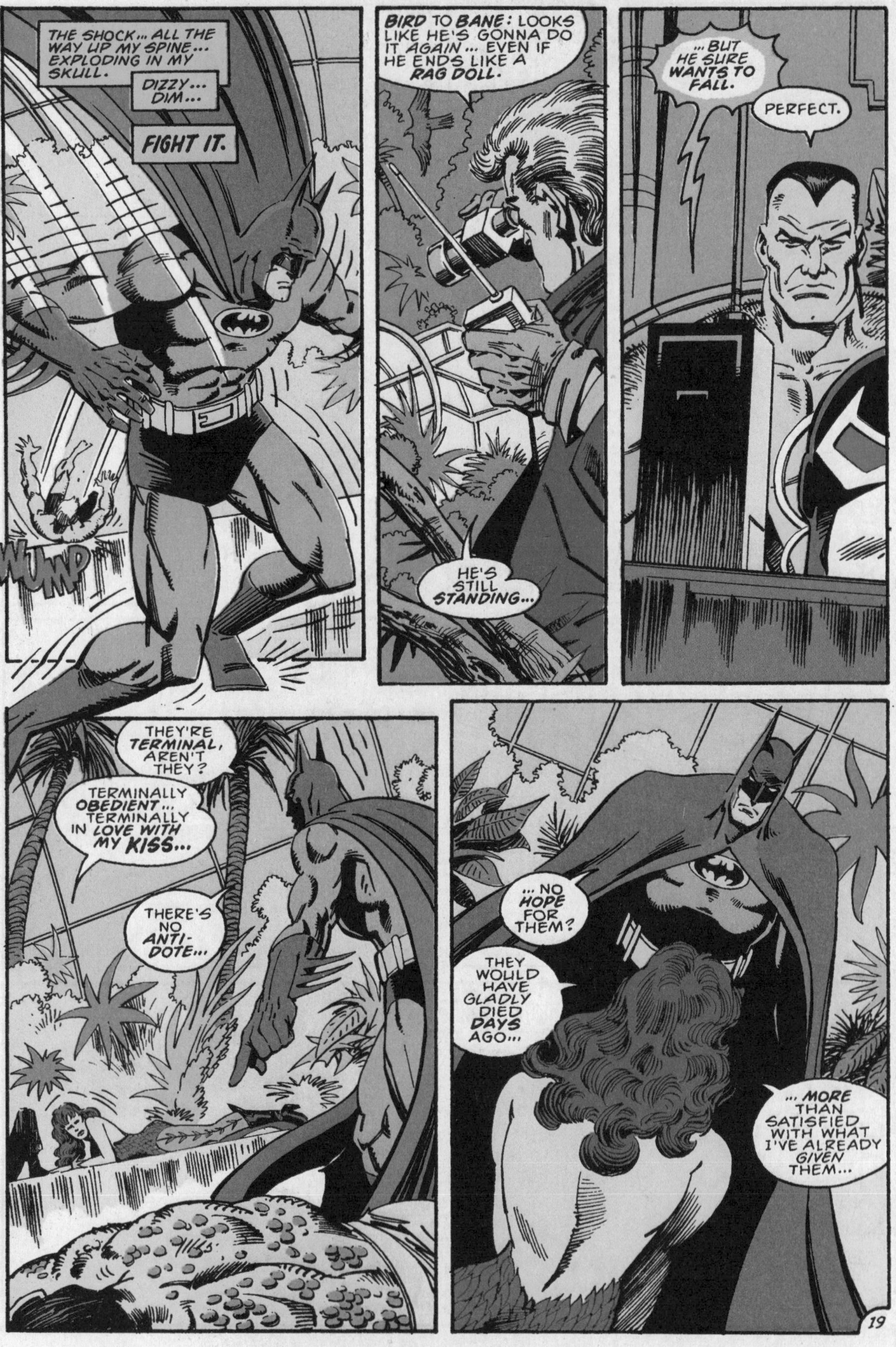
THE SHOCK... ALL THE WAY UP MY SPINE... EXPLODING IN MY SKULL.
DIZZY... DIM...
FIGHT IT.
WUMP
BIRD TO BANE: LOOKS LIKE HE'S GONNA DO IT AGAIN... EVEN IF HE ENDS LIKE A RAG DOLL.
HE'S STILL STANDING...
...BUT HE SURE WANTS TO FALL.
PERFECT.
THEY'RE TERMINAL, AREN'T THEY?
TERMINALLY OBEDIENT... TERMINALLY IN LOVE WITH MY KISS...
THERE'S NO ANTI-DOTE...
...NO HOPE FOR THEM?
THEY WOULD HAVE GLADLY DIED DAYS AGO...
...MORE THAN SATISFIED WITH WHAT I'VE ALREADY GIVEN THEM...
19

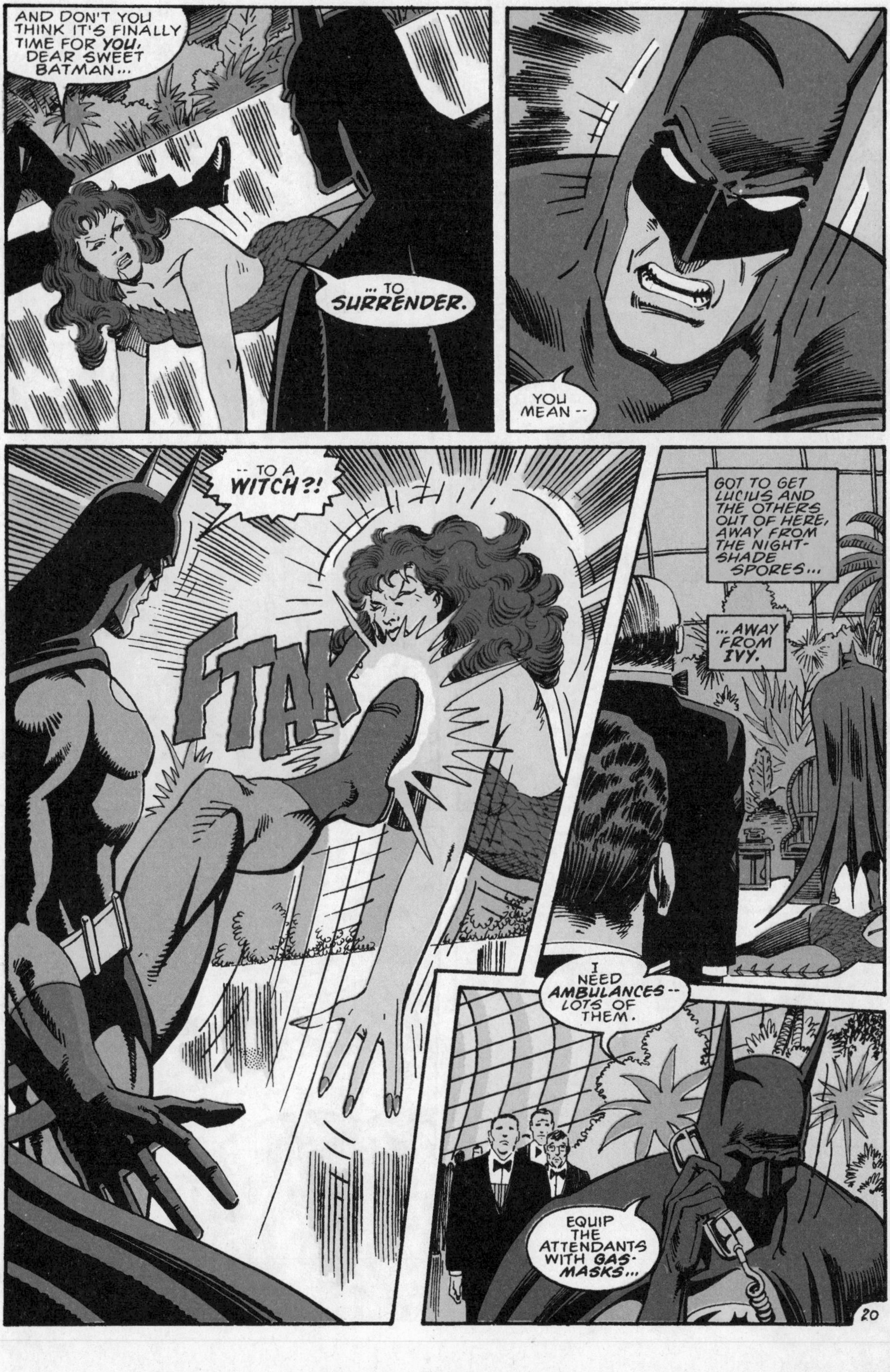
AND DON'T YOU THINK IT'S FINALLY TIME FOR YOU, DEAR SWEET BATMAN...
...TO SURRENDER.
YOU MEAN --
-- TO A WITCH?!
FTAK
GOT TO GET LUCIUS AND THE OTHERS OUT OF HERE, AWAY FROM THE NIGHT-SHADE SPORES...
...AWAY FROM IVY.
I NEED AMBULANCES -- LOTS OF THEM.
EQUIP THE ATTENDANTS WITH GAS-MASKS...
20

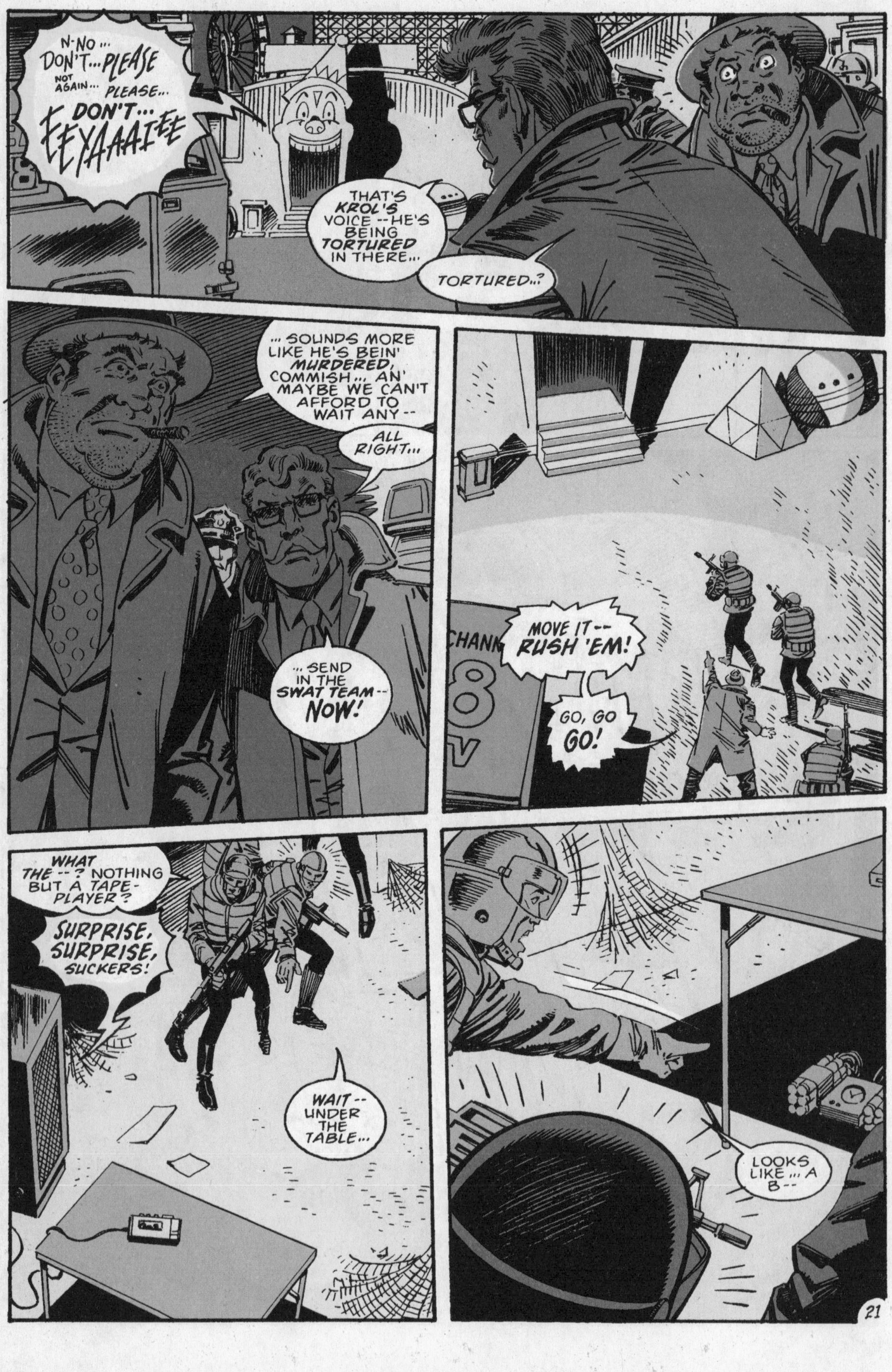
N-NO... DON'T...PLEASE NOT AGAIN... PLEASE... DON'T... EEYAAAIEE
THAT'S KROL'S VOICE --HE'S BEING TORTURED IN THERE...
TORTURED..?
... SOUNDS MORE LIKE HE'S BEIN' MURDERED, COMMISH... AN' MAYBE WE CAN'T AFFORD TO WAIT ANY --
ALL RIGHT...
... SEND IN THE SWAT TEAM -- NOW!
MOVE IT -- RUSH 'EM!
GO, GO GO!
CHANN
8
WHAT THE --? NOTHING BUT A TAPE-PLAYER?
SURPRISE, SURPRISE, SUCKERS!
WAIT -- UNDER THE TABLE...
LOOKS LIKE... A B --
21

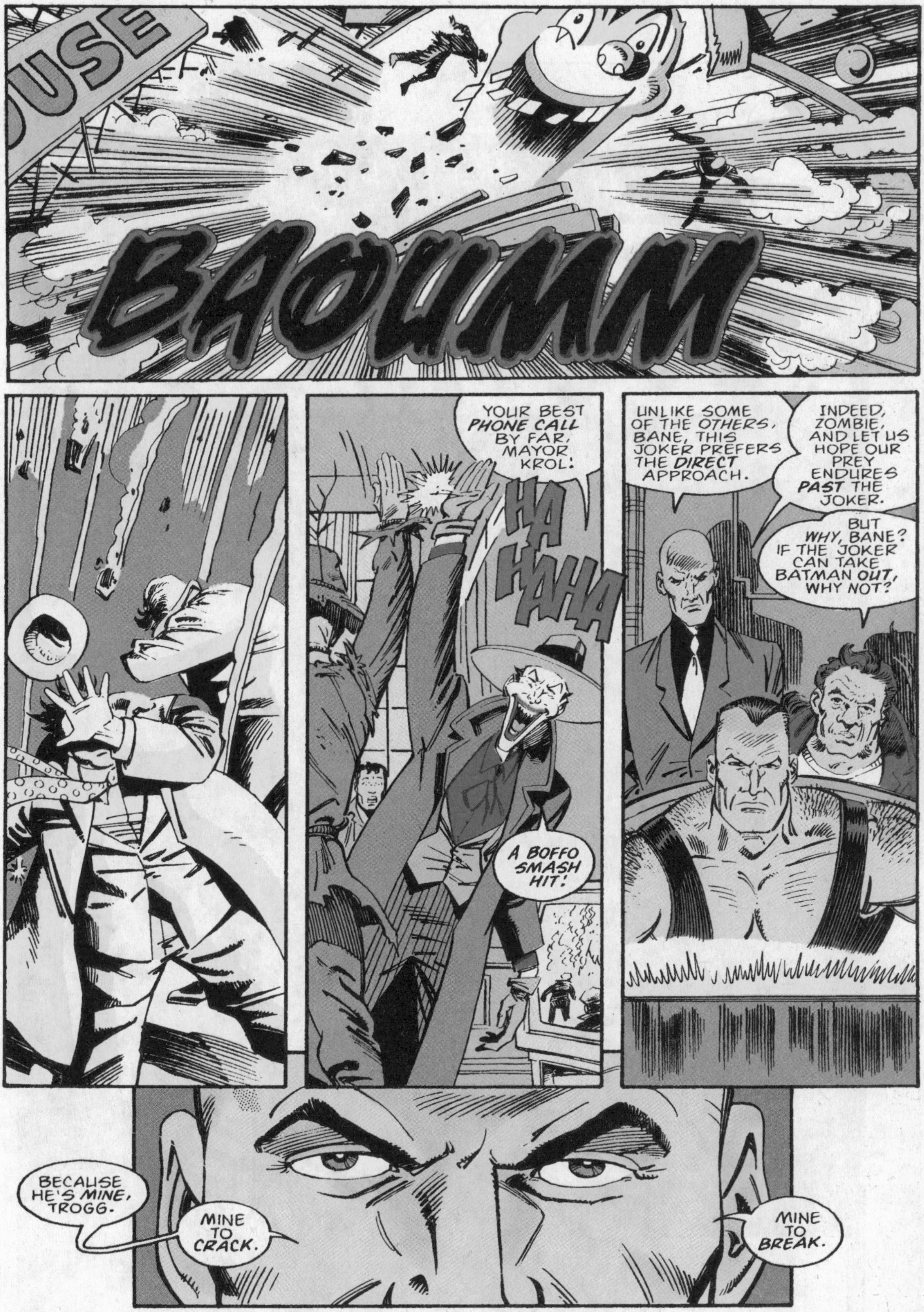

USE
BAOWMM
YOUR BEST PHONE CALL BY FAR, MAYOR KROL!
HA HAHAHA
A BOFFO SMASH HIT!
UNLIKE SOME OF THE OTHERS, BANE, THIS JOKER PREFERS THE DIRECT APPROACH.
INDEED, ZOMBIE, AND LET US HOPE OUR PREY ENDURES PAST THE JOKER.
BUT WHY, BANE? IF THE JOKER CAN TAKE BATMAN OUT, WHY NOT?
BECAUSE HE'S MINE, TROGG.
MINE TO CRACK.
MINE TO BREAK.

Cover art by SAM KIETH

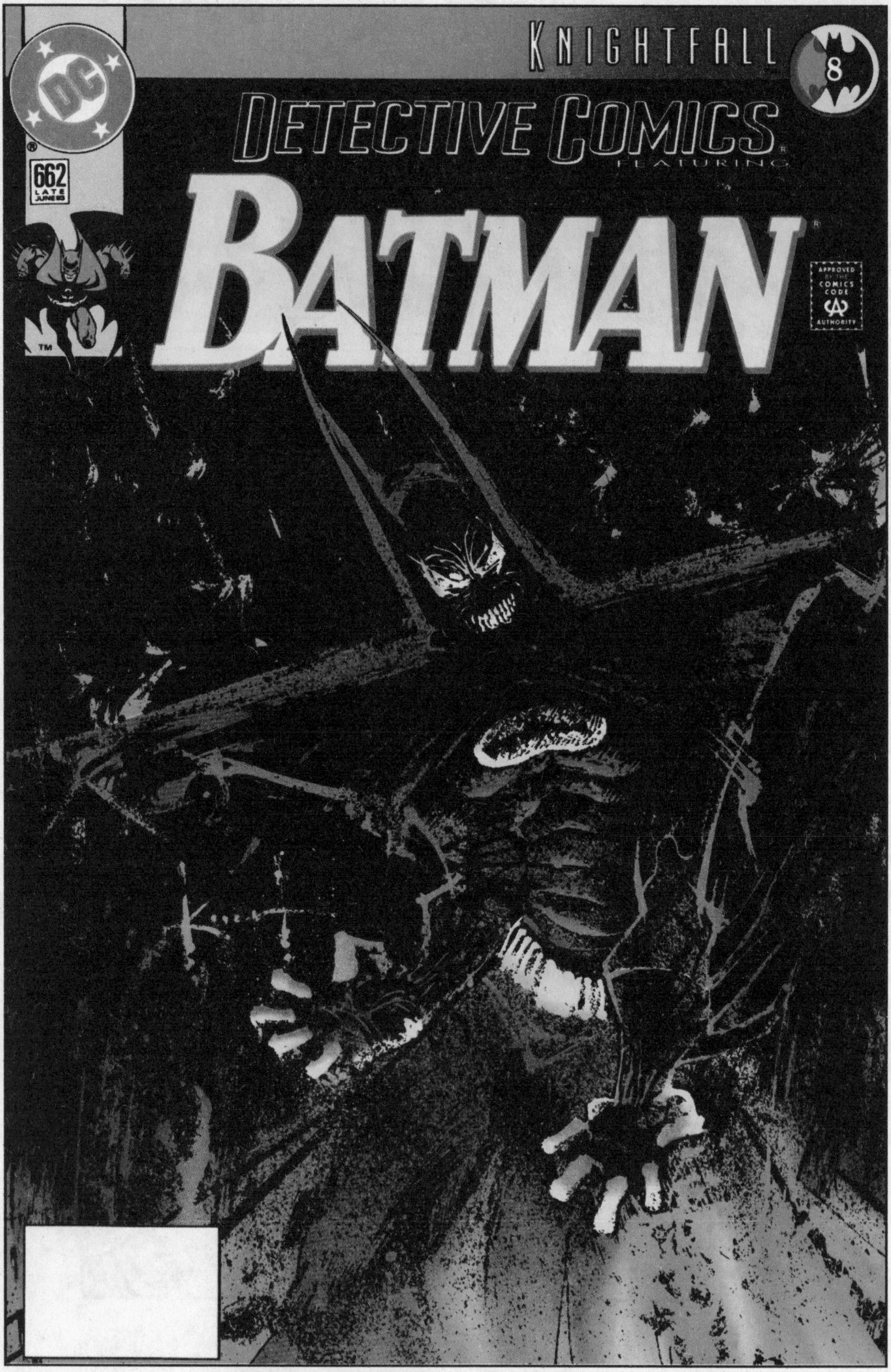
KNIGHTFALL
8
DC
DETECTIVE COMICS
FEATURING
662
LATE
BATMAN
APPROVED BY THE COMICS CODE AUTHORITY

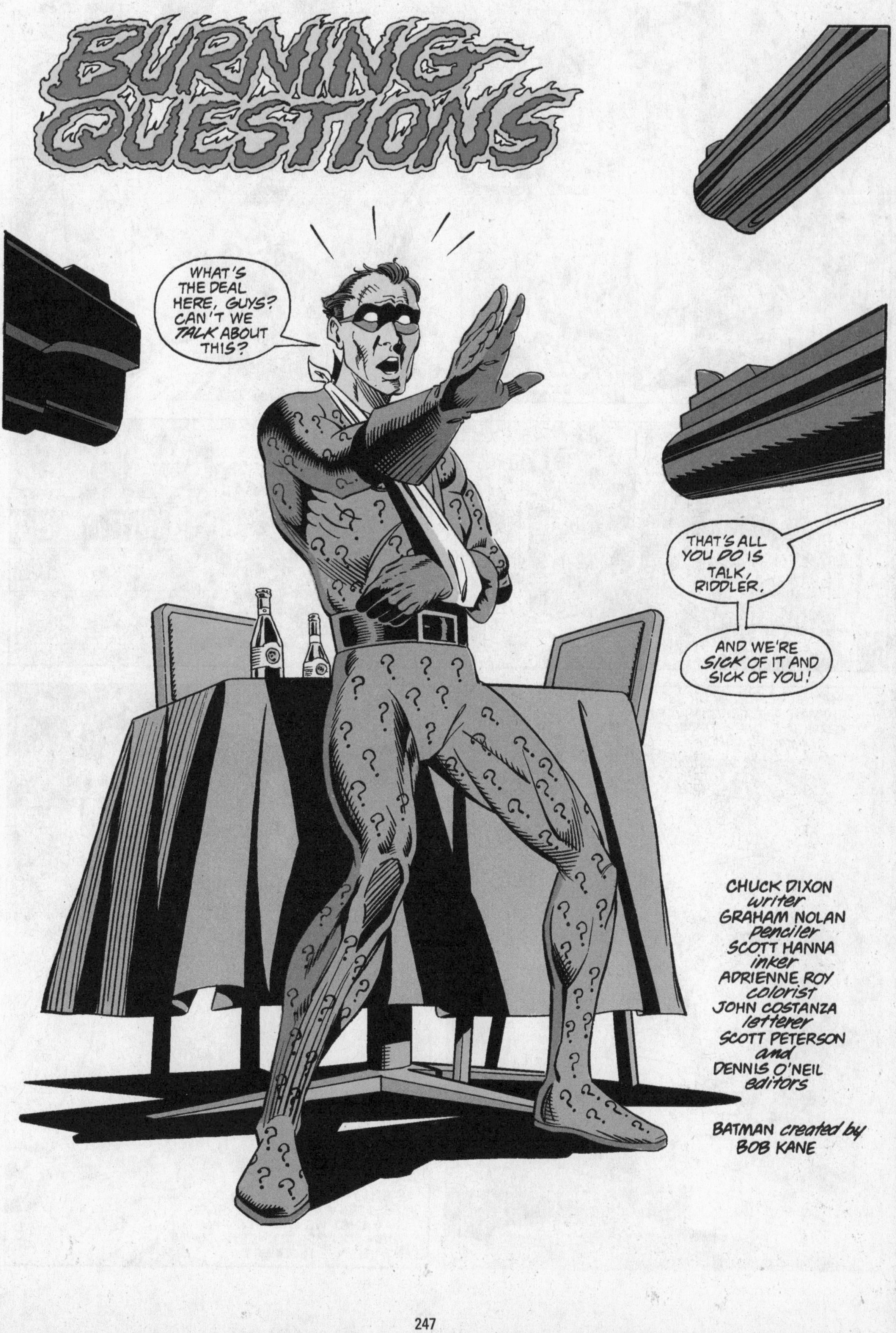
BURNING QUESTIONS
WHAT'S THE DEAL HERE, GUYS? CAN'T WE TALK ABOUT THIS?
THAT'S ALL YOU DO IS TALK, RIDDLER.
AND WE'RE SICK OF IT AND SICK OF YOU!
CHUCK DIXON writer
GRAHAM NOLAN penciler
SCOTT HANNA inker
ADRIENNE ROY colorist
JOHN COSTANZA letterer
SCOTT PETERSON and DENNIS O'NEIL editors
BATMAN created by BOB KANE

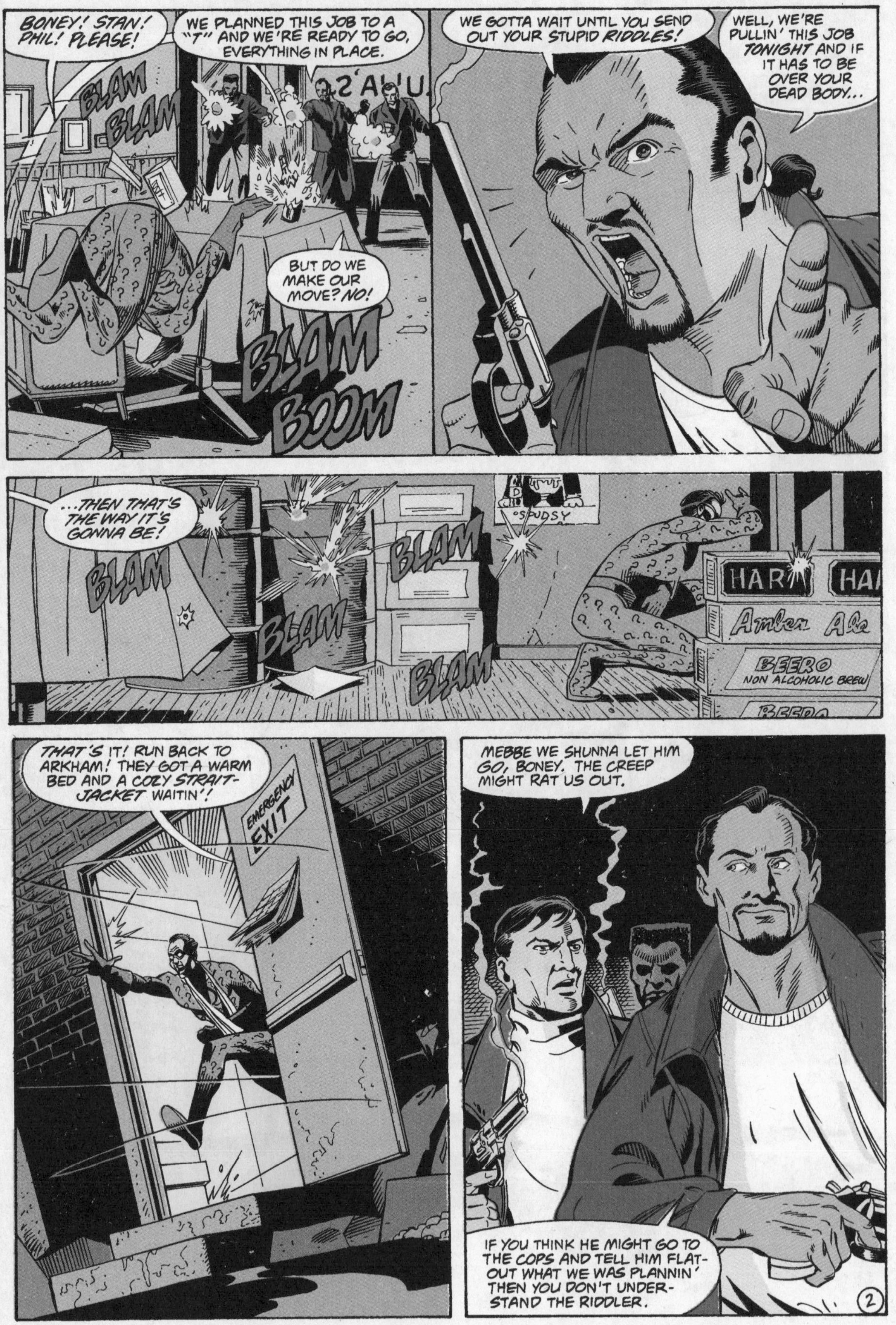
BONEY! STAN! PHIL! PLEASE!
WE PLANNED THIS JOB TO A "T" AND WE'RE READY TO GO, EVERYTHING IN PLACE.
BLAM
BLAM
BUT DO WE MAKE OUR MOVE? NO!
BLAM
BOOM
WE GOTTA WAIT UNTIL YOU SEND OUT YOUR STUPID RIDDLES!
WELL, WE'RE PULLIN' THIS JOB TONIGHT AND IF IT HAS TO BE OVER YOUR DEAD BODY...
...THEN THAT'S THE WAY IT'S GONNA BE!
BLAM
BLAM
BLAM
BLAM
BEERO
NON ALCOHOLIC BREW
Amber Ale
THAT'S IT! RUN BACK TO ARKHAM! THEY GOT A WARM BED AND A COZY STRAIT-JACKET WAITIN'!
EMERGENCY EXIT
MEBBE WE SHUNNA LET HIM GO, BONEY. THE CREEP MIGHT RAT US OUT.
IF YOU THINK HE MIGHT GO TO THE COPS AND TELL HIM FLAT-OUT WHAT WE WAS PLANNIN' THEN YOU DON'T UNDER-STAND THE RIDDLER.
2

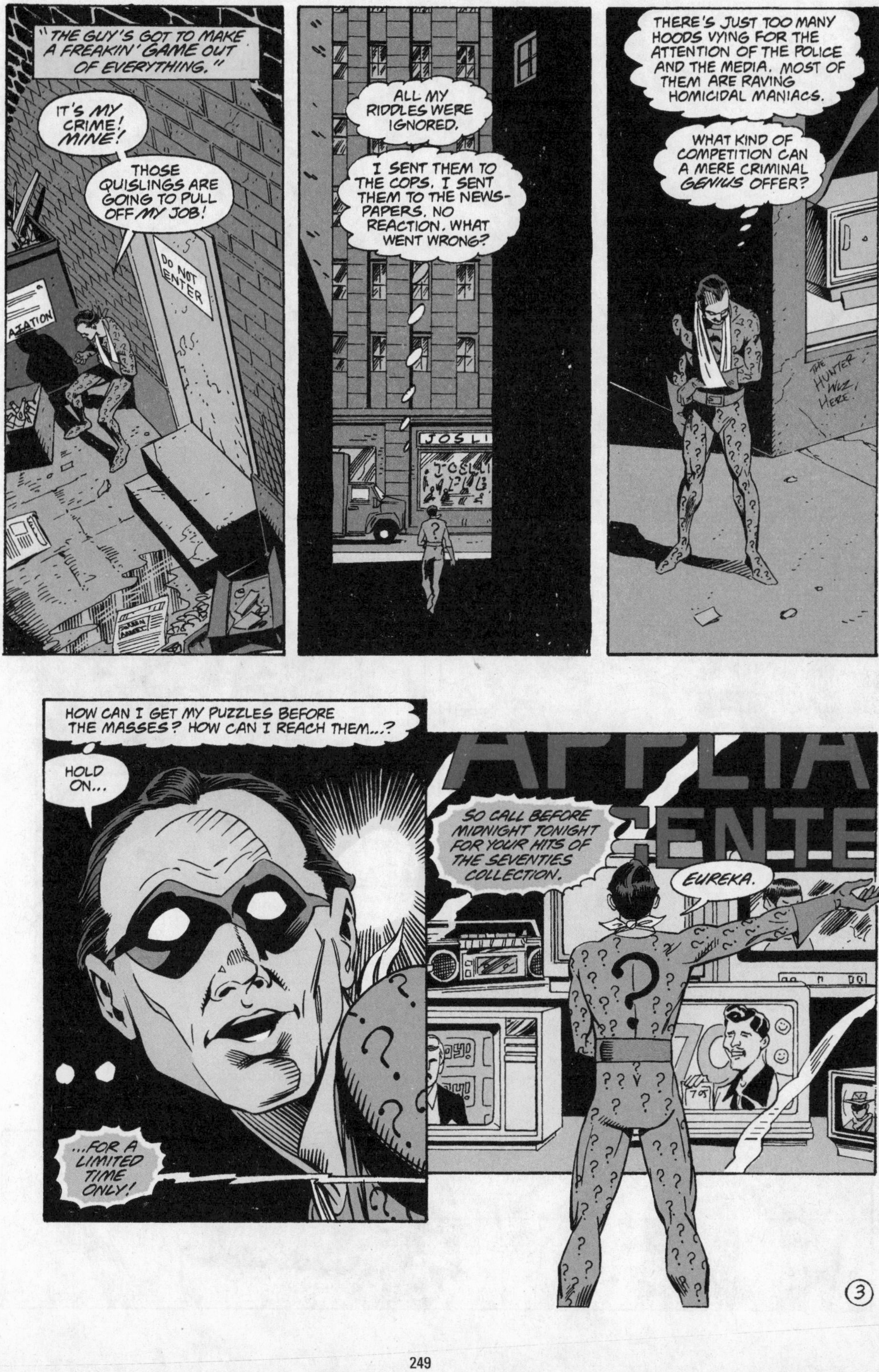

"THE GUY'S GOT TO MAKE A FREAKIN' GAME OUT OF EVERYTHING."
IT'S MY CRIME! MINE!
THOSE QUISLINGS ARE GOING TO PULL OFF MY JOB!
DO NOT ENTER
ALL MY RIDDLES WERE IGNORED.
I SENT THEM TO THE COPS. I SENT THEM TO THE NEWSPAPERS. NO REACTION. WHAT WENT WRONG?
THERE'S JUST TOO MANY HOODS VYING FOR THE ATTENTION OF THE POLICE AND THE MEDIA. MOST OF THEM ARE RAVING HOMICIDAL MANIACS.
WHAT KIND OF COMPETITION CAN A MERE CRIMINAL GENIUS OFFER?
THE HUNTER WUZ HERE.
HOW CAN I GET MY PUZZLES BEFORE THE MASSES? HOW CAN I REACH THEM...?
HOLD ON...
...FOR A LIMITED TIME ONLY!
SO CALL BEFORE MIDNIGHT TONIGHT FOR YOUR HITS OF THE SEVENTIES COLLECTION.
EUREKA.
3

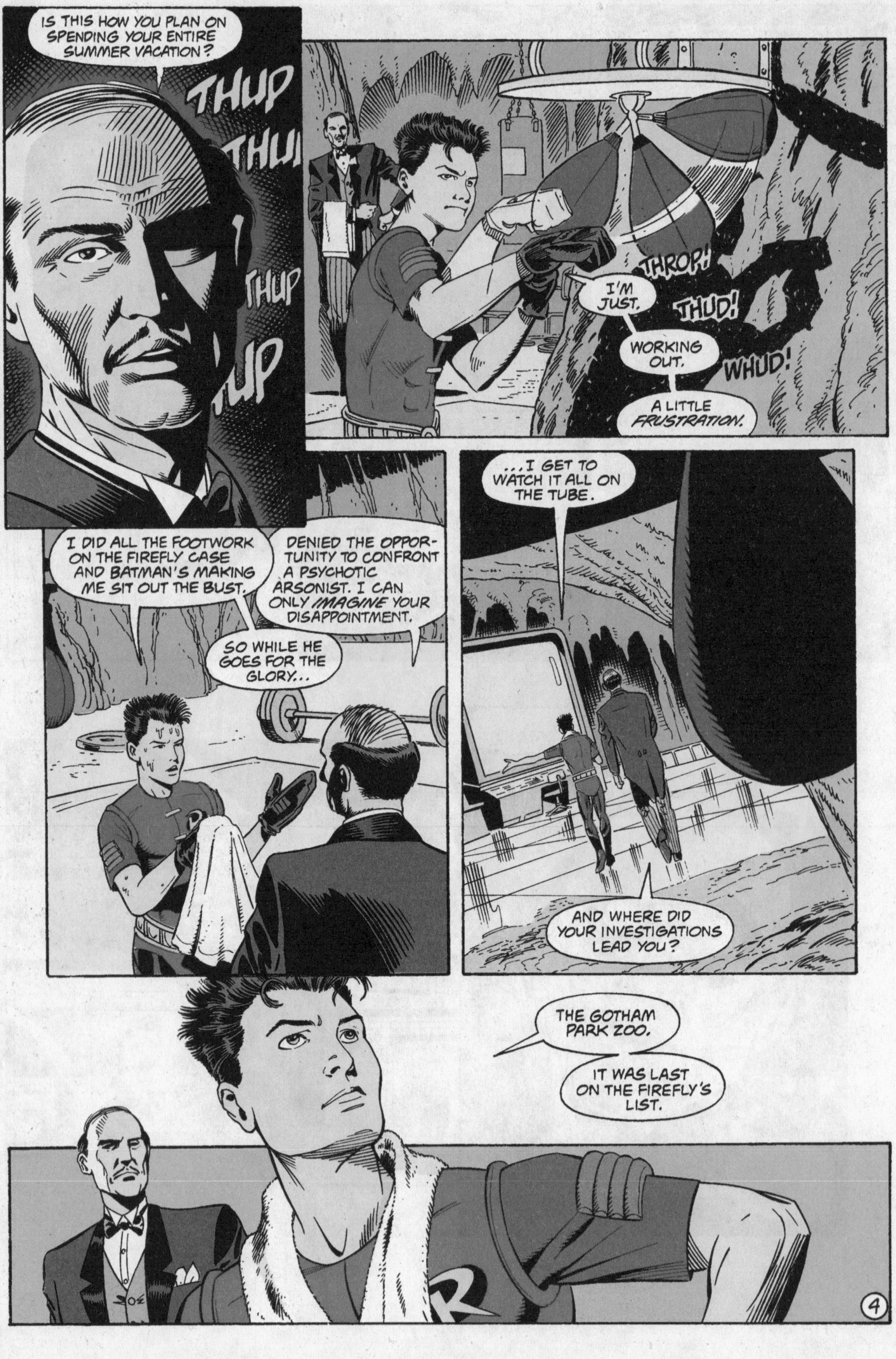
IS THIS HOW YOU PLAN ON SPENDING YOUR ENTIRE SUMMER VACATION?
THUP
THUP
THUP
THUP
I'M JUST.
WORKING OUT.
A LITTLE *FRUSTRATION.*
THROP!
THUD!
WHUD!
I DID ALL THE FOOTWORK ON THE FIREFLY CASE AND BATMAN'S MAKING ME SIT OUT THE BUST.
SO WHILE HE GOES FOR THE GLORY...
...I GET TO WATCH IT ALL ON THE TUBE.
DENIED THE OPPORTUNITY TO CONFRONT A PSYCHOTIC ARSONIST. I CAN ONLY *IMAGINE* YOUR DISAPPOINTMENT.
AND WHERE DID YOUR INVESTIGATIONS LEAD YOU?
THE GOTHAM PARK ZOO.
IT WAS LAST ON THE FIREFLY'S LIST.
4

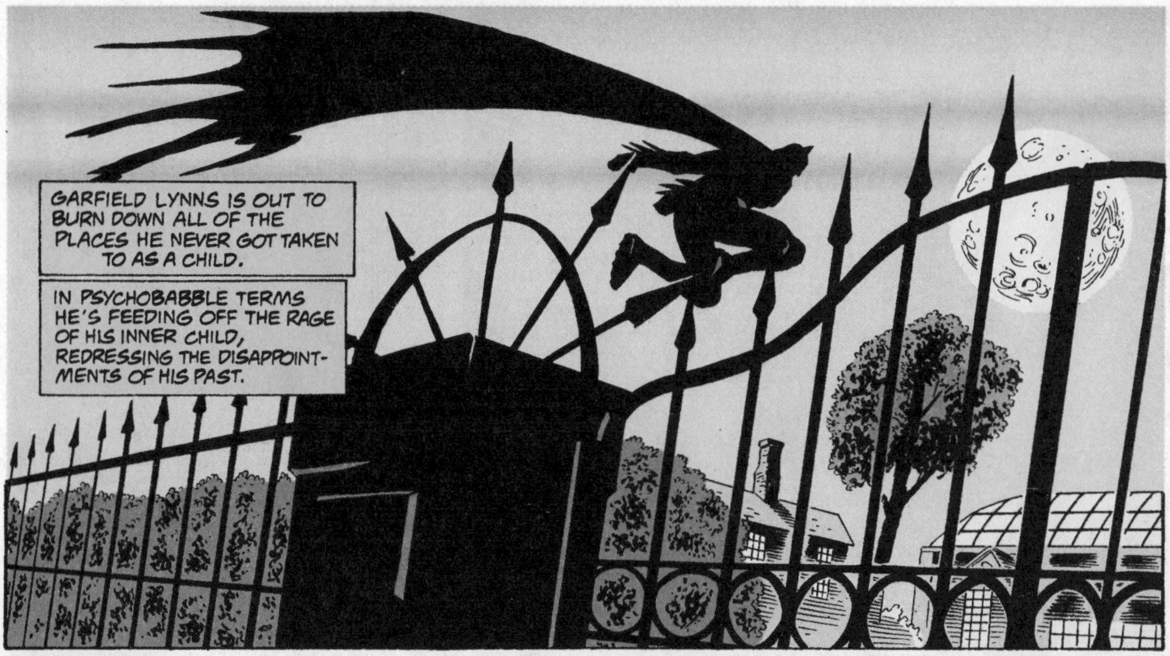
GARFIELD LYNNS IS OUT TO BURN DOWN ALL OF THE PLACES HE NEVER GOT TAKEN TO AS A CHILD.
IN PSYCHOBABBLE TERMS HE'S FEEDING OFF THE RAGE OF HIS INNER CHILD, REDRESSING THE DISAPPOINTMENTS OF HIS PAST.

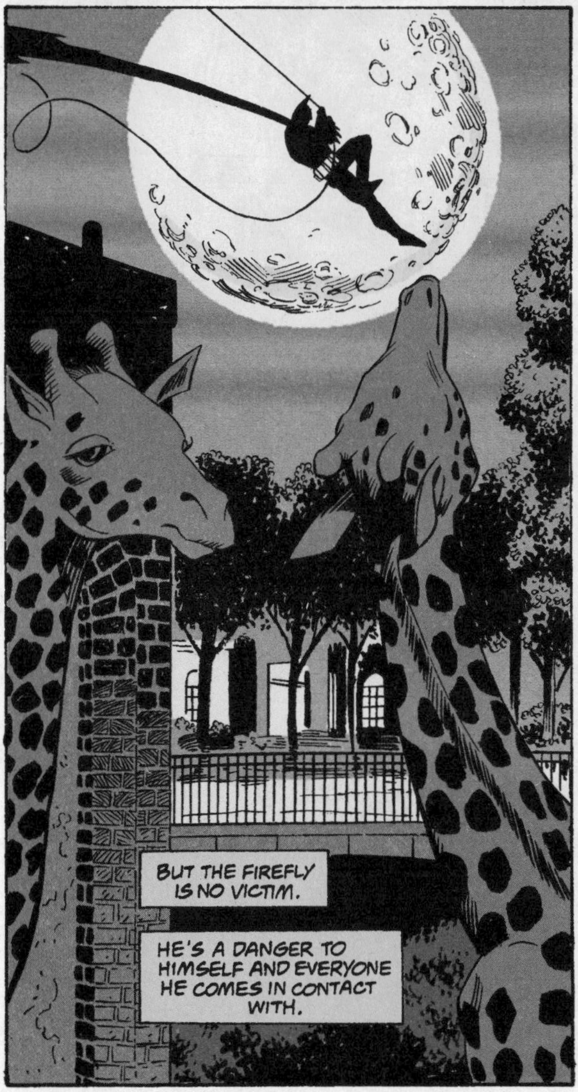
BUT THE FIREFLY IS NO VICTIM.
HE'S A DANGER TO HIMSELF AND EVERYONE HE COMES IN CONTACT WITH.

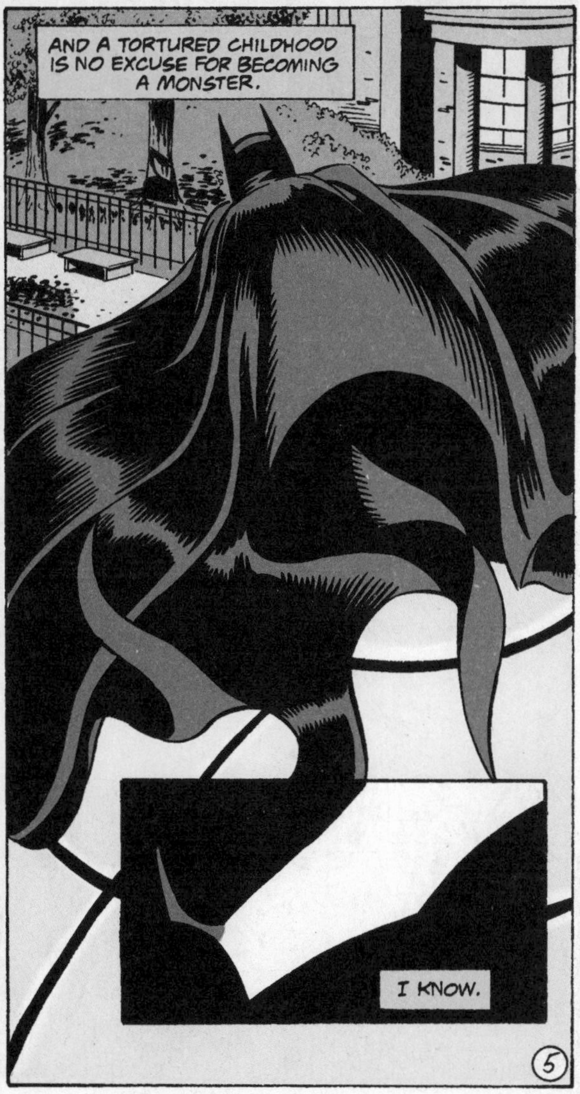
AND A TORTURED CHILDHOOD IS NO EXCUSE FOR BECOMING A MONSTER.
I KNOW.
5

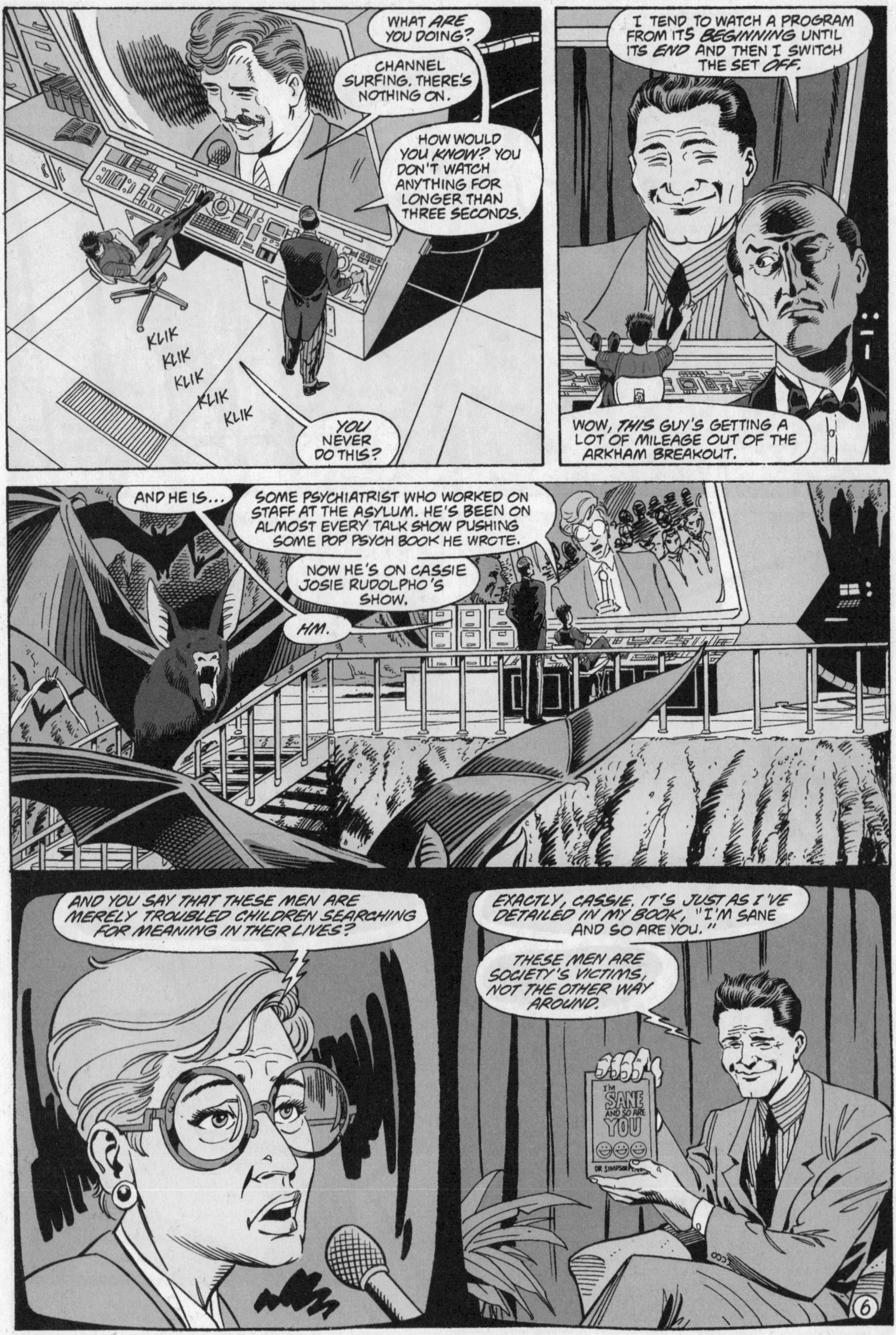
WHAT ARE YOU DOING?
CHANNEL SURFING. THERE'S NOTHING ON.
HOW WOULD YOU KNOW? YOU DON'T WATCH ANYTHING FOR LONGER THAN THREE SECONDS.
KLIK KLIK KLIK KLIK KLIK
YOU NEVER DO THIS?
I TEND TO WATCH A PROGRAM FROM ITS BEGINNING UNTIL ITS END AND THEN I SWITCH THE SET OFF.
WOW, THIS GUY'S GETTING A LOT OF MILEAGE OUT OF THE ARKHAM BREAKOUT.
AND HE IS...
SOME PSYCHIATRIST WHO WORKED ON STAFF AT THE ASYLUM. HE'S BEEN ON ALMOST EVERY TALK SHOW PUSHING SOME POP PSYCH BOOK HE WROTE.
NOW HE'S ON CASSIE JOSIE RUDOLPHO'S SHOW.
HM.
AND YOU SAY THAT THESE MEN ARE MERELY TROUBLED CHILDREN SEARCHING FOR MEANING IN THEIR LIVES?
EXACTLY, CASSIE. IT'S JUST AS I'VE DETAILED IN MY BOOK, "I'M SANE AND SO ARE YOU."
THESE MEN ARE SOCIETY'S VICTIMS, NOT THE OTHER WAY AROUND.
I'M SANE AND SO ARE YOU
6

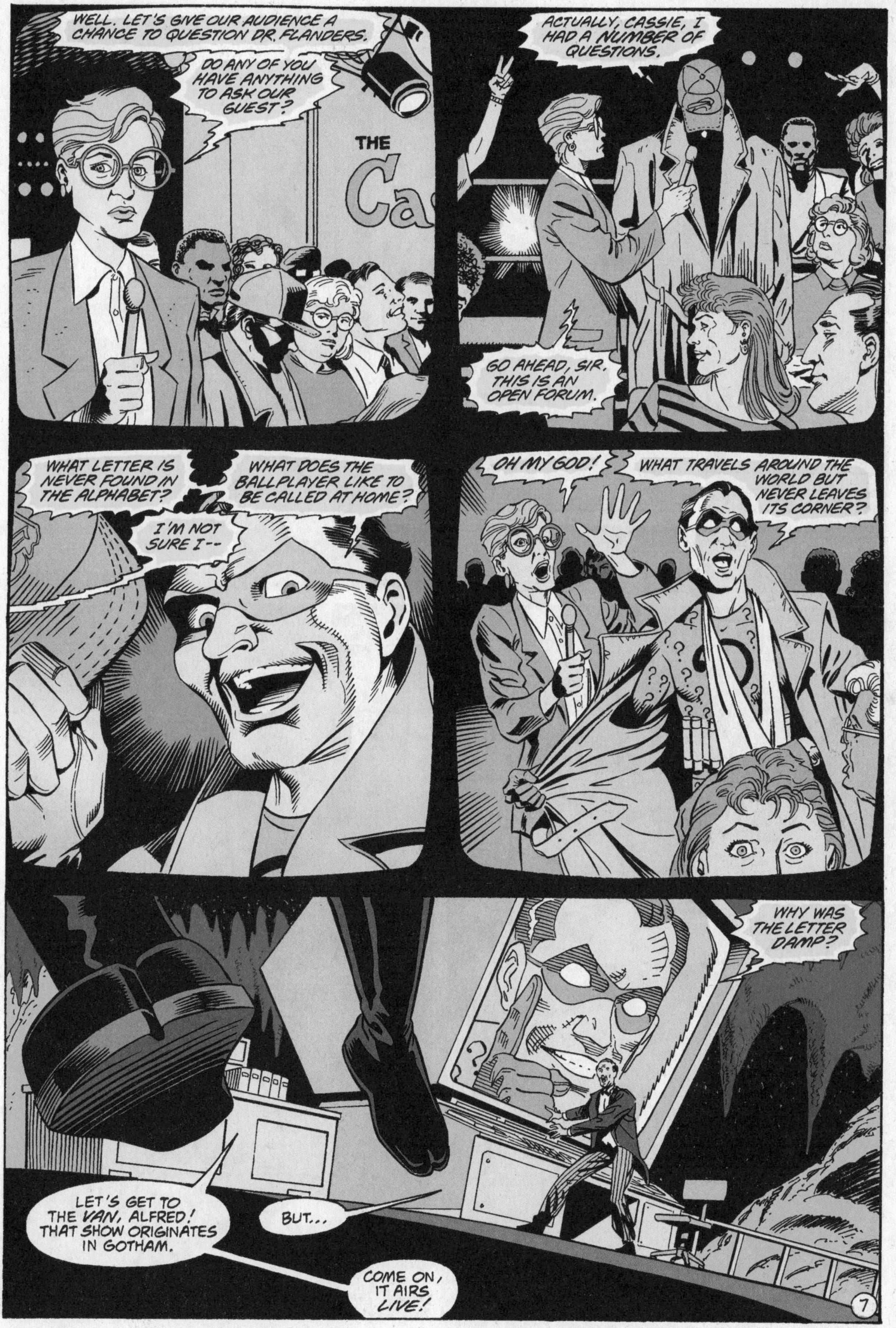
WELL. LET'S GIVE OUR AUDIENCE A CHANCE TO QUESTION DR. FLANDERS.
DO ANY OF YOU HAVE ANYTHING TO ASK OUR GUEST?
THE
ACTUALLY, CASSIE, I HAD A NUMBER OF QUESTIONS.
GO AHEAD, SIR. THIS IS AN OPEN FORUM.
WHAT LETTER IS NEVER FOUND IN THE ALPHABET?
WHAT DOES THE BALLPLAYER LIKE TO BE CALLED AT HOME?
I'M NOT SURE I--
OH MY GOD!
WHAT TRAVELS AROUND THE WORLD BUT NEVER LEAVES ITS CORNER?
WHY WAS THE LETTER DAMP?
LET'S GET TO THE VAN, ALFRED! THAT SHOW ORIGINATES IN GOTHAM.
BUT...
COME ON, IT AIRS LIVE!
7

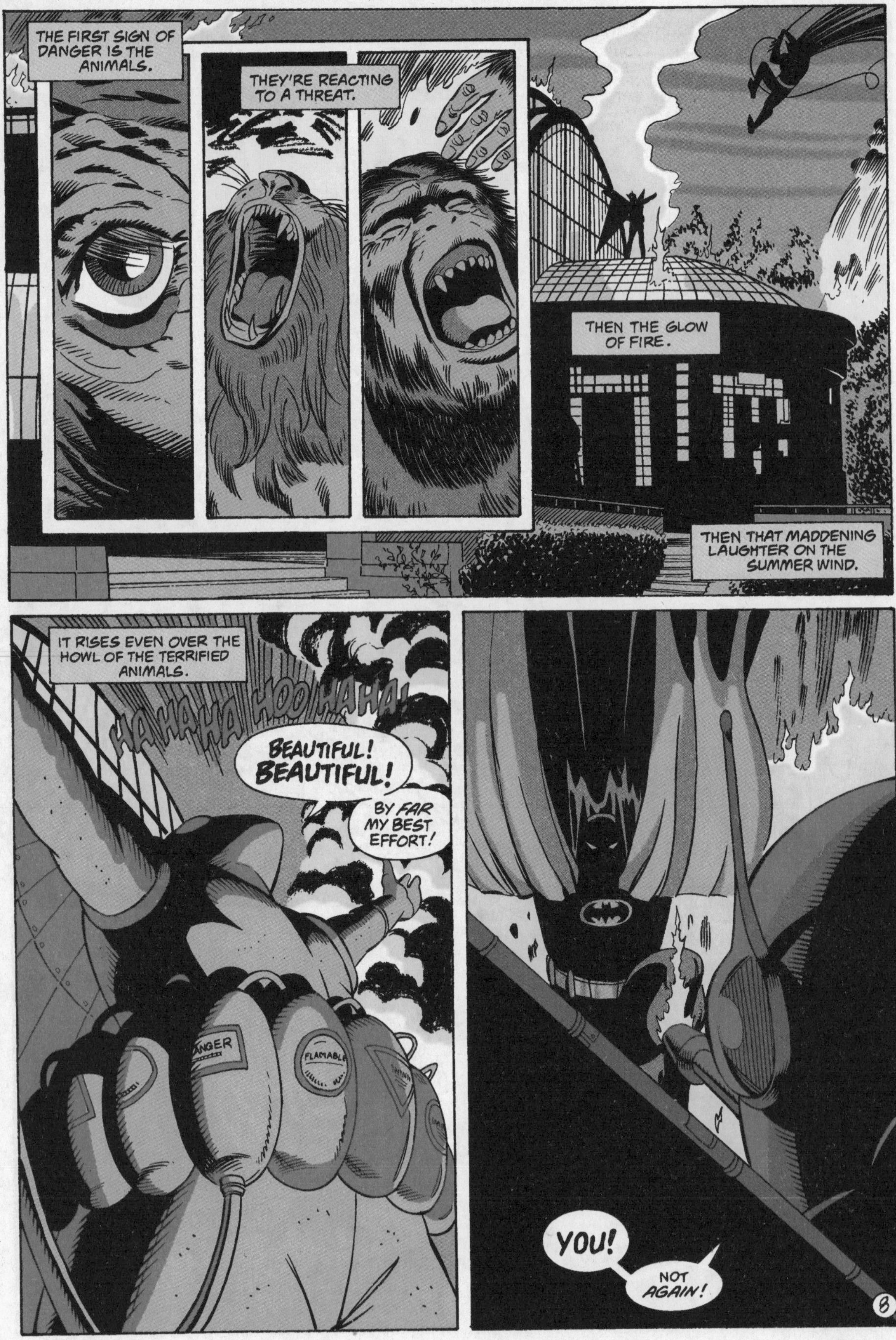

THE FIRST SIGN OF DANGER IS THE ANIMALS.
THEY'RE REACTING TO A THREAT.
THEN THE GLOW OF FIRE.
THEN THAT MADDENING LAUGHTER ON THE SUMMER WIND.
IT RISES EVEN OVER THE HOWL OF THE TERRIFIED ANIMALS.
HAHAHA HOO HAHA!
BEAUTIFUL! BEAUTIFUL!
BY FAR MY BEST EFFORT!
YOU!
NOT AGAIN!
8

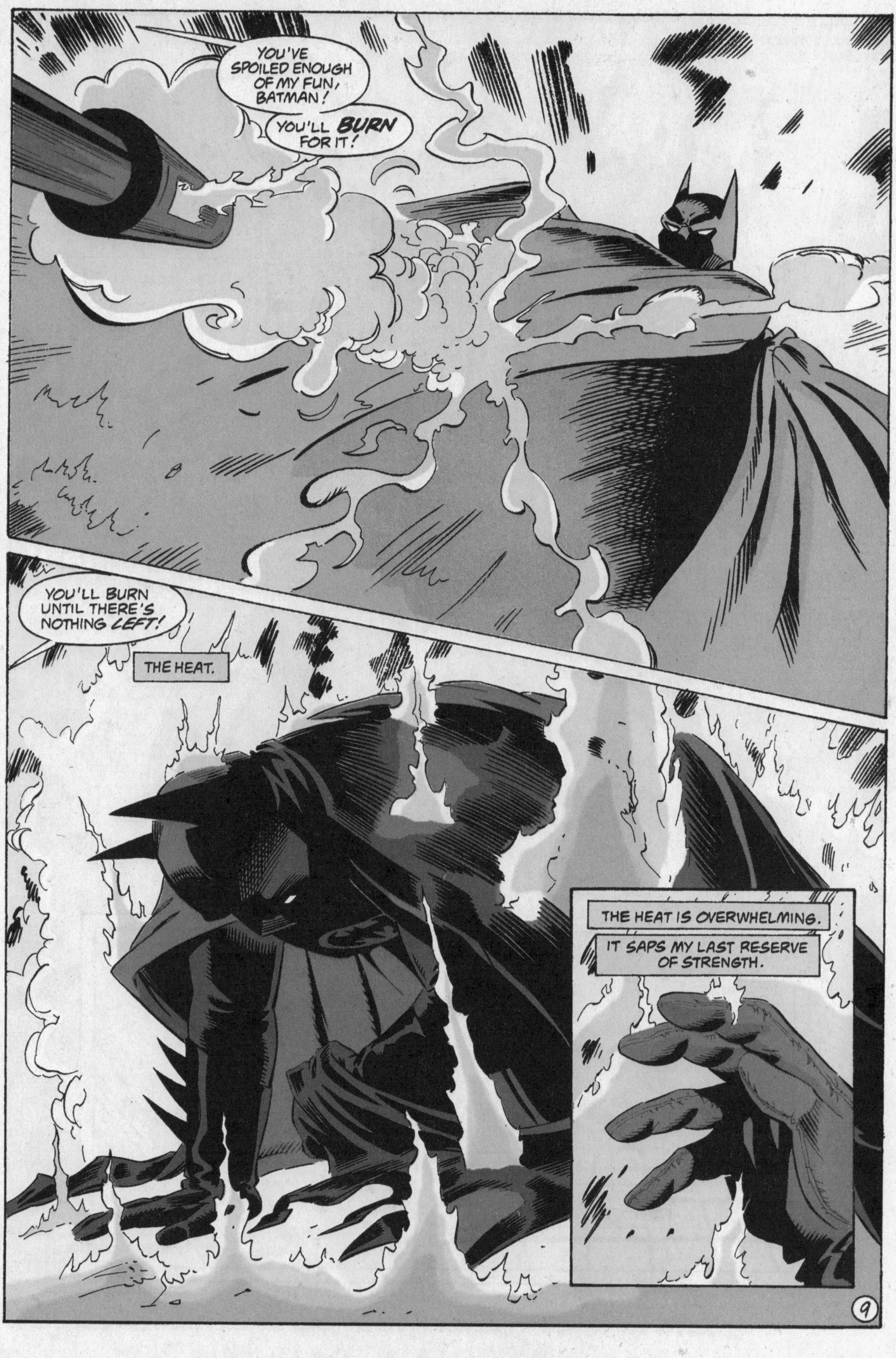
YOU'VE SPOILED ENOUGH OF MY FUN, BATMAN!
YOU'LL BURN FOR IT!
YOU'LL BURN UNTIL THERE'S NOTHING LEFT!
THE HEAT.
THE HEAT IS OVERWHELMING.
IT SAPS MY LAST RESERVE OF STRENGTH.
9

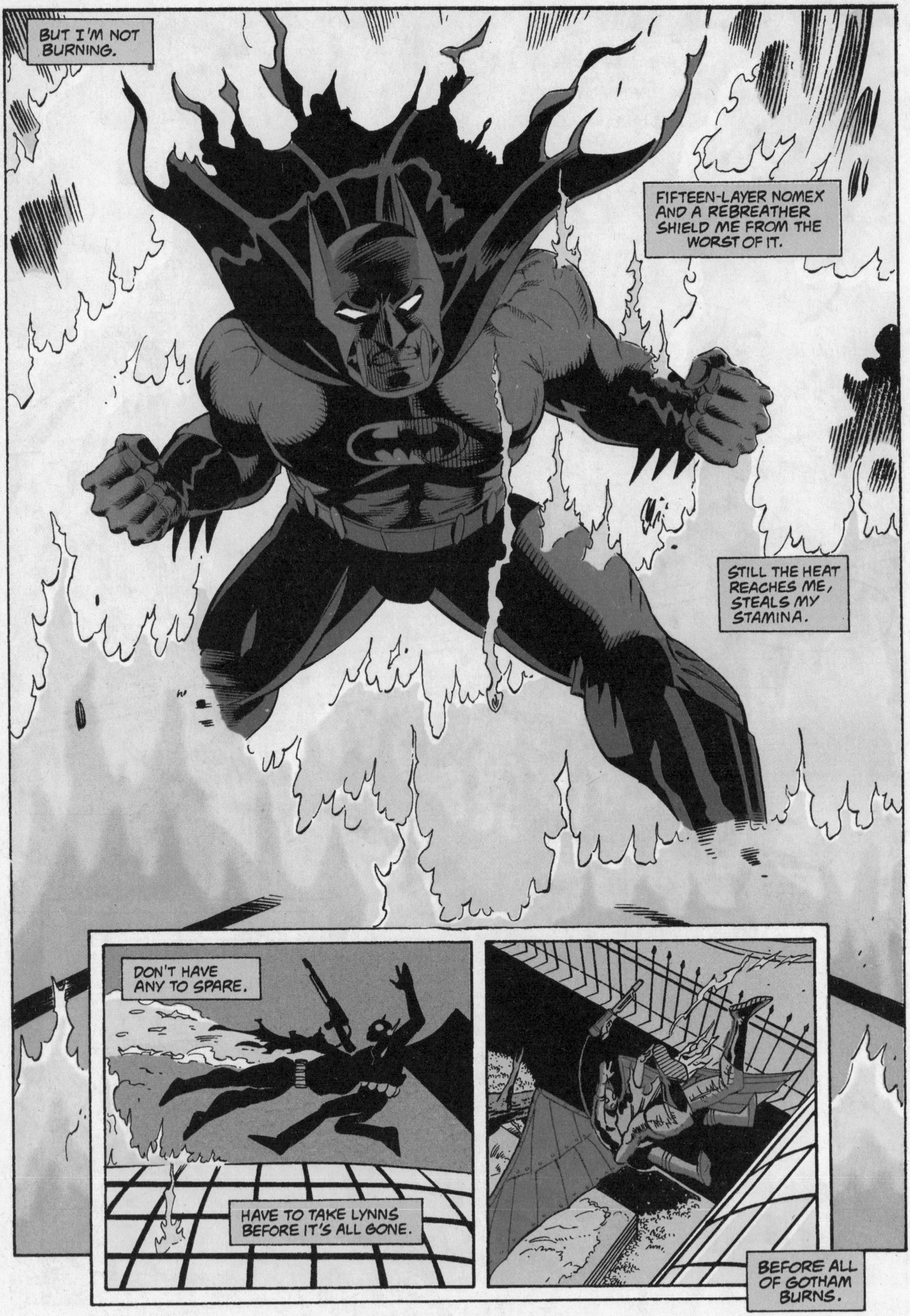
BUT I'M NOT BURNING.
FIFTEEN-LAYER NOMEX AND A REBREATHER SHIELD ME FROM THE WORST OF IT.
STILL THE HEAT REACHES ME, STEALS MY STAMINA.
DON'T HAVE ANY TO SPARE.
HAVE TO TAKE LYNNS BEFORE IT'S ALL GONE.
BEFORE ALL OF GOTHAM BURNS.

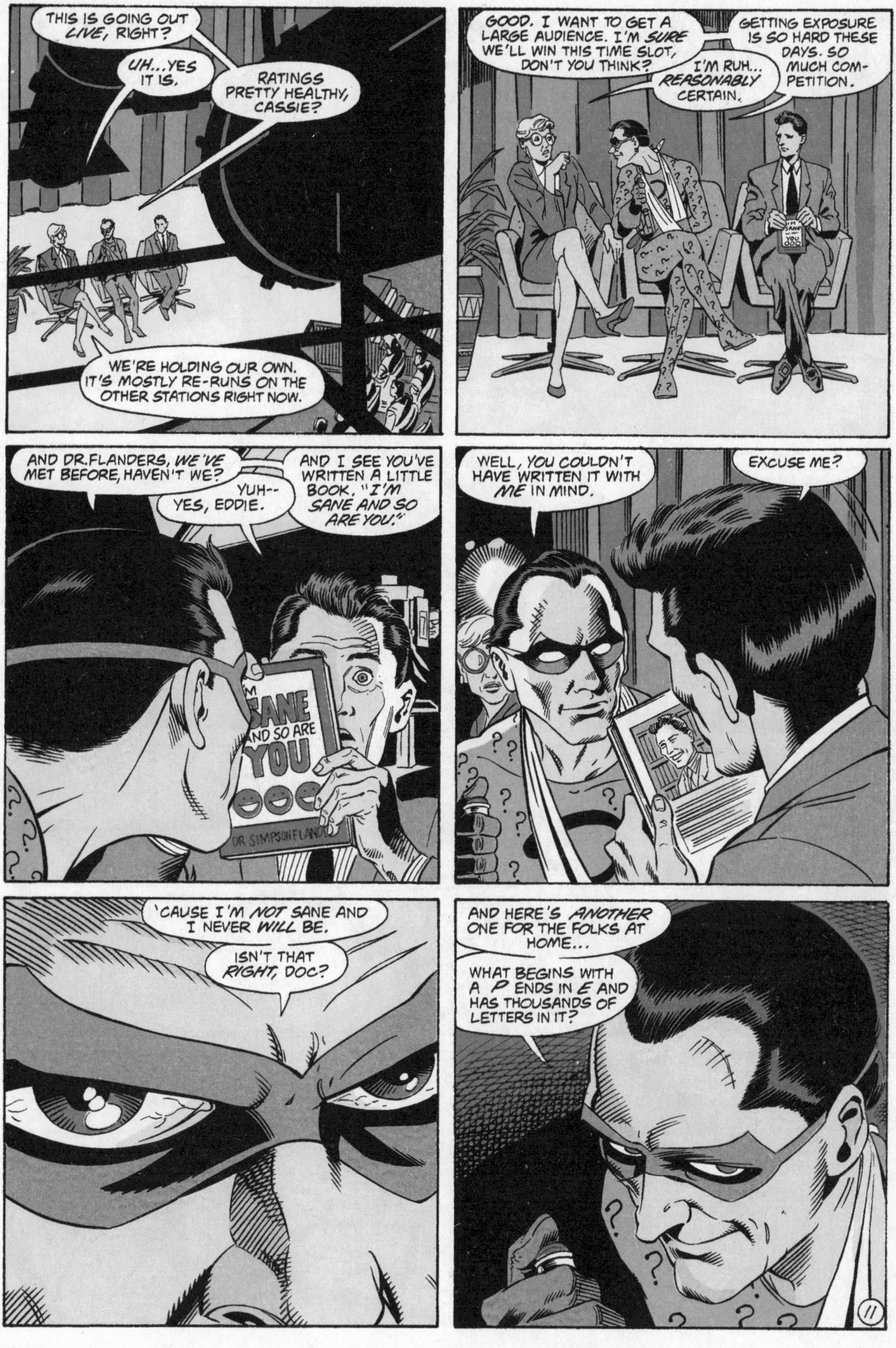
THIS IS GOING OUT LIVE, RIGHT?
UH...YES IT IS.
RATINGS PRETTY HEALTHY, CASSIE?
WE'RE HOLDING OUR OWN. IT'S MOSTLY RE-RUNS ON THE OTHER STATIONS RIGHT NOW.
GOOD. I WANT TO GET A LARGE AUDIENCE. I'M SURE WE'LL WIN THIS TIME SLOT, DON'T YOU THINK?
I'M RUH... REASONABLY CERTAIN.
GETTING EXPOSURE IS SO HARD THESE DAYS. SO MUCH COMPETITION.
AND DR.FLANDERS, WE'VE MET BEFORE, HAVEN'T WE?
YUH-- YES, EDDIE.
AND I SEE YOU'VE WRITTEN A LITTLE BOOK. "I'M SANE AND SO ARE YOU."
I'M SANE AND SO ARE YOU
DR SIMPSON FLAND
WELL, YOU COULDN'T HAVE WRITTEN IT WITH ME IN MIND.
EXCUSE ME?
'CAUSE I'M NOT SANE AND I NEVER WILL BE.
ISN'T THAT RIGHT, DOC?
AND HERE'S ANOTHER ONE FOR THE FOLKS AT HOME...
WHAT BEGINS WITH A P ENDS IN E AND HAS THOUSANDS OF LETTERS IN IT?
11

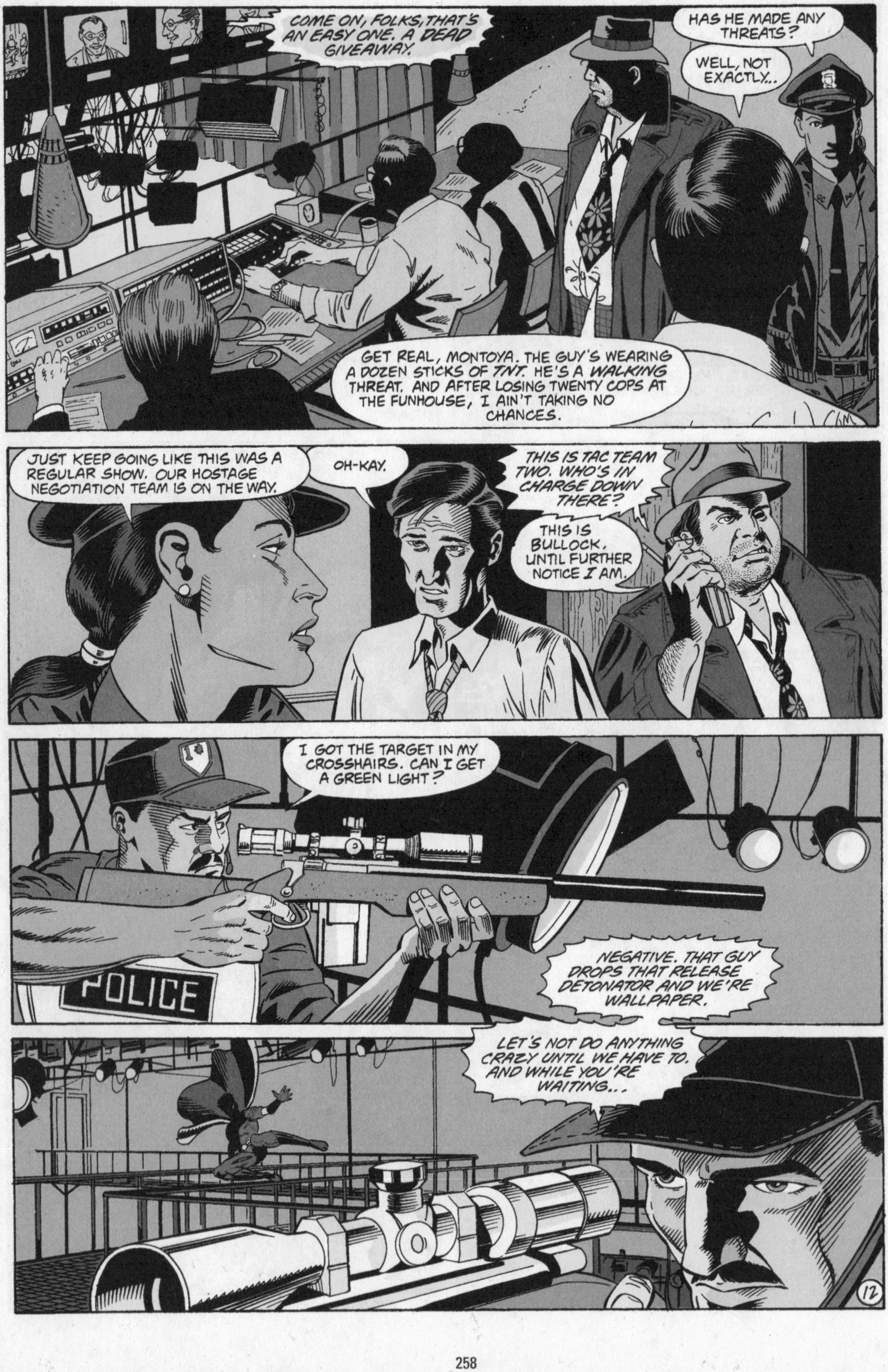

COME ON, FOLKS, THAT'S AN EASY ONE. A DEAD GIVEAWAY.
HAS HE MADE ANY THREATS?
WELL, NOT EXACTLY...
GET REAL, MONTOYA. THE GUY'S WEARING A DOZEN STICKS OF TNT. HE'S A WALKING THREAT. AND AFTER LOSING TWENTY COPS AT THE FUNHOUSE, I AIN'T TAKING NO CHANCES.
JUST KEEP GOING LIKE THIS WAS A REGULAR SHOW. OUR HOSTAGE NEGOTIATION TEAM IS ON THE WAY.
OH-KAY.
THIS IS TAC TEAM TWO. WHO'S IN CHARGE DOWN THERE?
THIS IS BULLOCK. UNTIL FURTHER NOTICE I AM.
I GOT THE TARGET IN MY CROSSHAIRS. CAN I GET A GREEN LIGHT?
POLICE
NEGATIVE. THAT GUY DROPS THAT RELEASE DETONATOR AND WE'RE WALLPAPER.
LET'S NOT DO ANYTHING CRAZY UNTIL WE HAVE TO. AND WHILE YOU'RE WAITING...
12

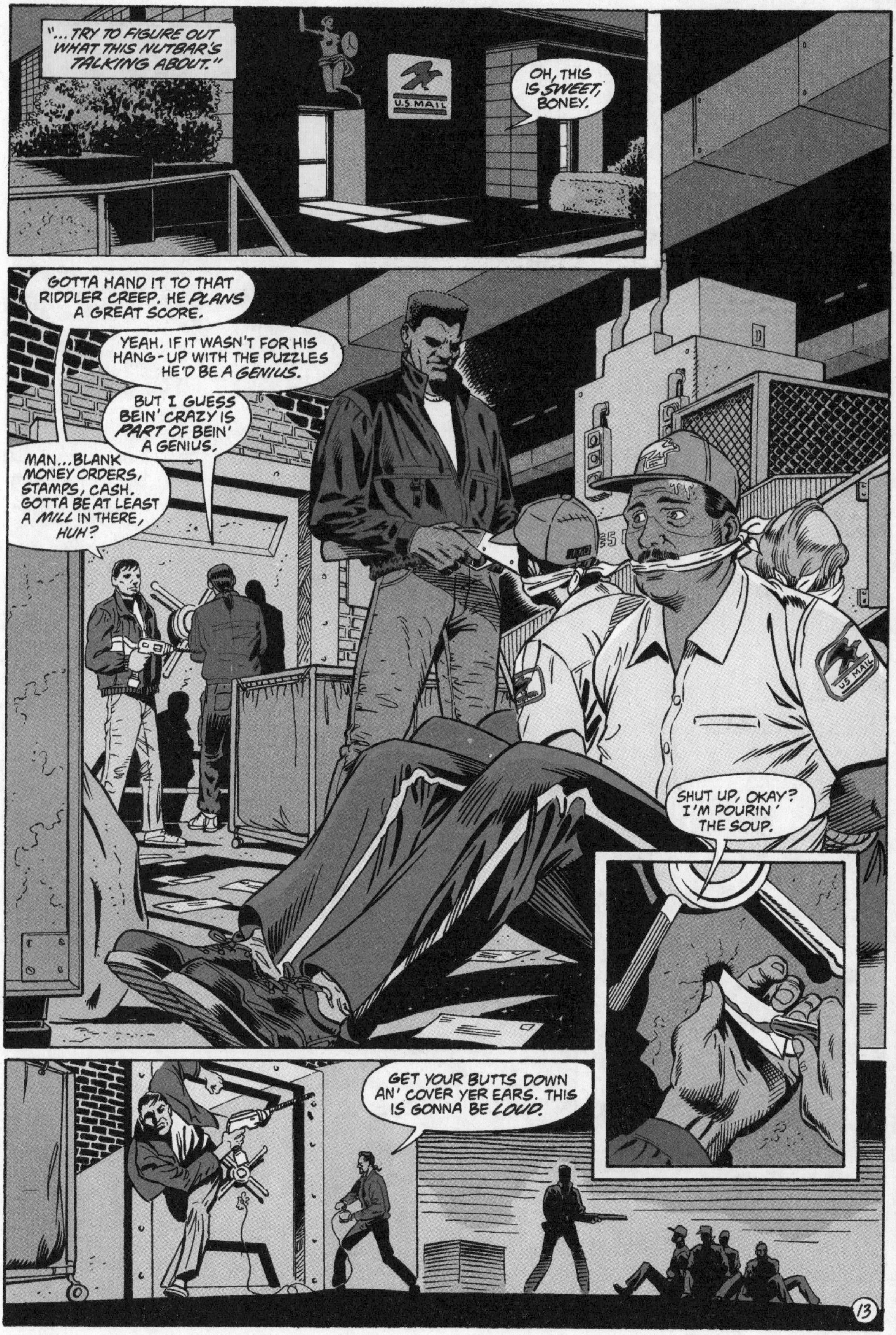
"...TRY TO FIGURE OUT WHAT THIS NUTBAR'S TALKING ABOUT."
U.S. MAIL
OH, THIS IS SWEET, BONEY.
GOTTA HAND IT TO THAT RIDDLER CREEP. HE PLANS A GREAT SCORE.
YEAH. IF IT WASN'T FOR HIS HANG-UP WITH THE PUZZLES HE'D BE A GENIUS.
BUT I GUESS BEIN' CRAZY IS PART OF BEIN' A GENIUS.
MAN...BLANK MONEY ORDERS, STAMPS, CASH. GOTTA BE AT LEAST A MILL IN THERE, HUH?
SHUT UP, OKAY? I'M POURIN' THE SOUP.
GET YOUR BUTTS DOWN AN' COVER YER EARS. THIS IS GONNA BE LOUD.
13

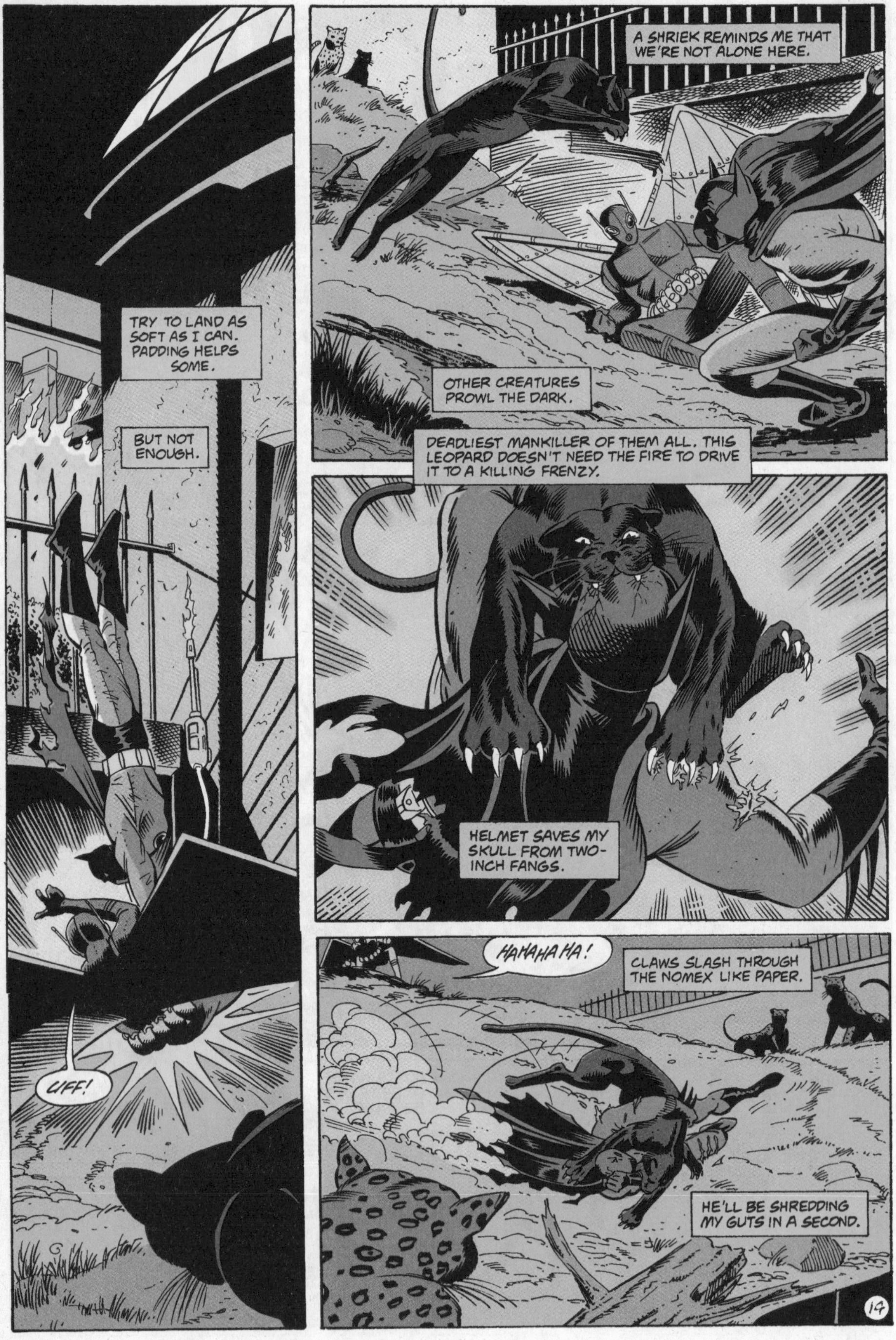
TRY TO LAND AS SOFT AS I CAN. PADDING HELPS SOME.
BUT NOT ENOUGH.
UFF!
A SHRIEK REMINDS ME THAT WE'RE NOT ALONE HERE.
OTHER CREATURES PROWL THE DARK.
DEADLIEST MANKILLER OF THEM ALL. THIS LEOPARD DOESN'T NEED THE FIRE TO DRIVE IT TO A KILLING FRENZY.
HELMET SAVES MY SKULL FROM TWO-INCH FANGS.
HAHAHAHA HA!
CLAWS SLASH THROUGH THE NOMEX LIKE PAPER.
HE'LL BE SHREDDING MY GUTS IN A SECOND.
17

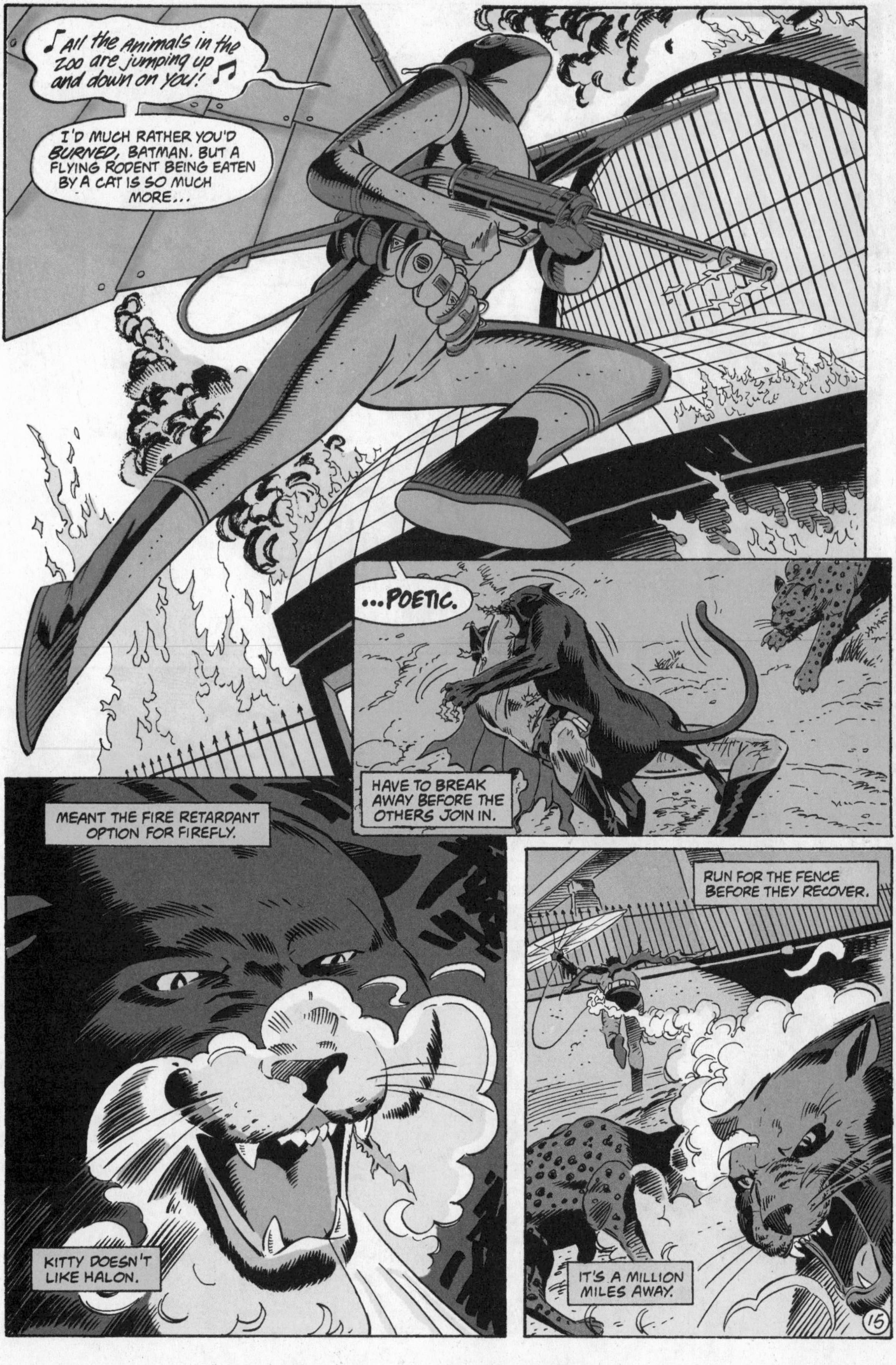
♪ All the Animals in the zoo are jumping up and down on you! ♫
I'D MUCH RATHER YOU'D BURNED, BATMAN. BUT A FLYING RODENT BEING EATEN BY A CAT IS SO MUCH MORE...
...POETIC.
HAVE TO BREAK AWAY BEFORE THE OTHERS JOIN IN.
MEANT THE FIRE RETARDANT OPTION FOR FIREFLY.
KITTY DOESN'T LIKE HALON.
RUN FOR THE FENCE BEFORE THEY RECOVER.
IT'S A MILLION MILES AWAY.
15

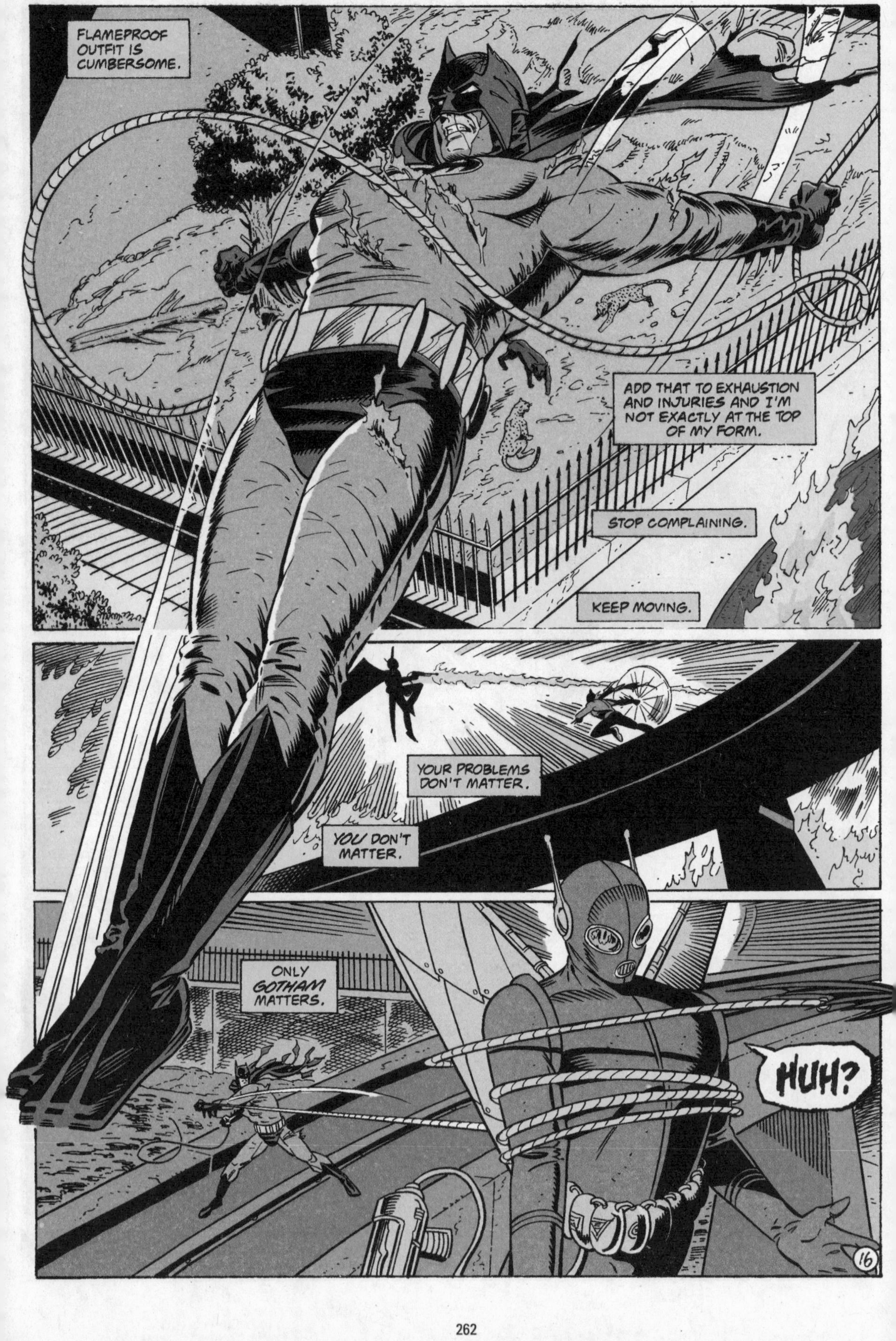
FLAMEPROOF OUTFIT IS CUMBERSOME.
ADD THAT TO EXHAUSTION AND INJURIES AND I'M NOT EXACTLY AT THE TOP OF MY FORM.
STOP COMPLAINING.
KEEP MOVING.
YOUR PROBLEMS DON'T MATTER.
YOU DON'T MATTER.
ONLY GOTHAM MATTERS.
HUH?
16

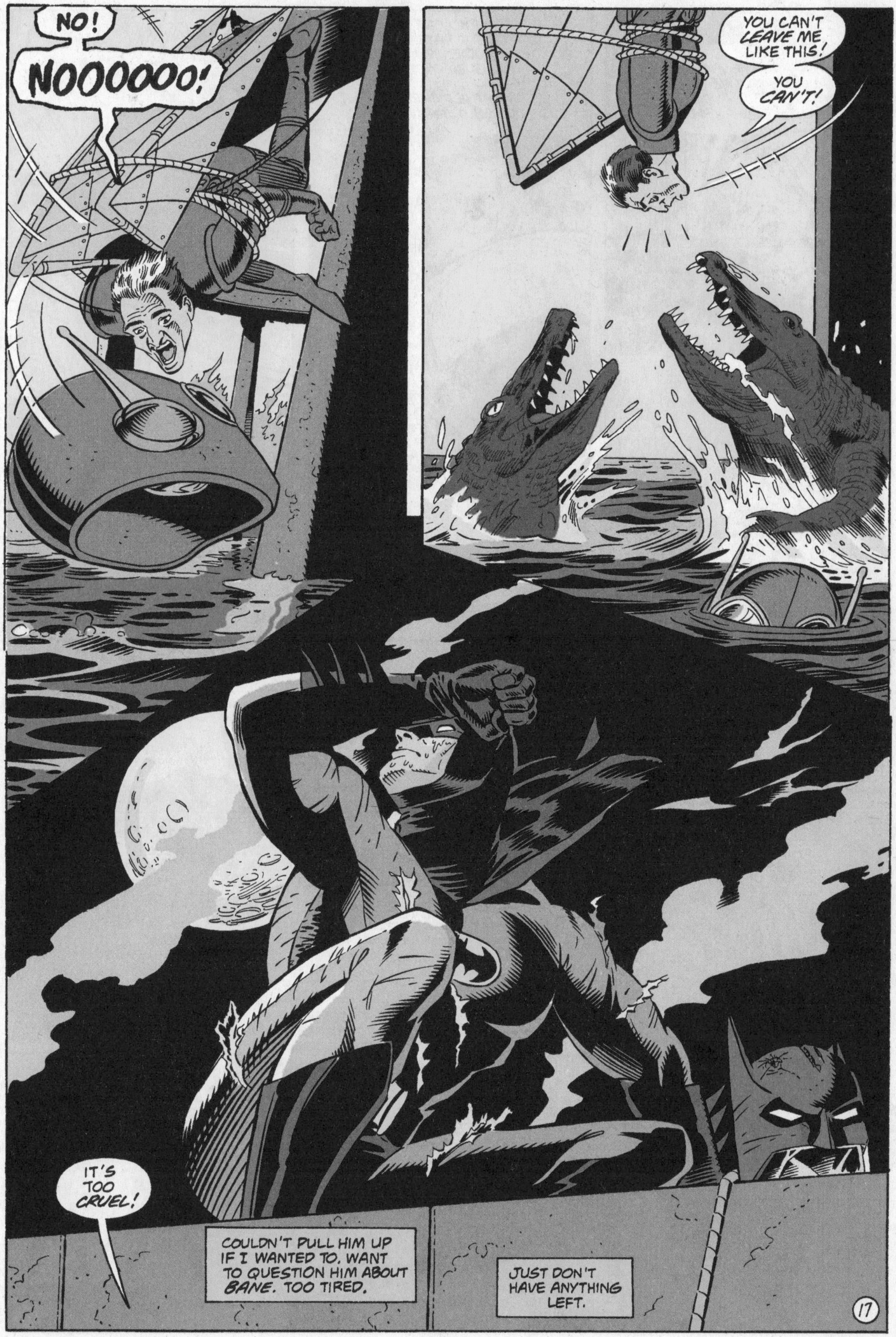
NO!
NOOOOOO!
YOU CAN'T LEAVE ME LIKE THIS!
YOU CAN'T!
IT'S TOO CRUEL!
COULDN'T PULL HIM UP IF I WANTED TO. WANT TO QUESTION HIM ABOUT BANE. TOO TIRED.
JUST DON'T HAVE ANYTHING LEFT.
17

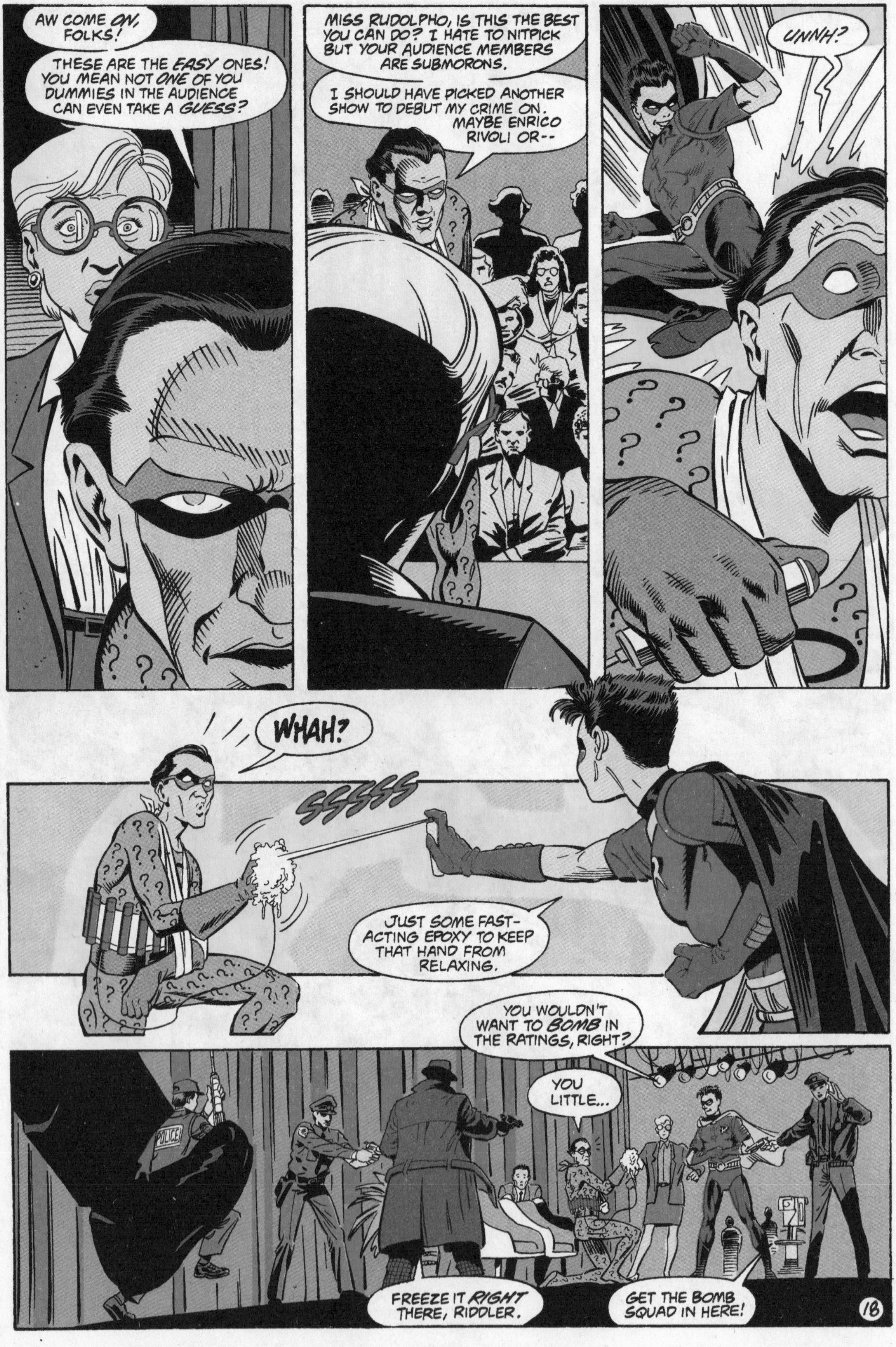
AW COME ON, FOLKS!
THESE ARE THE EASY ONES! YOU MEAN NOT ONE OF YOU DUMMIES IN THE AUDIENCE CAN EVEN TAKE A GUESS?
MISS RUDOLPHO, IS THIS THE BEST YOU CAN DO? I HATE TO NITPICK BUT YOUR AUDIENCE MEMBERS ARE SUBMORONS.
I SHOULD HAVE PICKED ANOTHER SHOW TO DEBUT MY CRIME ON. MAYBE ENRICO RIVOLI OR--
UNNH?
WHAH?
SSSSS
JUST SOME FAST-ACTING EPOXY TO KEEP THAT HAND FROM RELAXING.
YOU WOULDN'T WANT TO BOMB IN THE RATINGS, RIGHT?
YOU LITTLE...
POLICE
FREEZE IT RIGHT THERE, RIDDLER.
GET THE BOMB SQUAD IN HERE!
18

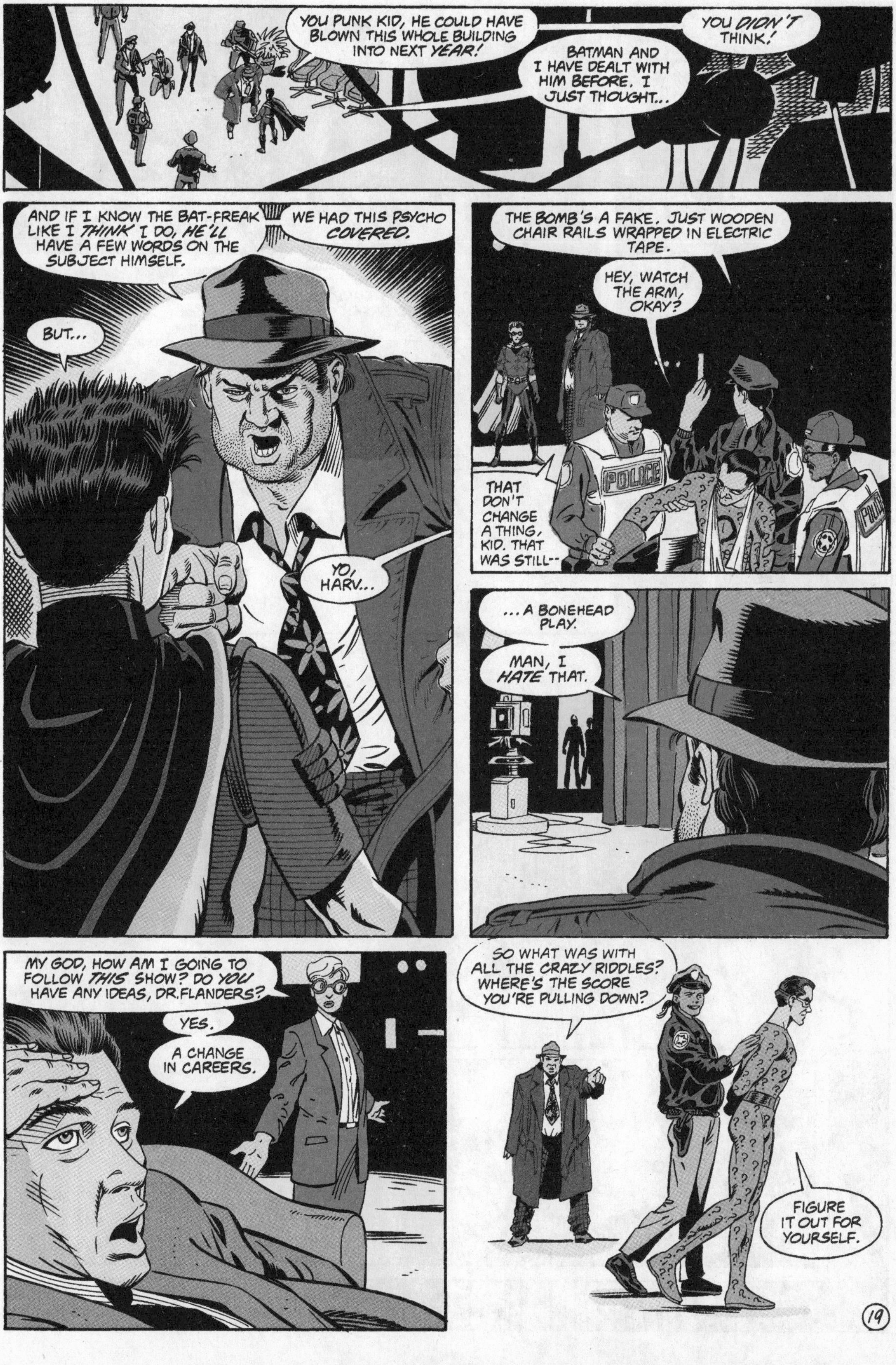

YOU PUNK KID, HE COULD HAVE BLOWN THIS WHOLE BUILDING INTO NEXT YEAR!
BATMAN AND I HAVE DEALT WITH HIM BEFORE. I JUST THOUGHT...
YOU DIDN'T THINK!
AND IF I KNOW THE BAT-FREAK LIKE I THINK I DO, HE'LL HAVE A FEW WORDS ON THE SUBJECT HIMSELF.
WE HAD THIS PSYCHO COVERED.
BUT...
YO, HARV...
THE BOMB'S A FAKE. JUST WOODEN CHAIR RAILS WRAPPED IN ELECTRIC TAPE.
HEY, WATCH THE ARM, OKAY?
POLICE
THAT DON'T CHANGE A THING, KID. THAT WAS STILL--
...A BONEHEAD PLAY.
MAN, I HATE THAT.
MY GOD, HOW AM I GOING TO FOLLOW THIS SHOW? DO YOU HAVE ANY IDEAS, DR. FLANDERS?
YES.
A CHANGE IN CAREERS.
SO WHAT WAS WITH ALL THE CRAZY RIDDLES? WHERE'S THE SCORE YOU'RE PULLING DOWN?
FIGURE IT OUT FOR YOURSELF.
19

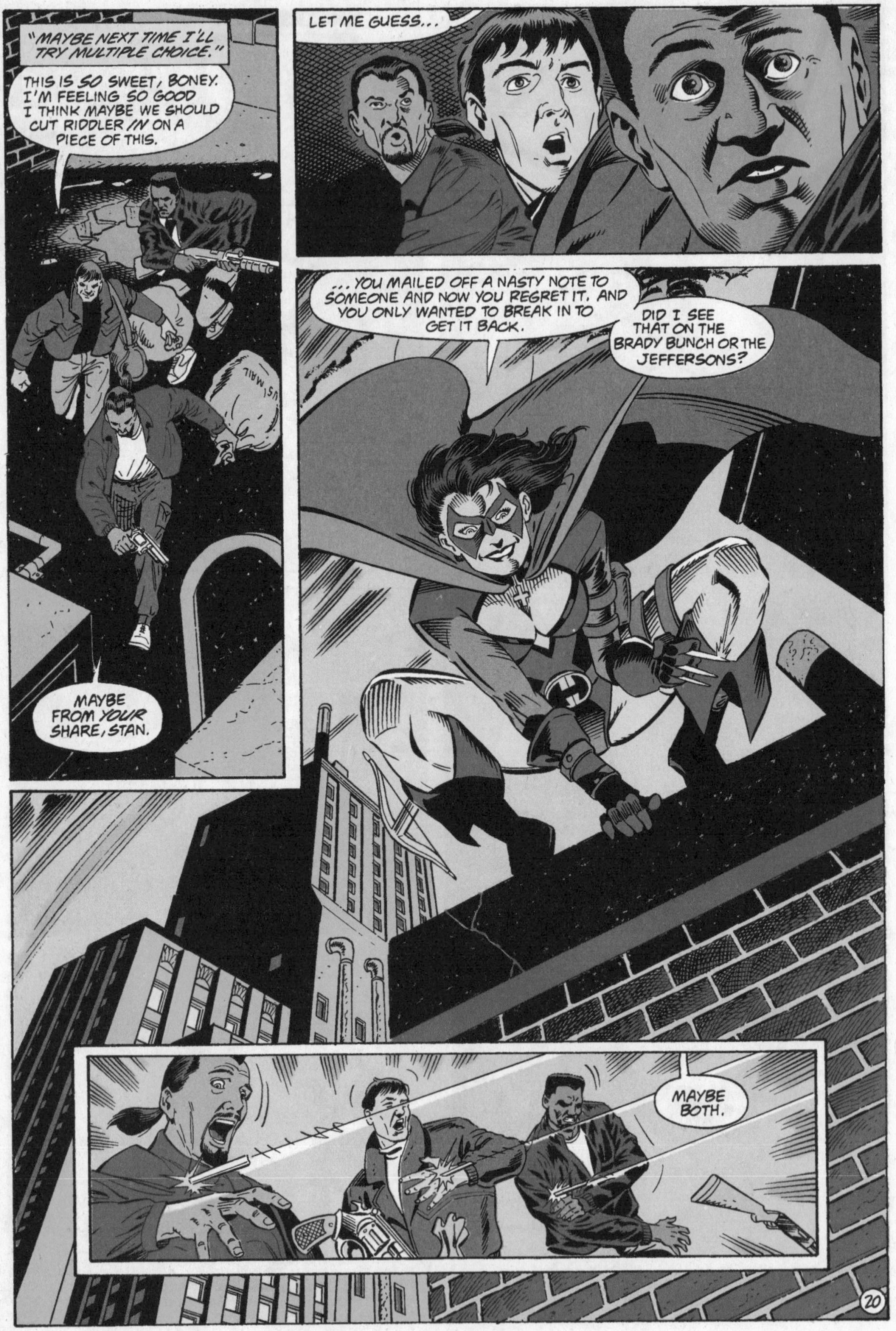
"MAYBE NEXT TIME I'LL TRY MULTIPLE CHOICE."
THIS IS SO SWEET, BONEY. I'M FEELING SO GOOD I THINK MAYBE WE SHOULD CUT RIDDLER IN ON A PIECE OF THIS.
U.S. MAIL
MAYBE FROM YOUR SHARE, STAN.
LET ME GUESS...
...YOU MAILED OFF A NASTY NOTE TO SOMEONE AND NOW YOU REGRET IT. AND YOU ONLY WANTED TO BREAK IN TO GET IT BACK.
DID I SEE THAT ON THE BRADY BUNCH OR THE JEFFERSONS?
MAYBE BOTH.
20

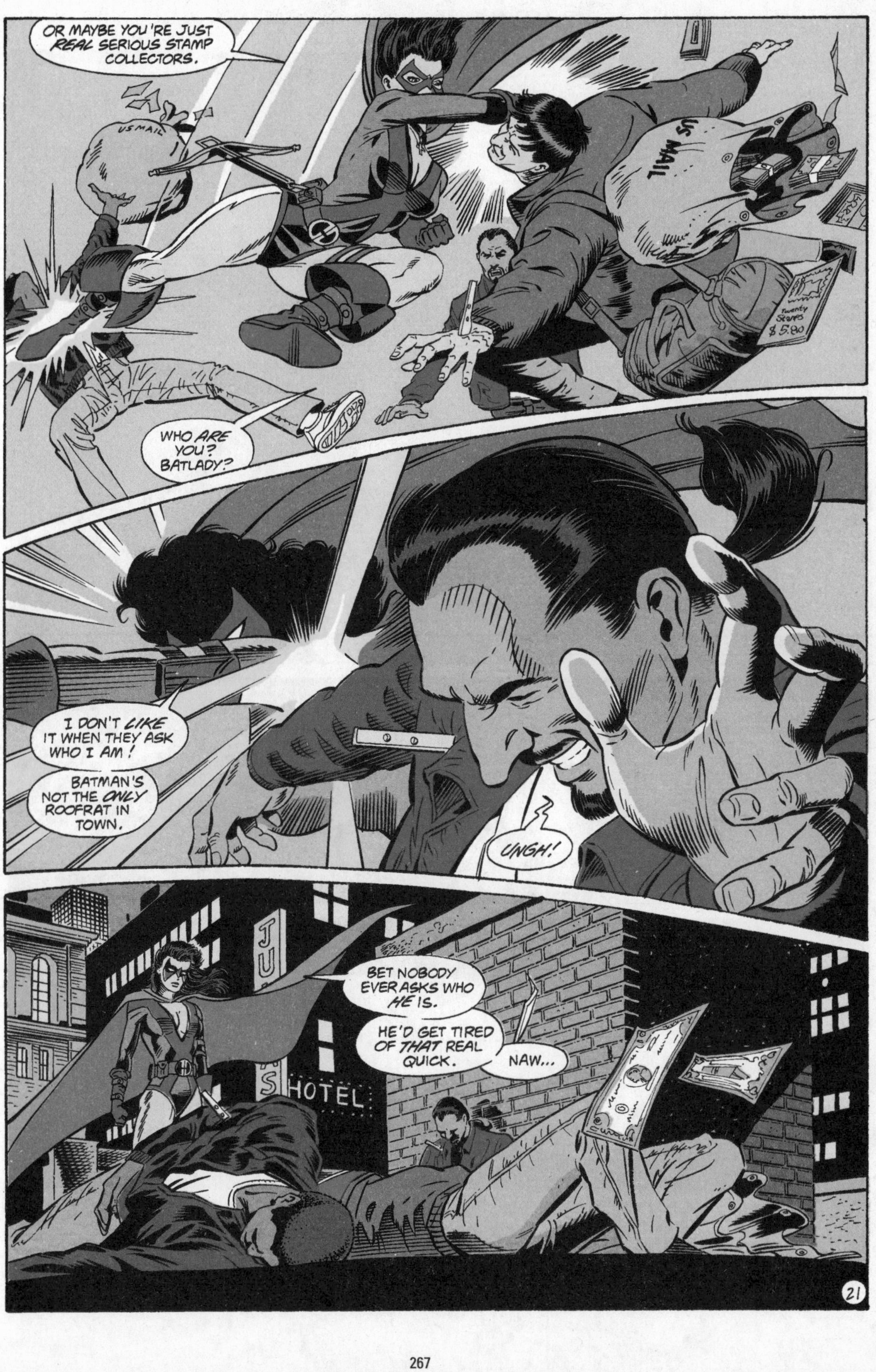
OR MAYBE YOU'RE JUST REAL SERIOUS STAMP COLLECTORS.
US MAIL
US MAIL
Twenty Stamps $5.80
WHO ARE YOU? BATLADY?
I DON'T LIKE IT WHEN THEY ASK WHO I AM!
BATMAN'S NOT THE ONLY ROOFRAT IN TOWN.
UNGH!
BET NOBODY EVER ASKS WHO HE IS.
HE'D GET TIRED OF THAT REAL QUICK.
NAW...
HOTEL
21

"...HE PROBABLY DOESN'T GET TIRED."

IT'S OVER.

FOR TONIGHT ANYWAY.

FIREFIGHTERS ARE HERE. THE ONES THAT AREN'T OUT ON STRIKE ANYWAY. THEY HAVE IT ALL IN HAND.

EIGHT DOWN. FIREFLY. ZSASZ. FILM FREAK. THE HATTER. CAVALIER. AMYGDALA. STIRK. POISON IVY.

MOSTLY SECOND-STRINGERS AND THEY NEARLY TOOK ME OUT.

THE *REALLY* DANGEROUS ONES ARE STILL ON THE STREET. SCARECROW. RIDDLER. JOKER.

HOW CAN I STAND AGAINST THEM WHEN I CAN'T EVEN STAND UP?

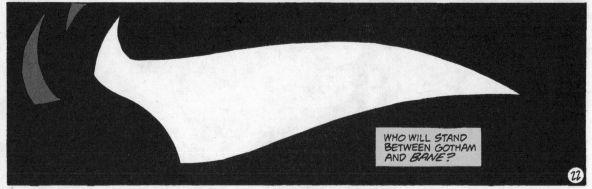

WHO WILL STAND BETWEEN GOTHAM AND *BANE?*

22

Cover art by KELLEY JONES

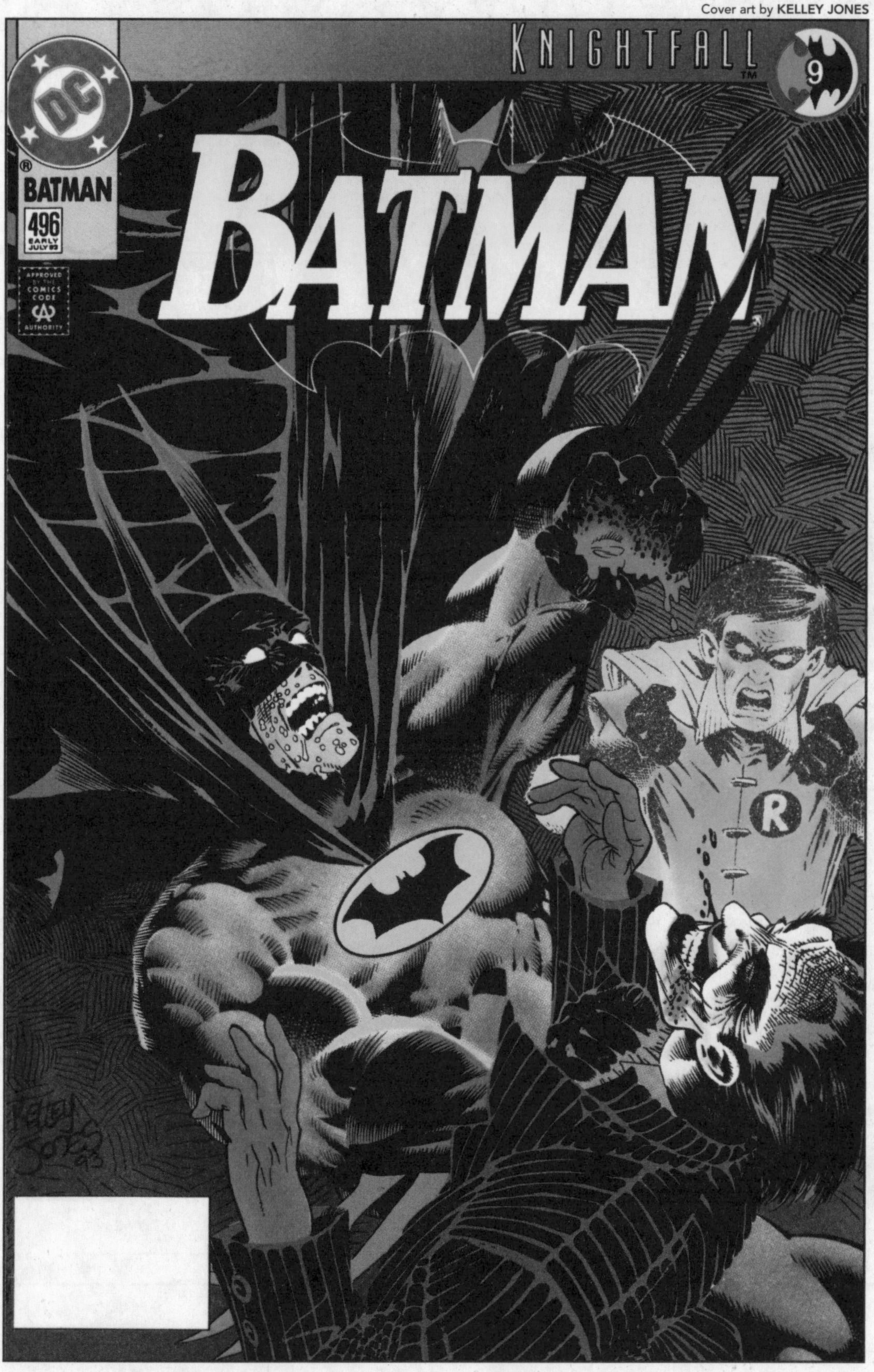
KNIGHTFALL
9
DC
BATMAN
496
EARLY JULY 93
APPROVED BY THE COMICS CODE AUTHORITY
BATMAN
R

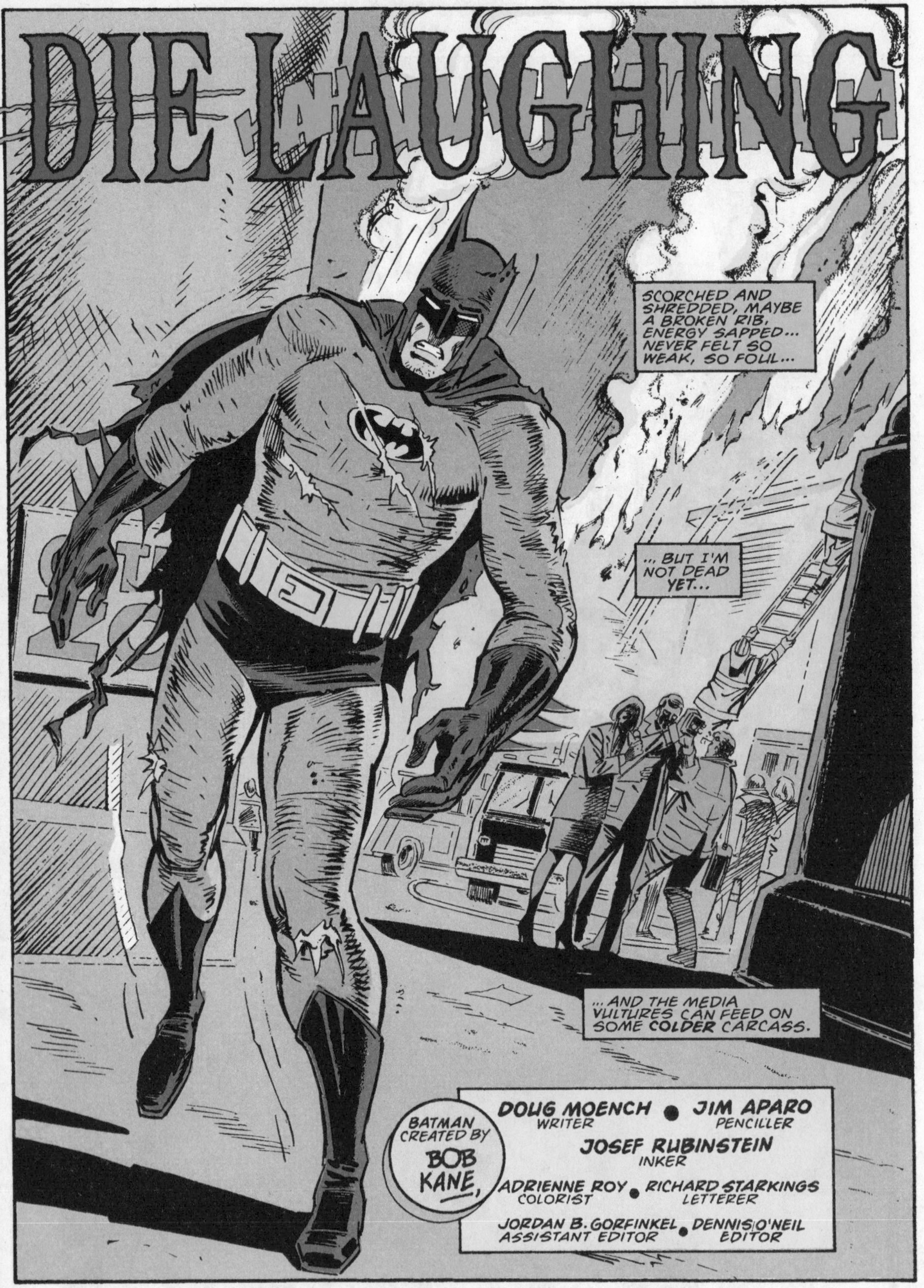
DIE LAUGHING
SCORCHED AND SHREDDED, MAYBE A BROKEN RIB. ENERGY SAPPED... NEVER FELT SO WEAK, SO FOUL...
...BUT I'M NOT DEAD YET...
...AND THE MEDIA VULTURES CAN FEED ON SOME COLDER CARCASS.
BATMAN CREATED BY BOB KANE,
DOUG MOENCH WRITER • JIM APARO PENCILLER
JOSEF RUBINSTEIN INKER
ADRIENNE ROY COLORIST • RICHARD STARKINGS LETTERER
JORDAN B. GORFINKEL ASSISTANT EDITOR • DENNIS O'NEIL EDITOR

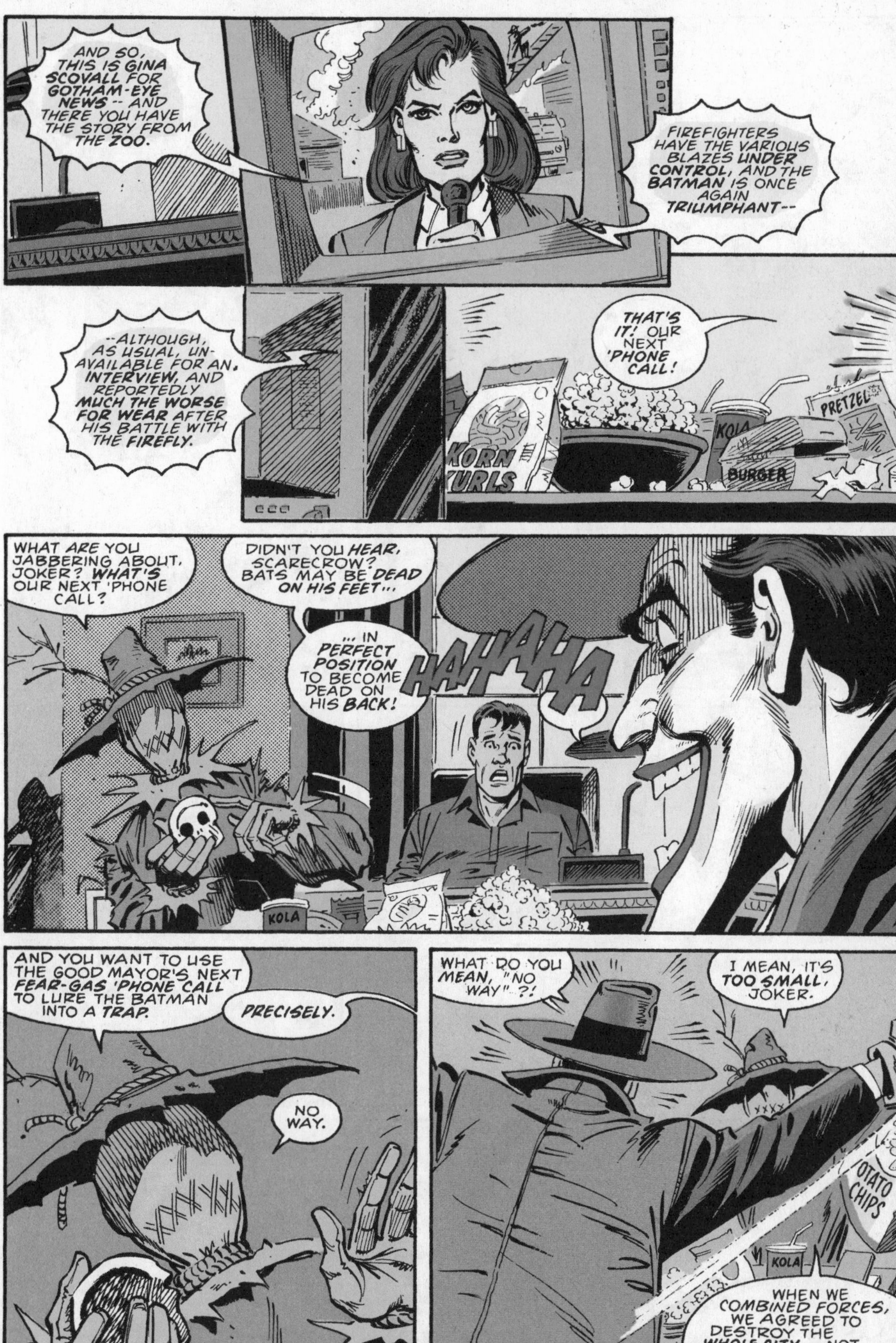
AND SO, THIS IS GINA SCOVALL FOR GOTHAM-EYE NEWS -- AND THERE YOU HAVE THE STORY FROM THE ZOO.
FIREFIGHTERS HAVE THE VARIOUS BLAZES UNDER CONTROL, AND THE BATMAN IS ONCE AGAIN TRIUMPHANT--
--ALTHOUGH, AS USUAL, UNAVAILABLE FOR AN INTERVIEW, AND REPORTEDLY MUCH THE WORSE FOR WEAR AFTER HIS BATTLE WITH THE FIREFLY.
THAT'S IT! OUR NEXT 'PHONE CALL!
KORN KURLS
KOLA
PRETZEL
BURGER
WHAT ARE YOU JABBERING ABOUT, JOKER? WHAT'S OUR NEXT 'PHONE CALL?
DIDN'T YOU HEAR, SCARECROW? BATS MAY BE DEAD ON HIS FEET...
... IN PERFECT POSITION TO BECOME DEAD ON HIS BACK!
HAHAHAHA
KOLA
AND YOU WANT TO USE THE GOOD MAYOR'S NEXT FEAR-GAS 'PHONE CALL TO LURE THE BATMAN INTO A TRAP.
PRECISELY.
NO WAY.
WHAT DO YOU MEAN, "NO WAY"-?!
I MEAN, IT'S TOO SMALL, JOKER.
OTATO CHIPS
KOLA
WHEN WE COMBINED FORCES, WE AGREED TO DESTROY THE WHOLE CITY -- NOT JUST ONE MAN.
2

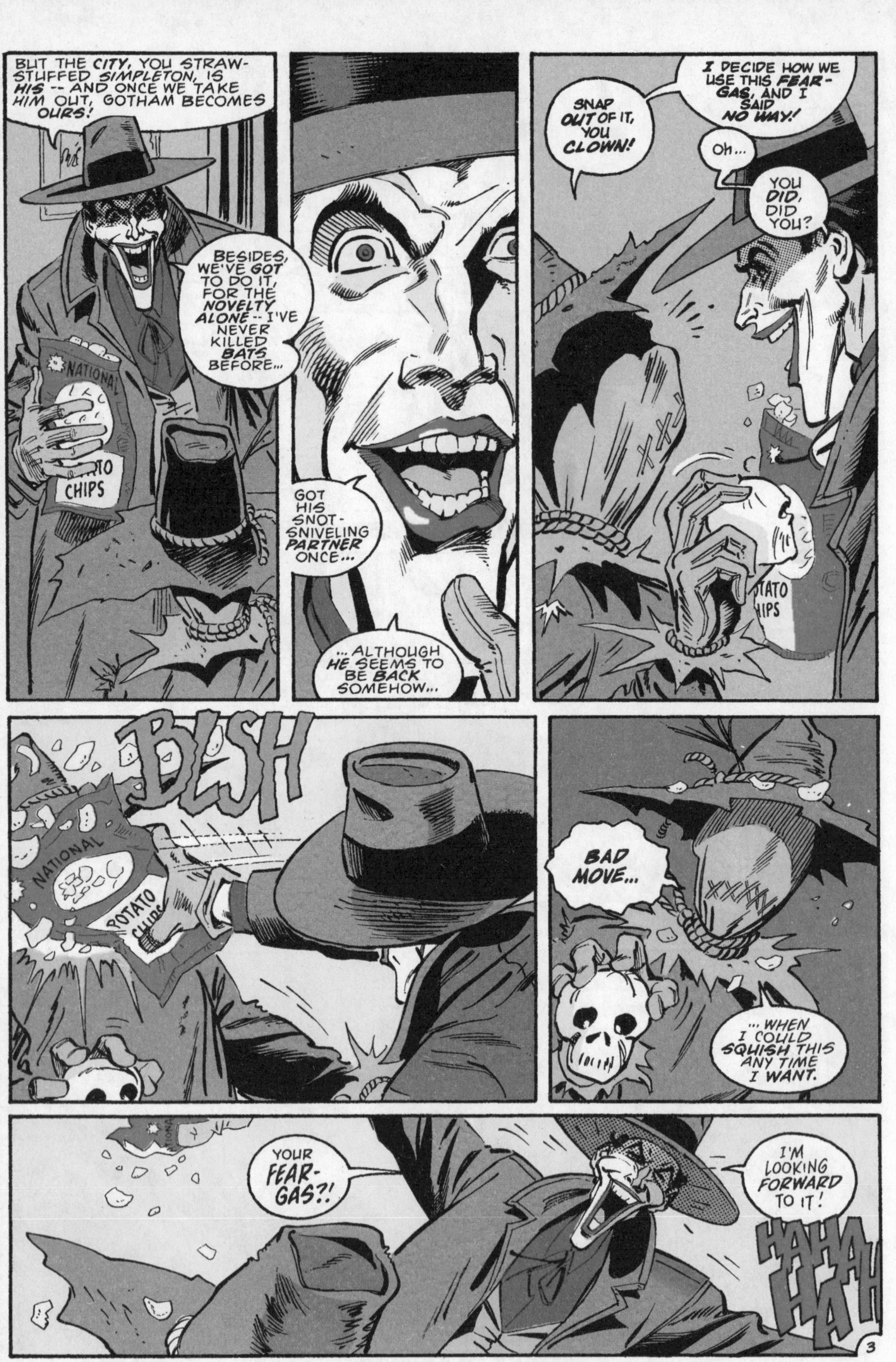
BUT THE CITY, YOU STRAW-STUFFED SIMPLETON, IS HIS -- AND ONCE WE TAKE HIM OUT, GOTHAM BECOMES OURS!
BESIDES, WE'VE GOT TO DO IT, FOR THE NOVELTY ALONE -- I'VE NEVER KILLED BATS BEFORE...
NATIONAL
POTATO CHIPS
GOT HIS SNOT-SNIVELING PARTNER ONCE...
...ALTHOUGH HE SEEMS TO BE BACK SOMEHOW...
SNAP OUT OF IT, YOU CLOWN!
I DECIDE HOW WE USE THIS FEAR-GAS, AND I SAID NO WAY!
Oh...
YOU DID, DID YOU?
BLSH
BAD MOVE...
...WHEN I COULD SQUISH THIS ANY TIME I WANT.
YOUR FEAR-GAS?!
I'M LOOKING FORWARD TO IT!
HAHAHAHA
3

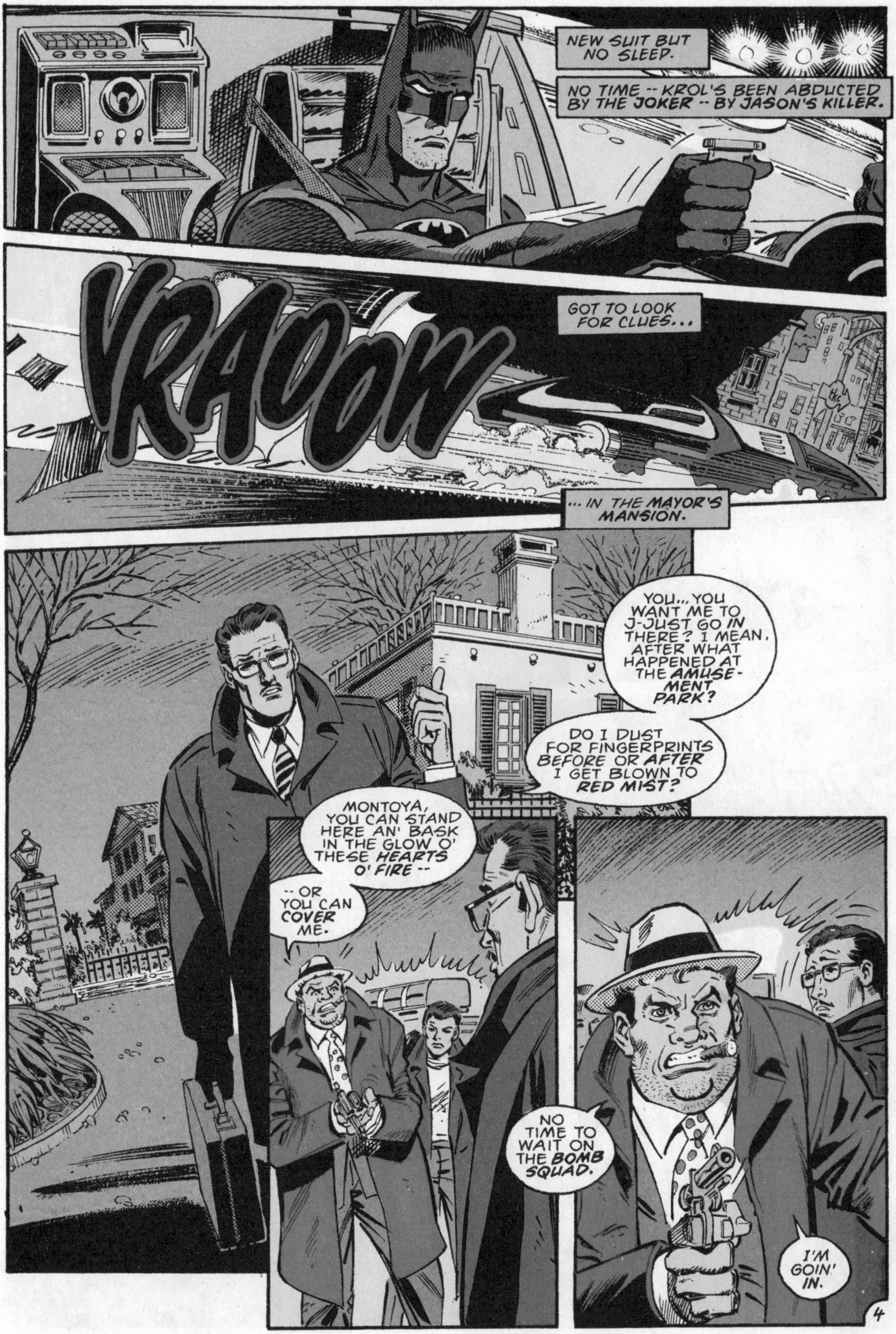
NEW SUIT BUT NO SLEEP.
NO TIME -- KROL'S BEEN ABDUCTED BY THE JOKER -- BY JASON'S KILLER.
VRAOOW
GOT TO LOOK FOR CLUES...
...IN THE MAYOR'S MANSION.
YOU... YOU WANT ME TO J-JUST GO IN THERE? I MEAN, AFTER WHAT HAPPENED AT THE AMUSEMENT PARK?
DO I DUST FOR FINGERPRINTS BEFORE OR AFTER I GET BLOWN TO RED MIST?
MONTOYA, YOU CAN STAND HERE AN' BASK IN THE GLOW O' THESE HEARTS O' FIRE --
-- OR YOU CAN COVER ME.
NO TIME TO WAIT ON THE BOMB SQUAD.
I'M GOIN' IN.
4

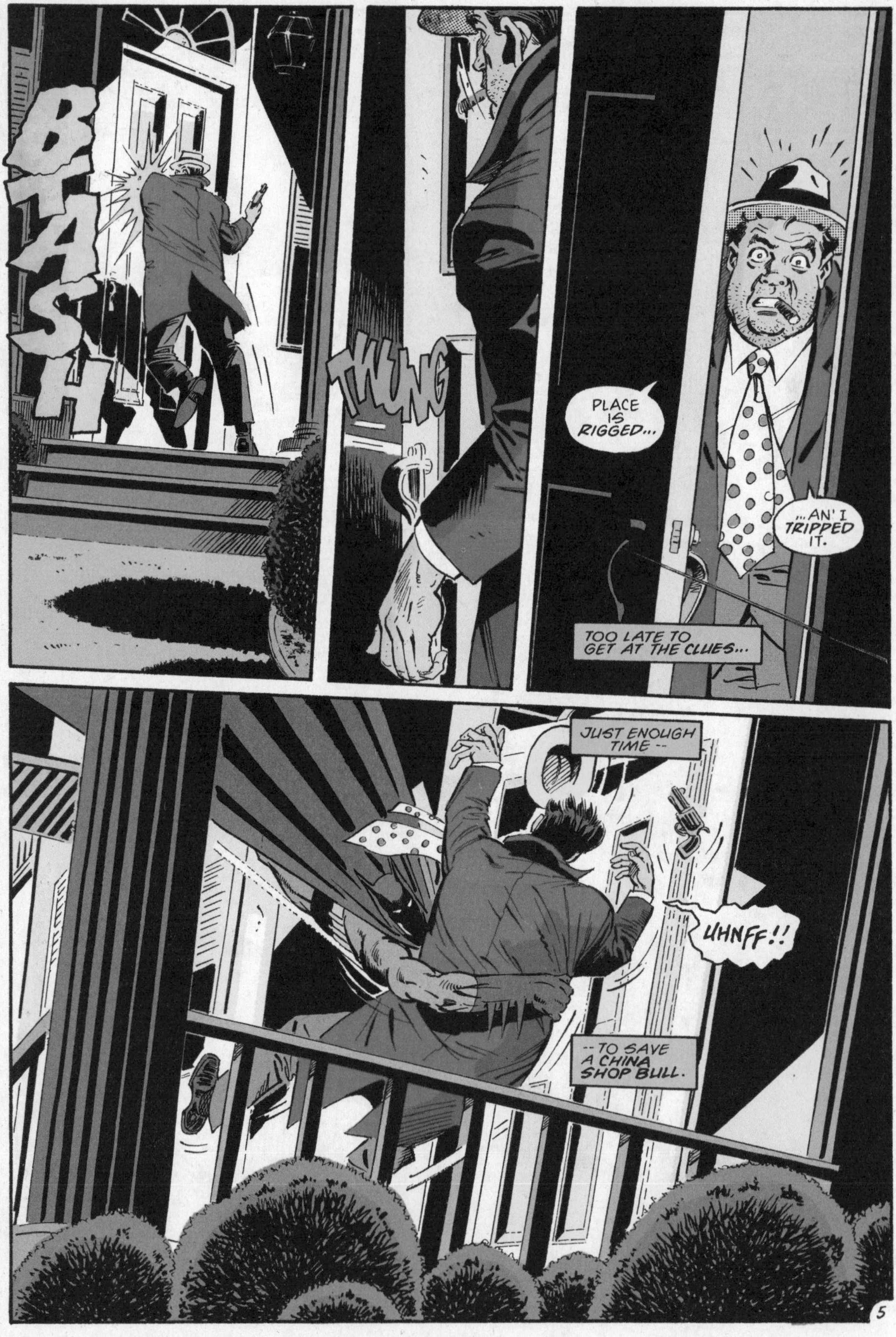
BLASH
THUNG
PLACE IS RIGGED...
...AN' I TRIPPED IT.
TOO LATE TO GET AT THE CLUES...
JUST ENOUGH TIME --
UHNFF!!
--TO SAVE A CHINA SHOP BULL.
5

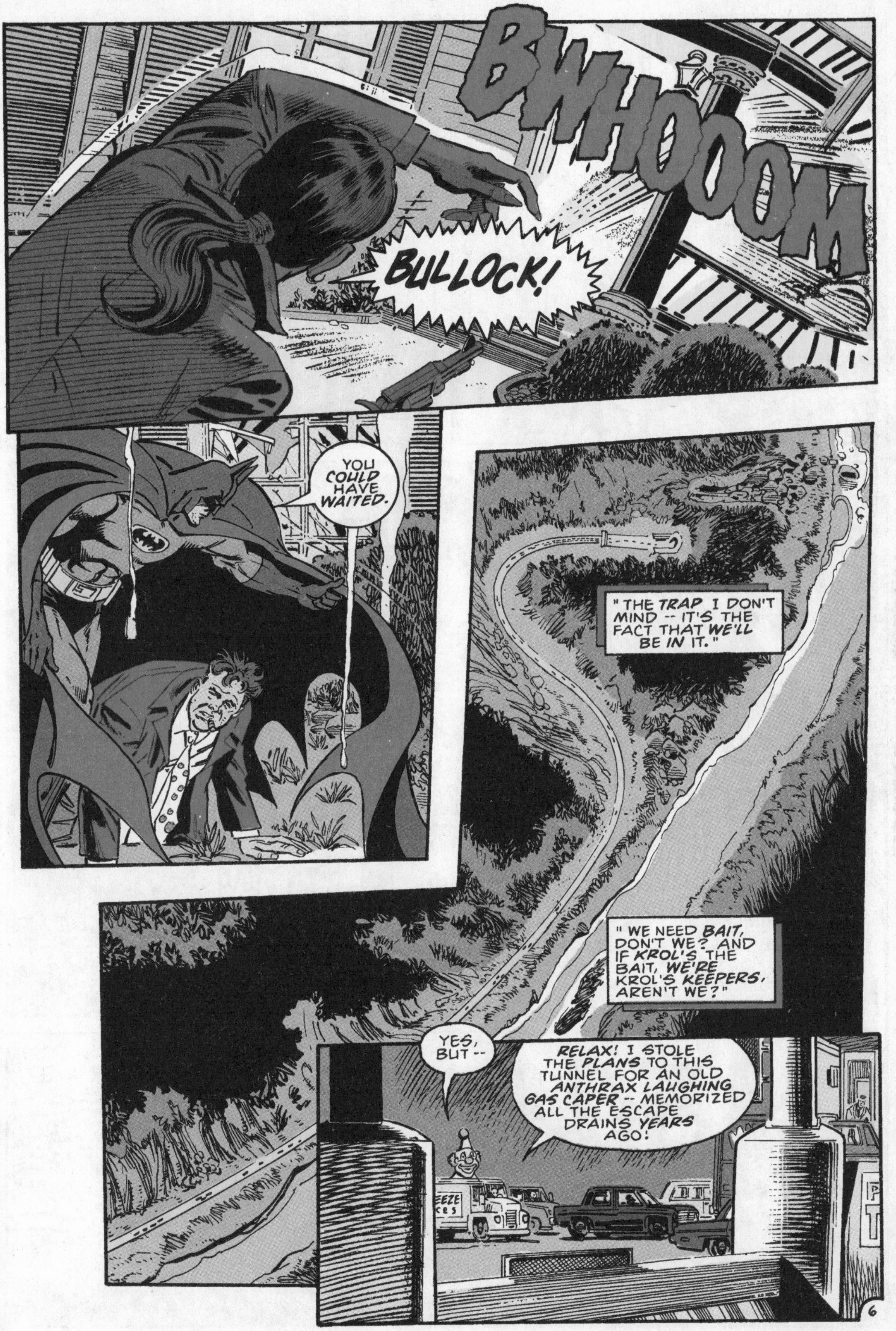
BWHOOOM
BULLOCK!
YOU COULD HAVE WAITED.
"THE TRAP I DON'T MIND -- IT'S THE FACT THAT WE'LL BE IN IT."
" WE NEED BAIT, DON'T WE? AND IF KROL'S THE BAIT, WE'RE KROL'S KEEPERS, AREN'T WE?"
YES, BUT --
RELAX! I STOLE THE PLANS TO THIS TUNNEL FOR AN OLD ANTHRAX LAUGHING GAS CAPER -- MEMORIZED ALL THE ESCAPE DRAINS YEARS AGO!
6

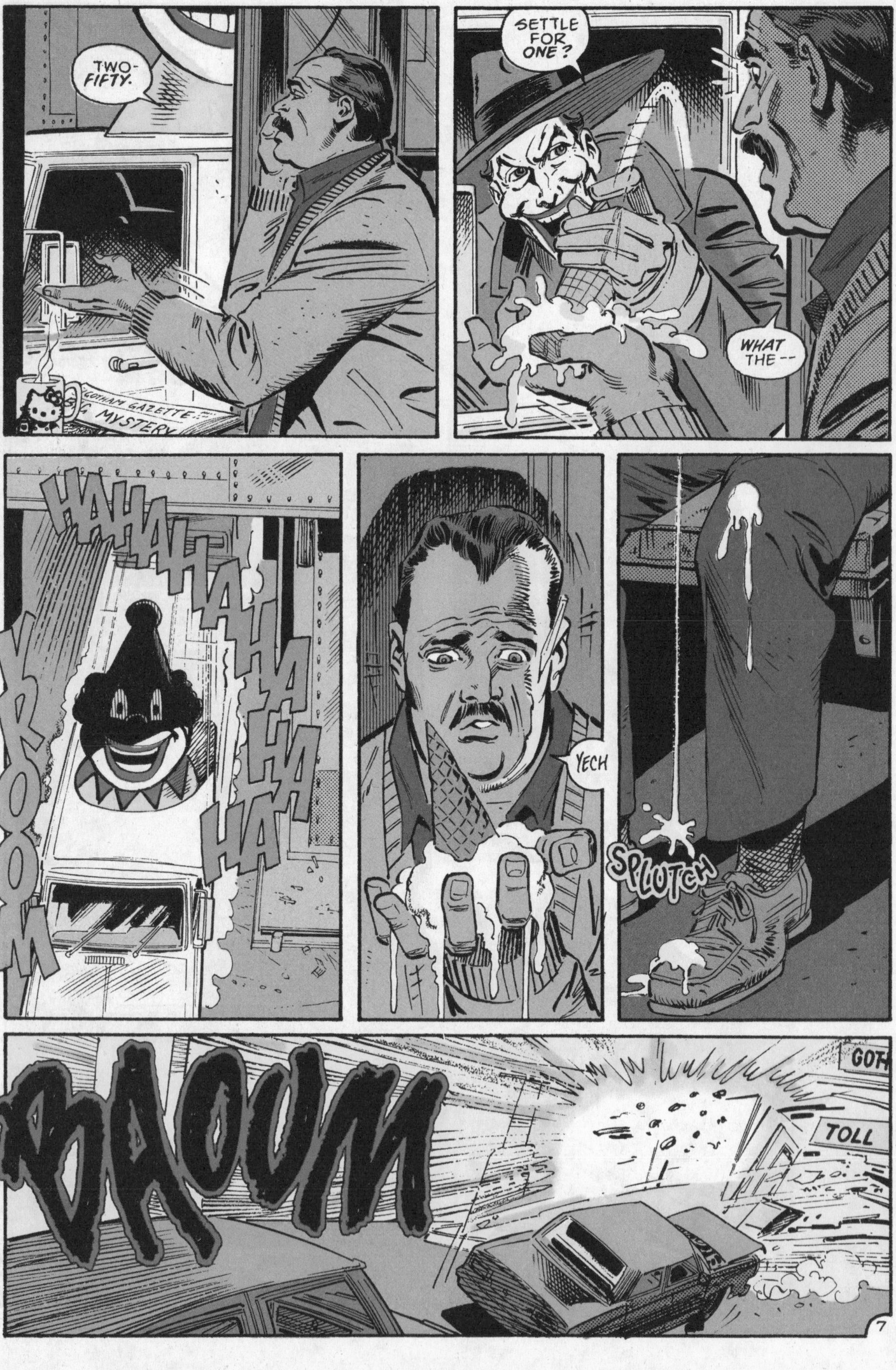
TWO-FIFTY.
GOTHAM GAZETTE
MYSTERY
SETTLE FOR ONE?
WHAT THE --
HAHAHAHAHAHAHAHA
KROOOM
YECH
SPLUTCH
BAOUM
GOTH
TOLL
7

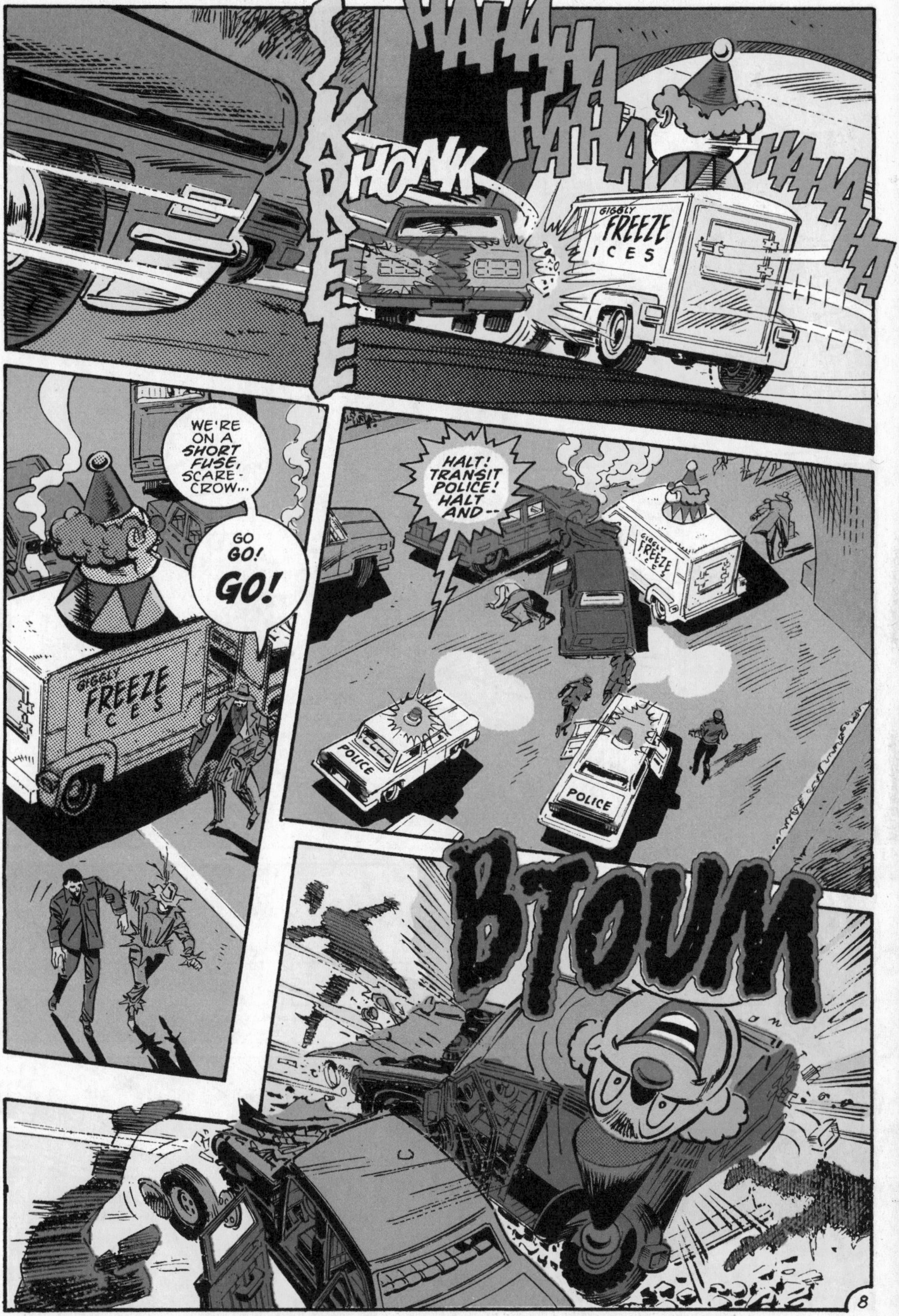
SKREEE
HONK
HAHAHAHA
HAHAHA
HAHAHAHA
GIGGLY FREEZE ICES
WE'RE ON A SHORT FUSE, SCARE-CROW...
GO GO! GO!
GIGGLY FREEZE ICES
HALT! TRANSIT POLICE! HALT AND--
POLICE
POLICE
BTOUM
8

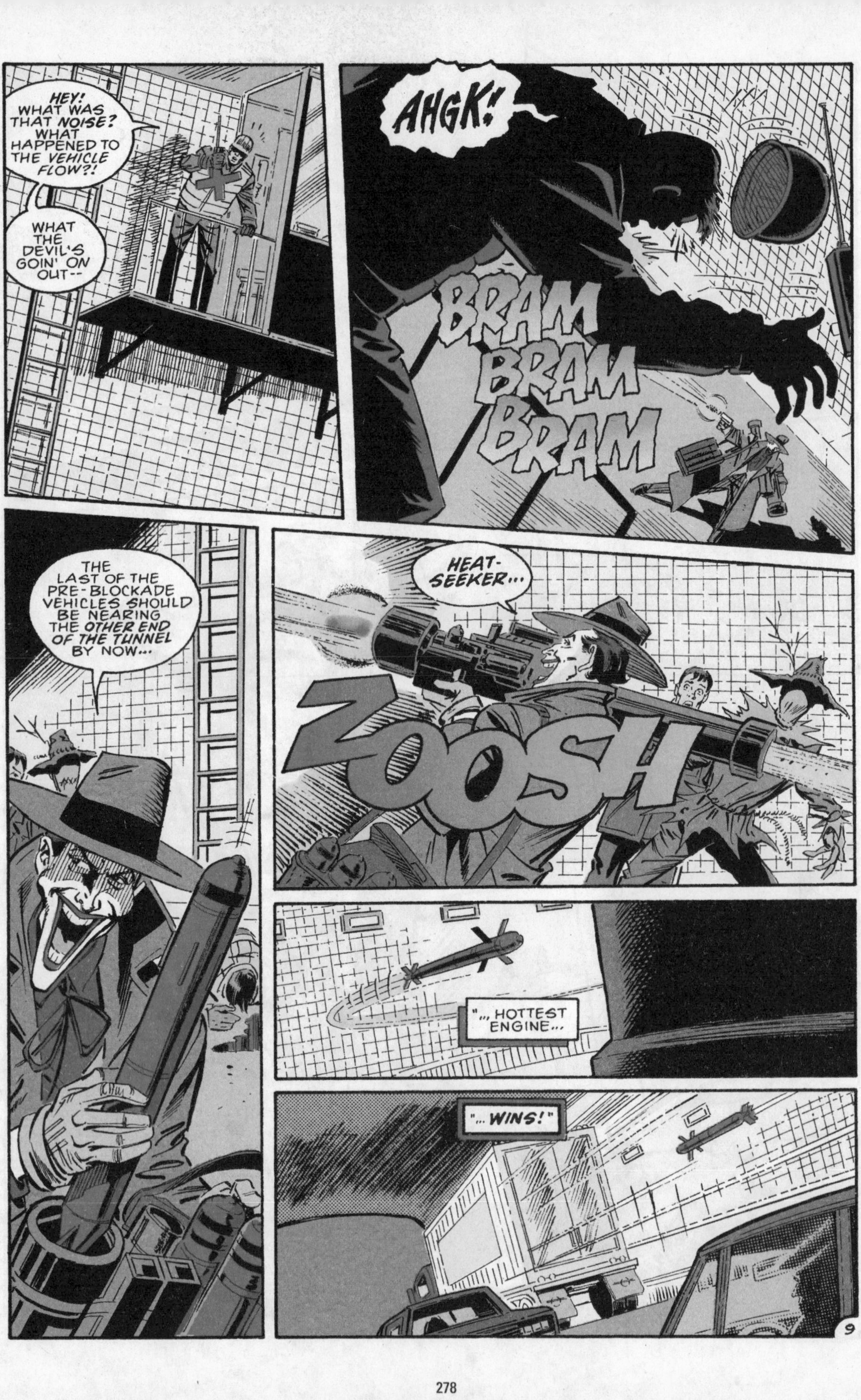
HEY! WHAT WAS THAT NOISE? WHAT HAPPENED TO THE VEHICLE FLOW?!
WHAT THE DEVIL'S GOIN' ON OUT--
AHGK!
BRAM BRAM BRAM
THE LAST OF THE PRE-BLOCKADE VEHICLES SHOULD BE NEARING THE OTHER END OF THE TUNNEL BY NOW...
HEAT-SEEKER...
ZOOSH
"... HOTTEST ENGINE...
"... WINS!"
9

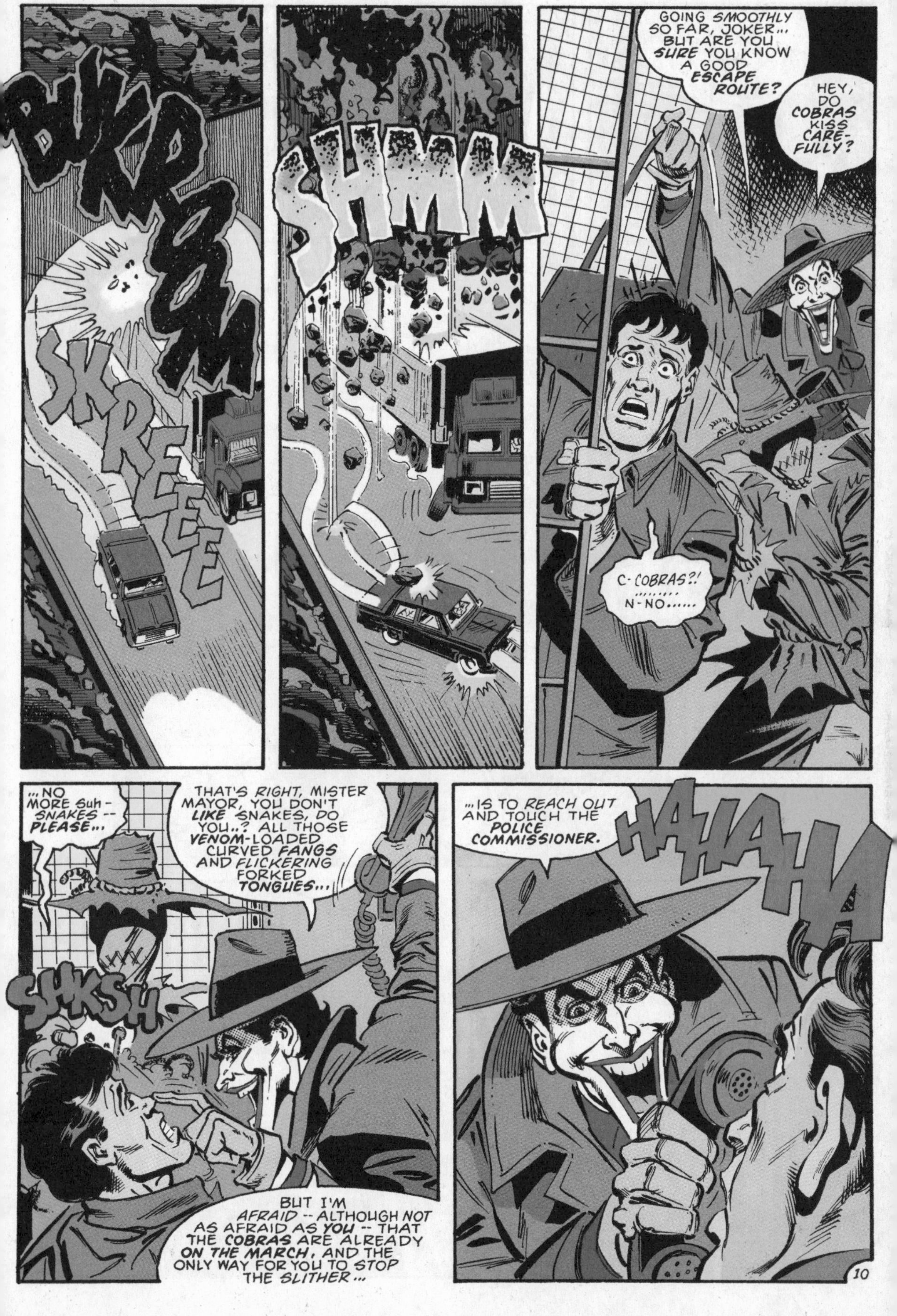
BAROOOM
SKREEEE
SHMMM
GOING SMOOTHLY SO FAR, JOKER... BUT ARE YOU SURE YOU KNOW A GOOD ESCAPE ROUTE?
HEY, DO COBRAS KISS CARE-FULLY?
C-COBRAS?! .... N-NO......
...NO MORE Suh-SNAKES -- PLEASE...
THAT'S RIGHT, MISTER MAYOR, YOU DON'T LIKE SNAKES, DO YOU..? ALL THOSE VENOM-LOADED CURVED FANGS AND FLICKERING FORKED TONGUES...
SHKSH
BUT I'M AFRAID -- ALTHOUGH NOT AS AFRAID AS YOU -- THAT THE COBRAS ARE ALREADY ON THE MARCH, AND THE ONLY WAY FOR YOU TO STOP THE SLITHER...
...IS TO REACH OUT AND TOUCH THE POLICE COMMISSIONER.
HAHAHAHA
10

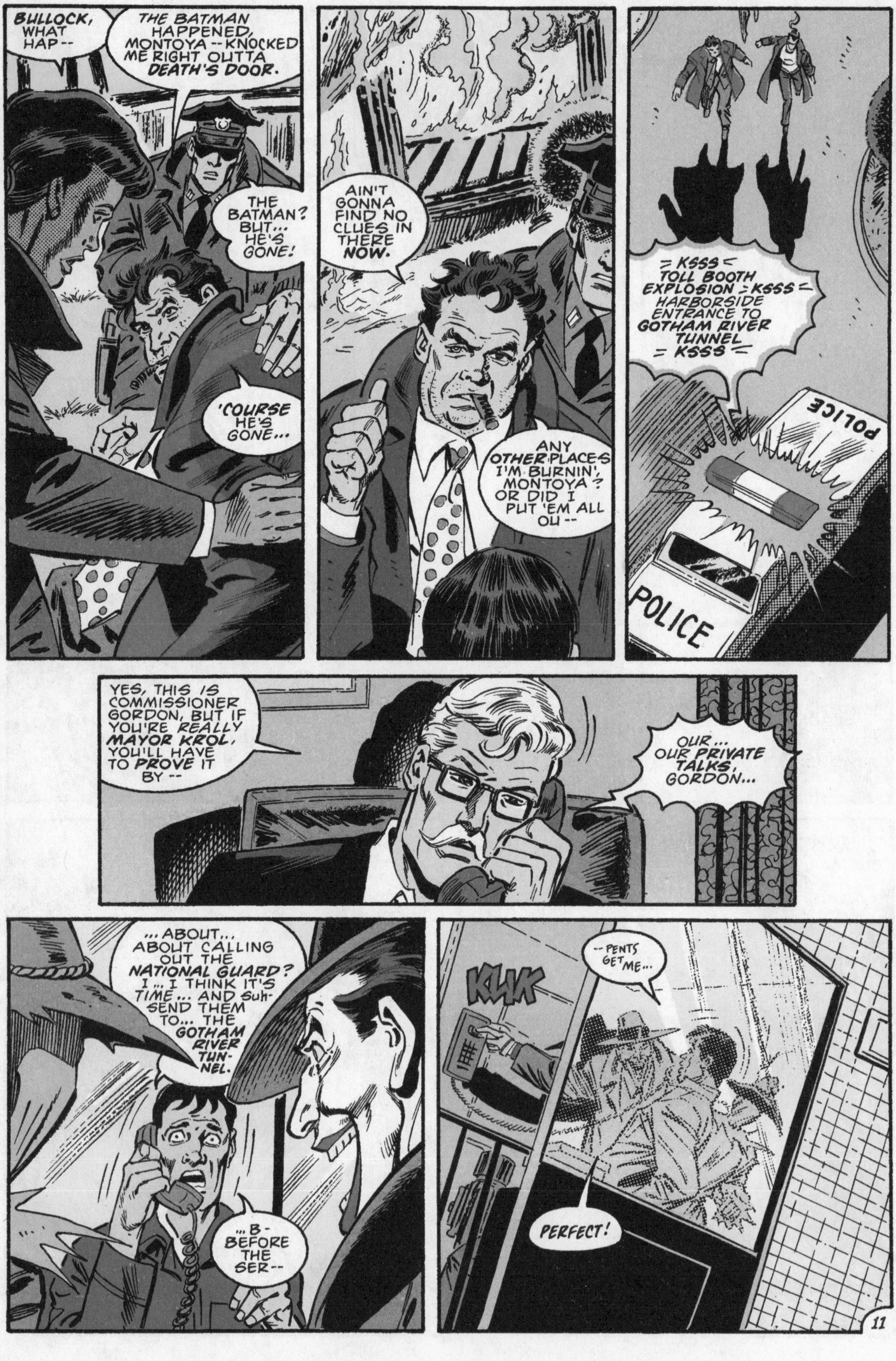
BULLOCK, WHAT HAP--
THE BATMAN HAPPENED, MONTOYA--KNOCKED ME RIGHT OUTTA DEATH'S DOOR.
THE BATMAN? BUT... HE'S GONE!
'COURSE HE'S GONE...
AIN'T GONNA FIND NO CLUES IN THERE NOW.
ANY OTHER PLACES I'M BURNIN', MONTOYA? OR DID I PUT 'EM ALL OU--
=KSSS= TOLL BOOTH EXPLOSION =KSSS= HARBORSIDE ENTRANCE TO GOTHAM RIVER TUNNEL KSSS
POLICE
POLICE
YES, THIS IS COMMISSIONER GORDON, BUT IF YOU'RE REALLY MAYOR KROL, YOU'LL HAVE TO PROVE IT BY--
OUR... OUR PRIVATE TALKS, GORDON...
...ABOUT... ABOUT CALLING OUT THE NATIONAL GUARD? I... I THINK IT'S TIME... AND Suh-SEND THEM TO... THE GOTHAM RIVER TUN-NEL.
...B-BEFORE THE SER--
KLIK
--PENTS GET ME...
PERFECT!
11

DID WE GET THE TRACE?!

CLAK

NO *WAY* THE NATIONAL GUARD -- OR *ANYONE ELSE* -- WILL BEAT *BATS* TO THE SCENE!

HA HA HA HA

SKSH

= SKSS = THIS IS GORDON -- EMERGENCY OVERRIDE = SKSS = WE'VE JUST TRACED A PHONE CALL FROM MAYOR KROL AT A SERVICE BOOTH INSIDE GOTHAM RIVER TUNNEL = SKSS =

ALL UNITS CONVERGE ON THE TUNNEL -- *BOTH* ENDS -- *BAYSIDE* AND *CENTER CITY* = SKSS =

THIS'S *BULLOCK*, COMMISH -- HALF THE UNITS ARE ALREADY ON THEIR WAY -- RESPONDIN' TO THE *EXPLOSIONS*...

= SKSS = WE'LL MEET YA THERE... = SKSS =

BANE -- IT'S BEEN *BANE* FROM THE *BEGINNING* -- BUT HE'S USING THE *JOKER* AGAIN...

SKREEEOW

12

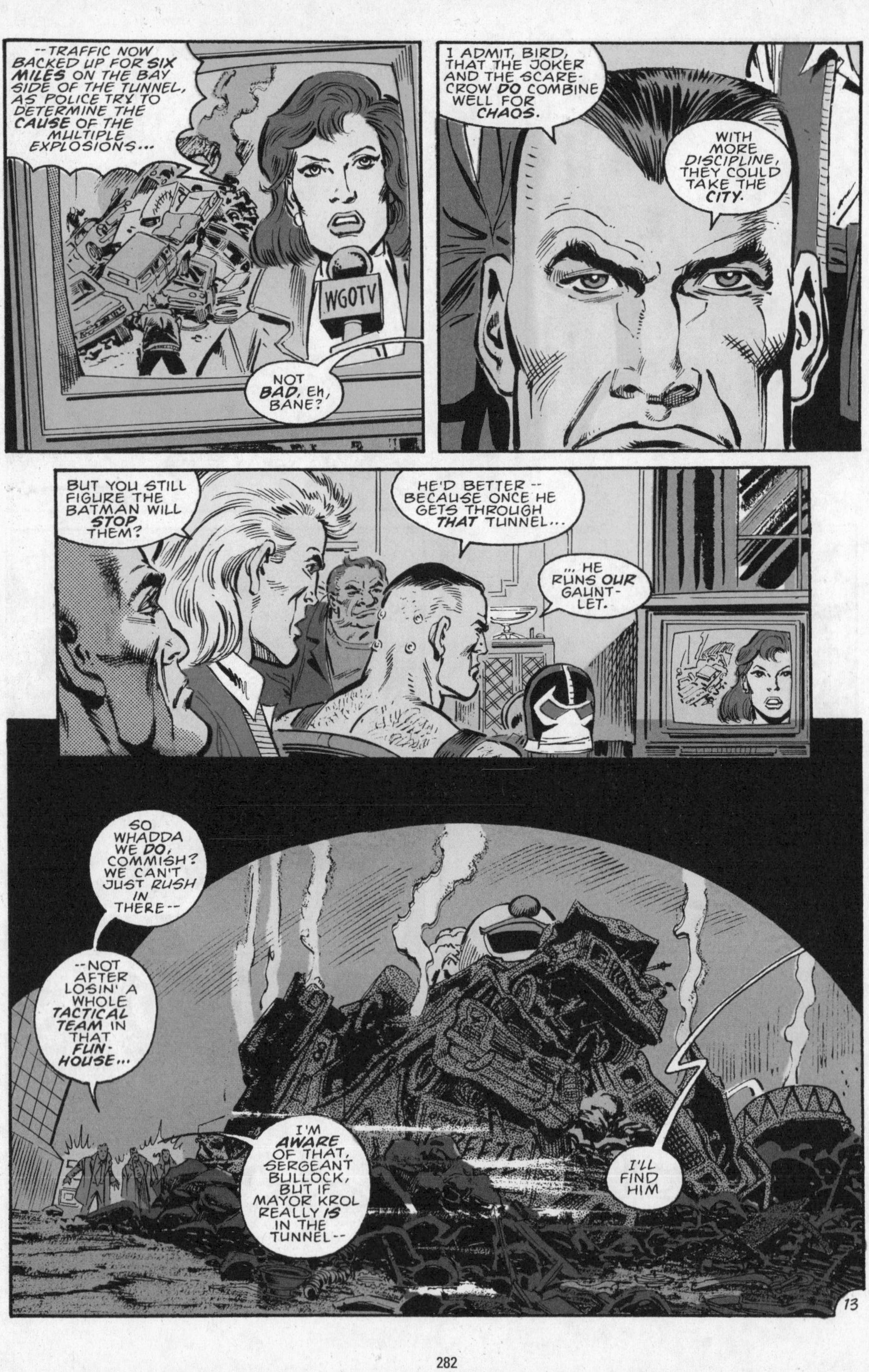
--TRAFFIC NOW BACKED UP FOR SIX MILES ON THE BAY SIDE OF THE TUNNEL, AS POLICE TRY TO DETERMINE THE CAUSE OF THE MULTIPLE EXPLOSIONS...
WGOTV
NOT BAD, Eh, BANE?
I ADMIT, BIRD, THAT THE JOKER AND THE SCARE-CROW DO COMBINE WELL FOR CHAOS.
WITH MORE DISCIPLINE, THEY COULD TAKE THE CITY.
BUT YOU STILL FIGURE THE BATMAN WILL STOP THEM?
HE'D BETTER -- BECAUSE ONCE HE GETS THROUGH THAT TUNNEL...
... HE RUNS OUR GAUNT-LET.
SO WHADDA WE DO, COMMISH? WE CAN'T JUST RUSH IN THERE--
--NOT AFTER LOSIN' A WHOLE TACTICAL TEAM IN THAT FUN-HOUSE...
I'M AWARE OF THAT, SERGEANT BULLOCK, BUT IF MAYOR KROL REALLY IS IN THE TUNNEL--
I'LL FIND HIM
13

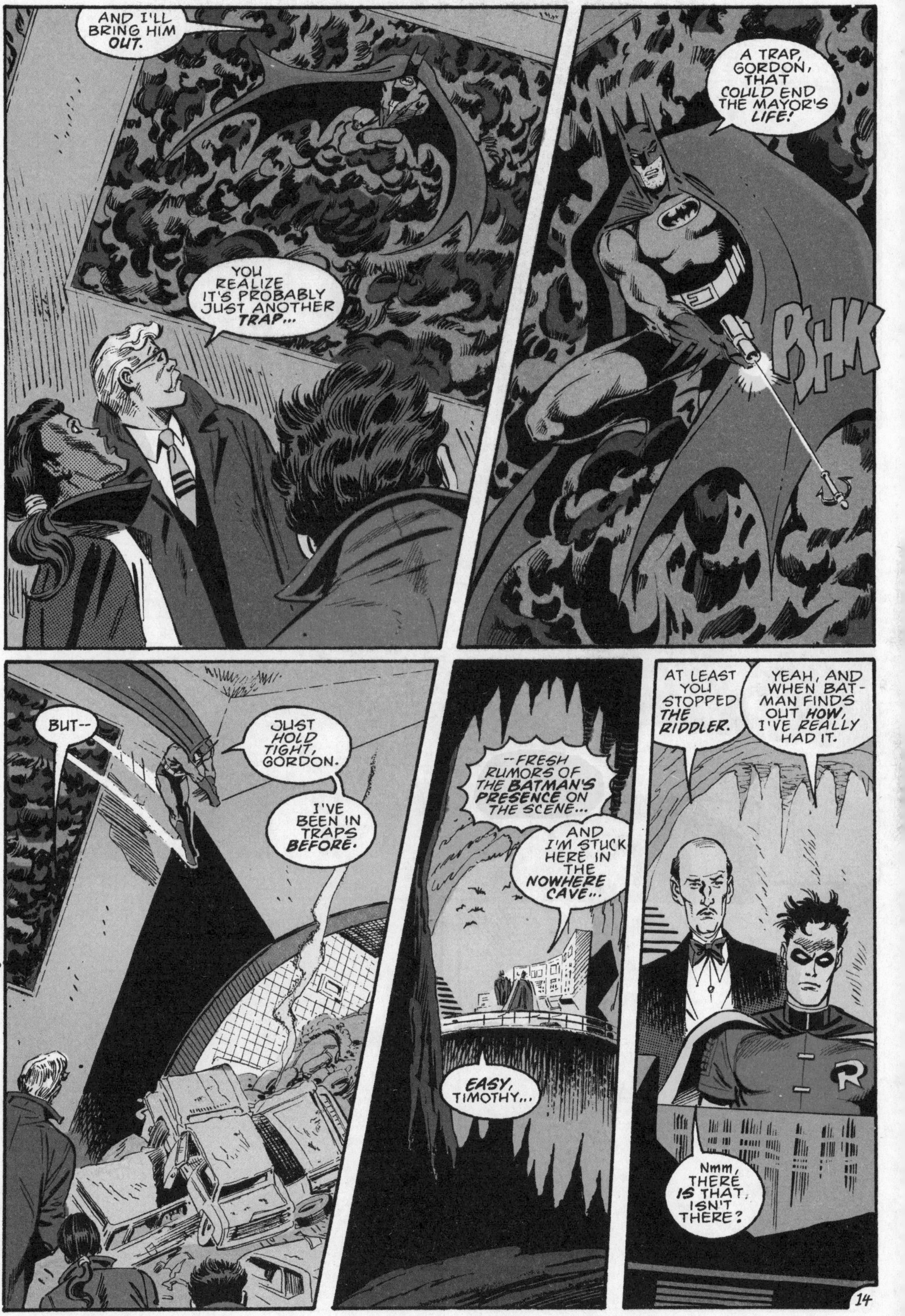
AND I'LL BRING HIM OUT.
YOU REALIZE IT'S PROBABLY JUST ANOTHER TRAP...
A TRAP, GORDON, THAT COULD END THE MAYOR'S LIFE!
PSHK
BUT--
JUST HOLD TIGHT, GORDON.
I'VE BEEN IN TRAPS BEFORE.
--FRESH RUMORS OF THE BATMAN'S PRESENCE ON THE SCENE...
AND I'M STUCK HERE IN THE NOWHERE CAVE...
EASY, TIMOTHY...
AT LEAST YOU STOPPED THE RIDDLER.
YEAH, AND WHEN BATMAN FINDS OUT HOW, I'VE REALLY HAD IT.
Nmm, THERE IS THAT, ISN'T THERE?
14

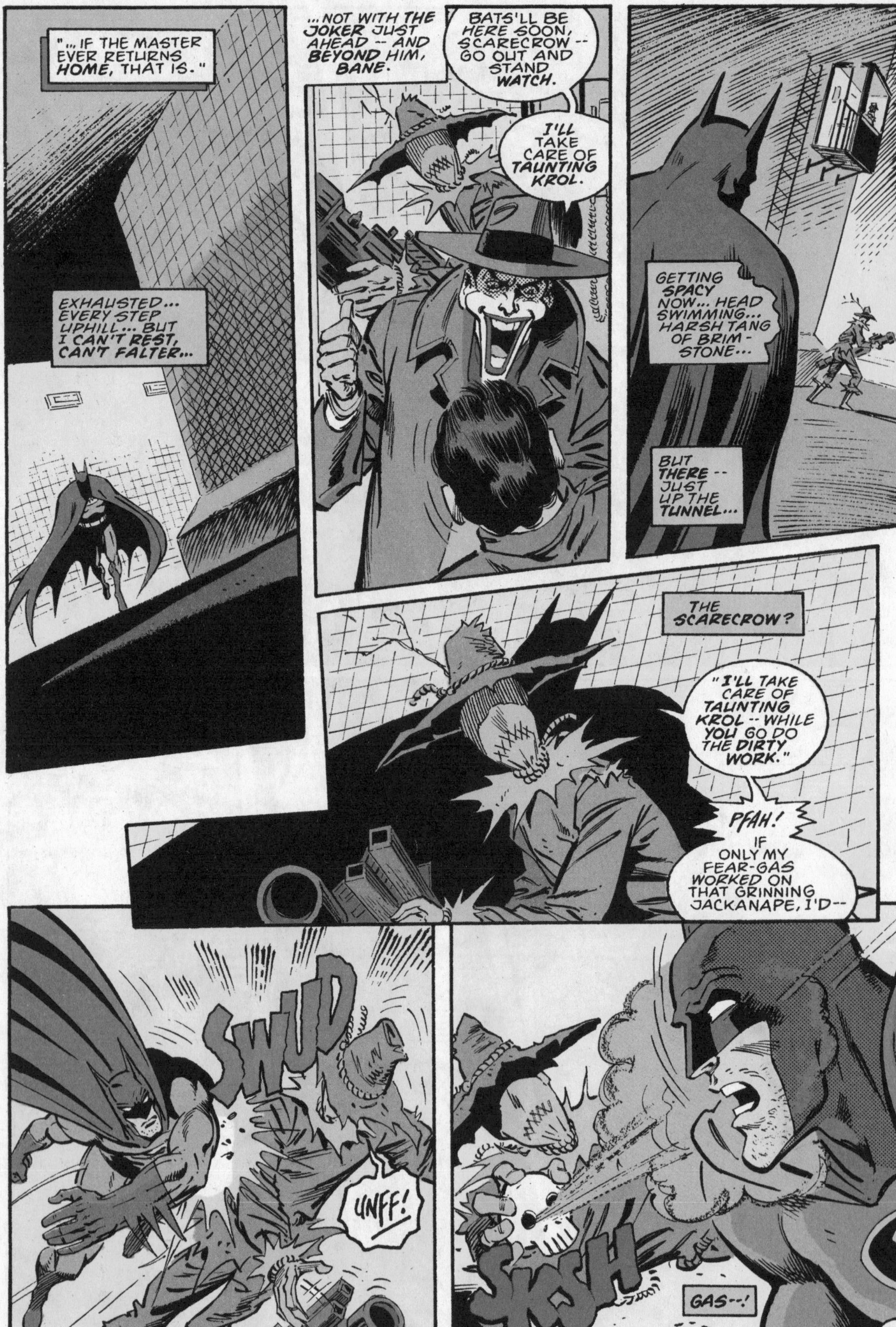
"... IF THE MASTER EVER RETURNS HOME, THAT IS."
EXHAUSTED... EVERY STEP UPHILL... BUT I CAN'T REST, CAN'T FALTER...
... NOT WITH THE JOKER JUST AHEAD -- AND BEYOND HIM, BANE.
BATS'LL BE HERE SOON, SCARECROW -- GO OUT AND STAND WATCH.
I'LL TAKE CARE OF TAUNTING KROL.
GETTING SPACY NOW... HEAD SWIMMING... HARSH TANG OF BRIM-STONE...
BUT THERE -- JUST UP THE TUNNEL...
THE SCARECROW?
"I'LL TAKE CARE OF TAUNTING KROL -- WHILE YOU GO DO THE DIRTY WORK."
PFAH!
IF ONLY MY FEAR-GAS WORKED ON THAT GRINNING JACKANAPE, I'D--
SWUD
UNFF!
SKSH
GAS--!
15

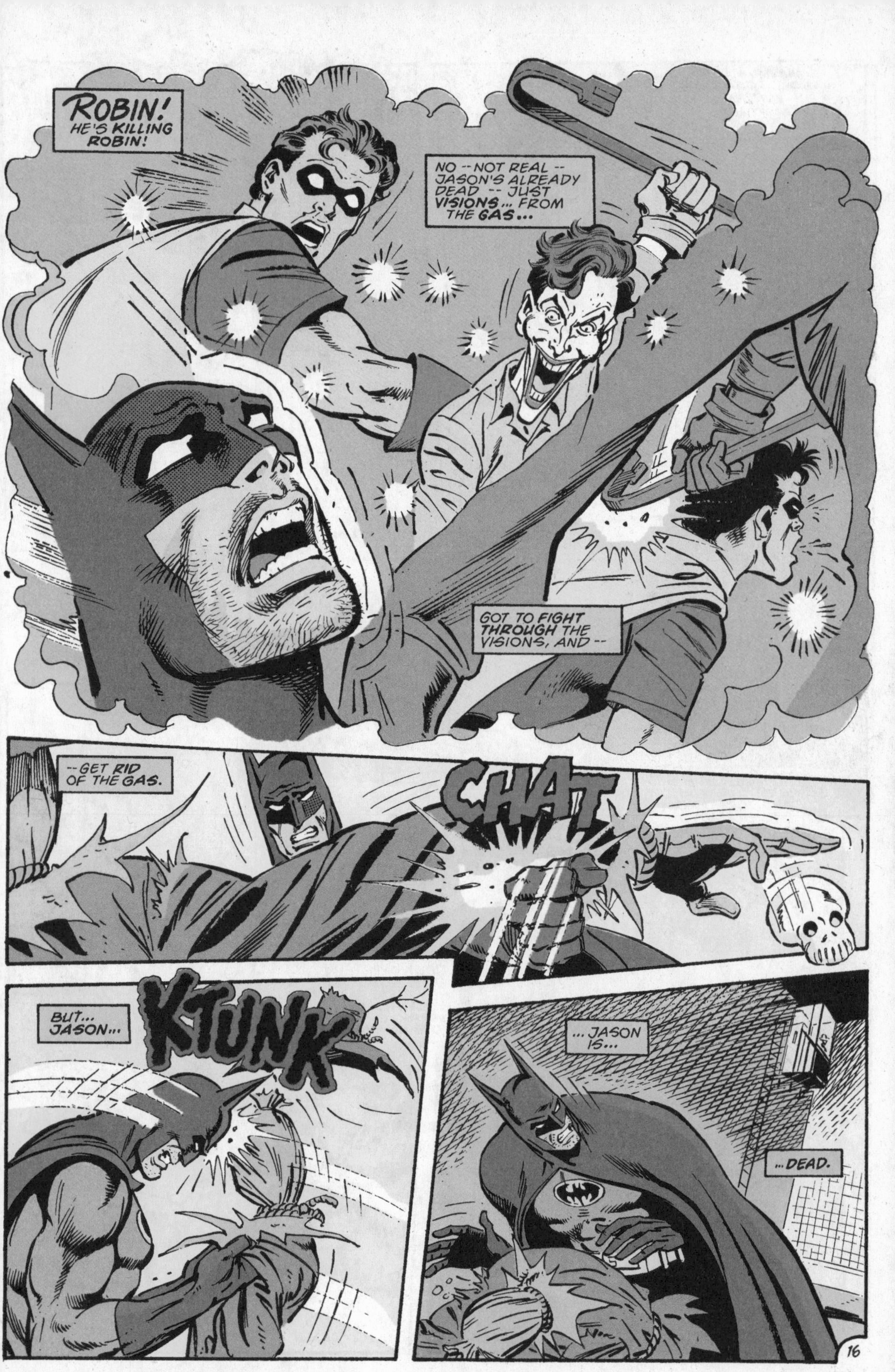
ROBIN! HE'S KILLING ROBIN!
NO -- NOT REAL -- JASON'S ALREADY DEAD -- JUST VISIONS... FROM THE GAS...
GOT TO FIGHT THROUGH THE VISIONS, AND --
-- GET RID OF THE GAS.
CHAT
BUT... JASON...
KTUNK
... JASON IS...
...DEAD.
16

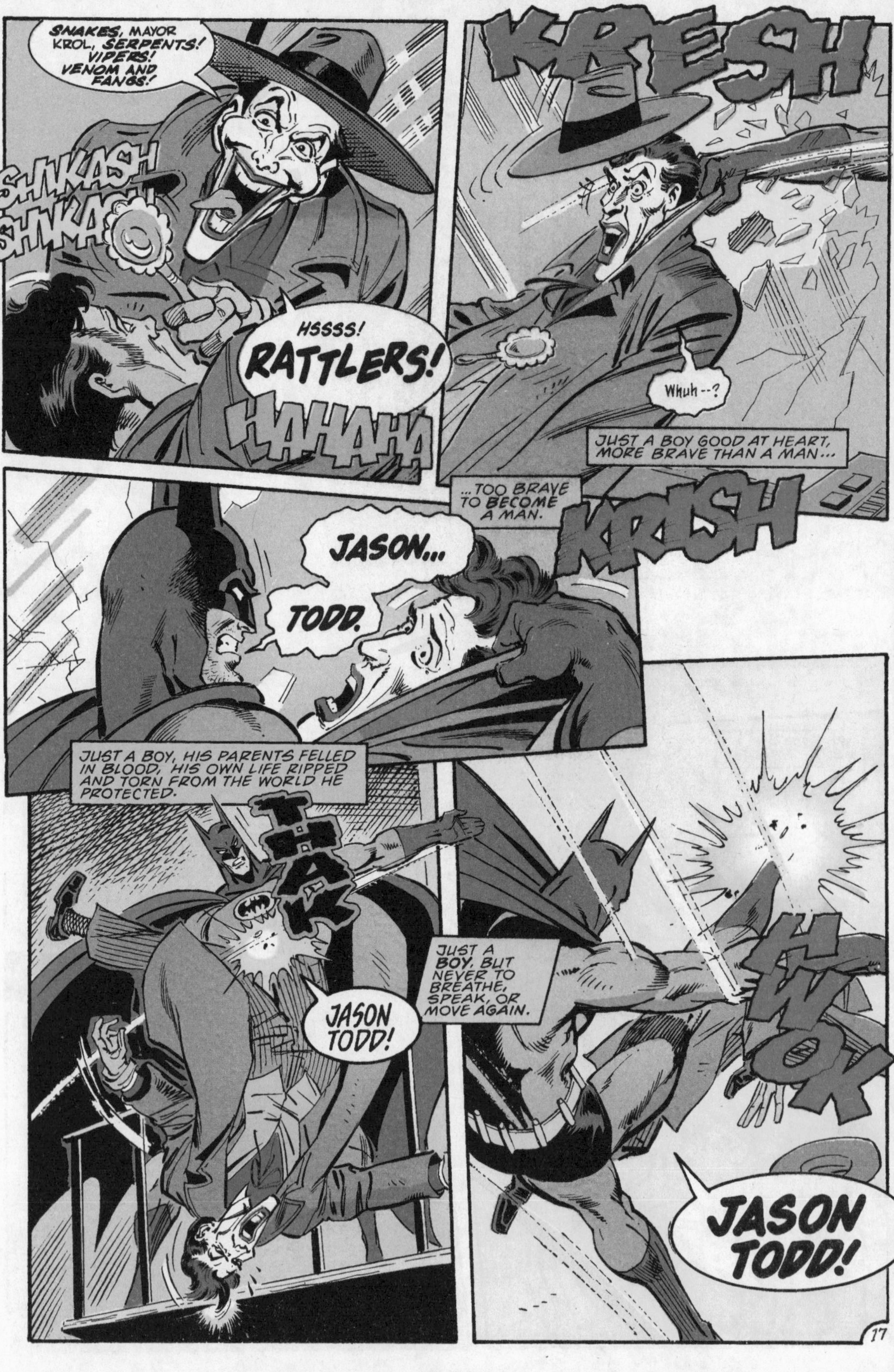
SNAKES, MAYOR KROL, SERPENTS! VIPERS! VENOM AND FANGS!
SHHKASH SHHKASH
HSSSS! RATTLERS!
HAHAHA
KRESH
Whuh --?
JUST A BOY GOOD AT HEART, MORE BRAVE THAN A MAN...
...TOO BRAVE TO BECOME A MAN.
KRASH
JASON...
TODD.
JUST A BOY, HIS PARENTS FELLED IN BLOOD, HIS OWN LIFE RIPPED AND TORN FROM THE WORLD HE PROTECTED.
THAK
JASON TODD!
JUST A BOY, BUT NEVER TO BREATHE, SPEAK, OR MOVE AGAIN.
WOK
JASON TODD!
17

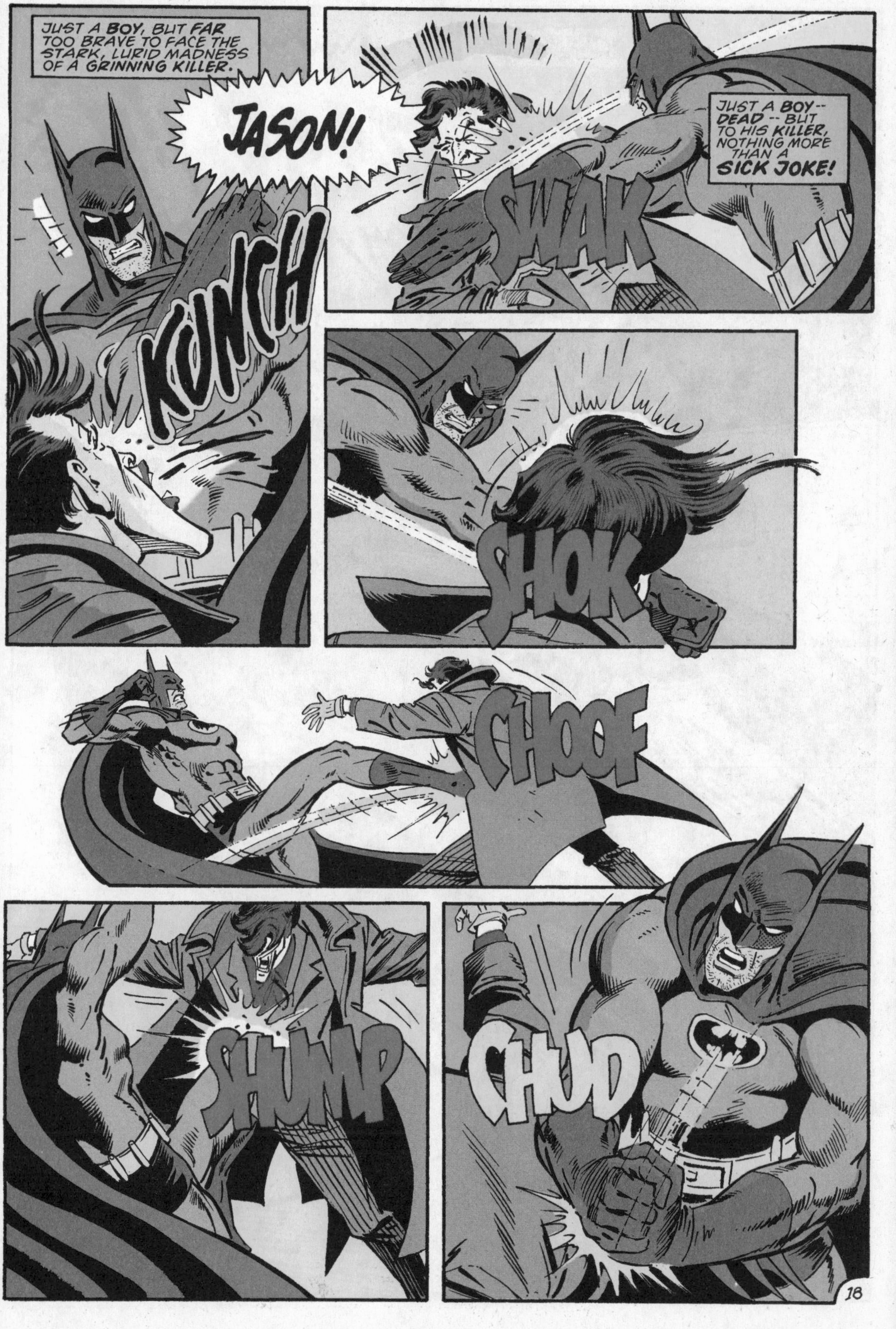
JUST A BOY, BUT FAR TOO BRAVE TO FACE THE STARK, LURID MADNESS OF A GRINNING KILLER.
JASON!
KUNCH
JUST A BOY-- DEAD -- BUT TO HIS KILLER, NOTHING MORE THAN A SICK JOKE!
SWAK
SHOK
CHOOF
SHUMP
CHUD
18

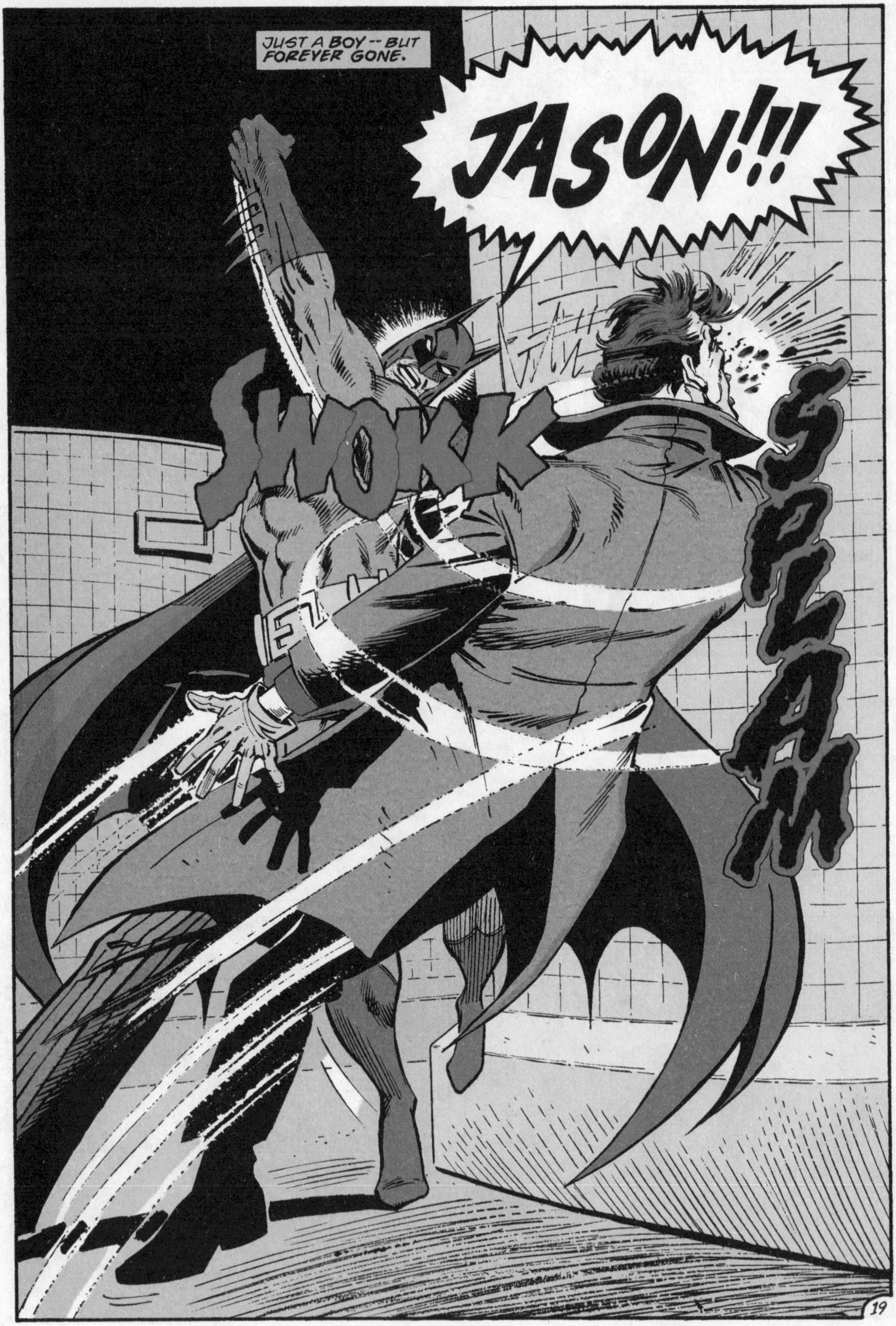
JUST A BOY -- BUT FOREVER GONE.
JASON!!!
SWOKK
SPLAM
19

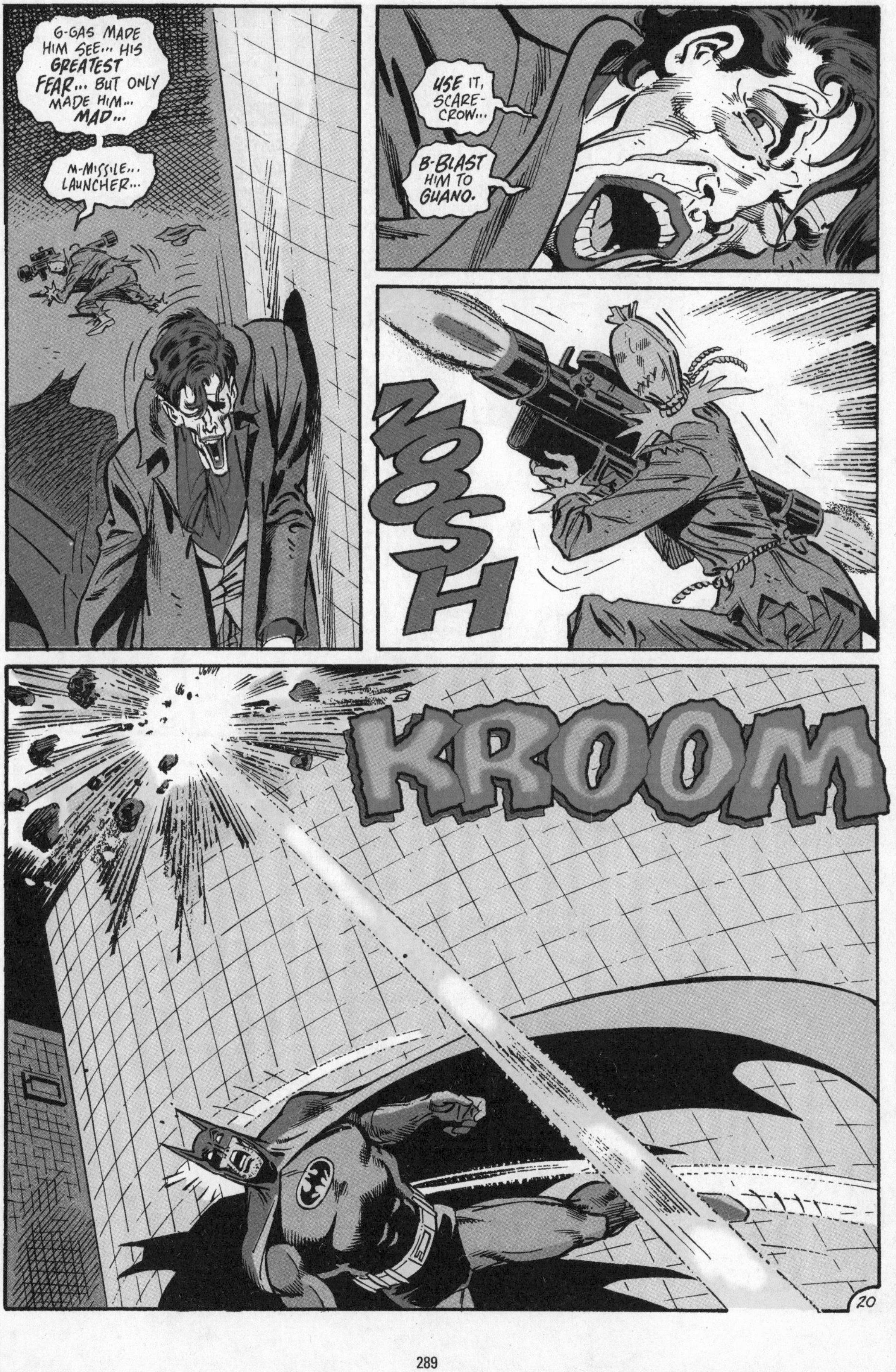
G-GAS MADE HIM SEE... HIS GREATEST FEAR... BUT ONLY MADE HIM... MAD...
M-MISSILE... LAUNCHER...
USE IT, SCARE-CROW...
B-BLAST HIM TO GUANO.
WOOSH
KROOM
20

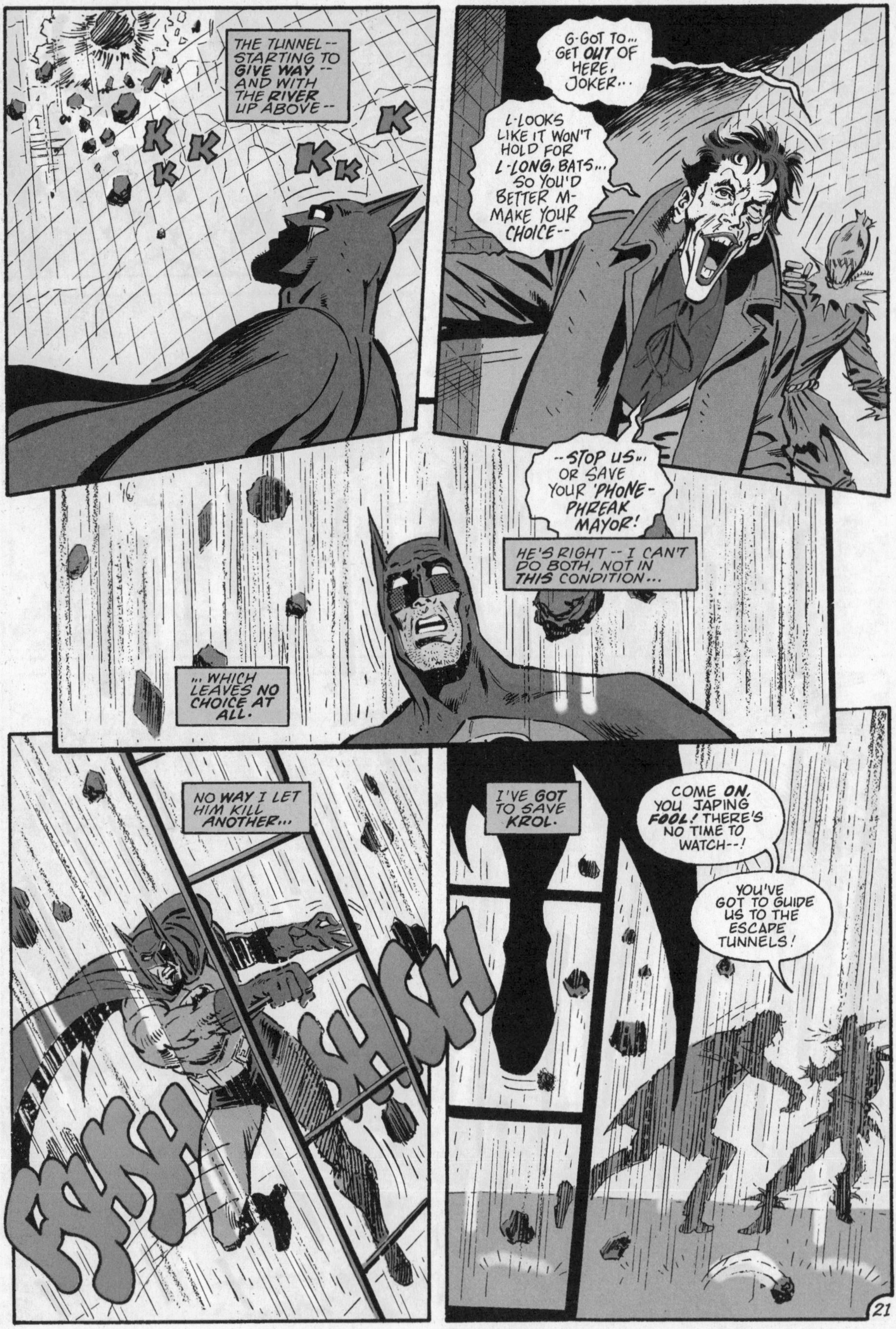
THE TUNNEL -- STARTING TO GIVE WAY -- AND WITH THE RIVER UP ABOVE --
KKKKKKK
G-GOT TO... GET OUT OF HERE, JOKER...
L-LOOKS LIKE IT WON'T HOLD FOR L-LONG, BATS... SO YOU'D BETTER M-MAKE YOUR CHOICE--
--STOP US... OR SAVE YOUR 'PHONE-PHREAK MAYOR!
HE'S RIGHT -- I CAN'T DO BOTH, NOT IN THIS CONDITION...
...WHICH LEAVES NO CHOICE AT ALL.
NO WAY I LET HIM KILL ANOTHER...
I'VE GOT TO SAVE KROL.
COME ON, YOU JAPING FOOL! THERE'S NO TIME TO WATCH--!
YOU'VE GOT TO GUIDE US TO THE ESCAPE TUNNELS!
SHSH
FSSH
21

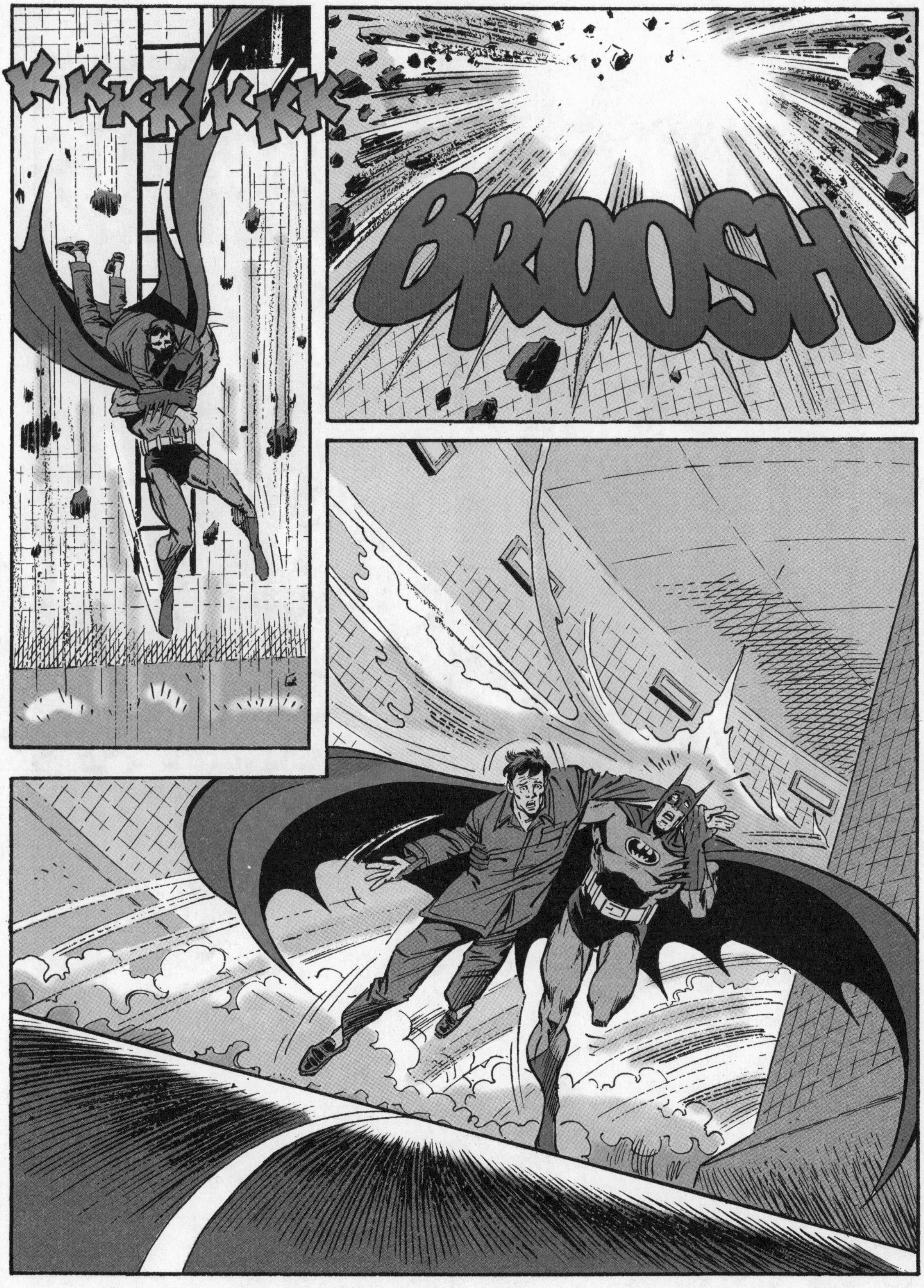
K KKK KKK
BROOSH

Cover art by KELLEY JONES

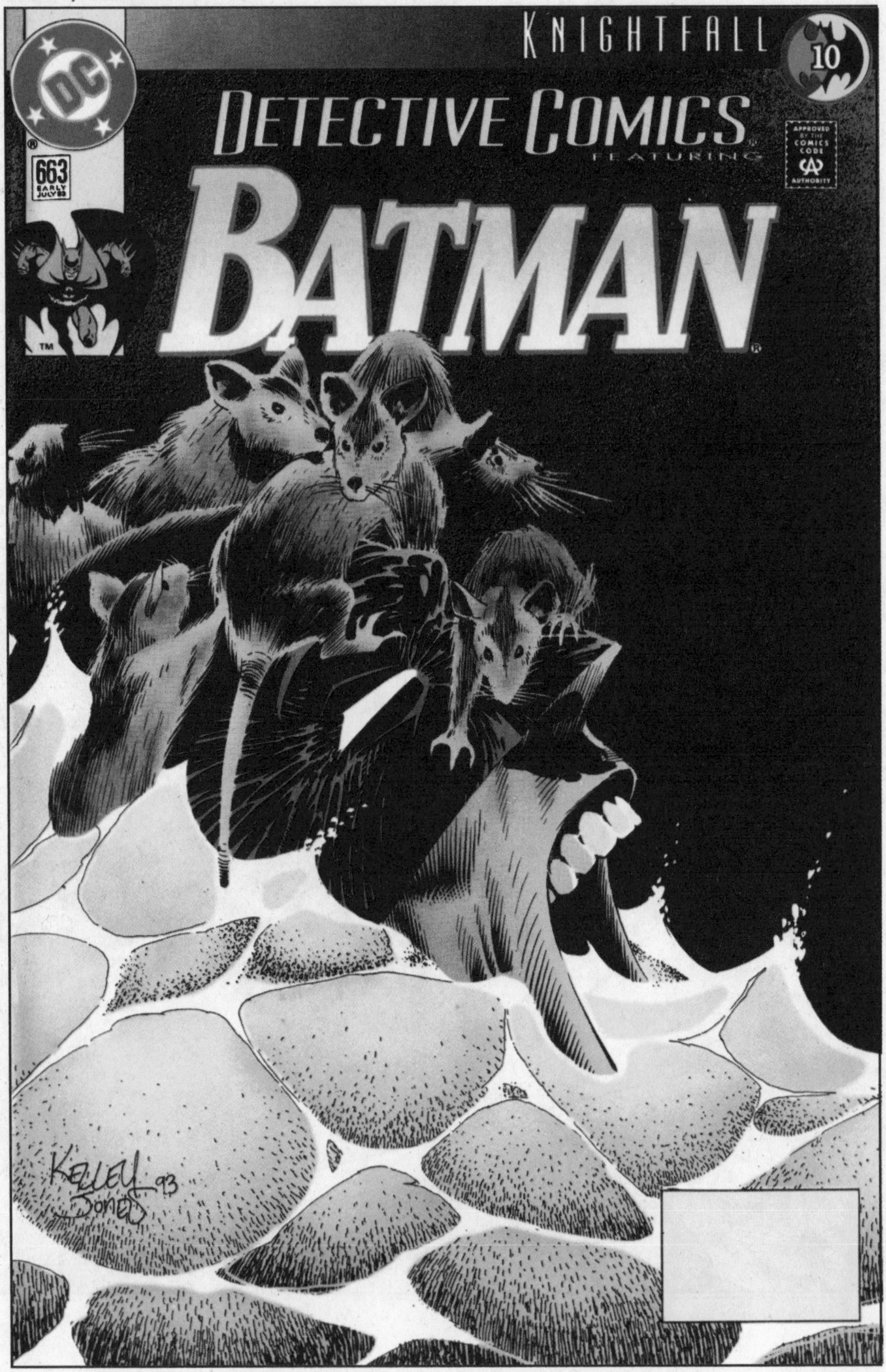
KNIGHTFALL
10
DC
DETECTIVE COMICS
FEATURING
BATMAN
663
EARLY JULY 93
APPROVED BY THE COMICS CODE AUTHORITY
KELLEY JONES '93

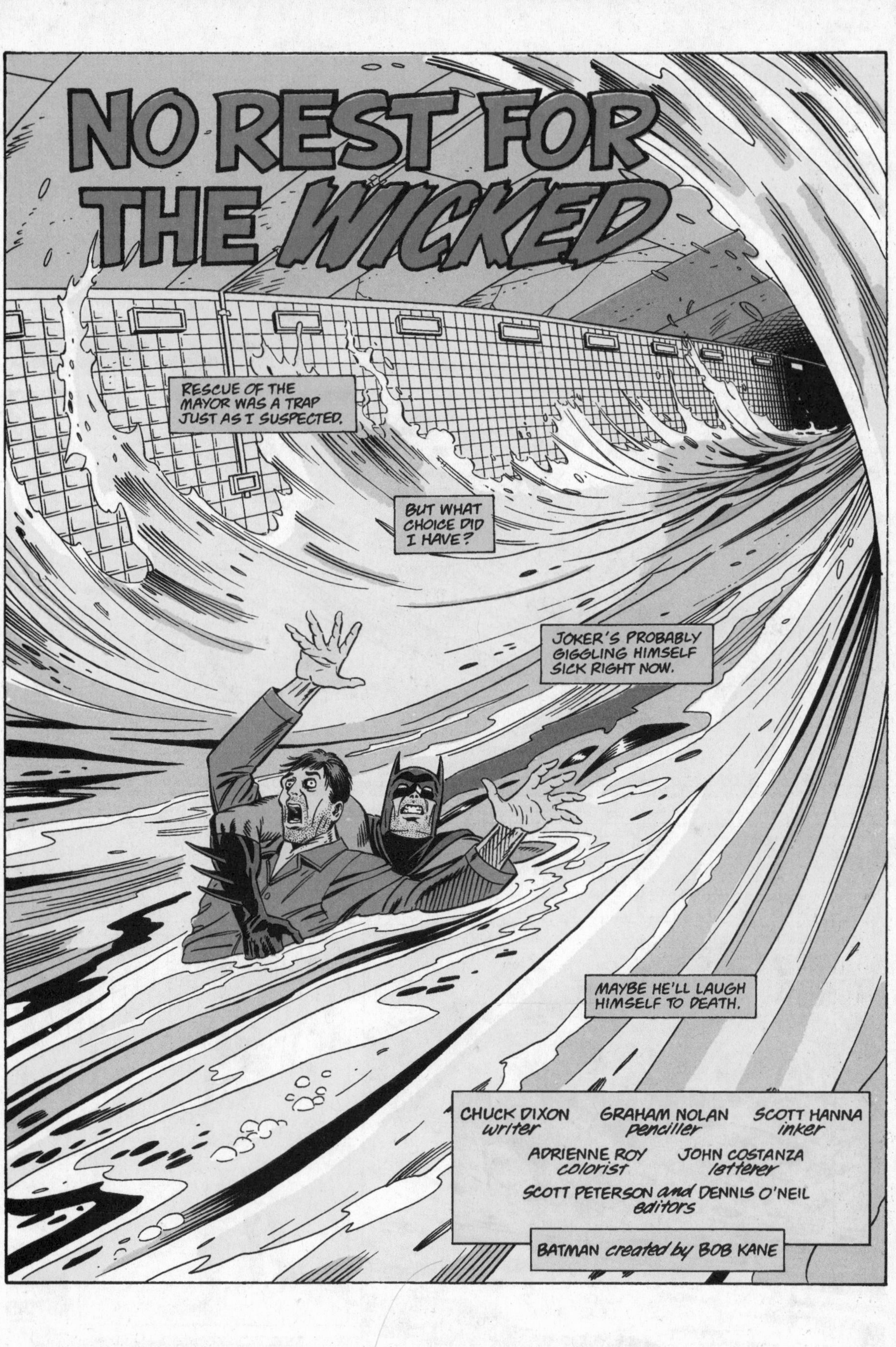
NO REST FOR THE WICKED
RESCUE OF THE MAYOR WAS A TRAP JUST AS I SUSPECTED.
BUT WHAT CHOICE DID I HAVE?
JOKER'S PROBABLY GIGGLING HIMSELF SICK RIGHT NOW.
MAYBE HE'LL LAUGH HIMSELF TO DEATH.
CHUCK DIXON writer
GRAHAM NOLAN penciller
SCOTT HANNA inker
ADRIENNE ROY colorist
JOHN COSTANZA letterer
SCOTT PETERSON and DENNIS O'NEIL editors
BATMAN created by BOB KANE

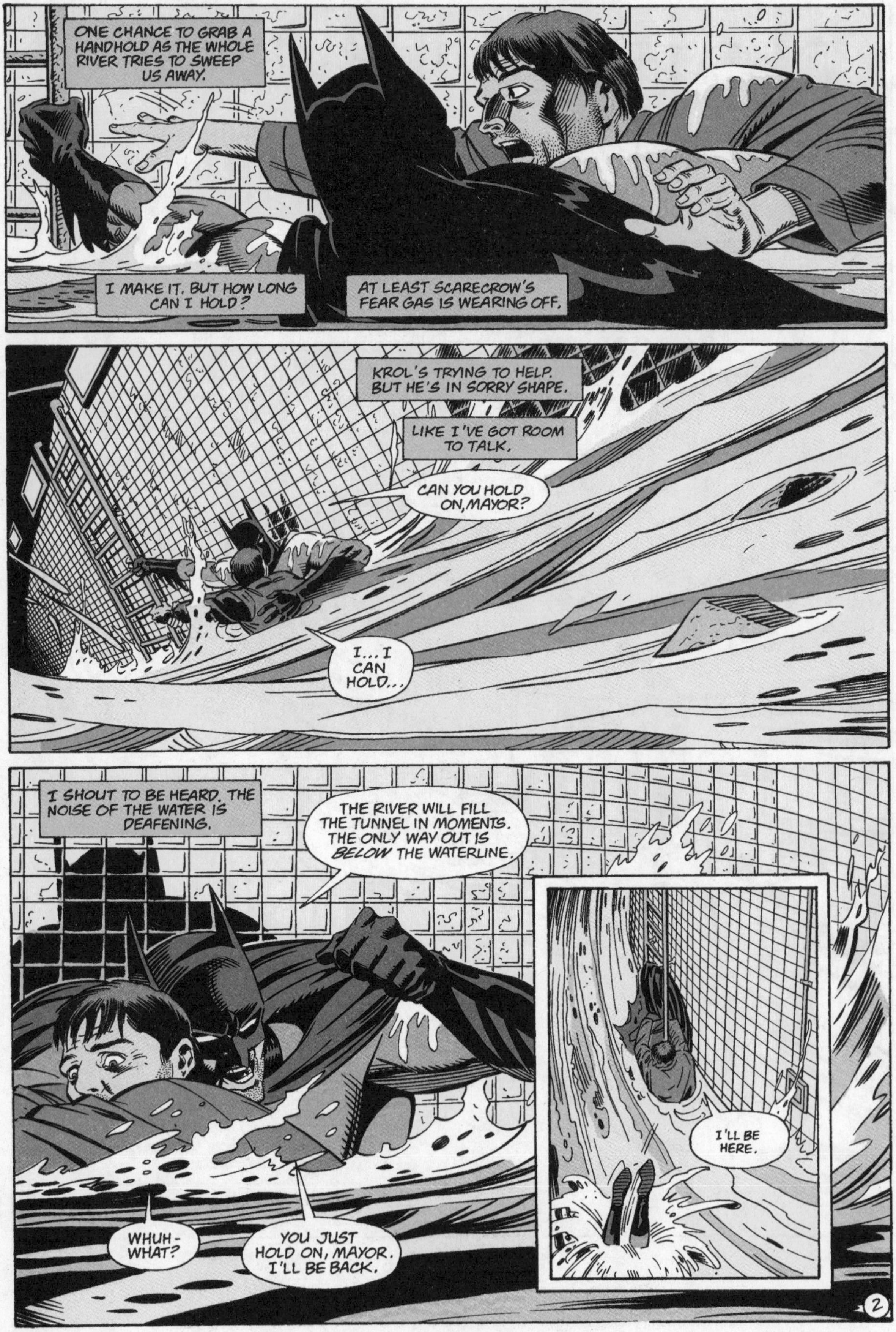

ONE CHANCE TO GRAB A HANDHOLD AS THE WHOLE RIVER TRIES TO SWEEP US AWAY.
I MAKE IT. BUT HOW LONG CAN I HOLD?
AT LEAST SCARECROW'S FEAR GAS IS WEARING OFF.
KROL'S TRYING TO HELP. BUT HE'S IN SORRY SHAPE.
LIKE I'VE GOT ROOM TO TALK.
CAN YOU HOLD ON, MAYOR?
I... I CAN HOLD...
I SHOUT TO BE HEARD. THE NOISE OF THE WATER IS DEAFENING.
THE RIVER WILL FILL THE TUNNEL IN MOMENTS. THE ONLY WAY OUT IS BELOW THE WATERLINE.
WHUH-WHAT?
YOU JUST HOLD ON, MAYOR. I'LL BE BACK.
I'LL BE HERE.
2

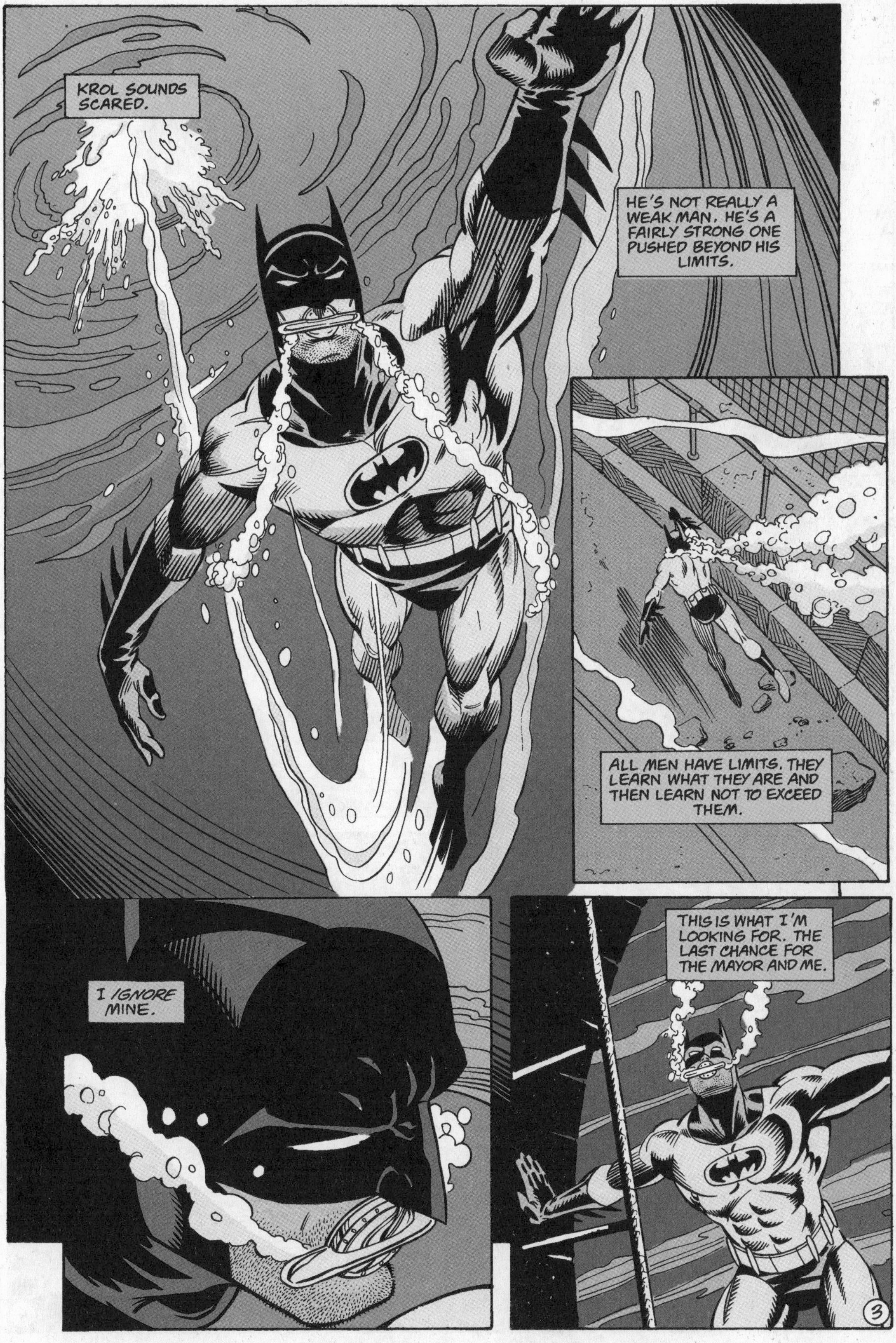
KROL SOUNDS SCARED.
HE'S NOT REALLY A WEAK MAN. HE'S A FAIRLY STRONG ONE PUSHED BEYOND HIS LIMITS.
ALL MEN HAVE LIMITS. THEY LEARN WHAT THEY ARE AND THEN LEARN NOT TO EXCEED THEM.
I IGNORE MINE.
THIS IS WHAT I'M LOOKING FOR. THE LAST CHANCE FOR THE MAYOR AND ME.
3

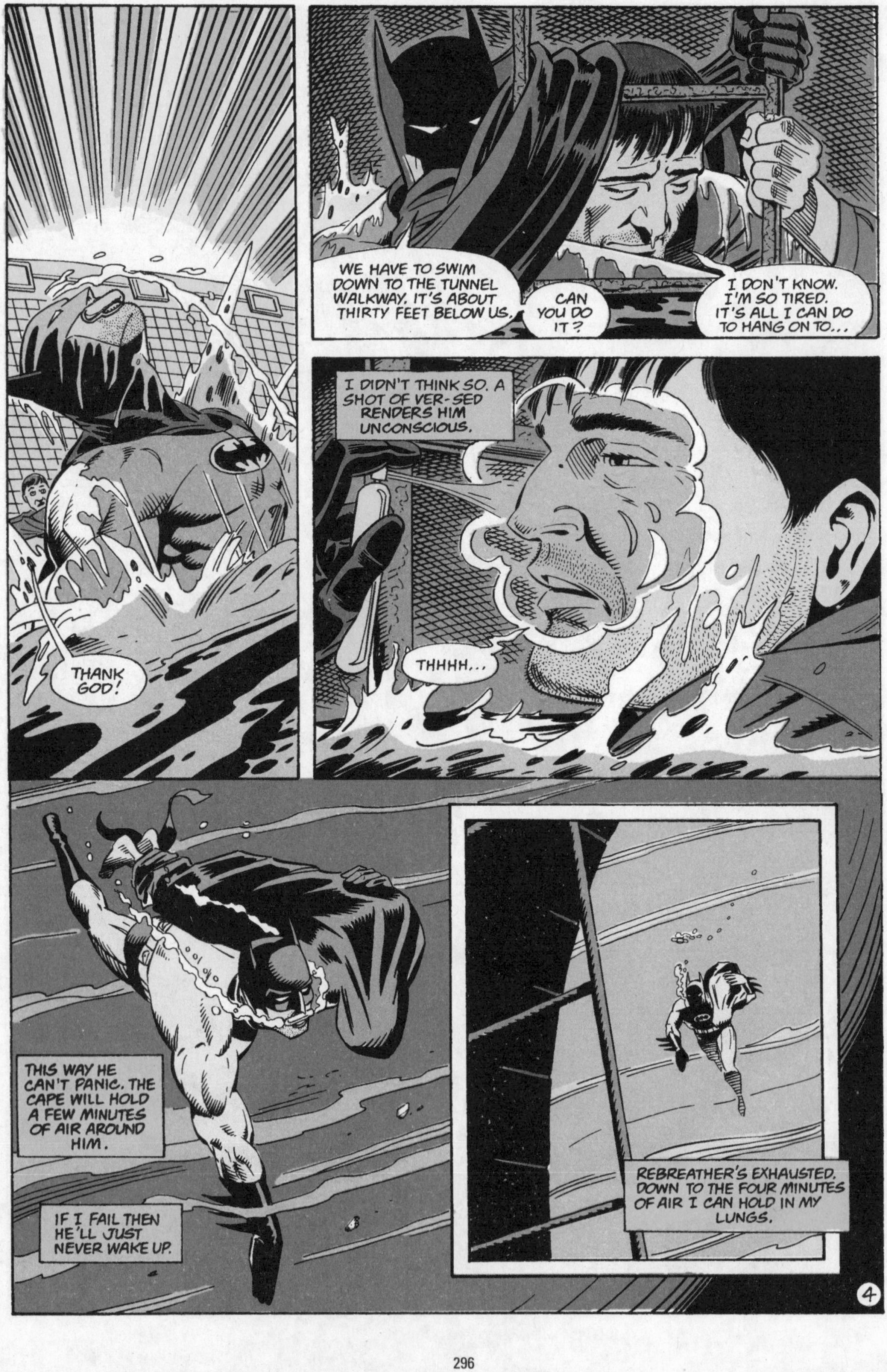
WE HAVE TO SWIM DOWN TO THE TUNNEL WALKWAY. IT'S ABOUT THIRTY FEET BELOW US.
CAN YOU DO IT?
I DON'T KNOW. I'M SO TIRED. IT'S ALL I CAN DO TO HANG ON TO...
THANK GOD!
I DIDN'T THINK SO. A SHOT OF VER-SED RENDERS HIM UNCONSCIOUS.
THHHH...
THIS WAY HE CAN'T PANIC. THE CAPE WILL HOLD A FEW MINUTES OF AIR AROUND HIM.
IF I FAIL THEN HE'LL JUST NEVER WAKE UP.
REBREATHER'S EXHAUSTED. DOWN TO THE FOUR MINUTES OF AIR I CAN HOLD IN MY LUNGS.
4

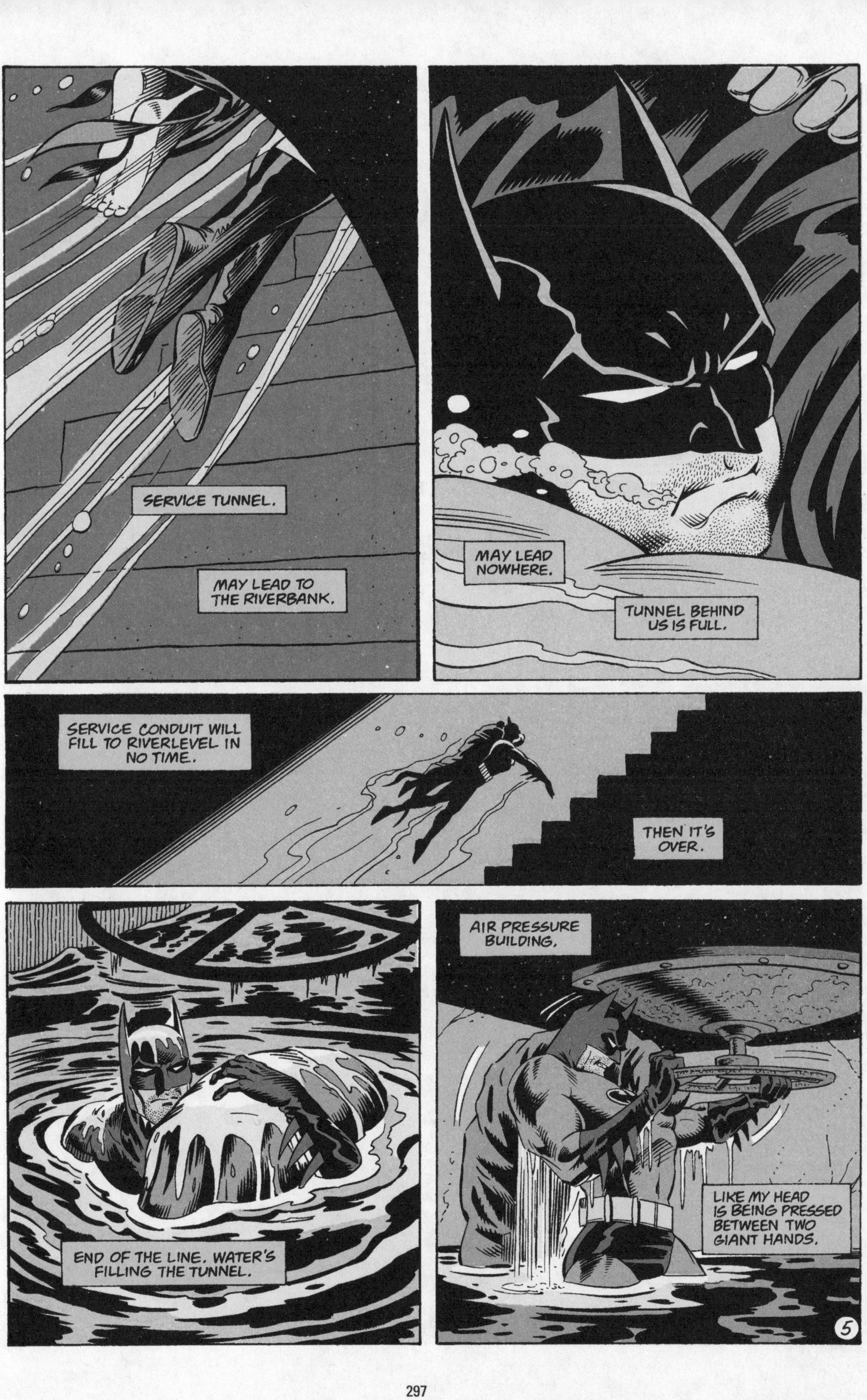
SERVICE TUNNEL.
MAY LEAD TO THE RIVERBANK.
MAY LEAD NOWHERE.
TUNNEL BEHIND US IS FULL.
SERVICE CONDUIT WILL FILL TO RIVERLEVEL IN NO TIME.
THEN IT'S OVER.
END OF THE LINE. WATER'S FILLING THE TUNNEL.
AIR PRESSURE BUILDING.
LIKE MY HEAD IS BEING PRESSED BETWEEN TWO GIANT HANDS.
5

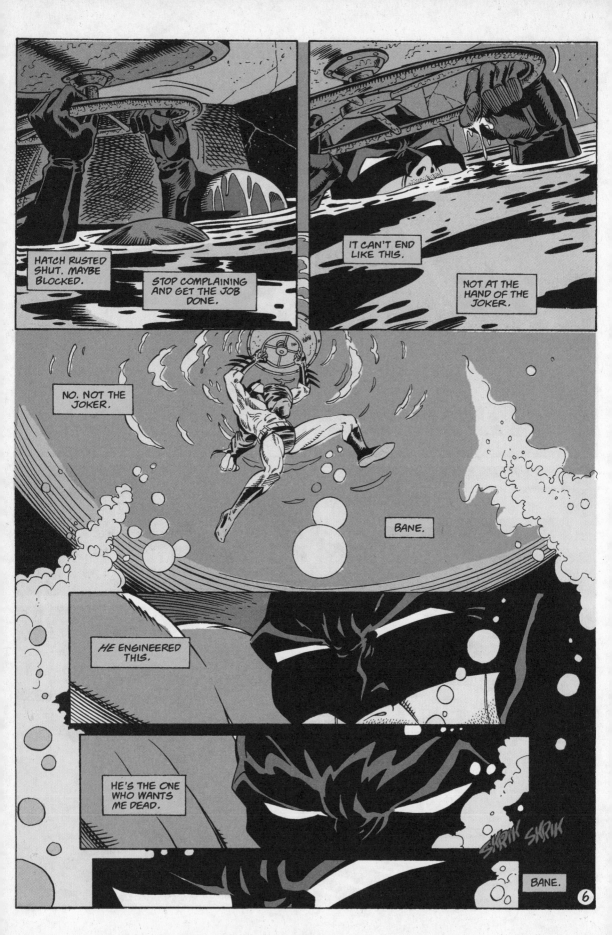

HATCH RUSTED SHUT. MAYBE BLOCKED.

STOP COMPLAINING AND GET THE JOB DONE.

IT CAN'T END LIKE THIS.

NOT AT THE HAND OF THE JOKER.

NO. NOT THE JOKER.

BANE.

HE ENGINEERED THIS.

HE'S THE ONE WHO WANTS ME DEAD.

SKRIK SKRIK

BANE.

6

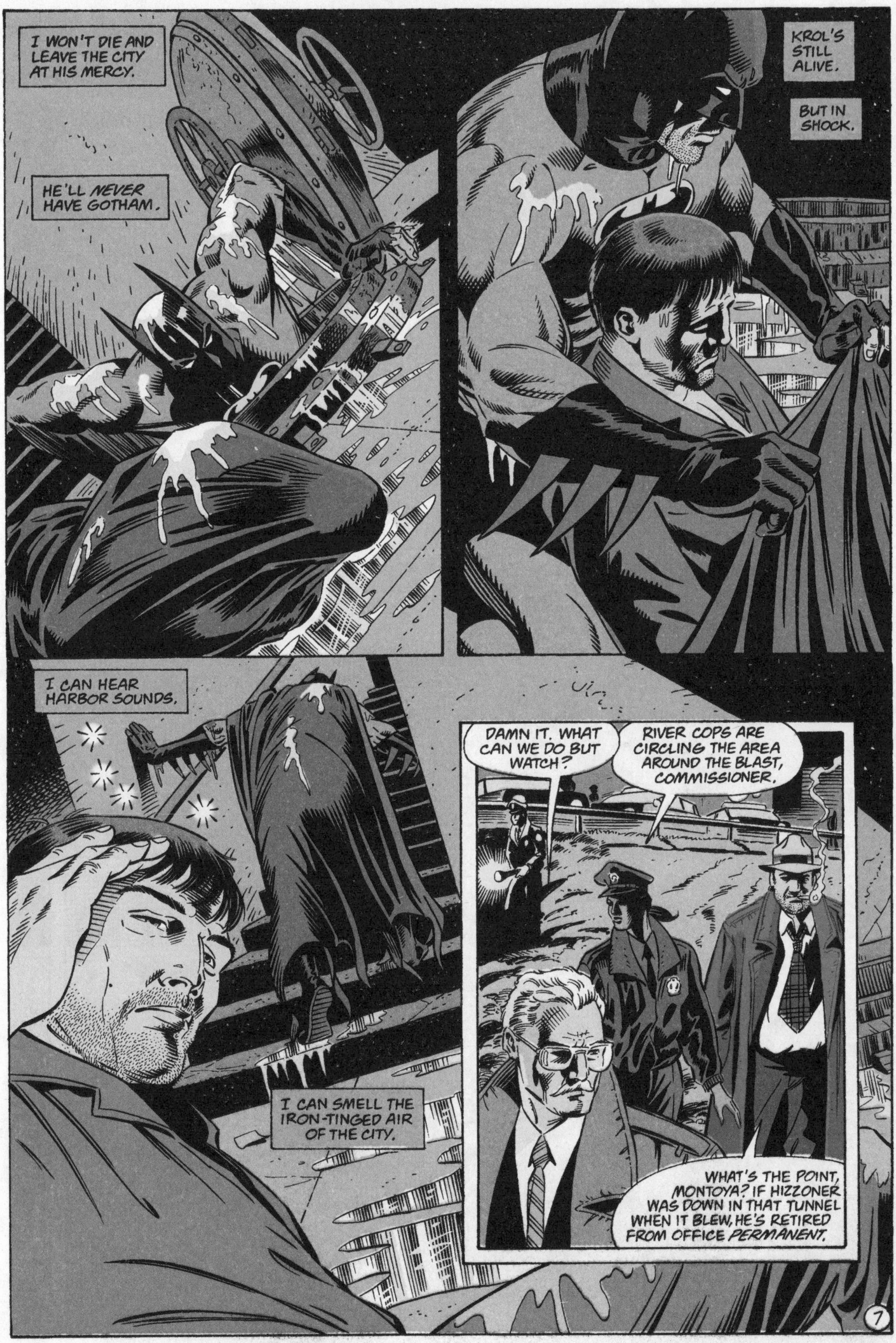
I WON'T DIE AND LEAVE THE CITY AT HIS MERCY.
HE'LL NEVER HAVE GOTHAM.
KROL'S STILL ALIVE.
BUT IN SHOCK.
I CAN HEAR HARBOR SOUNDS.
DAMN IT. WHAT CAN WE DO BUT WATCH?
RIVER COPS ARE CIRCLING THE AREA AROUND THE BLAST, COMMISSIONER.
I CAN SMELL THE IRON-TINGED AIR OF THE CITY.
WHAT'S THE POINT, MONTOYA? IF HIZZONER WAS DOWN IN THAT TUNNEL WHEN IT BLEW, HE'S RETIRED FROM OFFICE PERMANENT.
7

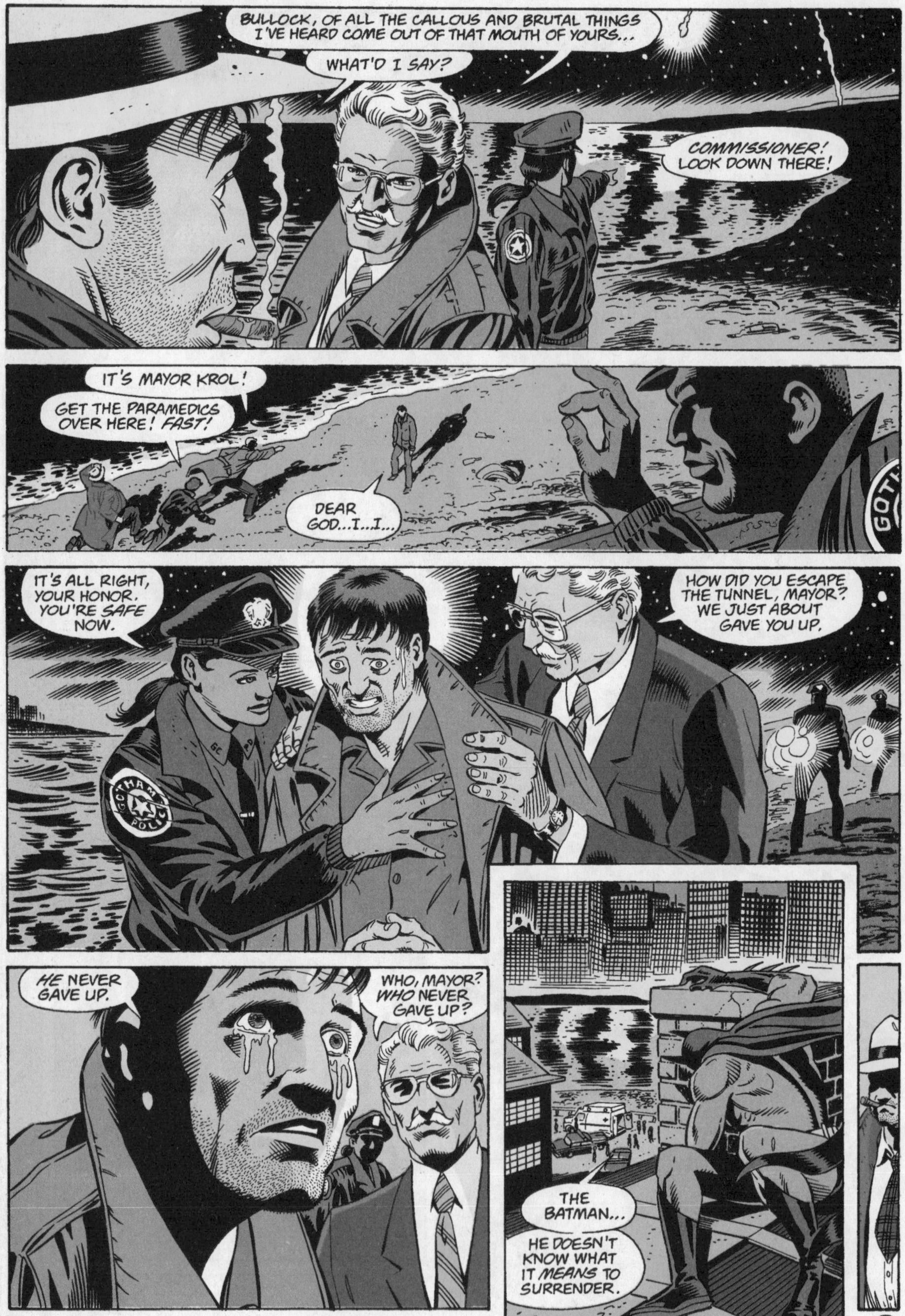
BULLOCK, OF ALL THE CALLOUS AND BRUTAL THINGS I'VE HEARD COME OUT OF THAT MOUTH OF YOURS...
WHAT'D I SAY?
COMMISSIONER! LOOK DOWN THERE!
IT'S MAYOR KROL!
GET THE PARAMEDICS OVER HERE! FAST!
DEAR GOD...I...I...
IT'S ALL RIGHT, YOUR HONOR. YOU'RE SAFE NOW.
HOW DID YOU ESCAPE THE TUNNEL, MAYOR? WE JUST ABOUT GAVE YOU UP.
HE NEVER GAVE UP.
WHO, MAYOR? WHO NEVER GAVE UP?
THE BATMAN...
HE DOESN'T KNOW WHAT IT MEANS TO SURRENDER.
8

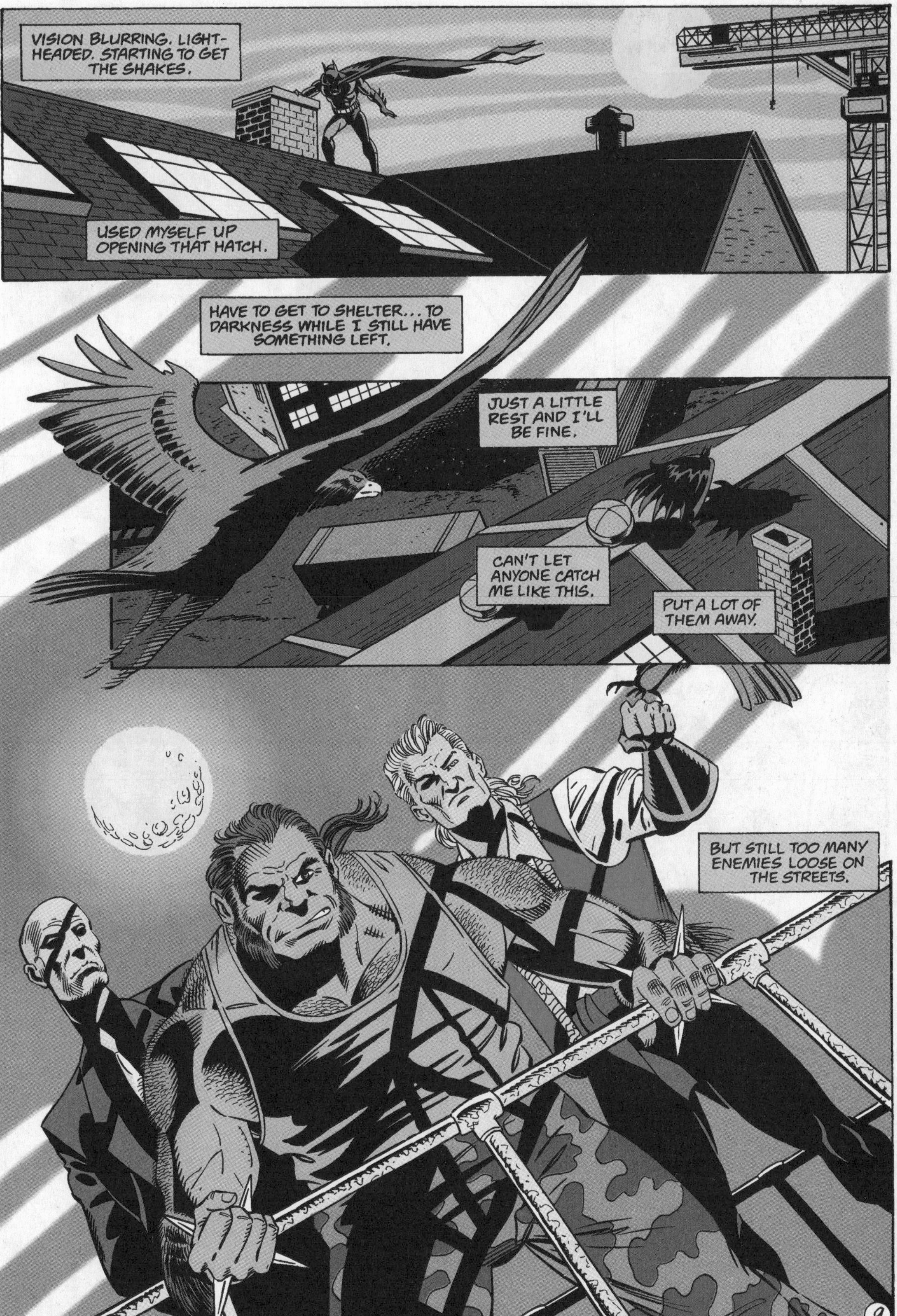
VISION BLURRING. LIGHT-HEADED. STARTING TO GET THE SHAKES.
USED MYSELF UP OPENING THAT HATCH.
HAVE TO GET TO SHELTER... TO DARKNESS WHILE I STILL HAVE SOMETHING LEFT.
JUST A LITTLE REST AND I'LL BE FINE.
CAN'T LET ANYONE CATCH ME LIKE THIS.
PUT A LOT OF THEM AWAY.
BUT STILL TOO MANY ENEMIES LOOSE ON THE STREETS.
9

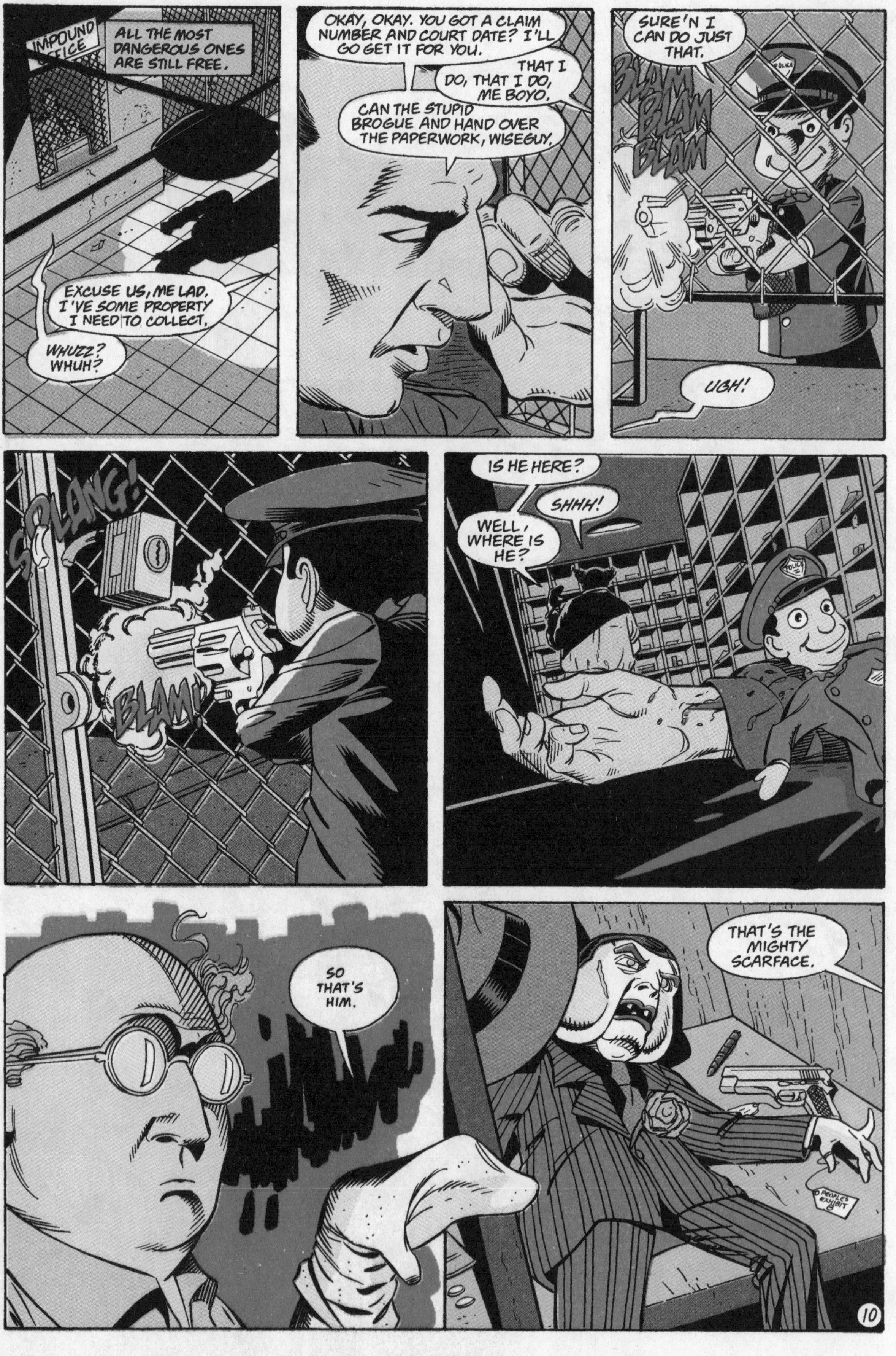
IMPOUND OFFICE
ALL THE MOST DANGEROUS ONES ARE STILL FREE.
EXCUSE US, ME LAD. I'VE SOME PROPERTY I NEED TO COLLECT.
WHUZZ? WHUH?
OKAY, OKAY. YOU GOT A CLAIM NUMBER AND COURT DATE? I'LL GO GET IT FOR YOU.
THAT I DO, THAT I DO, ME BOYO.
CAN THE STUPID BROGUE AND HAND OVER THE PAPERWORK, WISEGUY.
SURE'N I CAN DO JUST THAT.
BLAM BLAM BLAM
UGH!
SPLANG!
BLAM!
IS HE HERE?
SHHH!
WELL, WHERE IS HE?
SO THAT'S HIM.
THAT'S THE MIGHTY SCARFACE.
PEOPLES EXHIBIT
10

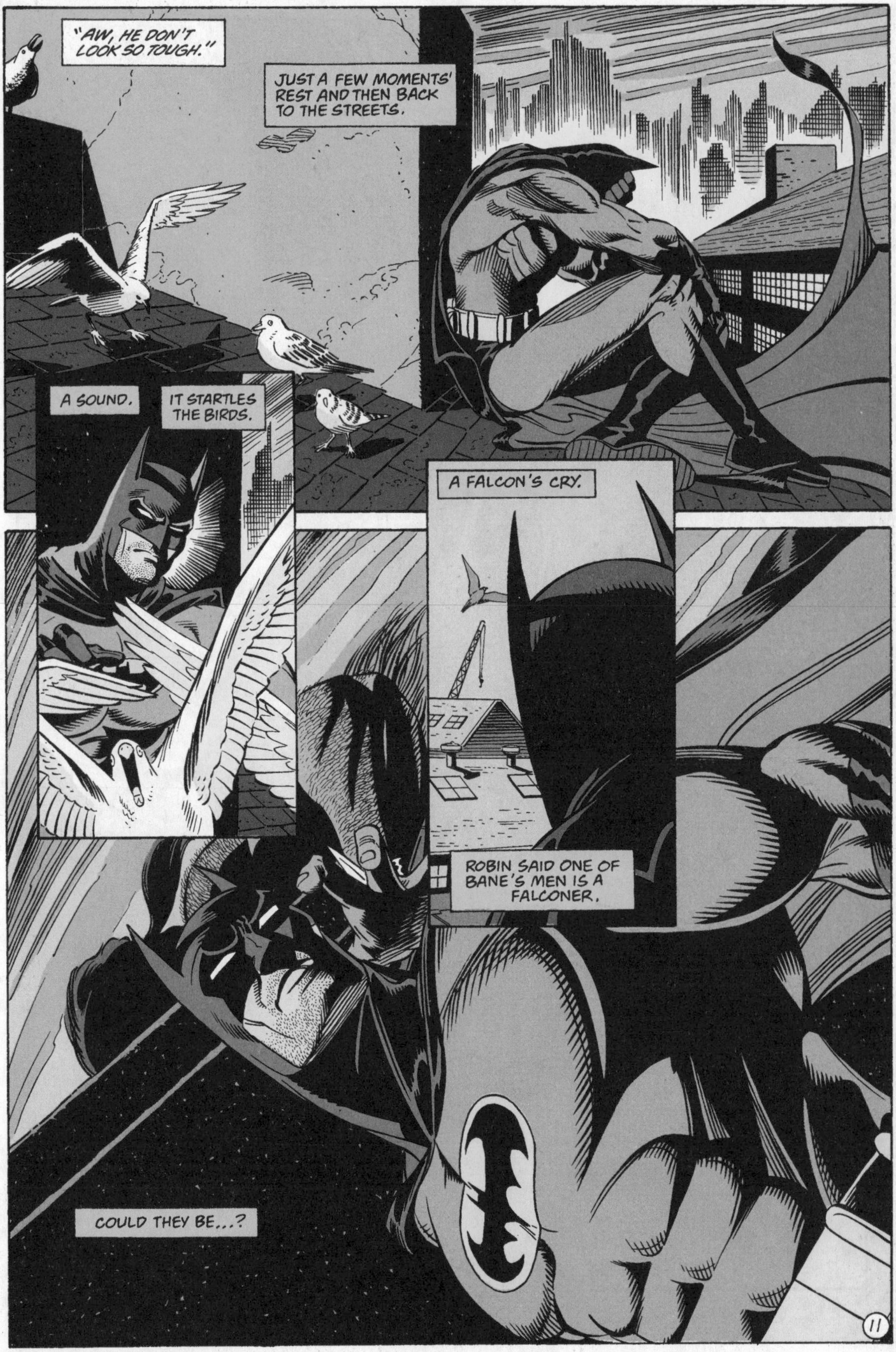
"AW, HE DON'T LOOK SO TOUGH."
JUST A FEW MOMENTS' REST AND THEN BACK TO THE STREETS.
A SOUND.
IT STARTLES THE BIRDS.
A FALCON'S CRY.
ROBIN SAID ONE OF BANE'S MEN IS A FALCONER.
COULD THEY BE...?
11

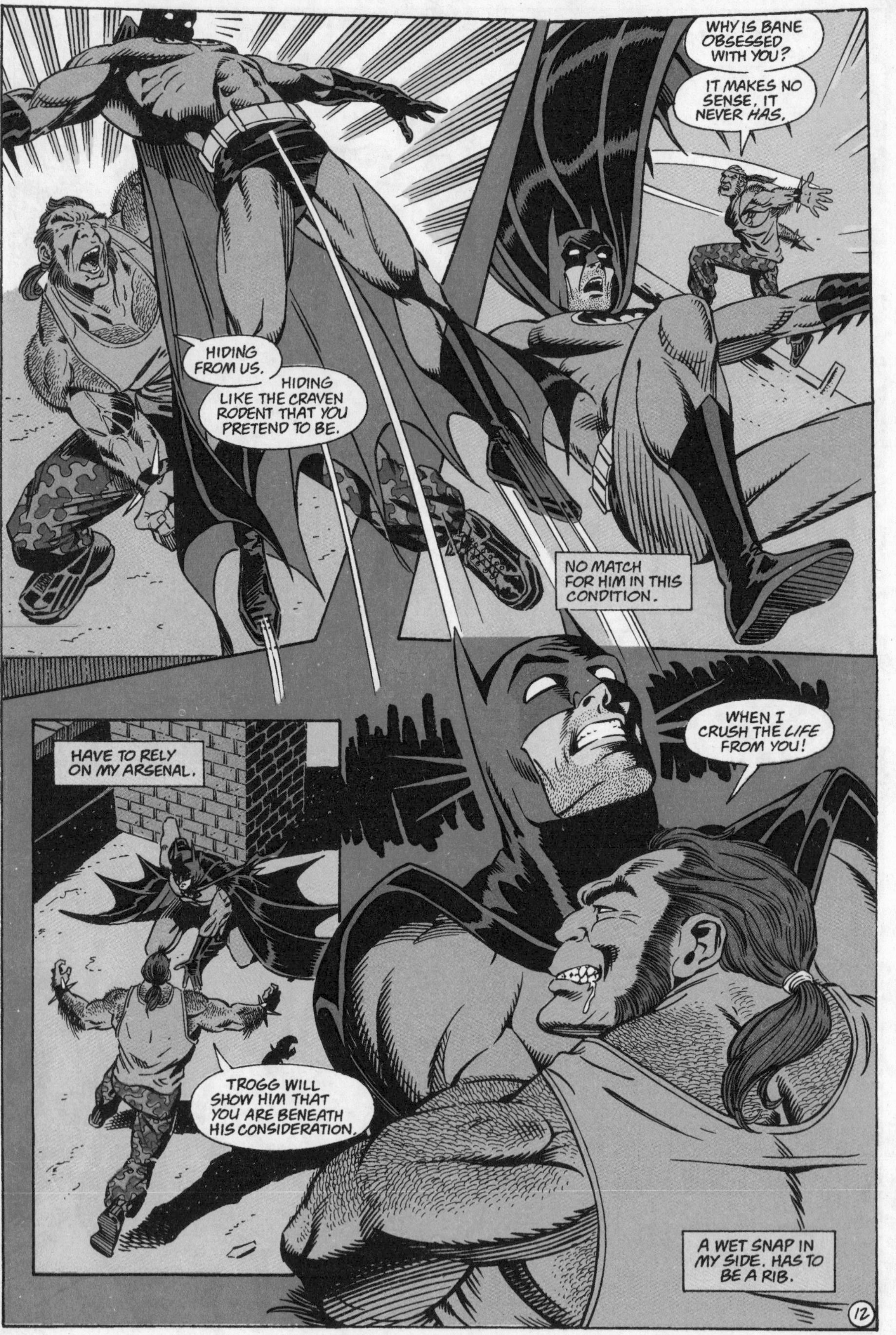
WHY IS BANE OBSESSED WITH YOU?
IT MAKES NO SENSE, IT NEVER HAS.
HIDING FROM US.
HIDING LIKE THE CRAVEN RODENT THAT YOU PRETEND TO BE.
NO MATCH FOR HIM IN THIS CONDITION.
HAVE TO RELY ON MY ARSENAL.
TROGG WILL SHOW HIM THAT YOU ARE BENEATH HIS CONSIDERATION.
WHEN I CRUSH THE LIFE FROM YOU!
A WET SNAP IN MY SIDE. HAS TO BE A RIB.
12

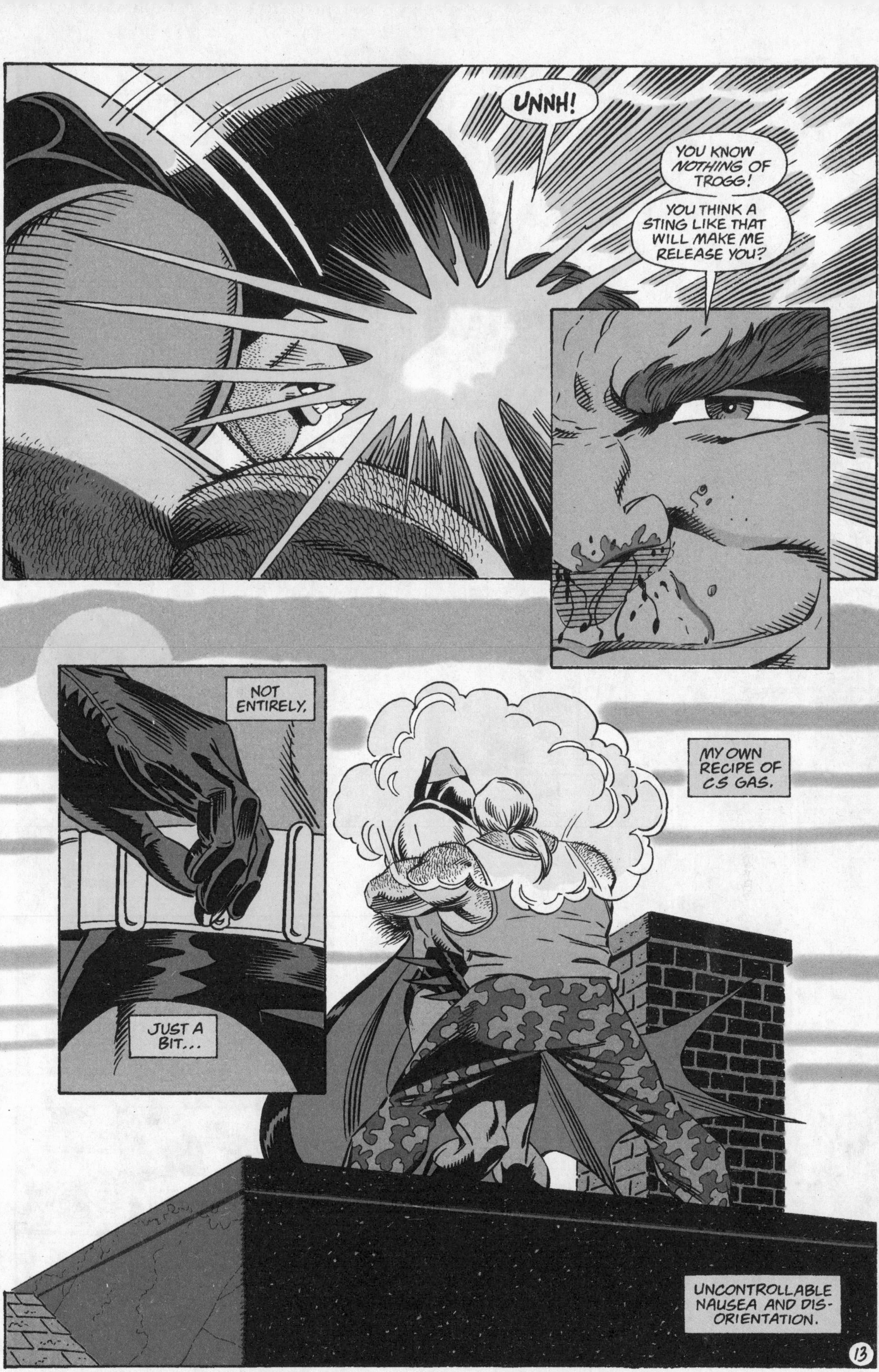
UNNH!
YOU KNOW NOTHING OF TROGG!
YOU THINK A STING LIKE THAT WILL MAKE ME RELEASE YOU?
NOT ENTIRELY.
JUST A BIT...
MY OWN RECIPE OF CS GAS.
UNCONTROLLABLE NAUSEA AND DIS-ORIENTATION.
13

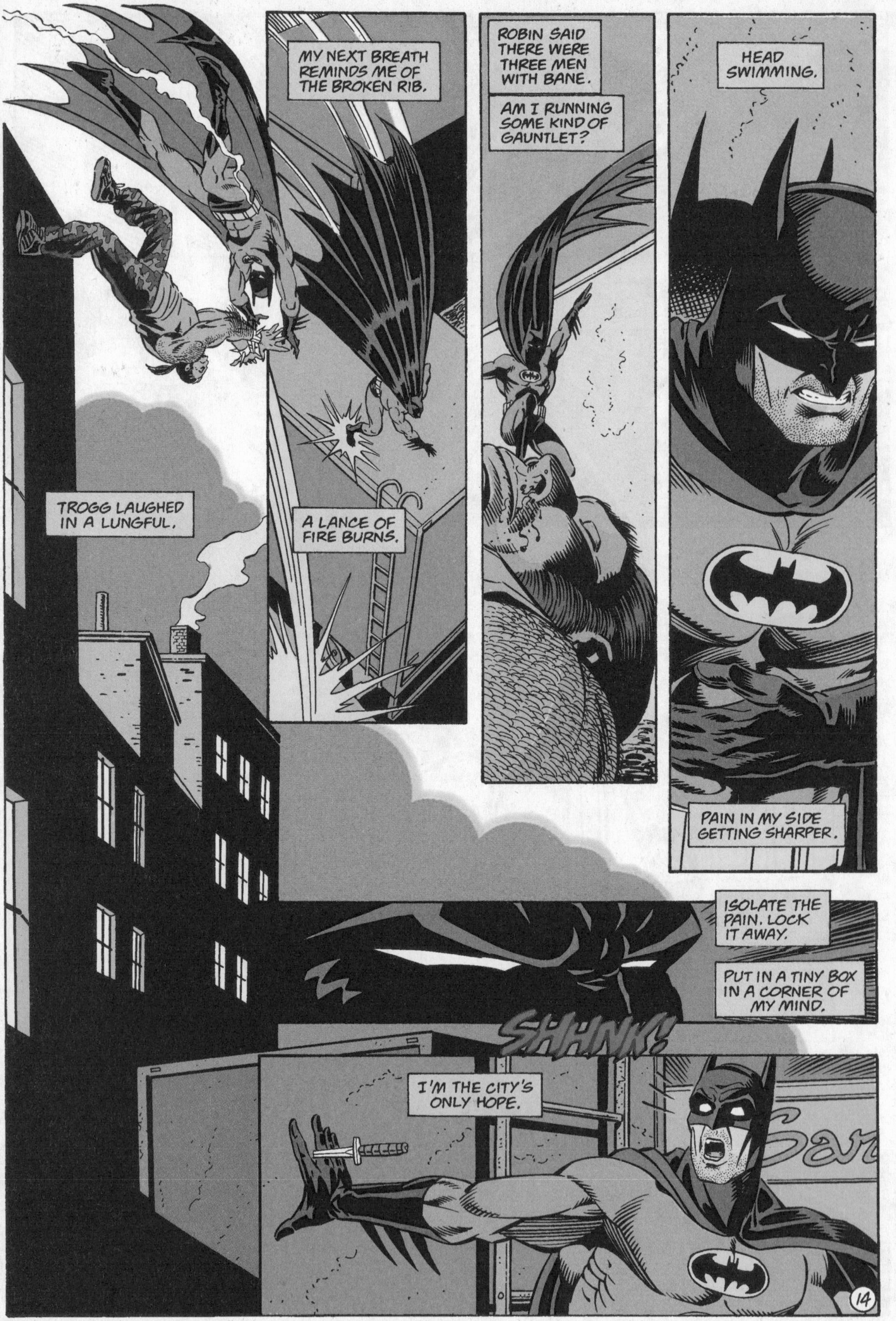

TROGG LAUGHED IN A LUNGFUL.
MY NEXT BREATH REMINDS ME OF THE BROKEN RIB.
A LANCE OF FIRE BURNS.
ROBIN SAID THERE WERE THREE MEN WITH BANE.
AM I RUNNING SOME KIND OF GAUNTLET?
HEAD SWIMMING.
PAIN IN MY SIDE GETTING SHARPER.
ISOLATE THE PAIN. LOCK IT AWAY.
PUT IN A TINY BOX IN A CORNER OF MY MIND.
SHHNK!
I'M THE CITY'S ONLY HOPE.
14

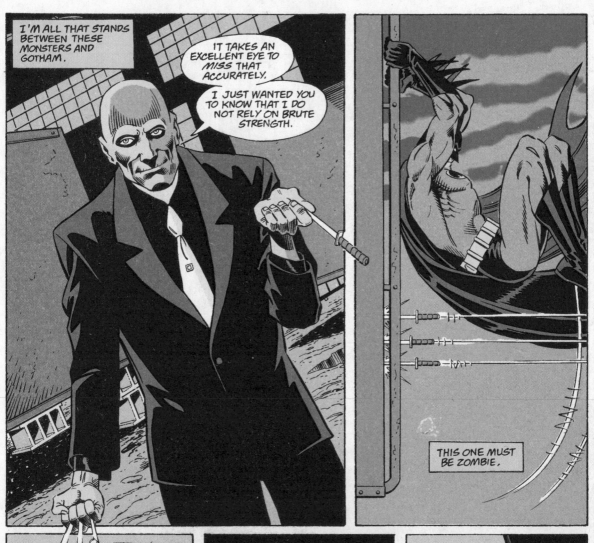

I'M ALL THAT STANDS BETWEEN THESE MONSTERS AND GOTHAM.

IT TAKES AN EXCELLENT EYE TO *MISS* THAT ACCURATELY.

I JUST WANTED YOU TO KNOW THAT I DO NOT RELY ON BRUTE STRENGTH.

THIS ONE MUST BE ZOMBIE.

SO IT'S ANOTHER TEST.

LIKE BREAKING THE INMATES OUT OF ARKHAM.

ALL TO TEST MY ABILITIES AND ENDURANCE.

AS THOUGH BANE WERE STUDYING ME.

TO WHAT END?

15

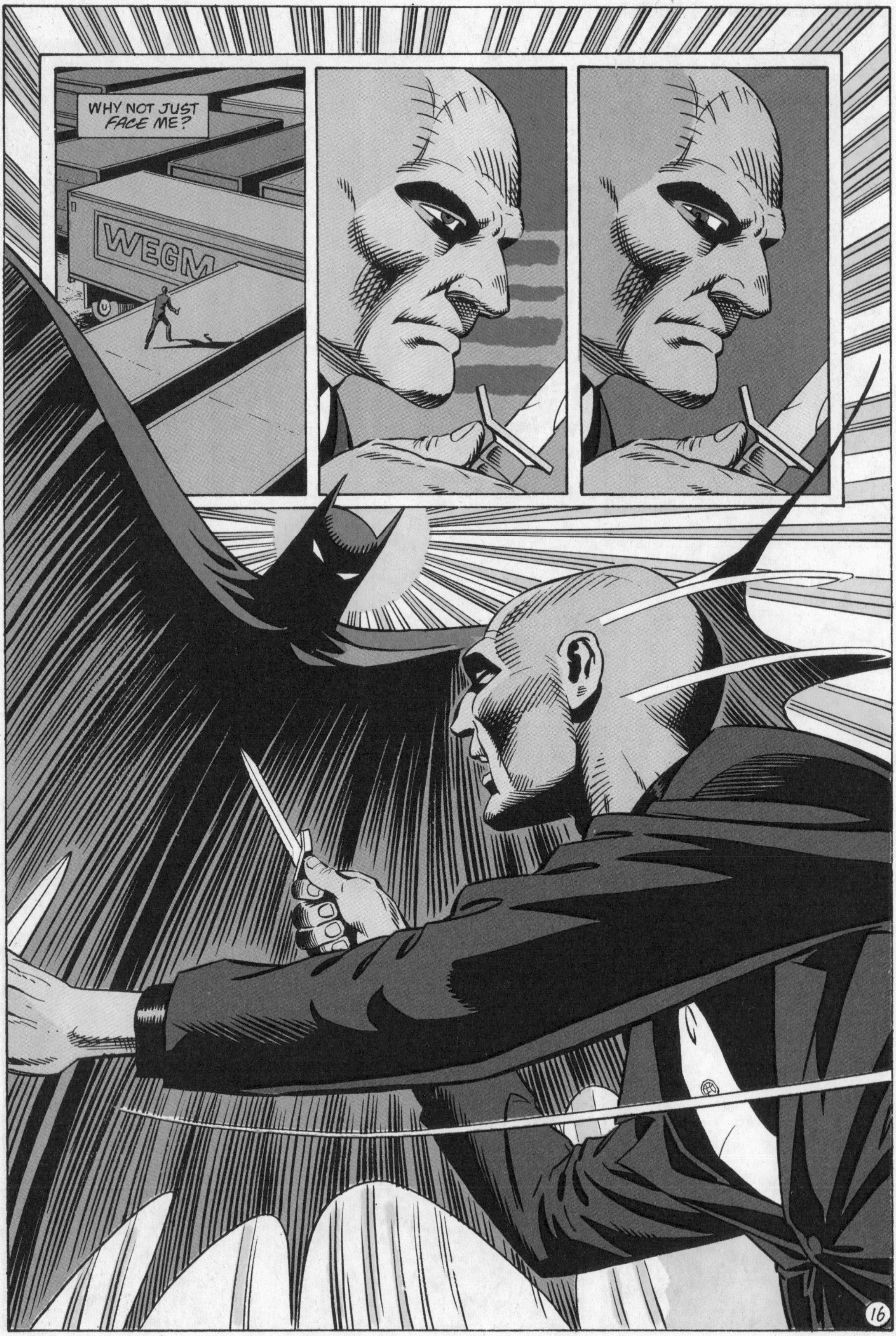
WHY NOT JUST FACE ME?
WEGM
16

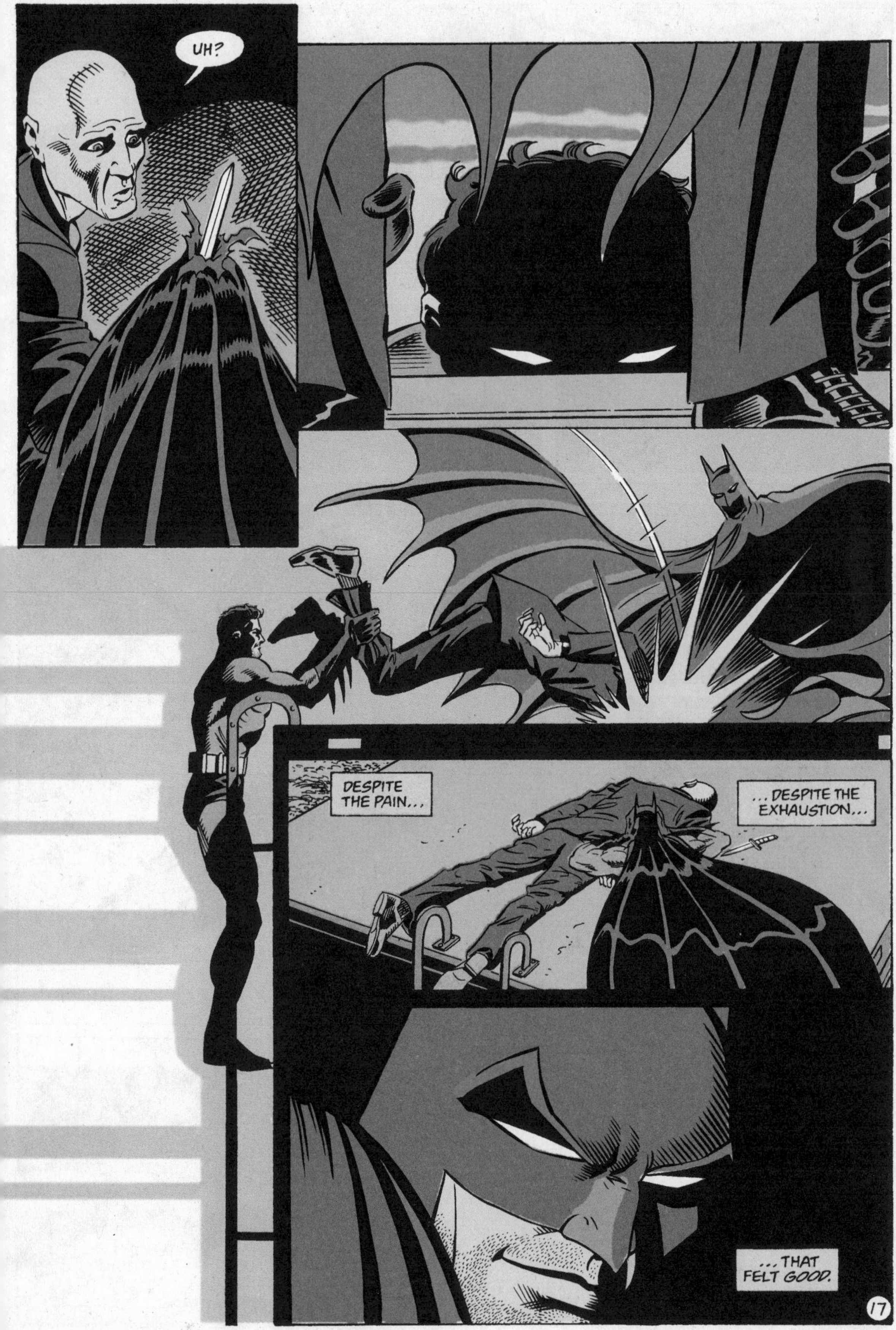
UH?
DESPITE THE PAIN...
...DESPITE THE EXHAUSTION...
...THAT FELT GOOD.
17

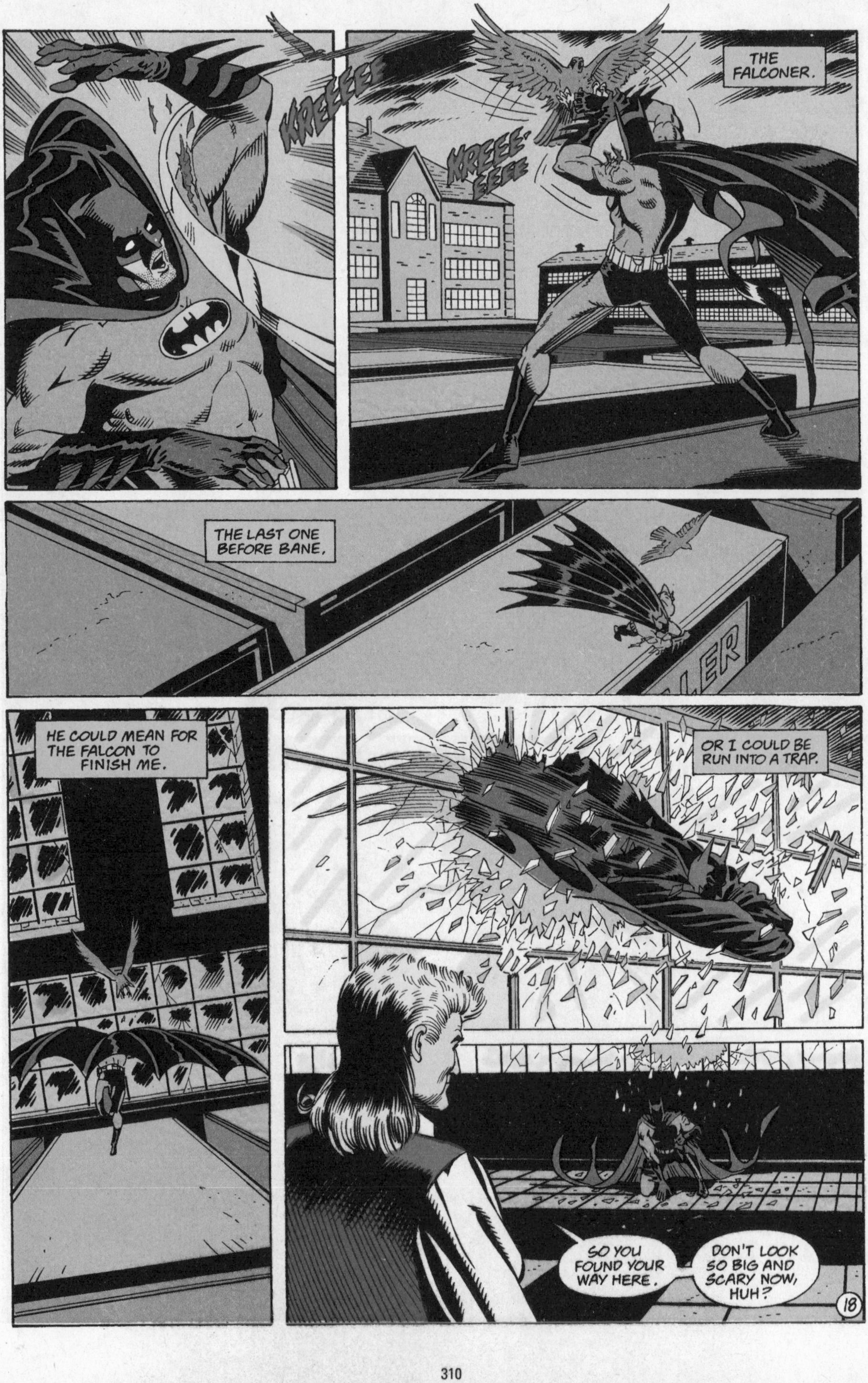
KREEEEE
KREEEE-EEEE
THE FALCONER.
THE LAST ONE BEFORE BANE.
HE COULD MEAN FOR THE FALCON TO FINISH ME.
OR I COULD BE RUN INTO A TRAP.
SO YOU FOUND YOUR WAY HERE.
DON'T LOOK SO BIG AND SCARY NOW, HUH?
18

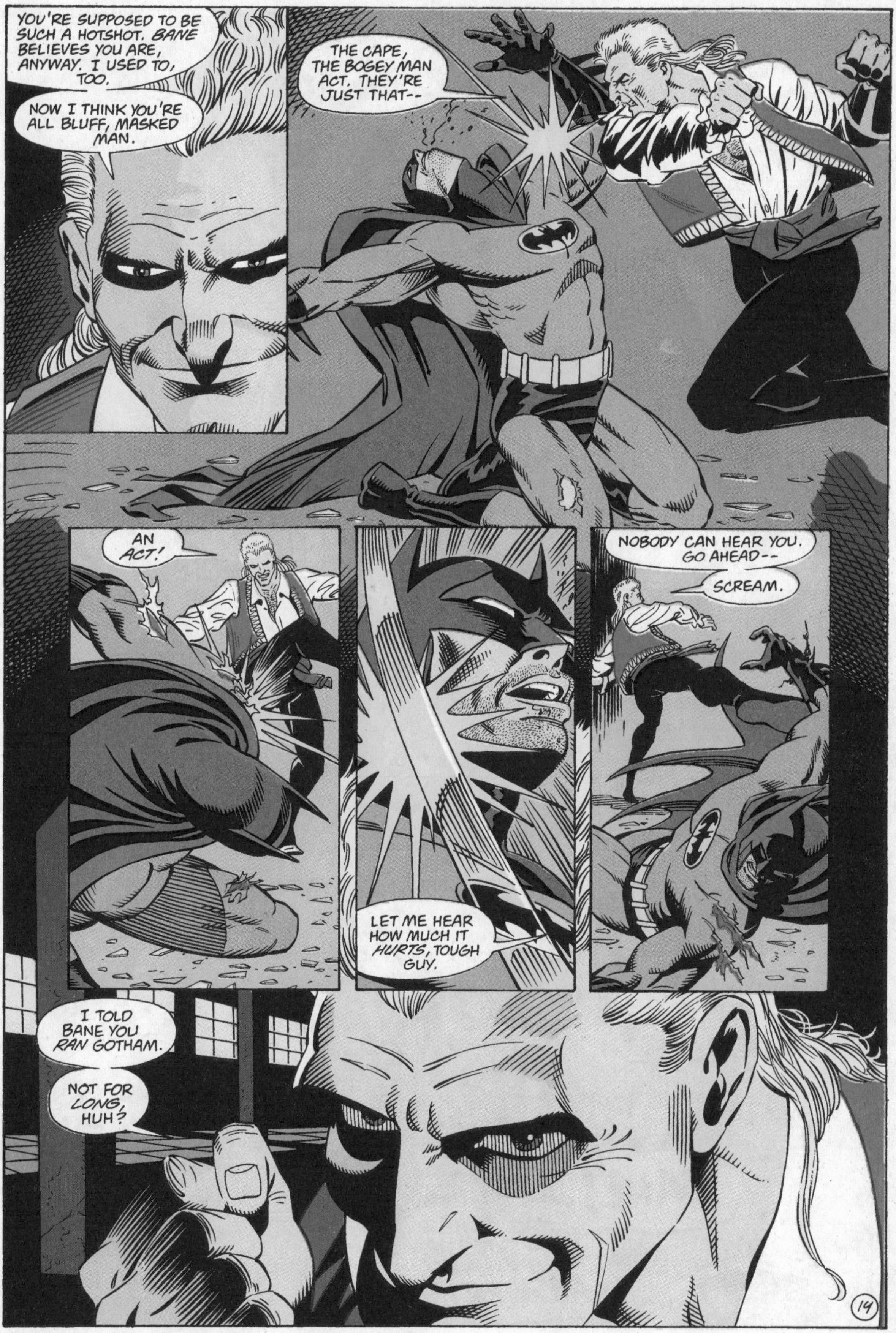

YOU'RE SUPPOSED TO BE SUCH A HOTSHOT. BANE BELIEVES YOU ARE, ANYWAY. I USED TO, TOO.
NOW I THINK YOU'RE ALL BLUFF, MASKED MAN.
THE CAPE, THE BOGEY MAN ACT. THEY'RE JUST THAT--
AN ACT!
NOBODY CAN HEAR YOU. GO AHEAD--
SCREAM.
LET ME HEAR HOW MUCH IT HURTS, TOUGH GUY.
I TOLD BANE YOU RAN GOTHAM.
NOT FOR LONG, HUH?
14

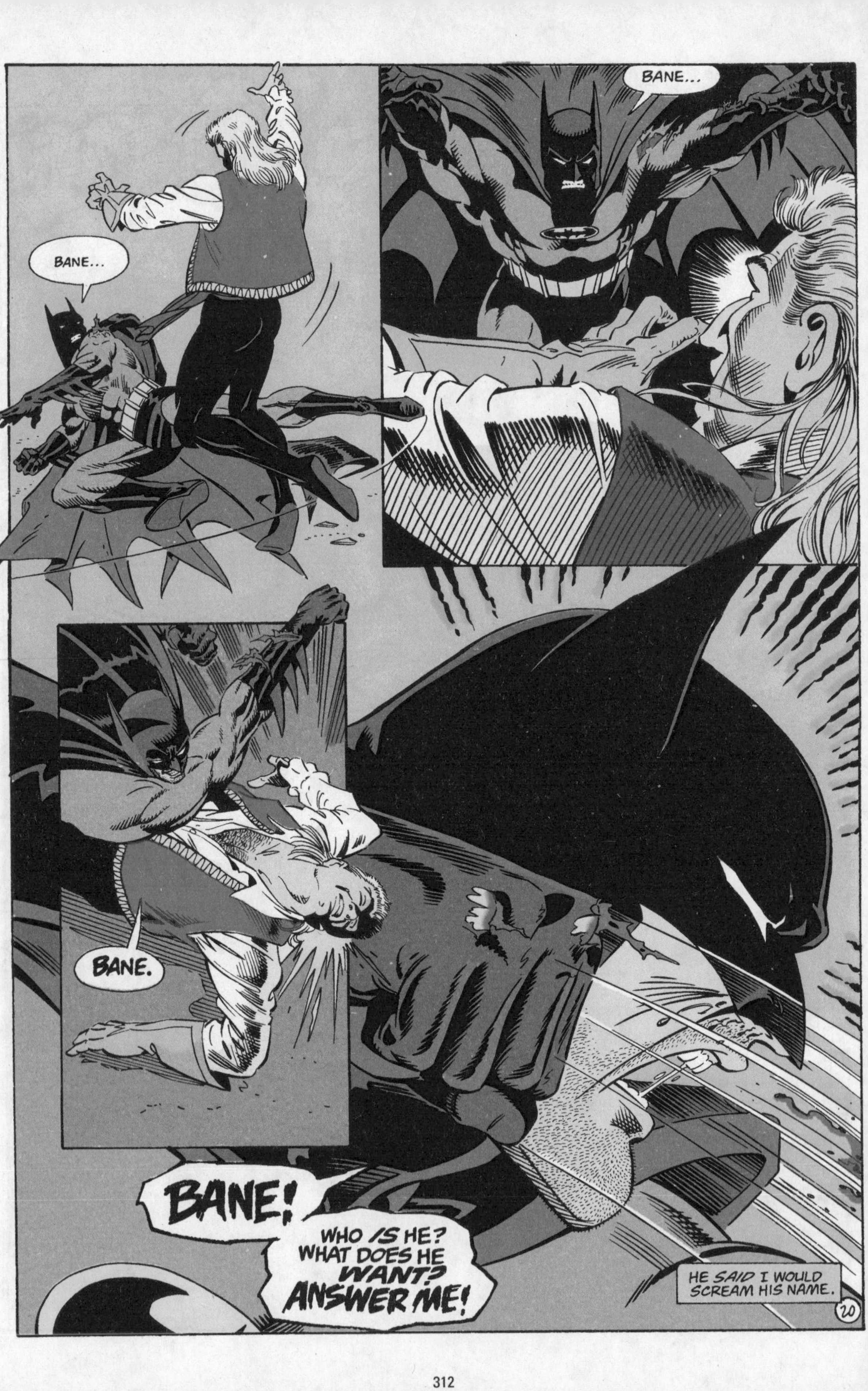
BANE...
BANE...
BANE.
BANE!
WHO IS HE? WHAT DOES HE WANT? ANSWER ME!
HE SAID I WOULD SCREAM HIS NAME.
20

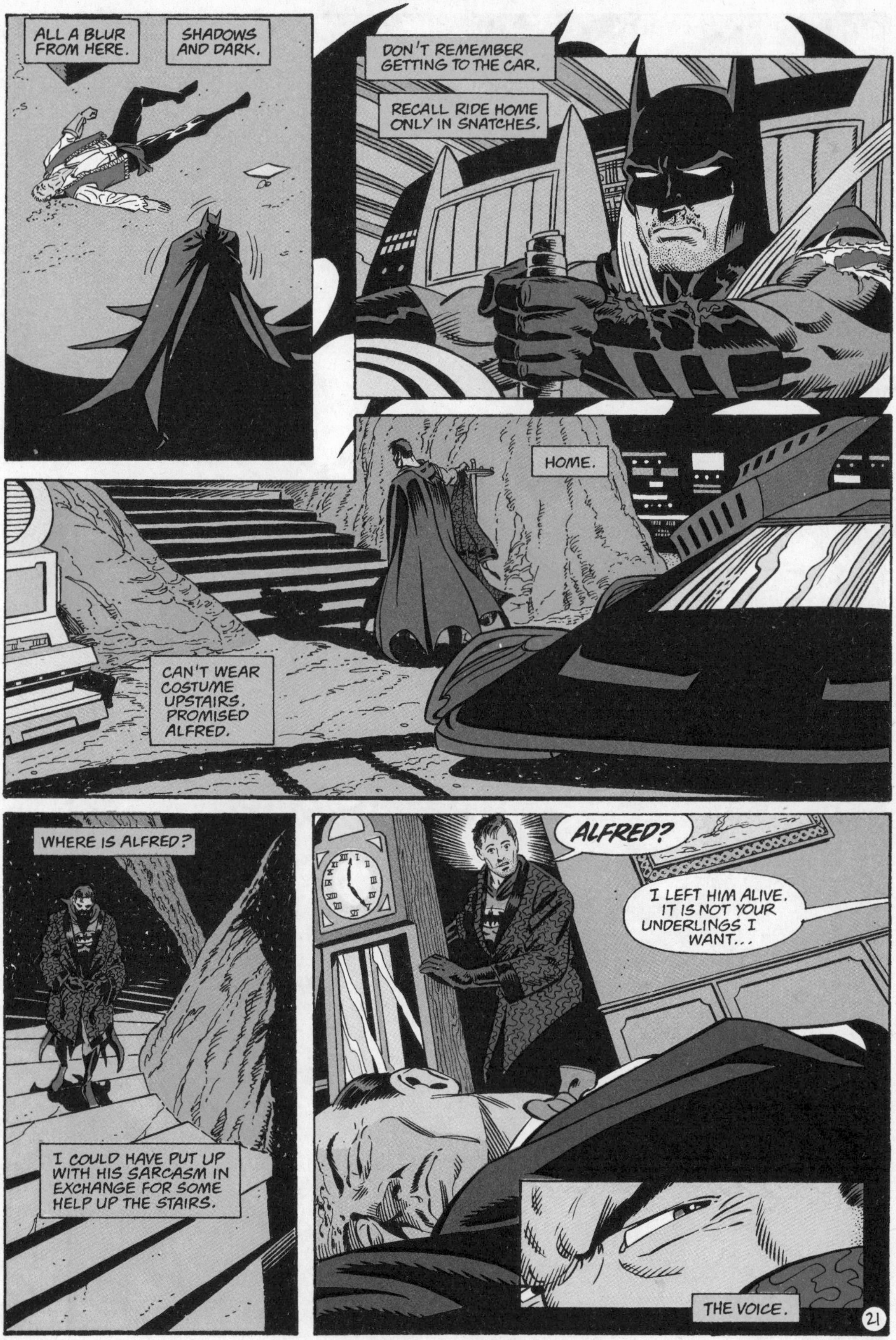
ALL A BLUR FROM HERE.
SHADOWS AND DARK.
DON'T REMEMBER GETTING TO THE CAR.
RECALL RIDE HOME ONLY IN SNATCHES.
HOME.
CAN'T WEAR COSTUME UPSTAIRS. PROMISED ALFRED.
WHERE IS ALFRED?
I COULD HAVE PUT UP WITH HIS SARCASM IN EXCHANGE FOR SOME HELP UP THE STAIRS.
ALFRED?
I LEFT HIM ALIVE. IT IS NOT YOUR UNDERLINGS I WANT...
THE VOICE.
21

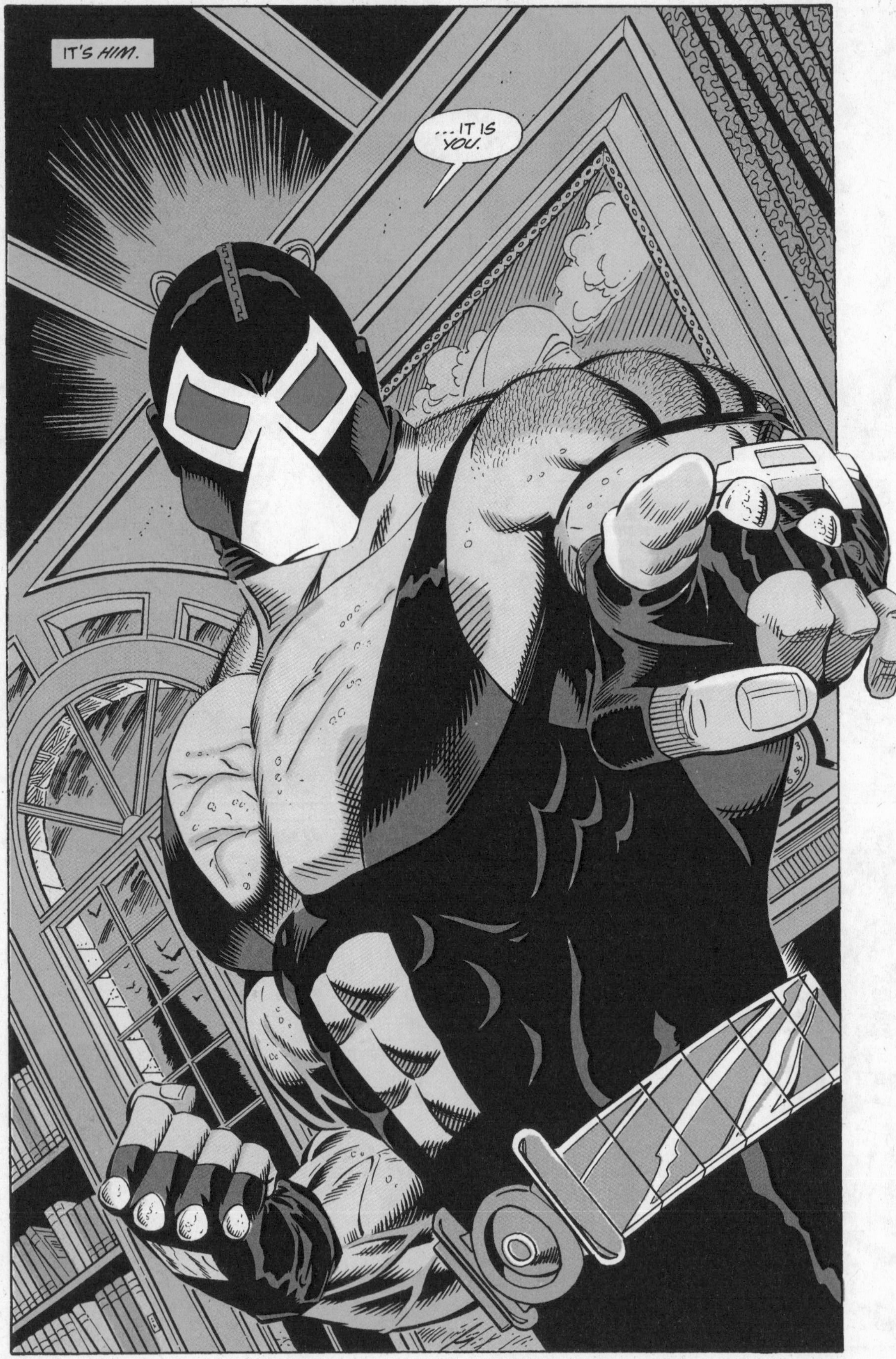
IT'S HIM.
...IT IS YOU.

Cover art by KELLEY JONES

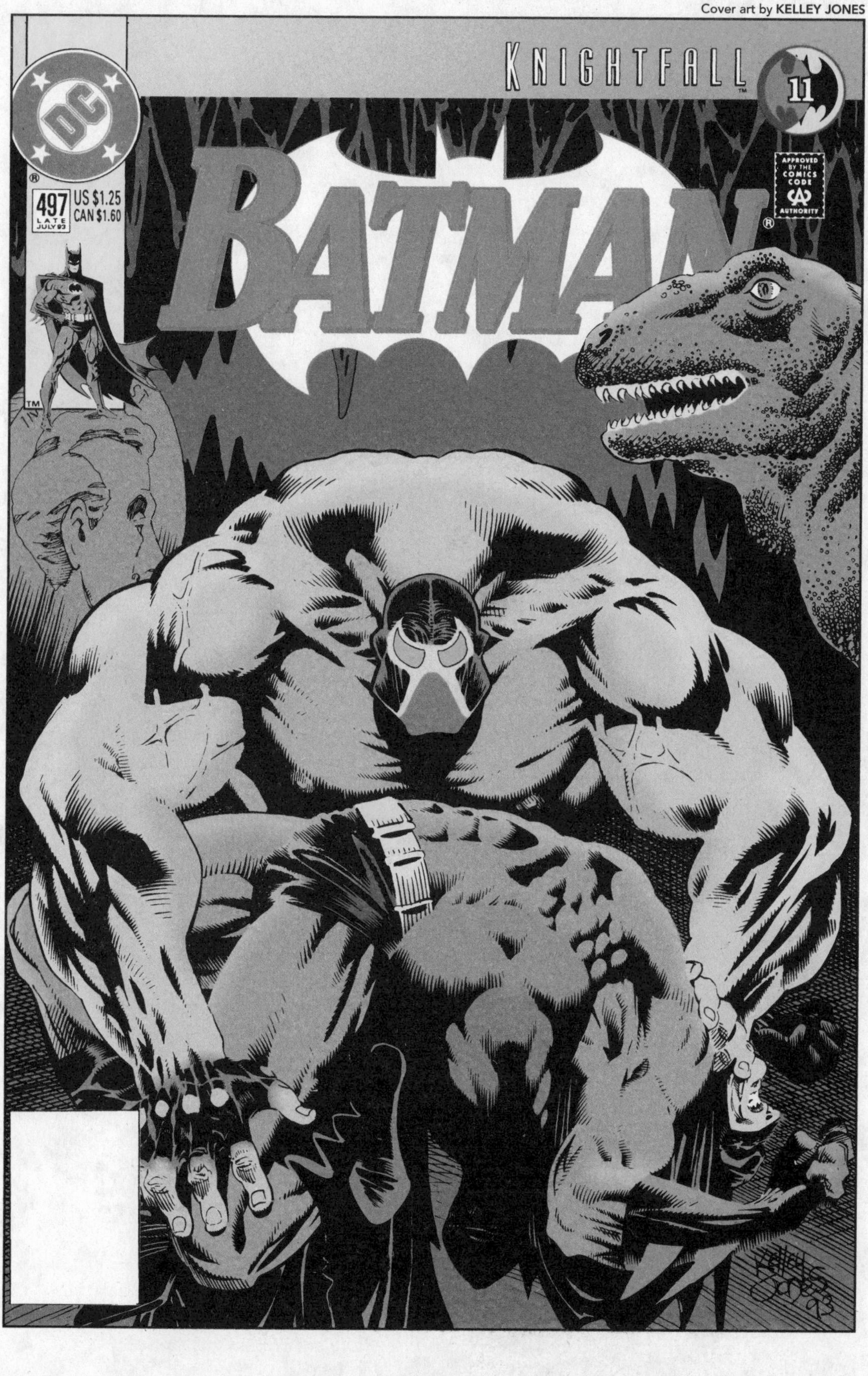

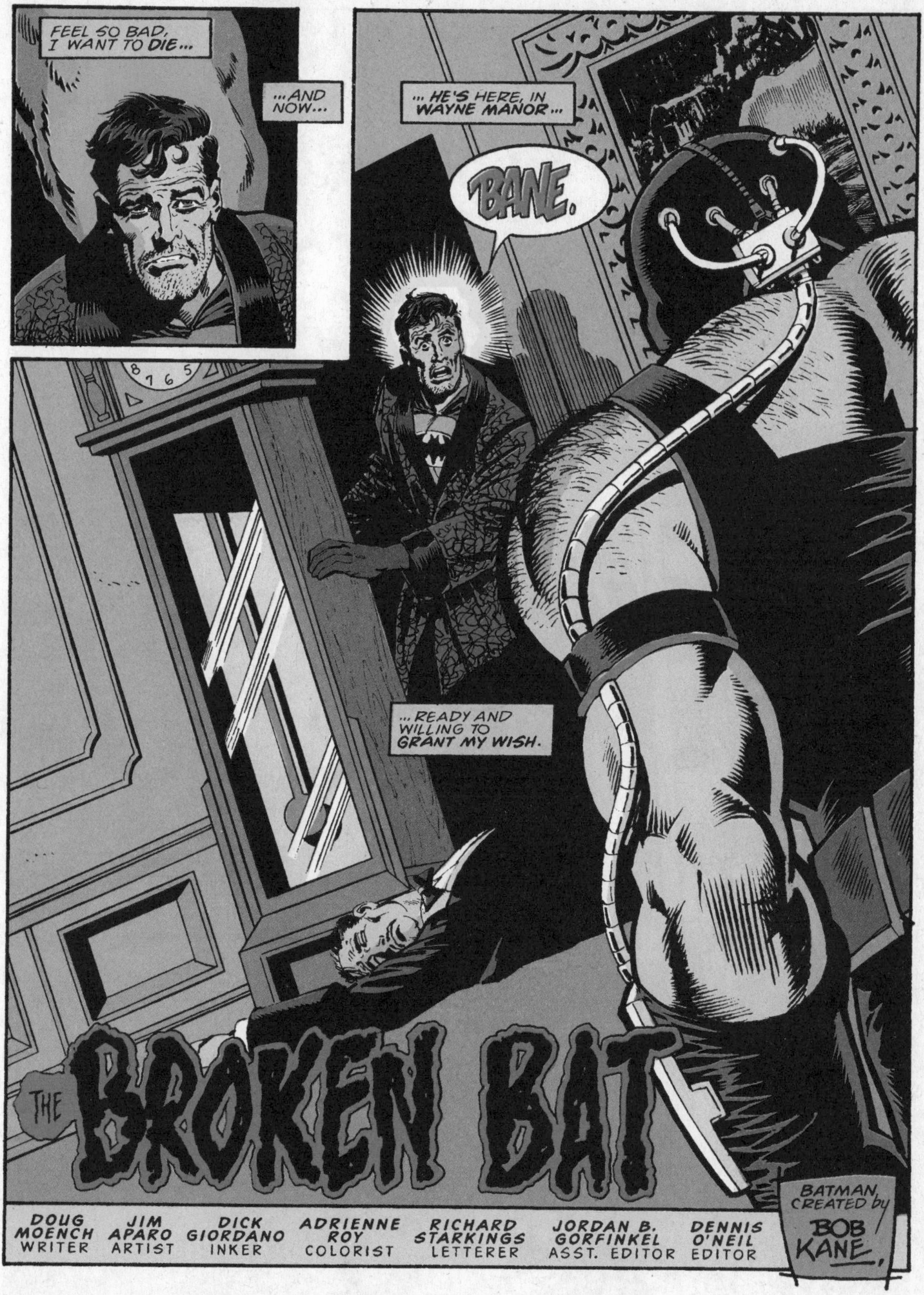
FEEL SO BAD, I WANT TO DIE...
...AND NOW...
...HE'S HERE, IN WAYNE MANOR...
BANE.
...READY AND WILLING TO GRANT MY WISH.
THE BROKEN BAT
DOUG MOENCH WRITER
JIM APARO ARTIST
DICK GIORDANO INKER
ADRIENNE ROY COLORIST
RICHARD STARKINGS LETTERER
JORDAN B. GORFINKEL ASST. EDITOR
DENNIS O'NEIL EDITOR
BATMAN CREATED by BOB KANE

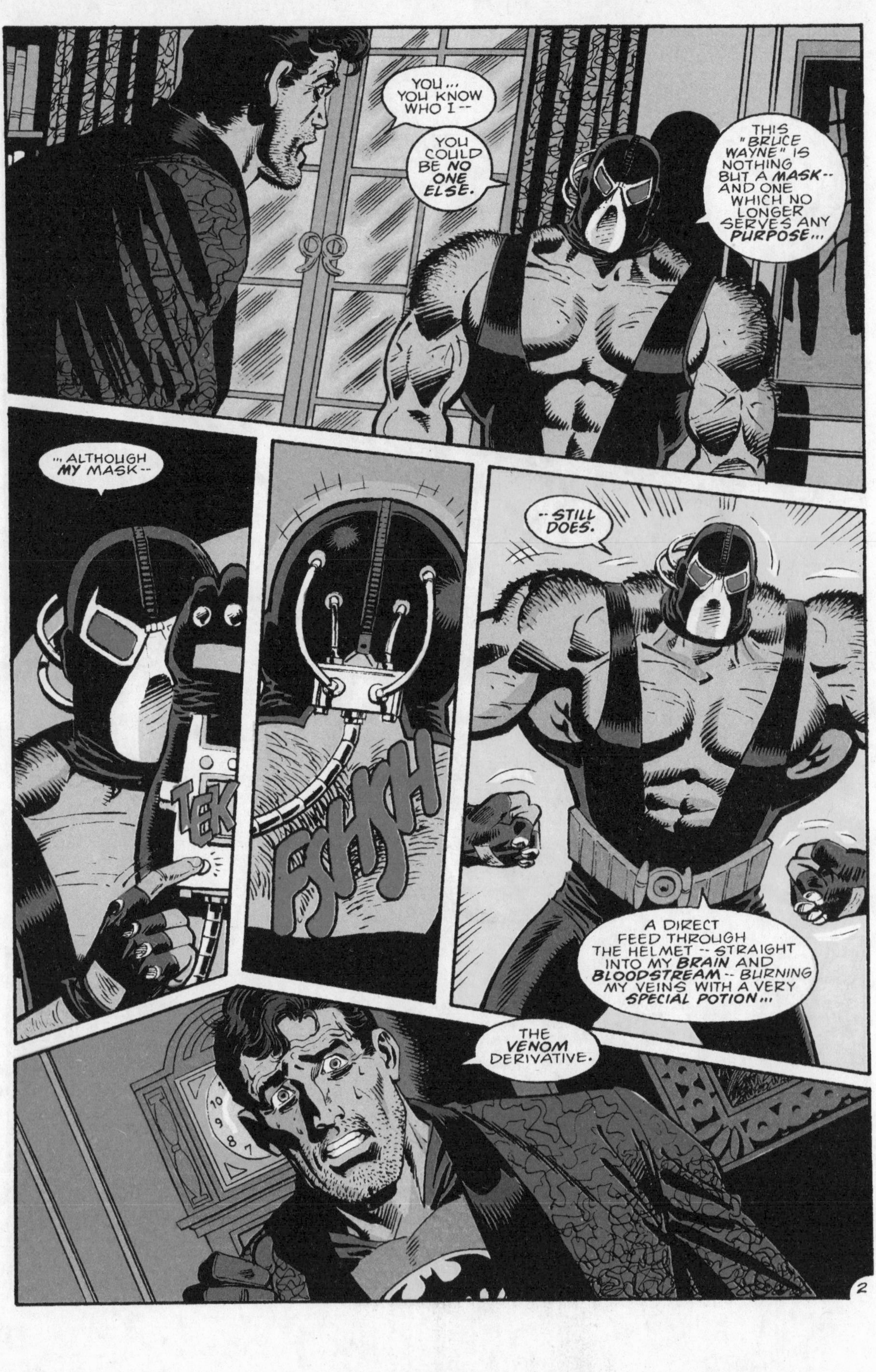
YOU... YOU KNOW WHO I --
YOU COULD BE NO ONE ELSE.
THIS "BRUCE WAYNE" IS NOTHING BUT A MASK -- AND ONE WHICH NO LONGER SERVES ANY PURPOSE...
...ALTHOUGH MY MASK --
TEK
FSHHH
-- STILL DOES.
A DIRECT FEED THROUGH THE HELMET -- STRAIGHT INTO MY BRAIN AND BLOODSTREAM -- BURNING MY VEINS WITH A VERY SPECIAL POTION...
THE VENOM DERIVATIVE.
2

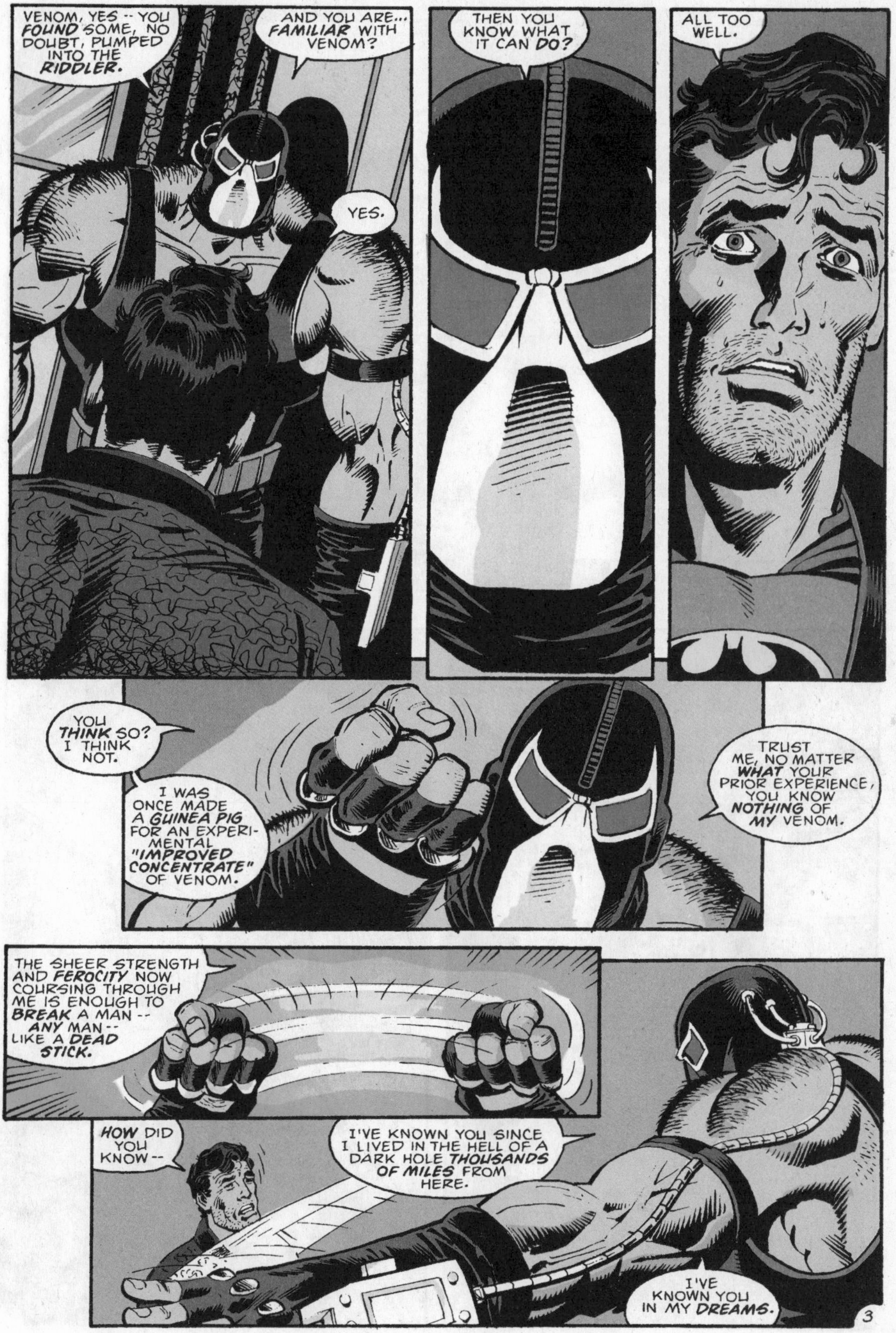
VENOM, YES -- YOU FOUND SOME, NO DOUBT, PUMPED INTO THE RIDDLER.
AND YOU ARE... FAMILIAR WITH VENOM?
YES.
THEN YOU KNOW WHAT IT CAN DO?
ALL TOO WELL.
YOU THINK SO? I THINK NOT.
I WAS ONCE MADE A GUINEA PIG FOR AN EXPERIMENTAL "IMPROVED CONCENTRATE" OF VENOM.
TRUST ME, NO MATTER WHAT YOUR PRIOR EXPERIENCE, YOU KNOW NOTHING OF MY VENOM.
THE SHEER STRENGTH AND FEROCITY NOW COURSING THROUGH ME IS ENOUGH TO BREAK A MAN -- ANY MAN -- LIKE A DEAD STICK.
HOW DID YOU KNOW --
I'VE KNOWN YOU SINCE I LIVED IN THE HELL OF A DARK HOLE THOUSANDS OF MILES FROM HERE.
I'VE KNOWN YOU IN MY DREAMS.
3

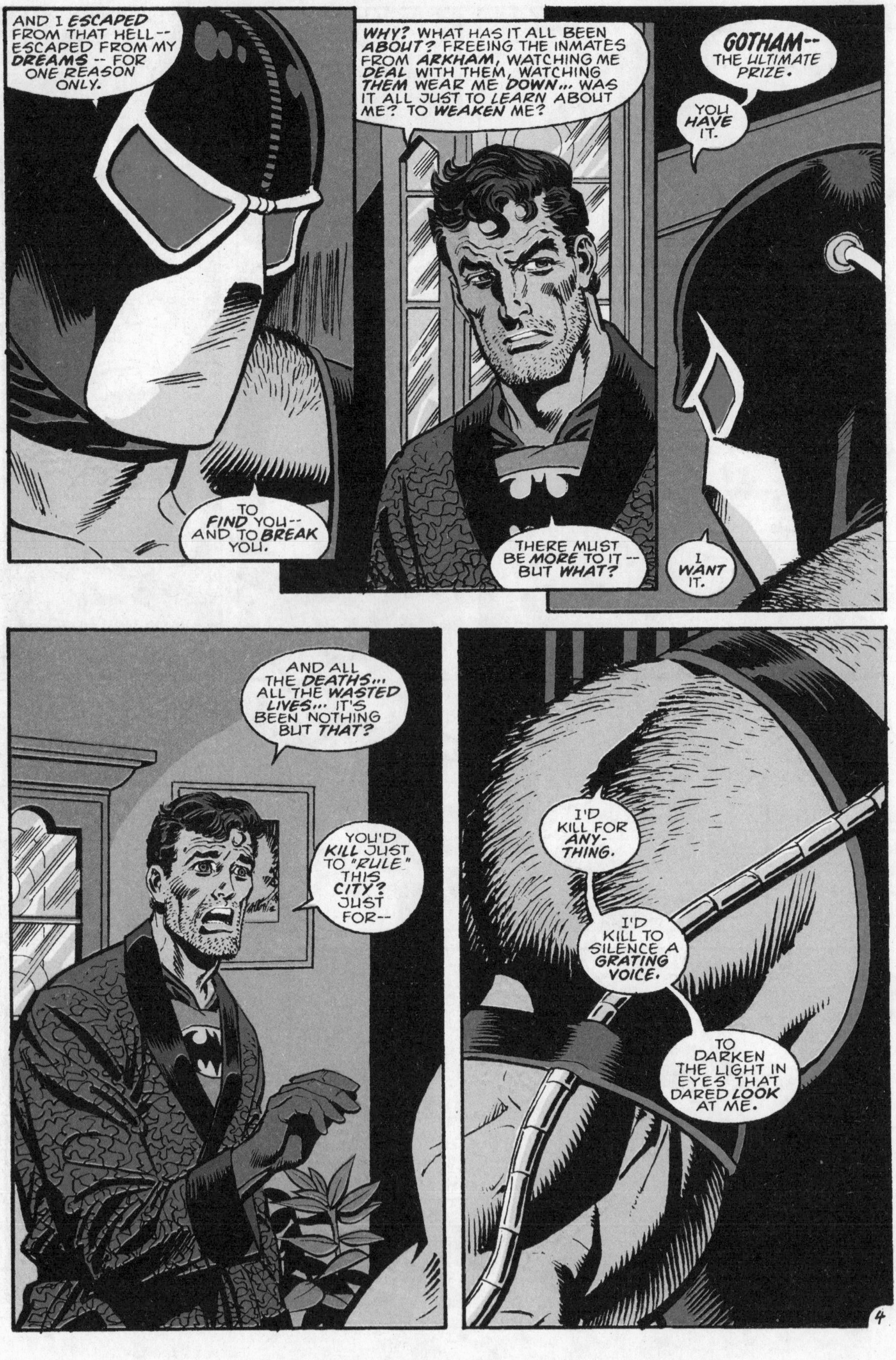
AND I ESCAPED FROM THAT HELL-- ESCAPED FROM MY DREAMS -- FOR ONE REASON ONLY.
TO FIND YOU-- AND TO BREAK YOU.
WHY? WHAT HAS IT ALL BEEN ABOUT? FREEING THE INMATES FROM ARKHAM, WATCHING ME DEAL WITH THEM, WATCHING THEM WEAR ME DOWN... WAS IT ALL JUST TO LEARN ABOUT ME? TO WEAKEN ME?
THERE MUST BE MORE TO IT -- BUT WHAT?
GOTHAM-- THE ULTIMATE PRIZE.
YOU HAVE IT.
I WANT IT.
AND ALL THE DEATHS... ALL THE WASTED LIVES... IT'S BEEN NOTHING BUT THAT?
YOU'D KILL JUST TO "RULE" THIS CITY? JUST FOR--
I'D KILL FOR ANY-THING.
I'D KILL TO SILENCE A GRATING VOICE.
TO DARKEN THE LIGHT IN EYES THAT DARED LOOK AT ME.
4

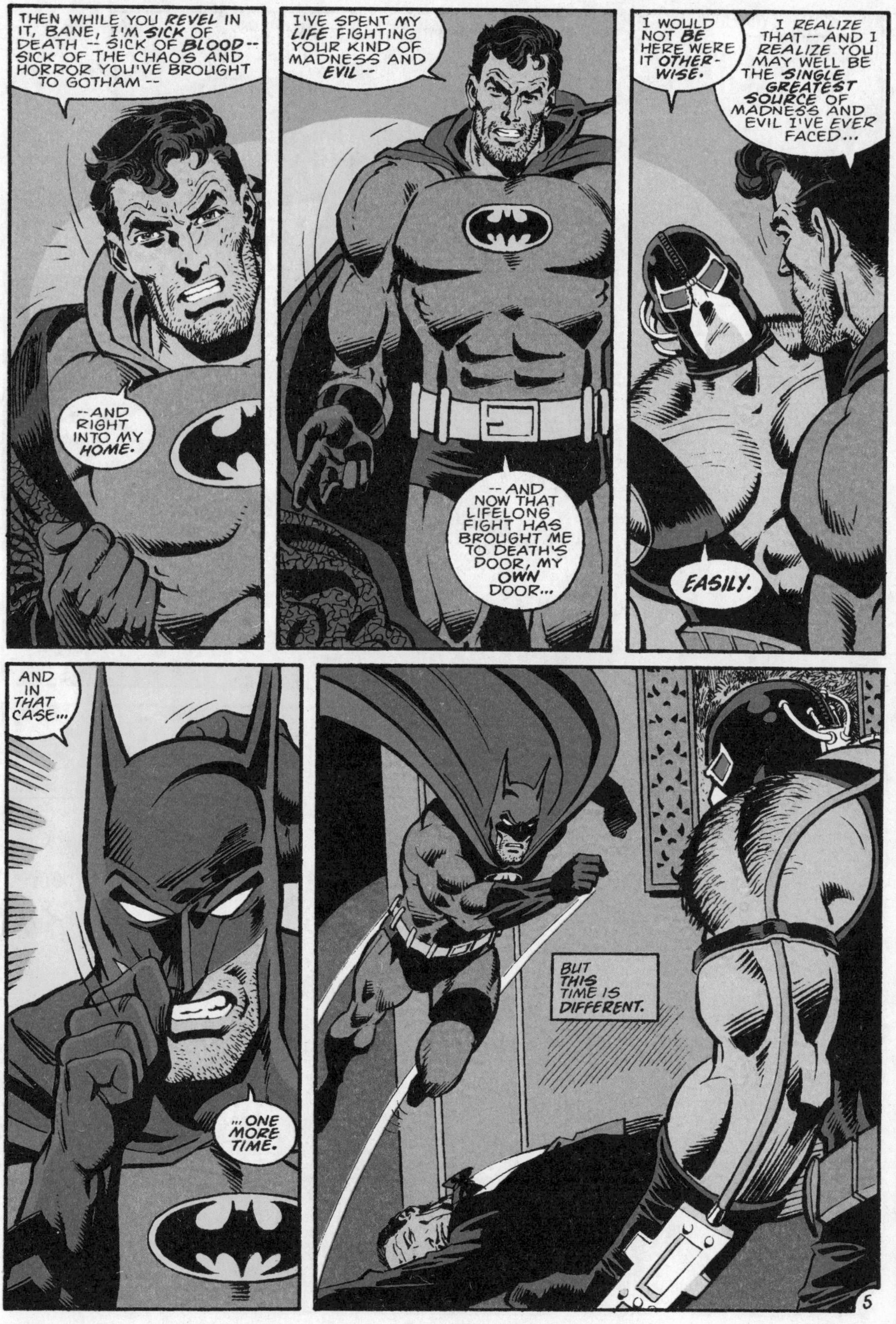
THEN WHILE YOU REVEL IN IT, BANE, I'M SICK OF DEATH -- SICK OF BLOOD -- SICK OF THE CHAOS AND HORROR YOU'VE BROUGHT TO GOTHAM --
--AND RIGHT INTO MY HOME.
I'VE SPENT MY LIFE FIGHTING YOUR KIND OF MADNESS AND EVIL --
--AND NOW THAT LIFELONG FIGHT HAS BROUGHT ME TO DEATH'S DOOR, MY OWN DOOR...
I WOULD NOT BE HERE WERE IT OTHERWISE.
I REALIZE THAT -- AND I REALIZE YOU MAY WELL BE THE SINGLE GREATEST SOURCE OF MADNESS AND EVIL I'VE EVER FACED...
EASILY.
AND IN THAT CASE...
...ONE MORE TIME.
BUT THIS TIME IS DIFFERENT.
5

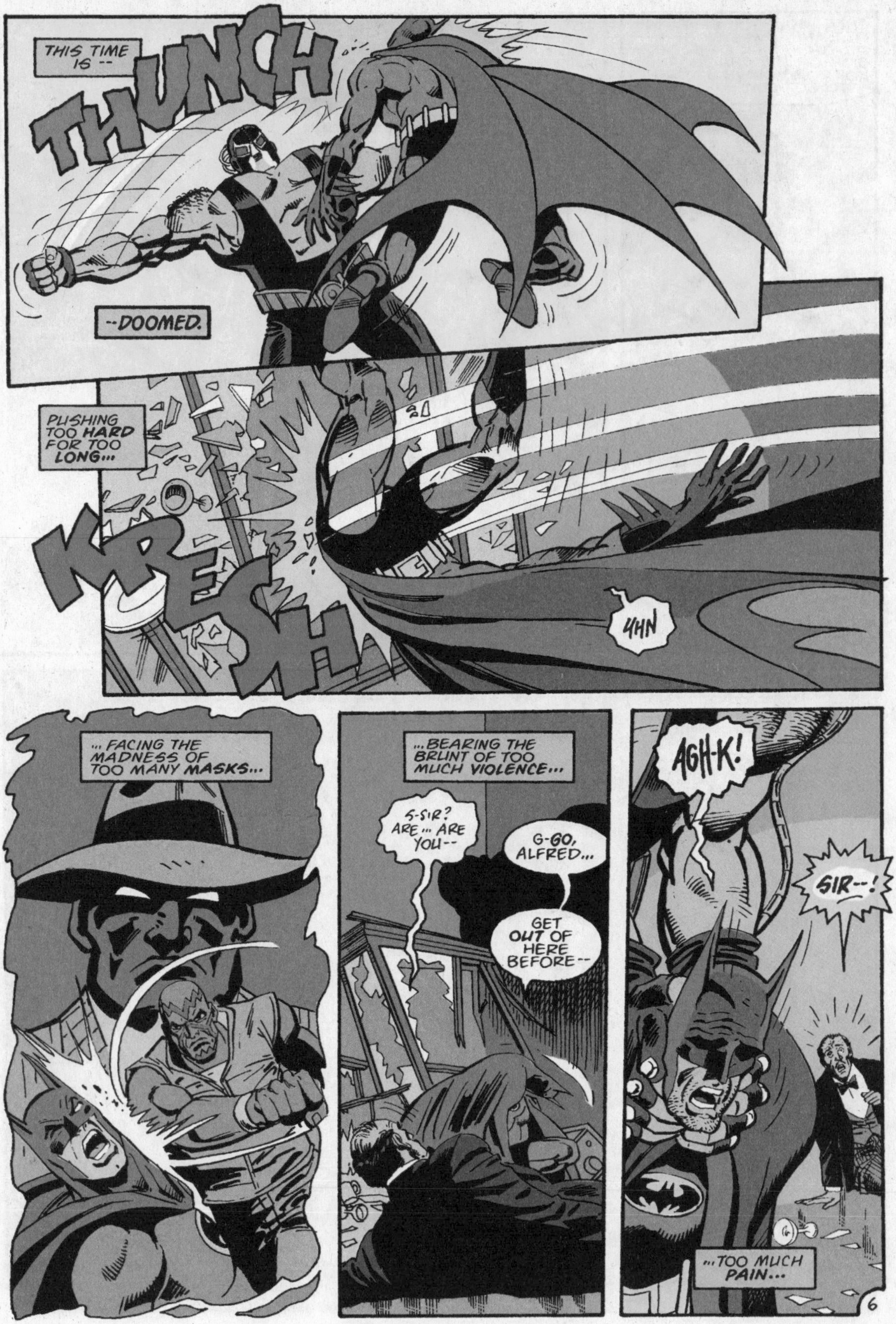
THIS TIME IS --
THUNCH
--DOOMED.
PUSHING TOO HARD FOR TOO LONG...
KRESSH
UHN
...FACING THE MADNESS OF TOO MANY MASKS...
...BEARING THE BRUNT OF TOO MUCH VIOLENCE...
S-SIR? ARE... ARE YOU--
G-GO, ALFRED...
GET OUT OF HERE BEFORE--
AGH-K!
SIR--!
...TOO MUCH PAIN...
6

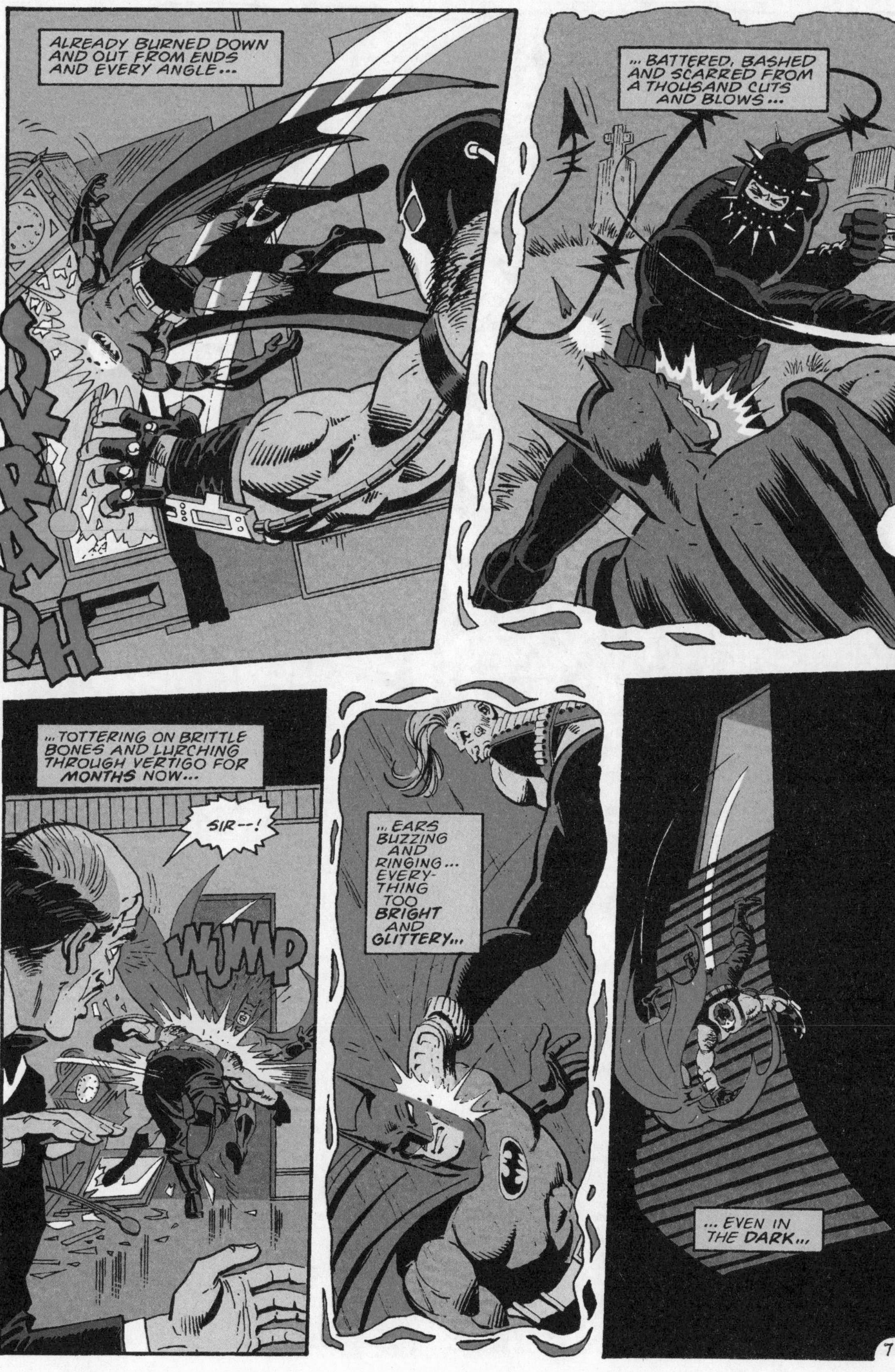
ALREADY BURNED DOWN AND OUT FROM ENDS AND EVERY ANGLE...
SMASH
...BATTERED, BASHED AND SCARRED FROM A THOUSAND CUTS AND BLOWS...
...TOTTERING ON BRITTLE BONES AND LURCHING THROUGH VERTIGO FOR MONTHS NOW...
SIR--!
WUMP
...EARS BUZZING AND RINGING... EVERY-THING TOO BRIGHT AND GLITTERY...
...EVEN IN THE DARK...
7

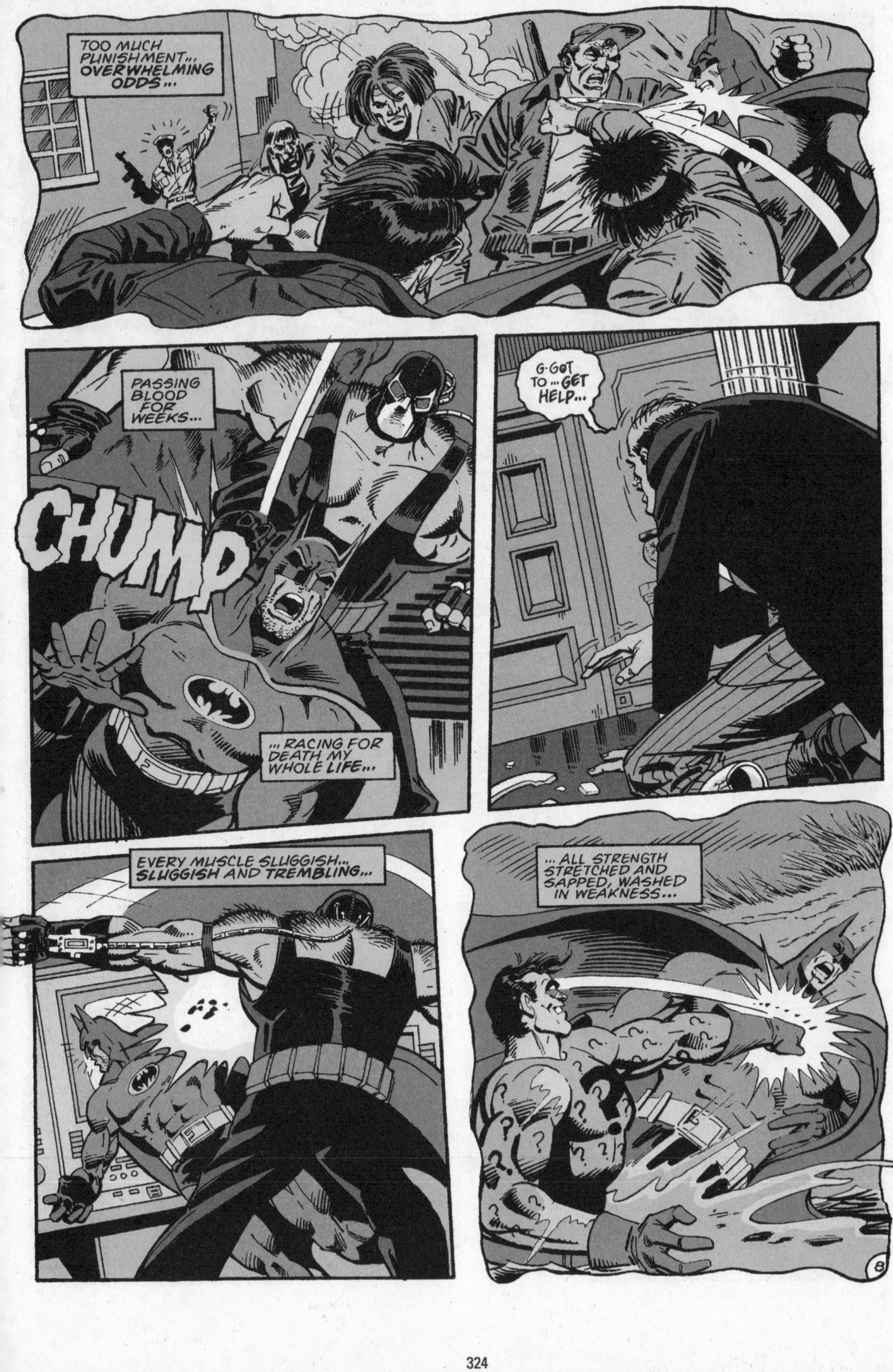
TOO MUCH PUNISHMENT... OVERWHELMING ODDS...
PASSING BLOOD FOR WEEKS...
CHUMP
...RACING FOR DEATH MY WHOLE LIFE...
G-GOT TO... GET HELP...
EVERY MUSCLE SLUGGISH... SLUGGISH AND TREMBLING...
...ALL STRENGTH STRETCHED AND SAPPED, WASHED IN WEAKNESS...
8

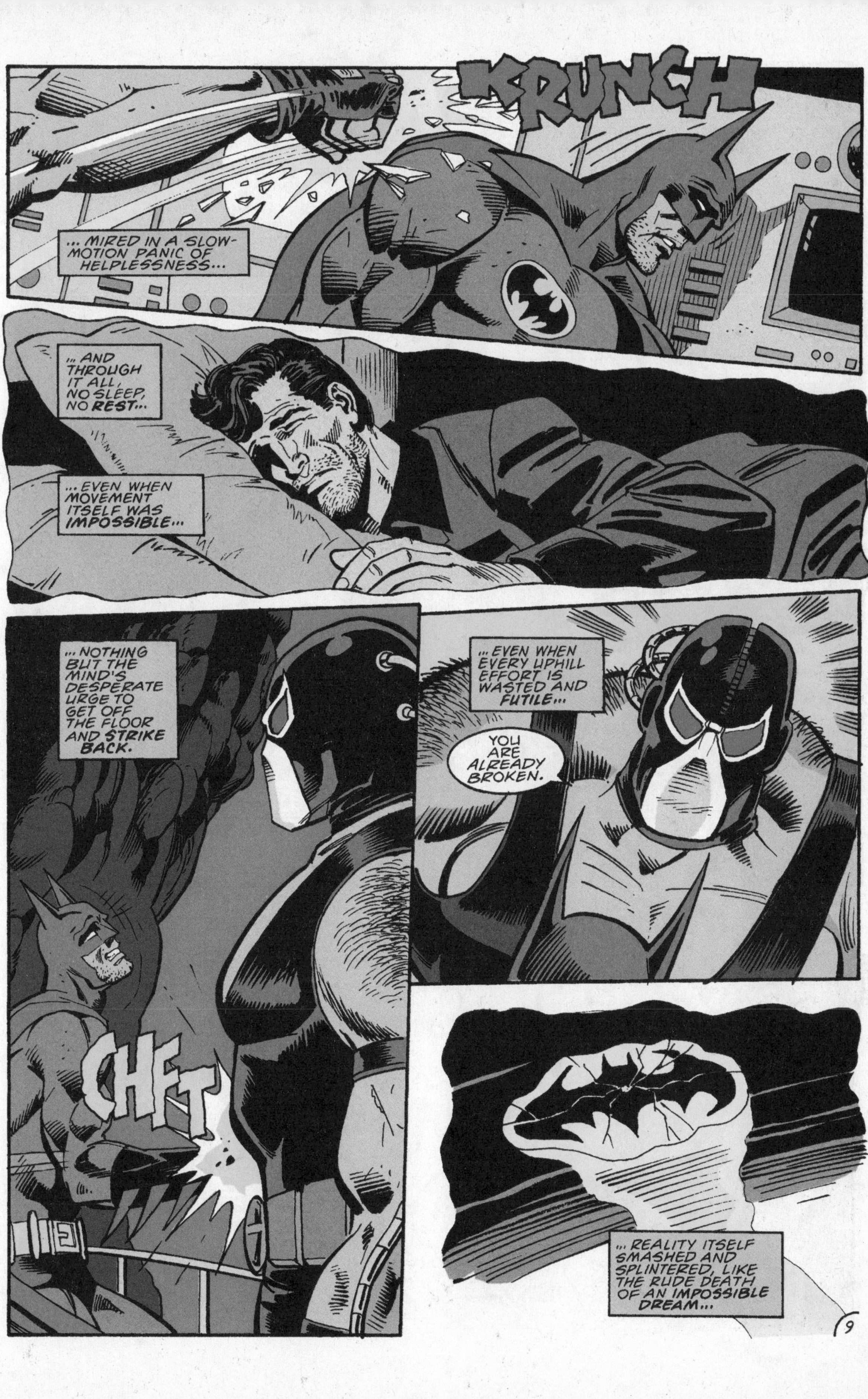
KRUNCH
...MIRED IN A SLOW-MOTION PANIC OF HELPLESSNESS...
...AND THROUGH IT ALL, NO SLEEP, NO REST...
...EVEN WHEN MOVEMENT ITSELF WAS IMPOSSIBLE...
...NOTHING BUT THE MIND'S DESPERATE URGE TO GET OFF THE FLOOR AND STRIKE BACK.
CHFT
...EVEN WHEN EVERY UPHILL EFFORT IS WASTED AND FUTILE...
YOU ARE ALREADY BROKEN.
...REALITY ITSELF SMASHED AND SPLINTERED, LIKE THE RUDE DEATH OF AN IMPOSSIBLE DREAM...
9

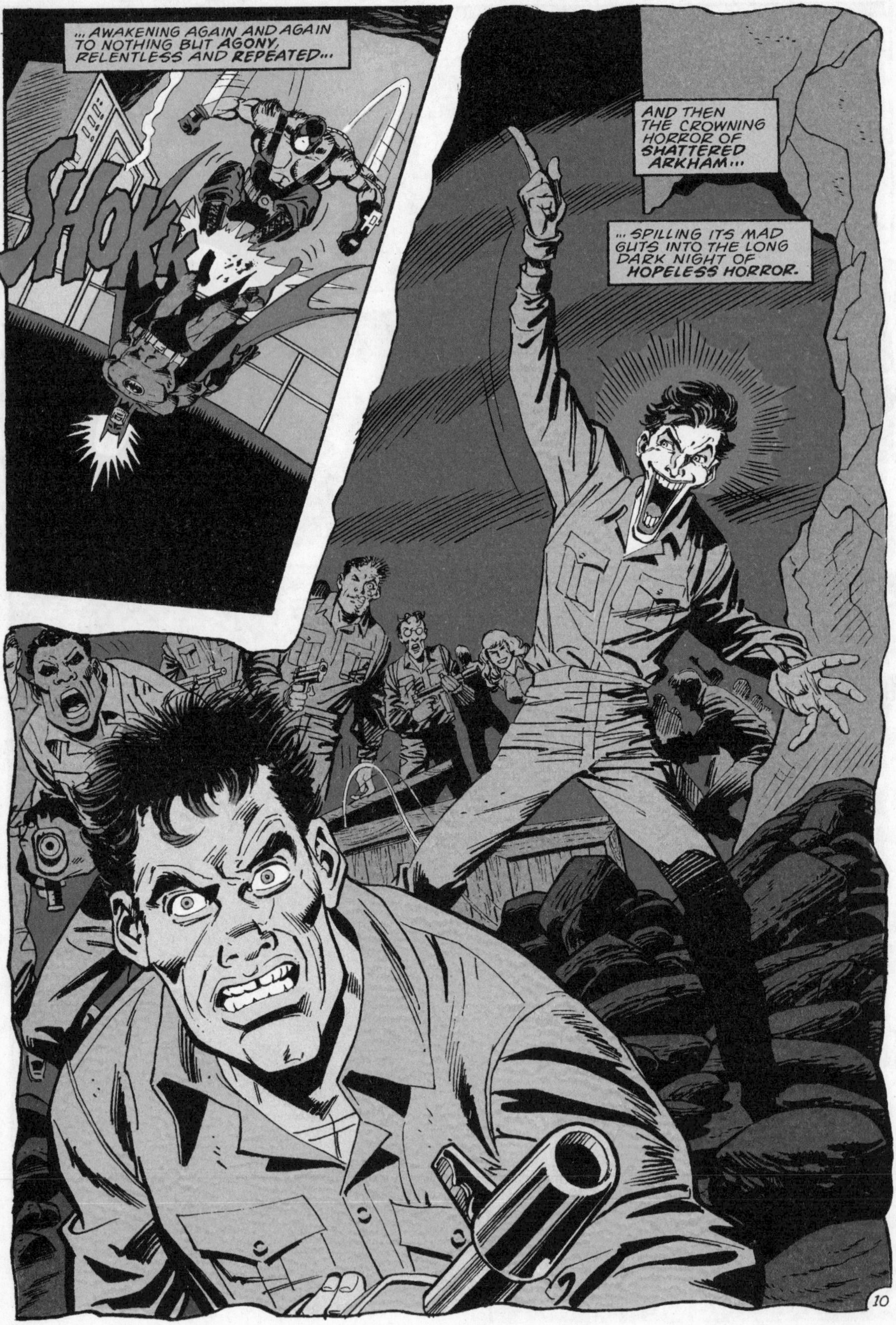
...AWAKENING AGAIN AND AGAIN TO NOTHING BUT AGONY, RELENTLESS AND REPEATED...
SHOKK
AND THEN THE CROWNING HORROR OF SHATTERED ARKHAM...
...SPILLING ITS MAD GUTS INTO THE LONG DARK NIGHT OF HOPELESS HORROR.
10

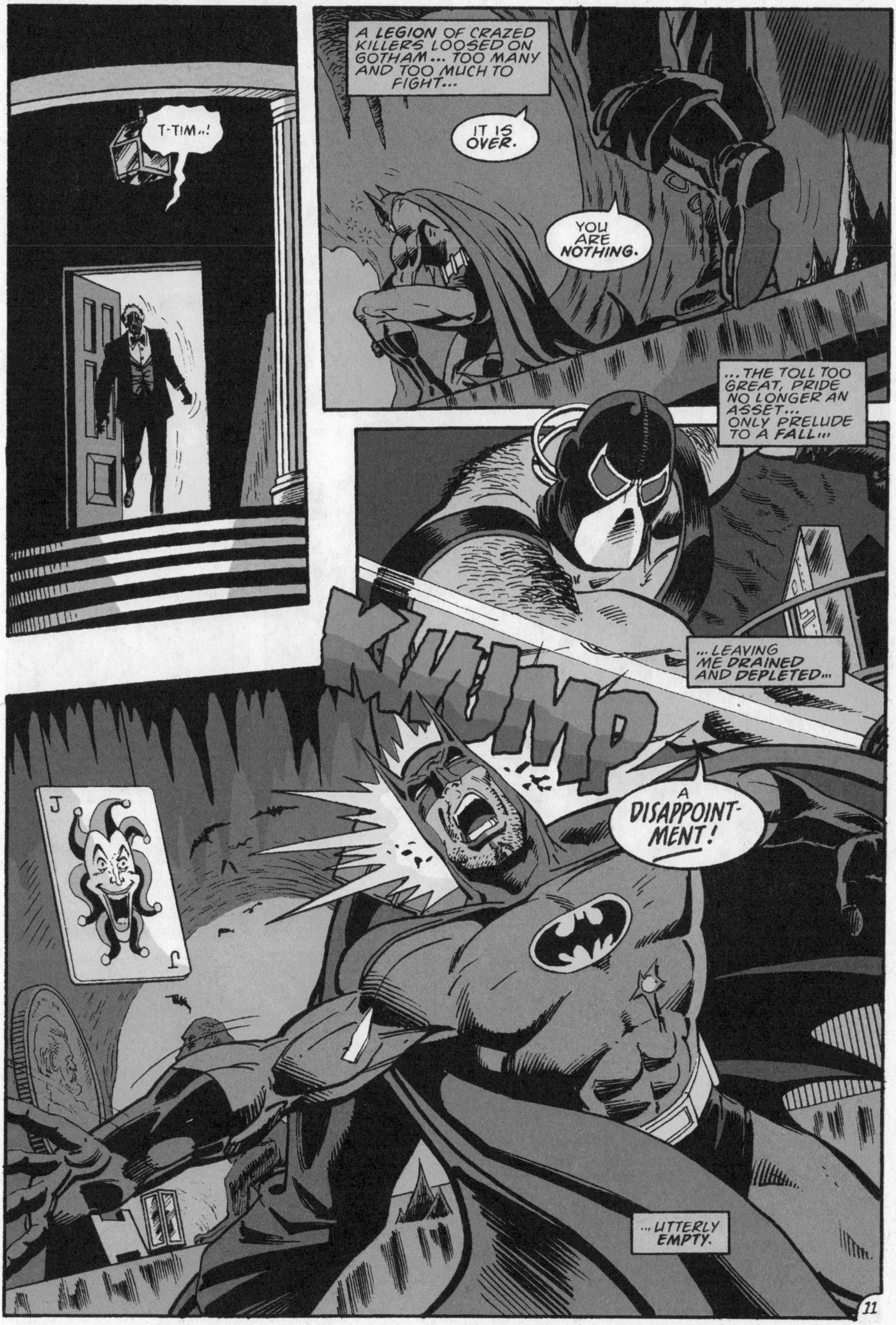
T-TIM..!
A LEGION OF CRAZED KILLERS LOOSED ON GOTHAM... TOO MANY AND TOO MUCH TO FIGHT...
IT IS OVER.
YOU ARE NOTHING.
...THE TOLL TOO GREAT, PRIDE NO LONGER AN ASSET... ONLY PRELUDE TO A FALL...
KWUMP
...LEAVING ME DRAINED AND DEPLETED...
A DISAPPOINTMENT!
...UTTERLY EMPTY.
11

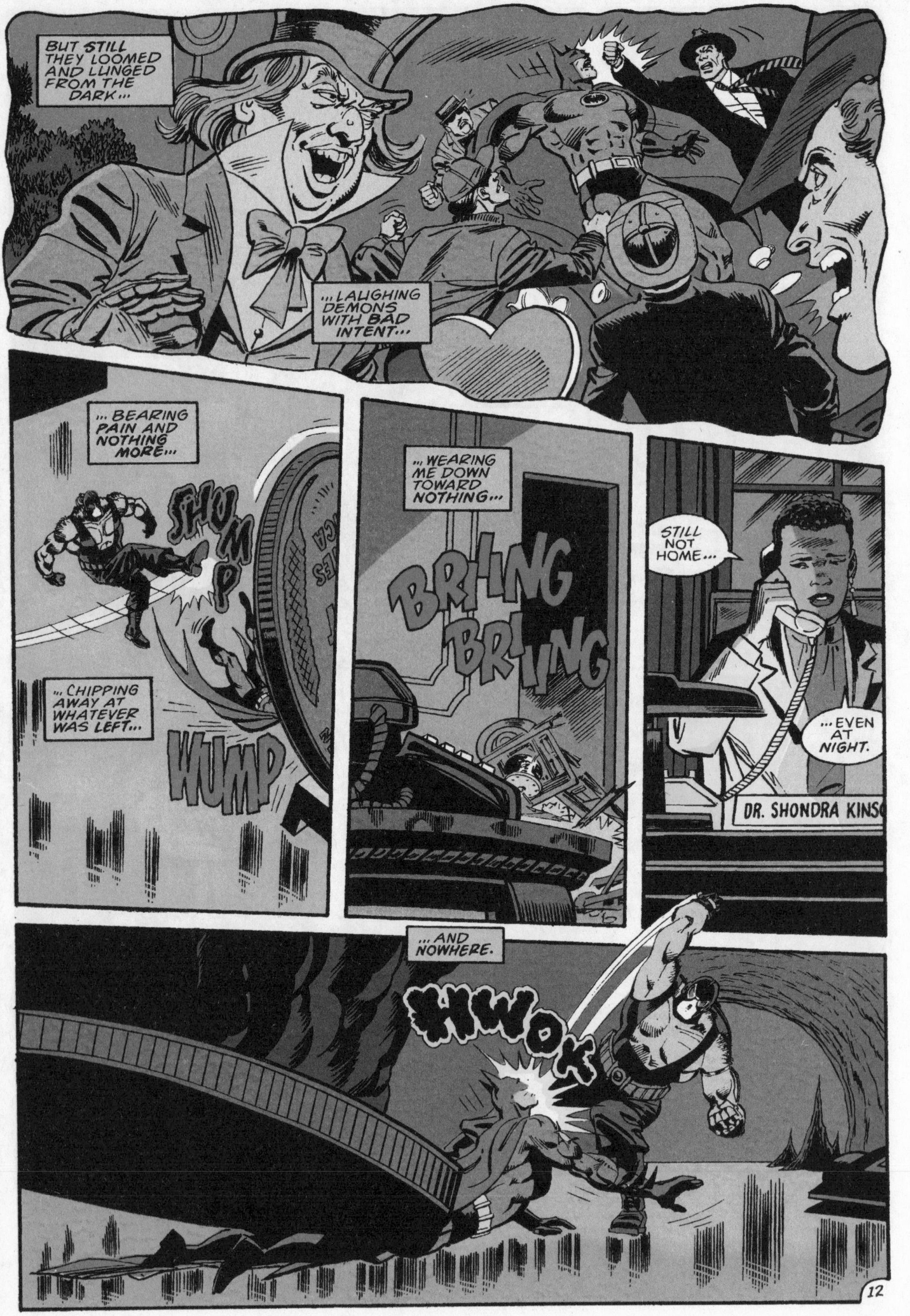
BUT STILL THEY LOOMED AND LUNGED FROM THE DARK...
...LAUGHING DEMONS WITH BAD INTENT...
...BEARING PAIN AND NOTHING MORE...
SHUMP
...CHIPPING AWAY AT WHATEVER WAS LEFT...
WUMP
...WEARING ME DOWN TOWARD NOTHING...
BRIIING
BRIIING
STILL NOT HOME...
...EVEN AT NIGHT.
DR. SHONDRA KINSO
...AND NOWHERE.
KWOK
12

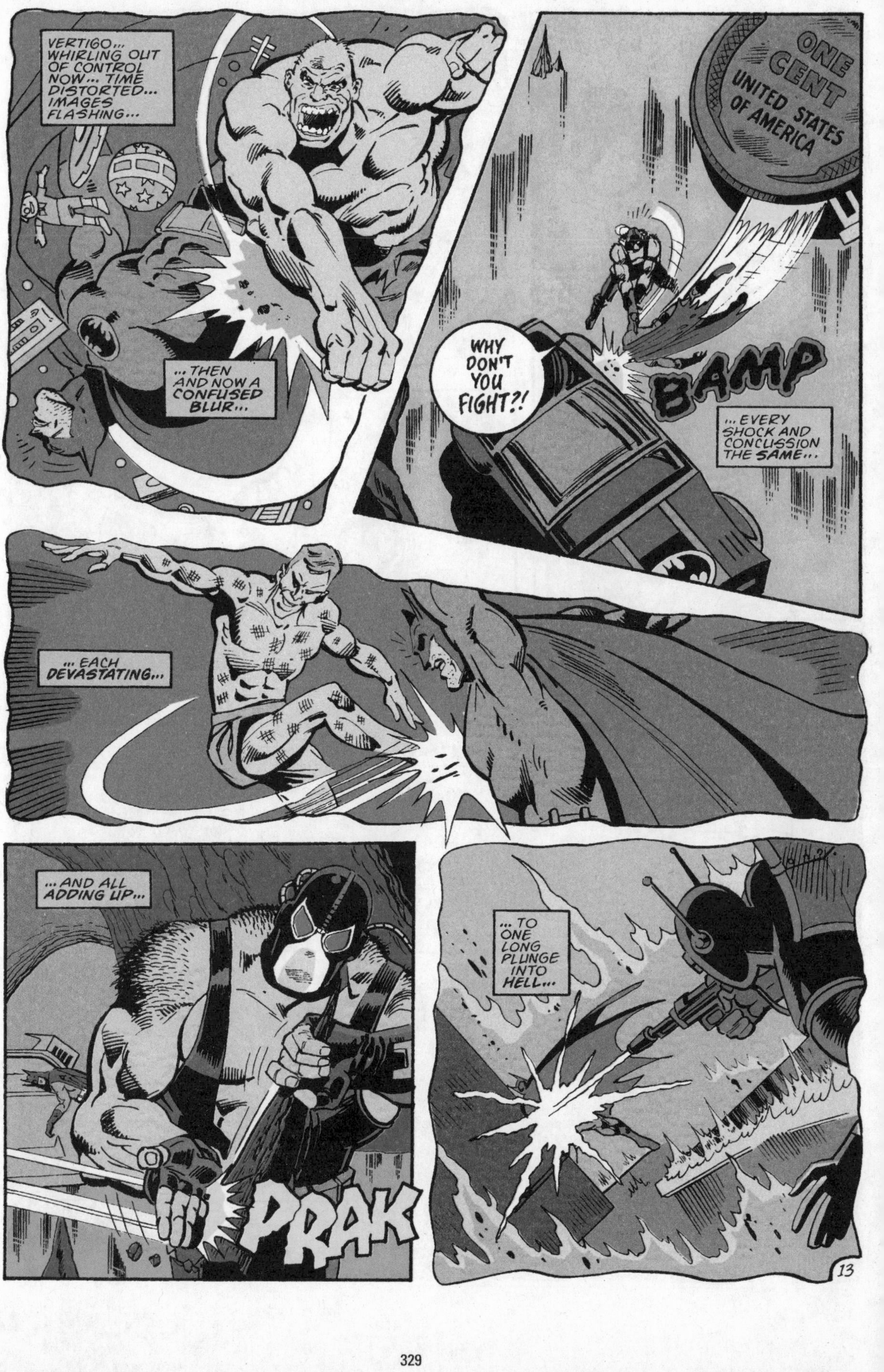
VERTIGO... WHIRLING OUT OF CONTROL NOW... TIME DISTORTED... IMAGES FLASHING...
...THEN AND NOW A CONFUSED BLUR...
ONE CENT
UNITED STATES OF AMERICA
WHY DON'T YOU FIGHT?!
BAMP
...EVERY SHOCK AND CONCUSSION THE SAME...
...EACH DEVASTATING...
...AND ALL ADDING UP...
PRAK
...TO ONE LONG PLUNGE INTO HELL...
13

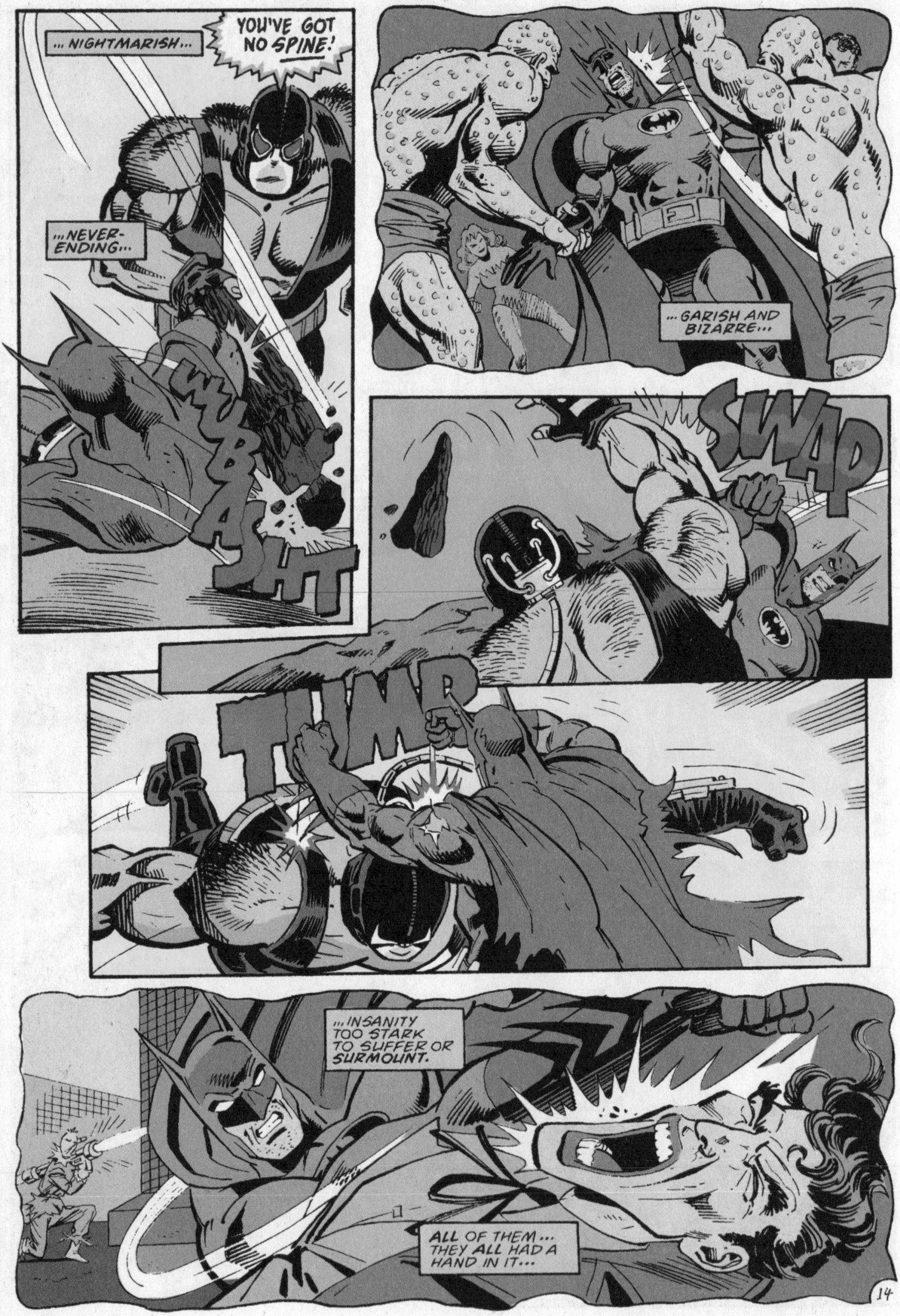

...NIGHTMARISH...
YOU'VE GOT NO SPINE!
...NEVER-ENDING...
WUBBASHT
...GARISH AND BIZARRE...
SWAP
THMP
...INSANITY TOO STARK TO SUFFER OR SURMOUNT.
ALL OF THEM... THEY ALL HAD A HAND IN IT...
14

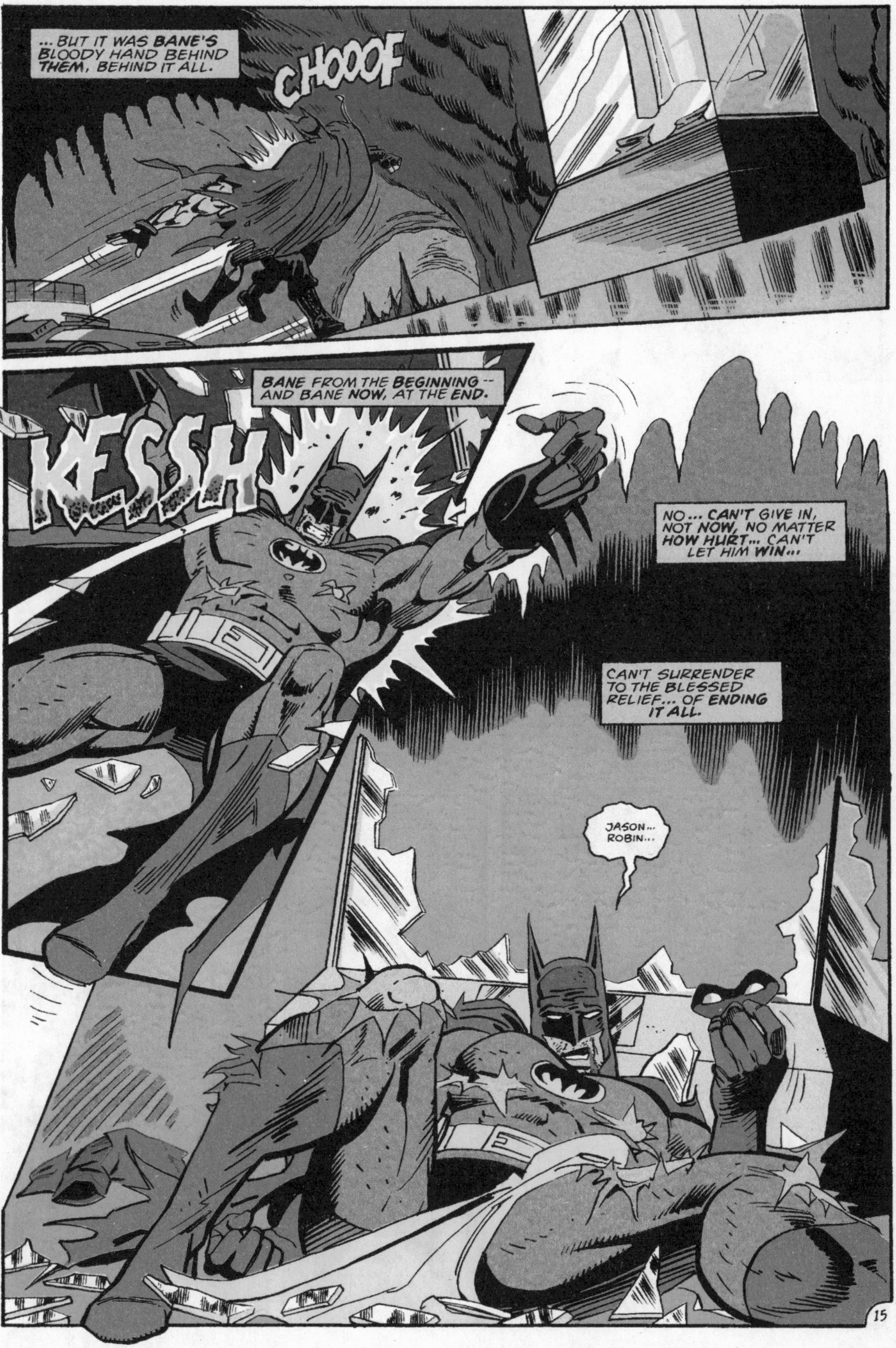
...BUT IT WAS BANE'S BLOODY HAND BEHIND THEM, BEHIND IT ALL.
CHOOOF
BANE FROM THE BEGINNING -- AND BANE NOW, AT THE END.
KESSH
NO... CAN'T GIVE IN, NOT NOW, NO MATTER HOW HURT... CAN'T LET HIM WIN...
CAN'T SURRENDER TO THE BLESSED RELIEF... OF ENDING IT ALL.
JASON... ROBIN...
15

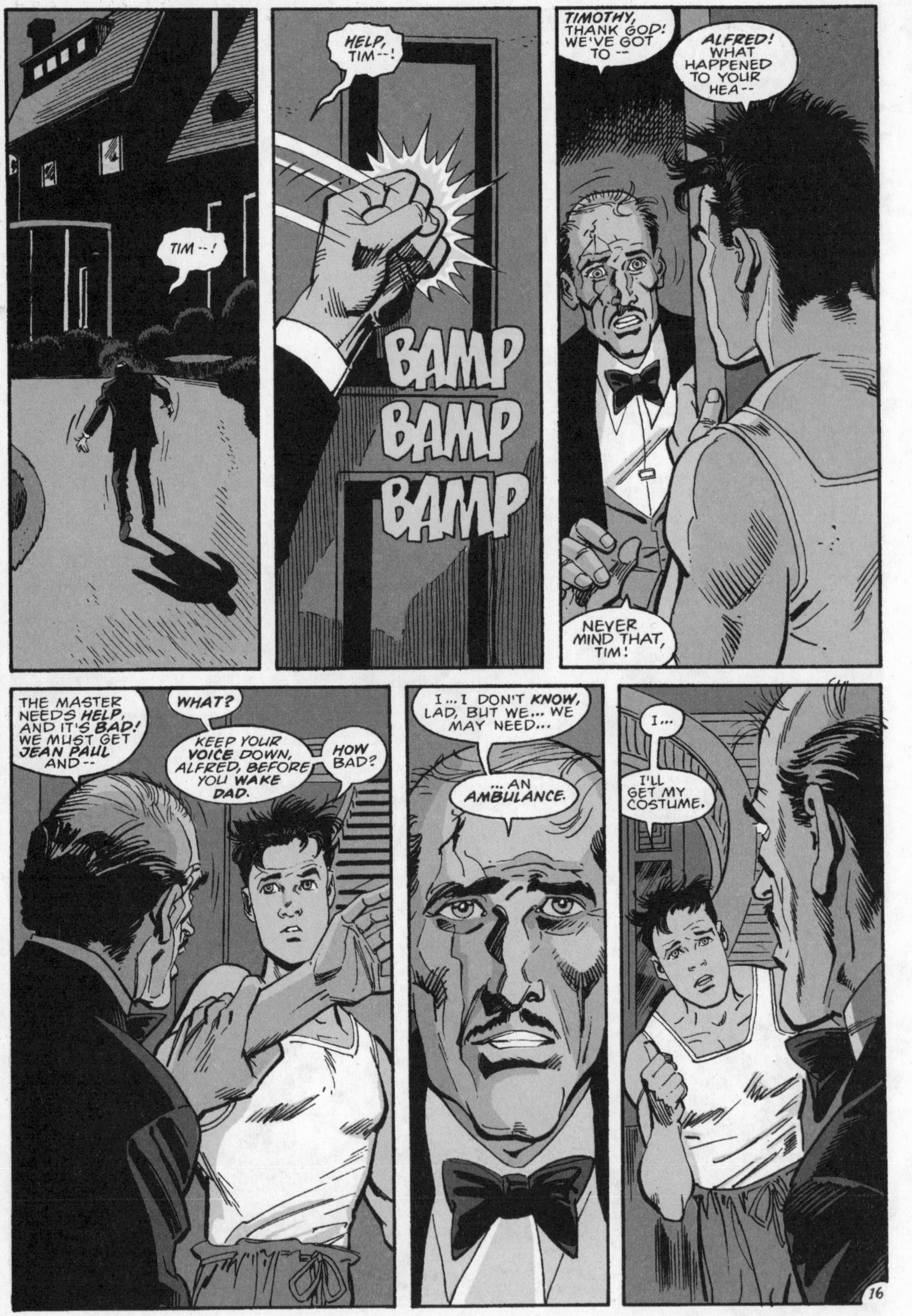
TIM--!
HELP, TIM--!
BAMP
BAMP
BAMP
TIMOTHY, THANK GOD! WE'VE GOT TO--
ALFRED! WHAT HAPPENED TO YOUR HEA--
NEVER MIND THAT, TIM!
THE MASTER NEEDS HELP, AND IT'S BAD! WE MUST GET JEAN PAUL AND--
WHAT?
KEEP YOUR VOICE DOWN, ALFRED, BEFORE YOU WAKE DAD.
HOW BAD?
I... I DON'T KNOW, LAD, BUT WE... WE MAY NEED...
...AN AMBULANCE.
I...
I'LL GET MY COSTUME.
16

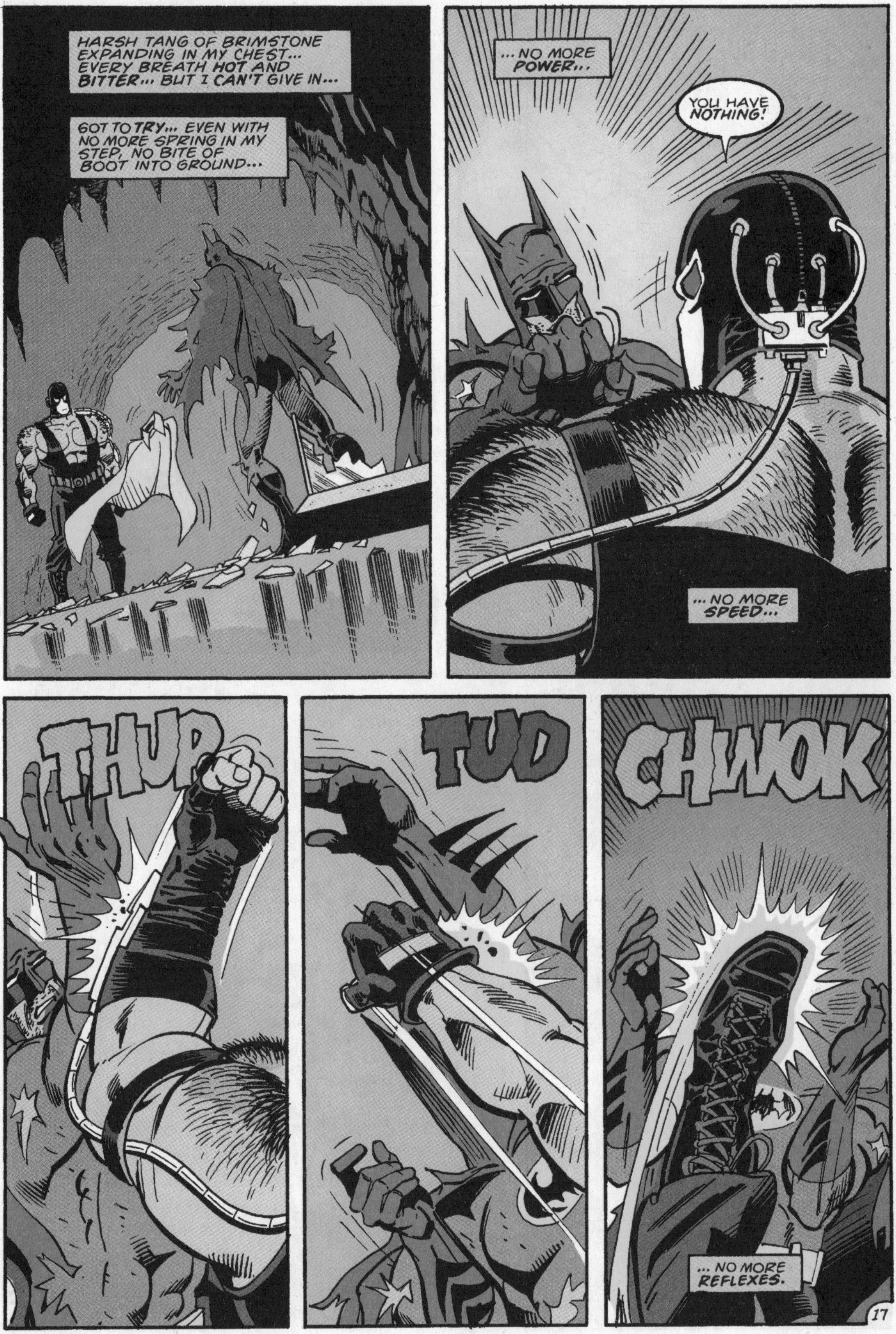
HARSH TANG OF BRIMSTONE EXPANDING IN MY CHEST... EVERY BREATH HOT AND BITTER... BUT I CAN'T GIVE IN...
GOT TO TRY... EVEN WITH NO MORE SPRING IN MY STEP, NO BITE OF BOOT INTO GROUND...
...NO MORE POWER...
YOU HAVE NOTHING!
...NO MORE SPEED...
THUP
TUD
CHWOK
...NO MORE REFLEXES.
17

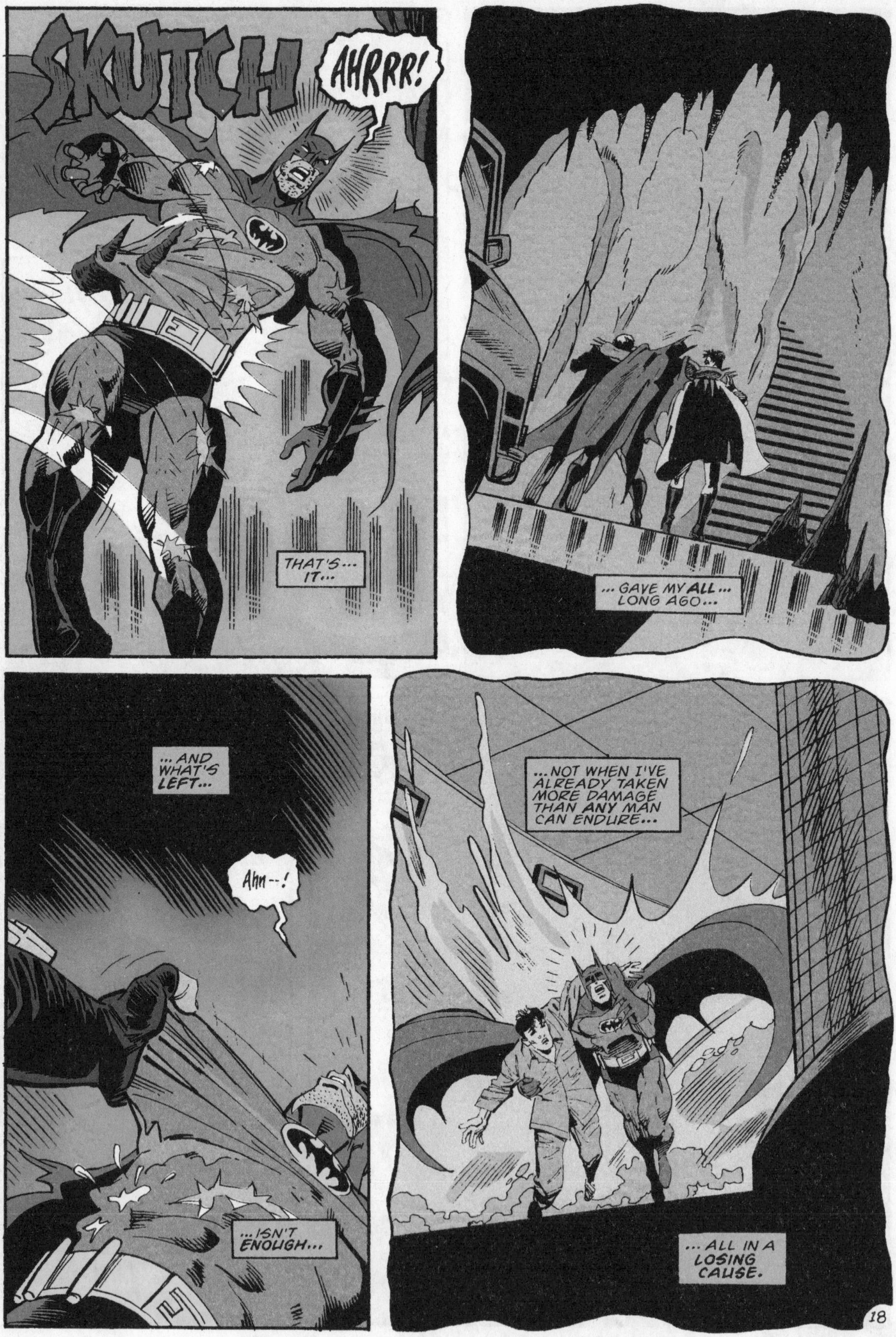
SKUTCH
AHRRR!
THAT'S... IT...
...GAVE MY ALL... LONG AGO...
...AND WHAT'S LEFT...
Ahn--!
...ISN'T ENOUGH...
...NOT WHEN I'VE ALREADY TAKEN MORE DAMAGE THAN ANY MAN CAN ENDURE...
...ALL IN A LOSING CAUSE.
18

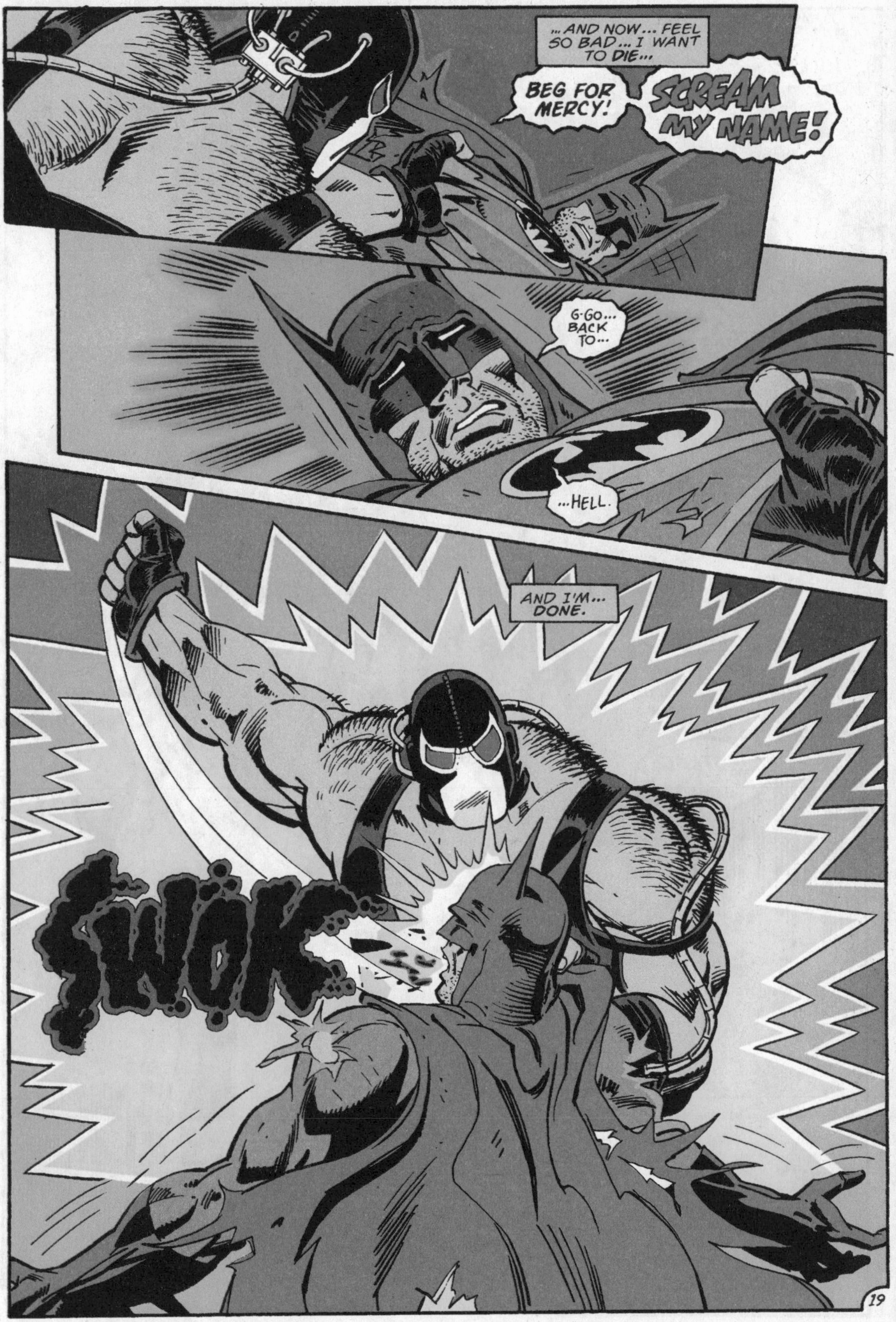
...AND NOW... FEEL SO BAD... I WANT TO DIE...
BEG FOR MERCY!
SCREAM MY NAME!
G-GO... BACK TO...
...HELL.
AND I'M... DONE.
SWOK
19

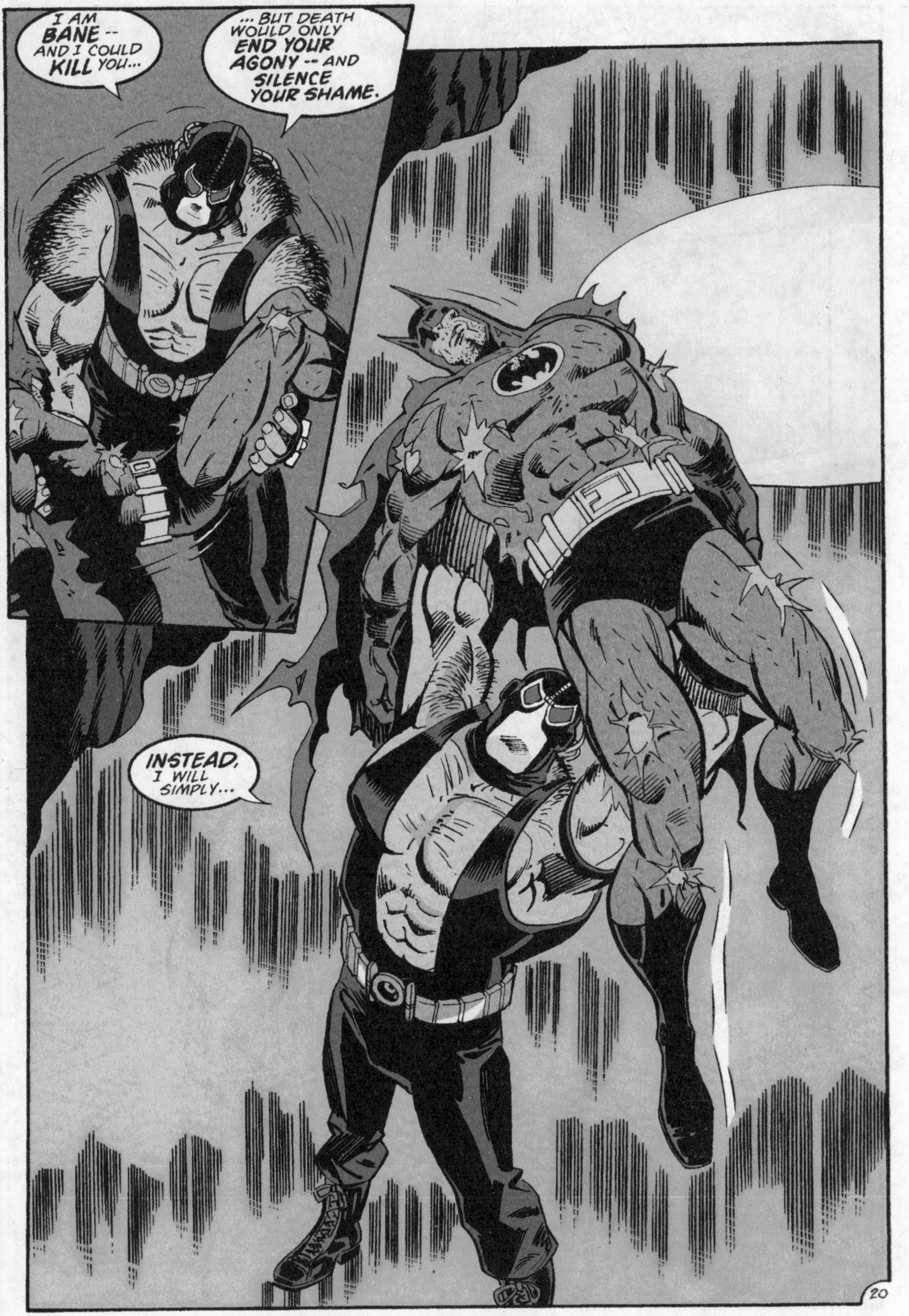
I AM BANE -- AND I COULD KILL YOU...
... BUT DEATH WOULD ONLY END YOUR AGONY -- AND SILENCE YOUR SHAME.
INSTEAD, I WILL SIMPLY...
20

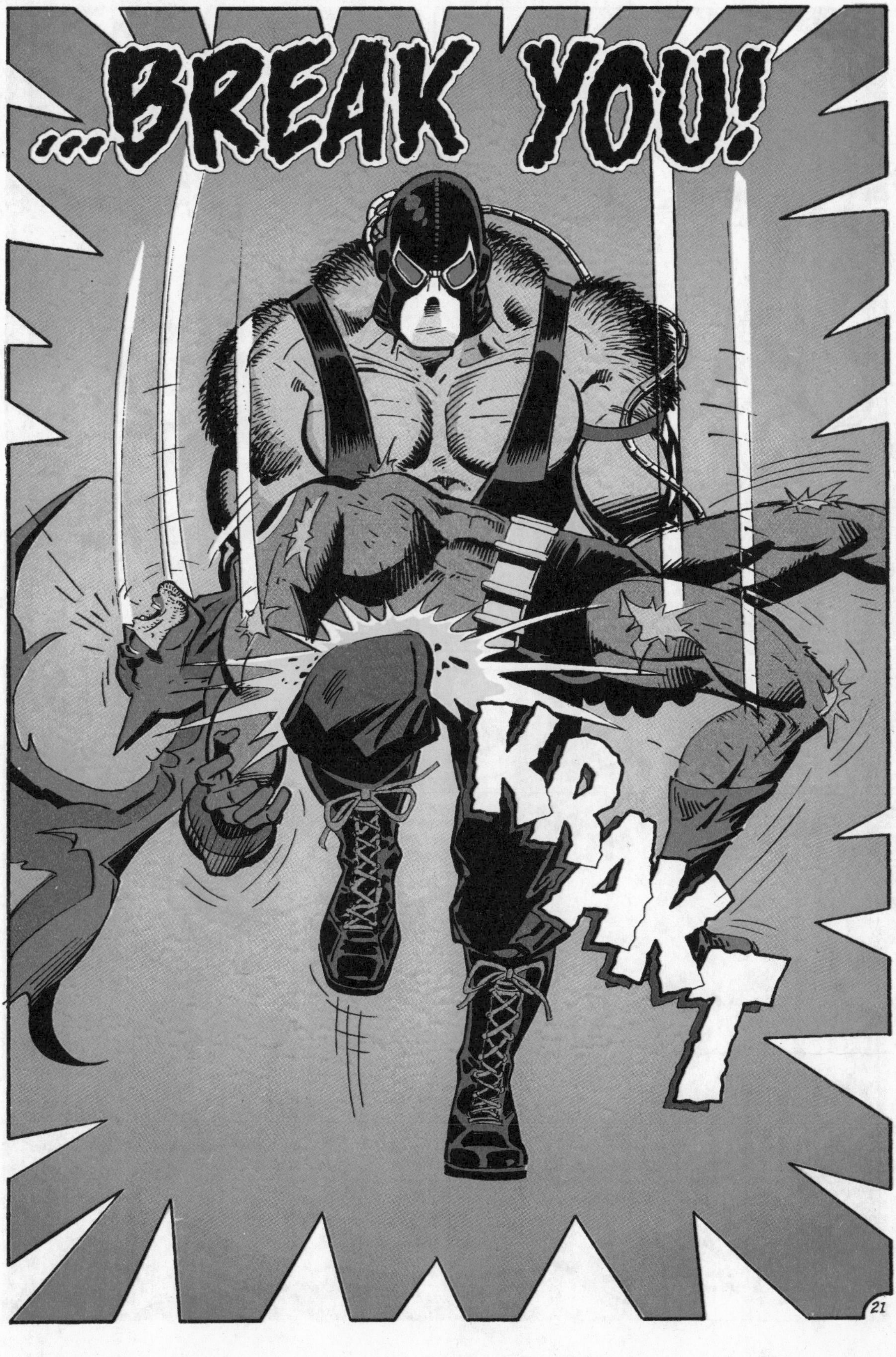
...BREAK YOU!
KRAKT
21

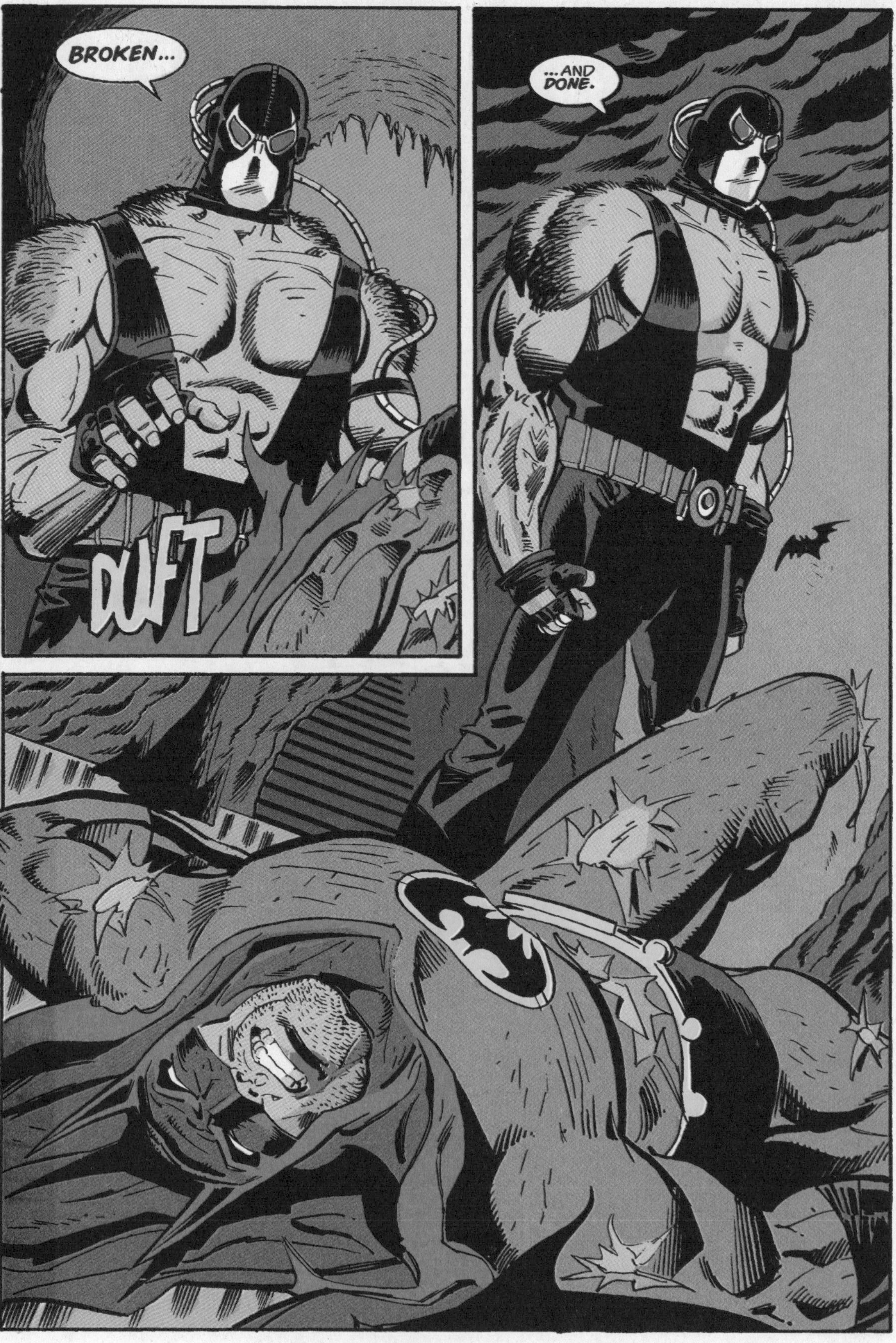
BROKEN...
DUFT
...AND DONE.

Cover art by **KELLEY JONES**

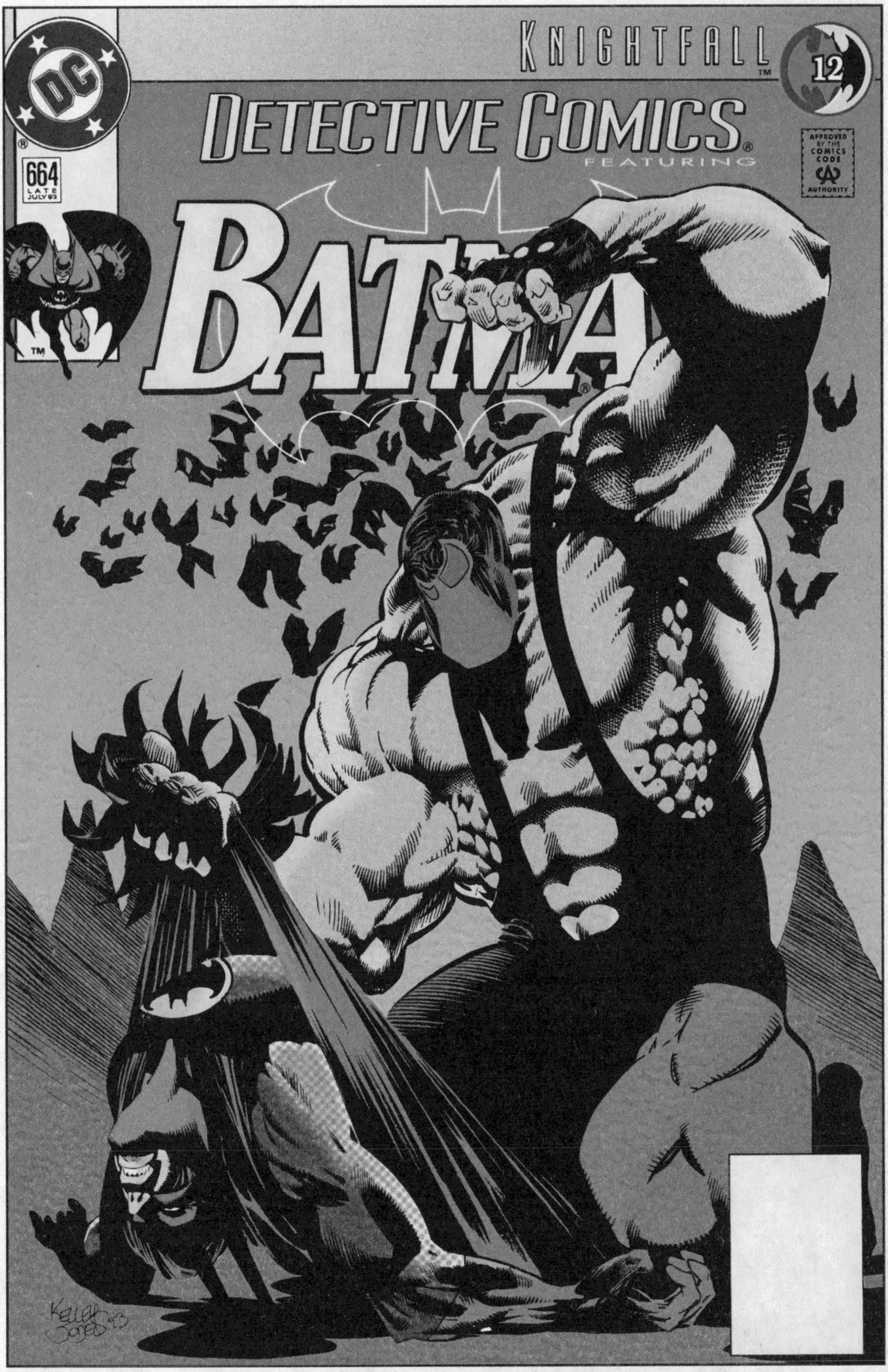
KNIGHTFALL
12
DETECTIVE COMICS
FEATURING
BATMAN
DC
664
LATE JULY 93
APPROVED BY THE COMICS CODE AUTHORITY
KELLEY JONES '93

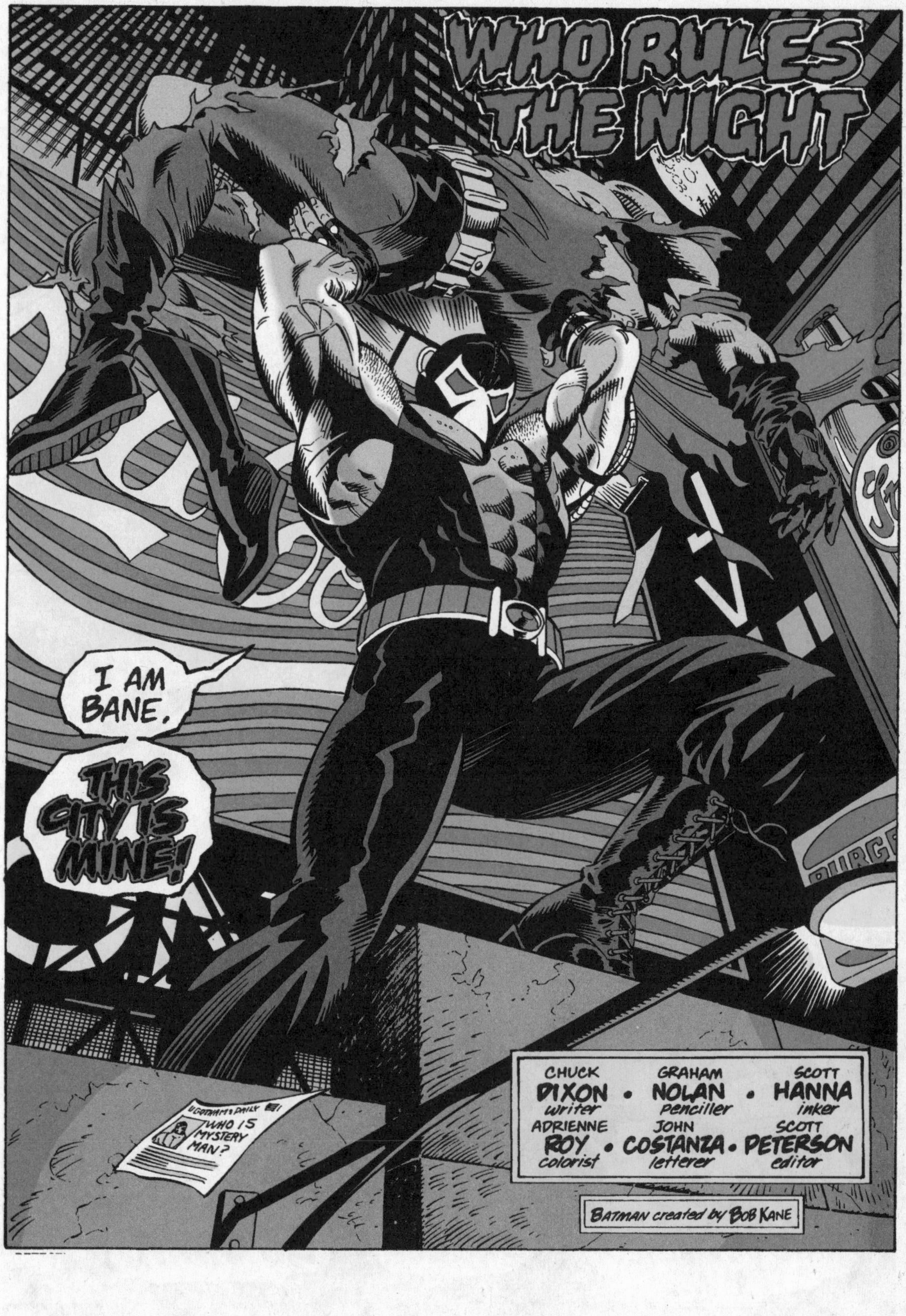
WHO RULES THE NIGHT
I AM BANE.
THIS CITY IS MINE!
GOTHAM DAILY
WHO IS MYSTERY MAN?
CHUCK DIXON writer • GRAHAM NOLAN penciller • SCOTT HANNA inker
ADRIENNE ROY colorist • JOHN COSTANZA letterer • SCOTT PETERSON editor
BATMAN created by BOB KANE

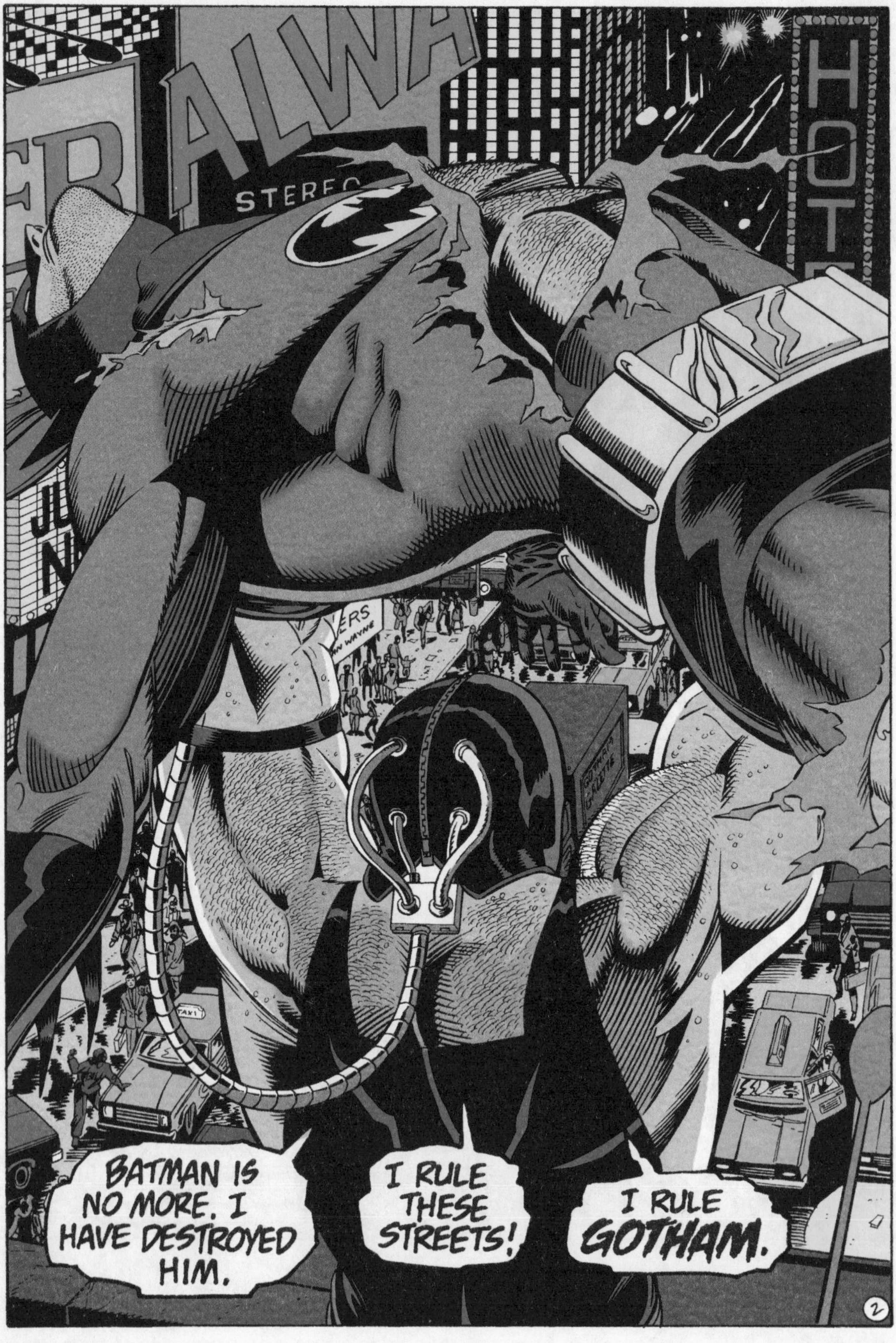
ALWA
STEREO
HOT
BATMAN IS NO MORE. I HAVE DESTROYED HIM.
I RULE THESE STREETS!
I RULE GOTHAM.
2

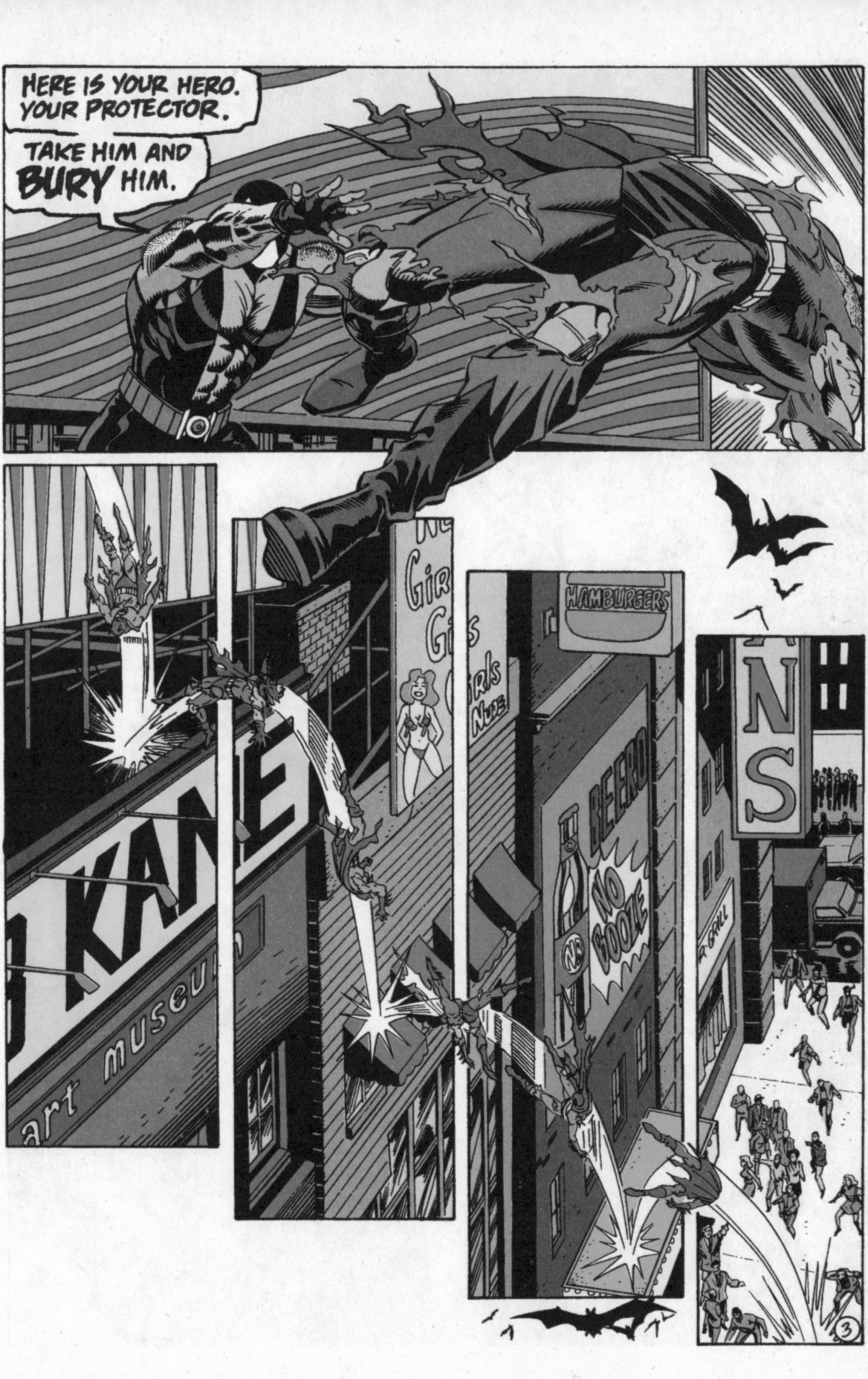
HERE IS YOUR HERO. YOUR PROTECTOR.
TAKE HIM AND BURY HIM.
HAMBURGERS
Girls Nude
BEER
NO BOOZE
KANE
art museu
3

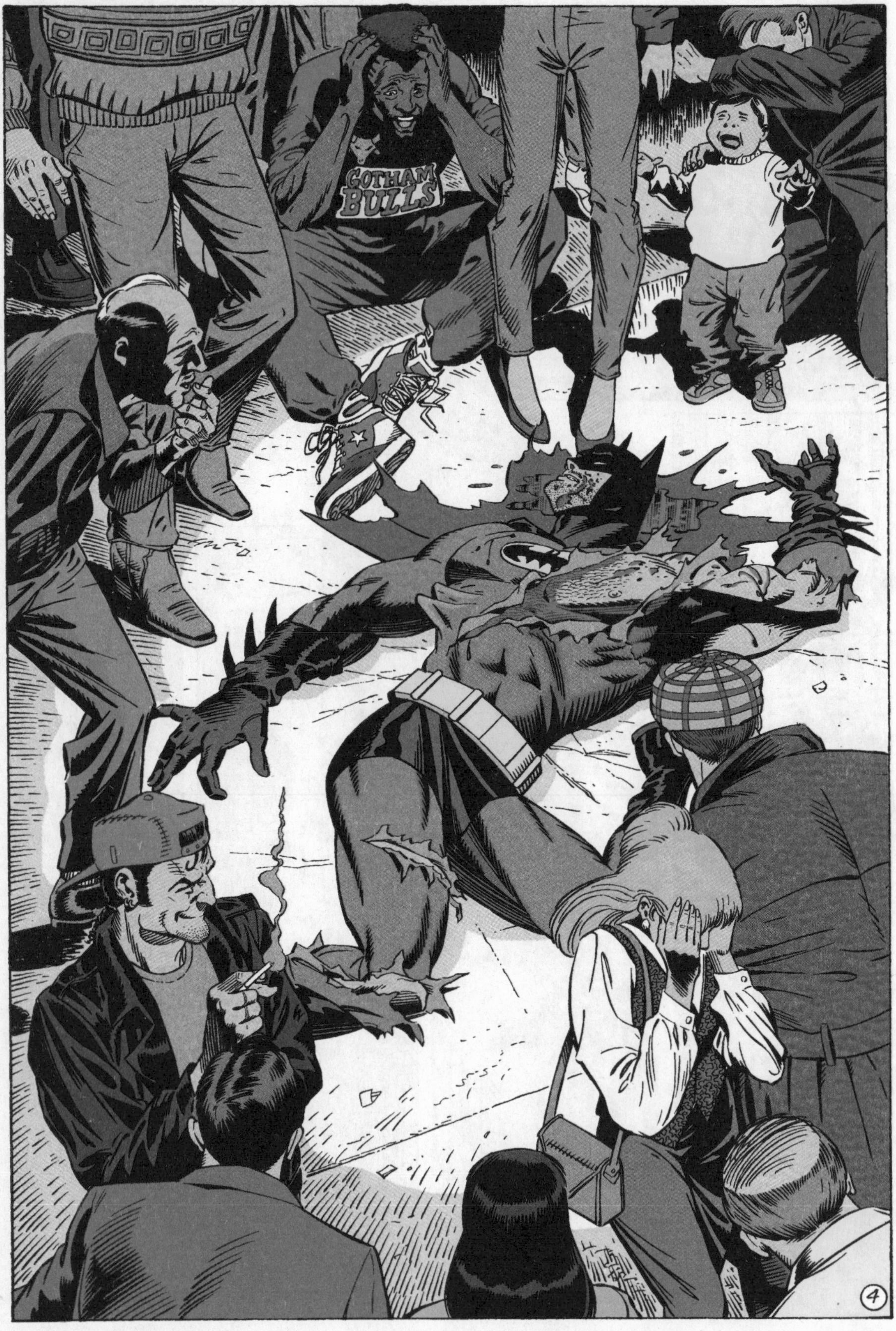
GOTHAM BULLS
4

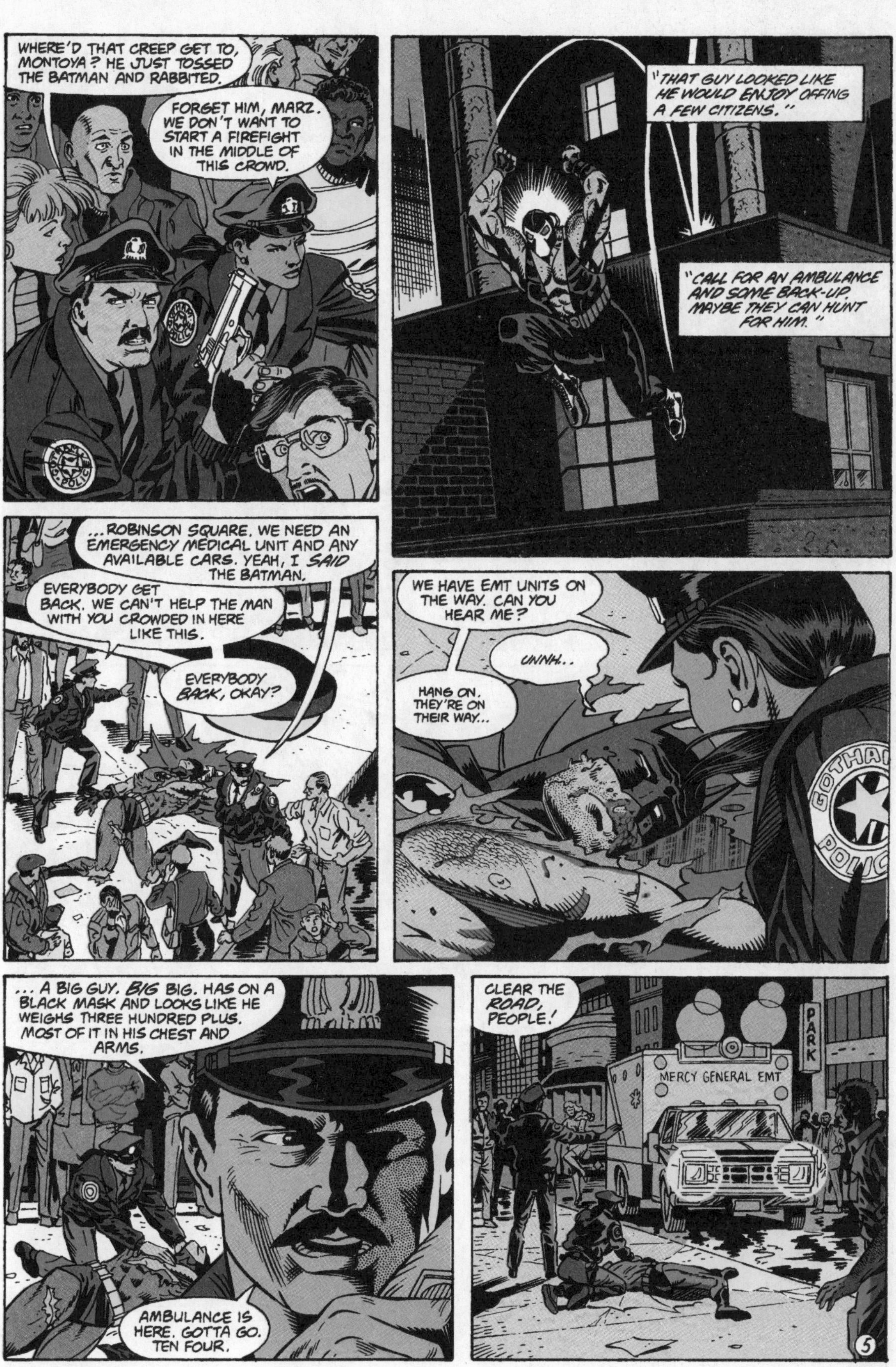
WHERE'D THAT CREEP GET TO, MONTOYA? HE JUST TOSSED THE BATMAN AND RABBITED.
FORGET HIM, MARZ. WE DON'T WANT TO START A FIREFIGHT IN THE MIDDLE OF THIS CROWD.
"THAT GUY LOOKED LIKE HE WOULD ENJOY OFFING A FEW CITIZENS."
"CALL FOR AN AMBULANCE AND SOME BACK-UP. MAYBE THEY CAN HUNT FOR HIM."
...ROBINSON SQUARE. WE NEED AN EMERGENCY MEDICAL UNIT AND ANY AVAILABLE CARS. YEAH, I SAID THE BATMAN.
EVERYBODY GET BACK. WE CAN'T HELP THE MAN WITH YOU CROWDED IN HERE LIKE THIS.
EVERYBODY BACK, OKAY?
WE HAVE EMT UNITS ON THE WAY. CAN YOU HEAR ME?
UNNH..
HANG ON. THEY'RE ON THEIR WAY...
GOTHAM POLICE
... A BIG GUY. BIG BIG. HAS ON A BLACK MASK AND LOOKS LIKE HE WEIGHS THREE HUNDRED PLUS. MOST OF IT IN HIS CHEST AND ARMS.
AMBULANCE IS HERE. GOTTA GO. TEN FOUR.
CLEAR THE ROAD, PEOPLE!
PARK
MERCY GENERAL EMT
5

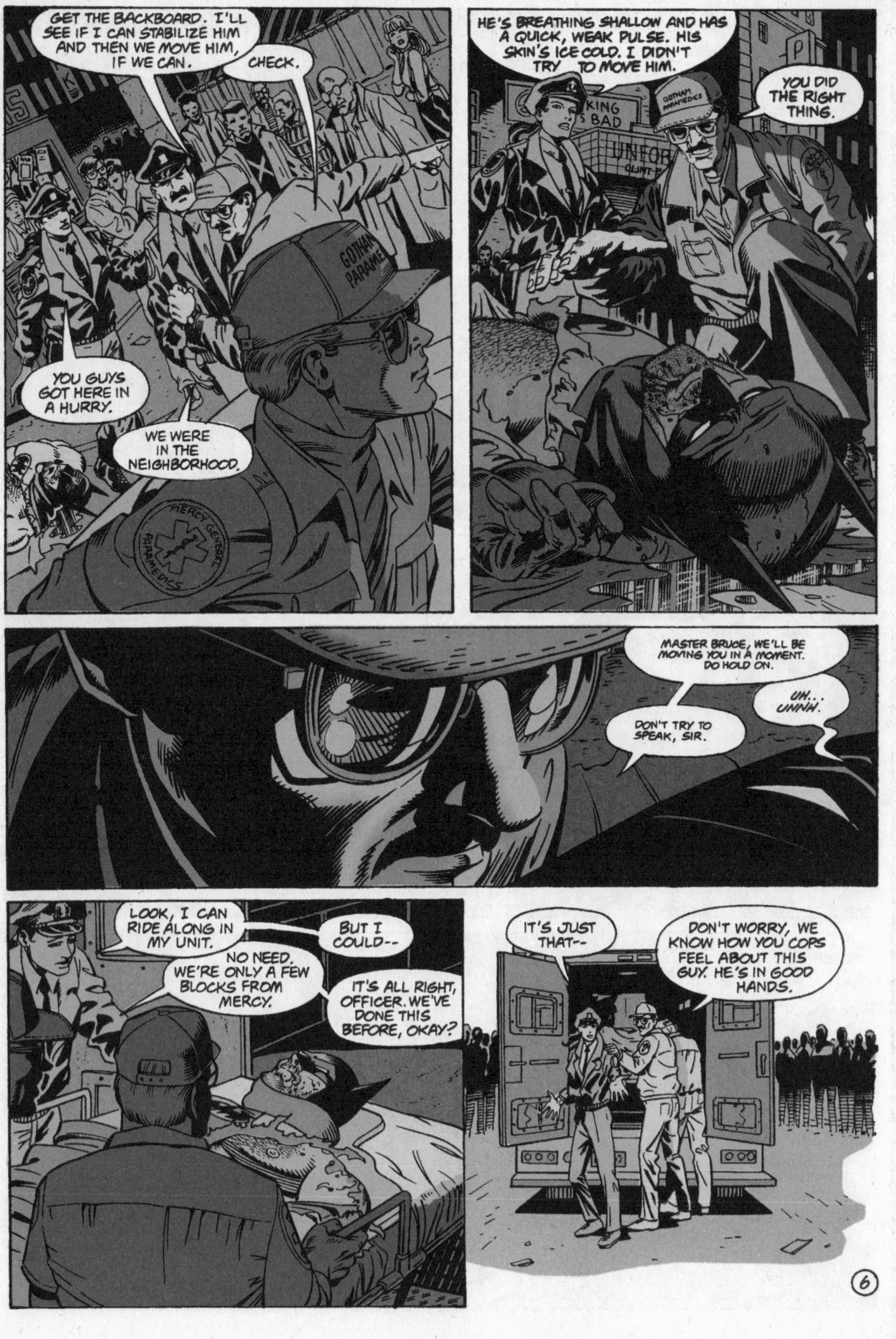
GET THE BACKBOARD. I'LL SEE IF I CAN STABILIZE HIM AND THEN WE MOVE HIM, IF WE CAN.
CHECK.
YOU GUYS GOT HERE IN A HURRY.
WE WERE IN THE NEIGHBORHOOD.
GOTHAM PARAME
MERCY GENERAL PARAMEDICS
HE'S BREATHING SHALLOW AND HAS A QUICK, WEAK PULSE. HIS SKIN'S ICE COLD. I DIDN'T TRY TO MOVE HIM.
YOU DID THE RIGHT THING.
GOTHAM PARAMEDICS
MASTER BRUCE, WE'LL BE MOVING YOU IN A MOMENT. DO HOLD ON.
UH... UNNH.
DON'T TRY TO SPEAK, SIR.
LOOK, I CAN RIDE ALONG IN MY UNIT.
BUT I COULD--
NO NEED. WE'RE ONLY A FEW BLOCKS FROM MERCY.
IT'S ALL RIGHT, OFFICER. WE'VE DONE THIS BEFORE, OKAY?
IT'S JUST THAT--
DON'T WORRY, WE KNOW HOW YOU COPS FEEL ABOUT THIS GUY. HE'S IN GOOD HANDS.
6

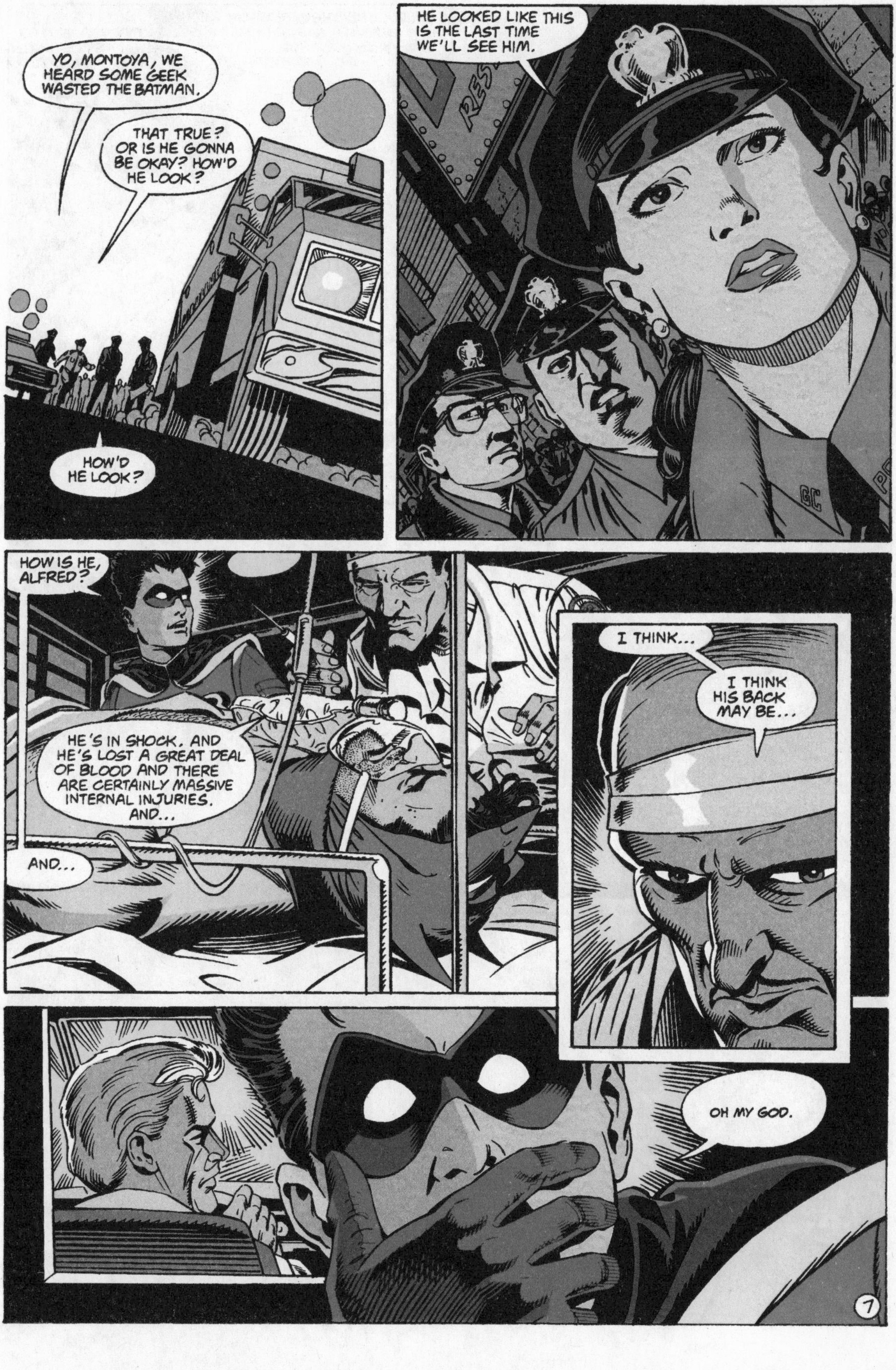
YO, MONTOYA, WE HEARD SOME GEEK WASTED THE BATMAN.
THAT TRUE? OR IS HE GONNA BE OKAY? HOW'D HE LOOK?
HOW'D HE LOOK?
HE LOOKED LIKE THIS IS THE LAST TIME WE'LL SEE HIM.
HOW IS HE, ALFRED?
HE'S IN SHOCK. AND HE'S LOST A GREAT DEAL OF BLOOD AND THERE ARE CERTAINLY MASSIVE INTERNAL INJURIES. AND...
AND...
I THINK...
I THINK HIS BACK MAY BE...
OH MY GOD.
7

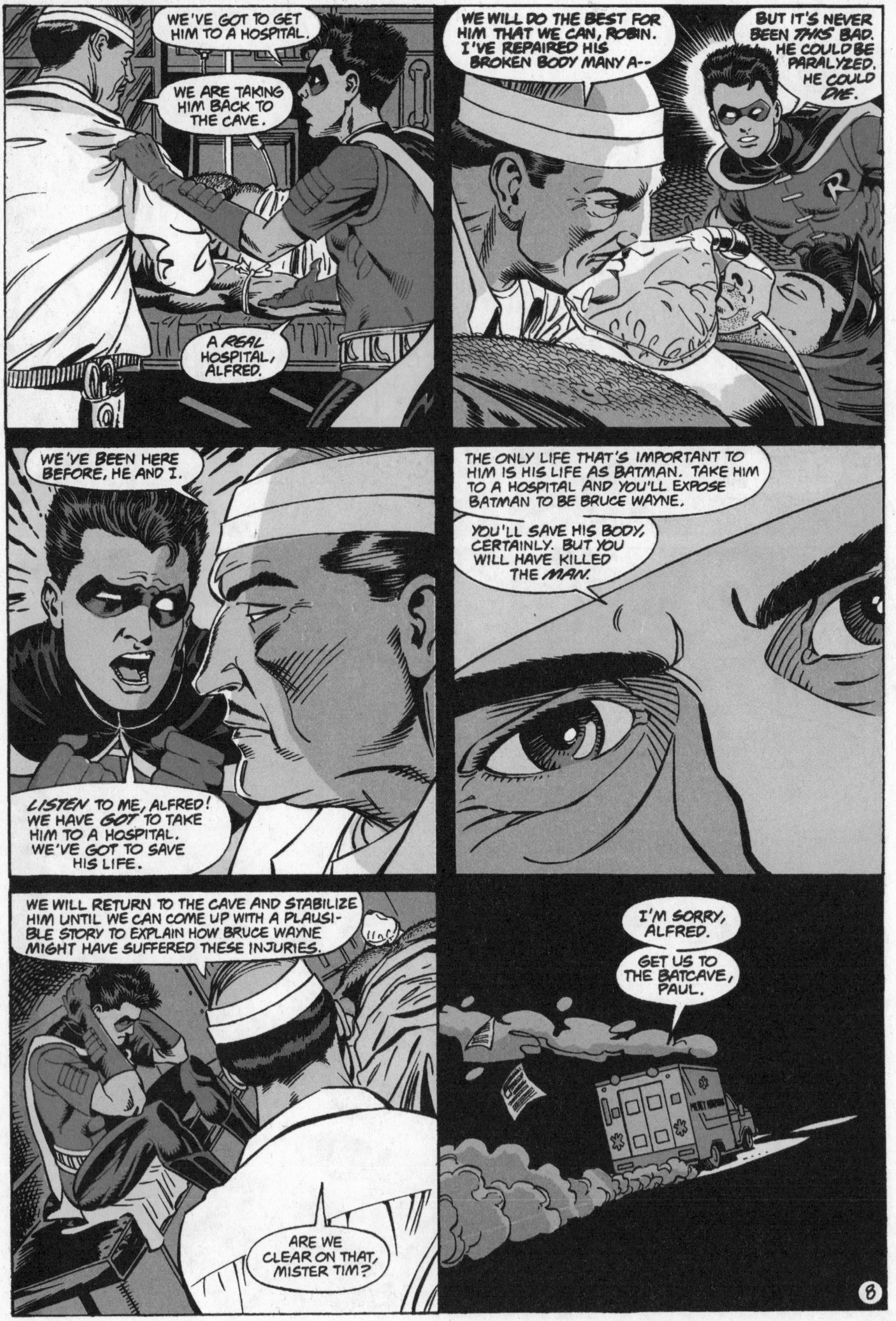
WE'VE GOT TO GET HIM TO A HOSPITAL.
WE ARE TAKING HIM BACK TO THE CAVE.
A REAL HOSPITAL, ALFRED.
WE WILL DO THE BEST FOR HIM THAT WE CAN, ROBIN. I'VE REPAIRED HIS BROKEN BODY MANY A--
BUT IT'S NEVER BEEN THIS BAD. HE COULD BE PARALYZED. HE COULD DIE.
WE'VE BEEN HERE BEFORE, HE AND I.
LISTEN TO ME, ALFRED! WE HAVE GOT TO TAKE HIM TO A HOSPITAL. WE'VE GOT TO SAVE HIS LIFE.
THE ONLY LIFE THAT'S IMPORTANT TO HIM IS HIS LIFE AS BATMAN. TAKE HIM TO A HOSPITAL AND YOU'LL EXPOSE BATMAN TO BE BRUCE WAYNE.
YOU'LL SAVE HIS BODY, CERTAINLY. BUT YOU WILL HAVE KILLED THE MAN.
WE WILL RETURN TO THE CAVE AND STABILIZE HIM UNTIL WE CAN COME UP WITH A PLAUSIBLE STORY TO EXPLAIN HOW BRUCE WAYNE MIGHT HAVE SUFFERED THESE INJURIES.
ARE WE CLEAR ON THAT, MISTER TIM?
I'M SORRY, ALFRED.
GET US TO THE BATCAVE, PAUL.
8

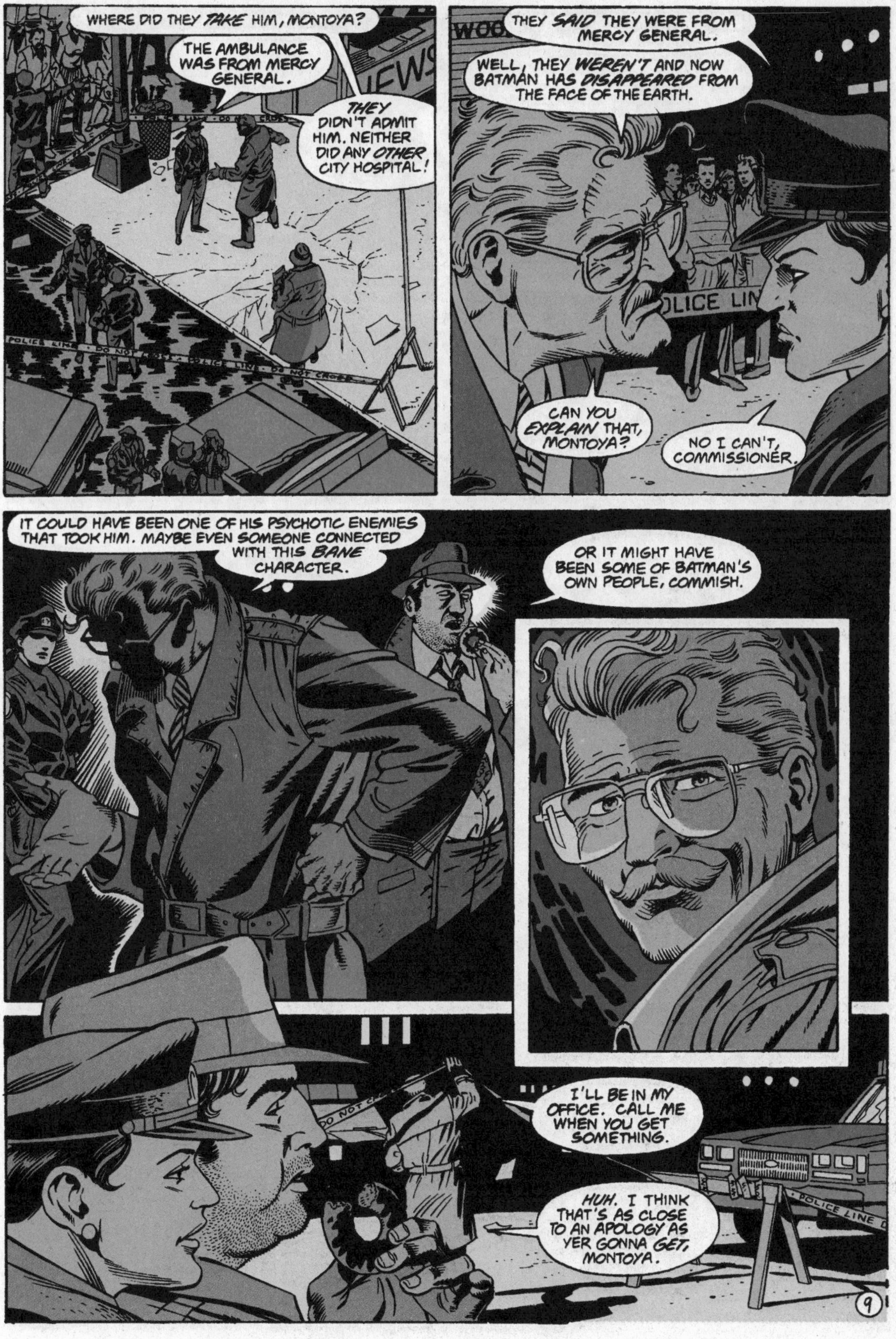
WHERE DID THEY TAKE HIM, MONTOYA?
THE AMBULANCE WAS FROM MERCY GENERAL.
THEY DIDN'T ADMIT HIM. NEITHER DID ANY OTHER CITY HOSPITAL!
THEY SAID THEY WERE FROM MERCY GENERAL.
WELL, THEY WEREN'T AND NOW BATMAN HAS DISAPPEARED FROM THE FACE OF THE EARTH.
CAN YOU EXPLAIN THAT, MONTOYA?
NO I CAN'T, COMMISSIONER.
IT COULD HAVE BEEN ONE OF HIS PSYCHOTIC ENEMIES THAT TOOK HIM. MAYBE EVEN SOMEONE CONNECTED WITH THIS BANE CHARACTER.
OR IT MIGHT HAVE BEEN SOME OF BATMAN'S OWN PEOPLE, COMMISH.
I'LL BE IN MY OFFICE. CALL ME WHEN YOU GET SOMETHING.
HUH. I THINK THAT'S AS CLOSE TO AN APOLOGY AS YER GONNA GET, MONTOYA.
9

...AND NOTHING IS KNOWN ABOUT THE WHEREABOUTS OF THE BATMAN OR THE MASKED STRANGER CALLING HIMSELF BANE.

OH, THIS IS RICH.

POLICE ARE STILL SCOURING THE ROBINSON SQUARE AREA AT THIS HOUR.

ISN'T IT *IRONIC*, SCARECROW? A *LEGION* OF BATTY'S BADDEST FOES TRY TO BRING HIM LOW AND SOME NEW *ROOKIE* COMES ALONG AND TRASHES HIM.

HILARIOUS.

WHY SO GLUM, SCARECHUM?

WE KIDNAP THE MAYOR, HOLD THE ENTIRE CITY AT BAY AND WHAT HAVE WE TO *SHOW* FOR IT?

NOTHING.

WELL, WE HAVE OUR BUDDING *FRIENDSHIP*, SCARY.

HUNH.

AND THIS MARVELOUS HIDEOUT, 'CROW.

A DUMP.

WATCH WHAT YOU SAY ABOUT LUCY. SHE HAS A LOOOOONG MEMORY.

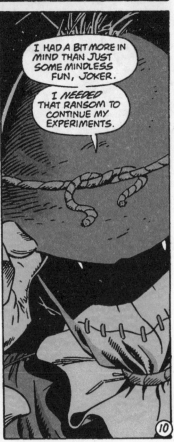

I HAD A BIT MORE IN MIND THAN JUST SOME MINDLESS FUN, JOKER.

I *NEEDED* THAT RANSOM TO CONTINUE MY EXPERIMENTS.

⑩

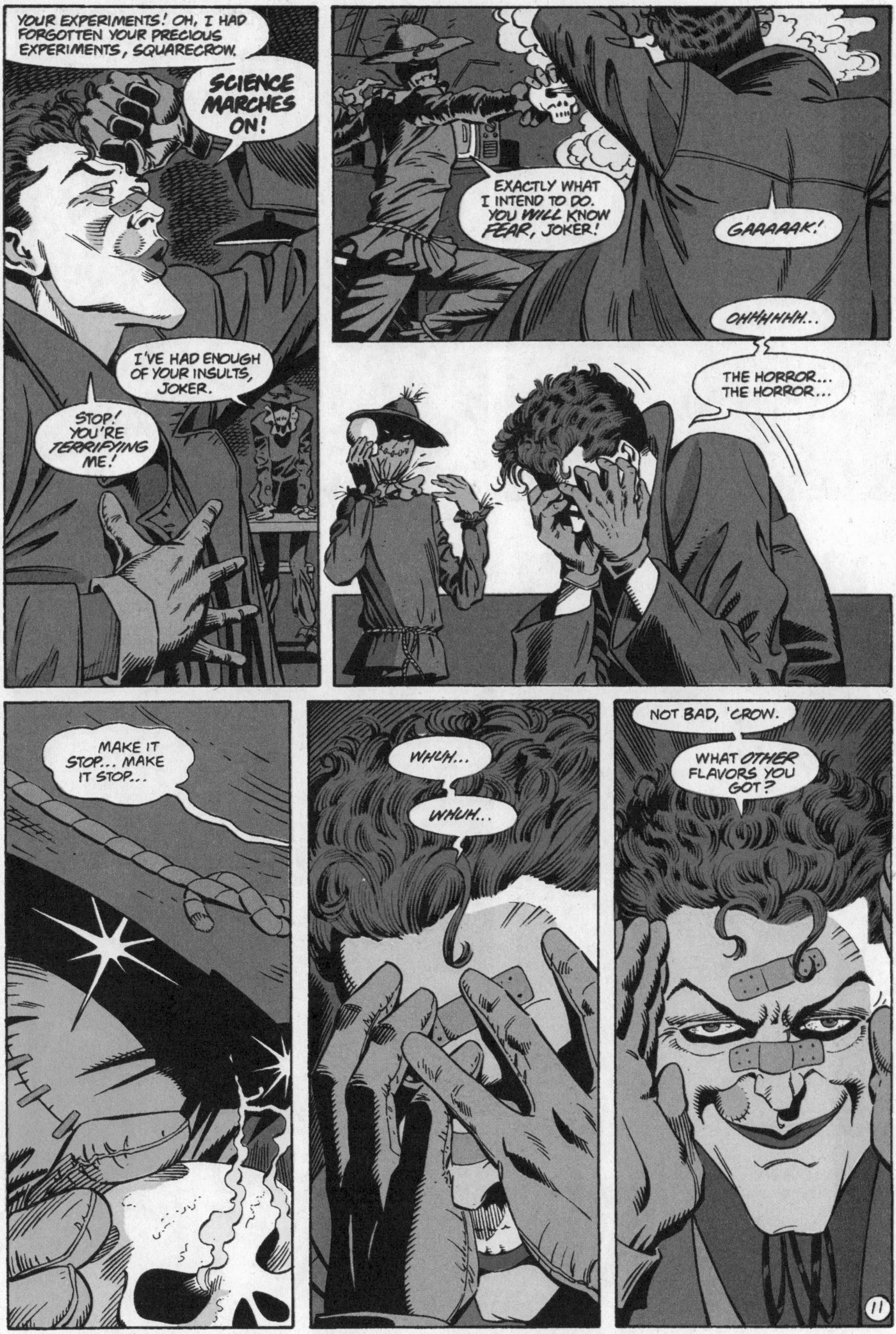
YOUR EXPERIMENTS! OH, I HAD FORGOTTEN YOUR PRECIOUS EXPERIMENTS, SQUARECROW.
SCIENCE MARCHES ON!
I'VE HAD ENOUGH OF YOUR INSULTS, JOKER.
STOP! YOU'RE TERRIFYING ME!
EXACTLY WHAT I INTEND TO DO. YOU WILL KNOW FEAR, JOKER!
GAAAAAK!
OHHHHHH...
THE HORROR... THE HORROR...
MAKE IT STOP... MAKE IT STOP...
WHUH...
WHUH...
NOT BAD, 'CROW.
WHAT OTHER FLAVORS YOU GOT?
11

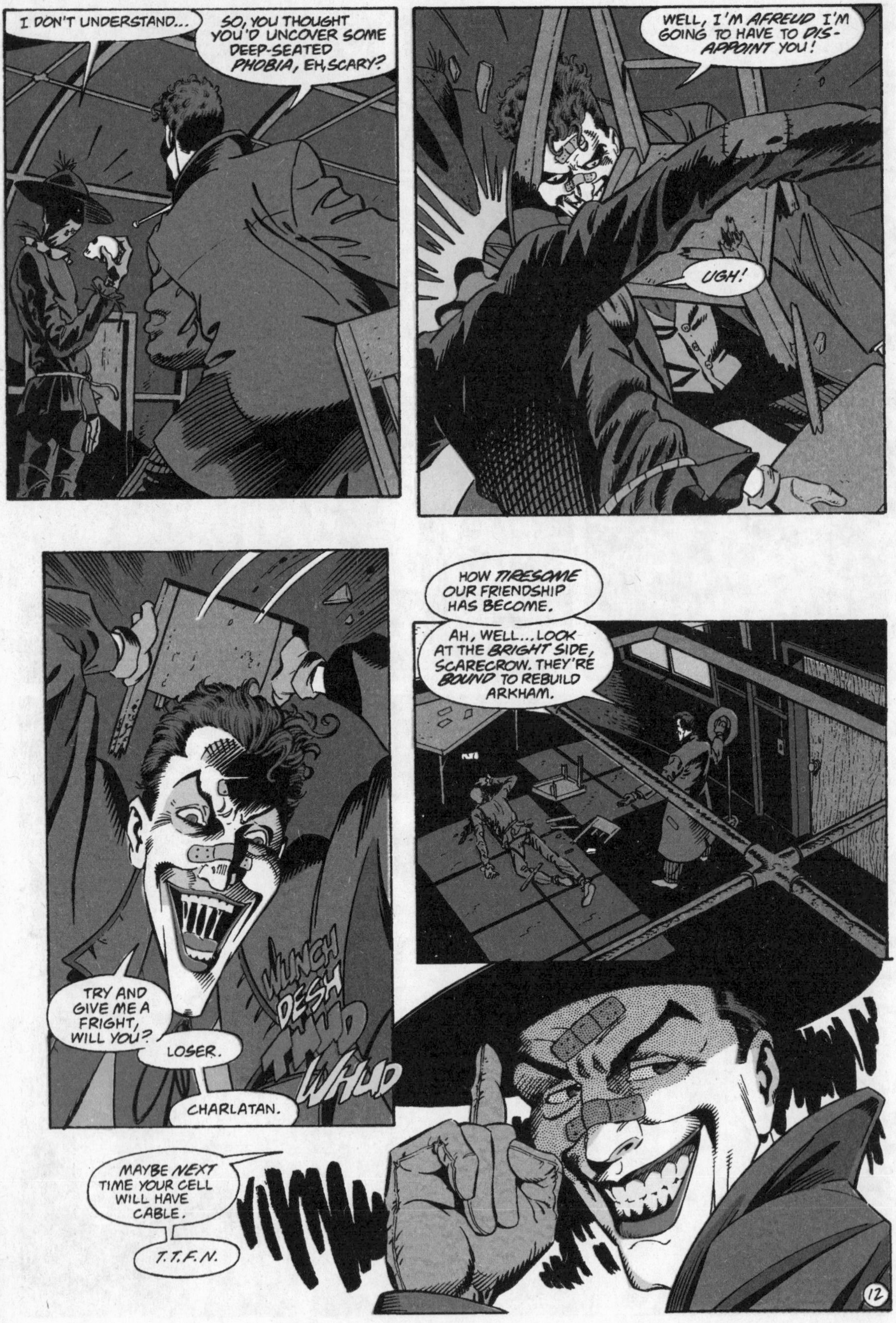
I DON'T UNDERSTAND...
SO, YOU THOUGHT YOU'D UNCOVER SOME DEEP-SEATED PHOBIA, EH, SCARY?
WELL, I'M AFREUD I'M GOING TO HAVE TO DIS-APPOINT YOU!
UGH!
TRY AND GIVE ME A FRIGHT, WILL YOU?
LOSER.
CHARLATAN.
WUNCH
DESH
THUD
WHUD
HOW TIRESOME OUR FRIENDSHIP HAS BECOME.
AH, WELL... LOOK AT THE BRIGHT SIDE, SCARECROW. THEY'RE BOUND TO REBUILD ARKHAM.
MAYBE NEXT TIME YOUR CELL WILL HAVE CABLE.
T.T.F.N.
12

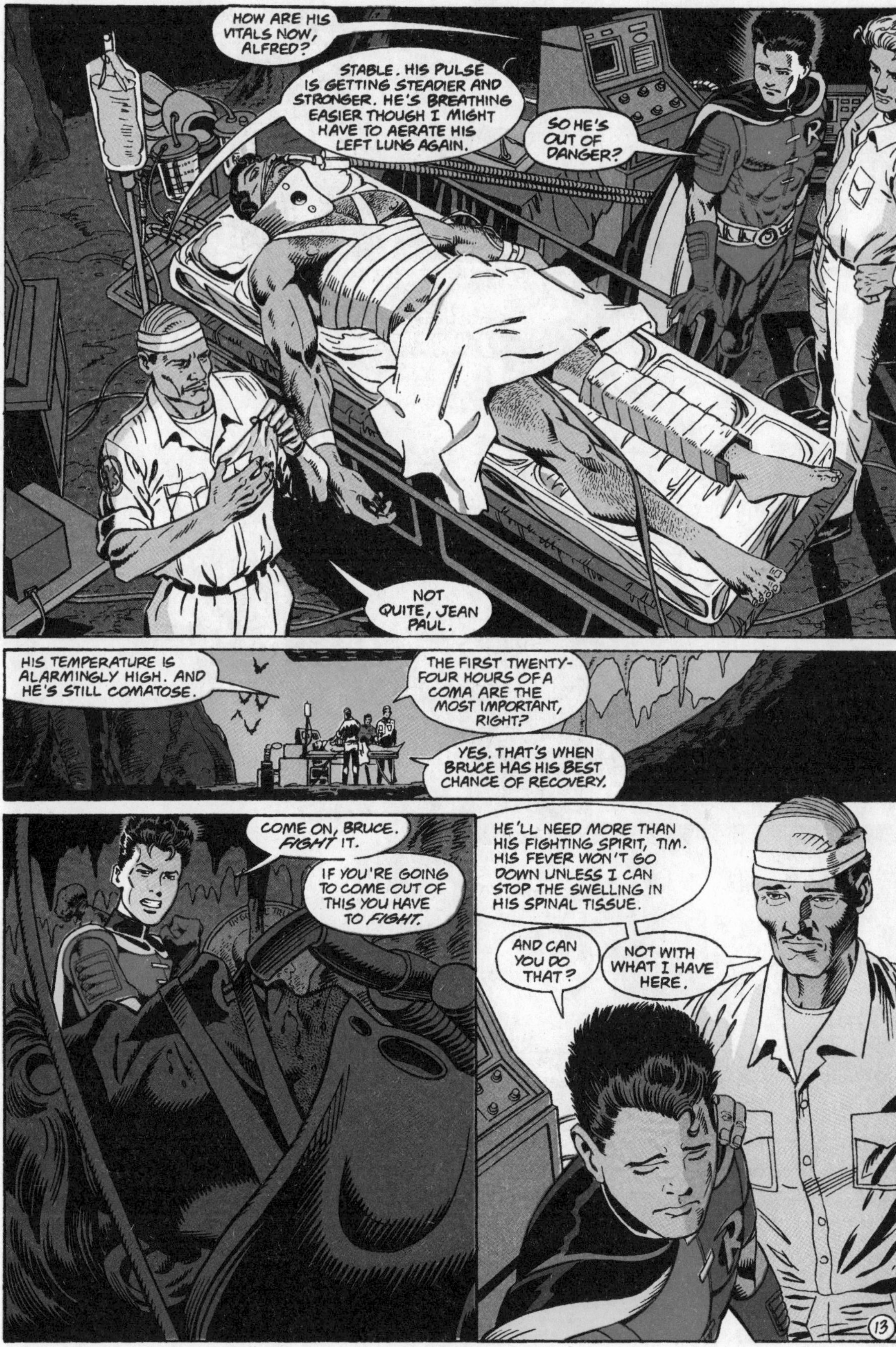
HOW ARE HIS VITALS NOW, ALFRED?
STABLE. HIS PULSE IS GETTING STEADIER AND STRONGER. HE'S BREATHING EASIER THOUGH I MIGHT HAVE TO AERATE HIS LEFT LUNG AGAIN.
SO HE'S OUT OF DANGER?
NOT QUITE, JEAN PAUL.
HIS TEMPERATURE IS ALARMINGLY HIGH. AND HE'S STILL COMATOSE.
THE FIRST TWENTY-FOUR HOURS OF A COMA ARE THE MOST IMPORTANT, RIGHT?
YES. THAT'S WHEN BRUCE HAS HIS BEST CHANCE OF RECOVERY.
COME ON, BRUCE. *FIGHT* IT.
IF YOU'RE GOING TO COME OUT OF THIS YOU HAVE TO *FIGHT*.
HE'LL NEED MORE THAN HIS FIGHTING SPIRIT, TIM. HIS FEVER WON'T GO DOWN UNLESS I CAN STOP THE SWELLING IN HIS SPINAL TISSUE.
AND CAN YOU DO THAT?
NOT WITH WHAT I HAVE HERE.
13

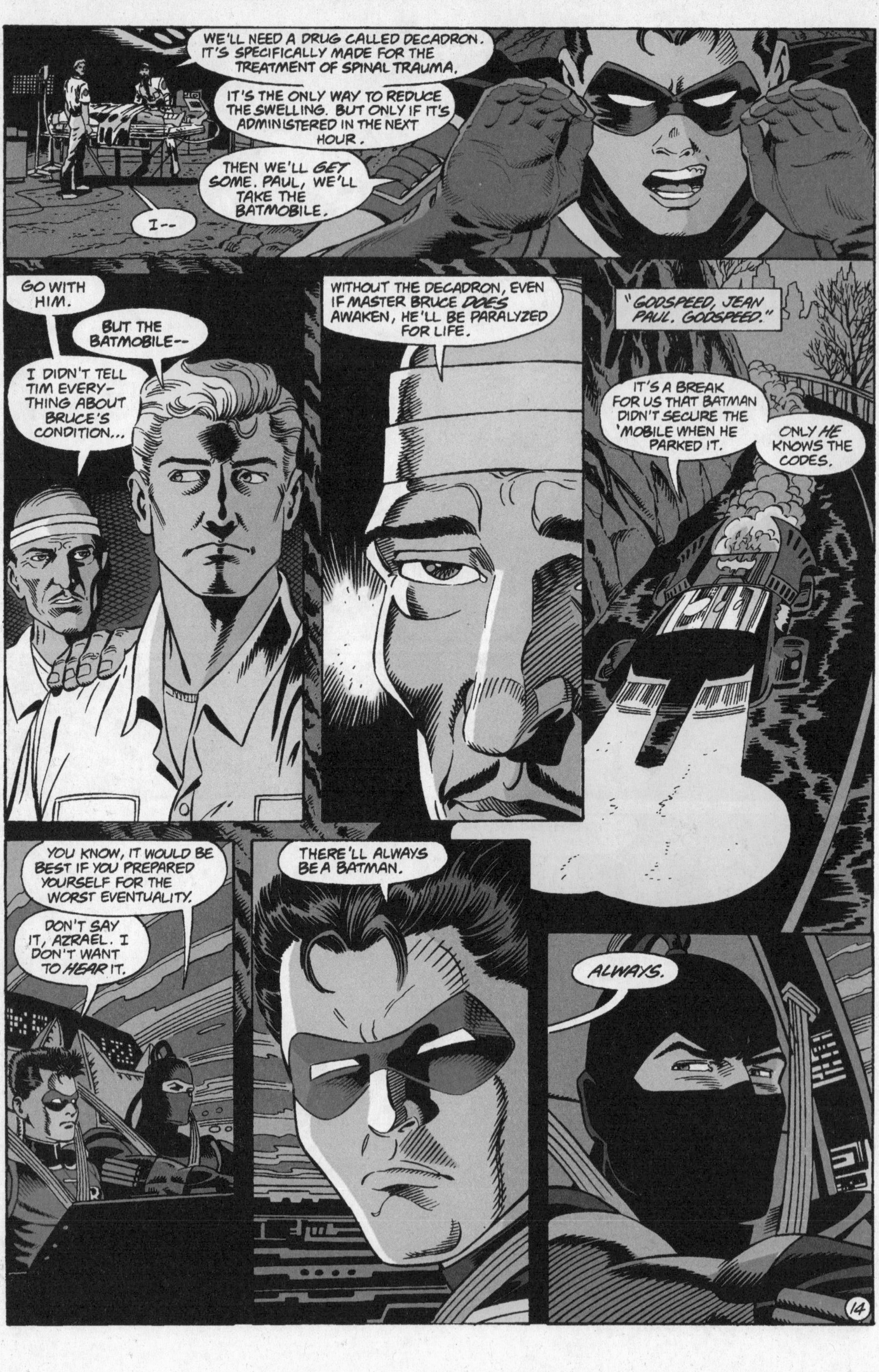

WE'LL NEED A DRUG CALLED DECADRON. IT'S SPECIFICALLY MADE FOR THE TREATMENT OF SPINAL TRAUMA.
IT'S THE ONLY WAY TO REDUCE THE SWELLING. BUT ONLY IF IT'S ADMINISTERED IN THE NEXT HOUR.
THEN WE'LL GET SOME. PAUL, WE'LL TAKE THE BATMOBILE.
I--
GO WITH HIM.
BUT THE BATMOBILE--
I DIDN'T TELL TIM EVERYTHING ABOUT BRUCE'S CONDITION...
WITHOUT THE DECADRON, EVEN IF MASTER BRUCE DOES AWAKEN, HE'LL BE PARALYZED FOR LIFE.
"GODSPEED, JEAN PAUL. GODSPEED."
IT'S A BREAK FOR US THAT BATMAN DIDN'T SECURE THE 'MOBILE WHEN HE PARKED IT.
ONLY HE KNOWS THE CODES.
YOU KNOW, IT WOULD BE BEST IF YOU PREPARED YOURSELF FOR THE WORST EVENTUALITY.
DON'T SAY IT, AZRAEL. I DON'T WANT TO HEAR IT.
THERE'LL ALWAYS BE A BATMAN.
ALWAYS.
14

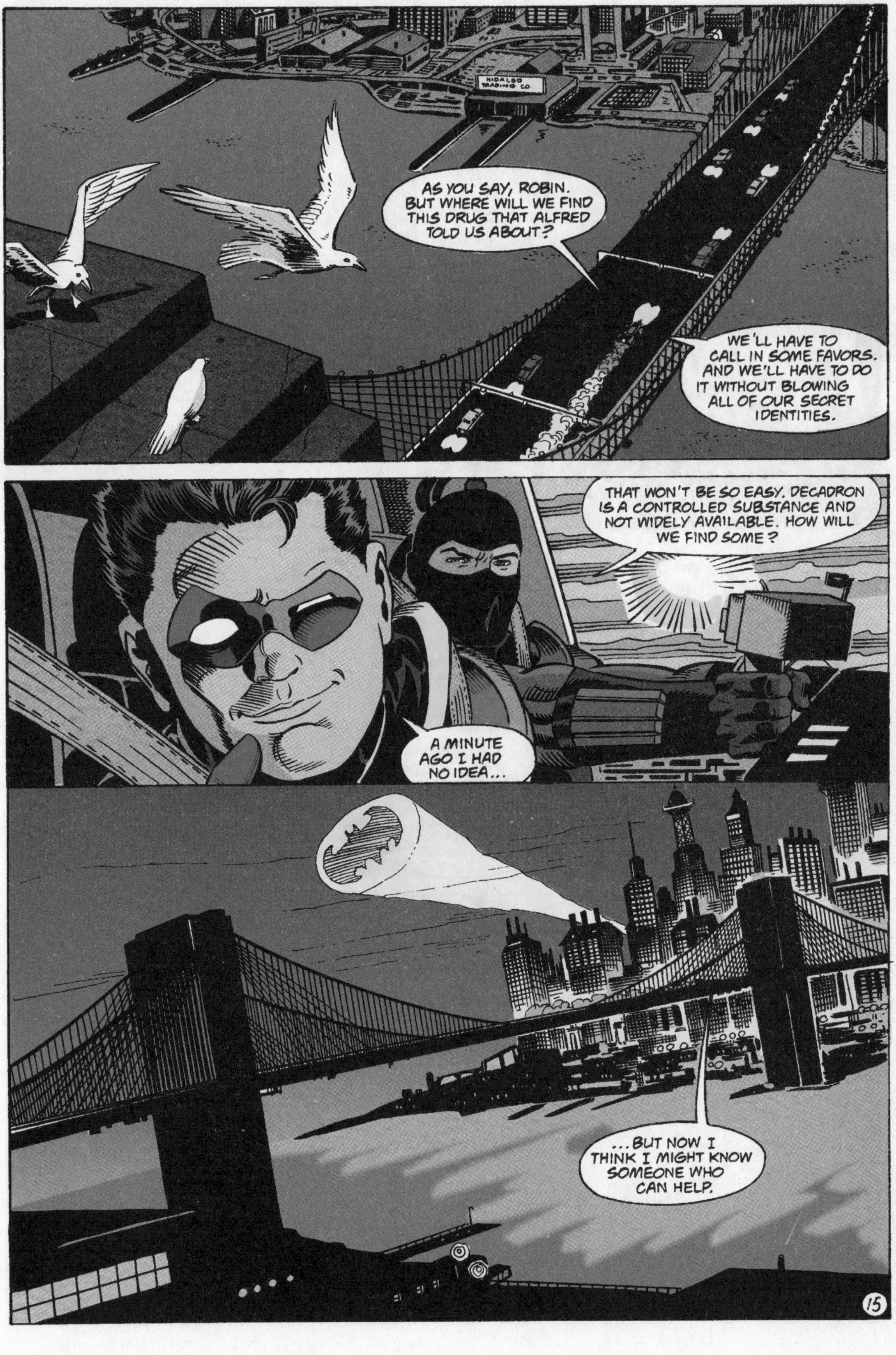
HIDALGO TRADING CO.
AS YOU SAY, ROBIN. BUT WHERE WILL WE FIND THIS DRUG THAT ALFRED TOLD US ABOUT?
WE'LL HAVE TO CALL IN SOME FAVORS. AND WE'LL HAVE TO DO IT WITHOUT BLOWING ALL OF OUR SECRET IDENTITIES.
THAT WON'T BE SO EASY. DECADRON IS A CONTROLLED SUBSTANCE AND NOT WIDELY AVAILABLE. HOW WILL WE FIND SOME?
A MINUTE AGO I HAD NO IDEA...
...BUT NOW I THINK I MIGHT KNOW SOMEONE WHO CAN HELP.
15

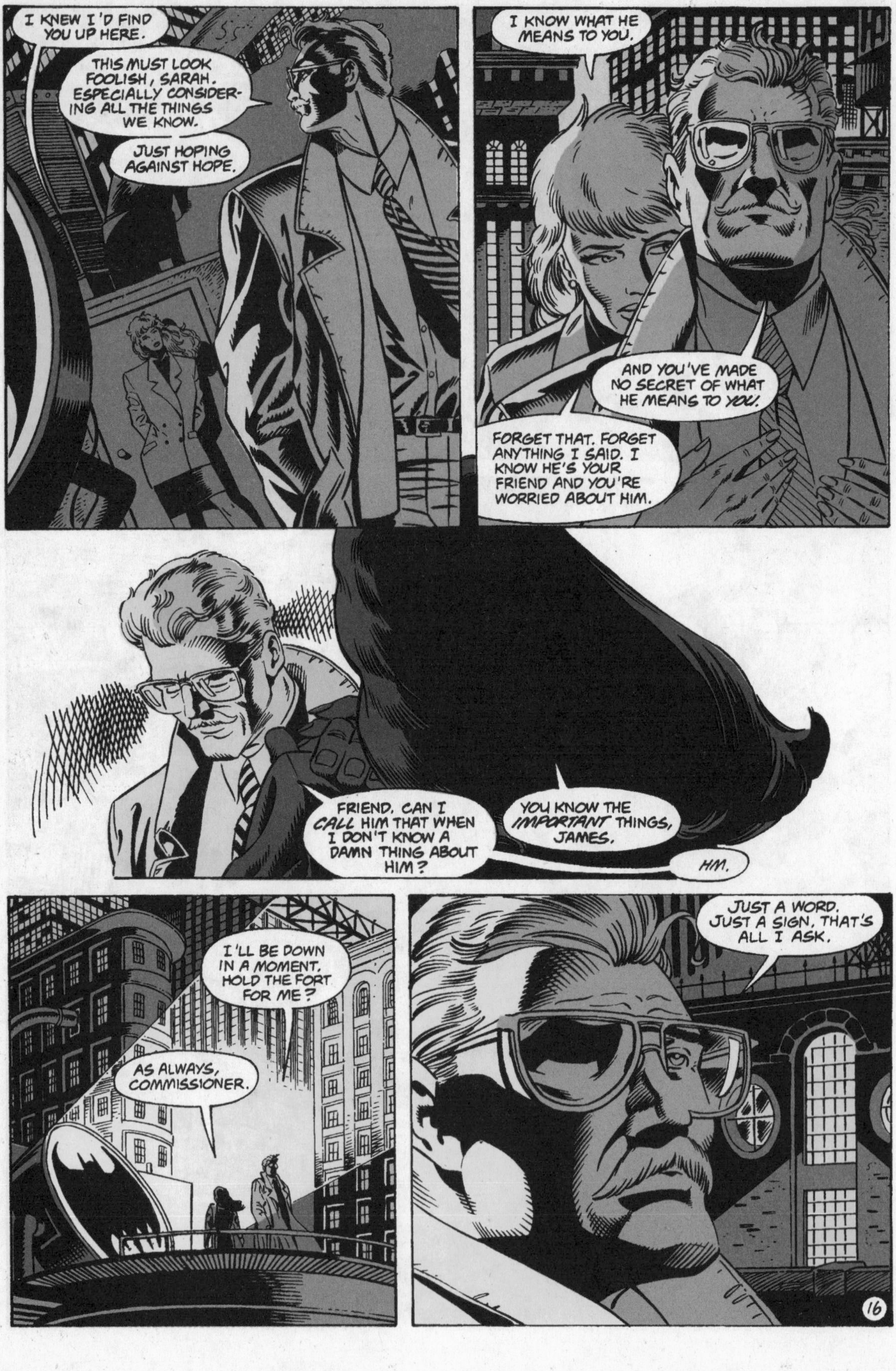
I KNEW I'D FIND YOU UP HERE.
THIS MUST LOOK FOOLISH, SARAH. ESPECIALLY CONSIDERING ALL THE THINGS WE KNOW.
JUST HOPING AGAINST HOPE.
I KNOW WHAT HE MEANS TO YOU.
AND YOU'VE MADE NO SECRET OF WHAT HE MEANS TO YOU.
FORGET THAT. FORGET ANYTHING I SAID. I KNOW HE'S YOUR FRIEND AND YOU'RE WORRIED ABOUT HIM.
FRIEND. CAN I CALL HIM THAT WHEN I DON'T KNOW A DAMN THING ABOUT HIM?
YOU KNOW THE IMPORTANT THINGS, JAMES.
HM.
I'LL BE DOWN IN A MOMENT. HOLD THE FORT FOR ME?
AS ALWAYS, COMMISSIONER.
JUST A WORD. JUST A SIGN, THAT'S ALL I ASK.
16

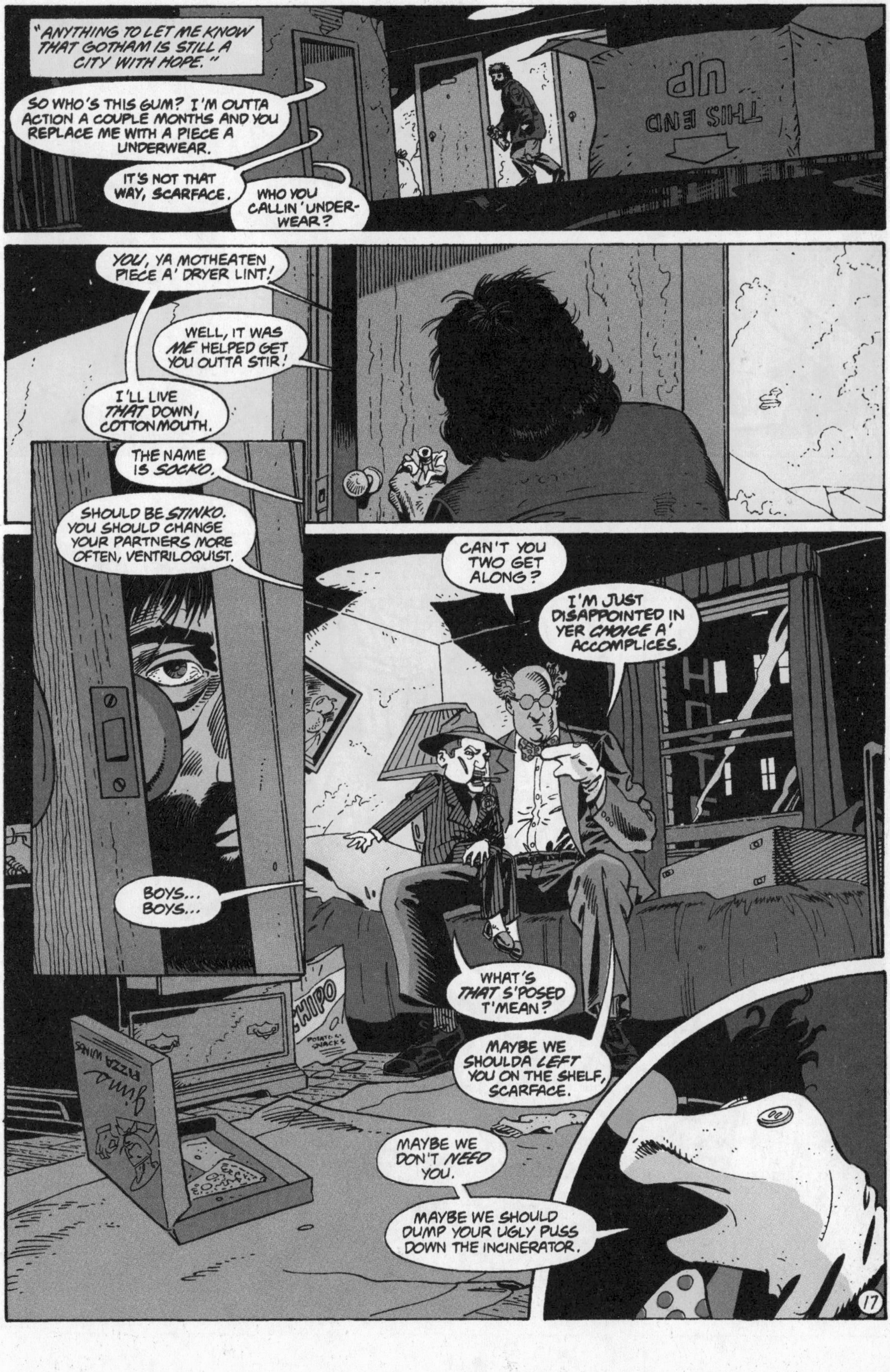
"ANYTHING TO LET ME KNOW THAT GOTHAM IS STILL A CITY WITH HOPE."
SO WHO'S THIS GUM? I'M OUTTA ACTION A COUPLE MONTHS AND YOU REPLACE ME WITH A PIECE A UNDERWEAR.
IT'S NOT THAT WAY, SCARFACE.
WHO YOU CALLIN' UNDER-WEAR?
THIS END UP
YOU, YA MOTHEATEN PIECE A' DRYER LINT!
WELL, IT WAS ME HELPED GET YOU OUTTA STIR!
I'LL LIVE THAT DOWN, COTTONMOUTH.
THE NAME IS SOCKO.
SHOULD BE STINKO. YOU SHOULD CHANGE YOUR PARTNERS MORE OFTEN, VENTRILOQUIST.
CAN'T YOU TWO GET ALONG?
I'M JUST DISAPPOINTED IN YER CHOICE A' ACCOMPLICES.
BOYS... BOYS...
WHAT'S THAT S'POSED T'MEAN?
MAYBE WE SHOULDA LEFT YOU ON THE SHELF, SCARFACE.
MAYBE WE DON'T NEED YOU.
MAYBE WE SHOULD DUMP YOUR UGLY PUSS DOWN THE INCINERATOR.
17

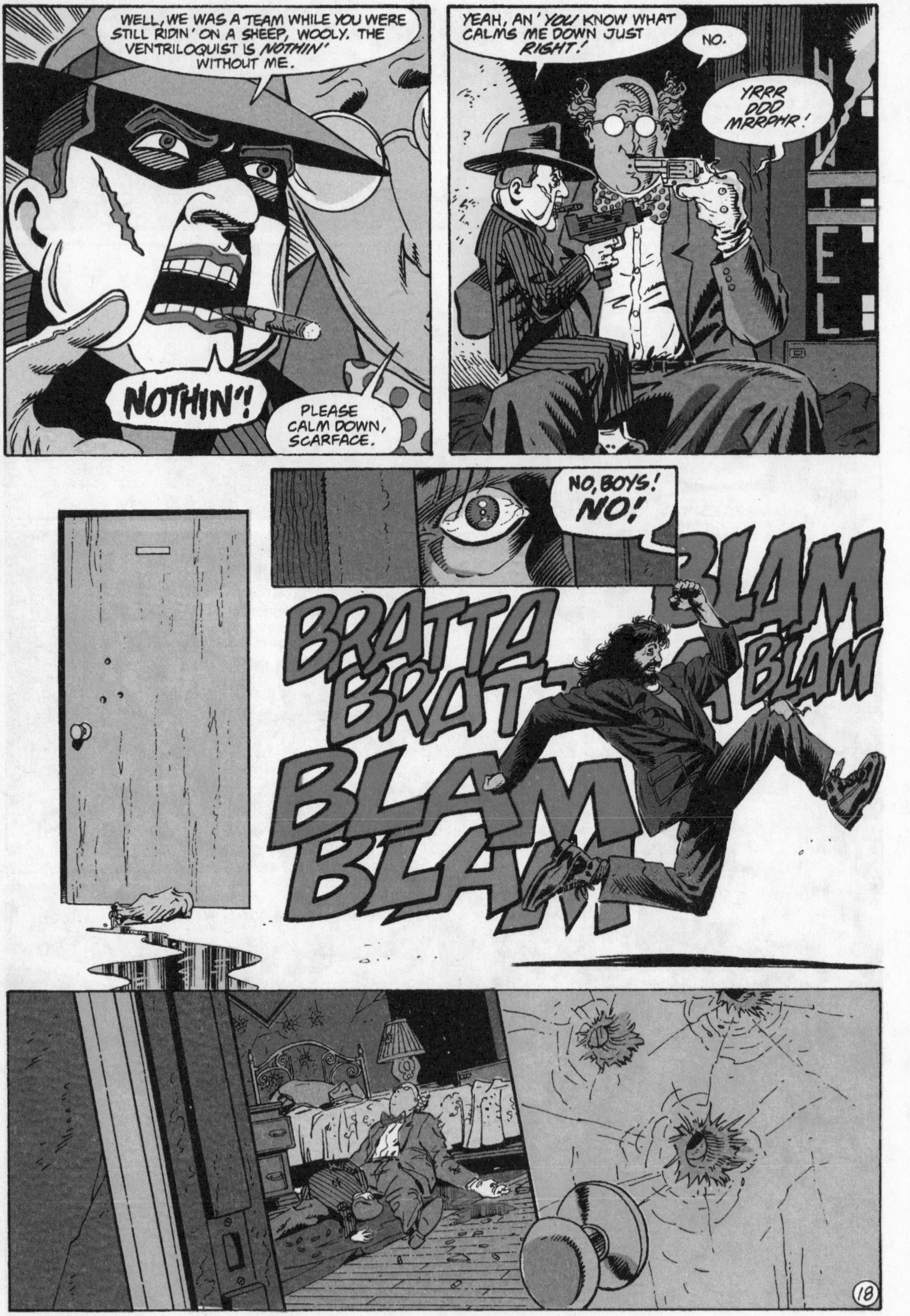
WELL, WE WAS A TEAM WHILE YOU WERE STILL RIDIN' ON A SHEEP, WOOLY. THE VENTRILOQUIST IS NOTHIN' WITHOUT ME.
NOTHIN'!
PLEASE CALM DOWN, SCARFACE.
YEAH, AN' YOU KNOW WHAT CALMS ME DOWN JUST RIGHT!
NO.
YRRR DDD MRRPHR!
NO, BOYS! NO!
BLAM
BLAM
BRATTA
BRATT
BLAM
BLAM
18

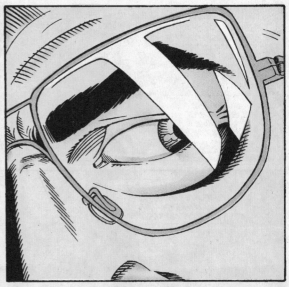

THANKS FOR LEAVING THE WINDOW OPEN.

YOU'RE ALONE.

I NEED YOUR HELP. *HE* NEEDS YOUR HELP.

ANYTHING.

A DRUG CALLED DECADRON. HE MIGHT DIE WITHOUT IT. WE NEED IT FAST.

WAIT HERE.

PATCH ME THROUGH TO BULLOCK'S UNIT.

BULLOCK, THIS IS THE COMMISSIONER, COME IN.

NO SIGN OF THIS BRAIN GUY, COMMISH. BUT HE CAN'T HIDE FOREVER.

IT'S *BANE*, HARV.

FORGET ABOUT THAT AND LISTEN UP...

19

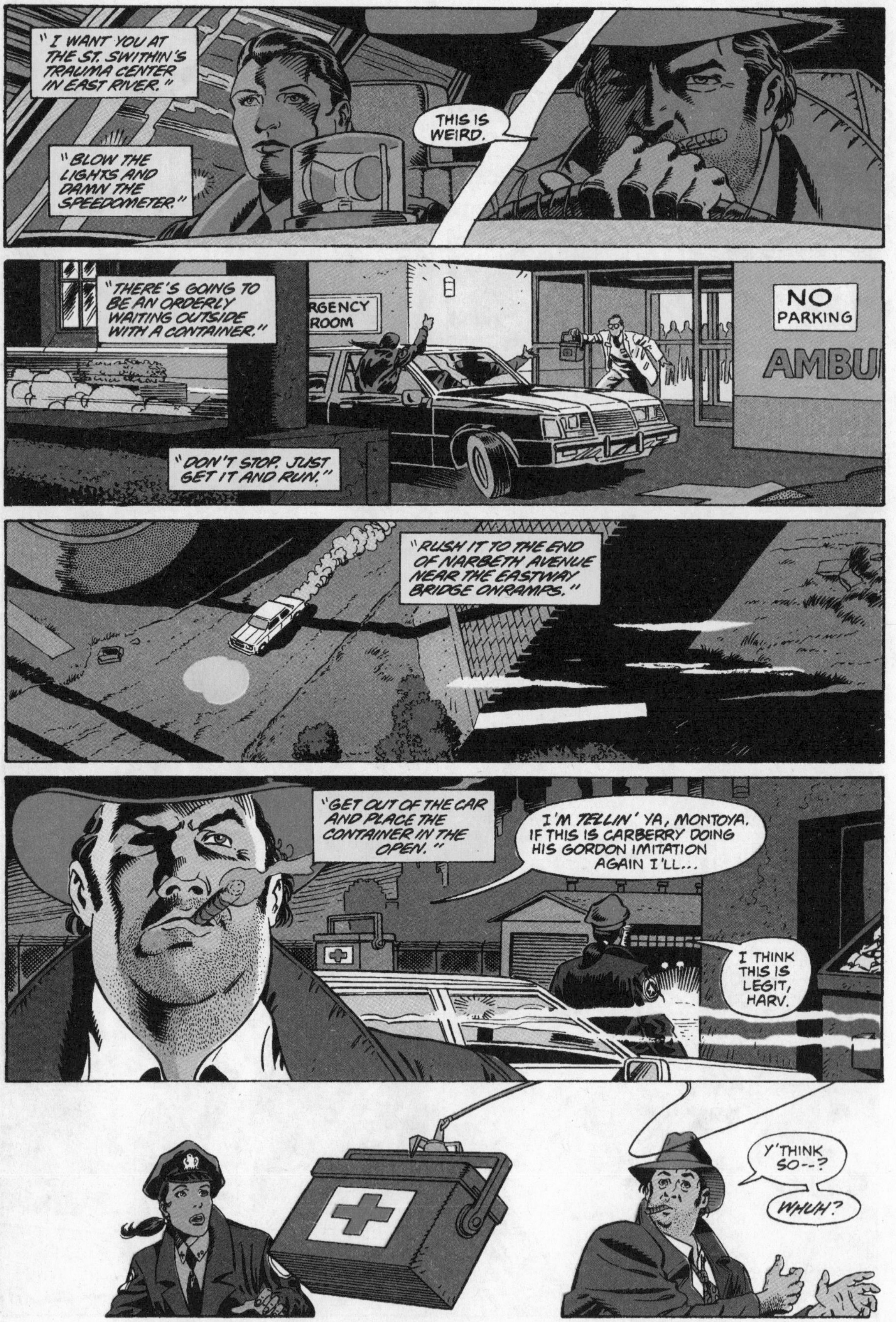
"I WANT YOU AT THE ST. SWITHIN'S TRAUMA CENTER IN EAST RIVER."
"BLOW THE LIGHTS AND DAMN THE SPEEDOMETER."
THIS IS WEIRD.
"THERE'S GOING TO BE AN ORDERLY WAITING OUTSIDE WITH A CONTAINER."
RGENCY ROOM
NO PARKING
AMBU
"DON'T STOP. JUST GET IT AND RUN."
"RUSH IT TO THE END OF NARBETH AVENUE NEAR THE EASTWAY BRIDGE ONRAMPS."
"GET OUT OF THE CAR AND PLACE THE CONTAINER IN THE OPEN."
I'M TELLIN' YA, MONTOYA. IF THIS IS CARBERRY DOING HIS GORDON IMITATION AGAIN I'LL...
I THINK THIS IS LEGIT, HARV.
Y'THINK SO--?
WHUH?

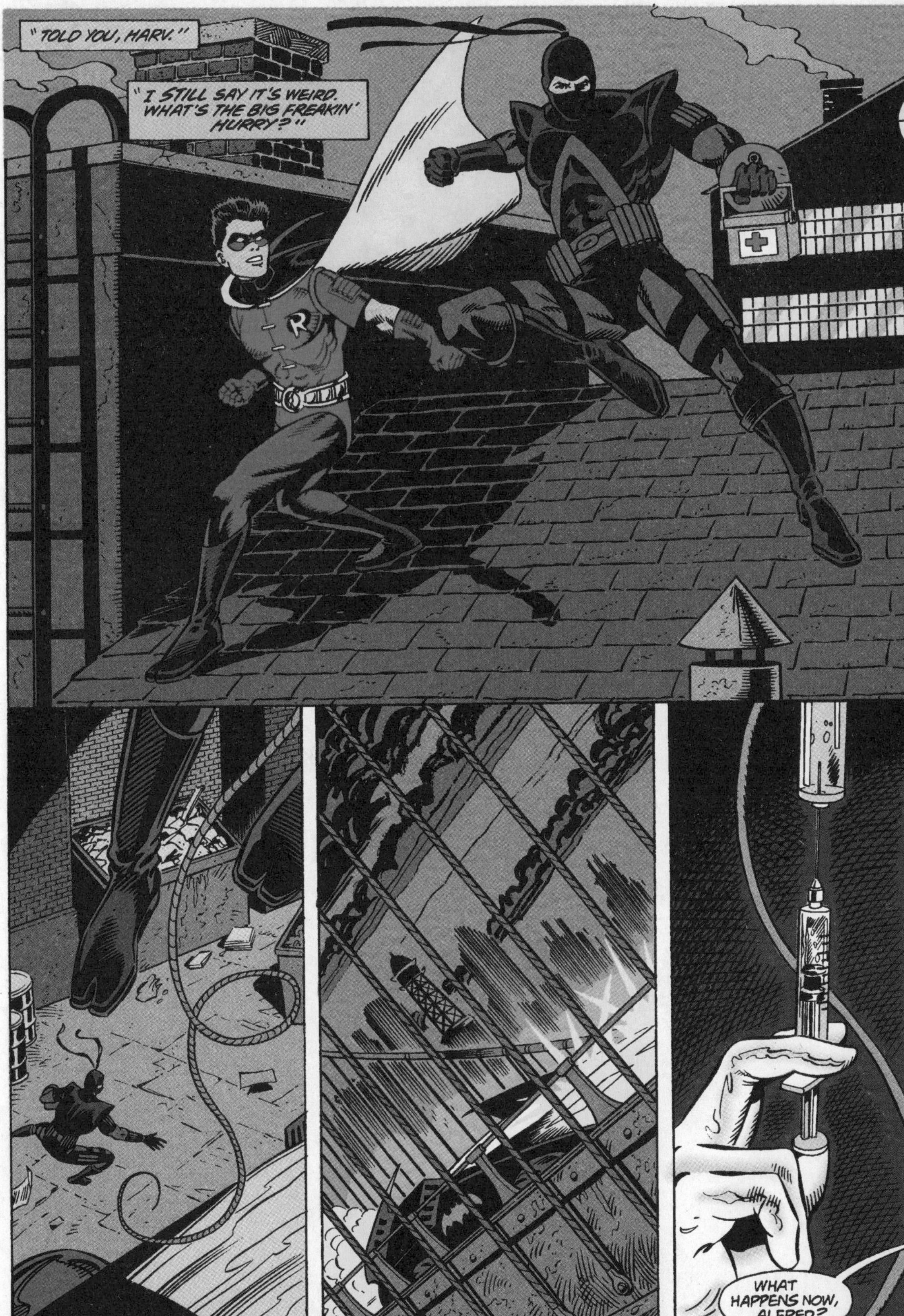
"TOLD YOU, HARV."
"I STILL SAY IT'S WEIRD. WHAT'S THE BIG FREAKIN' HURRY?"
WHAT HAPPENS NOW, ALFRED?
21

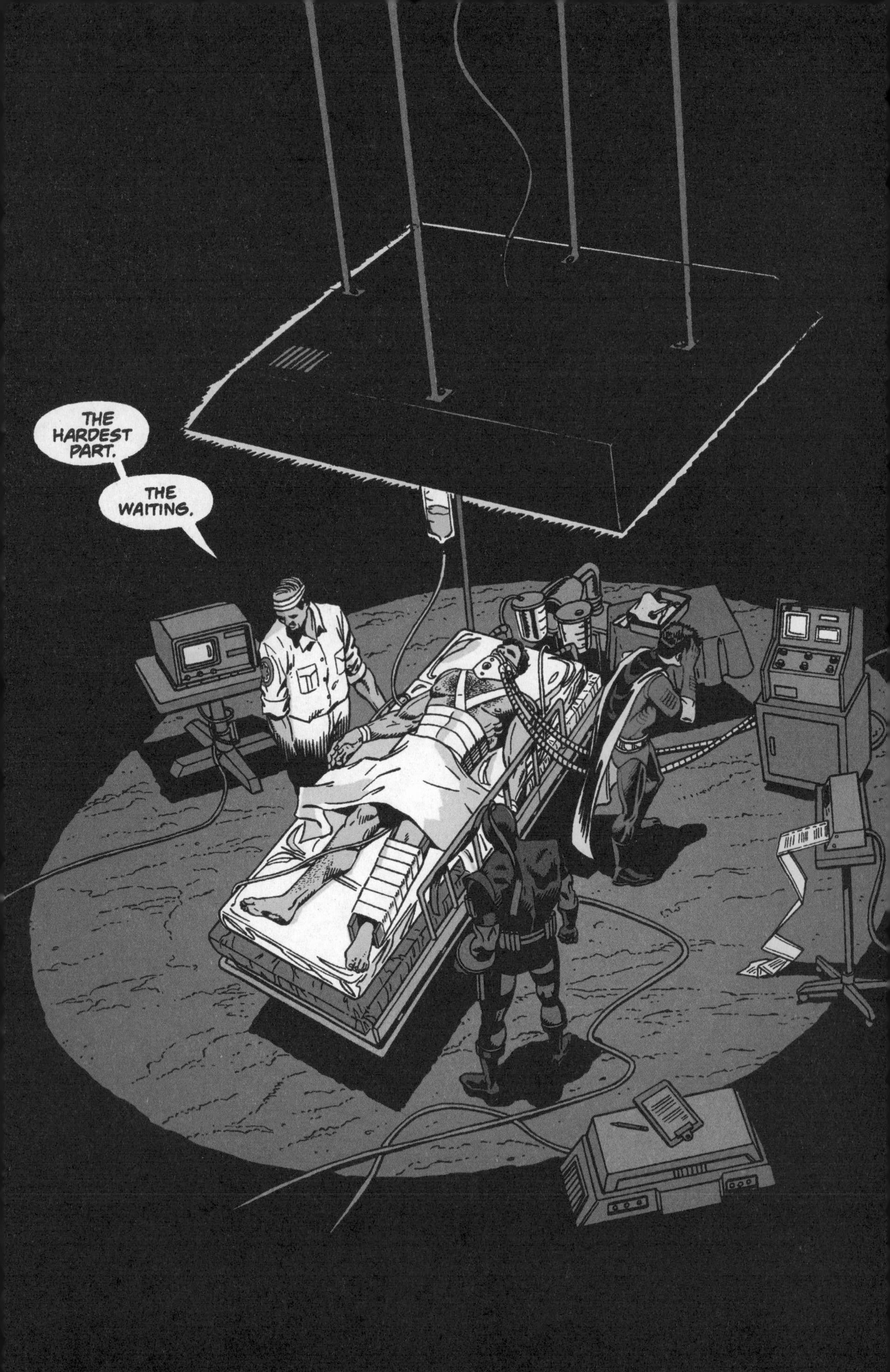
THE HARDEST PART.
THE WAITING.

Cover art by **BILL SIENKIEWICZ**

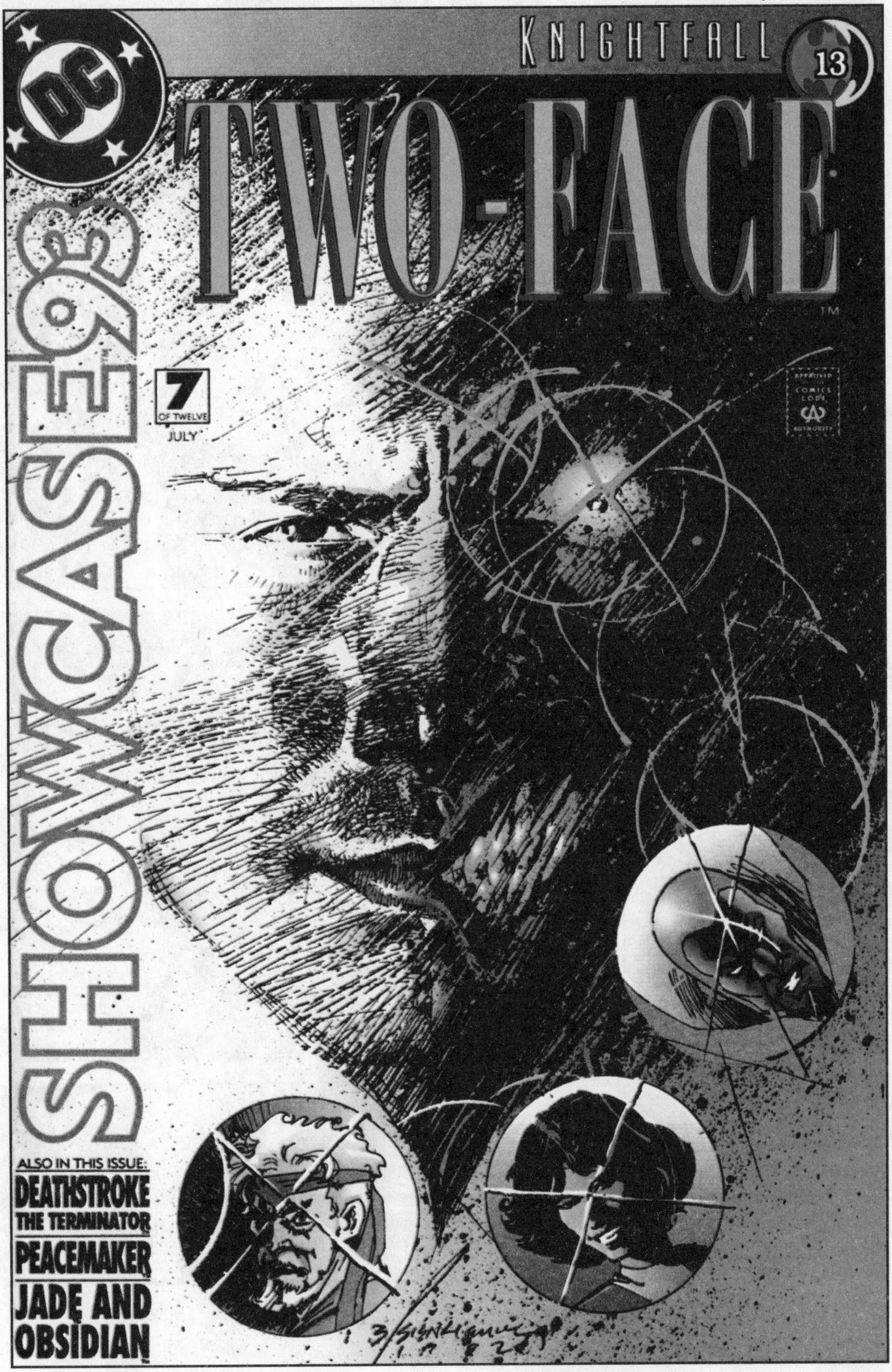
KNIGHTFALL
13
DC
TWO-FACE
SHOWCASE 93
7 OF TWELVE
JULY
APPROVED COMICS CODE AUTHORITY
ALSO IN THIS ISSUE:
DEATHSTROKE THE TERMINATOR
PEACEMAKER
JADE AND OBSIDIAN

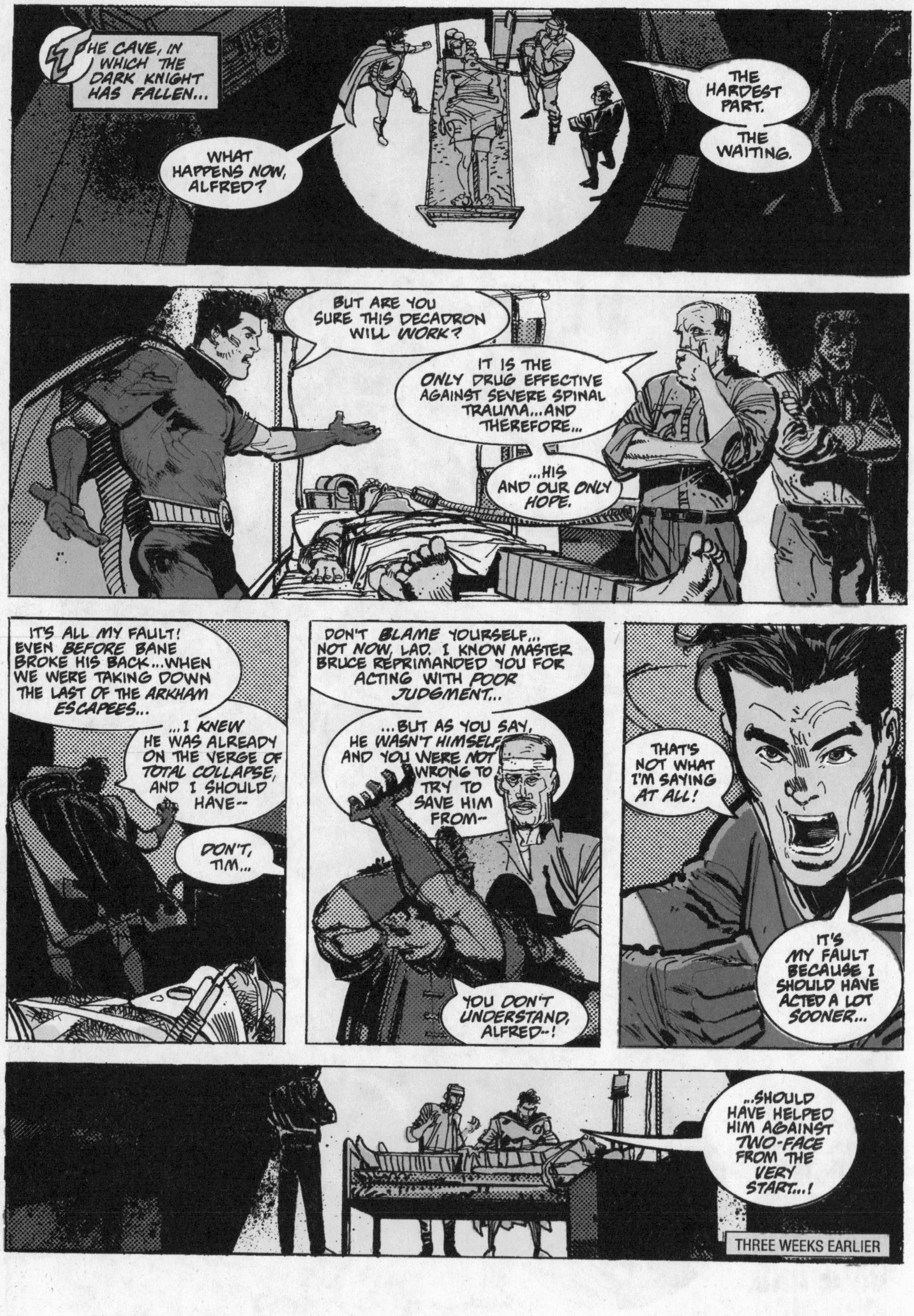
THE CAVE, IN WHICH THE DARK KNIGHT HAS FALLEN...
WHAT HAPPENS NOW, ALFRED?
THE HARDEST PART.
THE WAITING.
BUT ARE YOU SURE THIS DECADRON WILL WORK?
IT IS THE ONLY DRUG EFFECTIVE AGAINST SEVERE SPINAL TRAUMA...AND THEREFORE...
...HIS AND OUR ONLY HOPE.
IT'S ALL MY FAULT! EVEN BEFORE BANE BROKE HIS BACK...WHEN WE WERE TAKING DOWN THE LAST OF THE ARKHAM ESCAPEES...
...I KNEW HE WAS ALREADY ON THE VERGE OF TOTAL COLLAPSE, AND I SHOULD HAVE--
DON'T, TIM...
DON'T BLAME YOURSELF... NOT NOW, LAD. I KNOW MASTER BRUCE REPRIMANDED YOU FOR ACTING WITH POOR JUDGMENT...
...BUT AS YOU SAY, HE WASN'T HIMSELF, AND YOU WERE NOT WRONG TO TRY TO SAVE HIM FROM--
YOU DON'T UNDERSTAND, ALFRED--!
THAT'S NOT WHAT I'M SAYING AT ALL!
IT'S MY FAULT BECAUSE I SHOULD HAVE ACTED A LOT SOONER...
...SHOULD HAVE HELPED HIM AGAINST TWO-FACE FROM THE VERY START...!
THREE WEEKS EARLIER

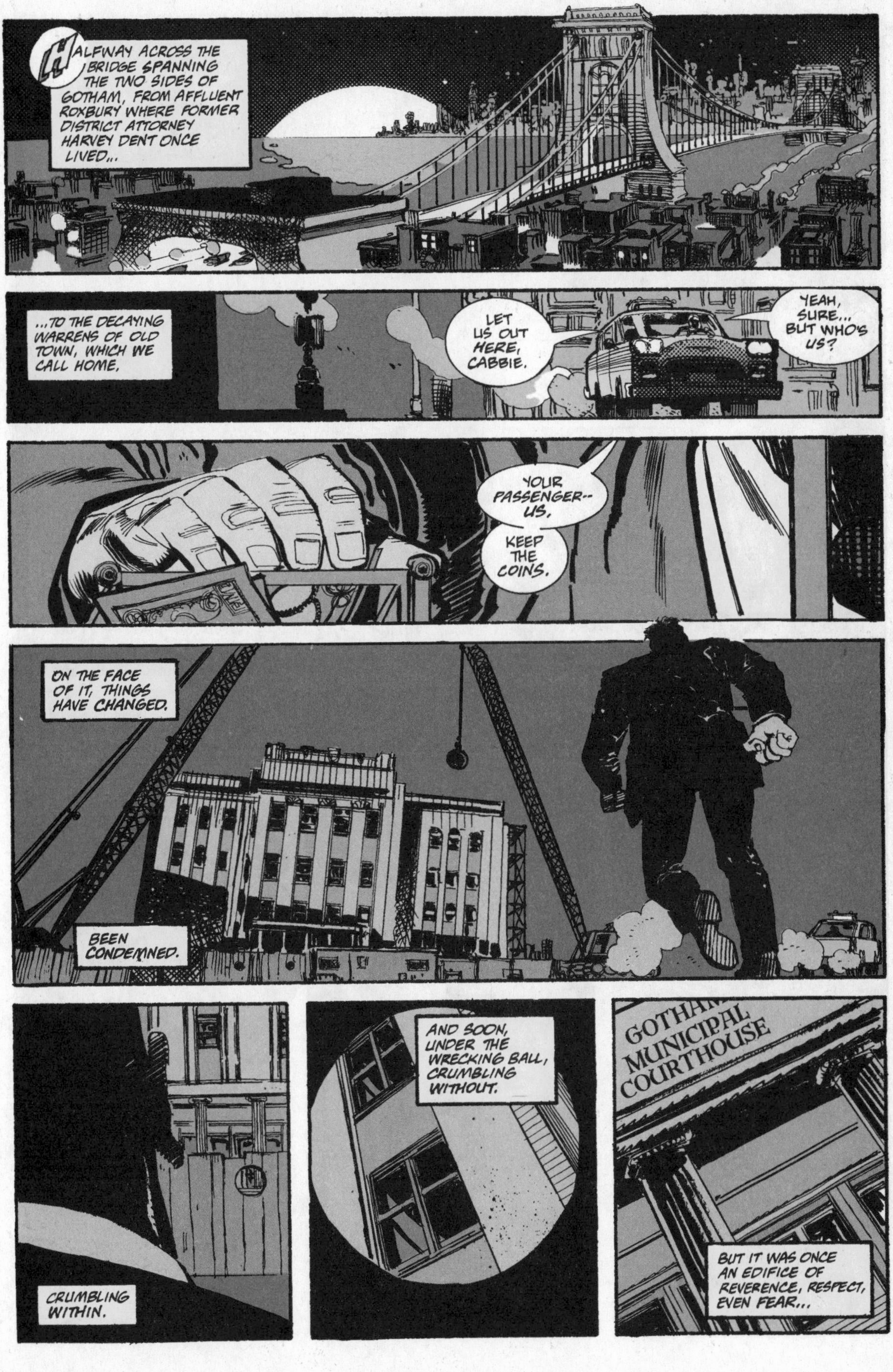
HALFWAY ACROSS THE BRIDGE SPANNING THE TWO SIDES OF GOTHAM, FROM AFFLUENT ROXBURY WHERE FORMER DISTRICT ATTORNEY HARVEY DENT ONCE LIVED...
...TO THE DECAYING WARRENS OF OLD TOWN, WHICH WE CALL HOME.
LET US OUT HERE, CABBIE.
YEAH, SURE... BUT WHO'S US?
YOUR PASSENGER-- US.
KEEP THE COINS.
ON THE FACE OF IT, THINGS HAVE CHANGED.
BEEN CONDEMNED.
CRUMBLING WITHIN.
AND SOON, UNDER THE WRECKING BALL, CRUMBLING WITHOUT.
GOTHAM MUNICIPAL COURTHOUSE
BUT IT WAS ONCE AN EDIFICE OF REVERENCE, RESPECT, EVEN FEAR...

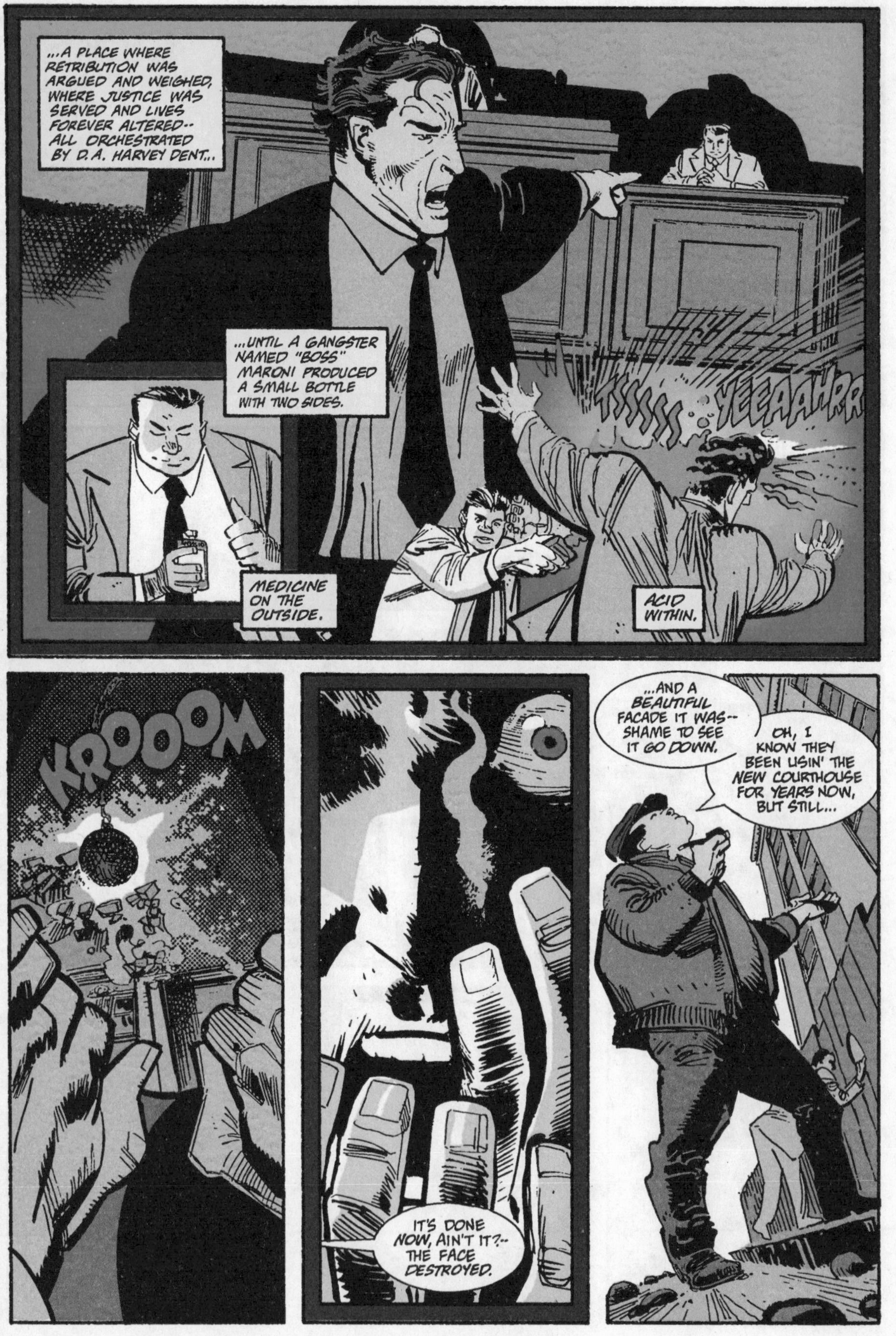
...A PLACE WHERE RETRIBUTION WAS ARGUED AND WEIGHED, WHERE JUSTICE WAS SERVED AND LIVES FOREVER ALTERED-- ALL ORCHESTRATED BY D.A. HARVEY DENT...
...UNTIL A GANGSTER NAMED "BOSS" MARONI PRODUCED A SMALL BOTTLE WITH TWO SIDES.
MEDICINE ON THE OUTSIDE.
TSSSS
YEEAAHRR
ACID WITHIN.
KROOOM
IT'S DONE NOW, AIN'T IT?-- THE FACE DESTROYED.
...AND A BEAUTIFUL FACADE IT WAS-- SHAME TO SEE IT GO DOWN.
OH, I KNOW THEY BEEN USIN' THE NEW COURTHOUSE FOR YEARS NOW, BUT STILL...

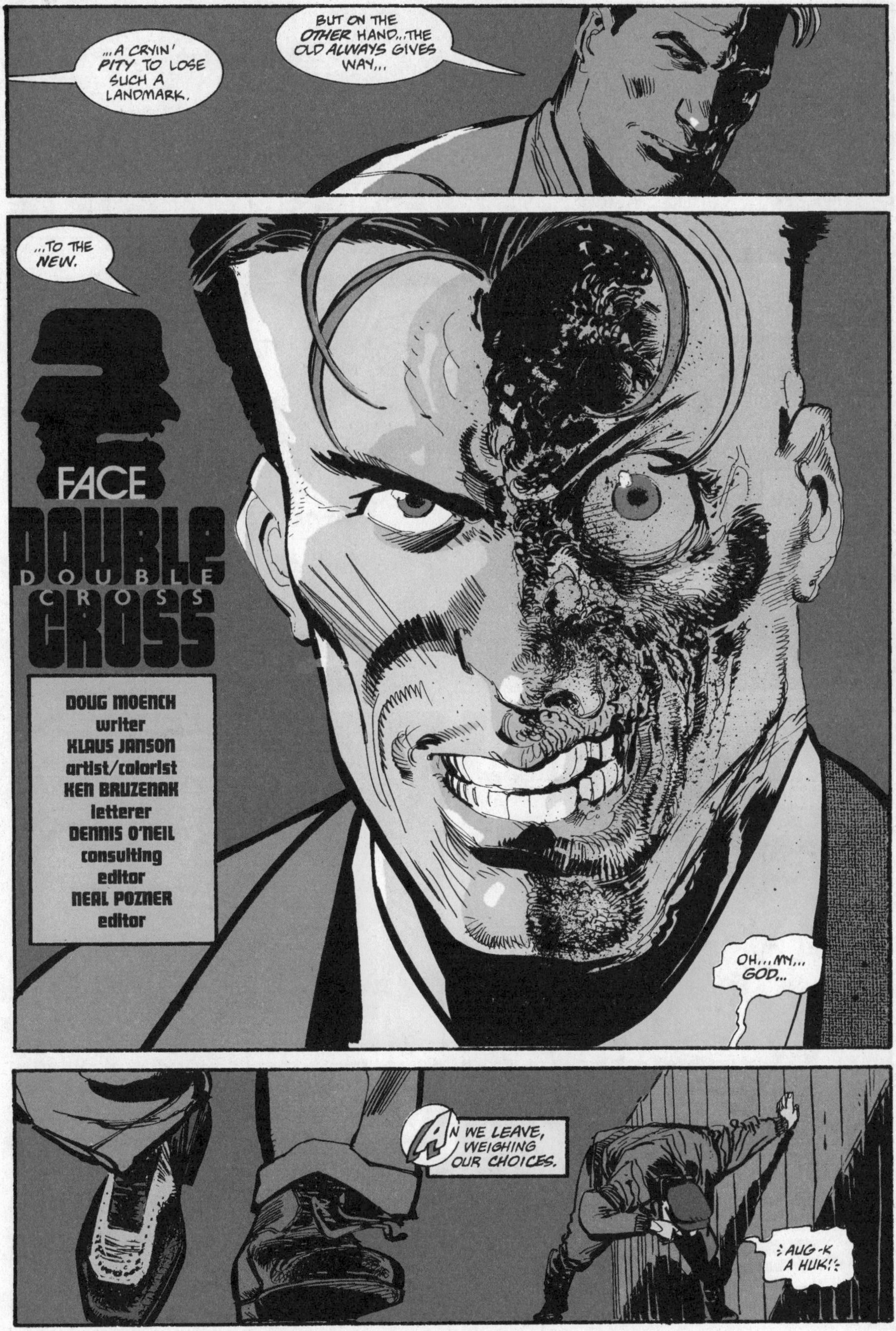
...A CRYIN' PITY TO LOSE SUCH A LANDMARK.
BUT ON THE OTHER HAND... THE OLD ALWAYS GIVES WAY...
...TO THE NEW.
2 FACE
DOUBLE DOUBLE CROSS CROSS
DOUG MOENCH writer
KLAUS JANSON artist/colorist
KEN BRUZENAK letterer
DENNIS O'NEIL consulting editor
NEAL POZNER editor
OH... MY... GOD...
AN WE LEAVE, WEIGHING OUR CHOICES.
AUG-K A HUK!

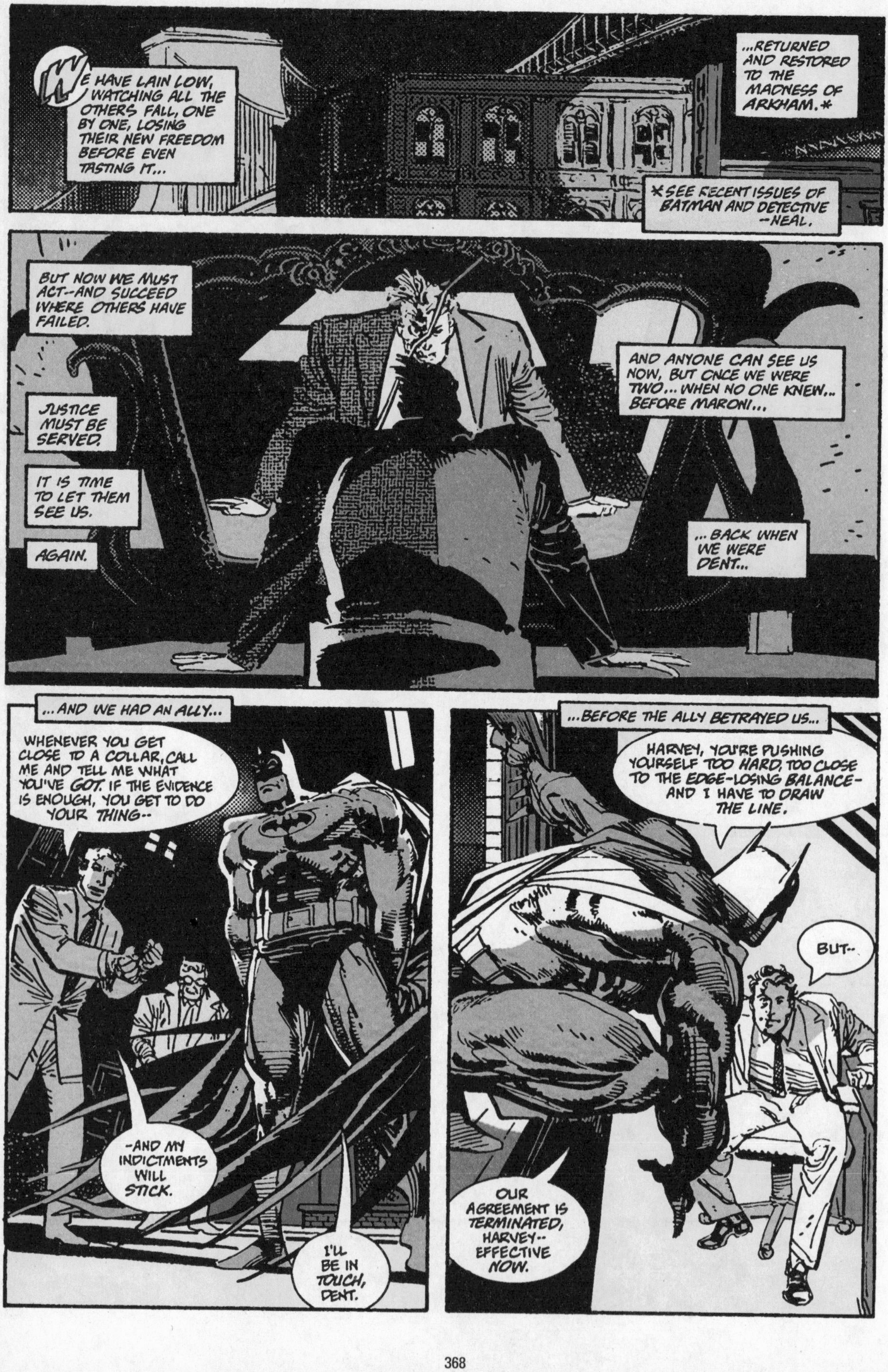
WE HAVE LAIN LOW, WATCHING ALL THE OTHERS FALL, ONE BY ONE, LOSING THEIR NEW FREEDOM BEFORE EVEN TASTING IT...
...RETURNED AND RESTORED TO THE MADNESS OF ARKHAM.*
*SEE RECENT ISSUES OF BATMAN AND DETECTIVE —NEAL.
BUT NOW WE MUST ACT--AND SUCCEED WHERE OTHERS HAVE FAILED.
JUSTICE MUST BE SERVED.
IT IS TIME TO LET THEM SEE US.
AGAIN.
AND ANYONE CAN SEE US NOW, BUT ONCE WE WERE TWO... WHEN NO ONE KNEW... BEFORE MARONI...
...BACK WHEN WE WERE DENT...
...AND WE HAD AN ALLY...
WHENEVER YOU GET CLOSE TO A COLLAR, CALL ME AND TELL ME WHAT YOU'VE GOT. IF THE EVIDENCE IS ENOUGH, YOU GET TO DO YOUR THING--
-AND MY INDICTMENTS WILL STICK.
I'LL BE IN TOUCH, DENT.
...BEFORE THE ALLY BETRAYED US...
HARVEY, YOU'RE PUSHING YOURSELF TOO HARD, TOO CLOSE TO THE EDGE-LOSING BALANCE- AND I HAVE TO DRAW THE LINE.
BUT--
OUR AGREEMENT IS TERMINATED, HARVEY-- EFFECTIVE NOW.

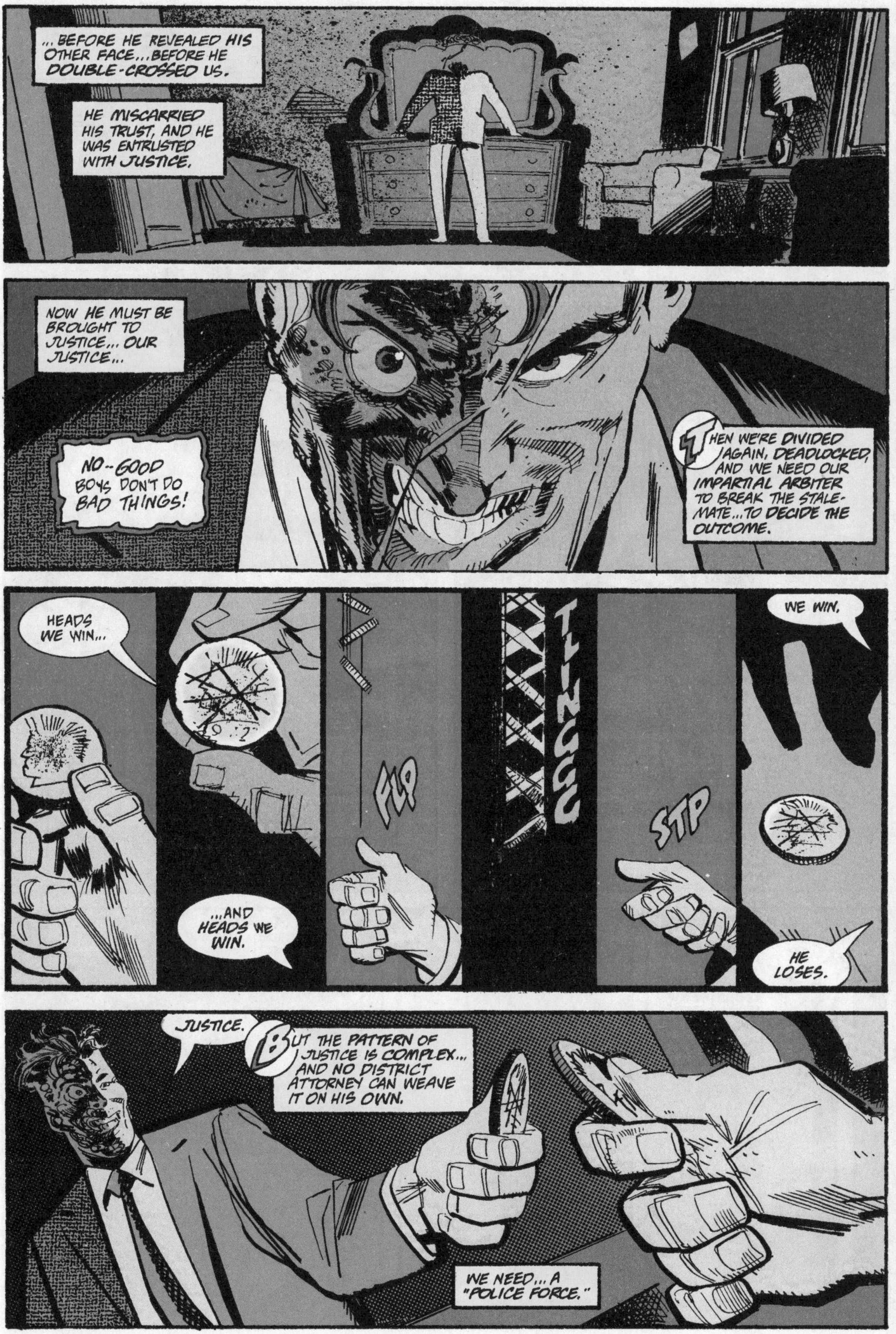
...BEFORE HE REVEALED HIS OTHER FACE...BEFORE HE DOUBLE-CROSSED US.
HE MISCARRIED HIS TRUST, AND HE WAS ENTRUSTED WITH JUSTICE.
NOW HE MUST BE BROUGHT TO JUSTICE... OUR JUSTICE...
NO--GOOD BOYS DON'T DO BAD THINGS!
THEN WE'RE DIVIDED AGAIN, DEADLOCKED, AND WE NEED OUR IMPARTIAL ARBITER TO BREAK THE STALE-MATE...TO DECIDE THE OUTCOME.
HEADS WE WIN...
...AND HEADS WE WIN.
FLP
TLINGGG
STP
WE WIN.
HE LOSES.
JUSTICE.
BUT THE PATTERN OF JUSTICE IS COMPLEX... AND NO DISTRICT ATTORNEY CAN WEAVE IT ON HIS OWN.
WE NEED... A "POLICE FORCE."

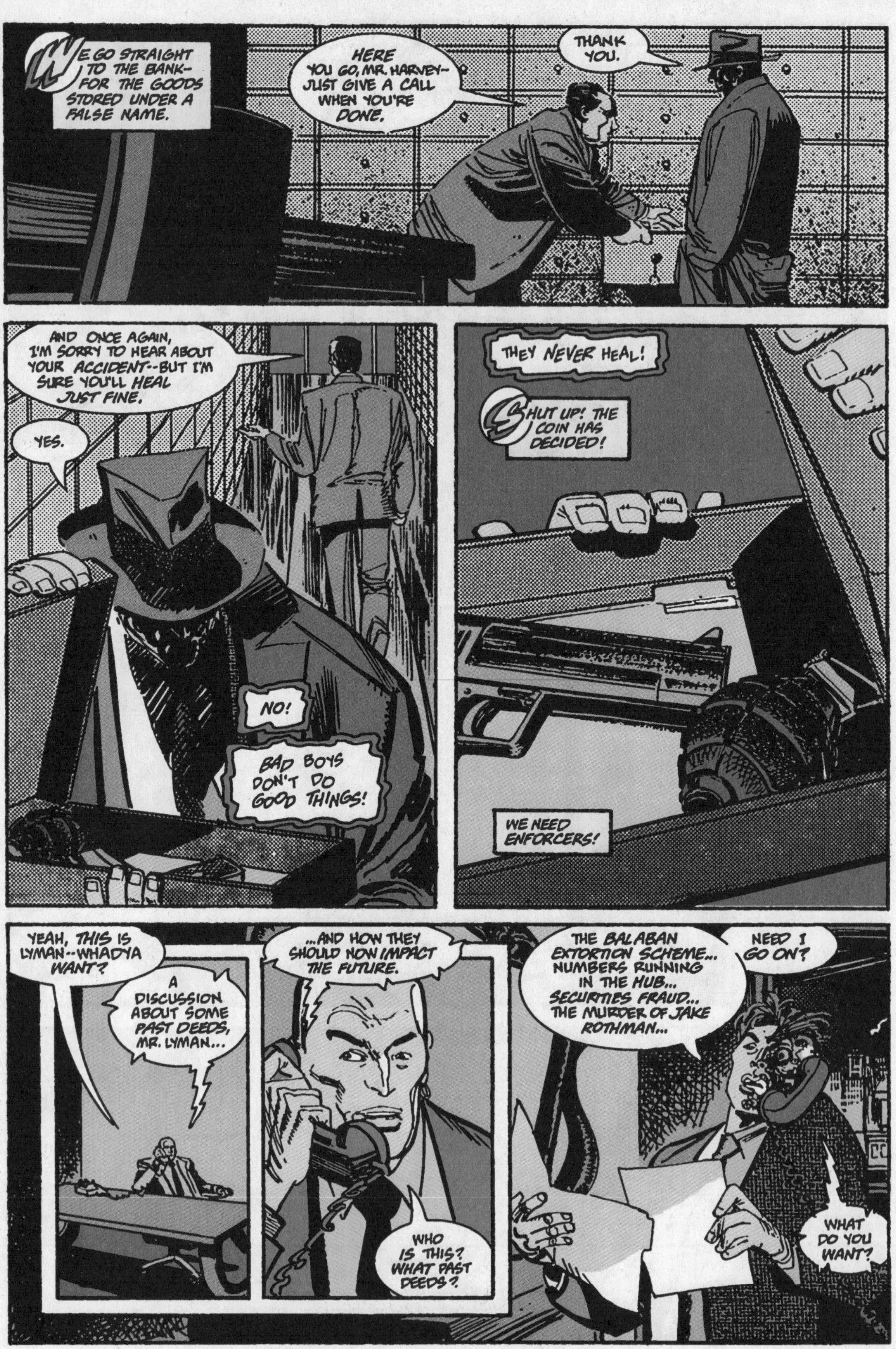
WE GO STRAIGHT TO THE BANK-- FOR THE GOODS STORED UNDER A FALSE NAME.
HERE YOU GO, MR. HARVEY-- JUST GIVE A CALL WHEN YOU'RE DONE.
THANK YOU.
AND ONCE AGAIN, I'M SORRY TO HEAR ABOUT YOUR ACCIDENT--BUT I'M SURE YOU'LL HEAL JUST FINE.
YES.
NO!
BAD BOYS DON'T DO GOOD THINGS!
THEY NEVER HEAL!
SHUT UP! THE COIN HAS DECIDED!
WE NEED ENFORCERS!
YEAH, THIS IS LYMAN--WHADYA WANT?
A DISCUSSION ABOUT SOME PAST DEEDS, MR. LYMAN...
...AND HOW THEY SHOULD NOW IMPACT THE FUTURE.
WHO IS THIS? WHAT PAST DEEDS?
THE BALABAN EXTORTION SCHEME... NUMBERS RUNNING IN THE HUB... SECURTIES FRAUD... THE MURDER OF JAKE ROTHMAN...
NEED I GO ON?
WHAT DO YOU WANT?

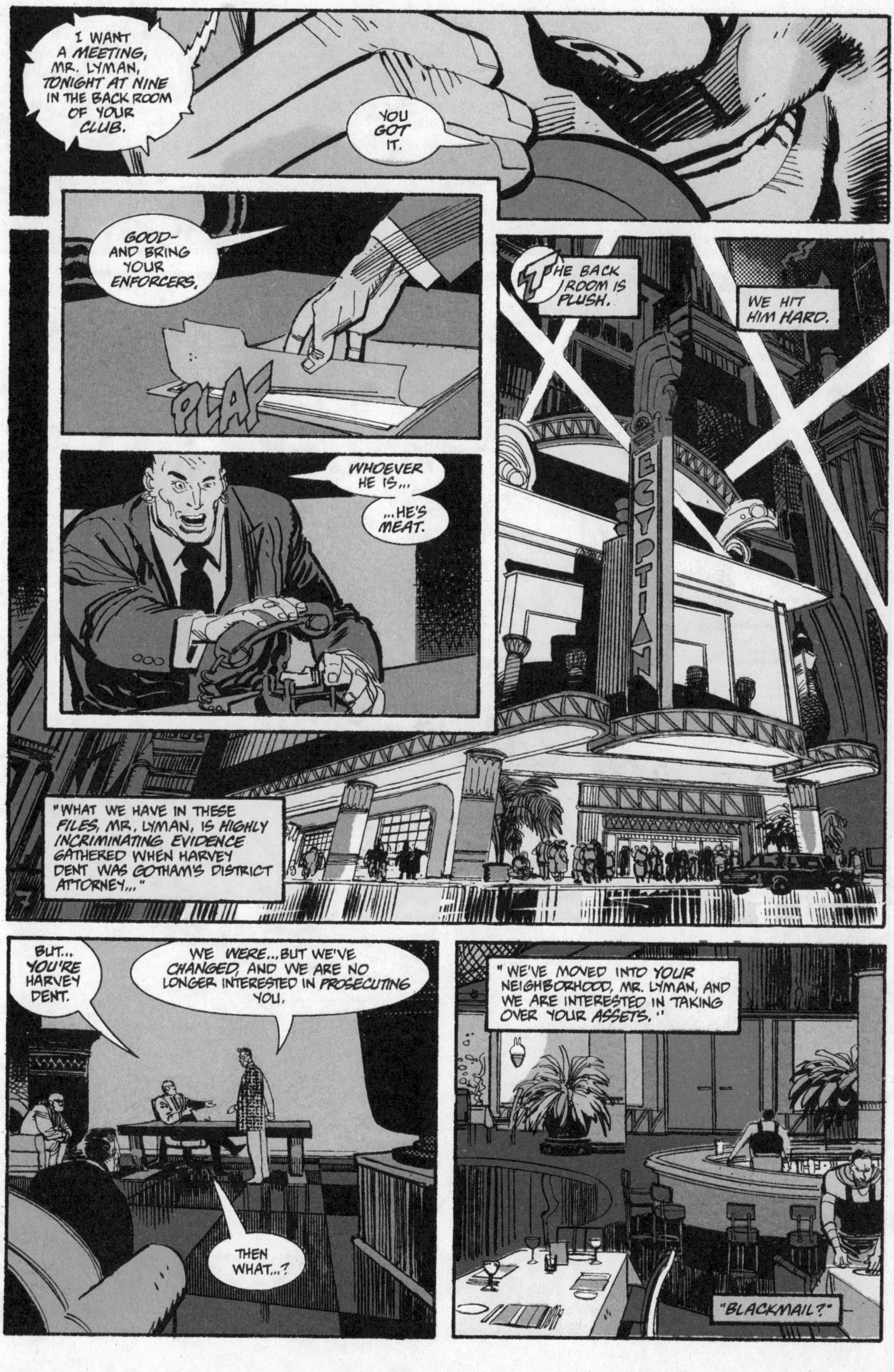
I WANT A MEETING, MR. LYMAN, TONIGHT AT NINE IN THE BACK ROOM OF YOUR CLUB.
YOU GOT IT.
GOOD-AND BRING YOUR ENFORCERS.
PLAF
WHOEVER HE IS...
...HE'S MEAT.
THE BACK ROOM IS PLUSH.
WE HIT HIM HARD.
EGYPTIAN
"WHAT WE HAVE IN THESE FILES, MR. LYMAN, IS HIGHLY INCRIMINATING EVIDENCE GATHERED WHEN HARVEY DENT WAS GOTHAM'S DISTRICT ATTORNEY..."
BUT... YOU'RE HARVEY DENT.
WE WERE...BUT WE'VE CHANGED, AND WE ARE NO LONGER INTERESTED IN PROSECUTING YOU.
THEN WHAT...?
"WE'VE MOVED INTO YOUR NEIGHBORHOOD, MR. LYMAN, AND WE ARE INTERESTED IN TAKING OVER YOUR ASSETS."
"BLACKMAIL?"

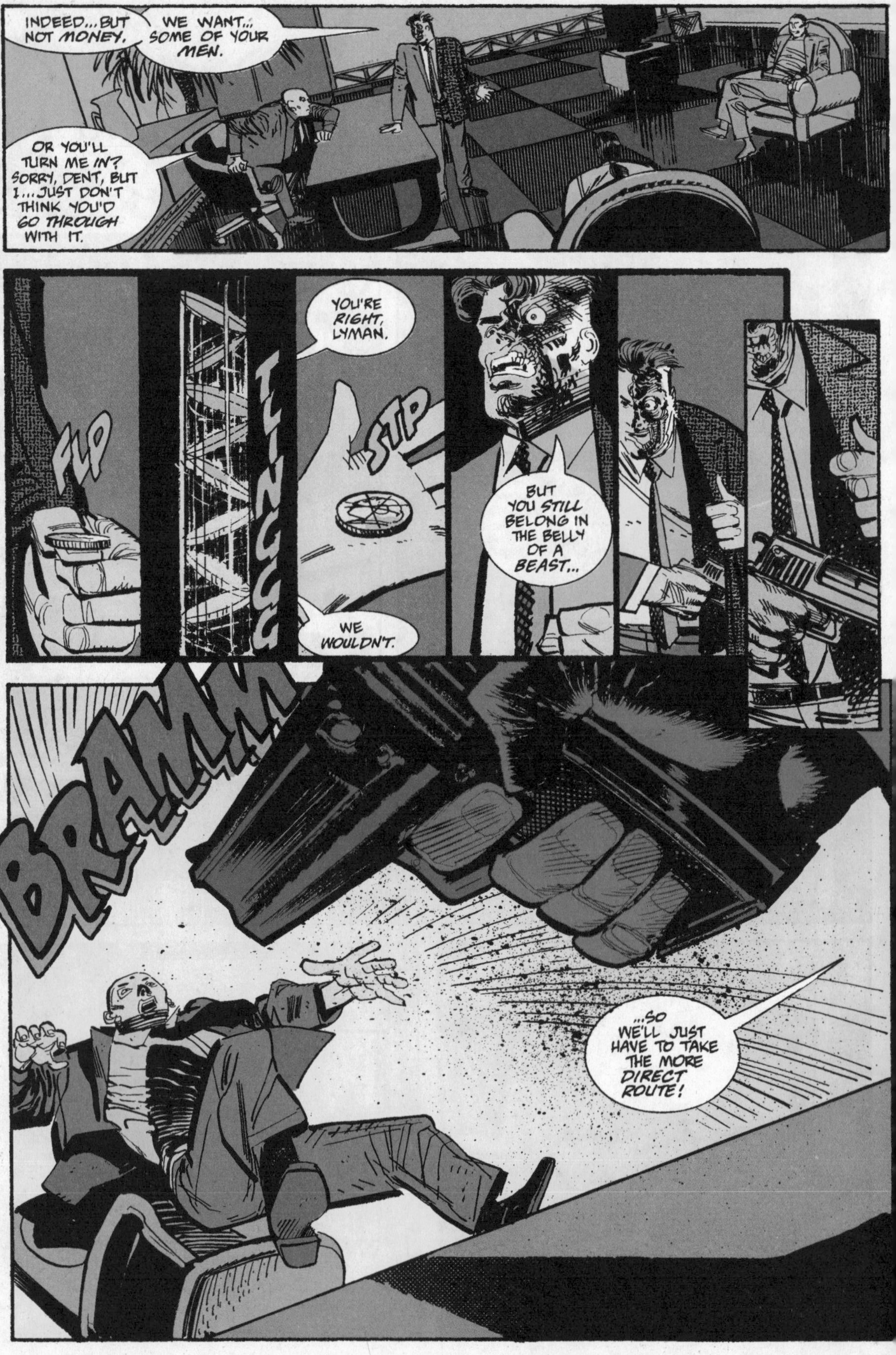
INDEED... BUT NOT MONEY.
WE WANT... SOME OF YOUR MEN.
OR YOU'LL TURN ME IN? SORRY, DENT, BUT I... JUST DON'T THINK YOU'D GO THROUGH WITH IT.
FLP
TLINGGG
YOU'RE RIGHT, LYMAN.
STP
WE WOULDN'T.
BUT YOU STILL BELONG IN THE BELLY OF A BEAST...
BRAMM
...SO WE'LL JUST HAVE TO TAKE THE MORE DIRECT ROUTE!

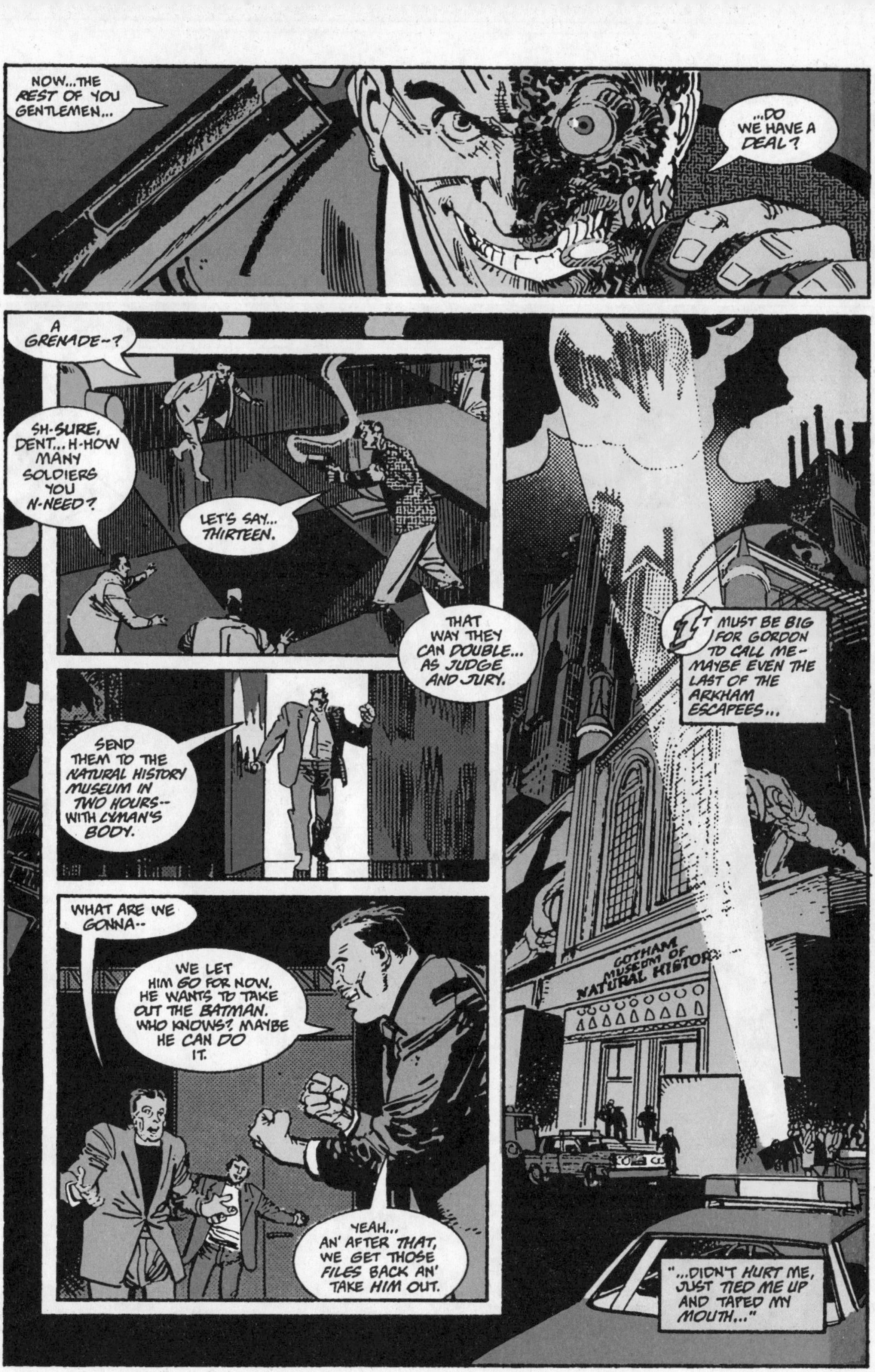

NOW... THE REST OF YOU GENTLEMEN...
...DO WE HAVE A DEAL?
A GRENADE--?
SH-SURE, DENT... H-HOW MANY SOLDIERS YOU N-NEED?
LET'S SAY... THIRTEEN.
THAT WAY THEY CAN DOUBLE... AS JUDGE AND JURY.
SEND THEM TO THE NATURAL HISTORY MUSEUM IN TWO HOURS-- WITH LYMAN'S BODY.
WHAT ARE WE GONNA--
WE LET HIM GO FOR NOW. HE WANTS TO TAKE OUT THE BATMAN. WHO KNOWS? MAYBE HE CAN DO IT.
YEAH... AN' AFTER THAT, WE GET THOSE FILES BACK AN' TAKE HIM OUT.
IT MUST BE BIG FOR GORDON TO CALL ME-- MAYBE EVEN THE LAST OF THE ARKHAM ESCAPEES...
GOTHAM MUSEUM OF NATURAL HISTOR
"...DIDN'T HURT ME, JUST TIED ME UP AND TAPED MY MOUTH..."

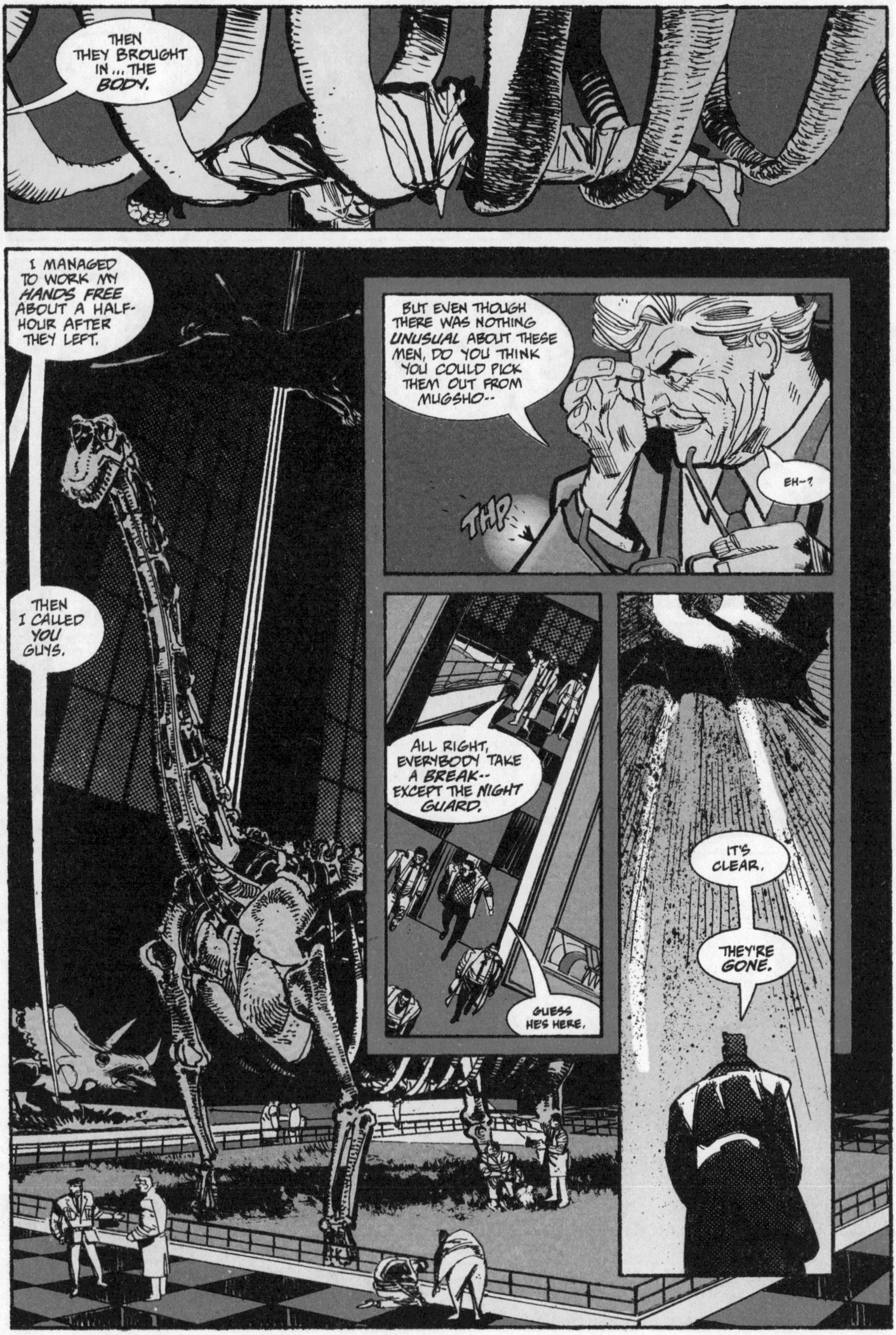

THEN THEY BROUGHT IN... THE BODY.
I MANAGED TO WORK MY HANDS FREE ABOUT A HALF-HOUR AFTER THEY LEFT.
THEN I CALLED YOU GUYS.
BUT EVEN THOUGH THERE WAS NOTHING UNUSUAL ABOUT THESE MEN, DO YOU THINK YOU COULD PICK THEM OUT FROM MUGSHO--
THP
EH--?
ALL RIGHT, EVERYBODY TAKE A BREAK-- EXCEPT THE NIGHT GUARD.
GUESS HE'S HERE.
IT'S CLEAR.
THEY'RE GONE.

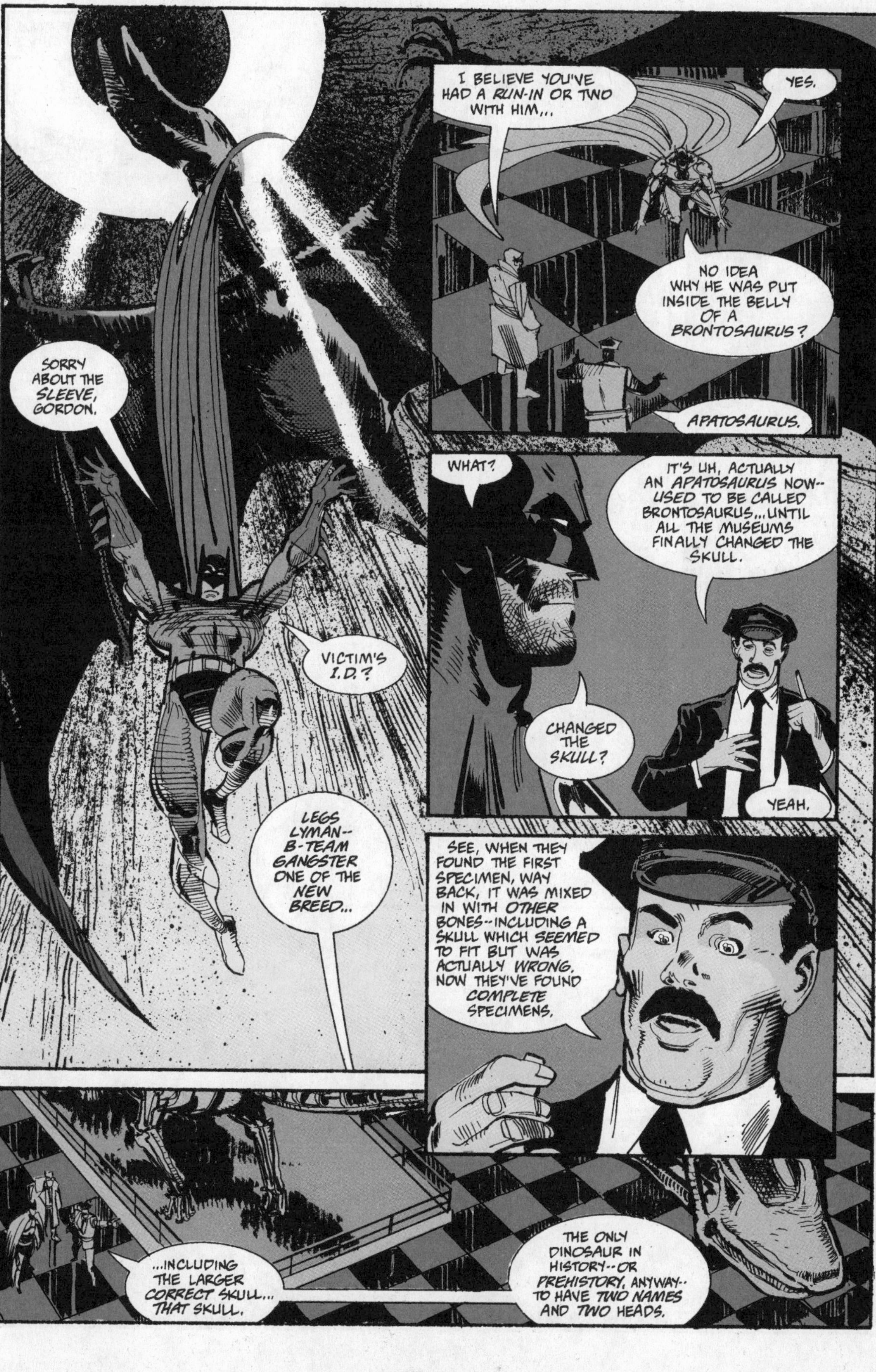

SORRY ABOUT THE SLEEVE, GORDON.
VICTIM'S I.D.?
LEGS LYMAN-- B-TEAM GANGSTER ONE OF THE NEW BREED...
I BELIEVE YOU'VE HAD A RUN-IN OR TWO WITH HIM...
YES.
NO IDEA WHY HE WAS PUT INSIDE THE BELLY OF A BRONTOSAURUS?
APATOSAURUS.
WHAT?
IT'S UH, ACTUALLY AN APATOSAURUS NOW-- USED TO BE CALLED BRONTOSAURUS...UNTIL ALL THE MUSEUMS FINALLY CHANGED THE SKULL.
CHANGED THE SKULL?
YEAH.
SEE, WHEN THEY FOUND THE FIRST SPECIMEN, WAY BACK, IT WAS MIXED IN WITH OTHER BONES--INCLUDING A SKULL WHICH SEEMED TO FIT BUT WAS ACTUALLY WRONG. NOW THEY'VE FOUND COMPLETE SPECIMENS.
...INCLUDING THE LARGER CORRECT SKULL... THAT SKULL.
THE ONLY DINOSAUR IN HISTORY--OR PREHISTORY, ANYWAY-- TO HAVE TWO NAMES AND TWO HEADS.

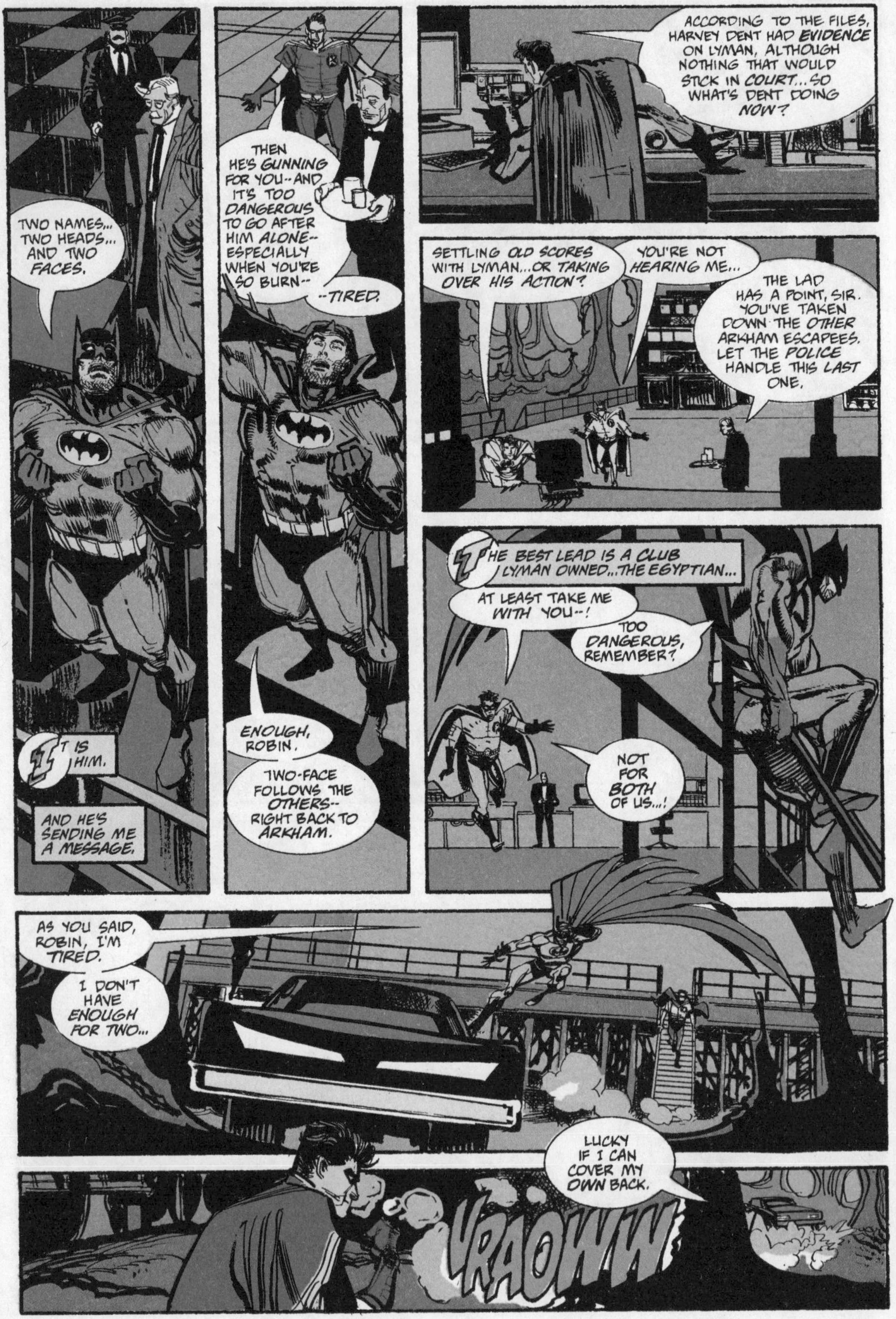
TWO NAMES... TWO HEADS... AND TWO FACES.
IT IS HIM.
AND HE'S SENDING ME A MESSAGE.
THEN HE'S GUNNING FOR YOU--AND IT'S TOO DANGEROUS TO GO AFTER HIM ALONE--ESPECIALLY WHEN YOU'RE SO BURN--
--TIRED.
ENOUGH, ROBIN.
TWO-FACE FOLLOWS THE OTHERS--RIGHT BACK TO ARKHAM.
ACCORDING TO THE FILES, HARVEY DENT HAD EVIDENCE ON LYMAN, ALTHOUGH NOTHING THAT WOULD STICK IN COURT... SO WHAT'S DENT DOING NOW?
SETTLING OLD SCORES WITH LYMAN... OR TAKING OVER HIS ACTION?
YOU'RE NOT HEARING ME...
THE LAD HAS A POINT, SIR. YOU'VE TAKEN DOWN THE OTHER ARKHAM ESCAPEES. LET THE POLICE HANDLE THIS LAST ONE.
THE BEST LEAD IS A CLUB LYMAN OWNED... THE EGYPTIAN...
AT LEAST TAKE ME WITH YOU--!
TOO DANGEROUS, REMEMBER?
NOT FOR BOTH OF US...!
AS YOU SAID, ROBIN, I'M TIRED.
I DON'T HAVE ENOUGH FOR TWO...
LUCKY IF I CAN COVER MY OWN BACK.
VRAOWW

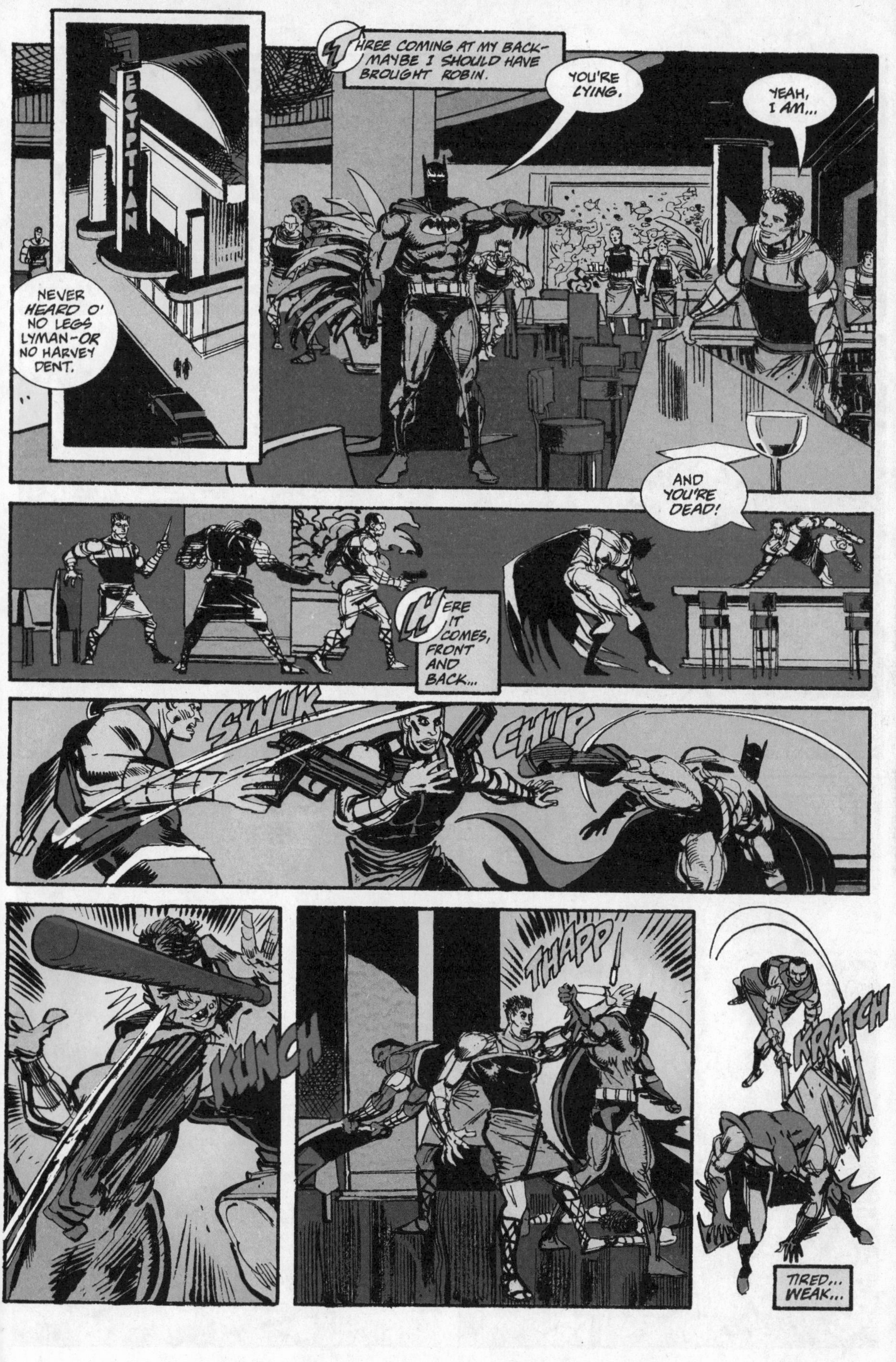
NEVER HEARD O' NO LEGS LYMAN-OR NO HARVEY DENT.
THREE COMING AT MY BACK-MAYBE I SHOULD HAVE BROUGHT ROBIN.
YOU'RE LYING.
YEAH, I AM...
AND YOU'RE DEAD!
HERE IT COMES, FRONT AND BACK...
SHUK
CHIP
KUNCH
THAPP
KRATCH
TIRED... WEAK...

By now, all four should be down to stay...

...the fight finished in seconds...

But instead--

UHN--!

SWOKK

KWUMP

--They just keep coming...

...big and clumsy...

CHUFT

SNKUEE

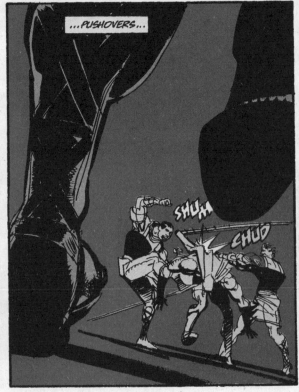

...pushovers...

SHUM

CHUD

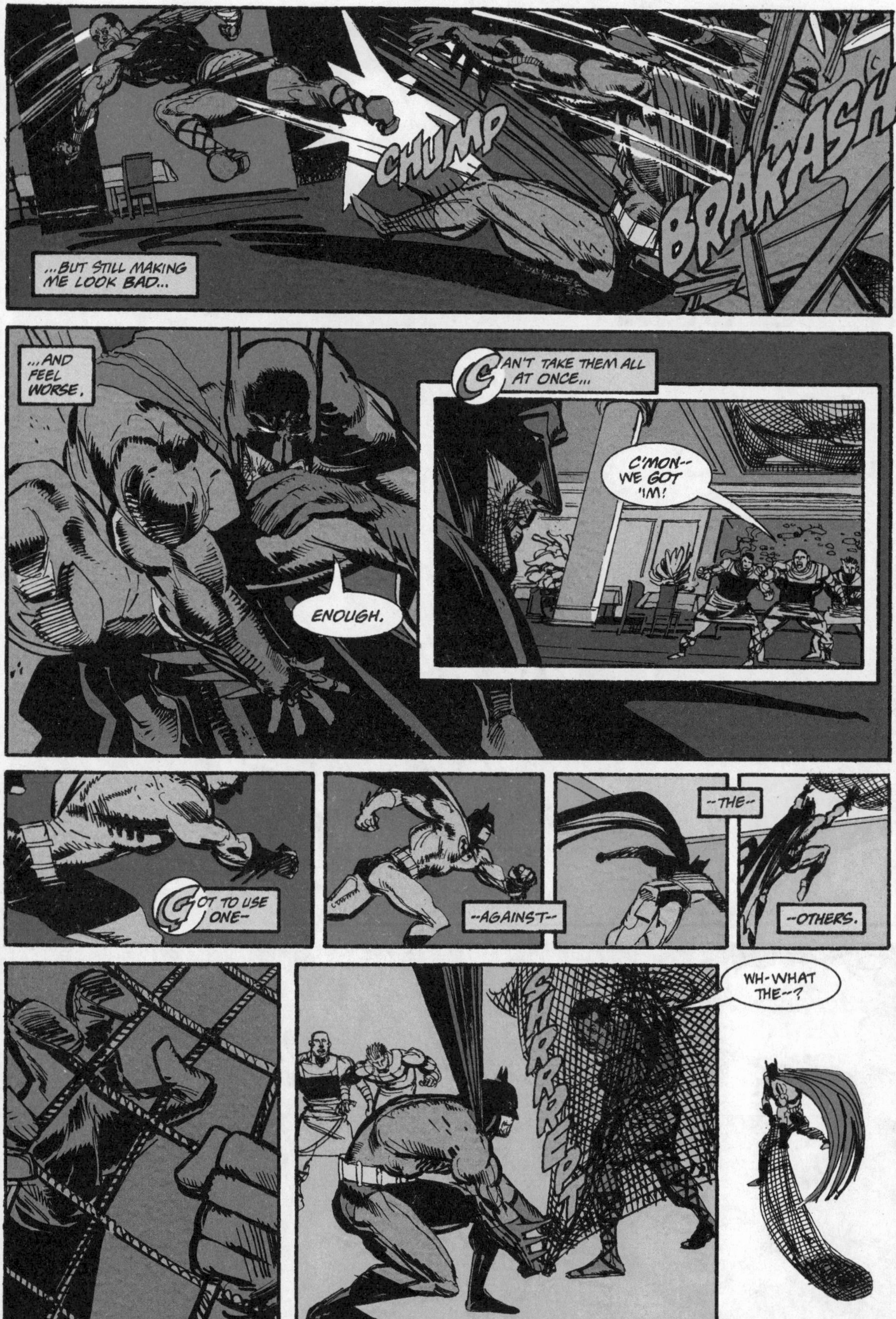

CHUMP
BRAKASH
...BUT STILL MAKING ME LOOK BAD...
...AND FEEL WORSE.
CAN'T TAKE THEM ALL AT ONCE...
C'MON-- WE GOT 'IM!
ENOUGH.
GOT TO USE ONE--
--AGAINST--
--THE--
--OTHERS.
WH-WHAT THE--?
SHRREPT

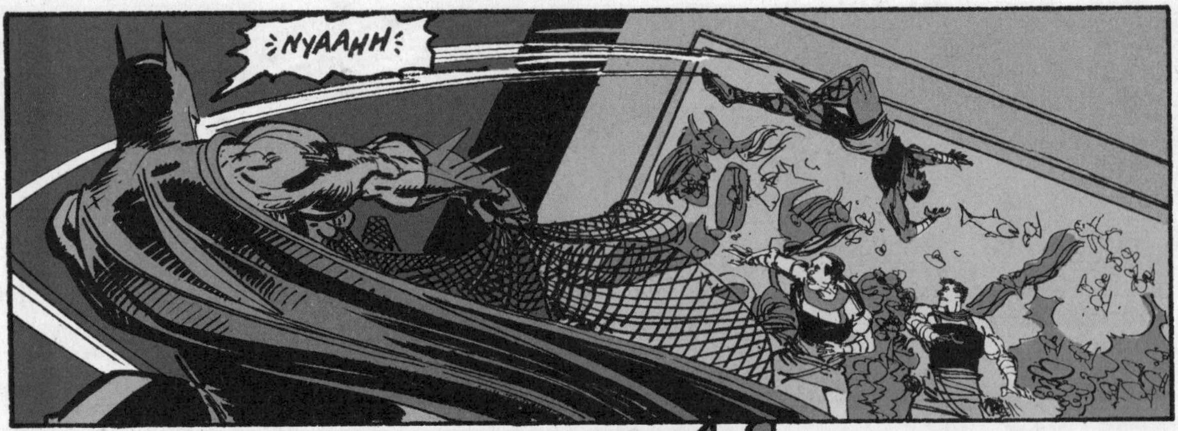
NYAAHH

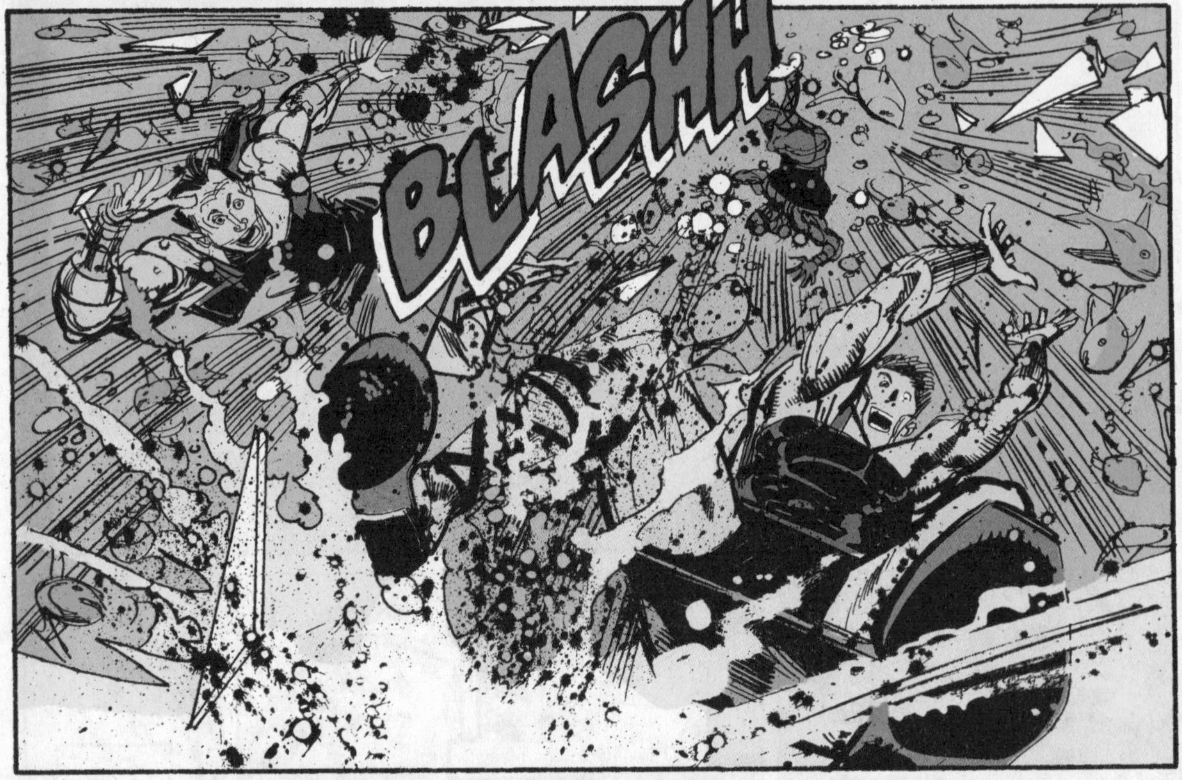
BLASHH

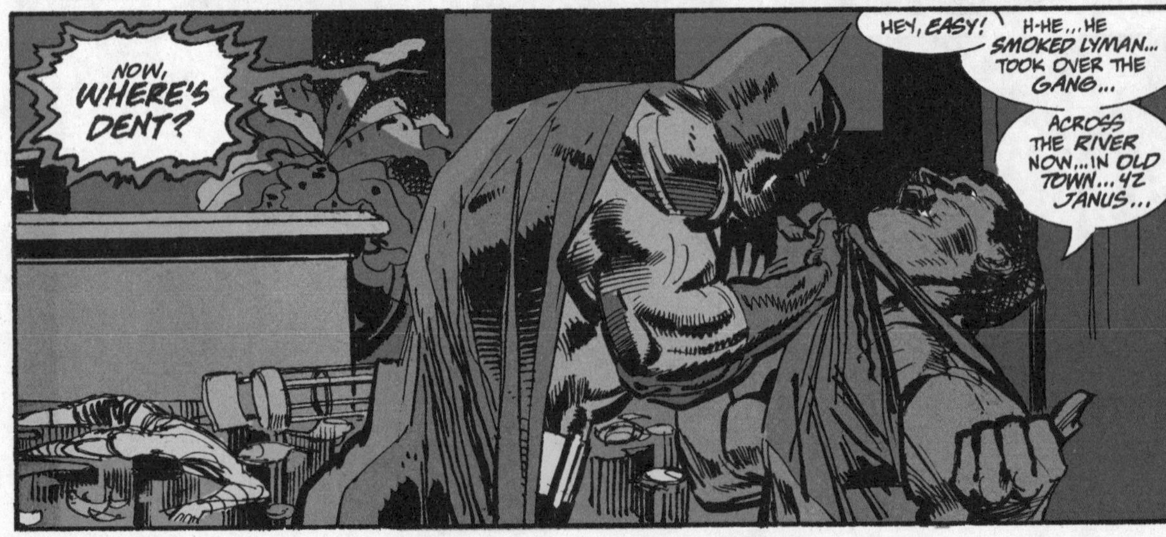
NOW, WHERE'S DENT?
HEY, EASY!
H-HE...HE SMOKED LYMAN... TOOK OVER THE GANG...
ACROSS THE RIVER NOW...IN OLD TOWN...42 JANUS...

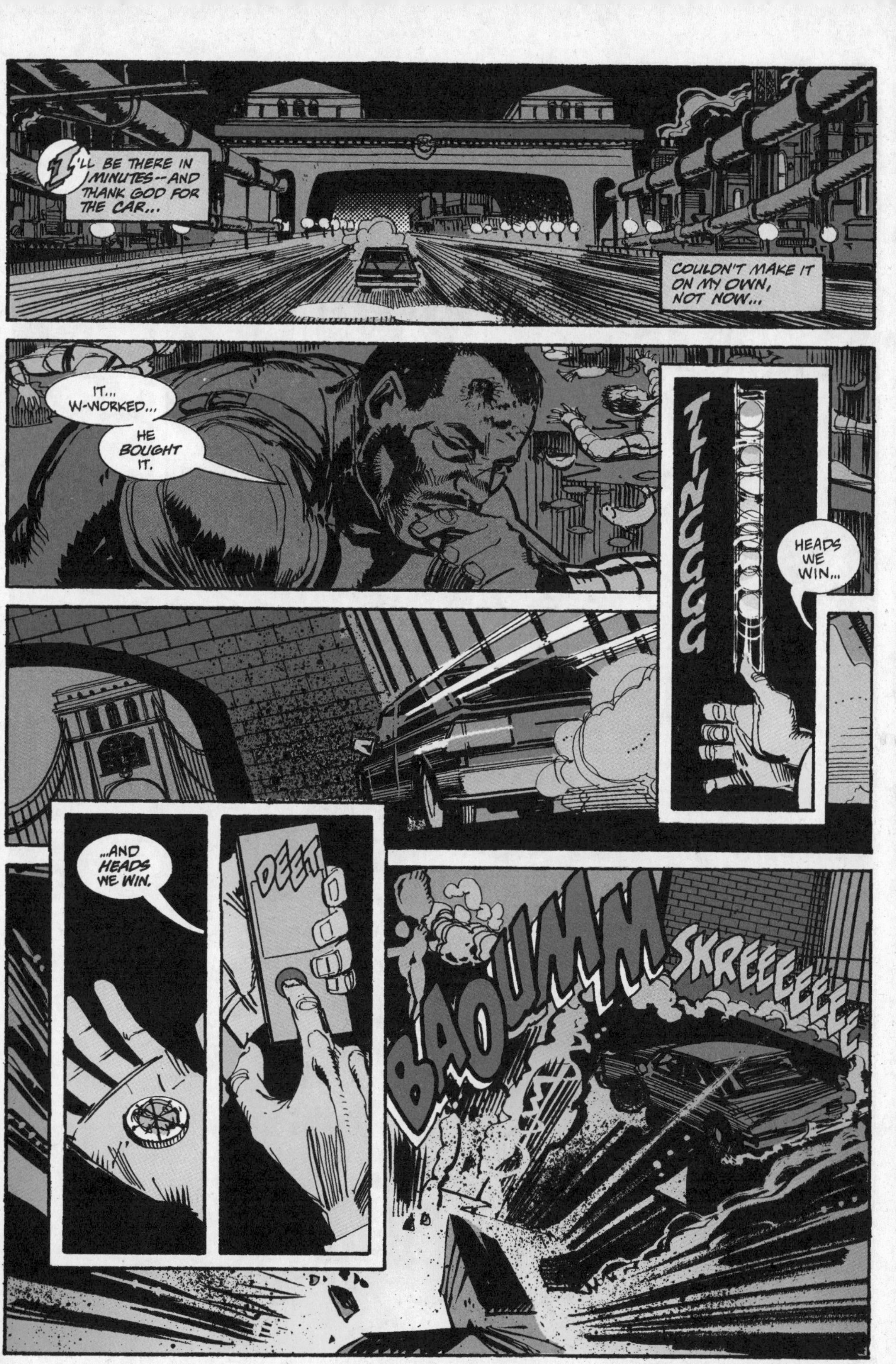
I'LL BE THERE IN MINUTES--AND THANK GOD FOR THE CAR...
COULDN'T MAKE IT ON MY OWN, NOT NOW...
IT... W-WORKED...
HE BOUGHT IT.
TLINGGGG
HEADS WE WIN...
...AND HEADS WE WIN.
DEET
BAOUMM
SKREEEEEEE

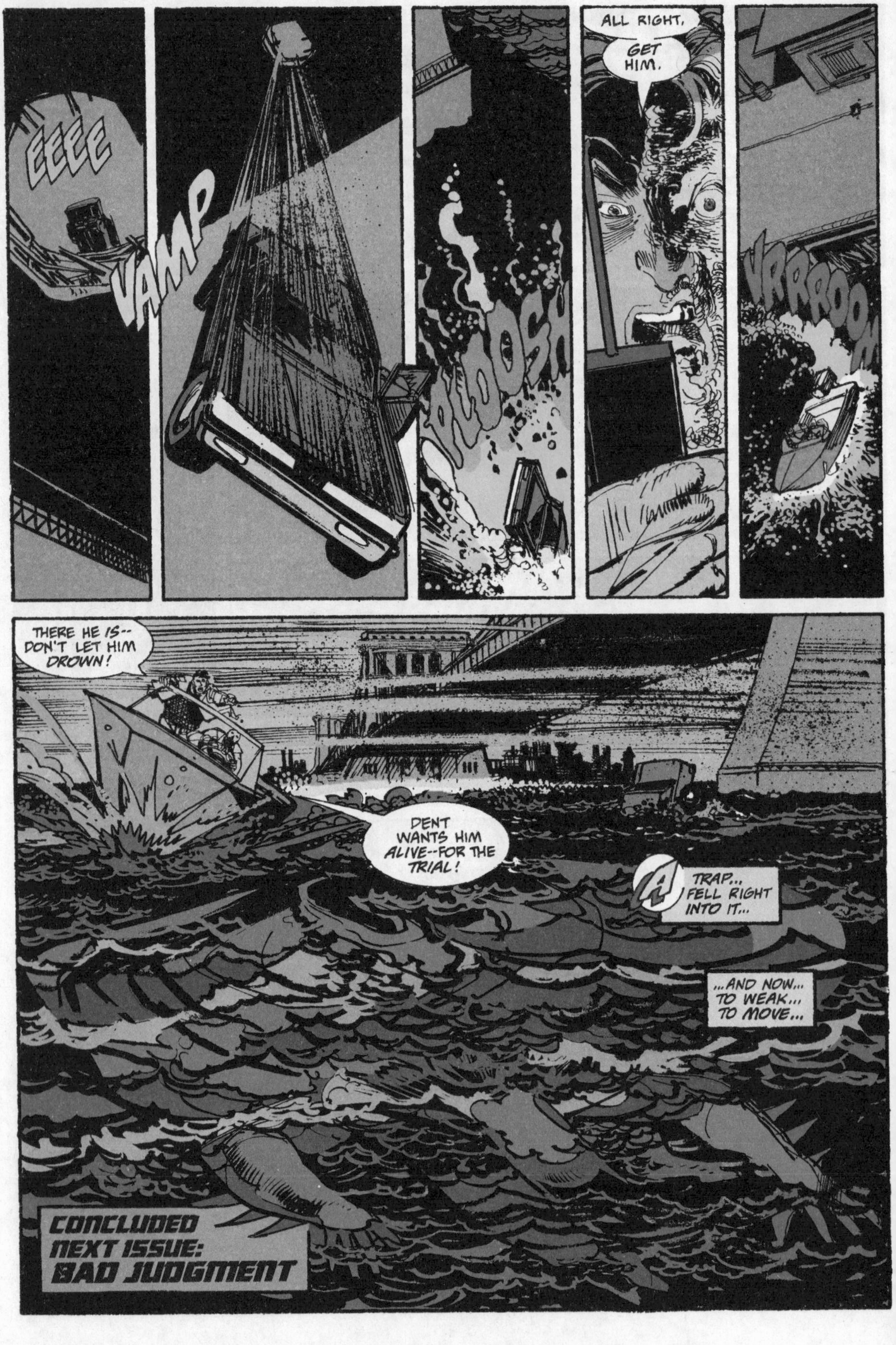
EEEE
VAMP
WHOOSH
ALL RIGHT,
GET HIM.
VRRROOM
THERE HE IS--
DON'T LET HIM
DROWN!
DENT
WANTS HIM
ALIVE--FOR THE
TRIAL!
A TRAP...
FELL RIGHT
INTO IT...
...AND NOW...
TO WEAK...
TO MOVE...
CONCLUDED
NEXT ISSUE:
BAD JUDGMENT

Cover art by GLENN FABRY

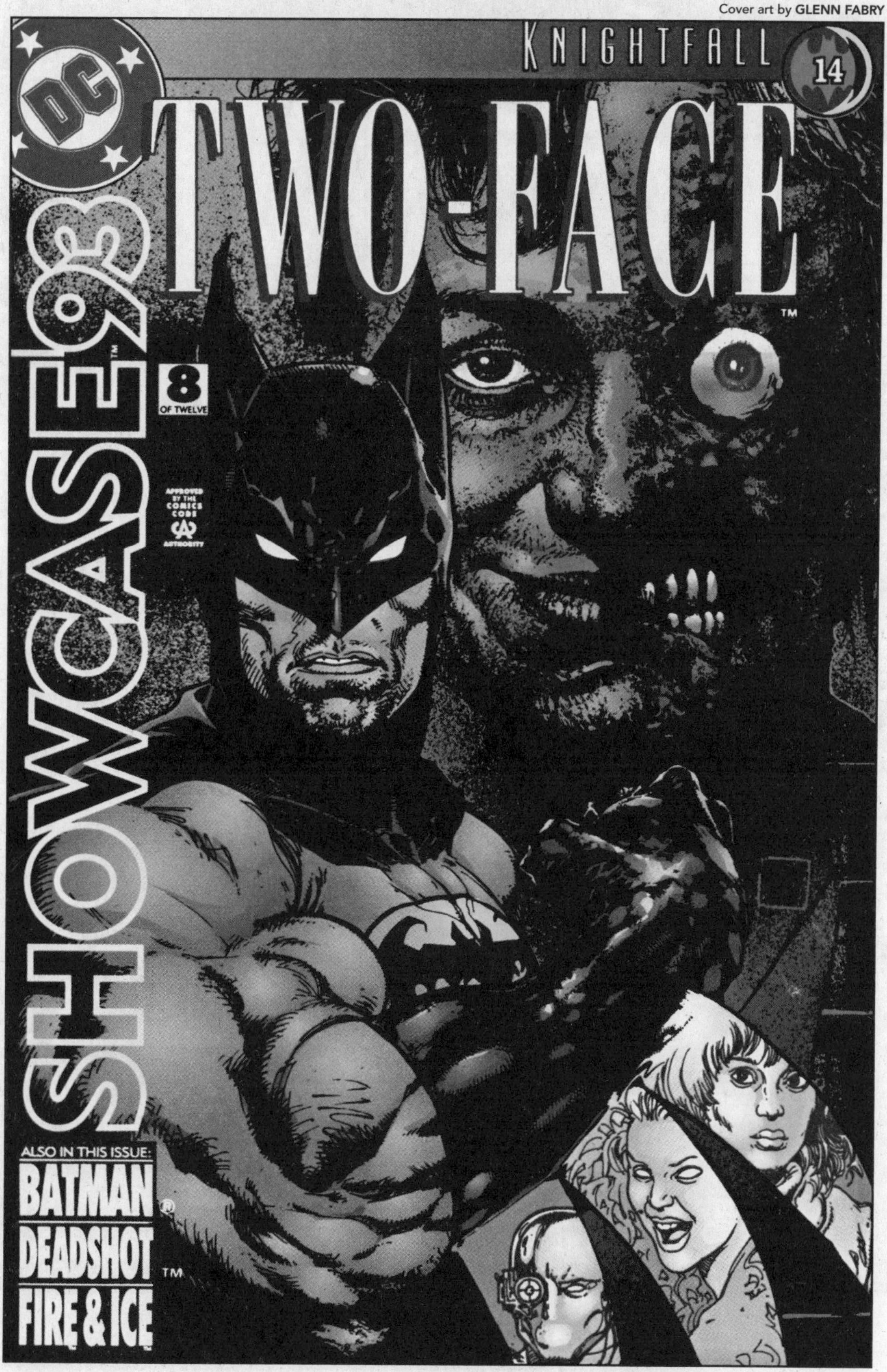
DC
KNIGHTFALL
14
TWO-FACE™
SHOWCASE'93™
8
OF TWELVE
APPROVED BY THE COMICS CODE AUTHORITY
ALSO IN THIS ISSUE:
BATMAN®
DEADSHOT™
FIRE & ICE

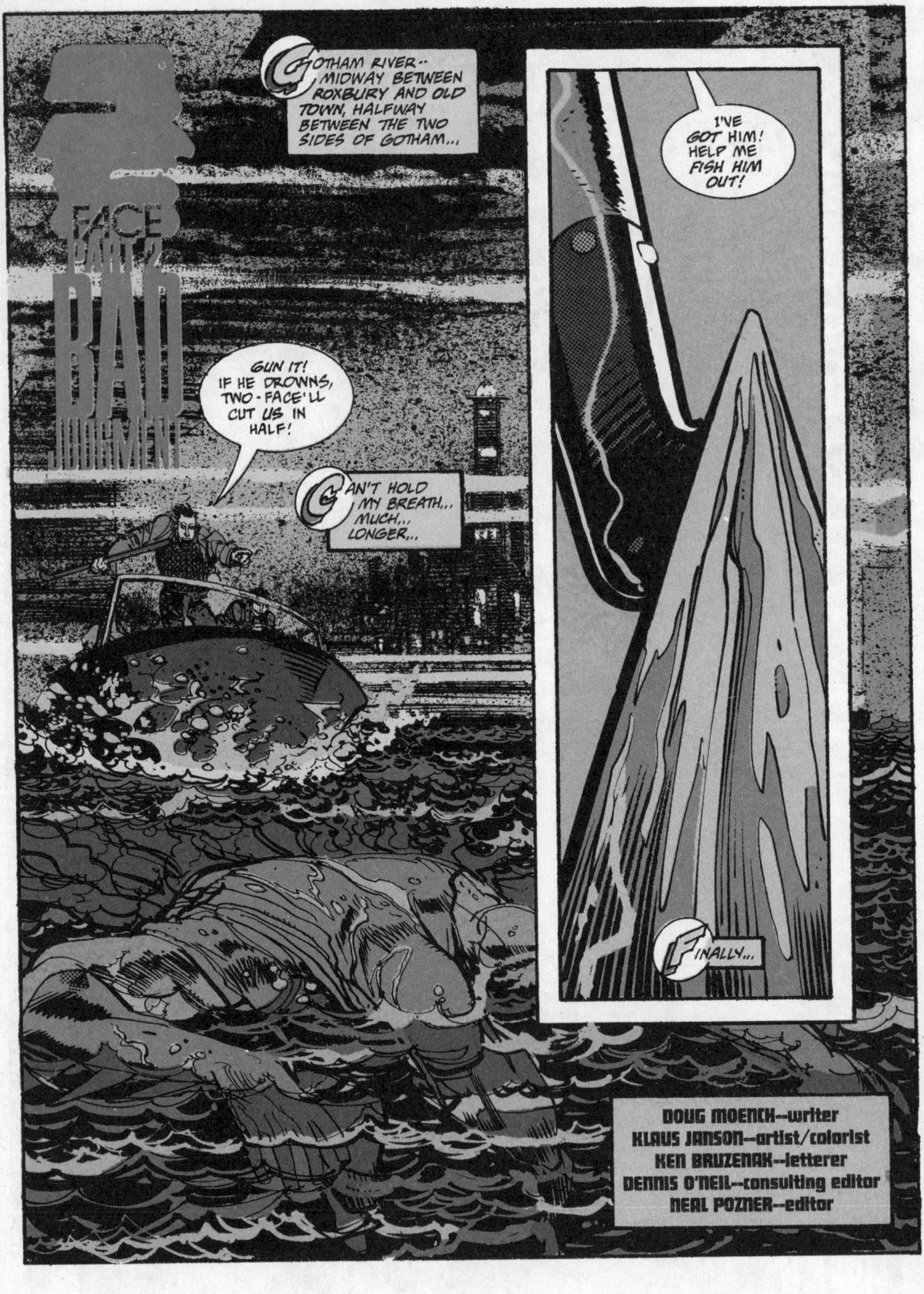
TWO FACE PART 2 BAD JUDGMENT
GOTHAM RIVER-- MIDWAY BETWEEN ROXBURY AND OLD TOWN, HALFWAY BETWEEN THE TWO SIDES OF GOTHAM...
I'VE GOT HIM! HELP ME FISH HIM OUT!
GUN IT! IF HE DROWNS, TWO-FACE'LL CUT US IN HALF!
CAN'T HOLD MY BREATH... MUCH... LONGER...
FINALLY...
DOUG MOENCH--writer
KLAUS JANSON--artist/colorist
KEN BRUZENAK--letterer
DENNIS O'NEIL--consulting editor
NEAL POZNER--editor

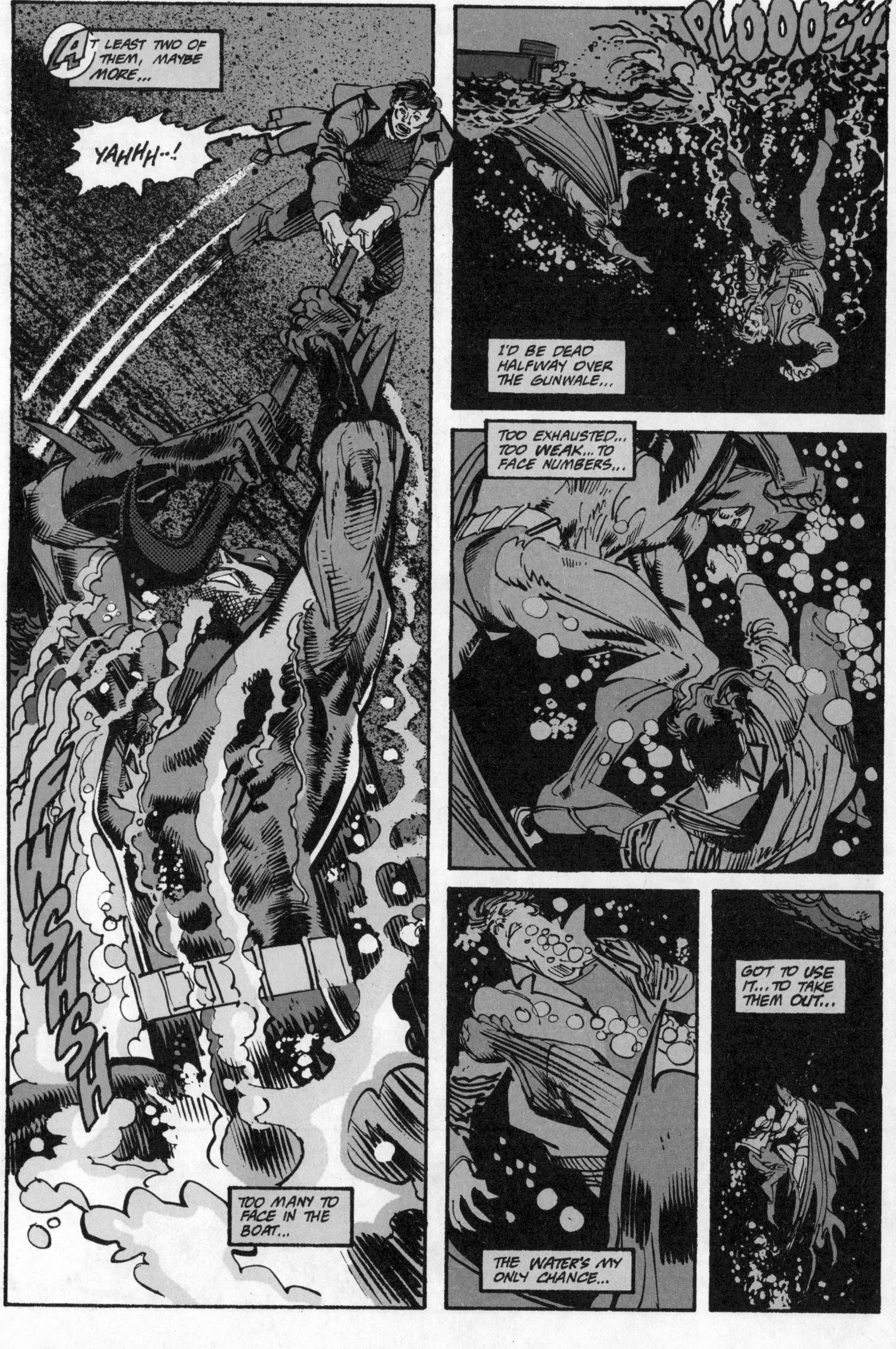
AT LEAST TWO OF THEM, MAYBE MORE...
YAHHH--!
PLOOOSH
I'D BE DEAD HALFWAY OVER THE GUNWALE...
TOO MANY TO FACE IN THE BOAT...
TOO EXHAUSTED... TOO WEAK... TO FACE NUMBERS...
THE WATER'S MY ONLY CHANCE...
GOT TO USE IT... TO TAKE THEM OUT...

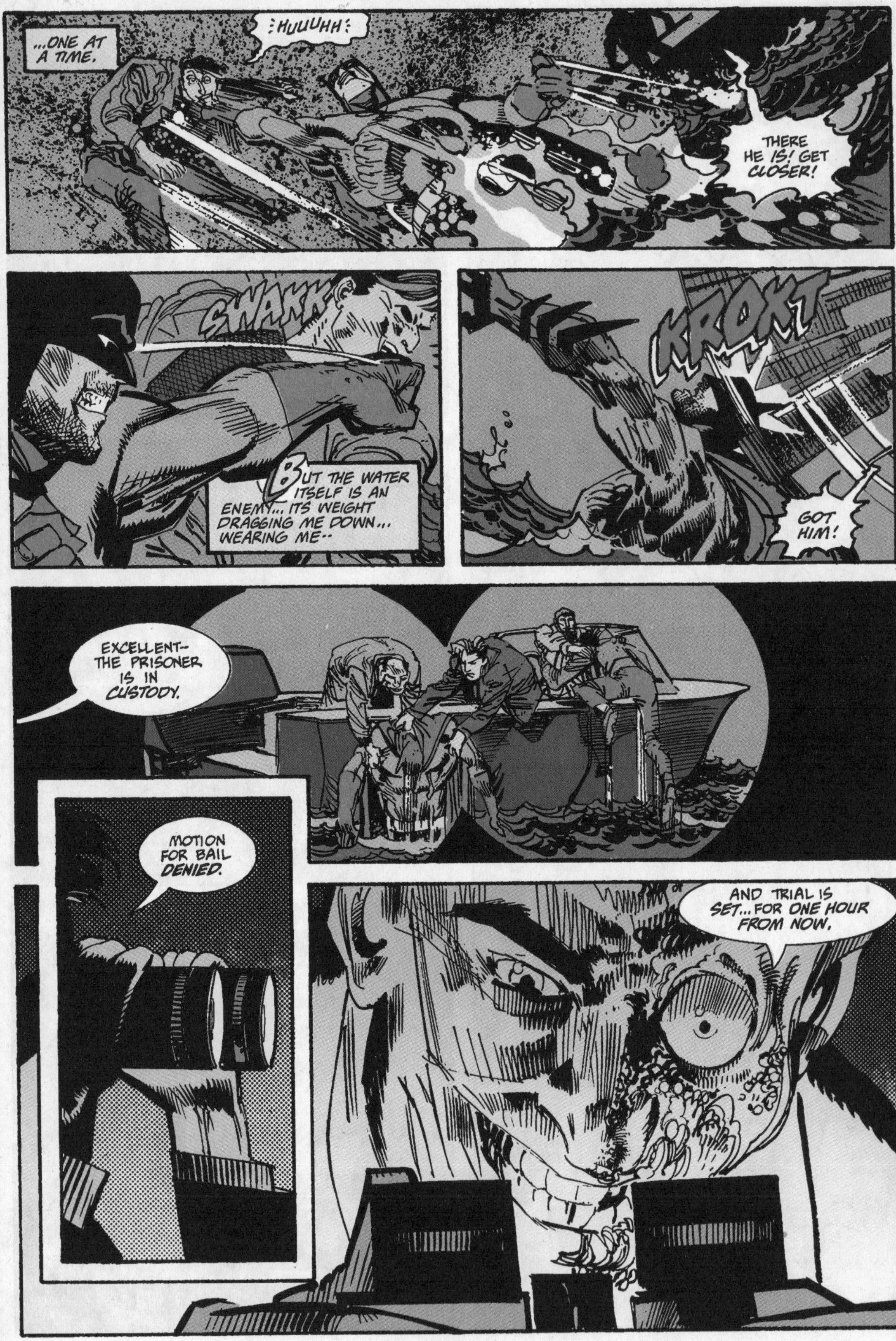
...ONE AT A TIME.
HUUUHH
THERE HE IS! GET CLOSER!
SHAKK
BUT THE WATER ITSELF IS AN ENEMY... ITS WEIGHT DRAGGING ME DOWN... WEARING ME--
KROKT
GOT HIM!
EXCELLENT-- THE PRISONER IS IN CUSTODY.
MOTION FOR BAIL DENIED.
AND TRIAL IS SET... FOR ONE HOUR FROM NOW.

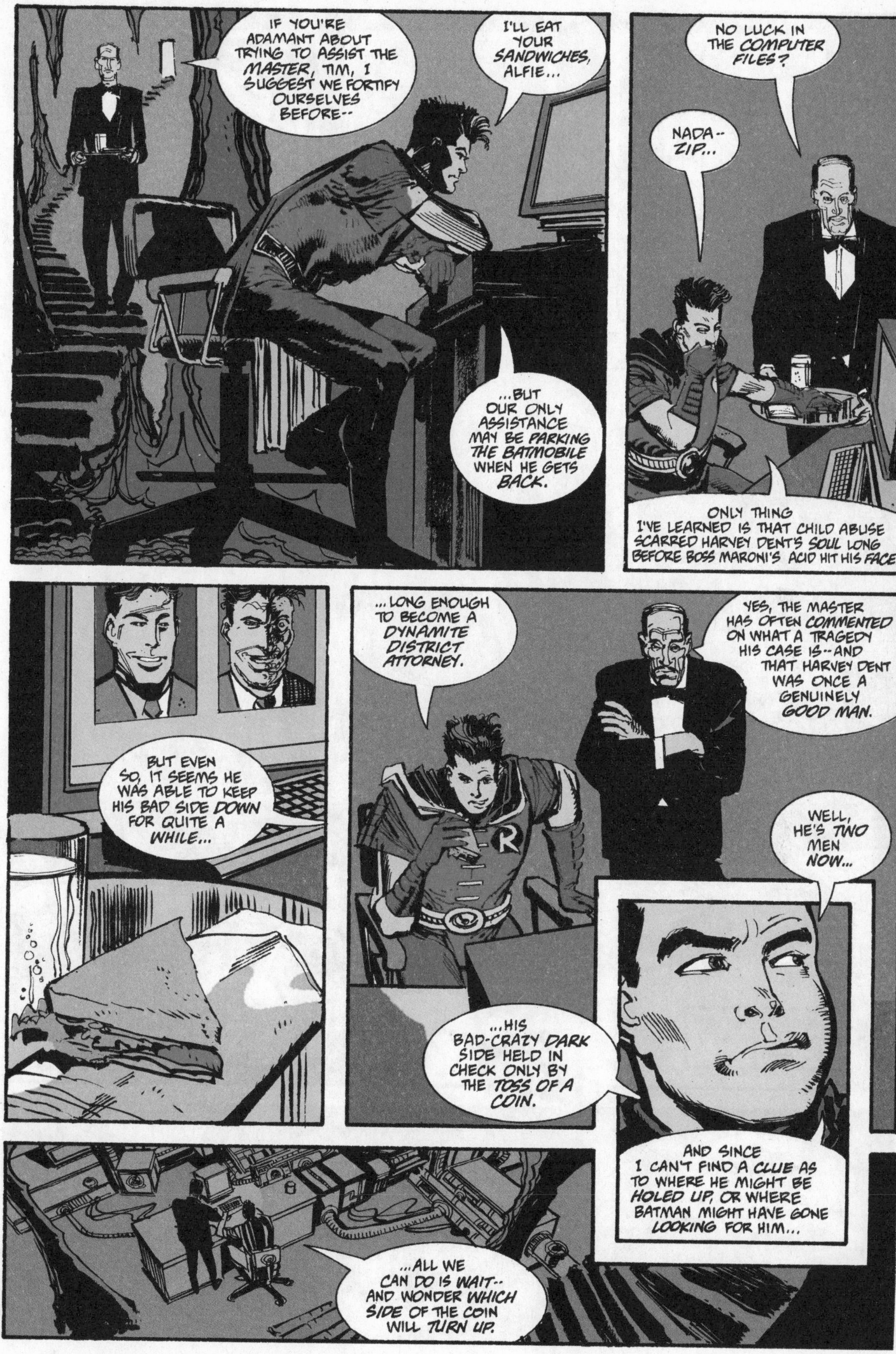

IF YOU'RE ADAMANT ABOUT TRYING TO ASSIST THE MASTER, TIM, I SUGGEST WE FORTIFY OURSELVES BEFORE--
I'LL EAT YOUR SANDWICHES, ALFIE...
...BUT OUR ONLY ASSISTANCE MAY BE PARKING THE BATMOBILE WHEN HE GETS BACK.
NO LUCK IN THE COMPUTER FILES?
NADA-- ZIP...
ONLY THING I'VE LEARNED IS THAT CHILD ABUSE SCARRED HARVEY DENT'S SOUL LONG BEFORE BOSS MARONI'S ACID HIT HIS FACE.
BUT EVEN SO, IT SEEMS HE WAS ABLE TO KEEP HIS BAD SIDE DOWN FOR QUITE A WHILE...
...LONG ENOUGH TO BECOME A DYNAMITE DISTRICT ATTORNEY.
YES, THE MASTER HAS OFTEN COMMENTED ON WHAT A TRAGEDY HIS CASE IS--AND THAT HARVEY DENT WAS ONCE A GENUINELY GOOD MAN.
WELL, HE'S TWO MEN NOW...
...HIS BAD-CRAZY DARK SIDE HELD IN CHECK ONLY BY THE TOSS OF A COIN.
AND SINCE I CAN'T FIND A CLUE AS TO WHERE HE MIGHT BE HOLED UP, OR WHERE BATMAN MIGHT HAVE GONE LOOKING FOR HIM...
...ALL WE CAN DO IS WAIT-- AND WONDER WHICH SIDE OF THE COIN WILL TURN UP.

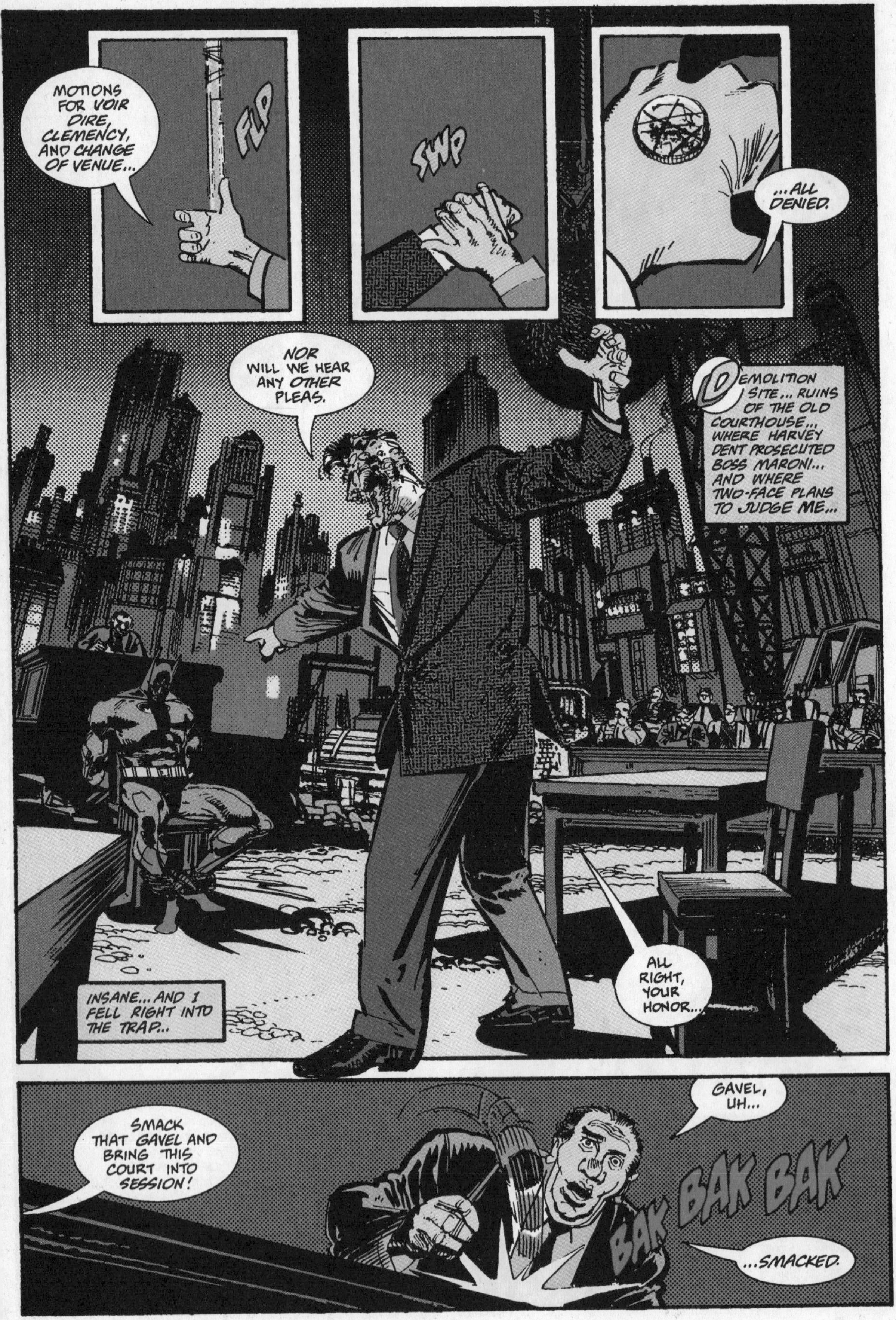
MOTIONS FOR VOIR DIRE, CLEMENCY, AND CHANGE OF VENUE...
FLP
SWP
...ALL DENIED.
NOR WILL WE HEAR ANY OTHER PLEAS.
DEMOLITION SITE... RUINS OF THE OLD COURTHOUSE... WHERE HARVEY DENT PROSECUTED BOSS MARONI... AND WHERE TWO-FACE PLANS TO JUDGE ME...
INSANE... AND I FELL RIGHT INTO THE TRAP...
ALL RIGHT, YOUR HONOR...
SMACK THAT GAVEL AND BRING THIS COURT INTO SESSION!
GAVEL, UH...
BAK BAK BAK
...SMACKED.

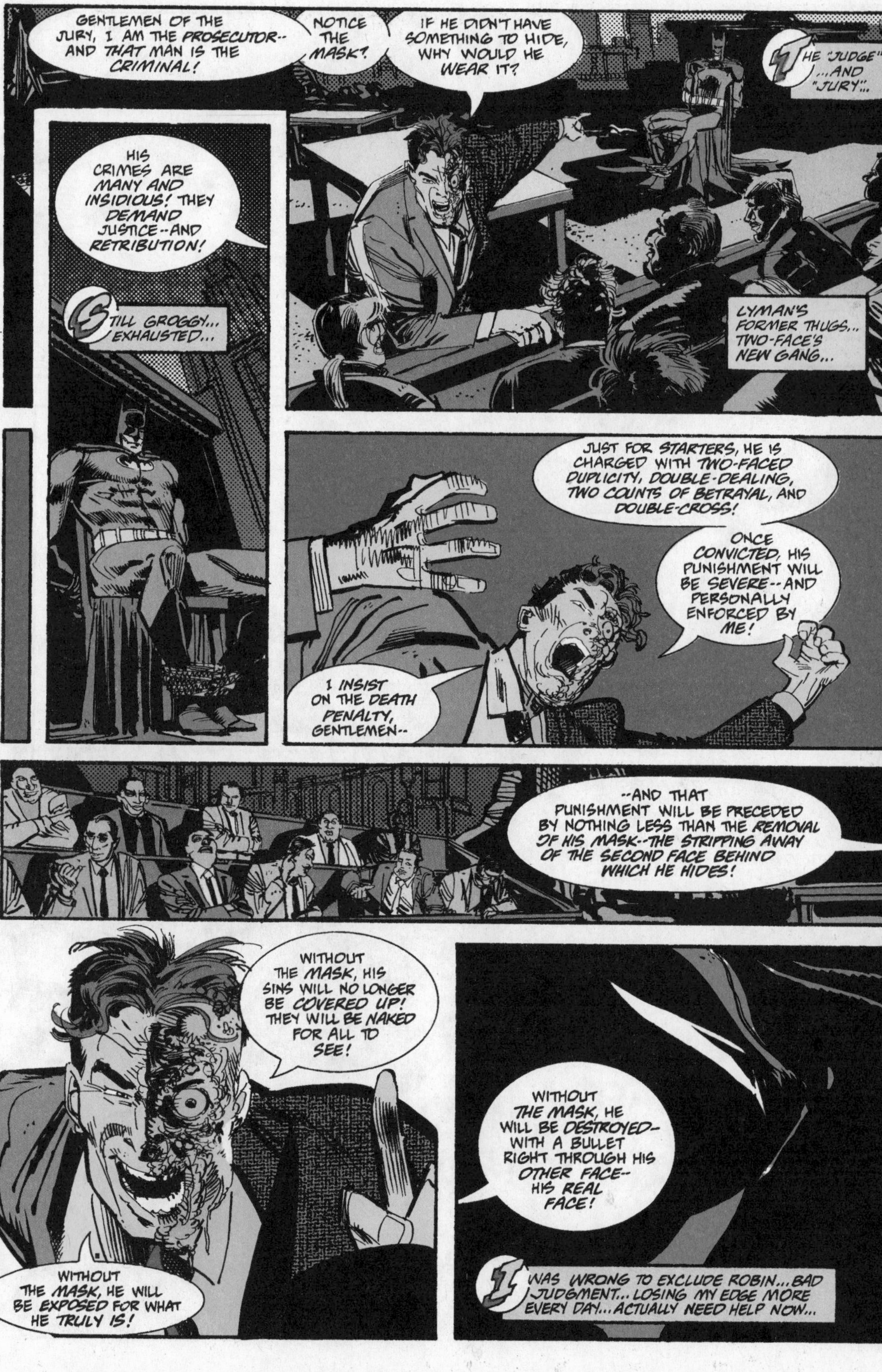
GENTLEMEN OF THE JURY, I AM THE PROSECUTOR--AND THAT MAN IS THE CRIMINAL!
NOTICE THE MASK?
IF HE DIDN'T HAVE SOMETHING TO HIDE, WHY WOULD HE WEAR IT?
THE "JUDGE" ...AND "JURY"...
HIS CRIMES ARE MANY AND INSIDIOUS! THEY DEMAND JUSTICE--AND RETRIBUTION!
STILL GROGGY... EXHAUSTED...
LYMAN'S FORMER THUGS... TWO-FACE'S NEW GANG...
JUST FOR STARTERS, HE IS CHARGED WITH TWO-FACED DUPLICITY, DOUBLE-DEALING, TWO COUNTS OF BETRAYAL, AND DOUBLE-CROSS!
ONCE CONVICTED, HIS PUNISHMENT WILL BE SEVERE--AND PERSONALLY ENFORCED BY ME!
I INSIST ON THE DEATH PENALTY, GENTLEMEN--
--AND THAT PUNISHMENT WILL BE PRECEDED BY NOTHING LESS THAN THE REMOVAL OF HIS MASK--THE STRIPPING AWAY OF THE SECOND FACE BEHIND WHICH HE HIDES!
WITHOUT THE MASK, HIS SINS WILL NO LONGER BE COVERED UP! THEY WILL BE NAKED FOR ALL TO SEE!
WITHOUT THE MASK, HE WILL BE EXPOSED FOR WHAT HE TRULY IS!
WITHOUT THE MASK, HE WILL BE DESTROYED-WITH A BULLET RIGHT THROUGH HIS OTHER FACE--HIS REAL FACE!
I WAS WRONG TO EXCLUDE ROBIN...BAD JUDGMENT... LOSING MY EDGE MORE EVERY DAY... ACTUALLY NEED HELP NOW...

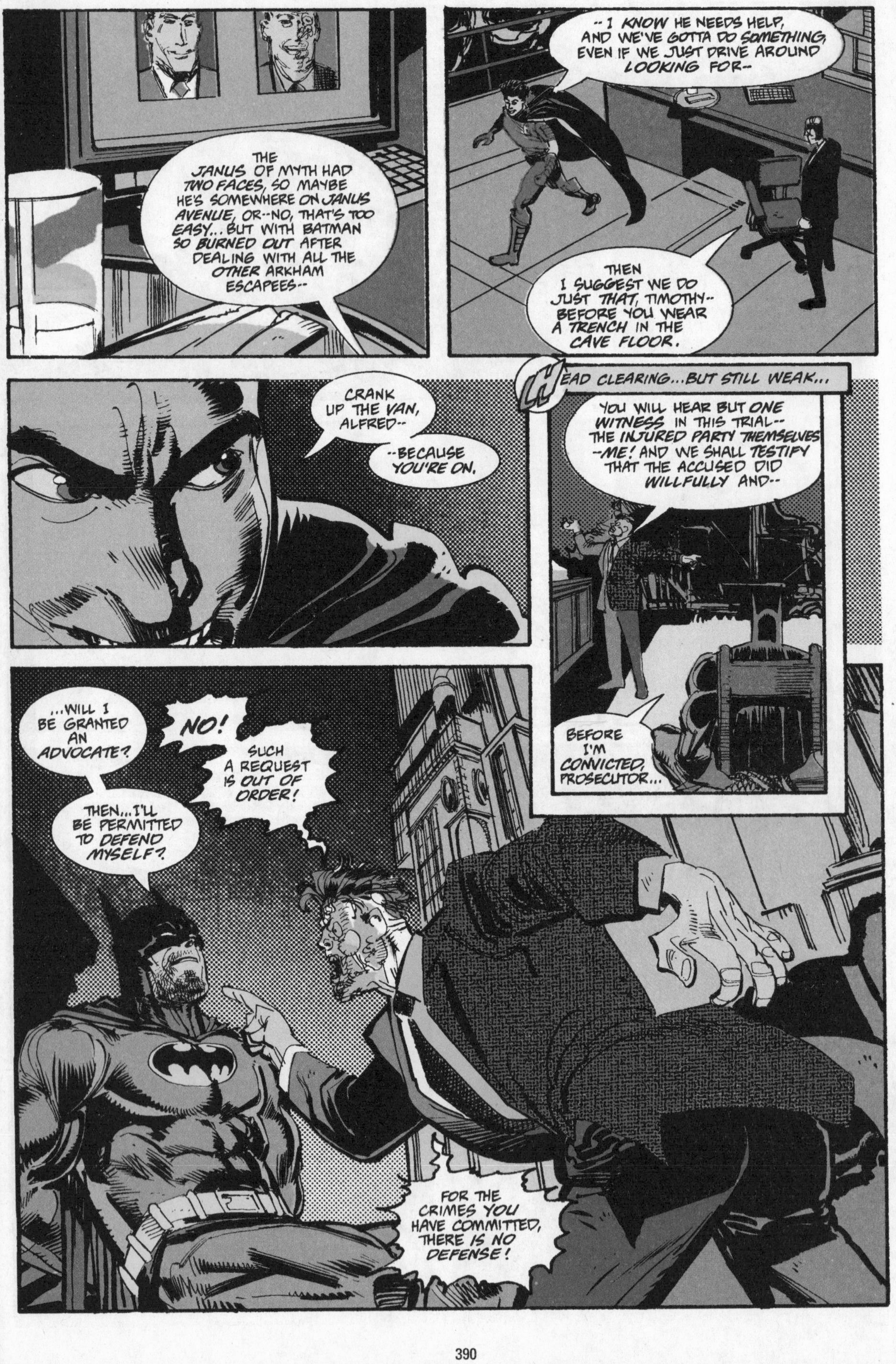
THE JANUS OF MYTH HAD TWO FACES, SO MAYBE HE'S SOMEWHERE ON JANUS AVENUE, OR--NO, THAT'S TOO EASY... BUT WITH BATMAN SO BURNED OUT AFTER DEALING WITH ALL THE OTHER ARKHAM ESCAPEES--
--I KNOW HE NEEDS HELP, AND WE'VE GOTTA DO SOMETHING, EVEN IF WE JUST DRIVE AROUND LOOKING FOR--
THEN I SUGGEST WE DO JUST THAT, TIMOTHY-- BEFORE YOU WEAR A TRENCH IN THE CAVE FLOOR.
CRANK UP THE VAN, ALFRED--
--BECAUSE YOU'RE ON.
HEAD CLEARING... BUT STILL WEAK...
YOU WILL HEAR BUT ONE WITNESS IN THIS TRIAL-- THE INJURED PARTY THEMSELVES --ME! AND WE SHALL TESTIFY THAT THE ACCUSED DID WILLFULLY AND--
BEFORE I'M CONVICTED, PROSECUTOR...
...WILL I BE GRANTED AN ADVOCATE?
NO!
SUCH A REQUEST IS OUT OF ORDER!
THEN... I'LL BE PERMITTED TO DEFEND MYSELF?
FOR THE CRIMES YOU HAVE COMMITTED, THERE IS NO DEFENSE!

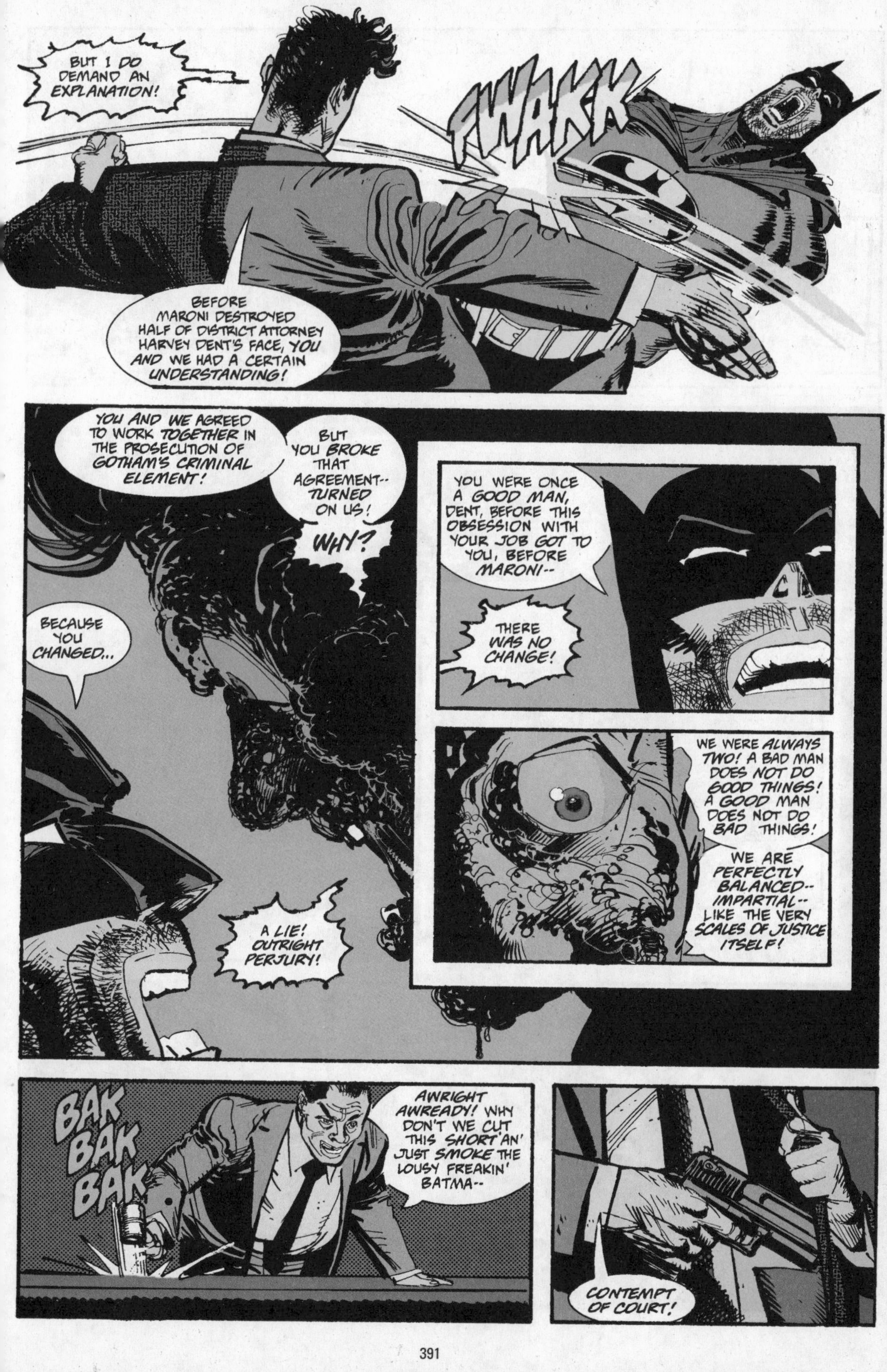

BUT I DO DEMAND AN EXPLANATION!
FWAKK
BEFORE MARONI DESTROYED HALF OF DISTRICT ATTORNEY HARVEY DENT'S FACE, YOU AND WE HAD A CERTAIN UNDERSTANDING!
YOU AND WE AGREED TO WORK TOGETHER IN THE PROSECUTION OF GOTHAM'S CRIMINAL ELEMENT!
BUT YOU BROKE THAT AGREEMENT-- TURNED ON US!
WHY?
BECAUSE YOU CHANGED...
YOU WERE ONCE A GOOD MAN, DENT, BEFORE THIS OBSESSION WITH YOUR JOB GOT TO YOU, BEFORE MARONI--
THERE WAS NO CHANGE!
WE WERE ALWAYS TWO! A BAD MAN DOES NOT DO GOOD THINGS! A GOOD MAN DOES NOT DO BAD THINGS!
WE ARE PERFECTLY BALANCED-- IMPARTIAL-- LIKE THE VERY SCALES OF JUSTICE ITSELF!
A LIE! OUTRIGHT PERJURY!
BAK BAK BAK
AWRIGHT AWREADY! WHY DON'T WE CUT THIS SHORT 'AN' JUST SMOKE THE LOUSY FREAKIN' BATMA--
CONTEMPT OF COURT!

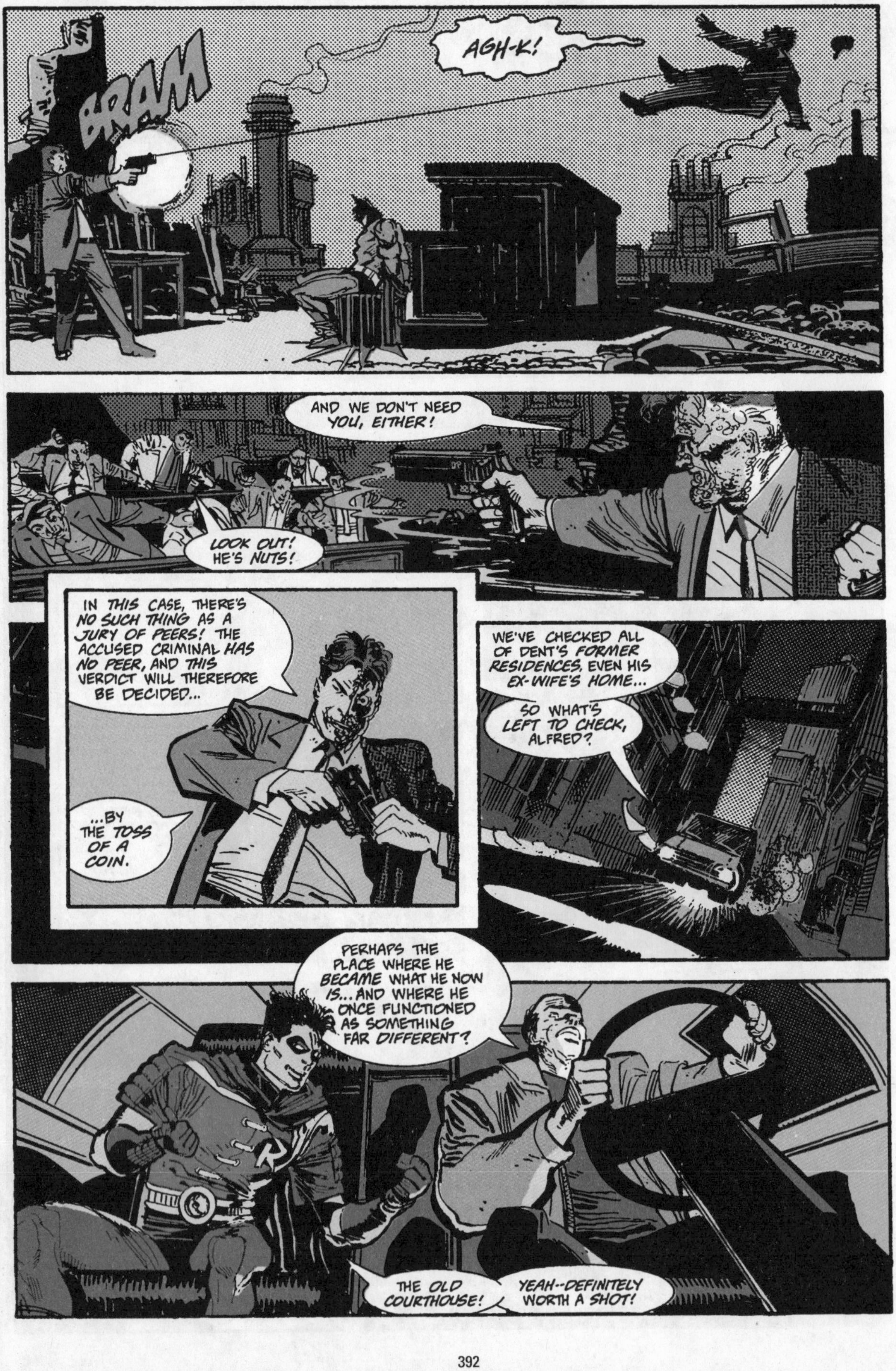
BRAM
AGH-K!
AND WE DON'T NEED YOU, EITHER!
LOOK OUT! HE'S NUTS!
IN THIS CASE, THERE'S NO SUCH THING AS A JURY OF PEERS! THE ACCUSED CRIMINAL HAS NO PEER, AND THIS VERDICT WILL THEREFORE BE DECIDED...
...BY THE TOSS OF A COIN.
WE'VE CHECKED ALL OF DENT'S FORMER RESIDENCES, EVEN HIS EX-WIFE'S HOME...
SO WHAT'S LEFT TO CHECK, ALFRED?
PERHAPS THE PLACE WHERE HE BECAME WHAT HE NOW IS...AND WHERE HE ONCE FUNCTIONED AS SOMETHING FAR DIFFERENT?
THE OLD COURTHOUSE!
YEAH--DEFINITELY WORTH A SHOT!

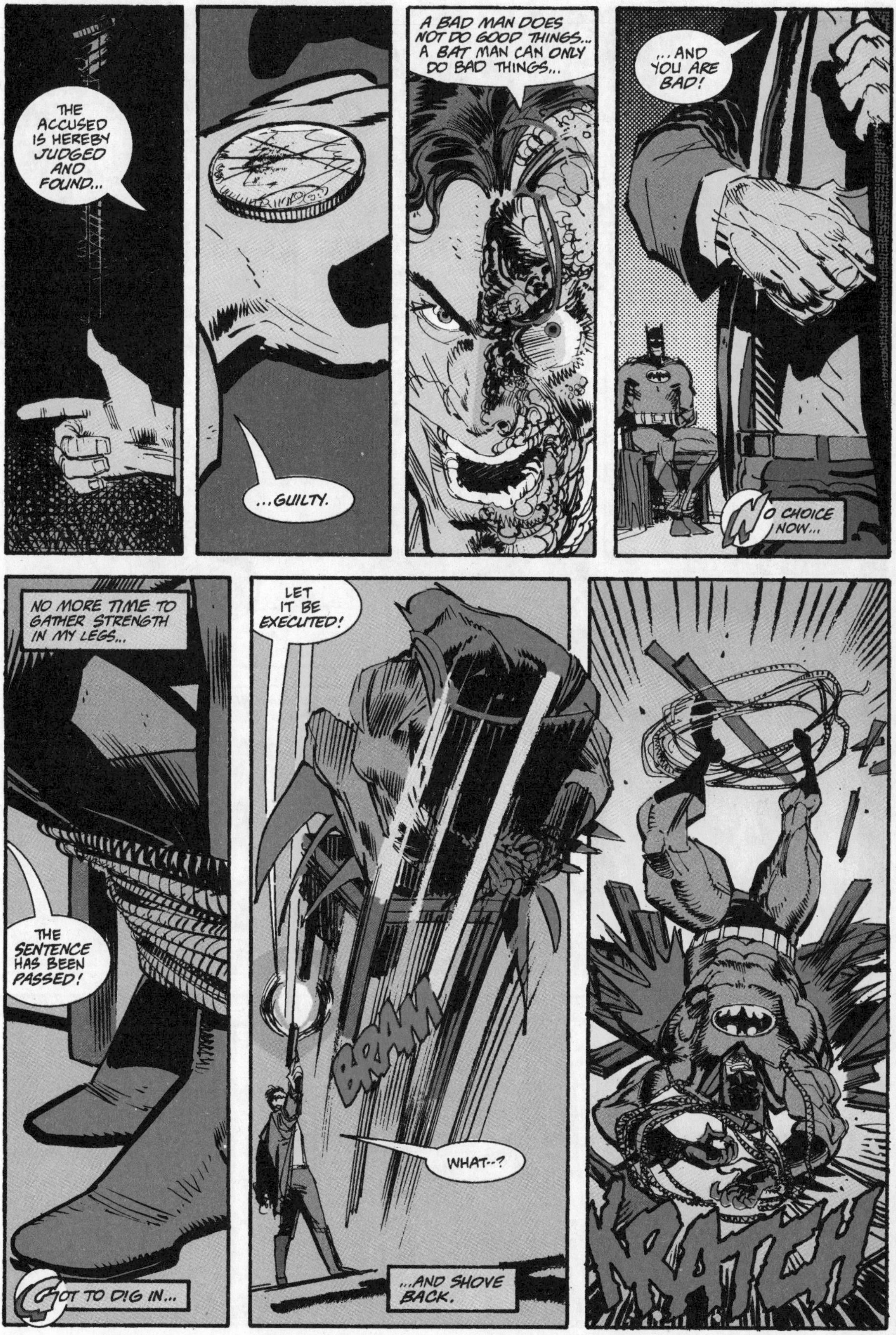
THE ACCUSED IS HEREBY JUDGED AND FOUND...
...GUILTY.
A BAD MAN DOES NOT DO GOOD THINGS... A BAT MAN CAN ONLY DO BAD THINGS...
...AND YOU ARE BAD!
NO CHOICE NOW...
NO MORE TIME TO GATHER STRENGTH IN MY LEGS...
THE SENTENCE HAS BEEN PASSED!
GOT TO DIG IN...
LET IT BE EXECUTED!
BRAAM
WHAT--?
...AND SHOVE BACK.
KRATCH

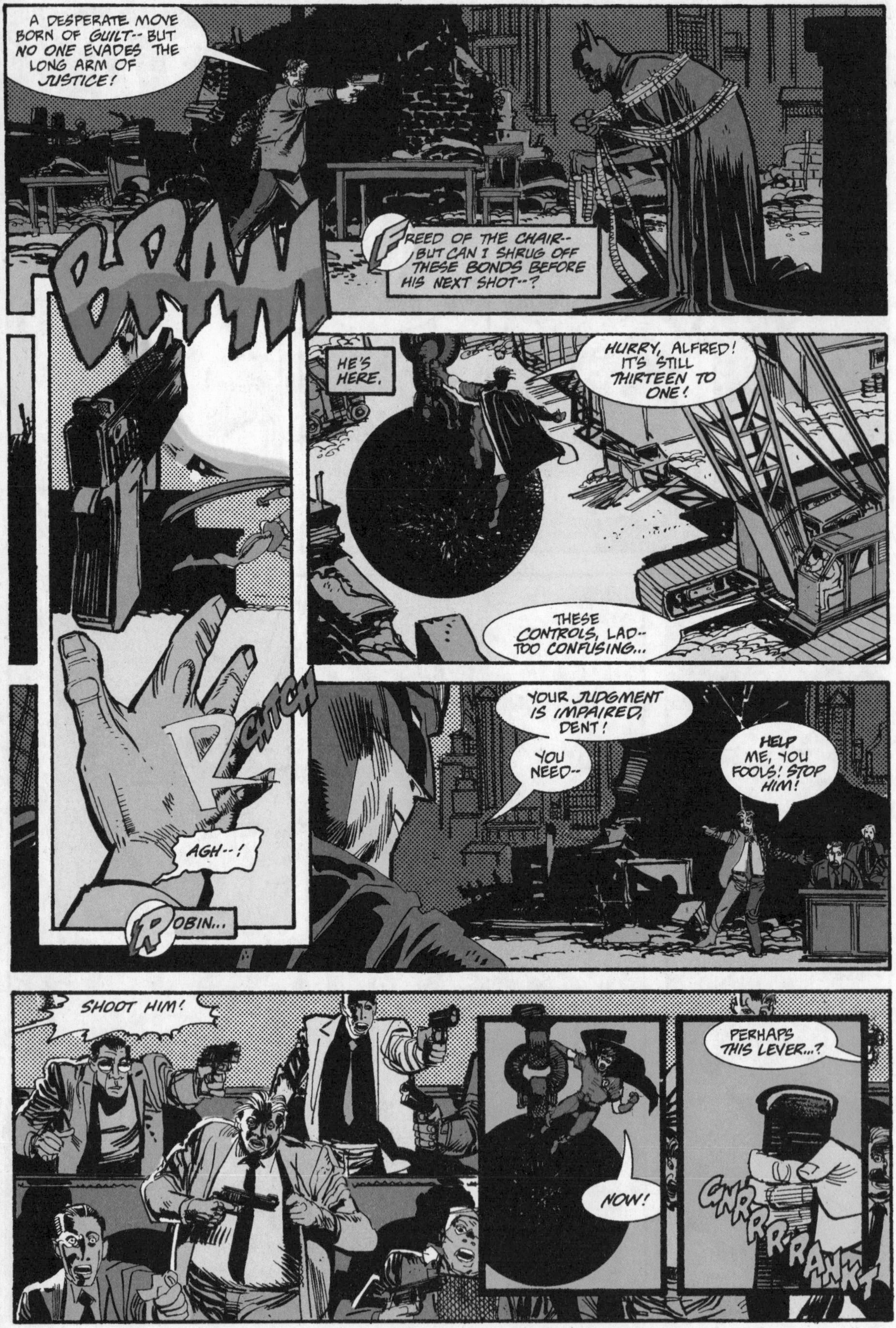
A DESPERATE MOVE BORN OF GUILT-- BUT NO ONE EVADES THE LONG ARM OF JUSTICE!
BRAM
FREED OF THE CHAIR-- BUT CAN I SHRUG OFF THESE BONDS BEFORE HIS NEXT SHOT--?
HE'S HERE.
HURRY, ALFRED! IT'S STILL THIRTEEN TO ONE!
THESE CONTROLS, LAD-- TOO CONFUSING...
RCHTCH
AGH--!
ROBIN...
YOUR JUDGMENT IS IMPAIRED, DENT!
YOU NEED--
HELP ME, YOU FOOLS! STOP HIM!
SHOOT HIM!
NOW!
PERHAPS THIS LEVER...?
GNRRRRANKT

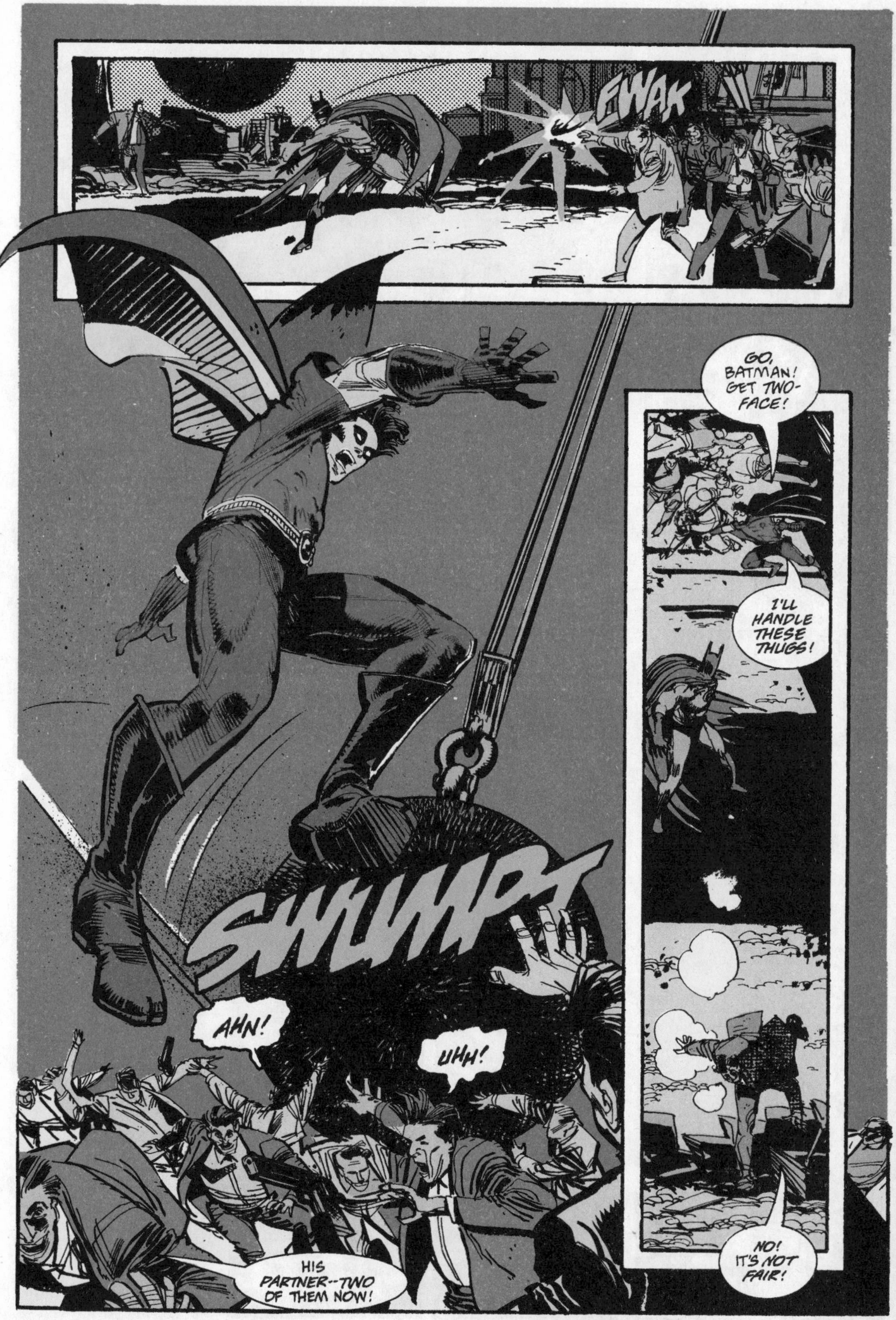

FWAK
GO, BATMAN! GET TWO-FACE!
I'LL HANDLE THESE THUGS!
SHUMPT
AHN!
UHH!
HIS PARTNER--TWO OF THEM NOW!
NO! IT'S NOT FAIR!

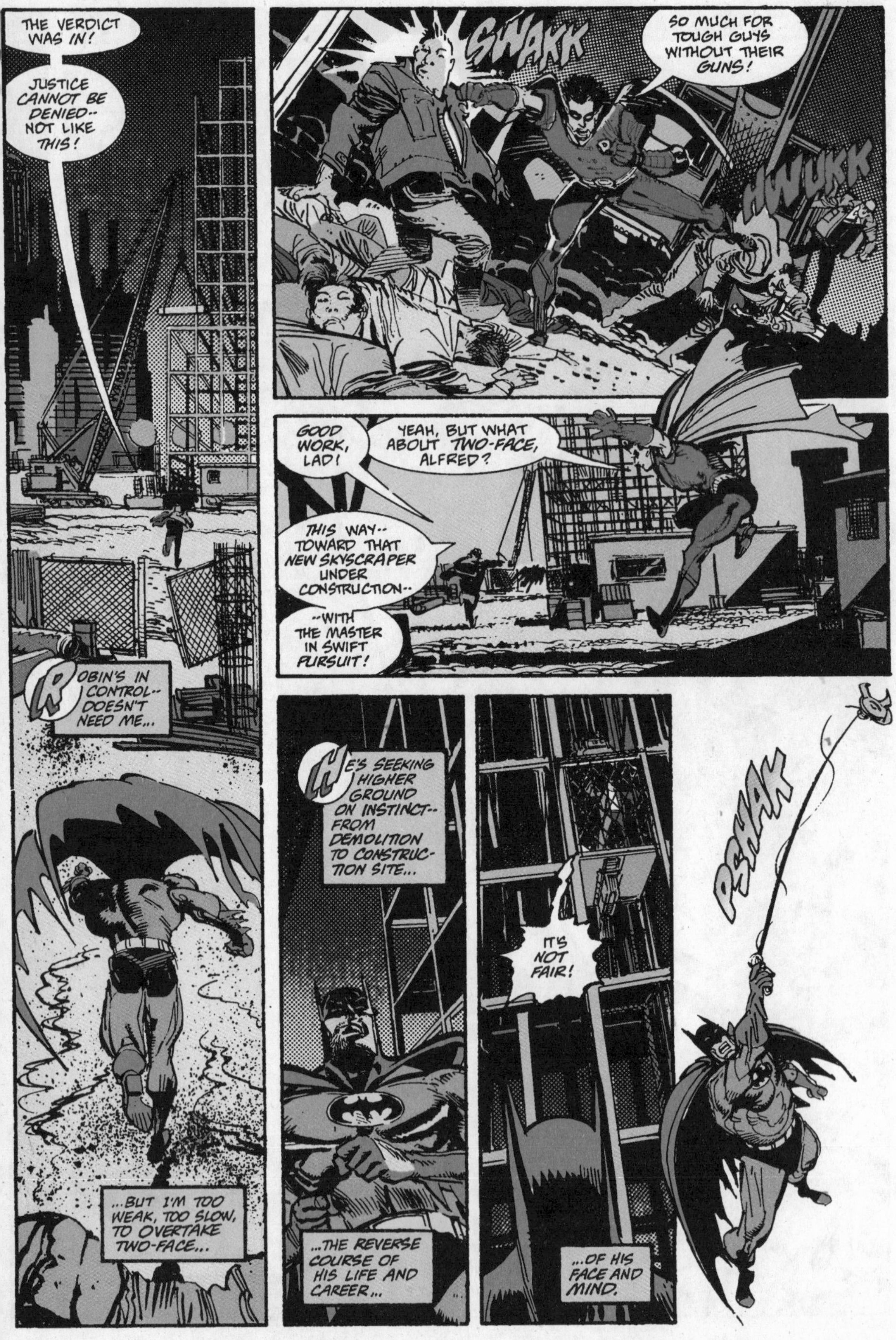
THE VERDICT WAS IN!
JUSTICE CANNOT BE DENIED-- NOT LIKE THIS!
SWAKK
SO MUCH FOR TOUGH GUYS WITHOUT THEIR GUNS!
HWUKK
GOOD WORK, LAD!
YEAH, BUT WHAT ABOUT TWO-FACE, ALFRED?
THIS WAY-- TOWARD THAT NEW SKYSCRAPER UNDER CONSTRUCTION--
--WITH THE MASTER IN SWIFT PURSUIT!
ROBIN'S IN CONTROL-- DOESN'T NEED ME...
...BUT I'M TOO WEAK, TOO SLOW, TO OVERTAKE TWO-FACE...
HE'S SEEKING HIGHER GROUND ON INSTINCT-- FROM DEMOLITION TO CONSTRUCTION SITE...
...THE REVERSE COURSE OF HIS LIFE AND CAREER...
IT'S NOT FAIR!
...OF HIS FACE AND MIND.
PSHAK

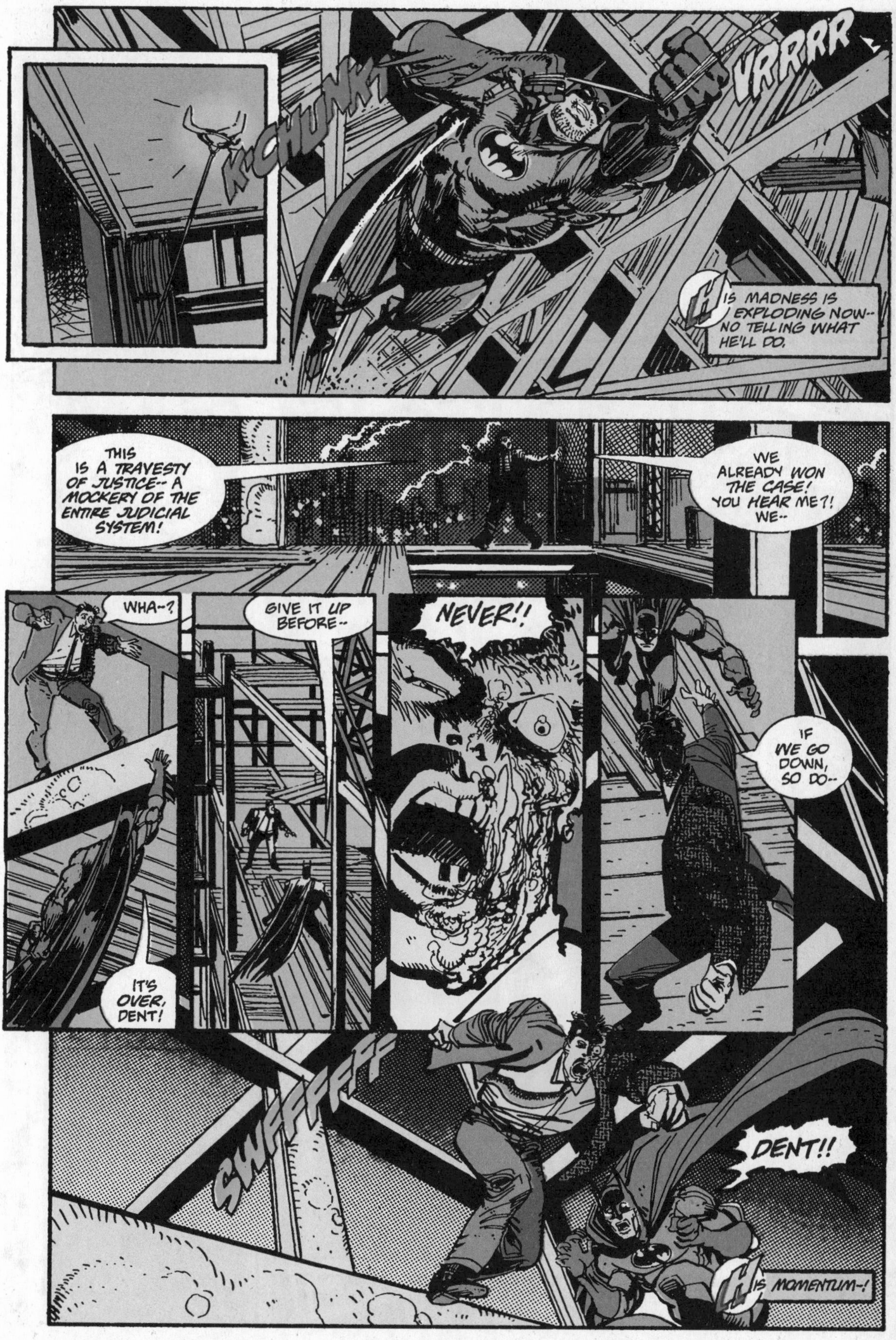
K-CHUNK!
VRRRR
HIS MADNESS IS EXPLODING NOW-- NO TELLING WHAT HE'LL DO.
THIS IS A TRAVESTY OF JUSTICE-- A MOCKERY OF THE ENTIRE JUDICIAL SYSTEM!
WE ALREADY WON THE CASE! YOU HEAR ME?! WE--
WHA--?
IT'S OVER, DENT!
GIVE IT UP BEFORE--
NEVER!!
IF WE GO DOWN, SO DO--
SWFFFFF
DENT!!
HIS MOMENTUM--!

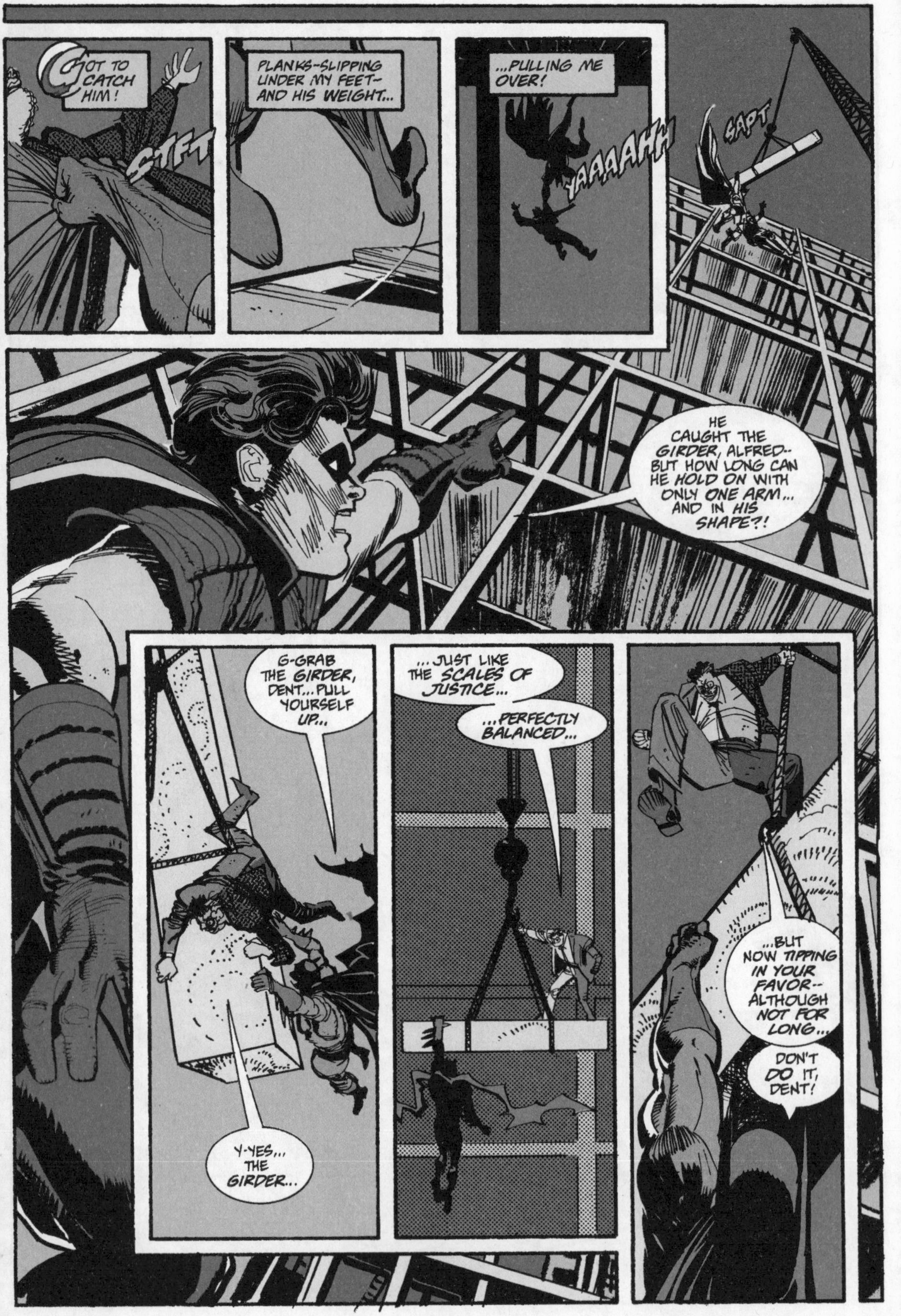
GOT TO CATCH HIM!
STFT
PLANKS-SLIPPING UNDER MY FEET- AND HIS WEIGHT...
...PULLING ME OVER!
YAAAAHH
SAPT
HE CAUGHT THE GIRDER, ALFRED-- BUT HOW LONG CAN HE HOLD ON WITH ONLY ONE ARM... AND IN HIS SHAPE?!
G-GRAB THE GIRDER, DENT...PULL YOURSELF UP...
Y-YES... THE GIRDER...
...JUST LIKE THE SCALES OF JUSTICE...
...PERFECTLY BALANCED...
...BUT NOW TIPPING IN YOUR FAVOR-- ALTHOUGH NOT FOR LONG...
DON'T DO IT, DENT!

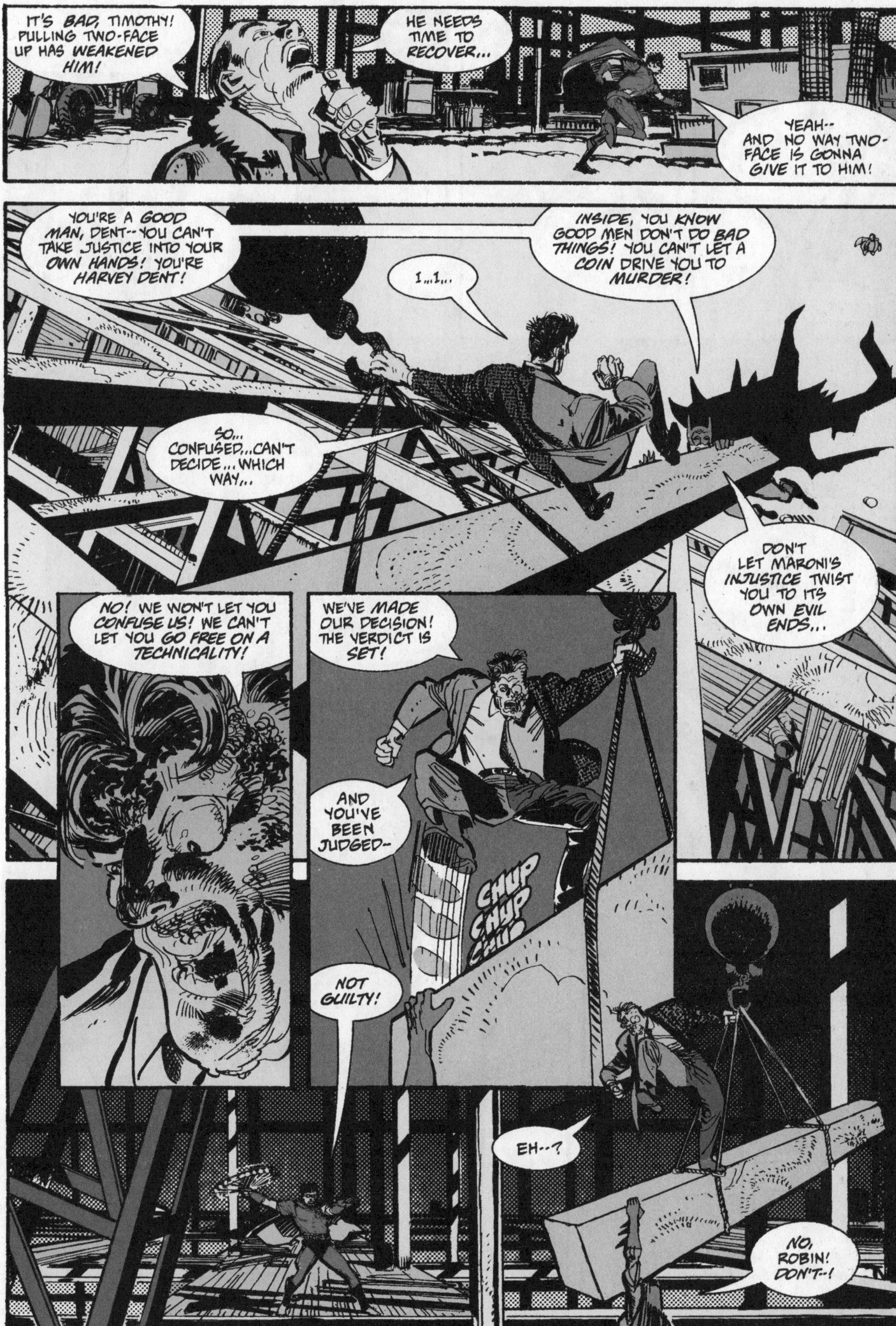
IT'S BAD, TIMOTHY! PULLING TWO-FACE UP HAS WEAKENED HIM!
HE NEEDS TIME TO RECOVER...
YEAH-- AND NO WAY TWO-FACE IS GONNA GIVE IT TO HIM!
YOU'RE A GOOD MAN, DENT-- YOU CAN'T TAKE JUSTICE INTO YOUR OWN HANDS! YOU'RE HARVEY DENT!
I...I...
INSIDE, YOU KNOW GOOD MEN DON'T DO BAD THINGS! YOU CAN'T LET A COIN DRIVE YOU TO MURDER!
SO... CONFUSED...CAN'T DECIDE... WHICH WAY...
DON'T LET MARONI'S INJUSTICE TWIST YOU TO ITS OWN EVIL ENDS...
NO! WE WON'T LET YOU CONFUSE US! WE CAN'T LET YOU GO FREE ON A TECHNICALITY!
WE'VE MADE OUR DECISION! THE VERDICT IS SET!
AND YOU'VE BEEN JUDGED--
CHUP CHUP CHUP
NOT GUILTY!
EH--?
NO, ROBIN! DON'T--!

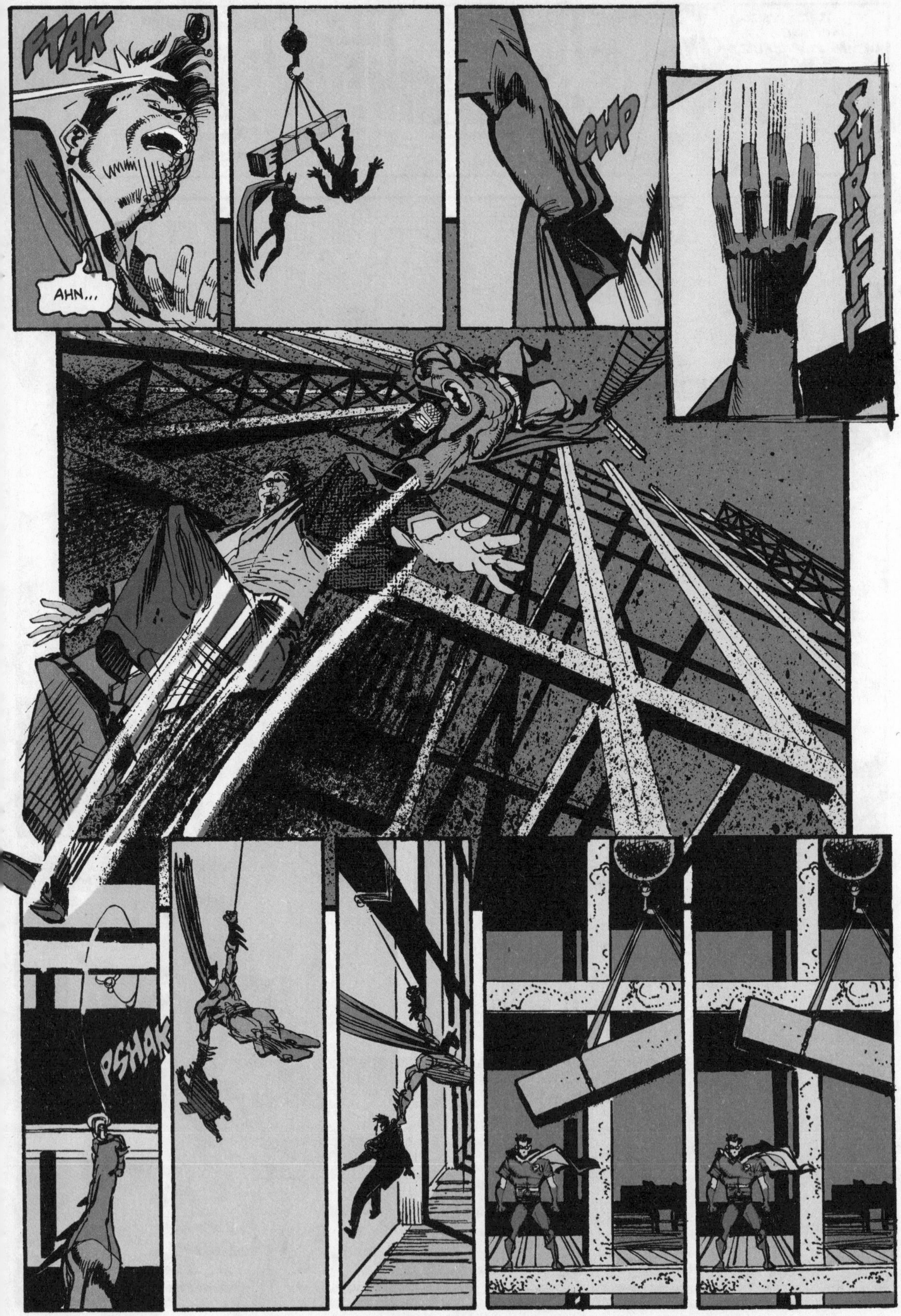
FTAK
AHN...
CHP
SHRFFF
PSHAK

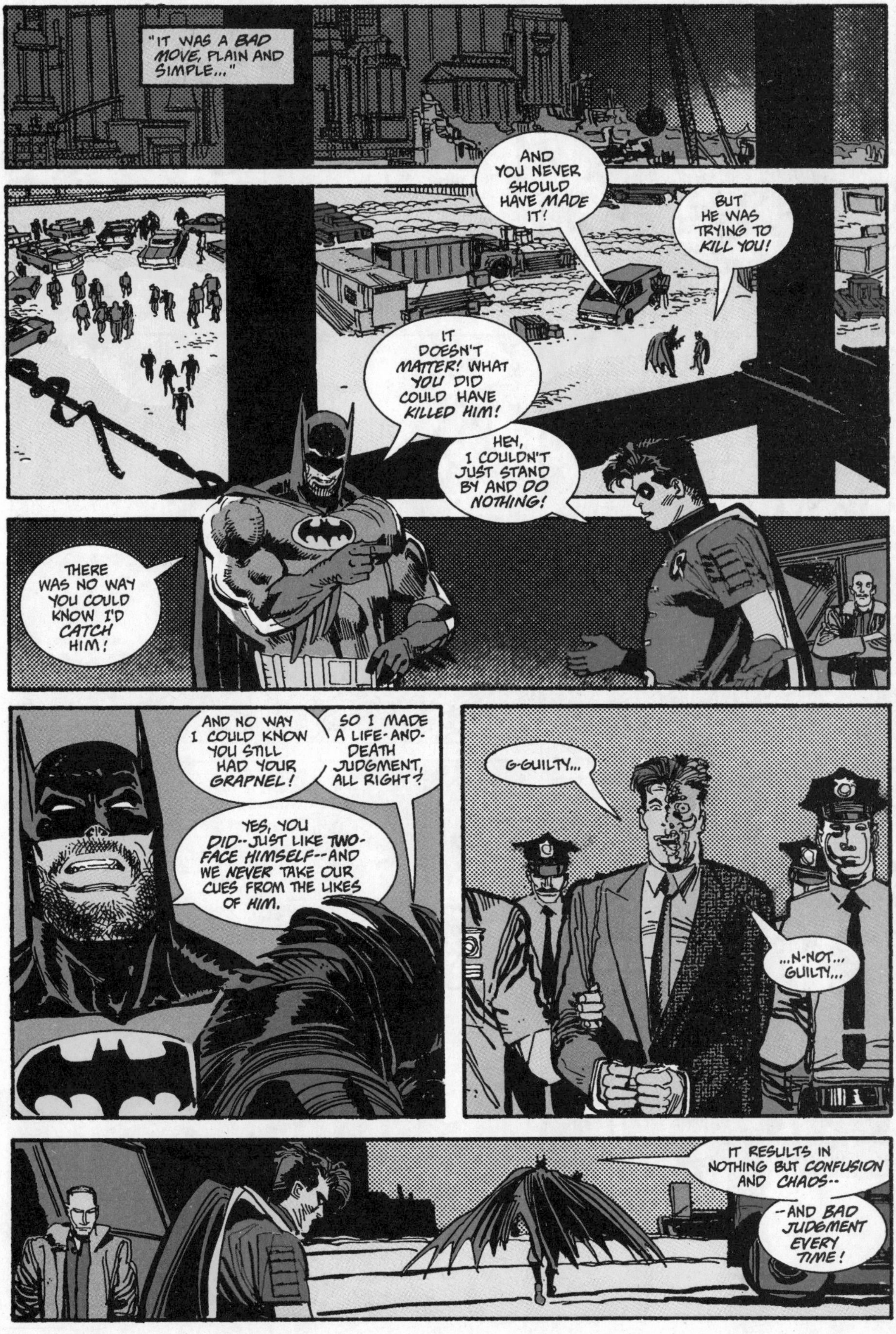
"IT WAS A BAD MOVE, PLAIN AND SIMPLE..."
AND YOU NEVER SHOULD HAVE MADE IT!
BUT HE WAS TRYING TO KILL YOU!
IT DOESN'T MATTER! WHAT YOU DID COULD HAVE KILLED HIM!
HEY, I COULDN'T JUST STAND BY AND DO NOTHING!
THERE WAS NO WAY YOU COULD KNOW I'D CATCH HIM!
AND NO WAY I COULD KNOW YOU STILL HAD YOUR GRAPNEL!
SO I MADE A LIFE-AND-DEATH JUDGMENT, ALL RIGHT?
YES, YOU DID--JUST LIKE TWO-FACE HIMSELF--AND WE NEVER TAKE OUR CUES FROM THE LIKES OF HIM.
G-GUILTY...
...N-NOT... GUILTY...
IT RESULTS IN NOTHING BUT CONFUSION AND CHAOS--
--AND BAD JUDGMENT EVERY TIME!

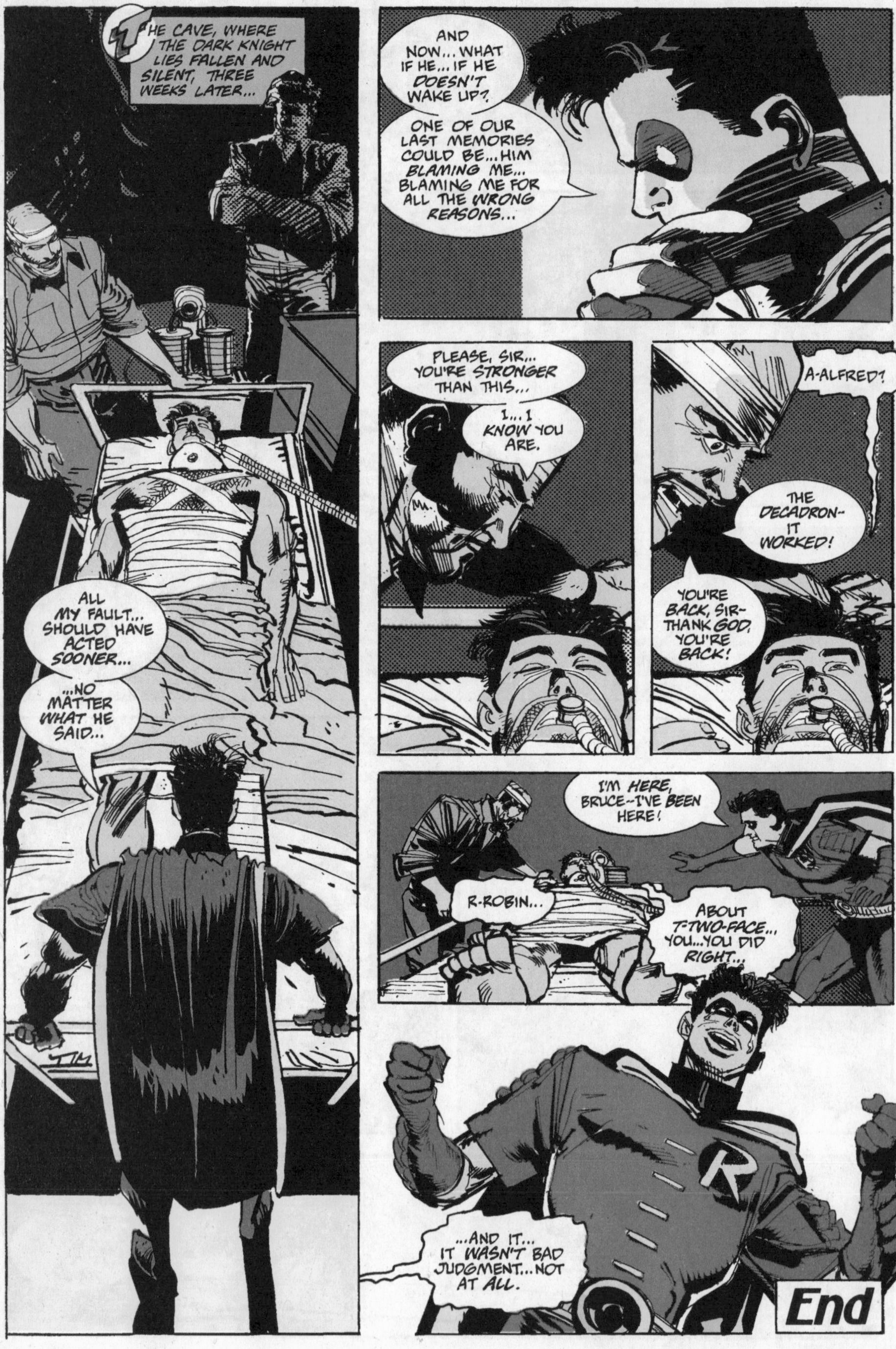
THE CAVE, WHERE THE DARK KNIGHT LIES FALLEN AND SILENT, THREE WEEKS LATER...
ALL MY FAULT... SHOULD HAVE ACTED SOONER...
...NO MATTER WHAT HE SAID...
AND NOW... WHAT IF HE... IF HE DOESN'T WAKE UP?
ONE OF OUR LAST MEMORIES COULD BE... HIM BLAMING ME... BLAMING ME FOR ALL THE WRONG REASONS...
PLEASE, SIR... YOU'RE STRONGER THAN THIS...
I... I KNOW YOU ARE.
A-ALFRED?
THE DECADRON-IT WORKED!
YOU'RE BACK, SIR-THANK GOD, YOU'RE BACK!
I'M HERE, BRUCE--I'VE BEEN HERE!
R-ROBIN...
ABOUT T-TWO-FACE... YOU... YOU DID RIGHT...
...AND IT... IT WASN'T BAD JUDGMENT... NOT AT ALL.
End

Cover art by KELLEY JONES

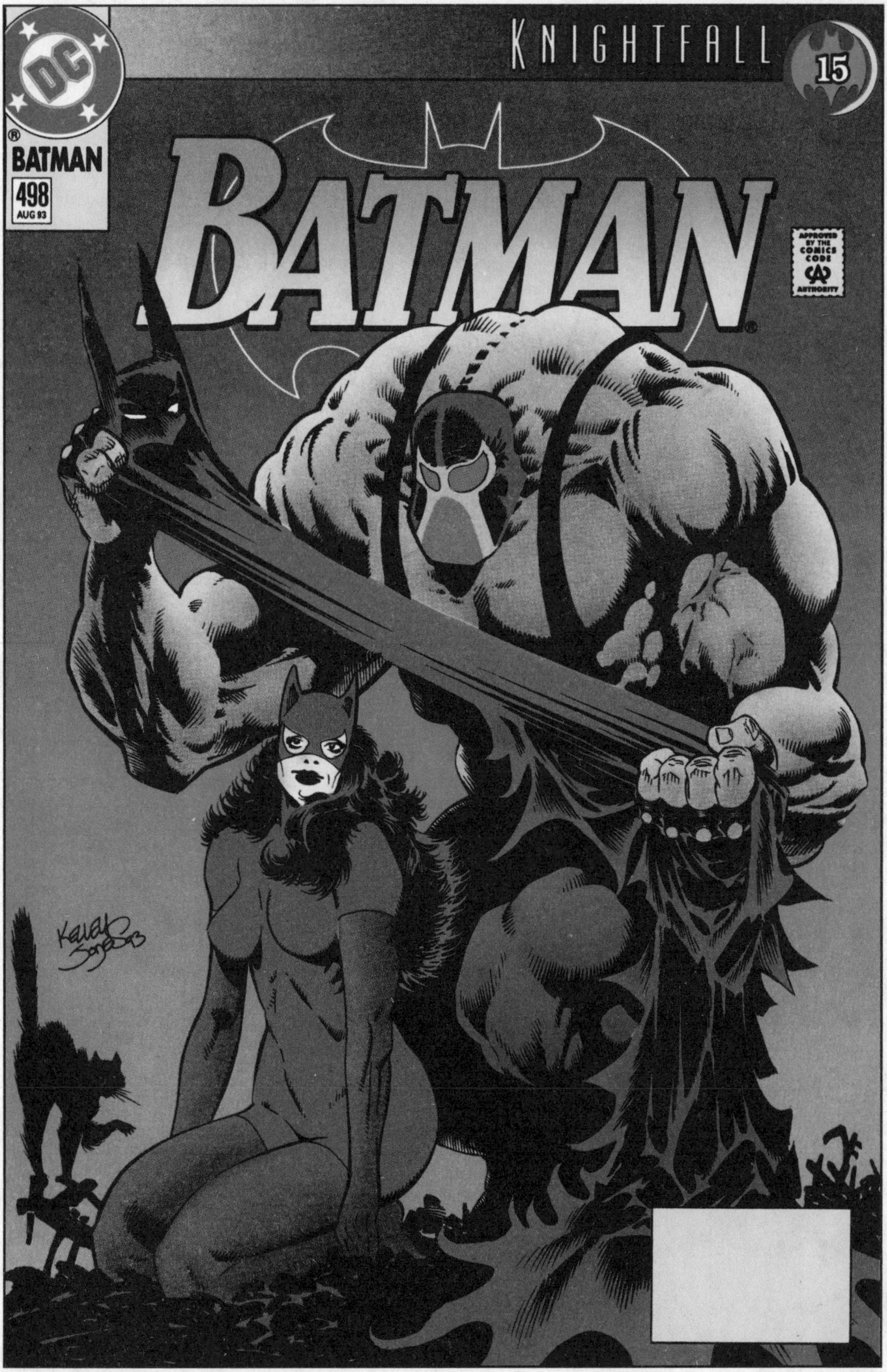
KNIGHTFALL
15
DC
BATMAN
498
AUG 93
BATMAN
APPROVED BY THE COMICS CODE AUTHORITY

KNIGHTS IN DARKNESS

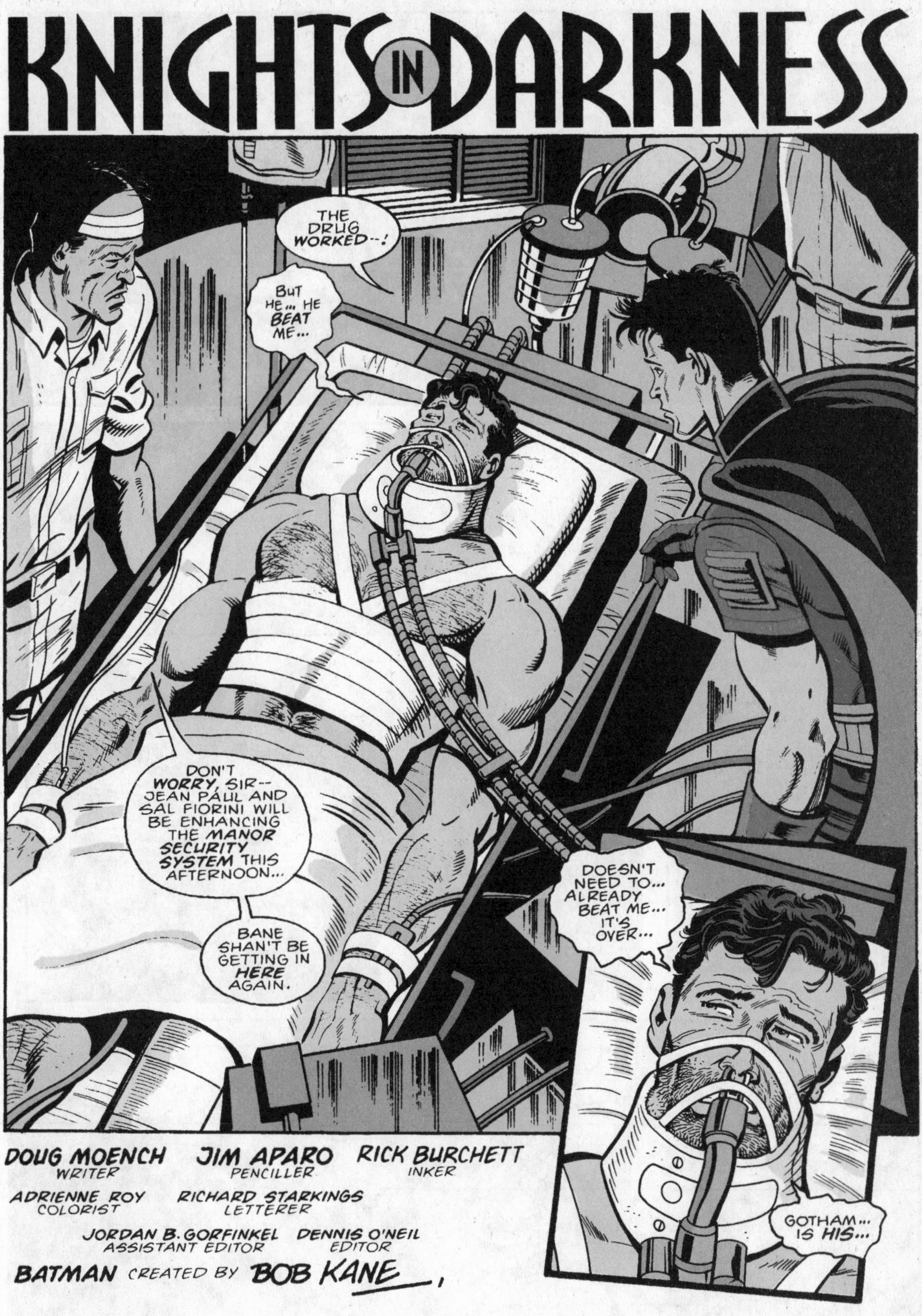

THE DRUG WORKED--!
BUT HE... HE BEAT ME...
DON'T WORRY, SIR-- JEAN PAUL AND SAL FIORINI WILL BE ENHANCING THE MANOR SECURITY SYSTEM THIS AFTERNOON...
BANE SHAN'T BE GETTING IN HERE AGAIN.
DOESN'T NEED TO... ALREADY BEAT ME... IT'S OVER...
GOTHAM... IS HIS...

DOUG MOENCH WRITER
JIM APARO PENCILLER
RICK BURCHETT INKER
ADRIENNE ROY COLORIST
RICHARD STARKINGS LETTERER
JORDAN B. GORFINKEL ASSISTANT EDITOR
DENNIS O'NEIL EDITOR
BATMAN CREATED BY BOB KANE

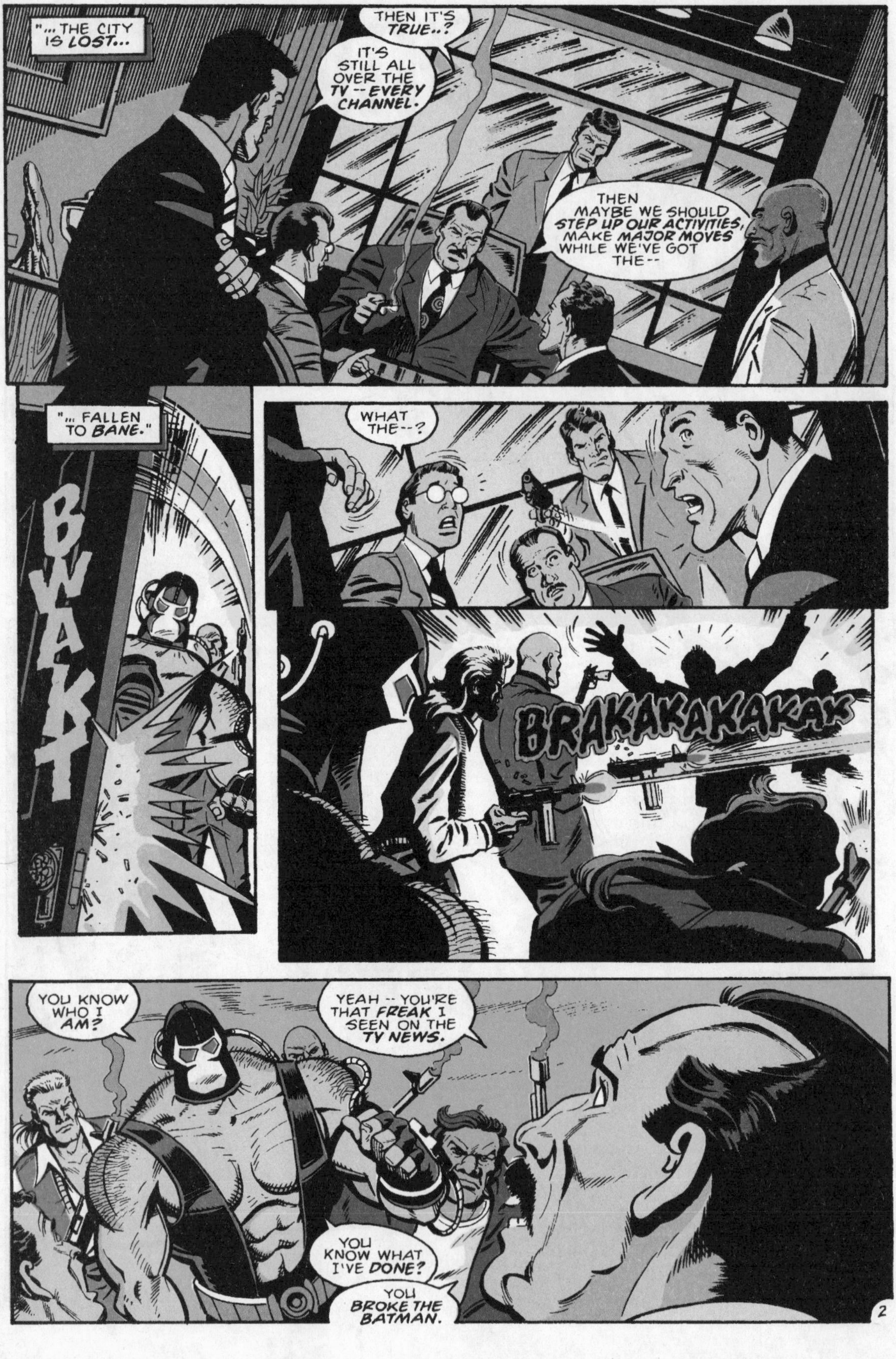
"...THE CITY IS LOST...
THEN IT'S TRUE..?
IT'S STILL ALL OVER THE TV -- EVERY CHANNEL.
THEN MAYBE WE SHOULD STEP UP OUR ACTIVITIES, MAKE MAJOR MOVES WHILE WE'VE GOT THE--
"...FALLEN TO BANE."
BWAKT
WHAT THE--?
BRAKAKAKAKAKAK
YOU KNOW WHO I AM?
YEAH -- YOU'RE THAT FREAK I SEEN ON THE TV NEWS.
YOU KNOW WHAT I'VE DONE?
YOU BROKE THE BATMAN.
2

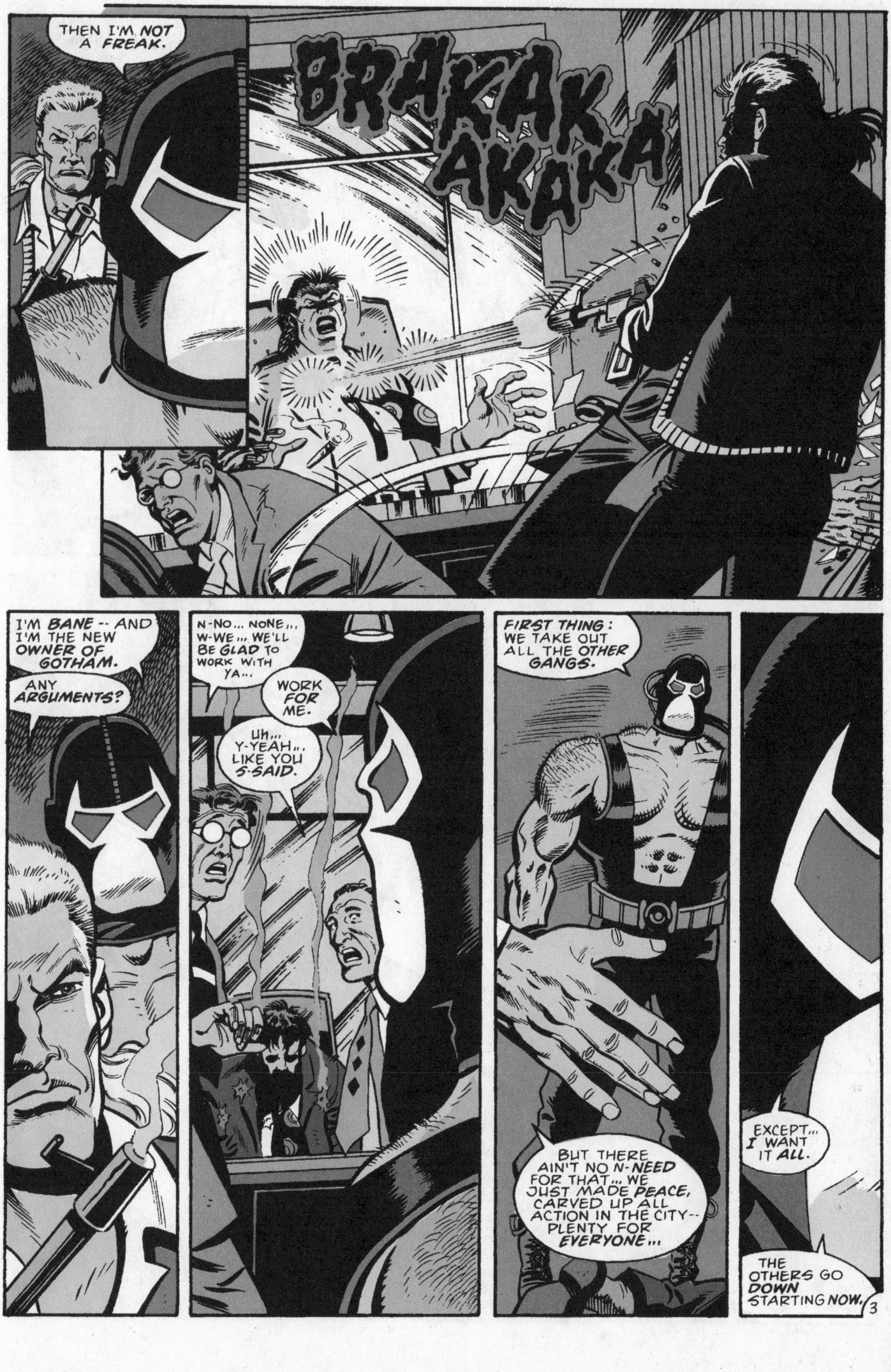
THEN I'M NOT A FREAK.
BRAKAKAKAKAKA
I'M BANE -- AND I'M THE NEW OWNER OF GOTHAM.
ANY ARGUMENTS?
N-NO... NONE... W-WE... WE'LL BE GLAD TO WORK WITH YA...
WORK FOR ME.
UH... Y-YEAH... LIKE YOU S-SAID.
FIRST THING: WE TAKE OUT ALL THE OTHER GANGS.
BUT THERE AIN'T NO N-NEED FOR THAT... WE JUST MADE PEACE, CARVED UP ALL ACTION IN THE CITY-- PLENTY FOR EVERYONE...
EXCEPT... I WANT IT ALL.
THE OTHERS GO DOWN STARTING NOW.
3

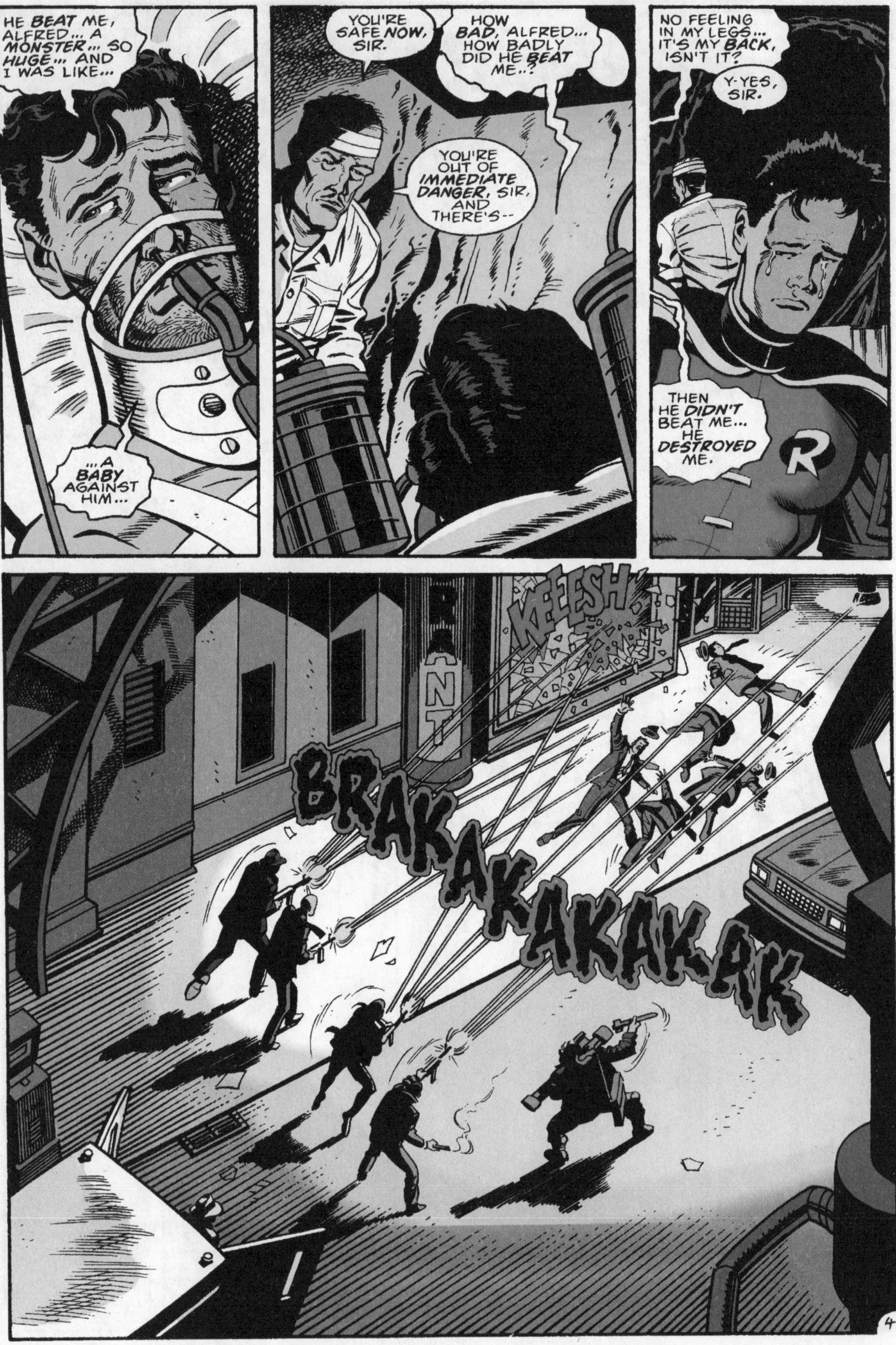
HE BEAT ME, ALFRED... A MONSTER... SO HUGE... AND I WAS LIKE...
...A BABY AGAINST HIM...
YOU'RE SAFE NOW, SIR.
HOW BAD, ALFRED... HOW BADLY DID HE BEAT ME...?
YOU'RE OUT OF IMMEDIATE DANGER, SIR, AND THERE'S--
NO FEELING IN MY LEGS... IT'S MY BACK, ISN'T IT?
Y-YES, SIR.
THEN HE DIDN'T BEAT ME... HE DESTROYED ME.
KEEESH
BRAKAKAKAKAKAK

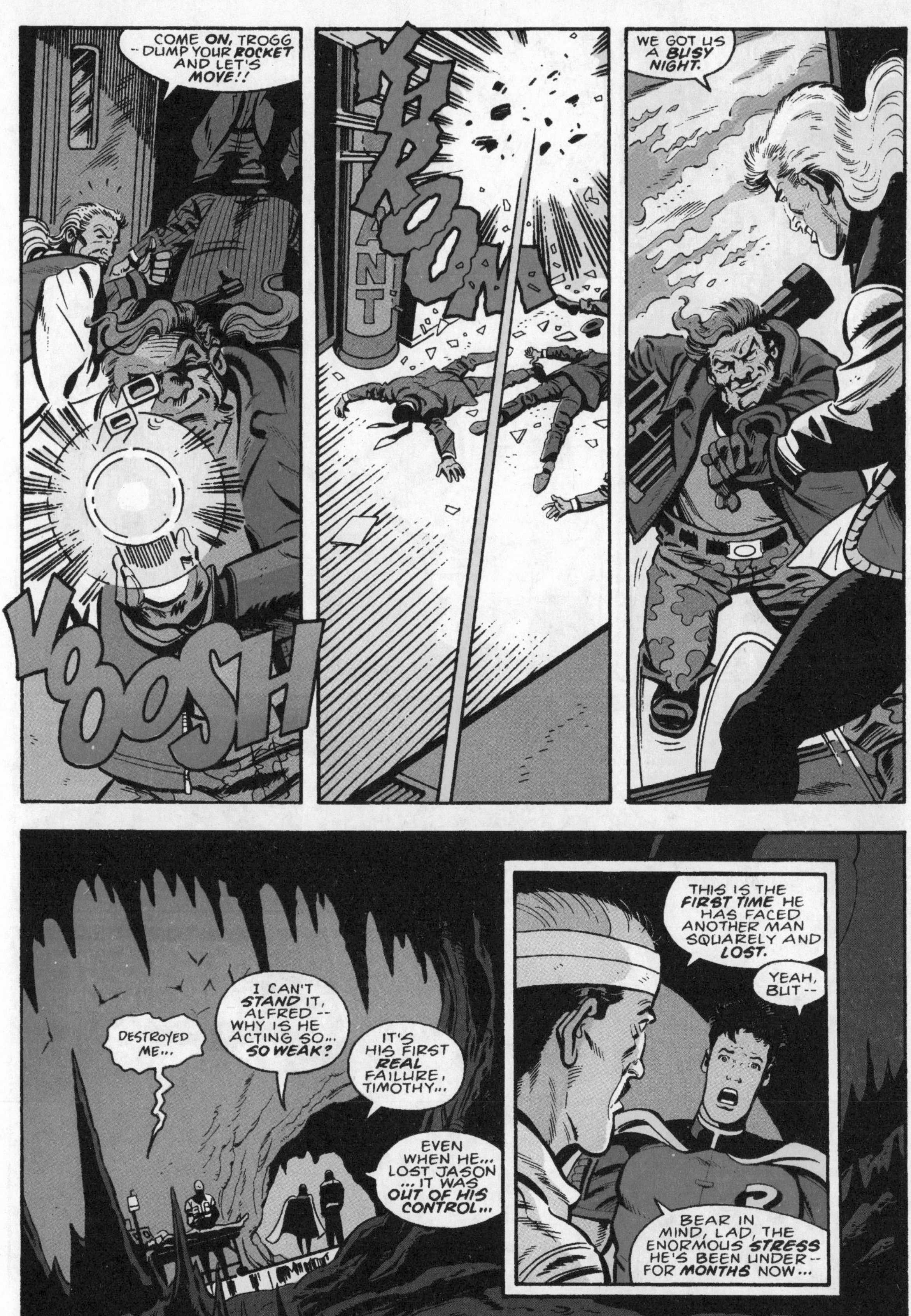
COME ON, TROGG -- DUMP YOUR ROCKET AND LET'S MOVE!!
WOOSH
KROOOM
WE GOT US A BUSY NIGHT.
DESTROYED ME...
I CAN'T STAND IT, ALFRED -- WHY IS HE ACTING SO... SO WEAK?
IT'S HIS FIRST REAL FAILURE, TIMOTHY...
EVEN WHEN HE... LOST JASON ... IT WAS OUT OF HIS CONTROL...
THIS IS THE FIRST TIME HE HAS FACED ANOTHER MAN SQUARELY AND LOST.
YEAH, BUT --
BEAR IN MIND, LAD, THE ENORMOUS STRESS HE'S BEEN UNDER -- FOR MONTHS NOW...
5

SUCH A PROLONGED ORDEAL *MUST* EXACT ITS TOLL -- ON *ANY* MAN.

NOT *HIM*, ALFRED! I CAN'T *BEAR* TO SEE HIM LIKE --

SNAP *OUT* OF IT, TIM! THE *IMMEDIATE* CRISIS MAY BE OVER, BUT THE MASTER STILL *NEEDS* US!

THERE'S MUCH *TO DO* -- AND I CAN'T DO IT WITHOUT *YOU!*

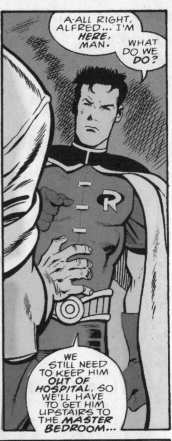

A-ALL RIGHT, ALFRED... I'M *HERE*, MAN. WHAT DO WE *DO?*

WE STILL NEED TO KEEP HIM *OUT* OF HOSPITAL, SO WE'LL HAVE TO GET HIM UPSTAIRS TO THE *MASTER BEDROOM...*

I'LL 'PHONE *LUCIUS FOX* AND HAVE HIM ARRANGE DELIVERY OF ALL THE *NECESSARY* EQUIPMENT...

STILL, ALL THE EQUIPMENT MONEY CAN BUY WON'T DO ONE *WHIT* OF GOOD WITHOUT A *DOCTOR...*

MY THOUGHTS *EXACTLY*, TIM.

WHAT THE *MASTER* REQUIRES EVIDENTLY GOES BEYOND MERE *PHYSICAL THERAPY* --

SHONDRA KINSOLVING!

SNAP

" -- AND IS PRECISELY THE SORT OF CARE DOCTOR KINSOLVING HAS GIVEN YOUR *FATHER...*

BROKE... ME...

"THE *WILL TO RECOVER.*"

6

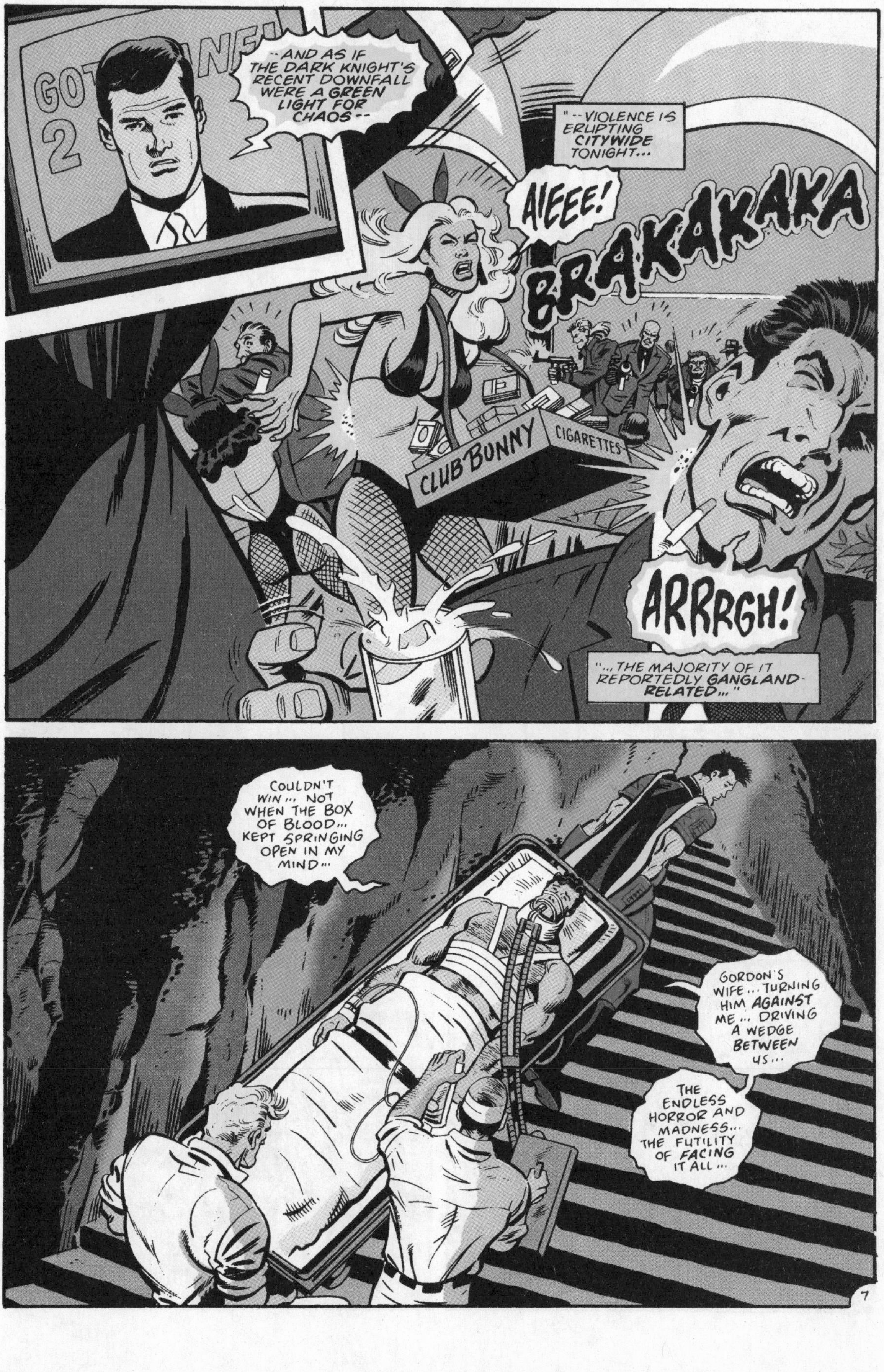
--AND AS IF THE DARK KNIGHT'S RECENT DOWNFALL WERE A GREEN LIGHT FOR CHAOS--
"--VIOLENCE IS ERUPTING CITYWIDE TONIGHT...
AIEEE!
BRAKAKAKA
CLUB BUNNY
CIGARETTES
ARRRGH!
"...THE MAJORITY OF IT REPORTEDLY GANGLAND-RELATED..."
COULDN'T WIN... NOT WHEN THE BOX OF BLOOD... KEPT SPRINGING OPEN IN MY MIND...
GORDON'S WIFE... TURNING HIM AGAINST ME... DRIVING A WEDGE BETWEEN US...
THE ENDLESS HORROR AND MADNESS... THE FUTILITY OF FACING IT ALL...
7

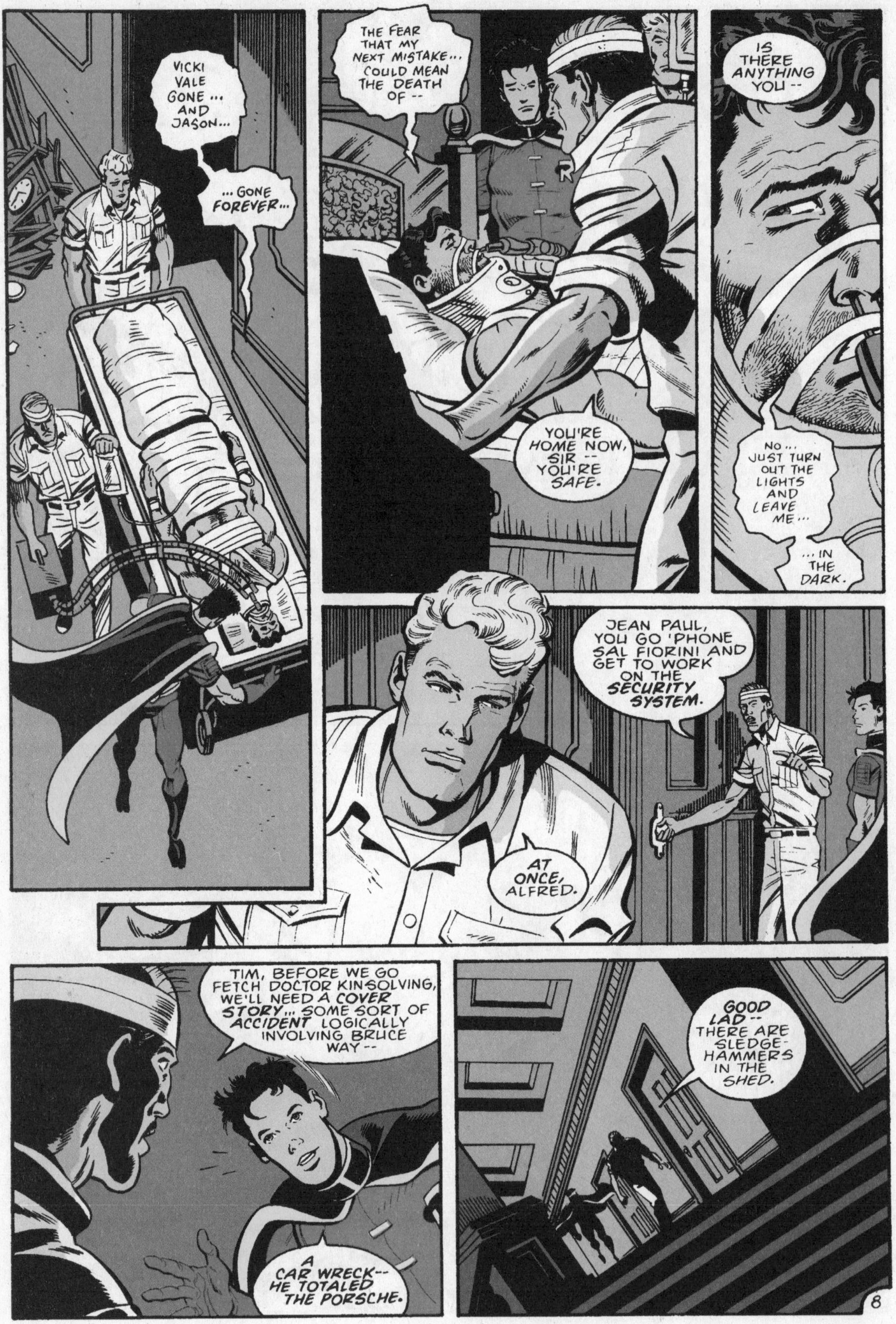
VICKI VALE GONE ... AND JASON...
... GONE FOREVER...
THE FEAR THAT MY NEXT MISTAKE... COULD MEAN THE DEATH OF --
YOU'RE HOME NOW, SIR -- YOU'RE SAFE.
IS THERE ANYTHING YOU --
NO... JUST TURN OUT THE LIGHTS AND LEAVE ME...
... IN THE DARK.
JEAN PAUL, YOU GO 'PHONE SAL FIORINI AND GET TO WORK ON THE SECURITY SYSTEM.
AT ONCE, ALFRED.
TIM, BEFORE WE GO FETCH DOCTOR KINSOLVING, WE'LL NEED A COVER STORY... SOME SORT OF ACCIDENT LOGICALLY INVOLVING BRUCE WAY --
A CAR WRECK-- HE TOTALED THE PORSCHE.
GOOD LAD -- THERE ARE SLEDGE-HAMMERS IN THE SHED.
8

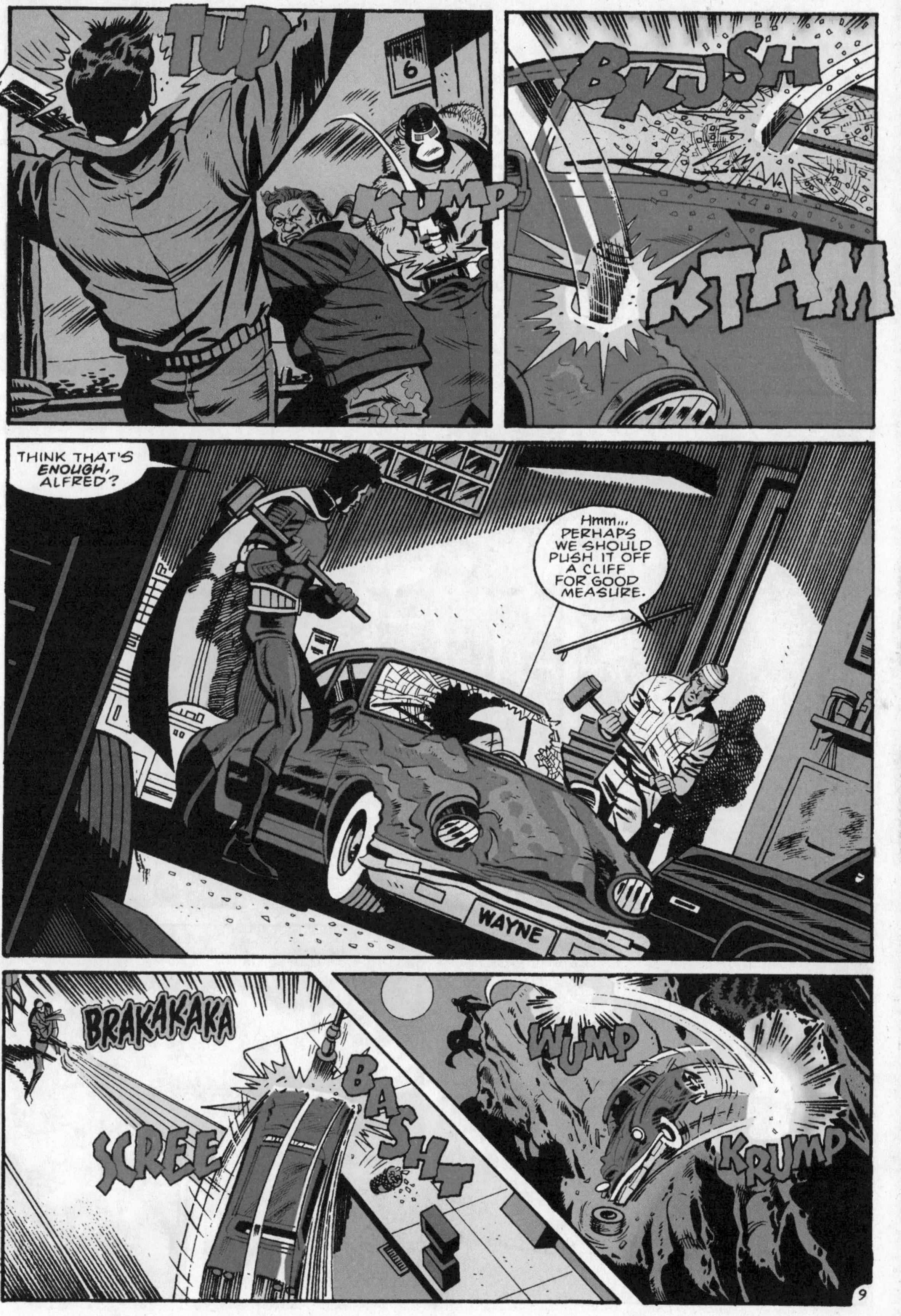
TUD
KUMP
BKJSH
KTAM
THINK THAT'S ENOUGH, ALFRED?
Hmm... PERHAPS WE SHOULD PUSH IT OFF A CLIFF FOR GOOD MEASURE.
WAYNE
BRAKAKAKA
SCREE
BASHT
WUMP
KRUMP
9

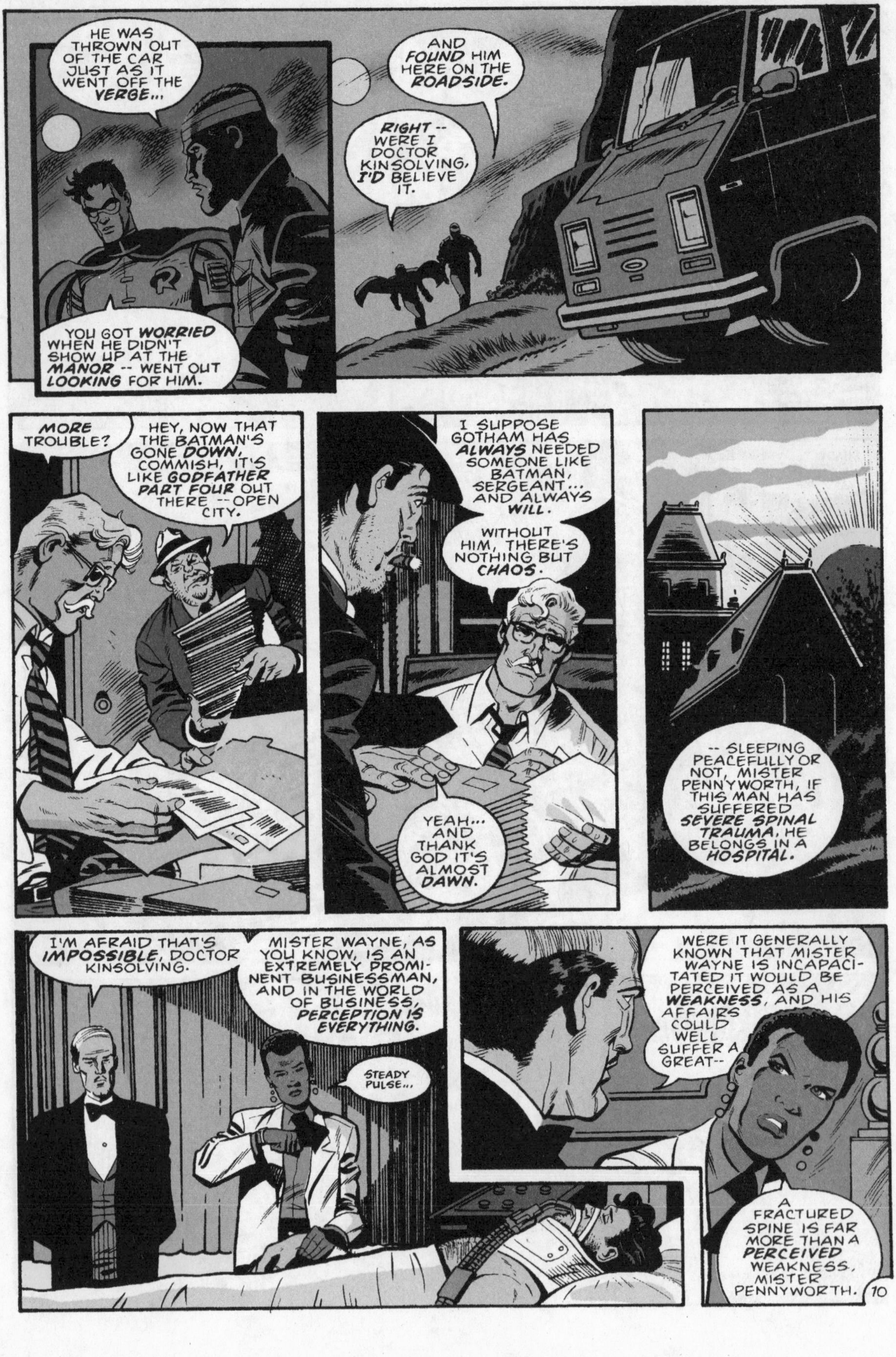
HE WAS THROWN OUT OF THE CAR JUST AS IT WENT OFF THE VERGE...
YOU GOT WORRIED WHEN HE DIDN'T SHOW UP AT THE MANOR -- WENT OUT LOOKING FOR HIM.
AND FOUND HIM HERE ON THE ROADSIDE.
RIGHT -- WERE I DOCTOR KINSOLVING, I'D BELIEVE IT.
MORE TROUBLE?
HEY, NOW THAT THE BATMAN'S GONE DOWN, COMMISH, IT'S LIKE GODFATHER PART FOUR OUT THERE -- OPEN CITY.
I SUPPOSE GOTHAM HAS ALWAYS NEEDED SOMEONE LIKE BATMAN, SERGEANT... AND ALWAYS WILL.
WITHOUT HIM, THERE'S NOTHING BUT CHAOS.
YEAH... AND THANK GOD IT'S ALMOST DAWN.
-- SLEEPING PEACEFULLY OR NOT, MISTER PENNYWORTH, IF THIS MAN HAS SUFFERED SEVERE SPINAL TRAUMA, HE BELONGS IN A HOSPITAL.
I'M AFRAID THAT'S IMPOSSIBLE, DOCTOR KINSOLVING.
MISTER WAYNE, AS YOU KNOW, IS AN EXTREMELY PROMINENT BUSINESSMAN, AND IN THE WORLD OF BUSINESS, PERCEPTION IS EVERYTHING.
STEADY PULSE...
WERE IT GENERALLY KNOWN THAT MISTER WAYNE IS INCAPACITATED IT WOULD BE PERCEIVED AS A WEAKNESS, AND HIS AFFAIRS COULD WELL SUFFER A GREAT--
A FRACTURED SPINE IS FAR MORE THAN A PERCEIVED WEAKNESS, MISTER PENNYWORTH.
10

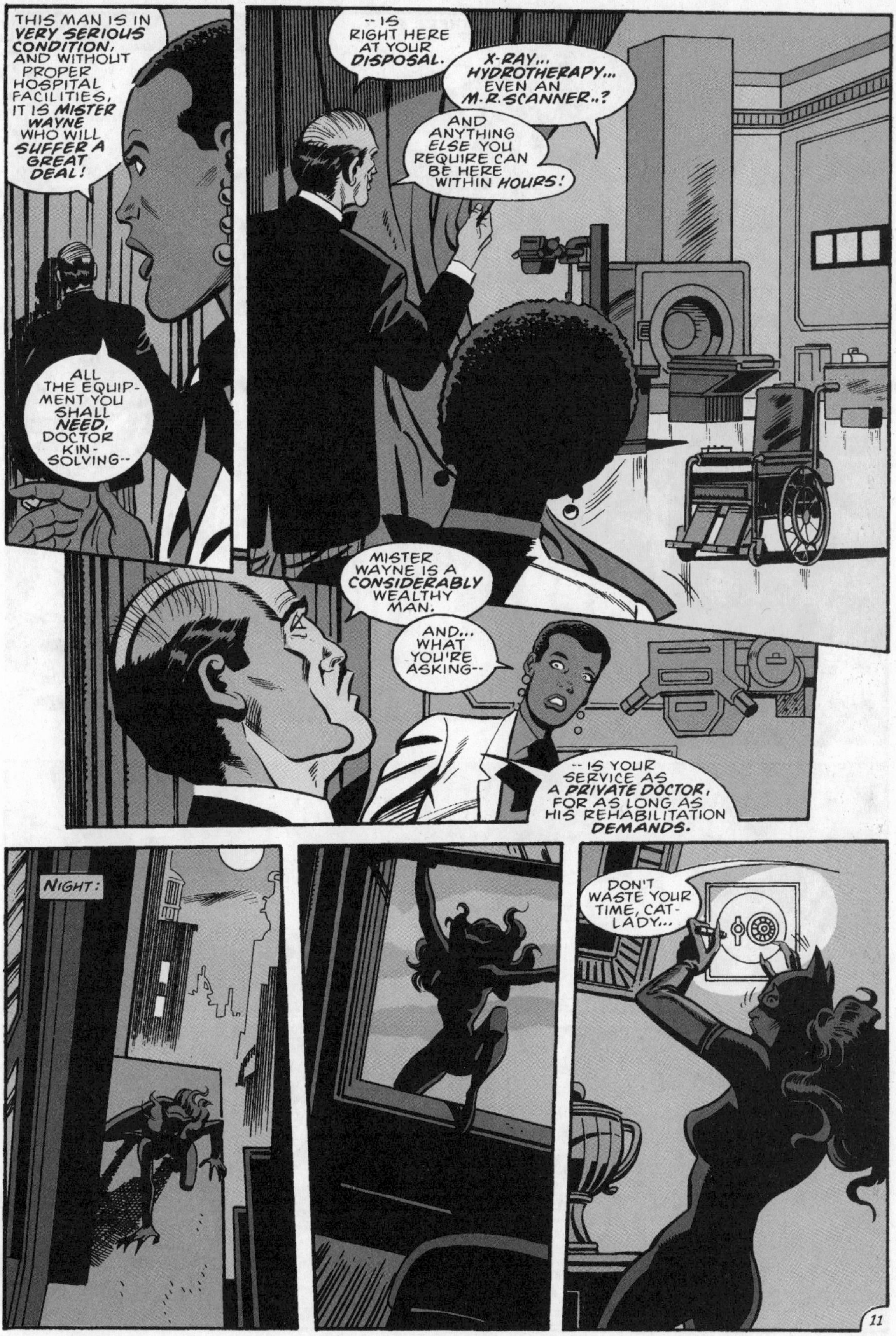
THIS MAN IS IN VERY SERIOUS CONDITION, AND WITHOUT PROPER HOSPITAL FACILITIES, IT IS MISTER WAYNE WHO WILL SUFFER A GREAT DEAL!
ALL THE EQUIPMENT YOU SHALL NEED, DOCTOR KINSOLVING--
--IS RIGHT HERE AT YOUR DISPOSAL.
X-RAY... HYDROTHERAPY... EVEN AN M.R. SCANNER..?
AND ANYTHING ELSE YOU REQUIRE CAN BE HERE WITHIN HOURS!
MISTER WAYNE IS A CONSIDERABLY WEALTHY MAN.
AND... WHAT YOU'RE ASKING--
--IS YOUR SERVICE AS A PRIVATE DOCTOR, FOR AS LONG AS HIS REHABILITATION DEMANDS.
NIGHT:
DON'T WASTE YOUR TIME, CAT-LADY...
11

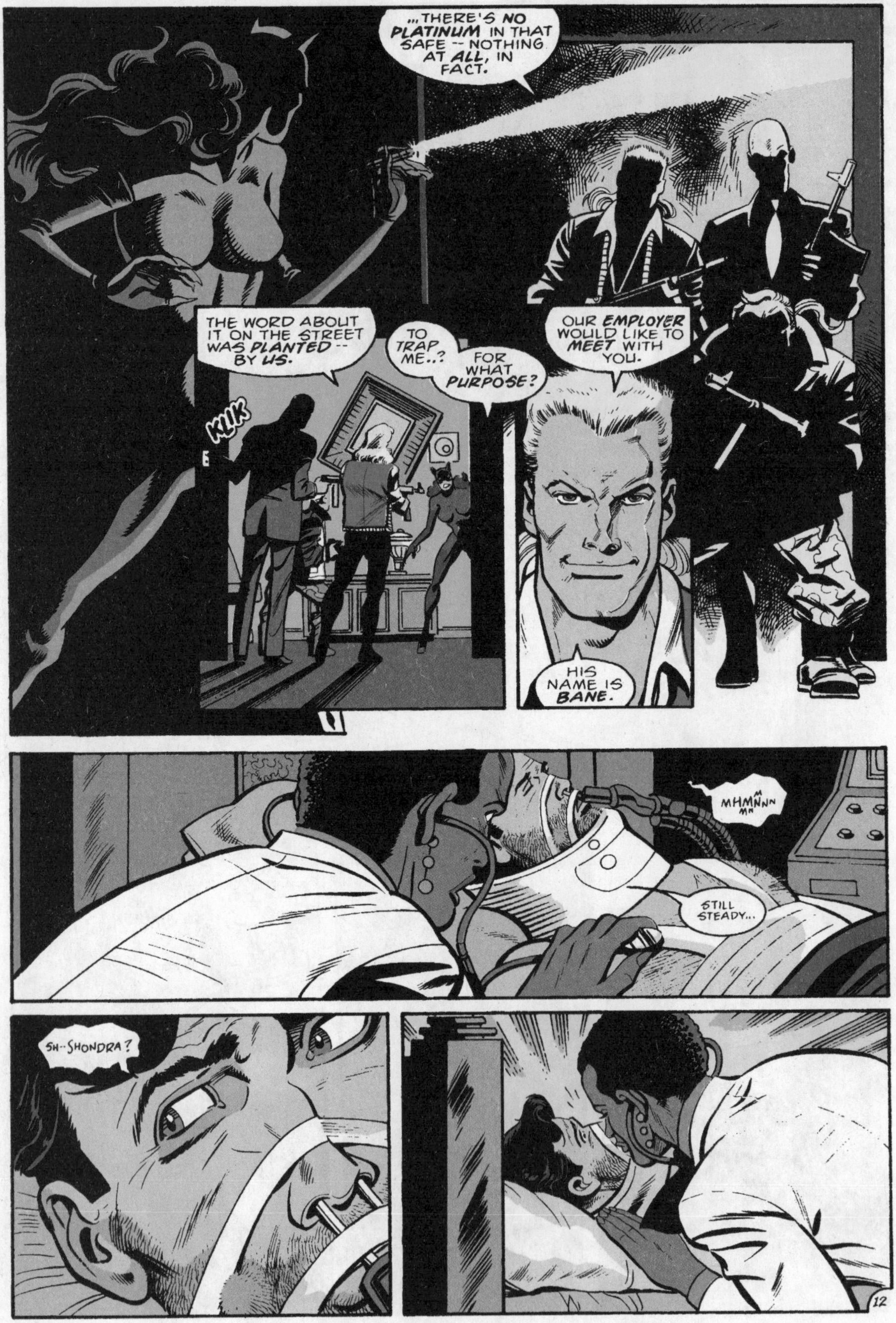
...THERE'S NO PLATINUM IN THAT SAFE -- NOTHING AT ALL, IN FACT.
THE WORD ABOUT IT ON THE STREET WAS PLANTED -- BY US.
TO TRAP ME..?
FOR WHAT PURPOSE?
OUR EMPLOYER WOULD LIKE TO MEET WITH YOU.
KLIK
HIS NAME IS BANE.
MHMNNN
STILL STEADY...
SH--SHONDRA?
12

STILL NO WORD ON WHERE HE **IS**, COMMISH?

NO.

GOIN' UP TO THE **ROOF**?

IT CAN'T **HURT**, SERGEANT, TO **TRY**.

ABOUT WHAT HAPPENED WHEN YOU **WOKE UP**, BRUCE, I ... WELL, I CAN'T REALLY **EXPLAIN** IT ...

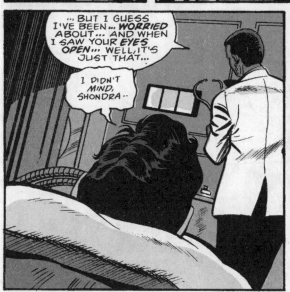

... BUT I GUESS I'VE BEEN ... **WORRIED** ABOUT ... AND WHEN I SAW YOUR **EYES OPEN** ... WELL, IT'S JUST THAT ...

I DIDN'T **MIND**, SHONDRA--

YOU **DIDN'T**?

OTHER THAN ... **WEAKNESS** AND **PAIN** ... IT WAS THE **FIRST TIME**, IN FAR TOO LONG, THAT I'VE FELT **ANYTHING**.

YES, ALFRED AND TIMOTHY TOLD ME YOU'RE EXPERIENCING SOME **DEPRESSION** ...

I'VE SUFFERED A ... **LOSS** ... BEYOND THE INJURY ...

I HOPE YOU'RE NOT TALKING ABOUT A MERE **CAR**.

CAR?!?

Ahem ...

THE **PORSCHE**, SIR.

YOU WERE IN **SHOCK** WHEN I **FOUND** YOU BY THE ROADSIDE, REMEMBER -- WITH LITTLE OR NO **MEMORY** OF YOUR ACCIDENT.

13

IT MAY TAKE A WHILE, DOCTOR, FOR MISTER WAYNE TO --

IF ANYONE CAN HEAL HIM, MISTER PENNYWORTH, *I WILL.*

MIGHTY CONFIDENT...

EXACTLY, BRUCE, AND THAT'S WHAT *YOU* MUST BE -- *BOTH* OF US -- *TOGETHER.*

FROM WHAT I *KNOW* OF YOU, YOU'RE NOT THE TYPE WHO *QUITS*... EVEN IF YOU ARE CAPABLE OF *LYING.*

LYING..?

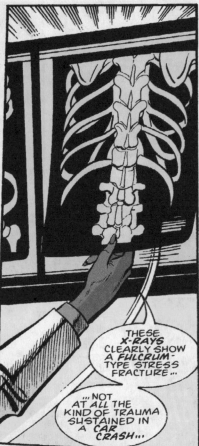

THESE *X-RAYS* CLEARLY SHOW A *FULCRUM-* TYPE STRESS FRACTURE...

...NOT AT ALL THE KIND OF TRAUMA SUSTAINED IN A *CAR CRASH*...

...WHICH, IN ANY CASE, WOULD HAVE SHATTERED YOUR *LEGS* BEFORE AFFECTING YOUR *BACK.*

I...

HE WAS *THROWN* FROM THE CAR -- BEFORE IT WENT OVER THE *VERGE* -- LANDED ON A LARGE *ROCK.*

THAT'S ALL RIGHT -- I *LIKE* IT.

YOU... *DO?!*

YOU'RE A *MYSTERY* TO ME, BRUCE -- AND THE FACT THAT YOU'RE *CLINGING* TO YOUR MYSTERY PROVES YOU *HAVEN'T* GIVEN UP!

BESIDES, THE DIAGNOSTICIAN IN ME ENJOYS PEELING MYSTERIES *OPEN*... ONE LAYER AT A *TIME.*

14

418

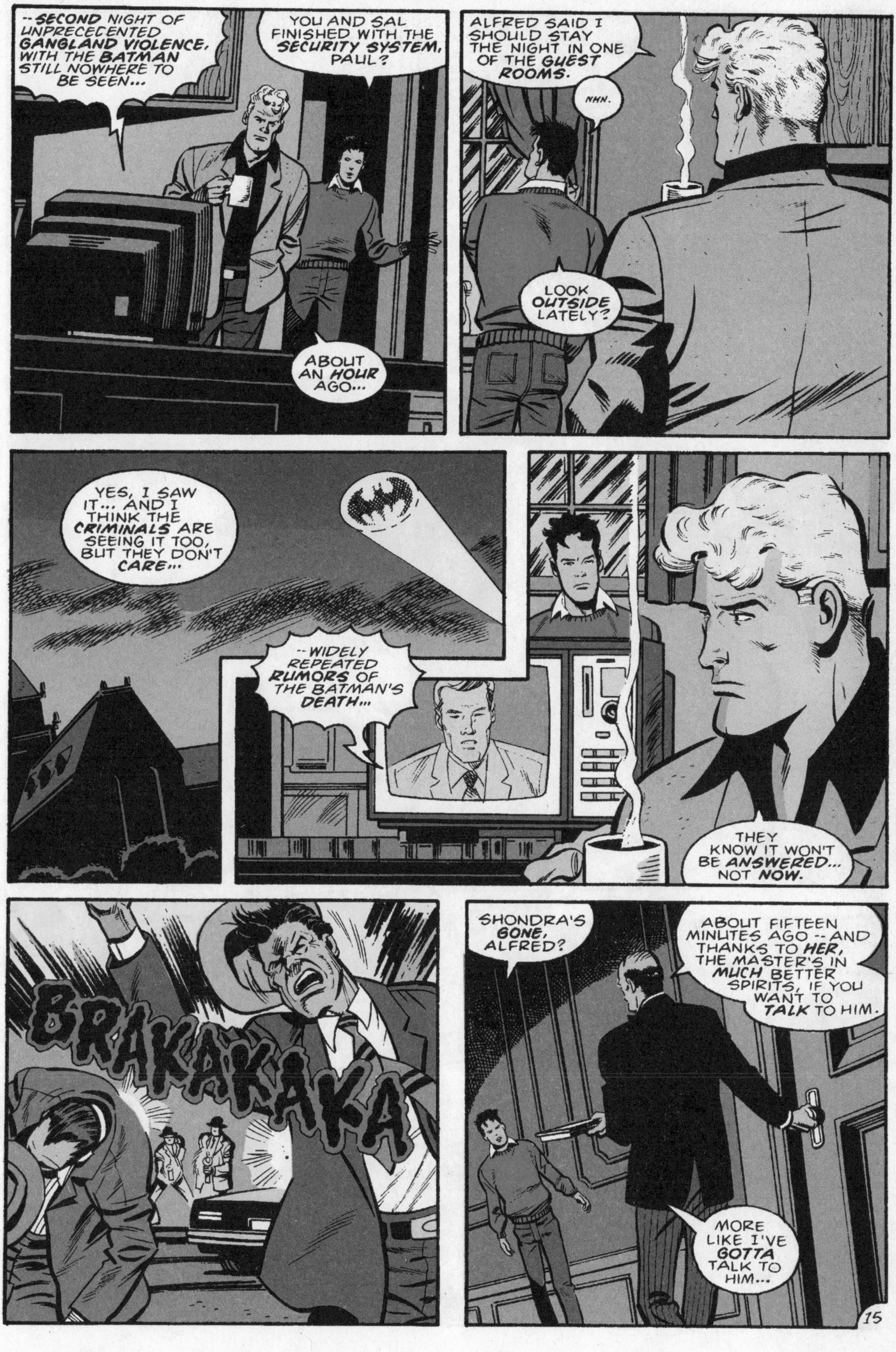
--SECOND NIGHT OF UNPRECEDENTED GANGLAND VIOLENCE, WITH THE BATMAN STILL NOWHERE TO BE SEEN...
YOU AND SAL FINISHED WITH THE SECURITY SYSTEM, PAUL?
ABOUT AN HOUR AGO...
ALFRED SAID I SHOULD STAY THE NIGHT IN ONE OF THE GUEST ROOMS.
NHN.
LOOK OUTSIDE LATELY?
YES, I SAW IT... AND I THINK THE CRIMINALS ARE SEEING IT TOO, BUT THEY DON'T CARE...
--WIDELY REPEATED RUMORS OF THE BATMAN'S DEATH...
THEY KNOW IT WON'T BE ANSWERED... NOT NOW.
BRAKAKAKAKA
SHONDRA'S GONE, ALFRED?
ABOUT FIFTEEN MINUTES AGO -- AND THANKS TO HER, THE MASTER'S IN MUCH BETTER SPIRITS, IF YOU WANT TO TALK TO HIM.
MORE LIKE I'VE GOTTA TALK TO HIM...
15

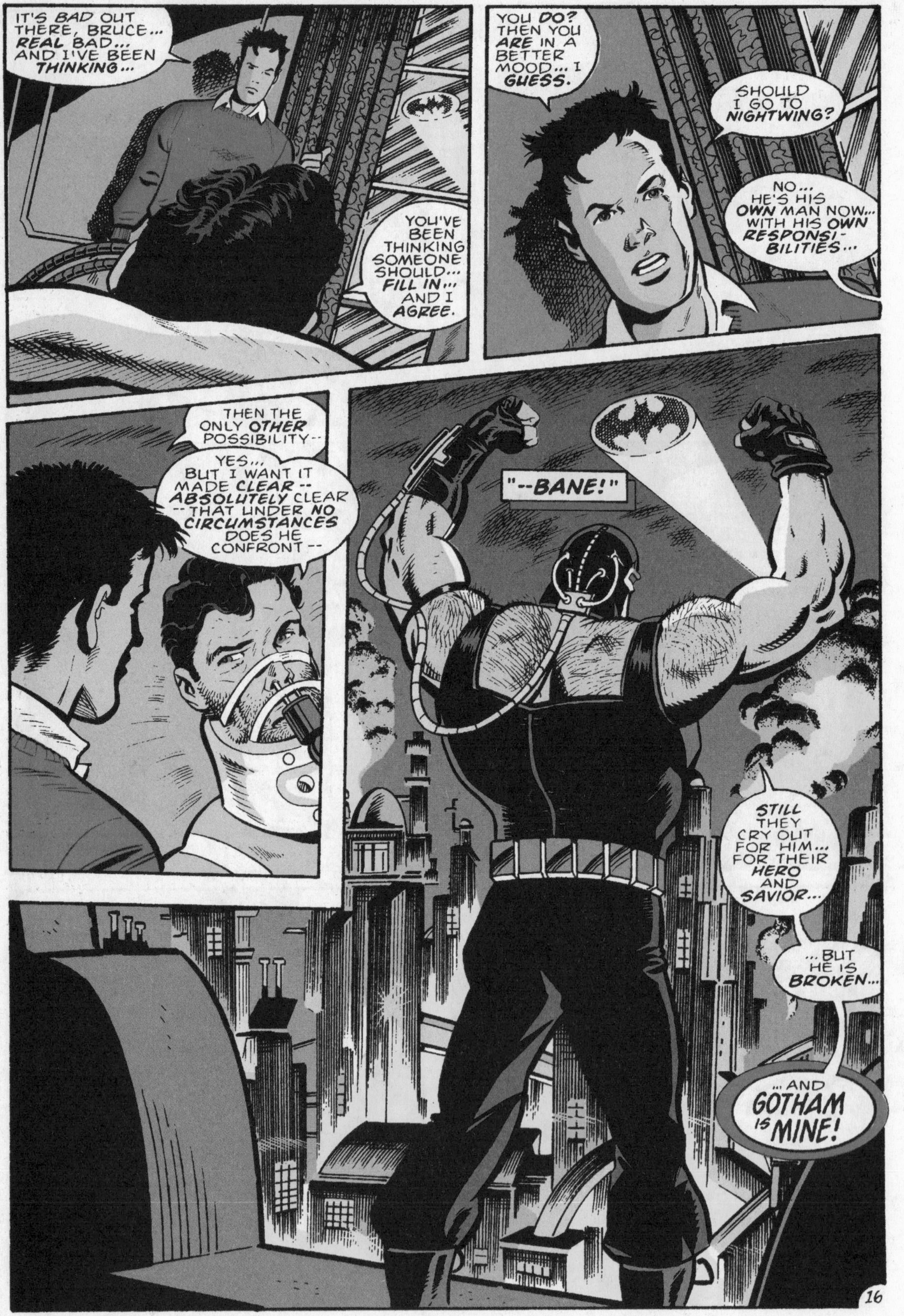
IT'S BAD OUT THERE, BRUCE... REAL BAD... AND I'VE BEEN THINKING...
YOU'VE BEEN THINKING SOMEONE SHOULD... FILL IN... AND I AGREE.
YOU DO? THEN YOU ARE IN A BETTER MOOD... I GUESS.
SHOULD I GO TO NIGHTWING?
NO... HE'S HIS OWN MAN NOW... WITH HIS OWN RESPONSI-BILITIES...
THEN THE ONLY OTHER POSSIBILITY--
YES... BUT I WANT IT MADE CLEAR-- ABSOLUTELY CLEAR --THAT UNDER NO CIRCUMSTANCES DOES HE CONFRONT--
"--BANE!"
STILL THEY CRY OUT FOR HIM... FOR THEIR HERO AND SAVIOR...
...BUT HE IS BROKEN...
...AND GOTHAM IS MINE!
16

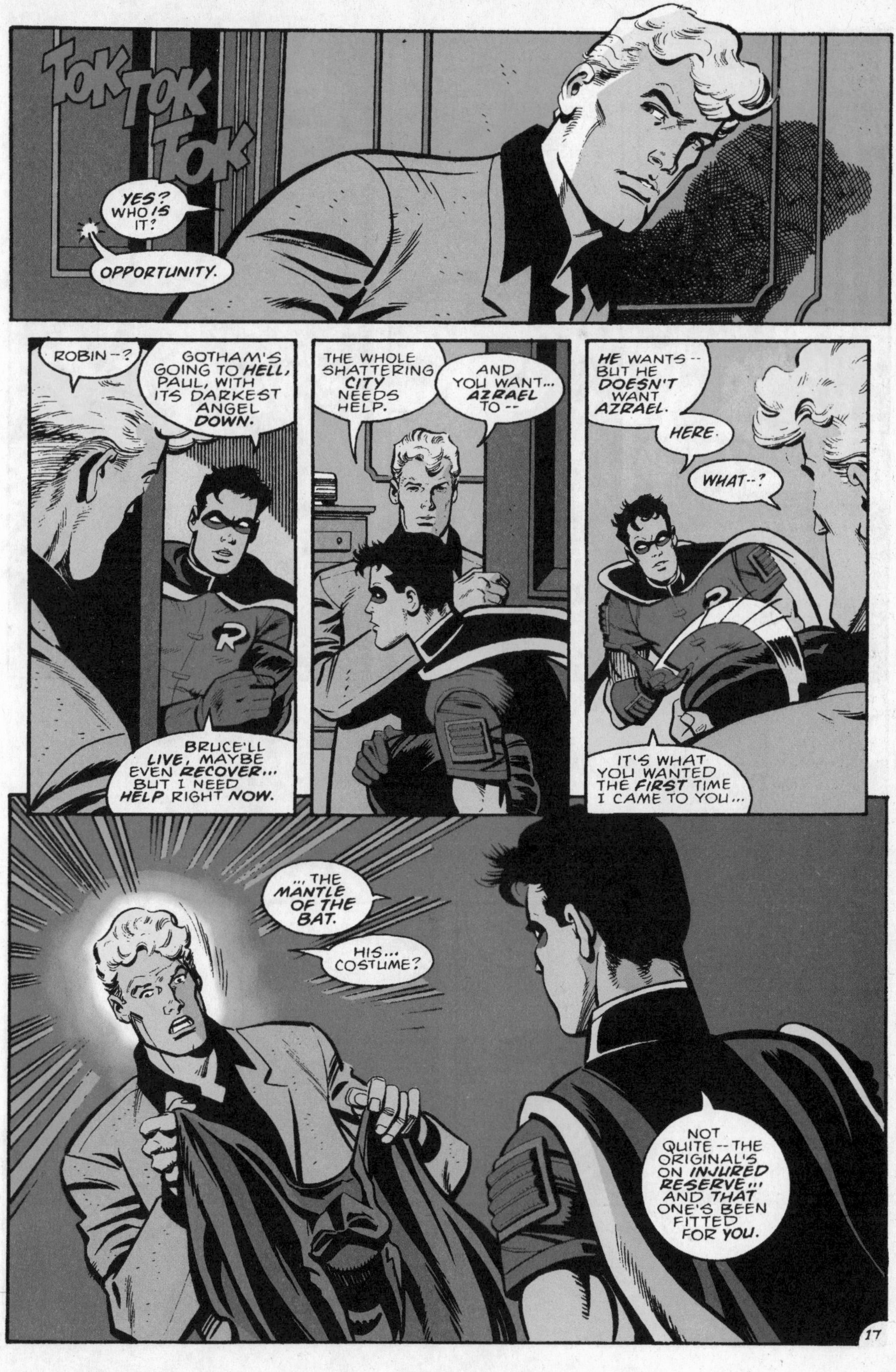
TOK TOK TOK
YES? WHO IS IT?
OPPORTUNITY.
ROBIN--?
GOTHAM'S GOING TO HELL, PAUL, WITH ITS DARKEST ANGEL DOWN.
BRUCE'LL LIVE, MAYBE EVEN RECOVER... BUT I NEED HELP RIGHT NOW.
THE WHOLE SHATTERING CITY NEEDS HELP.
AND YOU WANT... AZRAEL TO --
HE WANTS -- BUT HE DOESN'T WANT AZRAEL.
HERE.
WHAT--?
IT'S WHAT YOU WANTED THE FIRST TIME I CAME TO YOU...
..., THE MANTLE OF THE BAT.
HIS... COSTUME?
NOT QUITE -- THE ORIGINAL'S ON INJURED RESERVE... AND THAT ONE'S BEEN FITTED FOR YOU.
17

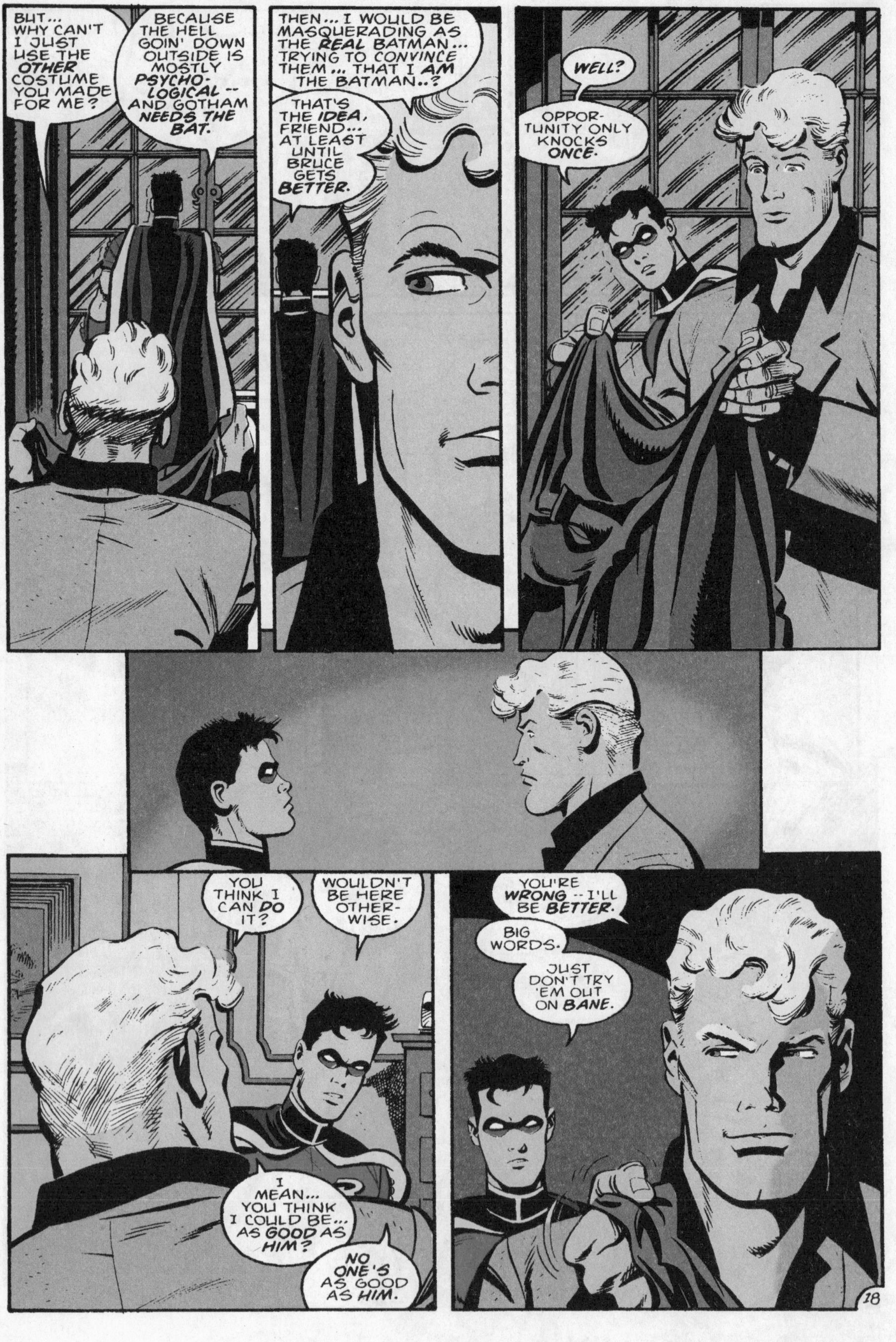
BUT... WHY CAN'T I JUST USE THE OTHER COSTUME YOU MADE FOR ME?
BECAUSE THE HELL GOIN' DOWN OUTSIDE IS MOSTLY PSYCHO-LOGICAL -- AND GOTHAM NEEDS THE BAT.
THEN... I WOULD BE MASQUERADING AS THE REAL BATMAN... TRYING TO CONVINCE THEM... THAT I AM THE BATMAN..?
THAT'S THE IDEA, FRIEND... AT LEAST UNTIL BRUCE GETS BETTER.
WELL?
OPPOR-TUNITY ONLY KNOCKS ONCE.
YOU THINK I CAN DO IT?
WOULDN'T BE HERE OTHER-WISE.
I MEAN... YOU THINK I COULD BE... AS GOOD AS HIM?
NO ONE'S AS GOOD AS HIM.
YOU'RE WRONG -- I'LL BE BETTER.
BIG WORDS.
JUST DON'T TRY 'EM OUT ON BANE.
18

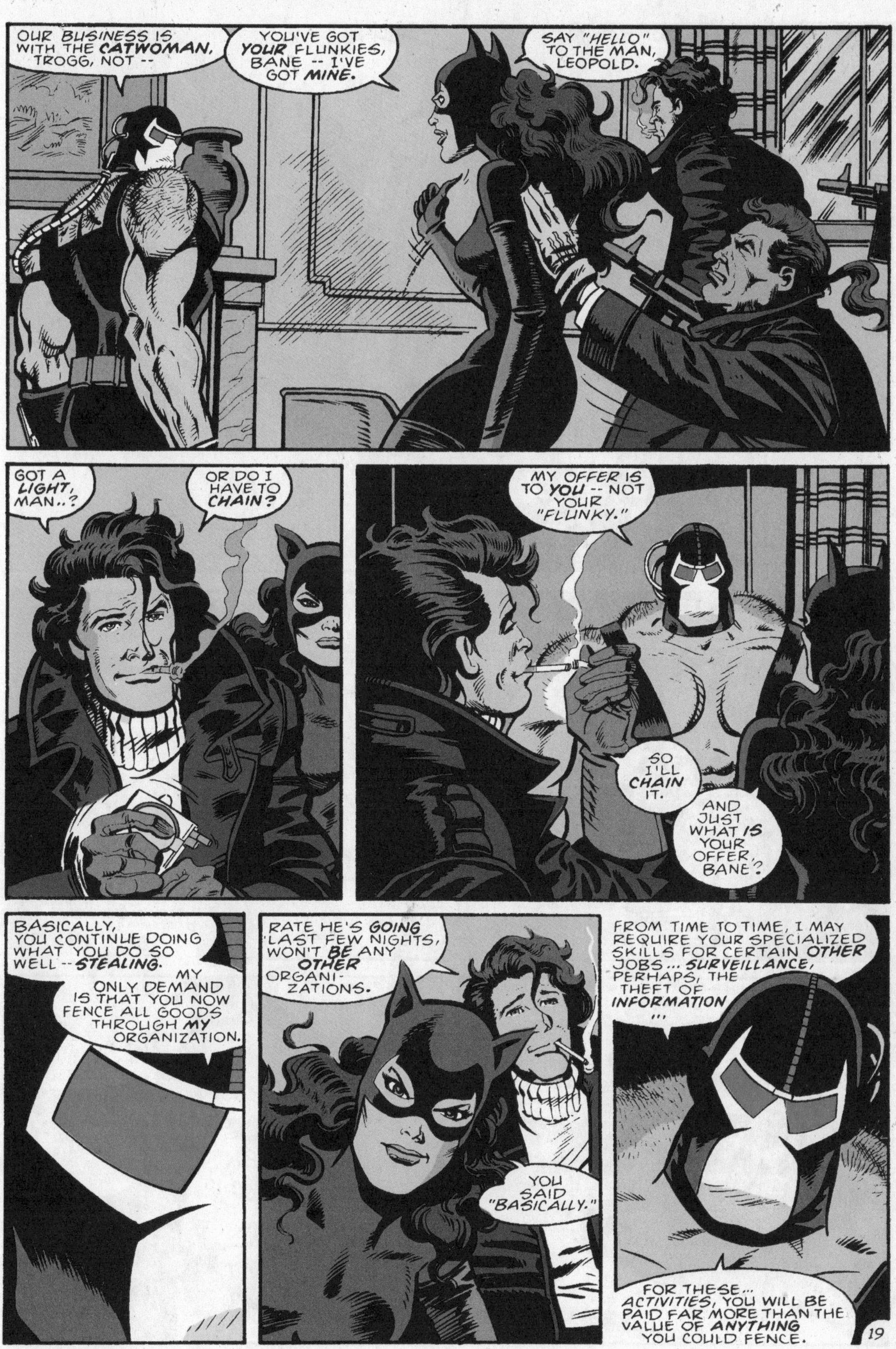
OUR BUSINESS IS WITH THE CATWOMAN, TROGG, NOT --
YOU'VE GOT YOUR FLUNKIES, BANE -- I'VE GOT MINE.
SAY "HELLO" TO THE MAN, LEOPOLD.
GOT A LIGHT, MAN..?
OR DO I HAVE TO CHAIN?
MY OFFER IS TO YOU -- NOT YOUR "FLUNKY."
SO I'LL CHAIN IT.
AND JUST WHAT IS YOUR OFFER, BANE?
BASICALLY, YOU CONTINUE DOING WHAT YOU DO SO WELL -- STEALING.
MY ONLY DEMAND IS THAT YOU NOW FENCE ALL GOODS THROUGH MY ORGANIZATION.
RATE HE'S GOING LAST FEW NIGHTS, WON'T BE ANY OTHER ORGANIZATIONS.
YOU SAID "BASICALLY."
FROM TIME TO TIME, I MAY REQUIRE YOUR SPECIALIZED SKILLS FOR CERTAIN OTHER JOBS... SURVEILLANCE, PERHAPS, THE THEFT OF INFORMATION...
FOR THESE... ACTIVITIES, YOU WILL BE PAID FAR MORE THAN THE VALUE OF ANYTHING YOU COULD FENCE.
19

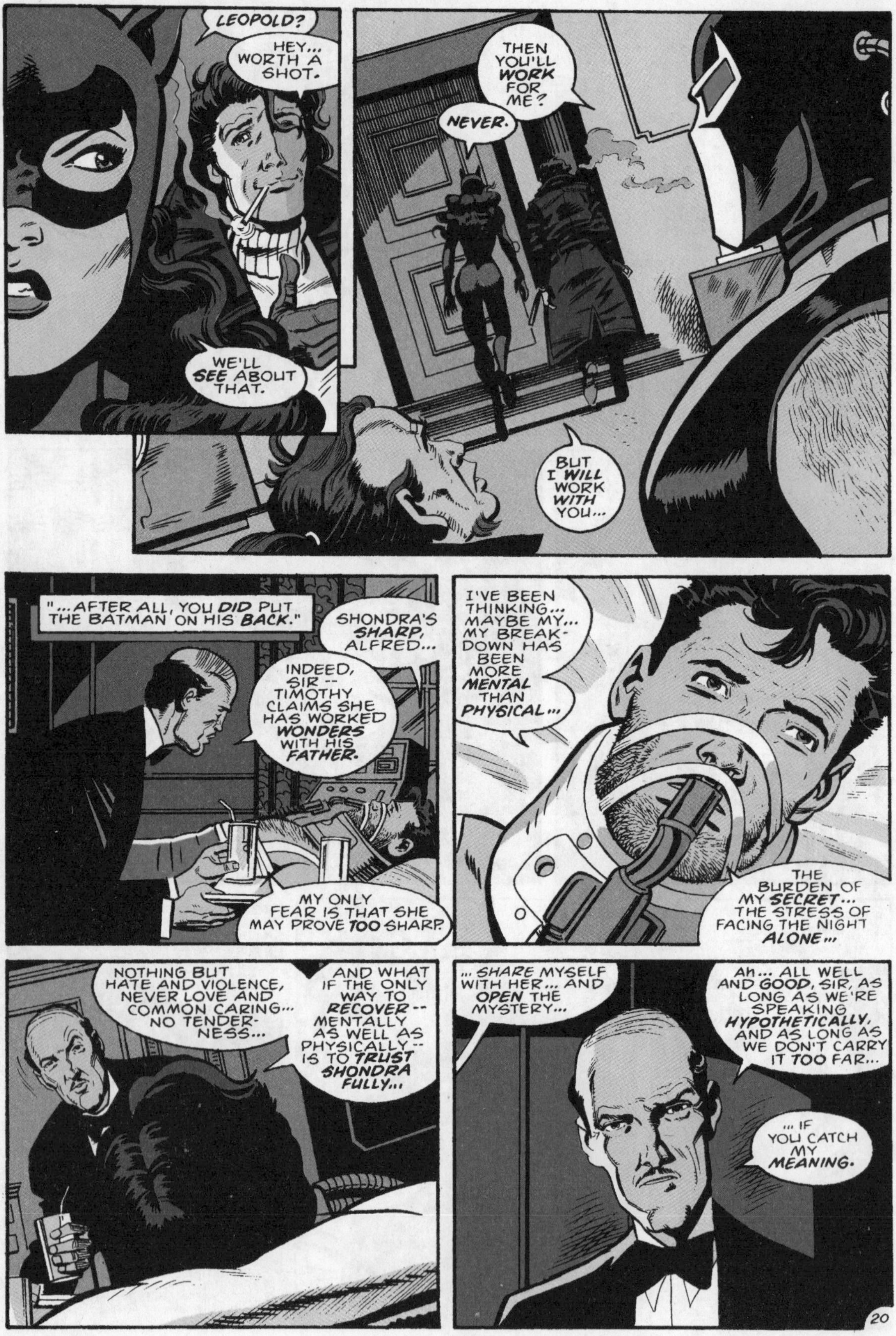
LEOPOLD?
HEY... WORTH A SHOT.
WE'LL SEE ABOUT THAT.
THEN YOU'LL WORK FOR ME?
NEVER.
BUT I WILL WORK WITH YOU...
"...AFTER ALL, YOU DID PUT THE BATMAN ON HIS BACK."
SHONDRA'S SHARP, ALFRED...
INDEED, SIR -- TIMOTHY CLAIMS SHE HAS WORKED WONDERS WITH HIS FATHER.
MY ONLY FEAR IS THAT SHE MAY PROVE TOO SHARP.
I'VE BEEN THINKING... MAYBE MY... MY BREAK-DOWN HAS BEEN MORE MENTAL THAN PHYSICAL...
THE BURDEN OF MY SECRET... THE STRESS OF FACING THE NIGHT ALONE...
NOTHING BUT HATE AND VIOLENCE, NEVER LOVE AND COMMON CARING... NO TENDER-NESS...
AND WHAT IF THE ONLY WAY TO RECOVER -- MENTALLY AS WELL AS PHYSICALLY -- IS TO TRUST SHONDRA FULLY...
...SHARE MYSELF WITH HER... AND OPEN THE MYSTERY...
Ah... ALL WELL AND GOOD, SIR, AS LONG AS WE'RE SPEAKING HYPOTHETICALLY, AND AS LONG AS WE DON'T CARRY IT TOO FAR...
...IF YOU CATCH MY MEANING.
20

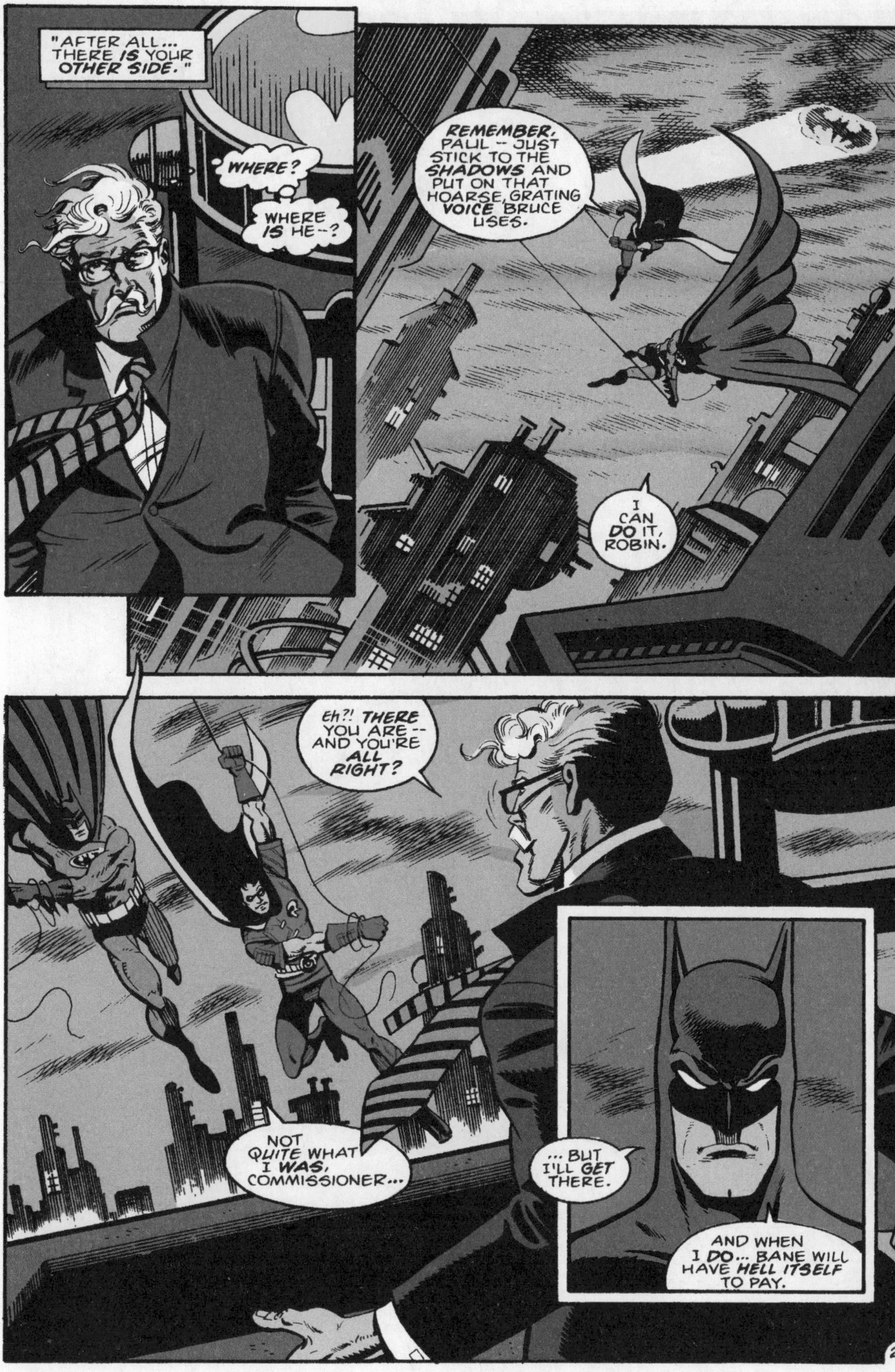

"AFTER ALL... THERE IS YOUR OTHER SIDE."
WHERE?
WHERE IS HE--?
REMEMBER, PAUL -- JUST STICK TO THE SHADOWS AND PUT ON THAT HOARSE, GRATING VOICE BRUCE USES.
I CAN DO IT, ROBIN.
Eh?! THERE YOU ARE -- AND YOU'RE ALL RIGHT?
NOT QUITE WHAT I WAS, COMMISSIONER...
...BUT I'LL GET THERE.
AND WHEN I DO... BANE WILL HAVE HELL ITSELF TO PAY.
21

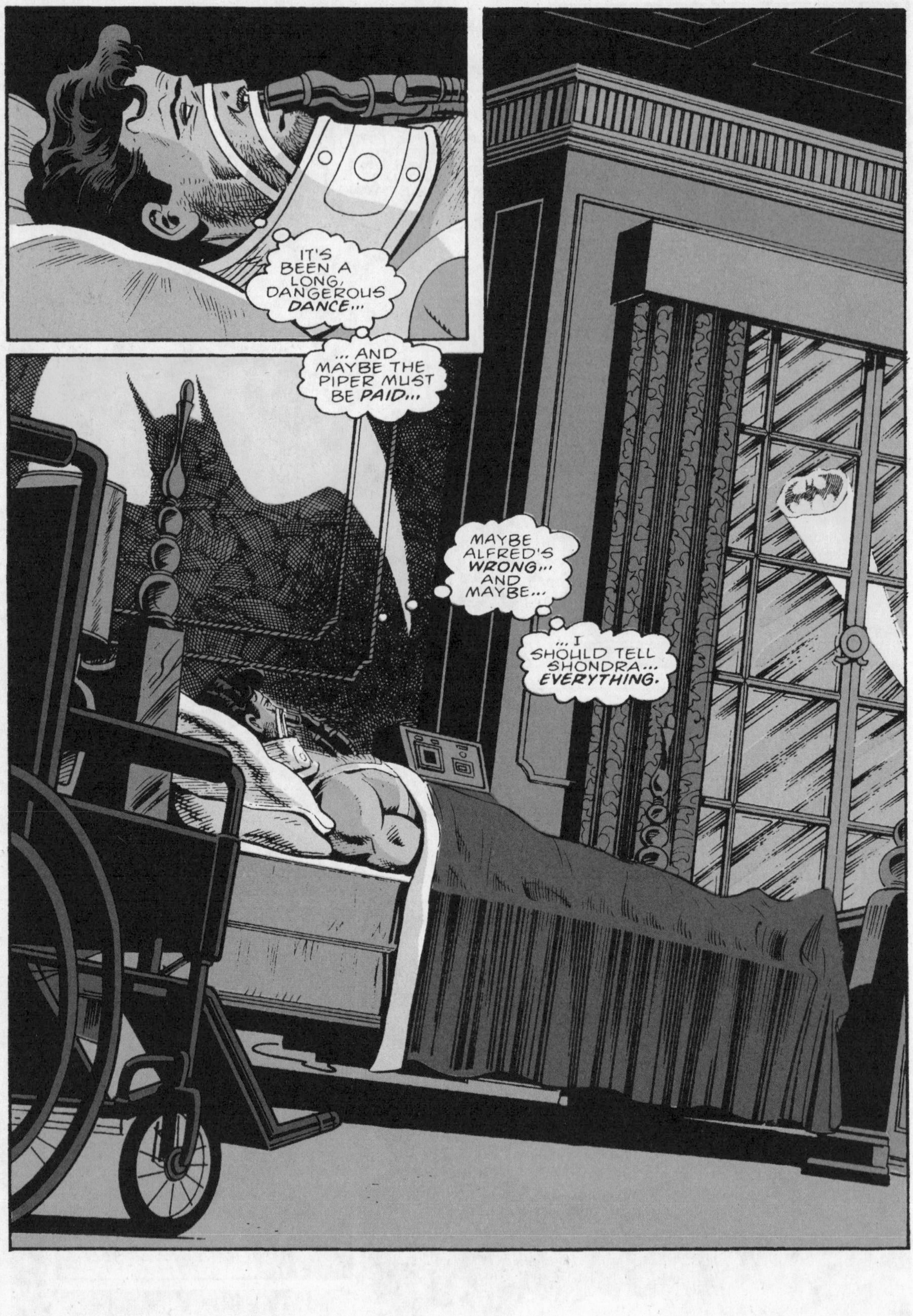
IT'S BEEN A LONG, DANGEROUS DANCE...
...AND MAYBE THE PIPER MUST BE PAID...
MAYBE ALFRED'S WRONG... AND MAYBE...
...I SHOULD TELL SHONDRA... EVERYTHING.

Cover art by **KELLEY JONES**

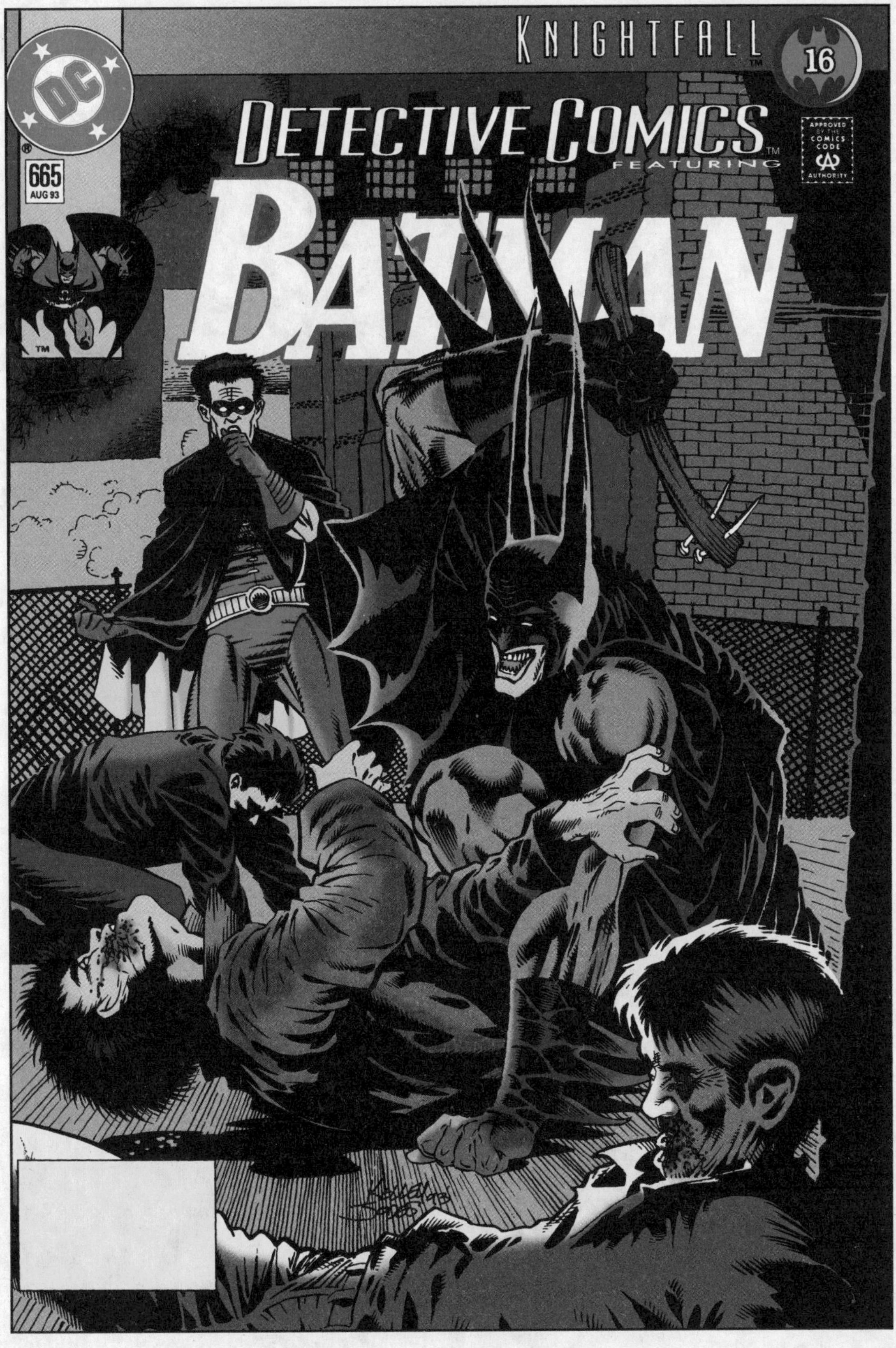
KNIGHTFALL
16
DC
665
AUG 93
DETECTIVE COMICS
FEATURING
BATMAN
APPROVED BY THE COMICS CODE AUTHORITY

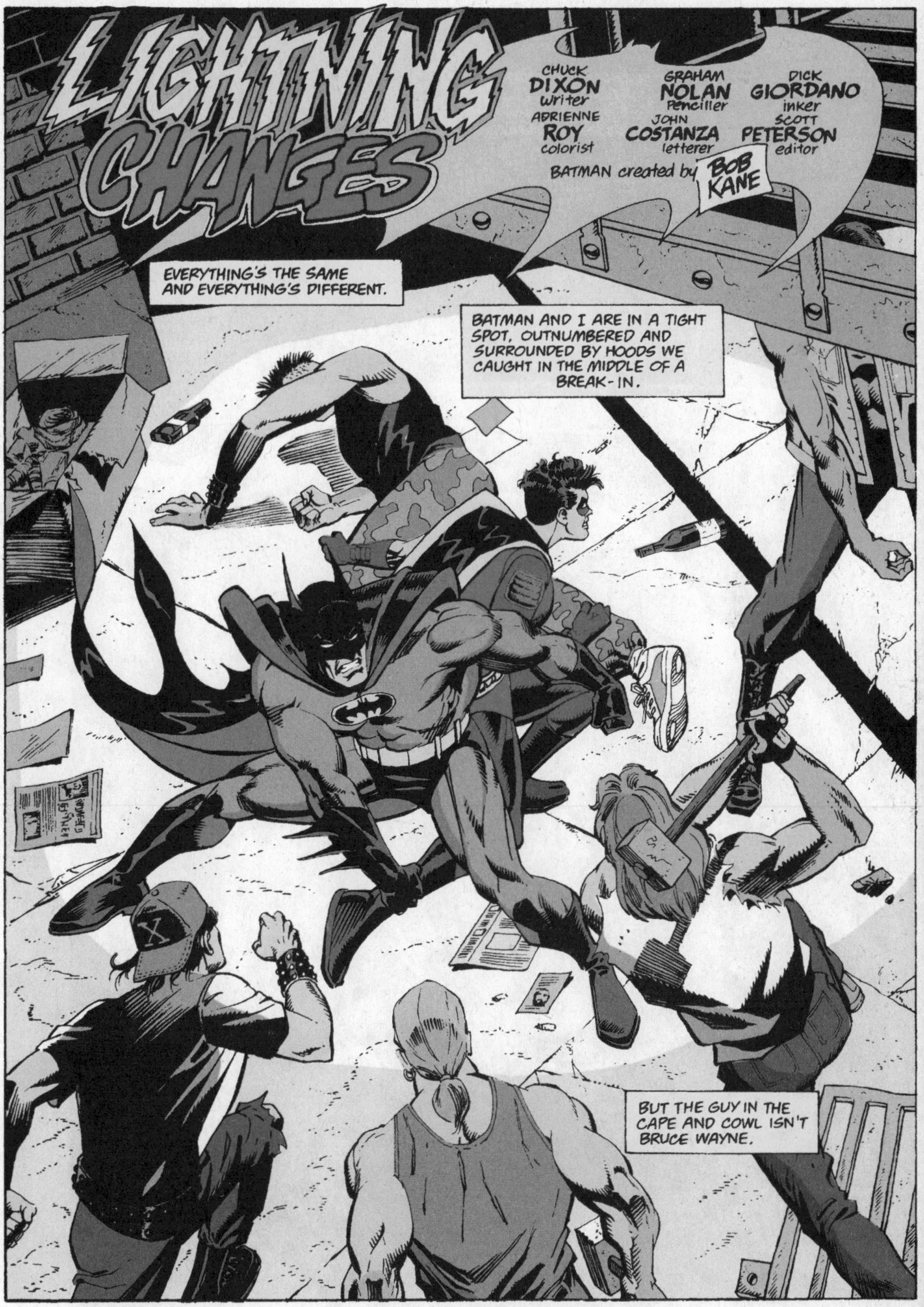
LIGHTNING CHANGES
CHUCK DIXON writer
GRAHAM NOLAN penciller
DICK GIORDANO inker
ADRIENNE ROY colorist
JOHN COSTANZA letterer
SCOTT PETERSON editor
BATMAN created by BOB KANE
EVERYTHING'S THE SAME AND EVERYTHING'S DIFFERENT.
BATMAN AND I ARE IN A TIGHT SPOT, OUTNUMBERED AND SURROUNDED BY HOODS WE CAUGHT IN THE MIDDLE OF A BREAK-IN.
BUT THE GUY IN THE CAPE AND COWL ISN'T BRUCE WAYNE.

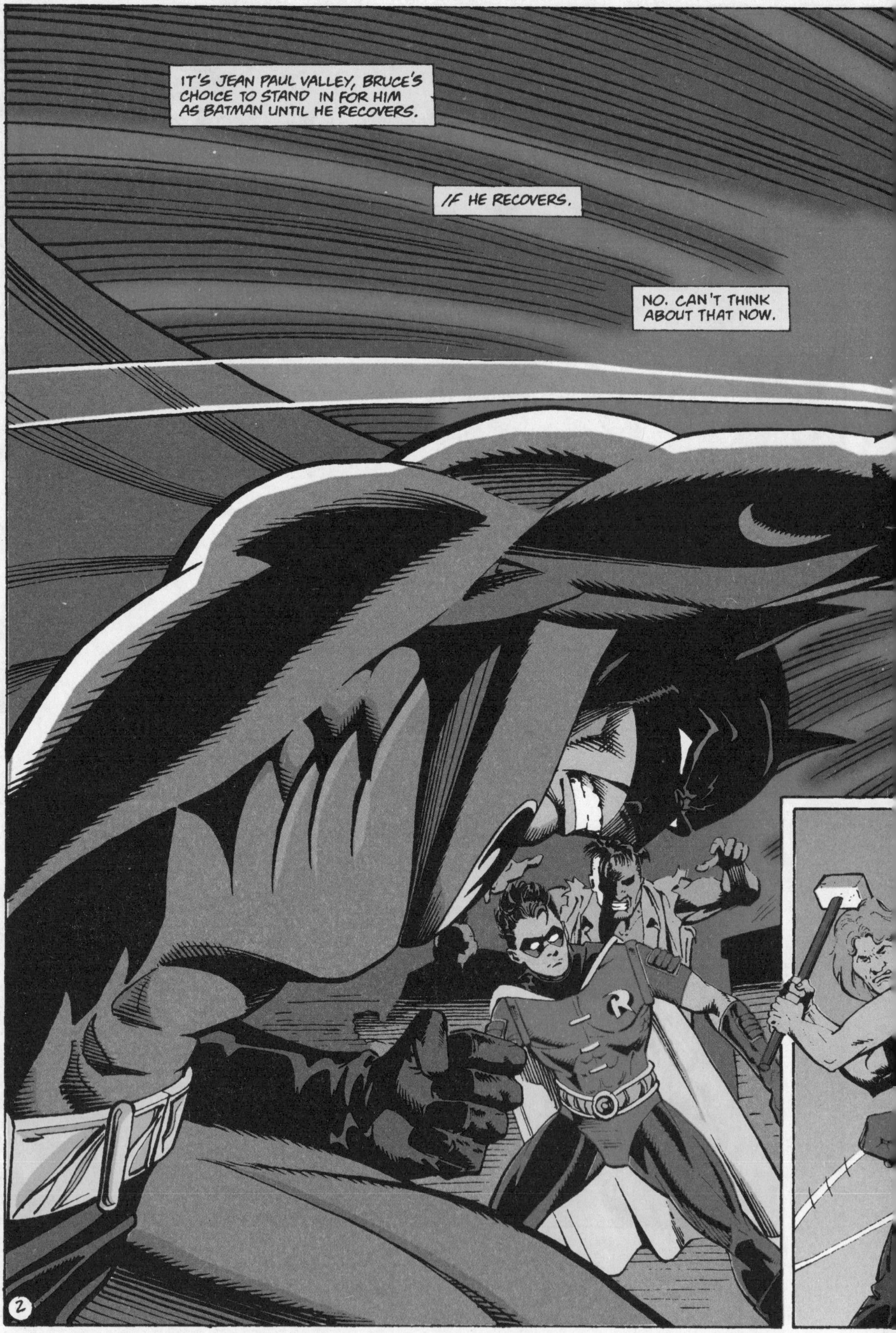
IT'S JEAN PAUL VALLEY, BRUCE'S CHOICE TO STAND IN FOR HIM AS BATMAN UNTIL HE RECOVERS.
IF HE RECOVERS.
NO. CAN'T THINK ABOUT THAT NOW.
2

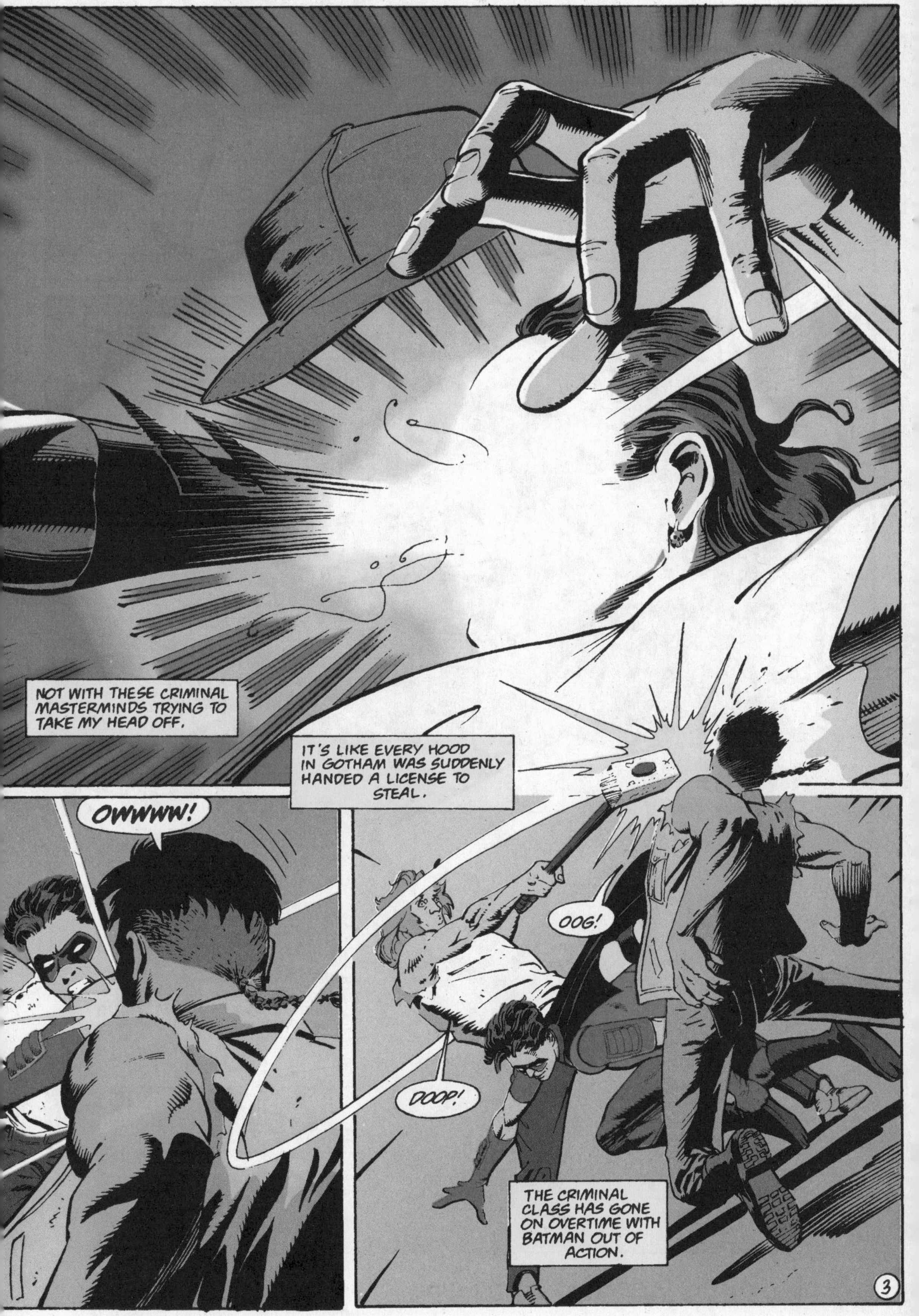
NOT WITH THESE CRIMINAL MASTERMINDS TRYING TO TAKE MY HEAD OFF.
IT'S LIKE EVERY HOOD IN GOTHAM WAS SUDDENLY HANDED A LICENSE TO STEAL.
OWWWW!
OOG!
DOOP!
THE CRIMINAL CLASS HAS GONE ON OVERTIME WITH BATMAN OUT OF ACTION.
3

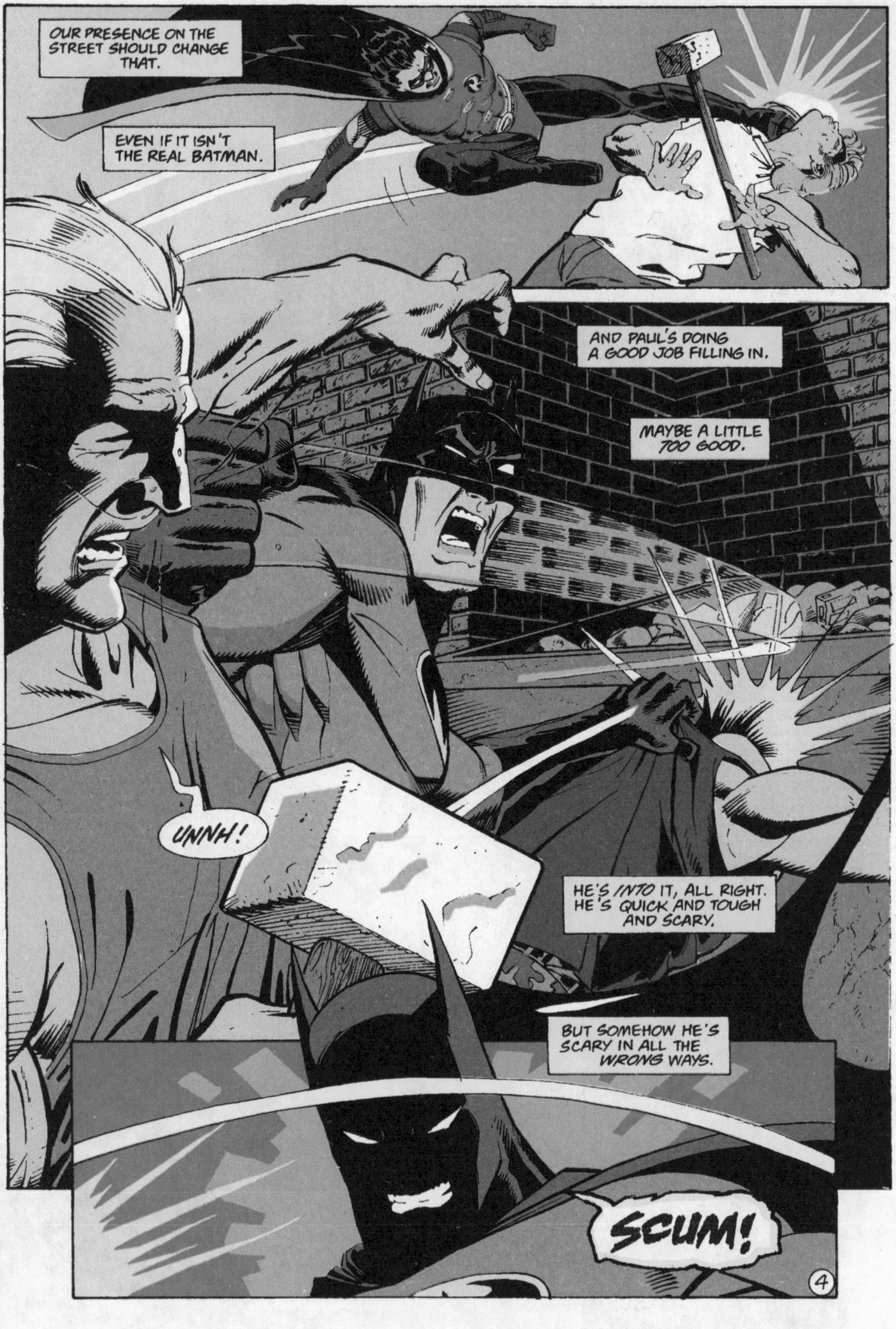
OUR PRESENCE ON THE STREET SHOULD CHANGE THAT.
EVEN IF IT ISN'T THE REAL BATMAN.
AND PAUL'S DOING A GOOD JOB FILLING IN.
MAYBE A LITTLE TOO GOOD.
UNNH!
HE'S INTO IT, ALL RIGHT. HE'S QUICK AND TOUGH AND SCARY.
BUT SOMEHOW HE'S SCARY IN ALL THE WRONG WAYS.
SCUM!
4

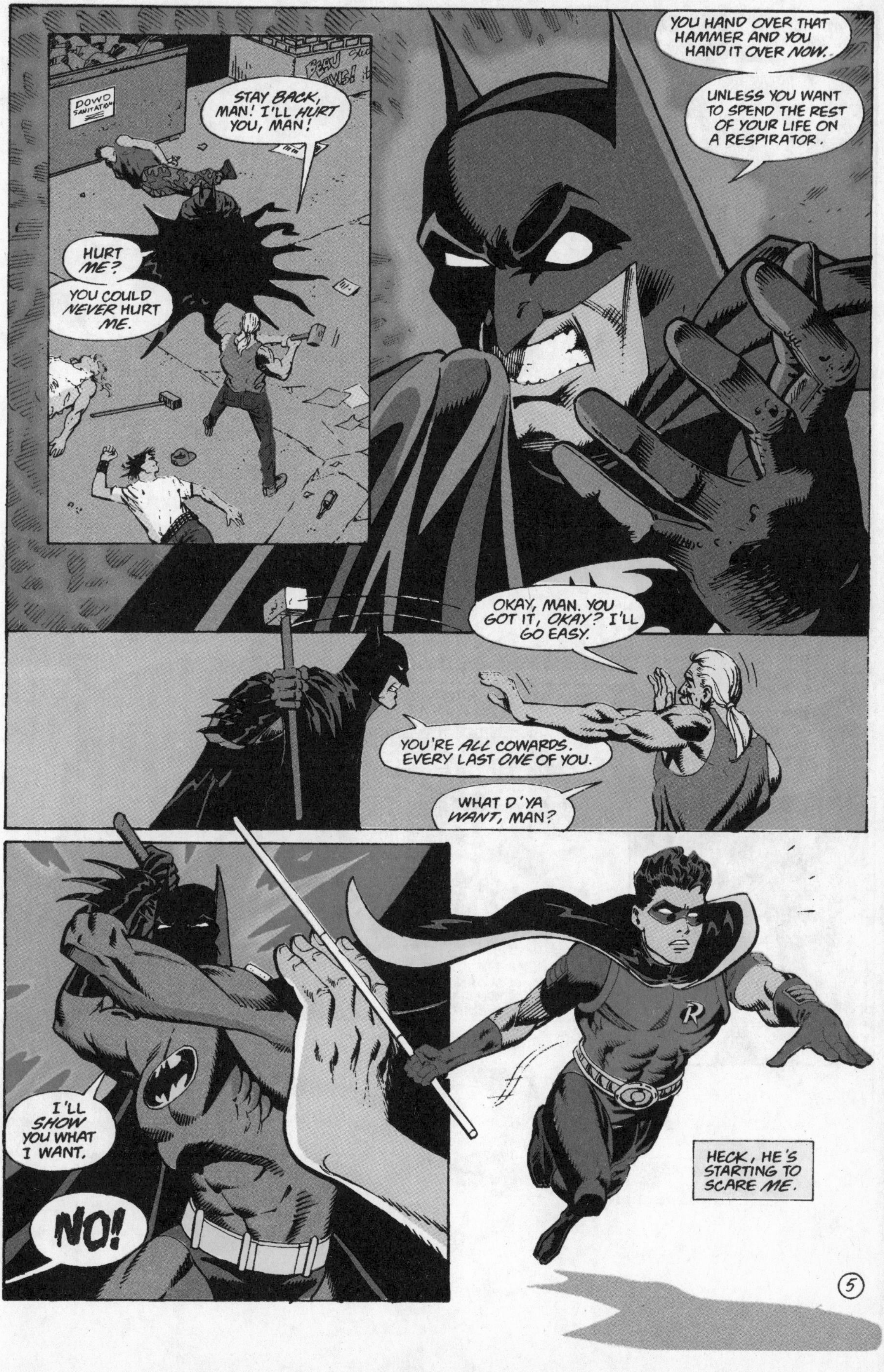
DOWD SANITATION
STAY BACK, MAN! I'LL HURT YOU, MAN!
HURT ME?
YOU COULD NEVER HURT ME.
YOU HAND OVER THAT HAMMER AND YOU HAND IT OVER NOW.
UNLESS YOU WANT TO SPEND THE REST OF YOUR LIFE ON A RESPIRATOR.
OKAY, MAN. YOU GOT IT, OKAY? I'LL GO EASY.
YOU'RE ALL COWARDS. EVERY LAST ONE OF YOU.
WHAT D'YA WANT, MAN?
I'LL SHOW YOU WHAT I WANT.
NO!
HECK, HE'S STARTING TO SCARE ME.
5

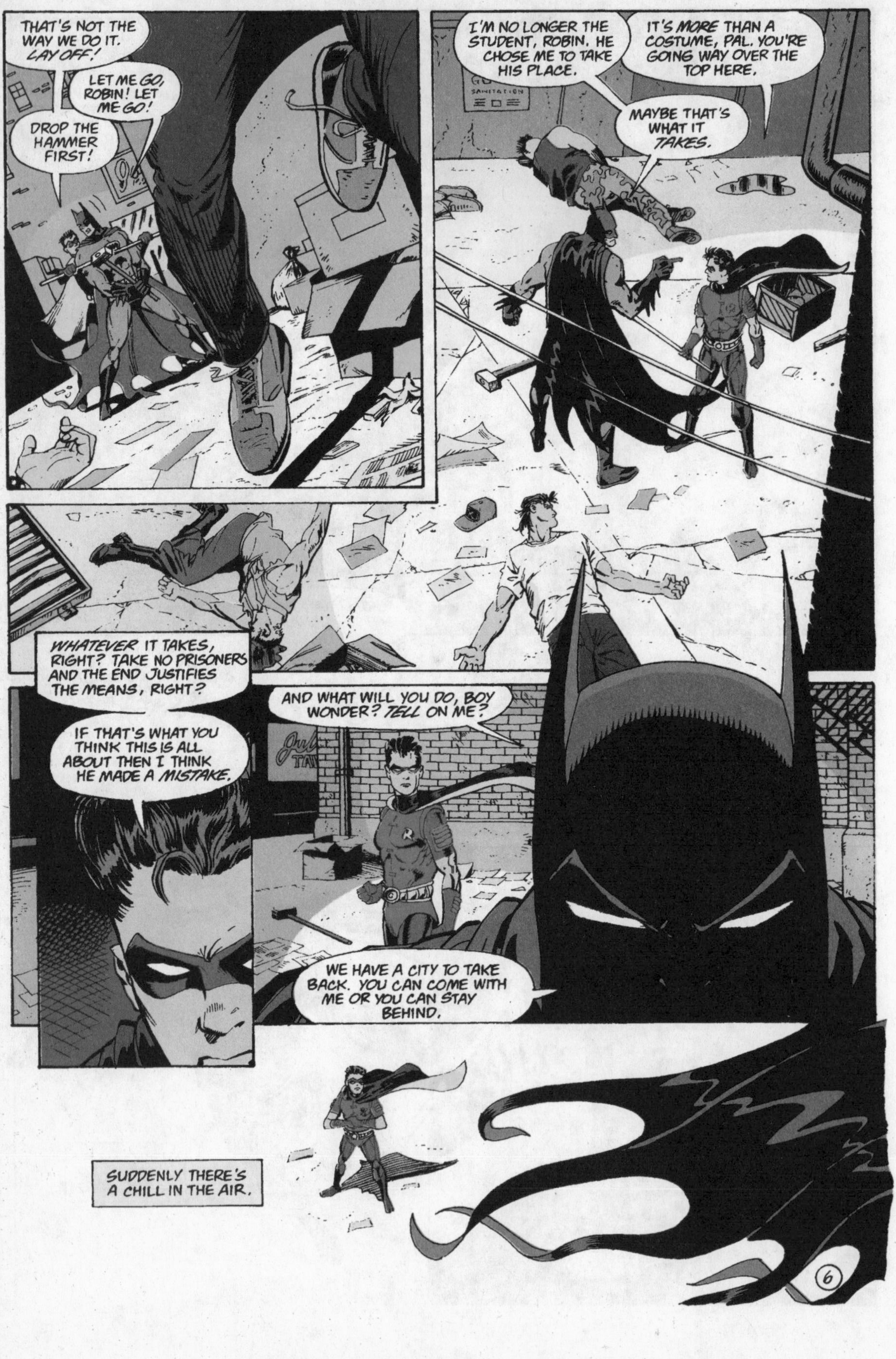

THAT'S NOT THE WAY WE DO IT. LAY OFF!
LET ME GO, ROBIN! LET ME GO!
DROP THE HAMMER FIRST!
I'M NO LONGER THE STUDENT, ROBIN. HE CHOSE ME TO TAKE HIS PLACE.
IT'S MORE THAN A COSTUME, PAL. YOU'RE GOING WAY OVER THE TOP HERE.
MAYBE THAT'S WHAT IT TAKES.
SANITATION
WHATEVER IT TAKES, RIGHT? TAKE NO PRISONERS AND THE END JUSTIFIES THE MEANS, RIGHT?
IF THAT'S WHAT YOU THINK THIS IS ALL ABOUT THEN I THINK HE MADE A MISTAKE.
AND WHAT WILL YOU DO, BOY WONDER? TELL ON ME?
WE HAVE A CITY TO TAKE BACK. YOU CAN COME WITH ME OR YOU CAN STAY BEHIND.
SUDDENLY THERE'S A CHILL IN THE AIR.
6

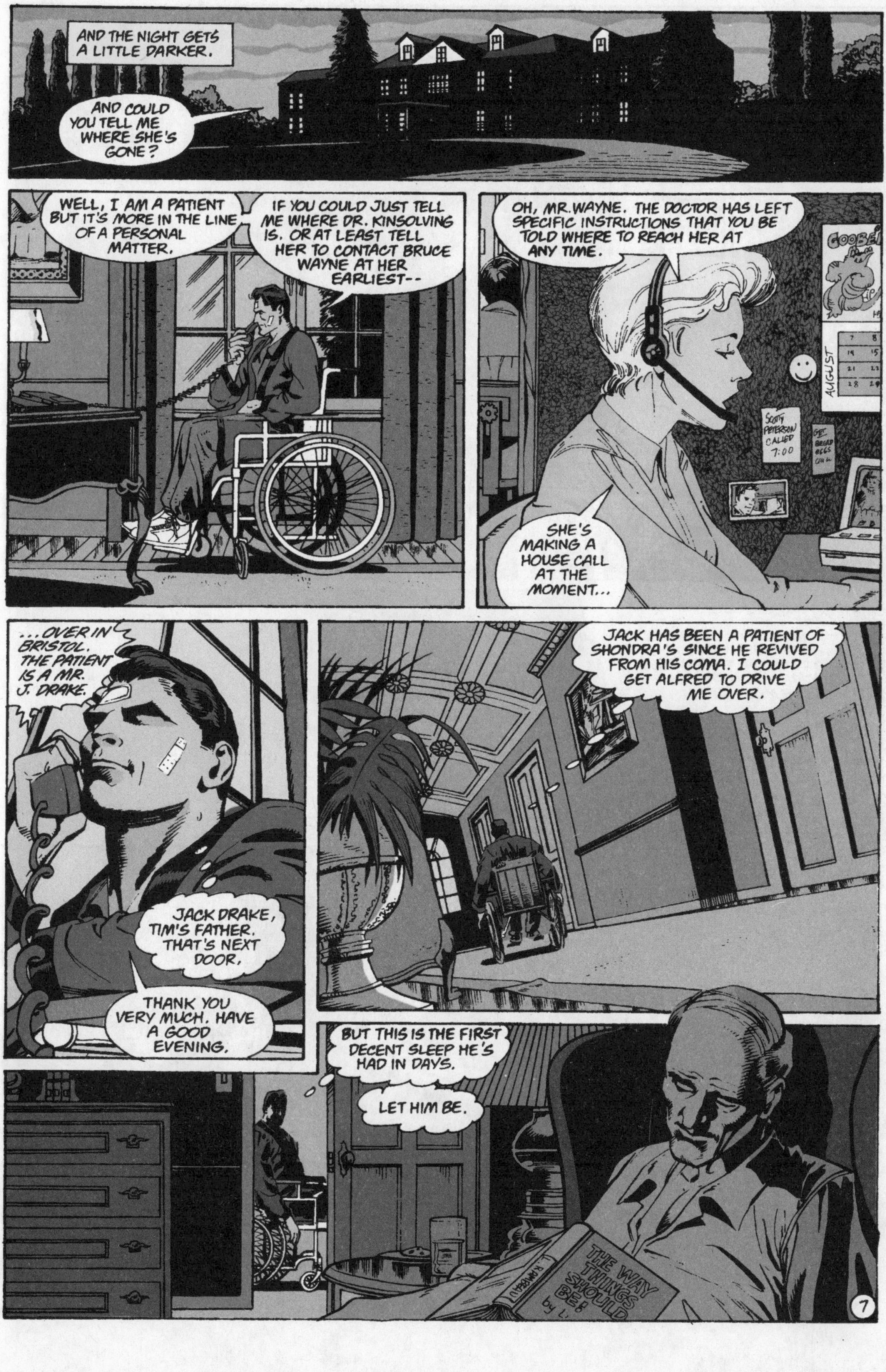
AND THE NIGHT GETS A LITTLE DARKER.
AND COULD YOU TELL ME WHERE SHE'S GONE?
WELL, I AM A PATIENT BUT IT'S MORE IN THE LINE OF A PERSONAL MATTER.
IF YOU COULD JUST TELL ME WHERE DR. KINSOLVING IS. OR AT LEAST TELL HER TO CONTACT BRUCE WAYNE AT HER EARLIEST--
OH, MR. WAYNE. THE DOCTOR HAS LEFT SPECIFIC INSTRUCTIONS THAT YOU BE TOLD WHERE TO REACH HER AT ANY TIME.
AUGUST
SCOTTY PETERSON CALLED 7:00
SHE'S MAKING A HOUSE CALL AT THE MOMENT...
...OVER IN BRISTOL. THE PATIENT IS A MR. J. DRAKE.
JACK DRAKE, TIM'S FATHER. THAT'S NEXT DOOR.
THANK YOU VERY MUCH. HAVE A GOOD EVENING.
JACK HAS BEEN A PATIENT OF SHONDRA'S SINCE HE REVIVED FROM HIS COMA. I COULD GET ALFRED TO DRIVE ME OVER.
BUT THIS IS THE FIRST DECENT SLEEP HE'S HAD IN DAYS.
LET HIM BE.
THE WAY THINGS SHOULD BE!
7

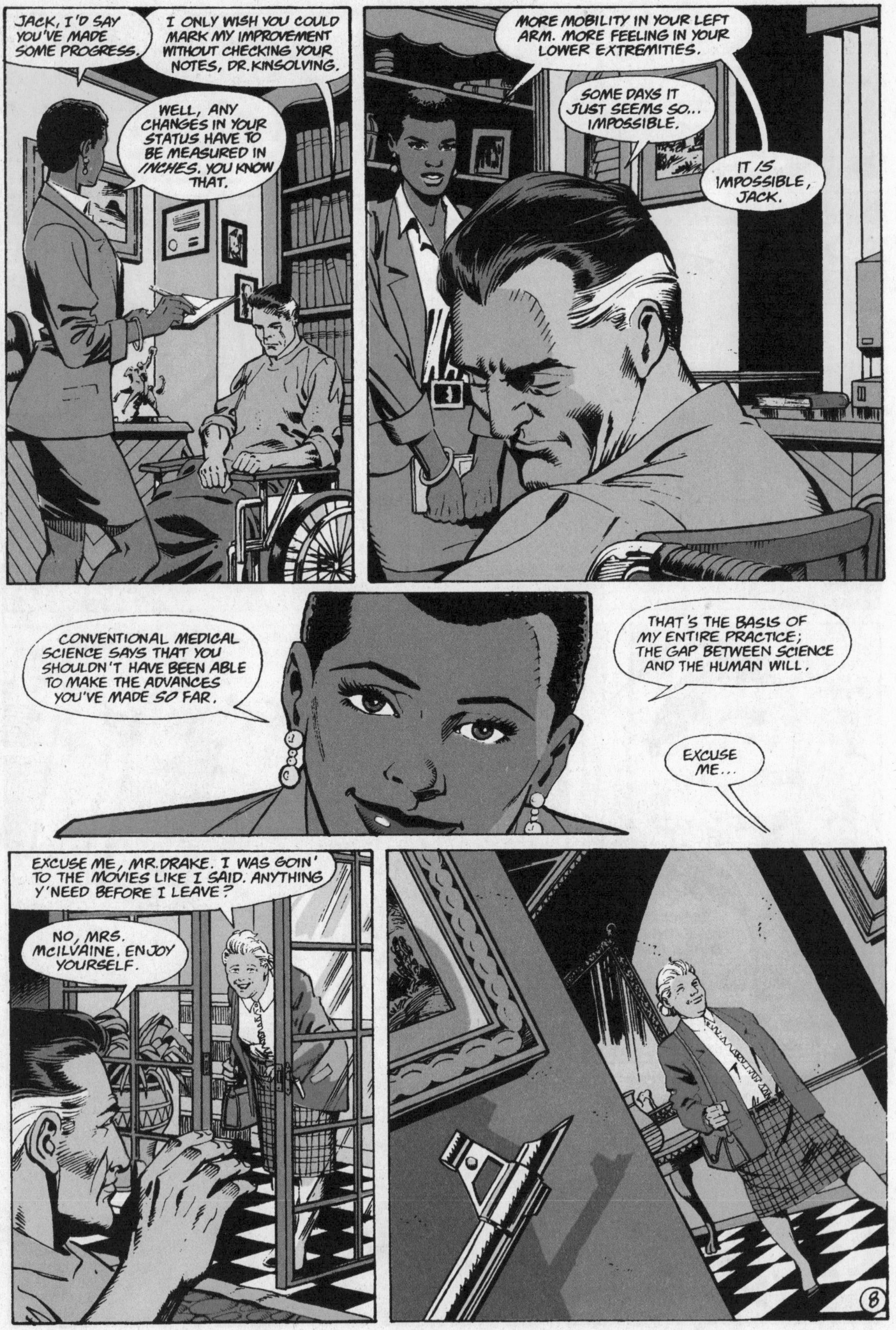
JACK, I'D SAY YOU'VE MADE SOME PROGRESS.
I ONLY WISH YOU COULD MARK MY IMPROVEMENT WITHOUT CHECKING YOUR NOTES, DR. KINSOLVING.
WELL, ANY CHANGES IN YOUR STATUS HAVE TO BE MEASURED IN INCHES. YOU KNOW THAT.
MORE MOBILITY IN YOUR LEFT ARM. MORE FEELING IN YOUR LOWER EXTREMITIES.
SOME DAYS IT JUST SEEMS SO... IMPOSSIBLE.
IT IS IMPOSSIBLE, JACK.
CONVENTIONAL MEDICAL SCIENCE SAYS THAT YOU SHOULDN'T HAVE BEEN ABLE TO MAKE THE ADVANCES YOU'VE MADE SO FAR.
THAT'S THE BASIS OF MY ENTIRE PRACTICE; THE GAP BETWEEN SCIENCE AND THE HUMAN WILL.
EXCUSE ME...
EXCUSE ME, MR. DRAKE. I WAS GOIN' TO THE MOVIES LIKE I SAID. ANYTHING Y'NEED BEFORE I LEAVE?
NO, MRS. McILVAINE. ENJOY YOURSELF.
8

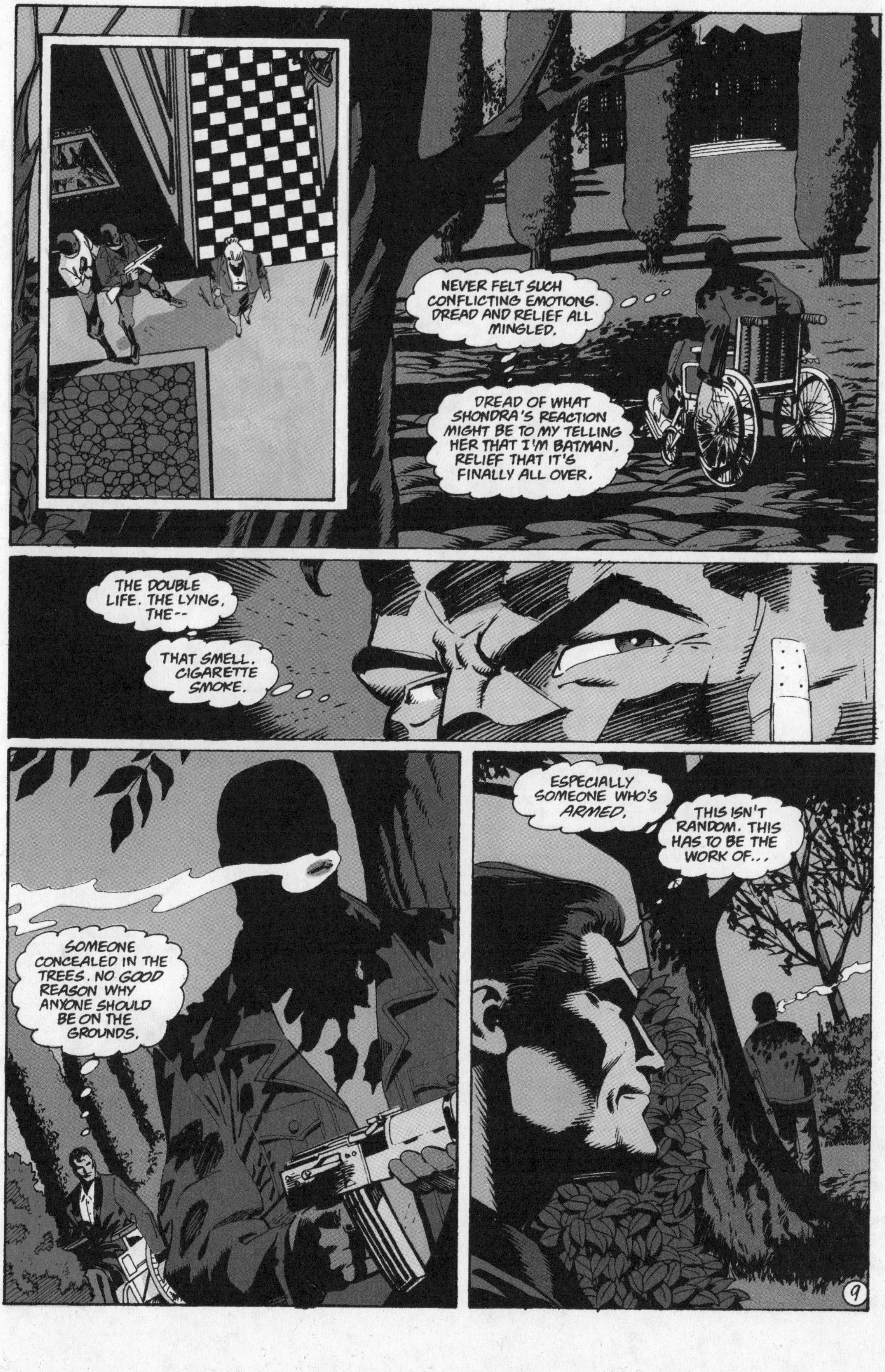
NEVER FELT SUCH CONFLICTING EMOTIONS. DREAD AND RELIEF ALL MINGLED.
DREAD OF WHAT SHONDRA'S REACTION MIGHT BE TO MY TELLING HER THAT I'M BATMAN. RELIEF THAT IT'S FINALLY ALL OVER.
THE DOUBLE LIFE. THE LYING, THE--
THAT SMELL. CIGARETTE SMOKE.
SOMEONE CONCEALED IN THE TREES. NO GOOD REASON WHY ANYONE SHOULD BE ON THE GROUNDS.
ESPECIALLY SOMEONE WHO'S ARMED.
THIS ISN'T RANDOM. THIS HAS TO BE THE WORK OF...
9

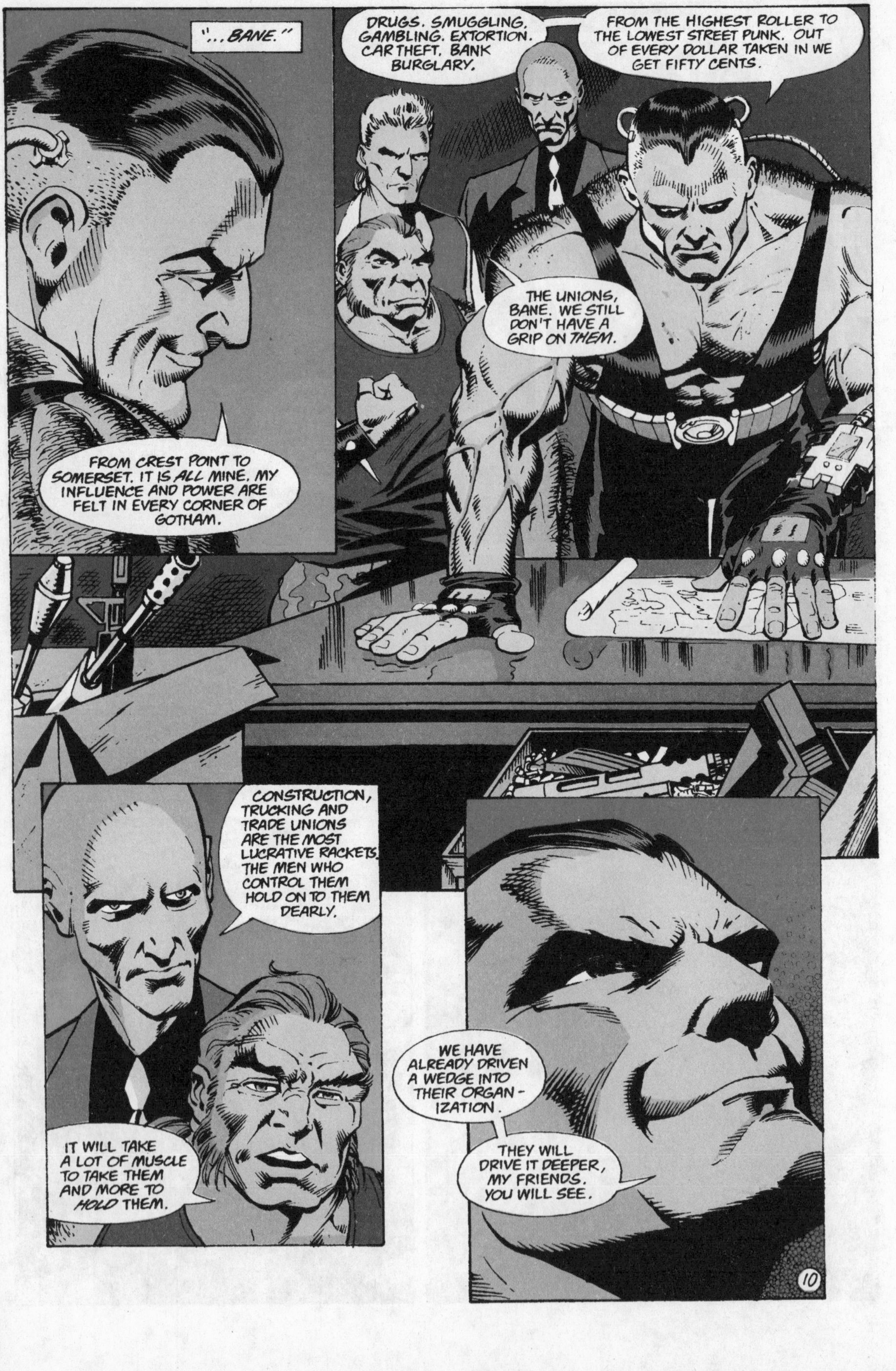
"...BANE."
DRUGS. SMUGGLING. GAMBLING. EXTORTION. CAR THEFT. BANK BURGLARY.
FROM THE HIGHEST ROLLER TO THE LOWEST STREET PUNK. OUT OF EVERY DOLLAR TAKEN IN WE GET FIFTY CENTS.
FROM CREST POINT TO SOMERSET. IT IS ALL MINE. MY INFLUENCE AND POWER ARE FELT IN EVERY CORNER OF GOTHAM.
THE UNIONS, BANE. WE STILL DON'T HAVE A GRIP ON THEM.
CONSTRUCTION, TRUCKING AND TRADE UNIONS ARE THE MOST LUCRATIVE RACKETS. THE MEN WHO CONTROL THEM HOLD ON TO THEM DEARLY.
IT WILL TAKE A LOT OF MUSCLE TO TAKE THEM AND MORE TO HOLD THEM.
WE HAVE ALREADY DRIVEN A WEDGE INTO THEIR ORGAN-IZATION.
THEY WILL DRIVE IT DEEPER, MY FRIENDS. YOU WILL SEE.
10

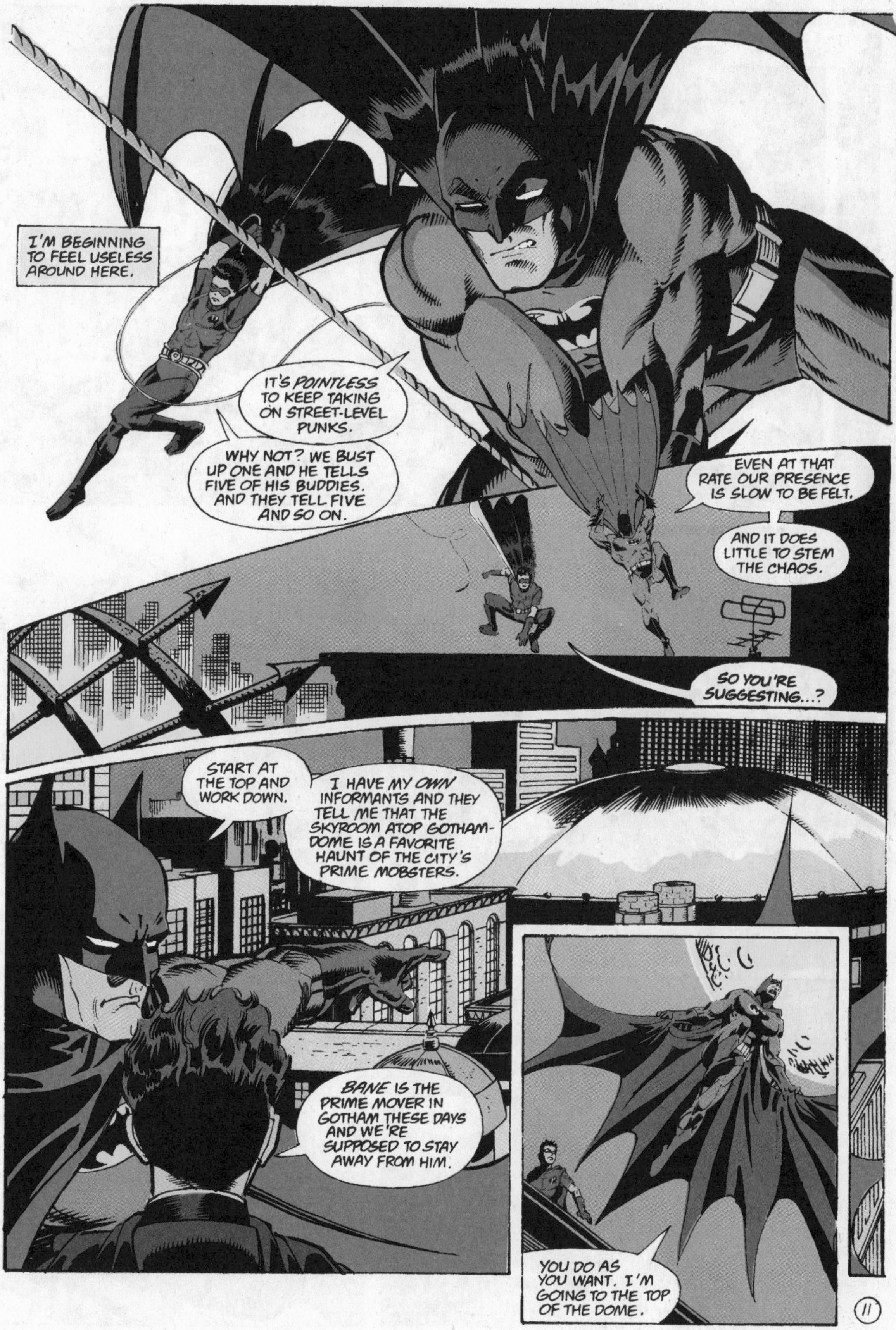
I'M BEGINNING TO FEEL USELESS AROUND HERE.
IT'S POINTLESS TO KEEP TAKING ON STREET-LEVEL PUNKS.
WHY NOT? WE BUST UP ONE AND HE TELLS FIVE OF HIS BUDDIES. AND THEY TELL FIVE AND SO ON.
EVEN AT THAT RATE OUR PRESENCE IS SLOW TO BE FELT.
AND IT DOES LITTLE TO STEM THE CHAOS.
SO YOU'RE SUGGESTING...?
START AT THE TOP AND WORK DOWN.
I HAVE MY OWN INFORMANTS AND THEY TELL ME THAT THE SKYROOM ATOP GOTHAM-DOME IS A FAVORITE HAUNT OF THE CITY'S PRIME MOBSTERS.
BANE IS THE PRIME MOVER IN GOTHAM THESE DAYS AND WE'RE SUPPOSED TO STAY AWAY FROM HIM.
YOU DO AS YOU WANT. I'M GOING TO THE TOP OF THE DOME.
11

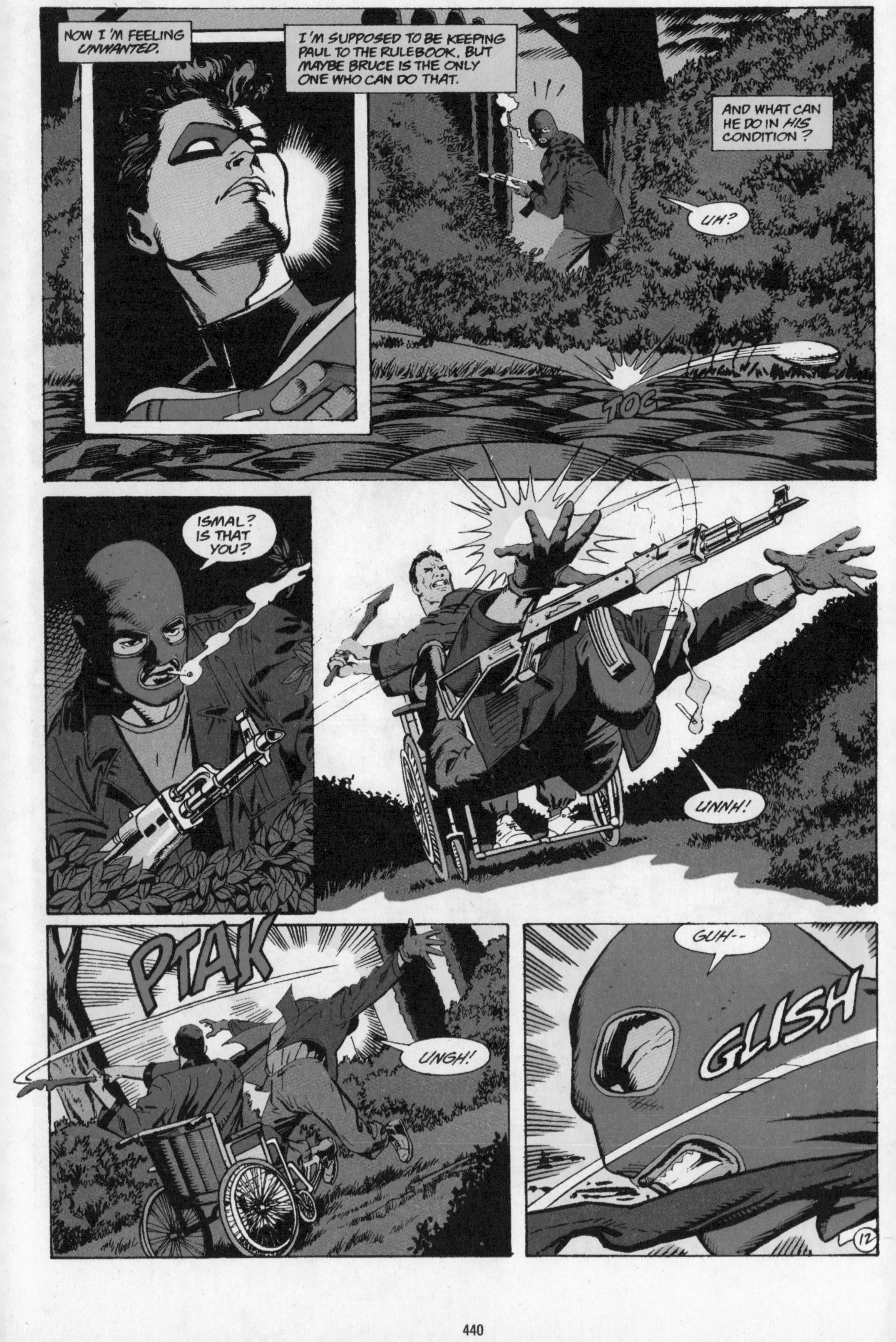
NOW I'M FEELING UNWANTED.
I'M SUPPOSED TO BE KEEPING PAUL TO THE RULEBOOK. BUT MAYBE BRUCE IS THE ONLY ONE WHO CAN DO THAT.
AND WHAT CAN HE DO IN HIS CONDITION?
UH?
TOC
ISMAL? IS THAT YOU?
UNNH!
PTAK
UNGH!
GUH--
GLISH
12

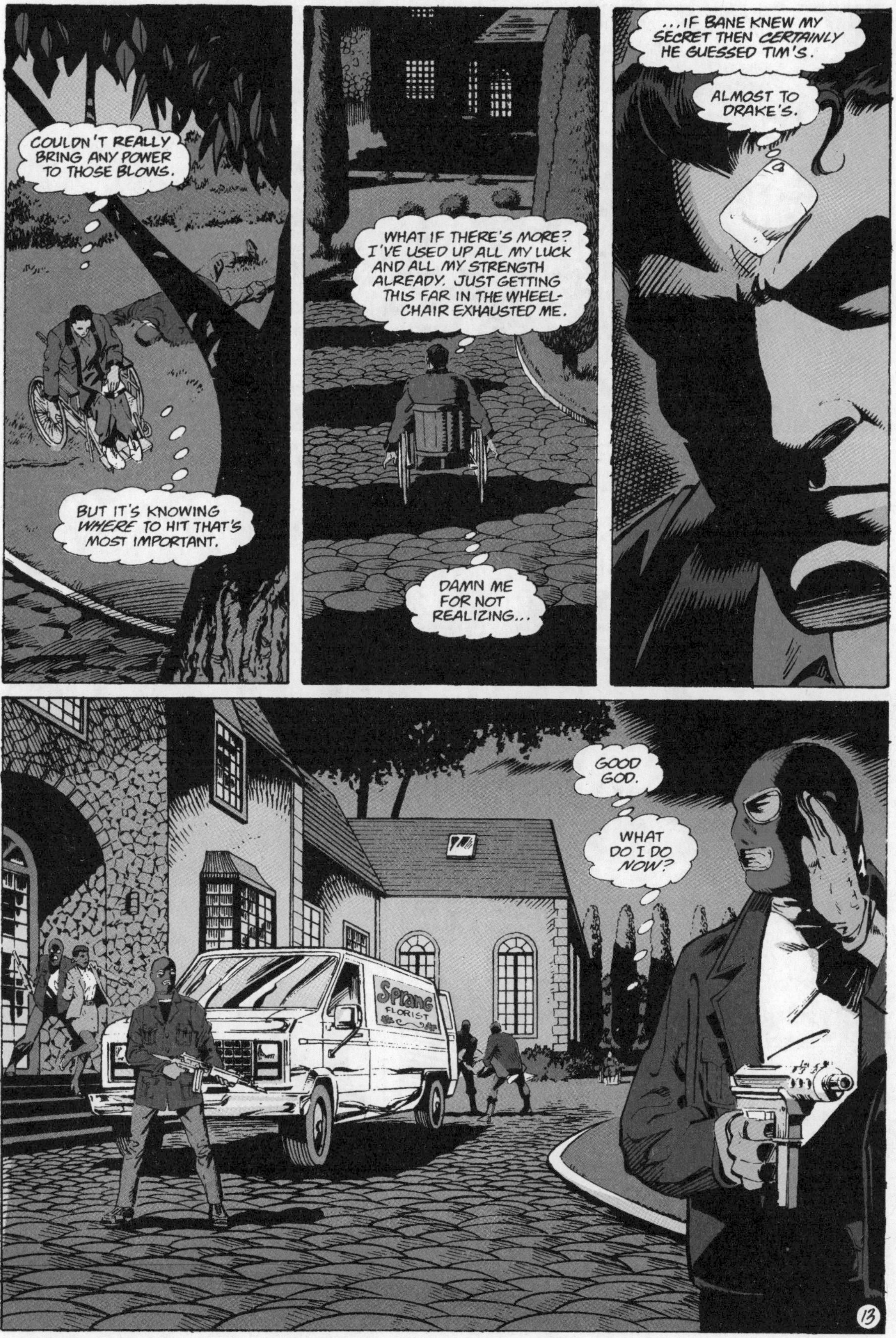
COULDN'T REALLY BRING ANY POWER TO THOSE BLOWS.
BUT IT'S KNOWING WHERE TO HIT THAT'S MOST IMPORTANT.
WHAT IF THERE'S MORE? I'VE USED UP ALL MY LUCK AND ALL MY STRENGTH ALREADY. JUST GETTING THIS FAR IN THE WHEEL-CHAIR EXHAUSTED ME.
DAMN ME FOR NOT REALIZING...
...IF BANE KNEW MY SECRET THEN CERTAINLY HE GUESSED TIM'S.
ALMOST TO DRAKE'S.
GOOD GOD.
WHAT DO I DO NOW?
SPRANG FLORIST
13

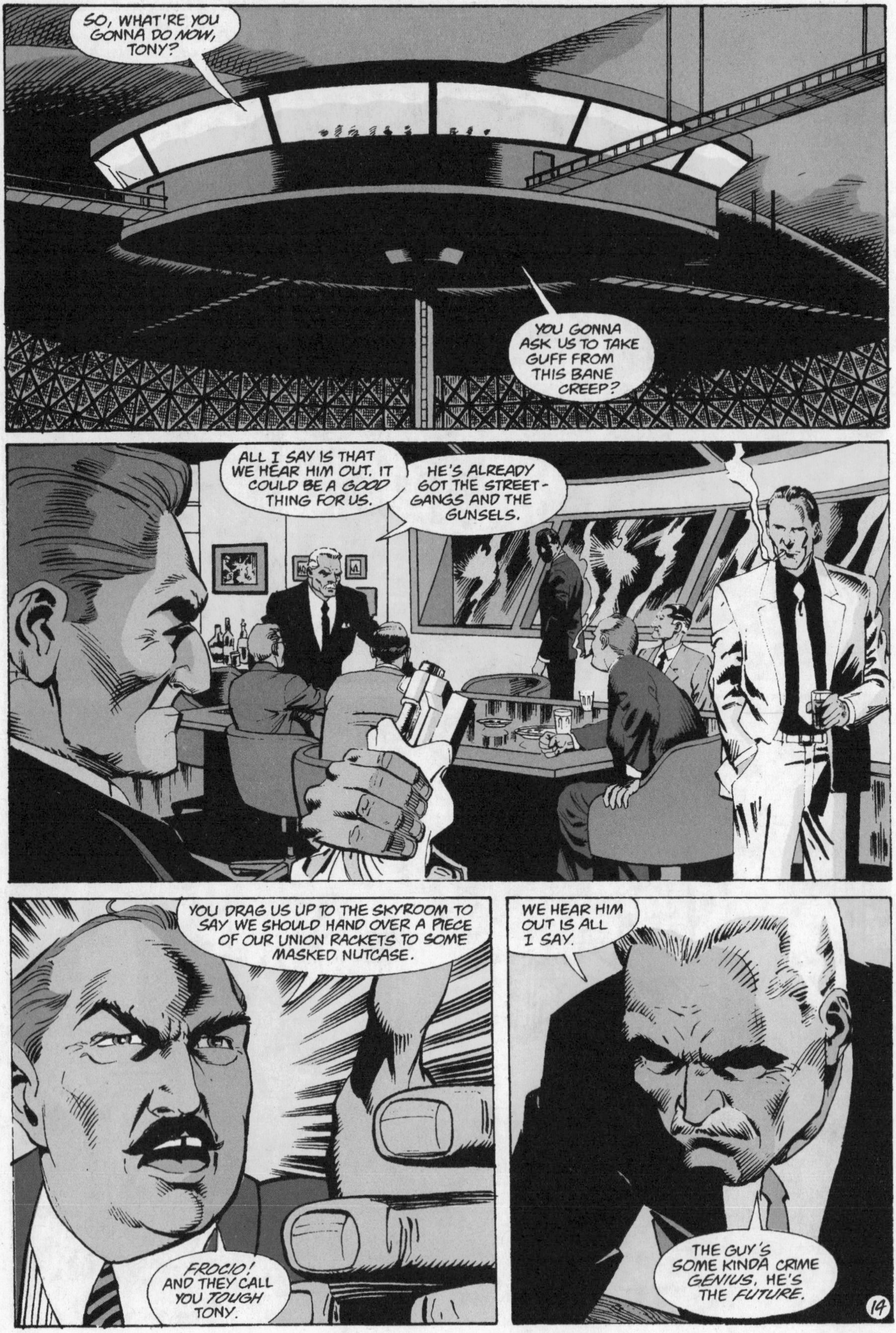
SO, WHAT'RE YOU GONNA DO NOW, TONY?
YOU GONNA ASK US TO TAKE GUFF FROM THIS BANE CREEP?
ALL I SAY IS THAT WE HEAR HIM OUT. IT COULD BE A GOOD THING FOR US.
HE'S ALREADY GOT THE STREET-GANGS AND THE GUNSELS.
YOU DRAG US UP TO THE SKYROOM TO SAY WE SHOULD HAND OVER A PIECE OF OUR UNION RACKETS TO SOME MASKED NUTCASE.
FROCIO! AND THEY CALL YOU TOUGH TONY.
WE HEAR HIM OUT IS ALL I SAY.
THE GUY'S SOME KINDA CRIME GENIUS, HE'S THE FUTURE.
14

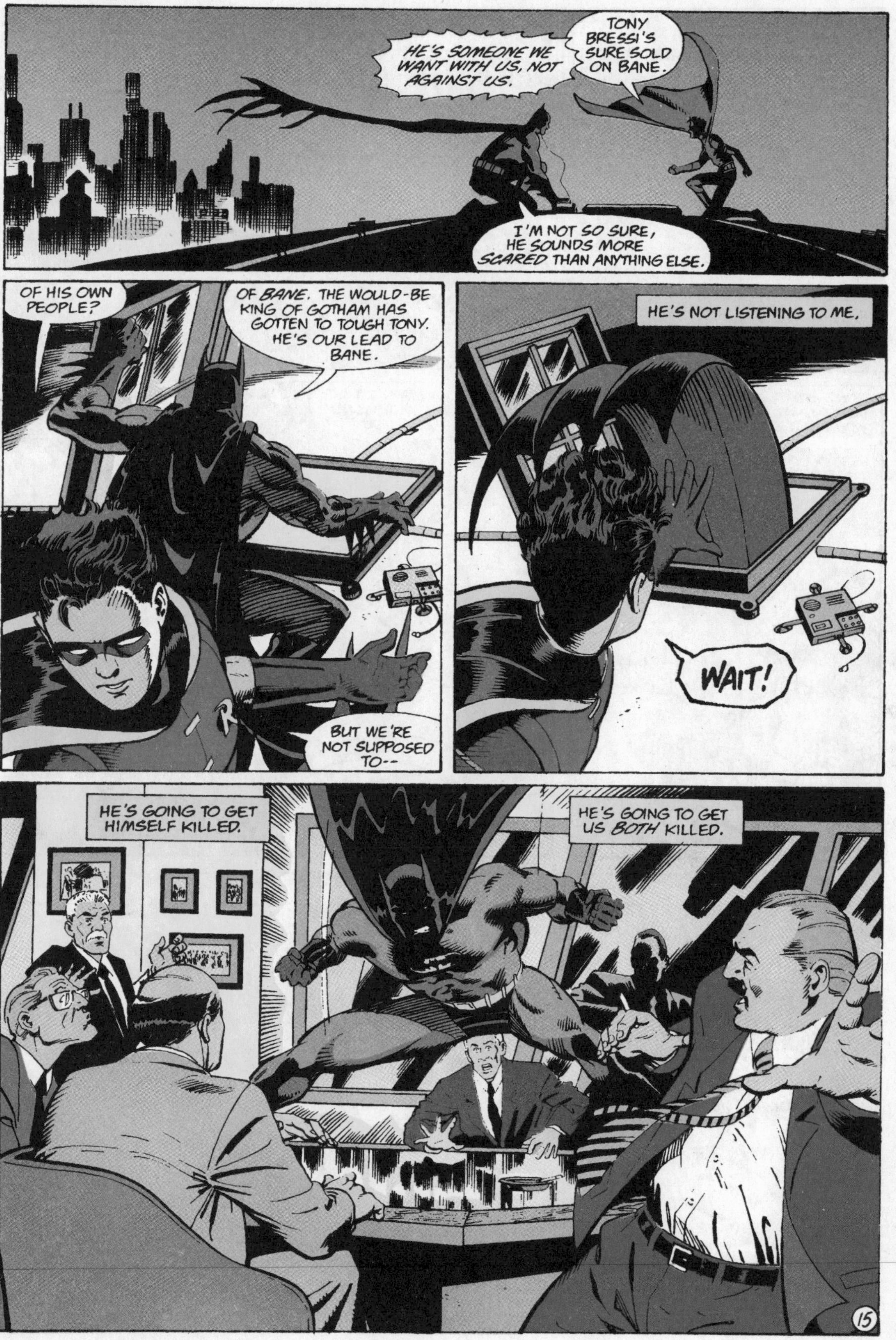
TONY BRESSI'S SURE SOLD ON BANE.
HE'S SOMEONE WE WANT WITH US, NOT AGAINST US.
I'M NOT SO SURE, HE SOUNDS MORE SCARED THAN ANYTHING ELSE.
OF HIS OWN PEOPLE?
OF BANE. THE WOULD-BE KING OF GOTHAM HAS GOTTEN TO TOUGH TONY. HE'S OUR LEAD TO BANE.
BUT WE'RE NOT SUPPOSED TO--
HE'S NOT LISTENING TO ME.
WAIT!
HE'S GOING TO GET HIMSELF KILLED.
HE'S GOING TO GET US BOTH KILLED.
15

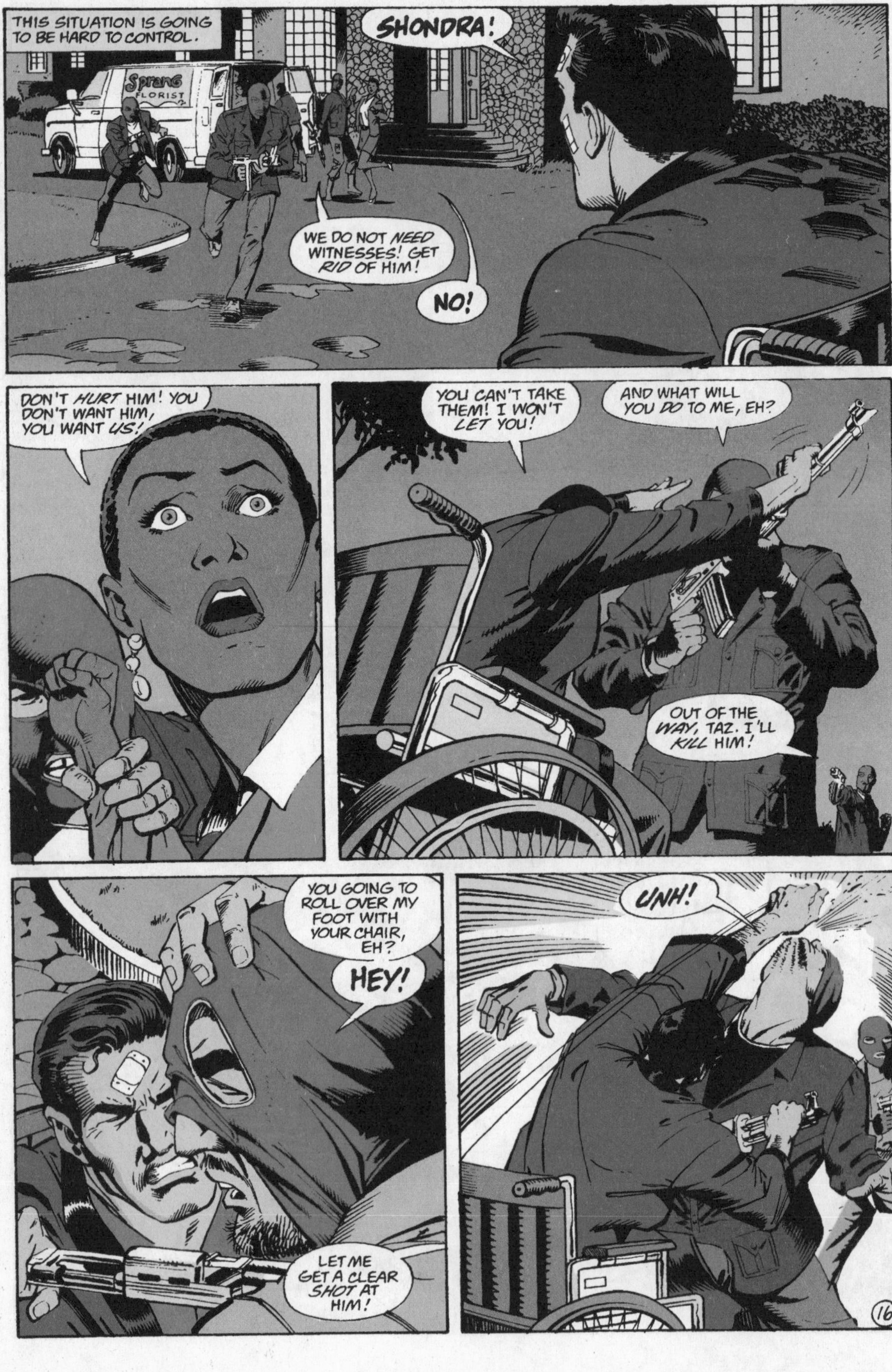
THIS SITUATION IS GOING TO BE HARD TO CONTROL.
SHONDRA!
Sprang FLORIST
WE DO NOT NEED WITNESSES! GET RID OF HIM!
NO!
DON'T HURT HIM! YOU DON'T WANT HIM, YOU WANT US!
YOU CAN'T TAKE THEM! I WON'T LET YOU!
AND WHAT WILL YOU DO TO ME, EH?
OUT OF THE WAY, TAZ. I'LL KILL HIM!
YOU GOING TO ROLL OVER MY FOOT WITH YOUR CHAIR, EH?
HEY!
LET ME GET A CLEAR SHOT AT HIM!
UNH!
16

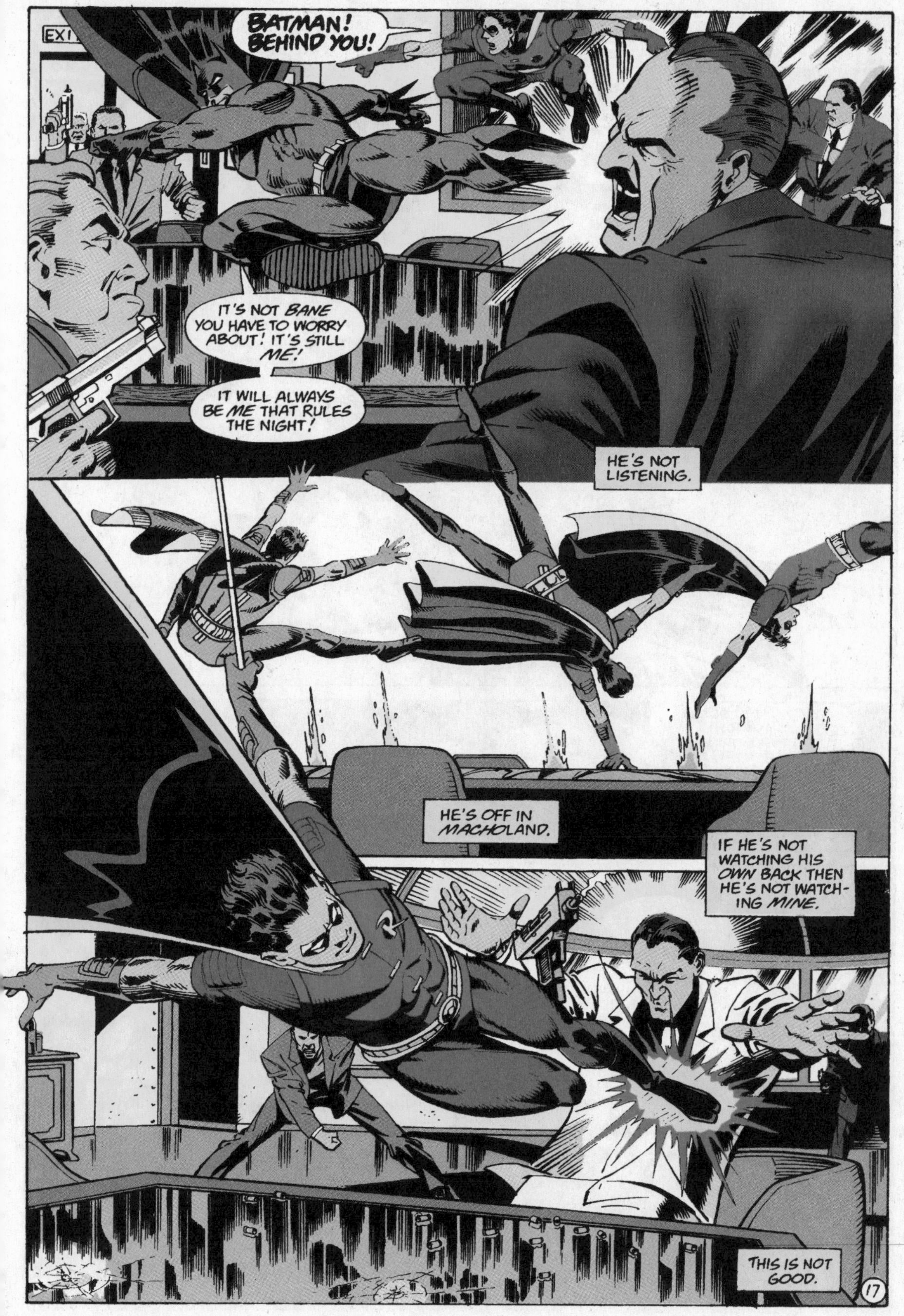
EXIT
BATMAN! BEHIND YOU!
IT'S NOT BANE YOU HAVE TO WORRY ABOUT! IT'S STILL ME!
IT WILL ALWAYS BE ME THAT RULES THE NIGHT!
HE'S NOT LISTENING.
HE'S OFF IN MACHOLAND.
IF HE'S NOT WATCHING HIS OWN BACK THEN HE'S NOT WATCHING MINE.
THIS IS NOT GOOD.
17

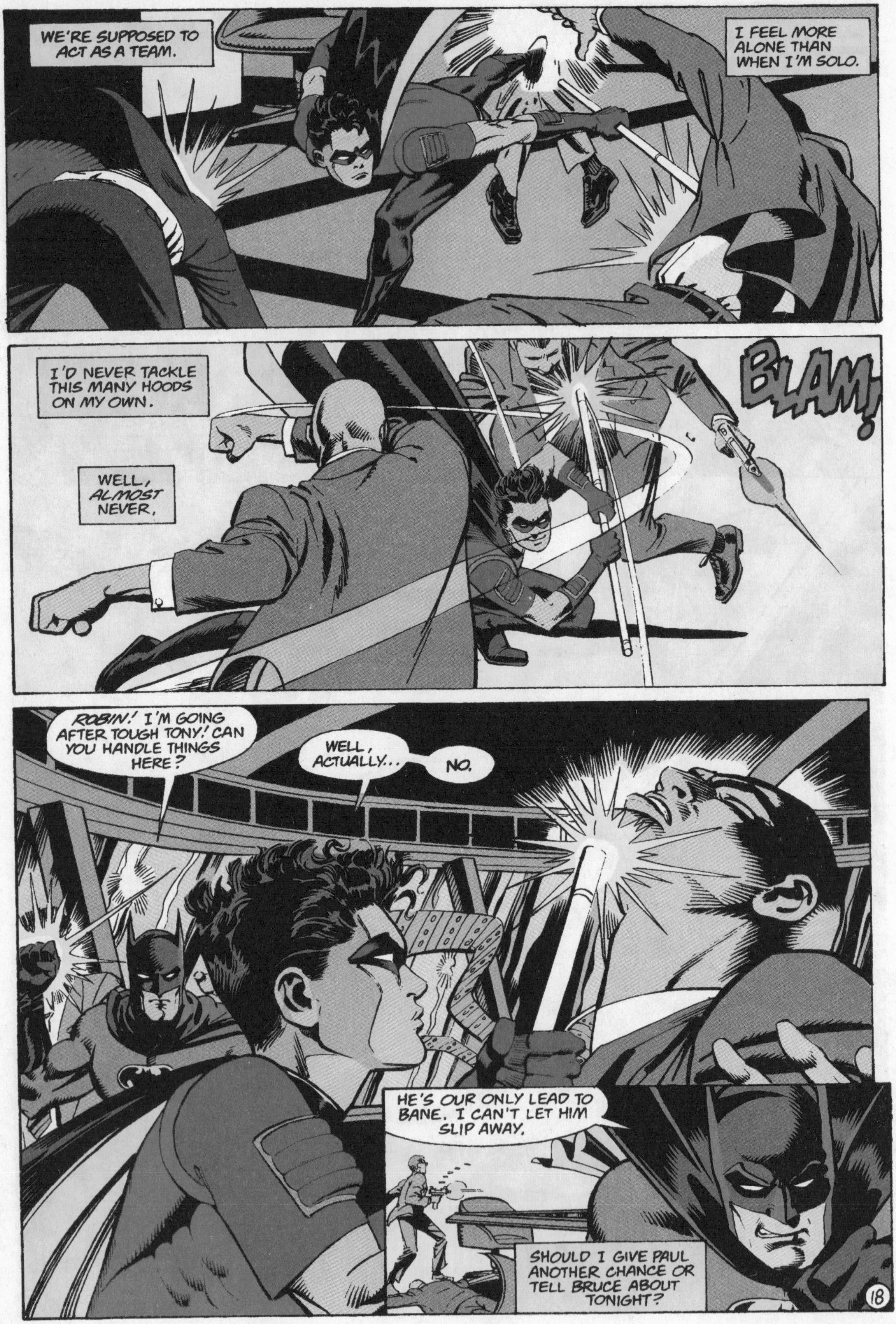
WE'RE SUPPOSED TO ACT AS A TEAM.
I FEEL MORE ALONE THAN WHEN I'M SOLO.
I'D NEVER TACKLE THIS MANY HOODS ON MY OWN.
WELL, *ALMOST* NEVER.
BLAM!
ROBIN! I'M GOING AFTER TOUGH TONY! CAN YOU HANDLE THINGS HERE?
WELL, ACTUALLY...
NO.
HE'S OUR ONLY LEAD TO BANE. I CAN'T LET HIM SLIP AWAY.
SHOULD I GIVE PAUL ANOTHER CHANCE OR TELL BRUCE ABOUT TONIGHT?
18

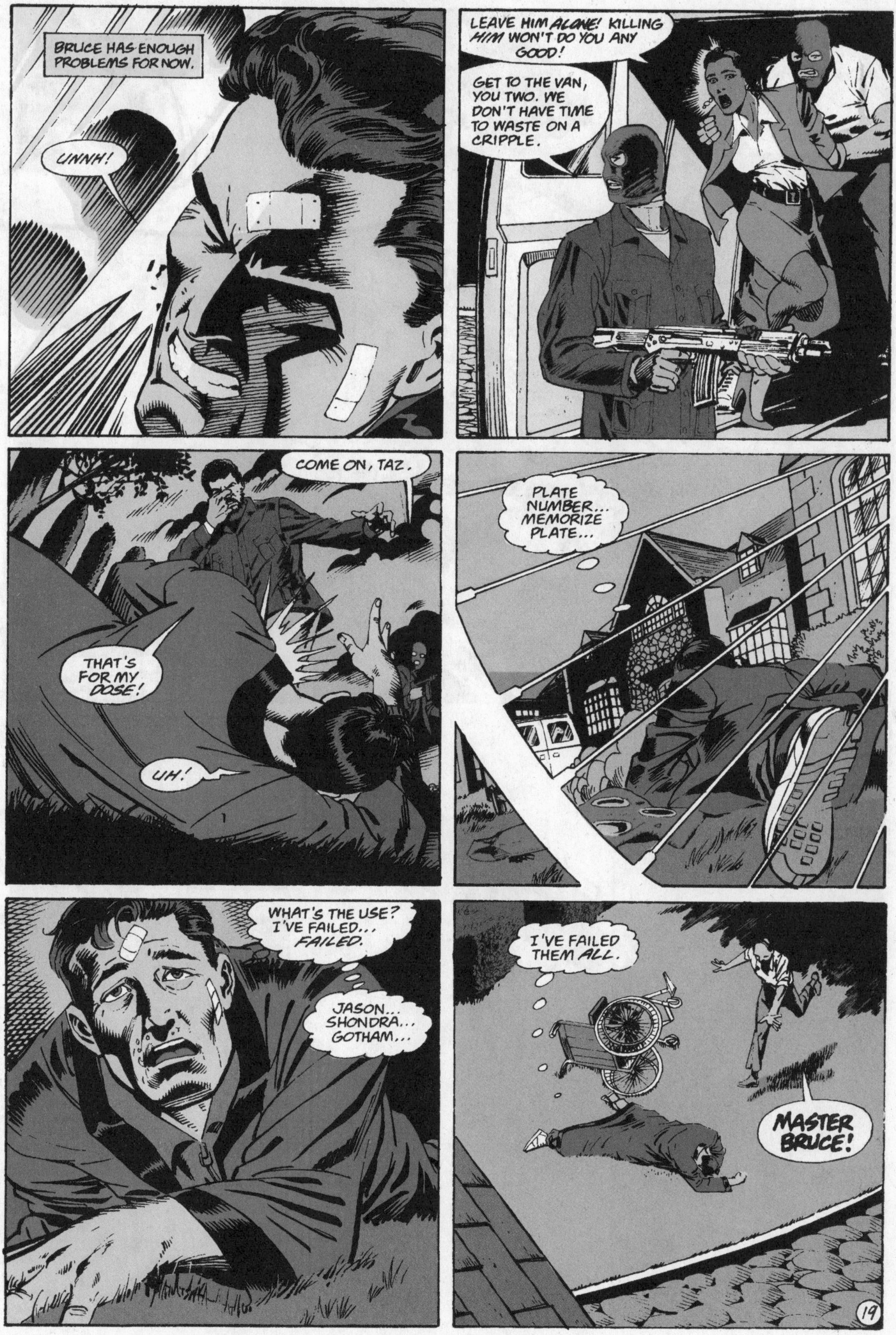

BRUCE HAS ENOUGH PROBLEMS FOR NOW.
UNNH!
LEAVE HIM ALONE! KILLING HIM WON'T DO YOU ANY GOOD!
GET TO THE VAN, YOU TWO. WE DON'T HAVE TIME TO WASTE ON A CRIPPLE.
COME ON, TAZ.
THAT'S FOR MY DOSE!
UH!
PLATE NUMBER... MEMORIZE PLATE...
WHAT'S THE USE? I'VE FAILED... FAILED.
JASON... SHONDRA... GOTHAM...
I'VE FAILED THEM ALL.
MASTER BRUCE!
19

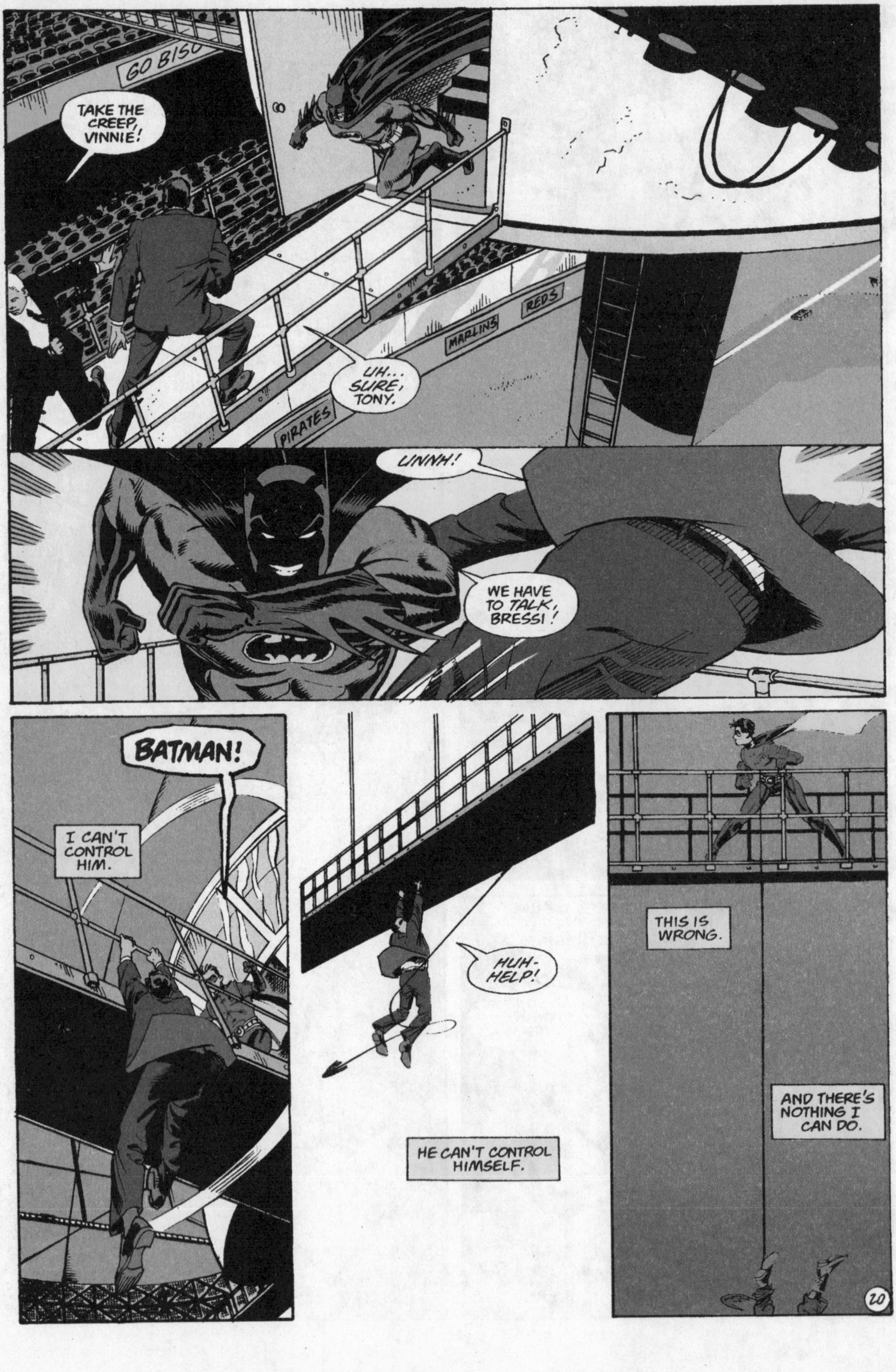
GO BISO
TAKE THE CREEP, VINNIE!
UH... SURE, TONY.
MARLINS
REDS
PIRATES
UNNH!
WE HAVE TO TALK, BRESSI!
BATMAN!
I CAN'T CONTROL HIM.
HUH-HELP!
HE CAN'T CONTROL HIMSELF.
THIS IS WRONG.
AND THERE'S NOTHING I CAN DO.
20

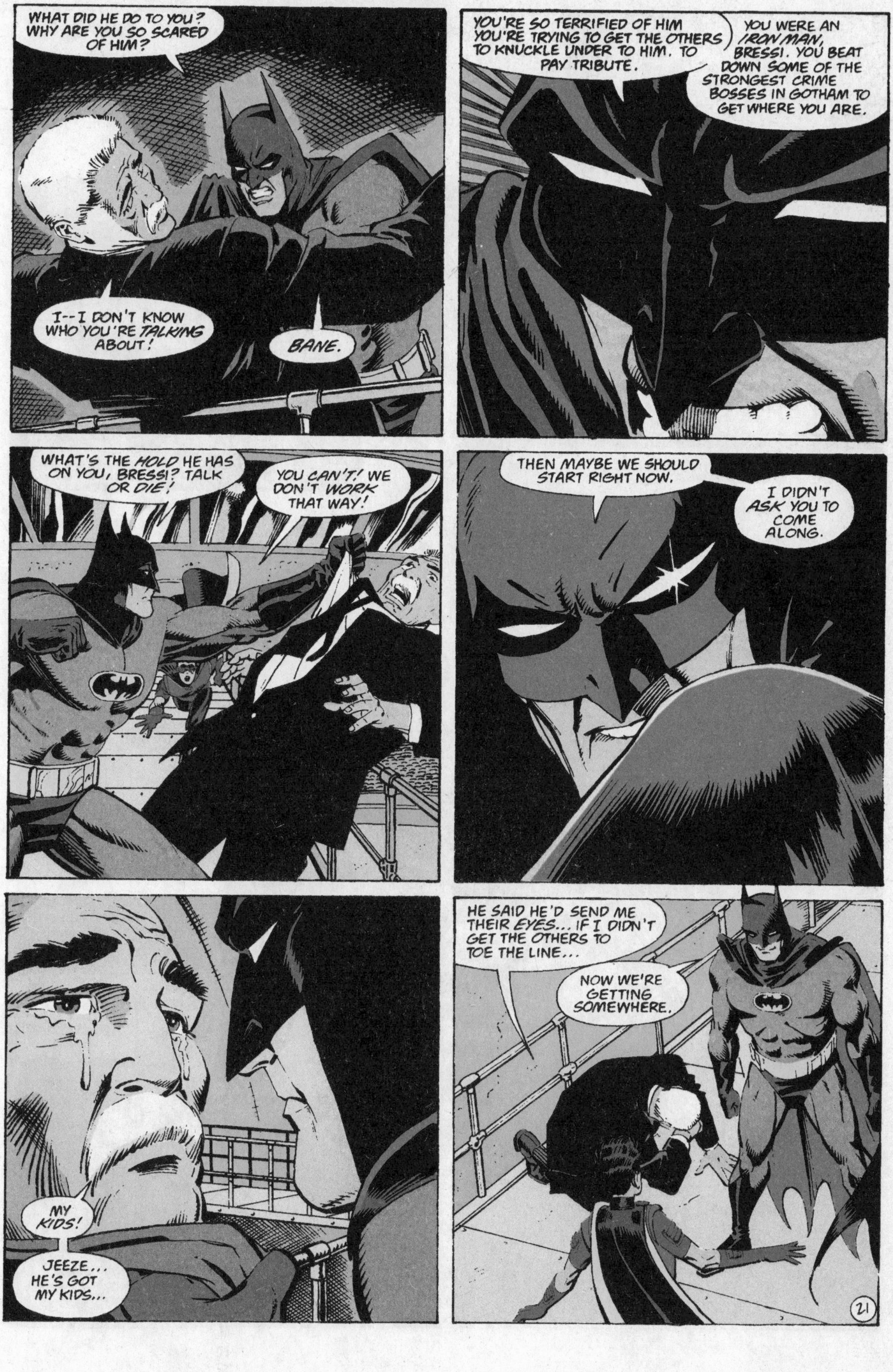
WHAT DID HE DO TO YOU? WHY ARE YOU SO SCARED OF HIM?
I--I DON'T KNOW WHO YOU'RE TALKING ABOUT!
BANE.
YOU'RE SO TERRIFIED OF HIM YOU'RE TRYING TO GET THE OTHERS TO KNUCKLE UNDER TO HIM. TO PAY TRIBUTE.
YOU WERE AN IRON MAN, BRESSI. YOU BEAT DOWN SOME OF THE STRONGEST CRIME BOSSES IN GOTHAM TO GET WHERE YOU ARE.
WHAT'S THE HOLD HE HAS ON YOU, BRESSI? TALK OR DIE!
YOU CAN'T! WE DON'T WORK THAT WAY!
THEN MAYBE WE SHOULD START RIGHT NOW.
I DIDN'T ASK YOU TO COME ALONG.
MY KIDS!
JEEZE... HE'S GOT MY KIDS...
HE SAID HE'D SEND ME THEIR EYES... IF I DIDN'T GET THE OTHERS TO TOE THE LINE...
NOW WE'RE GETTING SOMEWHERE.
21

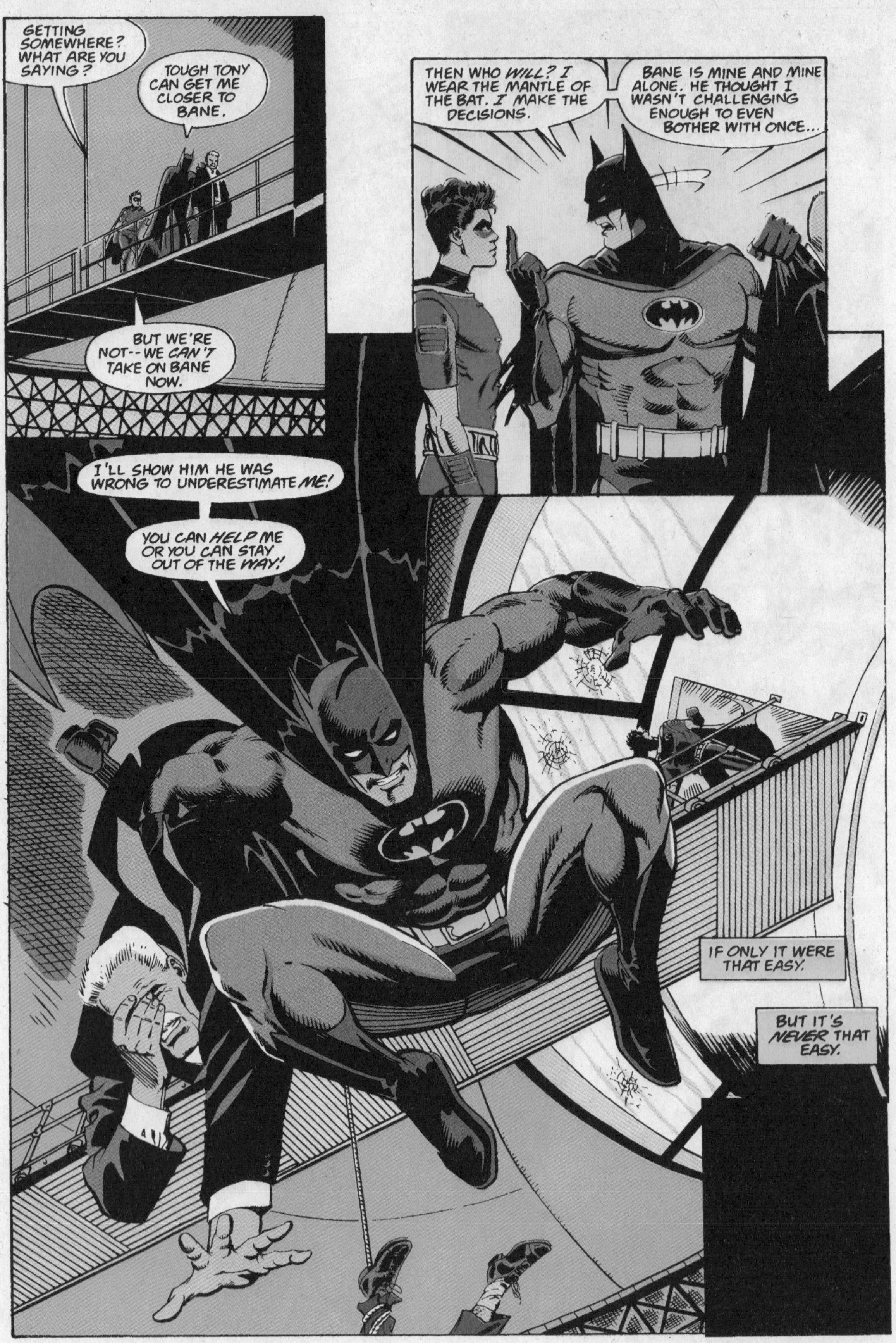
GETTING SOMEWHERE? WHAT ARE YOU SAYING?
TOUGH TONY CAN GET ME CLOSER TO BANE.
BUT WE'RE NOT--WE CAN'T TAKE ON BANE NOW.
THEN WHO WILL? I WEAR THE MANTLE OF THE BAT. I MAKE THE DECISIONS.
BANE IS MINE AND MINE ALONE. HE THOUGHT I WASN'T CHALLENGING ENOUGH TO EVEN BOTHER WITH ONCE...
I'LL SHOW HIM HE WAS WRONG TO UNDERESTIMATE ME!
YOU CAN HELP ME OR YOU CAN STAY OUT OF THE WAY!
IF ONLY IT WERE THAT EASY.
BUT IT'S NEVER THAT EASY.

Cover art by BRIAN STELFREEZE

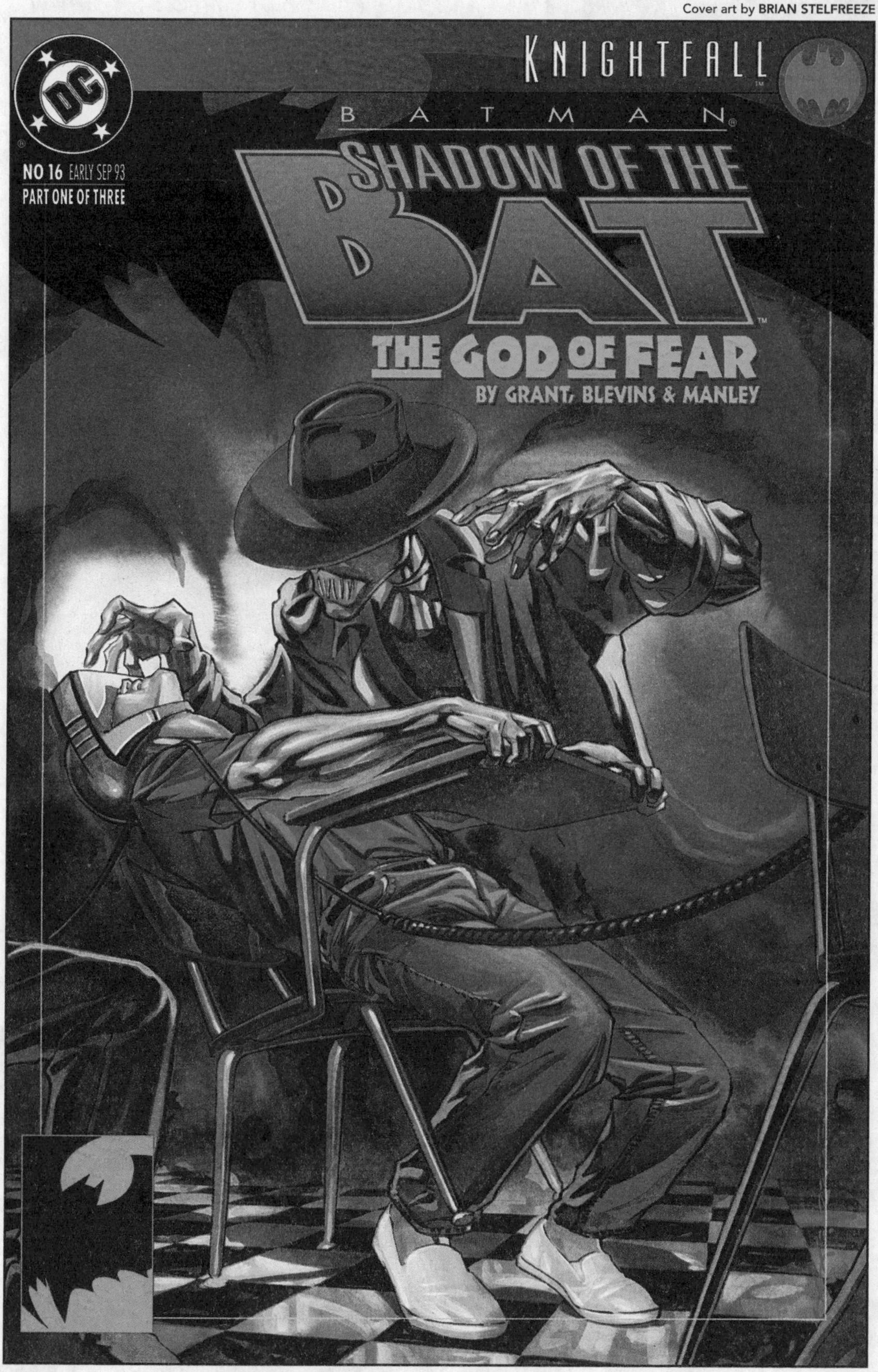
KNIGHTFALL
DC
NO 16 EARLY SEP 93
PART ONE OF THREE
BATMAN
SHADOW OF THE BAT
THE GOD OF FEAR
BY GRANT, BLEVINS & MANLEY

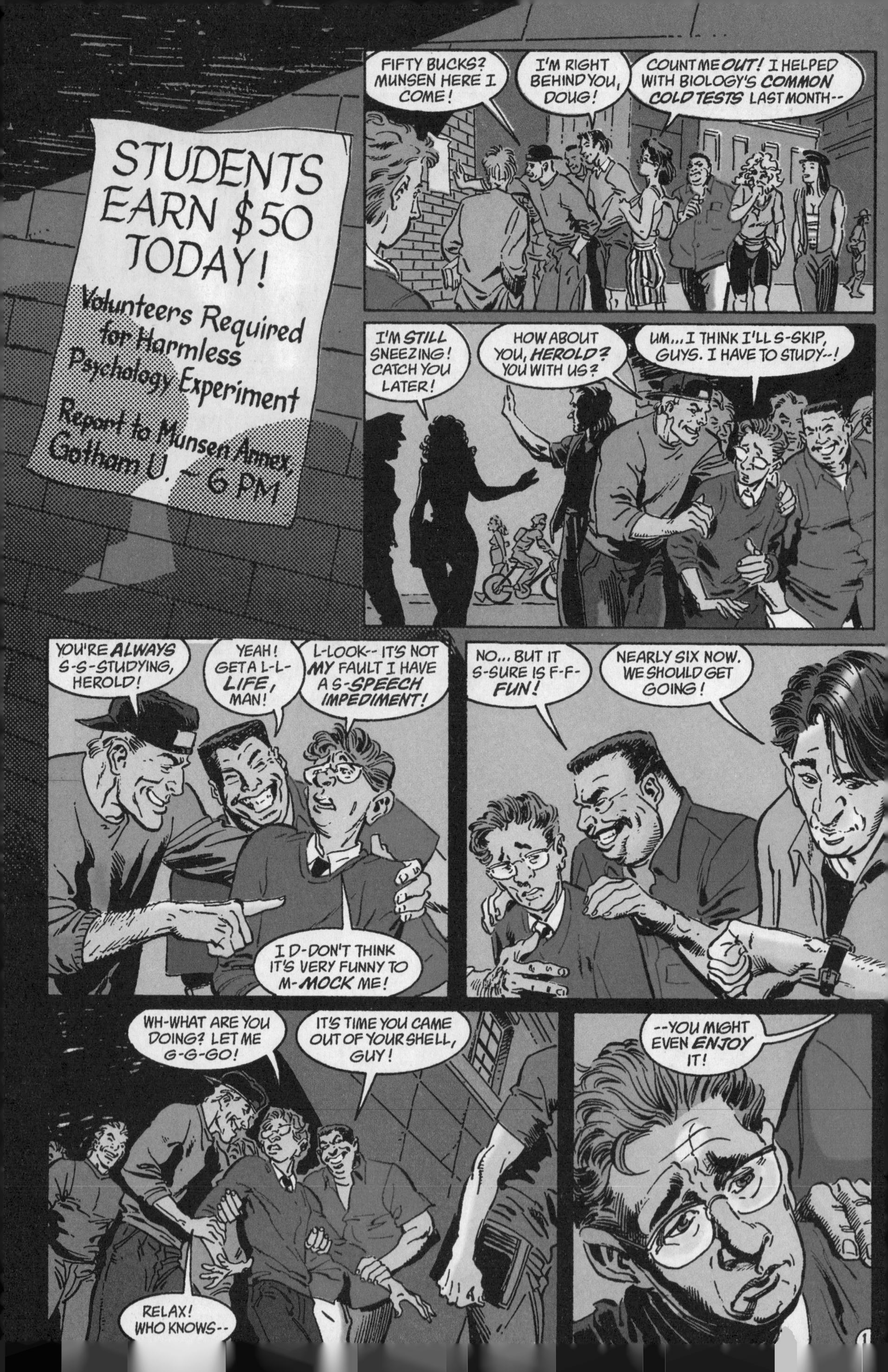
STUDENTS EARN $50 TODAY!
Volunteers Required for Harmless Psychology Experiment
Report to Munsen Annex, Gotham U. ~ 6 PM
FIFTY BUCKS? MUNSEN HERE I COME!
I'M RIGHT BEHIND YOU, DOUG!
COUNT ME OUT! I HELPED WITH BIOLOGY'S COMMON COLD TESTS LAST MONTH--
I'M STILL SNEEZING! CATCH YOU LATER!
HOW ABOUT YOU, HEROLD? YOU WITH US?
UM... I THINK I'LL S-SKIP, GUYS. I HAVE TO STUDY--!
YOU'RE ALWAYS S-S-STUDYING, HEROLD!
YEAH! GET A L-L-LIFE, MAN!
L-LOOK-- IT'S NOT MY FAULT I HAVE A S-SPEECH IMPEDIMENT!
I D-DON'T THINK IT'S VERY FUNNY TO M-MOCK ME!
NO... BUT IT S-SURE IS F-F-FUN!
NEARLY SIX NOW. WE SHOULD GET GOING!
WH-WHAT ARE YOU DOING? LET ME G-G-GO!
IT'S TIME YOU CAME OUT OF YOUR SHELL, GUY!
RELAX! WHO KNOWS--
--YOU MIGHT EVEN ENJOY IT!

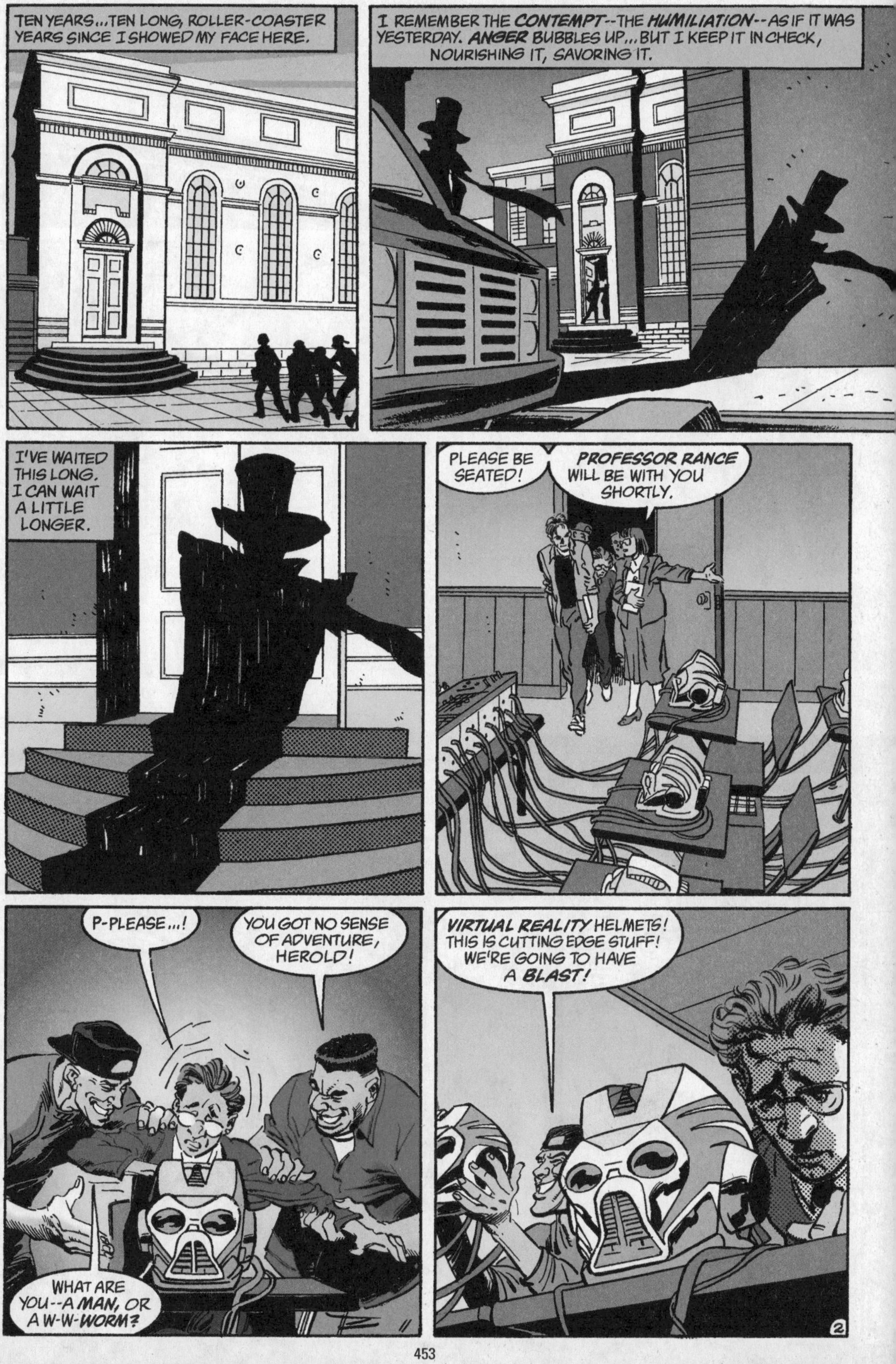
TEN YEARS...TEN LONG, ROLLER-COASTER YEARS SINCE I SHOWED MY FACE HERE.
I REMEMBER THE CONTEMPT--THE HUMILIATION--AS IF IT WAS YESTERDAY. ANGER BUBBLES UP... BUT I KEEP IT IN CHECK, NOURISHING IT, SAVORING IT.
I'VE WAITED THIS LONG. I CAN WAIT A LITTLE LONGER.
PLEASE BE SEATED!
PROFESSOR RANCE WILL BE WITH YOU SHORTLY.
P-PLEASE...!
YOU GOT NO SENSE OF ADVENTURE, HEROLD!
WHAT ARE YOU--A MAN, OR A W-W-WORM?
VIRTUAL REALITY HELMETS! THIS IS CUTTING EDGE STUFF! WE'RE GOING TO HAVE A BLAST!
2

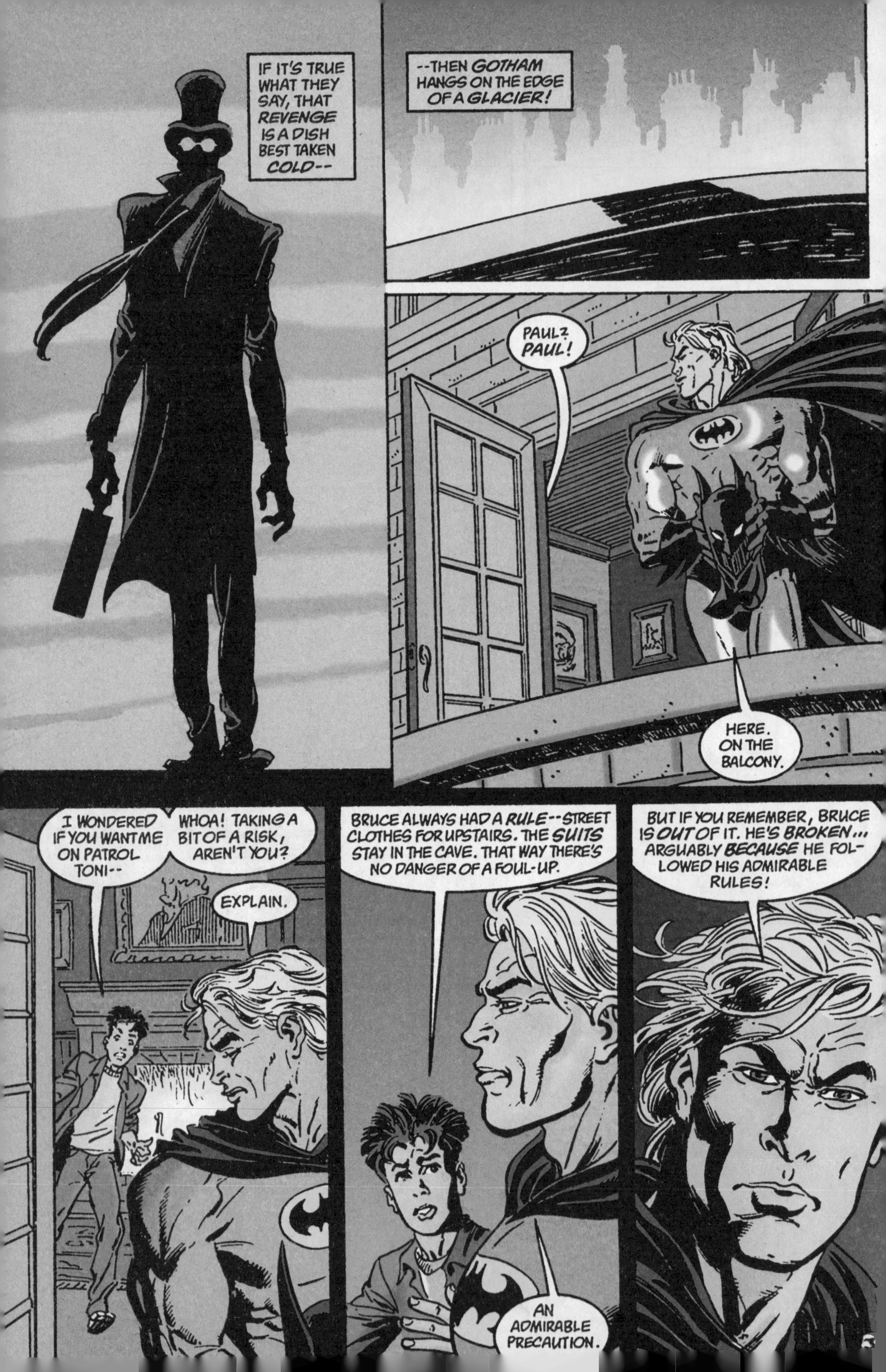
IF IT'S TRUE WHAT THEY SAY, THAT REVENGE IS A DISH BEST TAKEN COLD--
--THEN GOTHAM HANGS ON THE EDGE OF A GLACIER!
PAUL? PAUL!
HERE. ON THE BALCONY.
I WONDERED IF YOU WANT ME ON PATROL TONI--
WHOA! TAKING A BIT OF A RISK, AREN'T YOU?
EXPLAIN.
BRUCE ALWAYS HAD A RULE--STREET CLOTHES FOR UPSTAIRS. THE SUITS STAY IN THE CAVE. THAT WAY THERE'S NO DANGER OF A FOUL-UP.
AN ADMIRABLE PRECAUTION.
BUT IF YOU REMEMBER, BRUCE IS OUT OF IT. HE'S BROKEN... ARGUABLY BECAUSE HE FOLLOWED HIS ADMIRABLE RULES!

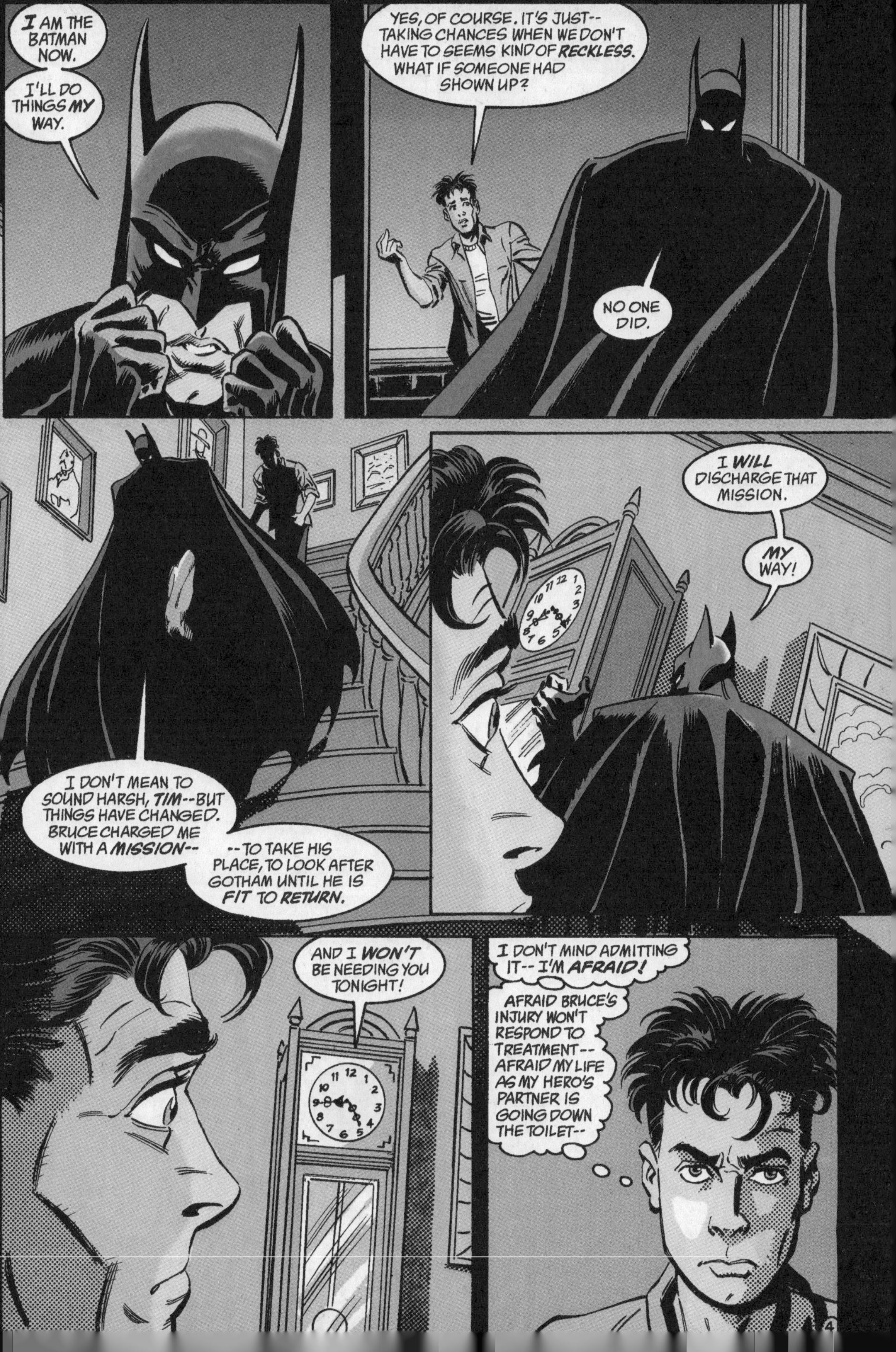
I AM THE BATMAN NOW.
I'LL DO THINGS MY WAY.
YES, OF COURSE. IT'S JUST-- TAKING CHANCES WHEN WE DON'T HAVE TO SEEMS KIND OF RECKLESS. WHAT IF SOMEONE HAD SHOWN UP?
NO ONE DID.
I DON'T MEAN TO SOUND HARSH, TIM--BUT THINGS HAVE CHANGED. BRUCE CHARGED ME WITH A MISSION--
--TO TAKE HIS PLACE, TO LOOK AFTER GOTHAM UNTIL HE IS FIT TO RETURN.
I WILL DISCHARGE THAT MISSION.
MY WAY!
AND I WON'T BE NEEDING YOU TONIGHT!
I DON'T MIND ADMITTING IT-- I'M AFRAID!
AFRAID BRUCE'S INJURY WON'T RESPOND TO TREATMENT-- AFRAID MY LIFE AS MY HERO'S PARTNER IS GOING DOWN THE TOILET--
4

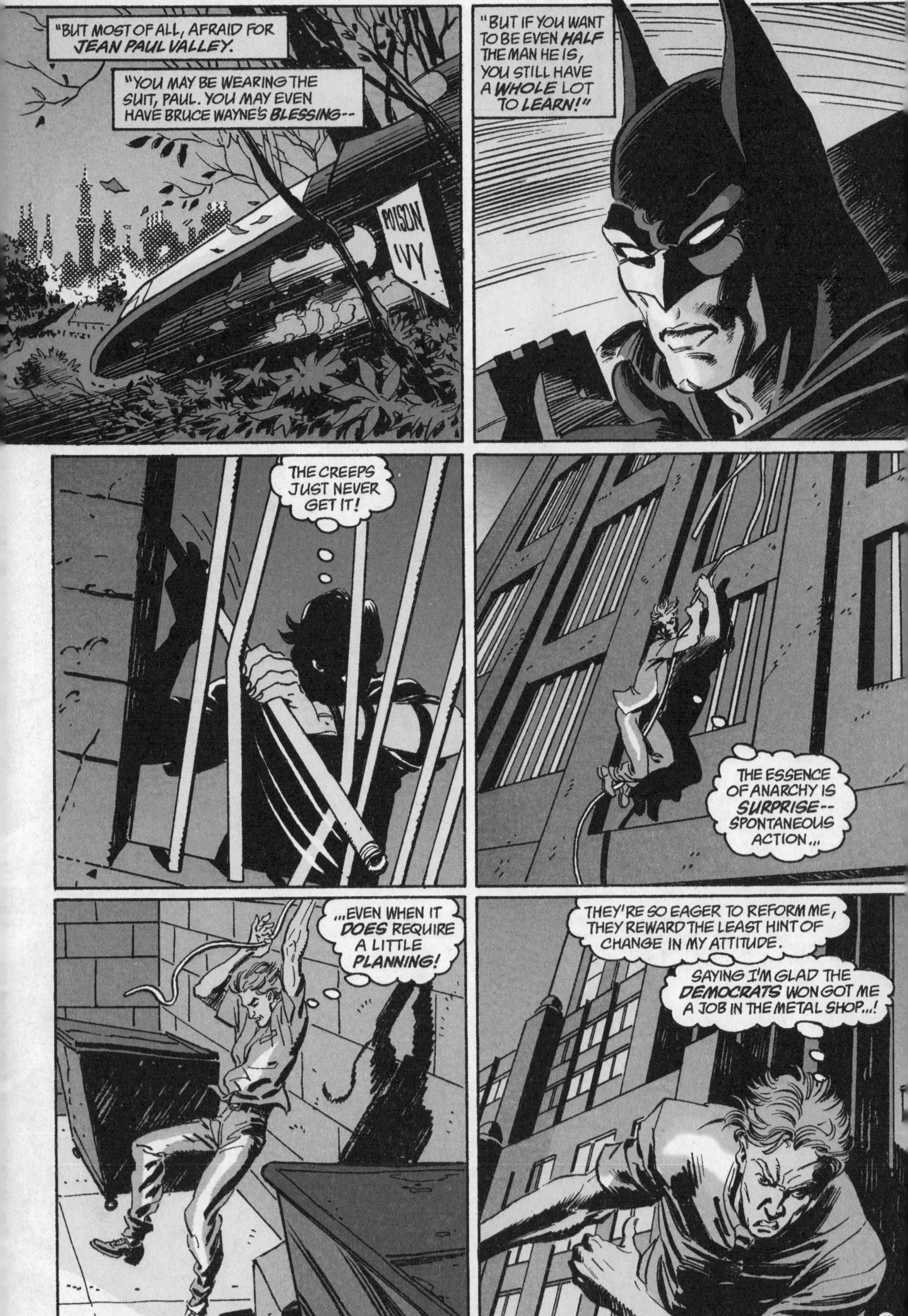
"BUT MOST OF ALL, AFRAID FOR JEAN PAUL VALLEY.
"YOU MAY BE WEARING THE SUIT, PAUL. YOU MAY EVEN HAVE BRUCE WAYNE'S BLESSING--
POISON IVY
"BUT IF YOU WANT TO BE EVEN HALF THE MAN HE IS, YOU STILL HAVE A WHOLE LOT TO LEARN!"
THE CREEPS JUST NEVER GET IT!
THE ESSENCE OF ANARCHY IS SURPRISE-- SPONTANEOUS ACTION...
...EVEN WHEN IT DOES REQUIRE A LITTLE PLANNING!
THEY'RE SO EAGER TO REFORM ME, THEY REWARD THE LEAST HINT OF CHANGE IN MY ATTITUDE.
SAYING I'M GLAD THE DEMOCRATS WON GOT ME A JOB IN THE METAL SHOP...!

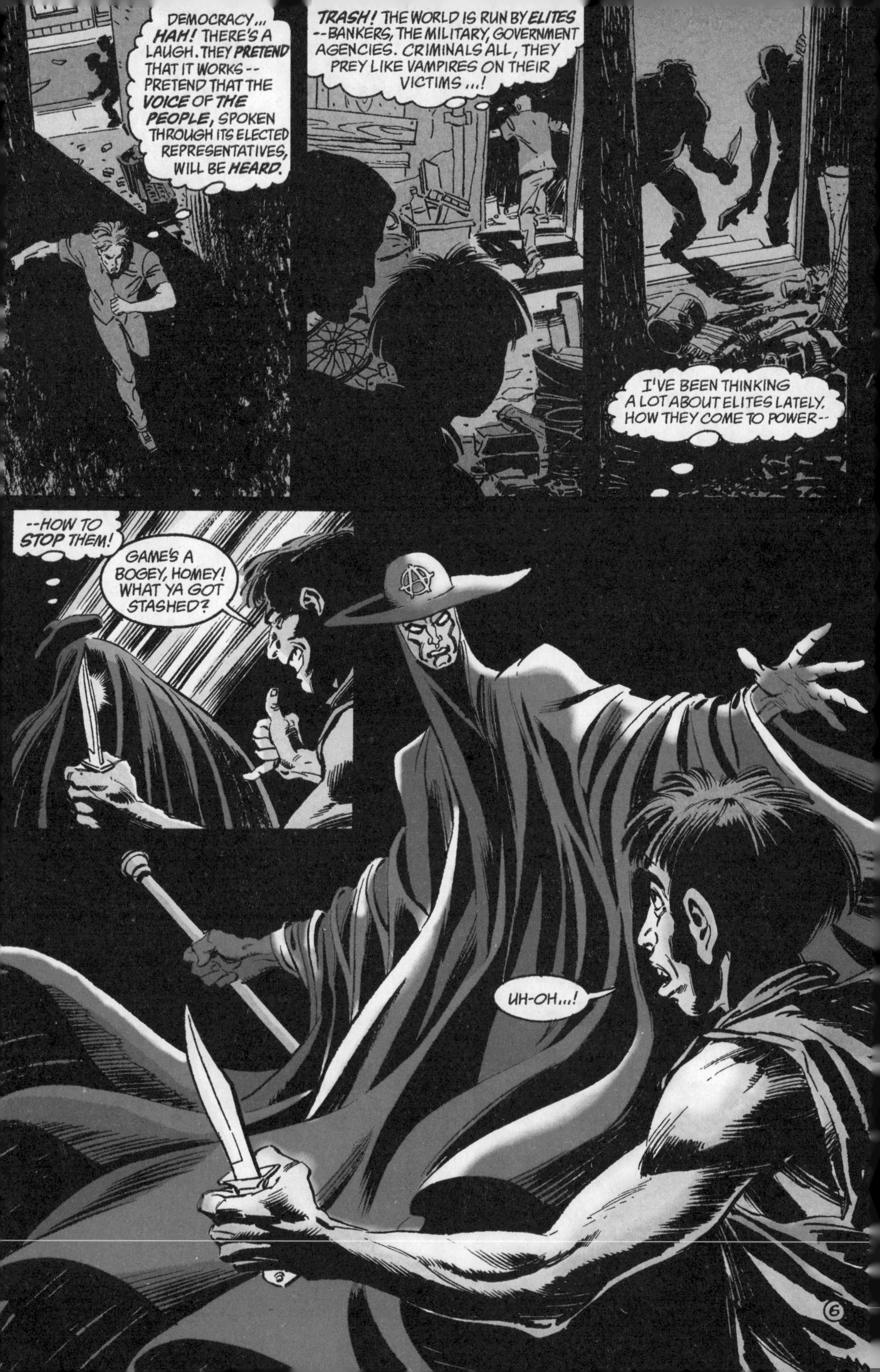
DEMOCRACY... HAH! THERE'S A LAUGH. THEY PRETEND THAT IT WORKS-- PRETEND THAT THE VOICE OF THE PEOPLE, SPOKEN THROUGH ITS ELECTED REPRESENTATIVES, WILL BE HEARD.
TRASH! THE WORLD IS RUN BY ELITES --BANKERS, THE MILITARY, GOVERNMENT AGENCIES. CRIMINALS ALL, THEY PREY LIKE VAMPIRES ON THEIR VICTIMS...!
I'VE BEEN THINKING A LOT ABOUT ELITES LATELY. HOW THEY COME TO POWER--
--HOW TO STOP THEM!
GAME'S A BOGEY, HOMEY! WHAT YA GOT STASHED?
UH-OH...!

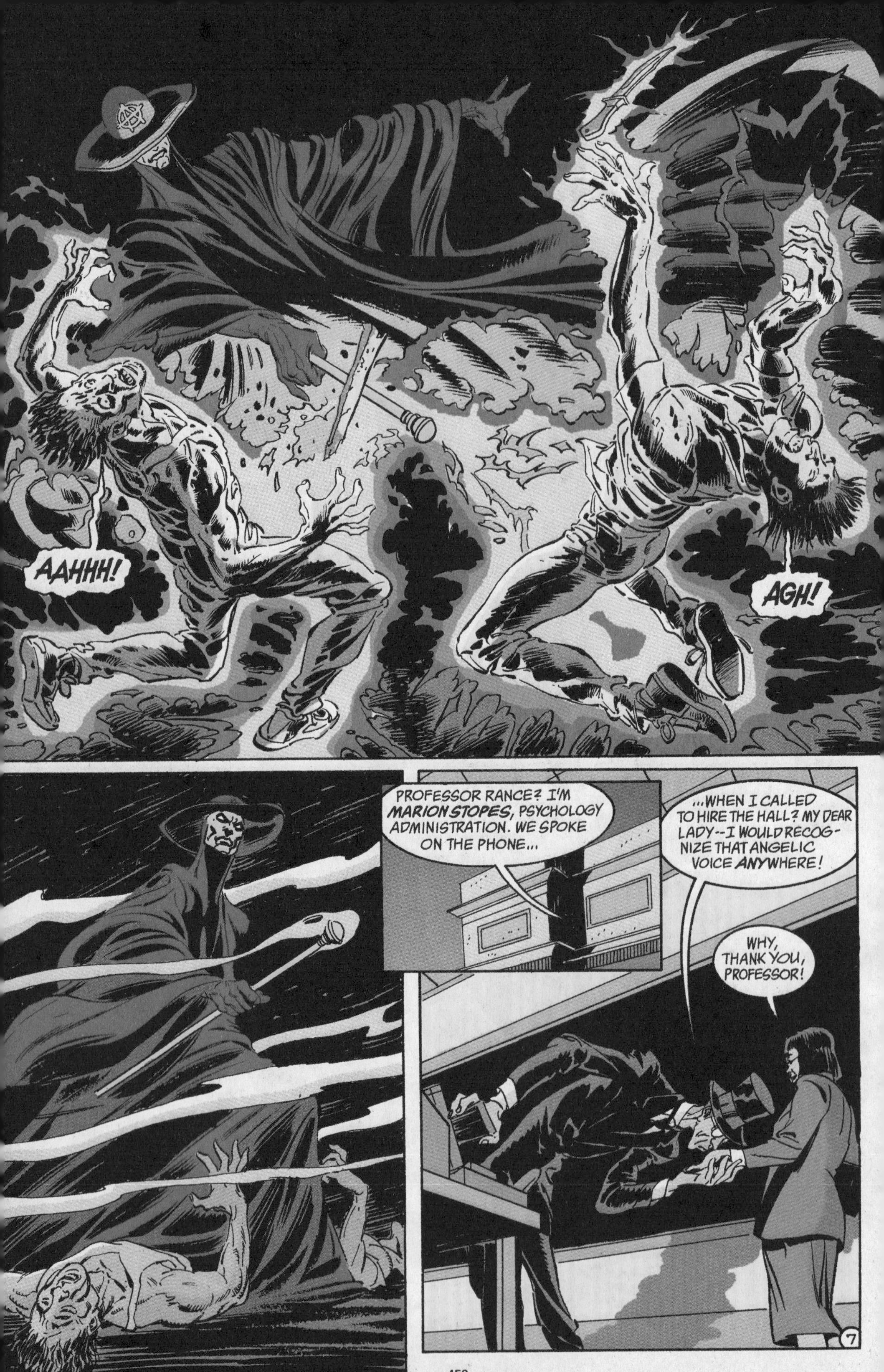
AAHHH!
AGH!
PROFESSOR RANCE? I'M MARION STOPES, PSYCHOLOGY ADMINISTRATION. WE SPOKE ON THE PHONE...
...WHEN I CALLED TO HIRE THE HALL? MY DEAR LADY--I WOULD RECOGNIZE THAT ANGELIC VOICE ANYWHERE!
WHY, THANK YOU, PROFESSOR!
7

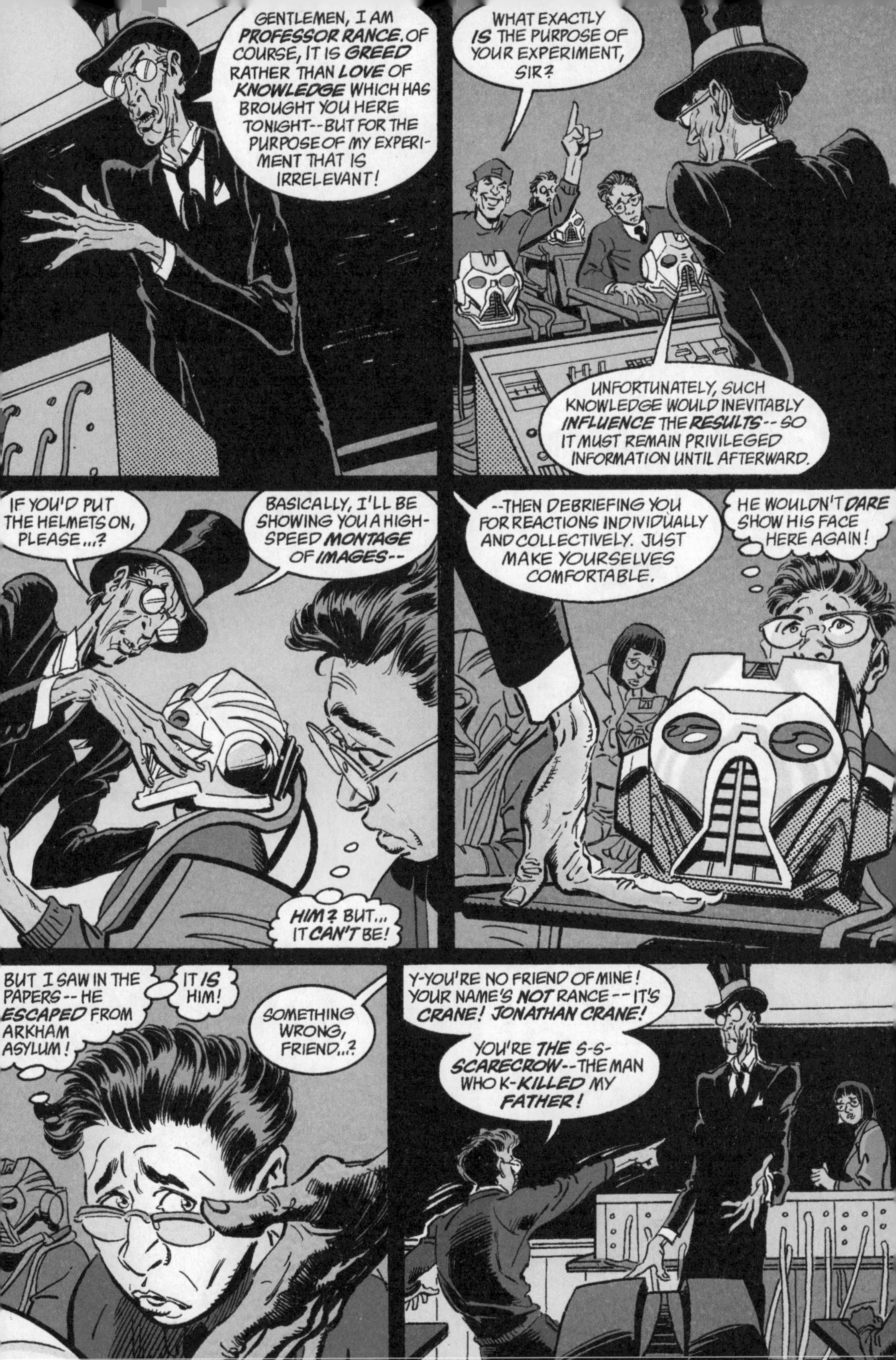
GENTLEMEN, I AM PROFESSOR RANCE. OF COURSE, IT IS GREED RATHER THAN LOVE OF KNOWLEDGE WHICH HAS BROUGHT YOU HERE TONIGHT--BUT FOR THE PURPOSE OF MY EXPERIMENT THAT IS IRRELEVANT!
WHAT EXACTLY IS THE PURPOSE OF YOUR EXPERIMENT, SIR?
UNFORTUNATELY, SUCH KNOWLEDGE WOULD INEVITABLY INFLUENCE THE RESULTS--SO IT MUST REMAIN PRIVILEGED INFORMATION UNTIL AFTERWARD.
IF YOU'D PUT THE HELMETS ON, PLEASE...?
BASICALLY, I'LL BE SHOWING YOU A HIGH-SPEED MONTAGE OF IMAGES--
HIM? BUT... IT CAN'T BE!
--THEN DEBRIEFING YOU FOR REACTIONS INDIVIDUALLY AND COLLECTIVELY. JUST MAKE YOURSELVES COMFORTABLE.
HE WOULDN'T DARE SHOW HIS FACE HERE AGAIN!
BUT I SAW IN THE PAPERS--HE ESCAPED FROM ARKHAM ASYLUM!
IT IS HIM!
SOMETHING WRONG, FRIEND...?
Y-YOU'RE NO FRIEND OF MINE! YOUR NAME'S NOT RANCE--IT'S CRANE! JONATHAN CRANE!
YOU'RE THE S-S-SCARECROW--THE MAN WHO K-KILLED MY FATHER!
8

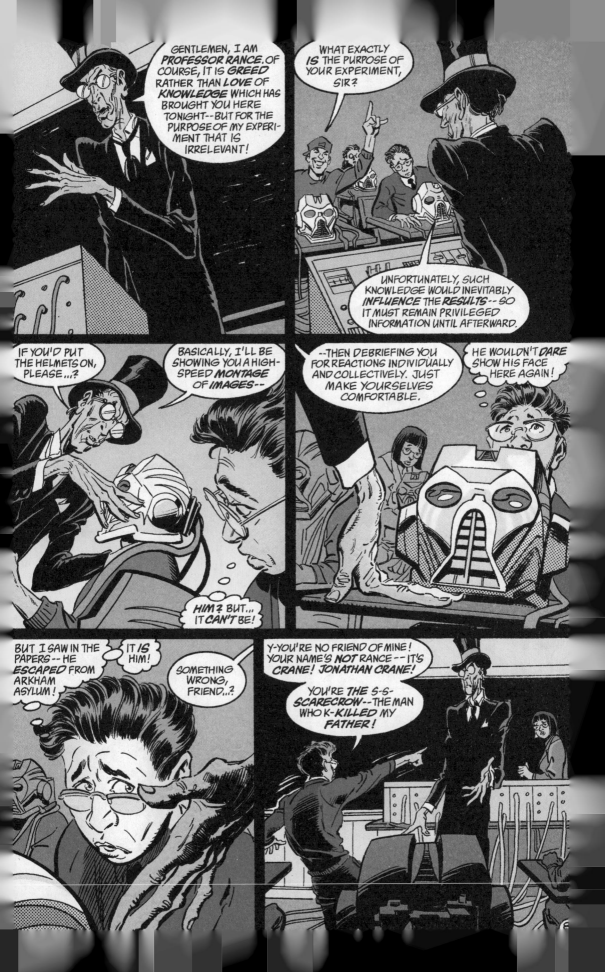

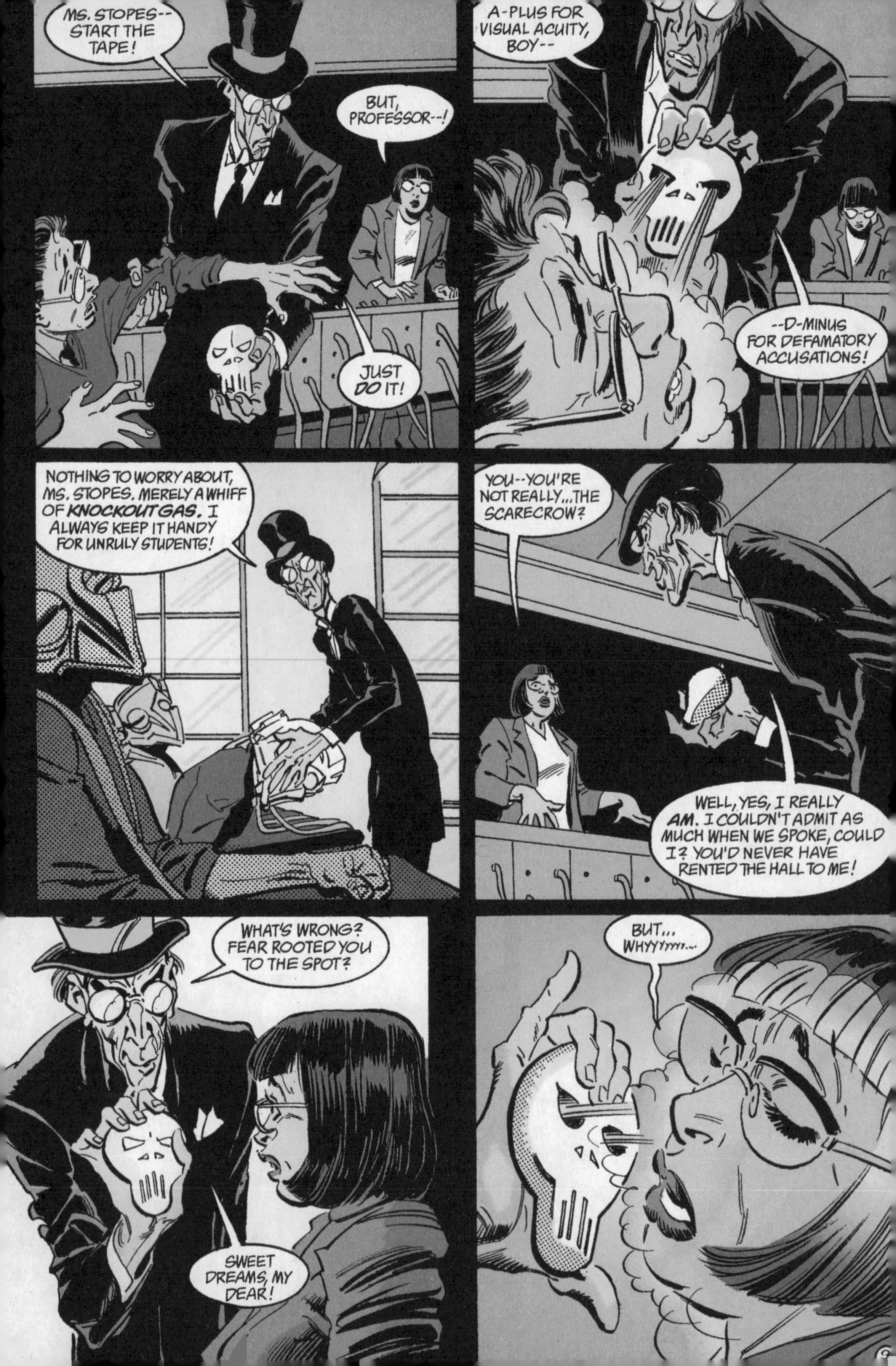
MS. STOPES-- START THE TAPE!
BUT, PROFESSOR--!
JUST DO IT!
A-PLUS FOR VISUAL ACUITY, BOY--
--D-MINUS FOR DEFAMATORY ACCUSATIONS!
NOTHING TO WORRY ABOUT, MS. STOPES. MERELY A WHIFF OF KNOCKOUT GAS. I ALWAYS KEEP IT HANDY FOR UNRULY STUDENTS!
YOU--YOU'RE NOT REALLY...THE SCARECROW?
WELL, YES, I REALLY AM. I COULDN'T ADMIT AS MUCH WHEN WE SPOKE, COULD I? YOU'D NEVER HAVE RENTED THE HALL TO ME!
WHAT'S WRONG? FEAR ROOTED YOU TO THE SPOT?
SWEET DREAMS, MY DEAR!
BUT... WHYYYyyyy...

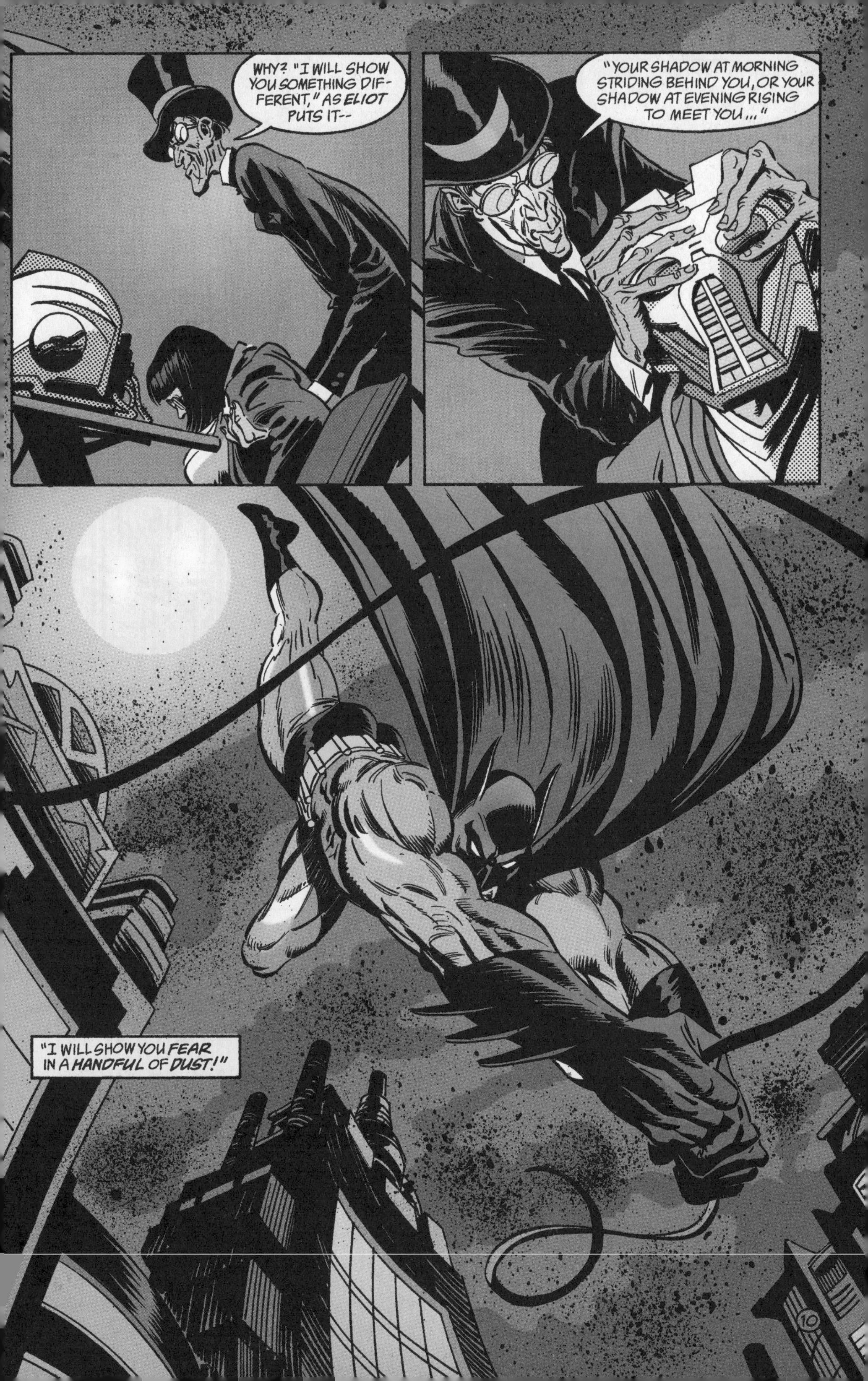
WHY? "I WILL SHOW YOU SOMETHING DIFFERENT," AS ELIOT PUTS IT--
"YOUR SHADOW AT MORNING STRIDING BEHIND YOU, OR YOUR SHADOW AT EVENING RISING TO MEET YOU..."
"I WILL SHOW YOU FEAR IN A HANDFUL OF DUST!"
10

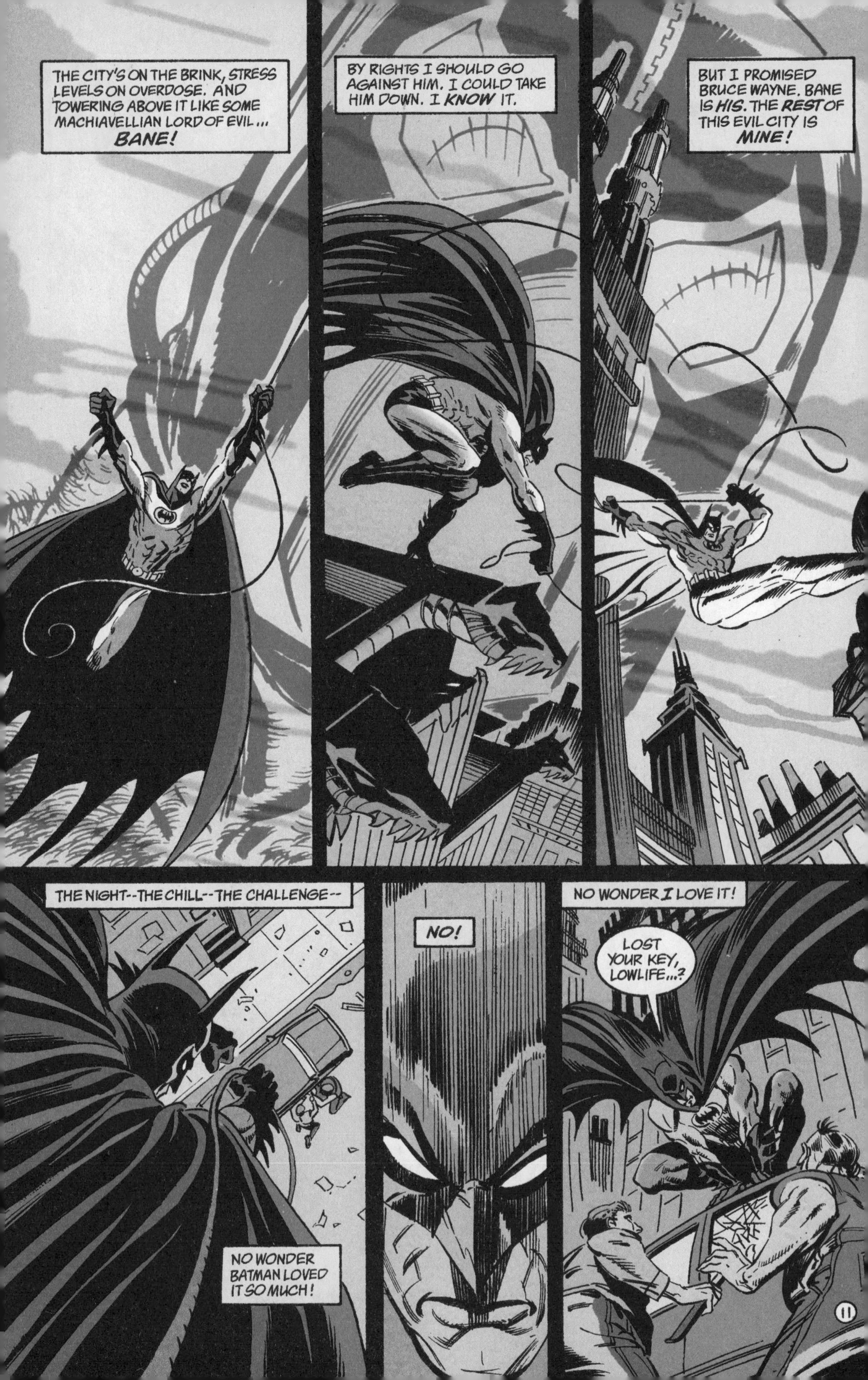

THE CITY'S ON THE BRINK, STRESS LEVELS ON OVERDOSE. AND TOWERING ABOVE IT LIKE SOME MACHIAVELLIAN LORD OF EVIL... BANE!
BY RIGHTS I SHOULD GO AGAINST HIM. I COULD TAKE HIM DOWN. I KNOW IT.
BUT I PROMISED BRUCE WAYNE. BANE IS HIS. THE REST OF THIS EVIL CITY IS MINE!
THE NIGHT--THE CHILL--THE CHALLENGE--
NO WONDER BATMAN LOVED IT SO MUCH!
NO!
NO WONDER I LOVE IT!
LOST YOUR KEY, LOWLIFE...?
11

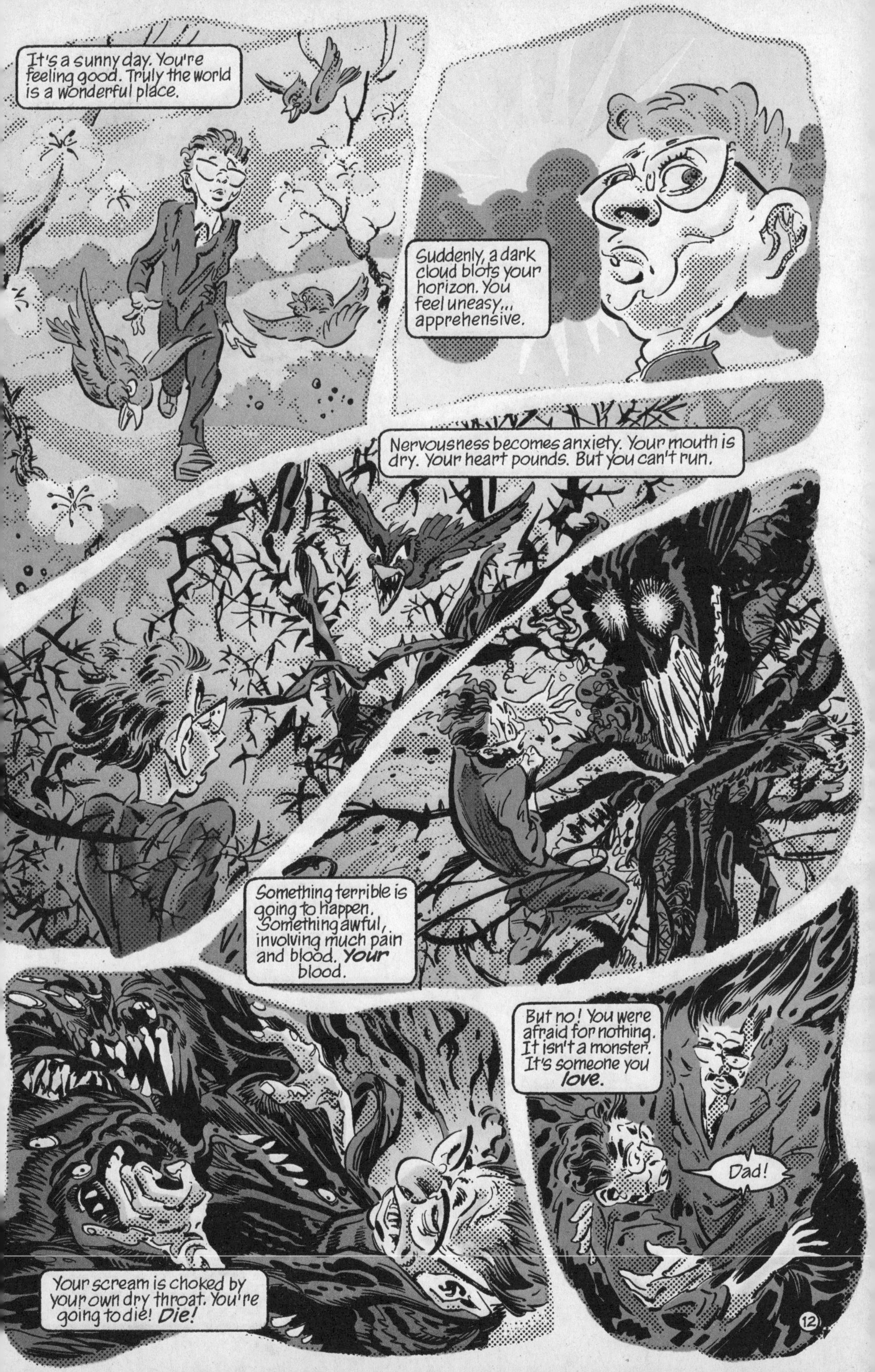
It's a sunny day. You're feeling good. Truly the world is a wonderful place.
Suddenly, a dark cloud blots your horizon. You feel uneasy... apprehensive.
Nervousness becomes anxiety. Your mouth is dry. Your heart pounds. But you can't run.
Something terrible is going to happen. Something awful, involving much pain and blood. *Your* blood.
Your scream is choked by your own dry throat. You're going to die! *Die!*
But no! You were afraid for nothing. It isn't a monster. It's someone you *love*.
Dad!

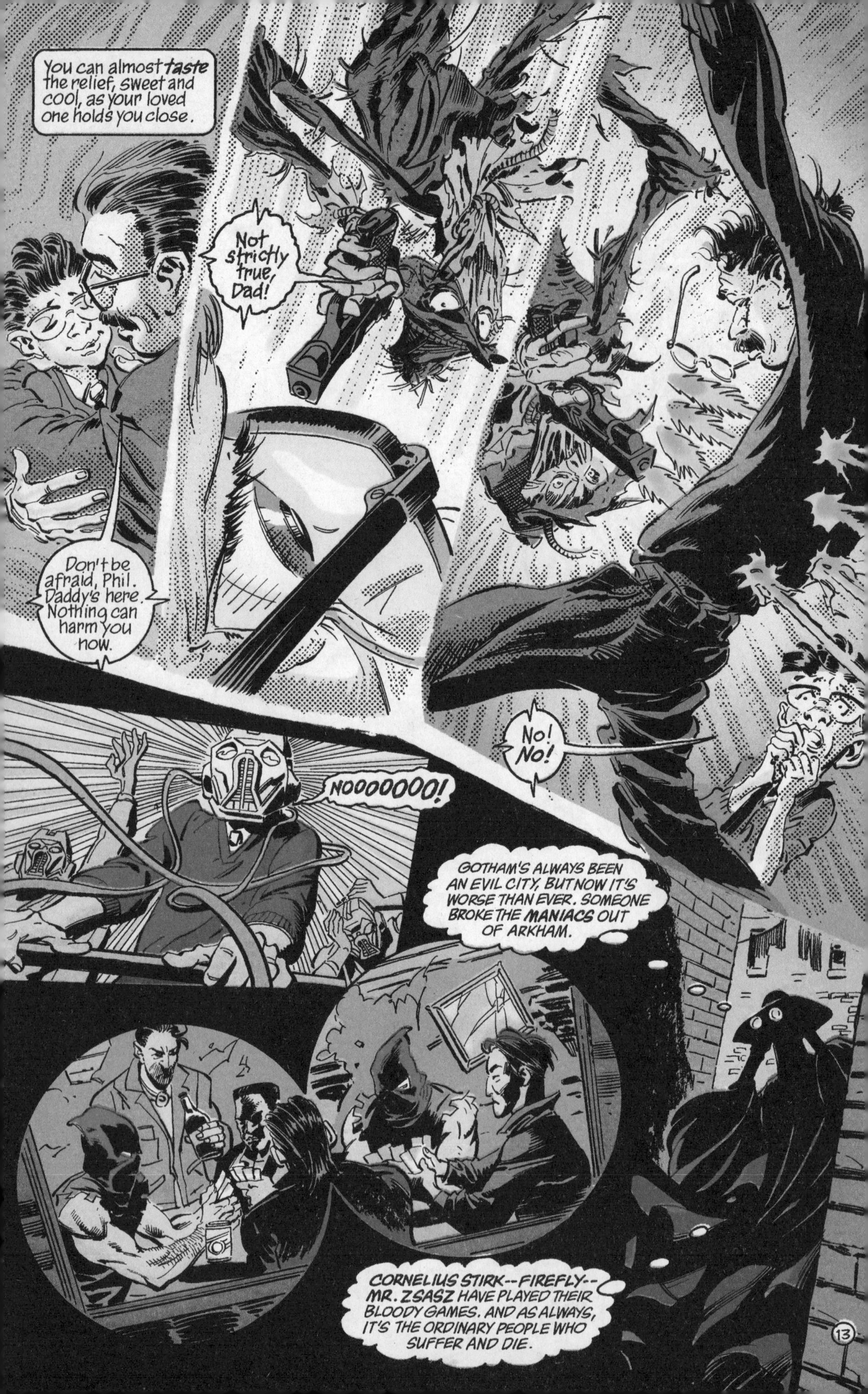
You can almost *taste* the relief, sweet and cool, as your loved one holds you close.
Not strictly true, Dad!
Don't be afraid, Phil. Daddy's here. Nothing can harm you now.
No! No!
NOOOOOOO!
GOTHAM'S ALWAYS BEEN AN EVIL CITY, BUT NOW IT'S WORSE THAN EVER. SOMEONE BROKE THE **MANIACS** OUT OF ARKHAM.
CORNELIUS STIRK--FIREFLY--MR. ZSASZ HAVE PLAYED THEIR BLOODY GAMES. AND AS ALWAYS, IT'S THE ORDINARY PEOPLE WHO SUFFER AND DIE.
13

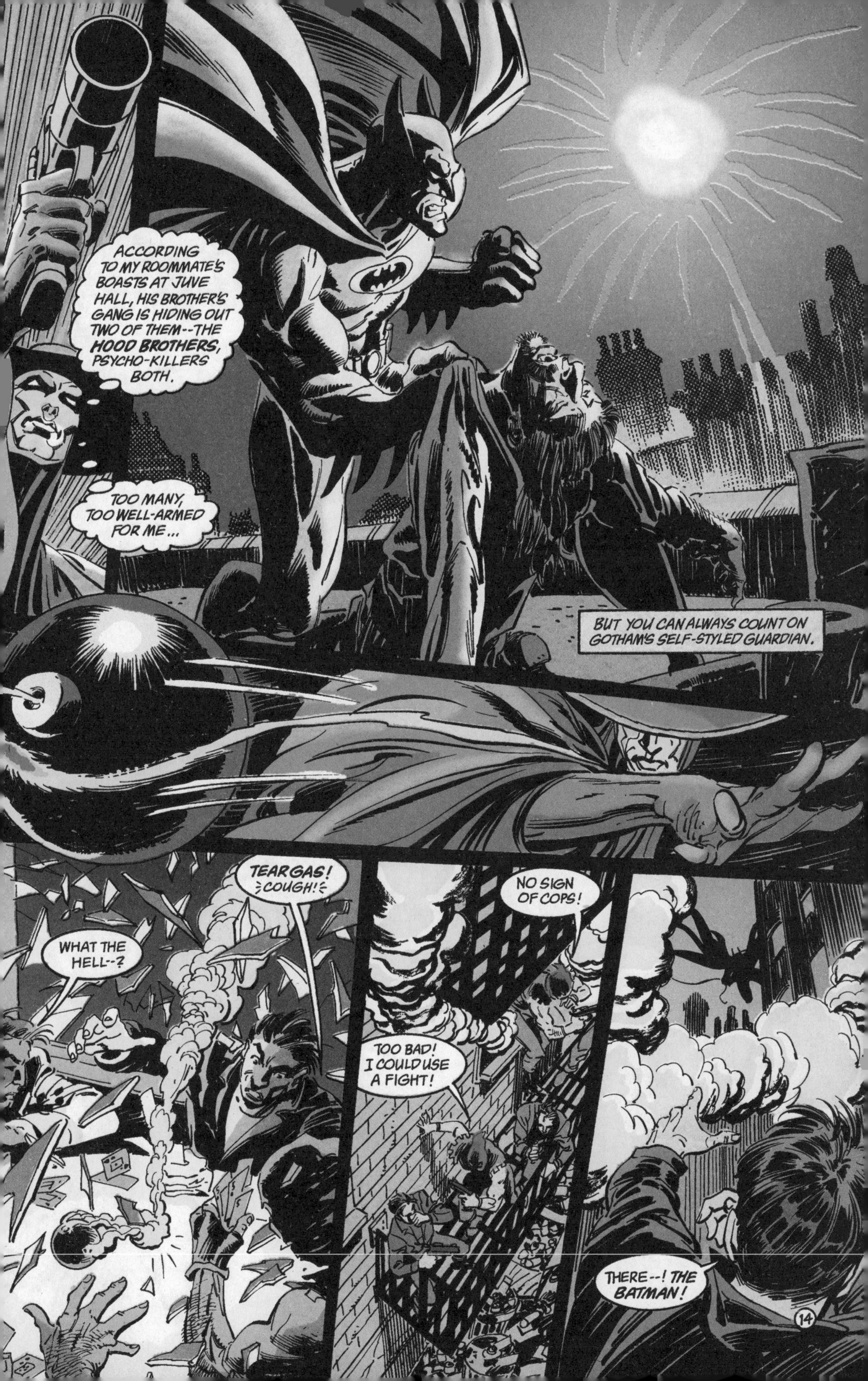
ACCORDING TO MY ROOMMATE'S BOASTS AT JUVE HALL, HIS BROTHER'S GANG IS HIDING OUT TWO OF THEM--THE HOOD BROTHERS, PSYCHO-KILLERS BOTH.
TOO MANY, TOO WELL-ARMED FOR ME...
BUT YOU CAN ALWAYS COUNT ON GOTHAM'S SELF-STYLED GUARDIAN.
WHAT THE HELL--?
TEAR GAS! COUGH!
NO SIGN OF COPS!
TOO BAD! I COULD USE A FIGHT!
THERE--! THE BATMAN!
14

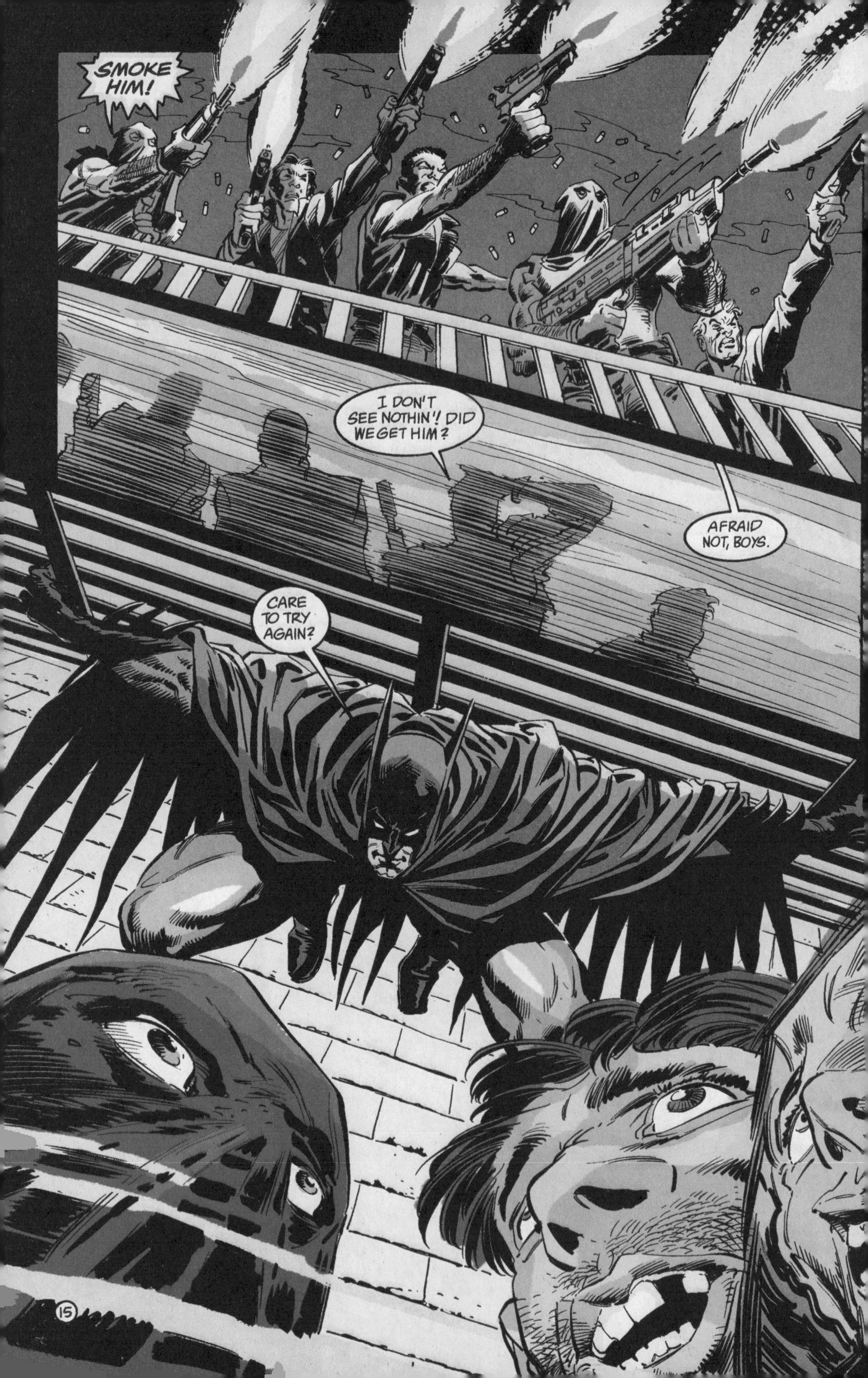
SMOKE HIM!
I DON'T SEE NOTHIN'! DID WE GET HIM?
AFRAID NOT, BOYS.
CARE TO TRY AGAIN?
15

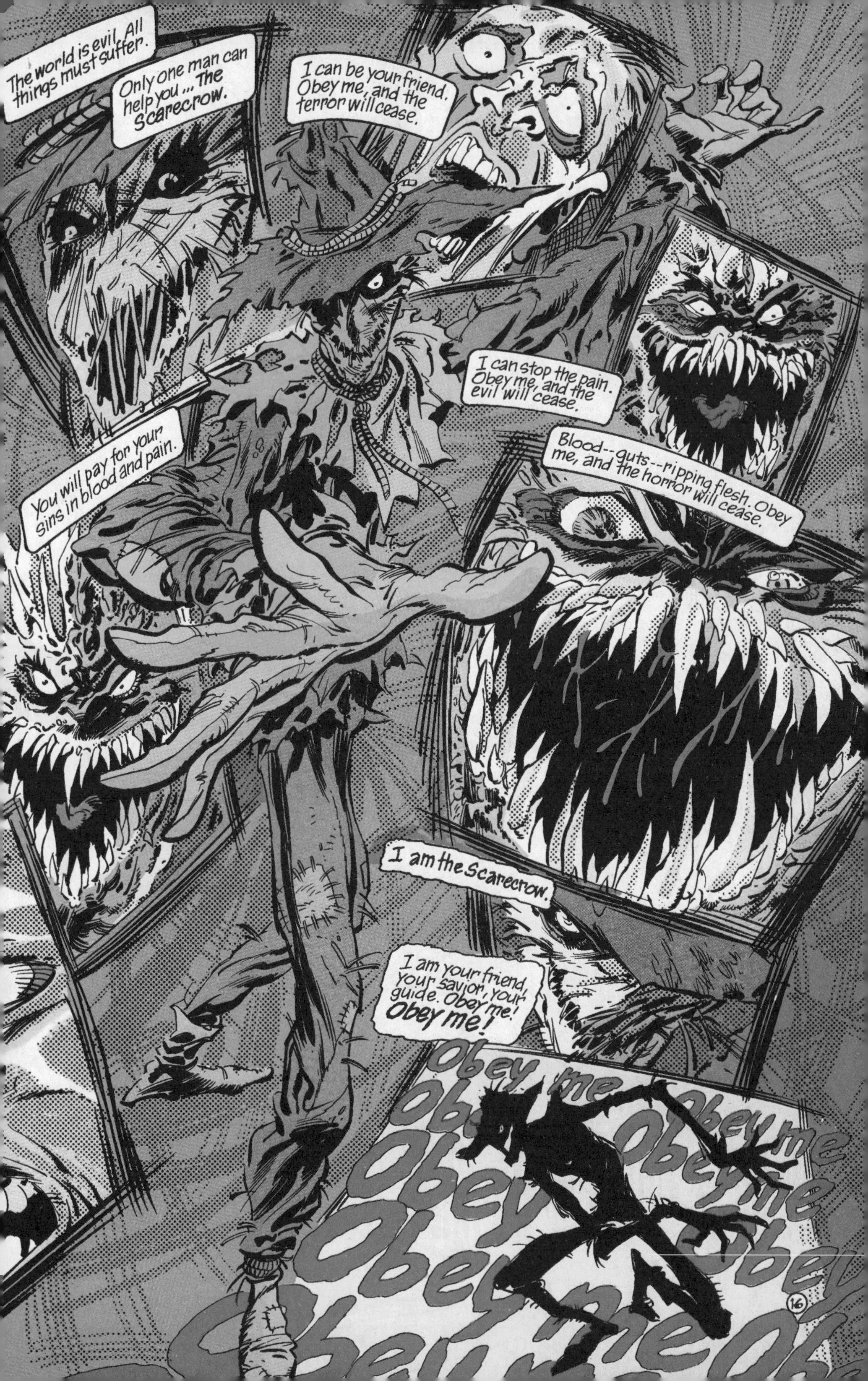

The world is evil. All things must suffer.
Only one man can help you ... The Scarecrow.
I can be your friend. Obey me, and the terror will cease.
I can stop the pain. Obey me, and the evil will cease.
You will pay for your sins in blood and pain.
Blood--guts--ripping flesh. Obey me, and the horror will cease.
I am the Scarecrow.
I am your friend, your savior, your guide. Obey me! Obey me!
Obey me
Obey me

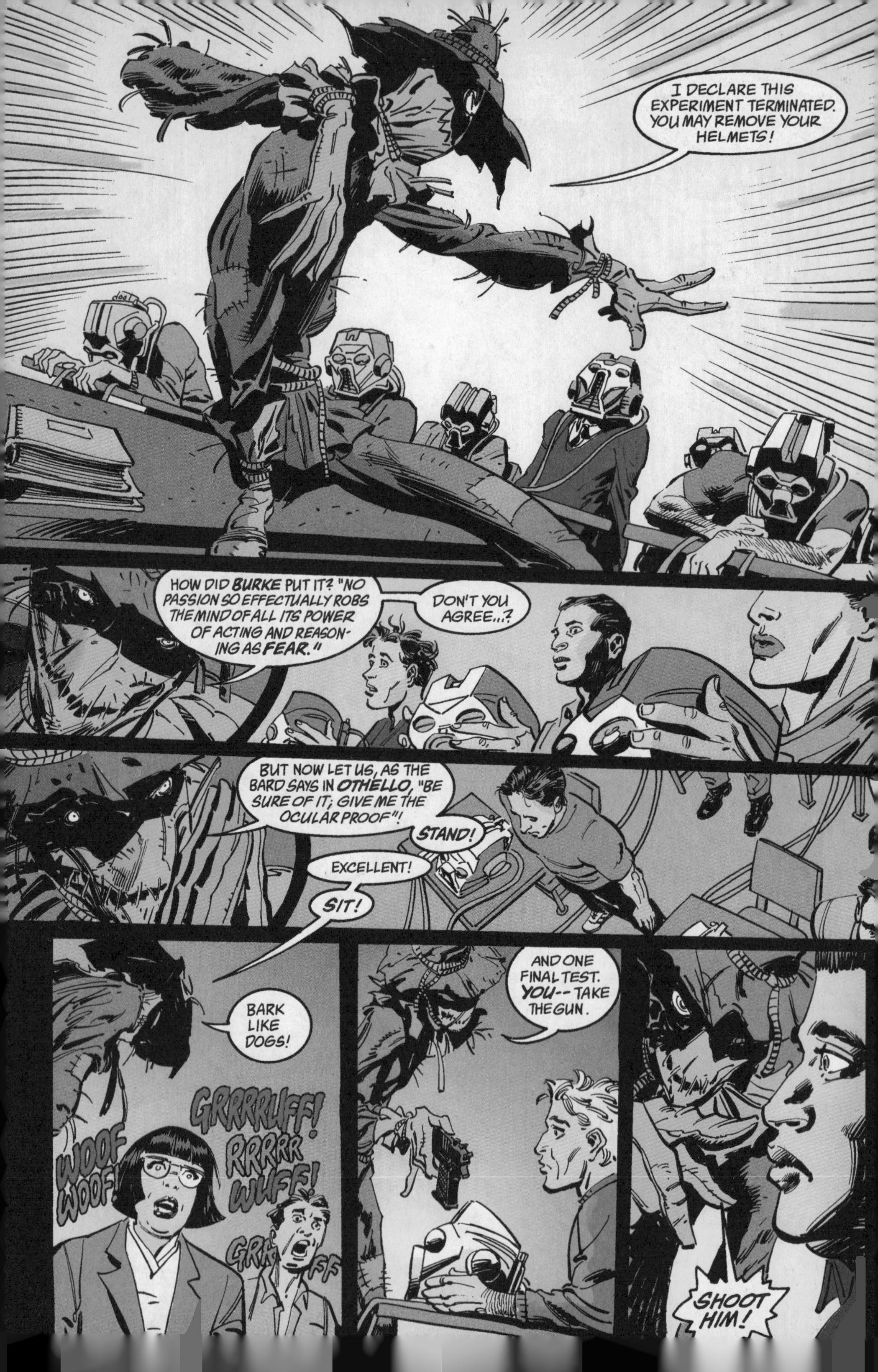

I DECLARE THIS EXPERIMENT TERMINATED. YOU MAY REMOVE YOUR HELMETS!
HOW DID BURKE PUT IT? "NO PASSION SO EFFECTUALLY ROBS THE MIND OF ALL ITS POWER OF ACTING AND REASONING AS FEAR."
DON'T YOU AGREE...?
BUT NOW LET US, AS THE BARD SAYS IN OTHELLO, "BE SURE OF IT; GIVE ME THE OCULAR PROOF"!
STAND!
EXCELLENT!
SIT!
BARK LIKE DOGS!
GRRRRUFF!
RRRRR WUFF!
WOOF WOOF!
GRRFF
AND ONE FINAL TEST. YOU-- TAKE THE GUN.
SHOOT HIM!

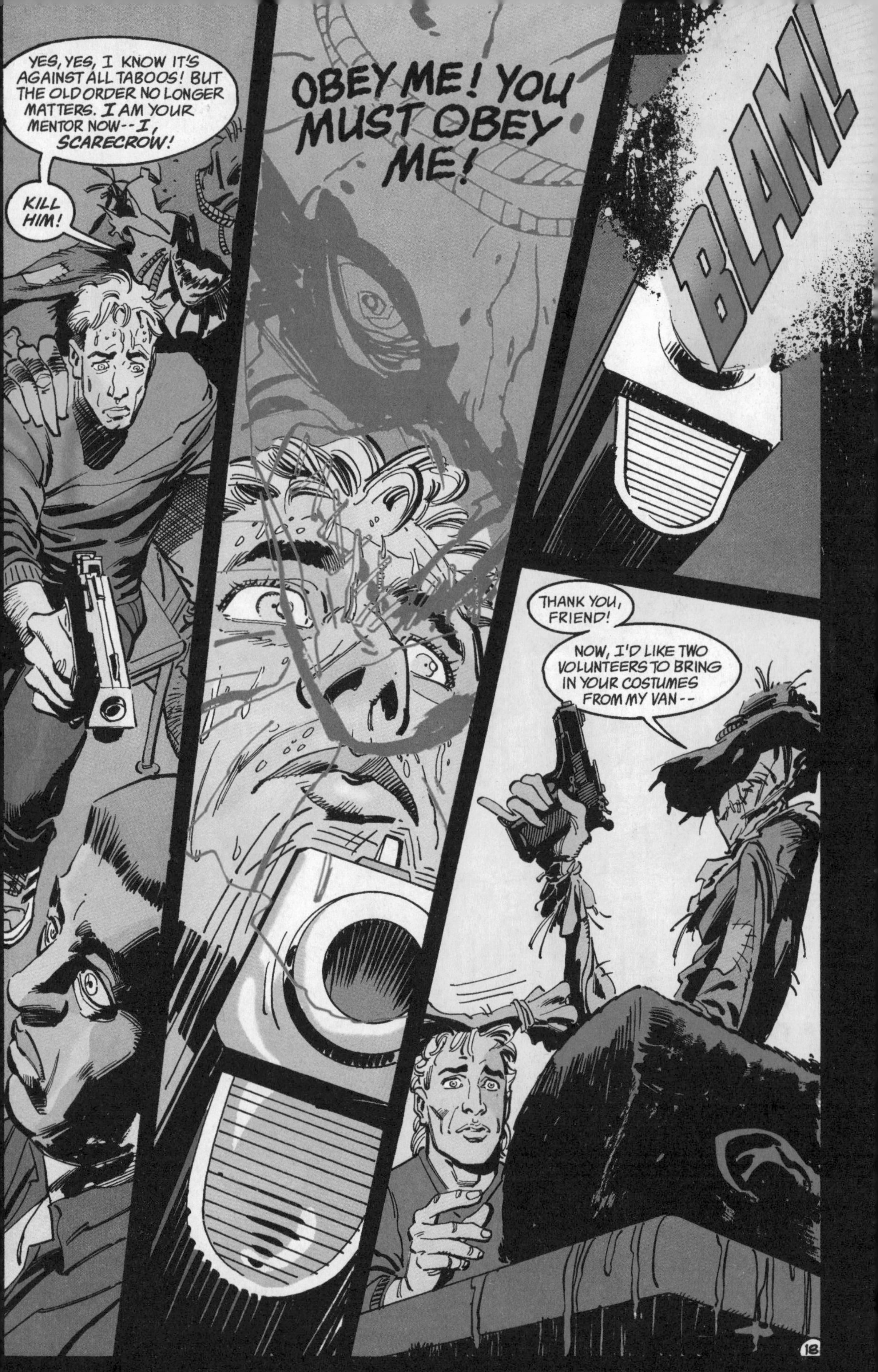
YES, YES, I KNOW IT'S AGAINST ALL TABOOS! BUT THE OLD ORDER NO LONGER MATTERS. I AM YOUR MENTOR NOW--I, SCARECROW!
KILL HIM!
OBEY ME! YOU MUST OBEY ME!
BLAM!
THANK YOU, FRIEND!
NOW, I'D LIKE TWO VOLUNTEERS TO BRING IN YOUR COSTUMES FROM MY VAN--
18

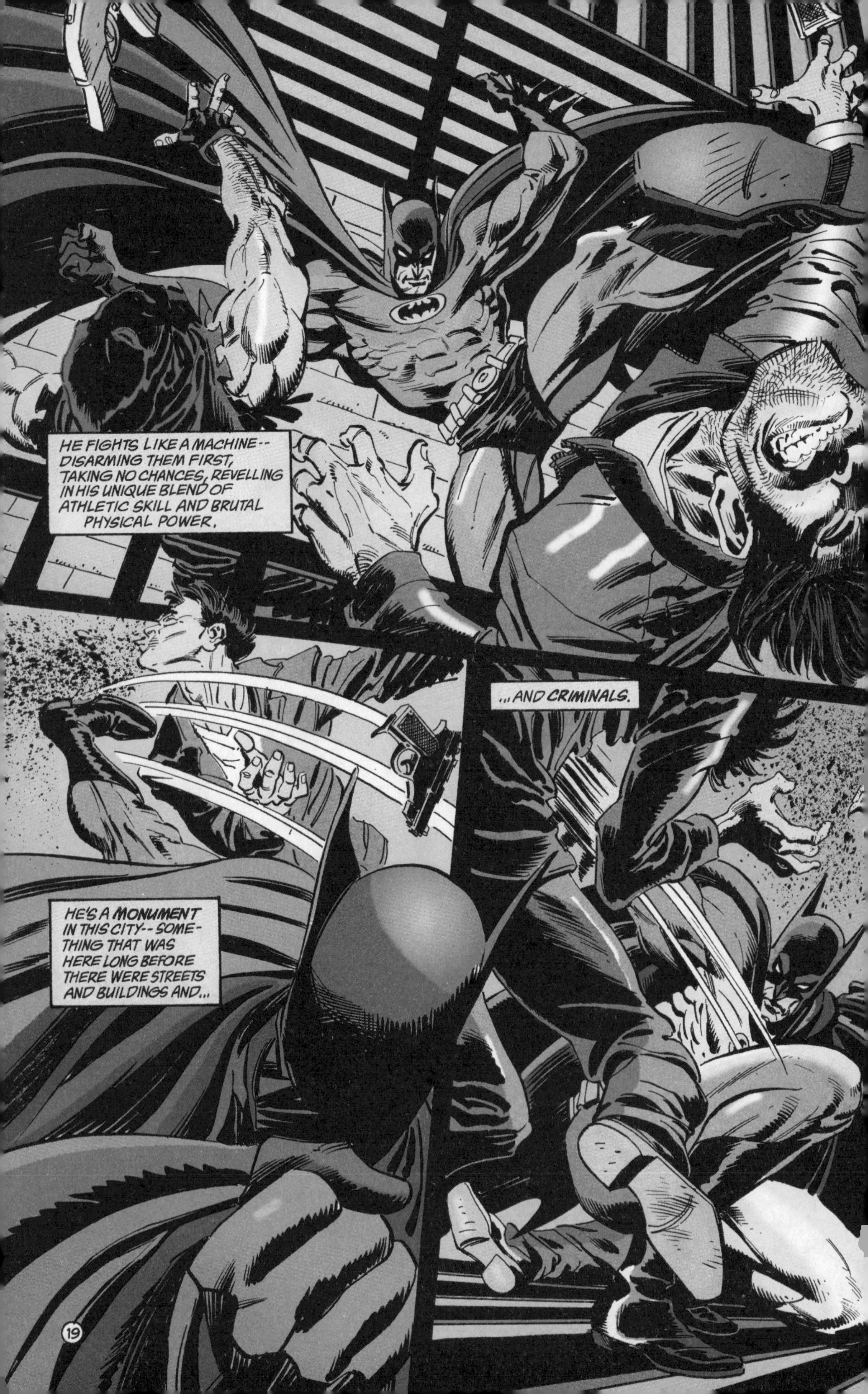
HE FIGHTS LIKE A MACHINE--DISARMING THEM FIRST, TAKING NO CHANCES, REVELLING IN HIS UNIQUE BLEND OF ATHLETIC SKILL AND BRUTAL PHYSICAL POWER.
HE'S A MONUMENT IN THIS CITY--SOMETHING THAT WAS HERE LONG BEFORE THERE WERE STREETS AND BUILDINGS AND...
...AND CRIMINALS.
19

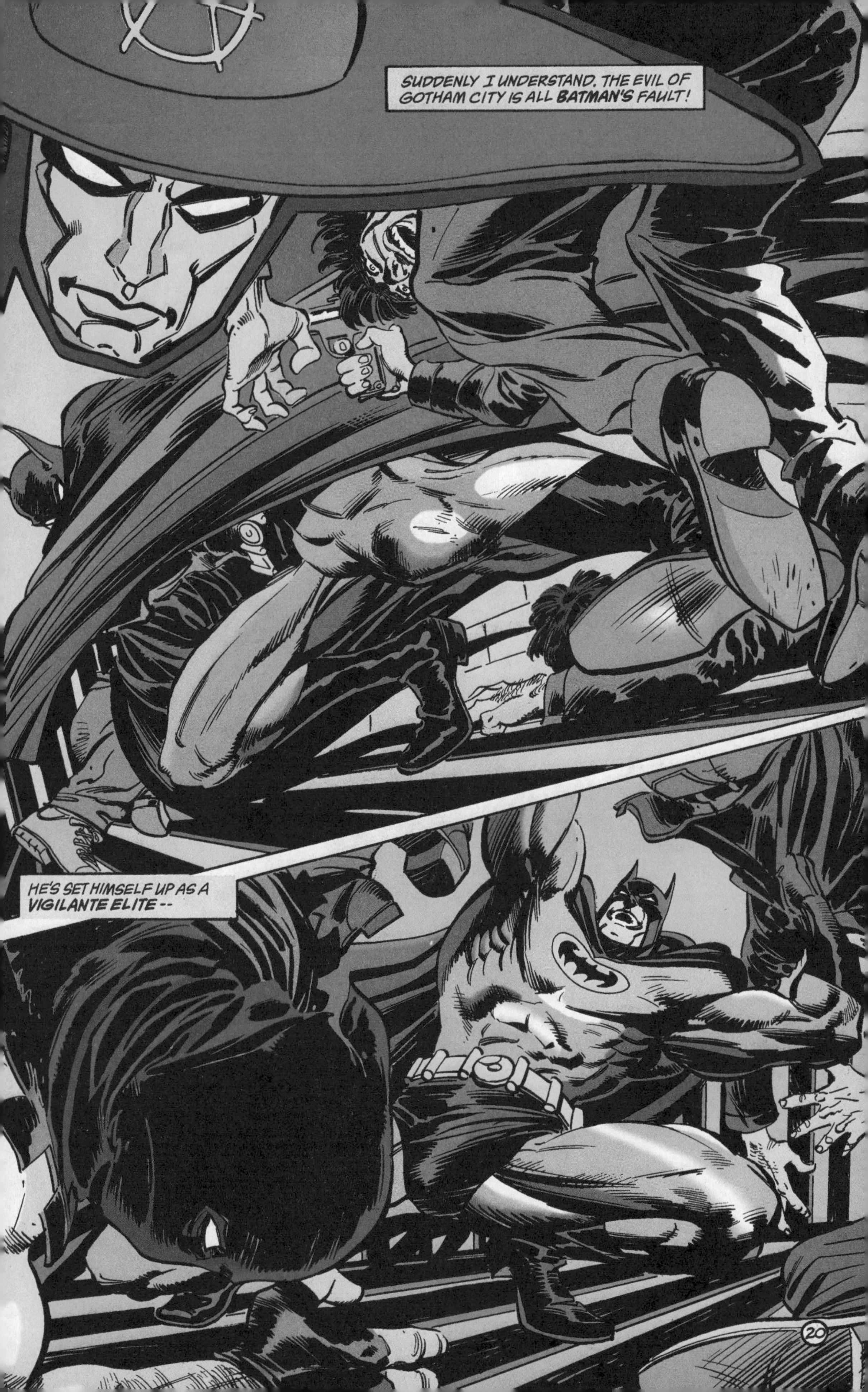
SUDDENLY I UNDERSTAND. THE EVIL OF GOTHAM CITY IS ALL BATMAN'S FAULT!
HE'S SET HIMSELF UP AS A VIGILANTE ELITE --
20

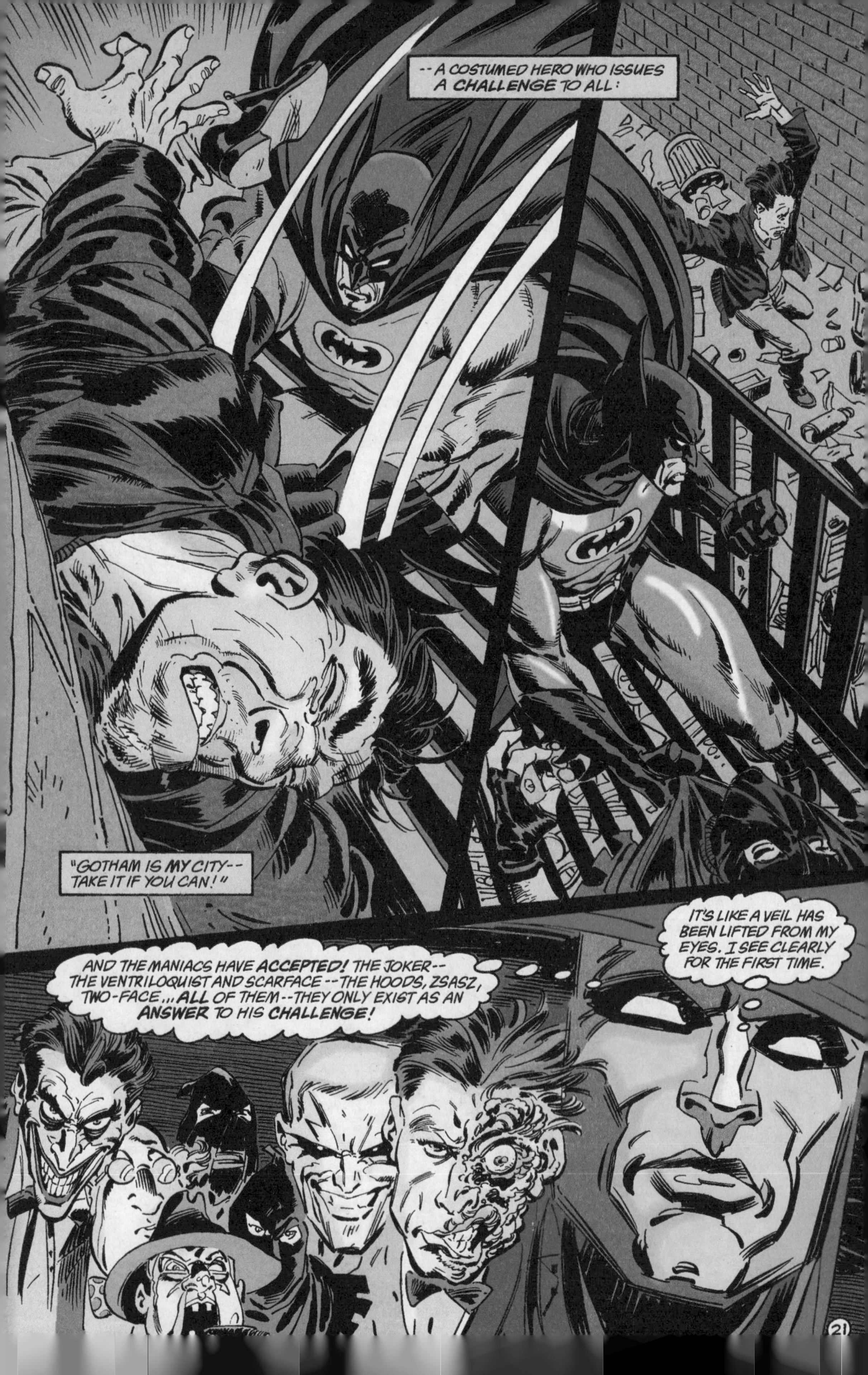
--A COSTUMED HERO WHO ISSUES A CHALLENGE TO ALL:
"GOTHAM IS MY CITY-- TAKE IT IF YOU CAN!"
AND THE MANIACS HAVE ACCEPTED! THE JOKER-- THE VENTRILOQUIST AND SCARFACE --THE HOODS, ZSASZ, TWO-FACE... ALL OF THEM--THEY ONLY EXIST AS AN ANSWER TO HIS CHALLENGE!
IT'S LIKE A VEIL HAS BEEN LIFTED FROM MY EYES. I SEE CLEARLY FOR THE FIRST TIME.

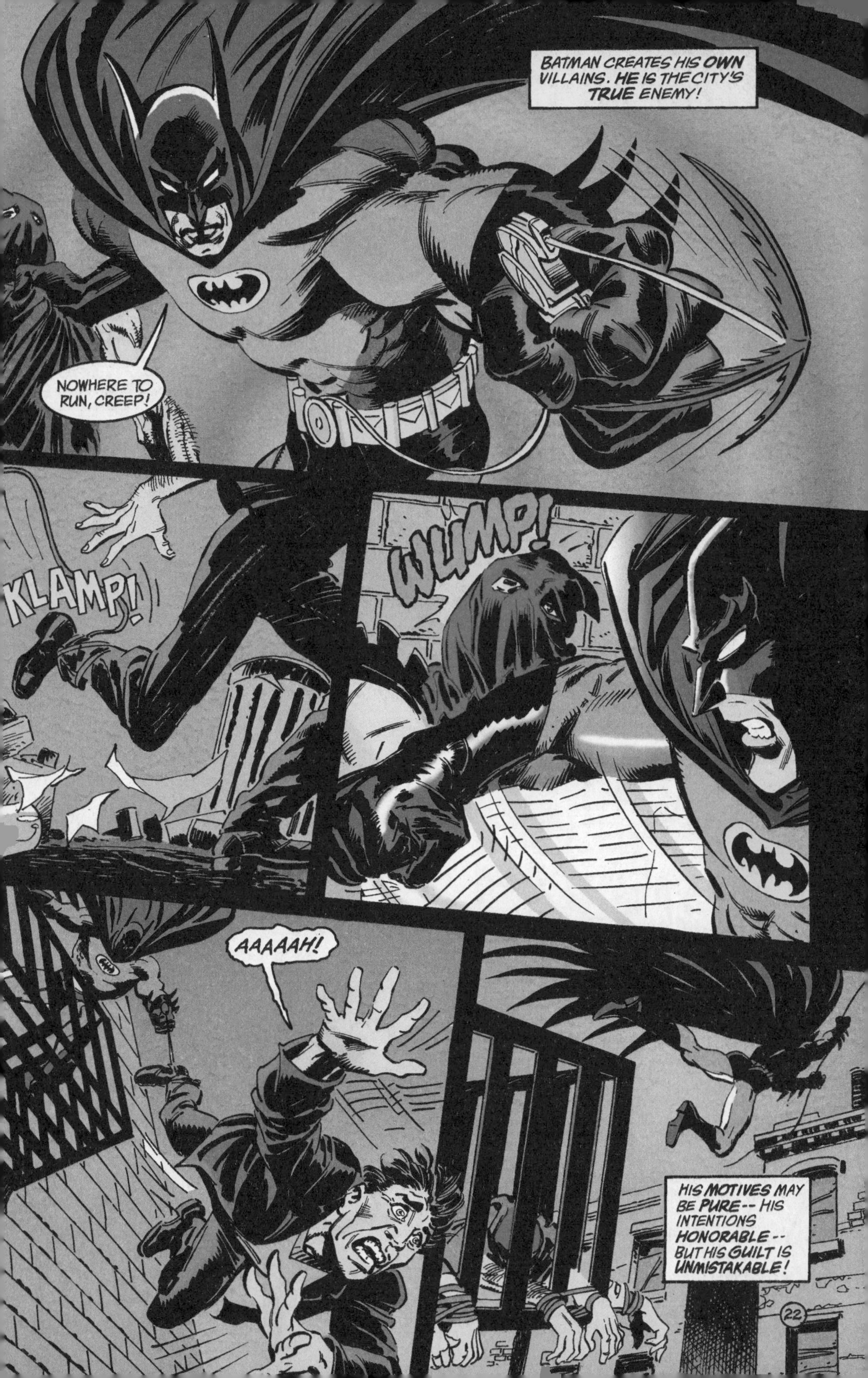
BATMAN CREATES HIS OWN VILLAINS. HE IS THE CITY'S TRUE ENEMY!
NOWHERE TO RUN, CREEP!
KLAMP!
WUMP!
AAAAAH!
HIS MOTIVES MAY BE PURE-- HIS INTENTIONS HONORABLE-- BUT HIS GUILT IS UNMISTAKABLE!
22

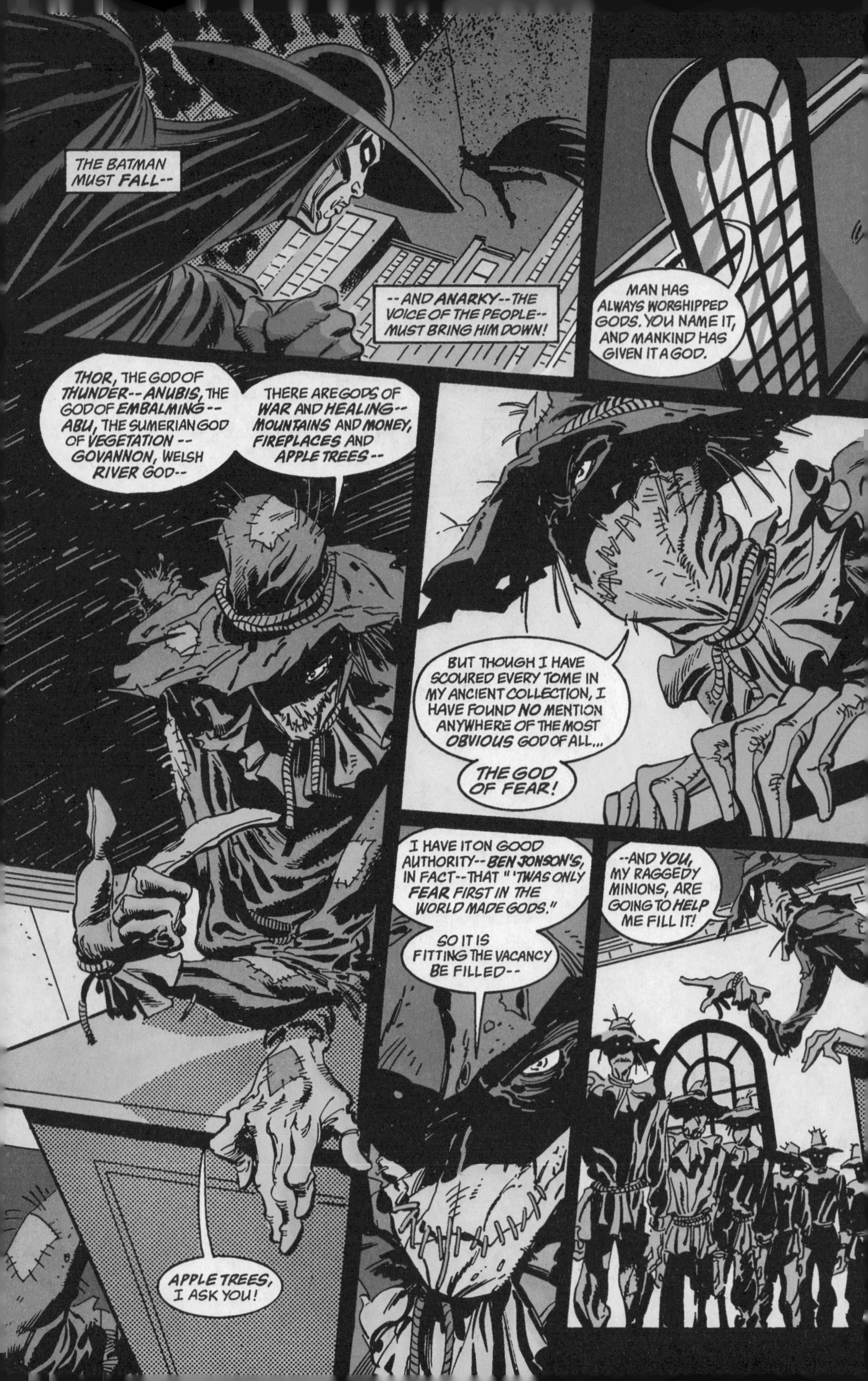
THE BATMAN MUST FALL--
--AND ANARKY--THE VOICE OF THE PEOPLE--MUST BRING HIM DOWN!
MAN HAS ALWAYS WORSHIPPED GODS. YOU NAME IT, AND MANKIND HAS GIVEN IT A GOD.
THOR, THE GOD OF THUNDER--ANUBIS, THE GOD OF EMBALMING--ABU, THE SUMERIAN GOD OF VEGETATION--GOVANNON, WELSH RIVER GOD--
THERE ARE GODS OF WAR AND HEALING--MOUNTAINS AND MONEY, FIREPLACES AND APPLE TREES--
APPLE TREES, I ASK YOU!
BUT THOUGH I HAVE SCOURED EVERY TOME IN MY ANCIENT COLLECTION, I HAVE FOUND NO MENTION ANYWHERE OF THE MOST OBVIOUS GOD OF ALL...
THE GOD OF FEAR!
I HAVE IT ON GOOD AUTHORITY--BEN JONSON'S, IN FACT--THAT "'TWAS ONLY FEAR FIRST IN THE WORLD MADE GODS."
SO IT IS FITTING THE VACANCY BE FILLED--
--AND YOU, MY RAGGEDY MINIONS, ARE GOING TO HELP ME FILL IT!

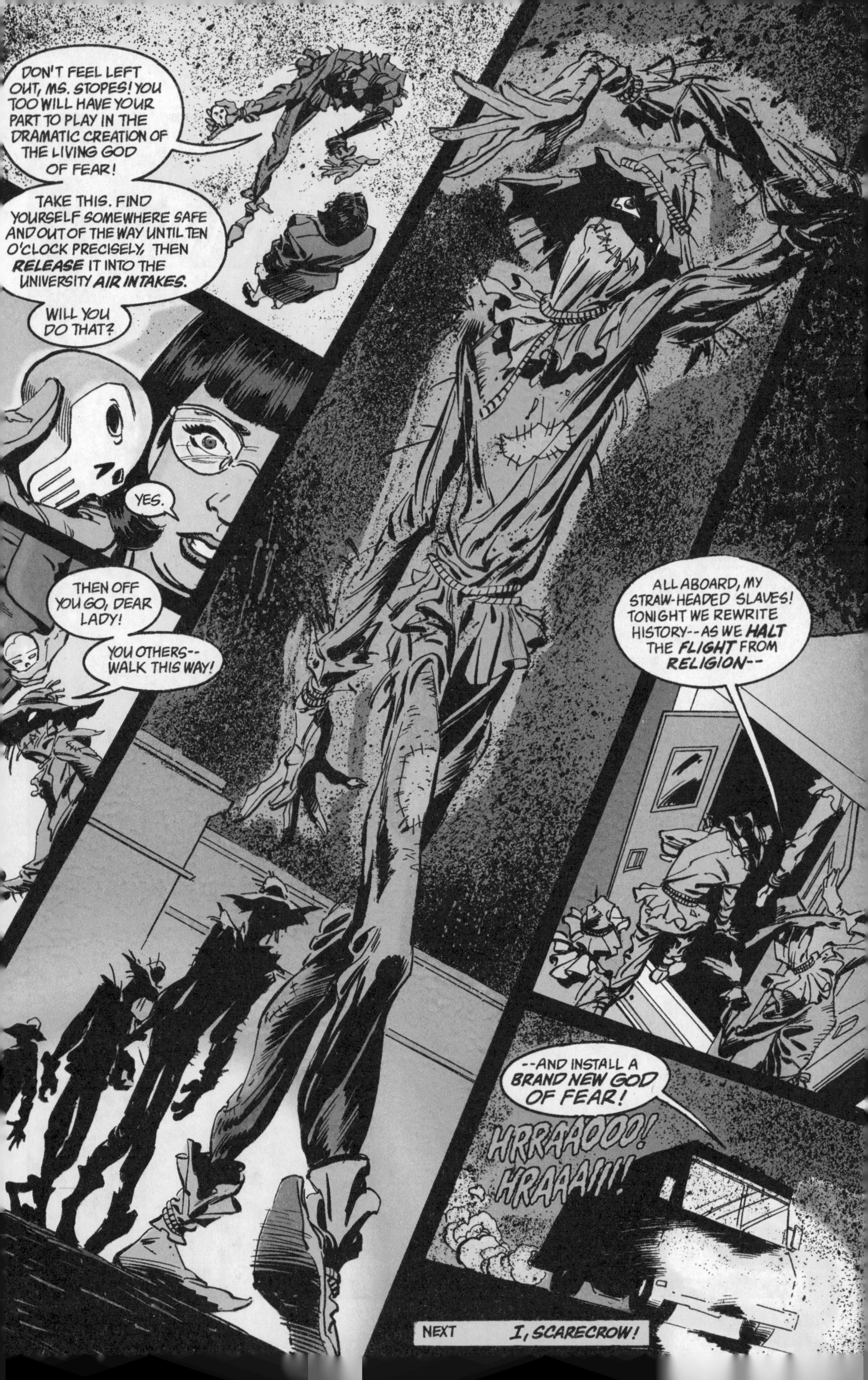
DON'T FEEL LEFT OUT, MS. STOPES! YOU TOO WILL HAVE YOUR PART TO PLAY IN THE DRAMATIC CREATION OF THE LIVING GOD OF FEAR!
TAKE THIS. FIND YOURSELF SOMEWHERE SAFE AND OUT OF THE WAY UNTIL TEN O'CLOCK PRECISELY, THEN RELEASE IT INTO THE UNIVERSITY AIR INTAKES.
WILL YOU DO THAT?
YES.
THEN OFF YOU GO, DEAR LADY!
YOU OTHERS-- WALK THIS WAY!
ALL ABOARD, MY STRAW-HEADED SLAVES! TONIGHT WE REWRITE HISTORY--AS WE HALT THE FLIGHT FROM RELIGION--
--AND INSTALL A BRAND NEW GOD OF FEAR!
HRRAAOOO! HRAAA!!!
NEXT I, SCARECROW!

Cover art by BRIAN STELFREEZE

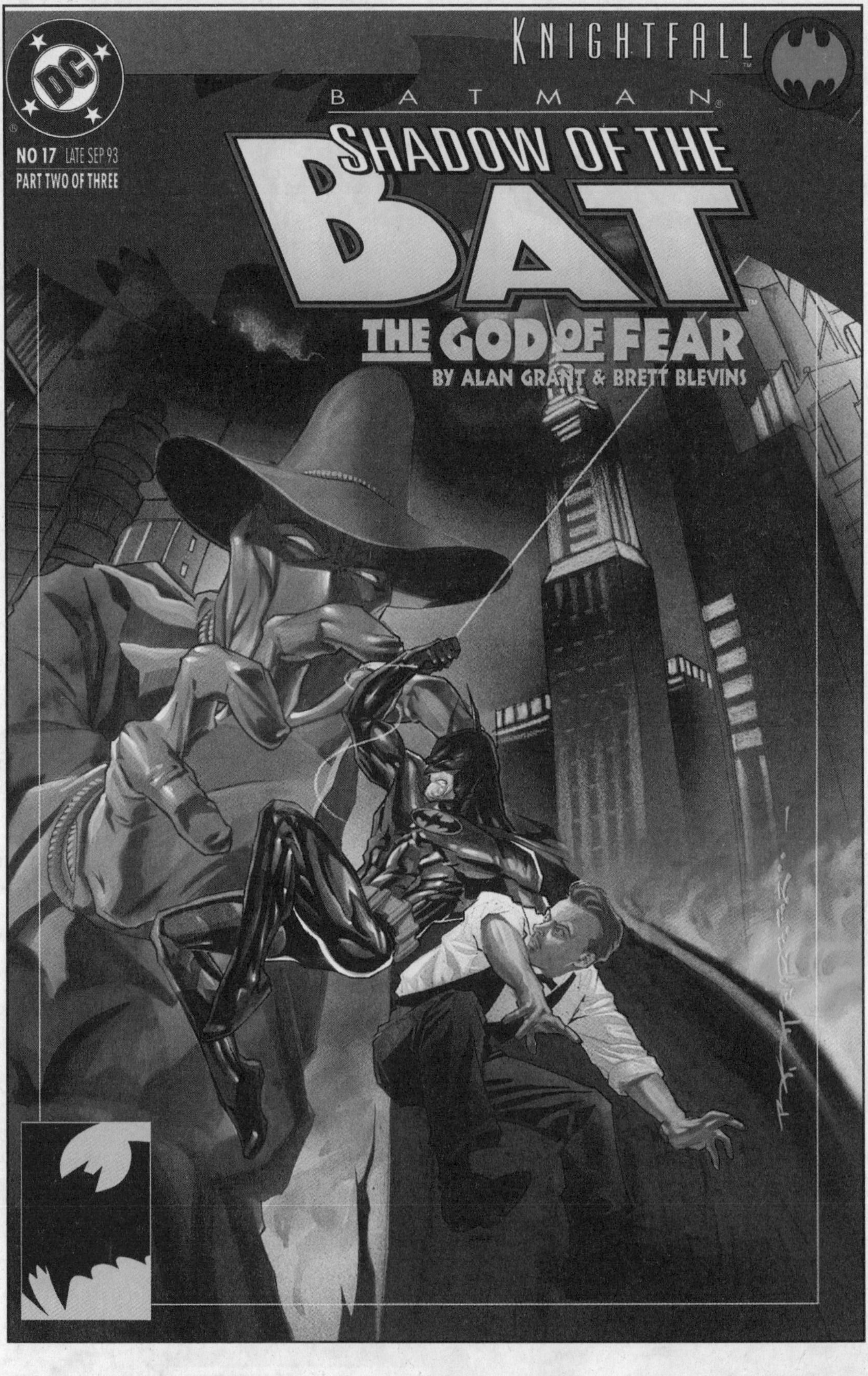
KNIGHTFALL
DC
BATMAN
NO 17 LATE SEP 93
PART TWO OF THREE
SHADOW OF THE BAT
THE GOD OF FEAR
BY ALAN GRANT & BRETT BLEVINS

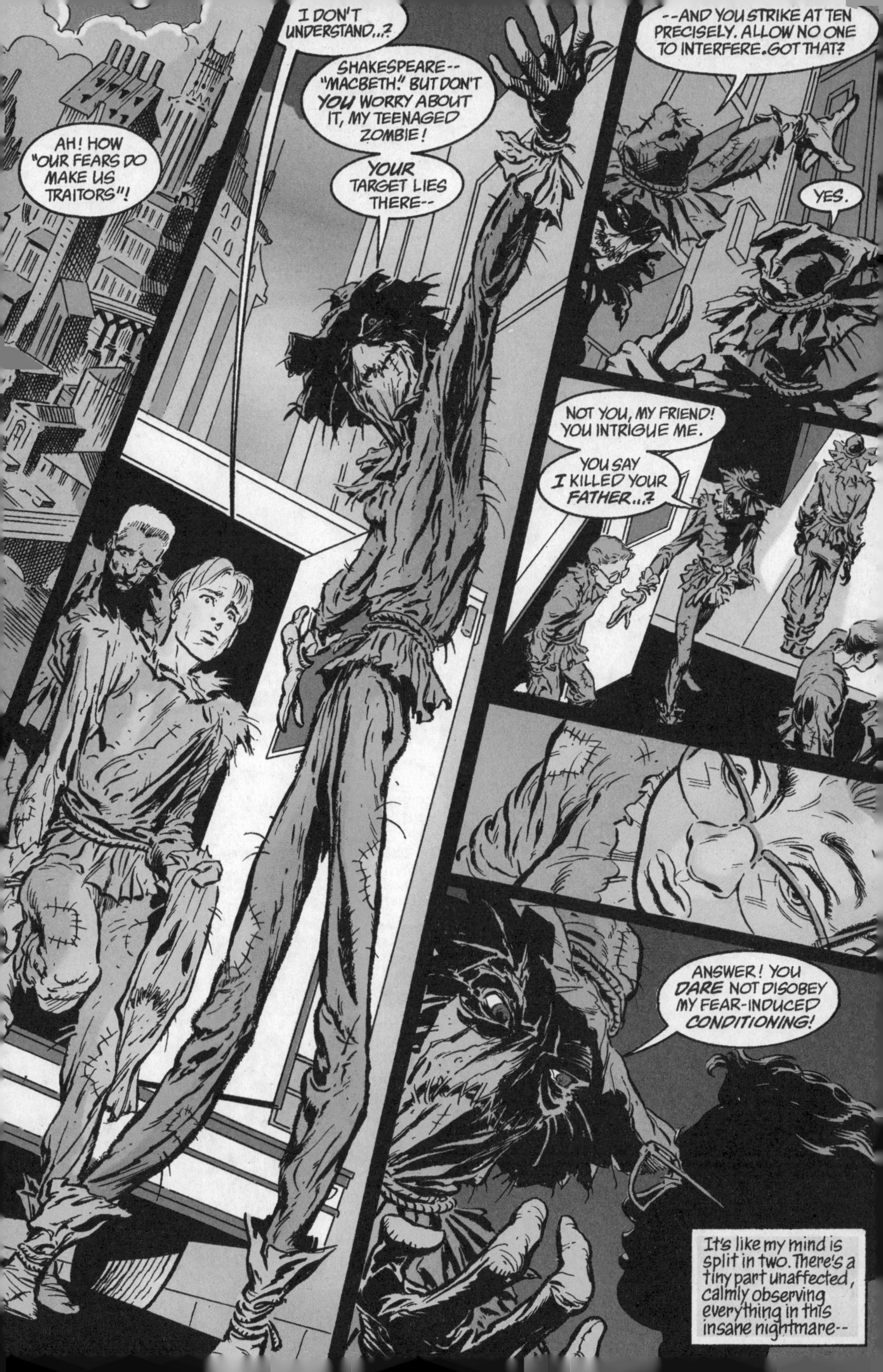
AH! HOW "OUR FEARS DO MAKE US TRAITORS"!
I DON'T UNDERSTAND...?
SHAKESPEARE-- "MACBETH." BUT DON'T YOU WORRY ABOUT IT, MY TEENAGED ZOMBIE!
YOUR TARGET LIES THERE--
--AND YOU STRIKE AT TEN PRECISELY. ALLOW NO ONE TO INTERFERE. GOT THAT?
YES.
NOT YOU, MY FRIEND! YOU INTRIGUE ME.
YOU SAY I KILLED YOUR FATHER...?
ANSWER! YOU DARE NOT DISOBEY MY FEAR-INDUCED CONDITIONING!
It's like my mind is split in two. There's a tiny part unaffected, calmly observing everything in this insane nightmare--

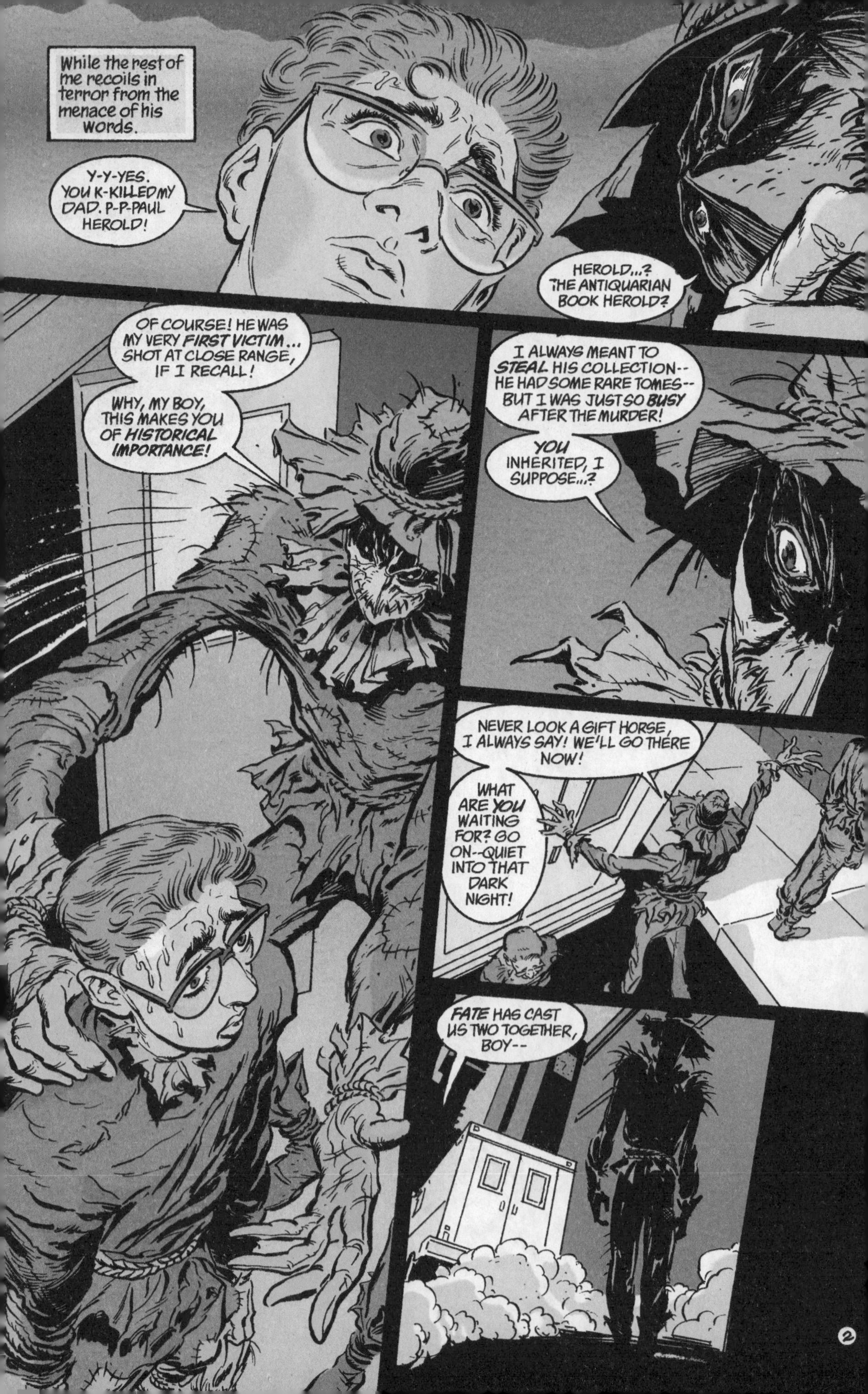
While the rest of me recoils in terror from the menace of his words.
Y-Y-YES. YOU K-KILLED MY DAD. P-P-PAUL HEROLD!
HEROLD...? THE ANTIQUARIAN BOOK HEROLD?
OF COURSE! HE WAS MY VERY FIRST VICTIM... SHOT AT CLOSE RANGE, IF I RECALL!
WHY, MY BOY, THIS MAKES YOU OF HISTORICAL IMPORTANCE!
I ALWAYS MEANT TO STEAL HIS COLLECTION-- HE HAD SOME RARE TOMES-- BUT I WAS JUST SO BUSY AFTER THE MURDER!
YOU INHERITED, I SUPPOSE...?
NEVER LOOK A GIFT HORSE, I ALWAYS SAY! WE'LL GO THERE NOW!
WHAT ARE YOU WAITING FOR? GO ON--QUIET INTO THAT DARK NIGHT!
FATE HAS CAST US TWO TOGETHER, BOY--
2

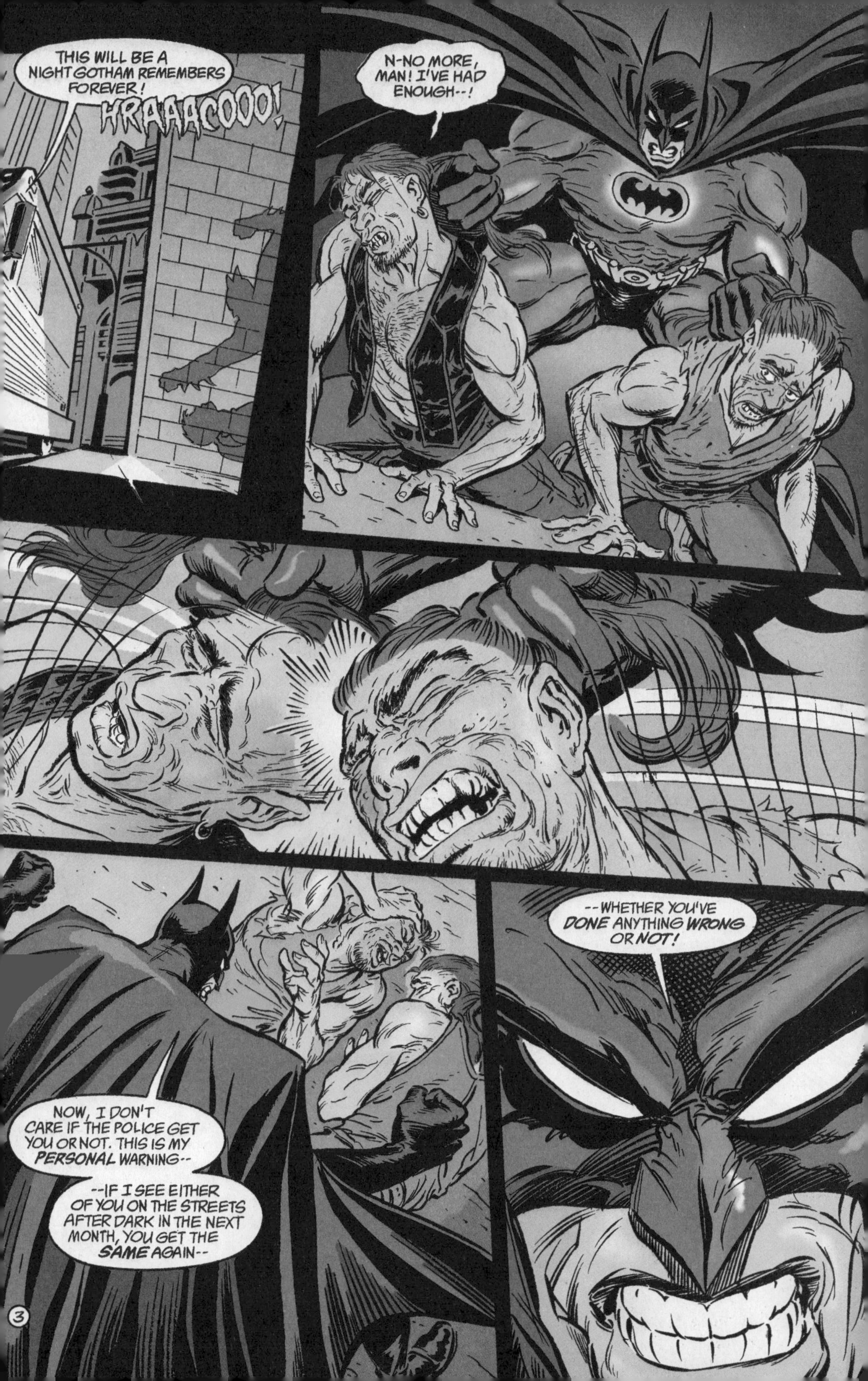
THIS WILL BE A NIGHT GOTHAM REMEMBERS FOREVER!
HRAAACOOO!
N-NO MORE, MAN! I'VE HAD ENOUGH--!
NOW, I DON'T CARE IF THE POLICE GET YOU OR NOT. THIS IS MY PERSONAL WARNING--
--IF I SEE EITHER OF YOU ON THE STREETS AFTER DARK IN THE NEXT MONTH, YOU GET THE SAME AGAIN--
--WHETHER YOU'VE DONE ANYTHING WRONG OR NOT!
3

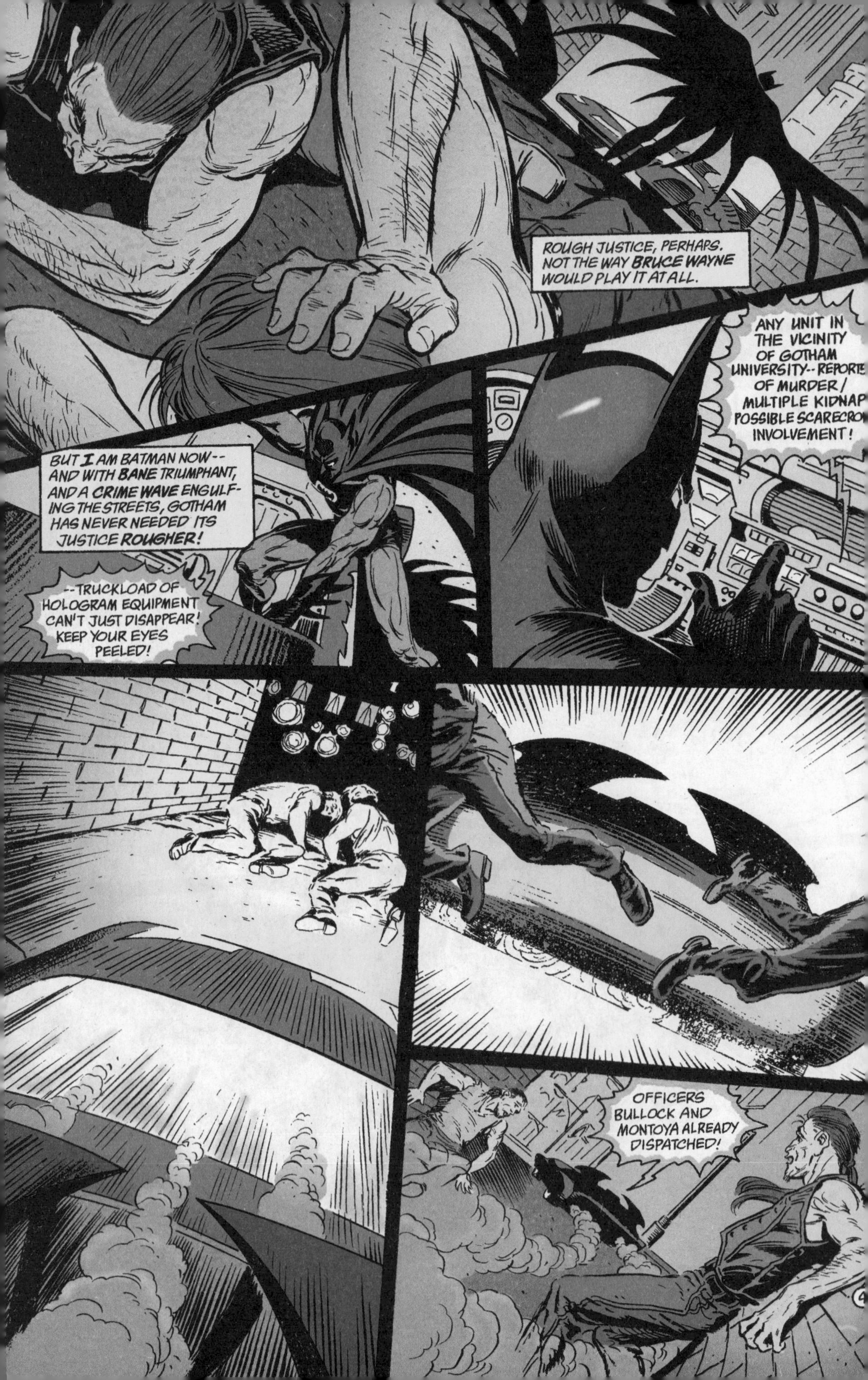
ROUGH JUSTICE, PERHAPS. NOT THE WAY BRUCE WAYNE WOULD PLAY IT AT ALL.
BUT I AM BATMAN NOW-- AND WITH BANE TRIUMPHANT, AND A CRIME WAVE ENGULFING THE STREETS, GOTHAM HAS NEVER NEEDED ITS JUSTICE ROUGHER!
ANY UNIT IN THE VICINITY OF GOTHAM UNIVERSITY-- REPORTE OF MURDER / MULTIPLE KIDNAP POSSIBLE SCARECRO INVOLVEMENT!
--TRUCKLOAD OF HOLOGRAM EQUIPMENT CAN'T JUST DISAPPEAR! KEEP YOUR EYES PEELED!
OFFICERS BULLOCK AND MONTOYA ALREADY DISPATCHED!
4

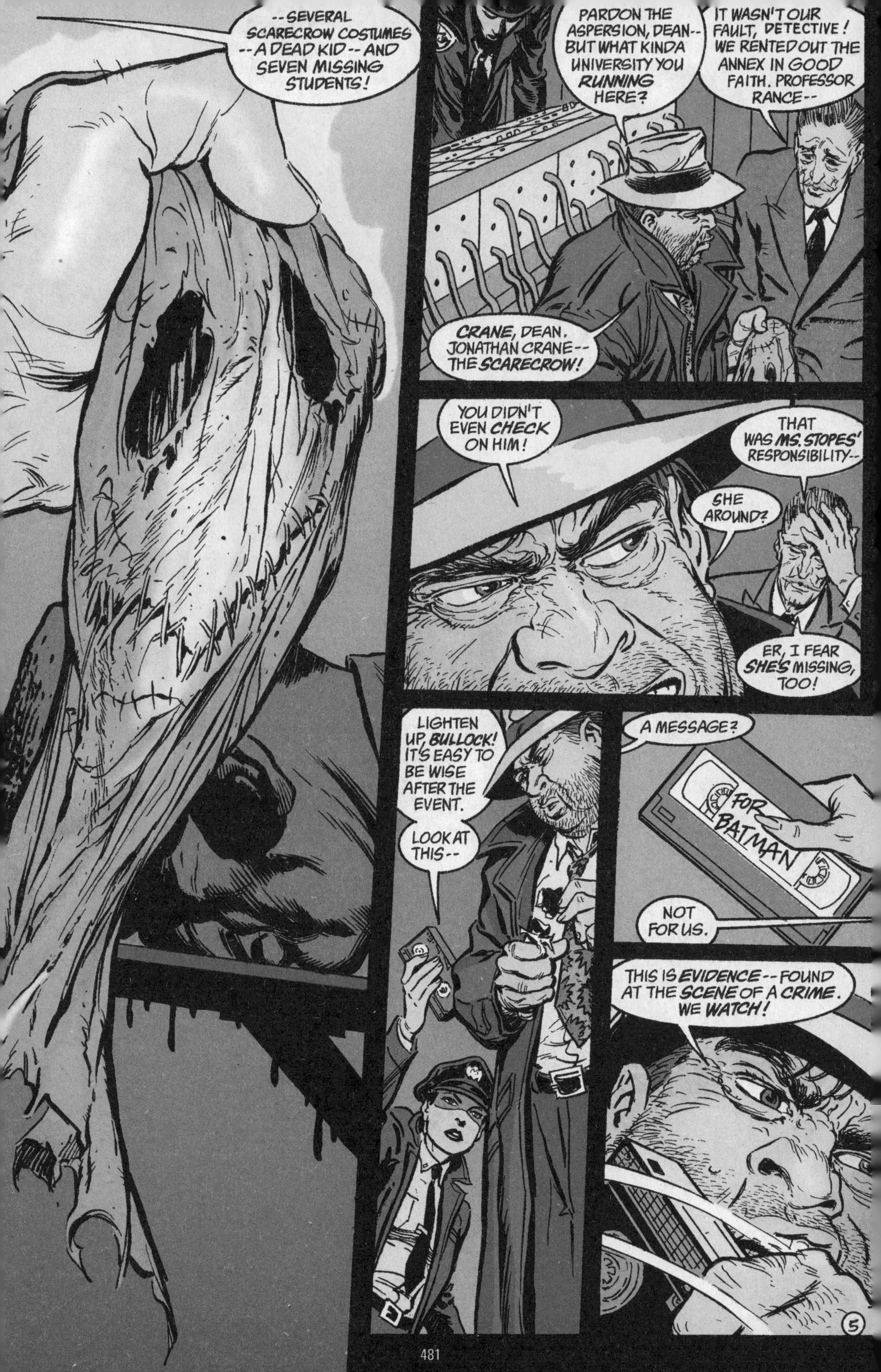
--SEVERAL SCARECROW COSTUMES --A DEAD KID--AND SEVEN MISSING STUDENTS!
PARDON THE ASPERSION, DEAN--BUT WHAT KINDA UNIVERSITY YOU RUNNING HERE?
IT WASN'T OUR FAULT, DETECTIVE! WE RENTED OUT THE ANNEX IN GOOD FAITH. PROFESSOR RANCE--
CRANE, DEAN. JONATHAN CRANE--THE SCARECROW!
YOU DIDN'T EVEN CHECK ON HIM!
THAT WAS MS. STOPES' RESPONSIBILITY--
SHE AROUND?
ER, I FEAR SHE'S MISSING, TOO!
LIGHTEN UP, BULLOCK! IT'S EASY TO BE WISE AFTER THE EVENT.
LOOK AT THIS--
A MESSAGE?
FOR BATMAN
NOT FOR US.
THIS IS EVIDENCE--FOUND AT THE SCENE OF A CRIME. WE WATCH!
5

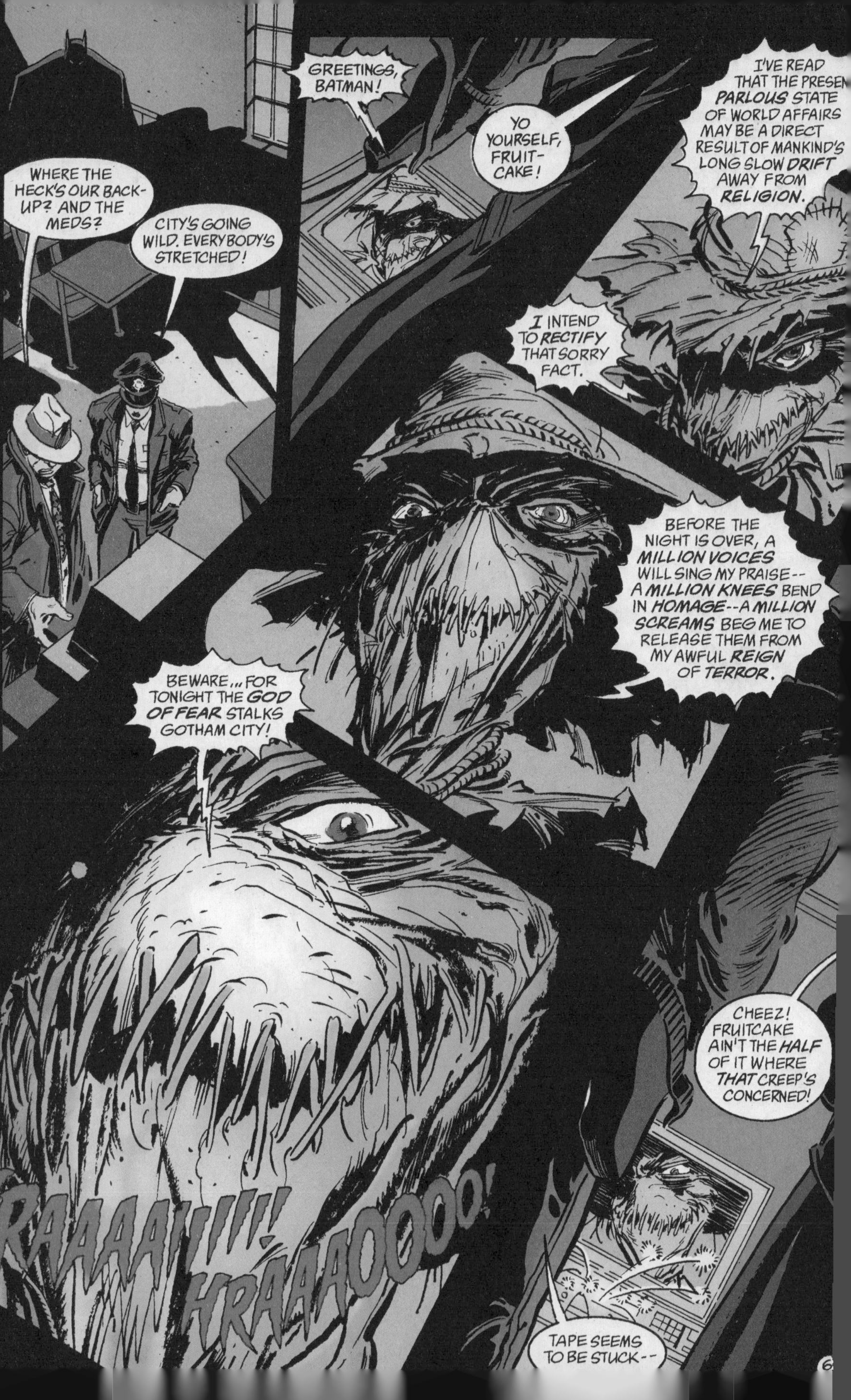
WHERE THE HECK'S OUR BACK-UP? AND THE MEDS?
CITY'S GOING WILD. EVERYBODY'S STRETCHED!
GREETINGS, BATMAN!
YO YOURSELF, FRUIT-CAKE!
I'VE READ THAT THE PRESEN PARLOUS STATE OF WORLD AFFAIRS MAY BE A DIRECT RESULT OF MANKIND'S LONG SLOW DRIFT AWAY FROM RELIGION.
I INTEND TO RECTIFY THAT SORRY FACT.
BEFORE THE NIGHT IS OVER, A MILLION VOICES WILL SING MY PRAISE-- A MILLION KNEES BEND IN HOMAGE--A MILLION SCREAMS BEG ME TO RELEASE THEM FROM MY AWFUL REIGN OF TERROR.
BEWARE... FOR TONIGHT THE GOD OF FEAR STALKS GOTHAM CITY!
RAAAAH!!!! HRAAAOOOOO!
CHEEZ! FRUITCAKE AIN'T THE HALF OF IT WHERE THAT CREEP'S CONCERNED!
TAPE SEEMS TO BE STUCK--

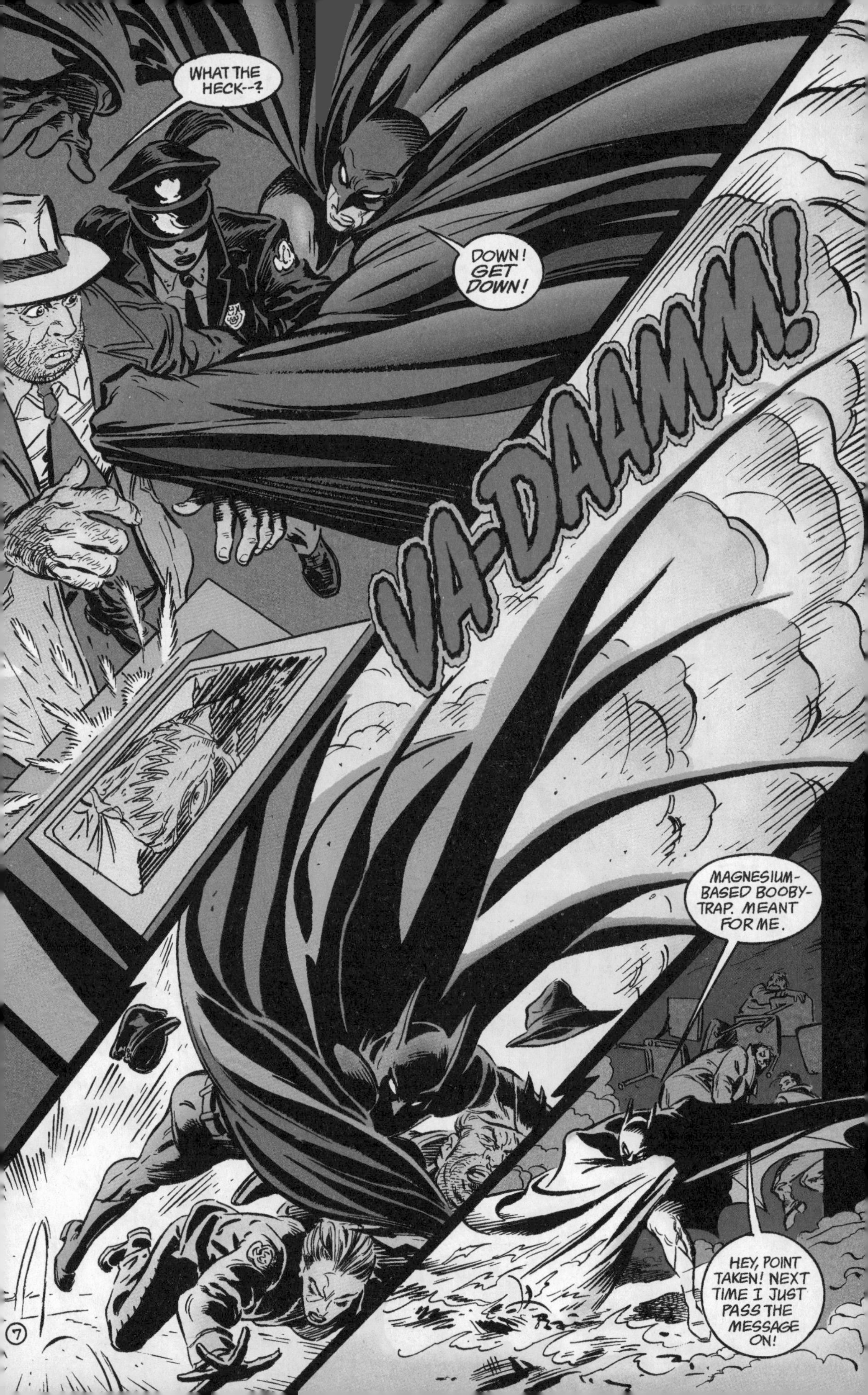
WHAT THE HECK--?
DOWN! GET DOWN!
VA-DAMM!
MAGNESIUM-BASED BOOBY-TRAP. MEANT FOR ME.
HEY, POINT TAKEN! NEXT TIME I JUST PASS THE MESSAGE ON!
7

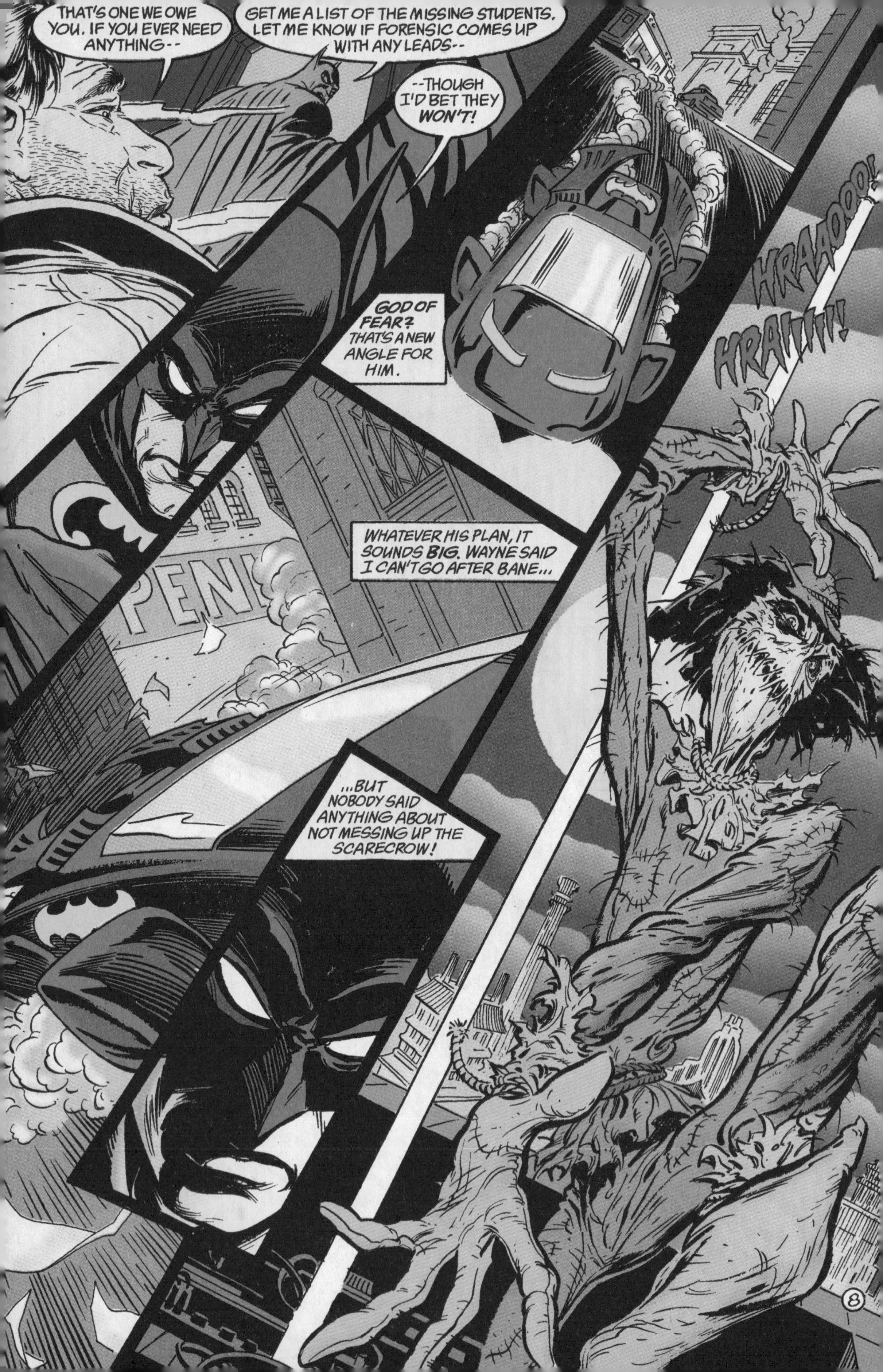
THAT'S ONE WE OWE YOU. IF YOU EVER NEED ANYTHING--
GET ME A LIST OF THE MISSING STUDENTS. LET ME KNOW IF FORENSIC COMES UP WITH ANY LEADS--
--THOUGH I'D BET THEY WON'T!
GOD OF FEAR? THAT'S A NEW ANGLE FOR HIM.
PEN
WHATEVER HIS PLAN, IT SOUNDS BIG. WAYNE SAID I CAN'T GO AFTER BANE...
...BUT NOBODY SAID ANYTHING ABOUT NOT MESSING UP THE SCARECROW!
HRAAOOO!
HRAIIIII!
8

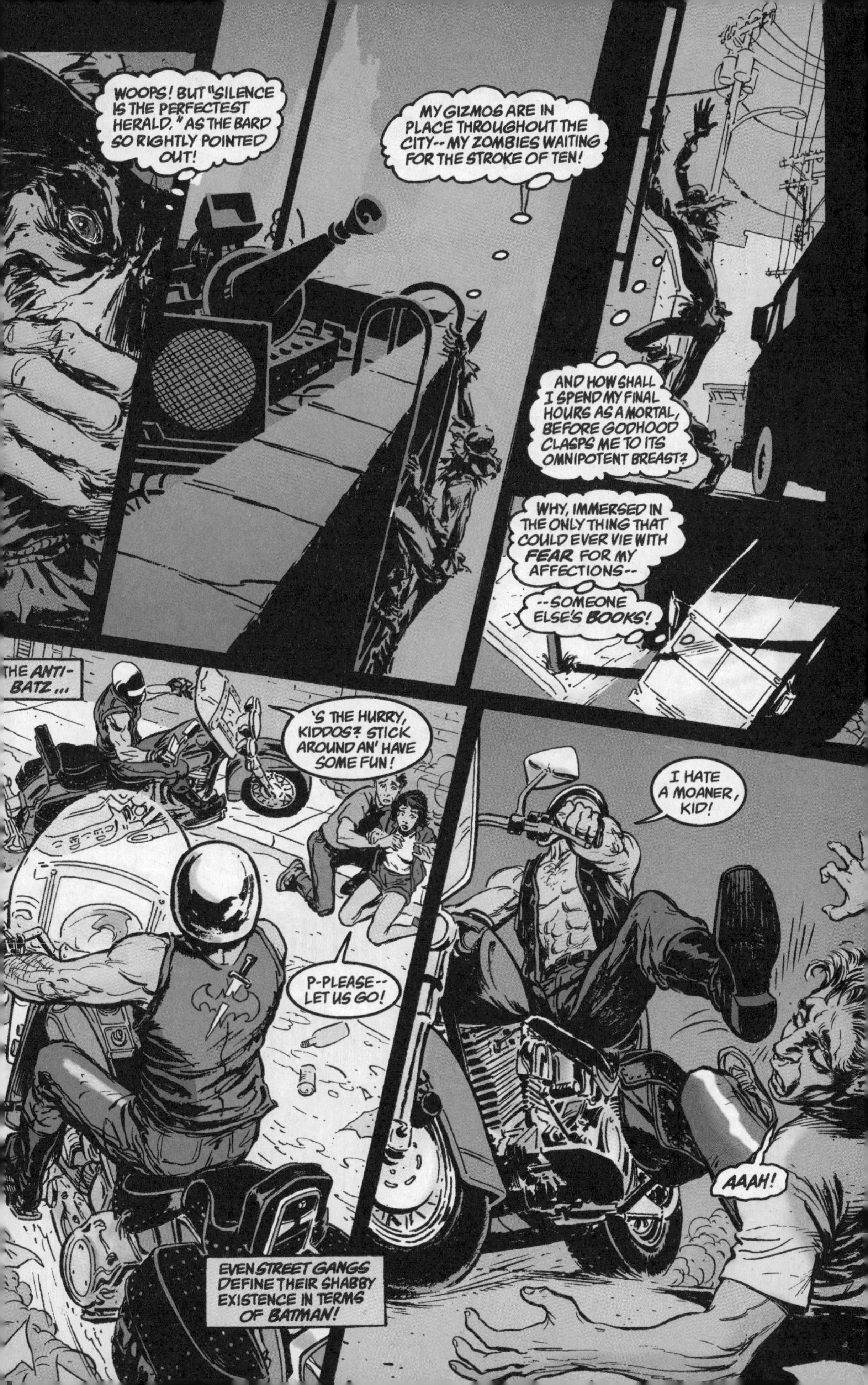
WOOPS! BUT "SILENCE IS THE PERFECTEST HERALD," AS THE BARD SO RIGHTLY POINTED OUT!
MY GIZMOS ARE IN PLACE THROUGHOUT THE CITY-- MY ZOMBIES WAITING FOR THE STROKE OF TEN!
AND HOW SHALL I SPEND MY FINAL HOURS AS A MORTAL, BEFORE GODHOOD CLASPS ME TO ITS OMNIPOTENT BREAST?
WHY, IMMERSED IN THE ONLY THING THAT COULD EVER VIE WITH FEAR FOR MY AFFECTIONS--
--SOMEONE ELSE'S BOOKS!
THE ANTI-BATZ...
'S THE HURRY, KIDDOS? STICK AROUND AN' HAVE SOME FUN!
P-PLEASE-- LET US GO!
EVEN STREET GANGS DEFINE THEIR SHABBY EXISTENCE IN TERMS OF BATMAN!
I HATE A MOANER, KID!
AAAH!

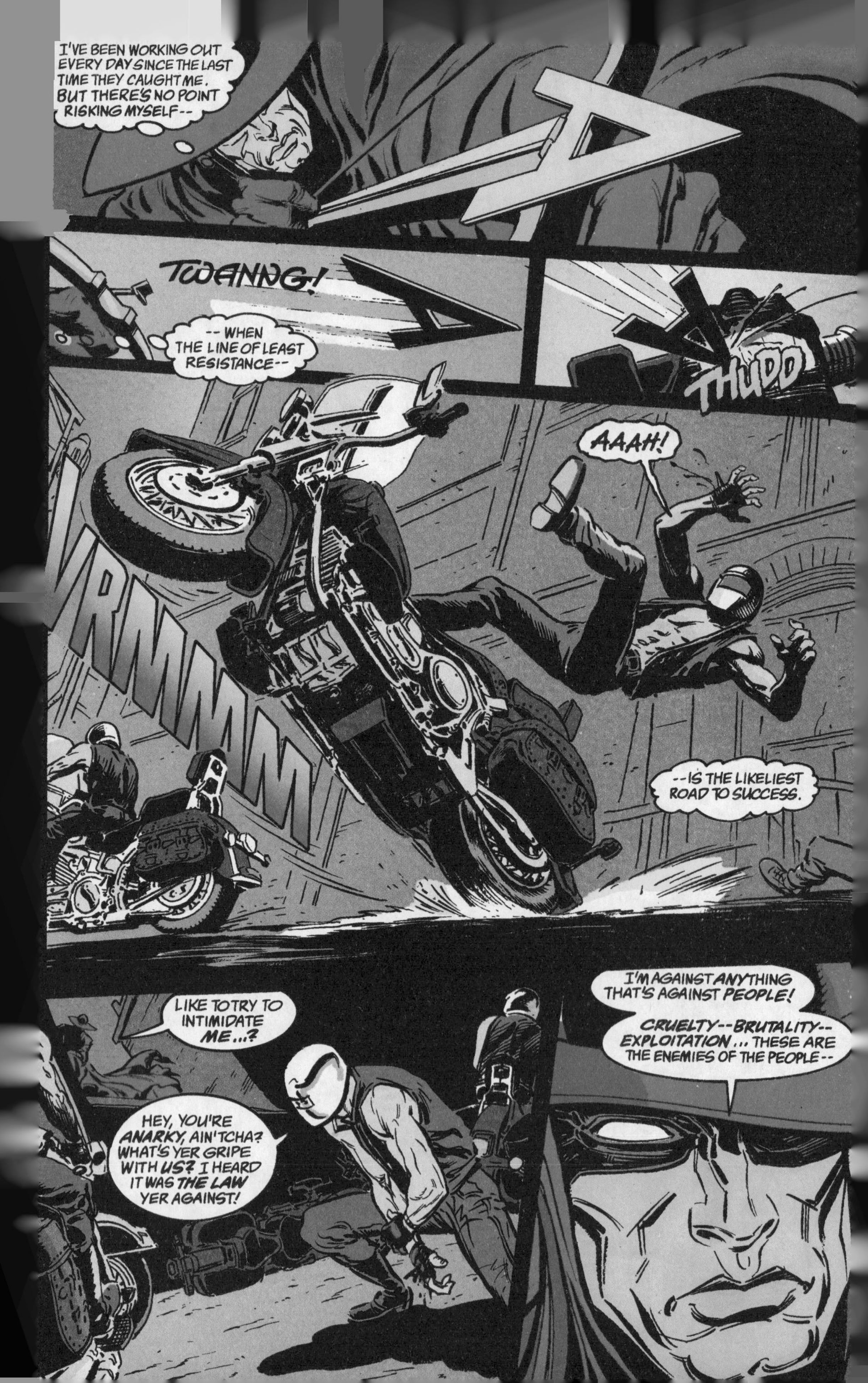

I'VE BEEN WORKING OUT EVERY DAY SINCE THE LAST TIME THEY CAUGHT ME. BUT THERE'S NO POINT RISKING MYSELF--
TWANNG!
--WHEN THE LINE OF LEAST RESISTANCE--
THUDD
AAAH!
VRMMMM
--IS THE LIKELIEST ROAD TO SUCCESS.
LIKE TO TRY TO INTIMIDATE ME...?
HEY, YOU'RE ANARKY, AIN'TCHA? WHAT'S YER GRIPE WITH US? I HEARD IT WAS THE LAW YER AGAINST!
I'M AGAINST ANYTHING THAT'S AGAINST PEOPLE!
CRUELTY--BRUTALITY--EXPLOITATION... THESE ARE THE ENEMIES OF THE PEOPLE--

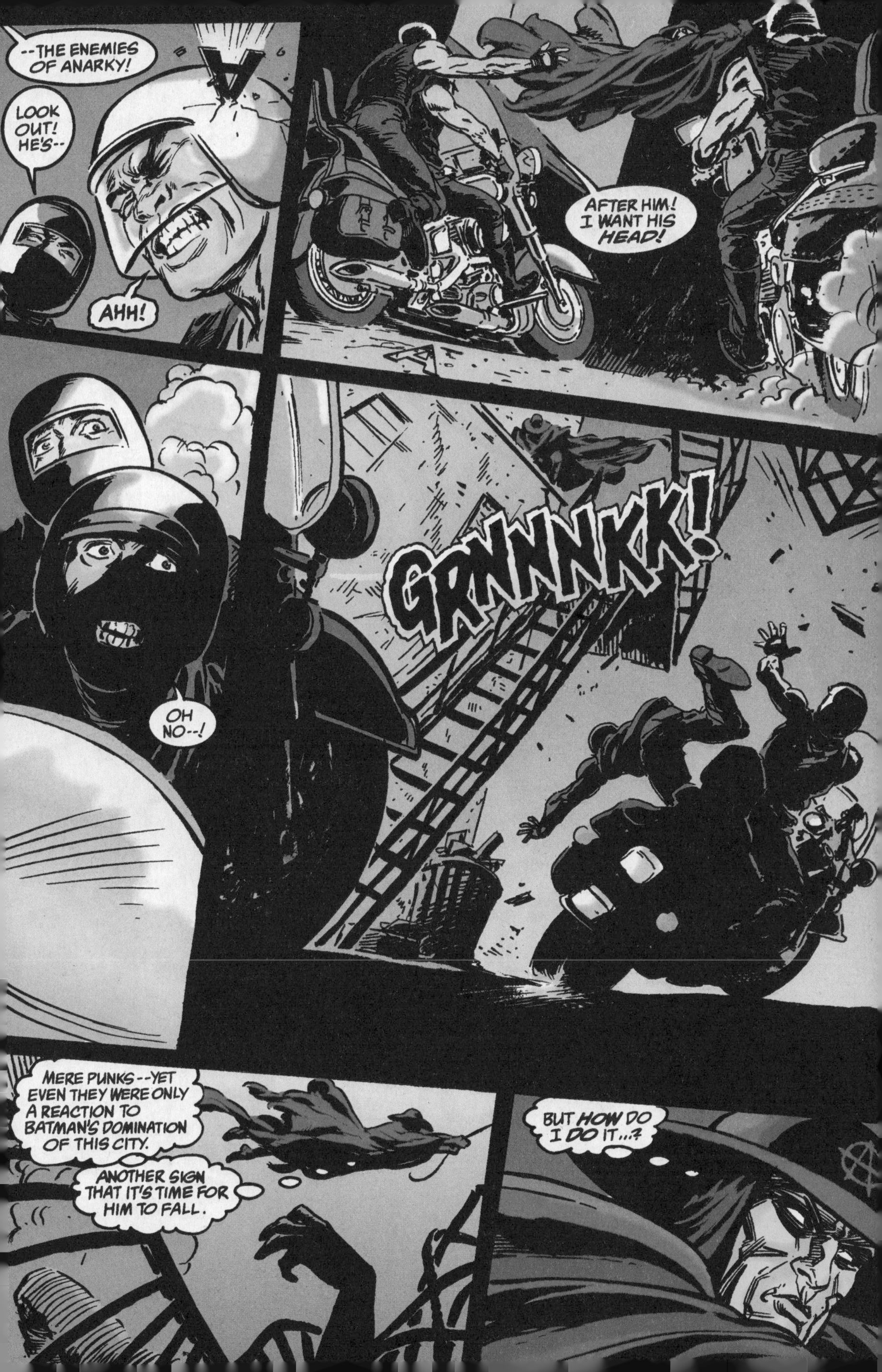
--THE ENEMIES OF ANARKY!
LOOK OUT! HE'S--
AHH!
AFTER HIM! I WANT HIS HEAD!
OH NO--!
GRNNNKK!
MERE PUNKS--YET EVEN THEY WERE ONLY A REACTION TO BATMAN'S DOMINATION OF THIS CITY.
ANOTHER SIGN THAT IT'S TIME FOR HIM TO FALL.
BUT HOW DO I DO IT...?

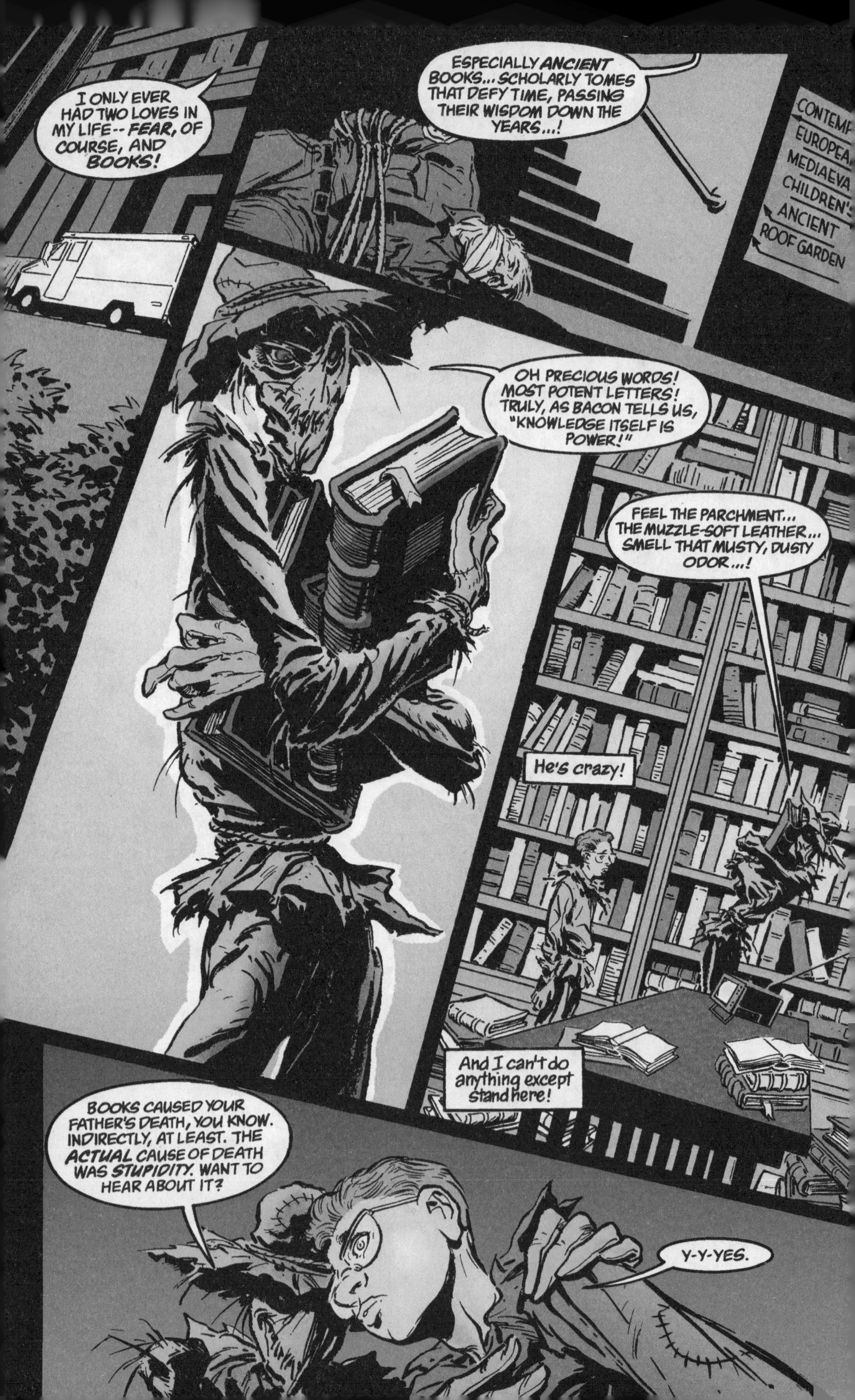
I ONLY EVER HAD TWO LOVES IN MY LIFE-- FEAR, OF COURSE, AND BOOKS!
ESPECIALLY ANCIENT BOOKS... SCHOLARLY TOMES THAT DEFY TIME, PASSING THEIR WISDOM DOWN THE YEARS...!
CONTEMP
EUROPEA
MEDIAEVA
CHILDREN'S
ANCIENT
ROOF GARDEN
OH PRECIOUS WORDS! MOST POTENT LETTERS! TRULY, AS BACON TELLS US, "KNOWLEDGE ITSELF IS POWER!"
FEEL THE PARCHMENT... THE MUZZLE-SOFT LEATHER... SMELL THAT MUSTY, DUSTY ODOR...!
He's crazy!
And I can't do anything except stand here!
BOOKS CAUSED YOUR FATHER'S DEATH, YOU KNOW. INDIRECTLY, AT LEAST. THE ACTUAL CAUSE OF DEATH WAS STUPIDITY. WANT TO HEAR ABOUT IT?
Y-Y-YES.

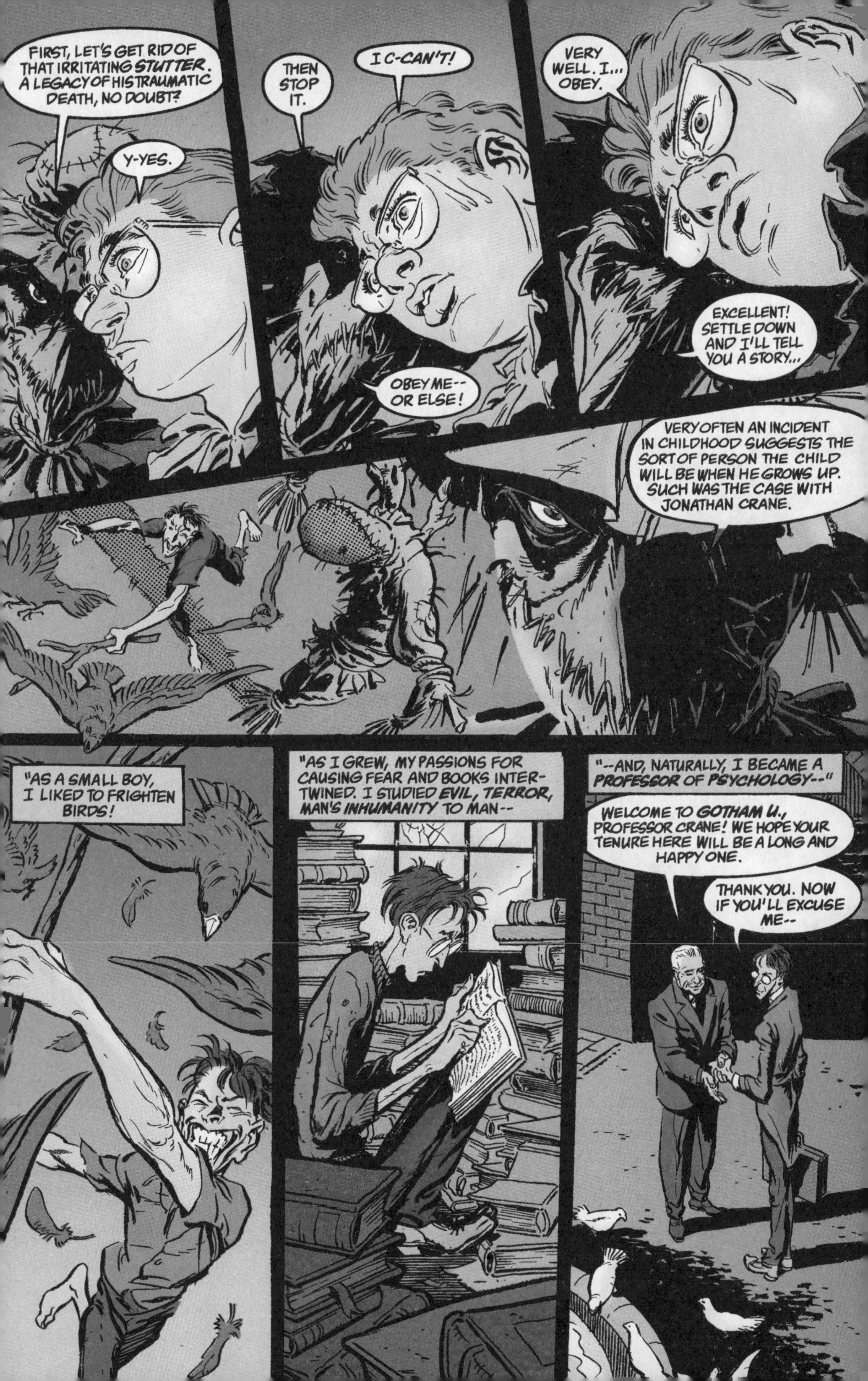
FIRST, LET'S GET RID OF THAT IRRITATING STUTTER. A LEGACY OF HIS TRAUMATIC DEATH, NO DOUBT?
Y-YES.
THEN STOP IT.
I C-CAN'T!
OBEY ME-- OR ELSE!
VERY WELL. I... OBEY.
EXCELLENT! SETTLE DOWN AND I'LL TELL YOU A STORY...
VERY OFTEN AN INCIDENT IN CHILDHOOD SUGGESTS THE SORT OF PERSON THE CHILD WILL BE WHEN HE GROWS UP. SUCH WAS THE CASE WITH JONATHAN CRANE.
"AS A SMALL BOY, I LIKED TO FRIGHTEN BIRDS!
"AS I GREW, MY PASSIONS FOR CAUSING FEAR AND BOOKS INTER-TWINED. I STUDIED EVIL, TERROR, MAN'S INHUMANITY TO MAN--
"--AND, NATURALLY, I BECAME A PROFESSOR OF PSYCHOLOGY--"
WELCOME TO GOTHAM U., PROFESSOR CRANE! WE HOPE YOUR TENURE HERE WILL BE A LONG AND HAPPY ONE.
THANK YOU. NOW IF YOU'LL EXCUSE ME--

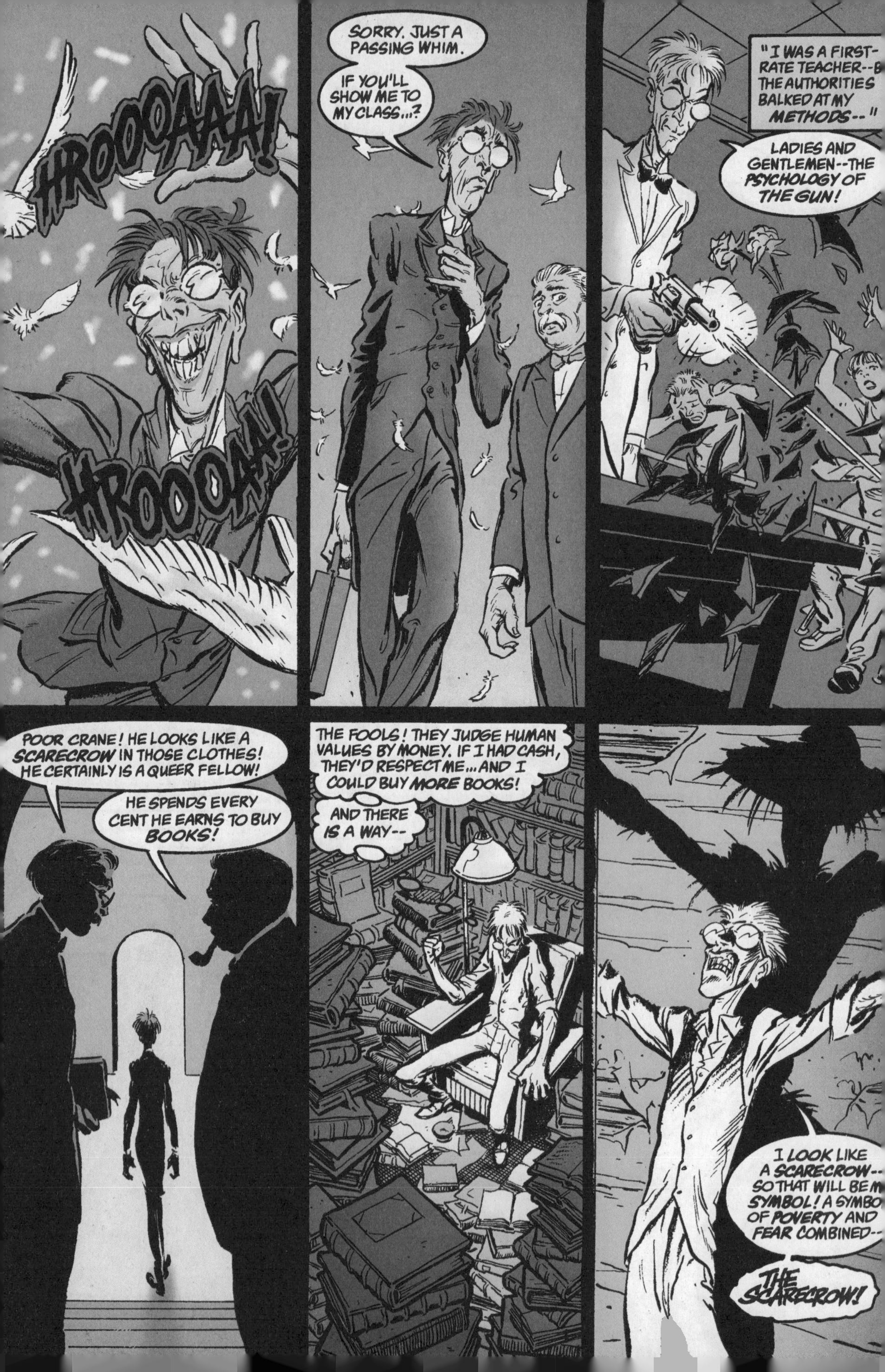
HROOOAAA!
HROOOAA!
SORRY. JUST A PASSING WHIM.
IF YOU'LL SHOW ME TO MY CLASS...?
"I WAS A FIRST-RATE TEACHER--B THE AUTHORITIES BALKED AT MY METHODS--"
LADIES AND GENTLEMEN--THE PSYCHOLOGY OF THE GUN!
POOR CRANE! HE LOOKS LIKE A SCARECROW IN THOSE CLOTHES! HE CERTAINLY IS A QUEER FELLOW!
HE SPENDS EVERY CENT HE EARNS TO BUY BOOKS!
THE FOOLS! THEY JUDGE HUMAN VALUES BY MONEY. IF I HAD CASH, THEY'D RESPECT ME... AND I COULD BUY MORE BOOKS!
AND THERE IS A WAY--
I LOOK LIKE A SCARECROW-- SO THAT WILL BE M SYMBOL! A SYMBO OF POVERTY AND FEAR COMBINED--
THE SCARECROW!

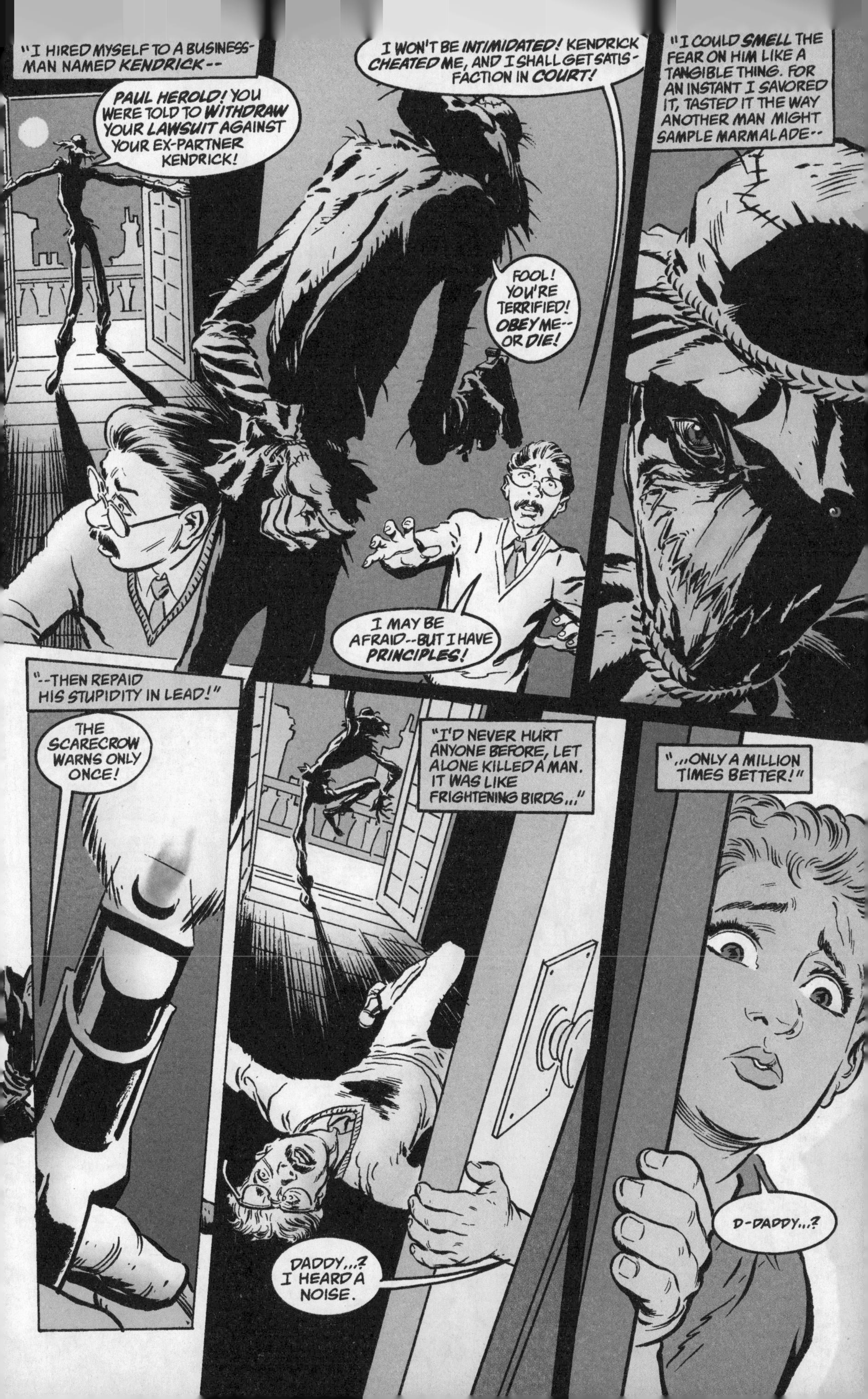
"I HIRED MYSELF TO A BUSINESS-MAN NAMED KENDRICK--
PAUL HEROLD! YOU WERE TOLD TO WITHDRAW YOUR LAWSUIT AGAINST YOUR EX-PARTNER KENDRICK!
I WON'T BE INTIMIDATED! KENDRICK CHEATED ME, AND I SHALL GET SATIS-FACTION IN COURT!
FOOL! YOU'RE TERRIFIED! OBEY ME--OR DIE!
I MAY BE AFRAID--BUT I HAVE PRINCIPLES!
"I COULD SMELL THE FEAR ON HIM LIKE A TANGIBLE THING. FOR AN INSTANT I SAVORED IT, TASTED IT THE WAY ANOTHER MAN MIGHT SAMPLE MARMALADE--
"--THEN REPAID HIS STUPIDITY IN LEAD!"
THE SCARECROW WARNS ONLY ONCE!
"I'D NEVER HURT ANYONE BEFORE, LET ALONE KILLED A MAN. IT WAS LIKE FRIGHTENING BIRDS..."
DADDY...? I HEARD A NOISE.
"...ONLY A MILLION TIMES BETTER!"
D-DADDY...?

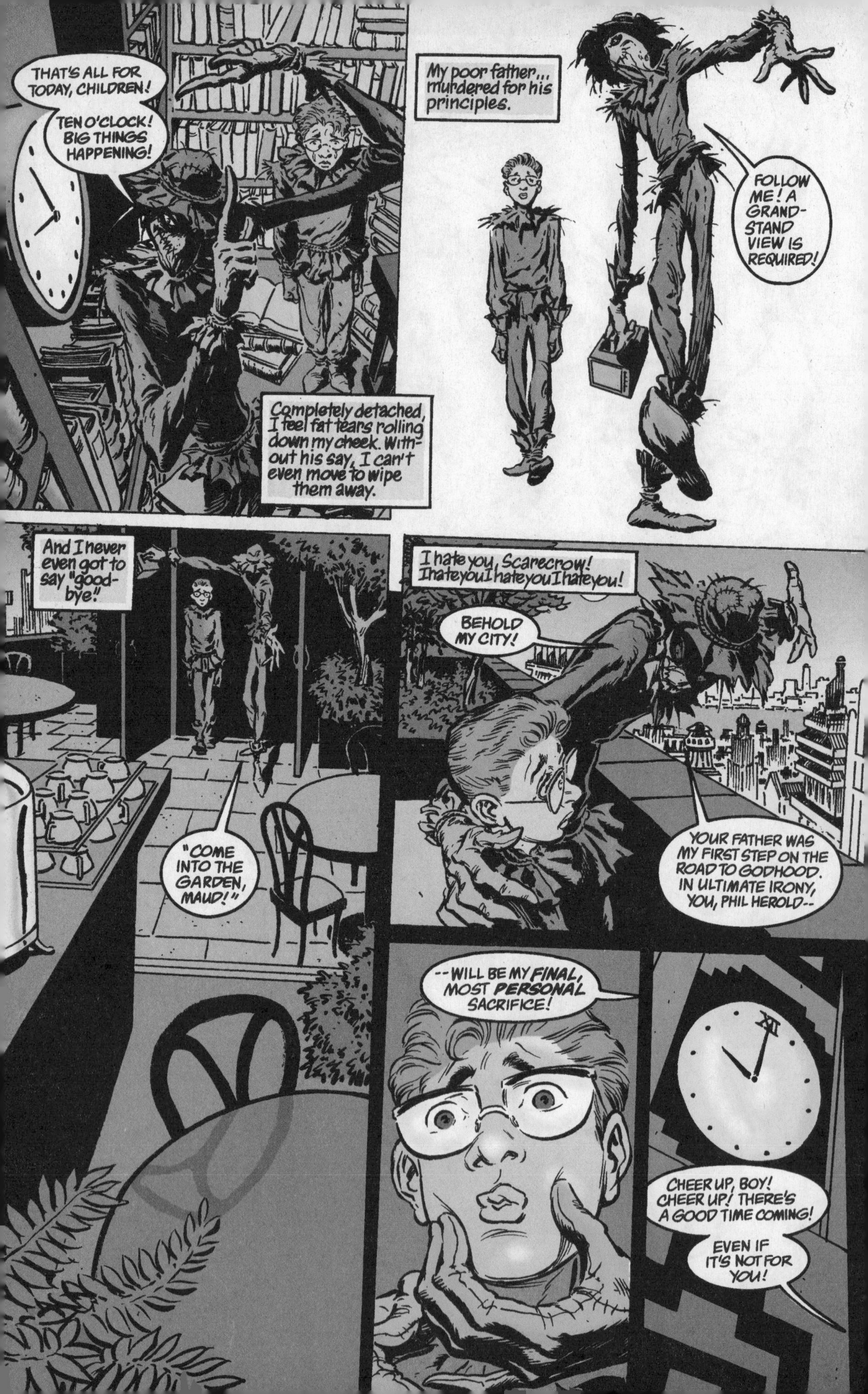
THAT'S ALL FOR TODAY, CHILDREN!
TEN O'CLOCK! BIG THINGS HAPPENING!
Completely detached, I feel fat tears rolling down my cheek. Without his say, I can't even move to wipe them away.
My poor father... murdered for his principles.
FOLLOW ME! A GRANDSTAND VIEW IS REQUIRED!
And I never even got to say "good-bye."
"COME INTO THE GARDEN, MAUD!"
I hate you, Scarecrow! I hate you I hate you I hate you!
BEHOLD MY CITY!
YOUR FATHER WAS MY FIRST STEP ON THE ROAD TO GODHOOD. IN ULTIMATE IRONY, YOU, PHIL HEROLD--
--WILL BE MY FINAL, MOST PERSONAL SACRIFICE!
CHEER UP, BOY! CHEER UP! THERE'S A GOOD TIME COMING!
EVEN IF IT'S NOT FOR YOU!

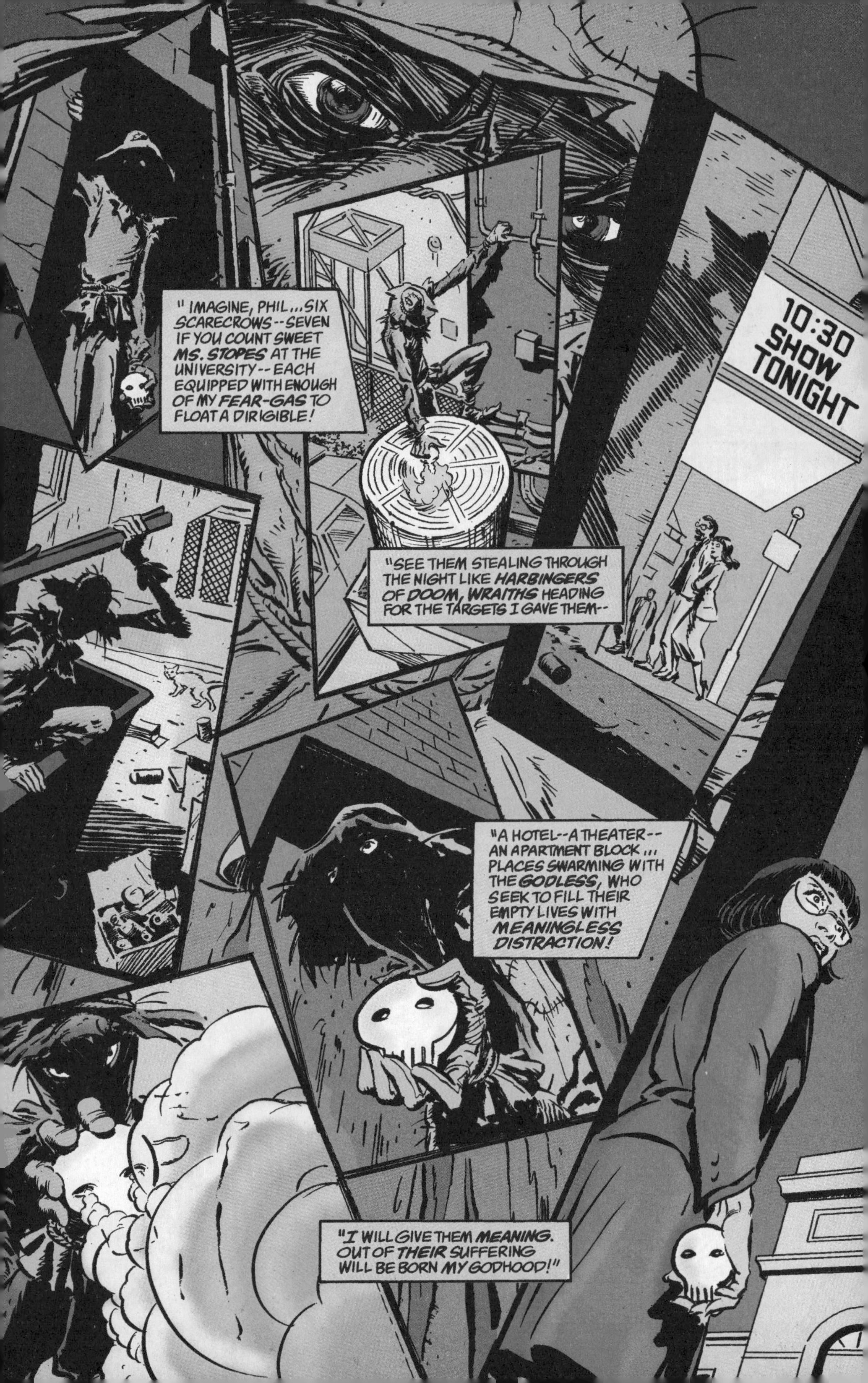
"IMAGINE, PHIL... SIX SCARECROWS--SEVEN IF YOU COUNT SWEET MS. STOPES AT THE UNIVERSITY--EACH EQUIPPED WITH ENOUGH OF MY FEAR-GAS TO FLOAT A DIRIGIBLE!
10:30 SHOW TONIGHT
"SEE THEM STEALING THROUGH THE NIGHT LIKE HARBINGERS OF DOOM, WRAITHS HEADING FOR THE TARGETS I GAVE THEM--
"A HOTEL--A THEATER--AN APARTMENT BLOCK... PLACES SWARMING WITH THE GODLESS, WHO SEEK TO FILL THEIR EMPTY LIVES WITH MEANINGLESS DISTRACTION!
"I WILL GIVE THEM MEANING. OUT OF THEIR SUFFERING WILL BE BORN MY GODHOOD!"

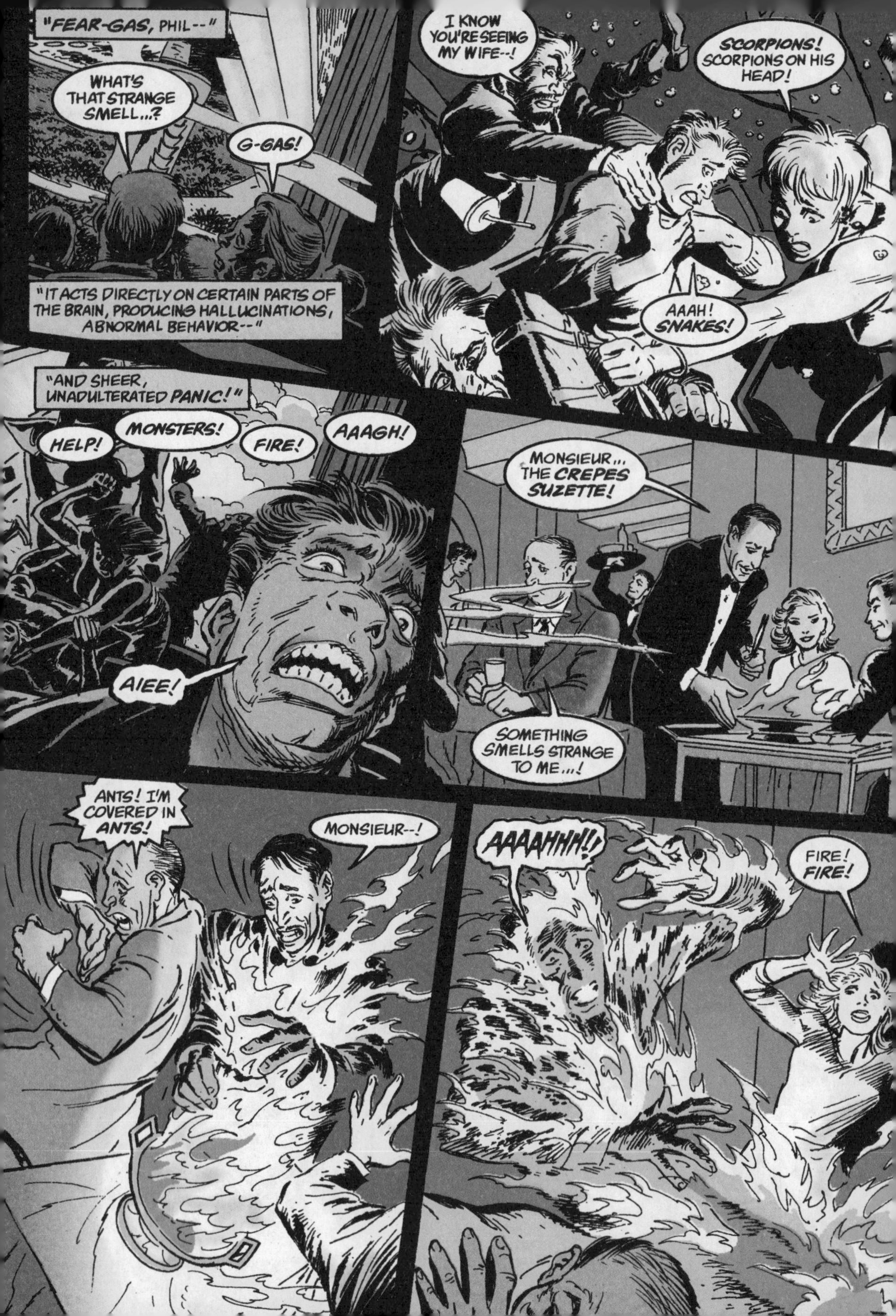
"FEAR-GAS, PHIL--"
WHAT'S THAT STRANGE SMELL...?
G-GAS!
I KNOW YOU'RE SEEING MY WIFE--!
SCORPIONS! SCORPIONS ON HIS HEAD!
"IT ACTS DIRECTLY ON CERTAIN PARTS OF THE BRAIN, PRODUCING HALLUCINATIONS, ABNORMAL BEHAVIOR--"
AAAH! SNAKES!
"AND SHEER, UNADULTERATED PANIC!"
HELP!
MONSTERS!
FIRE!
AAAGH!
AIEE!
MONSIEUR... THE CREPES SUZETTE!
SOMETHING SMELLS STRANGE TO ME...!
ANTS! I'M COVERED IN ANTS!
MONSIEUR--!
AAAAHHH!!
FIRE! FIRE!

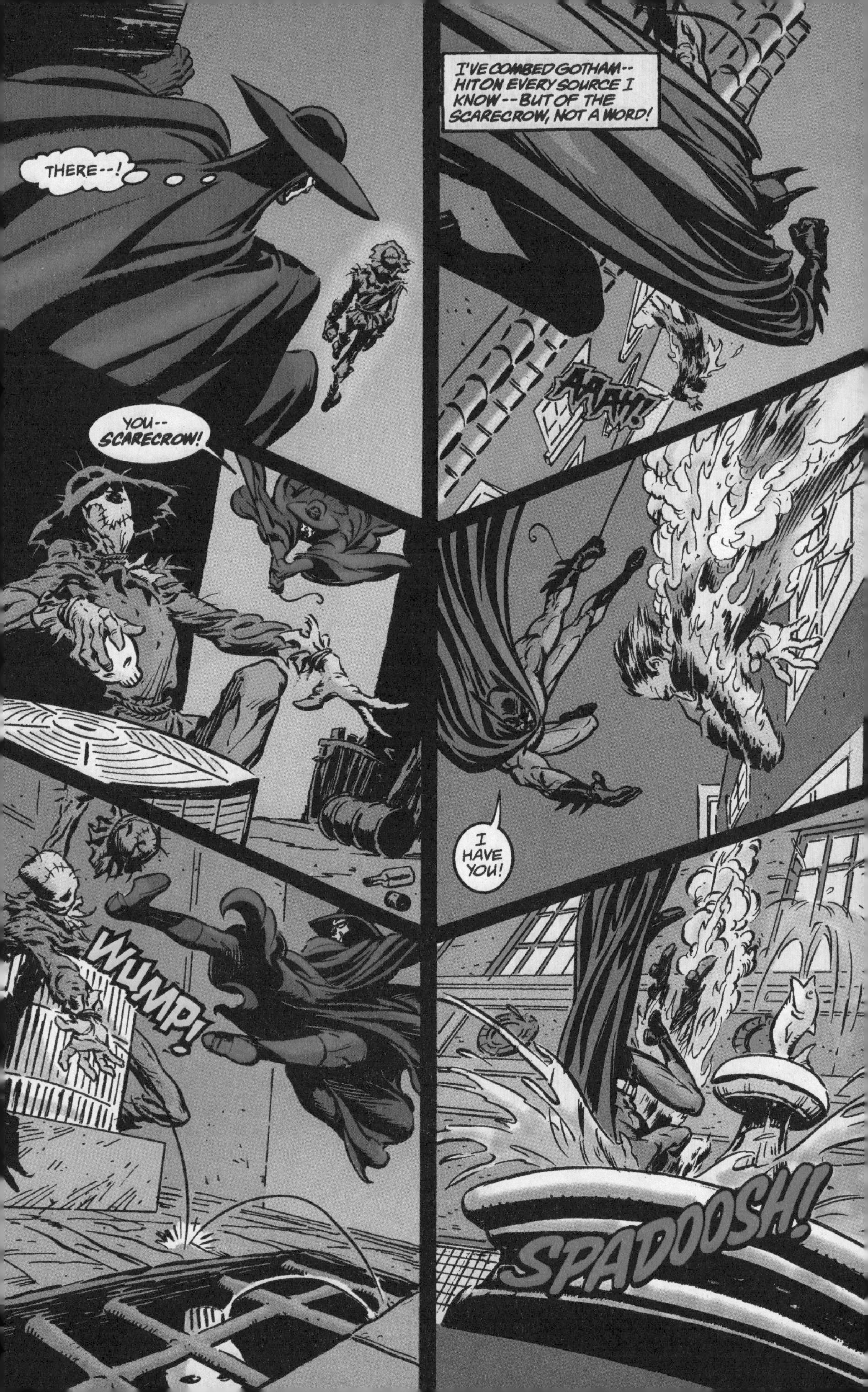
I'VE COMBED GOTHAM--HIT ON EVERY SOURCE I KNOW--BUT OF THE SCARECROW, NOT A WORD!
THERE--!
AAAHH!
YOU--SCARECROW!
I HAVE YOU!
WUMP!
SPADOOSH!

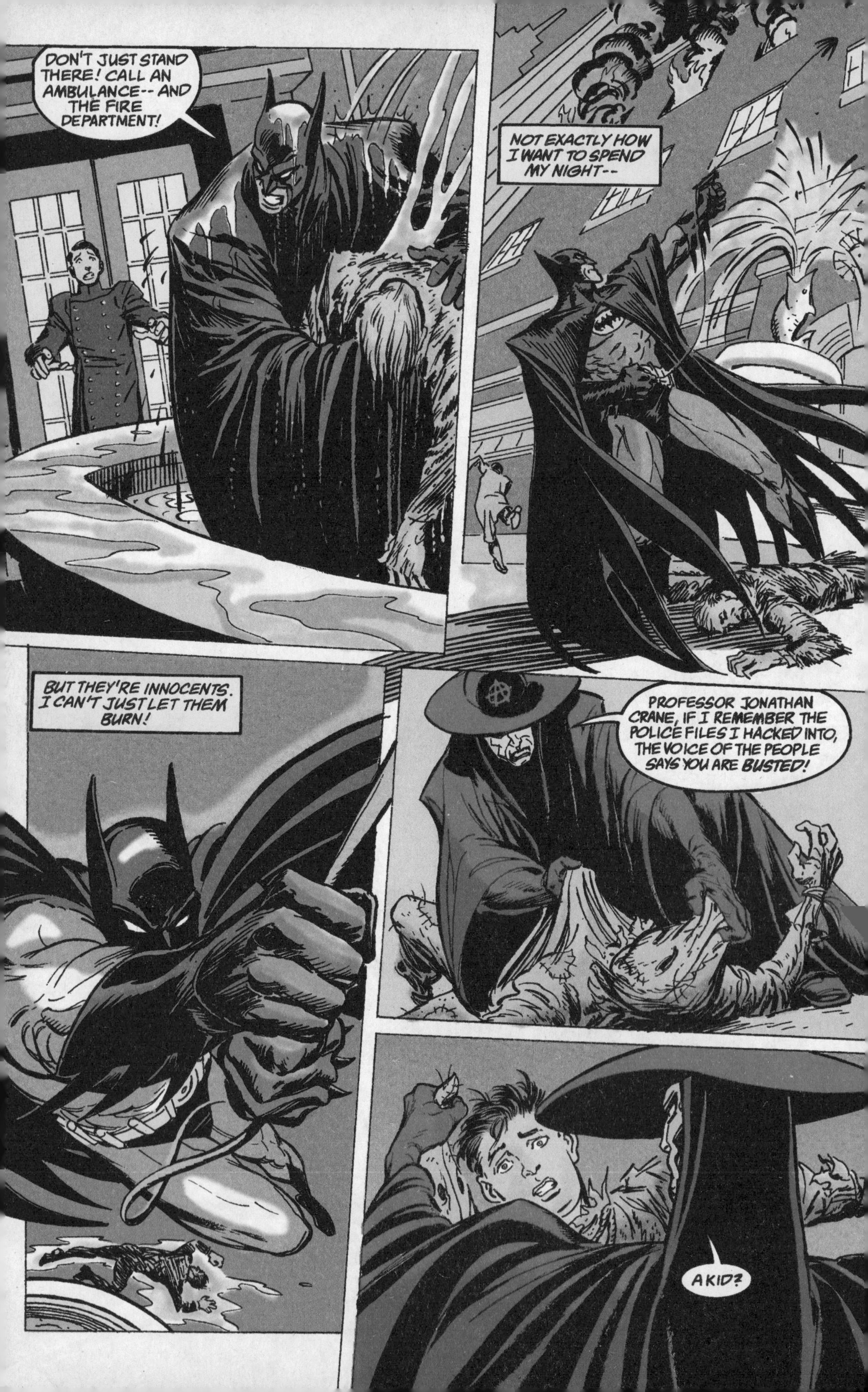
DON'T JUST STAND THERE! CALL AN AMBULANCE-- AND THE FIRE DEPARTMENT!
NOT EXACTLY HOW I WANT TO SPEND MY NIGHT--
BUT THEY'RE INNOCENTS. I CAN'T JUST LET THEM BURN!
PROFESSOR JONATHAN CRANE, IF I REMEMBER THE POLICE FILES I HACKED INTO, THE VOICE OF THE PEOPLE SAYS YOU ARE BUSTED!
A KID?

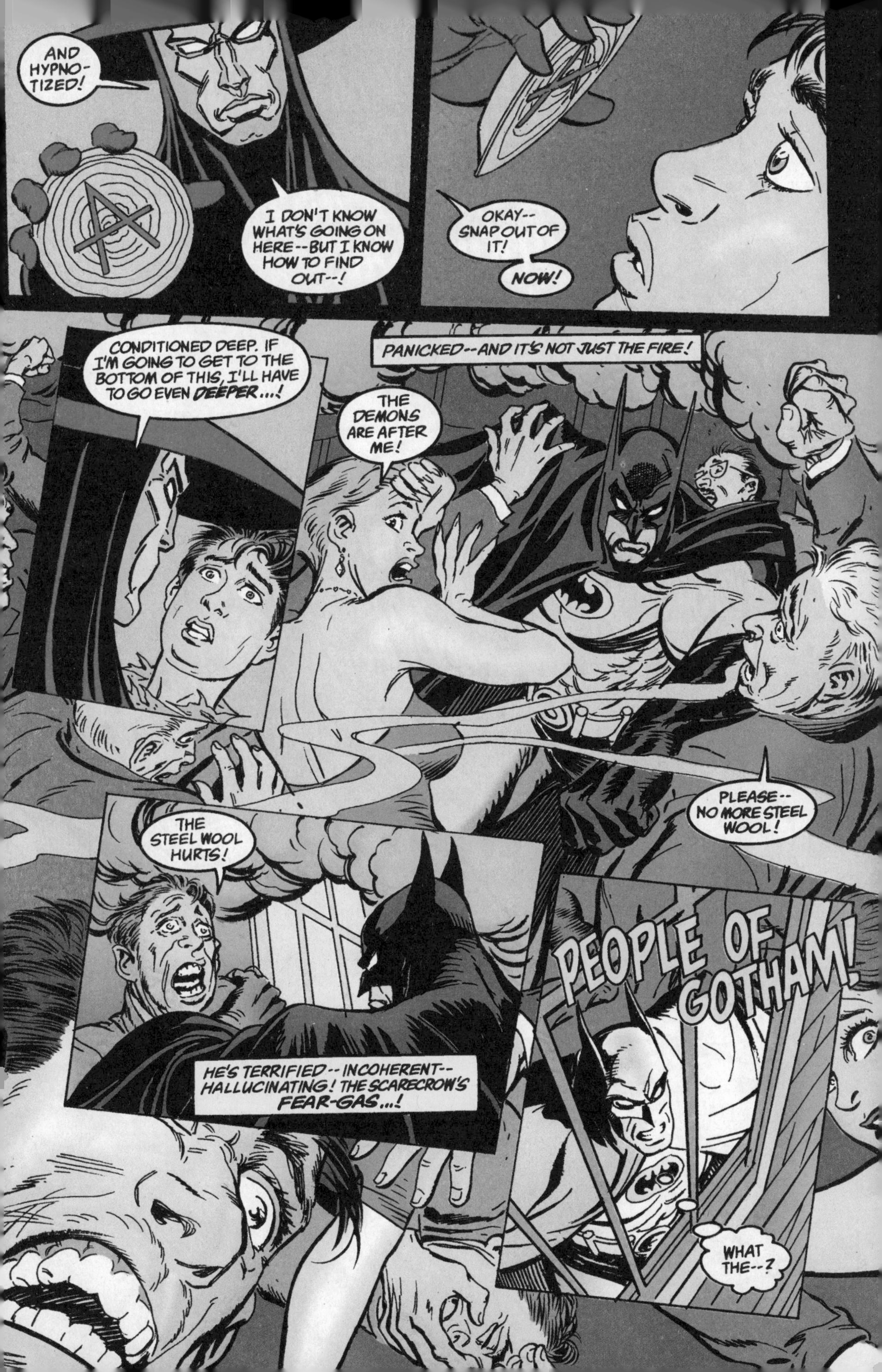
AND HYPNO-TIZED!
I DON'T KNOW WHAT'S GOING ON HERE--BUT I KNOW HOW TO FIND OUT--!
OKAY--SNAP OUT OF IT!
NOW!
CONDITIONED DEEP. IF I'M GOING TO GET TO THE BOTTOM OF THIS, I'LL HAVE TO GO EVEN DEEPER...!
PANICKED--AND IT'S NOT JUST THE FIRE!
THE DEMONS ARE AFTER ME!
PLEASE--NO MORE STEEL WOOL!
THE STEEL WOOL HURTS!
HE'S TERRIFIED--INCOHERENT--HALLUCINATING! THE SCARECROW'S FEAR-GAS...!
PEOPLE OF GOTHAM!
WHAT THE--?

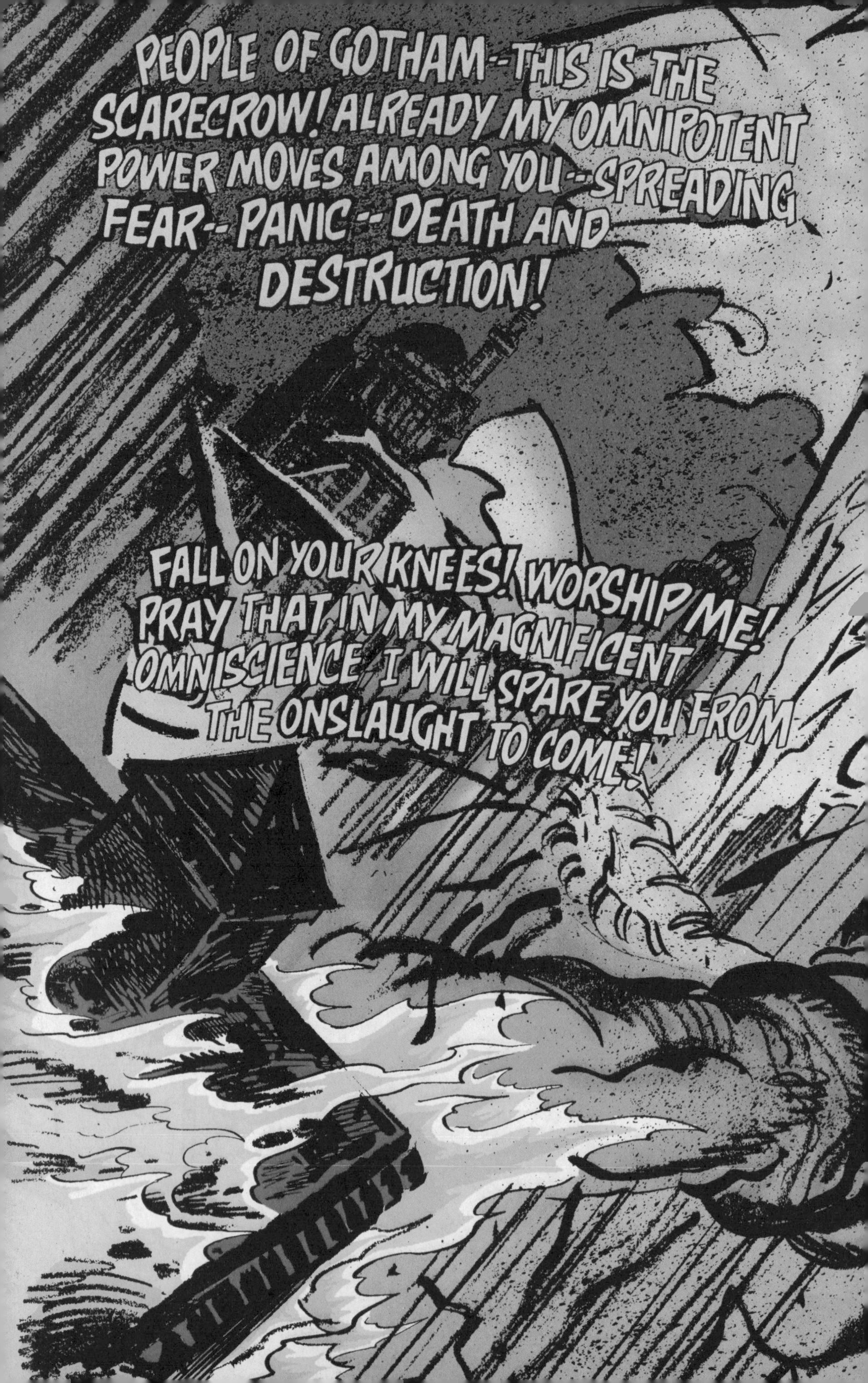
PEOPLE OF GOTHAM--THIS IS THE SCARECROW! ALREADY MY OMNIPOTENT POWER MOVES AMONG YOU--SPREADING FEAR--PANIC--DEATH AND DESTRUCTION!
FALL ON YOUR KNEES! WORSHIP ME! PRAY THAT IN MY MAGNIFICENT OMNISCIENCE I WILL SPARE YOU FROM THE ONSLAUGHT TO COME!

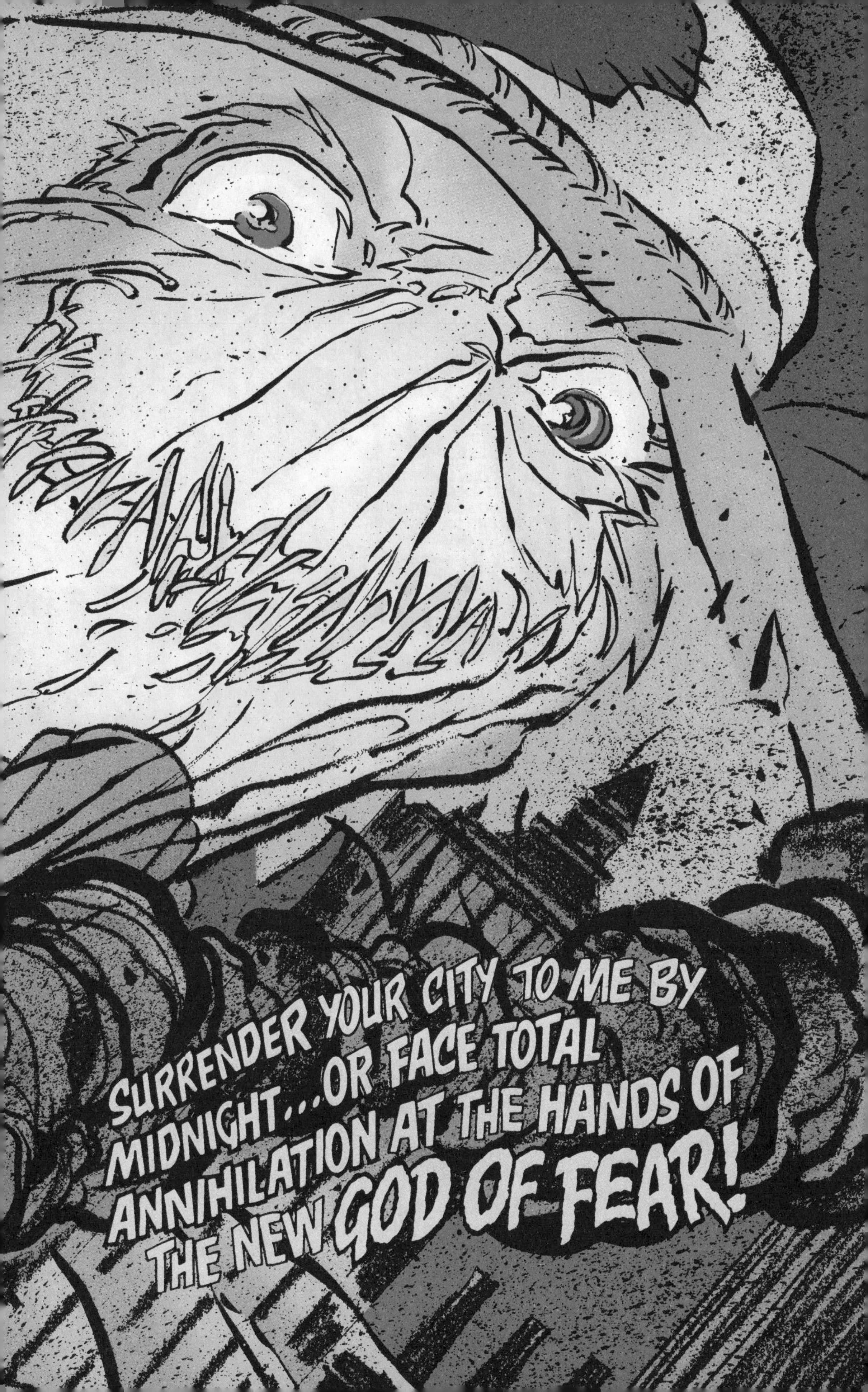
SURRENDER YOUR CITY TO ME BY MIDNIGHT...OR FACE TOTAL ANNIHILATION AT THE HANDS OF THE NEW GOD OF FEAR!

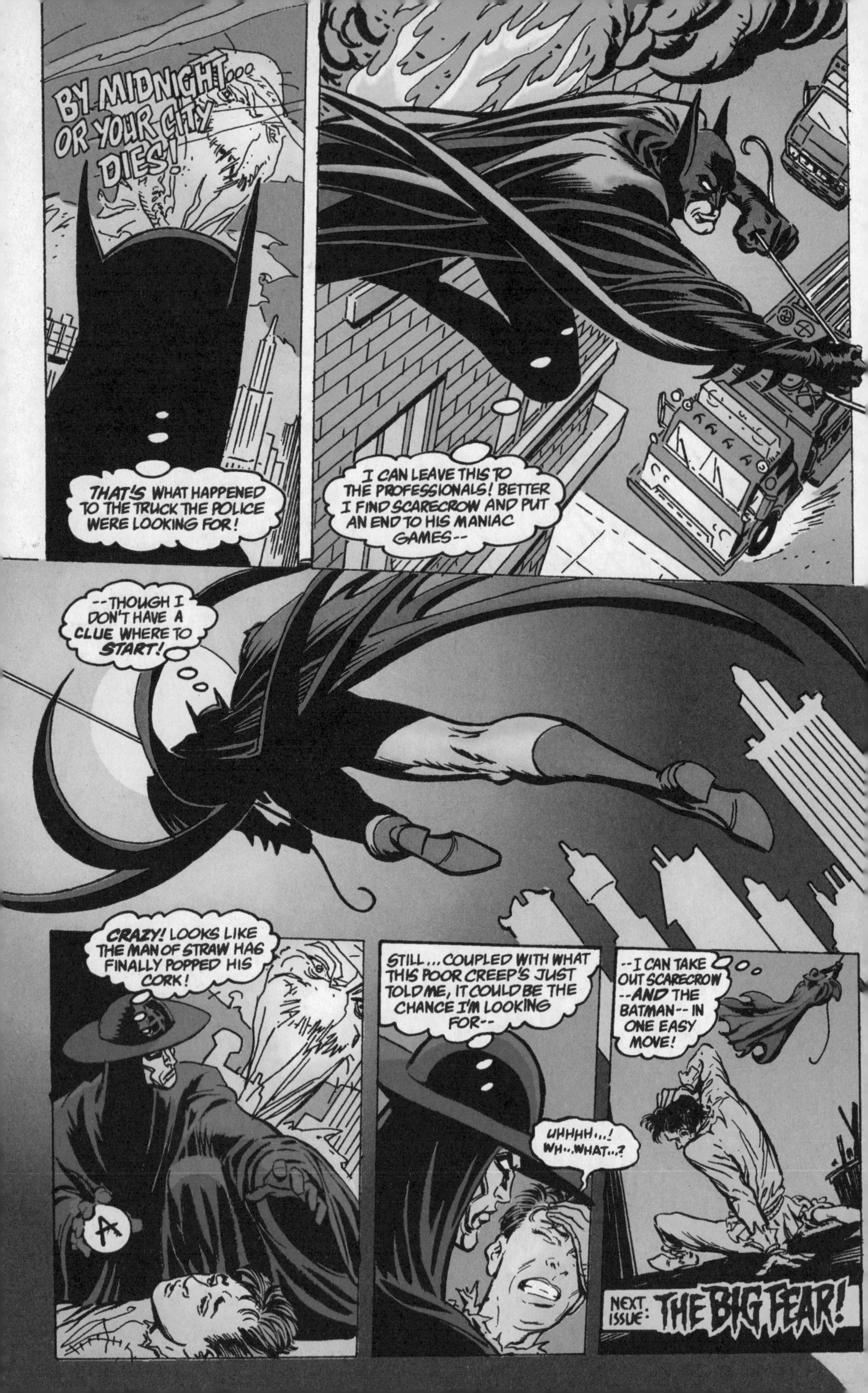
BY MIDNIGHT... OR YOUR CITY DIES!
THAT'S WHAT HAPPENED TO THE TRUCK THE POLICE WERE LOOKING FOR!
I CAN LEAVE THIS TO THE PROFESSIONALS! BETTER I FIND SCARECROW AND PUT AN END TO HIS MANIAC GAMES--
--THOUGH I DON'T HAVE A CLUE WHERE TO START!
CRAZY! LOOKS LIKE THE MAN OF STRAW HAS FINALLY POPPED HIS CORK!
STILL... COUPLED WITH WHAT THIS POOR CREEP'S JUST TOLD ME, IT COULD BE THE CHANCE I'M LOOKING FOR--
UHHHH...! WH...WHAT...?
--I CAN TAKE OUT SCARECROW --AND THE BATMAN-- IN ONE EASY MOVE!
NEXT ISSUE: THE BIG FEAR!

Cover art by BRIAN STELFREEZE

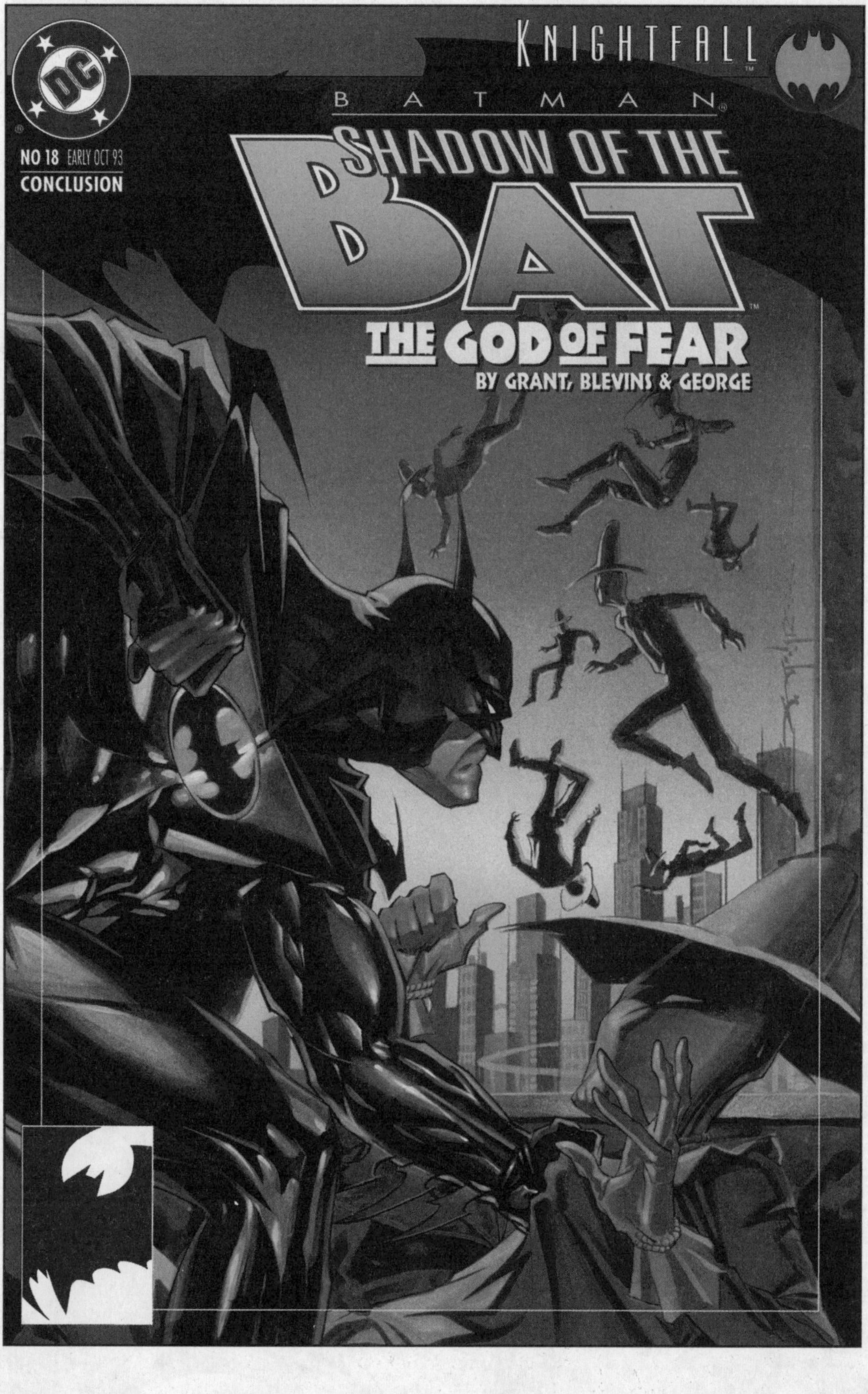

KNIGHTFALL
DC
NO 18 EARLY OCT 93
CONCLUSION
BATMAN
SHADOW OF THE BAT
THE GOD OF FEAR
BY GRANT, BLEVINS & GEORGE

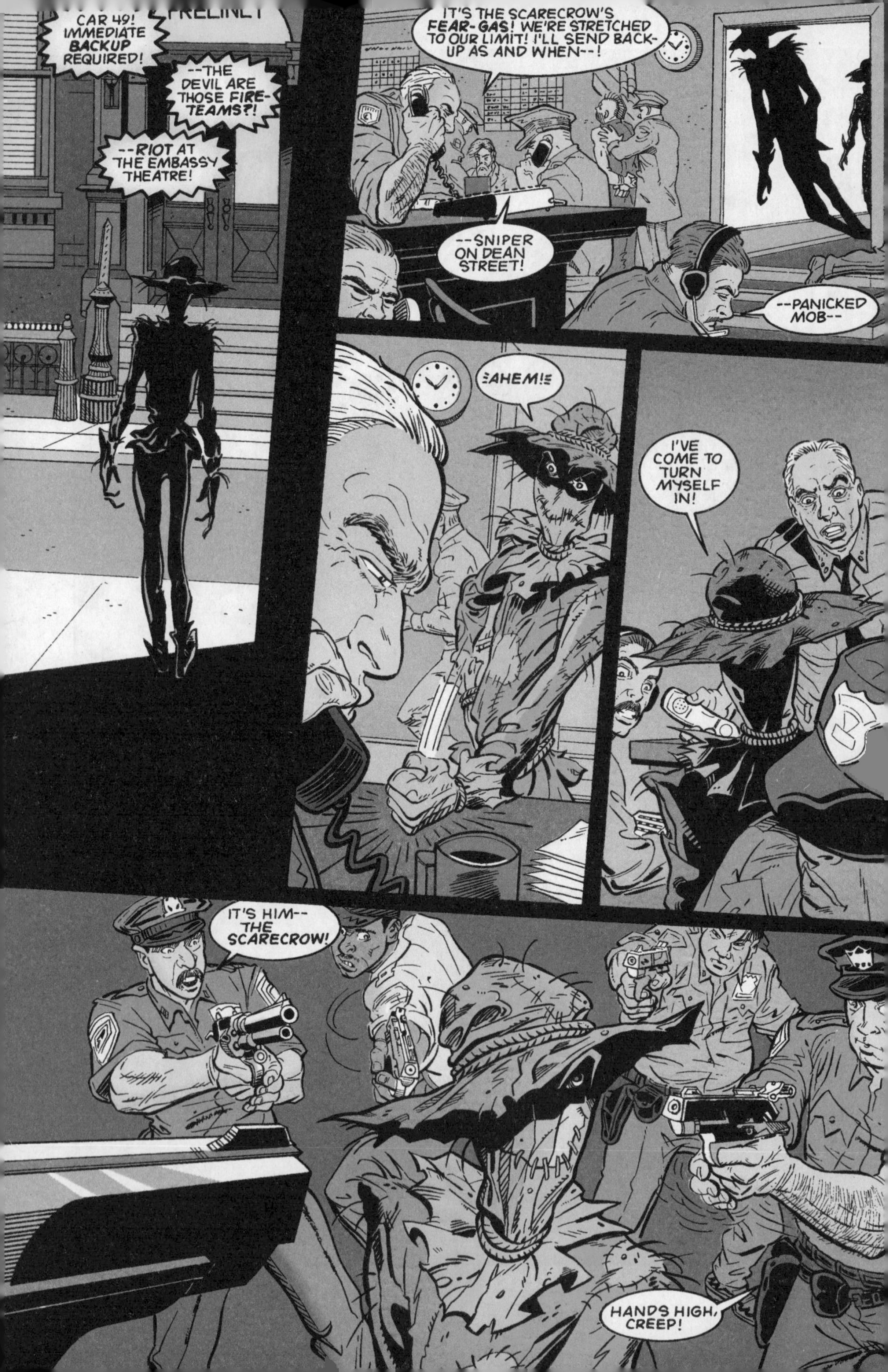
CAR 49! IMMEDIATE BACKUP REQUIRED!
--THE DEVIL ARE THOSE FIRE-TEAMS?!
--RIOT AT THE EMBASSY THEATRE!
IT'S THE SCARECROW'S FEAR-GAS! WE'RE STRETCHED TO OUR LIMIT! I'LL SEND BACK-UP AS AND WHEN--!
--SNIPER ON DEAN STREET!
--PANICKED MOB--
AHEM!
I'VE COME TO TURN MYSELF IN!
IT'S HIM--THE SCARECROW!
HANDS HIGH, CREEP!

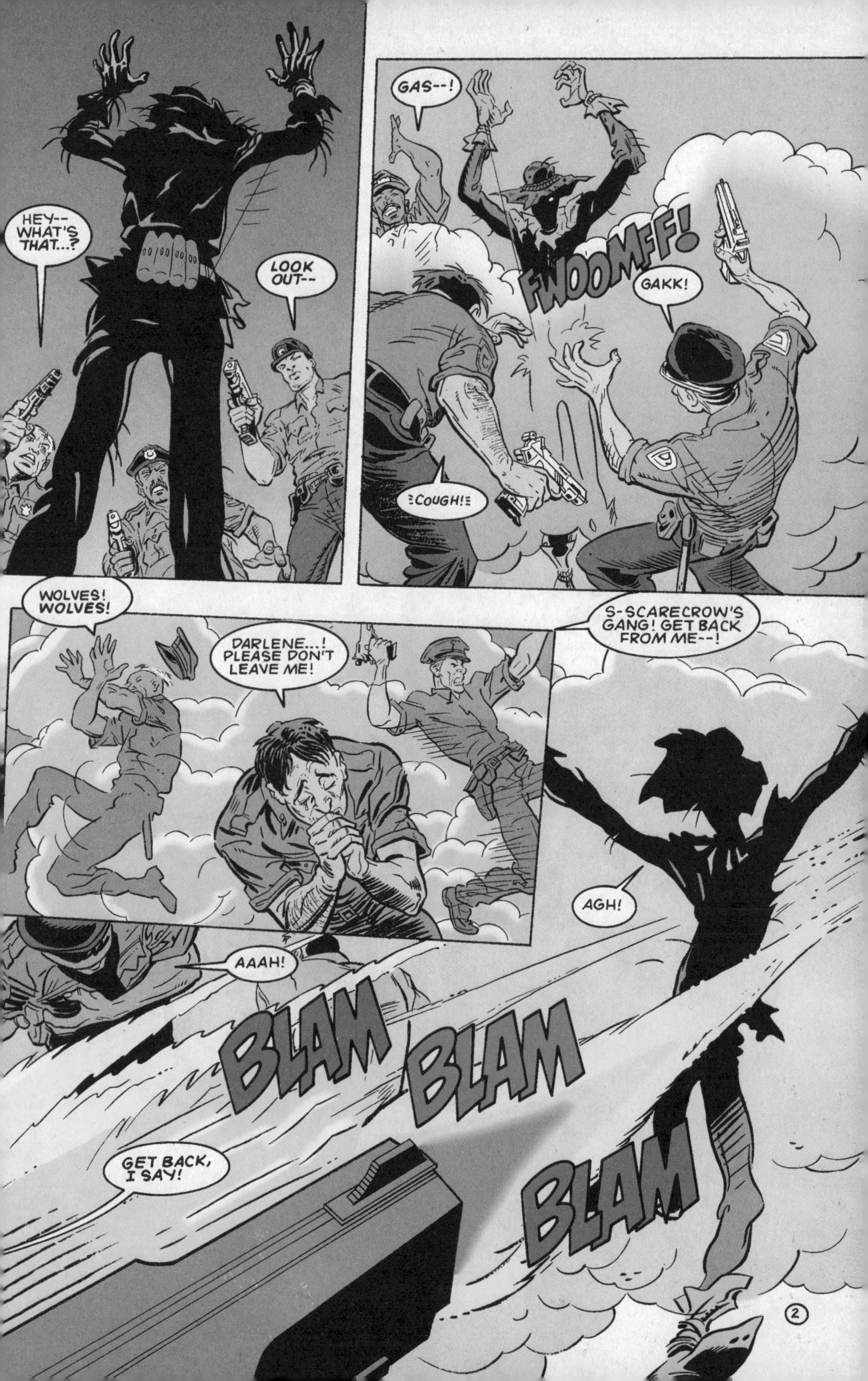
HEY-- WHAT'S THAT...?
LOOK OUT--
GAS--!
FWOOMFF!
GAKK!
COUGH!
WOLVES! WOLVES!
DARLENE...! PLEASE DON'T LEAVE ME!
S-SCARECROW'S GANG! GET BACK FROM ME--!
AGH!
AAAH!
BLAM
BLAM
GET BACK, I SAY!
BLAM

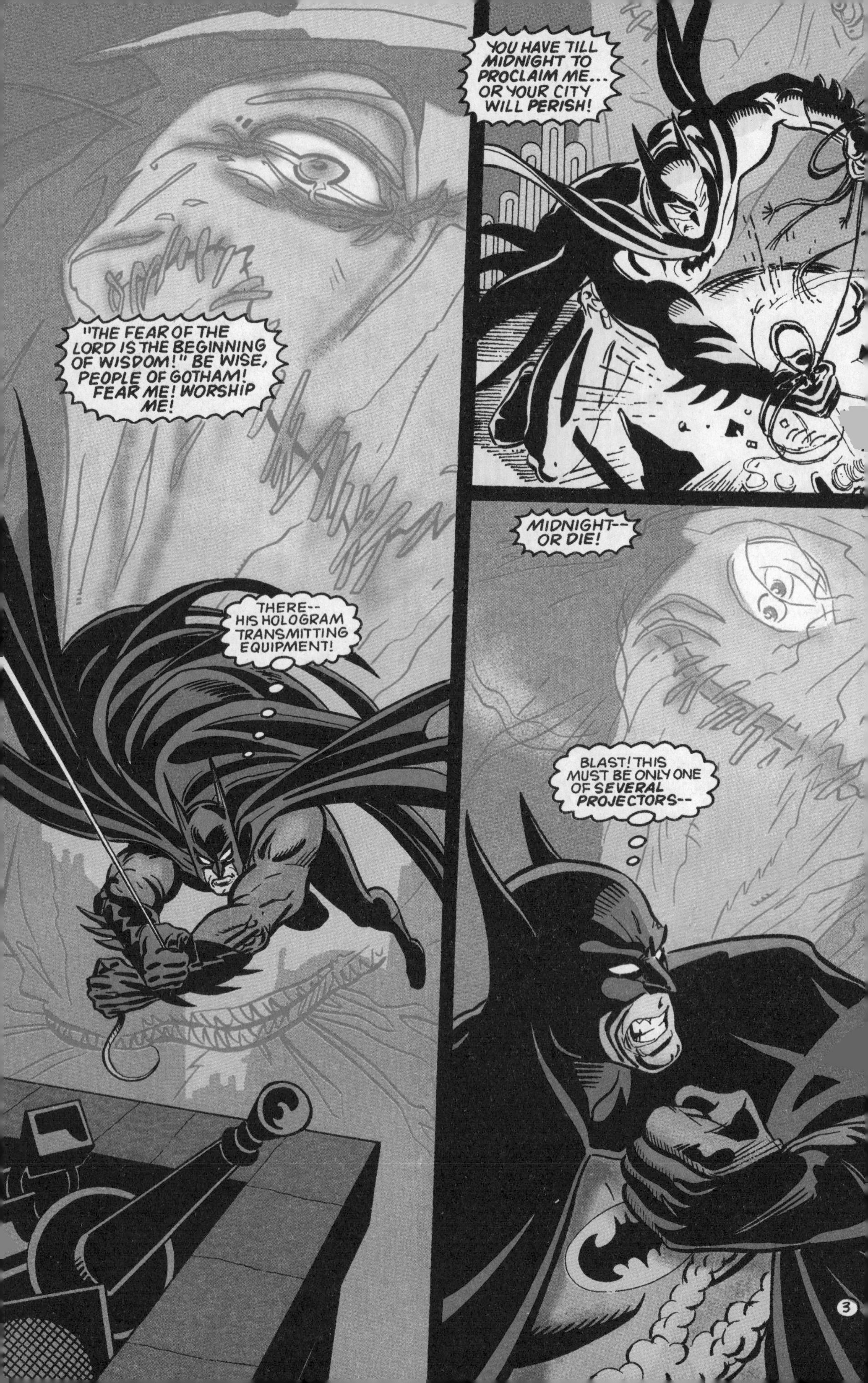
"THE FEAR OF THE LORD IS THE BEGINNING OF WISDOM!" BE WISE, PEOPLE OF GOTHAM! FEAR ME! WORSHIP ME!
YOU HAVE TILL MIDNIGHT TO PROCLAIM ME... OR YOUR CITY WILL PERISH!
THERE-- HIS HOLOGRAM TRANSMITTING EQUIPMENT!
MIDNIGHT-- OR DIE!
BLAST! THIS MUST BE ONLY ONE OF SEVERAL PROJECTORS--
3

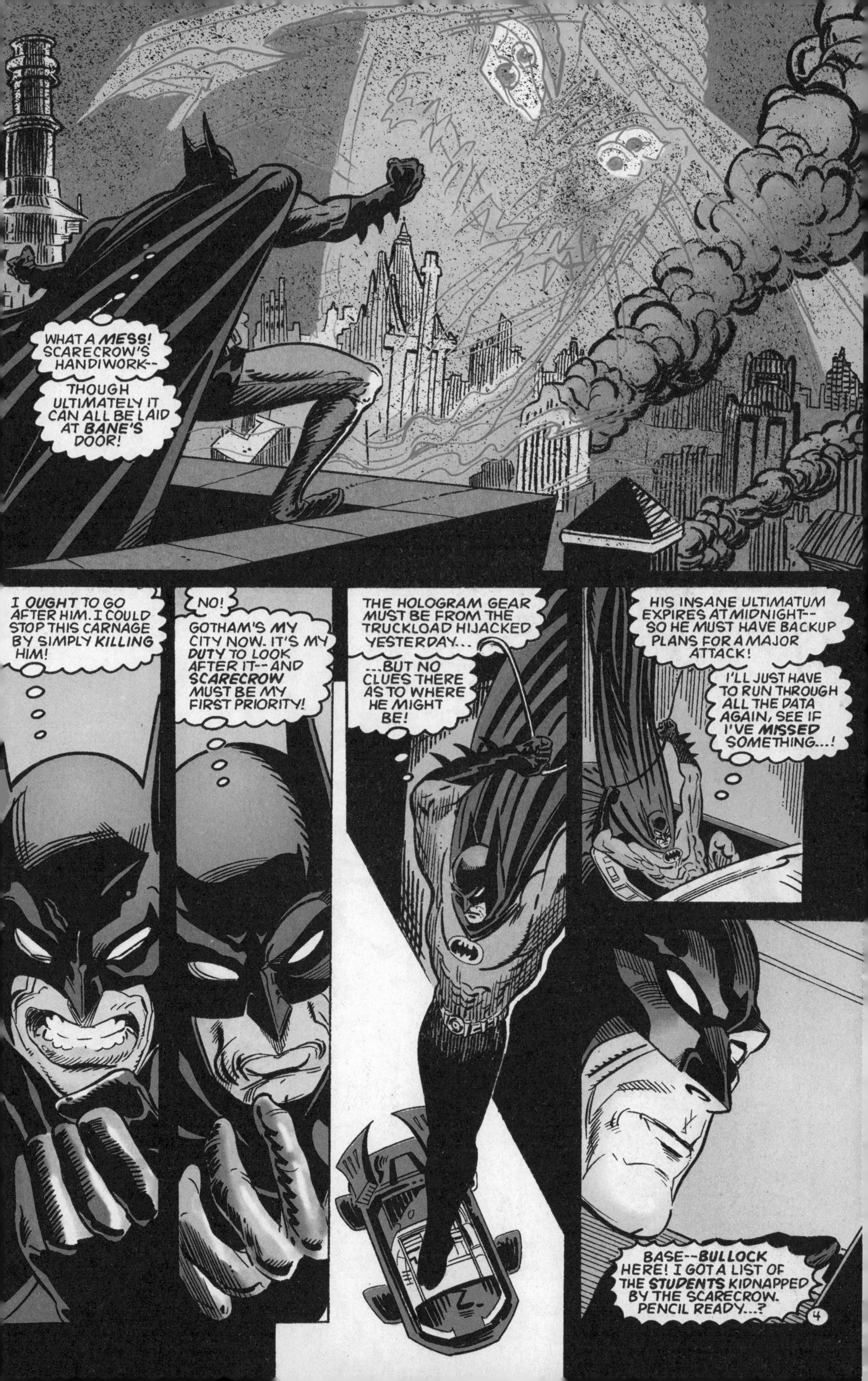
WHAT A MESS! SCARECROW'S HANDIWORK--
THOUGH ULTIMATELY IT CAN ALL BE LAID AT BANE'S DOOR!
I OUGHT TO GO AFTER HIM. I COULD STOP THIS CARNAGE BY SIMPLY KILLING HIM!
NO!
GOTHAM'S MY CITY NOW. IT'S MY DUTY TO LOOK AFTER IT-- AND SCARECROW MUST BE MY FIRST PRIORITY!
THE HOLOGRAM GEAR MUST BE FROM THE TRUCKLOAD HIJACKED YESTERDAY...
...BUT NO CLUES THERE AS TO WHERE HE MIGHT BE!
HIS INSANE ULTIMATUM EXPIRES AT MIDNIGHT-- SO HE MUST HAVE BACKUP PLANS FOR A MAJOR ATTACK!
I'LL JUST HAVE TO RUN THROUGH ALL THE DATA AGAIN, SEE IF I'VE MISSED SOMETHING...!
BASE--BULLOCK HERE! I GOT A LIST OF THE STUDENTS KIDNAPPED BY THE SCARECROW. PENCIL READY...?
4

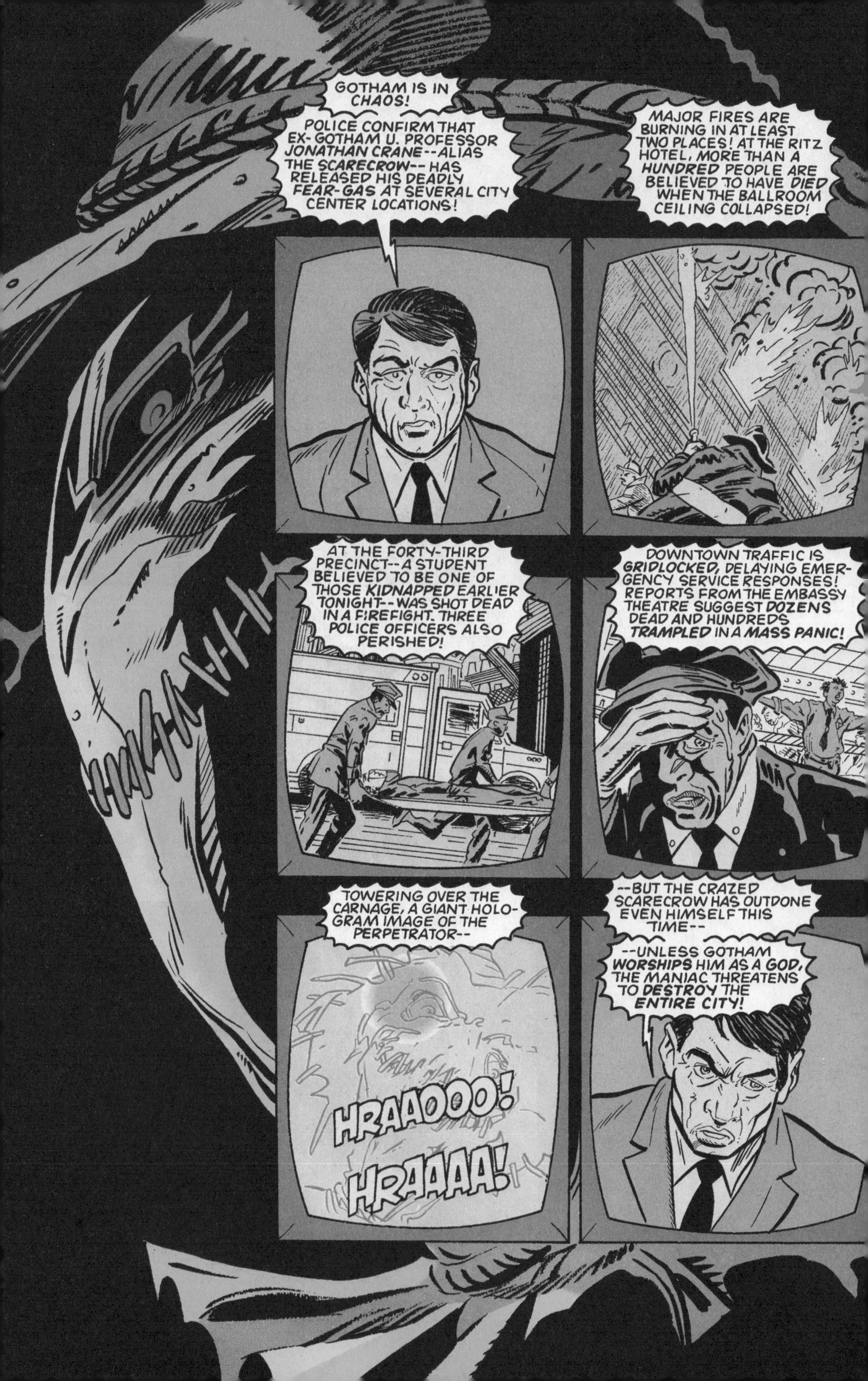
GOTHAM IS IN CHAOS!
POLICE CONFIRM THAT EX-GOTHAM U. PROFESSOR JONATHAN CRANE--ALIAS THE SCARECROW--HAS RELEASED HIS DEADLY FEAR-GAS AT SEVERAL CITY CENTER LOCATIONS!
MAJOR FIRES ARE BURNING IN AT LEAST TWO PLACES! AT THE RITZ HOTEL, MORE THAN A HUNDRED PEOPLE ARE BELIEVED TO HAVE DIED WHEN THE BALLROOM CEILING COLLAPSED!
AT THE FORTY-THIRD PRECINCT--A STUDENT BELIEVED TO BE ONE OF THOSE KIDNAPPED EARLIER TONIGHT--WAS SHOT DEAD IN A FIREFIGHT. THREE POLICE OFFICERS ALSO PERISHED!
DOWNTOWN TRAFFIC IS GRIDLOCKED, DELAYING EMERGENCY SERVICE RESPONSES! REPORTS FROM THE EMBASSY THEATRE SUGGEST DOZENS DEAD AND HUNDREDS TRAMPLED IN A MASS PANIC!
TOWERING OVER THE CARNAGE, A GIANT HOLOGRAM IMAGE OF THE PERPETRATOR--
HRAAOOO!
HRAAAA!
--BUT THE CRAZED SCARECROW HAS OUTDONE EVEN HIMSELF THIS TIME--
--UNLESS GOTHAM WORSHIPS HIM AS A GOD, THE MANIAC THREATENS TO DESTROY THE ENTIRE CITY!

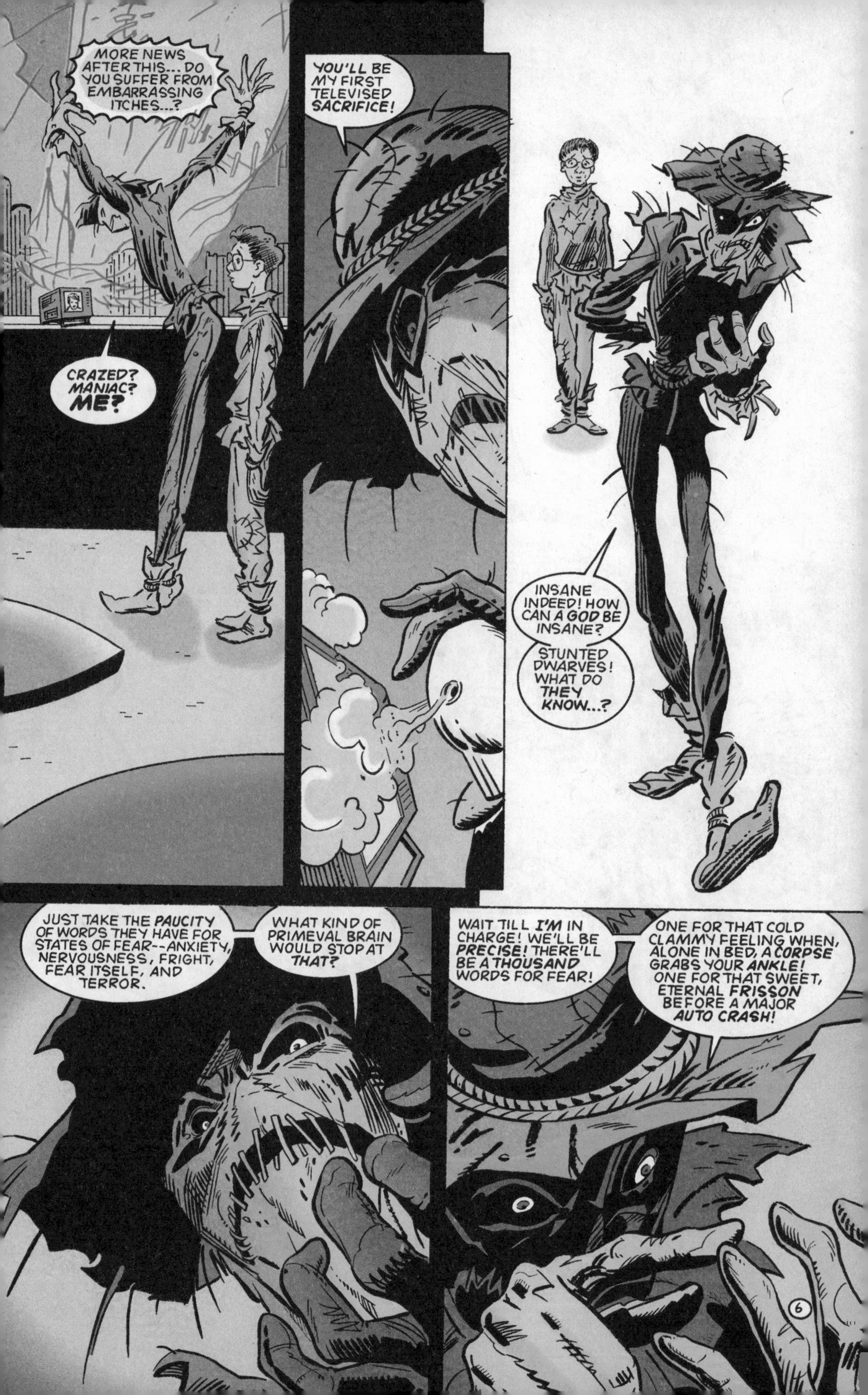

MORE NEWS AFTER THIS... DO YOU SUFFER FROM EMBARRASSING ITCHES...?
CRAZED? MANIAC? ME?
YOU'LL BE MY FIRST TELEVISED SACRIFICE!
INSANE INDEED! HOW CAN A GOD BE INSANE?
STUNTED DWARVES! WHAT DO THEY KNOW...?
JUST TAKE THE PAUCITY OF WORDS THEY HAVE FOR STATES OF FEAR--ANXIETY, NERVOUSNESS, FRIGHT, FEAR ITSELF, AND TERROR.
WHAT KIND OF PRIMEVAL BRAIN WOULD STOP AT THAT?
WAIT TILL I'M IN CHARGE! WE'LL BE PRECISE! THERE'LL BE A THOUSAND WORDS FOR FEAR!
ONE FOR THAT COLD CLAMMY FEELING WHEN, ALONE IN BED, A CORPSE GRABS YOUR ANKLE! ONE FOR THAT SWEET, ETERNAL FRISSON BEFORE A MAJOR AUTO CRASH!
6

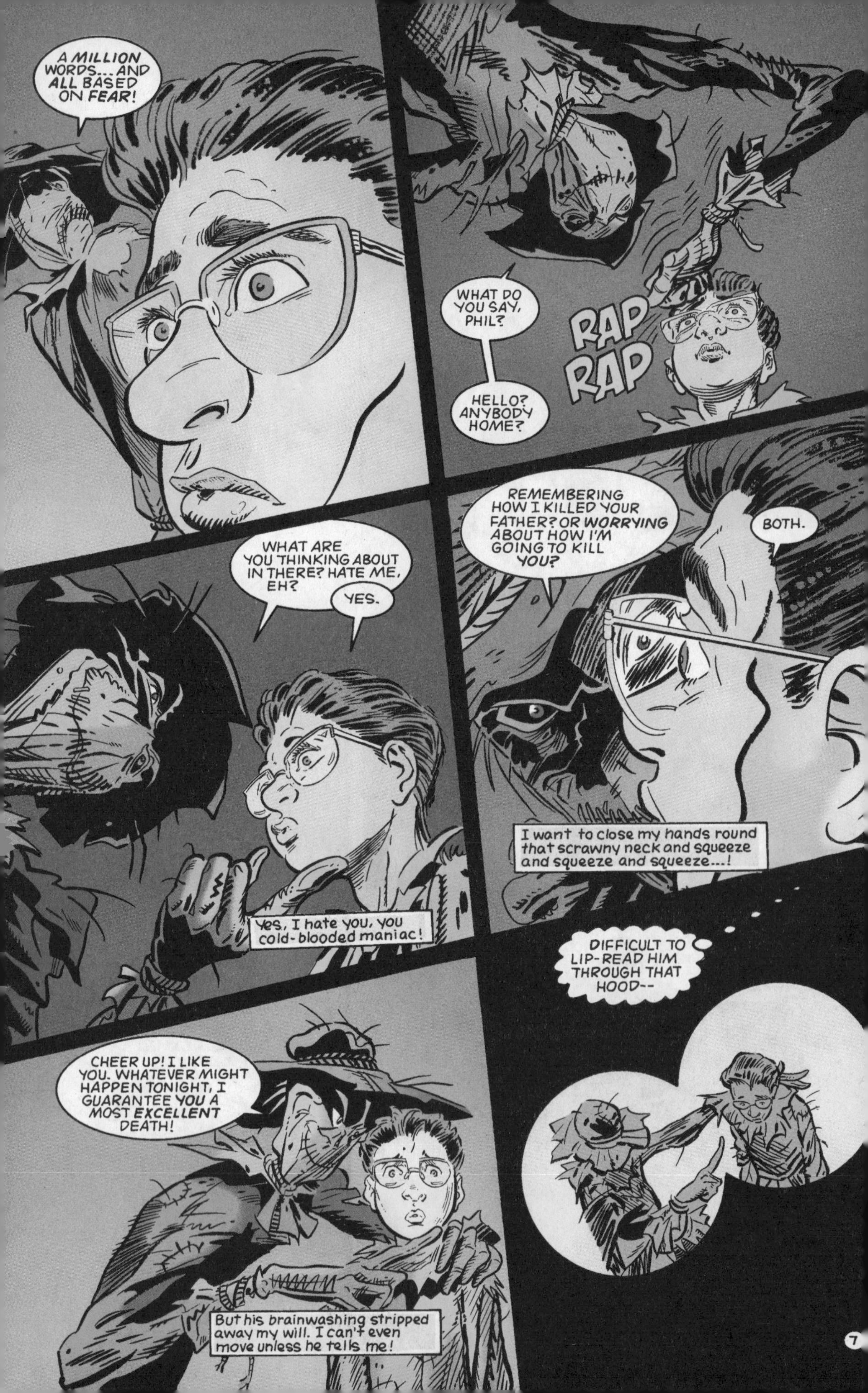
A MILLION WORDS... AND ALL BASED ON FEAR!
WHAT DO YOU SAY, PHIL?
HELLO? ANYBODY HOME?
RAP RAP
WHAT ARE YOU THINKING ABOUT IN THERE? HATE ME, EH?
YES.
Yes, I hate you, you cold-blooded maniac!
REMEMBERING HOW I KILLED YOUR FATHER? OR WORRYING ABOUT HOW I'M GOING TO KILL YOU?
BOTH.
I want to close my hands round that scrawny neck and squeeze and squeeze and squeeze...!
CHEER UP! I LIKE YOU. WHATEVER MIGHT HAPPEN TONIGHT, I GUARANTEE YOU A MOST EXCELLENT DEATH!
But his brainwashing stripped away my will. I can't even move unless he tells me!
DIFFICULT TO LIP-READ HIM THROUGH THAT HOOD--

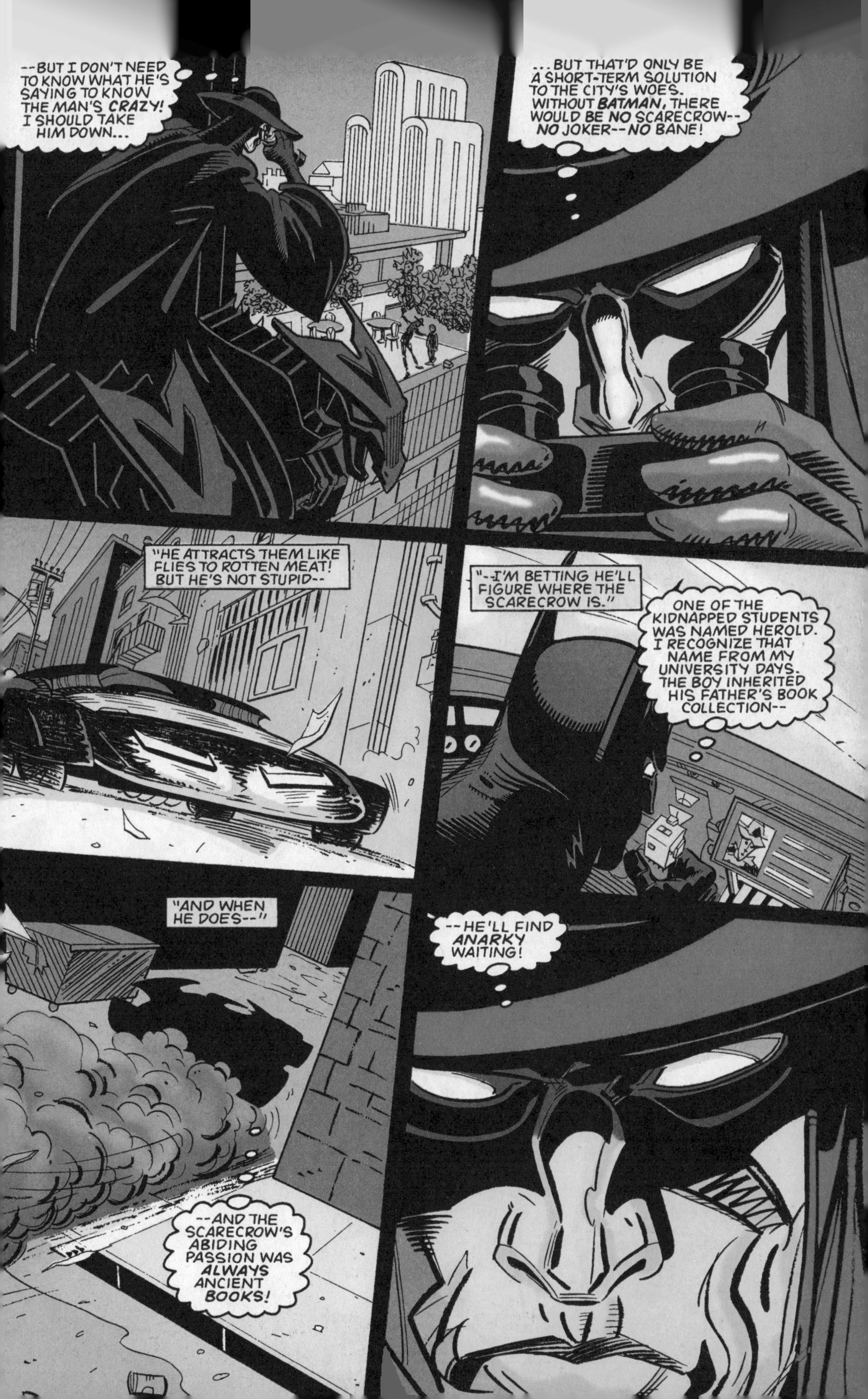
--BUT I DON'T NEED TO KNOW WHAT HE'S SAYING TO KNOW THE MAN'S CRAZY! I SHOULD TAKE HIM DOWN...
...BUT THAT'D ONLY BE A SHORT-TERM SOLUTION TO THE CITY'S WOES. WITHOUT BATMAN, THERE WOULD BE NO SCARECROW--NO JOKER--NO BANE!
"HE ATTRACTS THEM LIKE FLIES TO ROTTEN MEAT! BUT HE'S NOT STUPID--
"--I'M BETTING HE'LL FIGURE WHERE THE SCARECROW IS."
ONE OF THE KIDNAPPED STUDENTS WAS NAMED HEROLD. I RECOGNIZE THAT NAME FROM MY UNIVERSITY DAYS. THE BOY INHERITED HIS FATHER'S BOOK COLLECTION--
--AND THE SCARECROW'S ABIDING PASSION WAS ALWAYS ANCIENT BOOKS!
"AND WHEN HE DOES--"
--HE'LL FIND ANARKY WAITING!

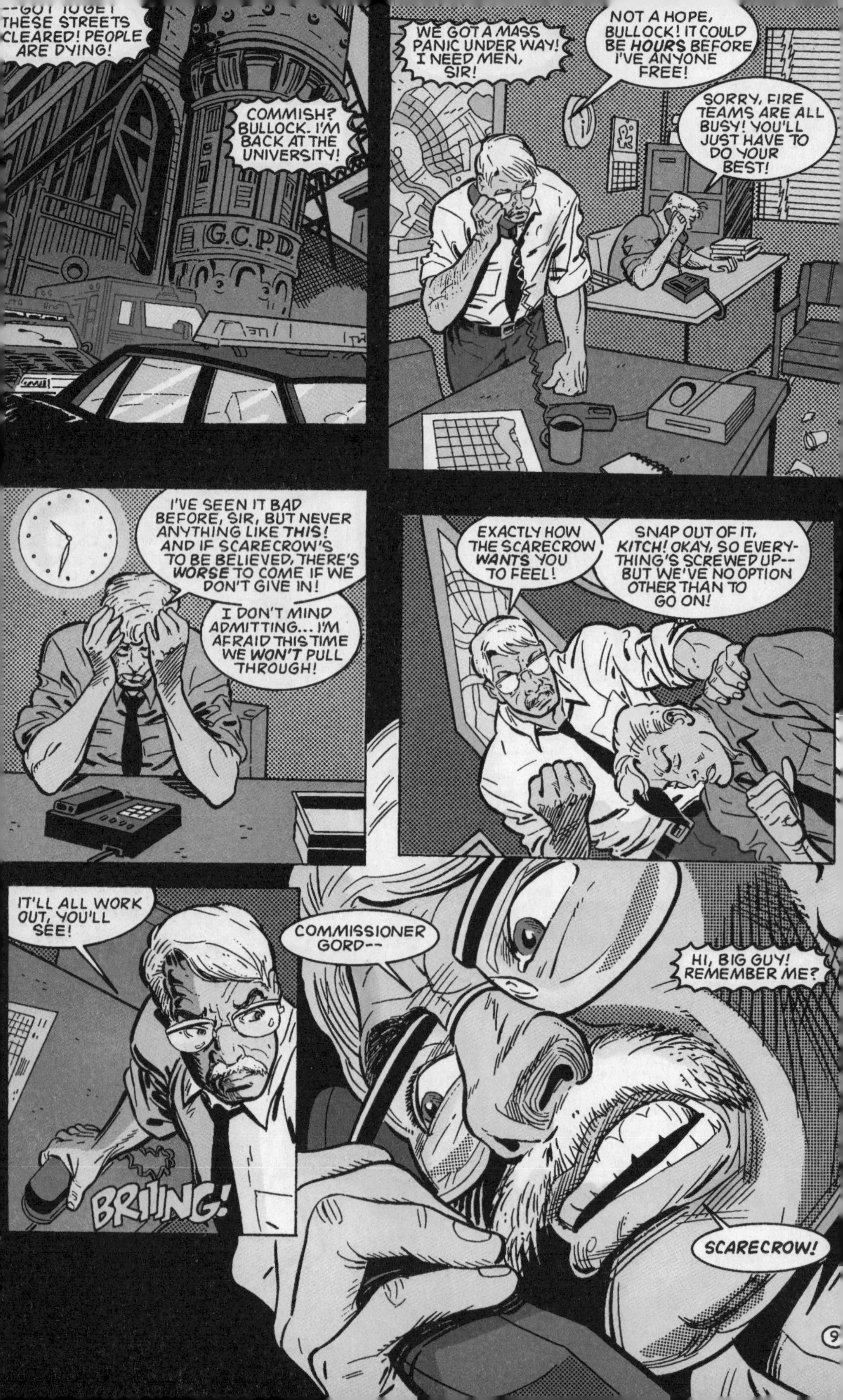
--GOT TO GET THESE STREETS CLEARED! PEOPLE ARE DYING!
COMMISH? BULLOCK. I'M BACK AT THE UNIVERSITY!
G.C.P.D.
WE GOT A MASS PANIC UNDER WAY! I NEED MEN, SIR!
NOT A HOPE, BULLOCK! IT COULD BE HOURS BEFORE I'VE ANYONE FREE!
SORRY, FIRE TEAMS ARE ALL BUSY! YOU'LL JUST HAVE TO DO YOUR BEST!
I'VE SEEN IT BAD BEFORE, SIR, BUT NEVER ANYTHING LIKE THIS! AND IF SCARECROW'S TO BE BELIEVED, THERE'S WORSE TO COME IF WE DON'T GIVE IN!
I DON'T MIND ADMITTING... I'M AFRAID THIS TIME WE WON'T PULL THROUGH!
EXACTLY HOW THE SCARECROW WANTS YOU TO FEEL!
SNAP OUT OF IT, KITCH! OKAY, SO EVERYTHING'S SCREWED UP--BUT WE'VE NO OPTION OTHER THAN TO GO ON!
IT'LL ALL WORK OUT, YOU'LL SEE!
BRIIING!
COMMISSIONER GORD--
HI, BIG GUY! REMEMBER ME?
SCARECROW!
9

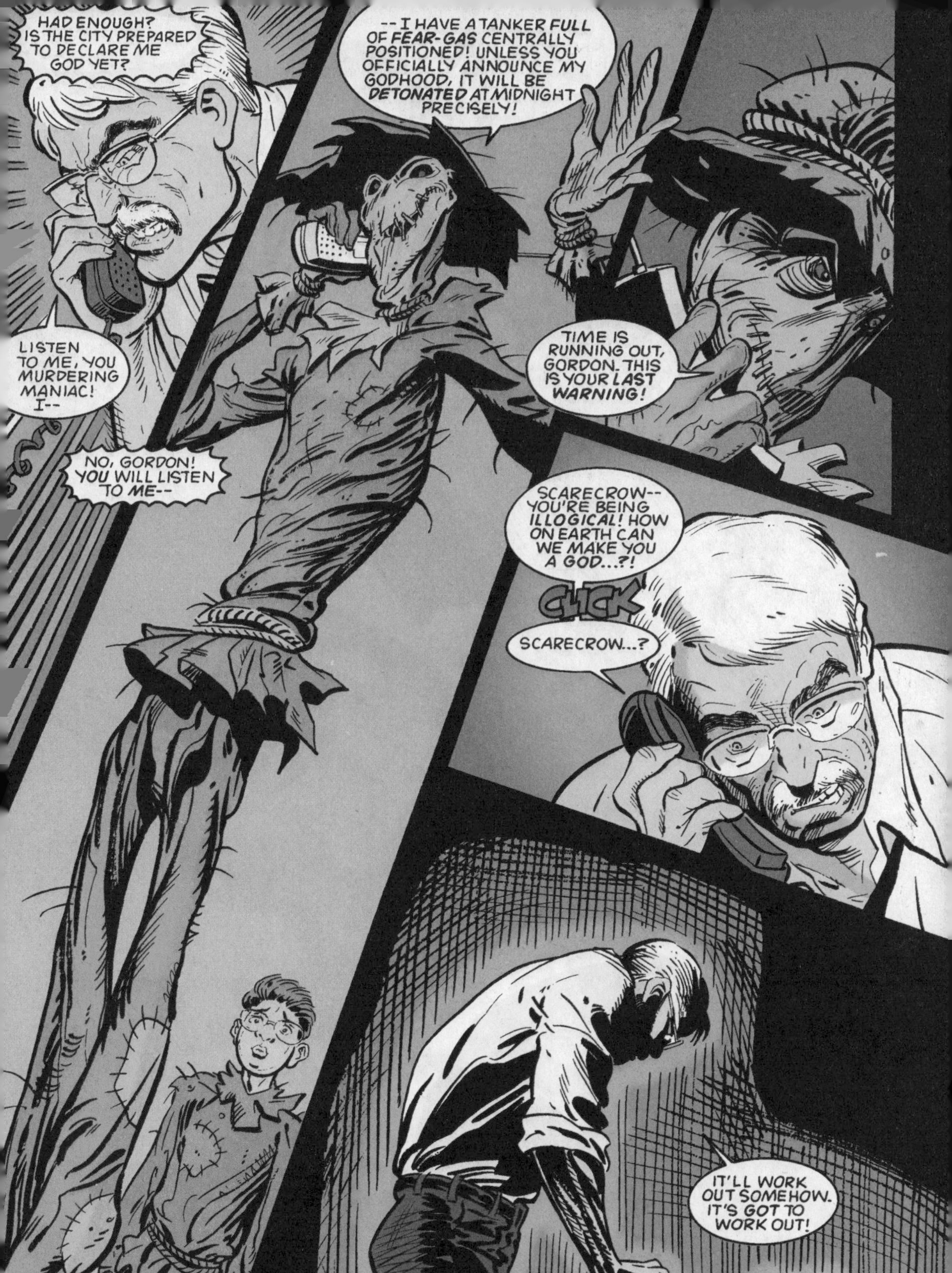
HAD ENOUGH? IS THE CITY PREPARED TO DECLARE ME GOD YET?
--I HAVE A TANKER FULL OF FEAR-GAS CENTRALLY POSITIONED! UNLESS YOU OFFICIALLY ANNOUNCE MY GODHOOD, IT WILL BE DETONATED AT MIDNIGHT PRECISELY!
LISTEN TO ME, YOU MURDERING MANIAC! I--
NO, GORDON! YOU WILL LISTEN TO ME--
TIME IS RUNNING OUT, GORDON. THIS IS YOUR LAST WARNING!
SCARECROW--YOU'RE BEING ILLOGICAL! HOW ON EARTH CAN WE MAKE YOU A GOD...?!
CLICK
SCARECROW...?
IT'LL WORK OUT SOMEHOW. IT'S GOT TO WORK OUT!

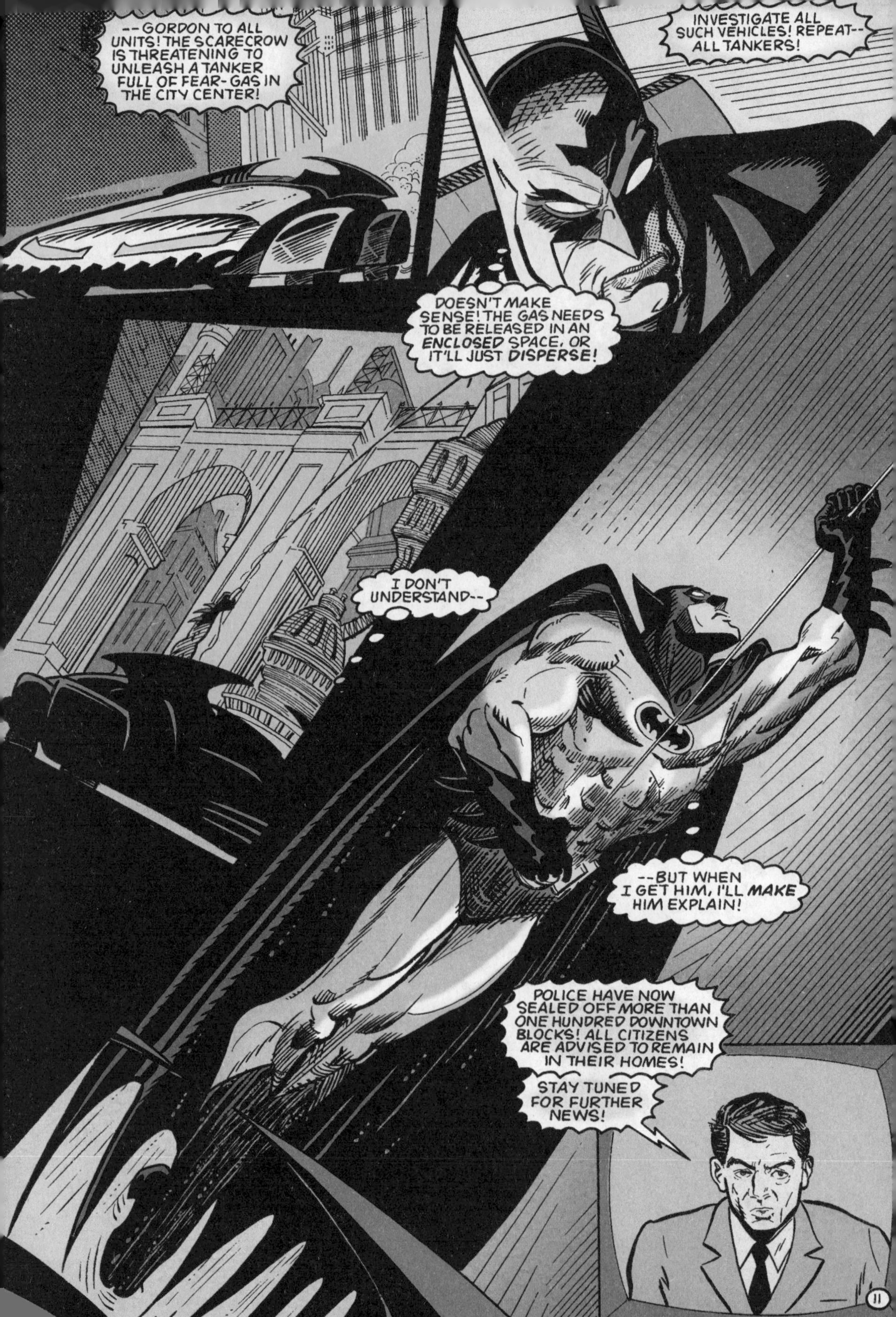
--GORDON TO ALL UNITS! THE SCARECROW IS THREATENING TO UNLEASH A TANKER FULL OF FEAR-GAS IN THE CITY CENTER!
INVESTIGATE ALL SUCH VEHICLES! REPEAT-- ALL TANKERS!
DOESN'T MAKE SENSE! THE GAS NEEDS TO BE RELEASED IN AN ENCLOSED SPACE, OR IT'LL JUST DISPERSE!
I DON'T UNDERSTAND--
--BUT WHEN I GET HIM, I'LL MAKE HIM EXPLAIN!
POLICE HAVE NOW SEALED OFF MORE THAN ONE HUNDRED DOWNTOWN BLOCKS! ALL CITIZENS ARE ADVISED TO REMAIN IN THEIR HOMES!
STAY TUNED FOR FURTHER NEWS!

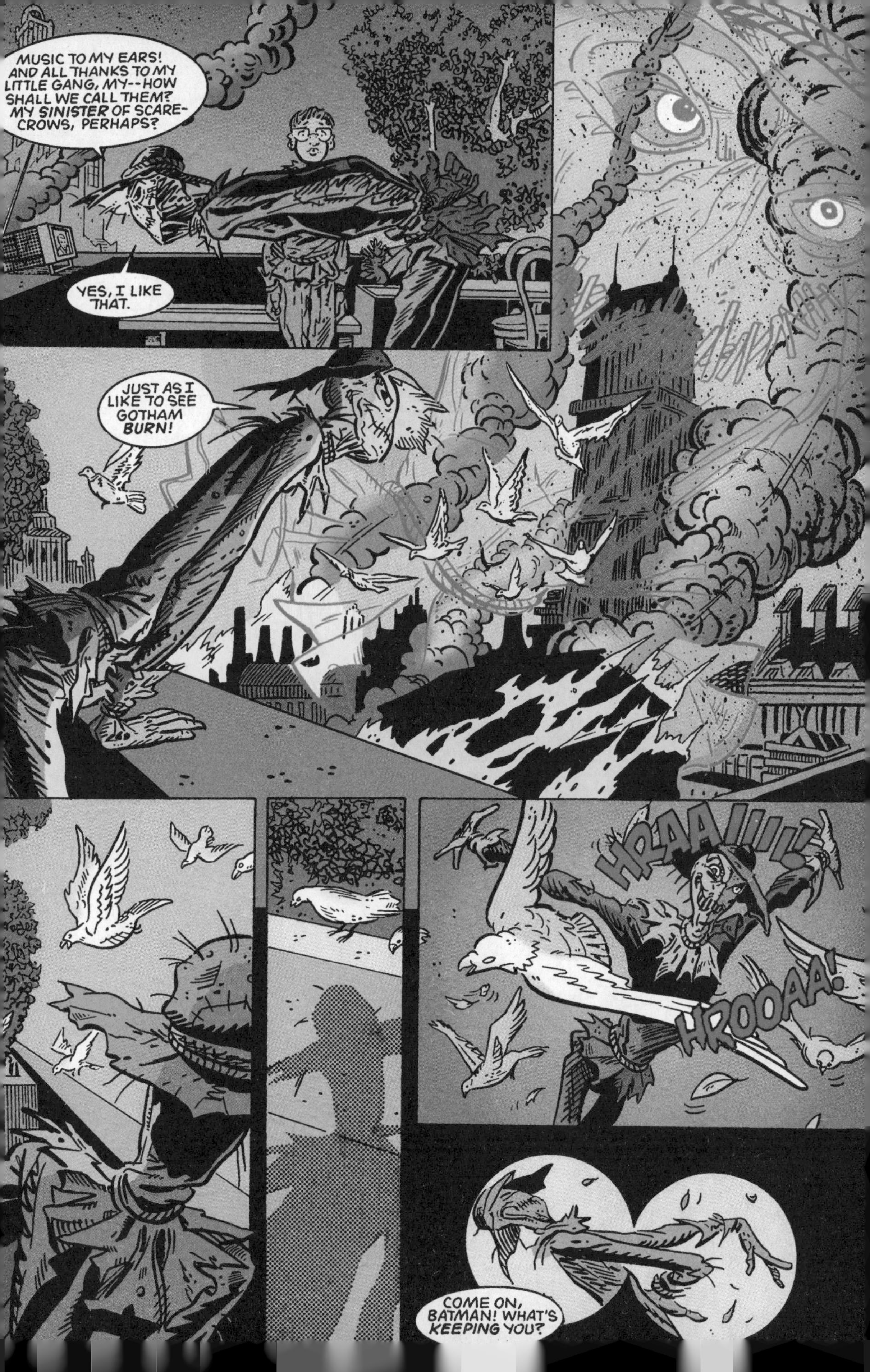
MUSIC TO MY EARS! AND ALL THANKS TO MY LITTLE GANG, MY--HOW SHALL WE CALL THEM? MY SINISTER OF SCARE-CROWS, PERHAPS?
YES, I LIKE THAT.
JUST AS I LIKE TO SEE GOTHAM BURN!
HRAAIIII!
HROOAA!
COME ON, BATMAN! WHAT'S KEEPING YOU?

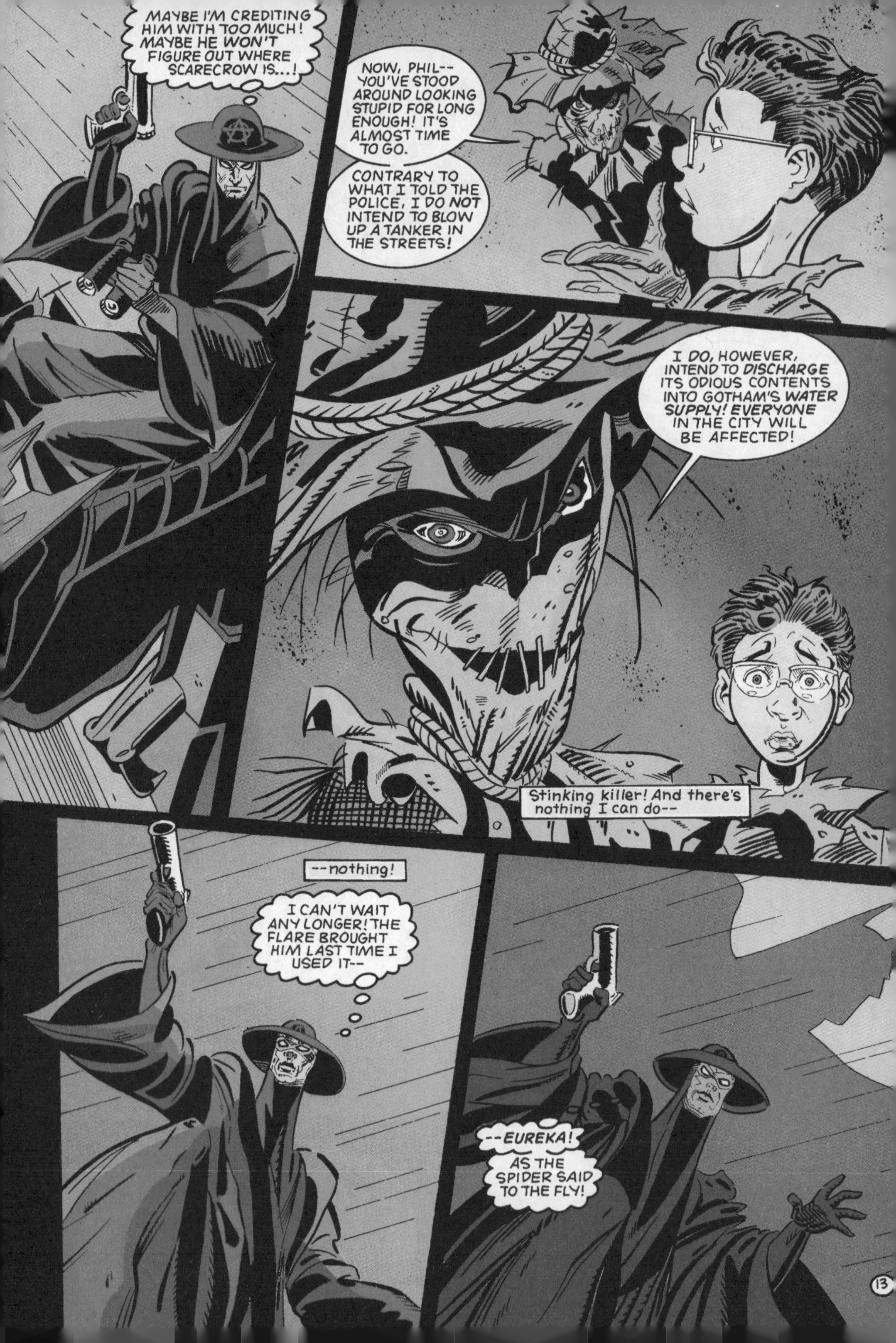
MAYBE I'M CREDITING HIM WITH TOO MUCH! MAYBE HE WON'T FIGURE OUT WHERE SCARECROW IS...!
NOW, PHIL--YOU'VE STOOD AROUND LOOKING STUPID FOR LONG ENOUGH! IT'S ALMOST TIME TO GO.
CONTRARY TO WHAT I TOLD THE POLICE, I DO NOT INTEND TO BLOW UP A TANKER IN THE STREETS!
I DO, HOWEVER, INTEND TO DISCHARGE ITS ODIOUS CONTENTS INTO GOTHAM'S WATER SUPPLY! EVERYONE IN THE CITY WILL BE AFFECTED!
Stinking killer! And there's nothing I can do--
--nothing!
I CAN'T WAIT ANY LONGER! THE FLARE BROUGHT HIM LAST TIME I USED IT--
--EUREKA!
AS THE SPIDER SAID TO THE FLY!

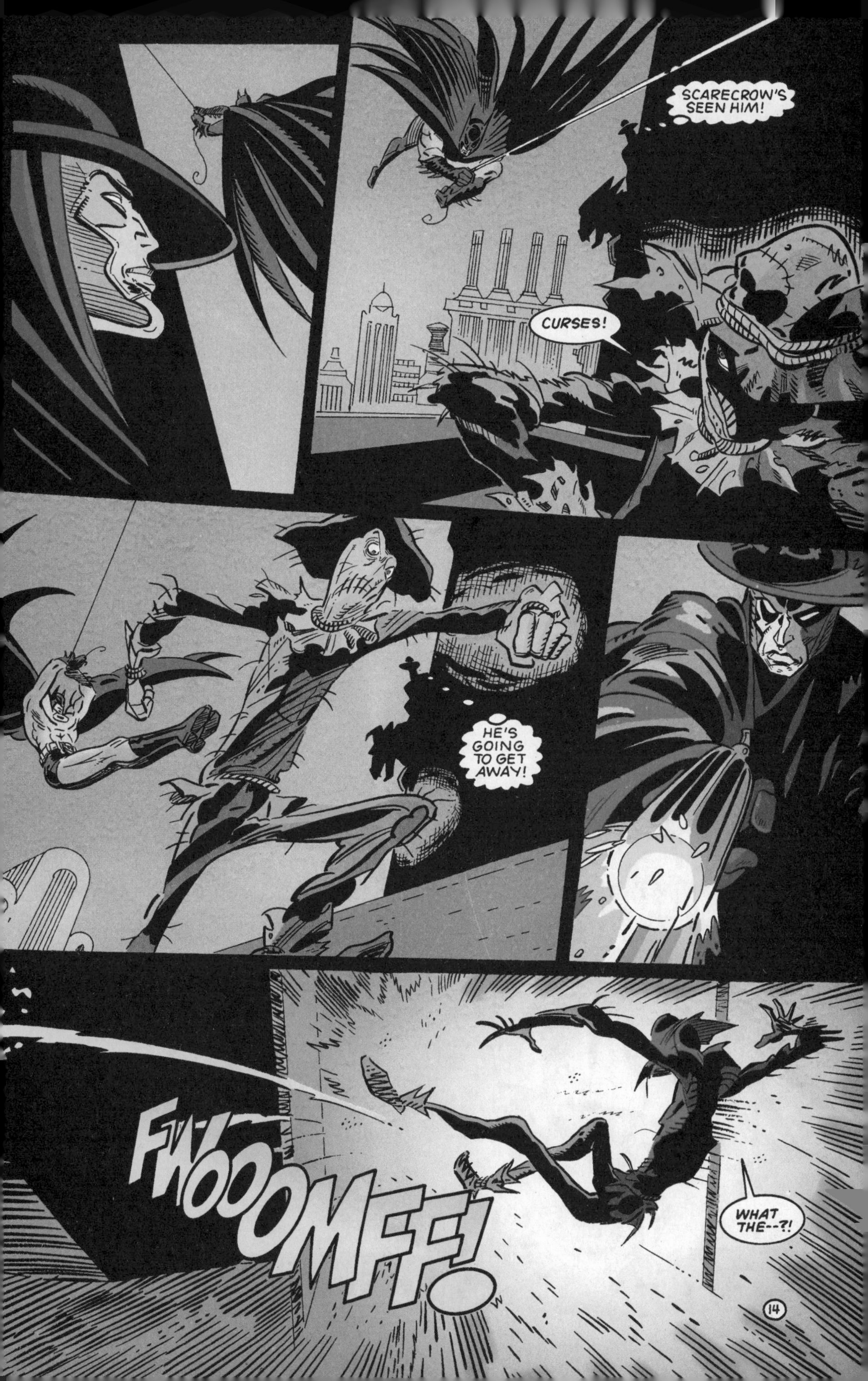
SCARECROW'S SEEN HIM!
CURSES!
HE'S GOING TO GET AWAY!
FWOOOMFF!
WHAT THE--?!
OW
14

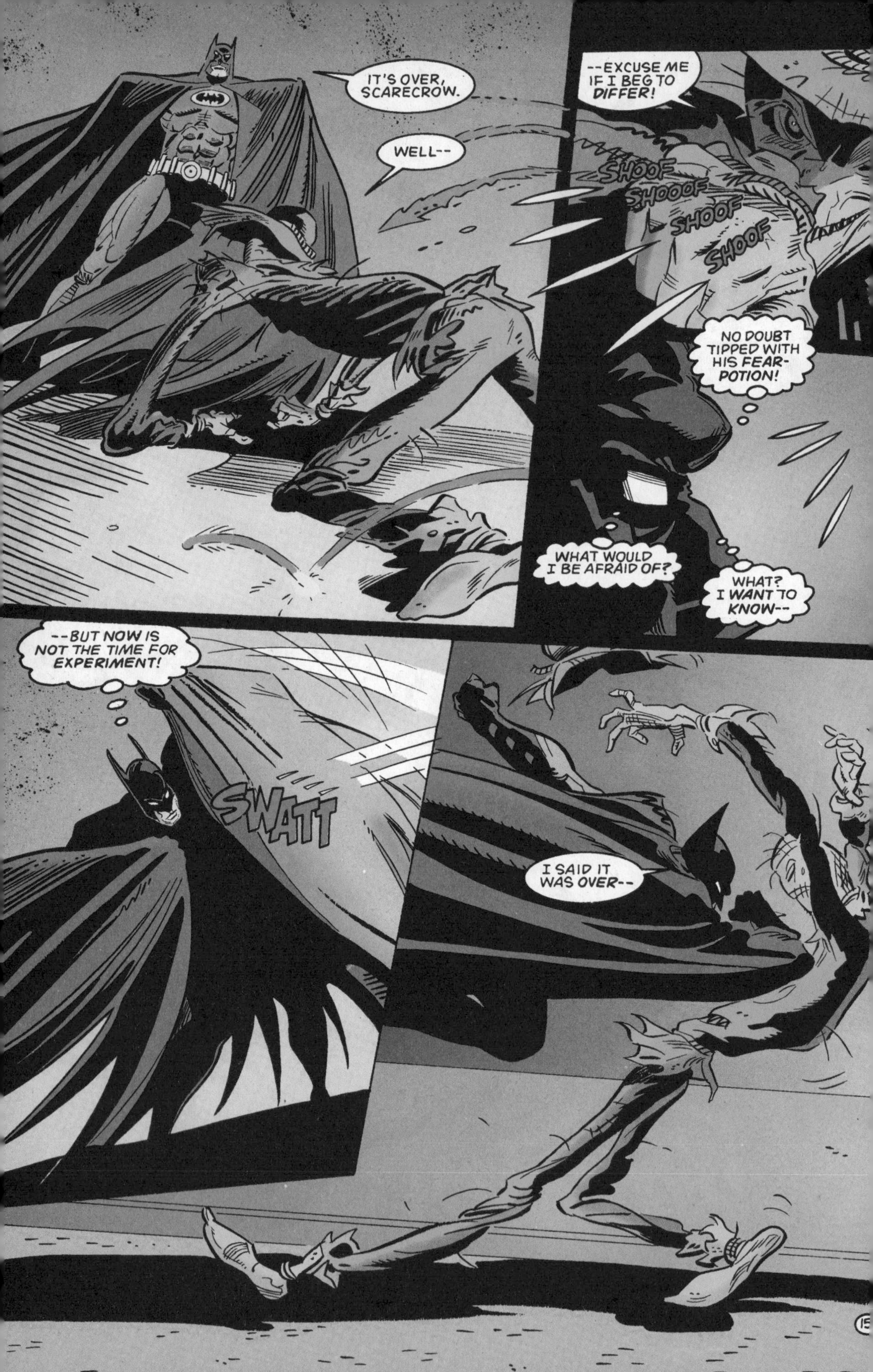
IT'S OVER, SCARECROW.
WELL--
--EXCUSE ME IF I BEG TO DIFFER!
SHOOF
SHOOOF
SHOOF
SHOOF
NO DOUBT TIPPED WITH HIS FEAR-POTION!
WHAT WOULD I BE AFRAID OF?
WHAT? I WANT TO KNOW--
--BUT NOW IS NOT THE TIME FOR EXPERIMENT!
SWATT
I SAID IT WAS OVER--

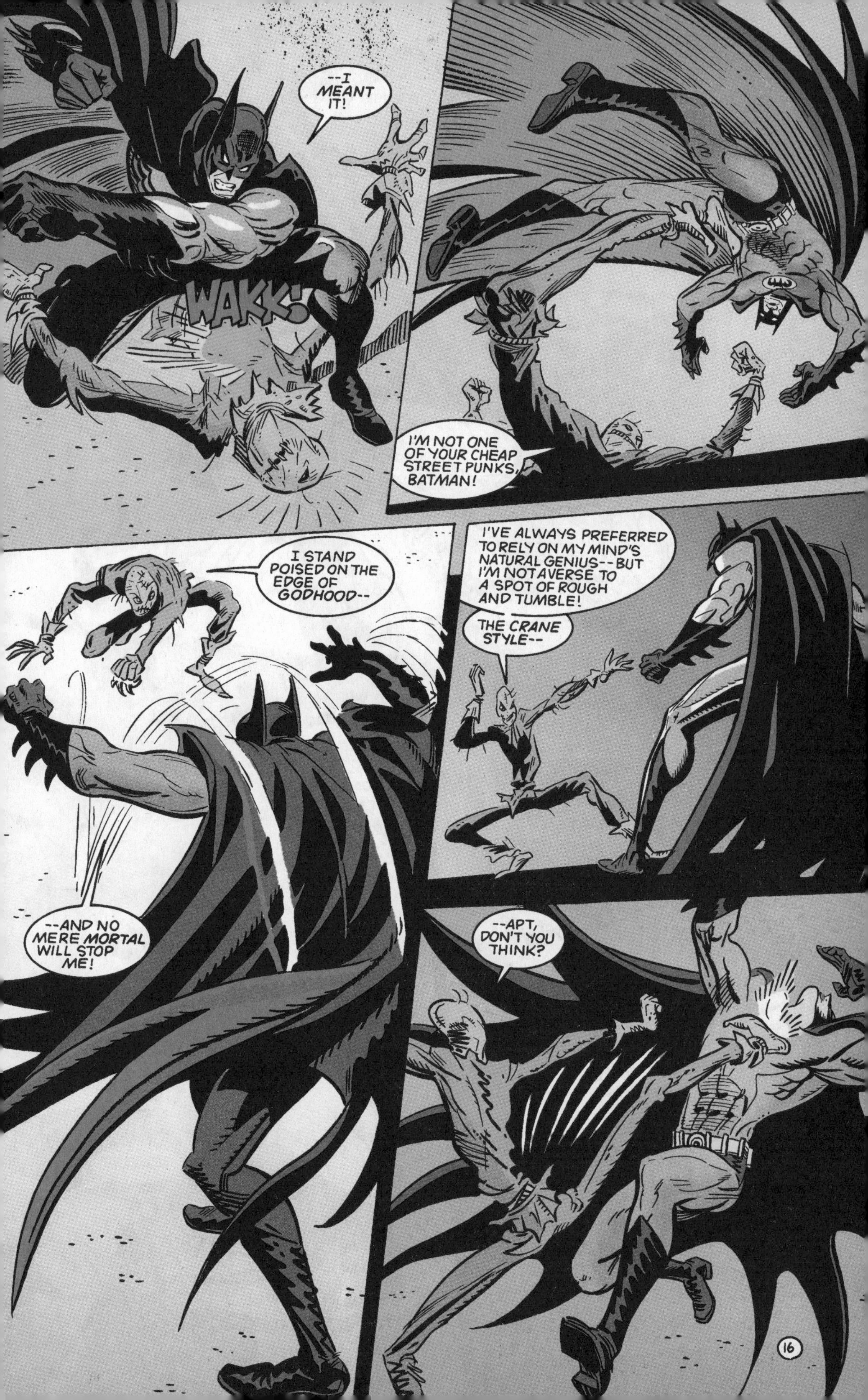
--I MEANT IT!
WAKK!
I'M NOT ONE OF YOUR CHEAP STREET PUNKS, BATMAN!
I STAND POISED ON THE EDGE OF GODHOOD--
--AND NO MERE MORTAL WILL STOP ME!
I'VE ALWAYS PREFERRED TO RELY ON MY MIND'S NATURAL GENIUS--BUT I'M NOT AVERSE TO A SPOT OF ROUGH AND TUMBLE!
THE CRANE STYLE--
--APT, DON'T YOU THINK?
16

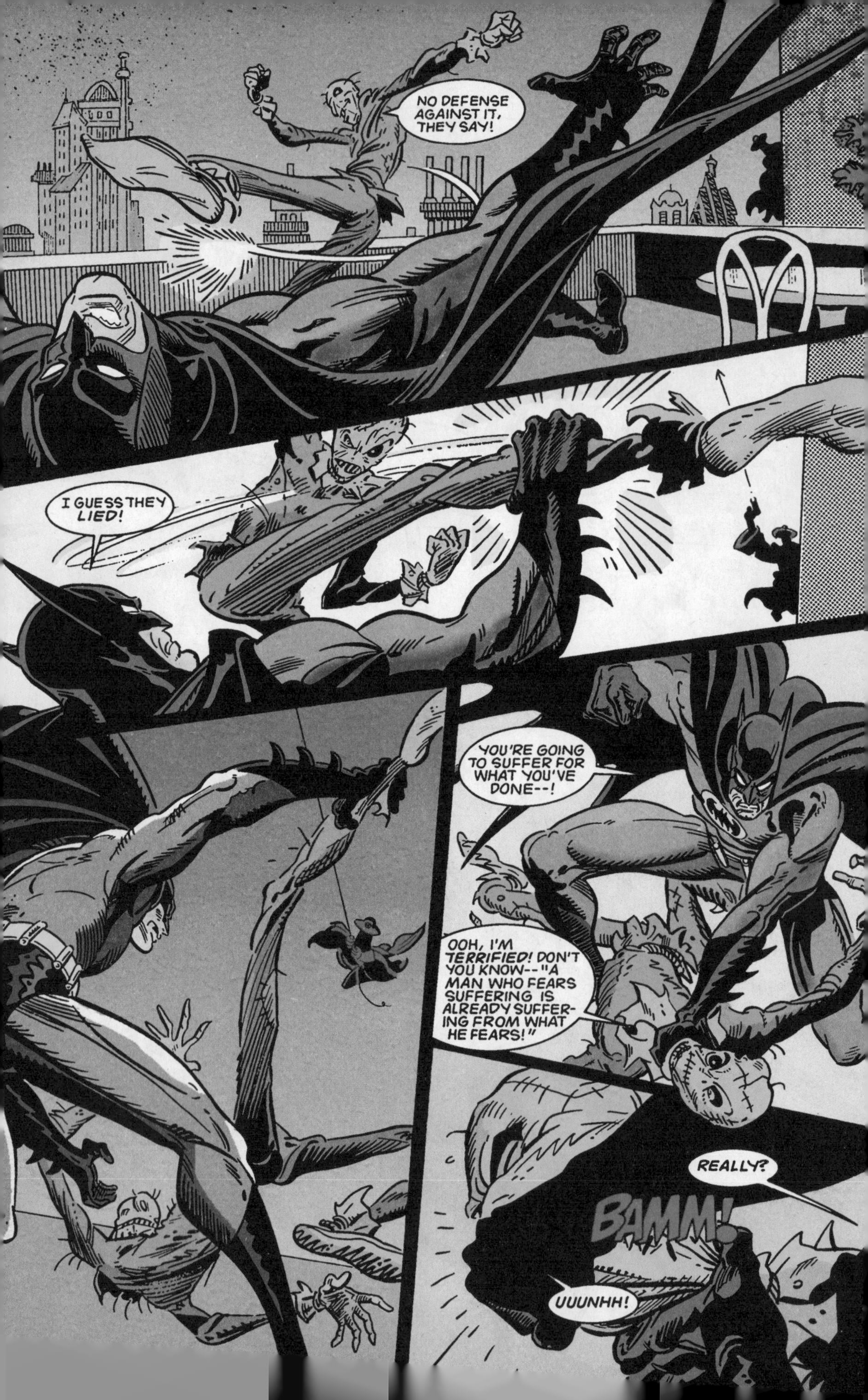
NO DEFENSE AGAINST IT, THEY SAY!
I GUESS THEY LIED!
YOU'RE GOING TO SUFFER FOR WHAT YOU'VE DONE--!
OOH, I'M TERRIFIED! DON'T YOU KNOW--"A MAN WHO FEARS SUFFERING IS ALREADY SUFFERING FROM WHAT HE FEARS!"
REALLY?
BAMM!
UUUNHH!

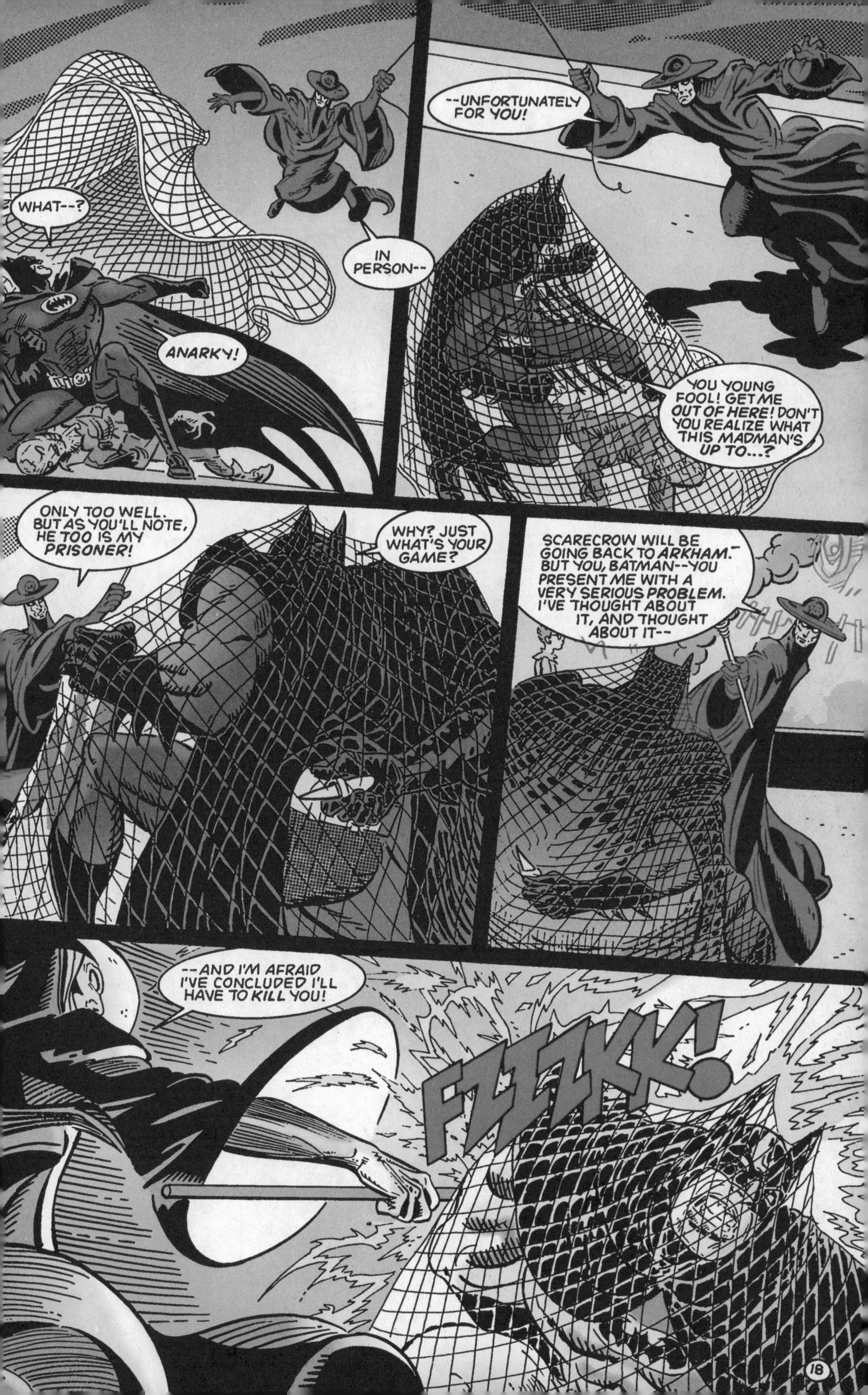
WHAT--?
IN PERSON--
ANARKY!
--UNFORTUNATELY FOR YOU!
YOU YOUNG FOOL! GET ME OUT OF HERE! DON'T YOU REALIZE WHAT THIS MADMAN'S UP TO...?
ONLY TOO WELL. BUT AS YOU'LL NOTE, HE TOO IS MY PRISONER!
WHY? JUST WHAT'S YOUR GAME?
SCARECROW WILL BE GOING BACK TO ARKHAM-- BUT YOU, BATMAN--YOU PRESENT ME WITH A VERY SERIOUS PROBLEM. I'VE THOUGHT ABOUT IT, AND THOUGHT ABOUT IT--
--AND I'M AFRAID I'VE CONCLUDED I'LL HAVE TO KILL YOU!
FZZKK!

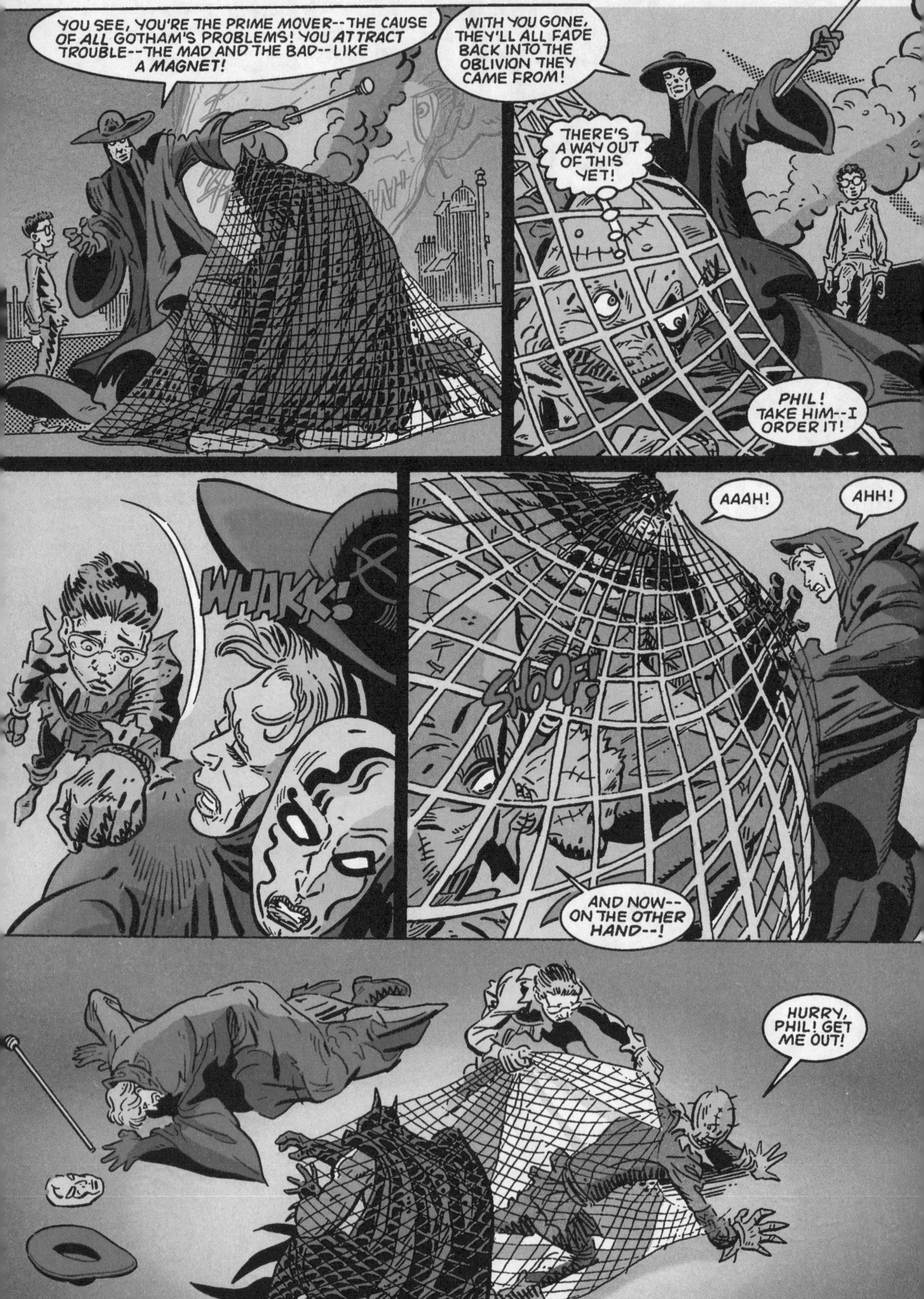
YOU SEE, YOU'RE THE PRIME MOVER--THE CAUSE OF ALL GOTHAM'S PROBLEMS! YOU ATTRACT TROUBLE--THE MAD AND THE BAD--LIKE A MAGNET!
WITH YOU GONE, THEY'LL ALL FADE BACK INTO THE OBLIVION THEY CAME FROM!
THERE'S A WAY OUT OF THIS YET!
PHIL! TAKE HIM--I ORDER IT!
WHAKK!
AAAH!
AHH!
SHOOF!
AND NOW--ON THE OTHER HAND--!
HURRY, PHIL! GET ME OUT!
19

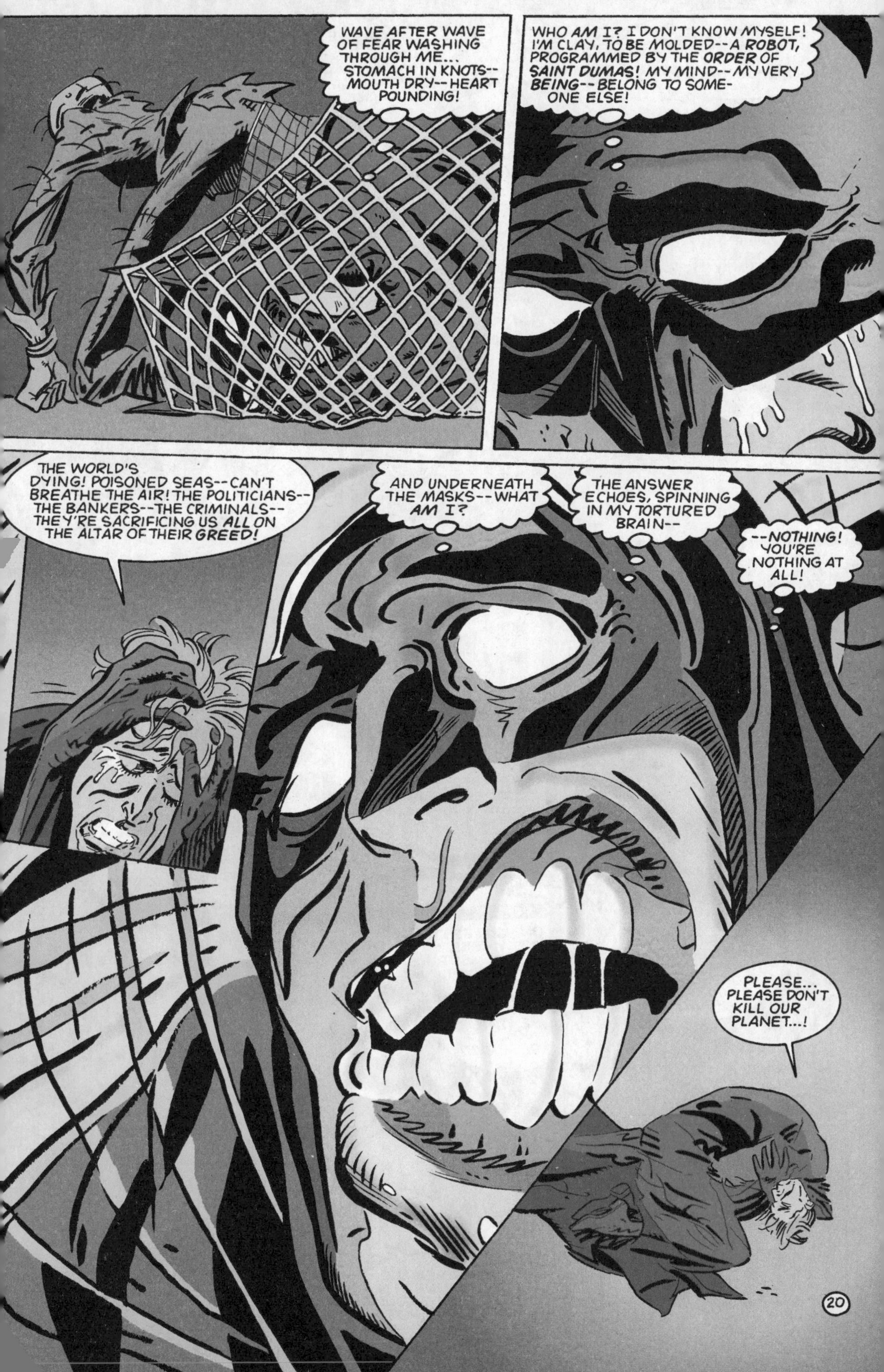
WAVE AFTER WAVE OF FEAR WASHING THROUGH ME... STOMACH IN KNOTS-- MOUTH DRY-- HEART POUNDING!
WHO AM I? I DON'T KNOW MYSELF! I'M CLAY, TO BE MOLDED-- A ROBOT, PROGRAMMED BY THE ORDER OF SAINT DUMAS! MY MIND-- MY VERY BEING-- BELONG TO SOMEONE ELSE!
THE WORLD'S DYING! POISONED SEAS--CAN'T BREATHE THE AIR! THE POLITICIANS-- THE BANKERS--THE CRIMINALS-- THEY'RE SACRIFICING US ALL ON THE ALTAR OF THEIR GREED!
AND UNDERNEATH THE MASKS-- WHAT AM I?
THE ANSWER ECHOES, SPINNING IN MY TORTURED BRAIN--
--NOTHING! YOU'RE NOTHING AT ALL!
PLEASE... PLEASE DON'T KILL OUR PLANET...!

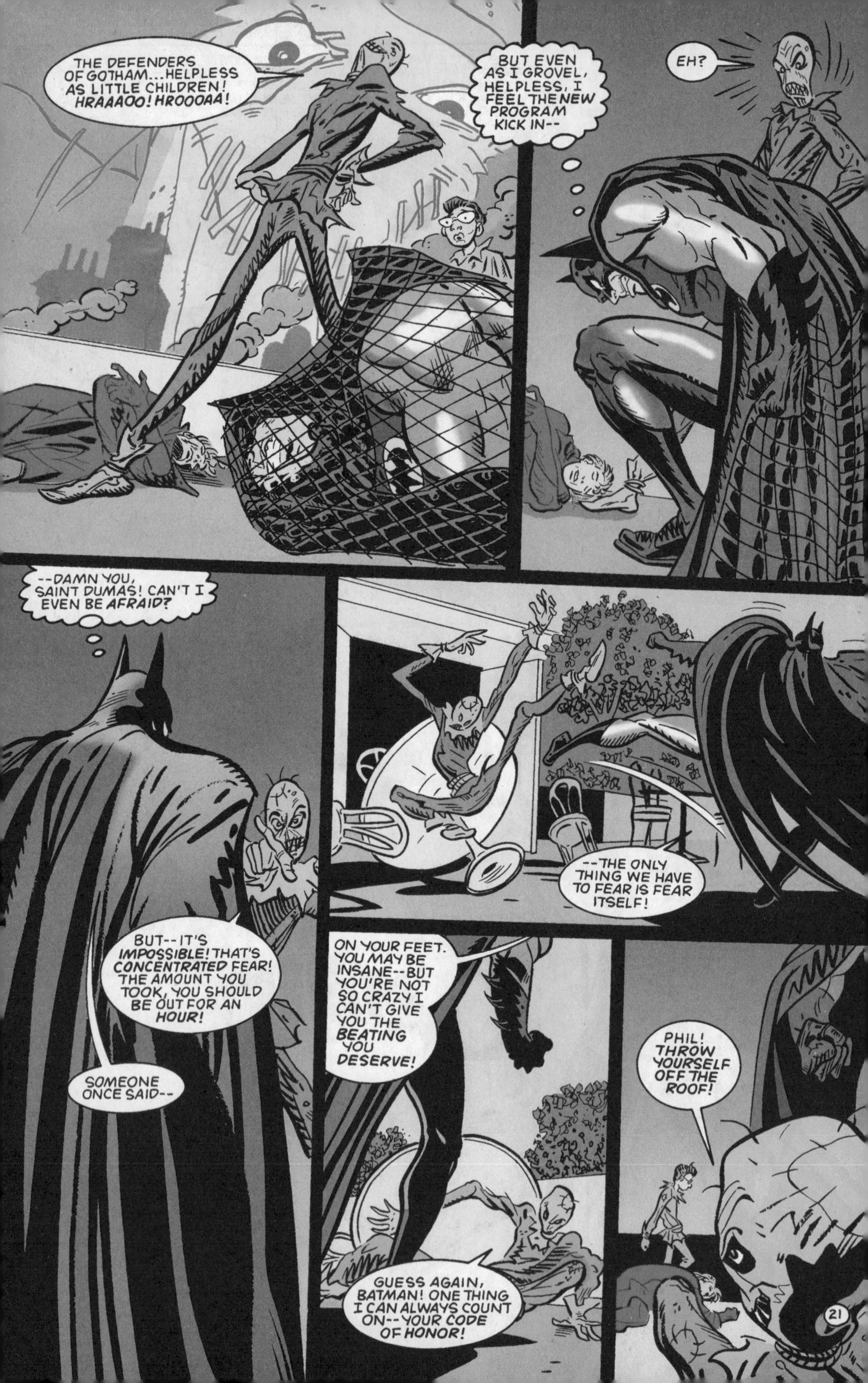
THE DEFENDERS OF GOTHAM... HELPLESS AS LITTLE CHILDREN! HRAAAOO! HROOOAA!
BUT EVEN AS I GROVEL, HELPLESS, I FEEL THE NEW PROGRAM KICK IN--
EH?
--DAMN YOU, SAINT DUMAS! CAN'T I EVEN BE AFRAID?
BUT--IT'S IMPOSSIBLE! THAT'S CONCENTRATED FEAR! THE AMOUNT YOU TOOK, YOU SHOULD BE OUT FOR AN HOUR!
SOMEONE ONCE SAID--
--THE ONLY THING WE HAVE TO FEAR IS FEAR ITSELF!
ON YOUR FEET. YOU MAY BE INSANE--BUT YOU'RE NOT SO CRAZY I CAN'T GIVE YOU THE BEATING YOU DESERVE!
GUESS AGAIN, BATMAN! ONE THING I CAN ALWAYS COUNT ON--YOUR CODE OF HONOR!
PHIL! THROW YOURSELF OFF THE ROOF!
21

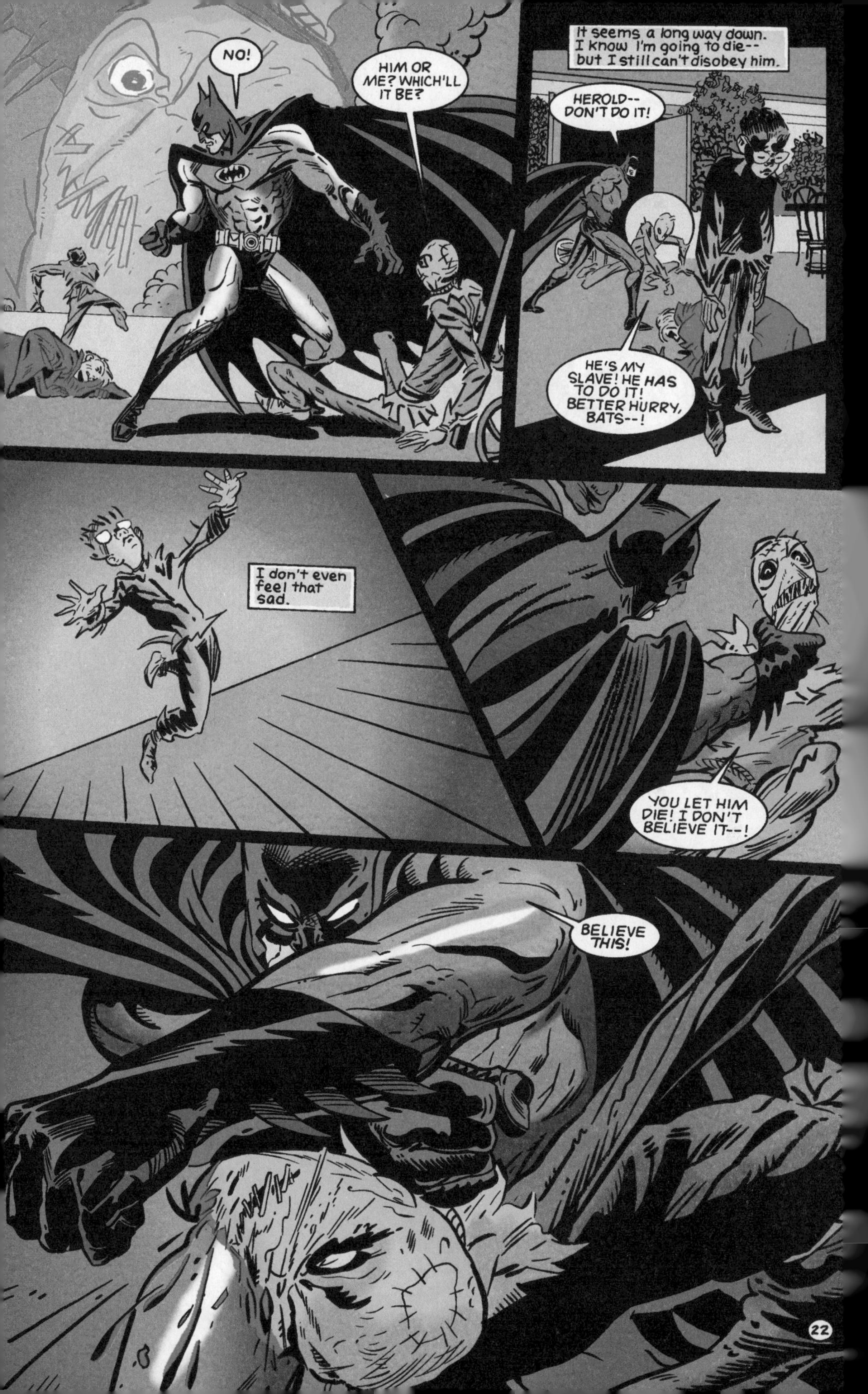
NO!
HIM OR ME? WHICH'LL IT BE?
It seems a long way down. I know I'm going to die-- but I still can't disobey him.
HEROLD-- DON'T DO IT!
HE'S MY SLAVE! HE HAS TO DO IT! BETTER HURRY, BATS--!
I don't even feel that sad.
YOU LET HIM DIE! I DON'T BELIEVE IT--!
BELIEVE THIS!

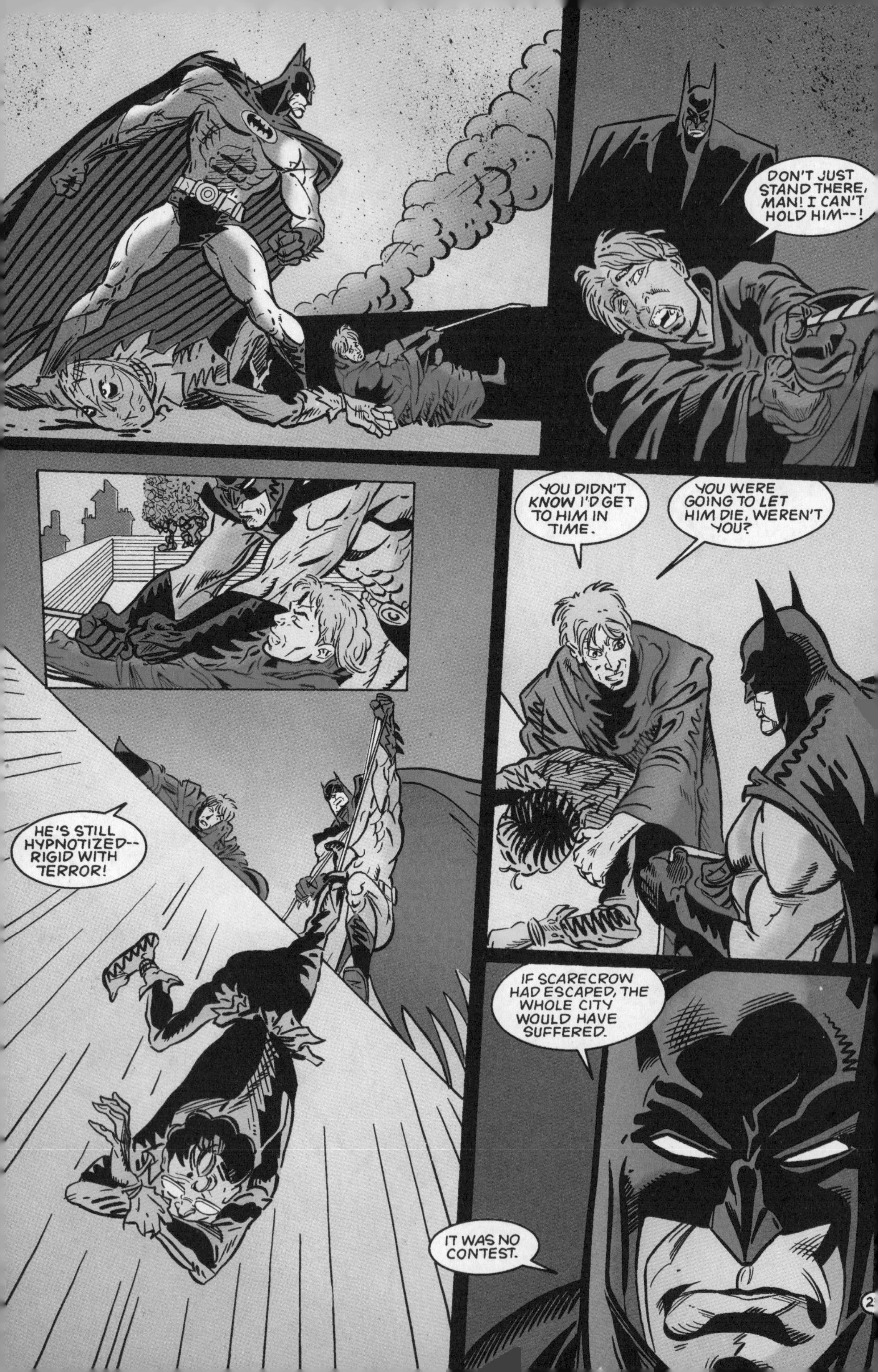
DON'T JUST STAND THERE, MAN! I CAN'T HOLD HIM--!
YOU DIDN'T KNOW I'D GET TO HIM IN TIME.
YOU WERE GOING TO LET HIM DIE, WEREN'T YOU?
HE'S STILL HYPNOTIZED-- RIGID WITH TERROR!
IF SCARECROW HAD ESCAPED, THE WHOLE CITY WOULD HAVE SUFFERED.
IT WAS NO CONTEST.
2

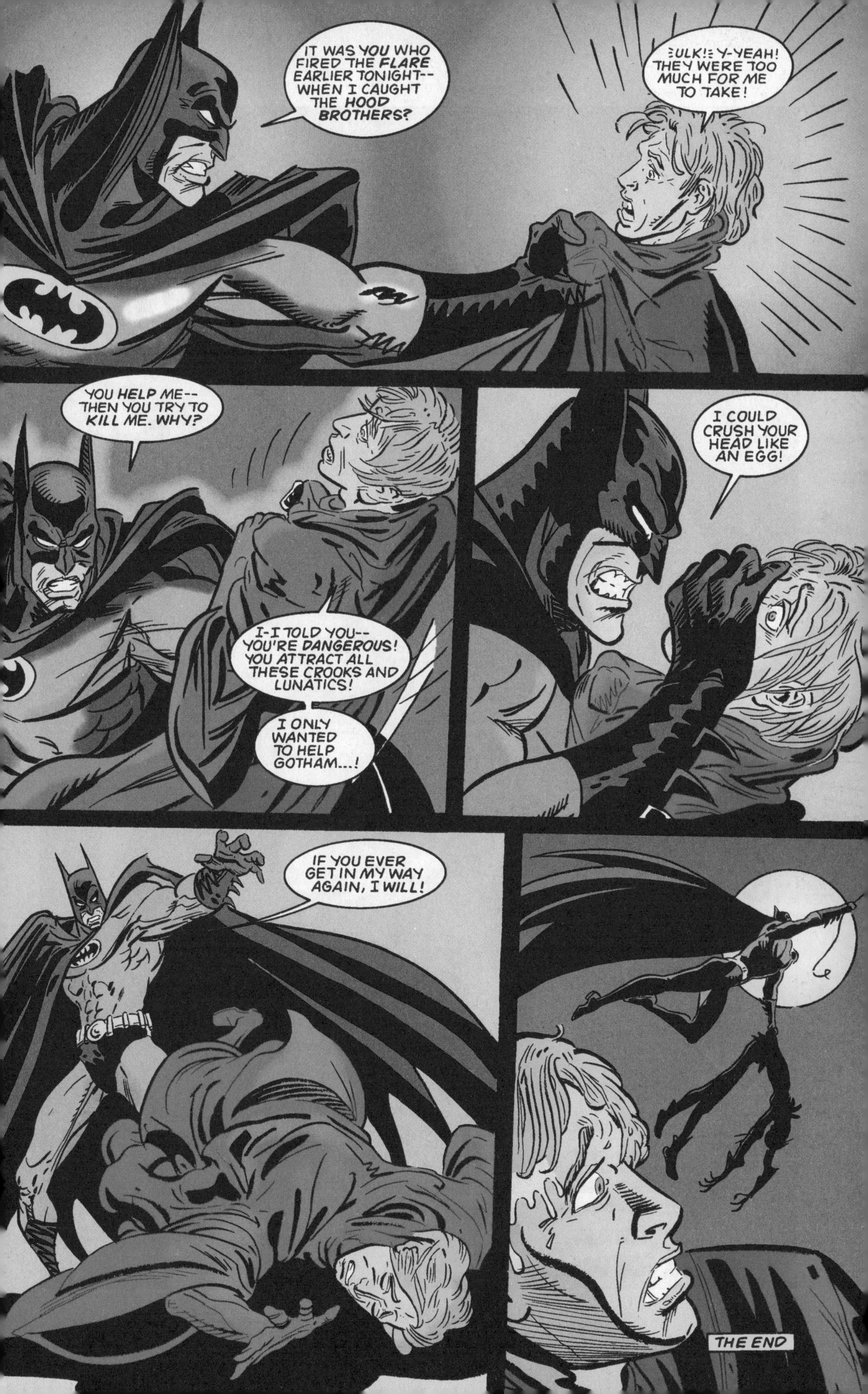
IT WAS YOU WHO FIRED THE FLARE EARLIER TONIGHT-- WHEN I CAUGHT THE HOOD BROTHERS?
ULK! Y-YEAH! THEY WERE TOO MUCH FOR ME TO TAKE!
YOU HELP ME-- THEN YOU TRY TO KILL ME. WHY?
I-I TOLD YOU-- YOU'RE DANGEROUS! YOU ATTRACT ALL THESE CROOKS AND LUNATICS!
I ONLY WANTED TO HELP GOTHAM...!
I COULD CRUSH YOUR HEAD LIKE AN EGG!
IF YOU EVER GET IN MY WAY AGAIN, I WILL!
THE END

Cover art by KELLEY JONES

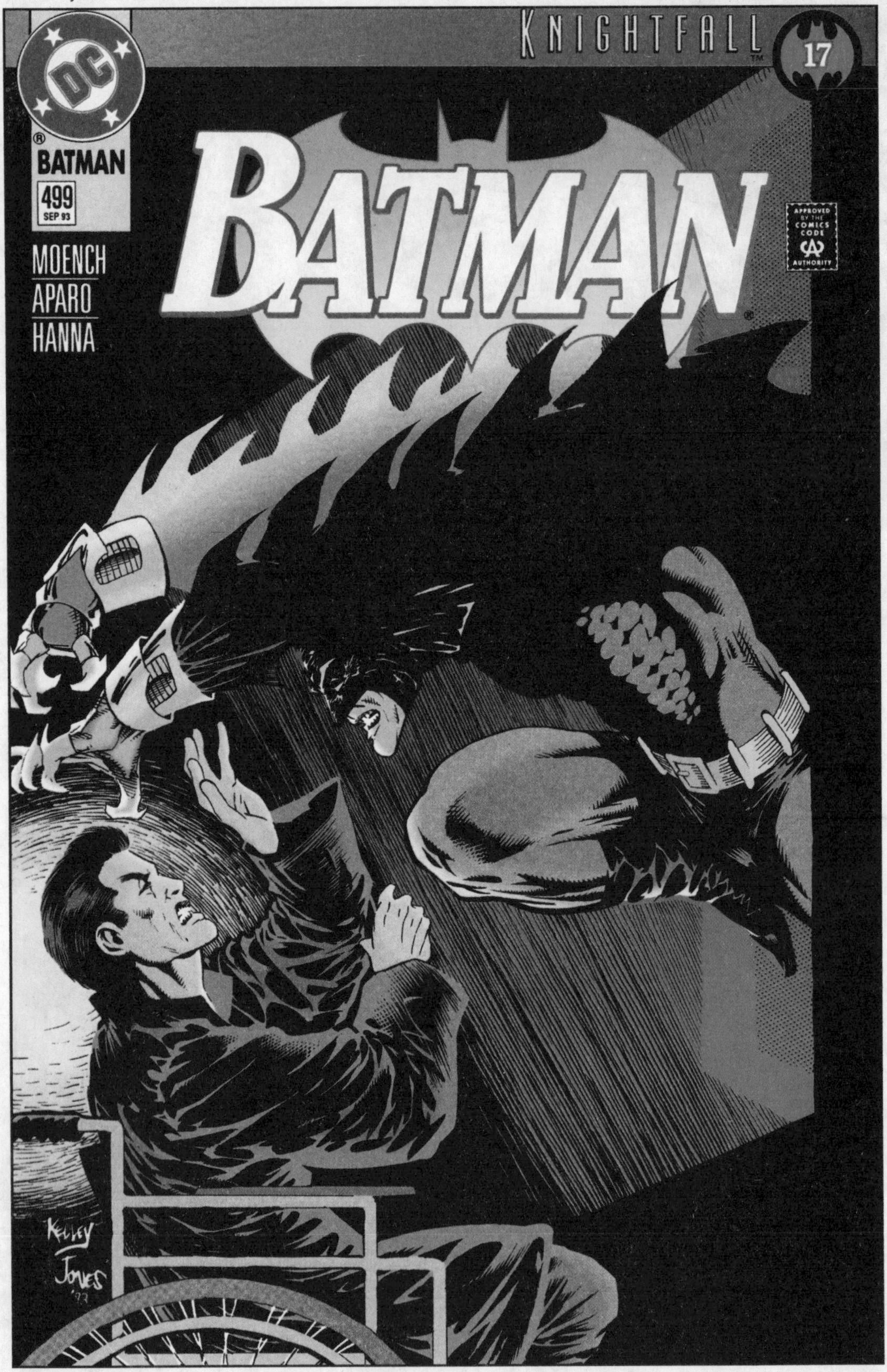

KNIGHTFALL
17
DC
BATMAN
499
SEP 93
MOENCH
APARO
HANNA
BATMAN
APPROVED BY THE COMICS CODE AUTHORITY
KELLEY JONES '93

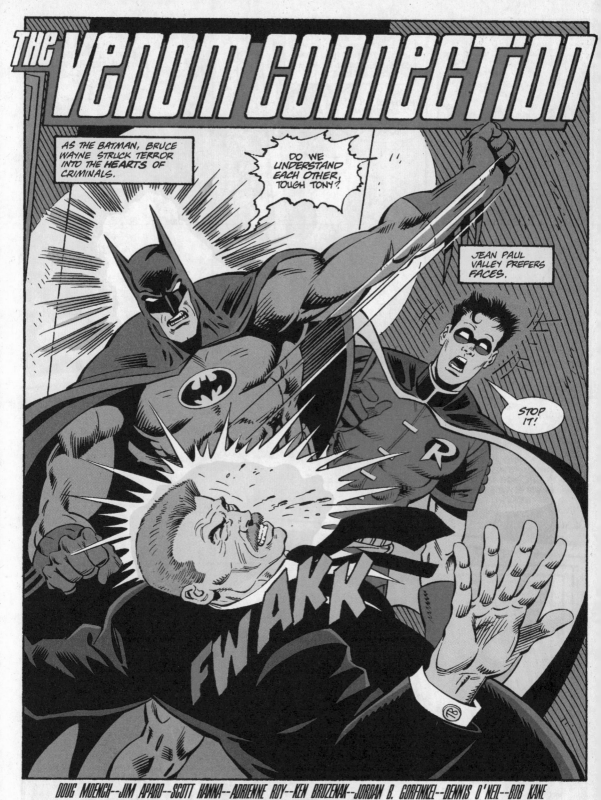

THE VENOM CONNECTION

AS THE BATMAN, BRUCE WAYNE STRUCK TERROR INTO THE HEARTS OF CRIMINALS.

DO WE UNDERSTAND EACH OTHER, TOUGH TONY?

JEAN PAUL VALLEY PREFERS FACES.

STOP IT!

FWAKK

DOUG MOENCH--JIM APARO--SCOTT HANNA--ADRIENNE ROY--KEN BRUZENAK--JORDAN B. GORFINKEL--DENNIS O'NEIL--BOB KANE

writer   artist   inker   colorist   letterer   vaccine creator   editor   Batman creator

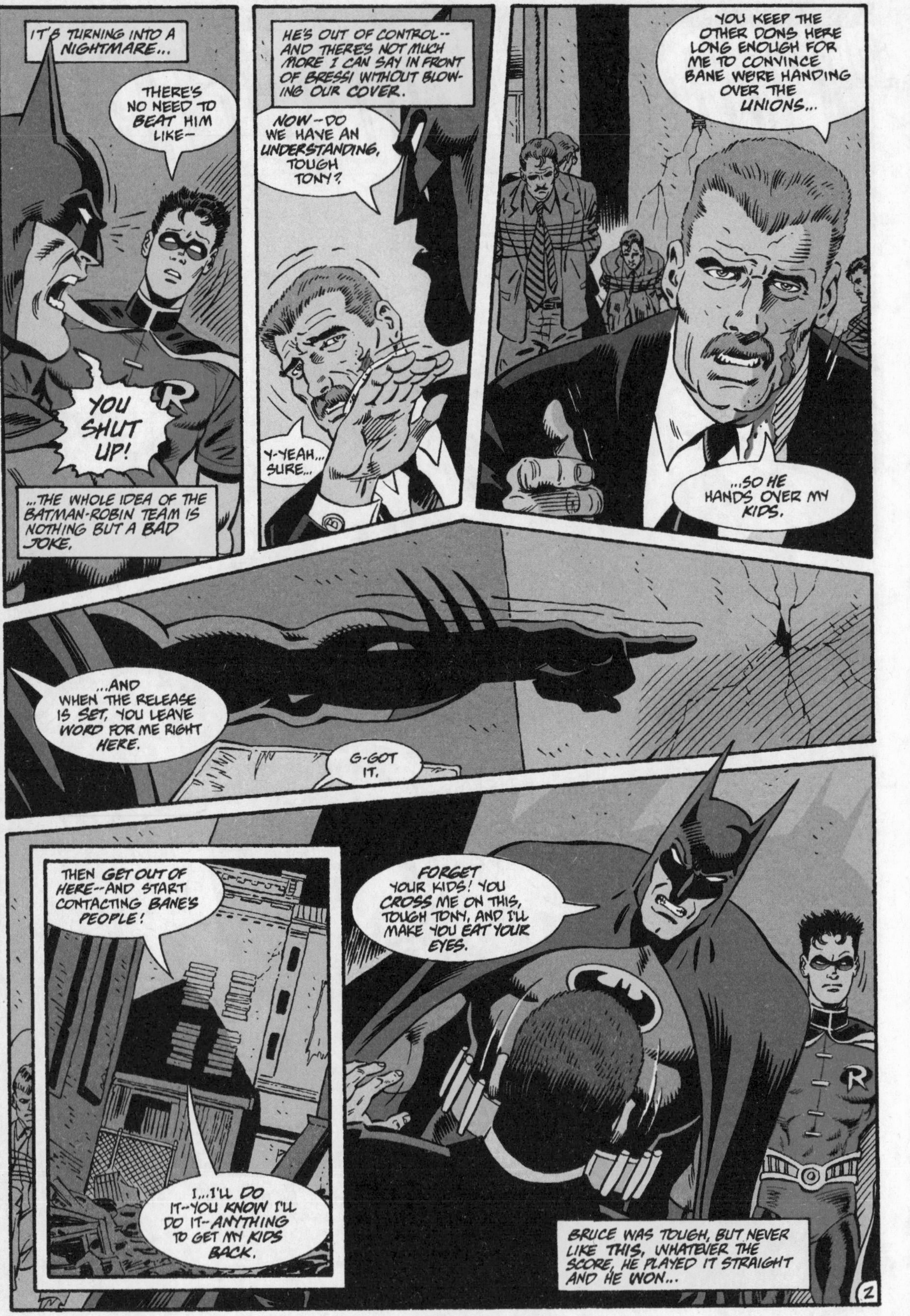

IT'S TURNING INTO A NIGHTMARE...
THERE'S NO NEED TO BEAT HIM LIKE—
YOU SHUT UP!
...THE WHOLE IDEA OF THE BATMAN-ROBIN TEAM IS NOTHING BUT A BAD JOKE.
HE'S OUT OF CONTROL-- AND THERE'S NOT MUCH MORE I CAN SAY IN FRONT OF BRESSI WITHOUT BLOWING OUR COVER.
NOW--DO WE HAVE AN UNDERSTANDING, TOUGH TONY?
Y-YEAH... SURE...
YOU KEEP THE OTHER DONS HERE LONG ENOUGH FOR ME TO CONVINCE BANE WE'RE HANDING OVER THE UNIONS...
...SO HE HANDS OVER MY KIDS.
...AND WHEN THE RELEASE IS SET, YOU LEAVE WORD FOR ME RIGHT HERE.
G-GOT IT.
THEN GET OUT OF HERE--AND START CONTACTING BANE'S PEOPLE!
I...I'LL DO IT--YOU KNOW I'LL DO IT--ANYTHING TO GET MY KIDS BACK.
FORGET YOUR KIDS! YOU CROSS ME ON THIS, TOUGH TONY, AND I'LL MAKE YOU EAT YOUR EYES.
BRUCE WAS TOUGH, BUT NEVER LIKE THIS. WHATEVER THE SCORE, HE PLAYED IT STRAIGHT AND HE WON...
2

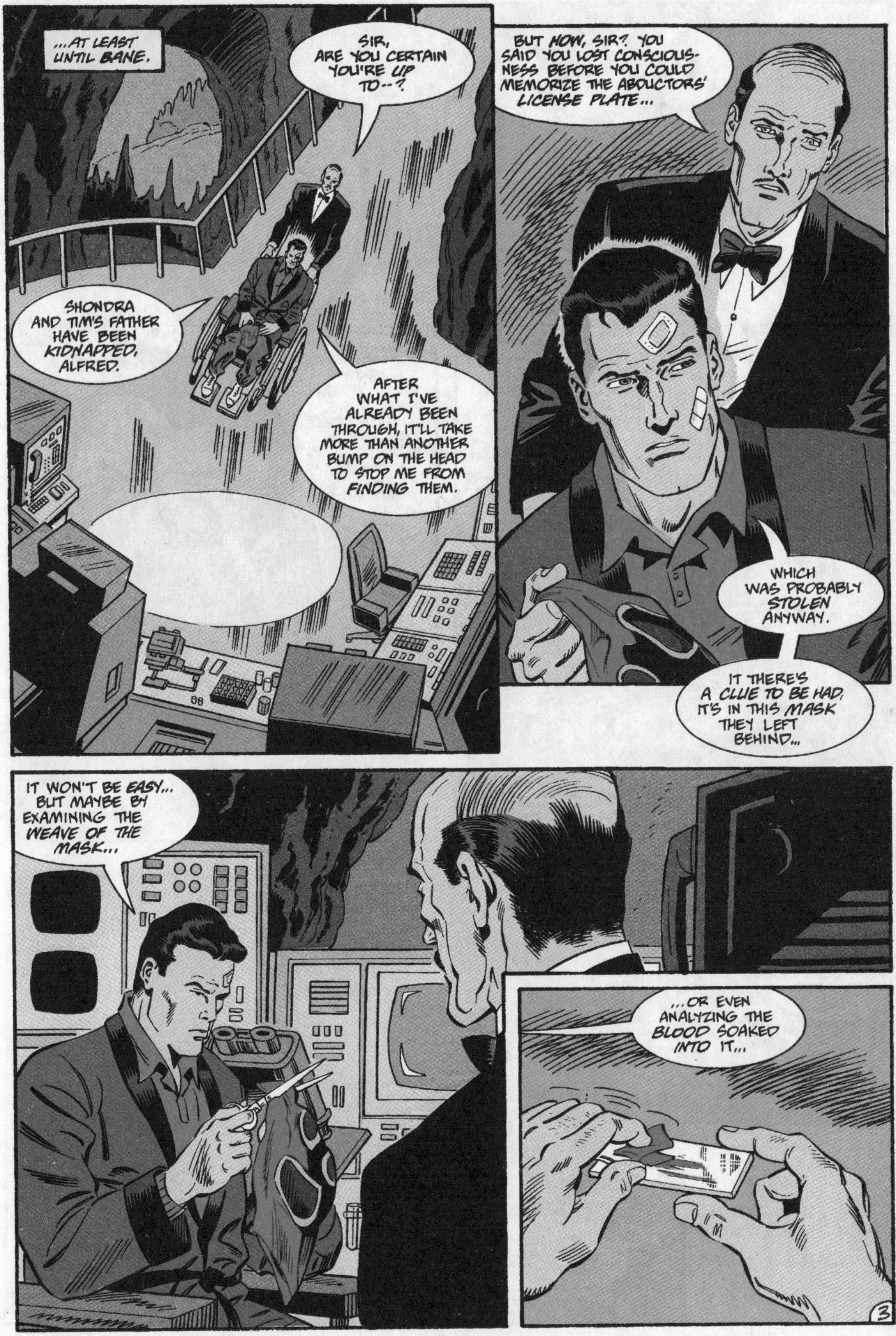
...AT LEAST UNTIL BANE.
SIR, ARE YOU CERTAIN YOU'RE UP TO--?
SHONDRA AND TIM'S FATHER HAVE BEEN KIDNAPPED, ALFRED.
AFTER WHAT I'VE ALREADY BEEN THROUGH, IT'LL TAKE MORE THAN ANOTHER BUMP ON THE HEAD TO STOP ME FROM FINDING THEM.
BUT HOW, SIR? YOU SAID YOU LOST CONSCIOUSNESS BEFORE YOU COULD MEMORIZE THE ABDUCTORS' LICENSE PLATE...
WHICH WAS PROBABLY STOLEN ANYWAY.
IT THERE'S A CLUE TO BE HAD, IT'S IN THIS MASK THEY LEFT BEHIND...
IT WON'T BE EASY... BUT MAYBE BY EXAMINING THE WEAVE OF THE MASK...
...OR EVEN ANALYZING THE BLOOD SOAKED INTO IT...
3

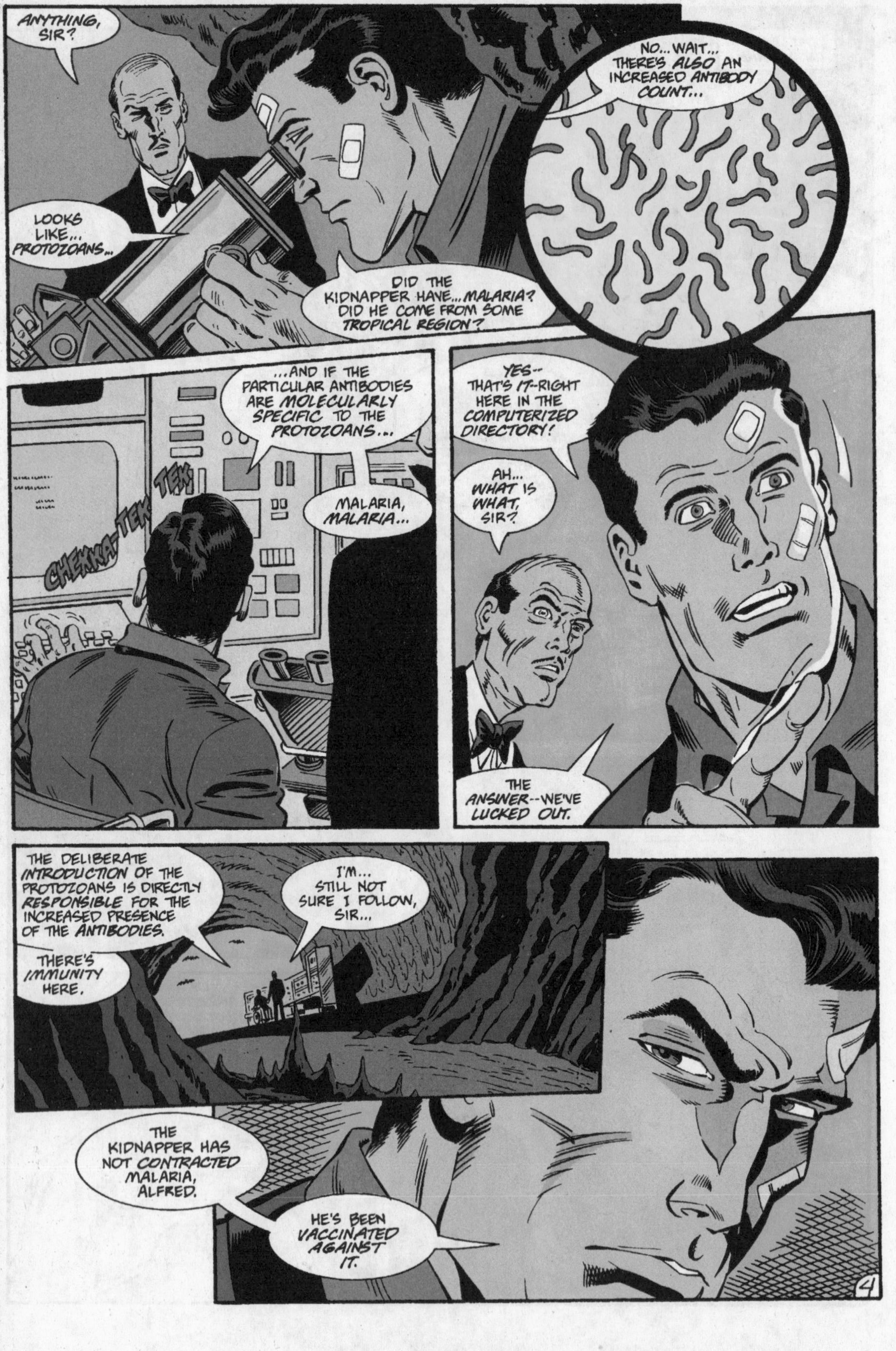
ANYTHING, SIR?
NO... WAIT... THERE'S ALSO AN INCREASED ANTIBODY COUNT...
LOOKS LIKE... PROTOZOANS...
DID THE KIDNAPPER HAVE... MALARIA? DID HE COME FROM SOME TROPICAL REGION?
...AND IF THE PARTICULAR ANTIBODIES ARE MOLECULARLY SPECIFIC TO THE PROTOZOANS...
TEK
CHEKKA-TEK
MALARIA, MALARIA...
YES-- THAT'S IT--RIGHT HERE IN THE COMPUTERIZED DIRECTORY!
AH... WHAT IS WHAT, SIR?
THE ANSWER--WE'VE LUCKED OUT.
THE DELIBERATE INTRODUCTION OF THE PROTOZOANS IS DIRECTLY RESPONSIBLE FOR THE INCREASED PRESENCE OF THE ANTIBODIES.
THERE'S IMMUNITY HERE.
I'M... STILL NOT SURE I FOLLOW, SIR...
THE KIDNAPPER HAS NOT CONTRACTED MALARIA, ALFRED.
HE'S BEEN VACCINATED AGAINST IT.
4

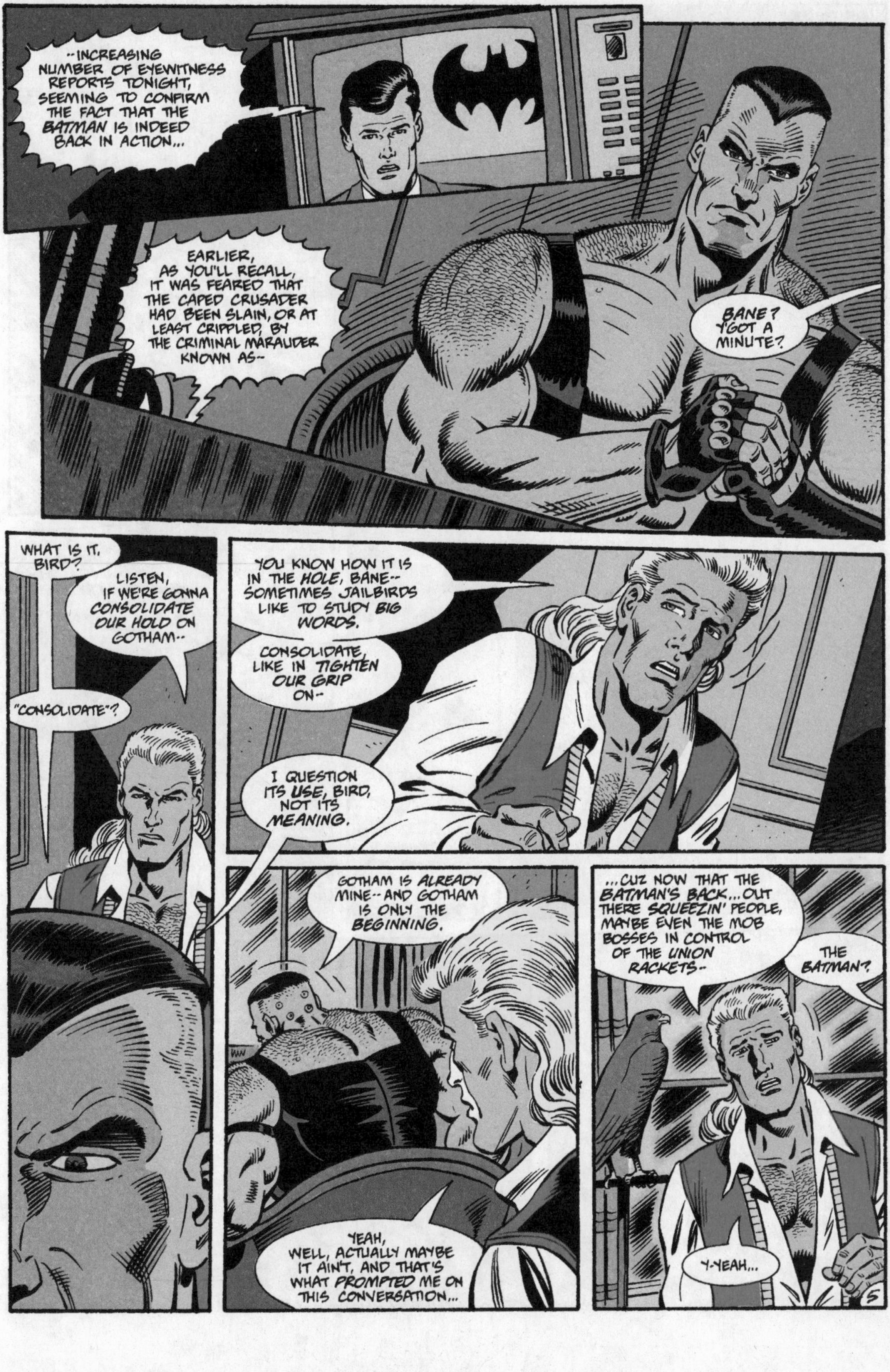
--INCREASING NUMBER OF EYEWITNESS REPORTS TONIGHT, SEEMING TO CONFIRM THE FACT THAT THE BATMAN IS INDEED BACK IN ACTION...
EARLIER, AS YOU'LL RECALL, IT WAS FEARED THAT THE CAPED CRUSADER HAD BEEN SLAIN, OR AT LEAST CRIPPLED, BY THE CRIMINAL MARAUDER KNOWN AS--
BANE? Y'GOT A MINUTE?
WHAT IS IT, BIRD?
LISTEN, IF WE'RE GONNA CONSOLIDATE OUR HOLD ON GOTHAM--
"CONSOLIDATE"?
YOU KNOW HOW IT IS IN THE HOLE, BANE-- SOMETIMES JAILBIRDS LIKE TO STUDY BIG WORDS.
CONSOLIDATE, LIKE IN TIGHTEN OUR GRIP ON--
I QUESTION ITS USE, BIRD, NOT ITS MEANING.
GOTHAM IS ALREADY MINE-- AND GOTHAM IS ONLY THE BEGINNING.
YEAH, WELL, ACTUALLY MAYBE IT AIN'T, AND THAT'S WHAT PROMPTED ME ON THIS CONVERSATION...
...CUZ NOW THAT THE BATMAN'S BACK... OUT THERE SQUEEZIN' PEOPLE, MAYBE EVEN THE MOB BOSSES IN CONTROL OF THE UNION RACKETS--
THE BATMAN?
Y-YEAH...
5

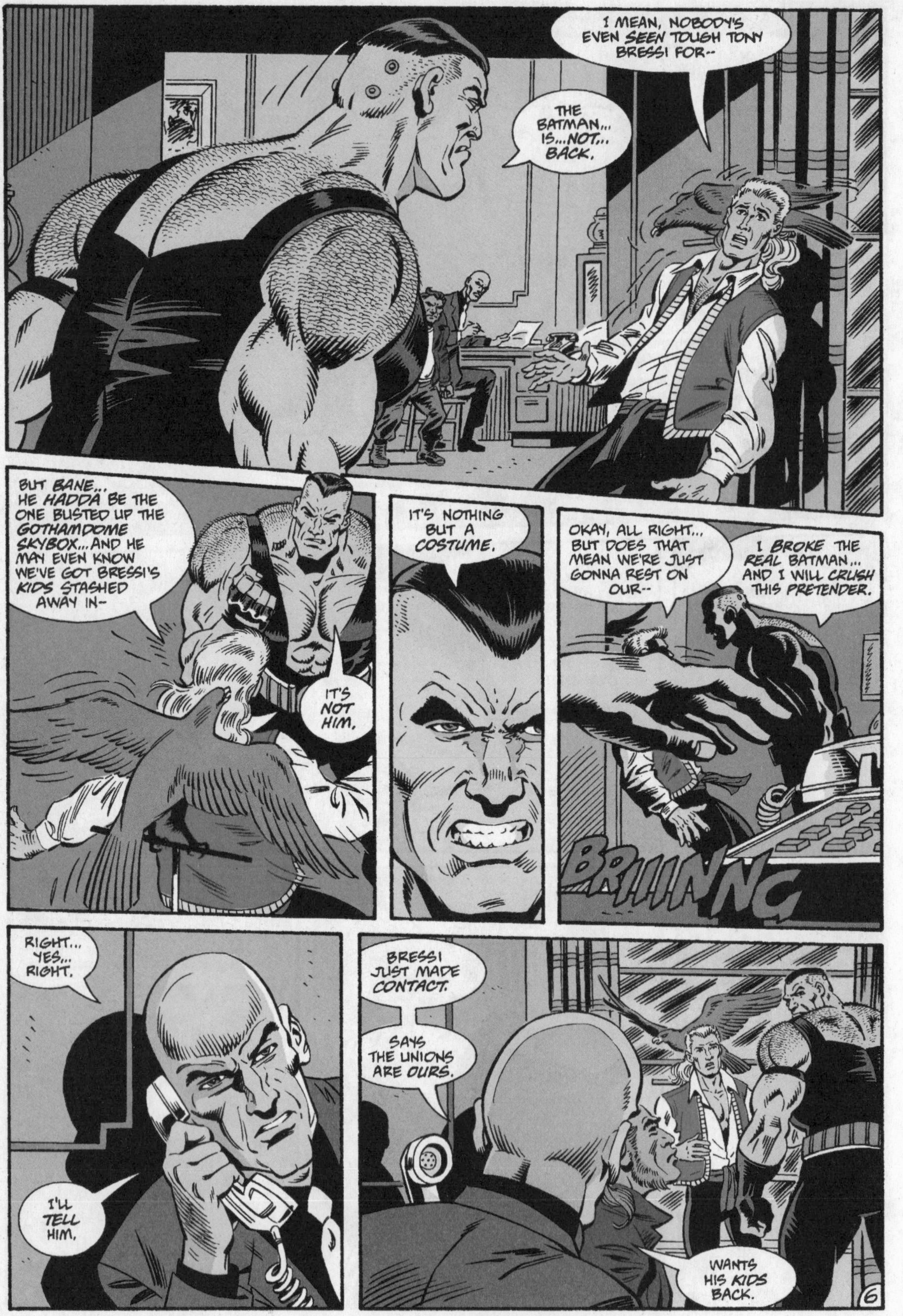
I MEAN, NOBODY'S EVEN SEEN TOUGH TONY BRESSI FOR--
THE BATMAN... IS...NOT... BACK.
BUT BANE... HE HADDA BE THE ONE BUSTED UP THE GOTHAMDOME SKYBOX...AND HE MAY EVEN KNOW WE'VE GOT BRESSI'S KIDS STASHED AWAY IN--
IT'S NOT HIM.
IT'S NOTHING BUT A COSTUME.
OKAY, ALL RIGHT... BUT DOES THAT MEAN WE'RE JUST GONNA REST ON OUR--
I BROKE THE REAL BATMAN... AND I WILL CRUSH THIS PRETENDER.
BRIIINNG
RIGHT... YES... RIGHT.
I'LL TELL HIM.
BRESSI JUST MADE CONTACT.
SAYS THE UNIONS ARE OURS.
WANTS HIS KIDS BACK.
6

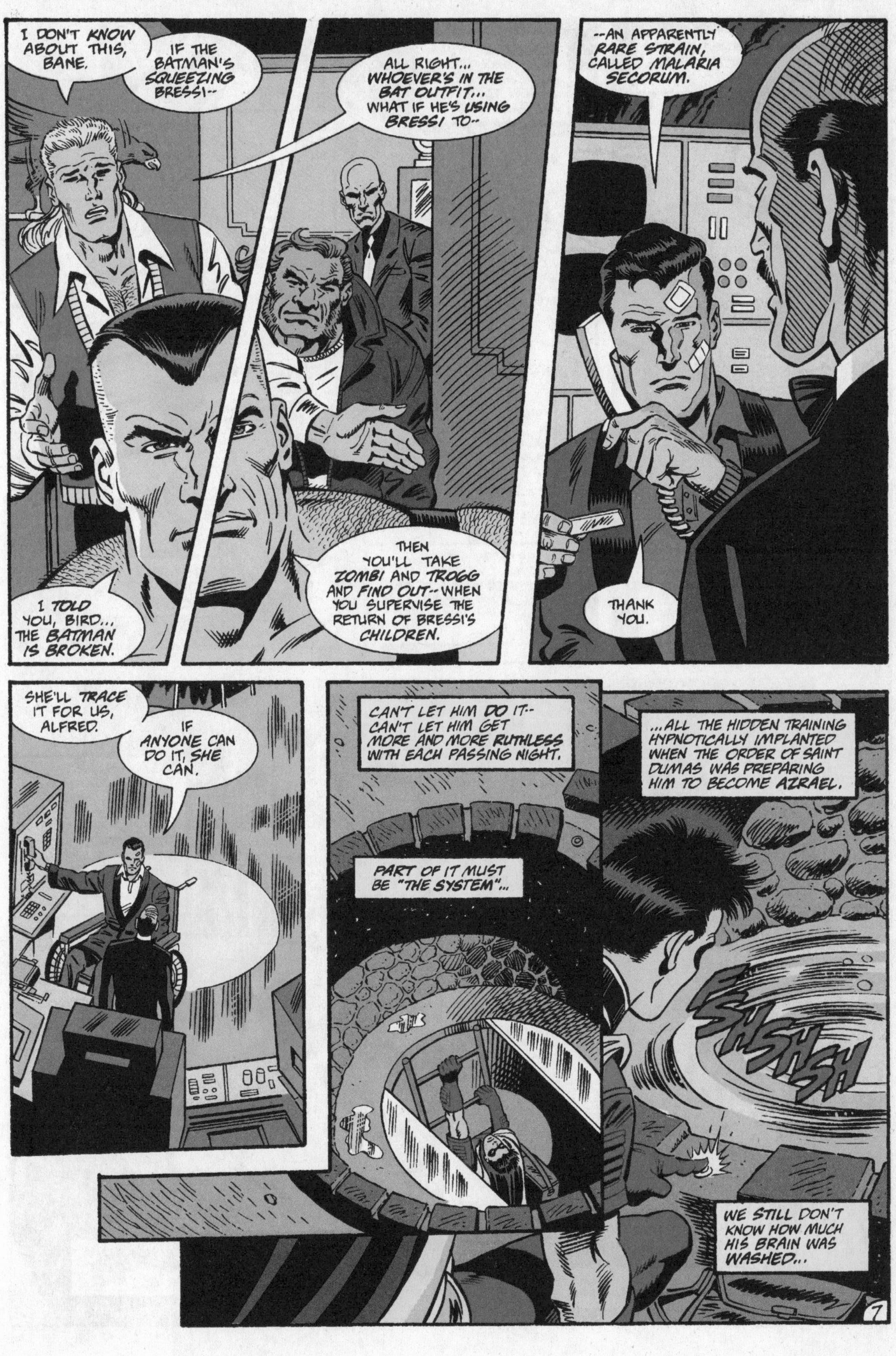

I DON'T KNOW ABOUT THIS, BANE.
IF THE BATMAN'S SQUEEZING BRESSI--
I TOLD YOU, BIRD... THE BATMAN IS BROKEN.
ALL RIGHT... WHOEVER'S IN THE BAT OUTFIT... WHAT IF HE'S USING BRESSI TO--
THEN YOU'LL TAKE ZOMBI AND TROGG AND FIND OUT-- WHEN YOU SUPERVISE THE RETURN OF BRESSI'S CHILDREN.
--AN APPARENTLY RARE STRAIN, CALLED MALARIA SECORUM.
THANK YOU.
SHE'LL TRACE IT FOR US, ALFRED.
IF ANYONE CAN DO IT, SHE CAN.
CAN'T LET HIM DO IT-- CAN'T LET HIM GET MORE AND MORE RUTHLESS WITH EACH PASSING NIGHT.
PART OF IT MUST BE "THE SYSTEM"...
...ALL THE HIDDEN TRAINING HYPNOTICALLY IMPLANTED WHEN THE ORDER OF SAINT DUMAS WAS PREPARING HIM TO BECOME AZRAEL.
SHSHSH
WE STILL DON'T KNOW HOW MUCH HIS BRAIN WAS WASHED...
7

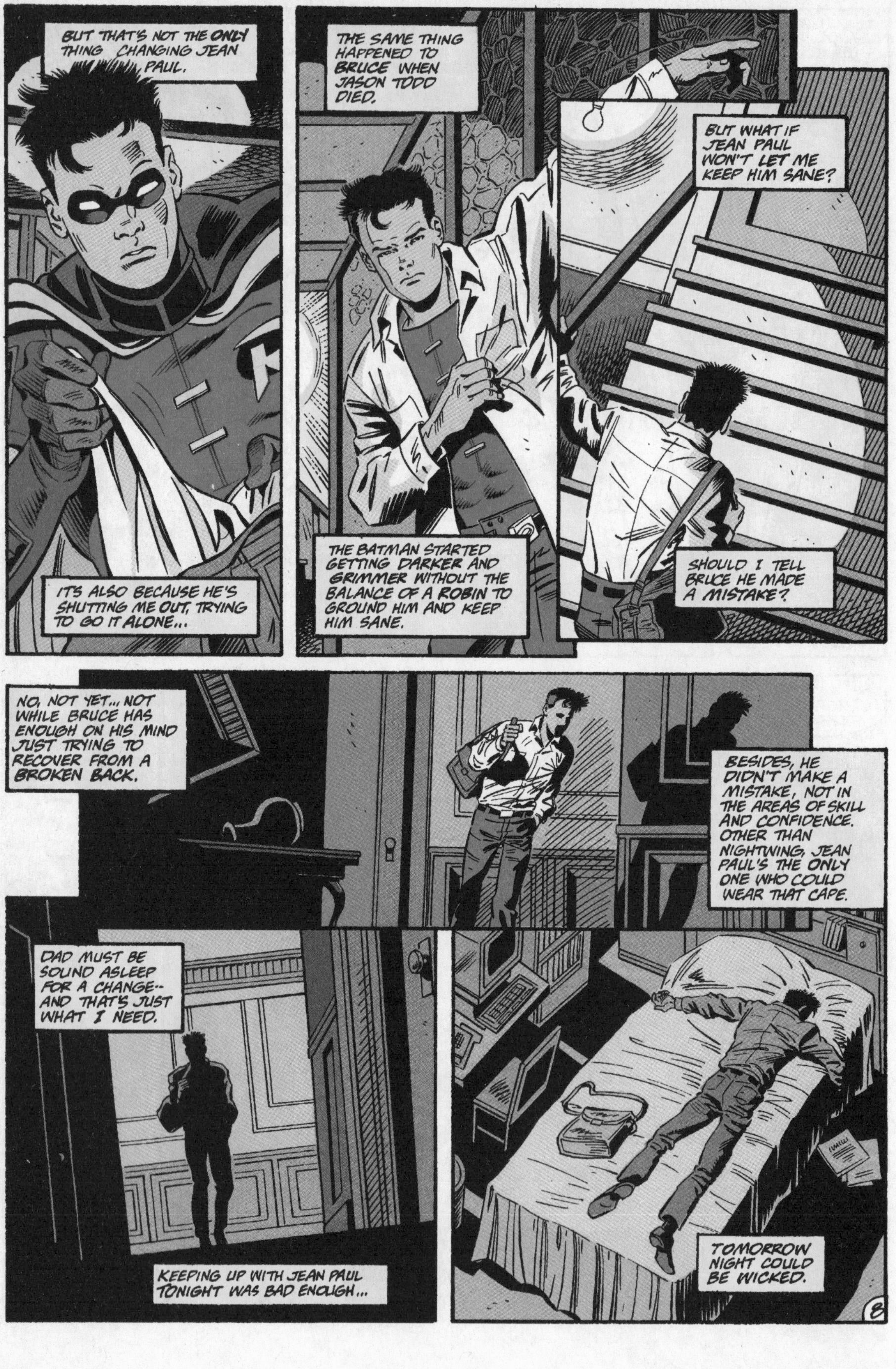
BUT THAT'S NOT THE ONLY THING CHANGING JEAN PAUL.
IT'S ALSO BECAUSE HE'S SHUTTING ME OUT, TRYING TO GO IT ALONE...
THE SAME THING HAPPENED TO BRUCE WHEN JASON TODD DIED.
THE BATMAN STARTED GETTING DARKER AND GRIMMER WITHOUT THE BALANCE OF A ROBIN TO GROUND HIM AND KEEP HIM SANE.
BUT WHAT IF JEAN PAUL WON'T LET ME KEEP HIM SANE?
SHOULD I TELL BRUCE HE MADE A MISTAKE?
NO, NOT YET... NOT WHILE BRUCE HAS ENOUGH ON HIS MIND JUST TRYING TO RECOVER FROM A BROKEN BACK.
BESIDES, HE DIDN'T MAKE A MISTAKE, NOT IN THE AREAS OF SKILL AND CONFIDENCE. OTHER THAN NIGHTWING, JEAN PAUL'S THE ONLY ONE WHO COULD WEAR THAT CAPE.
DAD MUST BE SOUND ASLEEP FOR A CHANGE-- AND THAT'S JUST WHAT I NEED.
KEEPING UP WITH JEAN PAUL TONIGHT WAS BAD ENOUGH...
TOMORROW NIGHT COULD BE WICKED.
8

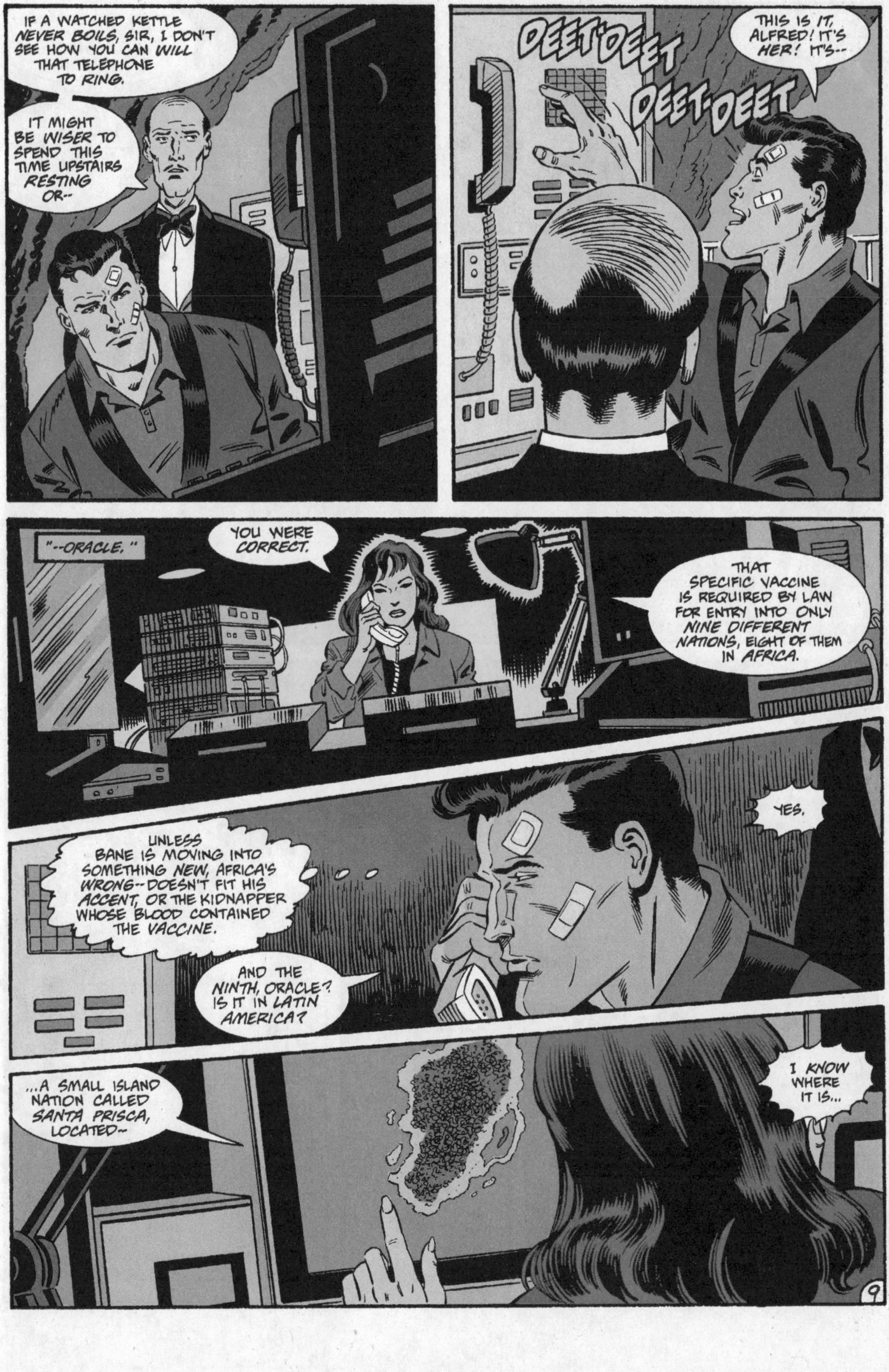
IF A WATCHED KETTLE NEVER BOILS, SIR, I DON'T SEE HOW YOU CAN WILL THAT TELEPHONE TO RING.
IT MIGHT BE WISER TO SPEND THIS TIME UPSTAIRS RESTING OR--
DEET DEET DEET DEET
THIS IS IT, ALFRED! IT'S HER! IT'S--
"--ORACLE."
YOU WERE CORRECT.
THAT SPECIFIC VACCINE IS REQUIRED BY LAW FOR ENTRY INTO ONLY NINE DIFFERENT NATIONS, EIGHT OF THEM IN AFRICA.
YES.
UNLESS BANE IS MOVING INTO SOMETHING NEW, AFRICA'S WRONG--DOESN'T FIT HIS ACCENT, OR THE KIDNAPPER WHOSE BLOOD CONTAINED THE VACCINE.
AND THE NINTH, ORACLE? IS IT IN LATIN AMERICA?
...A SMALL ISLAND NATION CALLED SANTA PRISCA, LOCATED--
I KNOW WHERE IT IS...
9

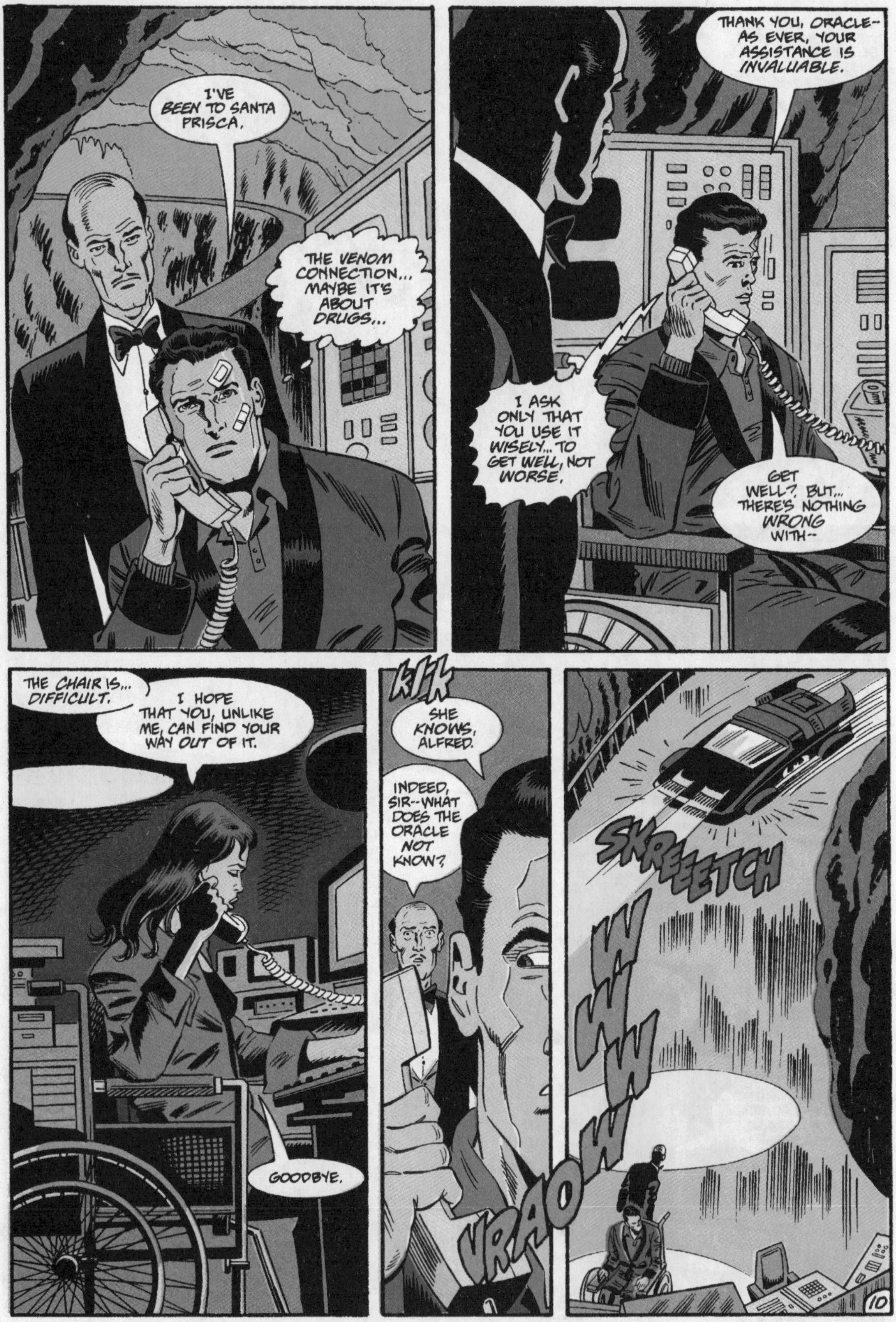
I'VE BEEN TO SANTA PRISCA.
THE VENOM CONNECTION... MAYBE IT'S ABOUT DRUGS...
THANK YOU, ORACLE-- AS EVER, YOUR ASSISTANCE IS INVALUABLE.
I ASK ONLY THAT YOU USE IT WISELY... TO GET WELL, NOT WORSE.
GET WELL? BUT... THERE'S NOTHING WRONG WITH--
THE CHAIR IS... DIFFICULT.
I HOPE THAT YOU, UNLIKE ME, CAN FIND YOUR WAY OUT OF IT.
GOODBYE.
KLIK
SHE KNOWS, ALFRED.
INDEED, SIR--WHAT DOES THE ORACLE NOT KNOW?
SKREEETCH
VRAOWWWWW
10

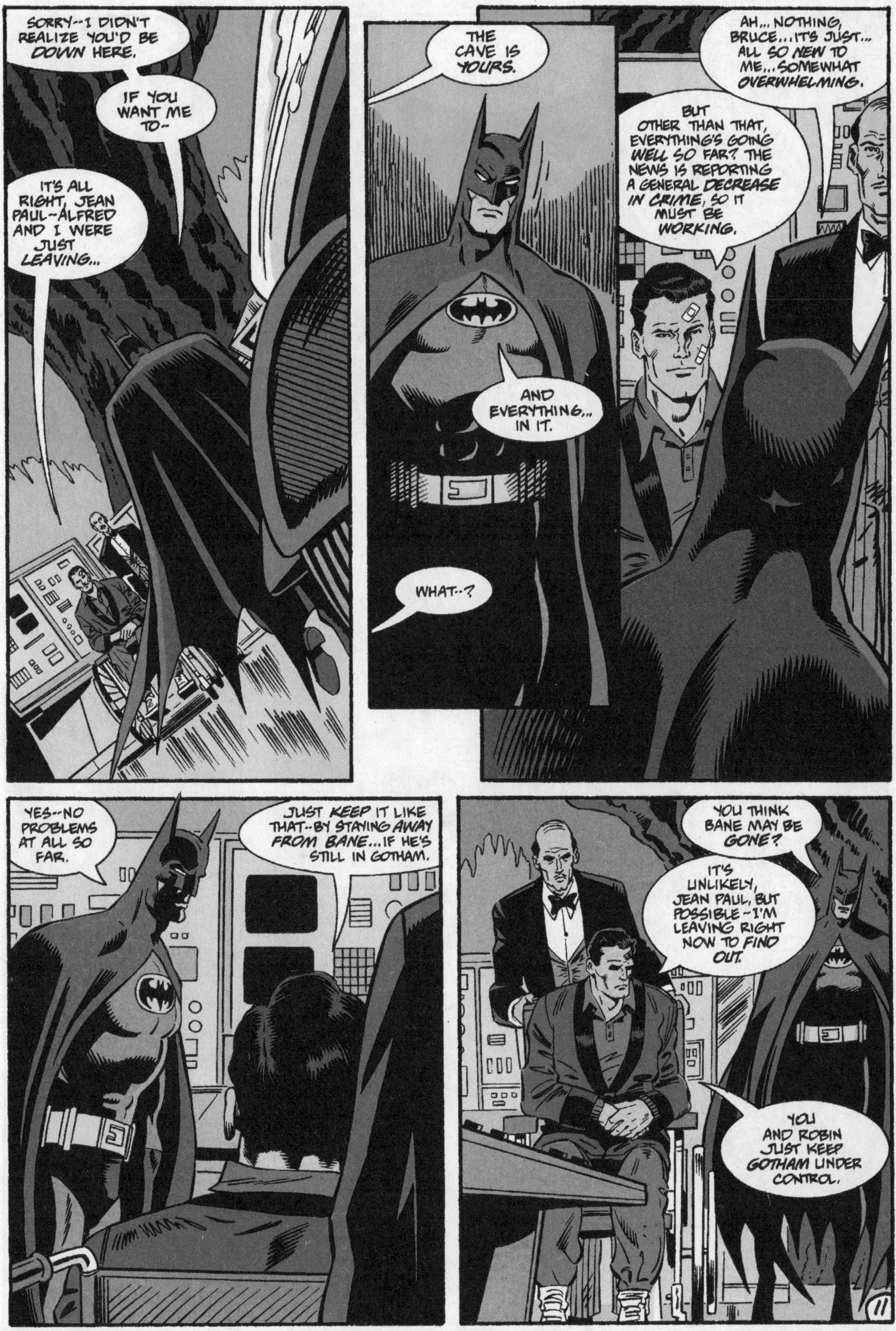
SORRY--I DIDN'T REALIZE YOU'D BE DOWN HERE.
IF YOU WANT ME TO--
IT'S ALL RIGHT, JEAN PAUL--ALFRED AND I WERE JUST LEAVING...
THE CAVE IS YOURS.
AND EVERYTHING... IN IT.
WHAT--?
AH... NOTHING, BRUCE... IT'S JUST... ALL SO NEW TO ME... SOMEWHAT OVERWHELMING.
BUT OTHER THAN THAT, EVERYTHING'S GOING WELL SO FAR? THE NEWS IS REPORTING A GENERAL DECREASE IN CRIME, SO IT MUST BE WORKING.
YES--NO PROBLEMS AT ALL SO FAR.
JUST KEEP IT LIKE THAT--BY STAYING AWAY FROM BANE... IF HE'S STILL IN GOTHAM.
YOU THINK BANE MAY BE GONE?
IT'S UNLIKELY, JEAN PAUL, BUT POSSIBLE--I'M LEAVING RIGHT NOW TO FIND OUT.
YOU AND ROBIN JUST KEEP GOTHAM UNDER CONTROL.
11

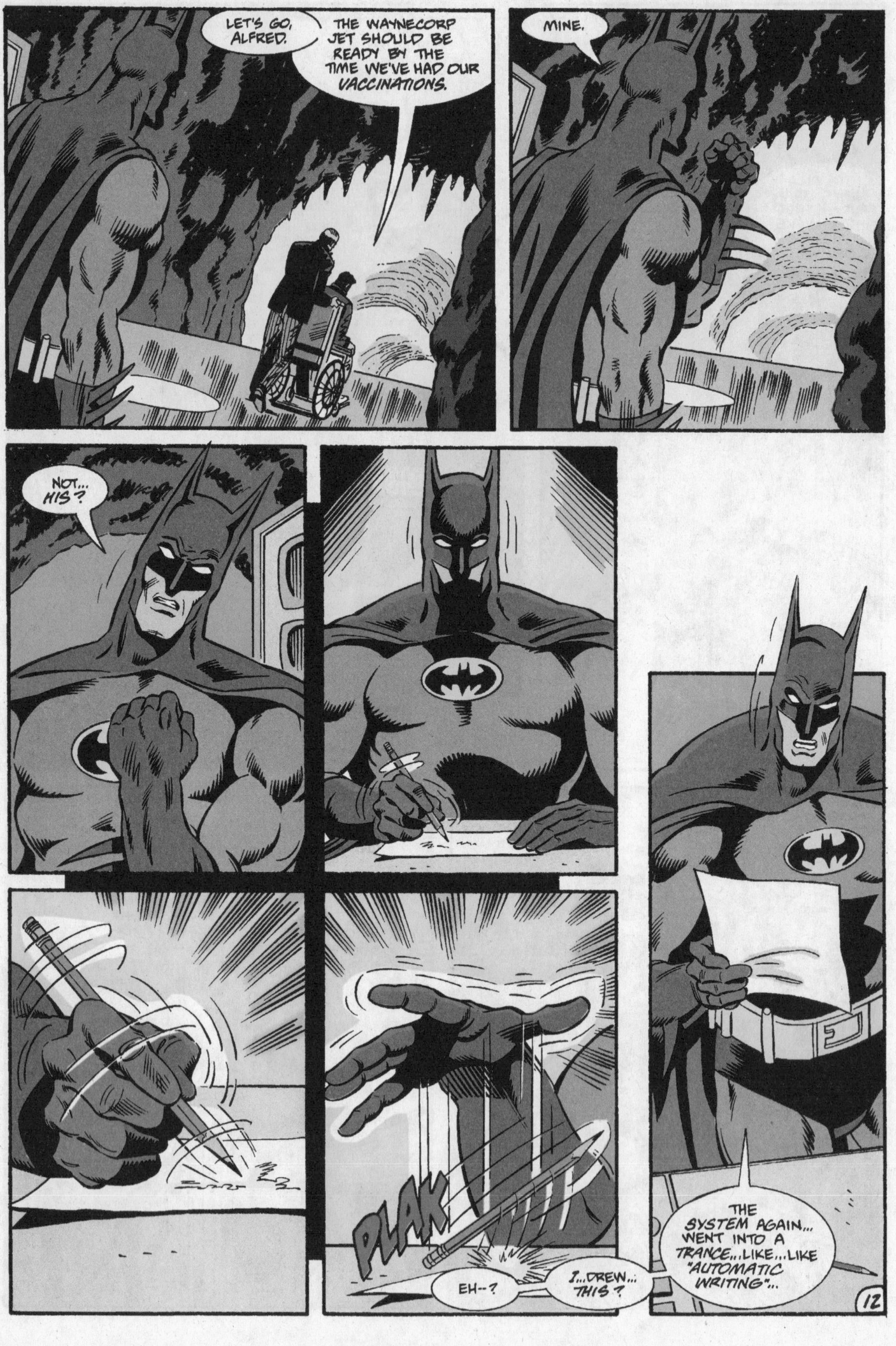
LET'S GO, ALFRED.
THE WAYNECORP JET SHOULD BE READY BY THE TIME WE'VE HAD OUR VACCINATIONS.
MINE.
NOT... HIS?
PLAK
EH--?
I...DREW... THIS?
THE SYSTEM AGAIN... WENT INTO A TRANCE...LIKE...LIKE "AUTOMATIC WRITING"...
12

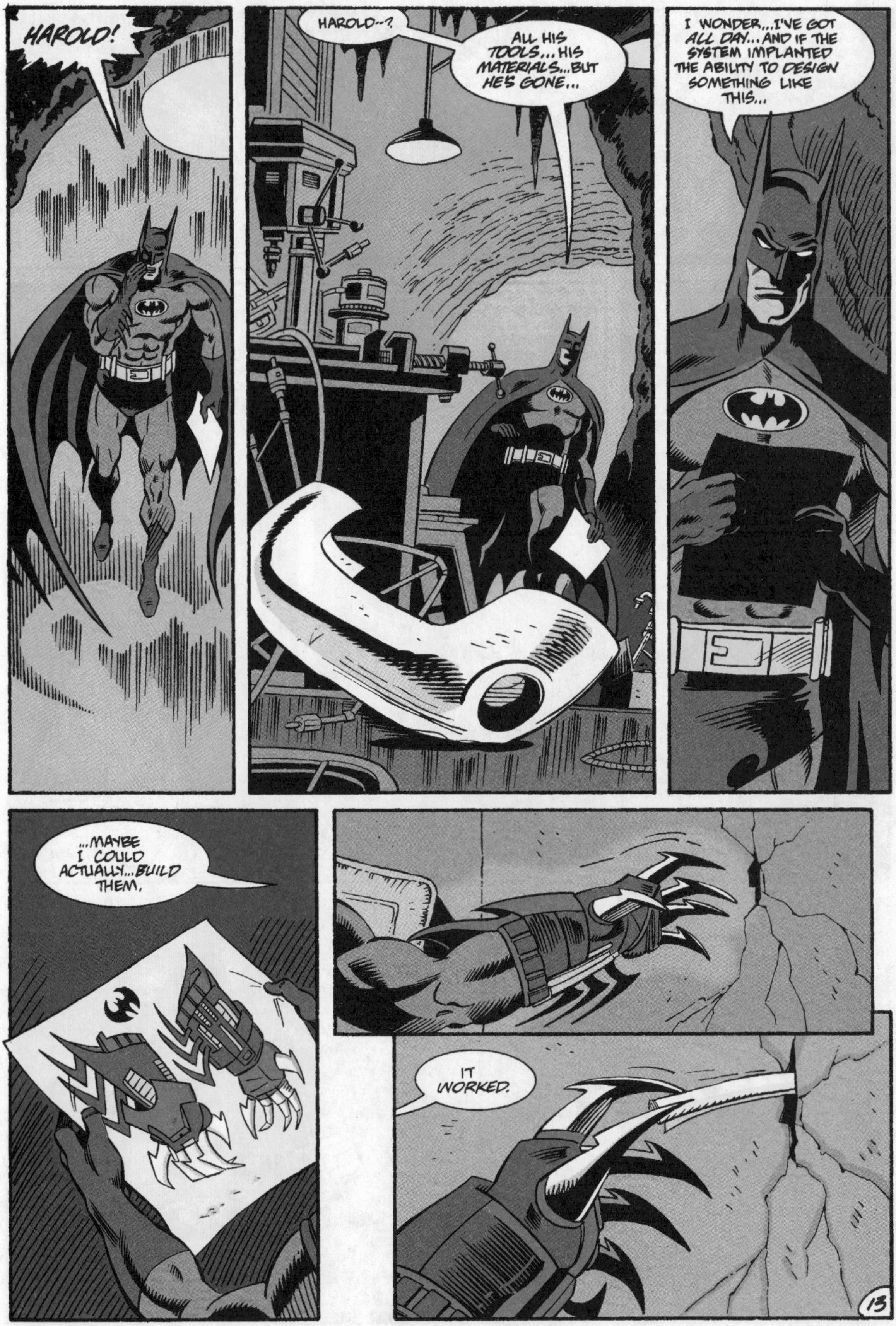
HAROLD!
HAROLD--?
ALL HIS TOOLS...HIS MATERIALS...BUT HE'S GONE...
I WONDER...I'VE GOT ALL DAY...AND IF THE SYSTEM IMPLANTED THE ABILITY TO DESIGN SOMETHING LIKE THIS...
...MAYBE I COULD ACTUALLY...BUILD THEM.
IT WORKED.
13

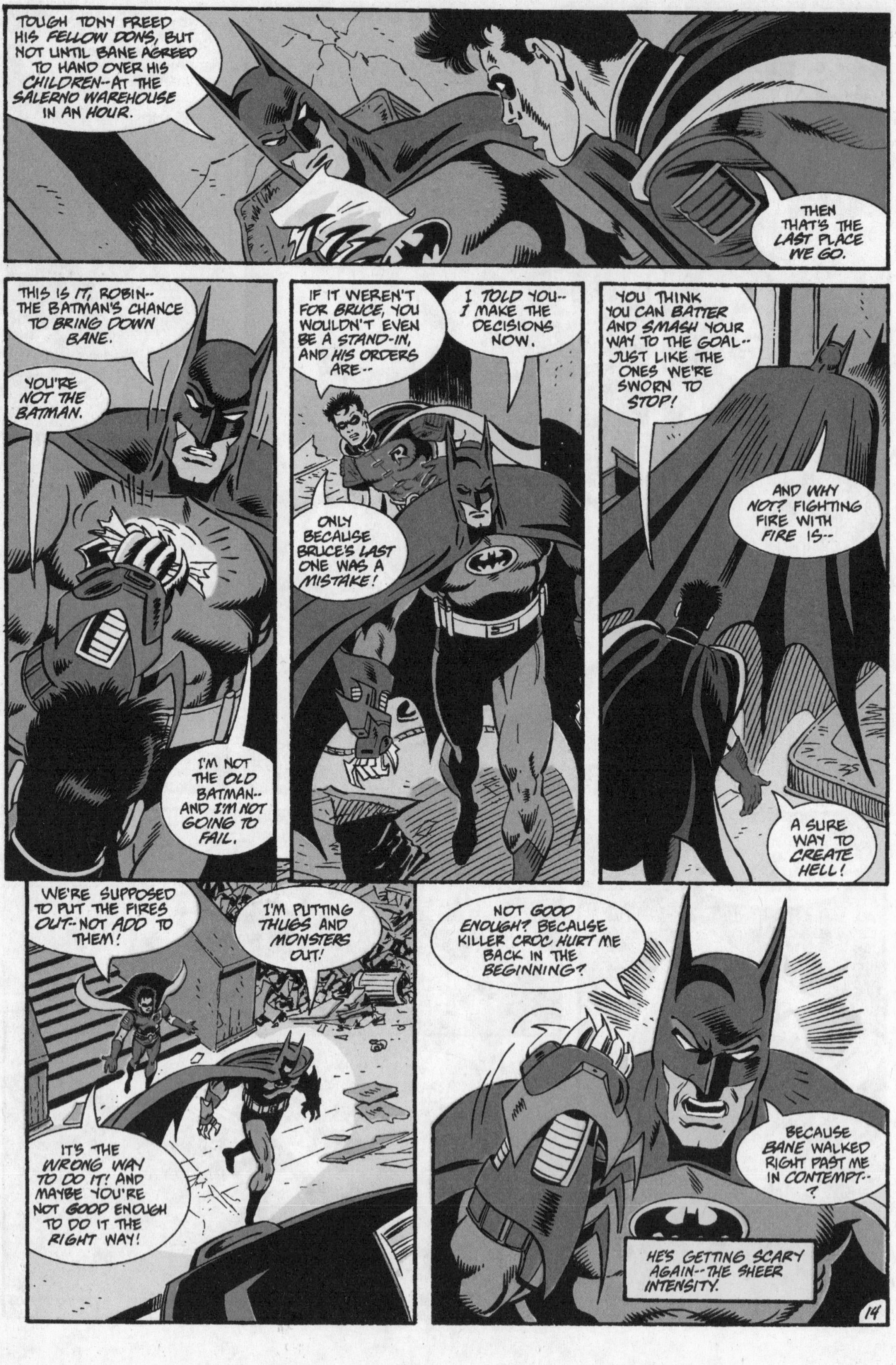
TOUGH TONY FREED HIS FELLOW DONS, BUT NOT UNTIL BANE AGREED TO HAND OVER HIS CHILDREN--AT THE SALERNO WAREHOUSE IN AN HOUR.
THEN THAT'S THE LAST PLACE WE GO.
THIS IS IT, ROBIN-- THE BATMAN'S CHANCE TO BRING DOWN BANE.
YOU'RE NOT THE BATMAN.
I'M NOT THE OLD BATMAN-- AND I'M NOT GOING TO FAIL.
IF IT WEREN'T FOR BRUCE, YOU WOULDN'T EVEN BE A STAND-IN, AND HIS ORDERS ARE--
I TOLD YOU-- I MAKE THE DECISIONS NOW.
ONLY BECAUSE BRUCE'S LAST ONE WAS A MISTAKE!
YOU THINK YOU CAN BATTER AND SMASH YOUR WAY TO THE GOAL-- JUST LIKE THE ONES WE'RE SWORN TO STOP!
AND WHY NOT? FIGHTING FIRE WITH FIRE IS--
A SURE WAY TO CREATE HELL!
WE'RE SUPPOSED TO PUT THE FIRES OUT--NOT ADD TO THEM!
I'M PUTTING THUGS AND MONSTERS OUT!
IT'S THE WRONG WAY TO DO IT! AND MAYBE YOU'RE NOT GOOD ENOUGH TO DO IT THE RIGHT WAY!
NOT GOOD ENOUGH? BECAUSE KILLER CROC HURT ME BACK IN THE BEGINNING?
BECAUSE BANE WALKED RIGHT PAST ME IN CONTEMPT-- ?
HE'S GETTING SCARY AGAIN--THE SHEER INTENSITY.
14

NEVER AGAIN, BOY WONDER...

NEVER AGAIN!

GREAT--NOW I HAVE TO RACE HIM TO THE WAREHOUSE ON FOOT...

VRRAOWN

...AND I HOPE I GET THERE BEFORE HE DESTROYS THE MANTLE OF THE BAT FOR GOOD.

I'M SORRY, MS. KYLE--BUT THERE ARE NO DEPARTURES FOR THAT DESTINATION--BY ANY AIRLINE--UNTIL WEDNESDAY.

BUT IT'S VITAL THAT I LEAVE FOR SANTA PRISCA IMMEDIATELY.

I'M SORRY, BUT--

GOTHAM INTERNATIONAL

SOUTHWAY AIRLINES

WHAT ABOUT A CHARTERED FLIGHT?

I'M AFRAID WITH ALL THE RECENT CUTBACKS AMONG THE INDEPEN--

THERE'S ABSOLUTELY NOTHING?

WELL, IT'S ODD...I MEAN, I'D BARELY HEARD OF SANTA PRISCA BEFORE TODAY, BUT...

BUT WHAT?

WELL, THERE IS A PRIVATE PLANE SCHEDULED TO USE ONE OF OUR RUNWAYS IN ABOUT AN HOUR...OWNED BY BRUCE WAYNE...BUT OF COURSE THERE'S NO WAY WE COULD BOOK YOU ON...

EH--?

15

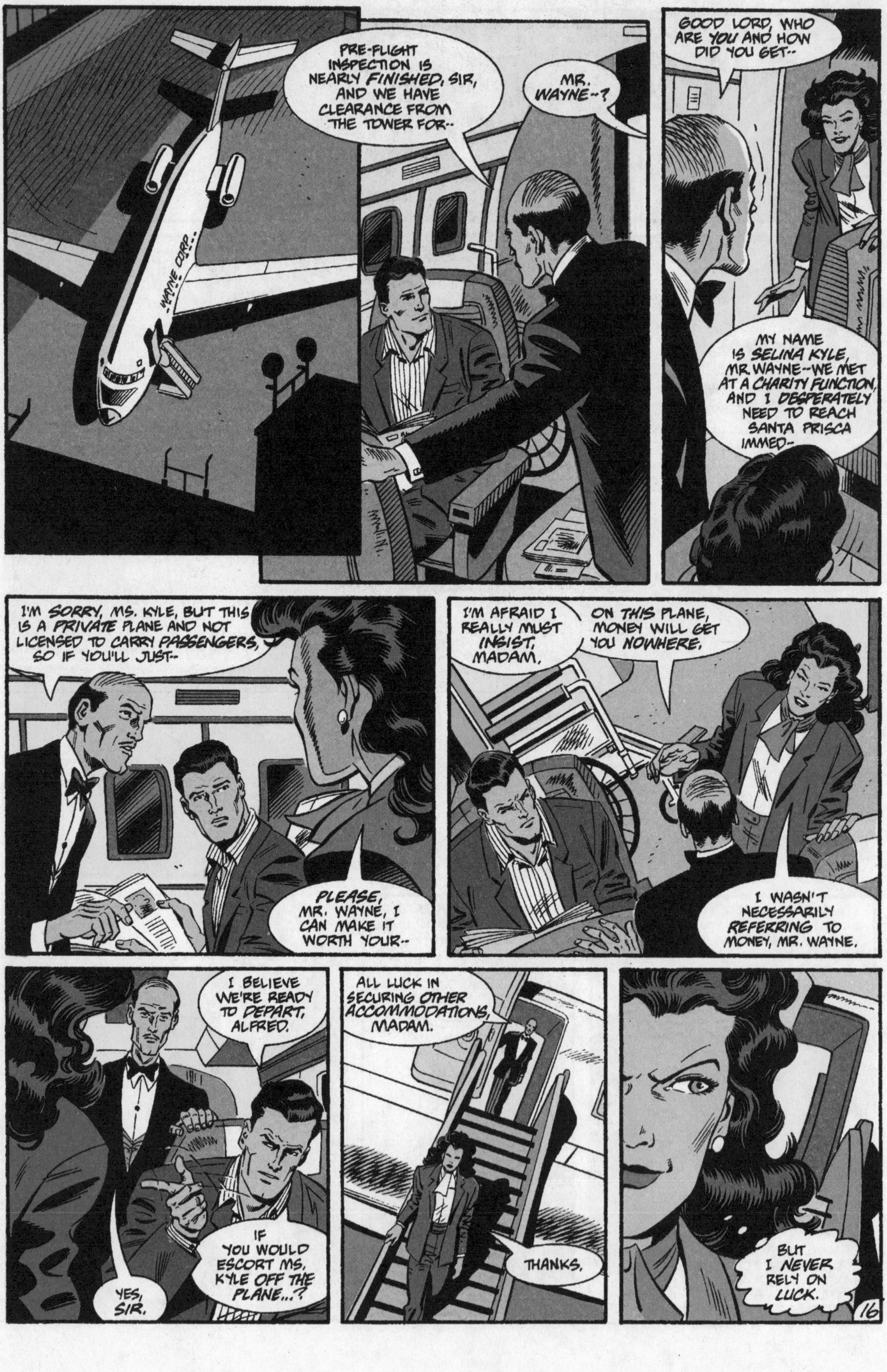
WAYNE CORP.
PRE-FLIGHT INSPECTION IS NEARLY FINISHED, SIR, AND WE HAVE CLEARANCE FROM THE TOWER FOR--
MR. WAYNE--?
GOOD LORD, WHO ARE YOU AND HOW DID YOU GET--
MY NAME IS SELINA KYLE, MR. WAYNE--WE MET AT A CHARITY FUNCTION, AND I DESPERATELY NEED TO REACH SANTA PRISCA IMMED--
I'M SORRY, MS. KYLE, BUT THIS IS A PRIVATE PLANE AND NOT LICENSED TO CARRY PASSENGERS, SO IF YOU'LL JUST--
PLEASE, MR. WAYNE, I CAN MAKE IT WORTH YOUR--
I'M AFRAID I REALLY MUST INSIST, MADAM.
ON THIS PLANE, MONEY WILL GET YOU NOWHERE.
I WASN'T NECESSARILY REFERRING TO MONEY, MR. WAYNE.
I BELIEVE WE'RE READY TO DEPART, ALFRED.
IF YOU WOULD ESCORT MS. KYLE OFF THE PLANE...?
YES, SIR.
ALL LUCK IN SECURING OTHER ACCOMMODATIONS, MADAM.
THANKS.
BUT I NEVER RELY ON LUCK.
16

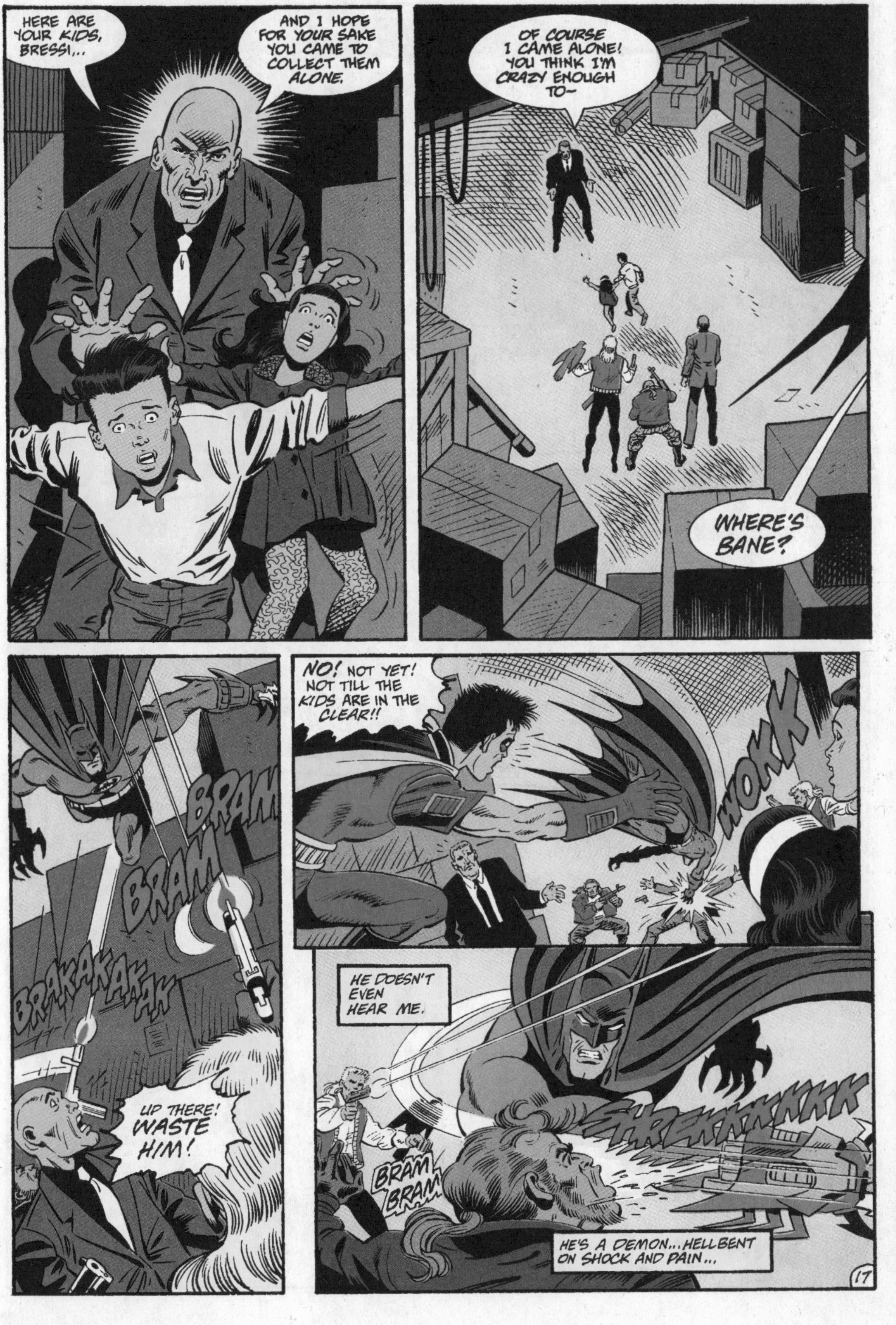
HERE ARE YOUR KIDS, BRESSI...
AND I HOPE FOR YOUR SAKE YOU CAME TO COLLECT THEM ALONE.
OF COURSE I CAME ALONE! YOU THINK I'M CRAZY ENOUGH TO–
WHERE'S BANE?
BRAM
BRAM
BRAKAKAKAKAK
UP THERE! WASTE HIM!
NO! NOT YET! NOT TILL THE KIDS ARE IN THE CLEAR!!
WOKK
HE DOESN'T EVEN HEAR ME.
SHREKKKKKKK
BRAM BRAM
HE'S A DEMON... HELLBENT ON SHOCK AND PAIN...
17

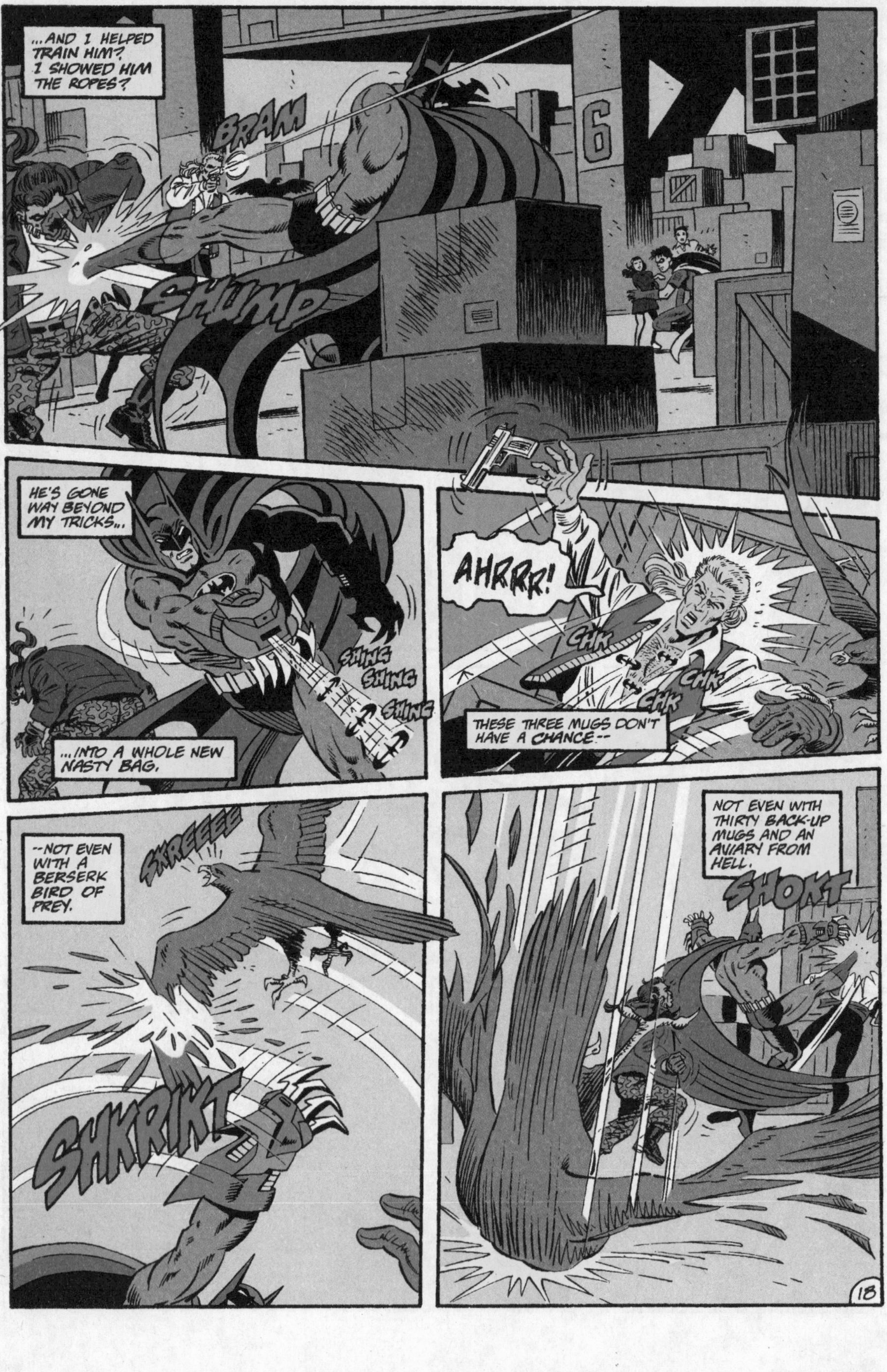
...AND I HELPED TRAIN HIM? I SHOWED HIM THE ROPES?
BRAM
SHUMP
HE'S GONE WAY BEYOND MY TRICKS...
SHING
SHING
SHING
...INTO A WHOLE NEW NASTY BAG.
AHRRR!
CHK
CHK
CHK
THESE THREE MUGS DON'T HAVE A CHANCE--
--NOT EVEN WITH A BERSERK BIRD OF PREY.
SKREEEE
SHKRIKT
NOT EVEN WITH THIRTY BACK-UP MUGS AND AN AVIARY FROM HELL.
SHOKT
18

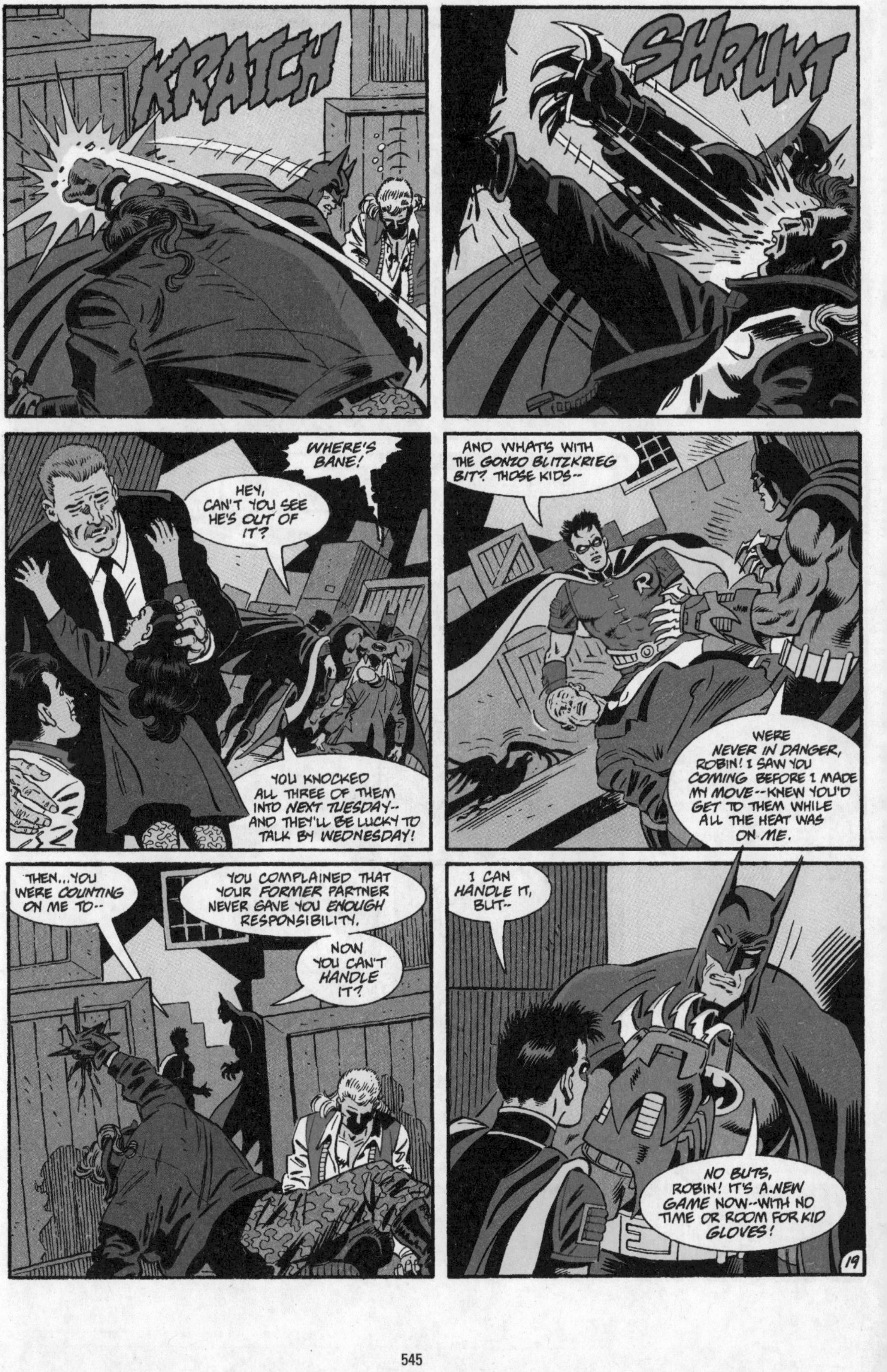
KRATCH
SHRUKT
WHERE'S BANE!
HEY, CAN'T YOU SEE HE'S OUT OF IT?
YOU KNOCKED ALL THREE OF THEM INTO NEXT TUESDAY-- AND THEY'LL BE LUCKY TO TALK BY WEDNESDAY!
AND WHAT'S WITH THE GONZO BLITZKRIEG BIT? THOSE KIDS--
WERE NEVER IN DANGER, ROBIN! I SAW YOU COMING BEFORE I MADE MY MOVE--KNEW YOU'D GET TO THEM WHILE ALL THE HEAT WAS ON ME.
THEN...YOU WERE COUNTING ON ME TO--
YOU COMPLAINED THAT YOUR FORMER PARTNER NEVER GAVE YOU ENOUGH RESPONSIBILITY.
NOW YOU CAN'T HANDLE IT?
I CAN HANDLE IT, BUT--
NO BUTS, ROBIN! IT'S A NEW GAME NOW--WITH NO TIME OR ROOM FOR KID GLOVES!
19

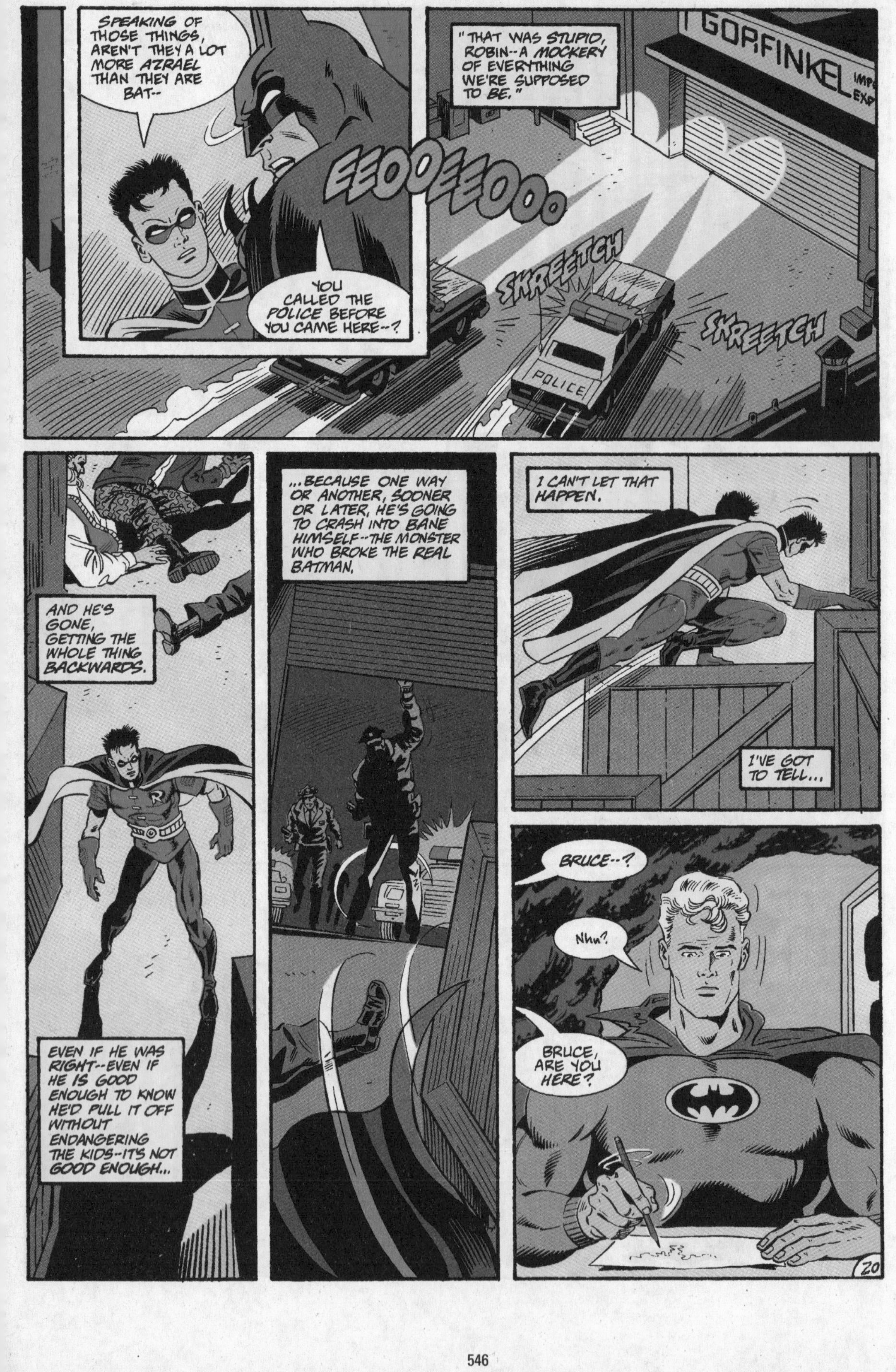
SPEAKING OF THOSE THINGS, AREN'T THEY A LOT MORE AZRAEL THAN THEY ARE BAT--
YOU CALLED THE POLICE BEFORE YOU CAME HERE--?
"THAT WAS STUPID, ROBIN--A MOCKERY OF EVERYTHING WE'RE SUPPOSED TO BE."
GORFINKEL
EEOOEEOOo
SKREETCH
SKREETCH
POLICE
AND HE'S GONE, GETTING THE WHOLE THING BACKWARDS.
EVEN IF HE WAS RIGHT--EVEN IF HE IS GOOD ENOUGH TO KNOW HE'D PULL IT OFF WITHOUT ENDANGERING THE KIDS--IT'S NOT GOOD ENOUGH...
...BECAUSE ONE WAY OR ANOTHER, SOONER OR LATER, HE'S GOING TO CRASH INTO BANE HIMSELF--THE MONSTER WHO BROKE THE REAL BATMAN.
I CAN'T LET THAT HAPPEN.
I'VE GOT TO TELL...
BRUCE--?
Nhn?
BRUCE, ARE YOU HERE?
20

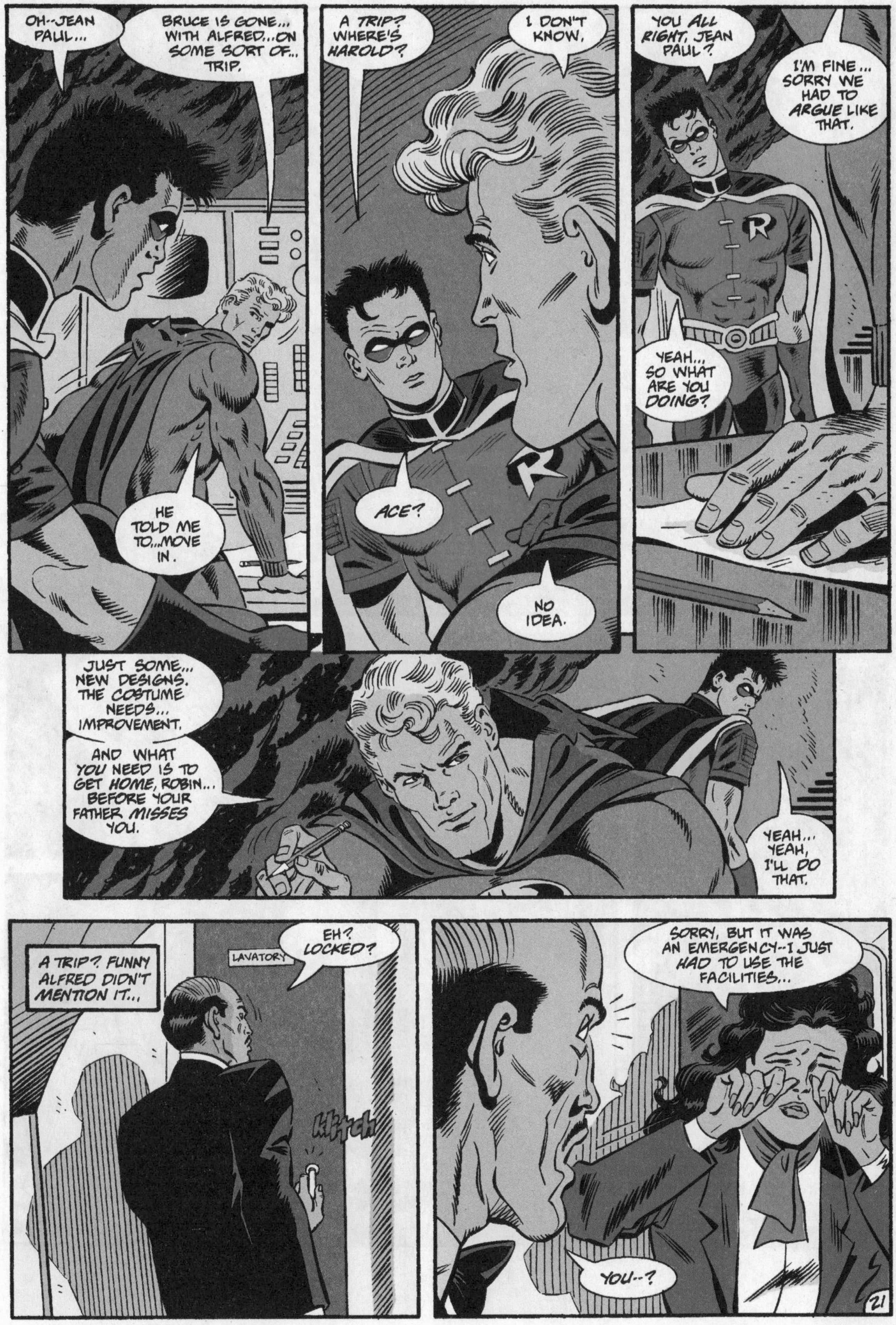
OH--JEAN PAUL...
BRUCE IS GONE... WITH ALFRED...ON SOME SORT OF... TRIP.
HE TOLD ME TO...MOVE IN.
A TRIP? WHERE'S HAROLD?
I DON'T KNOW.
ACE?
NO IDEA.
YOU ALL RIGHT, JEAN PAUL?
I'M FINE... SORRY WE HAD TO ARGUE LIKE THAT.
YEAH... SO WHAT ARE YOU DOING?
JUST SOME... NEW DESIGNS. THE COSTUME NEEDS... IMPROVEMENT.
AND WHAT YOU NEED IS TO GET HOME, ROBIN... BEFORE YOUR FATHER MISSES YOU.
YEAH... YEAH, I'LL DO THAT.
A TRIP? FUNNY ALFRED DIDN'T MENTION IT...
LAVATORY
EH? LOCKED?
klitch
SORRY, BUT IT WAS AN EMERGENCY--I JUST HAD TO USE THE FACILITIES...
YOU--?
21

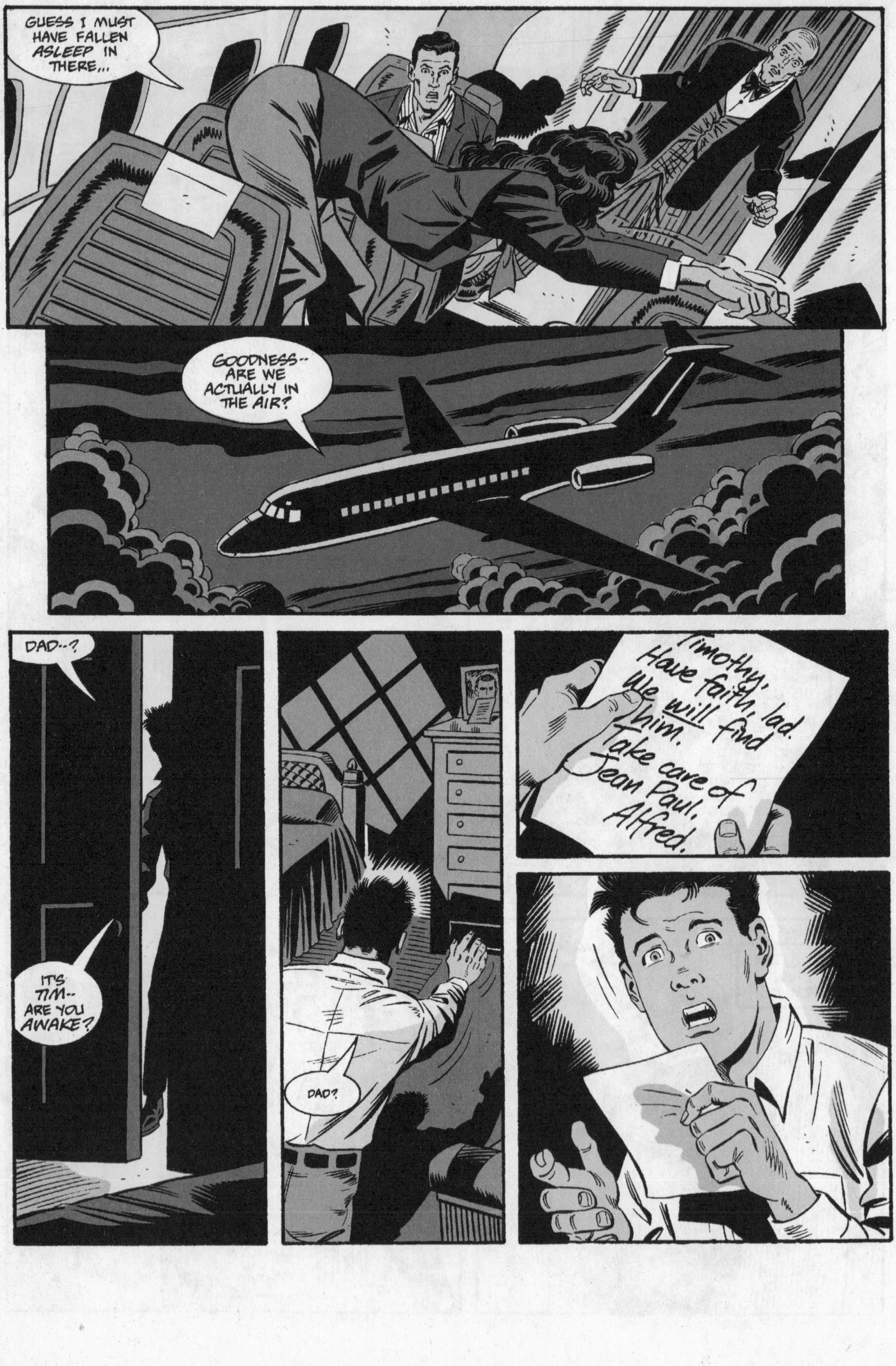
GUESS I MUST HAVE FALLEN ASLEEP IN THERE...
GOODNESS-- ARE WE ACTUALLY IN THE AIR?
DAD--?
IT'S TIM-- ARE YOU AWAKE?
DAD?
Timothy, Have faith, lad. We will find him. Take care of Jean Paul. Alfred.

Cover art by KELLEY JONES

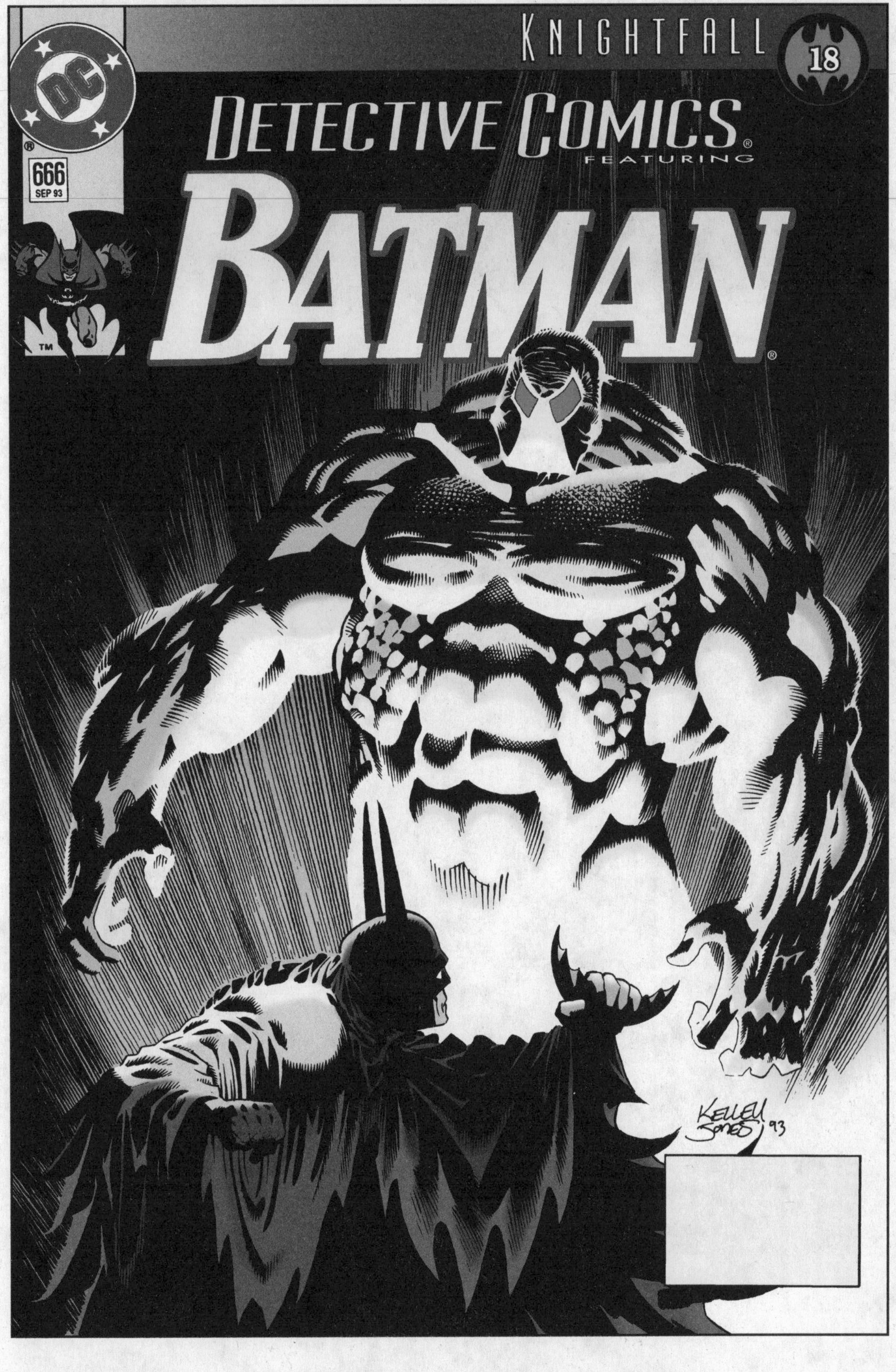
KNIGHTFALL
18
DC
666
SEP 93
DETECTIVE COMICS
FEATURING
BATMAN
KELLEY JONES '93

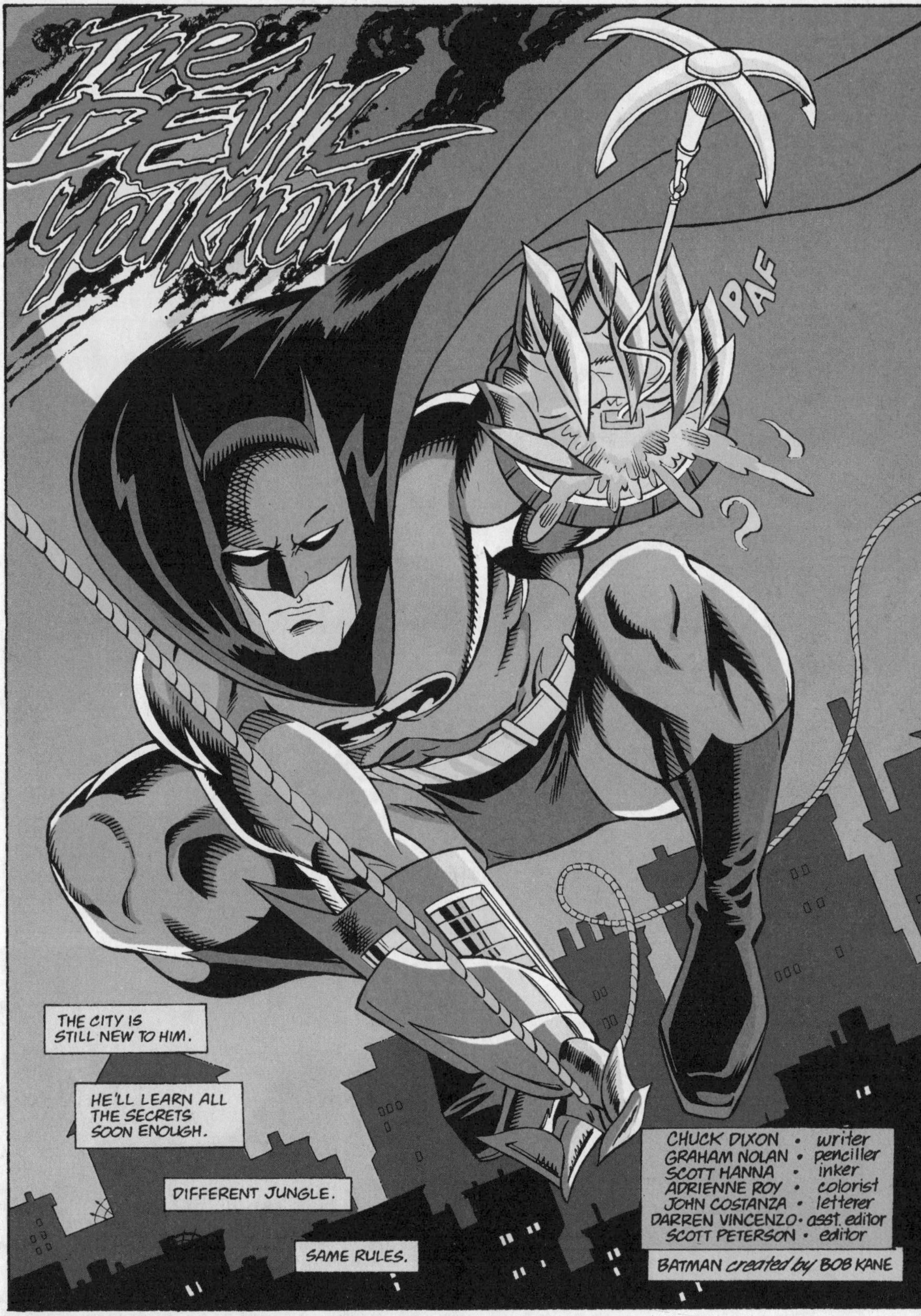
The Devil You Know
PAF
THE CITY IS STILL NEW TO HIM.
HE'LL LEARN ALL THE SECRETS SOON ENOUGH.
DIFFERENT JUNGLE.
SAME RULES.
CHUCK DIXON • writer
GRAHAM NOLAN • penciller
SCOTT HANNA • inker
ADRIENNE ROY • colorist
JOHN COSTANZA • letterer
DARREN VINCENZO • asst. editor
SCOTT PETERSON • editor
BATMAN created by BOB KANE

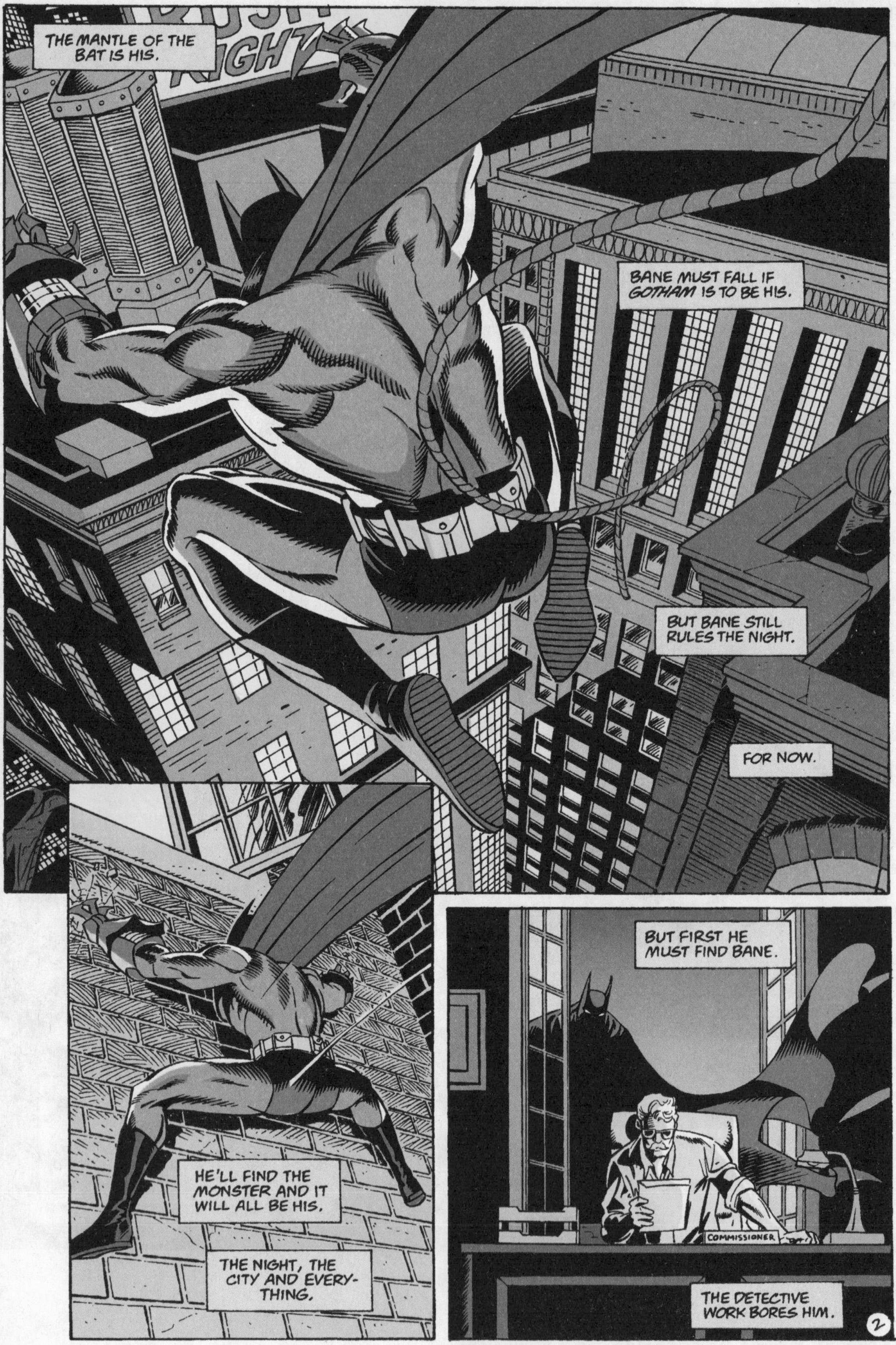
THE MANTLE OF THE BAT IS HIS.
BANE MUST FALL IF GOTHAM IS TO BE HIS.
BUT BANE STILL RULES THE NIGHT.
FOR NOW.
HE'LL FIND THE MONSTER AND IT WILL ALL BE HIS.
THE NIGHT, THE CITY AND EVERY-THING.
BUT FIRST HE MUST FIND BANE.
COMMISSIONER
THE DETECTIVE WORK BORES HIM.
2

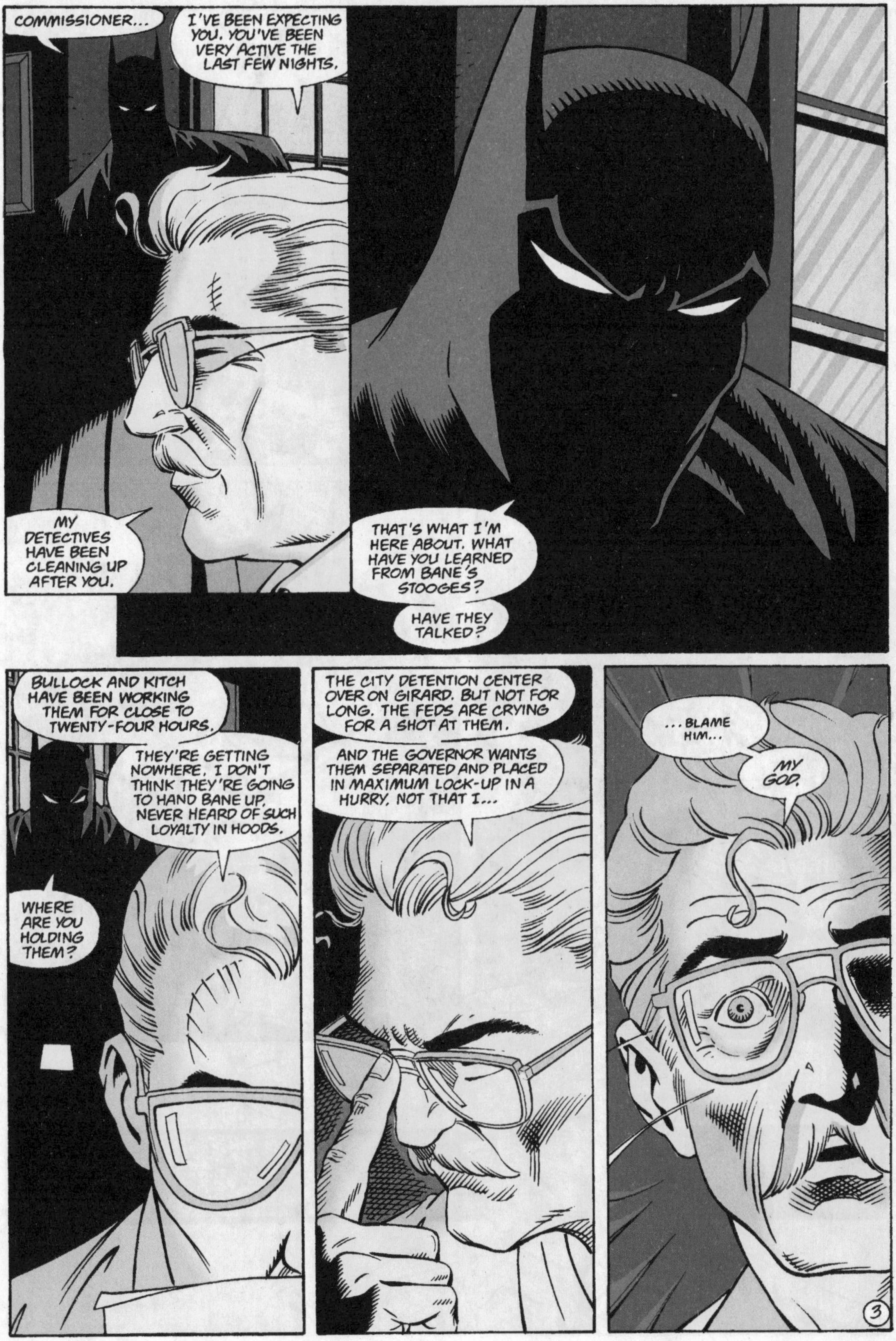
COMMISSIONER...
I'VE BEEN EXPECTING YOU. YOU'VE BEEN VERY ACTIVE THE LAST FEW NIGHTS.
MY DETECTIVES HAVE BEEN CLEANING UP AFTER YOU.
THAT'S WHAT I'M HERE ABOUT. WHAT HAVE YOU LEARNED FROM BANE'S STOOGES?
HAVE THEY TALKED?
BULLOCK AND KITCH HAVE BEEN WORKING THEM FOR CLOSE TO TWENTY-FOUR HOURS.
THEY'RE GETTING NOWHERE. I DON'T THINK THEY'RE GOING TO HAND BANE UP. NEVER HEARD OF SUCH LOYALTY IN HOODS.
WHERE ARE YOU HOLDING THEM?
THE CITY DETENTION CENTER OVER ON GIRARD. BUT NOT FOR LONG. THE FEDS ARE CRYING FOR A SHOT AT THEM.
AND THE GOVERNOR WANTS THEM SEPARATED AND PLACED IN MAXIMUM LOCK-UP IN A HURRY, NOT THAT I...
...BLAME HIM...
MY GOD.
3

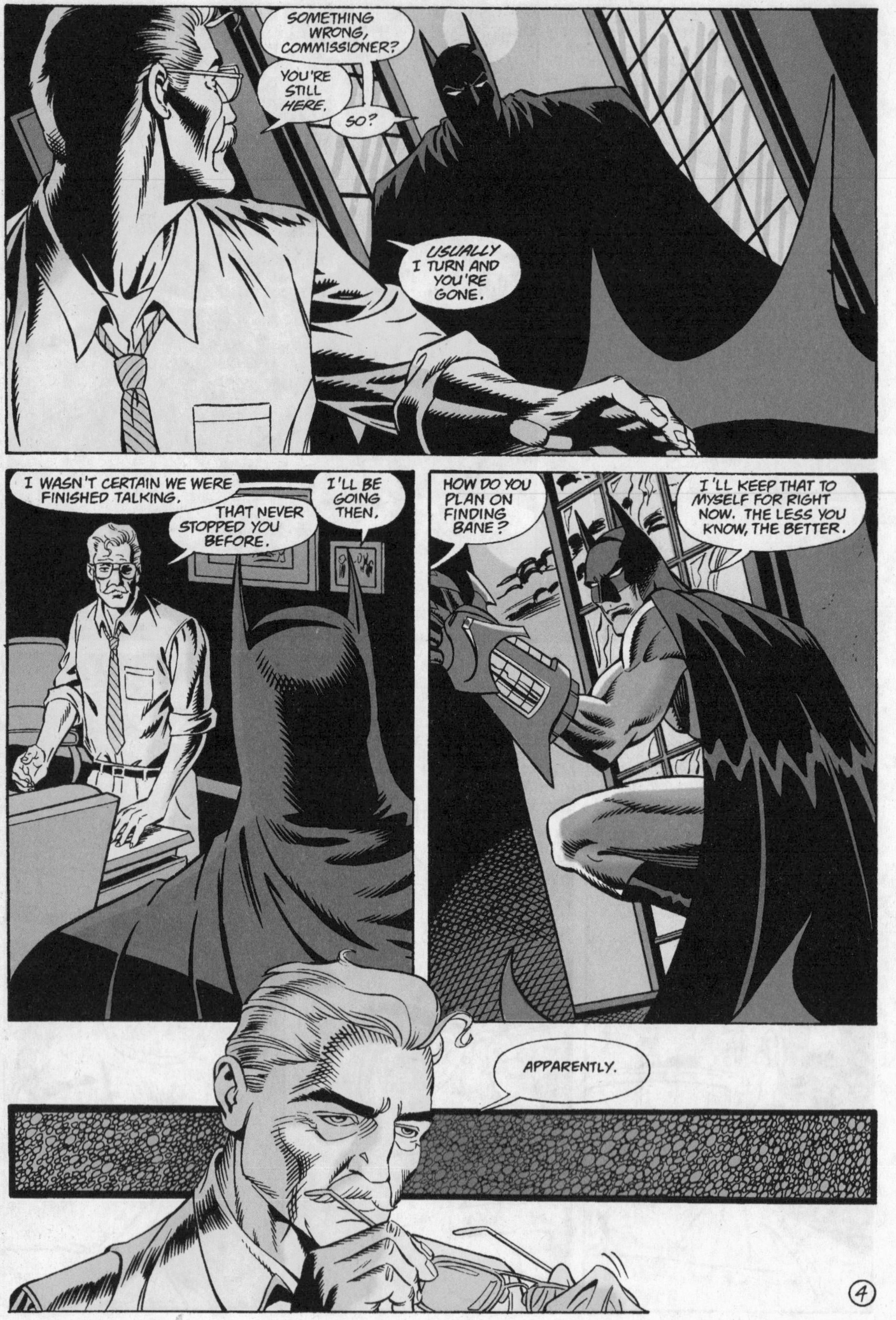

SOMETHING WRONG, COMMISSIONER?
YOU'RE STILL HERE.
SO?
USUALLY I TURN AND YOU'RE GONE.
I WASN'T CERTAIN WE WERE FINISHED TALKING.
THAT NEVER STOPPED YOU BEFORE.
I'LL BE GOING THEN.
HOW DO YOU PLAN ON FINDING BANE?
I'LL KEEP THAT TO MYSELF FOR RIGHT NOW. THE LESS YOU KNOW, THE BETTER.
APPARENTLY.
4

YOU GUYS ARE NEVER GONNA SEE THE LIGHT OF DAY, YOU KNOW THAT?

ARE YOU TRYING TO FRIGHTEN ME, SERGEANT?

WITH *WHAT*, SERGEANT? IMPRISONMENT?

I HAVE SERVED HARD TIME IN *PENA DURO*, THE HELLHOLE OF THE UNIVERSE. YOUR PRISONS ARE SOFT, EASY.

SURE. THEY'RE COUNTRY CLUBS.

BUT YOU'LL SERVE *ALONE*, ZOMBIE. THE FEDS ARE COMING TOMORROW AND SPLITTING YOU AND YOUR TWO BUNKIES UP. YOU'LL BE COUNTIN' THE YEARS IN THREE SEPARATE PENS.

HARD TIME IS *HARDER* WITHOUT FRIENDS.

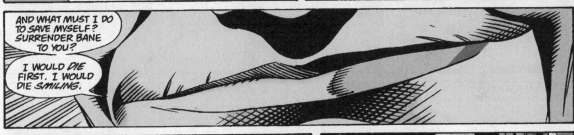

AND WHAT MUST I DO TO SAVE MYSELF? SURRENDER BANE TO YOU?

I WOULD *DIE* FIRST. I WOULD DIE *SMILING*.

GET THIS GOON OUTTA HERE BEFORE I PUT A SLUG IN HIM, LIEUTENANT.

LET'S GO, ZOMBIE, WE'RE FINISHED WITH YOU.

IMAGINE MY RELIEF.

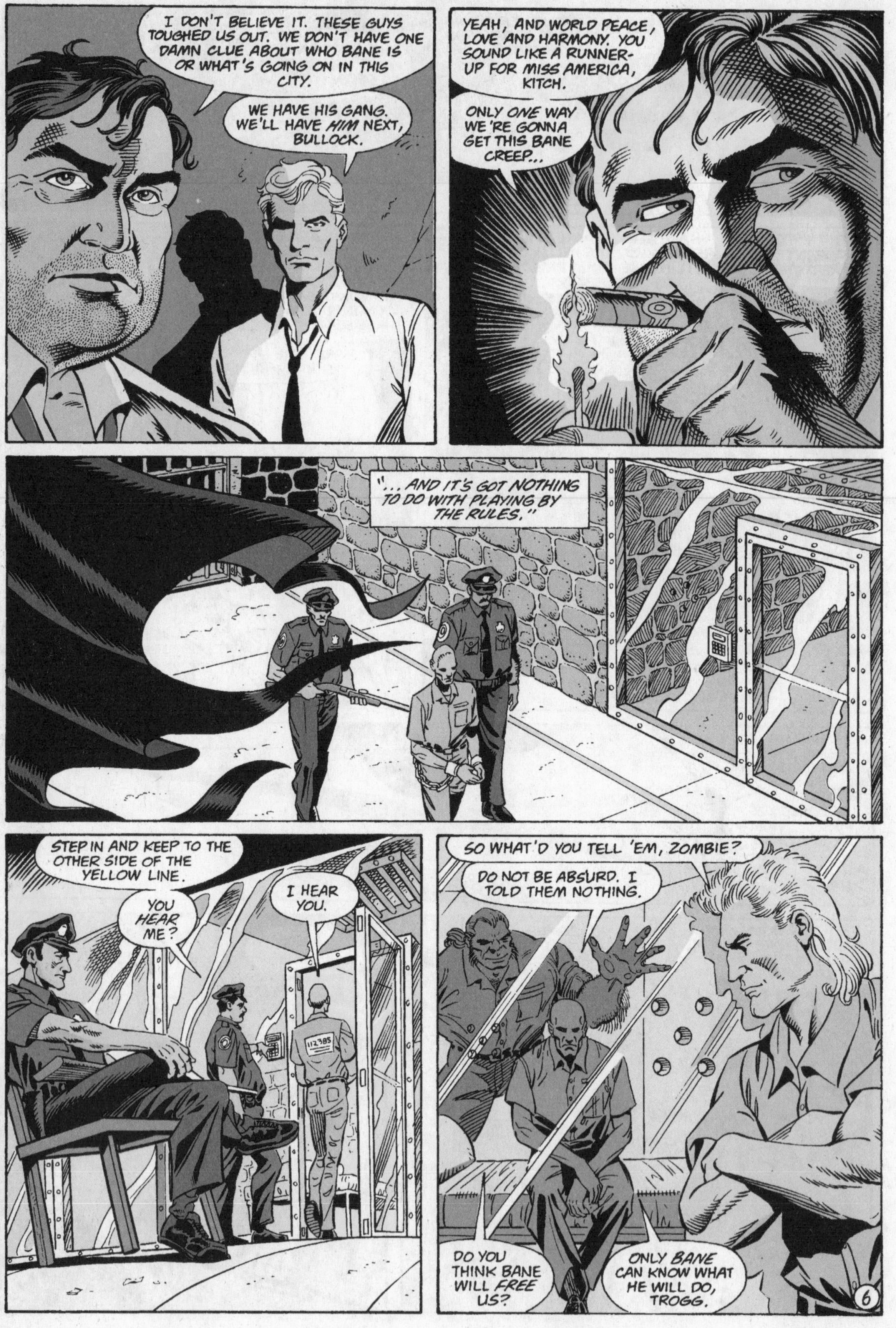
I DON'T BELIEVE IT. THESE GUYS TOUGHED US OUT. WE DON'T HAVE ONE DAMN CLUE ABOUT WHO BANE IS OR WHAT'S GOING ON IN THIS CITY.
WE HAVE HIS GANG. WE'LL HAVE HIM NEXT, BULLOCK.
YEAH, AND WORLD PEACE, LOVE AND HARMONY. YOU SOUND LIKE A RUNNER-UP FOR MISS AMERICA, KITCH.
ONLY ONE WAY WE'RE GONNA GET THIS BANE CREEP...
"...AND IT'S GOT NOTHING TO DO WITH PLAYING BY THE RULES."
STEP IN AND KEEP TO THE OTHER SIDE OF THE YELLOW LINE.
YOU HEAR ME?
I HEAR YOU.
112385
SO WHAT'D YOU TELL 'EM, ZOMBIE?
DO NOT BE ABSURD. I TOLD THEM NOTHING.
DO YOU THINK BANE WILL FREE US?
ONLY BANE CAN KNOW WHAT HE WILL DO, TROGG.
6

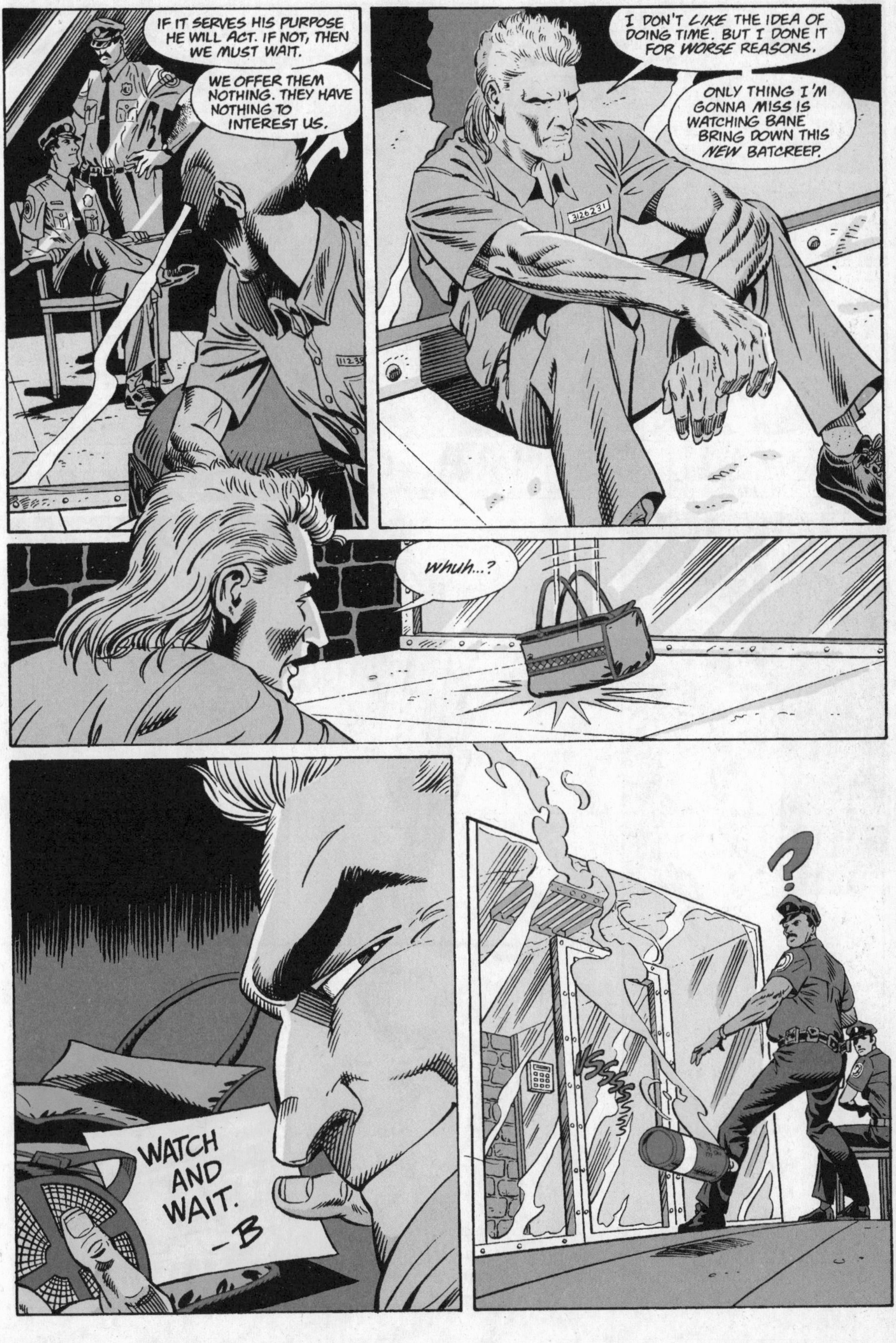
IF IT SERVES HIS PURPOSE HE WILL ACT. IF NOT, THEN WE MUST WAIT.
WE OFFER THEM NOTHING. THEY HAVE NOTHING TO INTEREST US.
I DON'T LIKE THE IDEA OF DOING TIME. BUT I DONE IT FOR WORSE REASONS.
ONLY THING I'M GONNA MISS IS WATCHING BANE BRING DOWN THIS NEW BATCREEP.
whuh...?
WATCH AND WAIT. -B
?
SSSSSS

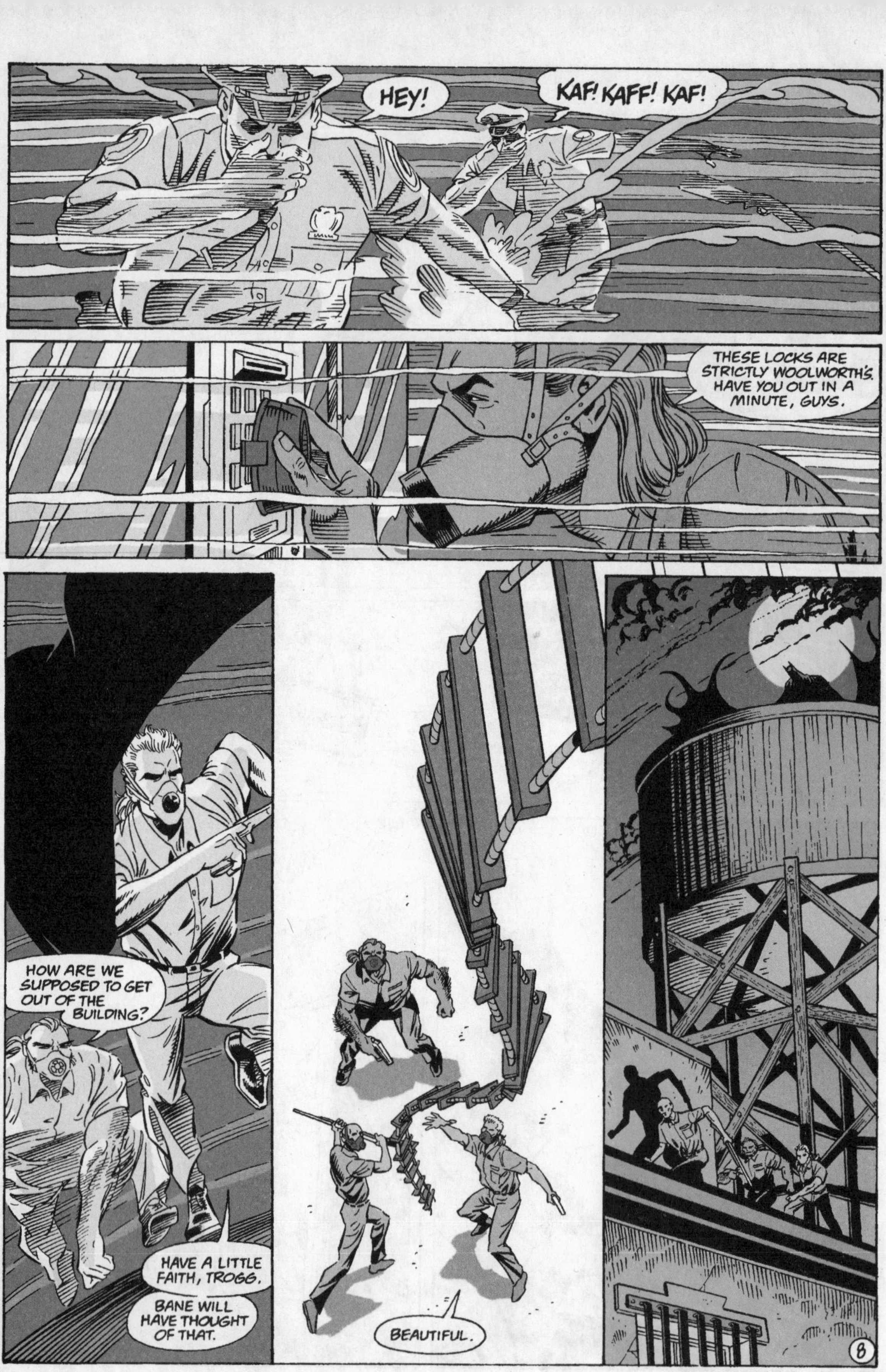
HEY!
KAF! KAFF! KAF!
THESE LOCKS ARE STRICTLY WOOLWORTH'S. HAVE YOU OUT IN A MINUTE, GUYS.
HOW ARE WE SUPPOSED TO GET OUT OF THE BUILDING?
HAVE A LITTLE FAITH, TROGG.
BANE WILL HAVE THOUGHT OF THAT.
BEAUTIFUL.
8

SO QUIET HERE WITH YOUR FATHER GONE AN' ALL, TIM.

YEAH, IT IS, MRS. MCILVAINE.

HE DIDN'T PACK ANY CLOTHES OR EVEN LET ME KNOW HE WAS GOIN'.

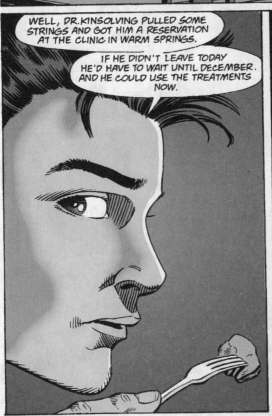

WELL, DR. KINSOLVING PULLED SOME STRINGS AND GOT HIM A RESERVATION AT THE CLINIC IN WARM SPRINGS.

IF HE DIDN'T LEAVE TODAY HE'D HAVE TO WAIT UNTIL DECEMBER. AND HE COULD USE THE TREATMENTS NOW.

I S'POSE. STRANGE HIM BEING HERE WHEN I WENT TO THE GROCERS AND BEIN' GONE WHEN I GOT BACK.

WILL YOU BE NEEDIN' ANYTHING ELSE, TIMOTHY?

UH... HAS BRUCE CALLED AT ALL TODAY? I WAS HOPING I'D HEAR FROM HIM.

NO. NOT A WORD FROM MR. WAYNE.

I GUESS NOT.

9

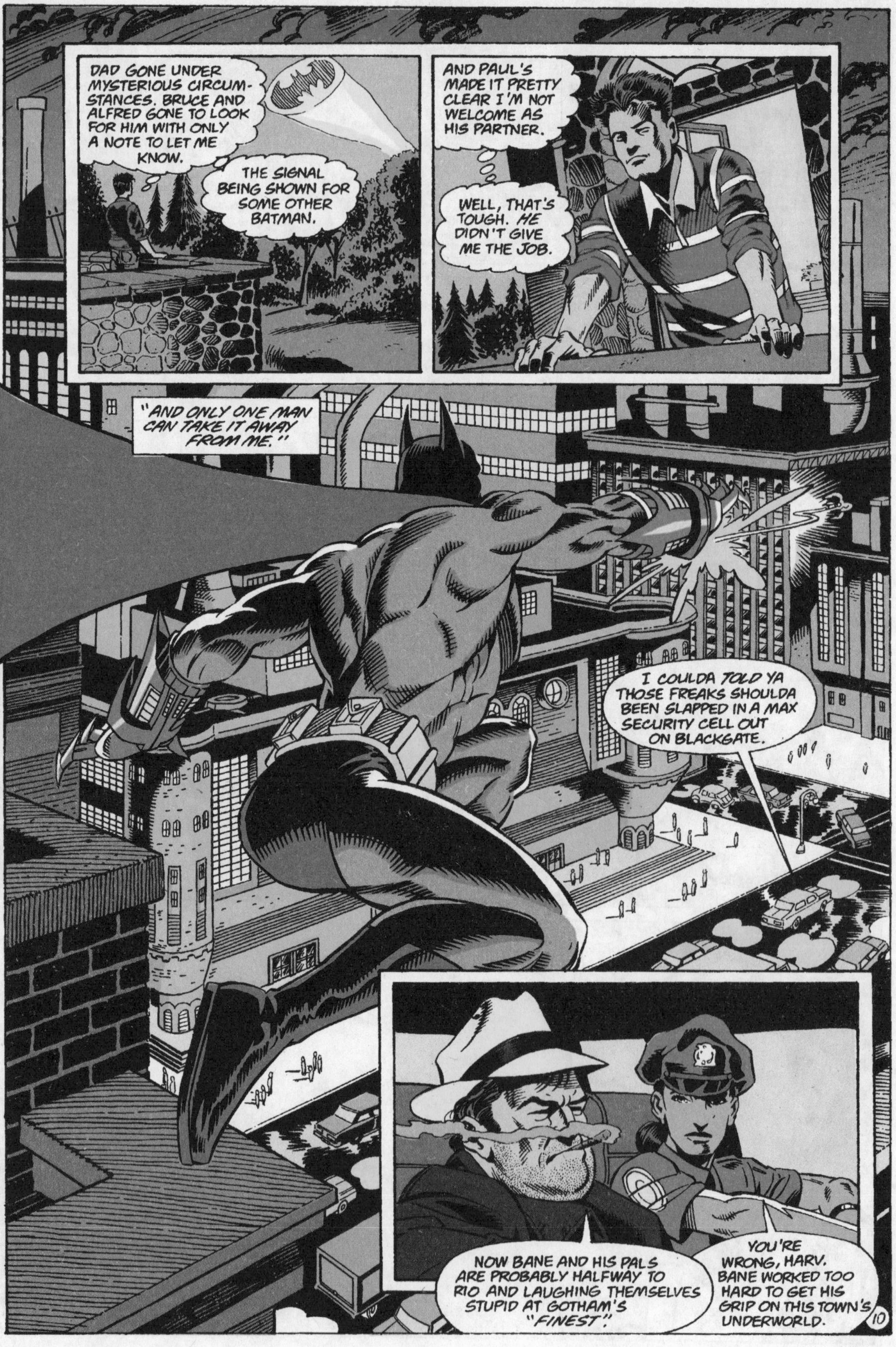
DAD GONE UNDER MYSTERIOUS CIRCUMSTANCES. BRUCE AND ALFRED GONE TO LOOK FOR HIM WITH ONLY A NOTE TO LET ME KNOW.
THE SIGNAL BEING SHOWN FOR SOME OTHER BATMAN.
AND PAUL'S MADE IT PRETTY CLEAR I'M NOT WELCOME AS HIS PARTNER.
WELL, THAT'S TOUGH. HE DIDN'T GIVE ME THE JOB.
"AND ONLY ONE MAN CAN TAKE IT AWAY FROM ME."
I COULDA TOLD YA THOSE FREAKS SHOULDA BEEN SLAPPED IN A MAX SECURITY CELL OUT ON BLACKGATE.
NOW BANE AND HIS PALS ARE PROBABLY HALFWAY TO RIO AND LAUGHING THEMSELVES STUPID AT GOTHAM'S "FINEST".
YOU'RE WRONG, HARV. BANE WORKED TOO HARD TO GET HIS GRIP ON THIS TOWN'S UNDERWORLD.
10

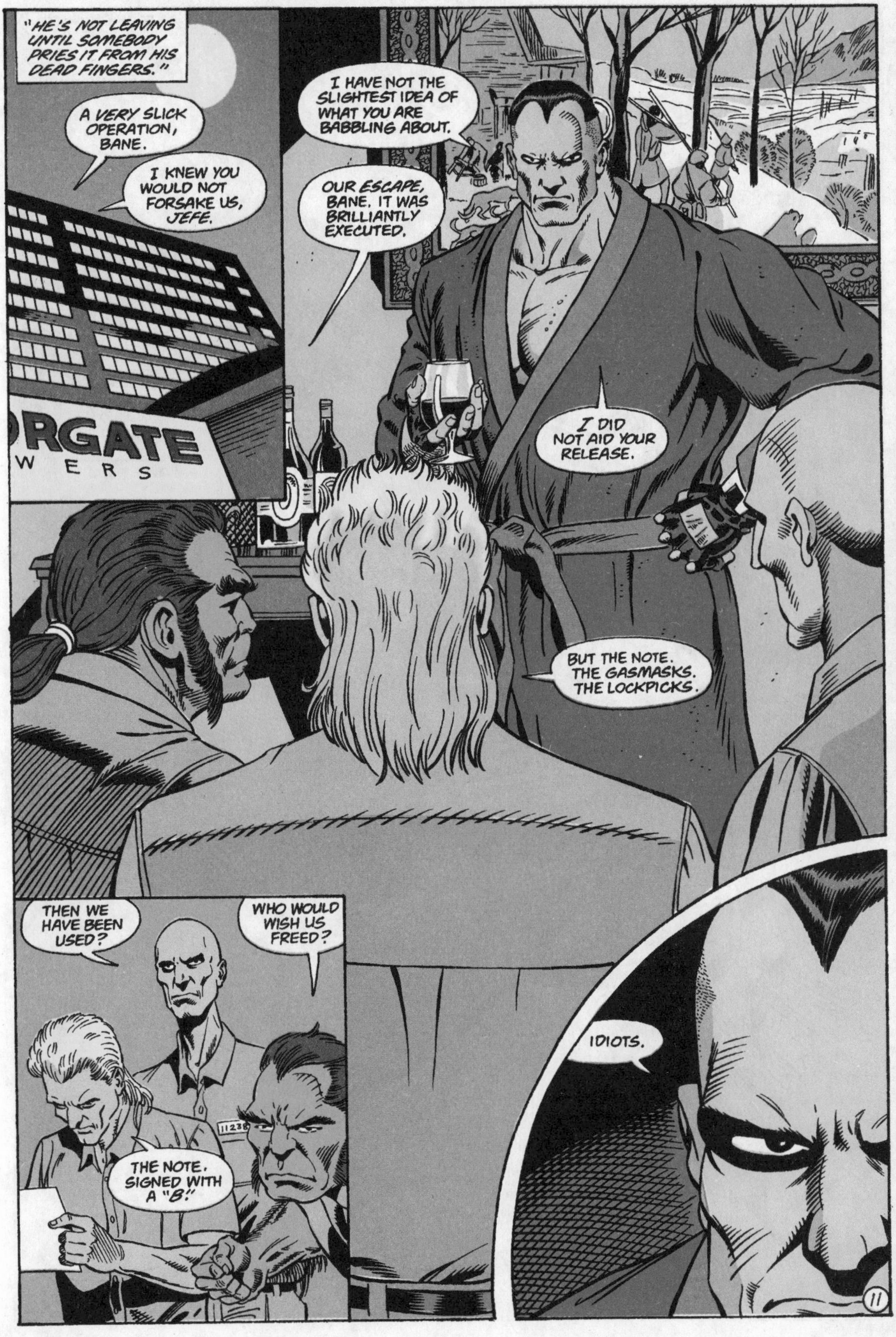
"HE'S NOT LEAVING UNTIL SOMEBODY PRIES IT FROM HIS DEAD FINGERS."
A VERY SLICK OPERATION, BANE.
I KNEW YOU WOULD NOT FORSAKE US, JEFE.
I HAVE NOT THE SLIGHTEST IDEA OF WHAT YOU ARE BABBLING ABOUT.
OUR ESCAPE, BANE. IT WAS BRILLIANTLY EXECUTED.
I DID NOT AID YOUR RELEASE.
BUT THE NOTE. THE GASMASKS. THE LOCKPICKS.
THEN WE HAVE BEEN USED?
WHO WOULD WISH US FREED?
THE NOTE. SIGNED WITH A "B!"
IDIOTS.
11

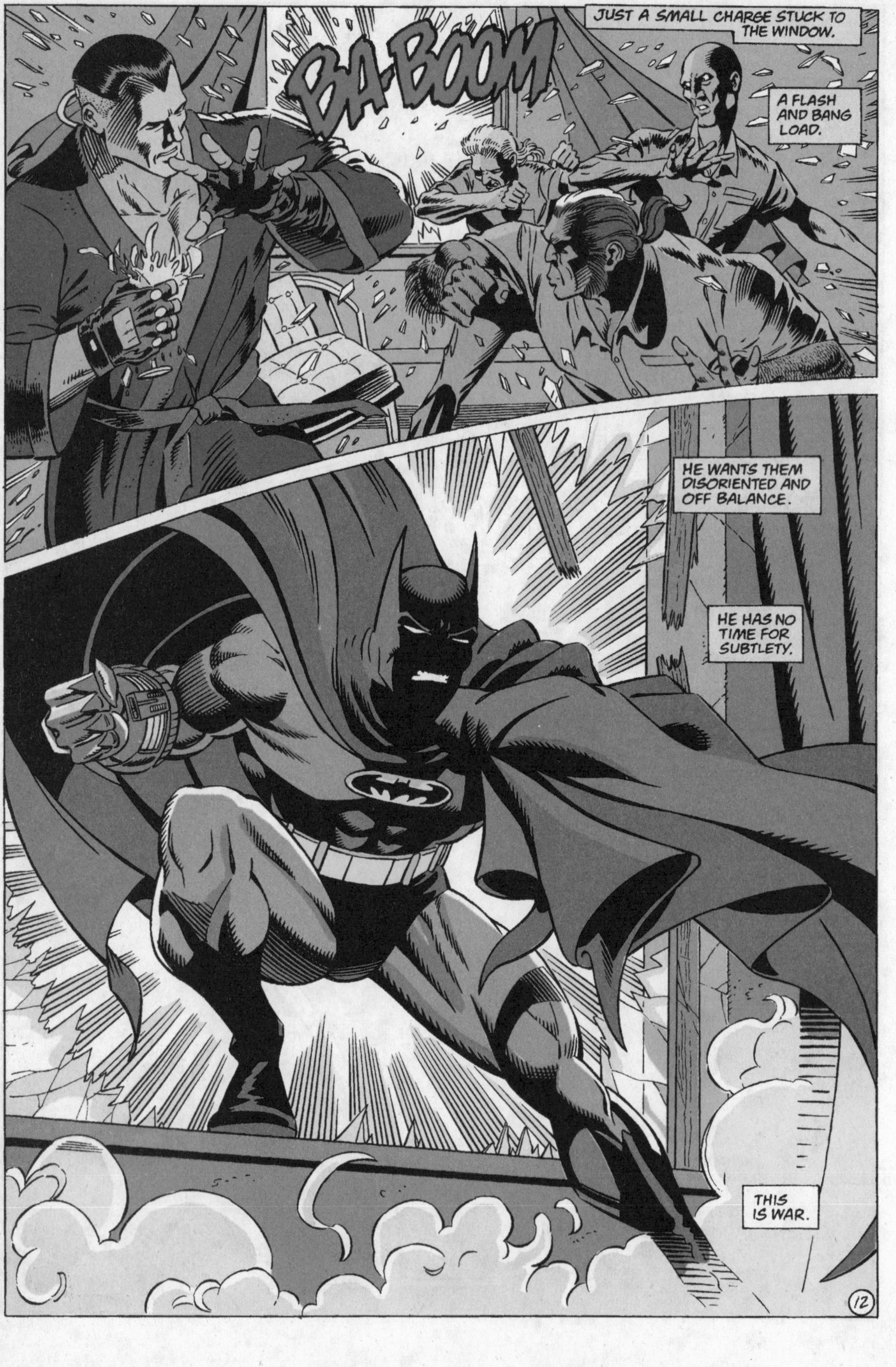
JUST A SMALL CHARGE STUCK TO THE WINDOW.
BA-BOOM
A FLASH AND BANG LOAD.
HE WANTS THEM DISORIENTED AND OFF BALANCE.
HE HAS NO TIME FOR SUBTLETY.
THIS IS WAR.
12

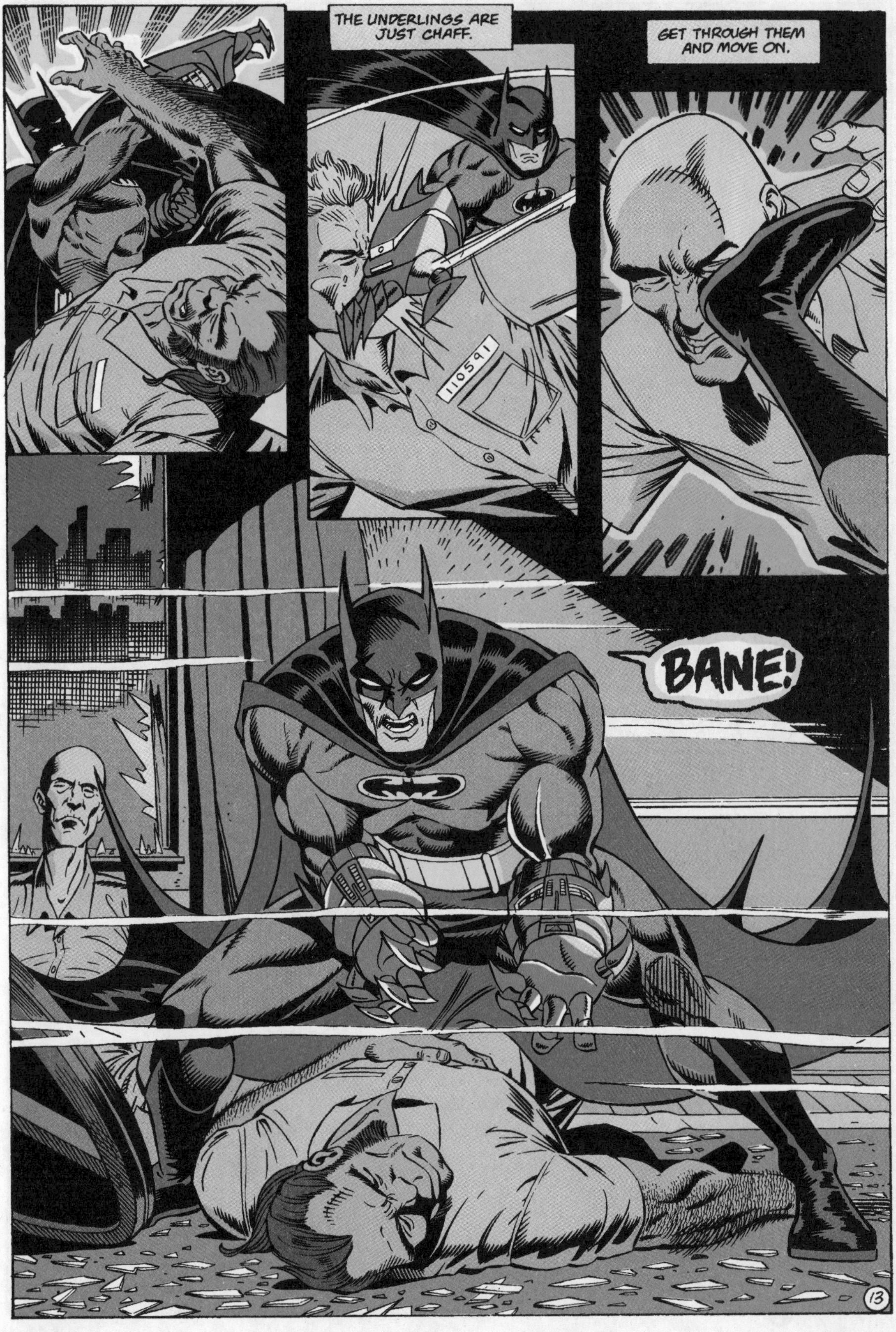
THE UNDERLINGS ARE JUST CHAFF.
GET THROUGH THEM AND MOVE ON.
110591
BANE!
13

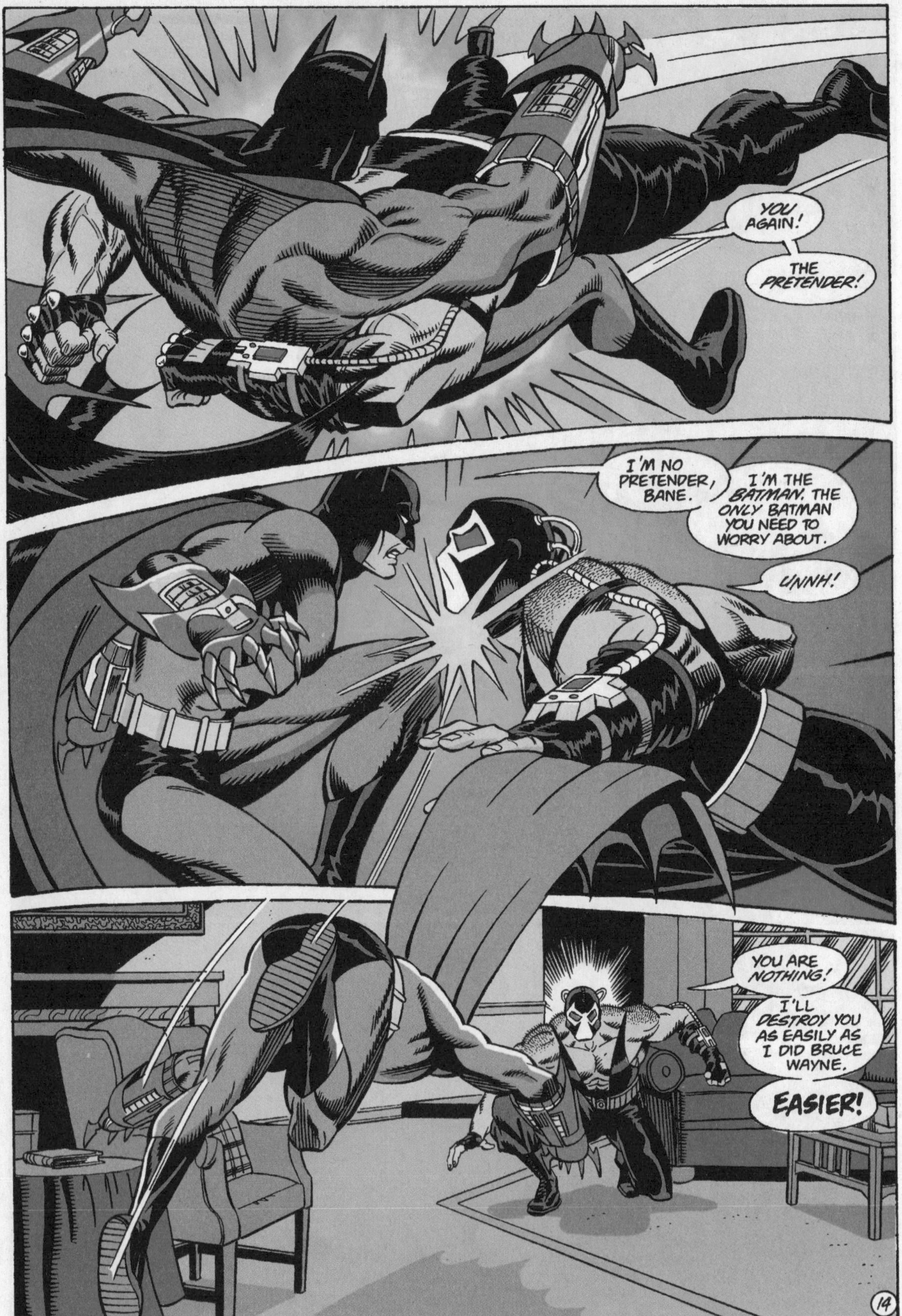
YOU AGAIN!
THE PRETENDER!
I'M NO PRETENDER, BANE.
I'M THE BATMAN. THE ONLY BATMAN YOU NEED TO WORRY ABOUT.
UNNH!
YOU ARE NOTHING!
I'LL DESTROY YOU AS EASILY AS I DID BRUCE WAYNE.
EASIER!
14

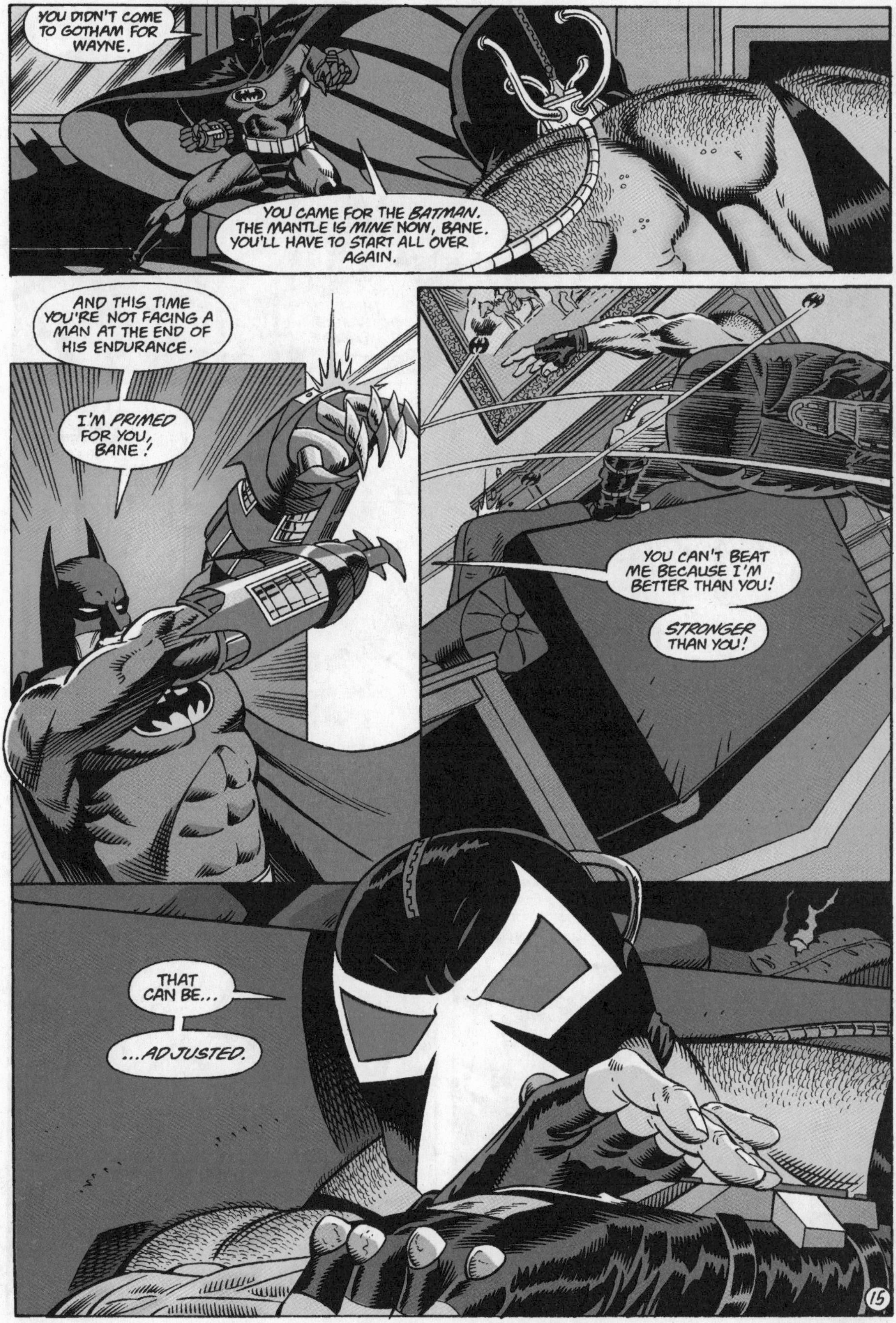

YOU DIDN'T COME TO GOTHAM FOR WAYNE.
YOU CAME FOR THE *BATMAN*. THE MANTLE IS *MINE* NOW, BANE. YOU'LL HAVE TO START ALL OVER AGAIN.
AND THIS TIME YOU'RE NOT FACING A MAN AT THE END OF HIS ENDURANCE.
I'M *PRIMED* FOR YOU, BANE!
YOU CAN'T BEAT ME BECAUSE I'M BETTER THAN YOU!
STRONGER THAN YOU!
THAT CAN BE...
...*ADJUSTED*.
15

HE'S ON VENOM NOW. THE DRUG COURSES THROUGH HIM LIKE FIRE.

SHRKKT

I WILL CRUSH THE LIFE FROM YOU AND BE RID OF BATMEN FOREVER!

THEN GOTHAM IS MINE ALONE!

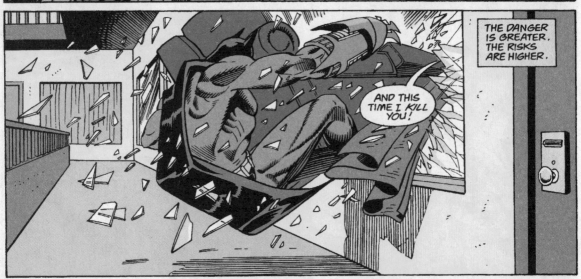

THE DANGER IS GREATER. THE RISKS ARE HIGHER.

AND THIS TIME I KILL YOU!

THE MONSTER IS AT THE HEIGHT OF HIS POWERS.

I WILL MAKE YOUR DEATH A MONUMENT.

HE SHOULD HAVE SKIPPED THE BRAVADO AND TAKEN BANE DOWN AT THE OUTSET.

THERE WILL BE NO MORE TO FOLLOW YOU! THE MANTLE OF THE BAT WILL BE A FUNERAL SHROUD!

16

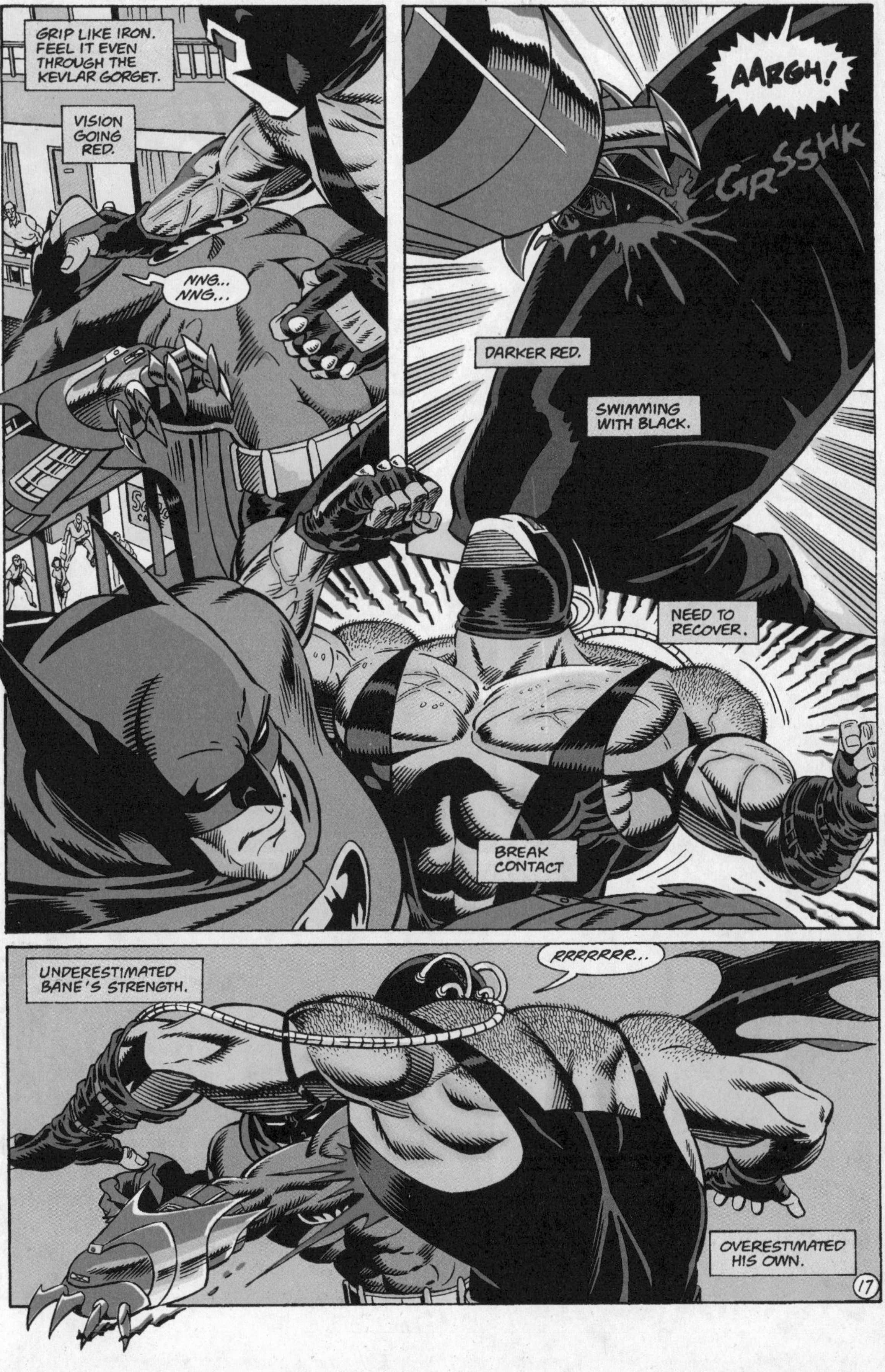
GRIP LIKE IRON. FEEL IT EVEN THROUGH THE KEVLAR GORGET.
VISION GOING RED.
NNG... NNG...
AARGH!
GRSSHK
DARKER RED.
SWIMMING WITH BLACK.
NEED TO RECOVER.
BREAK CONTACT
UNDERESTIMATED BANE'S STRENGTH.
RRRRRRR...
OVERESTIMATED HIS OWN.
17

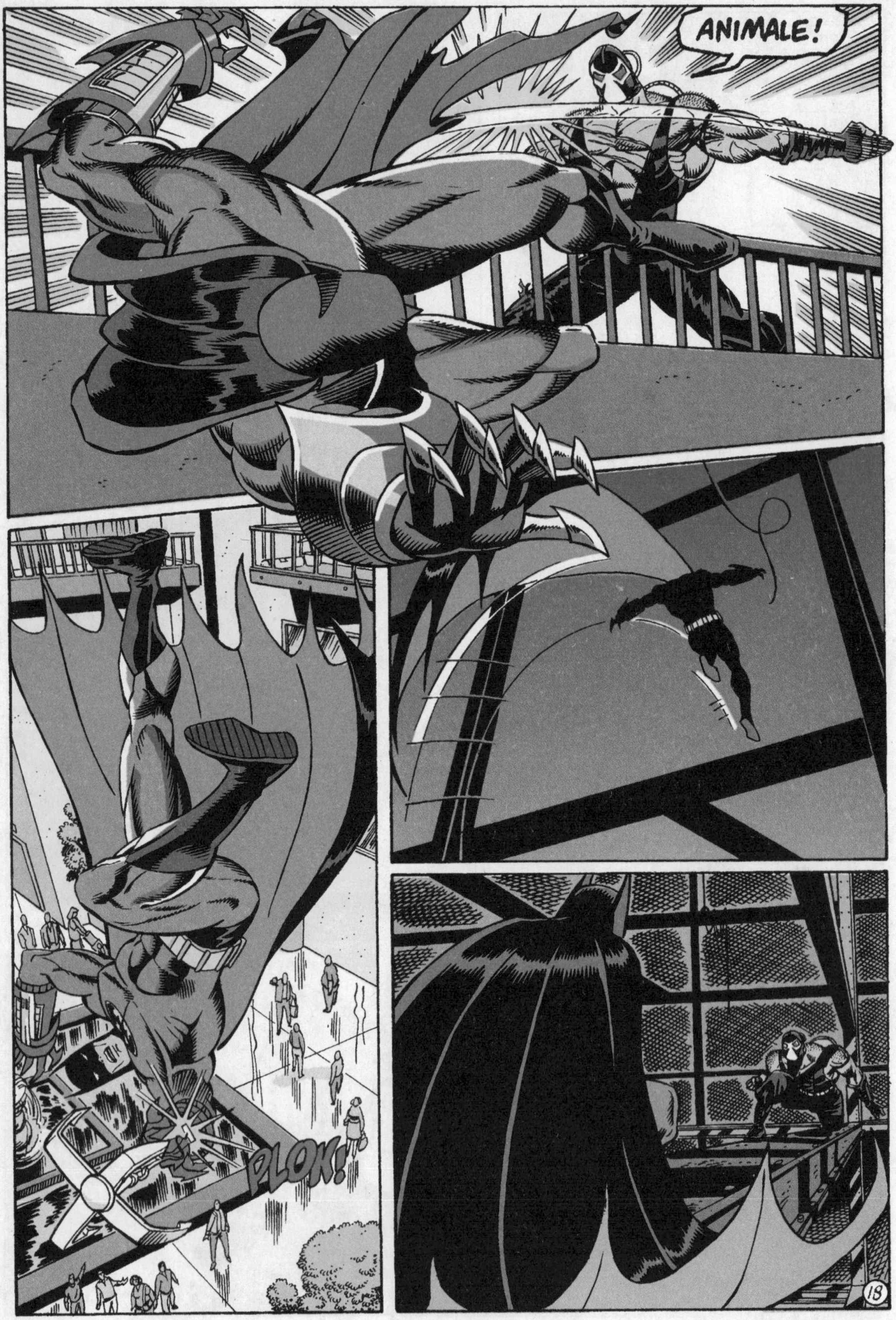
ANIMALE!
PLOK!
18

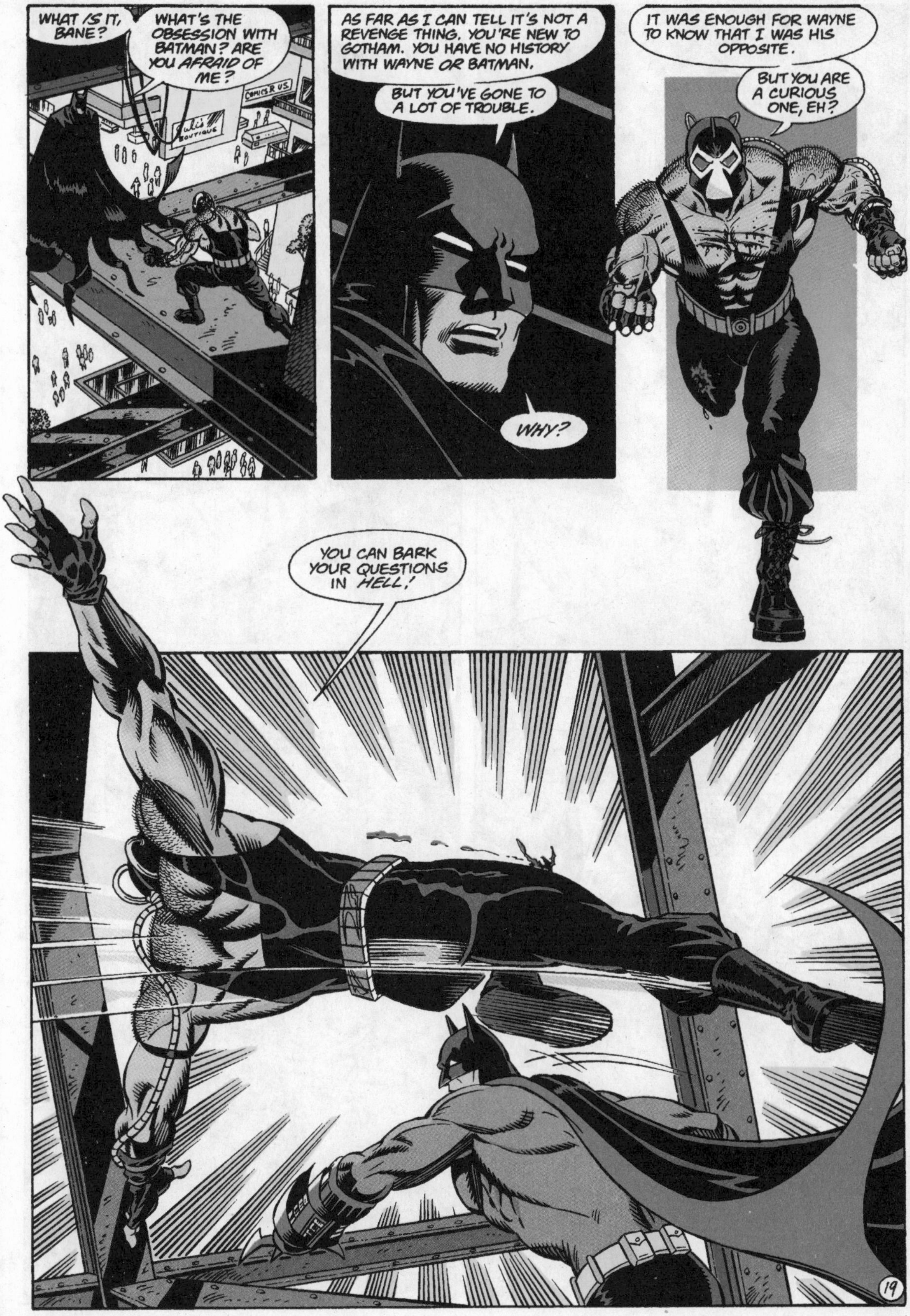
WHAT IS IT, BANE?
WHAT'S THE OBSESSION WITH BATMAN? ARE YOU AFRAID OF ME?
COMICS R US
AS FAR AS I CAN TELL IT'S NOT A REVENGE THING. YOU'RE NEW TO GOTHAM. YOU HAVE NO HISTORY WITH WAYNE OR BATMAN.
BUT YOU'VE GONE TO A LOT OF TROUBLE.
WHY?
IT WAS ENOUGH FOR WAYNE TO KNOW THAT I WAS HIS OPPOSITE.
BUT YOU ARE A CURIOUS ONE, EH?
YOU CAN BARK YOUR QUESTIONS IN HELL!
19

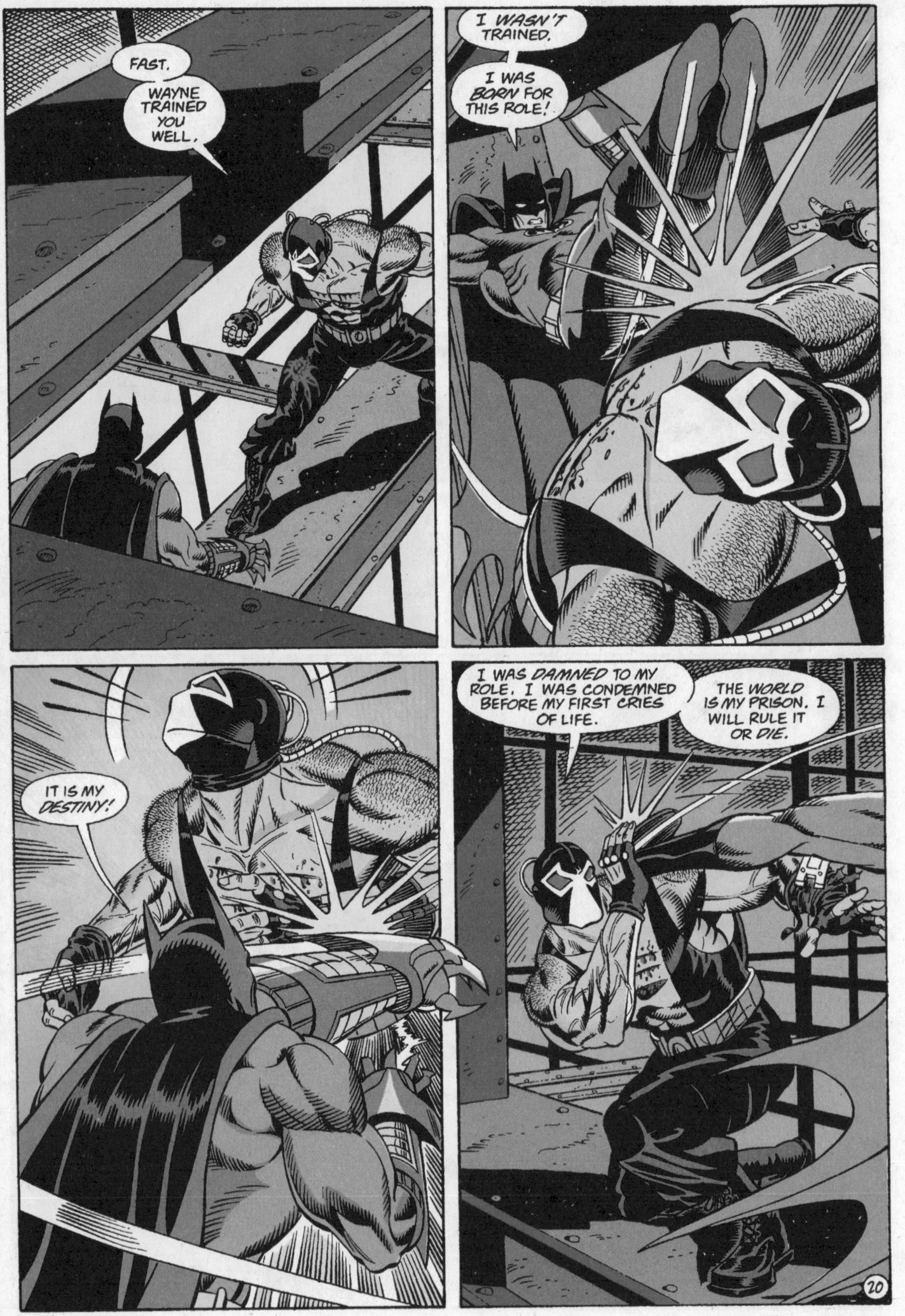
FAST.
WAYNE TRAINED YOU WELL.
I WASN'T TRAINED.
I WAS BORN FOR THIS ROLE!
IT IS MY DESTINY!
I WAS DAMNED TO MY ROLE. I WAS CONDEMNED BEFORE MY FIRST CRIES OF LIFE.
THE WORLD IS MY PRISON. I WILL RULE IT OR DIE.
20

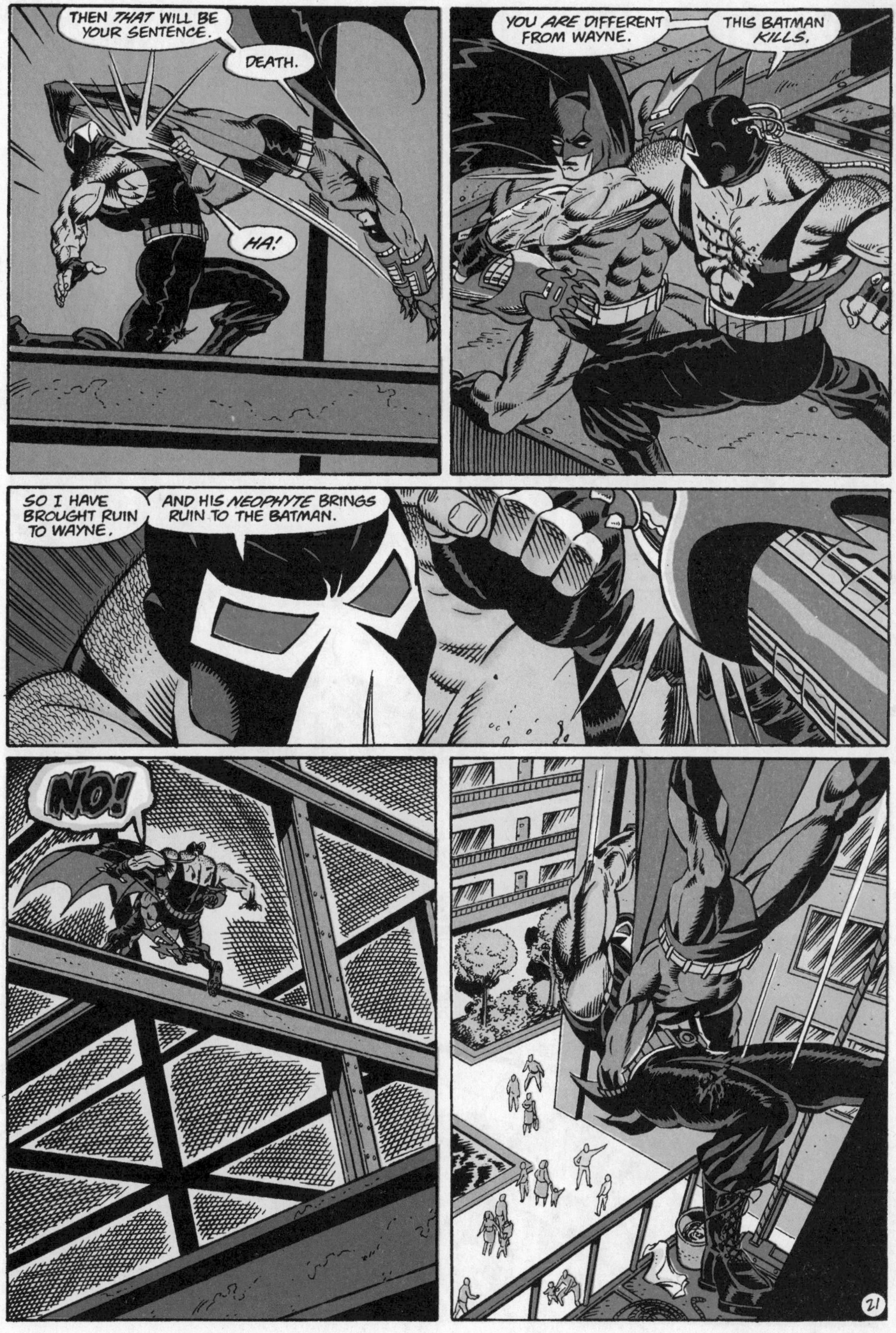
THEN THAT WILL BE YOUR SENTENCE.
DEATH.
HA!
YOU ARE DIFFERENT FROM WAYNE.
THIS BATMAN KILLS.
SO I HAVE BROUGHT RUIN TO WAYNE.
AND HIS NEOPHYTE BRINGS RUIN TO THE BATMAN.
NO!
21

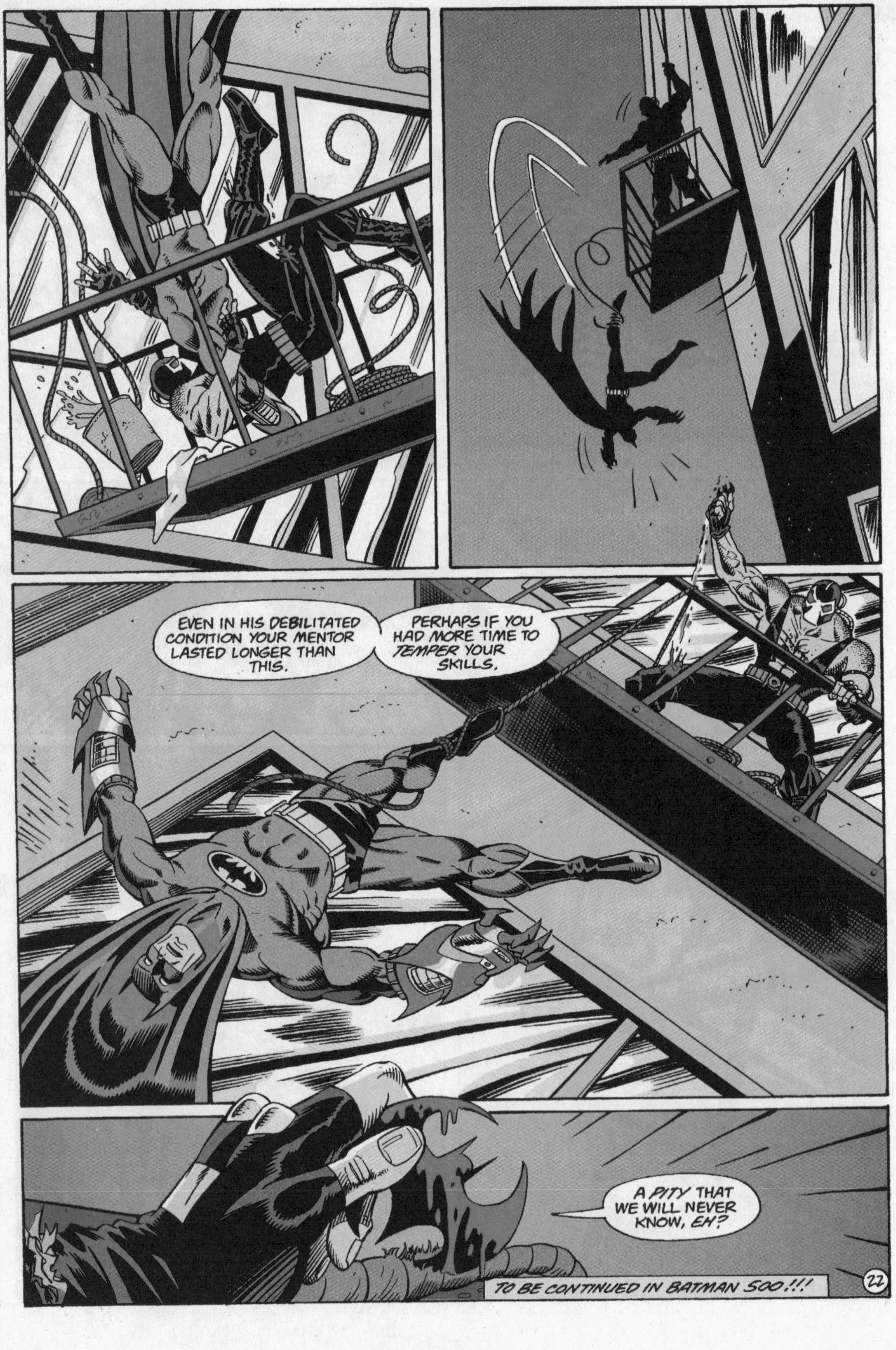
EVEN IN HIS DEBILITATED CONDITION YOUR MENTOR LASTED LONGER THAN THIS.
PERHAPS IF YOU HAD MORE TIME TO TEMPER YOUR SKILLS.
A PITY THAT WE WILL NEVER KNOW, EH?
TO BE CONTINUED IN BATMAN 500!!!
22

Cover art by **KELLEY JONES**

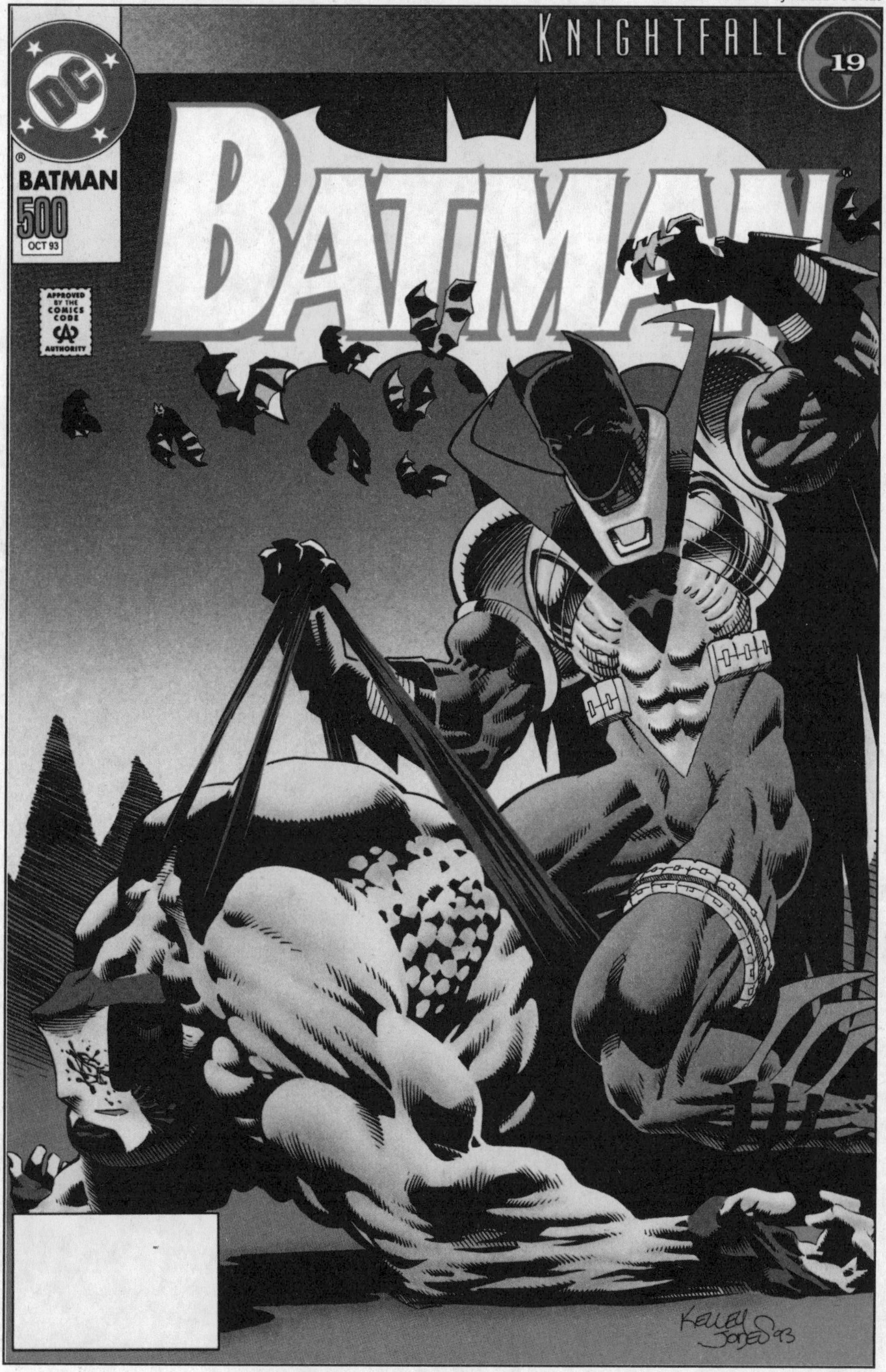
KNIGHTFALL
19
DC
BATMAN
500
OCT 93
BATMAN
APPROVED BY THE COMICS CODE AUTHORITY
KELLEY JONES '93

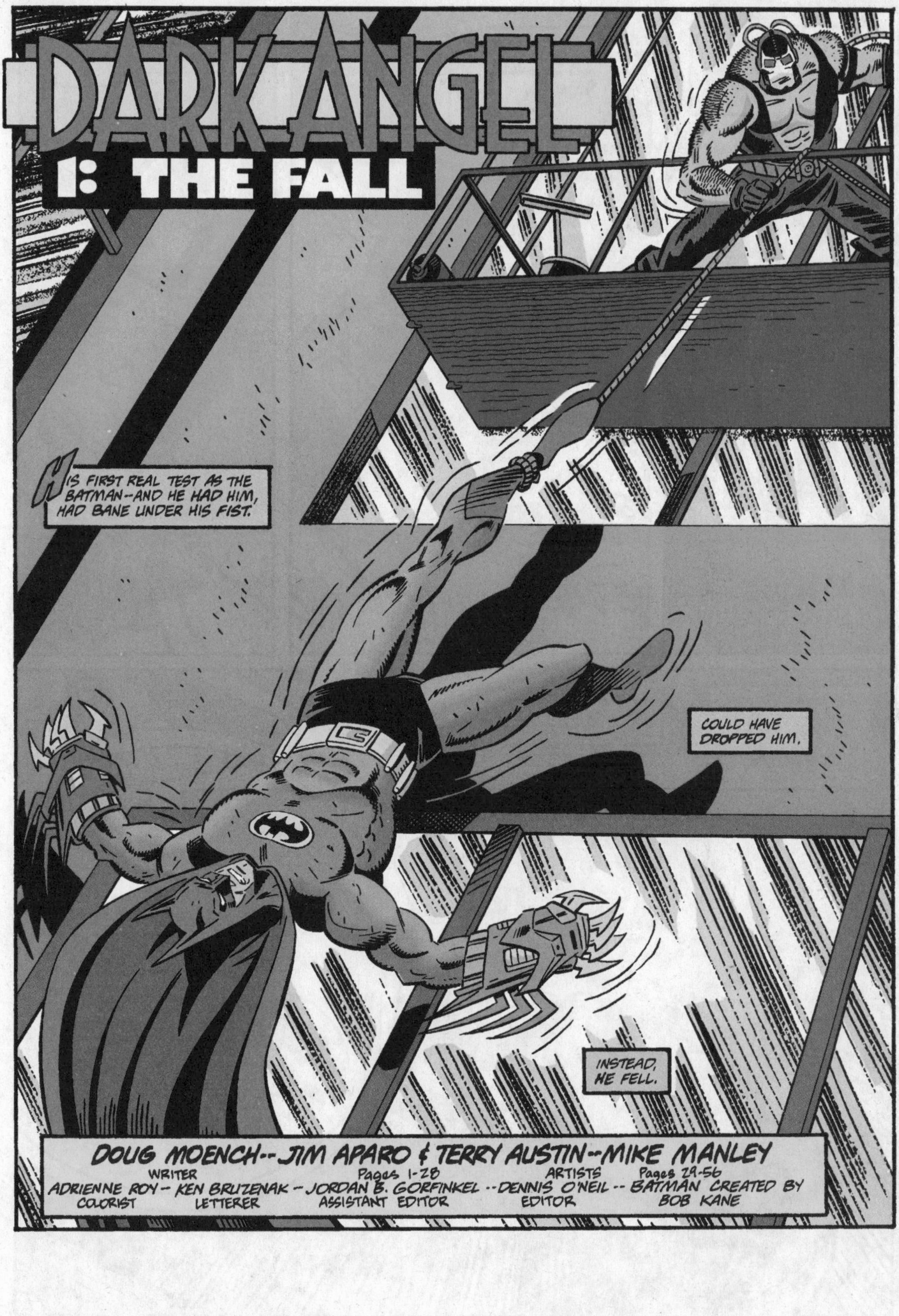
DARK ANGEL
1: THE FALL
HIS FIRST REAL TEST AS THE BATMAN--AND HE HAD HIM, HAD BANE UNDER HIS FIST.
COULD HAVE DROPPED HIM.
INSTEAD, HE FELL.
DOUG MOENCH--JIM APARO & TERRY AUSTIN--MIKE MANLEY
WRITER Pages 1-28 ARTISTS Pages 29-56
ADRIENNE ROY -- KEN BRUZENAK -- JORDAN B. GORFINKEL -- DENNIS O'NEIL -- BATMAN CREATED BY
COLORIST LETTERER ASSISTANT EDITOR EDITOR BOB KANE

AND NOW BANE IS USING A SHURIKEN-- ONE OF HIS OWN NEW WEAPONS--TO MAKE THE FALL PERMANENT.

VRNCH

RNCH

TO HELL WITH BUYING TIME.

HE TRIES TO SMASH AND GRAB IT, SHOOTING MORE OF THE BLADES.

SHING

SHING

SHING

DRIVING BANE BACK.

PRESERVING THE ROPE.

CHTCH

CHUT

STING

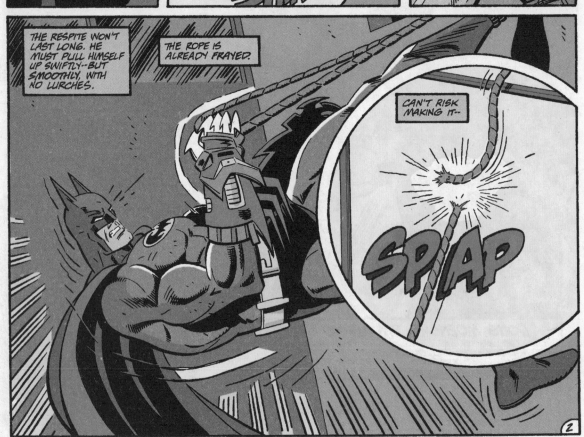

THE RESPITE WON'T LAST LONG. HE MUST PULL HIMSELF UP SWIFTLY--BUT SMOOTHLY, WITH NO LURCHES.

THE ROPE IS ALREADY FRAYED.

CAN'T RISK MAKING IT--

SPLAP

2

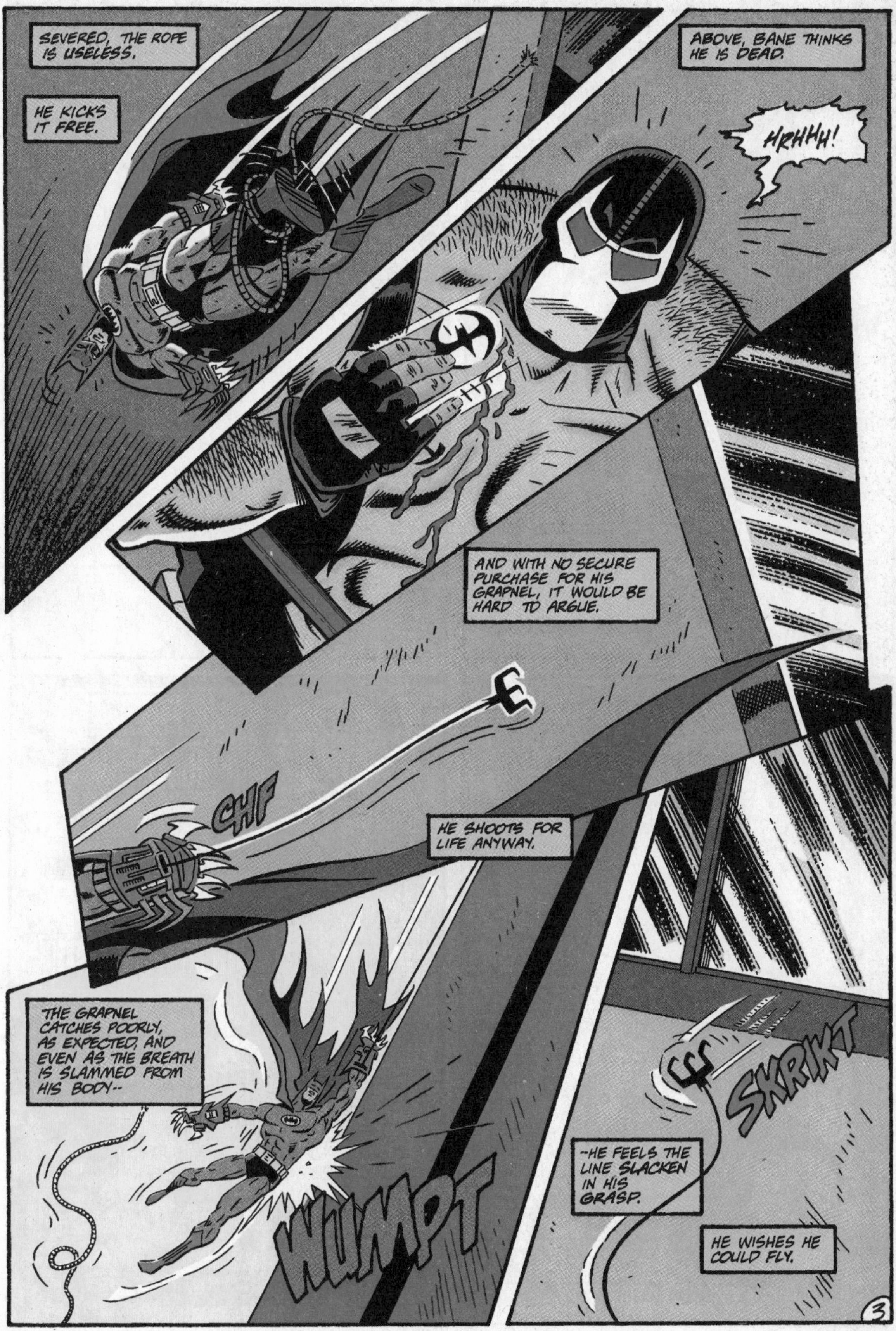

SEVERED, THE ROPE IS USELESS.
HE KICKS IT FREE.
ABOVE, BANE THINKS HE IS DEAD.
HRHHH!
AND WITH NO SECURE PURCHASE FOR HIS GRAPNEL, IT WOULD BE HARD TO ARGUE.
CHF
HE SHOOTS FOR LIFE ANYWAY.
THE GRAPNEL CATCHES POORLY, AS EXPECTED, AND EVEN AS THE BREATH IS SLAMMED FROM HIS BODY--
WUMPT
SKRIKT
--HE FEELS THE LINE SLACKEN IN HIS GRASP.
HE WISHES HE COULD FLY.
3

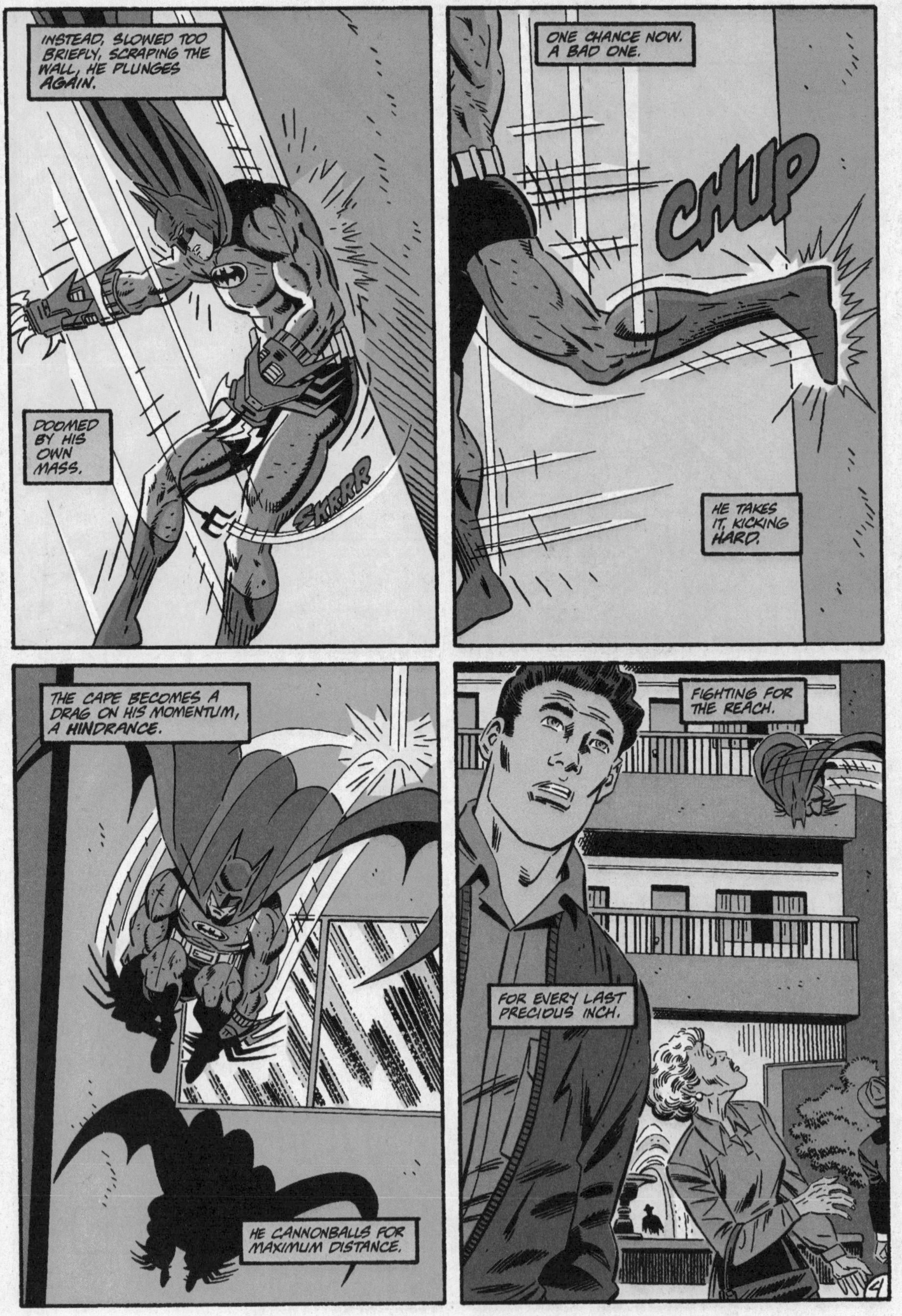
INSTEAD, SLOWED TOO BRIEFLY, SCRAPING THE WALL, HE PLUNGES AGAIN.
DOOMED BY HIS OWN MASS.
SKRRR
ONE CHANCE NOW. A BAD ONE.
CHUP
HE TAKES IT, KICKING HARD.
THE CAPE BECOMES A DRAG ON HIS MOMENTUM, A HINDRANCE.
HE CANNONBALLS FOR MAXIMUM DISTANCE.
FIGHTING FOR THE REACH.
FOR EVERY LAST PRECIOUS INCH.
4

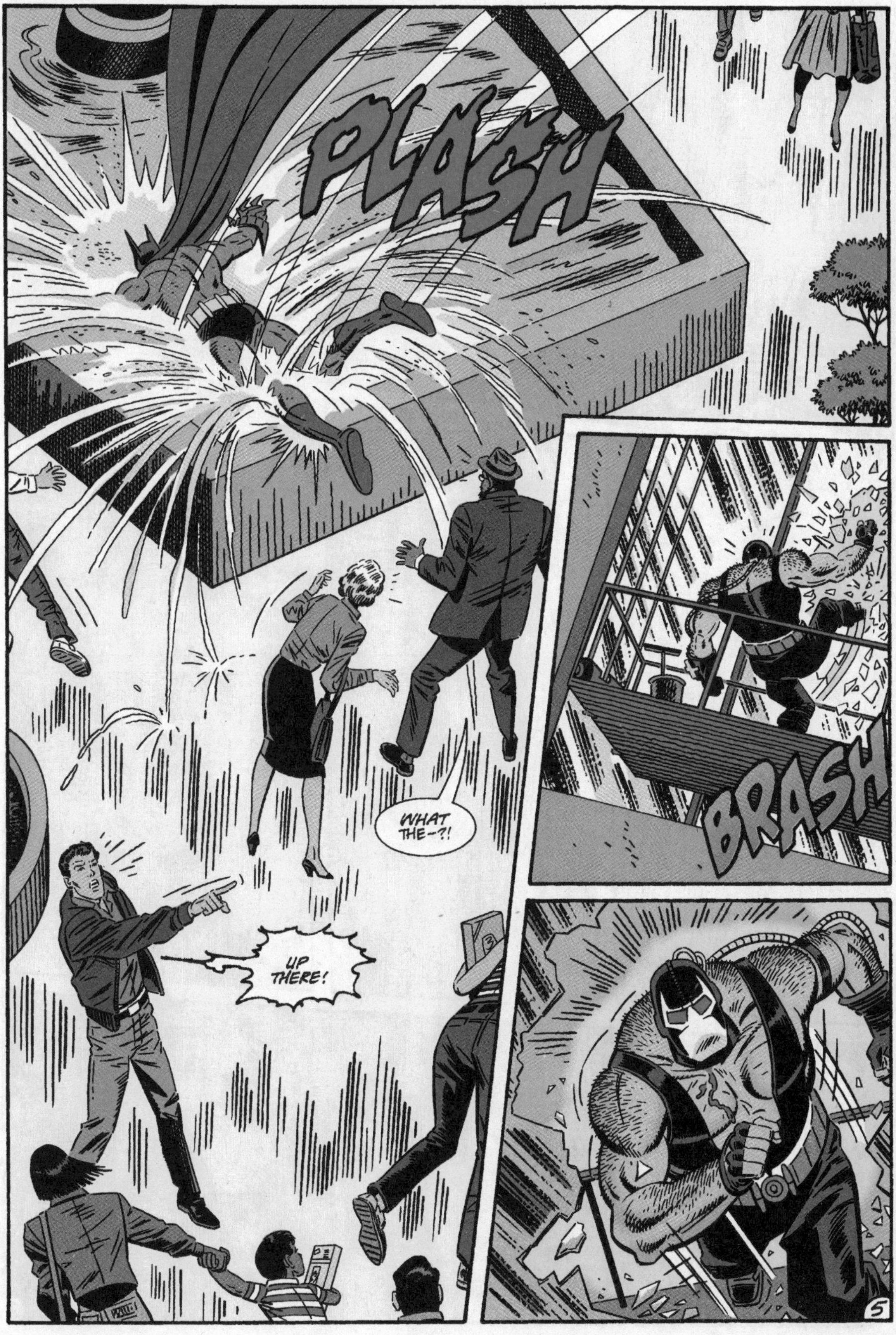
PLASH
BRASH
WHAT THE-?!
UP THERE!
5

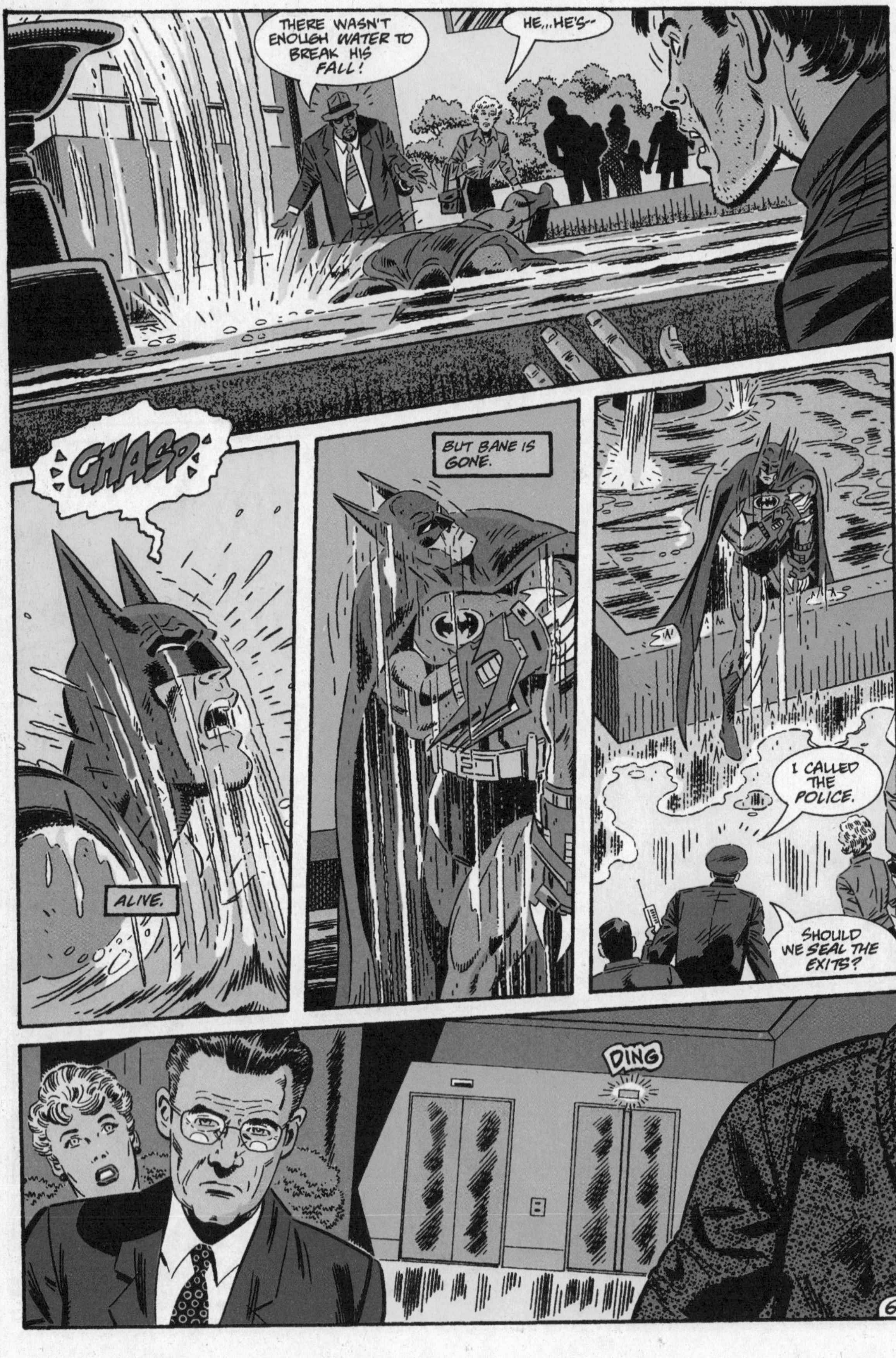
THERE WASN'T ENOUGH WATER TO BREAK HIS FALL!
HE...HE'S-
GHASP
ALIVE.
BUT BANE IS GONE.
I CALLED THE POLICE.
SHOULD WE SEAL THE EXITS?
DING
6

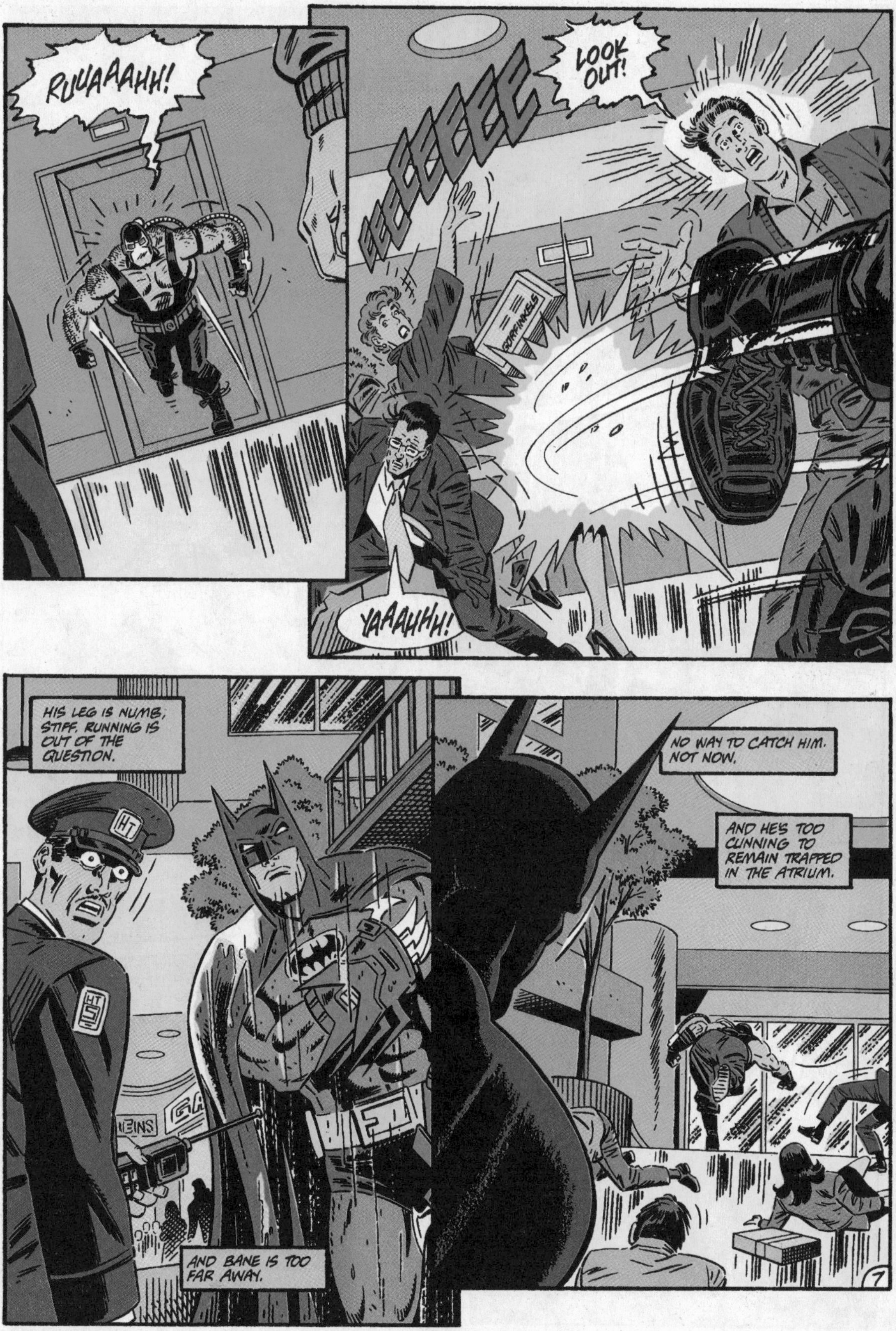

RUUAAAHH!
EEEEEEEEE
LOOK OUT!
YAAAHHH!
HIS LEG IS NUMB, STIFF. RUNNING IS OUT OF THE QUESTION.
AND BANE IS TOO FAR AWAY.
NO WAY TO CATCH HIM. NOT NOW.
AND HE'S TOO CUNNING TO REMAIN TRAPPED IN THE ATRIUM.

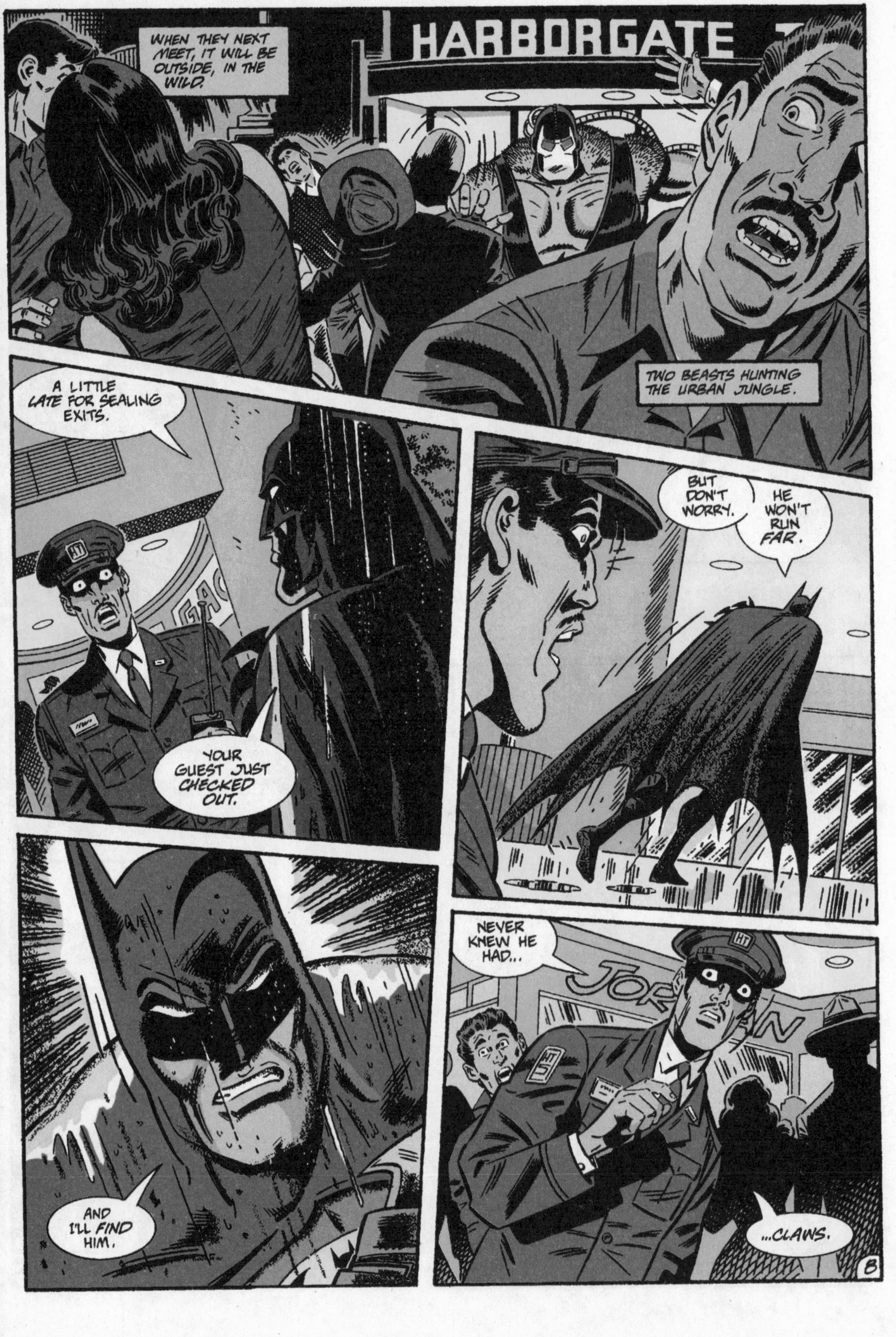
HARBORGATE
WHEN THEY NEXT MEET, IT WILL BE OUTSIDE, IN THE WILD.
TWO BEASTS HUNTING THE URBAN JUNGLE.
A LITTLE LATE FOR SEALING EXITS.
YOUR GUEST JUST CHECKED OUT.
BUT DON'T WORRY.
HE WON'T RUN FAR.
AND I'LL FIND HIM.
NEVER KNEW HE HAD...
...CLAWS.
8

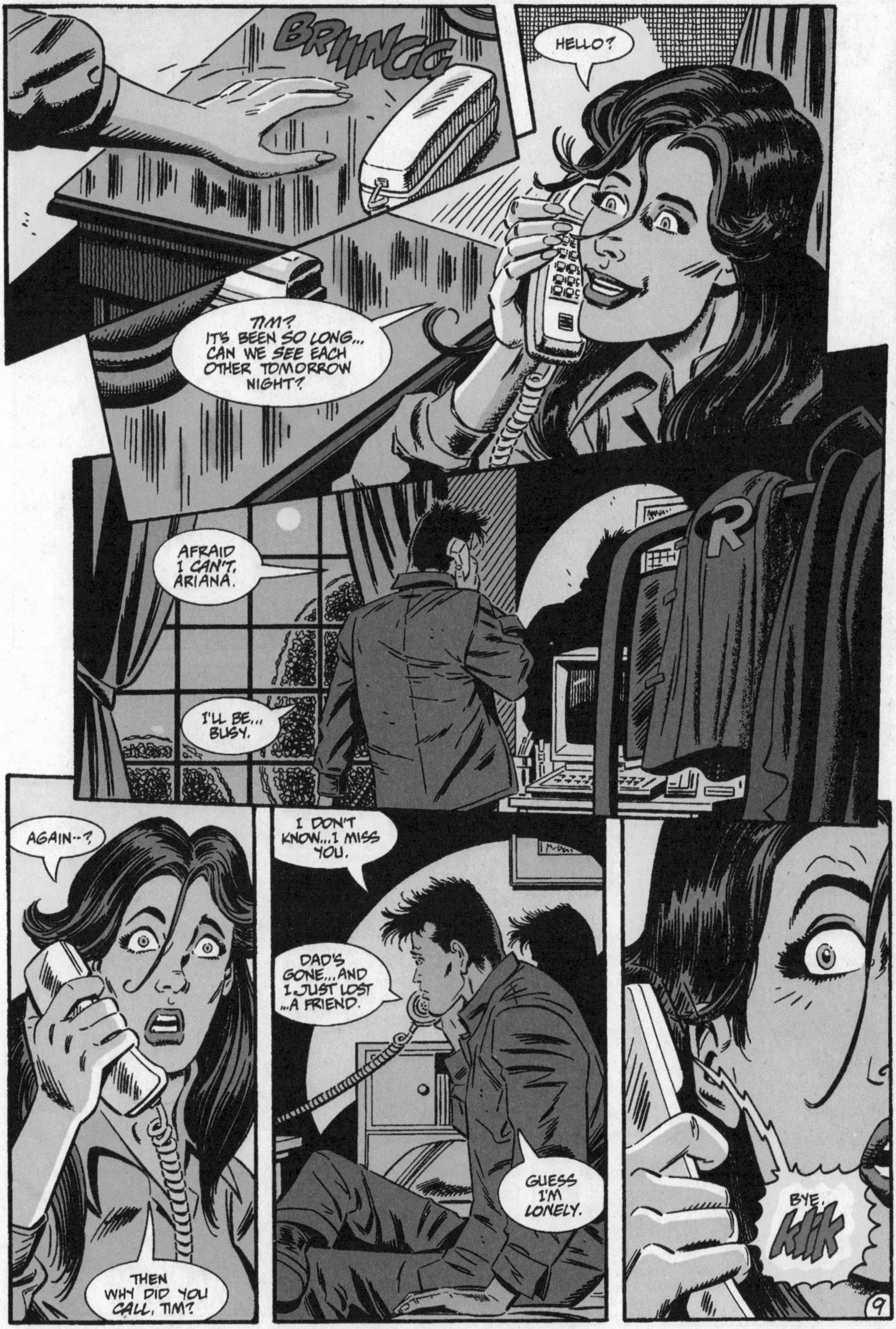
BRIIINGG
HELLO?
TIM? IT'S BEEN SO LONG... CAN WE SEE EACH OTHER TOMORROW NIGHT?
AFRAID I CAN'T, ARIANA.
I'LL BE... BUSY.
AGAIN--?
THEN WHY DID YOU CALL, TIM?
I DON'T KNOW...I MISS YOU.
DAD'S GONE...AND I JUST LOST ...A FRIEND.
GUESS I'M LONELY.
BYE.
klik
9

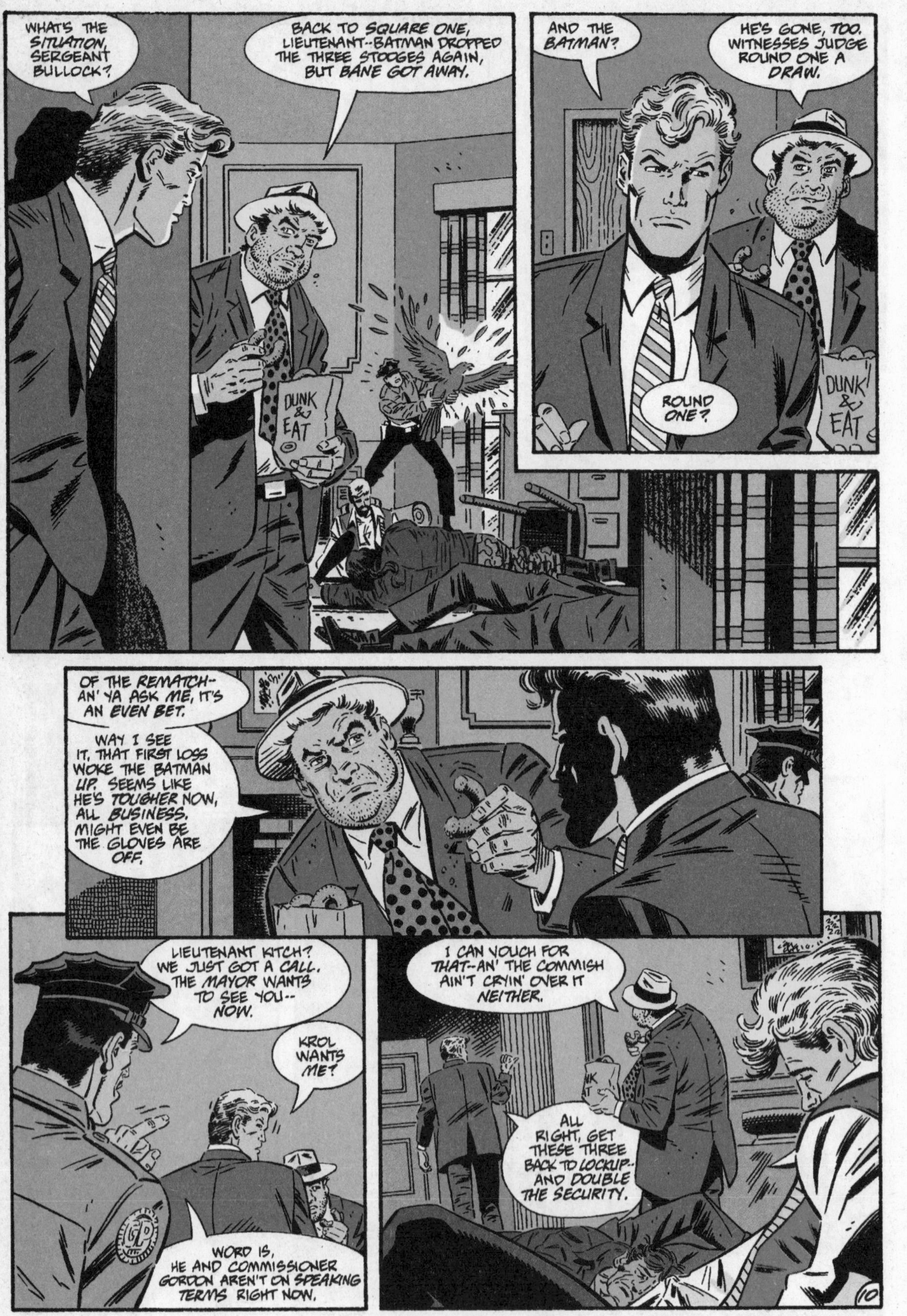
WHAT'S THE SITUATION, SERGEANT BULLOCK?
BACK TO SQUARE ONE, LIEUTENANT--BATMAN DROPPED THE THREE STOOGES AGAIN, BUT BANE GOT AWAY.
DUNK & EAT
AND THE BATMAN?
HE'S GONE, TOO. WITNESSES JUDGE ROUND ONE A DRAW.
ROUND ONE?
DUNK & EAT
OF THE REMATCH-- AN' YA ASK ME, IT'S AN EVEN BET.
WAY I SEE IT, THAT FIRST LOSS WOKE THE BATMAN UP. SEEMS LIKE HE'S TOUGHER NOW, ALL BUSINESS. MIGHT EVEN BE THE GLOVES ARE OFF.
LIEUTENANT KITCH? WE JUST GOT A CALL. THE MAYOR WANTS TO SEE YOU-- NOW.
KROL WANTS ME?
WORD IS, HE AND COMMISSIONER GORDON AREN'T ON SPEAKING TERMS RIGHT NOW.
I CAN VOUCH FOR THAT--AN' THE COMMISH AIN'T CRYIN' OVER IT NEITHER.
ALL RIGHT, GET THESE THREE BACK TO LOCKUP-- AND DOUBLE THE SECURITY.
10

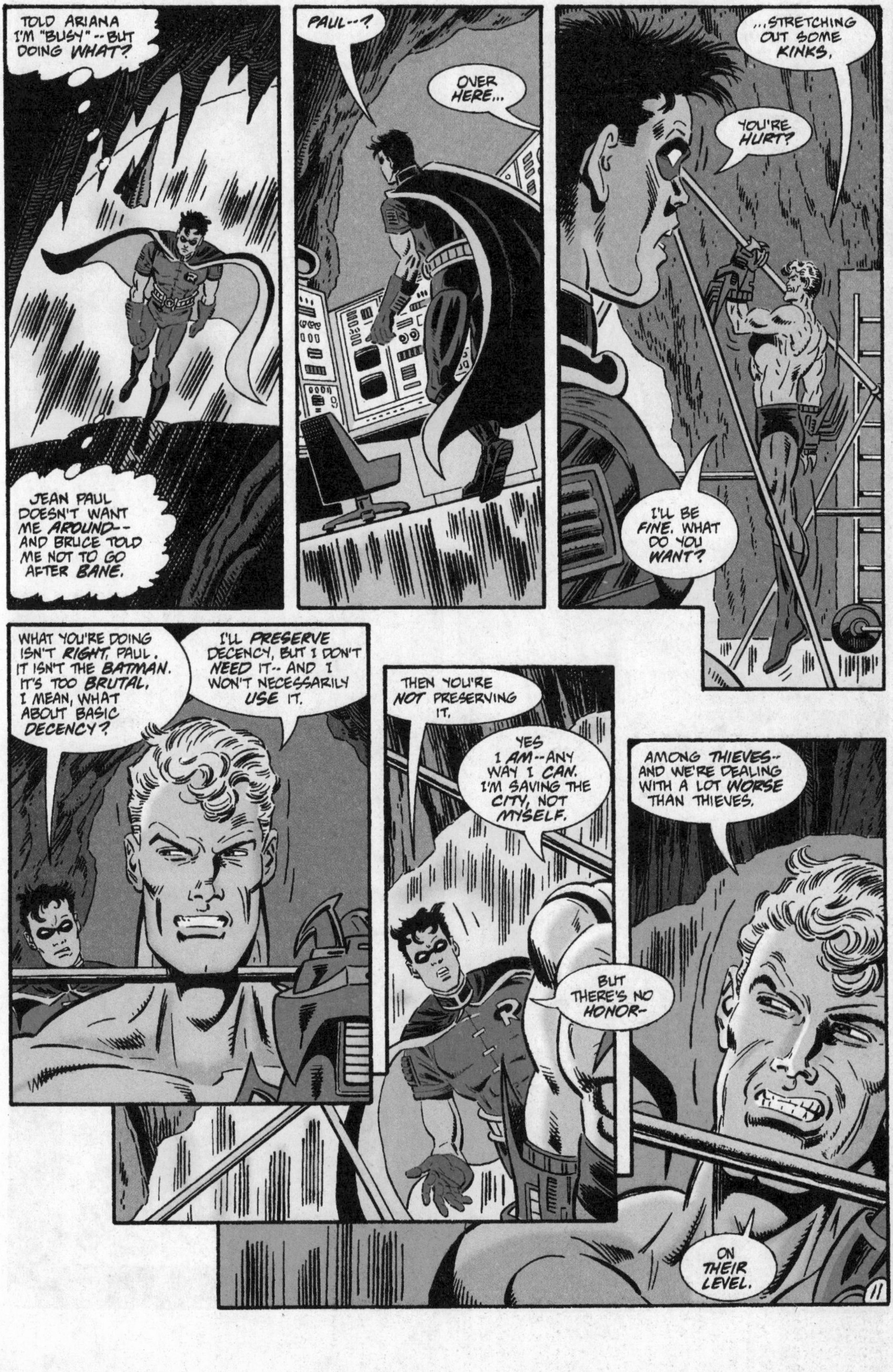
TOLD ARIANA I'M "BUSY" -- BUT DOING WHAT?
JEAN PAUL DOESN'T WANT ME AROUND-- AND BRUCE TOLD ME NOT TO GO AFTER BANE.
PAUL--?
OVER HERE...
...STRETCHING OUT SOME KINKS.
YOU'RE HURT?
I'LL BE FINE. WHAT DO YOU WANT?
WHAT YOU'RE DOING ISN'T RIGHT, PAUL. IT ISN'T THE BATMAN. IT'S TOO BRUTAL. I MEAN, WHAT ABOUT BASIC DECENCY?
I'LL PRESERVE DECENCY, BUT I DON'T NEED IT-- AND I WON'T NECESSARILY USE IT.
THEN YOU'RE NOT PRESERVING IT.
YES I AM--ANY WAY I CAN. I'M SAVING THE CITY, NOT MYSELF.
BUT THERE'S NO HONOR-
AMONG THIEVES-- AND WE'RE DEALING WITH A LOT WORSE THAN THIEVES.
ON THEIR LEVEL.
11

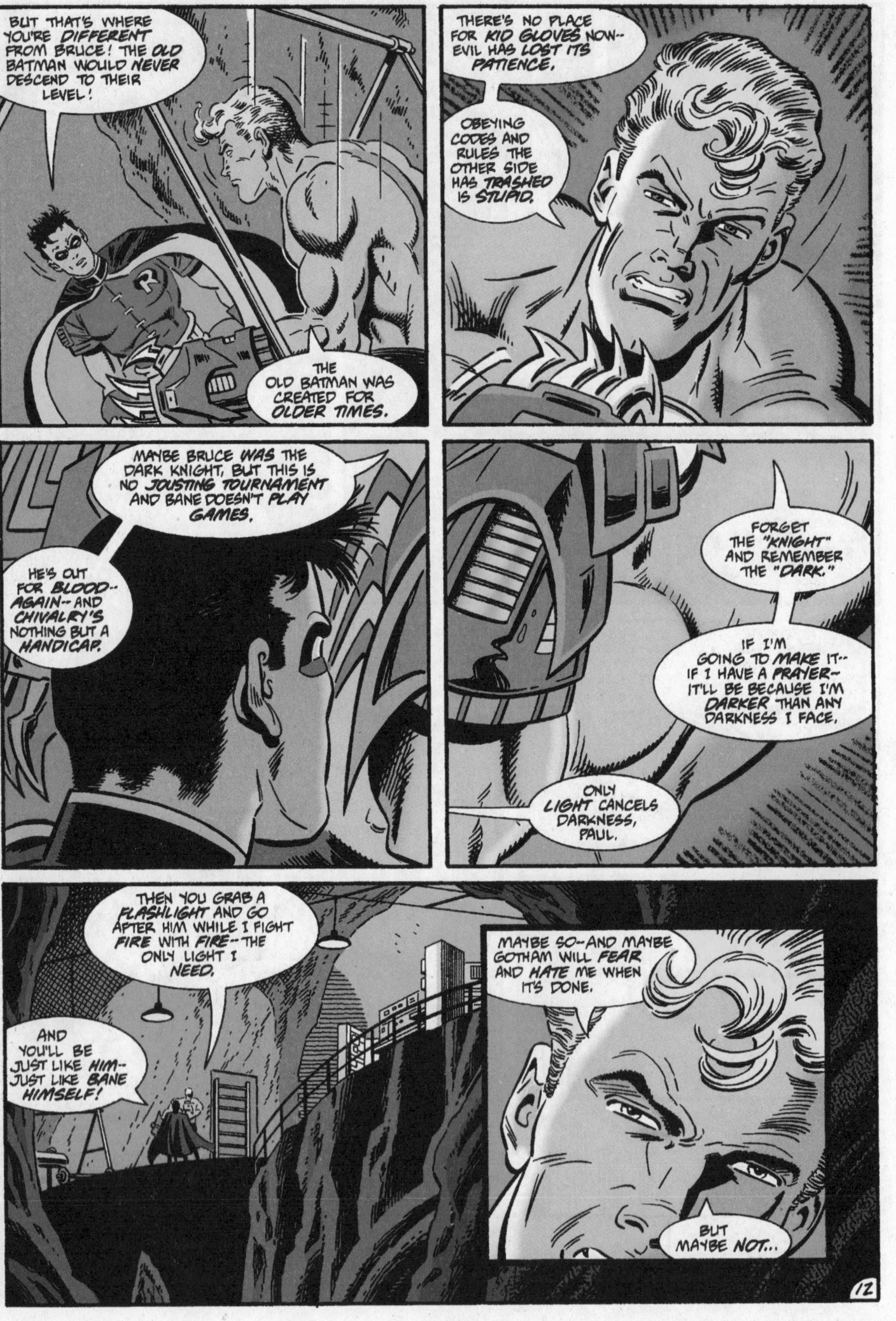
BUT THAT'S WHERE YOU'RE DIFFERENT FROM BRUCE! THE OLD BATMAN WOULD NEVER DESCEND TO THEIR LEVEL!
THE OLD BATMAN WAS CREATED FOR OLDER TIMES.
THERE'S NO PLACE FOR KID GLOVES NOW-- EVIL HAS LOST ITS PATIENCE.
OBEYING CODES AND RULES THE OTHER SIDE HAS TRASHED IS STUPID.
MAYBE BRUCE WAS THE DARK KNIGHT, BUT THIS IS NO JOUSTING TOURNAMENT AND BANE DOESN'T PLAY GAMES.
HE'S OUT FOR BLOOD-- AGAIN-- AND CHIVALRY'S NOTHING BUT A HANDICAP.
FORGET THE "KNIGHT" AND REMEMBER THE "DARK."
IF I'M GOING TO MAKE IT-- IF I HAVE A PRAYER-- IT'LL BE BECAUSE I'M DARKER THAN ANY DARKNESS I FACE.
ONLY LIGHT CANCELS DARKNESS, PAUL.
THEN YOU GRAB A FLASHLIGHT AND GO AFTER HIM WHILE I FIGHT FIRE WITH FIRE-- THE ONLY LIGHT I NEED.
AND YOU'LL BE JUST LIKE HIM-- JUST LIKE BANE HIMSELF!
MAYBE SO--AND MAYBE GOTHAM WILL FEAR AND HATE ME WHEN IT'S DONE.
BUT MAYBE NOT...
12

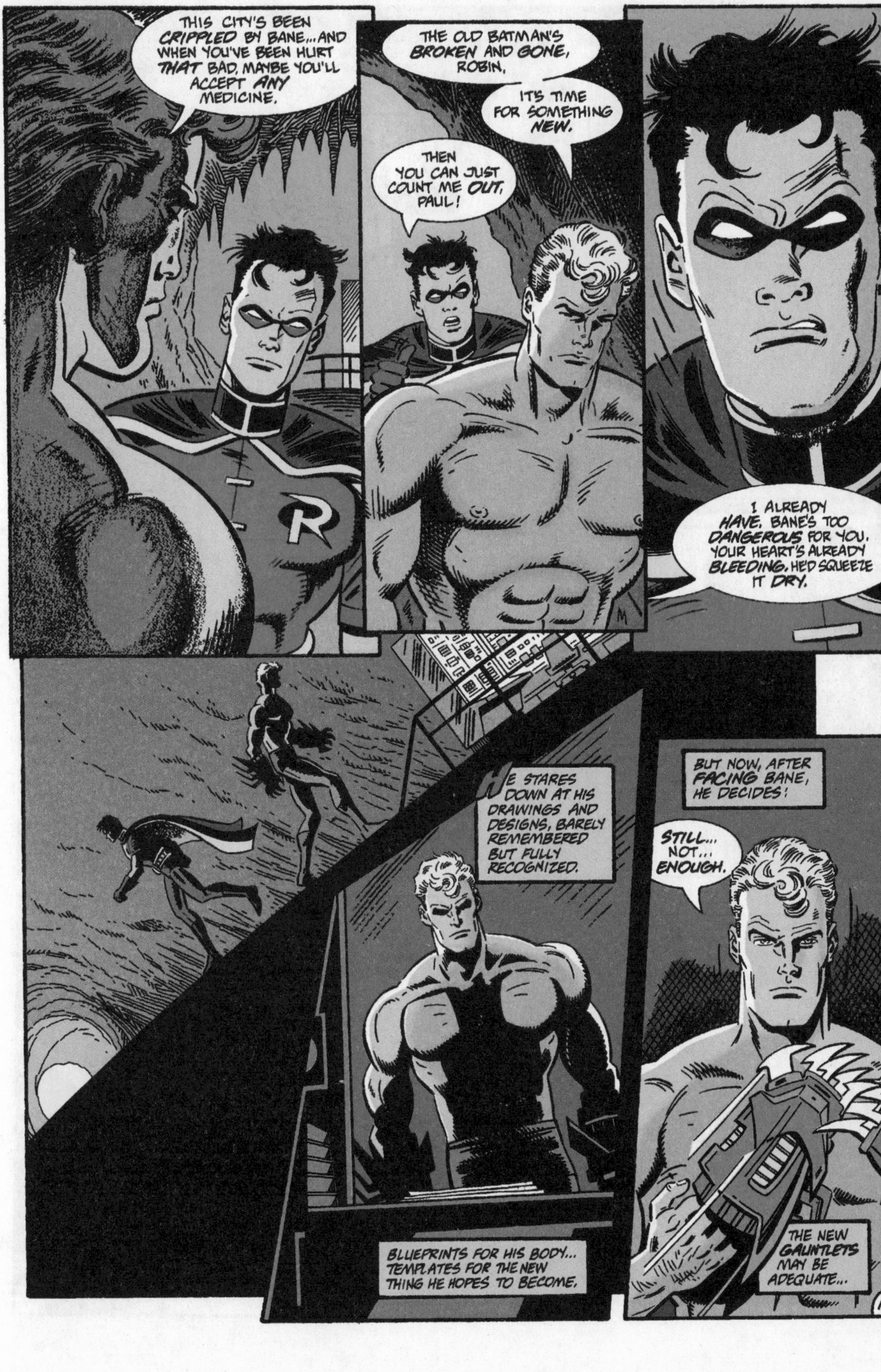
THIS CITY'S BEEN CRIPPLED BY BANE... AND WHEN YOU'VE BEEN HURT THAT BAD, MAYBE YOU'LL ACCEPT ANY MEDICINE.
THE OLD BATMAN'S BROKEN AND GONE, ROBIN.
IT'S TIME FOR SOMETHING NEW.
THEN YOU CAN JUST COUNT ME OUT, PAUL!
I ALREADY HAVE. BANE'S TOO DANGEROUS FOR YOU. YOUR HEART'S ALREADY BLEEDING. HE'D SQUEEZE IT DRY.
HE STARES DOWN AT HIS DRAWINGS AND DESIGNS, BARELY REMEMBERED BUT FULLY RECOGNIZED.
BLUEPRINTS FOR HIS BODY... TEMPLATES FOR THE NEW THING HE HOPES TO BECOME.
BUT NOW, AFTER FACING BANE, HE DECIDES:
STILL... NOT... ENOUGH.
THE NEW GAUNTLETS MAY BE ADEQUATE...
13

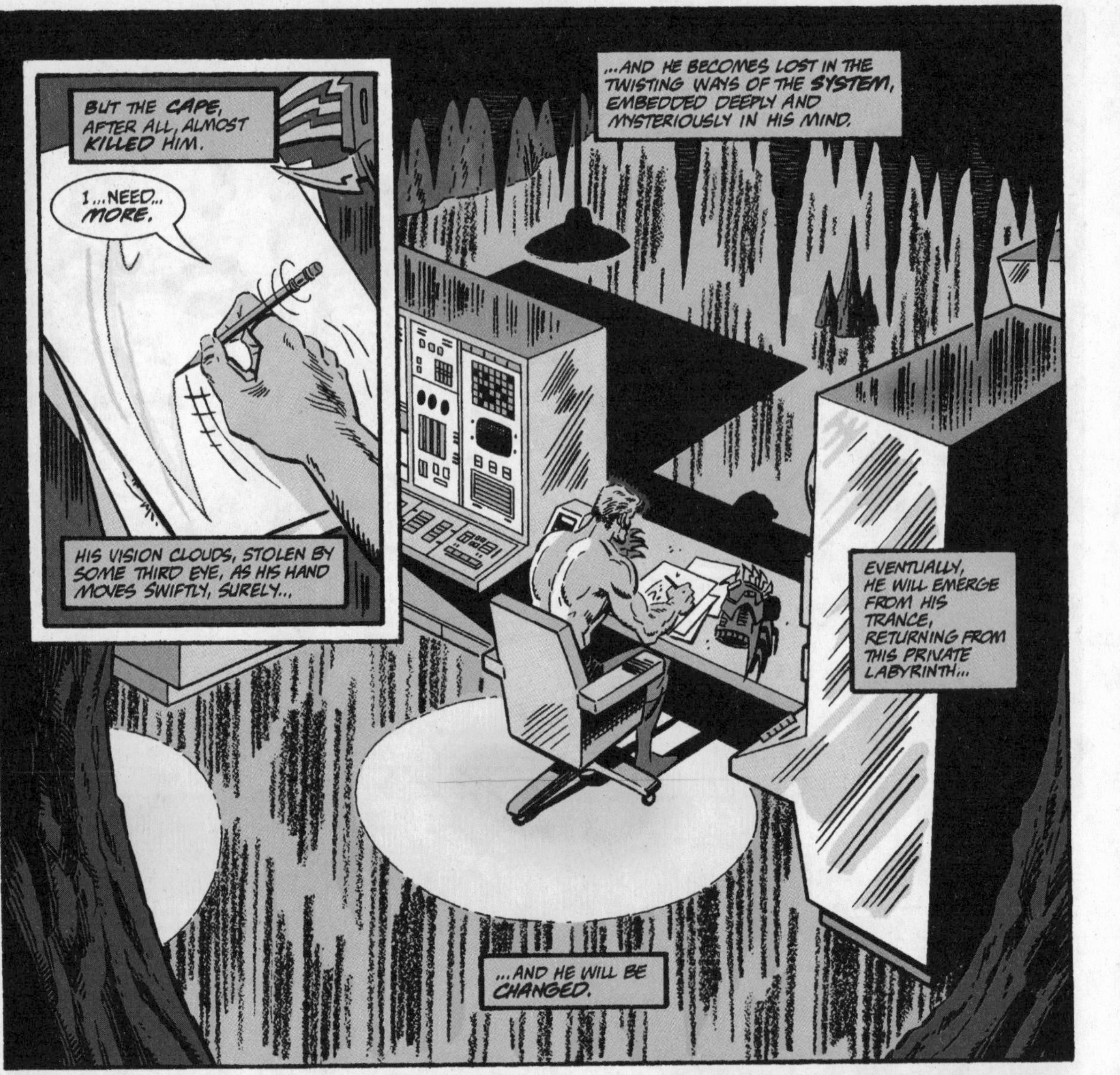
BUT THE CAPE, AFTER ALL, ALMOST KILLED HIM.
I...NEED... MORE.
HIS VISION CLOUDS, STOLEN BY SOME THIRD EYE, AS HIS HAND MOVES SWIFTLY, SURELY...
...AND HE BECOMES LOST IN THE TWISTING WAYS OF THE SYSTEM, EMBEDDED DEEPLY AND MYSTERIOUSLY IN HIS MIND.
EVENTUALLY, HE WILL EMERGE FROM HIS TRANCE, RETURNING FROM THIS PRIVATE LABYRINTH...
...AND HE WILL BE CHANGED.

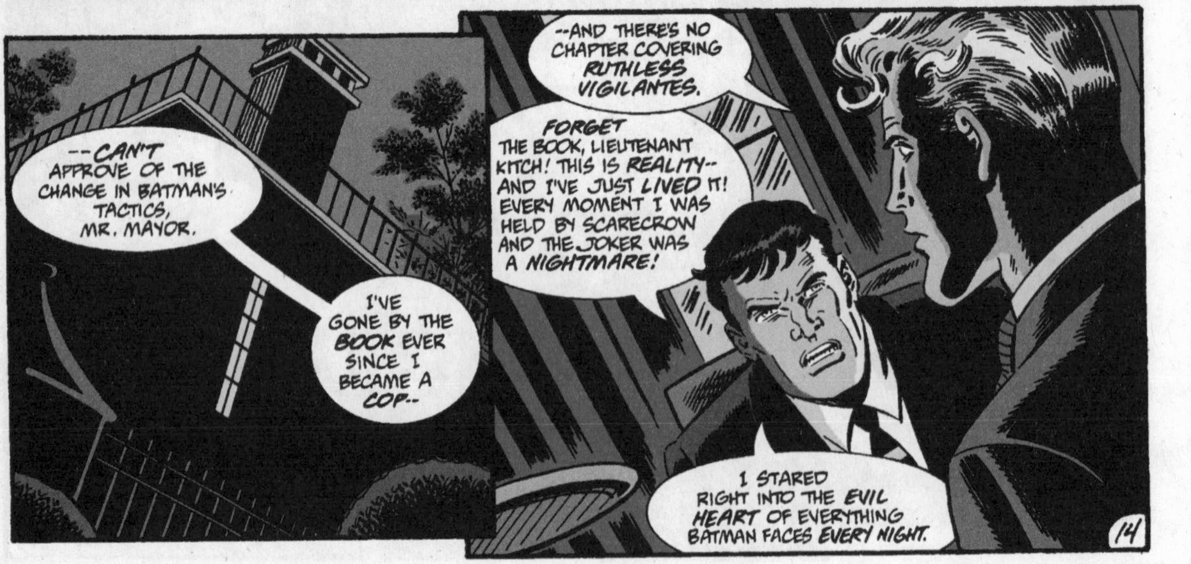
--CAN'T APPROVE OF THE CHANGE IN BATMAN'S TACTICS, MR. MAYOR.
I'VE GONE BY THE BOOK EVER SINCE I BECAME A COP--
--AND THERE'S NO CHAPTER COVERING RUTHLESS VIGILANTES.
FORGET THE BOOK, LIEUTENANT KITCH! THIS IS REALITY--AND I'VE JUST LIVED IT! EVERY MOMENT I WAS HELD BY SCARECROW AND THE JOKER WAS A NIGHTMARE!
I STARED RIGHT INTO THE EVIL HEART OF EVERYTHING BATMAN FACES EVERY NIGHT.
14

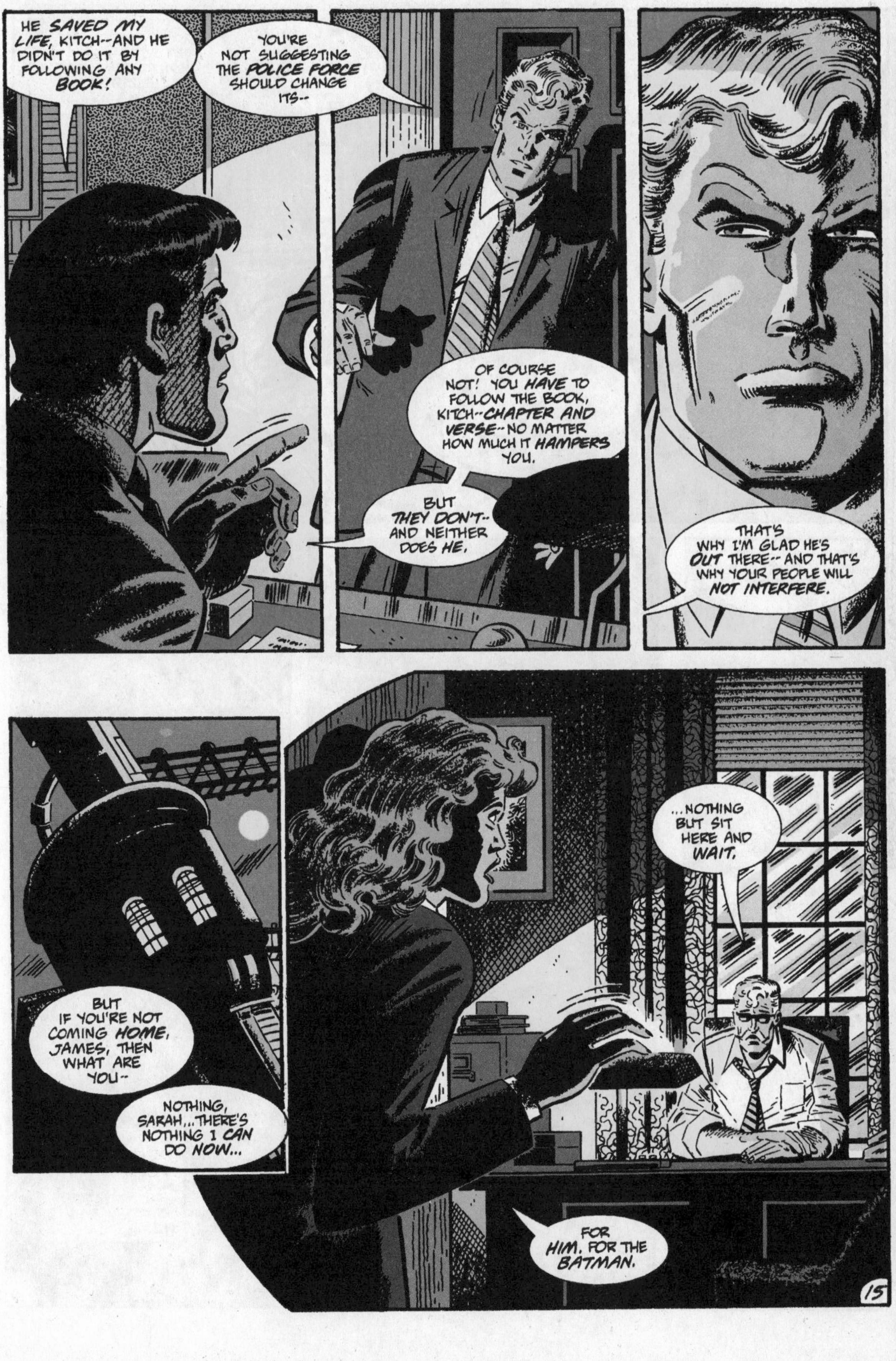

HE SAVED MY LIFE, KITCH--AND HE DIDN'T DO IT BY FOLLOWING ANY BOOK!
YOU'RE NOT SUGGESTING THE POLICE FORCE SHOULD CHANGE ITS--
OF COURSE NOT! YOU HAVE TO FOLLOW THE BOOK, KITCH--CHAPTER AND VERSE--NO MATTER HOW MUCH IT HAMPERS YOU.
BUT THEY DON'T--AND NEITHER DOES HE.
THAT'S WHY I'M GLAD HE'S OUT THERE--AND THAT'S WHY YOUR PEOPLE WILL NOT INTERFERE.
BUT IF YOU'RE NOT COMING HOME, JAMES, THEN WHAT ARE YOU--
NOTHING, SARAH... THERE'S NOTHING I CAN DO NOW...
...NOTHING BUT SIT HERE AND WAIT.
FOR HIM. FOR THE BATMAN.
15

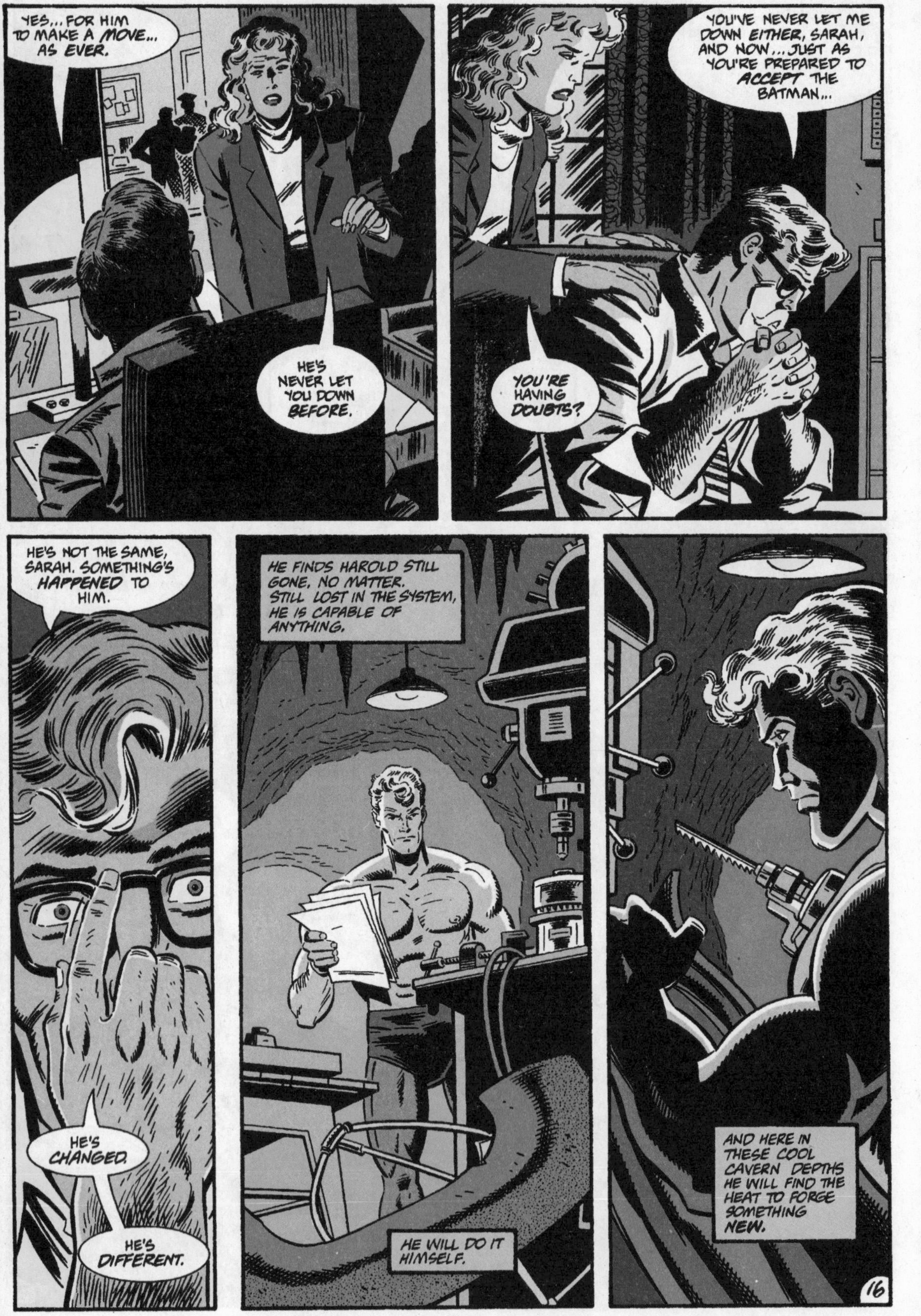
YES... FOR HIM TO MAKE A MOVE... AS EVER.
HE'S NEVER LET YOU DOWN BEFORE.
YOU'VE NEVER LET ME DOWN EITHER, SARAH, AND NOW... JUST AS YOU'RE PREPARED TO ACCEPT THE BATMAN...
YOU'RE HAVING DOUBTS?
HE'S NOT THE SAME, SARAH. SOMETHING'S HAPPENED TO HIM.
HE'S CHANGED.
HE'S DIFFERENT.
HE FINDS HAROLD STILL GONE. NO MATTER. STILL LOST IN THE SYSTEM, HE IS CAPABLE OF ANYTHING.
HE WILL DO IT HIMSELF.
AND HERE IN THESE COOL CAVERN DEPTHS HE WILL FIND THE HEAT TO FORGE SOMETHING NEW.
16

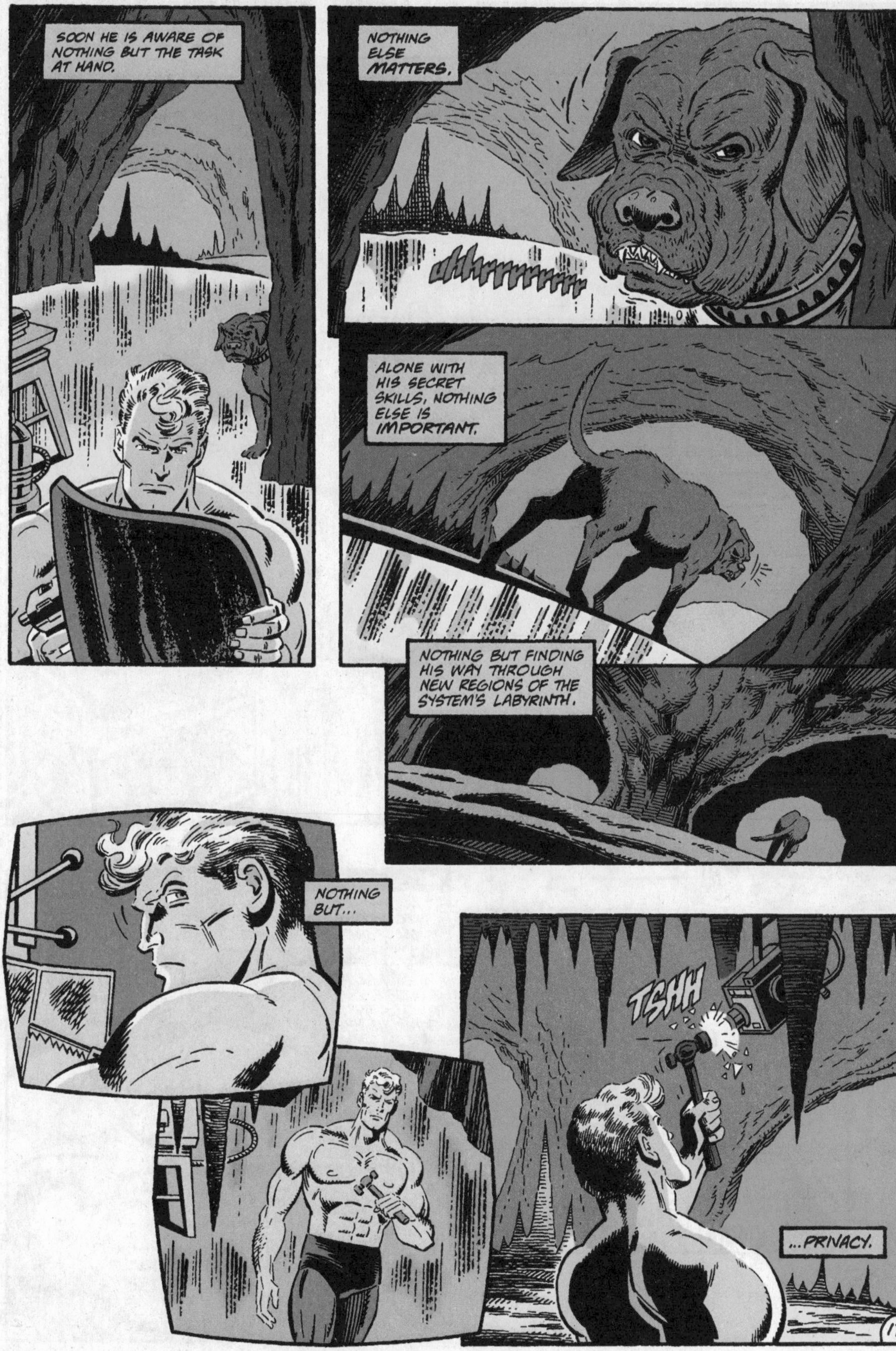
SOON HE IS AWARE OF NOTHING BUT THE TASK AT HAND.
NOTHING ELSE MATTERS.
uhhrrrrrrrrr
ALONE WITH HIS SECRET SKILLS, NOTHING ELSE IS IMPORTANT.
NOTHING BUT FINDING HIS WAY THROUGH NEW REGIONS OF THE SYSTEM'S LABYRINTH.
NOTHING BUT...
TSHH
...PRIVACY.
17

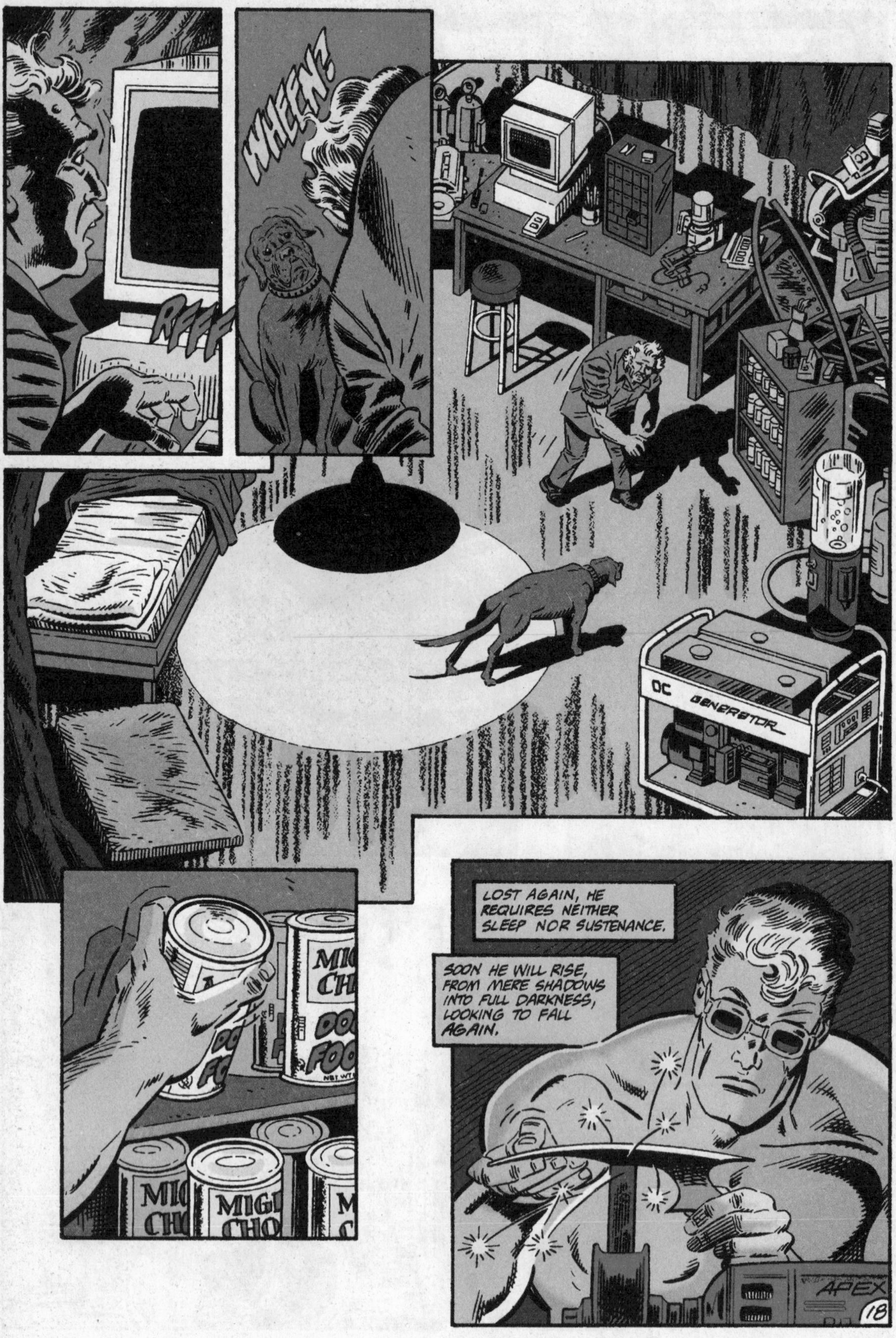
WHEEN?
RFFF
DC GENERATOR
MIGHTY CHOW DOG FOOD
LOST AGAIN, HE REQUIRES NEITHER SLEEP NOR SUSTENANCE.
SOON HE WILL RISE, FROM MERE SHADOWS INTO FULL DARKNESS, LOOKING TO FALL AGAIN.
APEX
18

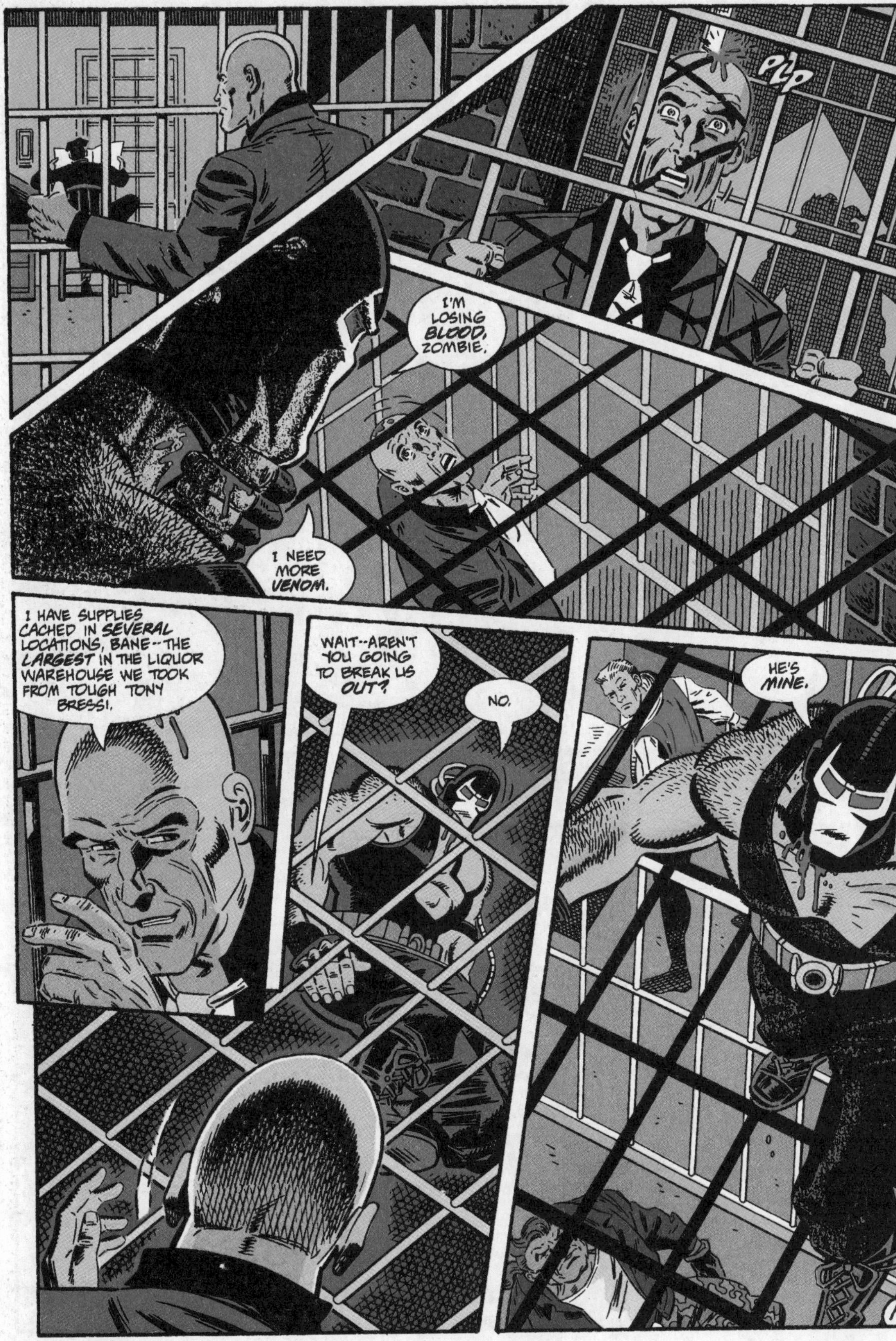
PLIP
I'M LOSING BLOOD, ZOMBIE.
I NEED MORE VENOM.
I HAVE SUPPLIES CACHED IN SEVERAL LOCATIONS, BANE--THE LARGEST IN THE LIQUOR WAREHOUSE WE TOOK FROM TOUGH TONY BRESSI.
WAIT--AREN'T YOU GOING TO BREAK US OUT?
NO.
HE'S MINE.
19

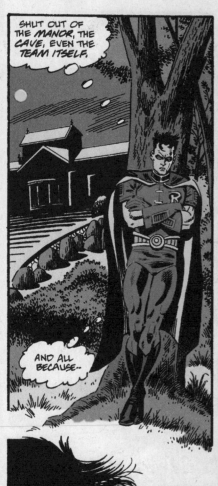

SHUT OUT OF THE MANOR, THE CAVE, EVEN THE TEAM ITSELF.

AND ALL BECAUSE--

BRUCE IS OUT OF DANGER.

NIGHTWING--!

HOW DID YOU KNOW HE WAS--

I HAD TO LEARN IT FROM ORACLE.

UH, SORRY... BUT BRUCE FIGURED IT'D BE BEST TO KEEP IT SECRET.

EVEN FROM ME?

HEY, IT'S BEEN KINDA FRANTIC AROUND HERE.

NO DOUBT--BUT I'LL LET BRUCE TELL ME ABOUT IT.

HE'S NOT HERE-- AND NEITHER IS ALFRED.

AND YET THE BATMAN LOOMS LARGE IN TODAY'S NEWS.

IT'S NOT HIM, NIGHTWING.

HE'S OUT OF DANGER, BUT... HE'S STILL IN A WHEELCHAIR.

20

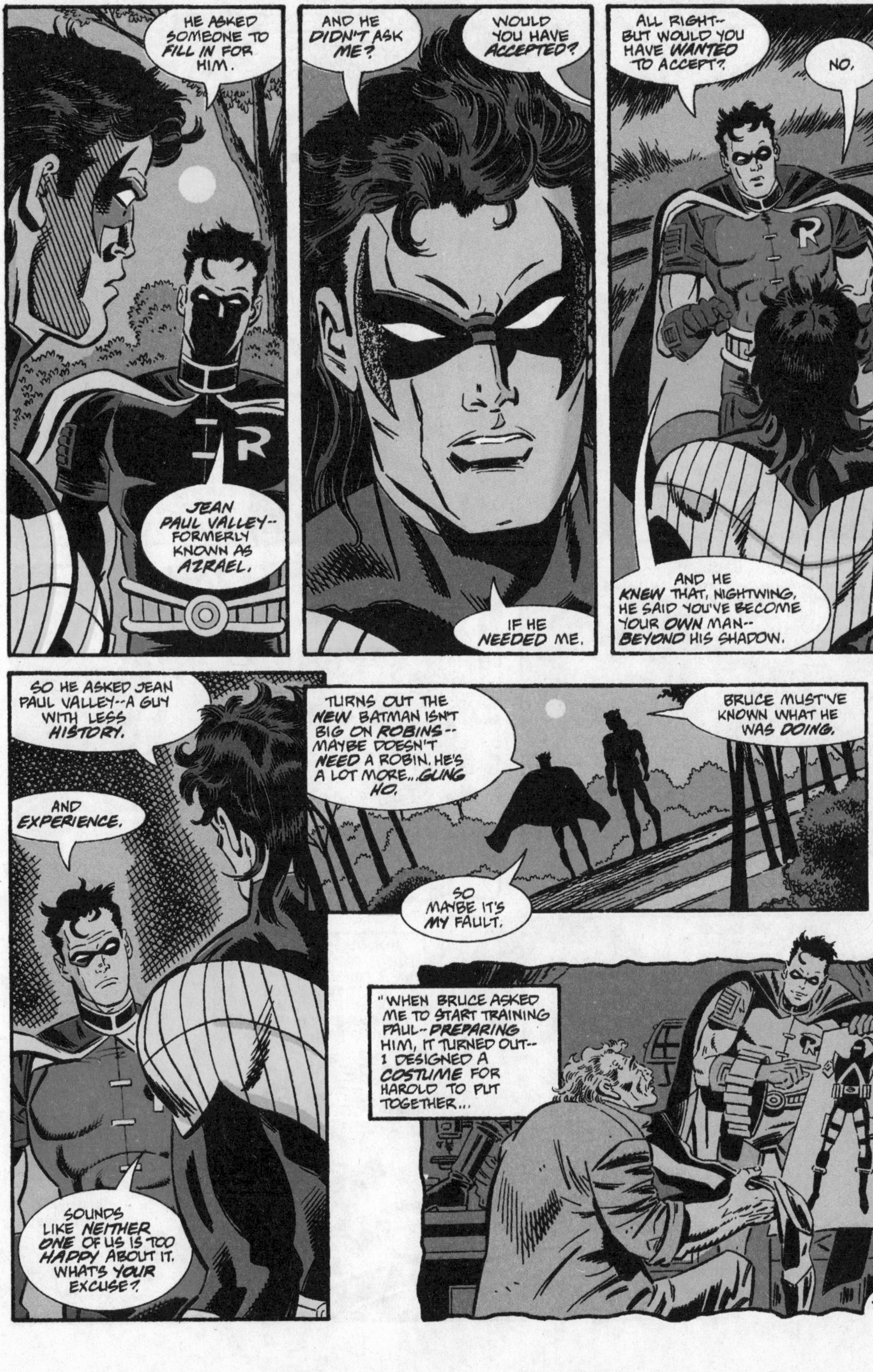
HE ASKED SOMEONE TO FILL IN FOR HIM.
JEAN PAUL VALLEY-- FORMERLY KNOWN AS AZRAEL.
AND HE DIDN'T ASK ME?
WOULD YOU HAVE ACCEPTED?
IF HE NEEDED ME.
ALL RIGHT-- BUT WOULD YOU HAVE WANTED TO ACCEPT?
NO.
AND HE KNEW THAT, NIGHTWING. HE SAID YOU'VE BECOME YOUR OWN MAN-- BEYOND HIS SHADOW.
SO HE ASKED JEAN PAUL VALLEY--A GUY WITH LESS HISTORY.
AND EXPERIENCE.
SOUNDS LIKE NEITHER ONE OF US IS TOO HAPPY ABOUT IT. WHAT'S YOUR EXCUSE?
TURNS OUT THE NEW BATMAN ISN'T BIG ON ROBINS-- MAYBE DOESN'T NEED A ROBIN. HE'S A LOT MORE...GUNG HO.
BRUCE MUST'VE KNOWN WHAT HE WAS DOING.
SO MAYBE IT'S MY FAULT.
"WHEN BRUCE ASKED ME TO START TRAINING PAUL--PREPARING HIM, IT TURNED OUT-- I DESIGNED A COSTUME FOR HAROLD TO PUT TOGETHER...
21

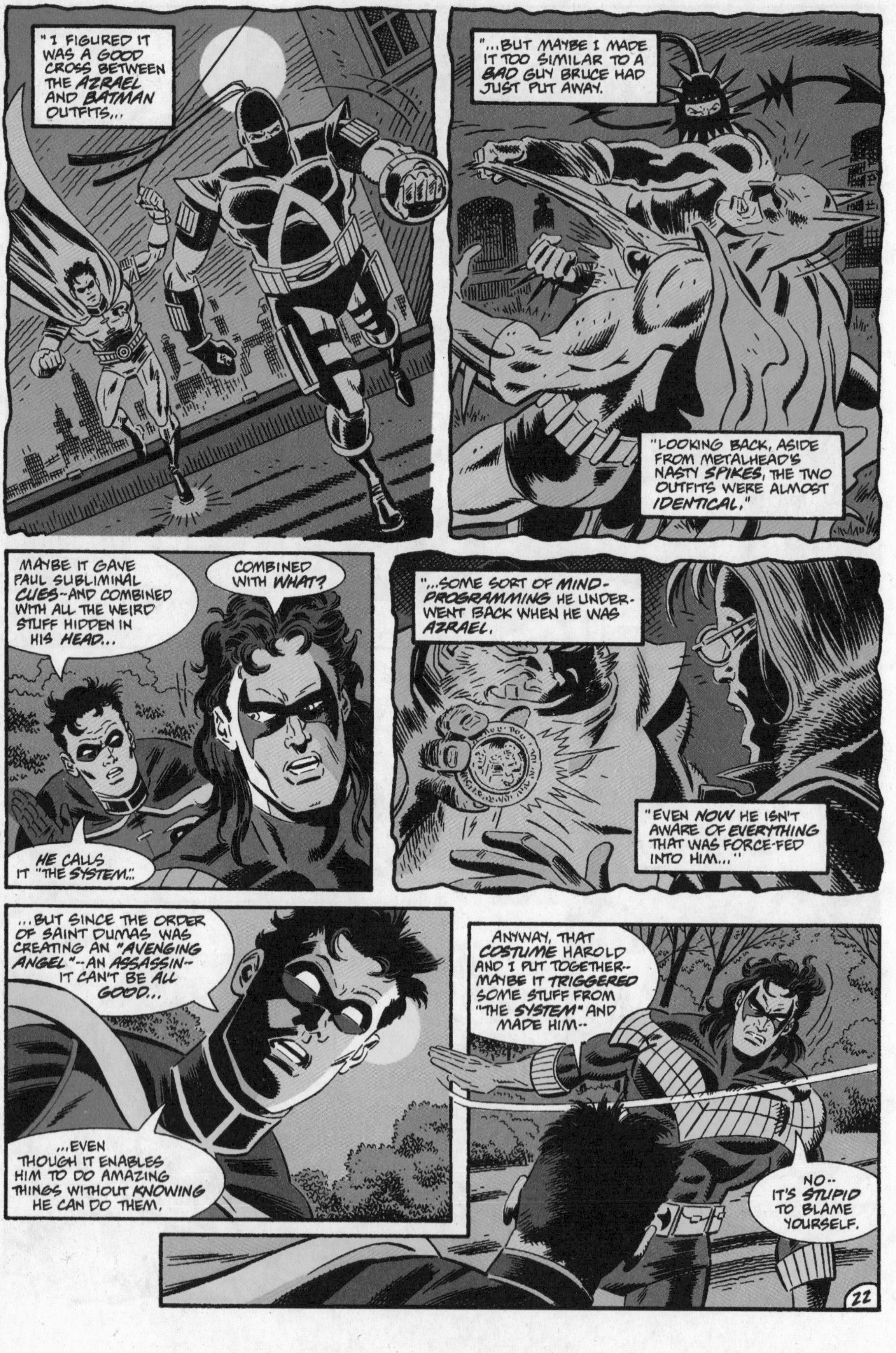
"I FIGURED IT WAS A GOOD CROSS BETWEEN THE AZRAEL AND BATMAN OUTFITS...
"...BUT MAYBE I MADE IT TOO SIMILAR TO A BAD GUY BRUCE HAD JUST PUT AWAY.
"LOOKING BACK, ASIDE FROM METALHEAD'S NASTY SPIKES, THE TWO OUTFITS WERE ALMOST IDENTICAL."
MAYBE IT GAVE PAUL SUBLIMINAL CUES--AND COMBINED WITH ALL THE WEIRD STUFF HIDDEN IN HIS HEAD...
COMBINED WITH WHAT?
HE CALLS IT "THE SYSTEM."
"...SOME SORT OF MIND-PROGRAMMING HE UNDERWENT BACK WHEN HE WAS AZRAEL.
"EVEN NOW HE ISN'T AWARE OF EVERYTHING THAT WAS FORCE-FED INTO HIM..."
...BUT SINCE THE ORDER OF SAINT DUMAS WAS CREATING AN "AVENGING ANGEL"--AN ASSASSIN--IT CAN'T BE ALL GOOD...
...EVEN THOUGH IT ENABLES HIM TO DO AMAZING THINGS WITHOUT KNOWING HE CAN DO THEM.
ANYWAY, THAT COSTUME HAROLD AND I PUT TOGETHER--MAYBE IT TRIGGERED SOME STUFF FROM "THE SYSTEM" AND MADE HIM--
NO--IT'S STUPID TO BLAME YOURSELF.
22

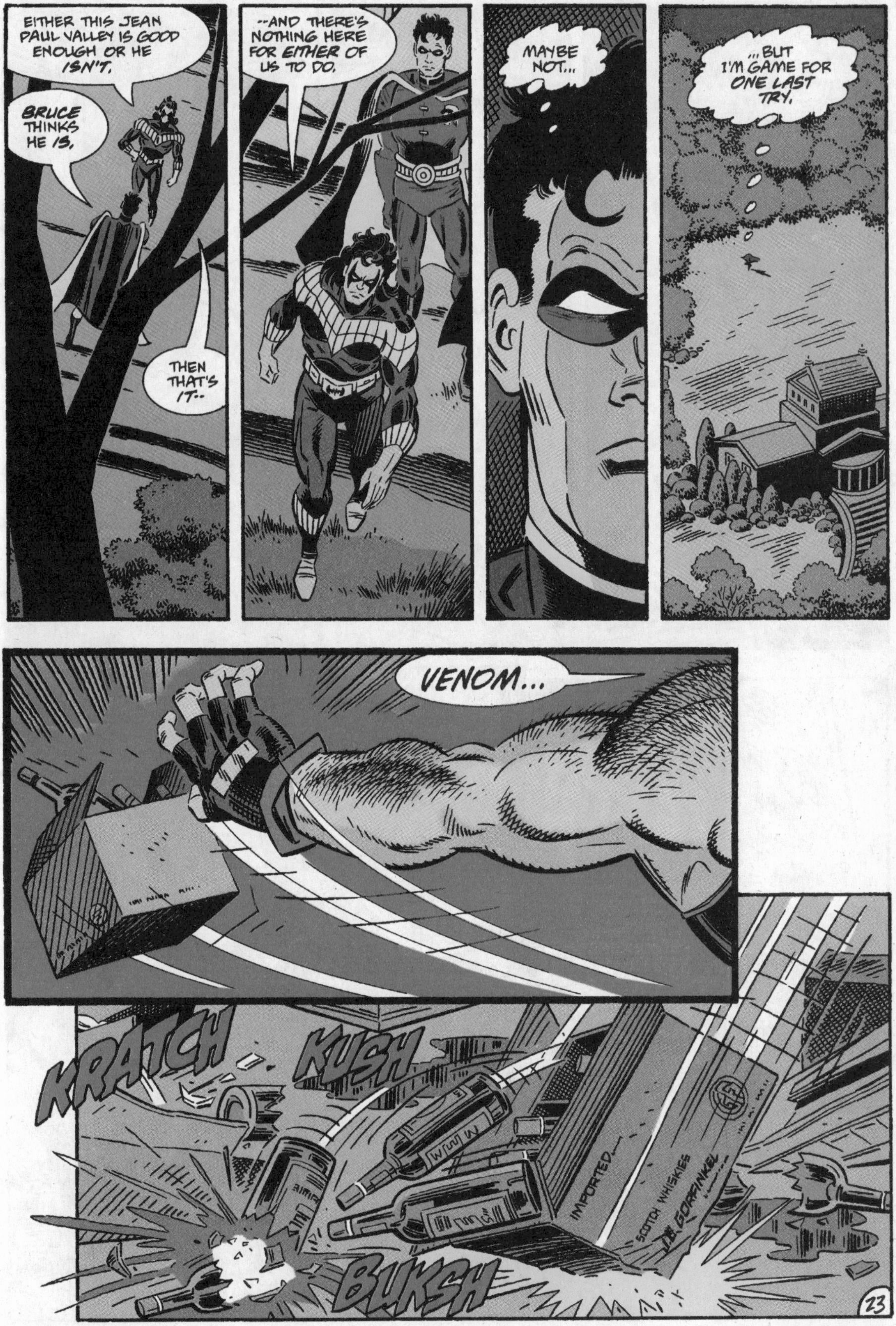
EITHER THIS JEAN PAUL VALLEY IS GOOD ENOUGH OR HE ISN'T.
BRUCE THINKS HE IS.
THEN THAT'S IT--
--AND THERE'S NOTHING HERE FOR EITHER OF US TO DO.
MAYBE NOT...
...BUT I'M GAME FOR ONE LAST TRY.
VENOM...
KRATCH
KUSH
BUKSH
IMPORTED
SCOTCH WHISKIES
J.B. GORFINKEL
23

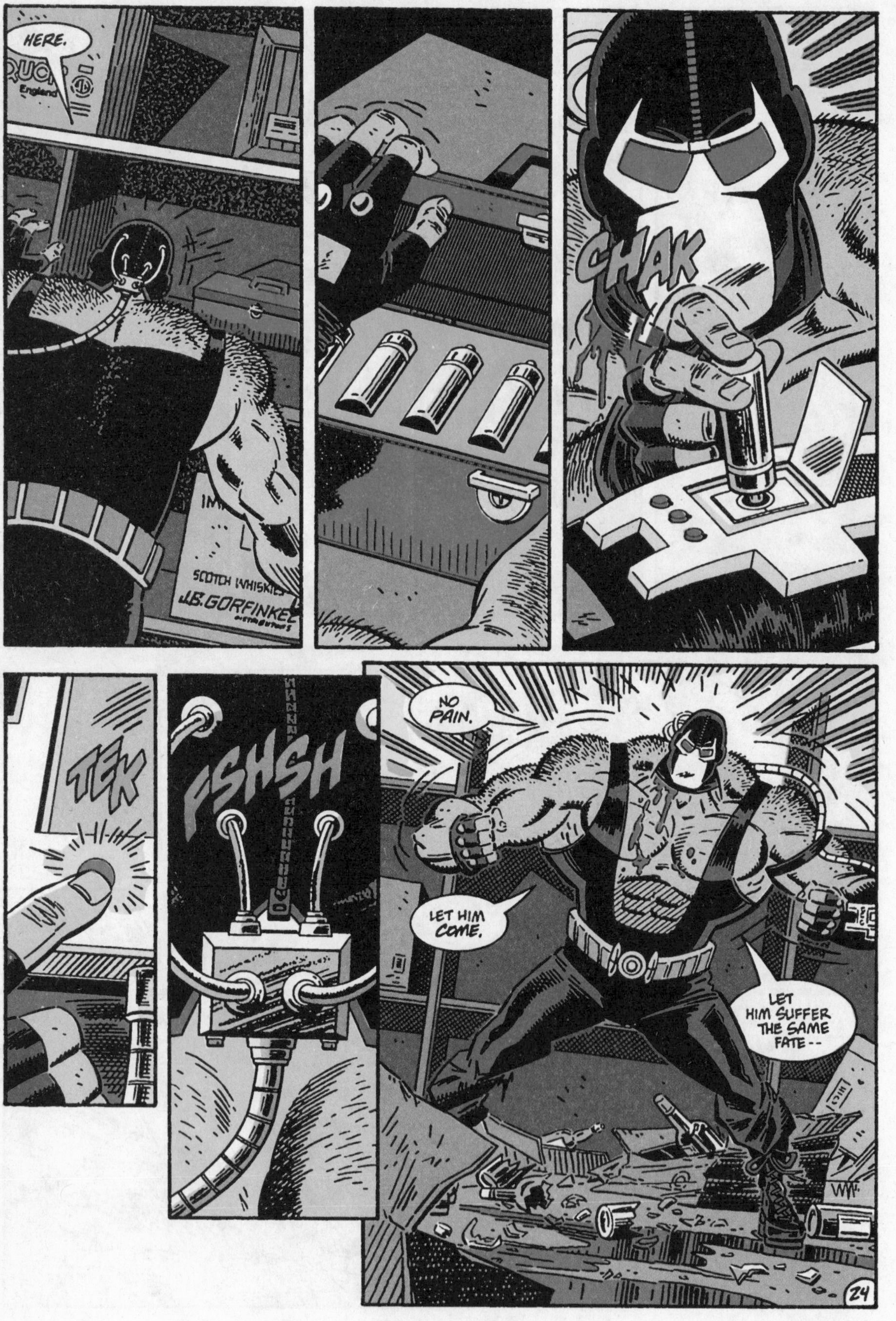
HERE.
England
SCOTCH WHISKIES
J.B. GORFINKEL
CHAK
TEK
FSHSH
NO PAIN.
LET HIM COME.
LET HIM SUFFER THE SAME FATE--
24

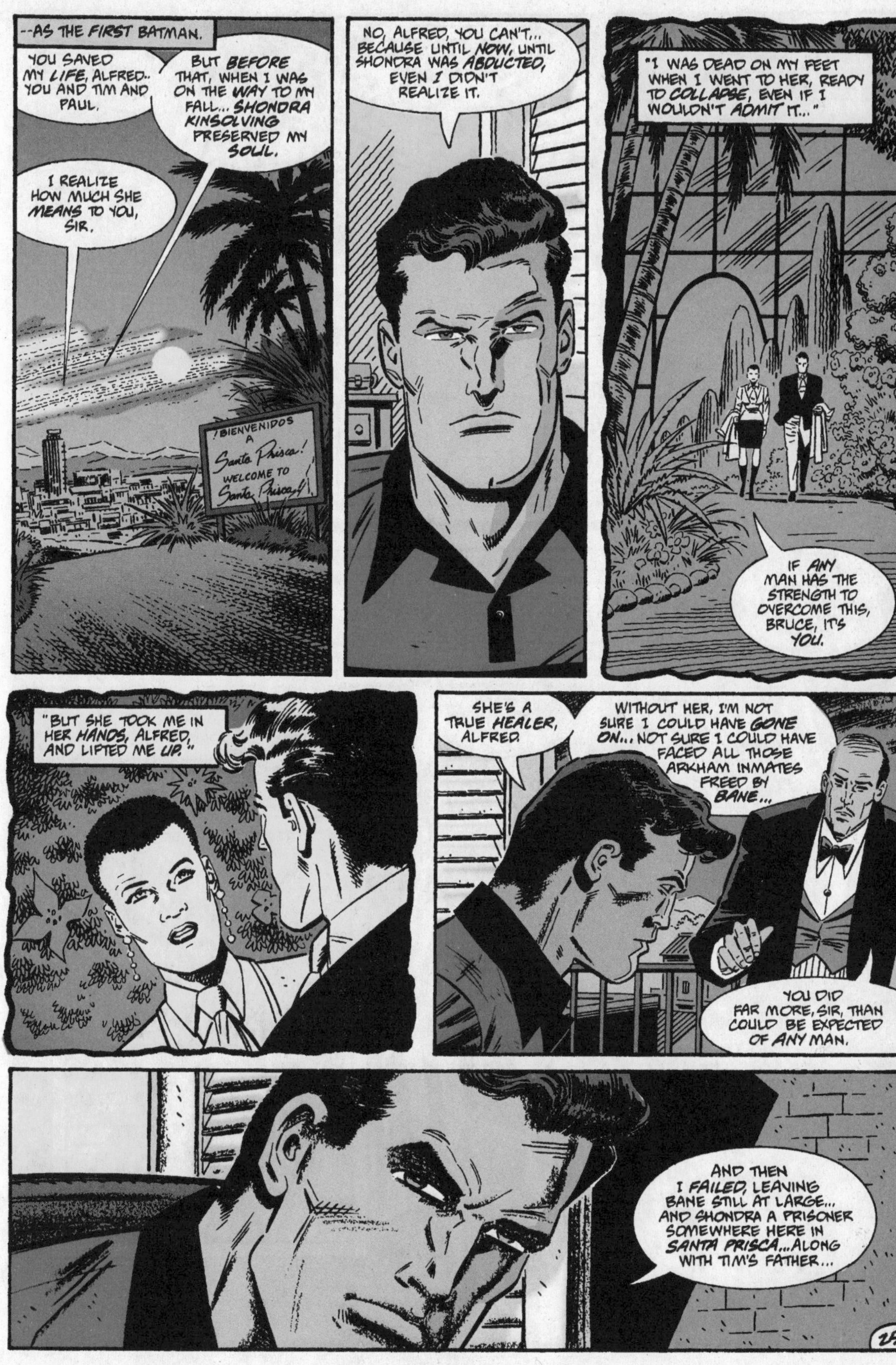
--AS THE FIRST BATMAN.
YOU SAVED MY LIFE, ALFRED.. YOU AND TIM AND PAUL.
BUT BEFORE THAT, WHEN I WAS ON THE WAY TO MY FALL... SHONDRA KINSOLVING PRESERVED MY SOUL.
I REALIZE HOW MUCH SHE MEANS TO YOU, SIR.
!BIENVENIDOS A Santa Prisca! WELCOME TO Santa Prisca!
NO, ALFRED, YOU CAN'T... BECAUSE UNTIL NOW, UNTIL SHONDRA WAS ABDUCTED, EVEN I DIDN'T REALIZE IT.
"I WAS DEAD ON MY FEET WHEN I WENT TO HER, READY TO COLLAPSE, EVEN IF I WOULDN'T ADMIT IT..."
IF ANY MAN HAS THE STRENGTH TO OVERCOME THIS, BRUCE, IT'S YOU.
"BUT SHE TOOK ME IN HER HANDS, ALFRED, AND LIFTED ME UP."
SHE'S A TRUE HEALER, ALFRED.
WITHOUT HER, I'M NOT SURE I COULD HAVE GONE ON... NOT SURE I COULD HAVE FACED ALL THOSE ARKHAM INMATES FREED BY BANE...
YOU DID FAR MORE, SIR, THAN COULD BE EXPECTED OF ANY MAN.
AND THEN I FAILED, LEAVING BANE STILL AT LARGE... AND SHONDRA A PRISONER SOMEWHERE HERE IN SANTA PRISCA... ALONG WITH TIM'S FATHER...
25

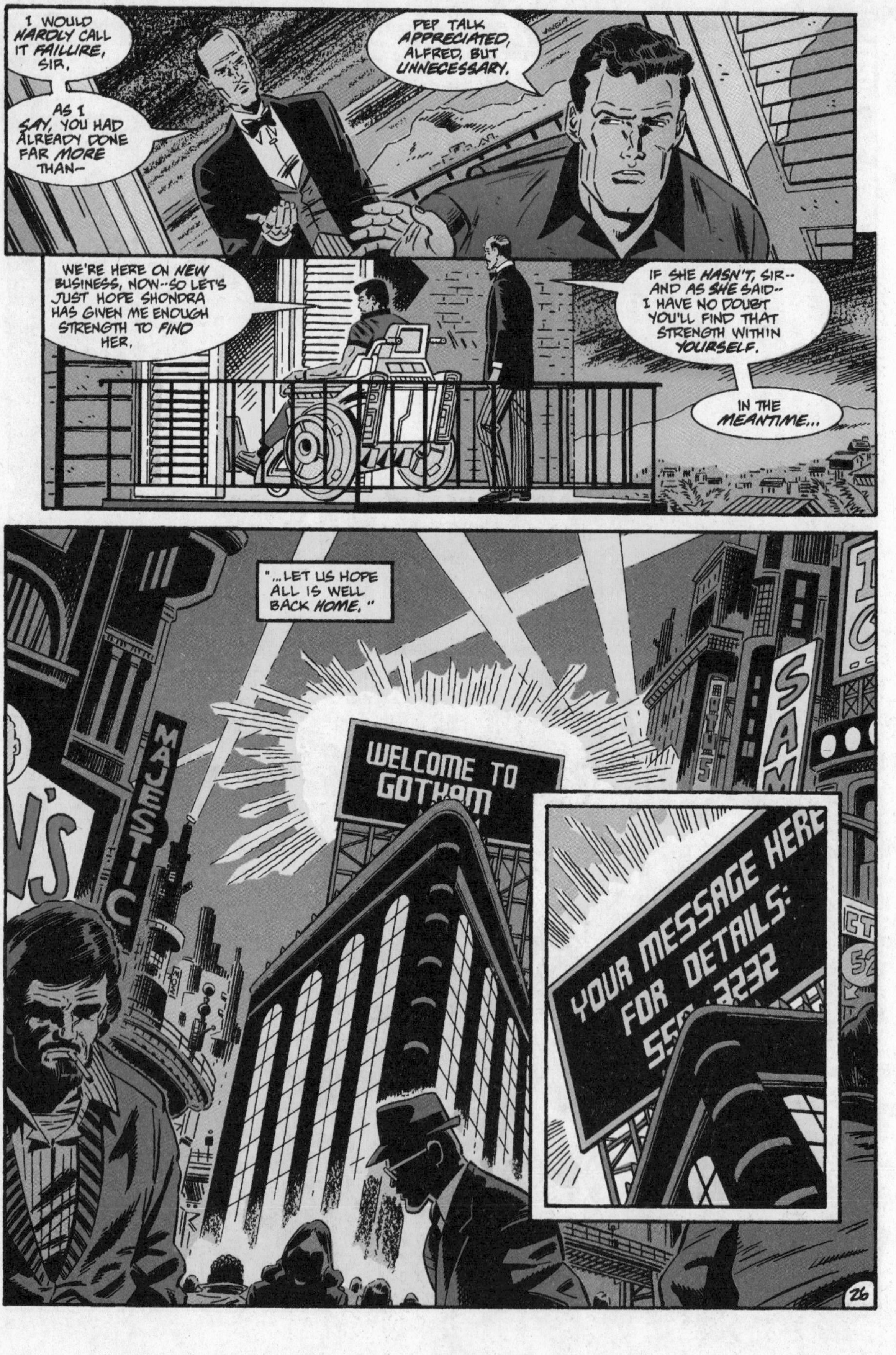
I WOULD HARDLY CALL IT FAILURE, SIR.
AS I SAY, YOU HAD ALREADY DONE FAR MORE THAN-
PEP TALK APPRECIATED, ALFRED, BUT UNNECESSARY.
WE'RE HERE ON NEW BUSINESS, NOW--SO LET'S JUST HOPE SHONDRA HAS GIVEN ME ENOUGH STRENGTH TO FIND HER.
IF SHE HASN'T, SIR-- AND AS SHE SAID-- I HAVE NO DOUBT YOU'LL FIND THAT STRENGTH WITHIN YOURSELF.
IN THE MEANTIME...
"...LET US HOPE ALL IS WELL BACK HOME."
MAJESTIC
WELCOME TO GOTHAM
YOUR MESSAGE HERE
FOR DETAILS:
26

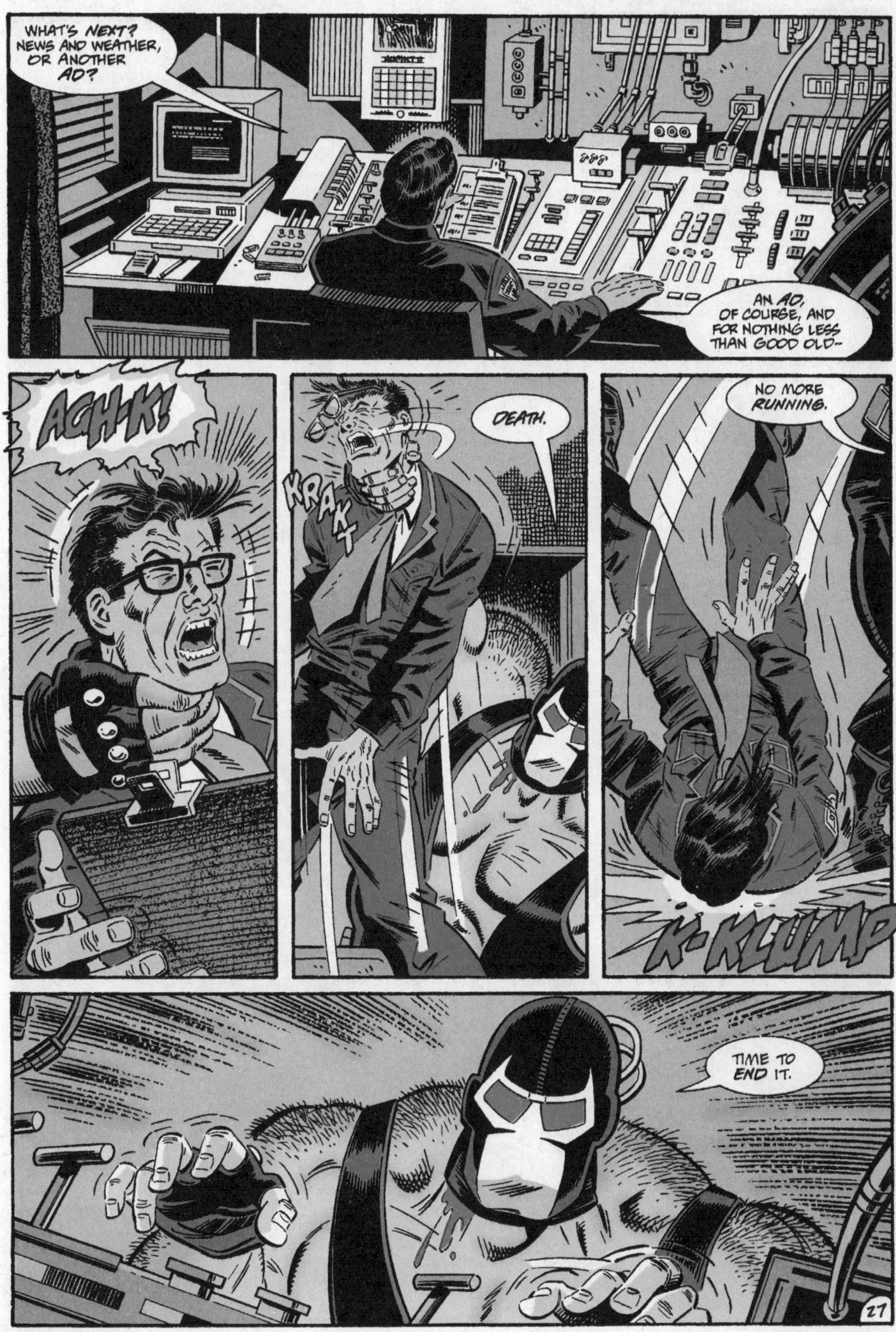
WHAT'S NEXT? NEWS AND WEATHER, OR ANOTHER AD?
AN AD, OF COURSE, AND FOR NOTHING LESS THAN GOOD OLD--
AGH-K!
KRAKT
DEATH.
NO MORE RUNNING.
K-KLUMP
TIME TO END IT.
27

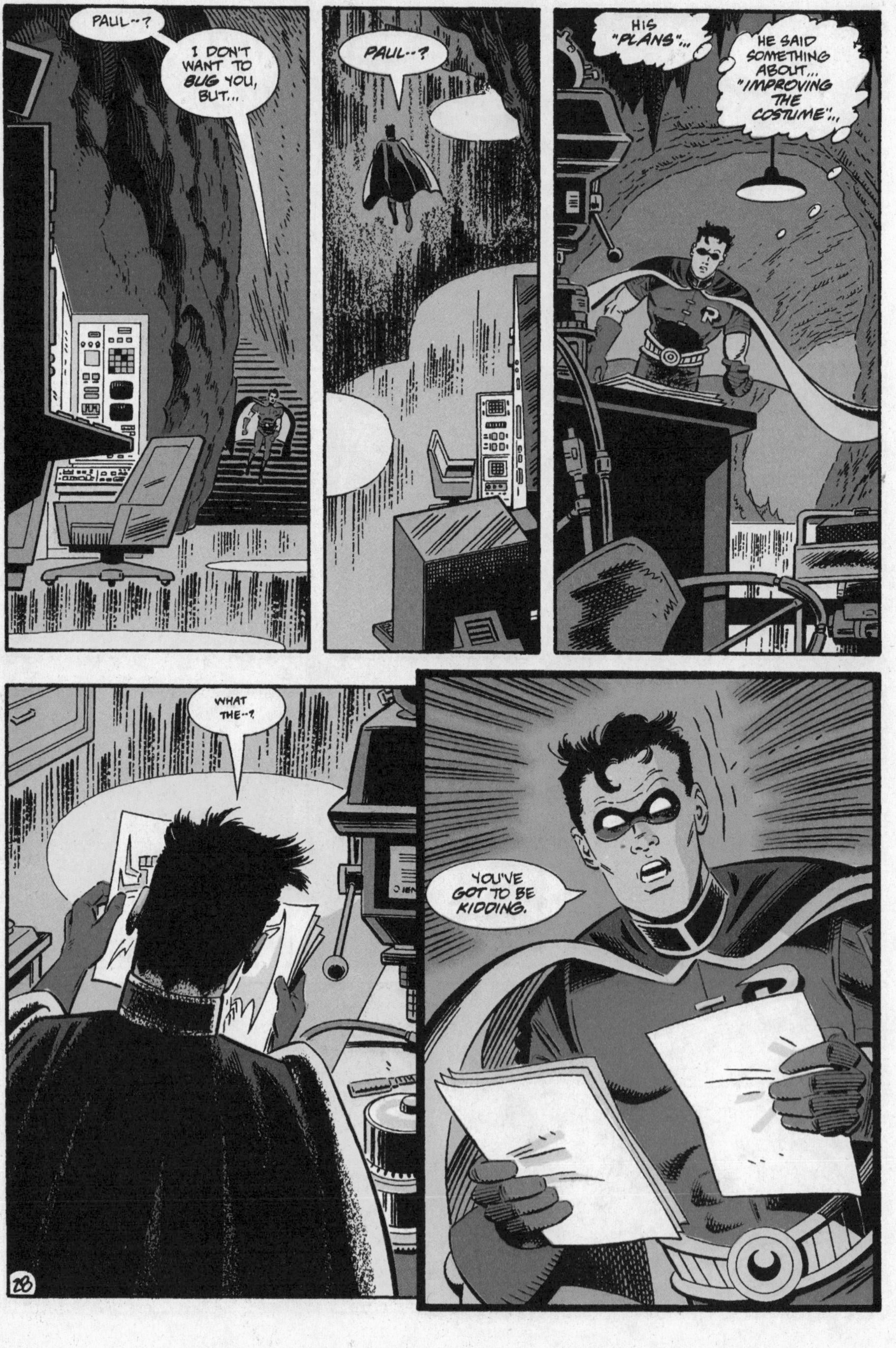
PAUL--?
I DON'T WANT TO BUG YOU, BUT...
PAUL--?
HIS "PLANS"...
HE SAID SOMETHING ABOUT... "IMPROVING THE COSTUME"...
WHAT THE--?
YOU'VE GOT TO BE KIDDING.
28

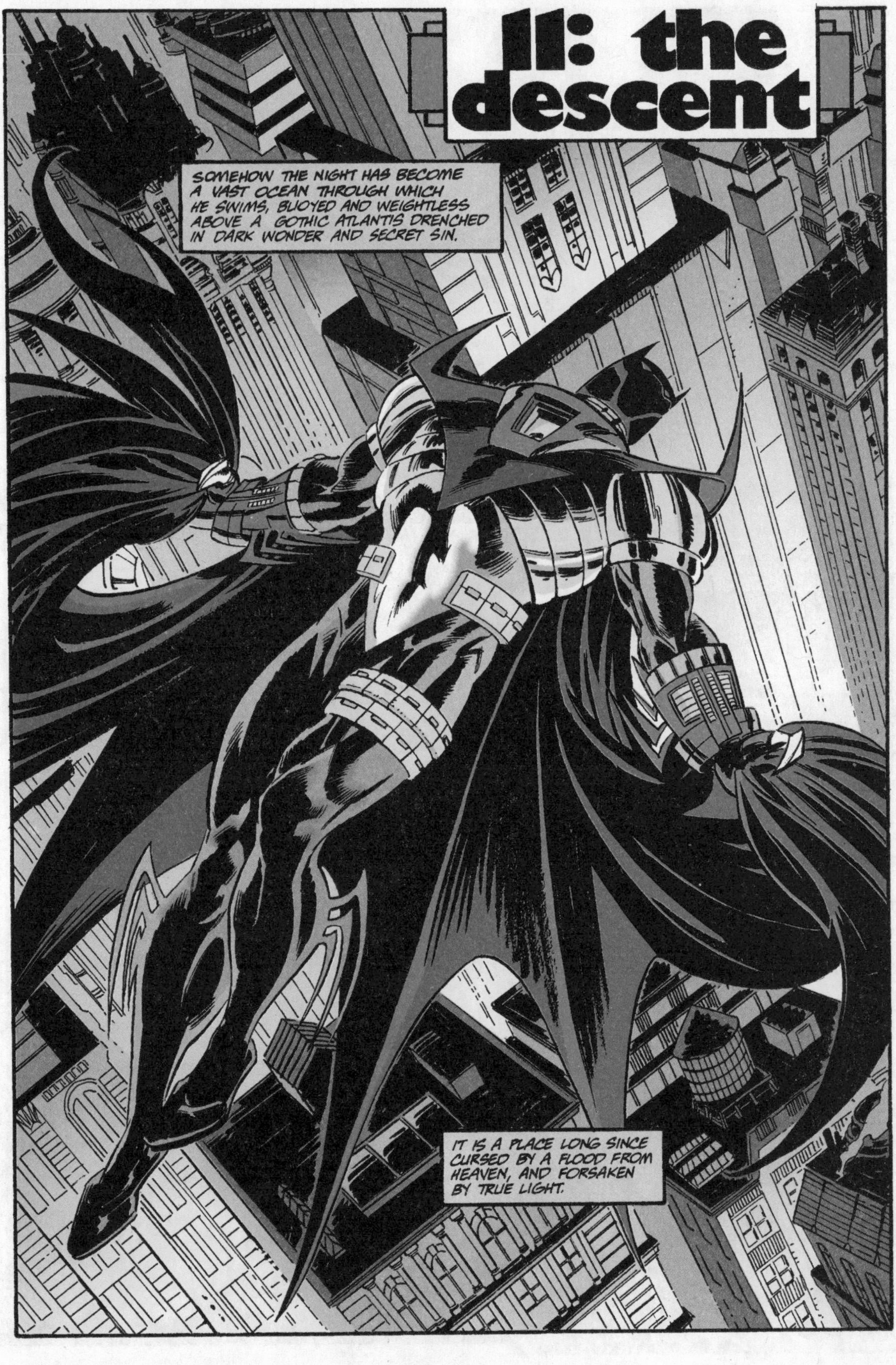
II: the descent
SOMEHOW THE NIGHT HAS BECOME A VAST OCEAN THROUGH WHICH HE SWIMS, BUOYED AND WEIGHTLESS ABOVE A GOTHIC ATLANTIS DRENCHED IN DARK WONDER AND SECRET SIN.
IT IS A PLACE LONG SINCE CURSED BY A FLOOD FROM HEAVEN, AND FORSAKEN BY TRUE LIGHT.

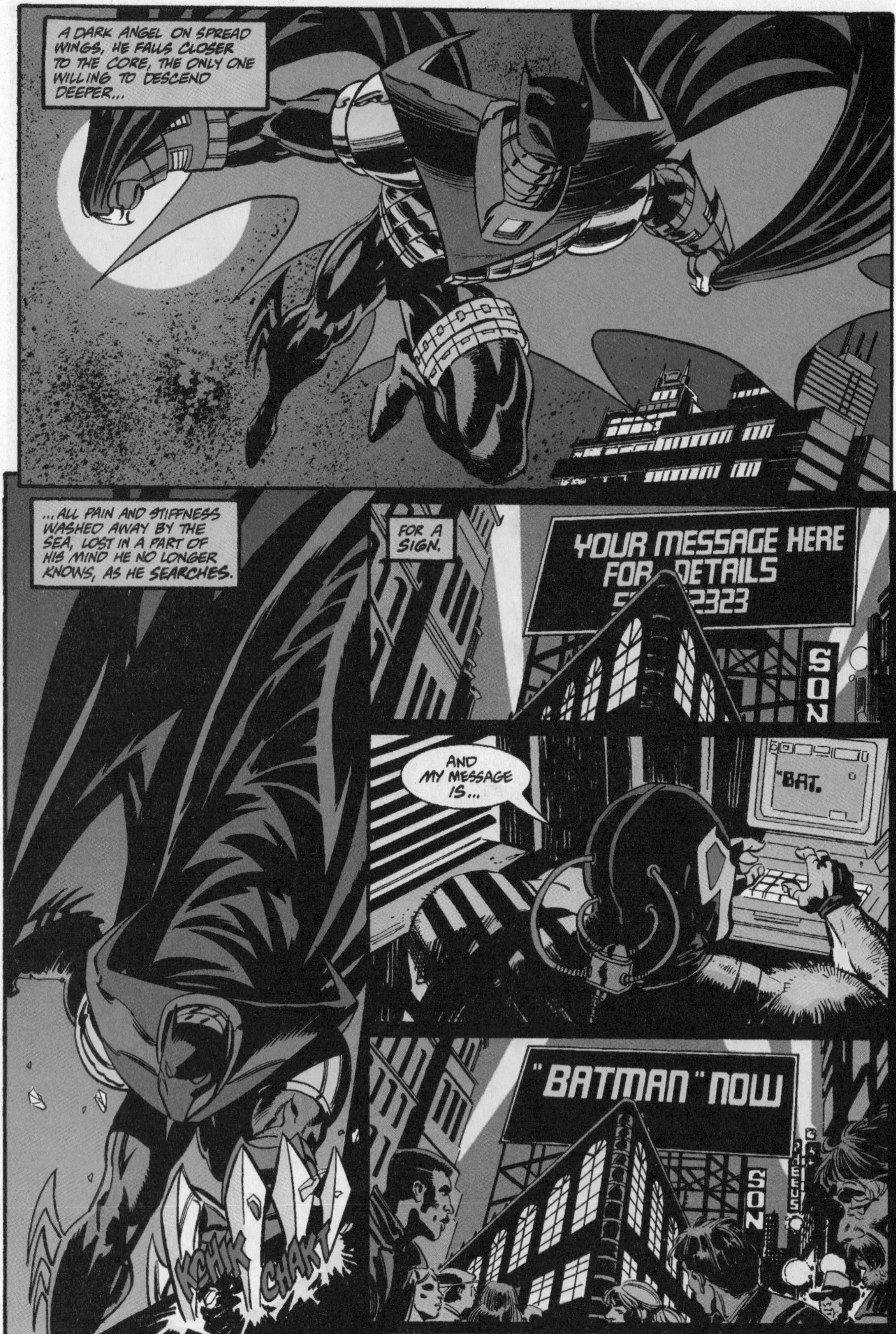

A DARK ANGEL ON SPREAD WINGS, HE FALLS CLOSER TO THE CORE, THE ONLY ONE WILLING TO DESCEND DEEPER...
...ALL PAIN AND STIFFNESS WASHED AWAY BY THE SEA, LOST IN A PART OF HIS MIND HE NO LONGER KNOWS, AS HE SEARCHES.
FOR A SIGN.
YOUR MESSAGE HERE
FOR DETAILS
2323
SON
AND MY MESSAGE IS...
"BAT.
"BATMAN" NOW
SON
KCHIK
CHAKT

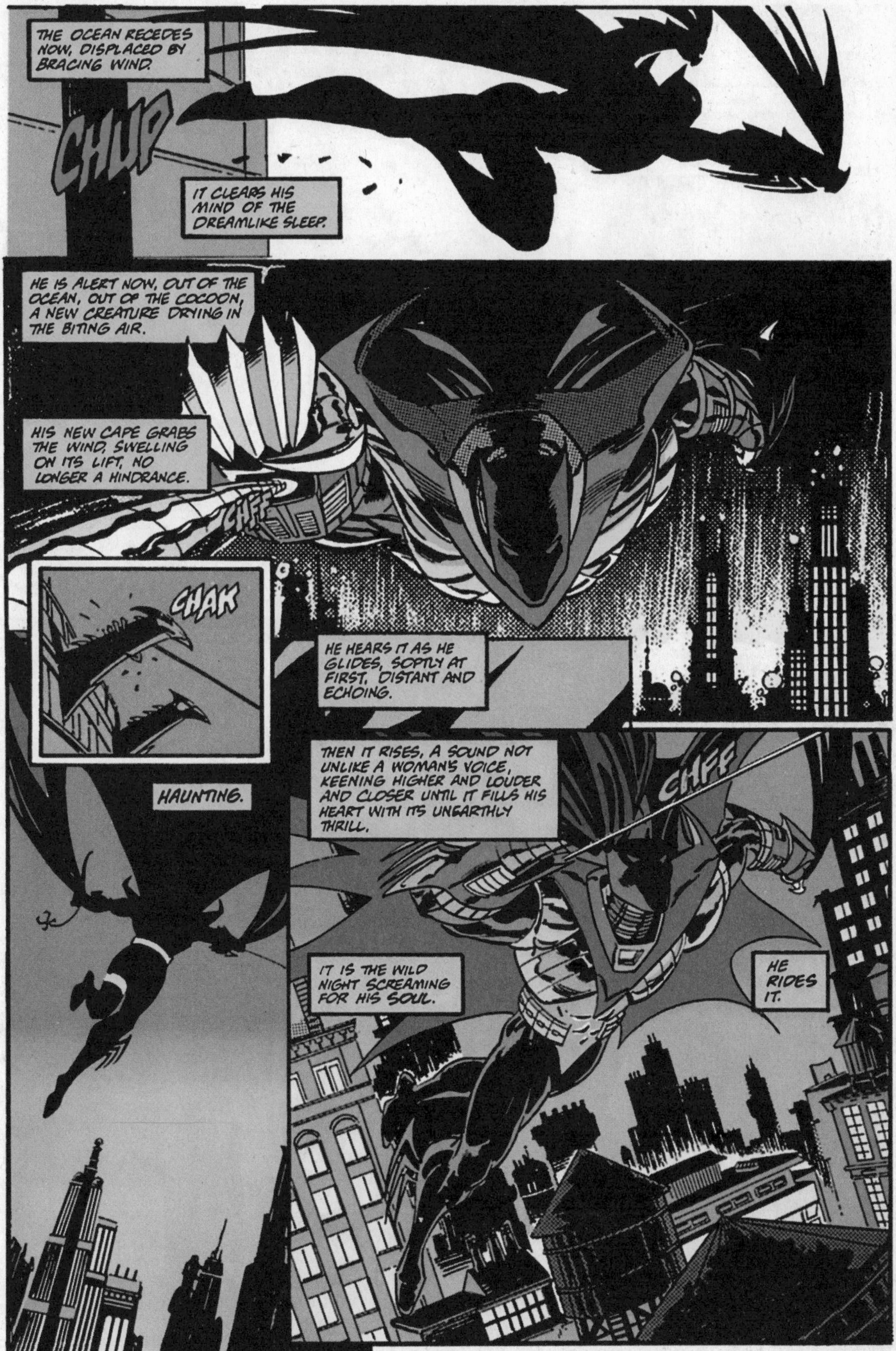
THE OCEAN RECEDES NOW, DISPLACED BY BRACING WIND.
CHUP
IT CLEARS HIS MIND OF THE DREAMLIKE SLEEP.
HE IS ALERT NOW, OUT OF THE OCEAN, OUT OF THE COCOON, A NEW CREATURE DRYING IN THE BITING AIR.
HIS NEW CAPE GRABS THE WIND, SWELLING ON ITS LIFT, NO LONGER A HINDRANCE.
CHFF
CHAK
HE HEARS IT AS HE GLIDES, SOFTLY AT FIRST, DISTANT AND ECHOING.
HAUNTING.
THEN IT RISES, A SOUND NOT UNLIKE A WOMAN'S VOICE, KEENING HIGHER AND LOUDER AND CLOSER UNTIL IT FILLS HIS HEART WITH ITS UNEARTHLY THRILL.
CHFF
IT IS THE WILD NIGHT SCREAMING FOR HIS SOUL.
HE RIDES IT.

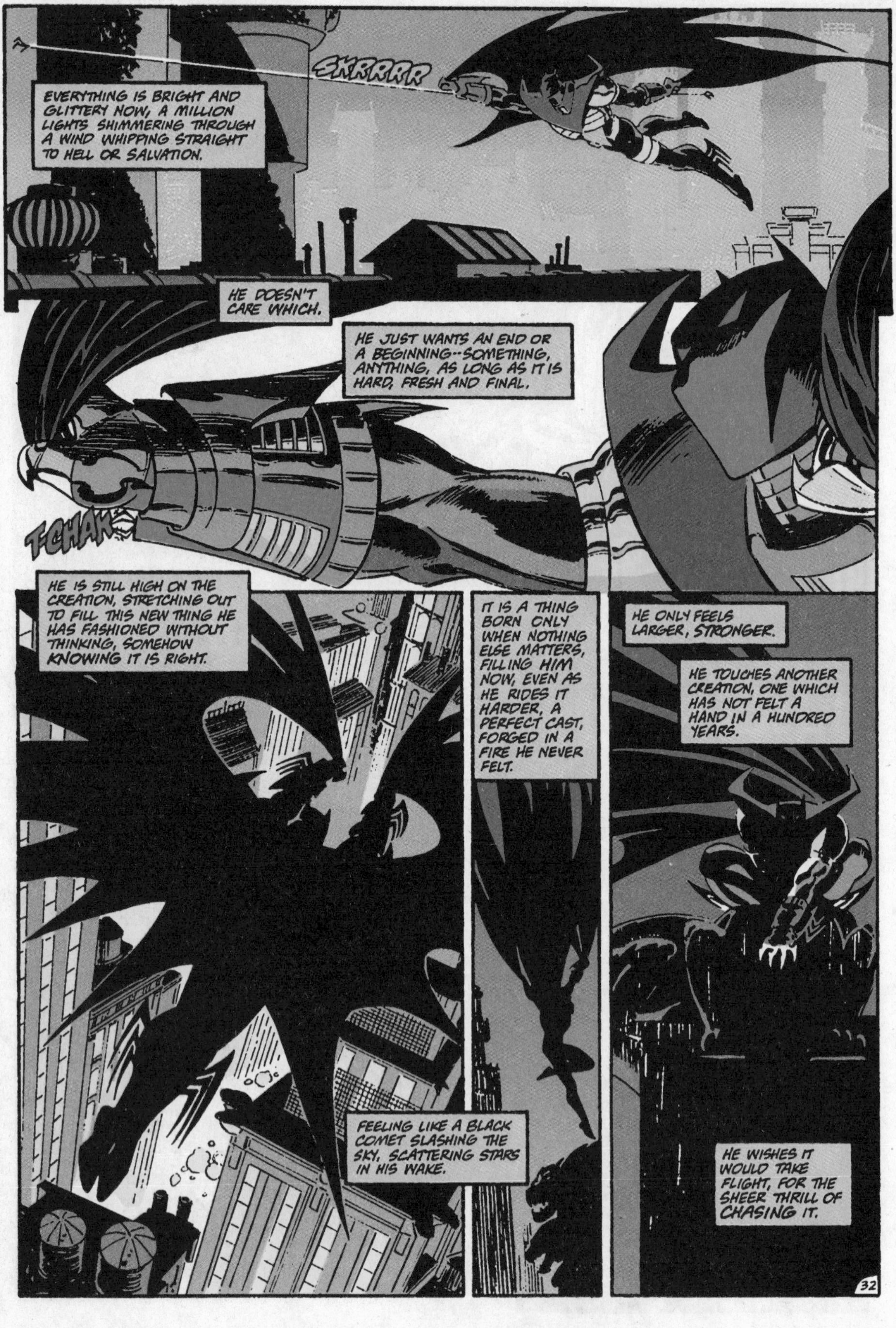
SKRRRR
EVERYTHING IS BRIGHT AND GLITTERY NOW, A MILLION LIGHTS SHIMMERING THROUGH A WIND WHIPPING STRAIGHT TO HELL OR SALVATION.
HE DOESN'T CARE WHICH.
HE JUST WANTS AN END OR A BEGINNING--SOMETHING, ANYTHING, AS LONG AS IT IS HARD, FRESH AND FINAL.
T-CHAK
HE IS STILL HIGH ON THE CREATION, STRETCHING OUT TO FILL THIS NEW THING HE HAS FASHIONED WITHOUT THINKING, SOMEHOW KNOWING IT IS RIGHT.
FEELING LIKE A BLACK COMET SLASHING THE SKY, SCATTERING STARS IN HIS WAKE.
IT IS A THING BORN ONLY WHEN NOTHING ELSE MATTERS, FILLING HIM NOW, EVEN AS HE RIDES IT HARDER, A PERFECT CAST, FORGED IN A FIRE HE NEVER FELT.
HE ONLY FEELS LARGER, STRONGER.
HE TOUCHES ANOTHER CREATION, ONE WHICH HAS NOT FELT A HAND IN A HUNDRED YEARS.
HE WISHES IT WOULD TAKE FLIGHT, FOR THE SHEER THRILL OF CHASING IT.
32

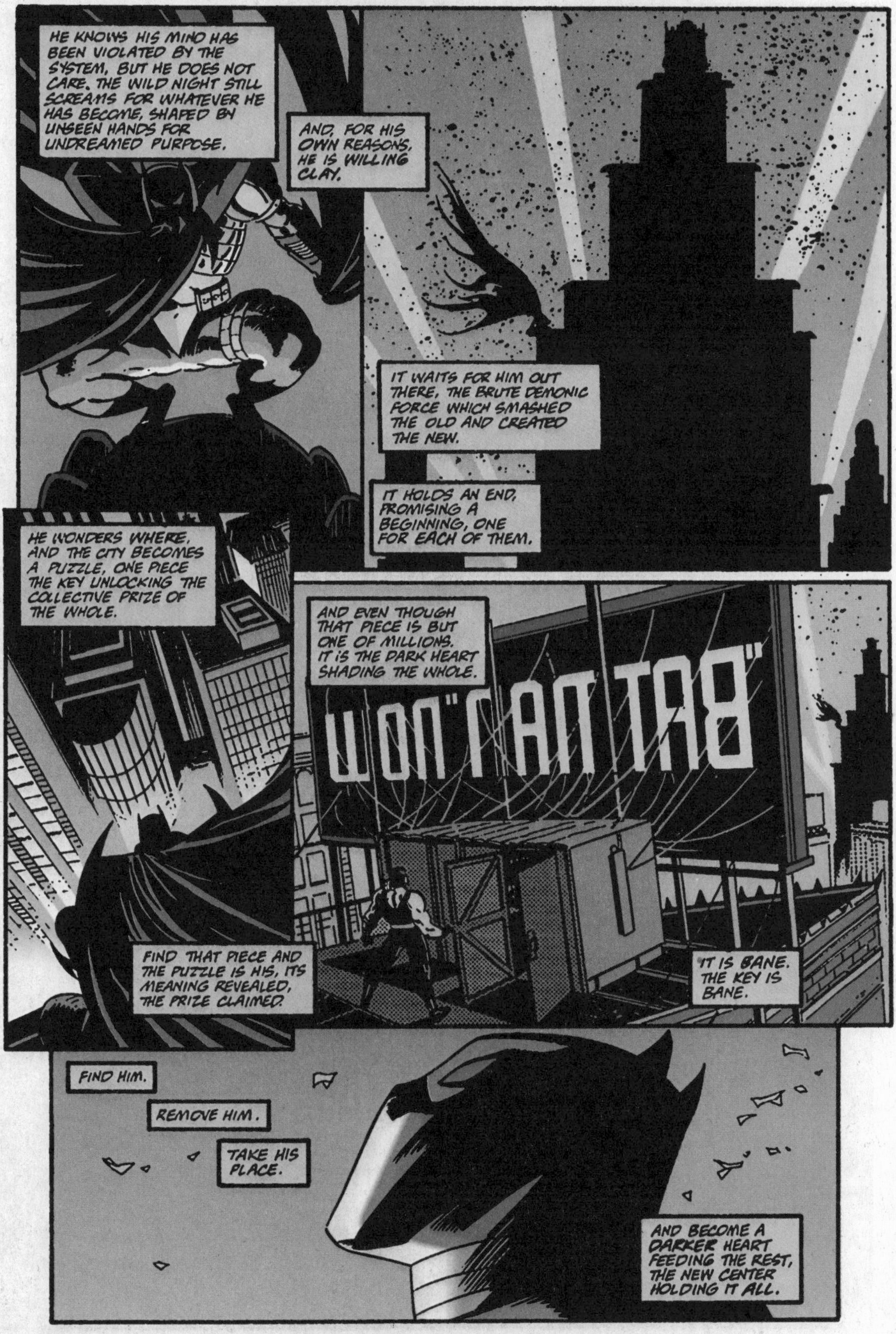
HE KNOWS HIS MIND HAS BEEN VIOLATED BY THE SYSTEM, BUT HE DOES NOT CARE. THE WILD NIGHT STILL SCREAMS FOR WHATEVER HE HAS BECOME, SHAPED BY UNSEEN HANDS FOR UNDREAMED PURPOSE.
AND, FOR HIS OWN REASONS, HE IS WILLING CLAY.
IT WAITS FOR HIM OUT THERE, THE BRUTE DEMONIC FORCE WHICH SMASHED THE OLD AND CREATED THE NEW.
IT HOLDS AN END, PROMISING A BEGINNING, ONE FOR EACH OF THEM.
HE WONDERS WHERE. AND THE CITY BECOMES A PUZZLE, ONE PIECE THE KEY UNLOCKING THE COLLECTIVE PRIZE OF THE WHOLE.
FIND THAT PIECE AND THE PUZZLE IS HIS, ITS MEANING REVEALED, THE PRIZE CLAIMED.
AND EVEN THOUGH THAT PIECE IS BUT ONE OF MILLIONS, IT IS THE DARK HEART SHADING THE WHOLE.
WON" I AN TAB"
IT IS BANE. THE KEY IS BANE.
FIND HIM.
REMOVE HIM.
TAKE HIS PLACE.
AND BECOME A DARKER HEART FEEDING THE REST, THE NEW CENTER HOLDING IT ALL.

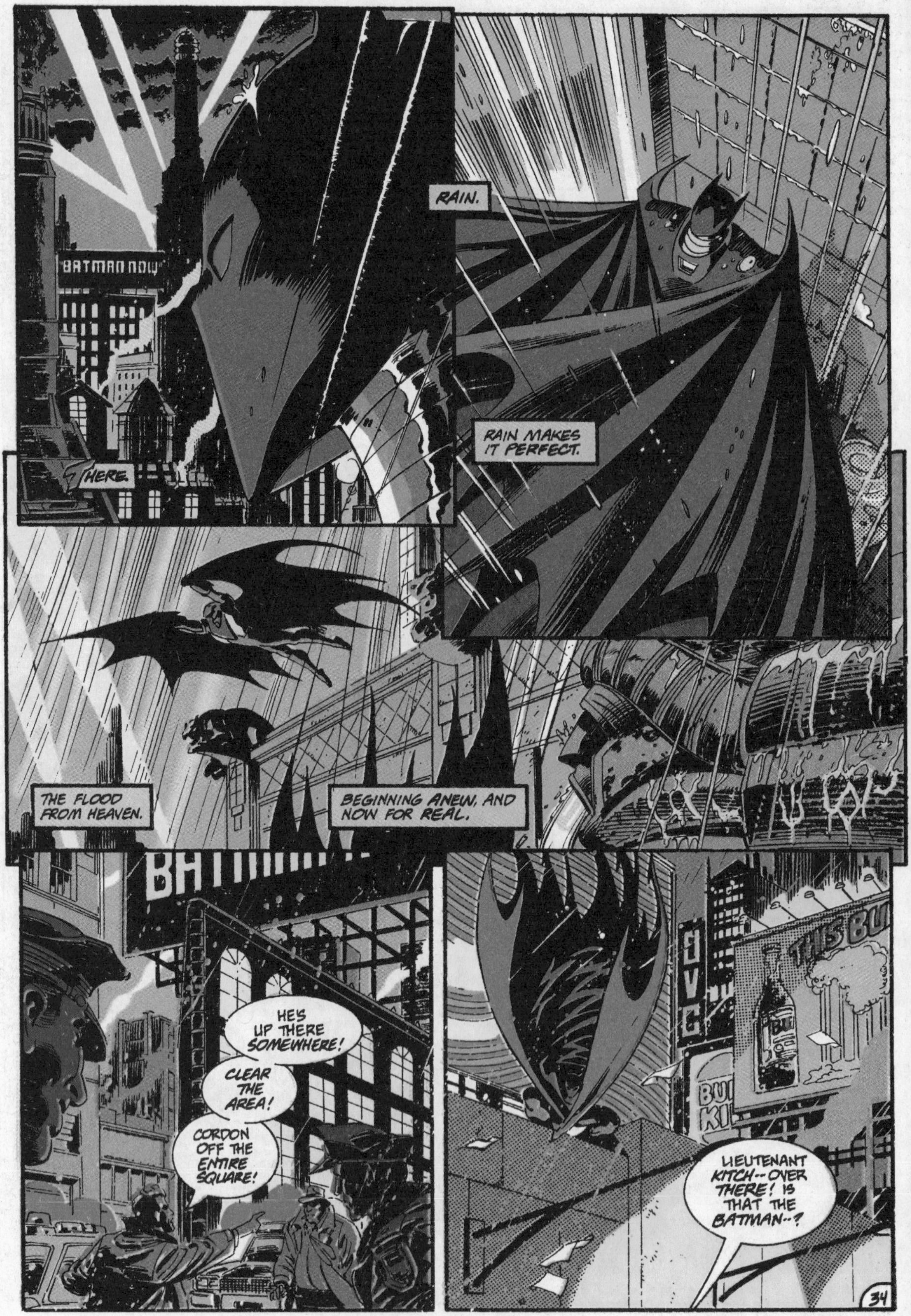
BATMAN NOW
THERE.
RAIN.
RAIN MAKES IT PERFECT.
THE FLOOD FROM HEAVEN.
BEGINNING ANEW, AND NOW FOR REAL.
HE'S UP THERE SOMEWHERE!
CLEAR THE AREA!
CORDON OFF THE ENTIRE SQUARE!
LIEUTENANT KITCH-- OVER THERE! IS THAT THE BATMAN--?
34

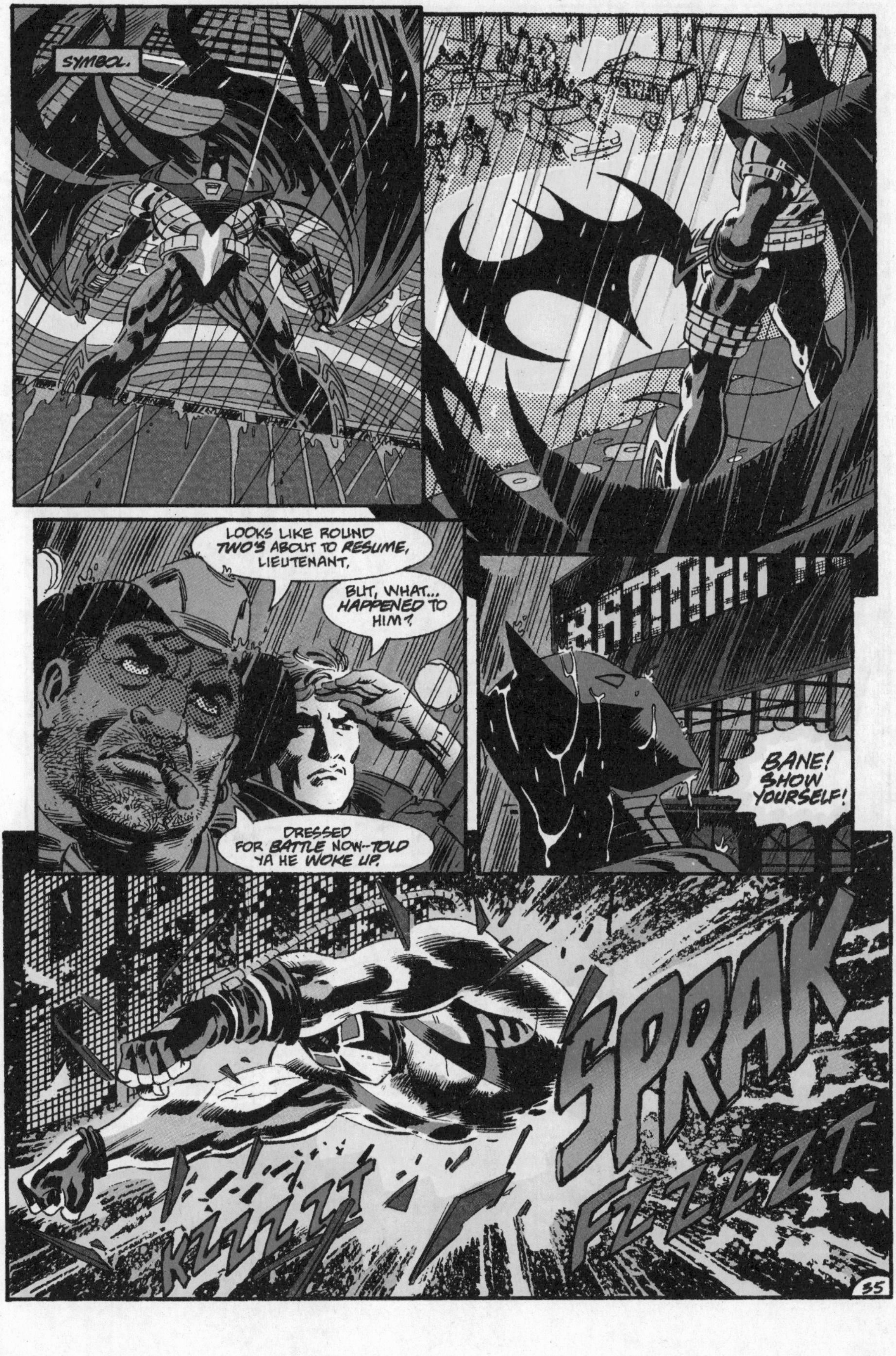
SYMBOL.
LOOKS LIKE ROUND TWO'S ABOUT TO RESUME, LIEUTENANT,
BUT, WHAT... HAPPENED TO HIM?
DRESSED FOR BATTLE NOW--TOLD YA HE WOKE UP.
BANE! SHOW YOURSELF!
SPRAK
KZZZZT
FZZZZZT
35

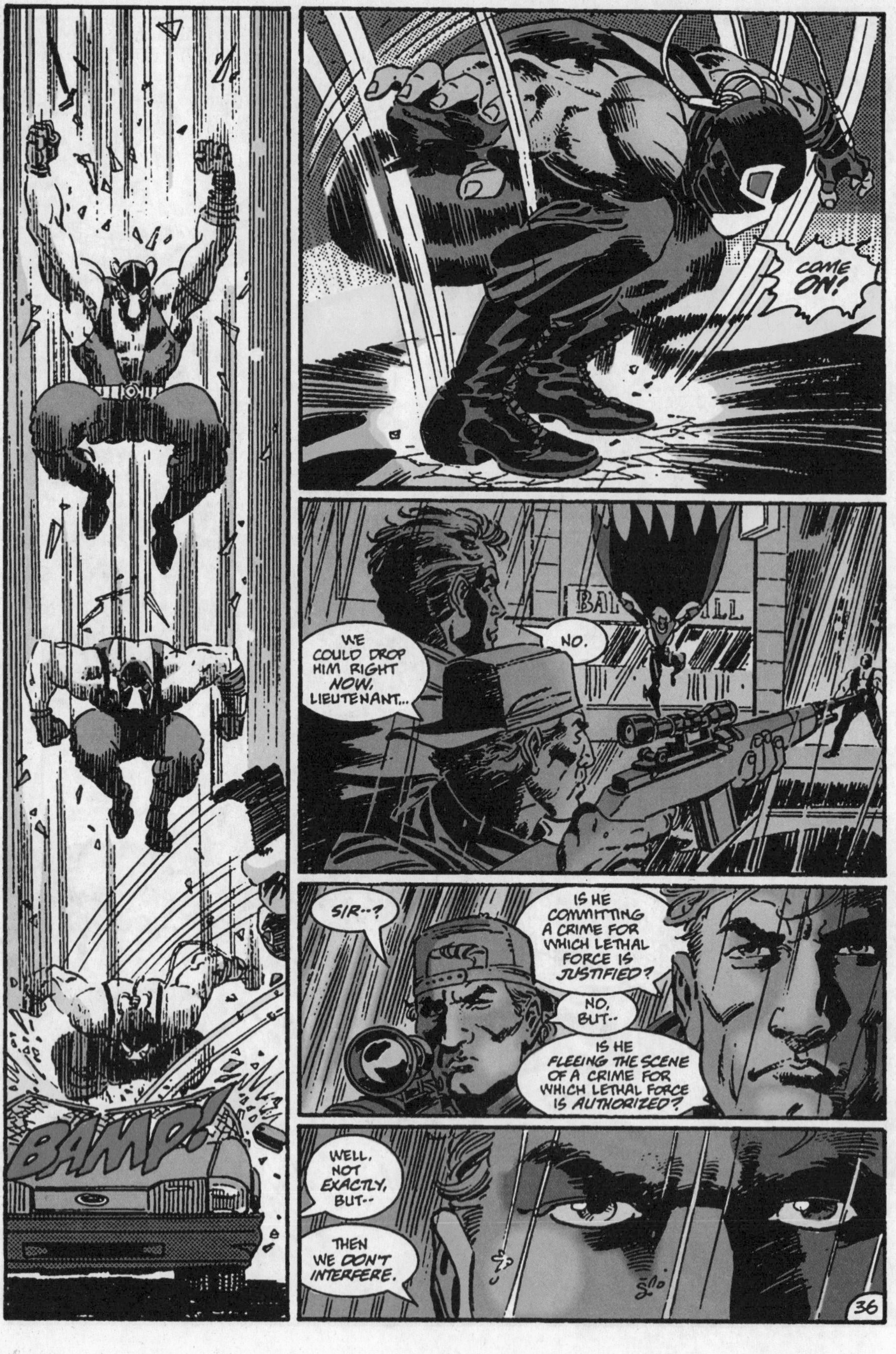
COME ON!
WE COULD DROP HIM RIGHT NOW, LIEUTENANT...
NO.
SIR--?
IS HE COMMITTING A CRIME FOR WHICH LETHAL FORCE IS JUSTIFIED?
NO, BUT--
IS HE FLEEING THE SCENE OF A CRIME FOR WHICH LETHAL FORCE IS AUTHORIZED?
WELL, NOT EXACTLY, BUT--
THEN WE DON'T INTERFERE.
BAMP!
36

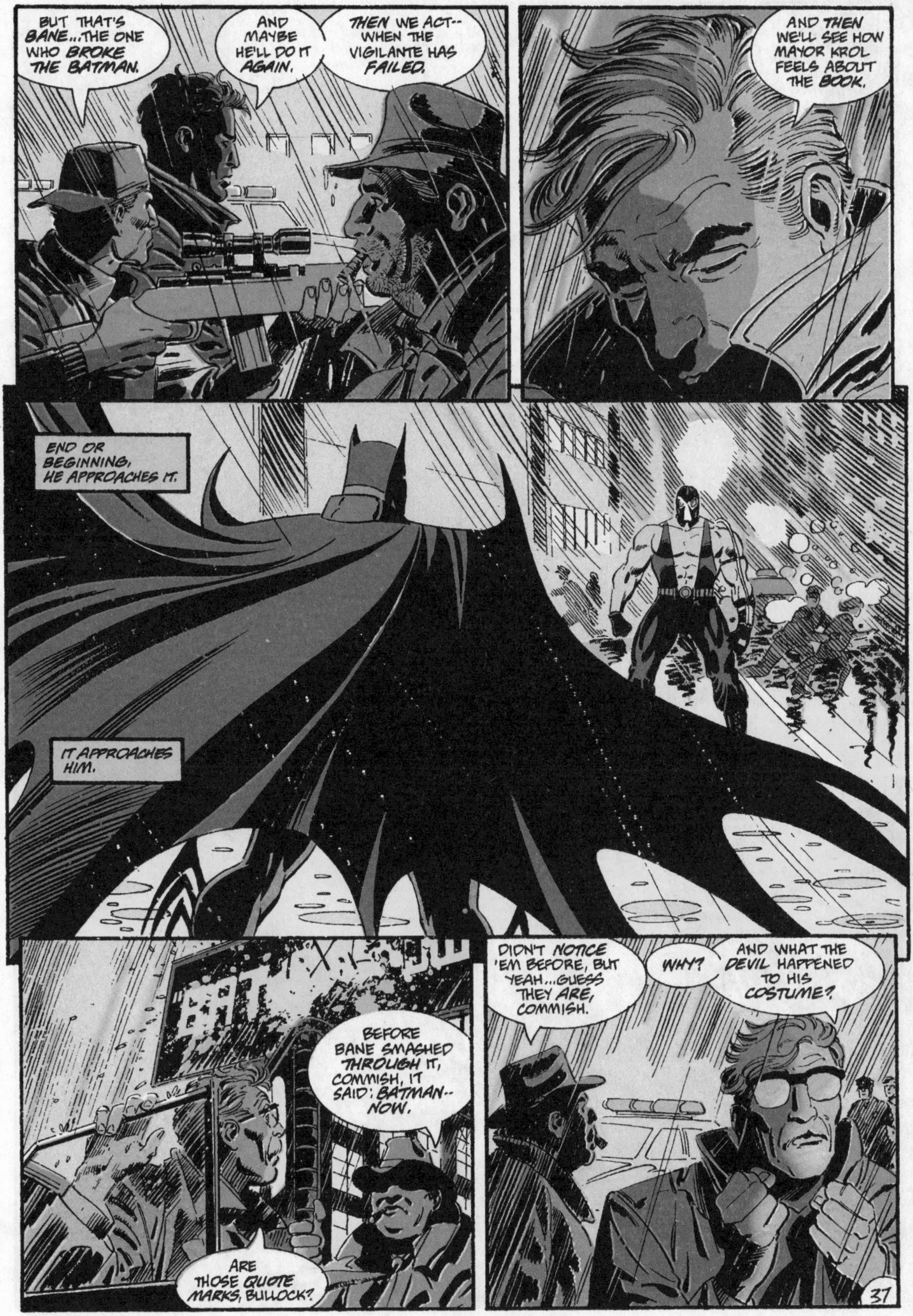
BUT THAT'S BANE...THE ONE WHO BROKE THE BATMAN.
AND MAYBE HE'LL DO IT AGAIN.
THEN WE ACT-- WHEN THE VIGILANTE HAS FAILED.
AND THEN WE'LL SEE HOW MAYOR KROL FEELS ABOUT THE BOOK.
END OR BEGINNING, HE APPROACHES IT.
IT APPROACHES HIM.
BEFORE BANE SMASHED THROUGH IT, COMMISH, IT SAID: BATMAN-- NOW.
ARE THOSE QUOTE MARKS, BULLOCK?
DIDN'T NOTICE 'EM BEFORE, BUT YEAH...GUESS THEY ARE, COMMISH.
WHY?
AND WHAT THE DEVIL HAPPENED TO HIS COSTUME?
37

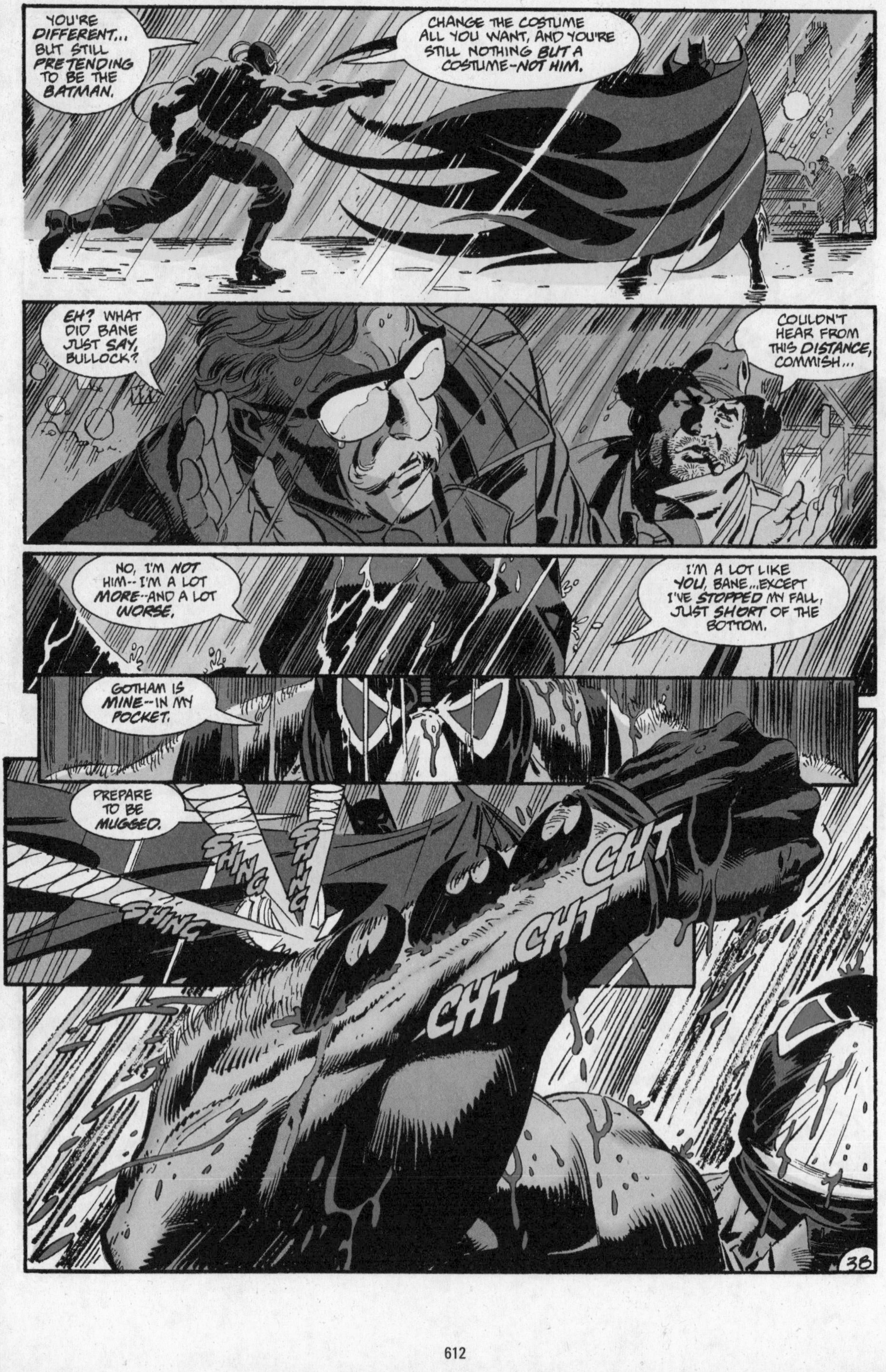
YOU'RE DIFFERENT... BUT STILL PRETENDING TO BE THE BATMAN.
CHANGE THE COSTUME ALL YOU WANT, AND YOU'RE STILL NOTHING BUT A COSTUME--NOT HIM.
EH? WHAT DID BANE JUST SAY, BULLOCK?
COULDN'T HEAR FROM THIS DISTANCE, COMMISH...
NO, I'M NOT HIM--I'M A LOT MORE--AND A LOT WORSE.
I'M A LOT LIKE YOU, BANE...EXCEPT I'VE STOPPED MY FALL, JUST SHORT OF THE BOTTOM.
GOTHAM IS MINE--IN MY POCKET.
PREPARE TO BE MUGGED.
SHING
SHING
SHING
CHT
CHT
CHT
38

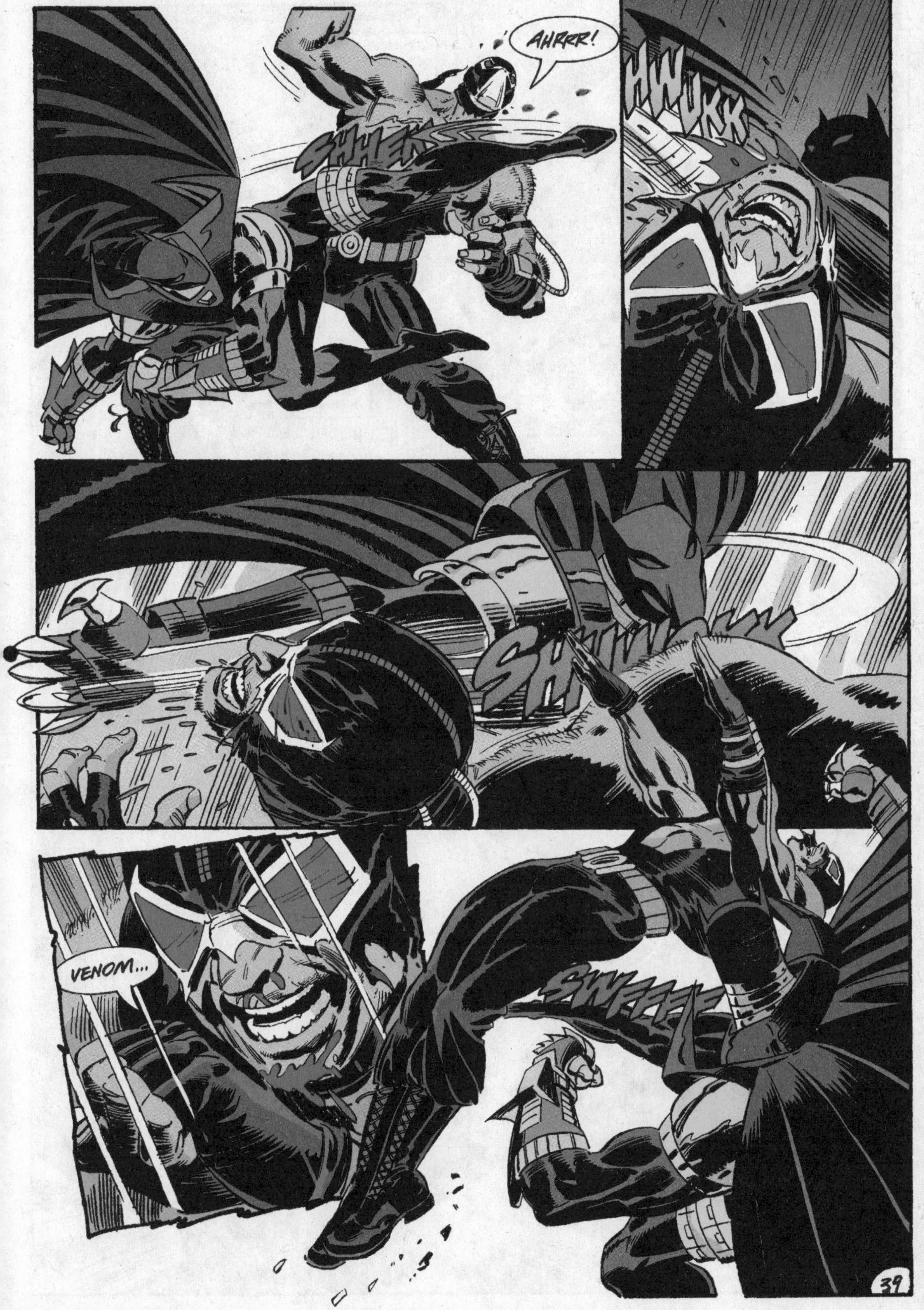
AHRRR!
SHHEK
HWUKK
SHWWWM
VENOM...
SWFFF
39

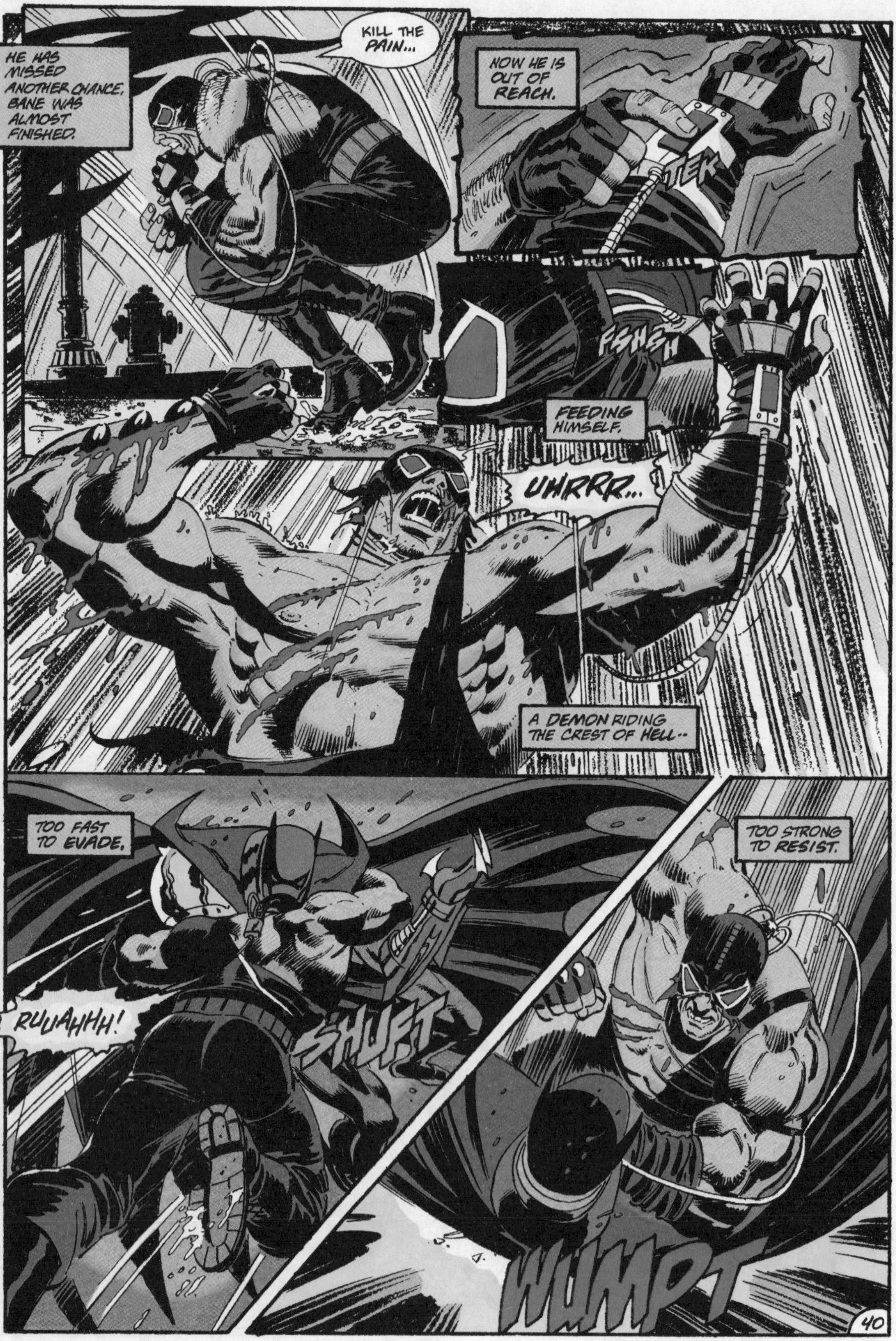
HE HAS MISSED ANOTHER CHANCE. BANE WAS ALMOST FINISHED.
KILL THE PAIN...
NOW HE IS OUT OF REACH.
PSHSH
FEEDING HIMSELF.
UHRRR...
A DEMON RIDING THE CREST OF HELL--
TOO FAST TO EVADE.
RUUAHHH!
SHUFT
TOO STRONG TO RESIST.
WUMPT
40

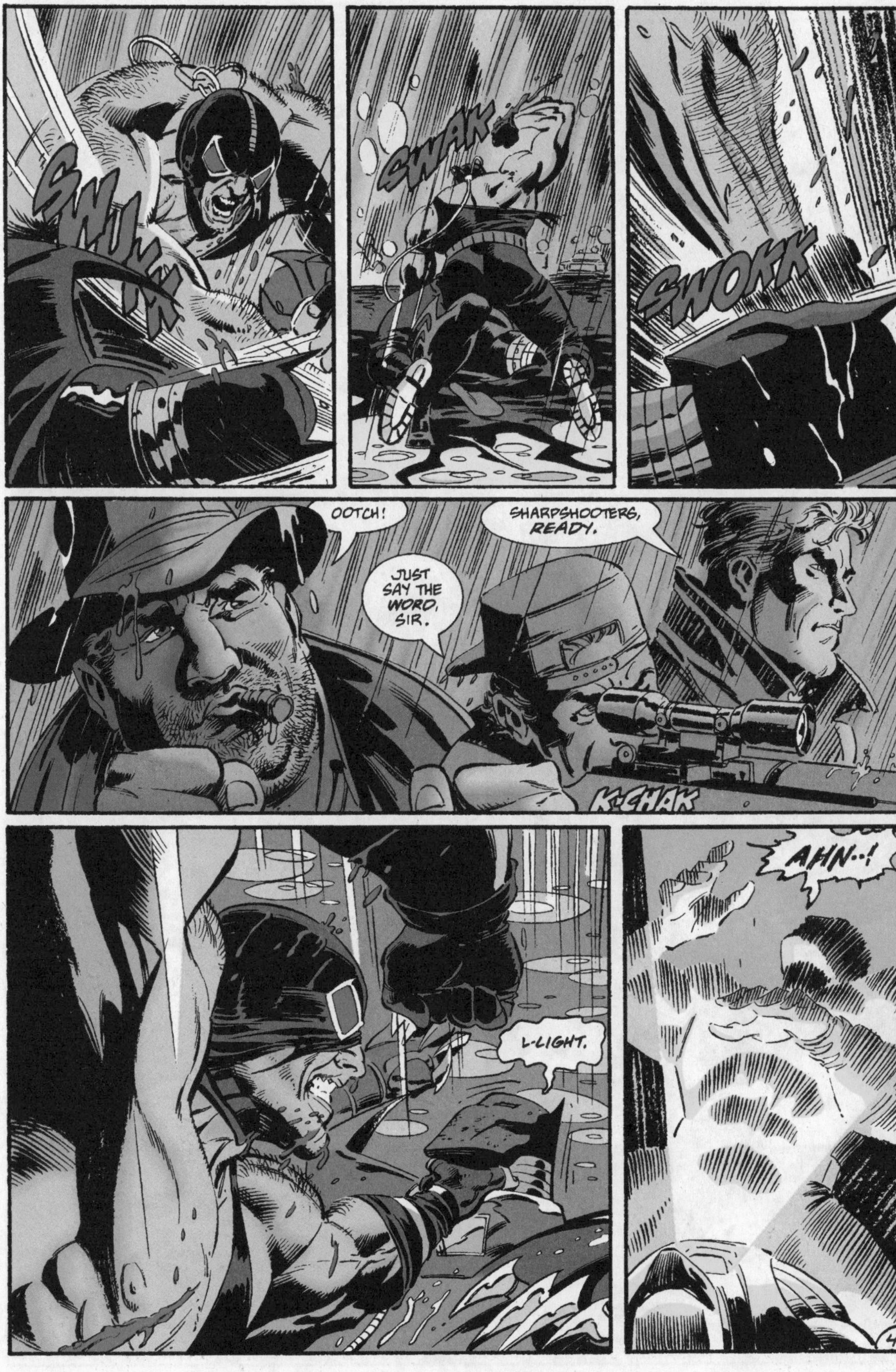
SWUNK
SWAK
SWOKK
OOTCH!
SHARPSHOOTERS, READY.
JUST SAY THE WORD, SIR.
K-CHAK
L-LIGHT.
AHN..!
41

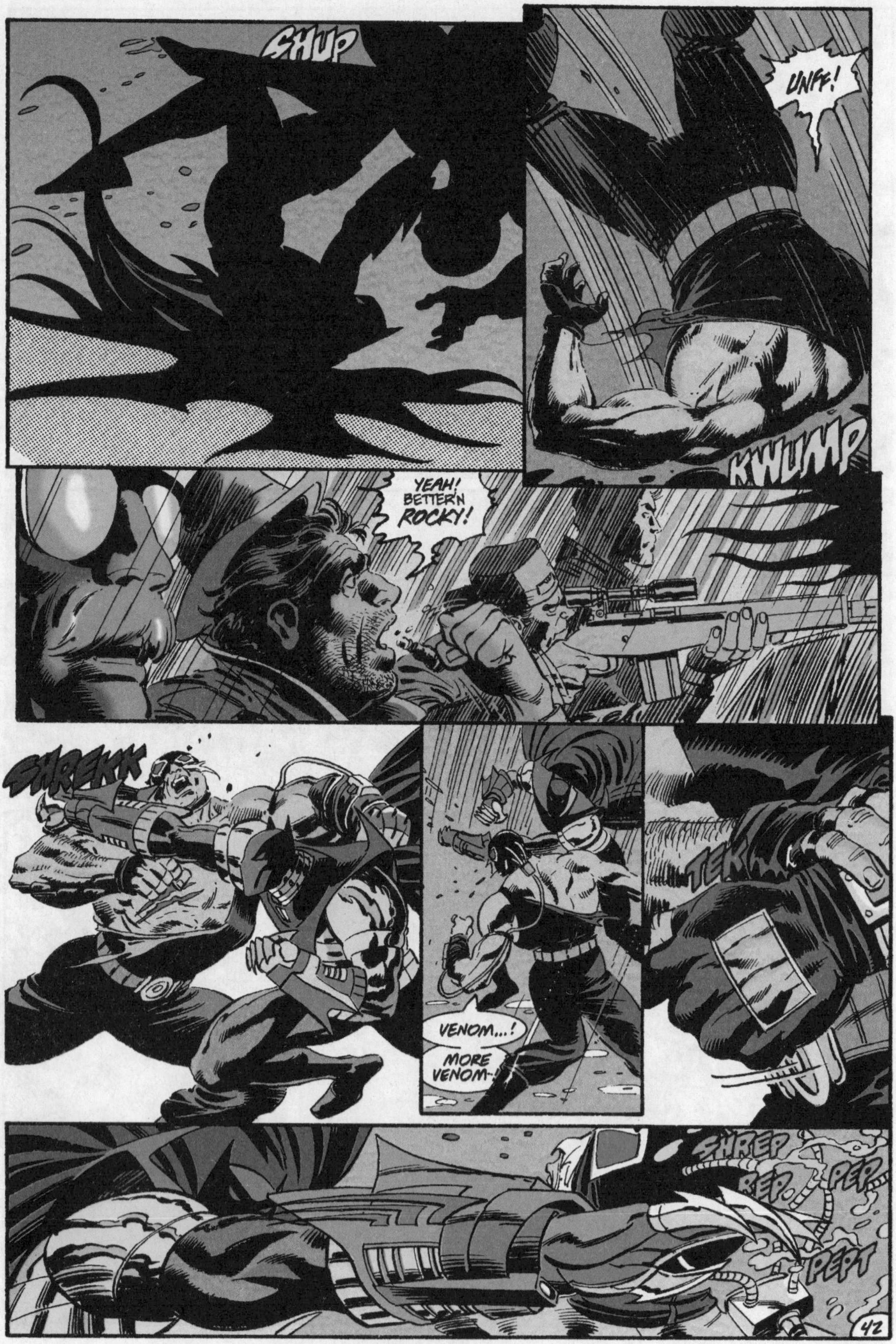
SHUP
UNFF!
KWUMP
YEAH! BETTER'N ROCKY!
SHREKK
TEK
VENOM...!
MORE VENOM-!
SHREP
PEP
PEP
PEPT
42

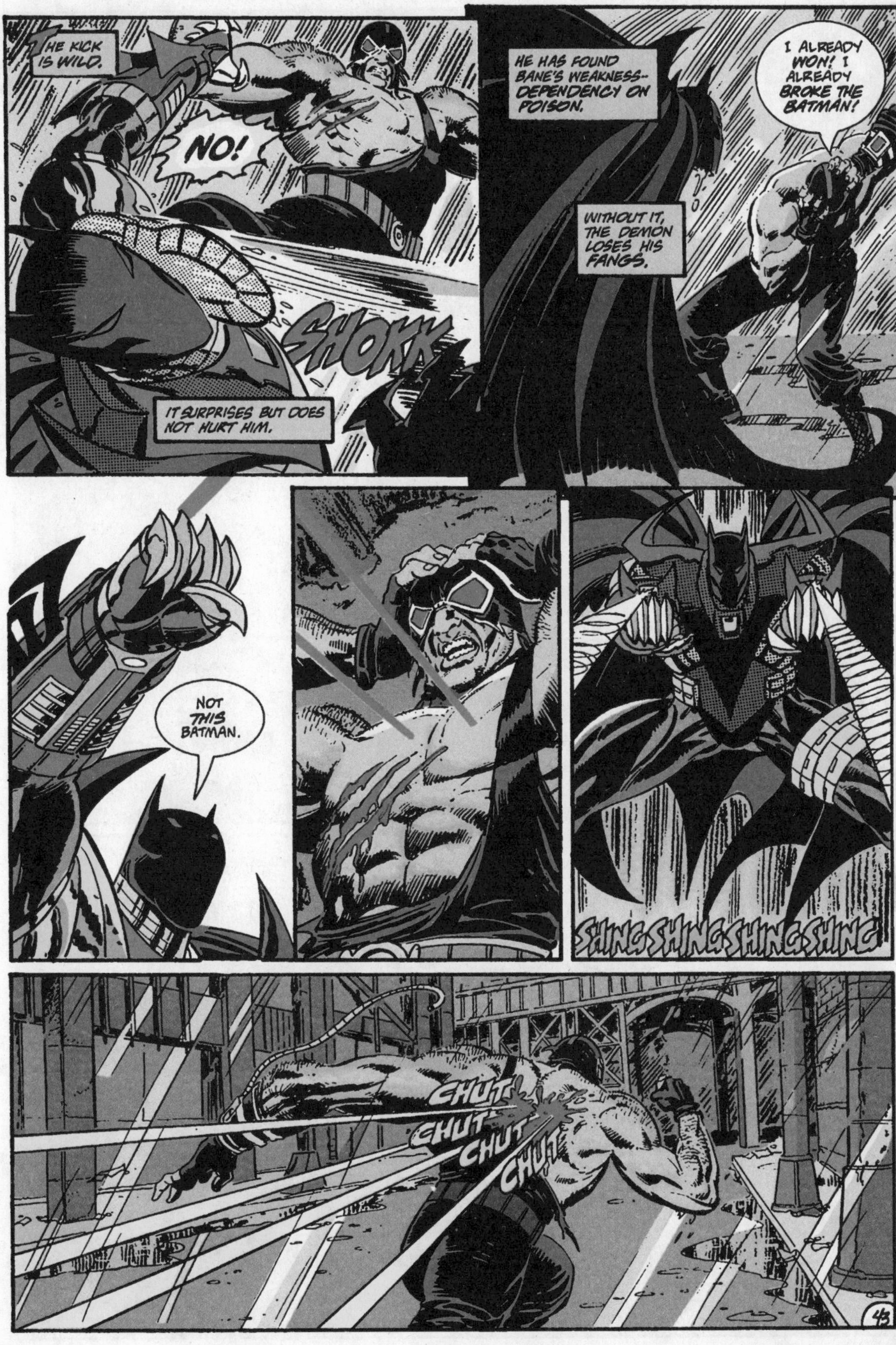

HE KICK IS WILD.
NO!
SHOKK
IT SURPRISES BUT DOES NOT HURT HIM.
HE HAS FOUND BANE'S WEAKNESS-- DEPENDENCY ON POISON.
WITHOUT IT, THE DEMON LOSES HIS FANGS.
I ALREADY WON! I ALREADY BROKE THE BATMAN!
NOT THIS BATMAN.
SHING SHING SHING SHING
CHUT
CHUT
CHUT
CHUT
43

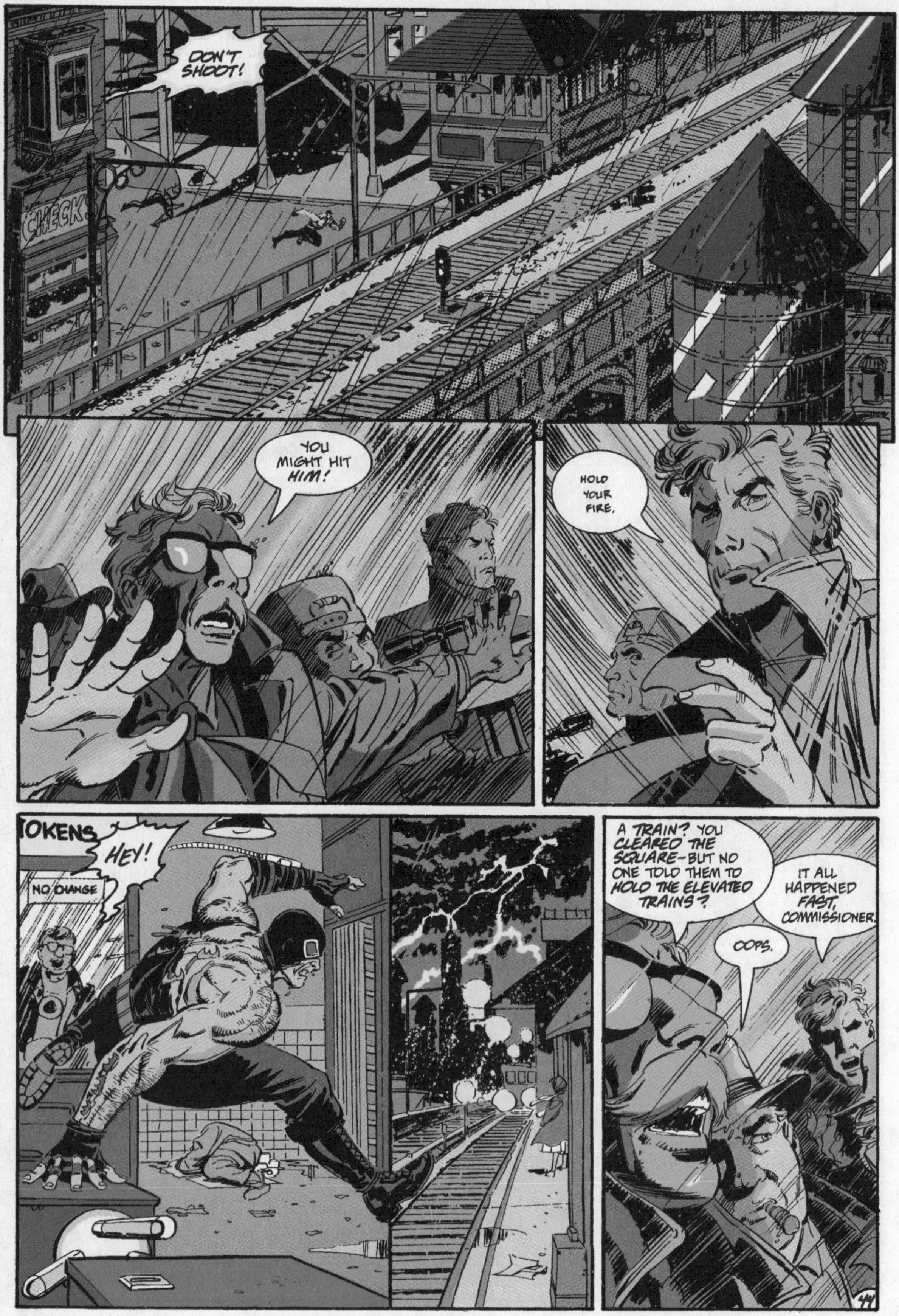
DON'T SHOOT!
CHECKS
YOU MIGHT HIT HIM!
HOLD YOUR FIRE.
TOKENS
HEY!
NO CHANGE
A TRAIN? YOU CLEARED THE SQUARE-BUT NO ONE TOLD THEM TO HOLD THE ELEVATED TRAINS?
IT ALL HAPPENED FAST, COMMISSIONER.
OOPS.
44

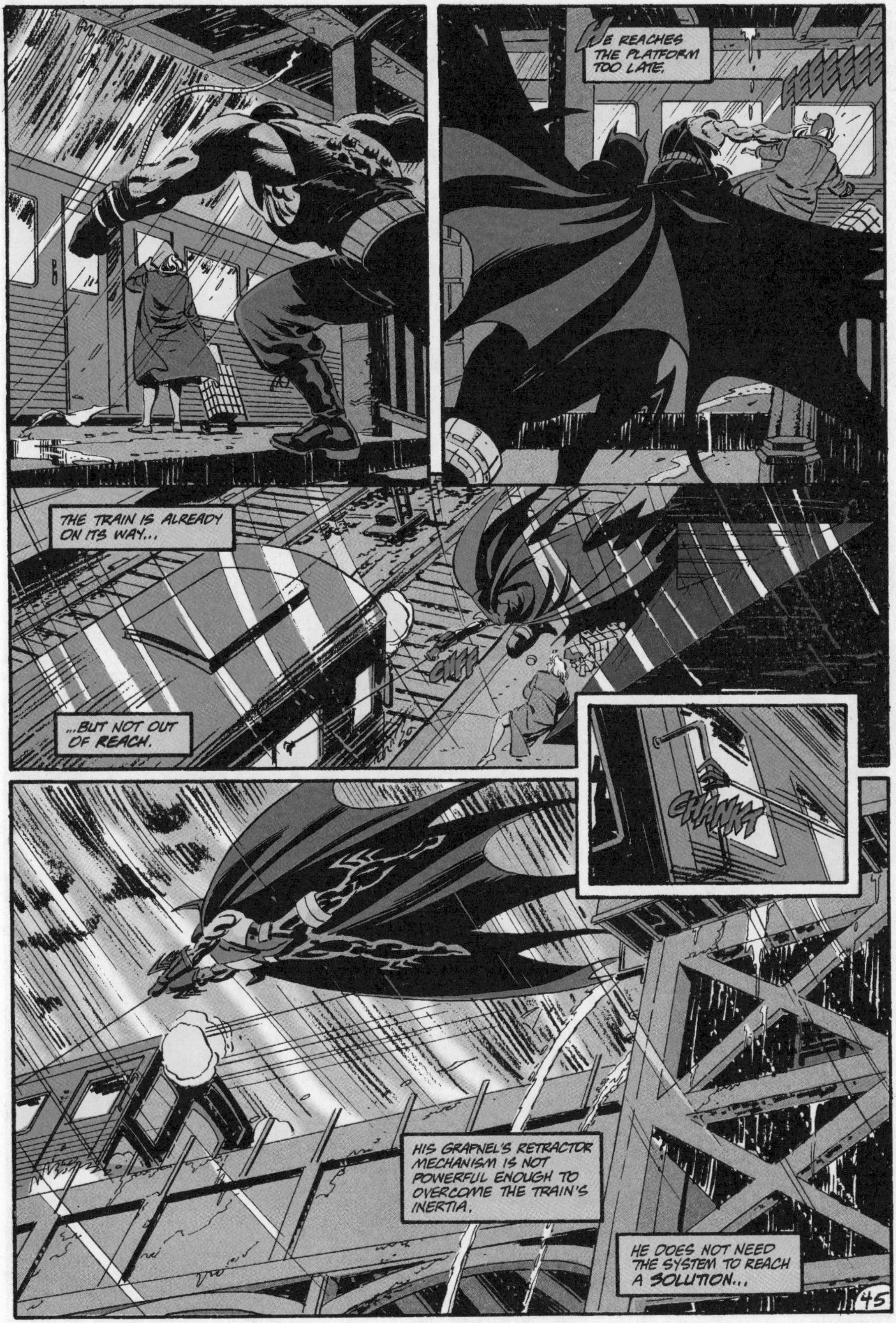
HE REACHES THE PLATFORM TOO LATE.
EEEEEEE
THE TRAIN IS ALREADY ON ITS WAY...
...BUT NOT OUT OF REACH.
CHUNK
HIS GRAPNEL'S RETRACTOR MECHANISM IS NOT POWERFUL ENOUGH TO OVERCOME THE TRAIN'S INERTIA.
HE DOES NOT NEED THE SYSTEM TO REACH A SOLUTION...
45

HE SIMPLY DIGS IN.

SPRONT

PRONT

AND HAULS.

EVERYONE OUT-- INTO THE NEXT CAR! NOW!!

WHAT THE--? ONE OF THE HEADLIGHTS JUST WENT OU--

CHUSH

46

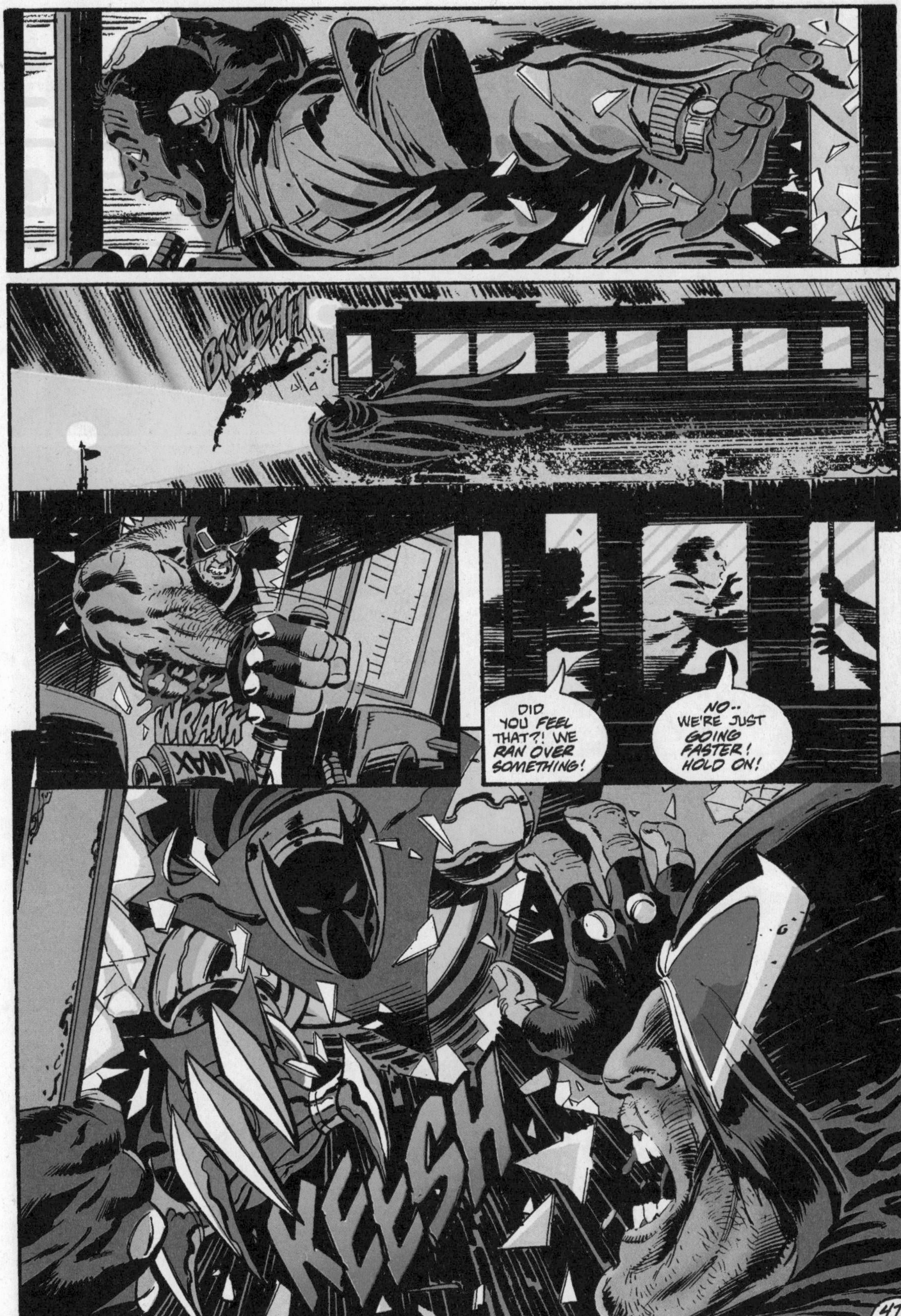
BKLSHH
WRAKK
DID YOU FEEL THAT?! WE RAN OVER SOMETHING!
NO.. WE'RE JUST GOING FASTER! HOLD ON!
KEESH
47

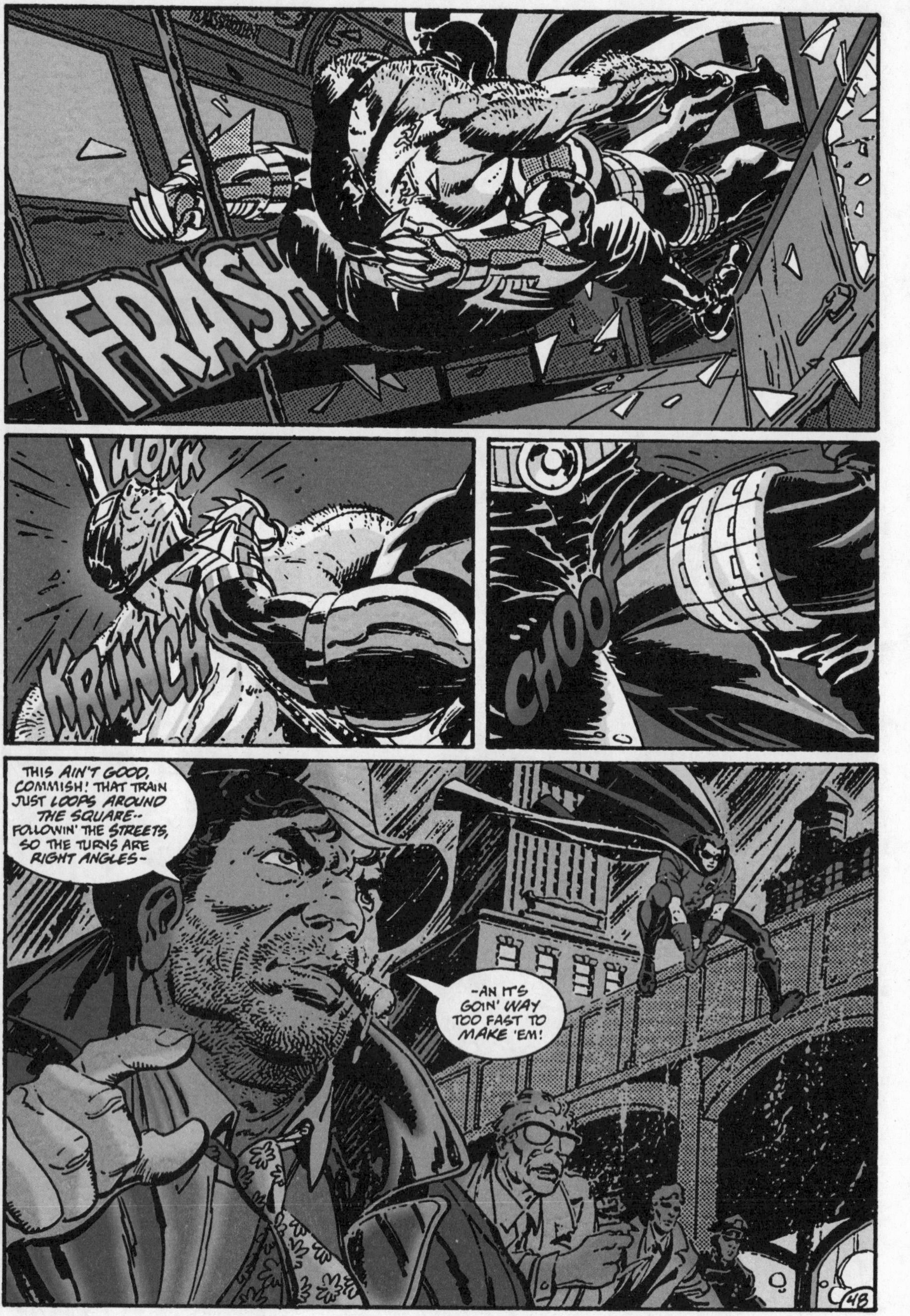
FRASH
WOKK
KRUNCH
CHOOK
THIS AIN'T GOOD, COMMISH! THAT TRAIN JUST LOOPS AROUND THE SQUARE-- FOLLOWIN' THE STREETS, SO THE TURNS ARE RIGHT ANGLES-
-AN IT'S GOIN' WAY TOO FAST TO MAKE 'EM!
48

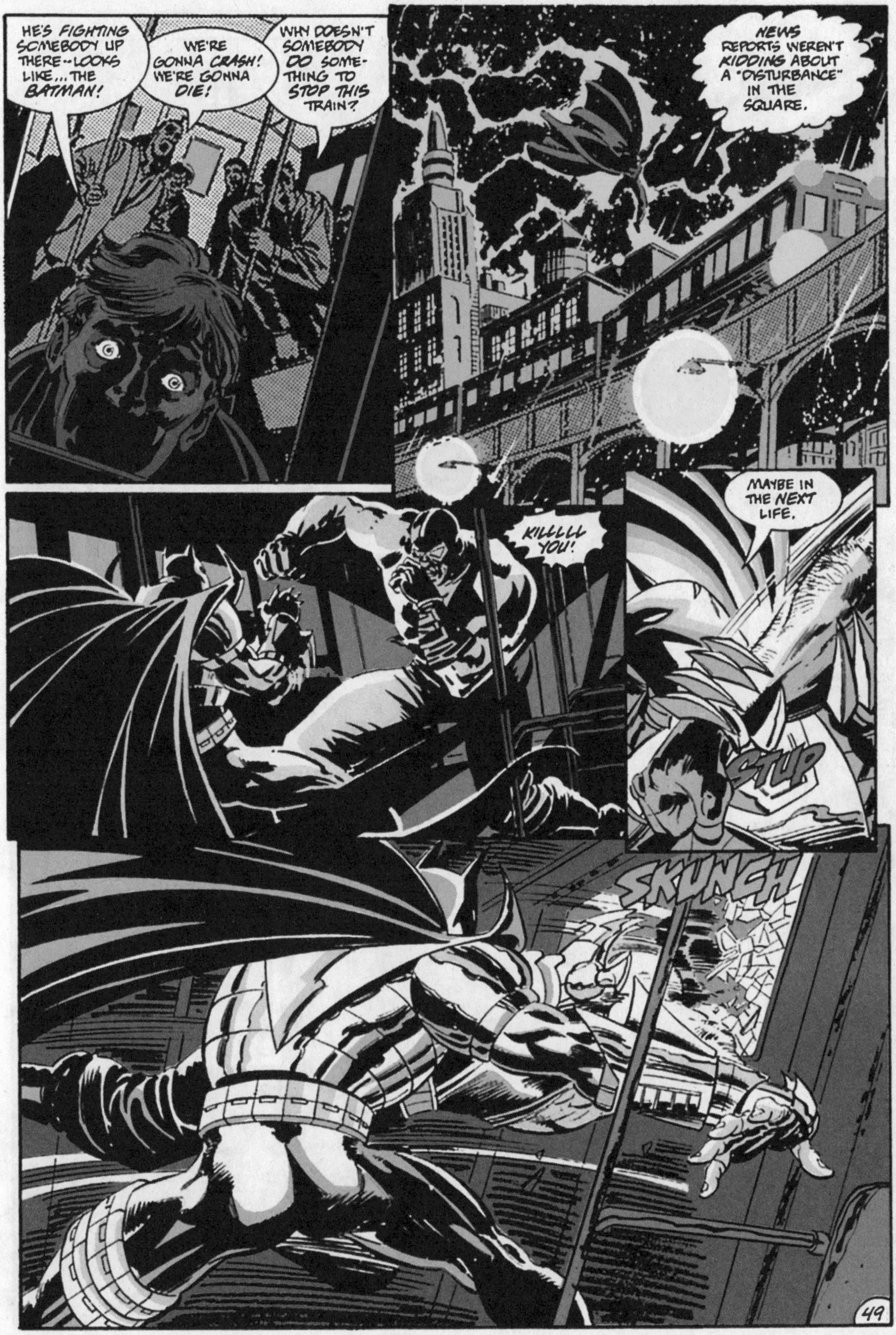
HE'S FIGHTING SOMEBODY UP THERE--LOOKS LIKE... THE BATMAN!
WE'RE GONNA CRASH! WE'RE GONNA DIE!
WHY DOESN'T SOMEBODY DO SOMETHING TO STOP THIS TRAIN?
NEWS REPORTS WEREN'T KIDDING ABOUT A "DISTURBANCE" IN THE SQUARE.
KILLLLL YOU!
MAYBE IN THE NEXT LIFE.
STUP
SKUNCH
49

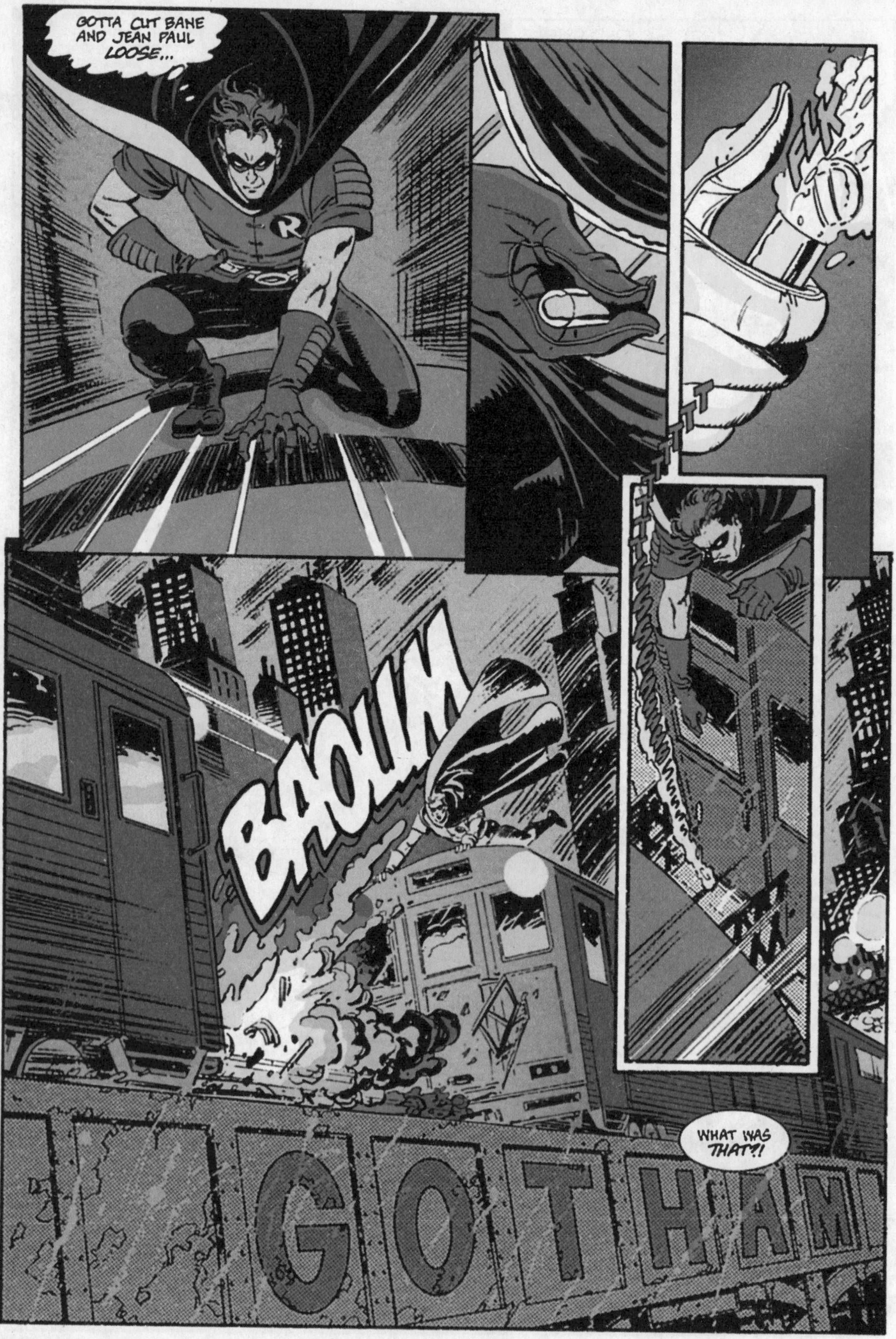
GOTTA CUT BANE AND JEAN PAUL LOOSE...
FLIK
BAOUM
WHAT WAS THAT?!
GOTHAM

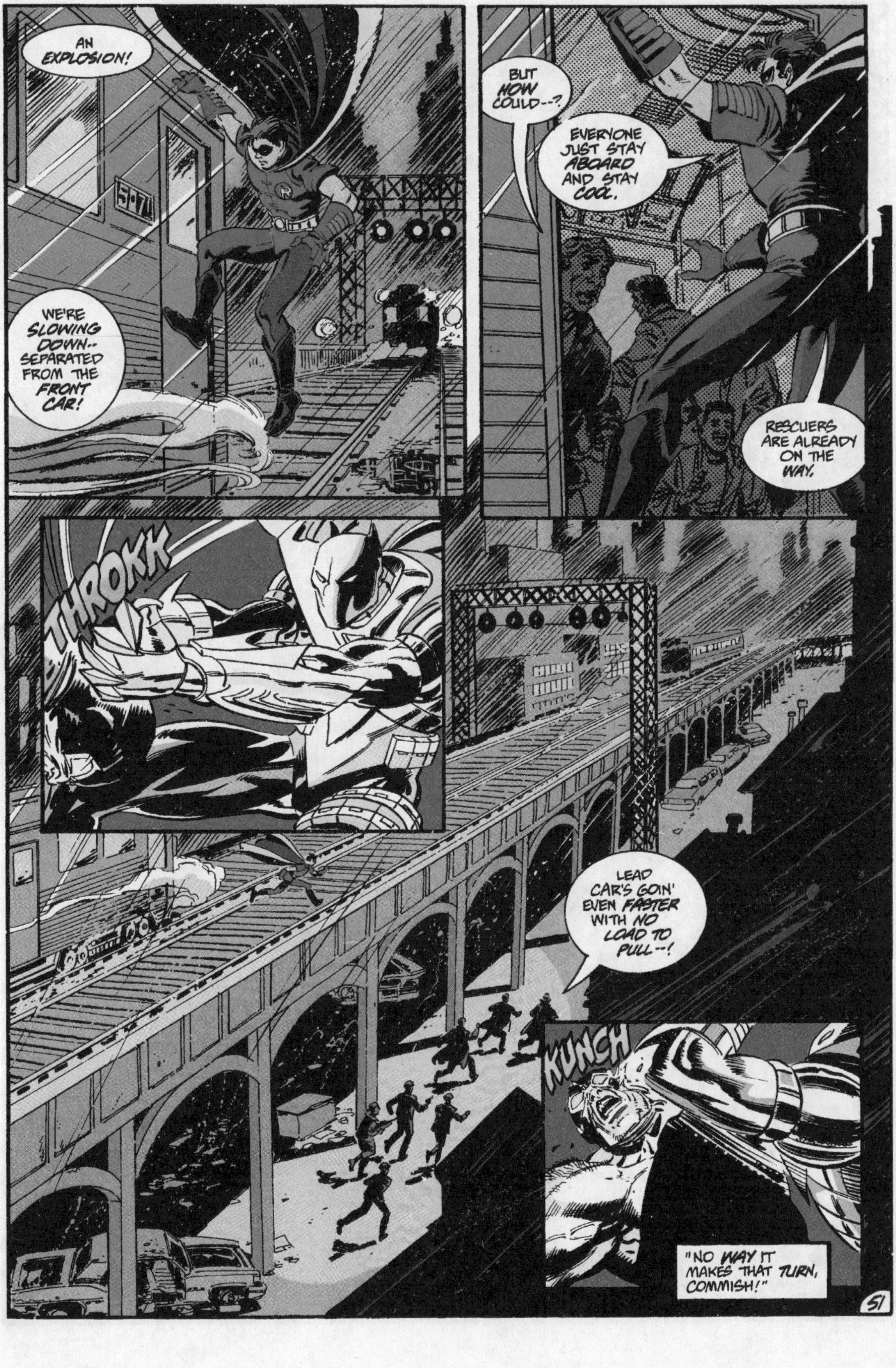
AN EXPLOSION!
WE'RE SLOWING DOWN.. SEPARATED FROM THE FRONT CAR!
BUT HOW COULD--?
EVERYONE JUST STAY ABOARD AND STAY COOL.
RESCUERS ARE ALREADY ON THE WAY.
THROKK
LEAD CAR'S GOIN' EVEN FASTER WITH NO LOAD TO PULL--!
KUNCH
"NO WAY IT MAKES THAT TURN, COMMISH!"
51

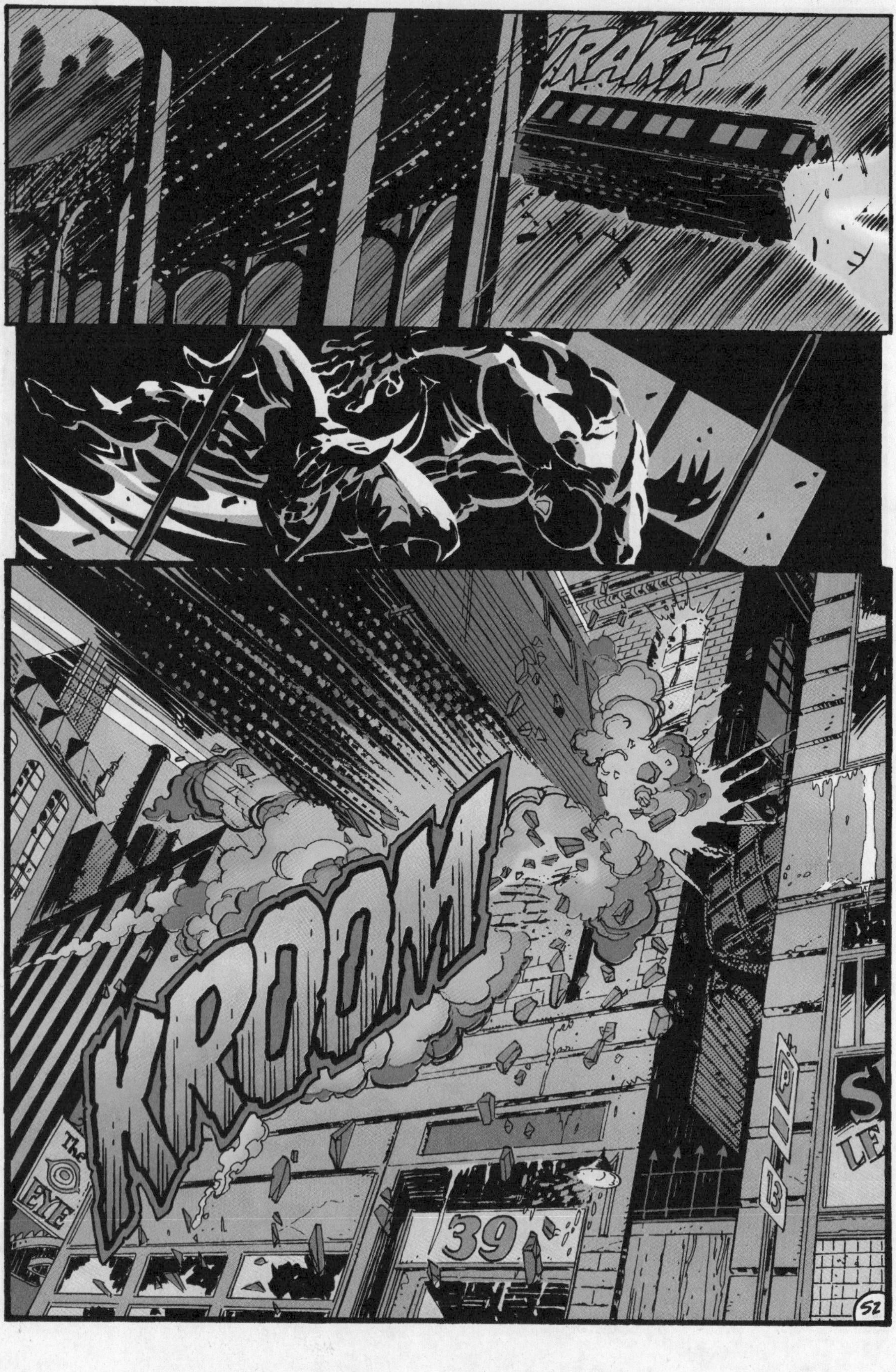

KRAKK
KRA-KOOM
The EYE
39
P
13
SL
LE
52

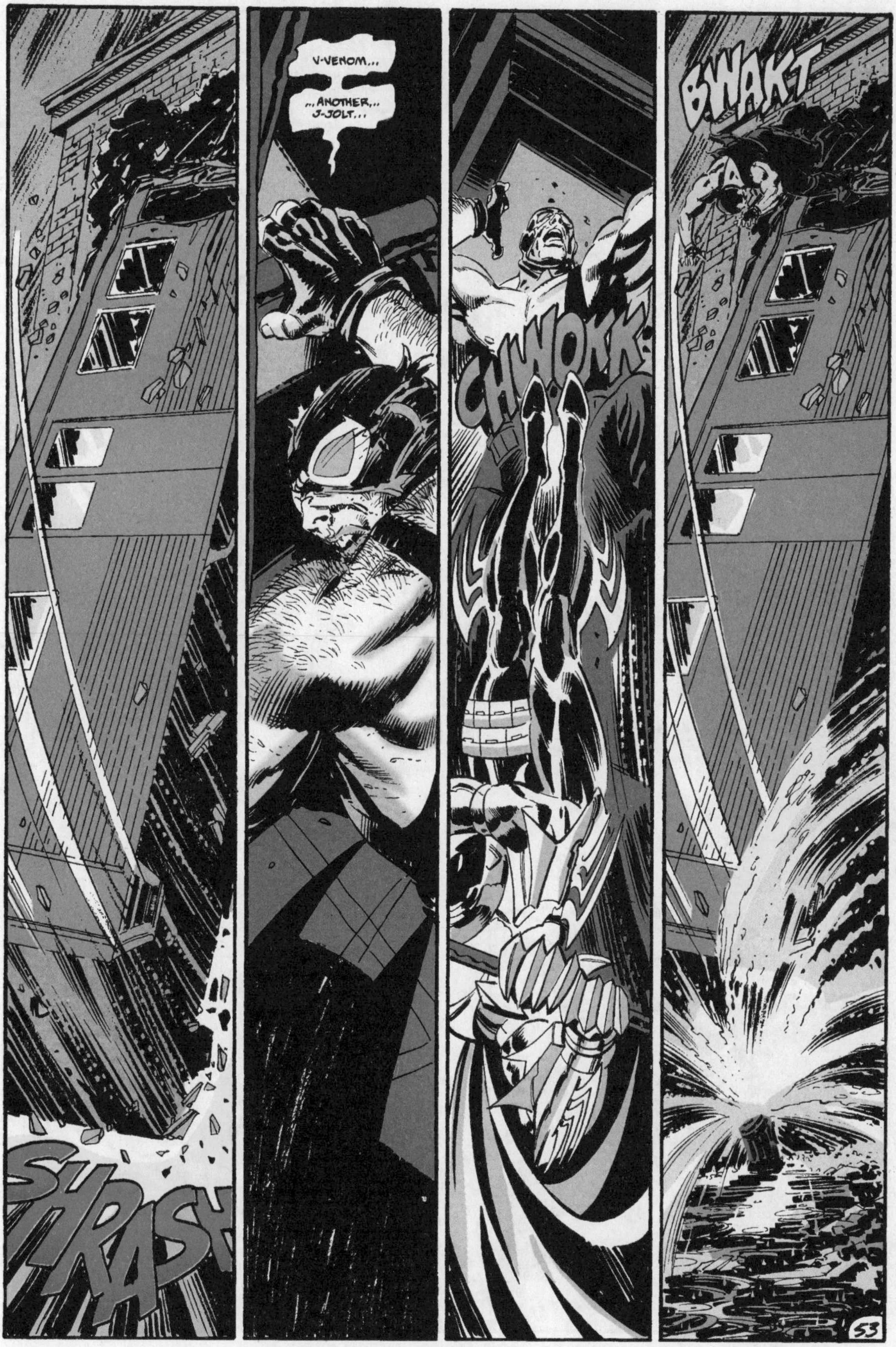
SHRASH
V-VENOM...
...ANOTHER... J-JOLT...
CHWOKK
BWAKT
53

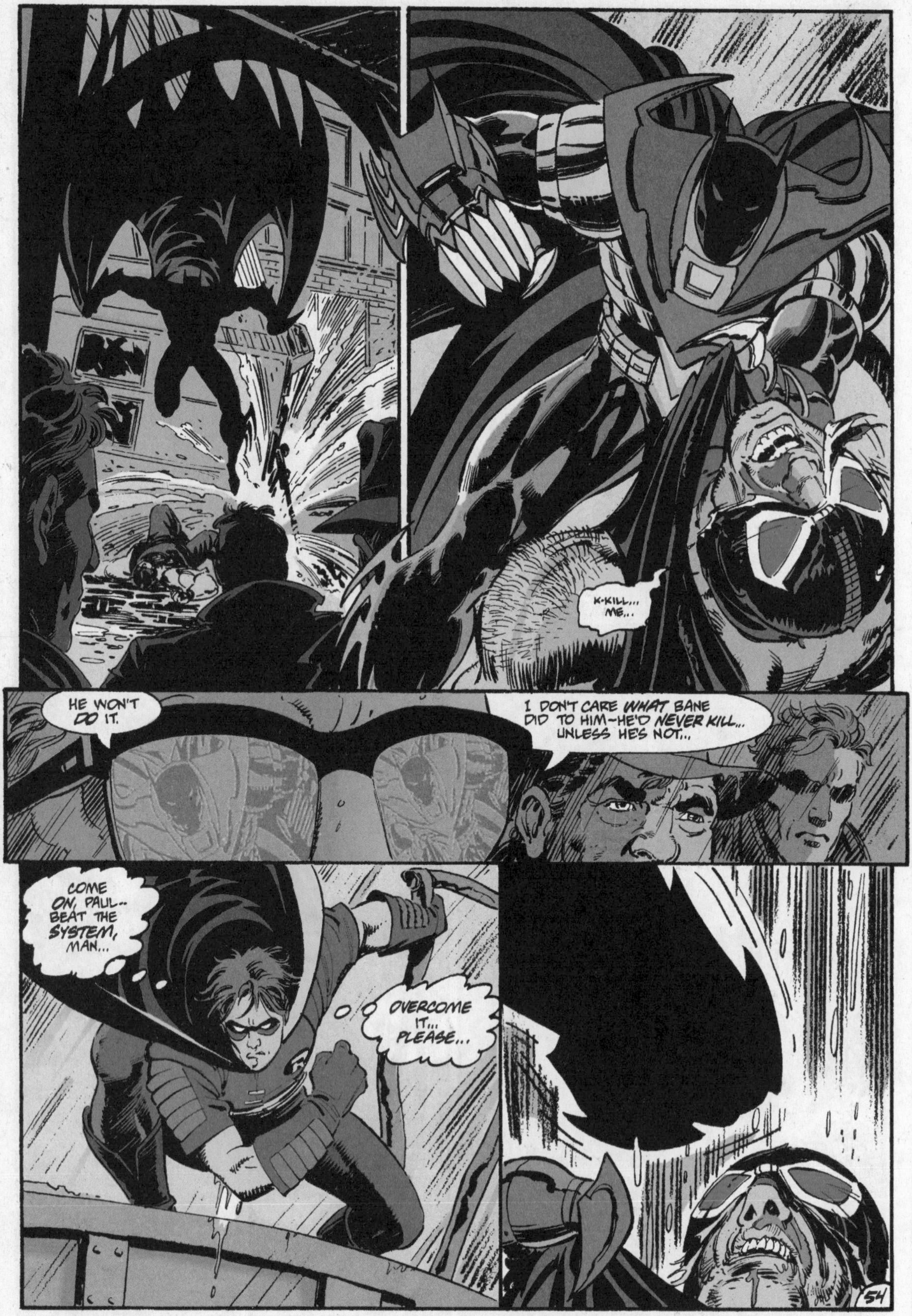
K-KILL... ME...
HE WON'T DO IT.
I DON'T CARE WHAT BANE DID TO HIM--HE'D NEVER KILL... UNLESS HE'S NOT...
COME ON, PAUL... BEAT THE SYSTEM, MAN...
OVERCOME IT... PLEASE...
54

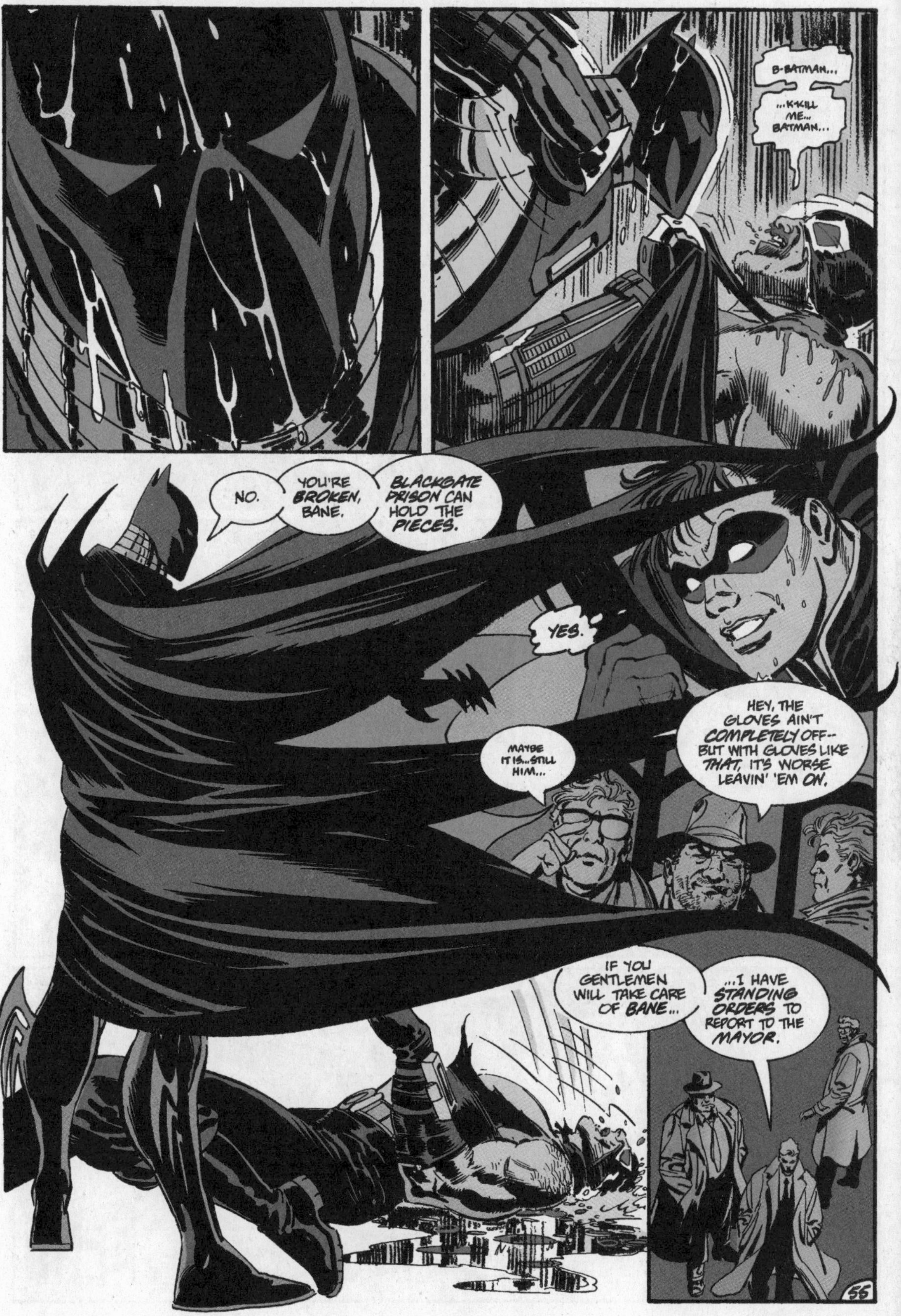
B-BATMAN...
...K-KILL ME... BATMAN...
NO.
YOU'RE BROKEN, BANE.
BLACKGATE PRISON CAN HOLD THE PIECES.
YES.
MAYBE IT IS...STILL HIM...
HEY, THE GLOVES AIN'T COMPLETELY OFF-- BUT WITH GLOVES LIKE THAT, IT'S WORSE LEAVIN' 'EM ON.
IF YOU GENTLEMEN WILL TAKE CARE OF BANE...
...I HAVE STANDING ORDERS TO REPORT TO THE MAYOR.
56

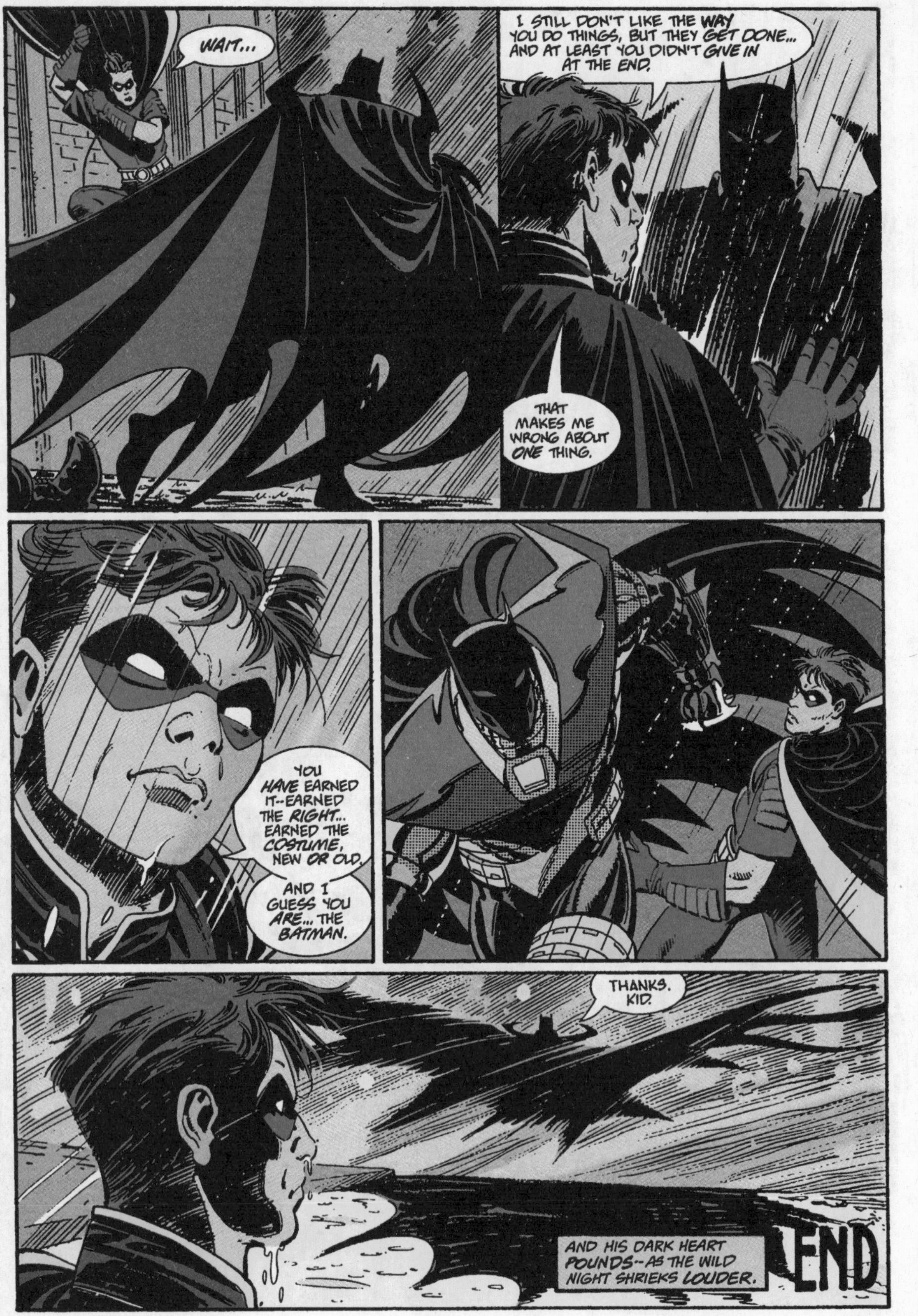
WAIT...
I STILL DON'T LIKE THE WAY YOU DO THINGS, BUT THEY GET DONE... AND AT LEAST YOU DIDN'T GIVE IN AT THE END.
THAT MAKES ME WRONG ABOUT ONE THING.
YOU HAVE EARNED IT--EARNED THE RIGHT... EARNED THE COSTUME, NEW OR OLD.
AND I GUESS YOU ARE... THE BATMAN.
THANKS. KID.
AND HIS DARK HEART POUNDS--AS THE WILD NIGHT SHRIEKS LOUDER.
END

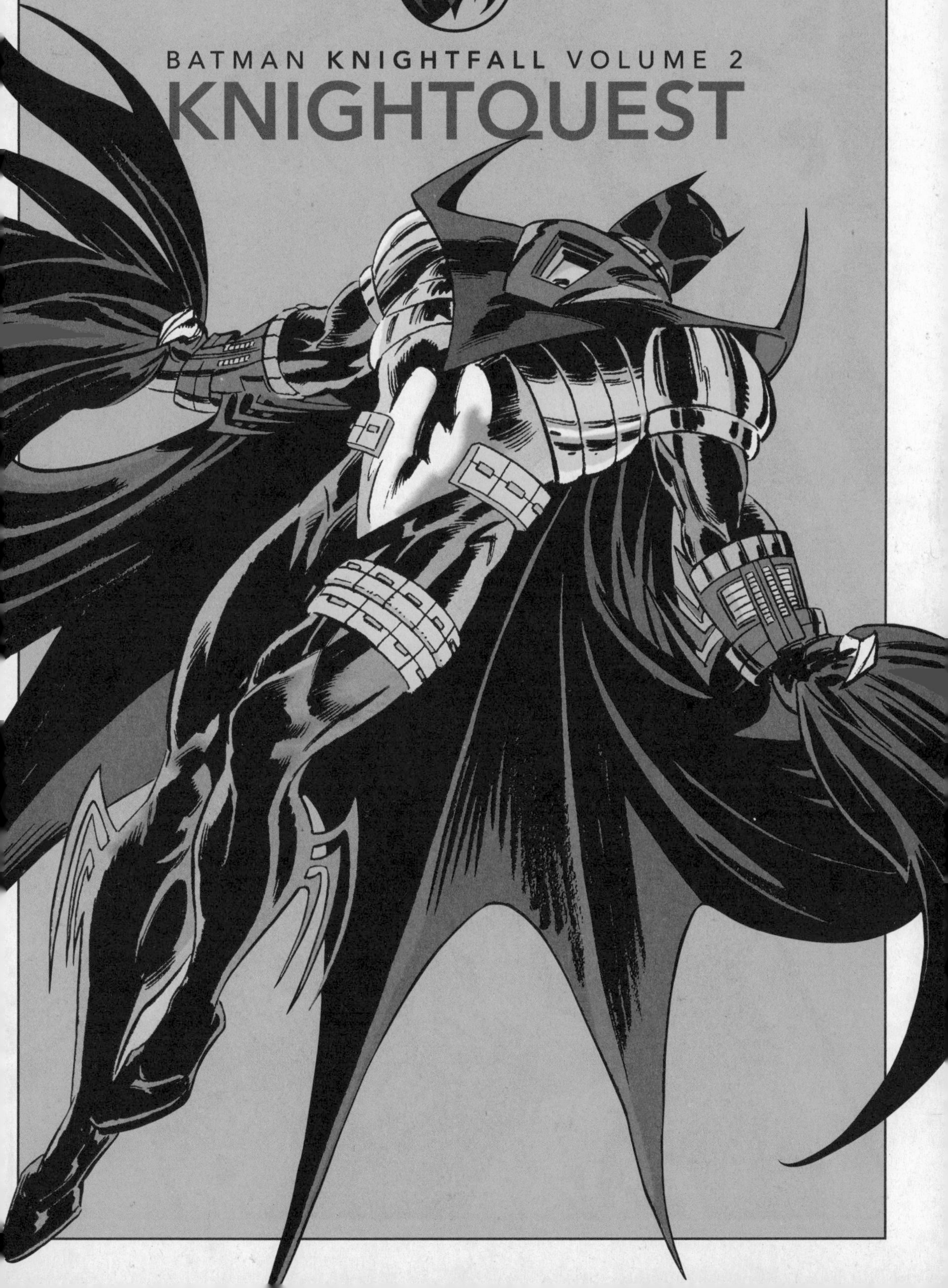

BATMAN #500 variant cover art by **JOE QUESADA** and **KEVIN NOWLAN**

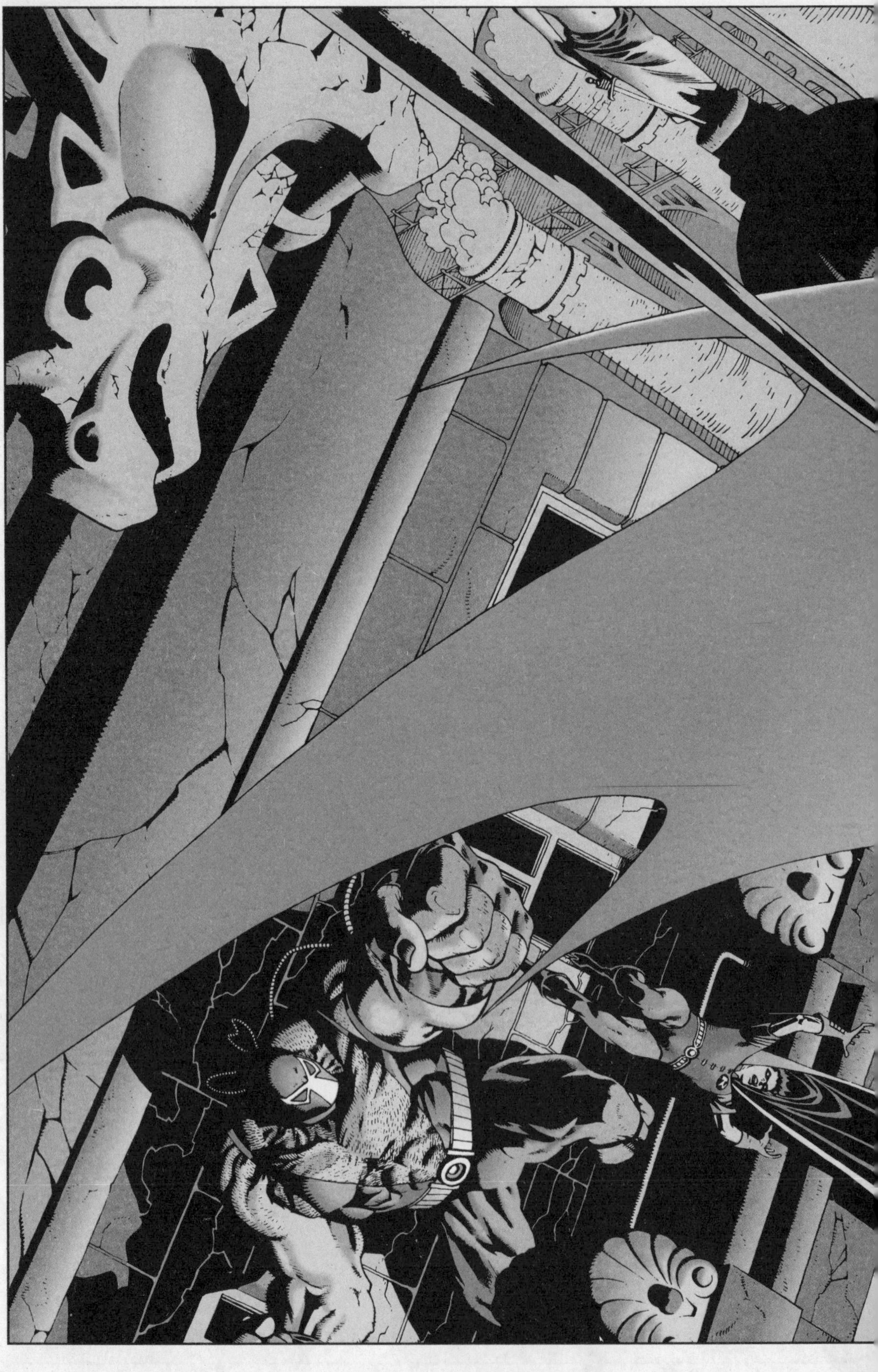

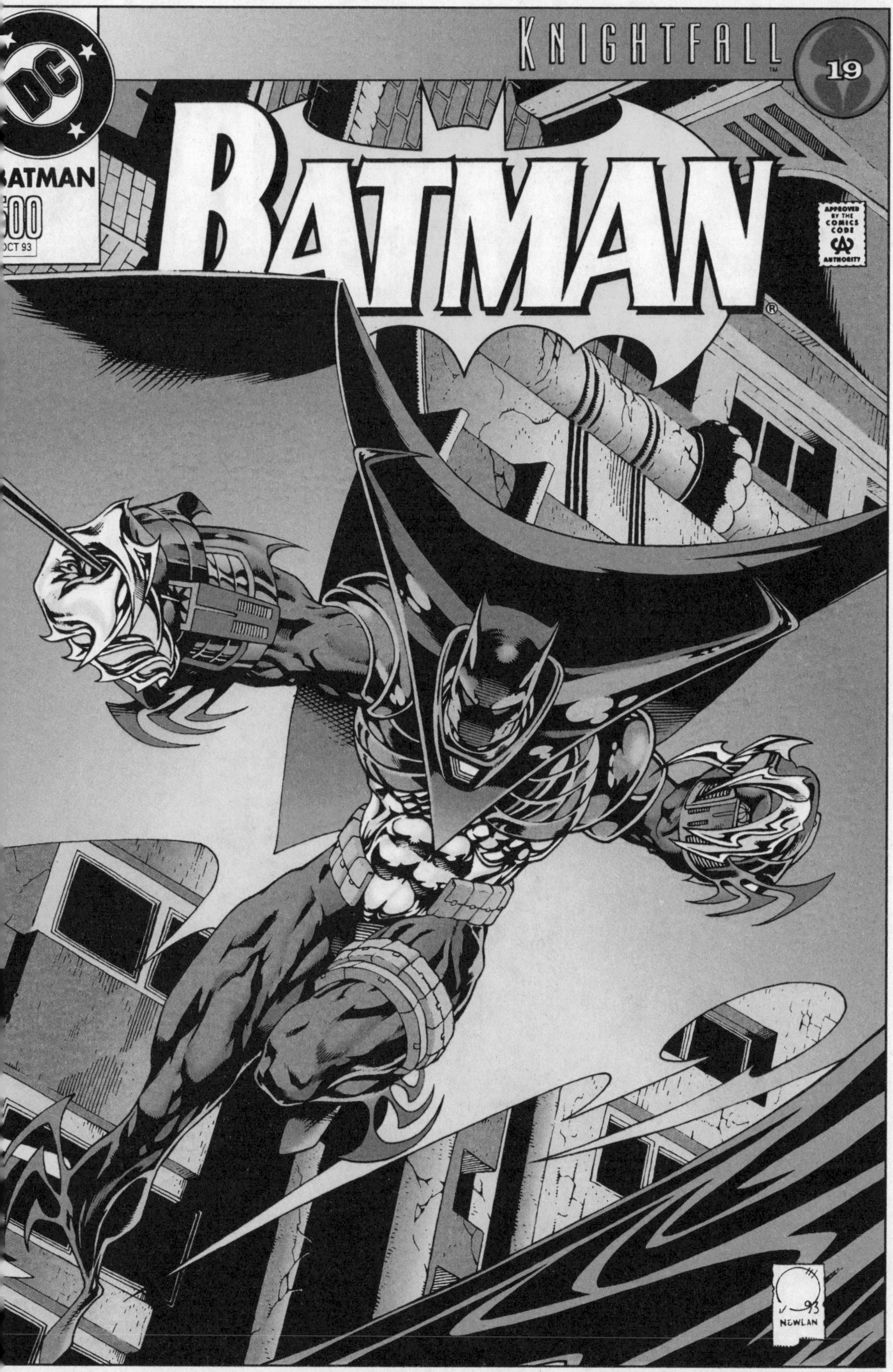

DC
BATMAN
500
OCT 93
KNIGHTFALL
19
BATMAN
APPROVED BY THE COMICS CODE AUTHORITY
NEWLAN

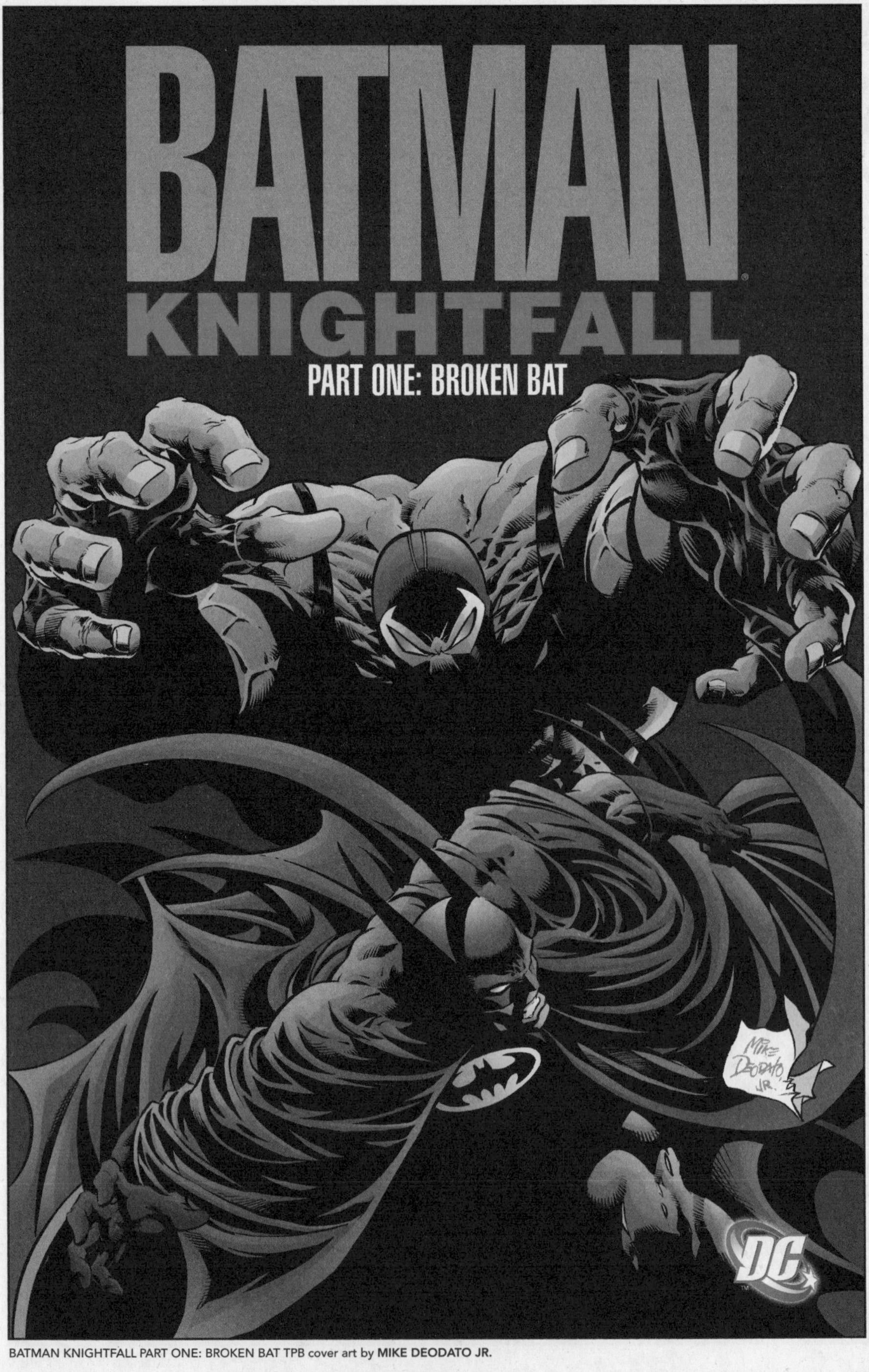
BATMAN
KNIGHTFALL
PART ONE: BROKEN BAT
MIKE DEODATO, JR.

BATMAN KNIGHTFALL PART ONE: BROKEN BAT TPB cover art by **MIKE DEODATO JR.**

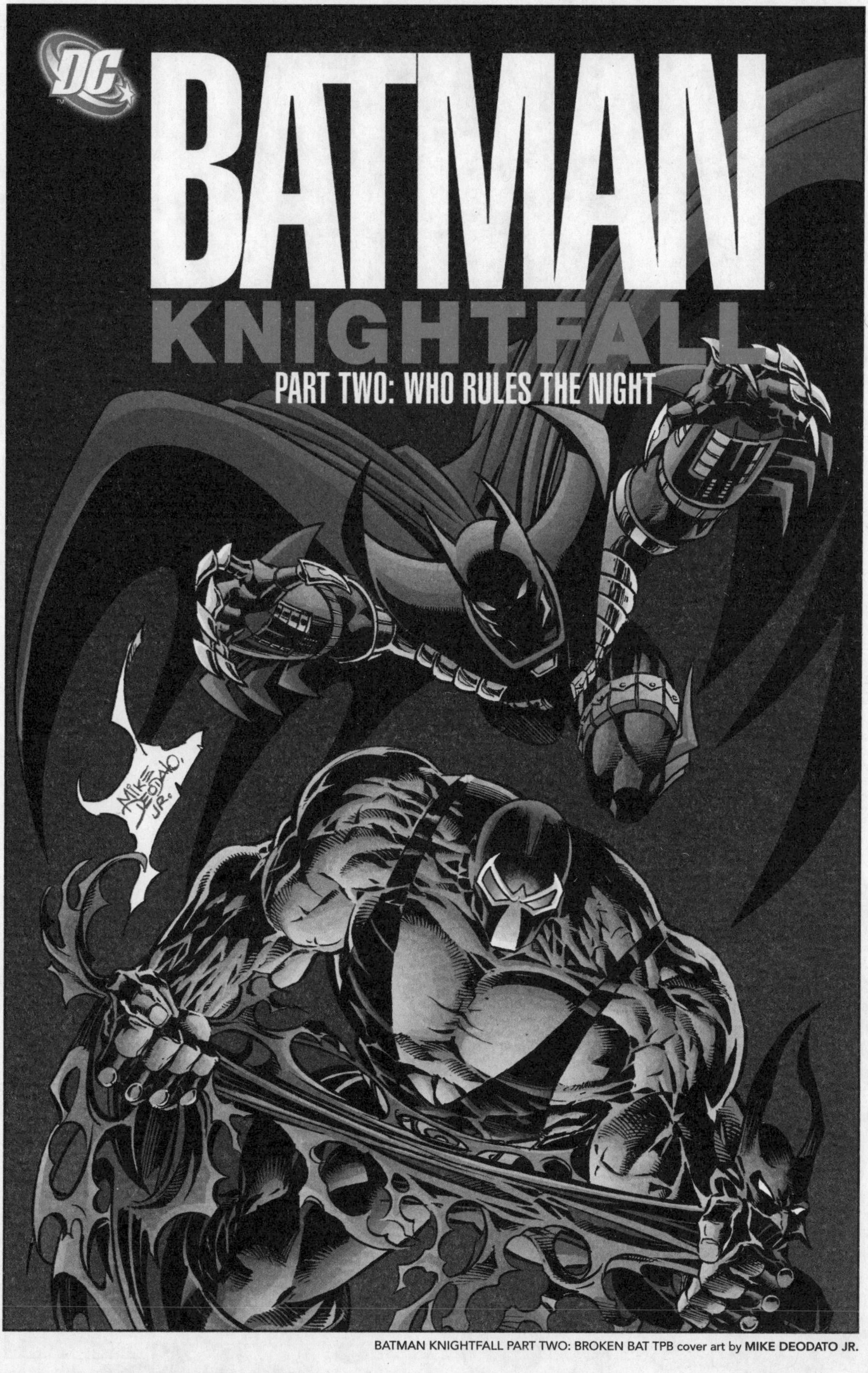

BATMAN

KNIGHTFALL

PART TWO: WHO RULES THE NIGHT

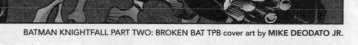

BATMAN KNIGHTFALL PART TWO: BROKEN BAT TPB cover art by MIKE DEODATO JR.

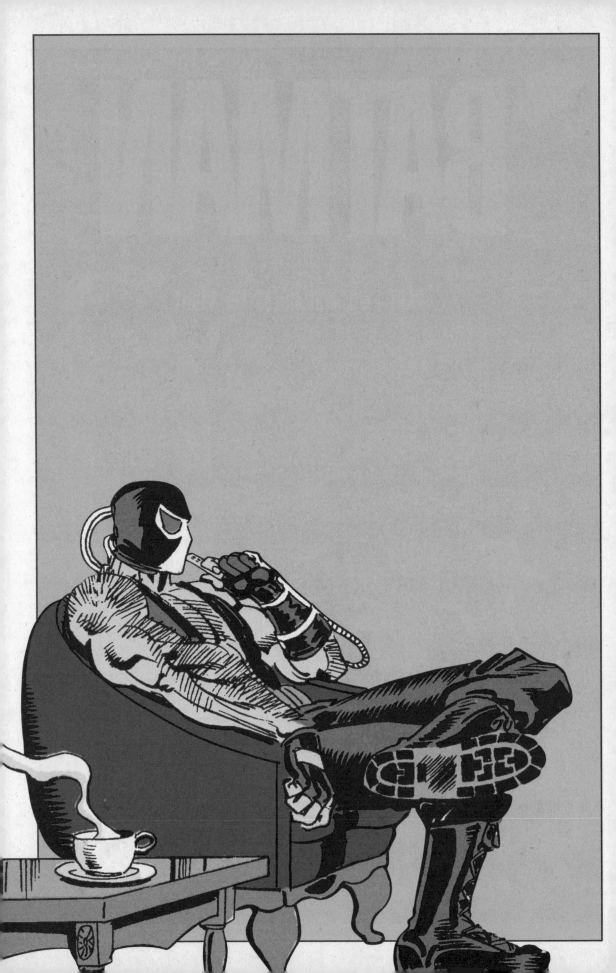

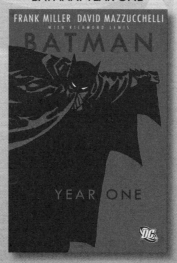

FROM THE WRITER OF
ALL-STAR SUPERMAN & JLA

GRANT MORRISON

with ANDY KUBERT

"Terrifically exciting." VARIETY
GRANT MORRISON
ANDY KUBERT
JESSE DELPERDANG
BATMAN AND SON

"As good as superhero comics get."
– IGN

"Morrison and Quitely have the magic touch."
– MTV SPLASH PAGE

"The best title that DC Comics is currently publishing."
– CRAVE ONLINE

BATMAN:
THE BLACK GLOVE

GRANT MORRISON
J.H. WILLIAMS III
TONY S. DANIEL
BATMAN THE BLACK GLOVE

with
**J.H. WILLIAMS III
& TONY DANIEL**

BATMAN:
R.I.P.

GRANT MORRISON
TONY S. DANIEL
BATMAN
R.I.P.

with
TONY DANIEL

BATMAN AND ROBIN
VOL. 1: BATMAN REBORN

grant morrison
frank quitely philip tan
BATMAN
& ROBIN
THE DELUXE EDITION
BATMAN REBORN

with
**FRANK QUITELY
& PHILIP TAN**

BATMAN AND ROBIN
VOL. 2: BATMAN VS. ROBIN

grant morrison
cameron stewart andy clarke
BATMAN
& ROBIN
THE DELUXE EDITION
BATMAN VS. ROBIN

with
**CAMERON STEWART,
ANDY CLARKE
& DUSTIN NGUYEN**

SEARCH THE GRAPHIC NOVELS SECTION OF
DCCOMICS.COM
FOR ART AND INFORMATION ON ALL OF OUR BOOKS!

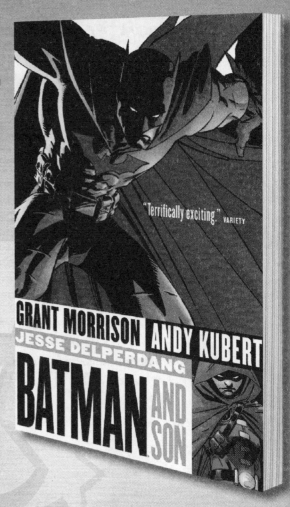